"[The Metrics chapter] is a very strong differentiating feature. The concept itself is new, and very workable in the classroom because it is intuitively clear."

–Johny Johansson
Georgetown Univ.

"Marshall & Johnston have responded to the emerging need in business programs to be more action oriented and to emphasize how marketing is really practiced."

–Dennis Pitta
Univ. of Baltimore

"[The CRM chapter] is a welcome addition to the text that reflects the application of technology to marketing management."

–Craig Gustin
American InterContinental University

"I like the practical hands-on approach the book takes. It puts the principles into practice by having the "executive perspective," which is unique, in my opinion."

–Vanessa Patrick
University of Georgia

"The integration of marketing plan elements in the chapters will greatly enhance the appeal of the book. In our marketing management course, we frequently require students to develop a marketing plan. The fact that the text makes it apparent how they could apply course material to the marketing plan is simply terrific."

–Hope Torkornoo
Kennesaw State University

MARKETING MANAGEMENT

MARKETING MANAGEMENT

Greg W. Marshall
ROLLINS COLLEGE

Mark W. Johnston
ROLLINS COLLEGE

 **McGraw-Hill Irwin**

Boston   Burr Ridge, IL   Dubuque, IA   New York   San Francisco   St. Louis
Bangkok   Bogotá   Caracas   Kuala Lumpur   Lisbon   London   Madrid   Mexico City
Milan   Montreal   New Delhi   Santiago   Seoul   Singapore   Sydney   Taipei   Toronto

McGraw-Hill
Irwin

MARKETING MANAGEMENT

Published by McGraw-Hill/Irwin, a business unit of The McGraw-Hill Companies, Inc., 1221 Avenue of the Americas, New York, NY, 10020. Copyright © 2010 by The McGraw-Hill Companies, Inc. All rights reserved. No part of this publication may be reproduced or distributed in any form or by any means, or stored in a database or retrieval system, without the prior written consent of The McGraw-Hill Companies, Inc., including, but not limited to, in any network or other electronic storage or transmission, or broadcast for distance learning.

Some ancillaries, including electronic and print components, may not be available to customers outside the United States.

This book is printed on acid-free paper.

1 2 3 4 5 6 7 8 9 0 WCK/WCK 0 9 8

ISBN 978-0-07-352979-0
MHID 0-07-352979-6

Vice president and editor-in-chief: *Brent Gordon*
Publisher: *Paul Ducham*
Executive editor: *Doug Hughes*
Editorial coordinator: *Devon Raemisch*
Marketing manager: *Katie Mergen*
Project manager: *Dana M. Pauley*
Lead production supervisor: *Carol A. Bielski*
Interior designer: *Cara Hawthorne, cara david DESIGN*
Senior photo research coordinator: *Lori Kramer*
Photo researcher: *Robin Sand*
Senior media project manager: *Brian Nacik*
Cover design: *Cara Hawthorne, cara david DESIGN*
Typeface: *10/12 Palatino LT Std. Roman*
Compositor: *Laserwords Private Limited*
Printer: *Quebecor World Versailles Inc.*

Library of Congress Cataloging-in-Publication Data
Marshall, Greg W.
  Marketing management / Greg Marshall, Mark Johnston.
    p. cm.
  Includes index.
  ISBN-13: 978-0-07-352979-0 (alk. paper)
  ISBN-10: 0-07-352979-6 (alk. paper)
  1. Marketing—Management. I. Johnston, Mark W. II. Title.
HF5415.13.M3699 2010
  658.8—dc22

                                        2008045879

To Patti and Justin

-Greg

To Susan, my love and Grace, my joy, thank you

-Mark

Greg W. Marshall

Greg W. Marshall is the Charles Harwood Professor of Marketing and Strategy in the Roy E. Crummer Graduate School of Business at Rollins College in Winter Park, Florida. He also serves as vice president for strategic marketing for Rollins College. He earned his Ph.D. in Business Administration from Oklahoma State University, taking a marketing major and management minor, and holds a BSBA in marketing and MBA from the University of Tulsa. Before joining Rollins, Greg was on the faculty at the University of South Florida, Texas Christian University, and Oklahoma State University.

Prior to returning to school for his doctorate, Greg's managerial industry experience included 13 years in consumer packaged goods and retailing with companies such as Warner Lambert, Mennen, and Target Corporation. He also has considerable experience as a consultant and trainer for a variety of organizations in industries such as hospitality, financial services/insurance, defense contracting, consumer products, information technology, government, and not-for-profit. Greg has been heavily involved in teaching Marketing Management at multiple universities to both MBA and undergraduate students and has been the recipient of several teaching awards both within his schools and within the marketing discipline.

He is editor of the *Journal of Marketing Theory and Practice* and from 2002–2005 was editor of the *Journal of Personal Selling & Sales Management.* Greg serves on the editorial review boards of the *Journal of the Academy of Marketing Science, Industrial Marketing Management,* and *Journal of Business Research,* among others. Greg's published research focuses on the areas of decision making by marketing managers, intraorganizational relationships, and sales force performance.

Greg is past president of the American Marketing Association Academic Division and also was a founder and served for five years on its Strategic Planning Group. He is a Fellow and past-president of the Society for Marketing Advances, presently serves as president-elect for the Academy of Marketing Science, and is a member of the board of directors of the Direct Selling Education Foundation.

Mark W. Johnston

Mark W. Johnston is the Alan and Sandra Gerry Professor of Marketing and Ethics in the Roy E. Crummer Graduate School of Business at Rollins College in Winter Park, Florida. He earned his Ph.D. in Marketing in 1986 from Texas A&M University. Before receiving his doctorate, he worked in industry as a sales representative for a leading distributor of photographic equipment. His research has been published in a number of professional journals including *Journal of Marketing Research, Journal of Applied Psychology, Journal of Business Ethics, Journal of Marketing Education, Journal of Personal Selling & Sales Management,* and many others. Mark is also an active member in the American Marketing Association and Academy of Marketing Science.

Mark has been retained as a consultant for firms in a number of industries including personal health care, chemical, transportation, hospitality, and telecommunications. He has consulted on a wide range of issues involving strategic business development, sales force structure and performance, international market opportunities, and ethical decision making. Mark also works with MBA students on consulting projects around the world for companies such as Tupperware, Disney, and Johnson & Johnson.

He has conducted seminars globally on a range of topics including the strategic role of selling in the organization, developing an ethical framework for decision making, improving business unit performance, and structuring an effective international marketing department. Mark continues to provide specialized seminars to top managers on strategic marketing issues.

For more than two decades Mark has taught Marketing Management working with thousands of students. His hands-on, real-world approach to marketing management has earned him a number of teaching awards.

In addition to working together on *Marketing Management,* Greg and Mark are the co-authors of two other McGraw-Hill/ Irwin titles: *Relationship Selling,* 3rd edition, and *Churchill/ Ford/Walker's Sales Force Management,* 9th edition.

INTRODUCTION

No doubt about it, the field of marketing is *really changing*—so much so that the American Marketing Association recently unveiled a change in the "official definition" of marketing:

> Marketing is the activity, set of institutions, and processes for creating, communicating, delivering, and exchanging offerings that have value for customers, clients, partners, and society at large.

Recent changes in the practice of marketing management are dramatic and important, and call attention to a number of organizational issues in today's business milieu that differ from the past. In general, marketing management today is:

- Very strategic—customer centricity is now a core *organizational* value.
- Focused on facilitating value for the customer.
- Concerned with internal alignment of people, processes, systems, and strategies to effectively compete through a customer focus.
- Accountable to top management through diligent attention to metrics and measurement.
- Oriented toward service as the driver of product.
- Long-term customer relationship-centered understanding of the need to develop deep commitments from current profitable customers while also cultivating new ones.
- "Owned" by everybody in the firm, to one degree or another.
- Critically committed to exhibiting the utmost ethical behavior in all dealings.

In contrast, marketing management in the past has been:

- Much less strategic in nature.
- Very 4Ps oriented—more tactical.
- Less relationship-centered, thus focused on shorter time horizon decision making.
- Less focused on the ability to facilitate value for the customer.
- Oriented toward product as the core deliverable.
- Done by marketing *departments*.
- Much less accountable to upper management in terms of measurement of marketing success.

WHY WE WROTE THIS BOOK

Given the dramatic changes in the field of marketing, it is a sure bet that the job of leading and managing marketing's contributions to (quoting from the last line of the AMA definition) "customers, clients, partners, and society at large" has changed at a concurrent level. Yet, no marketing management book on the market today fully and effectively captures and communicates to students how marketing management is really practiced in the 21st century world of business. Clearly, it was time for an updated approach to teaching and learning within the field. This book is designed to fulfill this need.

We hear it from colleagues all the time—the complaint that the book they are using in their marketing management course "doesn't say what I believe the students need to hear" or that it "doesn't match what my MBAs actually do on the job" or that it "reads like an encyclopedia of marketing" or that it "has too much about everything and not enough focus on anything." During the development process for this book we've heard comments like these and others from hundreds of colleagues in focus groups, in written reviewer comments, and in numerous casual conversations about the course. We've become convinced that such comments truly are pervasive among instructors who teach marketing management, whether as the introductory MBA course, capstone undergraduate course, or first focal course after the undergraduate marketing principles course. Many marketing management instructors are looking for a book that is:

- Written for today's students in an up-to-date, user-friendly, yet professional and thorough, style.
- Able to strike an effective balance between presenting the new world order of marketing at the strategic, operational, and tactical levels.
- A step up from the previous norm in terms of support materials for the classroom.

Marshall/Johnston's *Marketing Management* has taken great effort to represent marketing management the way it is actually practiced in successful organizations today. In our view, leading and managing the aspects of marketing to improve individual, unit, and organizational performance—**marketing management**—is a *core business activity.* Its relevance is not limited to just marketing departments or marketing majors. And business students of all backgrounds should appreciate the impact of effective marketing management on their own professional careers as well on as the overall success of their organizations. Bottom line, the ability to do great marketing management is relevant to *everyone in a firm.*

The content of the book reflects the major trends in the managerial practice of marketing, and the pedagogy is crafted around *learning and teaching preferences in today's classroom.* Above all, it is written in a style that is appealing for both students and instructors so that students will actually enjoy reading the material and instructors will be proud to teach from it and confident about presenting its up-to-date, professional, and thorough approach to their courses.

STRUCTURE OF THE BOOK

Marshall/Johnston's *Marketing Management* has four major parts, reflective of the logical sequence of building blocks for the course.

- **Part One: Introduction to Marketing Management.** In this part, students gain an understanding of the dynamics of the field. Significant attention is paid to framing the importance of studying marketing to future success as a manager. Global marketplace issues are presented early in the book based on the idea that today, truly *all marketing is global.* And to kick off the marketing planning theme early in the course, comprehensive coverage of this aspect along with an example marketing plan appears in Part One.

- **Part Two: Information Drives Marketing Decision Making.** It has often been said that information is the fuel that fires the engine of marketing management decision making. With this in mind, Part Two begins with a unique and highly useful treatment of customer relationship management (CRM), presented in the context of connecting CRM capabilities with other relevant competencies and capabilities of successful marketers. The remainder of this part focuses on effective management of information to better understand competitors and customers, both in the consumer and business marketplaces.

- **Part Three: Developing the Value Offering.** Effective segmentation, target marketing, and positioning are at the core of successful marketing and this part provides a modern managerial treatment of these critical topics, followed by a comprehensive drill-down into today's world of product strategy, branding, and new-product development. Reflective of the notion that service is a key driver of product success, a separate chapter makes important links between service and the overall offering. Part Three concludes with a fresh, managerially relevant treatment of pricing decision making.

- **Part Four: Communicating and Delivering the Value Offering.** This part takes an integrative approach to the multitude of modes at a manager's disposal today by which an offering can be made available to customers as well as the array of new-age and traditional marketing communication vehicles. The final chapter in the book is unique in marketing management books, in that it is the first of its kind to focus on comprehensive approaches to selecting and executing marketing metrics for decision making. As such, it is useful as a resource chapter for numerous other topics in the course including the development of a marketing plan.

EXECUTIVE PERSPECTIVE

A feature box kicks off each chapter introducing students to a marketing executive, who presents his or her situation and answers questions relevant to key chapter material.

ETHICAL DIMENSION

Reflective of the centrality of ethical practices to marketing management, each chapter includes a real-world example of business ethics related to chapter material. These lively boxed features highlight how ethical issues permeate every marketing decision.

POP-OUT EXAMPLES

Each chapter contains numerous pop-out examples so that students can immediately connect chapter content to real-world application.

FYIs

FYIs are more extended examples of current, cutting-edge marketing management topics and ideas that influence marketing decision makers.

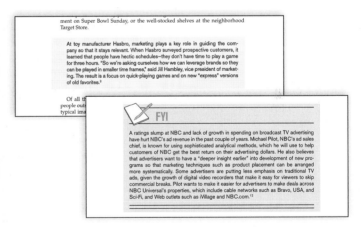

MANAGEMENT DECISION CASE

At the end of each chapter is a case drawn and developed from recent *BusinessWeek* headlines. Students are engaged by the currency of the problem and asked to develop solutions using chapter material. The cases are just the right size for today's classroom use—not too short but not too long!

MARKETING PLAN EXERCISES

ACTIVITY 1: Elements of a Marketing Plan

In the chapter, you learned that marketing planning drives the activities of the marketing manager and you were provided a framework for marketing planning. Before you move further through this course, it is important to be sure that you understand the flow and content of a typical marketing plan.

1. Read the annotated marketing plan example presented in the appendix to this chapter.

2. Make notes about any questions you may have about the example plan, and be prepared to bring those questions to class for clarification.

3. If you are going to be using Marketing Plan Pro Software to develop your marketing plan, take this opportunity to open your copy of the software and familiarize yourself with its functionality. An electronic template for your marketing plan that follows Exhibit 2.2 in the chapter (which is the same format used in the CloudCab Small Jet Taxi Service example in the Appendix) can be accessed at www.mhhe.com/marshall1e.

If you are using Marketing Plan Pro, a template for this assignment can be accessed at www.mhhe.com/marshall1e.

MARKETING PLAN EXERCISE

Each chapter connects that chapter's key content to a semester-long marketing plan project activity, augmented by Marketing Plan Pro software. Marshall/Johnston's *Marketing Management* is the only marketing management book to effectively thread a marketing planning focus throughout the textbook itself. Whether or not a semester marketing plan project is used by the instructor, the marketing plan exercise feature does a great job of tying together important planning concepts for students.

GLOSSARY OF TERMS

A complete glossary of key terms and definitions is provided at the end of the book. The glossary serves as an important reference as well as a handy study aid for students preparing for exams.

OTHER FEATURES IN EACH CHAPTER

- *Learning objectives:* set the stage for what students will achieve by reading and studying the chapter.
- *Summary:* at the end of each chapter, reminds students of the highlighted topics.
- *Key terms:* bolded throughout the chapter and connected with definitions in the Glossary.
- *Application questions:* These engaging questions at the end of each chapter are designed to direct students' thinking about the topics to the next level of application. Throughout the book all of these questions have been specially designed to simulate managerial decision making.
- *Recommended readings:* provides a short list of the most compelling additional readings on the topics at hand.

LEARNING OBJECTIVES

- Examine the concept of value and the elements and role of the value chain.
- Understand the conditions required for successful marketing planning, that marketing planning is focused on the value proposition, and that marketing planning is a dynamic process.
- Identify various types of organizational strategies.
- Conduct a situation analysis.
- Use the framework provided for marketing planning, along with the content in future chapters, to build a marketing plan.

Assurance of Learning Ready

Assurance of learning is an important element of many accreditation standards. Marshall/Johnston's *Marketing Management* is designed specifically to support your assurance of learning initiatives. Each chapter in the book begins with a list of learning objectives, which are then addressed throughout the chapter, as well as in the end-of-chapter problems and exercises. Every test bank question is also linked to one of these objectives, in addition to level of difficulty, topic area, Bloom's Taxonomy level, and AACSB skill area. EZ Test, McGraw-Hill's easy-to-use test bank software, can search the test bank by these and other categories, providing an engine for targeted Assurance of Learning analysis and assessment.

AACSB Statement

The McGraw-Hill Companies is a proud corporate member of AACSB International. Understanding the importance and value of AACSB accreditation, Marshall/Johnston's *Marketing Management* has sought to recognize the curricula guidelines detailed in the AACSB standards for business accreditation by connecting selected questions in the test bank to the general knowledge and skill guidelines found in the AACSB standards.

The statements contained in Marshall/Johnston's *Marketing Management* are provided only as a guide for the users of this text. The AACSB leaves content coverage and assessment within the purview of individual schools, the mission of the school, and the faculty. While Marshall/Johnston's *Marketing Management* and the teaching package make no claim of any specific AACSB qualification or evaluation, we have labeled selected questions according to the six general knowledge and skills areas.

SUPPLEMENT PACKAGE

Marshall/Johnston's *Marketing Management* is committed to having the best supplement package in the marketing management textbook arena.

MARKETING PLAN PRO

Marketing Plan Pro is the most widely used marketing plan software program in the industry, and it includes everything students need to create professional, complete, and accurate marketing plans. Marketing Plan Pro can be packaged with Marshall/Johnston's *Marketing Management* for a nominal fee (approximately $20). In addition, Marshall/ Johnston's *Marketing Management* will have a Correlation Guide provided at no extra cost linking the Marketing Plan Exercises at the end of each chapter to the Marketing Plan Pro software. This eliminates the need for instructors to spend time in office hours and in class showing how to use this program.

BUSINESSWEEK VIDEO MONTHLY NEWSLETTER

Each month you will receive an electronic newsletter from the authors including synopses of current *BusinessWeek* videos as well as discussion questions that correlate to relevant topics in the textbook.

INSTRUCTOR'S RESOURCE CD

The Instructor's Resource CD contains instructor supplements including the Instructor's Manual, PowerPoint slides, and Test Bank. These supplements are also available on the password-protected Instructor Online Learning Center.

- The Instructor's Manual contains a chapter outline for each of the 19 chapters in the text as well as PowerPoint thumbnail references, sample syllabi, and end-of-chapter text solutions.

- The PowerPoint slides include examples from the text and additional lecture support.

- The Test Bank contains true/false, multiple-choice, short answer, and essay questions that are tagged to the appropriate Learning Objective within each chapter as well as applicable AACSB Learning Outcomes.

ONLINE LEARNING CENTER

Students using Marshall/Johnston's *Marketing Management* will have access to resources located on the Online Learning Center, including Chapter Quizzes and a Marketing Plan Guide. The Marketing Plan Guide is a correlation guide linking the Marketing Plan Exercises at the end of each chapter to the Marketing Plan Pro software. This guide walks students through the Marketing Plan Pro software, providing direct correlations to show how to complete the marketing plan exercises using the online software.

CONCLUSION

Our overarching goal is to introduce the first really new marketing management book in over a decade—one that truly captures the managerial practice of marketing in a way that is fully relevant to today's business students, professors, and managers. As stated earlier, we strongly believe that leading and managing the aspects of marketing to improve individual, unit, and organizational performance—**marketing management**—is a core business activity that is relevant to any MBA or undergraduate business student, regardless of their functional area of focus. At the end of the course, we want this book to allow marketing management instructors to have accomplished these key objectives:

- Clearly bring knowledge leadership in managerial aspects of marketing into the classroom, especially focusing on marketing management decision making in this new era of marketing.

- At the same time, cover the core areas of day-to-day management of marketing functions, but with a focus always on application and managerial decision making.

- Integrate the following themes as systematic focal areas of the course experience: marketing planning, leadership, metrics, value, customer centricity, globalization, ethics, technology and data-driven marketing, and marketing's interface with other business functions.

- Speak to today's students in an up-to-date, user-friendly, yet professional and thorough writing style with vivid examples of actual marketing managers and leaders doing their jobs and making decisions about marketing problems and opportunities.

- Provide a state-of-the-art supplement package that enhances instructional effectiveness and the student's learning experience.

- Ultimately, provide a book today's instructor's will be proud to teach from, secure in the knowledge that students will *want* to read it and that it represents the field of marketing management the way it is practiced in today's business milieu.

Acknowledgments

The task of writing a first edition textbook requires the talents of many dedicated people. First and foremost, we want to thank the McGraw-Hill/Irwin team for sharing the vision of this project with us from the very beginning. Particularly given the dynamic nature of marketing management both as a professional field and as a course of study, it was critically important that throughout the development process the authors and the editorial, production, and marketing team remain steadfast in believing in the vision of the project. The high level of mutual enthusiasm never waned, and we commend McGraw-Hill/Irwin for this.

In particular, we want to recognize and thank the following individuals at McGraw-Hill/Irwin who played a significant part in the successful development of Marshall/Johnston's *Marketing Management*. A few of these people have moved on to other professional opportunities, but their role in the success of the project deserves mention just the same. Credit for understanding and embracing the original conceptualization of the project goes to John Biernat and Barrett Koger. Other key contributors on the publisher's side include Sarah Crago, Paul Ducham, Doug Hughes, Katie Mergen, Devon Raemisch and Andy Winston. We would also like to thank Carol Bielski, Cara Hawthorne, Brian Nacik, and Dana Pauley for their substantial contributions. All of these great professionals made our job as authors much more enjoyable, and we are indebted to them for their significant contributions to the project.

In addition, we appreciate the contributions by several members of the Rollins College Crummer Graduate School of Business family. Paul Borges developed the marketing budget spreadsheets that are on the book's Web site and linked to Chapter 19. He also developed the Glossary, played a significant role in sourcing references for many of the chapters, and correlated the Marketing Plan Exercises to the Marketing Plan Pro software. Harry Antonio and Alexandra Edgar created the marketing audit instrument that appears in Chapter 19, and Harry also created the abbreviated marketing plan example that appears as the appendix to Chapter 2.

Leroy Robinson, Jr., at the University of Houston—Clear Lake did a masterful job in creating and managing the supplements program for the book. Leroy, you have our utmost thanks for a job exceptionally well done! Likewise, Jill Solomon at the University of South Florida developed an outstanding set of testing materials to accompany the book, and without your exceptional contribution the value of the overall course package would not be what it is. Thank you so much.

Many colleagues participated in the developmental process of Marshall/ Johnston *Marketing Management* through focus groups and chapter reviews. Thanks go to each of the following people for their guidance and suggestions through this process:

Kalthom Abdullah, *INTERNATIONAL ISLAMIC UNIVERSITY OF MALAYSIA*

Denise Ammirato, *WESTFIELD STATE COLLEGE*

David Amponsah, *TROY UNIVERSITY MONTGOMERY*

David Andrus, *KANSAS STATE UNIVERSITY*

Paul Arsenault, *WEST CHESTER UNIVERSITY OF PENNSYLVANIA*

Semih Arslanoglu, *BOSTON UNIVERSITY*

Parimal Baghat, *INDIANA UNIVERSITY OF PENNSYLVANIA*

William Baker, *SAN DIEGO STATE UNIVERSITY–SAN DIEGO*

Roger Baran, *DEPAUL UNIVERSITY*

Danny Bellenger, *GEORGIA STATE UNIVERSITY*

John Bellenoit, *WESTFIELD STATE COLLEGE*

Parimal Bhagat, *INDIANA UNIVERSITY OF PENNSYLVANIA*

Subodh Bhat, *SAN FRANCISCO STATE UNIVERSITY*

Carol Bienstock, *RADFORD UNIVERSITY*

Diedre Bird, *PROVIDENCE COLLEGE*

Douglas Boyd, *JAMES MADISON UNIVERSITY*

Steve Brokaw, *UNIVERSITY OF WISCONSIN–LACROSSE*

Laura Buckner, *MIDDLE TENNESSEE STATE UNIVERSITY*

Tim Calkins, *NORTHWESTERN UNIVERSITY*

Barb Casey, *DOWLING COLLEGE*

Bob Cline, *UNIVERSITY OF IOWA*

Cathy Cole, *UNIVERSITY OF IOWA*

Mark Collins, *UNIVERSITY OF TENNESSEE–KNOXVILLE*

David Conrad, *AUGSBURG COLLEGE*

Bob Cutler, *CLEVELAND STATE UNIVERSITY*

Geoffrey Da Silva, *TEMASEK POLYTECHNIC*

Lorie Darche, *SOUTHWEST FLORIDA COLLEGE*

F. Robert Dwyer, *UNIVERSITY OF CINCINNATI*

Michael Edwards, *UNIVERSITY OF ST. THOMAS*

Ken Fairweather, *LETOURNEAU UNIVERSITY*

Bagher Fardanesh, *JOHNS HOPKINS UNIVERSITY*

Andrew Forman, *HOFSTRA UNIVERSITY*

Fred Fusting, *LOYOLA COLLEGE OF MARYLAND*

Mahesh Gopinath, *OLD DOMINION UNIVERSITY*

Shiv Gupta, *UNIVERSITY OF FINDLAY*

Liz Hafer, *UNIVERSITY OF COLORADO–BOULDER*

Angela Hausman, *UNIVERSITY OF NORTH CAROLINA AT PEMBROKE*

Chuck Hermans, *MISSOURI STATE UNIVERSITY*

Asep Hermawan, *UNIVERSITAS TRISAKTI*

Mahmood Hussain, *SAN FRANCISCO STATE UNIVERSITY*

Donna Rue Jenkins, *WARREN NATIONAL UNIVERSITY*

Johny Johansson, *GEORGETOWN UNIVERSITY*

Amit Joshi, *UNIVERSITY OF CENTRAL FLORIDA*

Fred Katz, *JOHNS HOPKINS UNIVERSITY*

Craig Kelley, *CALIFORNIA STATE UNIVERSITY–SACRAMENTO*

Elias Konwufine, *KEISER UNIVERSITY*

Robert Kopp, *BABSON COLLEGE*

Michael Levens, *WALSH COLLEGE*

Cesar Maloles, *CALIFORNIA STATE UNIVERSITY–EAST BAY*

Avinash Malshe, *UNIVERSITY OF ST. THOMAS*

Susan Mantel, *INDIANA UNIVERSITY–PURDUE UNIVERSITY–INDIANAPOLIS*

Norton Marks, *CALIFORNIA STATE UNIVERSITY–SAN BERNARDINO*

Thomas Maronick, *TOWSON UNIVERSITY*

H. Lee Mathews, *OHIO STATE UNIVERSITY*

Melvin Mattson, *RADFORD UNIVERSITY*

Denny McCorkle, *UNIVERSITY OF NORTHERN COLORADO*

Michael Menasco, *CALIFORNIA STATE UNIVERSITY–SAN BERNADINO*

Morgan Miles, *GEORGIA SOUTHERN UNIVERSITY*

Chad Milewicz, *UNIVERSITY OF CENTRAL FLORIDA*

Herb Miller, *UNIVERSITY OF TEXAS*

Mark Mitchell, *COASTAL CAROLINA UNIVERSITY*

Thomas Noordewier, *UNIVERSITY OF VERMONT*

Nicholas Nugent, *SOUTHERN NEW HAMPSHIRE UNIVERSITY*

Carl Obermiller, *SEATTLE UNIVERSITY*

Azizah Omar, *UNIVERSITI SAINS MALAYSIA*

Barnett Parker, *PFEIFFER UNIVERSITY*

Vanessa Patrick, *UNIVERSITY OF GEORGIA*

Dennis Pitta, *UNIVERSITY OF BALTIMORE*

Salim Qureshi, *BLOOMSBURG UNIVERSITY*

Pushkala Raman, *TEXAS WOMANS UNIVERSITY–DENTON*

K. Ramakrishna Rao, *MULTIMEDIA UNIVERSITY*

Molly Rapert, *UNIVERSITY OF ARKANSAS–FAYETTEVILLE*

Richard Rexeisen, *UNIVERSITY OF SAINT THOMAS*

Subom Rhee, *SANTA CLARA UNIVERSITY*

Robert Richey, *UNIVERSITY OF ALABAMA–TUSCALOOSA*

Torsten Ringberg, *UNIVERSITY OF WISCONSIN–MILWAUKEE*

Ann Root, *FLORIDA ATLANTIC UNIVERSITY–BOCA RATON*

David Rylander, *TEXAS WOMANS UNIVERSITY–DENTON*

Mahmod Sabri Haron, *UNIVERSITI SAINS MALAYSIA*

Dennis Sandler, *PACE UNIVERSITY*

Matt Sarkees, *PENNSYLVANIA STATE UNIVERSITY*

Linda Saytes, *UNIVERSITY OF SAN FRANCISCO*

Shahid Sheikh, *AMERICAN INTERCONTINENTAL UNIVERSITY*

Susan Sieloff, *NORTHEASTERN UNIVERSITY*

Karen Smith, *COLUMBIA SOUTHERN UNIVERSITY*

Sharon Smith, *DEPAUL UNIVERSITY*

Jill Solomon, *UNIVERSITY OF SOUTH FLORIDA*

Ashish Sood, *EMORY UNIVERSITY*

Robert Spekman, *UNIVERSITY OF VIRGINIA*

James Spiers, *ARIZONA STATE UNIVERSITY–TEMPE*

Thomas Steenburgh, *HARVARD BUSINESS SCHOOL*

Geoffrey Stewart, *UNIVERSITY OF LOUISIANA–LAFAYETTE*

John Stovall, *GEORGIA SOUTHWESTERN STATE UNIVERSITY*

Ziad Swaidan, *UNIVERSITY OF HOUSTON AT VICTORIA*

Michael Swenson, *BRIGHAM YOUNG UNIVERSITY*

Leona Tam, *OLD DOMINION UNIVERSITY*

Niwet Thamma, *RAMKHAMHEANG UNIVERSITY*

Meg Thams, *REGIS UNIVERSITY*

Rungting Tu, *PEKING UNIVERSITY*

Bronislaw Verhage, *GEORGIA STATE UNIVERSITY*

Guangping Wang, *PENNSYLVANIA STATE UNIVERSITY*

Cathy Waters, *BOSTON COLLEGE*

Art Weinstein, *NOVA SOUTHEASTERN UNIVERSITY*

Darin White, *UNION UNIVERSITY–JACKSON*

Ken Williamson, *JAMES MADISON UNIVERSITY*

Dale Wilson, *MICHIGAN STATE UNIVERSITY*

Walter Wochos, *CARDINAL STRITCH UNIVERSITY*

Khanchitpol Yousapronpaiboon, *KHONKHEN UNIVERSITY*

Yong Zhang, *HOFSTRA UNIVERSITY*

Shaoming Zou, *UNIVERSITY OF MISSOURI–COLUMBIA*

And finally, we want to offer a very special and heartfelt note of appreciation to our families and friends. Their encouragement and good humor throughout this process were integral to the end result.

Greg W. Marshall, *ROLLINS COLLEGE*

Mark W. Johnston, *ROLLINS COLLEGE*

January 2009

BRIEF TABLE OF CONTENTS

TABLE OF CONTENTS

part THREE
Developing the Value Offering 235

part ONE

Introduction to Marketing Management

chapter 01
MARKETING IN TODAY'S BUSINESS MILIEU

chapter 02
ELEMENTS OF MARKETING STRATEGY AND PLANNING

chapter 03
UNDERSTANDING THE GLOBAL MARKETPLACE: MARKETING WITHOUT BORDERS

MARKETING IN TODAY'S BUSINESS MILIEU

LEARNING OBJECTIVES

- Identify typical misconceptions about marketing, why they persist, and the resulting challenges for marketing management.

- Define what marketing and marketing management really are and how they contribute to a firm's success.

- Appreciate how marketing has evolved from its early roots to be practiced as it is today .

- Recognize the impact of key change drivers on the future of marketing.

EXECUTIVE PERSPECTIVE

Executive Rick Rotondo, Chief Marketing Officer

Company Spectrum Bridge Inc.

Business Start-up high-tech telecom solutions

Why is great marketing essential to business success today?

The growth of the Internet and global competition has resulted in a flood of products, information, and claims that often overwhelm your prospects and customers. The volume of information makes it difficult for customers to find you. Getting your message to stand out so your products can lead the industry and your company can beat the competition requires great marketing.

What is great marketing? Great marketing starts by talking in the language of the customer, not about technology or features. It makes it clear that you understand your customers and that you alone can best address their desires and pain points. It makes it easy too for your customers to figure out what to buy and even easier for them to buy it from you. Great marketing finds customers instead of waiting for them to come to you.

Finally, great marketing listens. It listens to how your customers want to use your product, it listens to trends in the marketplace, and it listens to your competitors in its quest to improve its messaging, product, and service.

"Everyone in the firm owns marketing" is a phrase heard a lot these days. What does this mean to you and why is it important?

As an entrepreneur, you can only dream of having an adequate marketing staff, so you have to leverage and equip everybody in your company to be able to carry out critical marketing functions. Your engineering, finance, and even administrative staffs are interacting with potential customers and buyers on a daily basis.

By instilling basic marketing techniques and knowledge into everyone in the firm, you can immensely enhance your marketing results. Marketing professionals must understand and embrace the responsibility to make this a reality. This goes for entrepreneurs as well as for Fortune 500 firms.

It is up to you to be sure that everyone understands your company's and products' value propositions and can articulate them clearly. They must also know how to recognize a prospect and what to do with leads so that they can be turned into customers. Keep in mind that anyone in the firm can be a potential source of valuable customer and competitive information.

What are a few tips you would like to give somebody just starting out as a marketing manager?

Make your customers famous and let them sell for you. Real customers have great "street cred" and can market to new prospects better than anyone in your company. Give them the support and venue to tell the world why they were smart to buy your product and why your prospects should too. If you do, they will.

Never stop marketing. You may think that after months or years of marketing your product everybody must know about you. The fact is, even with great marketing, vast numbers of potential customers have still never heard of you. The next marketing campaign, trade show, or seminar may be the one to reach them. And that makes it all worth it.

WELCOME TO MARKETING MANAGEMENT

Welcome to the world of marketing management! In late 2007, the American Marketing Association announced a new "official" definition of marketing as follows: **marketing** is the activity, set of institutions, and processes for creating, communicating, delivering, and exchanging offerings that have value for customers, clients, partners, and society at large.[1]

An exciting aspect of modern marketing is that it is an inherently global enterprise. Chapter 3 will present strong evidence that today marketing and global marketing are basically synonymous.

Now is a great time to be studying about marketing. In fact, marketing as a field of study has much to offer everyone, regardless of whether or not the word "marketing" appears in their job title. Whether your interest and training is in engineering, accounting, finance, information technology, or fields outside business, marketing is relevant to you. You can be confident that, when finished with this course about marketing management, you will emerge with a set of knowledge and skills that will not only enhance your personal effectiveness as a leader and manager regardless of area of responsibility or job title, but will also positively impact the performance of your work group and firm. Mastering great marketing is useful for anyone!

Despite the strong case for the value of learning about marketing, marketing is often misunderstood for a variety of reasons. So let's start by clearing the air. Before you learn about great marketing and how to successfully manage it, it is important to address some misconceptions and stereotypes about marketing. Getting these out in the open will give you the opportunity to challenge your own perceptions of the field. After this section, attention will quickly turn from marketing misconceptions to *marketing realities* in today's business milieu.

MARKETING MISCONCEPTIONS

When you think of *marketing*, what sorts of ideas and images initially come to mind? Close your eyes and think about the essence of the word. What images flow in? The images will vary depending on your age, professional background, and whether you have worked in some aspect of the marketing field. Here is a short list of perceptions commonly conjured up about marketing:

- Catchy and entertaining advertisements—or perhaps the opposite, incessant and boring advertisements.
- Pushy salespeople trying to persuade someone to *buy it right now.*
- Famous brands and their celebrity spokespeople, such as Nike's athlete endorsers.
- Product claims that turn out to be overstated or just plain false, causing doubt about the trustworthiness of a company.
- Marketing departments "own" an organization's marketing initiative.

Exhibit 1.1 expands on these examples of common stereotypes and misconceptions about marketing.

Behind the Misconceptions

Several important factors have contributed to the development of these misconceptions: marketing's inherent visibility and its tendency toward buzzwords and "spin."

| EXHIBIT 1.1 | Marketing Misconceptions: What Marketing Is *Not* |

MISCONCEPTION NO. 1: Marketing is all about advertising.

THE REALITY: Advertising is just one way that marketing is communicated to potential customers. Advertising is highly visible to the general public, so many people naturally think of advertising when they think of marketing. A famous axiom: *Good advertising makes a bad product fail faster.*

MISCONCEPTION NO. 2: Marketing is all about selling.

THE REALITY: The general public also experiences a lot of selling. Much of this day-to-day selling is in retail store environments. Selling, or more correctly "personal selling," is simply another method of marketing communication. Marketers have to decide on a mix of marketing communication approaches that (in addition to advertising and personal selling) might also include public relations/publicity, sales promotion, and direct marketing. Later chapters discuss how and when each might be most effective in communicating the message.

MISCONCEPTION NO. 3: Marketing is all about the *sizzle*.

THE REALITY: Yes, some aspects of marketing are inherently fun and glitzy. Hiring Tiger Woods as a celebrity spokesperson had to be a real thrill for everybody at Nike, not to mention the pleasure and fun it gave Nike fans. But marketing also has aspects that involve sophisticated research, detailed analysis, careful decision making, and thoughtful development of strategies and plans. For many organizations, marketing represents a major investment and firms are naturally reluctant to invest major resources without a reasonable level of assurance of a satisfactory payback.

MISCONCEPTION NO. 4: Marketing is inherently unethical and harmful to society.

THE REALITY: Marketing is no more inherently unethical than other business areas. The accounting scandals at Enron, WorldCom, and other firms in the early 2000s show that to be true. However, when some element of marketing proves to be unethical (or even illegal), it tends to be visible to the general public. Untrue advertising claims, arm-twisting sales tactics, and nonenvironmentally friendly product packaging are a few very visible examples of marketing not behaving at its best.

MISCONCEPTION NO. 5: Only marketers market.

THE REALITY: Everybody does marketing. Everybody has a stake in the success of marketing. Regardless of your position in a firm or job title, learning how to do great marketing is a key professional asset. People with strong marketing skills achieve greater success—both on the job and off. If you've never thought of yourself in the context of being a "personal brand" that needs to be effectively communicated, just consider how useful such an approach could be in job seeking or positioning yourself for a promotion.

MISCONCEPTION NO. 6: Marketing is just another cost center in a firm.

THE REALITY: The mind-set that marketing is a cost, rather than an investment, is deadly in a firm because costs are inherently to be reduced or avoided. When management doesn't view marketing as earning its keep—that is, marketing being able to pay back its investment over the long term—it becomes very easy for firms to suboptimize their success in the long run by avoiding investment in brand and product development in favor of cutting costs. This is the classic argument that successful firms must simultaneously monitor costs to ensure short-term financial performance while also investing in marketing to ensure long-term competitive strength.

Marketing Is Highly Visible by Nature

Unlike most other key areas of business, marketing as a field is highly public and readily visible outside the confines of the internal business operation. Think of it this way: Most aspects of financial management, accounting, information technology, production, operations management, and human resource management take place behind the curtain of an organization, out of the general public's sight. But marketing is very different. A good portion of marketing is very public. Marketing is seen through the Web page that stimulates interest in seeking more product information, the (hopefully) good service received from the salesperson representing a firm's products, the enjoyment and interest generated from a clever advertisement on Super Bowl Sunday, or the well-stocked shelves at the neighborhood Target Store.

> At toy manufacturer Hasbro, marketing plays a key role in guiding the company so that it stays relevant. When Hasbro surveyed prospective customers, it learned that people have hectic schedules—they don't have time to play a game for three hours. "So we're asking ourselves how we can leverage brands so they can be played in smaller time frames," said Jill Hambley, vice president of marketing. The result is a focus on quick-playing games and on new "express" versions of old favorites.[2]

Of all the business fields, marketing is almost certainly the most visible to people outside the organization. While the other fields also have negative stereotypical images (think accountants with green eyeshades or IT computer geeks), you'd be hard pressed to identify another business field about which nearly everyone has formed a deeply held set of images and opinions or about which nearly everybody thinks they know enough to confidently offer advice! Think about how many times casual conversation in a social setting turns to something marketing related. Have you ever had similar social exchanges about the ins and outs of financial management or the complexities of computerized production systems? Of course not, but it seems almost anybody is comfortable talking about elements of marketing—from the week's advertised specials at the supermarket to this year's fashion for kids heading back to school to the service received at a favorite vacation hotel—marketing is a topic everyone can discuss!

> One topic of conversation these days is the marketing of luxury goods to teenagers. Teens today are much more brand-aware because they're surrounded by brand references from Web sites, rap music, movies, magazines, and MTV. Many are showered with the best of everything from their baby boomer parents. Leather-goods maker Dooney & Bourke has developed a line of purses aimed squarely at teens. The "It" collection of purses ranges from $65 for a "bitsy" bag to $225 for a gym bag.[3]

Why is the notion that marketing is visible and accessible to nearly everyone so important to students of marketing management? The truth is, despite the fact that much of marketing is easily observable to just about anyone, marketing as a professional field worthy of serious study doesn't always get the respect it deserves, maybe in part because of its overexposure. The business functions of financial management, operations, IT, and the rest seem to be viewed by many MBA and undergraduate students (and also unfortunately by managers in many firms) as the more "serious" parts of an enterprise—topics that are perceived as more concrete, more scientific, and more analytical than marketing, thus implying they are topics worthy of more substantial investment in time, money, and other resources.[4] In the past, marketing has had few useful metrics or measures to gauge the performance impact of a firm's marketing investment, while other areas of the firm have historically been much more driven by measurement of results. The old adage "if it can't be measured, it can't be managed" has plagued marketing for years. This is changing, and today measurement of marketing's performance and contribution is a focal point in many firms.[5] In fact, so many great marketing metrics are available that we've included a whole chapter on the topic at the end of the book.

Marketing Is More Than Buzzwords

Given the inherently transparent nature of marketing and the prior lack of ways to effectively measure its impact on a firm's success, it should be no surprise that some managers consider marketing to be little more than a necessary evil—a *cost* they reluctantly have to incur.[6] They're not sure *how* marketing works, or even *if* marketing really does work, but for competitive reasons—or maybe just because it's always been done—they continue to invest large sums of money in its many facets including market research, brand development, advertising, salespeople, public relations, and so forth. With so much ambiguity historically surrounding the management and control of marketing, a "flavor of the month" club mentality has developed around the field of marketing, often promoted by consultants and authors looking to make a quick buck by selling their latest and greatest ideas complete with their own catchy buzzwords for the program.

Anyone who doubts the pervasiveness of quick-fix approaches to marketing should visit a bookstore or online bookseller. Go to the business section and look at the marketing titles. Among the buzzwords right in the book titles are such gems as *guerilla marketing, permission marketing, holistic marketing, marketing warfare, marketing rainmaking, buzz marketing, integrated marketing* . . . the list goes on and on. While there be some germ of usefulness in each of these approaches, the circus-like atmosphere surrounding the field has detracted from its position as a respectable business function.

Hilton communicates its image as a customer-friendly company by its "Be Hospitable Index."

Beyond the Misconceptions and Toward the *Reality* of Modern Marketing

Of course, buzzwords are just window dressing, and most popular press prescription approaches to marketing don't do much to improve the *long-term* performance of an organization. Effective marketing management isn't about buzzwords or quick fixes. Nor is the essence of marketing really about the kinds of stereotypical viewpoints identified earlier in this section. In today's business milieu, marketing is a central function and set of processes essential to any enterprise.[7] Moreover, leading and managing the facets of marketing to improve individual, unit, and organizational performance—**marketing management**—is a *core business activity,* worthy of any student's study and mastery.

> Chinese audio manufacturers offer great sound at great prices. Their products, such as CD players, are attracting attention. But Chinese companies are realizing that ultimately marketing determines success, says Ling Junyan, chief designer with Chengu Xindak Electronic, which makes amplifiers and CD players. "Our products are strong, but our marketing is weak," says Ling. "That's what we need to do, market—not just sell our image but build up service centers, improve our reliability, build quality, and learn what Western listeners want."[8]

The chapters that follow lay the groundwork for developing the knowledge and skills around marketing that will allow you to build a more successful career as a leader and manager, regardless of department, area of specialization, level in the organization, or job title. Is marketing relevant to *you?* You bet it is, because *everyone* in an organization does marketing in some way and must share ownership of its success or failure.

Learning about marketing management is not just about reading a book or taking a course, although dedication to these activities is a great starting point. Instead, great marketing is a lifelong journey that requires dedication to continuous learning and improvement of your knowledge and skills as a leader and manager. It is in this spirit that we enthusiastically invite you to begin your journey into the field of marketing management!

DEFINING MARKETING

Over 50 years ago, the late management guru Peter Drucker, often referred to as the father of modern management, set the stage for defining contemporary marketing and conceiving of its potential power. Consider this quote from Drucker, circa 1954 (emphasis added):

> If we want to know what a business is we have to start with its *purpose*. There is only one valid definition of business purpose: *to create a customer*. It is the customer who determines what a business is. For it is the customer, and he alone, who through being willing to pay for a good or service, converts economic resources into wealth, things into goods. What the business thinks it produces is not of first importance—especially not to the future of the business and its success. What the customer thinks he is buying, what he considers "value" is decisive. . . . Because it is the [purpose of a business] to create a customer, [the] business enterprise has two—and only two—business functions: *marketing* and *innovation*.[9]

Consider the power of these ideas: a business built around the customer with resources and processes aligned to maximize customer value. Within this context, Drucker is not talking just about "marketing departments," but rather marketing in much broader terms. More on that distinction later. For now, consider this subsequent quote from Drucker circa 1973:

> Marketing is so basic that it cannot be considered a separate function (i.e., a separate skill or work) within the business . . . it is, first, a central dimension of the entire business. It is the *whole business* . . . seen from the *customer's* point of view. Concern and responsibility for marketing must, therefore, permeate all areas of the enterprise.[10]

Clearly, Peter Drucker was a man whose business philosophy was way ahead of his time. Now fast forward to this decade. In late 2007, after numerous iterations and refinements with input from literally hundreds of marketers, the American Marketing Association unveiled its new official definition of marketing, which you saw at the very beginning of this chapter: Marketing is the activity, set of institutions, and processes for creating, communicating, delivering, and exchanging offerings that have value for customers, clients, partners, and society at large.

Exhibit 1.2 provides two prior AMA marketing definitions. It is interesting to compare them.

In general, when compared to the earlier definitions of marketing in Exhibit 1.2, the 2007 definition:

- Focuses on the more *strategic* aspects of marketing, which positions marketing as a core contributor to overall firm success.
- Recognizes marketing as an activity, set of institutions, and processes—that is, marketing is not just a "department" in an organization.
- Shifts the areas of central focus of marketing to *value*—creating, communicating, delivering, and exchanging offerings of value to various stakeholders.

Just who are the relevant stakeholders of marketing? **Marketing's stakeholders** include any person or entity inside or outside a firm with whom marketing interacts, impacts, and is impacted by. For example, internal stakeholders—those

EXHIBIT 1.2	Historical Definitions of Marketing

AMA OFFICIAL DEFINITION—1948; REAFFIRMED 1960

Marketing is the performance of business activities that direct the flow of goods and services from producers to consumers.

Comment:

This definition reflects marketing's roots in physical distribution. Historically, marketing as a recognized field originally emanated from the movement of agricultural commodities from farmer through intermediaries to end-user consumers. Over the years the concept was expanded to include all kinds of goods and services, agricultural and otherwise.

AMA OFFICIAL DEFINITION—1985

Marketing is the process of planning and executing the conception, pricing, promotion, and distribution of ideas, goods, and services to create exchanges that satisfy individual and organizational objectives.

Comment:

This definition is highly reflective of the 4Ps, or *marketing mix*, approach to marketing—product (here "conception"), pricing, promotion, and place (distribution). Note the emphasis on "creating exchange." *Exchange* as a central role in marketing gained prominence during the 1980s and 1990s. That is, marketing is the facilitating force of exchange of something of value between two or more parties.

---

inside a firm—include other organizational units that marketing interacts with in the course of business. Strong, productive relationships between marketing and finance, accounting, production, quality control, engineering, human resources, and many other areas in a firm are necessary in order for a firm to do business successfully.[11] The range of external stakeholders—those outside a firm—is even broader and includes customers, vendors, governmental bodies, labor unions, and many others. One important challenge in marketing management is deciding how to prioritize these internal and external stakeholders in terms of their relevance and importance to the firm.[12] Most firms place the customer first, but a key question is: how do you decide which of the others deserve the most attention?

At the broadest conceptual level, members of society at large can be viewed as a stakeholder for marketing, a concept called **societal marketing.** As one example, the concept of environmentally friendly marketing, or *green marketing,* has been a growing trend in socially responsible companies. Today the movement has evolved into a part of the philosophical and strategic core of many firms under the label **sustainability,** which refers to business practices that meet humanity's needs without harming future generations.[13] Sustainability practices have helped socially responsible organizations incorporate *doing well by doing good* into their overarching business models so that both the success of the firm and the success of society at large are sustained over the long term. Ethical Dimension 1 takes a look at environmentally friendly marketing at several firms.

Green marketing isn't a theme one might expect to see Waste Management, Inc., conveying, yet they have a powerful environmental message.

ETHICAL DIMENSION 1

The Green Product Challenge

Environmental awareness coupled with a sense of social responsibility is leading many companies to assess their environmental policies and business practices. Some companies such as General Electric are developing environmentally sensitive products while others such as Starbucks have adopted tough recycling programs that minimize environmental waste. Companies worldwide acknowledge a concern for the environment, seek to minimize environmental damage, and commit resources to their environmental programs.

One challenge for manufacturers around the world is to transform environmentally harmful products into environmentally friendly products. In some industries, making products more environmentally safe has been relatively straightforward. For instance, air conditioner manufacturers moved from the refrigerant known by the brand name Freon to a more environmental friendly product, Puron, that reduced chlorine emissions and depletion of the ozone layer.

In other situations, it is more difficult to create environmentally sensitive products. Consider Nike, a company that built its running shoe business through outstanding products and creative marketing communications. A key product feature for Nike has been a small pocket of air in its Nike Air shoes. The extra cushion was a significant product innovation when it was introduced and proved to be a major market differentiator for the company. However, the pocket of "air" was not just air; it also contained a small amount of sulfur hexafluoride or SF6, a gas that damages the ozone layer.

In 1992 questions about Nike's use of SF6 gas became public. While the Nike air cushion was a key factor in the company's success, Nike realized that continued use of SF6 posed an environmental problem.

Unfortunately, replacing SF6 with a solution that minimized environmental damage while providing the same product benefits (long-lasting cushion and support) proved challenging.

After millions of dollars and 14 years, a team of 60 Nike engineers replaced the old product with a new, greener solution using sophisticated manufacturing techniques to replace the SR6 with nitrogen. The AirMax 360 was the first shoe to incorporate the new technology. Interestingly, the new shoe actually increases comfort and weighs less than older models, making the environmentally sensitive solution the best business solution as well. Nike's focus on product performance and technical innovation created a better, environmentally friendly product that is successful in the marketplace.

As part of the product development process, Nike kept environmental groups informed of the progress. While there were tensions as the process took longer than anyone planned (14 years), the communication between Nike and stakeholders helped minimize long-term negative publicity. The challenge for marketers is finding the right balance between consumer demand and environmental stewardship.[14]

Ethical Perspective

1. **Nike:** How would you prioritize what are often two conflicting demands: consumer product performance expectations and the demand for eco-friendly products?

2. **Consumers:** Would you choose a Nike shoe that provided less comfort but was more environmentally friendly? Would you pay a premium for an environmentally friendly Nike shoe?

3. **Environmental groups:** Nike took 14 years to create a new sole for its air cushion; would you allow a company that much time to deal with an environmentally damaging product?

Value and Exchange Are Core Marketing Concepts

Throughout the various topics encompassed within this book, the idea of value as a core concept in marketing will be a central theme. From a customer's perspective, we define **value** as a ratio of the bundle of benefits a customer receives from an offering compared to the costs incurred by the customer in acquiring that bundle of benefits.[15] Another central tenet of marketing is the concept of **exchange,** in which a person gives up something of value to them for something else they desire to have.[16] Usually an exchange is facilitated by money, but not always. Sometimes people trade or barter nonmonetary resources such as time, skill, expertise, intellectual capital, and other things of value for something else they want. For any exchange to take place, the following five conditions must be present:

1. There must be at least two parties.
2. Each party has something that might be of value to the other party.
3. Each party is capable of communication and delivery.
4. Each party is free to accept or reject the exchange offer.
5. Each party believes it is appropriate or desirable to deal with the other party.

Just because these conditions exist does not guarantee that an exchange will take place. The parties must come to an agreement that results in both being better off, hence the phrase in the AMA definition of marketing "... exchanging offerings that *have value*...(emphasis added)." Value implies that both parties win from the exchange.

> "Our job in marketing is to define what value we are providing," said Randy Susan Wagner, CMO of Orbitz. Orbitz sells airline tickets, but it also sells hotel and car rentals as part of the package. The value comes in the whole package, like an "extra value meal" at McDonald's, Wagner says.[17]

The AMA definition of marketing highlights marketing's central role in creating, communicating, delivering, and exchanging offerings that have value. But marketing's central focus hasn't always been on value and customer relationships, and the truth is that even today some firms lag in these areas. The next section offers perspectives on marketing's roots and evolution, and explains why some firms today are frozen in past approaches to marketing.

MARKETING'S ROOTS AND EVOLUTION

In the spirit of the old adage that he who ignores history is doomed to repeat its mistakes, here's a short marketing history lesson. Exhibit 1.3 illustrates the flow of marketing's evolution as a field.

Pre-Industrial Revolution

Before Henry Ford and his contemporaries created assembly lines and mass production, marketing was done very much on a one-to-one basis between firms and customers, although the word *marketing* wasn't really used. Consider what happened when a person needed a new pair of shoes, pre-industrial revolution. One would likely go visit the village cobbler, who would take precise measurements and then send the customer away with instructions to return in a week or so to pick up the new shoes. Materials, styles, and colors would be limited, but customers likely would get a great fit since the cobbler created a customized pair of shoes for

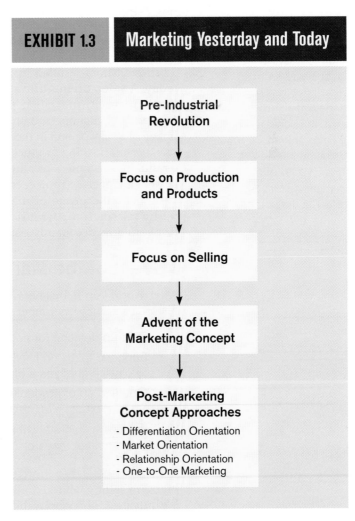

| EXHIBIT 1.3 | Marketing Yesterday and Today |

Pre-Industrial Revolution

↓

Focus on Production and Products

↓

Focus on Selling

↓

Advent of the Marketing Concept

↓

Post-Marketing Concept Approaches
- Differentiation Orientation
- Market Orientation
- Relationship Orientation
- One-to-One Marketing

each person. And if they didn't fit just right, the cobbler would adjust the shoes to a customer's liking—right on the spot.

Focus on Production and Products

The industrial revolution changed nearly everything in business by shifting the focus from meeting demand one item at a time to mass production via assembly line. Maximizing production capacity utilization became a predominant concern. For the early part of the 20th century, the focus was on this **production orientation** of improving products and production efficiency without much regard for what was going on in the marketplace. In fact, consumers snapped up this new pipeline of reasonably priced goods, even if the products didn't give much choice in style or function. Having a Ford Model T was great, but as Henry Ford himself said, "People can have the Model T in any color—so long that it's black."[18]

A production orientation assumes that customers will beat a path to your door just because you have a great product that functions nicely; build a better mousetrap and they will come. You will learn throughout your study of marketing management that great products alone do not assure success. Unfortunately, firms that are stuck in a production orientation mentality likely will have great difficulty competing successfully for customers.

Focus on Selling

Around the end of World War I, production capacity utilization began to decline for several reasons. First, capacity had been increased greatly for the war. Second, a number of firms that had dominated their respective industries before the war now found themselves with stiff competition for sales because many new competitors had flooded into the marketplace. And third, financial markets were becoming more sophisticated and were placing more pressure on firms to continually increase sales volume and profits.

These factors resulted in the rise of many of the great sales organizations of today. A **sales orientation** suggests that, to increase sales and consequently production capacity utilization, professional salespeople need to "push" product into the hands of customers, both businesses and end users. For years, the most vivid image of a salesperson in the public eye was that of the peddler, the classic outside salesperson pushing product on customers with a smile, promise, and handshake. Gradually, customers of all kinds grew wary of high-pressure selling, sparking laws at all levels to protect consumers from unscrupulous salespeople. For many customers, the image of marketing became permanently frozen as that of the pushy salesperson. And just as with the production orientation, to this day some firms still practice mainly a sales-oriented approach to their business.

Advent of the Marketing Concept

After World War II, business began to change in many long-lasting ways. Business historians point to a number of reasons for this shift, including:

- Pent-up demand for consumer goods and services after the war.
- Euphoric focus on family and a desperate need to regain a normalcy of day-to-day life after years of war (which produced the baby boomer generation).
- Opening up of production capacity dominated for years by war production.
- Advent of readily available mainframe computing capability, and especially the associated statistical analytic techniques that allowed for more sophisticated market research.

In the 1950s, these forces, combined with growing frustration with high-pressure selling, sparked a shift in the focus of American business. The resulting business philosophy has been labeled the **marketing concept,** which is an organization-wide customer orientation with the objective of achieving long-run profits.[19] General Electric's *1952 Annual Report* is often cited as the first time the marketing concept was articulated in writing by a major corporation. Clearly delighted to herald its new-age management philosophy, GE wrote the following to stockholders in its *1952 Annual Report* (in this historical period, the assumption was that business professionals would be male):

> [The marketing concept]. . .introduces the marketing man at the beginning rather than at the end of the production cycle and integrates marketing into each phase of the business. Thus, marketing, through its studies and research, will establish for the engineer, the design and manufacturing man, what the customer wants in a given product, what price he is willing to pay, and where and when it will be wanted. Marketing will have authority in product planning, production scheduling, and inventory control, as well as in sales distribution and servicing of the product.[20]

The articulation of the marketing concept was a major breakthrough in business, and in the 1960s and '70s it spread like wildfire throughout companies of all kinds. Soon firms everywhere were adopting the practice of letting the market decide what products to offer. Such an approach required substantial investment in ongoing market and consumer research and also necessitated an organization-wide commitment to marketing planning. As a result, the idea of the marketing plan became codified in most organizations' business processes. We'll come back to the idea of marketing planning in Chapter 2.

Charitable organizations like AIDS awareness group UNTIL.org often use celebrities and sophisticated imagery in their approach to gaining loyal donors.

The Marketing Mix

The articulation of the marketing concept and its quick adoption across a gamut of industries quickly led to a major focus on teaching marketing courses in colleges and universities. In the mid-1960s, a convenient way of teaching the key components was developed with the advent of the **marketing mix,** or **4Ps of marketing,** originally for *product*, *price*, *place*, and *promotion*.[21] The idea was that these fundamental elements comprise the marketer's "tool kit" to be applied in carrying out the job. It is referred to as a "mix" because, by developing unique combinations of these elements, marketers set their product or brand apart from the competition. Also, an important rubric in marketing is the following: making a change in any one of the marketing mix elements tends to result in a domino effect on the others.

Today, the basic concept of the marketing mix still persists but with considerably greater sophistication than in the 1960s. The product is now regarded broadly in the context of an overall *offering*, which could include a bundle of goods, services, ideas (for example, intellectual property), and other components, often represented by strong overarching branding. Many marketers today are more focused on *solutions* than products—the characterization of an offering as a solution is nice because of the implication that a solution has been developed in conjunction with specific, well-understood customer wants and needs.[22] Price today is largely regarded in relationship to the concept of value. *Place* has undergone tremendous change. Rather than just connoting the process of getting goods from Point A to Point B, firms now understand that sophisticated, integrated supply chain approaches are a crucial component of business success.[23] And finally, to grasp the magnitude of changes in *promotion* since the 1960s one need only consider the proliferation of high-tech media options available to marketers today, from the Internet to cell phones and beyond.

Over the years some authors have proposed various additions to the original marketing mix—that is, adding "more Ps." Especially outside the setting of marketing physical goods, as in the context of marketing services or ideas, the case is frequently made for the need to add more elements to the marketer's tool kit.[24] This issue has been hotly debated for years. You will find as you progress in your reading of this book that we follow the basic topical flow of creating, communicating, delivering, and exchanging offerings that have value. Thus, in terms of the marketing mix, Part 3 of the book focuses on *creating* the value offering through positioning, product development and branding, attention to service, and effective pricing. Then, Part 4 focuses on communicating and delivering the value offering through effective supply chain management and retailing and via integrated marketing communication. Thus, the core elements of the original 4Ps of marketing are there, but presented within the context of the terminology and work processes used by *today's* marketing managers.

Beyond the Marketing Concept

Close perusal of the definition of the marketing concept reveals several issues that still resonate widely in today's business milieu. The decision to place the customer at the core of the enterprise (often referred to as a **customer-centric** approach to business), focus on investment in customers over the *long term*, and marketing as an *organization-wide* issue (that is, not just relegated to a "marketing department") are all relevant and important topics in business classes and boardrooms today, and each will be discussed further in later chapters.[25] Referring again to Exhibit 1.3, the four evolutionary steps beyond the original marketing concept warrant further discussion now: differentiation orientation, market orientation, relationship orientation, and one-to-one marketing.

FYI

What does it mean to be customer-centric? For one thing, it means that top management devotes time and attention to customers. At retailer Cabela's, for example, Vice Chairman James W. Cabela spends hours each morning reading through customer comments and hand-delivering them to each department. He circles the issues that he wants resolved. This focus on the customer from the top signals to everyone in the organization that customer service is important. As Cabela's Vice President of Customer Relations Ron Spath says, "When Jim Cabela puts them on your desk, you pay attention."[26]

Differentiation Orientation

More sophisticated research and analytical approaches have made it possible to do increasingly precise refinement of market segmentation, target marketing, and positioning of products to serve very specific customer groups, processes you will learn more about in Chapter 9. The idea is to create and communicate **differentiation,** or what clearly distinguishes your products from those of competitors in the minds of customers.[27] The ability for marketers to tailor and deliver different product messages to different groups also has been greatly enhanced by the proliferation of multiple types of media that can be used with great precision to communicate to very specifically defined customer groups.

VF, manufacturer of Lee and Wrangler jeans, began seeing that its customers wanted more personal brands—brands that said something about who the customer was and what they do. For example, the brand should make a statement that the wearer is an outdoor adventurer. Of VF's Reef brand, Chairman and CEO Mackey McDonald says, "When you think of Reef, you think surfing. You think of the whole attitude and lifestyle of surfing. It gives you the opportunity to emotionally connect with the consumer."[28]

Market Orientation

A great deal of research has been devoted to learning how a firm can successfully put the marketing concept into practice. Think of **market orientation** as the implementation of the marketing concept. The notion of market orientation, one component of which is **customer orientation**—placing the customer at the core of all aspects of the enterprise—takes the guiding business philosophy of the marketing concept and works to more usefully define just how to implement it within a firm.[29] A central purpose of this book is to aid managers (and future managers) in adopting and implementing a market orientation in their firms.

Relationship Orientation

Marketing managers today recognize the power of securing, building, and maintaining long-term relationships with profitable customers.[30] The original marketing concept clearly recognized the need for an orientation toward the longer term in marketing—that is, not just making the next quarter's financial projections but rather cultivating customers for the long haul. The move toward a **relationship orientation** by firms has been driven by the realization that it is far more efficient and effective to invest in keeping and cultivating profitable current customers instead of constantly having to invest in gaining new customers that come with unknown return on investment.[31] Certainly most firms simultaneously focus on both current and new customers, but no company wants to be in a position of losing great customers and having to scramble to replace the associated lost revenue.

One way to build a long-term relationship with a customer is to imbue the brand with a more emotional tie to the consumer. Procter & Gamble is doing just that with its Tide brand of laundry detergent. Laundry detergent is a mundane product, but Tide's ads convey that women can focus on other things in their lives because they can rely on Tide to take care of the laundry. This elevates Tide "out of the laundry basket and into her life," says P&G's fabric care manager Kevin Burke.[32]

A relationship orientation draws its power from the firm's capability to effectively collect and use ongoing, real-time information on customers in marketing management decision making. Implementation of a relationship orientation is discussed in Chapter 4 in the context of customer relationship management (CRM). Much of CRM is designed to facilitate higher levels of customer satisfaction and loyalty, as well as to provide a means for identifying the most profitable customers—those worthy of the most marketing investment.[33]

One-to-One Marketing

Remember the earlier example of the pre-industrial revolution cobbler who would customize a pair of shoes for each customer? In many ways marketing's evolution has come full circle back to a focus on creating capabilities for such customization. In their books and articles, Don Peppers and Martha Rogers have popularized the term **one-to-one marketing,** which advocates that firms should direct energy and resources into establishing a learning relationship with each customer and

WHY FARMERS WITH DAUGHTERS OWN SHOTGUNS.

Pa won't like this one bit: Pure Sportster™ styling with a taste of the outlaw thrown in. A sound that could curdle the milk in a cow's udder. And 1200cc of Harley-Davidson® V-Twin built to roam far and wide. The Sportster 1200 Custom. All that. Plus plenty of torque for a quick getaway should the need ever arise. 1-800-443-2153 or www.harley-davidson.com. **The Legend Rolls On.™**

Harley markets itself as much more than just the physical motocycle it sells – instead, it's all about the experience and the community of those owning one.

then connect that knowledge with the firm's production and service capabilities to fulfill that customer's needs in as custom a manner as possible.[34]

Some firms come close to one-to-one marketing by employing **mass customization,** in which they combine flexible manufacturing with flexible marketing to greatly enhance customer choices.[35] The most famous example is Dell's Web site, which allows the customer to build a seemingly endless variety of combinations of features into a laptop or desktop to create a computer that, if not perfectly customized, certainly gives the buyer the strong impression of creating his or her very own machine.[36]

So far in this chapter we have explored common misconceptions about marketing and then moved well past the stereotypes to begin to gain a solid foundation for understanding what marketing management really is about today. Given the increasingly rapid pace of changes in today's business environment, it's highly likely that marketing's role will evolve even more rapidly than in the past. Let's look to the future to identify important change drivers that are sure to impact marketing over the next decade and beyond.

CHANGE DRIVERS IMPACTING THE FUTURE OF MARKETING

A great way to systematically explore the future of marketing is by considering several well-documented broad trends that are likely to impact the future of the field. These trends are well under way, but their ultimate impact on marketing and on business in general is not yet fully known. Five areas of shift are:

- Shift to product glut and customer shortage.
- Shift in information power from marketer to customer.
- Shift in generational values and preferences.
- Shift to demanding return on marketing investment.
- Shift to distinguishing Marketing ("Big M") from marketing ("little m").

Shift to Product Glut and Customer Shortage

Fred Wiersema, in his book *The New Market Leaders,* builds a powerful case that the balance of power is shifting between marketers and their customers, both in business-to-consumer (B2C/end user) markets and business-to-business (B2B) markets. He identifies "six new market realities" in support of this trend: Competitors proliferate, all secrets are open secrets, innovation is universal, information overwhelms and depreciates, easy growth makes hard times, and customers have less time than ever.[37] Wiersema's ideas are expanded in Exhibit 1.4.

The typical consumer is exposed to between 600 and 3,000 paid messages each day. Chipotle Mexican Grill founder M. Steven Ells decided to focus his advertising budget on giving away free samples. His rationale: Most people would enjoy the food and tell their friends. When Chipotle opened its midtown Manhattan restaurant, for example, it gave free burritos to 6,000 people at a cost of $35,000. In return, it got 6,000 "spokespeople" to talk about the restaurant to their friends.[38]

| EXHIBIT 1.4 | Fred Wiersema's New Market Realities |

Fred Wiersema has identified several factors, which he calls "new market realities," contributing to the shift to product glut and customer shortage.

COMPETITORS PROLIFERATE

Most companies are facing ever accelerating competition—sometimes referred to as *hypercompetition* because of the speed at which competitors and their products enter and leave markets. And this competition often comes from unexpected sources. For example, Boeing now lends money to customers to buy its planes, thus making Boeing a competitor of banks. And McDonald's famously missed for several years the trend of full-service restaurants such as Outback Steakhouse and TGI Friday's offering call-ahead drive-up food pickup, which in essence made this genre of restaurant faster and more convenient than the supposedly "fast-food" outlets like McDonald's.

ALL SECRETS ARE OPEN SECRETS

Today no company can expect its best practices to remain proprietary very long. Firms are becoming more adept at learning competitors' secrets and adapting them for their own purposes. Everybody seems to be imitating everybody else. The acceleration of technology and proliferation of information only exacerbate this process.

INNOVATION IS UNIVERSAL

Product life cycles keep getting shorter and continuous innovation is now *expected* and even common. It has gotten so frantic that customers are inundated with products (over 25,000 new packaged goods in a typical year) and suppliers are dizzy from pursuit of "the next best thing." Today, innovation is not optional; firms either innovate or perish.

INFORMATION OVERWHELMS AND DEPRECIATES

Everyone is swamped with information. Quoting Wiersema: "Junk mail fills mailboxes; magazines stuffed with ads run as long as 500 pages . . . advertisers stamp their logos on every conceivable surface, from cruising blimps and ski-lift towers to e-mail screens and bus roofs. Some television markets offer 200 cable channels. An Internet surfer discovers a Milky Way of random data, much of it conflicting and some of it stupefying." Our problem as managers today isn't how to generate and disseminate information, it's how to screen and prioritize it, digest the relevant portions, and make sense of how to apply it to our business challenges.

EASY GROWTH MAKES HARD TIMES

Growth as the overarching mantra of business has its drawbacks. U.S. carmakers routinely produce 30 to 40 percent more cars than can be readily sold. Airlines keep squeezing costs to pack more and more passengers into fewer and fewer planes and routes. The cellular phone industry continues to condense the number of providers to take advantage of network infrastructure and increased bandwidths. In industry after industry, technology and other factors make it possible to make more things faster. Yes, in business, growth *is* sacred but it can also lead to overcapacity, a shortage of customers, fewer sales, lowering prices, and ultimately falling margins and profits, especially when a focus on cost cutting for profit growth diminishes new product development.

CUSTOMERS HAVE LESS TIME THAN EVER

For a host of cultural and workplace-related reasons, many people today simply have very little time left in their daily lives for watching an ad or even shopping for a product! A company's biggest threat might not be its competitive rival, but rather the escalating demands on customers' time. Pressed for time and overstimulated by too many choices, people cope by tuning out. Brands and their messages have to catch people's attention in a nanosecond because that's all the time they will give. They are not paying attention; they are scanning. And this is going to keep getting much worse!

Wiersema's central point is that not only is a customer orientation desirable, but also in today's market it is a *necessity for survival.* Coming to grips with the impact of his six market realities greatly heightens the role of marketing in the firm as the nexus of an organization's customer-focused strategies.

What's the typical McDonald's customer like? Whether she's a working mom or a single man in his 20s, McDonald's "heavy user" customers have one thing in common: they're busy, busy, busy. "People don't sit down and have an organized meal today," says Marlene Schwartz of Yale University. "Eating is something you check off." The average American now eats out five times a week. Since 2003, 90 percent of McDonald's restaurants in the United States have extended their hours beyond the basic 6 a.m. to 11 p.m. daily, and 40 percent operate nonstop.[39]

Shift in Information Power from Marketer to Customer

Nowadays, customers of all kinds have nearly limitless access to information about companies, products, competitors, other customers, and even detailed elements of marketing plans and strategies. This is analogous to Wiersema's "All Secrets Are Open Secrets," but here we're talking about the customer's perspective. For decades, marketers held a degree of information power over their customers because firms had access to detailed and sophisticated information about their products and services that customers couldn't get without the help of somebody in the firm (usually a salesperson). Now, customers are empowered to access boundless information about all kinds of products and services on the Internet.[40]

For competitive reasons, firms have no choice but to be more open about their businesses and products. Even if they wanted to, firms can't stop chat rooms, independent Web sites, Web logs or blogs, and other customer-generated modes of communication from filling Web page after Web page with information,

State Farm and other traditional insurance firms are working hard to increase their appeal to younger customers that are focused on price and convenience.

disinformation, and opinions about a company's products, services, and even company dirty laundry. Consider Wal-Mart, one of the world's most successful companies. In recent years Wal-Mart has been caught off guard by the number and voracity of uncontrollable information sources about it and its activities. Another example of this shift in information power is the physician/patient relationship. Between open direct-to-consumer advertising by pharmaceutical companies and innumerable Web sites devoted to every medical malady, more and more patients arrive at the doctor's office self-diagnosed and ready to self-prescribe![41]

The trend toward more information in the hands of the customer is not going to diminish. Marketing approaches must be altered to reflect and respond to this important change.

Shift in Generational Values and Preferences

Aspects of generational marketing will be discussed in more detail in Chapter 9. For now, the inexorable shift in values and preferences from generation to generation deserves mention as one of the key trends affecting the future of marketing. One clear impact is on the firm's message and the method by which that message is communicated. For example, GenY consumers tend to be much more receptive to electronic commerce as a primary mode of receiving marketing communication and ultimately purchasing than are prior generations.[42] Yet, many of the big insurance firms continue to rely on face-to-face selling as their primary business model. State Farm, Allstate, and Farmers Insurance Group all have been affected by upstarts such as Progressive and GEICO, who appeal to a younger customer who is disinterested in being sold in person by an agent and more inclined to engage in a quick in-and-out transaction online or by phone—and often at a lower price. This preference has clear implications for how marketing carries out its management of customer relationships across generations and also calls into question how much *value* younger customers derive from the different approaches to relationships. That is, do members of the younger generation appreciate, or even need, the kinds of close personal relationships companies like State Farm provide through their agents, or are they perfectly happy to interact with firms exclusively through electronic means.

Generational shifts also impact marketing in terms of human resources. Consider how generational differences in attitudes toward work life versus family life, expectations about job satisfaction and rewards, and preferred modes of learning and working (e.g., electronic versus face-to-face) affect the ability of firms to hire people into various marketing-related positions. For example, firms often wish to differentiate themselves by offering great service to their

FYI

Michael Patrick Duffy, the CEO of the Financial Center Credit Union, wants to increase the number of 20-somethings who are customers of his credit union. To do so, he's talking with these future customers and listening to their needs. He created a series of podcasts called "Talkin' About the Benjamins" to offer financial advice. The segments are chatty, not preachy, and they offer tips on managing money. Duffy's approach seems to be working: The podcasts get more than 1,000 hits each month, and the number of customers age 18 to 29 has increased 6 percent in one year.[43]

customers. Yet, nearly all organizations are severely challenged today in hiring and keeping high-quality customer service personnel because of a severe shortage of capable, qualified customer care personnel.[44]

Generational changes are nothing new. Both in the context of customers and organization members, understanding the generational differences and how to work to appeal to different generations' values and preferences is a critical part of marketing management. Today, the importance of this issue is accentuated and accelerated in marketing due to propensities among generational groups to differentially use technology and the impact of generational differences on workplace design and management practice.

Shift to Distinguishing Marketing (Big M) from marketing (little m)

Earlier it was established that the marketing concept is intended to be an overarching business philosophy in which firms place the customer at the core of the enterprise. Also, you have learned through reading some of the stereotypical impressions of what marketing is (and is not) that marketing—at least the *image* of marketing—can be fairly fragmented and often quite tactical in nature. How can marketing as a discipline that is both strategic and tactical be rectified?

Begin by thinking of marketing as occurring on two dimensions within an organization. These dimensions exist in tandem, and even intersect on occasion, but still hold fundamental differences in goals and properties. For convenience, we can distinguish these dimensions by capitalizing the word for one ("Marketing"—"Big M") and leaving the word in lower case for the other ("marketing"—"little m"). Exhibit 1.5 portrays this relationship. Let's investigate these concepts further.

Marketing (Big M)

Marketing (Big M) serves as a core driver of business strategy. That is, an understanding of markets, competitors, and other external forces, coupled with attention to internal capabilities, allows a firm to successfully develop strategies for the future. This approach is often referred to as **strategic marketing,** which means a long-term, firm-level commitment to investing in marketing—supported at the highest organization level—for the purpose of enhancing organizational performance.

EXHIBIT 1.5 **Strategic and Tactical Marketing**

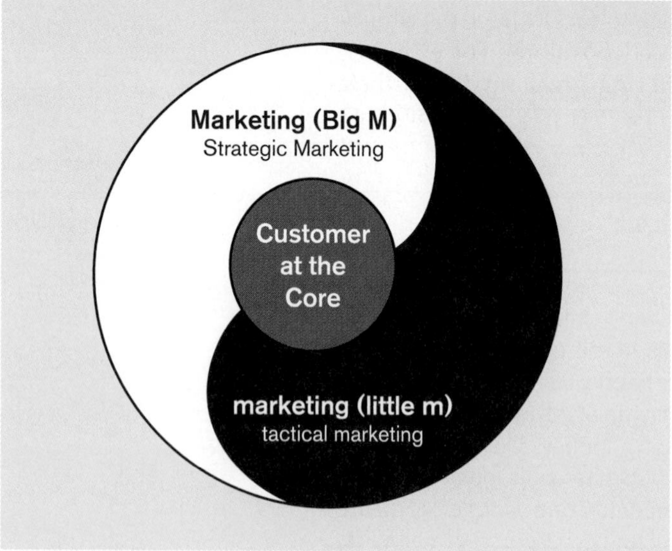

Marketing (Big M)
Strategic Marketing

Customer at the Core

marketing (little m)
tactical marketing

Going back to the AMA definition, marketing's focus as ". . . the activity, set of institutions, and processes for creating, communicating, delivering, and exchanging offerings that have value for customers, clients, partners, and society at large," contains substantial elements of Marketing (Big M): The core concepts of customer value, exchange, customer relationships, and benefit to the organization and its stakeholders are all very strategic in nature and help form the core business philosophy of a firm. Earlier we saw that the marketing concept includes a strong Marketing (Big M) thrust: ". . . an organization-wide customer orientation with the objective of achieving long-run profits." Certainly the core marketing concept characteristics of an organization-wide customer orientation and long-run profits are very strategic. Both the

AMA definition of marketing and the long-standing marketing concept provide evidence of the centrality of Marketing (Big M) to the firm as a core business philosophy.

The concept of Marketing (Big M) necessitates several important actions on the part of the organization to maximize marketing's impact. Consider these action elements required for successful Marketing (Big M):

- Make sure *everyone* in an organization, regardless of their position or title, understands the concept of customer orientation, which places the customer at the core of all aspects of the enterprise. It doesn't matter whether or not the organization member directly interfaces with customers outside the firm. The point is that everybody has customers within the organization, and through the process of effectively serving those internal customers, the firm can better serve its external customers. In this way, everyone in the firm has a stake in the success of Marketing (Big M).

- Align all internal organizational processes and systems around the customer. Don't let the IT system, telecommunications system, billing system, or any other internal process or system become an impediment to a customer orientation. If the people inside a firm understand the power of a customer-centric business approach, but the internal systems don't support it, Marketing (Big M) won't be successful.

- Find somebody at the top of the firm to consistently champion this Marketing (Big M) business philosophy. The CEO is the most appropriate person for this role, perhaps manifest through the CMO (chief marketing officer). Like anything else of importance in a business organization, Marketing (Big M) takes resources, patience, and time to acculturate and implement, and it won't happen unless someone at the top is consistently supportive, both with resources and leadership.

- Forget the concept that the marketing department is where Marketing (Big M) takes place. Marketing (Big M) is not about what one department does or does not do. Marketing (Big M) is the basis on which an organization approaches its whole enterprise—remember Peter Drucker's words: "[Marketing] is the *whole business* . . . seen from the *customer's* point of view. Concern and responsibility for marketing must, therefore, permeate all areas of the enterprise." Drucker was right!

- Create *market-driving*, not just *market-driven*, strategies. It is imperative to study the market and competition as part of the marketing planning process. Firms today must break out of linear thinking when developing new products and markets. Certainly research on markets and customers can uncover unmet needs and offer guidance on designing products to fulfill those needs. But the process contributes little toward **market creation**—approaches that drive the market toward fulfilling a whole new set of needs that customers did not realize was possible or feasible before. Classic examples of market creation include Microsoft's revolution of the information field, Disney's creation of the modern theme park industry, and Apple's revolution in integrated telecommunications via the iPhone. These were all market-driving strategies that created really new markets.

marketing (little m)

In contrast, **marketing (little m)** serves the firm and its stakeholders at a functional or operational level; hence, marketing (little m) is often thought of as **tactical marketing.** In fact, marketing (little m) almost always takes place at the functional or operational level of a firm. Specific programs and tactics aimed at customers and other stakeholder groups tend to emanate from marketing (little m).[45] But marketing (little m) always needs to be couched within the philosophy, culture, and strategies of the firm's Marketing (Big M). In this way, Marketing (Big M) and marketing (little m) should be quite naturally connected within a firm, as the latter tends to represent the day-to-day operationalization and implementation of the former. Everything from brand image, to the message salespeople and advertisements deliver, to customer service, to packaging and product features, to the chosen distribution channel—in fact, all elements of the marketing mix and beyond—exemplify marketing (little m).

Understanding these two dimensions of marketing helps clarify much of the confusion surrounding the field today. It certainly helps explain much of the confusion surrounding what marketing management is supposed to be, and how and why the field tends to have a bit of an identity crisis both inside firms and with the public at large. Occasionally throughout this book, the Marketing (Big M), marketing (little m) notion will be brought up to add explanatory power to important points. But for the most part, we'll just use one version of the word, assuming we all understand it contains both levels.

Shift to Justifying the Relevance and Payback of the Marketing Investment

The final change driver affecting the future of marketing is a topic on the minds of many CEOs and CMOs today. The issue is how management can effectively measure and assess the level of success a firm's investment in various aspects of marketing has had. Appropriate and effective **marketing metrics** must be designed to identify, track, evaluate, and provide key benchmarks for improvement just as various financial metrics guide the financial management of the firm.[46] The Marketing Science Institute (MSI) has commissioned research for the marketing field funded by a number of large companies. Every two years, MSI publishes a list of research priorities that top organizations are willing to fund with large sums of money to further the practice of marketing management. In recent years, the topic of marketing metrics has been one of the highest priorities for most MSI member companies, especially connecting appropriate metrics to marketing management decision making.[47]

Why the intense focus on metrics? Here are several important reasons:

- *Marketing is a fuzzy field.* Marketing has often historically viewed itself as working within gray area comfort zones of a business. That is, if what marketing contributed was mostly creative in nature, how can the impact of such activities effectively be measured? For the marketer, this can be a somewhat attractive position to be in, and historically many marketers probably took advantage of the idea that their activities were above measurement. Those days are over.

- *If it can't be measured, it can't be managed.* As with all aspects of business, effective management of the various aspects of marketing requires quantification of objectives and results. The marketing plan is one of the most important elements of a business plan. Effective planning requires metrics.

"The pharmaceutical industry has had very bad information on what drives prescribing, and what doesn't," said Mike Luby, president and CEO of TargetRx. "Most companies haven't had information to quantify the [marketing] impact, so they don't measure it, and so then they can't really manage it." Putting numbers to marketing means figuring out not only what is and isn't effective, but also why.[48]

- *Is marketing an expense or an investment?* Practicing marketers tend to pitch marketing internally as an investment in the future success of the organization. As an investment, it is not unreasonable that expected returns be identified and measured.[49]

- *CEOs and stockholders expect marketing accountability.* A few years ago, MSI published a report with the provocative title "Can Marketing Regain Its Seat at the Table?" The report centered on the fragmentation of marketing and ways marketing can recover its relevance in firms where it has become underutilized and undervalued, and has therefore lost its seat on the executive committee. One of the major conclusions of the report is that marketers need to create tools for ongoing, meaningful measurement of marketing productivity. More and more, CMOs are being held accountable for marketing performance in the same manner as are CFOs and leaders of other functional aspects of the business.[50]

This section has identified and examined several core change drivers that are sure to impact the future of marketing. Clearly, many other trends in the macro-level environment of business also affect marketing, including the obvious examples of globalization, ethnic diversification, and the growth and proliferation of technology.

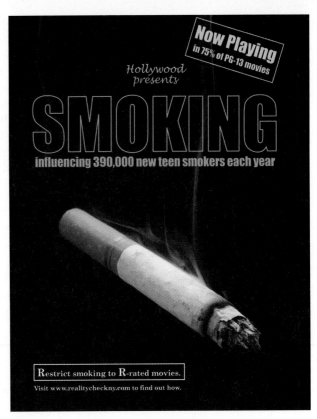

Marketing is a powerful tool in gaining regulatory changes.

Courtesy Tobacco Control Program, New York State Department of Health.

YOUR MARKETING MANAGEMENT JOURNEY BEGINS

Some students take the marketing management course because they "have to," not necessarily because they see inherent value in marketing for their career as a leader and manager. It is our hope that if you initially fell into this category, you can now see that gaining the knowledge and skills required for marketing management will increase your worth as an asset to any firm, regardless of your position or job title.

As you progress through this course, keep in mind that marketing management is not so much a position or a job title as it is a process and a way of approaching decision making about important business opportunities and challenges. Our presumption throughout this book is that you are seeking knowledge and skills that will enable you to use marketing to its fullest potential to positively impact organizational performance. Be assured from the outset that a high level of personal and career value can be derived by investing time and energy now in mastering the leadership and management of marketing.

SUMMARY

Marketing as an activity, set of institutions, and processes adds value to a firm and its internal and external stakeholders in many ways. For a marketing manager to be successful he or she must approach the job with a strong understanding of what it takes to do great marketing *today,* which because of a variety of change drivers is very different from doing marketing in the past. Leading and managing the facets of marketing in order to improve individual, unit, and organizational performance—marketing management—is a core business activity in today's business milieu, worthy of study and mastery by any student of business regardless of job title or professional or educational background.

KEY TERMS

marketing 4

marketing management 7

marketing's stakeholders 8

societal marketing 9

sustainability 9

value 10

exchange 10

production orientation 12

sales orientation 12

marketing concept 12

marketing mix (4Ps of marketing) 13

customer-centric 14

differentiation 14

market orientation 15

customer orientation 15

relationship orientation 15

one-to-one marketing 15

mass customization 16

Marketing (Big M) 20

strategic marketing 20

market creation 21

marketing (little m) 21

tactical marketing 21

marketing metrics 22

APPLICATION QUESTIONS

1. Consider the various marketing misconceptions introduced in this chapter.
   a. Pick any two of the misconceptions and develop a specific example of each from your own experience with firms and brands.
   b. How will it be beneficial for a new marketing manager to understand the misconceptions that exist about marketing?
   c. Can you come up with some other marketing misconceptions of your own—ones that are not addressed in the chapter?

2. In the chapter we make a strong case for the relevance of Peter Drucker's key themes today, even though much of his writing was done decades ago. Do you agree that his message was ahead of its time and is still relevant? Why or why not? Assume you are the CEO of a firm that wants to practice a market orientation. How will Drucker's advice help you to accomplish this goal?

3. Put yourself in the role of a marketing manager. From this perspective, do you agree with the concepts of societal marketing and sustainability? Why or why not? How does a focus on sustainability affect the marketing manager's role and activities? Identify two organizations that you believe do a great job of paying attention to sustainability and present the evidence that leads you to this conclusion.

4. Review the section on change drivers, including Fred Wiersema's list of new market realities. Select any two of the key change drivers (these can include any from Wiersema's list or any of the others) within the section. Pick an organization of your choice and answer the following questions:
   a. In what ways do each of the change drivers impact the firm's ability to successfully do marketing?
   b. How is the firm responding to the change drivers in the way it approaches its business? What should it be doing that it is not doing at present?

c. What role do you believe the marketing manager has in proactively preparing for these and future change drivers?

5. In the chapter you learned that harmonious performance of Marketing (big M) and marketing (little m) within a firm can lead to greater levels of success. Why is this true? What does it mean that these two need to be "harmonious"? What would be some likely negative consequences if they were out of sync?

MANAGEMENT DECISION CASE: Unilever Makes *Sustainability* "Business as Usual"

Standard b-school case drill would have presumed that in his former role as CEO of Unilever, Patrick Cescau would be totally fixated on finding new ways to sell more soap and shampoo than archrival P&G. But if you ask Cescau (who retired at the end of 2008) about the $52 billion Dutch-British consumer product conglomerate's biggest strategic challenge during his tenure, his reply is likely to be about water-starved villages in Africa or the planet's warming climate. A CEO off-message? Not hardly.

Unilever is but one example of best-practice companies that have moved past the tacit attention firms paid to "green marketing" in the 1990s (often largely more PR-focused than sincere changes in organizational culture) and on to an emerging global movement of *sustainability*—put simply, an enterprise doing well by doing good. Sustainability is an old ideal, broadly endorsed by economic development experts, environmentalists, and human rights activists, but until now too touchy-feely for most U.S. CEOs.

For firms with a sustainability focus, the entire planning approach to their business changes. Sustainability is at once a business philosophy, organizational culture, and overarching strategy. It frames the way business planning is done and impacts the relationships that customers (and employees) have with an organization and its brands. CEOs used to frame such initiatives in the context of social or moral responsibility, but now as Cescau says, "It's all about growth and innovation. In the future, it will be the only way to do business."

The world is Unilever's laboratory. In Brazil, the company operates a free community laundry in a São Paulo slum, provides financing to help tomato growers convert to eco-friendly "drip" irrigation, and recycles 17 tons of waste annually at a toothpaste factory. Unilever funds a floating hospital that offers free medical care in Bangladesh, a nation with just 20 doctors for every 10,000 people. In Ghana, it teaches palm oil producers to reuse plant waste while providing potable water to deprived communities. In India, Unilever employees help thousands of women in remote villages start micro-enterprises. And responding to green activists, the company discloses how much carbon dioxide and hazardous waste its factories discharge around the world.

As Cescau sees it, helping such nations wrestle with poverty, water scarcity, and the effects of climate change is vital to staying competitive in coming decades. Some 40 percent of the company's sales and most of its growth now occur in developing nations. Unilever food products account for roughly 10 percent of the world's crops of tea and 30 percent of all spinach. It is also one of the world's biggest buyers of fish. As environmental regulations grow tighter around the world, Unilever must invest in environmentally friendly technologies or its leadership in packaged foods, soaps, and other consumable goods could be imperiled.

Even in the "what have you done for me this quarter" obsessed U.S. executive suites, sustainability has moved past the stereotypical tree-hugger mind-set and into mainstream business planning. New sets of metrics designed to measure sustainability efforts have helped convince CEOs and boards that major investments in such initiatives pay off. Until recently, few Wall Street analysts, for example, have tried to assess how much damage Wal-Mart's reputation for poor labor and environmental practices did to the company's stock price. But New York's Communications Consulting Worldwide (CCW), which studies issues such as reputation, puts it in stark dollars and cents. CCW calculates that if Wal-Mart had a reputation like that of rival Target Corp., its stock would be worth over 8 percent more, adding $16 billion in market capitalization! This is not an isolated result; numbers for return-on-sustainability-investment show stronger financial performance nearly universally for sustainability-focused firms within any given competitive set.

According to the McKinsey Global Institute, more U.S. CEOs, especially younger ones, have sustainability at the top of their planning agendas. Concurrently, serious investment money is lining up behind the initiative. Assets of mutual funds that are designed to invest in sustainability-enlightened companies swelled from $12 billion in 1995 to nearly $200 billion in 2007. Today, business planning decisions have to include sustainability in the mix, for as Unilever's Cescau says, "You can't ignore the impact your company has on the community and environment."

Questions for Consideration

1. What stakeholders are served by sustainability efforts?

2. What are the advantages to the organization itself by investing in sustainability? What are potential downsides of not doing so?

3. How could a firm potentially measure the profit impact of its sustainability strategies?

Source: Pete Engardio, "Beyond the Green Corporation," *Business-Week*, January 29, 2007, pp. 50–60.

RECOMMENDED READINGS

1. Jim Collins, *Good to Great: Why Some Companies Make the Leap . . . and Others Don't* (New York: Collins, 2001).
2. Malcolm Gladwell, *The Tipping Point: How Little Things Can Make a Big Difference* (New York: Back Bay Books, 2002).
3. Chip Heath and Dan Heath, *Made to Stick: Why Some Ideas Survive and Others Die* (New York: Random House, 2007).
4. Chris Murray, *The Marketing Gurus: Lessons from the Best Marketing Books of All Time* (New York: Portfolio Hardcover, 2006).

CHAPTER 02

ELEMENTS OF MARKETING STRATEGY AND PLANNING

LEARNING OBJECTIVES

- Examine the concept of value and the elements and role of the value chain.

- Understand the conditions required for successful marketing planning, that marketing planning is focused on the value proposition, and that marketing planning is a dynamic process.

- Identify various types of organizational strategies.

- Conduct a situation analysis.

- Use the framework provided for marketing planning, along with the content in future chapters, to build a marketing plan.

EXECUTIVE PERSPECTIVE

Executive Robert D. Finfrock

Company Finfrock Design-Manufacture-Construct

Business Designer/builder of commercial buildings and manufacturer of precast/prestressed concrete structures

How does your company add value in the marketplace?

Our company adds value in the marketplace by lowering cost and lowering risk for our customers. We're in the construction industry, and we offer our customers something that's unique: We design commercial buildings for customers, manufacture the structures of these buildings, and also act as the general contractor. That combination is unique in our industry because typically one company does the design but a different company does the construction.

When separate companies are involved in these elements, the customer's risks and costs go up. Our company integrates the design, manufacture, and construction for customers, which means we save the customer money and can guarantee that the building can be built for a specific cost. We specialize in certain market sectors, particularly parking structures, student housing, and mixed-use buildings. By specializing in these sectors, we've developed deep experience to know how much it will cost to build one of these structures. We then use our manufactured product—precast/prestressed concrete—for the structures of all of these buildings.

How do you conduct marketing planning?

Our executive committee has biweekly meetings. One of the major topics of discussion is our strategic plan. The strategic plan lays out what we're going to do and where we're going and of course includes our marketing plan. We define our target markets, our reason for targeting them, and the logic behind our marketing strategy. We ask ourselves, "Where can we be competitive?" and "Is our approach consistent with good marketing?" From the marketing strategy, we move down to specific marketing tactics. For example, for us, our marketing tactics include using newsletters and attending trade shows in specific industries. The newsletters help our customers keep us in mind, and the trade shows introduce us to new customers.

Why is effectively developing and executing marketing strategies and tactics so critical to a firm's success today?

To be successful today, companies need to *differentiate* themselves from the competition. Developing and executing a marketing strategy, backed up by strong tactics, means thinking through what makes your company different and how it adds value to customers. A marketing strategy is not just about crafting an advertising message; it's about knowing what your value proposition is and creating that value in the first place. You can't just come up with a clever slogan; you have to execute on it on a daily basis. You have to *really deliver* the value proposition consistently to customers. Advertising is to differentiation what painting a house is to its design and construction. No matter how great the paint job, the paint can't hide the flaws of a home that is poorly designed and constructed.

Shop and not drop.

9 essential nutrients
active bodies need.
Perfect for 1-day sales.

got milk?

America's Milk Producers continue to market their product through strong personal appeals.

VALUE IS AT THE CORE OF MARKETING

In Chapter 1, the concept of value was introduced as a core element of marketing. Value was defined from a customer's perspective as a ratio of the bundle of benefits a customer receives from an offering compared to the costs incurred by the customer in acquiring that bundle of benefits. From the late management guru Peter Drucker's early writings in the 1950s through to the recently updated American Marketing Association official definition of marketing, it is clear that marketing plays a central role in creating, communicating, delivering, and exchanging offerings that have value.

Let's examine the idea of value a bit more carefully now. One can think of value as a ratio of benefits to costs, as viewed from the eyes of the beholder (the customer). That is, customers incur a variety of costs in doing business with any firm, be those costs financial, time, opportunity costs, or otherwise. For the investment of these costs, the customer has a right to expect a certain bundle of benefits in return. A **benefit** is some type of utility that a company and its products (and services) provide its customers. **Utility** is the want-satisfying power of a good or service.[1] Four major kinds of utility exist: form, time, place, and ownership. *Form utility* is created when the firm converts raw materials into finished products that are desired by the market. The other three utilities—*time, place,* and *ownership*— are created by marketing. They are created when products are available to customers at a convenient location when they want to purchase them, and facilities of *exchange* are available that allow for transfer of the product ownership from seller to buyer. Chapter 1 mentioned that facilitating exchange between buyers and sellers is another core element of marketing.

Since value is a ratio of benefits to costs, a firm can impact the customer's perceptions of value by altering the benefits, the costs, or both. Assume that a person is faced with the decision of buying one of two automobiles. One should expect that a purchase decision will be greatly influenced by the ratio of costs (not just monetary) versus benefits for each model. That is, it is not just pure price that drives the decision. It is price compared with all the various benefits (or utilities) that Car 1 brings versus Car 2.[2] These benefits could relate to availability, style, prestige, features—all sorts of factors beyond mere price.

What's the value proposition of a Jimmy Dean food product? It's not just a quick meal. Jimmy Dean marketers learned that customers want more than convenience; they want a homemade touch, even though they don't have a lot of time to cook. The company introduced Jimmy Dean Skillets, which combine different meats with potatoes, vegetables, and seasonings. Consumers simply add eggs, and they give a home-cooked feeling to the meal in under 10 minutes.[3]

Recall that marketing is charged not just with *creating* offerings that have value, but also with *communicating, delivering,* and *exchanging* those offerings. When a firm communicates the **value proposition** of its products to customers, the value message may include the whole bundle of benefits the company promises to deliver, not just the benefits of the product itself.[4] For example, when South Korean-based Samsung first brought its brand to the United States, it communicated a message centered primarily on functionality at a moderate price—a strategy designed to provide an advantage over pricier Japanese brands. But over time, Samsung's value proposition has expanded to include innovativeness, style, and dependability—the latter of which was helped significantly by high ratings of many of the company's products by sources such as *Consumer Reports.*[5]

For years, firms have been preoccupied with measuring **customer satisfaction,** which at its most fundamental level means how much the customer likes the product. However, for firms interested in building long-term customer relationships, having satisfied customers is not enough to ensure the relationship is going to last. A firm's value proposition must be strong enough to move customers past mere satisfaction and into a commitment to a company and its products and brands for the long run. Such a commitment reflects a high level of **customer loyalty,** which increases **customer retention** and reduces **customer switching.**[6]

Washington Mutual Bank (known as WaMu), which is now part of JPMorgan Chase, measures customer satisfaction at each of its branch locations, but it doesn't stop there. It also focuses on fostering loyalty. One way that WaMu encourages customer loyalty is by having "concierge" greeters at the entrance of each branch. The greeters, dressed in colorful shirts, make eye contact and help customers find where they need to go. Some branches even have a play area for kids.[7]

Customer loyalty almost always is directly related to the various sources of value the customer is presently deriving from the relationship with the company and its brands. Except in situations of monopoly (which creates forced loyalty), loyal customers by definition tend to also experience a high level of satisfaction.[8] However, not all satisfied customers are loyal. If a competitor comes along with a better value proposition, or if a value proposition begins to slip or is not effectively communicated, customers who are presently satisfied become good candidates for switching to another company's products.[9]

Hertz Rental Car reduces customer switching by being proactive. When long lines start to build at the counter, Hertz employees go out into the line with laptops to help customers rent cars quickly. Frequent Hertz customers can join Hertz's "#1 CLUB GOLD" and can skip the rental counter completely. Customers rated Hertz's car pick-up process significantly higher than the industry average.[10]

The Value Chain

A highly useful approach to bringing together and understanding the concepts of customer value, satisfaction, and loyalty is the **value chain.** Created by Michael Porter in his classic book *Competitive Advantage,* the value chain serves as a means for firms to identify ways to create, communicate, and deliver more customer value within a firm.[11] Exhibit 2.1 portrays Porter's value chain concept.

Basically, the value chain concept holds that every organization represents a synthesis of activities involved in designing, producing, marketing, delivering, and supporting its products. The value chain identifies nine relevant strategic activities the organization can engage in that create/impact both sides of the value equation: benefits and costs. Porter's nine **value-creating activities** include five primary activities and four support activities.[12]

The five *primary activities* in the value chain are:

1. *Inbound logistics*—how the firm goes about sourcing raw materials for production.

2. *Operations*—how the firm converts the raw materials into final products.

EXHIBIT 2.1   Porter's Value Chain

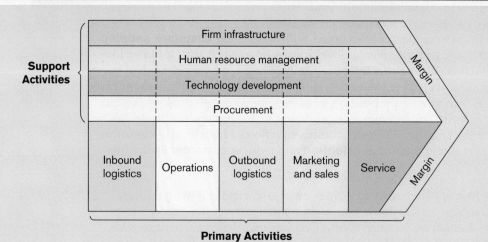

3. *Outbound logistics*—how the firm transports and distributes the final products to the marketplace.

4. *Marketing and sales*—how the firm communicates the value proposition to the marketplace.

5. *Service*—how the firm supports customers during and after the sale.

The four *support activities* in the value chain are:

1. *Firm infrastructure*—how the firm is set up for doing business; are the internal processes aligned and efficient.

2. *Human resource management*—how the firm ensures it has the right people in place, trains them, and keeps them.

3. *Technology development*—how the firm embraces technology usage for the benefit of customers.

4. *Procurement*—how the firm deals with vendors and quality issues.

The value chain concept is highly useful in understanding the major activities through which a firm creates, communicates, and delivers value for its customers. CEOs in recent years have been concentrating on *aligning* the various elements of the value chain, meaning that all facets of the company are working together to ensure that no snags will negatively impact the firm's value proposition.[13] From a customer's perspective, when the supplier's value chain is working well, all the customer tends to see are the *results* of a well-aligned value chain: quality products, good salespeople, on-time delivery, prompt service after the sale, and so on. However, it takes only one weak link in the value chain and the whole process of cultivating satisfied and loyal customers can be circumvented.

Consider, for example, what happens if a glitch in the value chain of one of Wal-Mart's vendors delays delivery of products at the peak selling season, resulting in stock-outs in Wal-Mart stores. If this happens repeatedly, it can damage the overall relationship Wal-Mart enjoys with its customers as well as the relationship between Wal-Mart and that supplier. To minimize the potential for this happening, Wal-Mart, as well as a growing list of other firms, requires all vendors to link with its IT system so that the whole process of order fulfillment and inventory management is as seamless as possible.[14]

One final element depicted at the end of the value chain is margin, which refers to profit made by the firm. Intelligent investment in the primary and support activities within the value chain should positively enhance profit margin through more efficient and effective firm performance.[15]

Planning for the Value Offering

The remainder of this chapter presents the approach that marketing managers use to plan for creating, communicating, and delivering the value offering. This is often referred to as **marketing planning**—the ongoing process of developing and implementing market-driven strategies for an organization—and the resulting document that records the marketing planning process in a useful framework is the **marketing plan.**[16]

MARKETING PLANNING IS BOTH STRATEGIC AND TACTICAL

Recall that one key trend identified in Chapter 1 was the practice of marketing on two dimensions or levels within an organization. Although these dimensions exist in tandem and even intersect on occasion, each holds fundamental differences in goals and properties. At the strategic level, Marketing (Big M) serves as a core driver of business strategy. That is, an understanding of markets, competitors, and other external forces, coupled with attention to internal capabilities, allows a firm to successfully develop strategies for the future. At the functional or operational level, marketing (little m) represents the specific programs and tactics aimed at customers and other stakeholder groups and includes everything from brand image, to the message salespeople and advertisements deliver, to customer service, to packaging and product features —in fact, all elements of operationalizing the marketing mix and beyond.[17]

Governmental entities such as the U.S. Army often do sophisticated marketing planning, as evidenced by this ad.

Marketing messages play to many stakeholders, including environmental regulators. The European Association of Communications Agencies, an association that represents Europe's leading advertising agencies, recognizes the need for good corporate citizenship. Therefore, it provides guidelines to ad agencies about marketing messages. For example, it suggests, "Speed or acceleration claims should not be the main message of an [automobile] advertisement." EACA wants to be proactive on issues of public interest, like global warming.[18]

Although these two levels of marketing are distinctly different in scope and activities, the common link is in the process of marketing planning. Marketing managers must be able to grasp both the big picture of strategy formulation and the details of tactical implementation. In fact, many a marketing plan has failed because either the formulation of the strategies was flawed or their implementation was poorly executed. A well-written marketing plan must fully address both Marketing (Big M) and marketing (little m) elements. Ultimately, the following must be in place for effective marketing planning to occur:

• *Everyone* in an organization, regardless of their position or title, must understand and support the concept of customer orientation, which places the customer at the core of all aspects of the enterprise. Firms who promote and practice a high level of customer focus are often referred to as *customer-centric* organizations.[19]

- To operationalize a customer-centric approach, all internal organizational processes and systems must be aligned around the customer. A firm's internal structure and systems cannot be allowed to become an impediment to a customer orientation.[20] Anyone who has ever placed a phone call for service and been driven through a maze of phone transfers with a string of people (or machines) unable to help knows how poor structure and systems can impact customer satisfaction and loyalty!

Enterprise Rent-A-Car is a customer-centric company. It measures customer satisfaction continuously using an "Enterprise Service Quality index" (ESQi). Enterprise ensures that its employees are aligned on customer service goals by tying employee rewards and promotions to customer satisfaction. For example, branch managers with a below-average score say they're in "ESQi jail" because they can't get promoted until their scores rise.[21]

- The CEO and others at the top of the organization must consistently set the tone for market-driven strategic planning through the customer-centric business philosophy. As with a firm's internal structure and systems, its culture must be supportive of such an approach in order for a marketing plan to be successful. Upper management must also support the process through consistent investment of resources necessary to make it work. Marketing planning is not a "sometimes" process; rather, it should be a driving force in the firm day in and day out.[22]

At this point in the learning process about marketing management, you may begin to feel concerned that you are getting a lot of structure for marketing planning but not enough specific content to fill in the elements of the marketing plan template. That reaction is quite natural, as by design the depth of content for most of the various sections of a marketing plan is covered later in the book. Your next task is to familiarize yourself with the overall process and framework for marketing planning so that as the content pieces unfold chapter by chapter, it will be very clear how those pieces fit together into a complete marketing plan. Beginning with this one, each chapter ends with an activity called "Building a Marketing Plan." These are designed to help you make the connections between the content in each chapter and the requirements of your marketing plan template.

ELEMENTS OF MARKETING PLANNING

To get you started, we'll first walk through the process and content involved in marketing planning. A condensed framework for this process is presented in Exhibit 2.2. Then at the end of this chapter you'll find an abbreviated marketing plan example for the fictitious company CloudCab Small Jet Taxi Service. You'll want to look at that appendix for an example of what the key elements of a marketing plan look like in practice.

Connecting the Marketing Plan to the Firm's Business Plan

How does a marketing plan fit into a firm's overall business planning process? As we have learned, marketing is somewhat unique among the functional areas of business in that it has the properties of being both a core business philosophy (Marketing, Big M) and a functional/operational part of the business (marketing,

EXHIBIT 2.2 | **Condensed Framework for Marketing Planning**

- Ensure the marketing plan is connected to the firm's business plan including organizational-level mission, vision, goals, objectives, and strategies.
- Conduct a situation analysis.
  - Macro-level external environment
  - Competitive environment
  - Internal environment
- Perform any needed market research.
- Establish marketing goals and objectives.
- Develop marketing strategies.
  - Product-market combinations
  - Market segmentation, target marketing, positioning

- Marketing mix strategies:
  - Product/branding strategies
  - Service strategies
  - Pricing strategies
  - Supply chain strategies
  - Integrated marketing communication strategies
- Develop implementation plans.
  - Programs/action plans for each strategy including timetable, assignment of responsibilities, and resources required
  - Forecasting and budgets
  - Metrics for marketing control
  - Provide for contingency planning.

little m). As such, all business-level strategy must be market-driven in order to be successful. Hence, the term **market-driven strategic planning** is often used to describe the process at the corporate or strategic business unit (SBU) level of marshaling the various resource and functional areas of the firm toward a central purpose around the customer.[23]

A great example of how these levels of planning fit together is General Electric. GE contains numerous SBUs that compete in very different markets, from lighting to jet engines to financial services. CEO Jeff Immelt oversees a **corporate-level strategic plan** to serve as an umbrella plan for the overall direction of the corporation, but the real action in marketing planning at GE is at the individual SBU level. Each GE business has its own **SBU-level strategic plan,** and part of GE's historical leadership culture has been to turn SBU management loose to run their own businesses under their own plans, so long as they meet their performance requirements and contribute satisfactorily to the overall corporate plan.

Portfolio Analysis

Portfolio analysis, which views SBUs and sometimes even product lines as a series of investments from which it expects maximization of returns, is one tool that can contribute to strategic planning in a multi-business corporation. Two of the most popular approaches are the **Boston Consulting Group (BCG) Growth-Share Matrix** and the **GE Business Screen.** These are portrayed in Exhibits 2.3 and 2.4.

The concept of the BCG approach to portfolio analysis is to position each SBU within a firm on the two-dimensional matrix shown in Exhibit 2.3. The competitive market-share dimension is the ratio of share to that of the largest competitor. The growth dimension is intended as a strong indicator of overall market attractiveness. Within the BCG matrix you find four cells, each representing strategy recommendations:

- *Stars* (high share, high growth): important to building the future of the business and deserving any needed investment.
- *Cash Cows* (high share, low growth): key sources of internal cash generation for the firm.

EXHIBIT 2.3

Boston Consulting Group Growth-Share Matrix

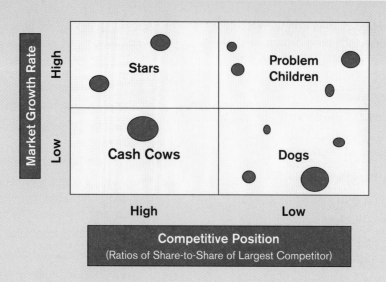

Market Growth Rate

High

Low

Stars

Problem Children

Cash Cows

Dogs

High

Low

Competitive Position
(Ratios of Share-to-Share of Largest Competitor)

EXHIBIT 2.4

GE Business Screen

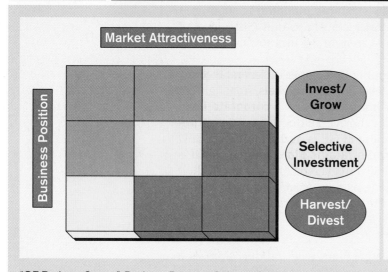

Market Attractiveness

Business Position

Invest/ Grow

Selective Investment

Harvest/ Divest

Business Position (high, medium, and low): Assess the firm's ability to compete. Factors include organization, growth, market share by segment, customer loyalty, margins, distribution, technology skills, patents, marketing, and flexibility, among others.

Market Attractiveness (high, medium, and low): For the market, assess size, growth, customer satisfaction levels, competition (quantity, types, effectiveness, commitment), price levels, profitability, technology, governmental regulations, sensitivity to economic trends, among others.[24]

"GE Business Screen," *Business Resource Software Online,* www.brs-inc.com/pwxcharts.asp?32, accessed May 16, 2008.

- *Dogs* (low share, low growth): potential high cash users and prime candidates for liquidation.
- *Problem Children,* or Question Marks (low share, high growth): high cash needs that, if properly nurtured, can convert into stars.[25]

For purposes of strategy development, the BCG matrix approach is seductively simple and has contributed to decision making about internal cash generation and usage across SBUs. It has also morphed in application downward to often be applied to product lines and product groups, which is nominally possible so long as costs and returns can be properly isolated for investment decisions. But by nature of simplicity, BCG ignores other important factors that should go into this decision making and also ignores the viability of generating cash externally.

The GE Business Screen, shown in Exhibit 2.4, is a more realistic and complex portfolio model. It also evaluates the business on two dimensions—market attractiveness and business position, which refers to its ability to compete. The investment decision is again suggested by the position on a matrix. A business that is favorable on both dimensions should usually be a candidate to grow. When both market attractiveness and business position evaluations are unfavorable, the harvest or divest options should be raised. When the matrix position is neither unambiguously positive nor negative, the investment decision will require more analysis.

For now, it is important to note that portfolio analysis does not offer a panacea for corporate strategy formulation. In fact, since the heyday of the use of portfolio analysis in the 1970s and 1980s, firms are more cautious in its application and recognize that it is but one approach to strategy decision making.[26]

Functional Level Plans

A firm's SBU plans all incorporate **functional-level plans** from operations, marketing, finance, and the other operational areas. Just as the individual SBU CEOs are held accountable for their unit's performance to Jeff Immelt within the context of GE's plan, each SBUs chief marketing officer, chief financial officer, and other operational-level executive is held accountable for the performance of his or her portion of the SBU plan to their own business unit CEO.[27] While GE's system certainly may be larger in scope and complexity than many business planning situations, the logic is the same regardless of the type or size of an organization. Hence, the marketing plan is nested within the context of an overall corporate and/or business-level strategic plan.

Before each of the sections of the marketing plan is identified and described, you are referred to Jet-Blue Airways as an example of a firm that has become noted for successful marketing planning. Why JetBlue as an example? Clearly, JetBlue's not perfect, and in the turbulent airline industry it's really tough to do great marketing planning. In Chapter 1 we discussed Fred Wiersema's "new market realities," one of which is "all secrets are open secrets." During his tenure as Chairman and CEO, JetBlue founder David Neeleman was quite transparent about his strategies and plans for the company, not only discussing them openly with the business press but also placing a substantial amount of organizational information on the company Web site. This approach has continued in the post-Neeleman era of the firm. And when JetBlue has made missteps, the company has been forthright in recognizing and addressing the errors. As each of the elements of the marketing planning process is described below, JetBlue will be used as a thematic example of each piece in practice.

Organizational Mission, Vision, Goals, and Objectives

Marketing planning does not occur in a vacuum; it must connect with the firm's overall mission and vision. A **mission statement** articulates an organization's purpose, or reason for existence. A well-conceived mission statement defines the fundamental, unique purpose that sets a company apart from other firms of its type and identifies the scope of a company's operations, products, and markets.[28]

Marketing planning and strategy, while analytical in nature, often yield very funny marketing communication programs.

FRESH STEP ® is a registered trademark of the Clorox Pet Products Company. Used with permission. FRESH STEP ® advertisement. © 2009 The Pet Products Clorox Company. Reprinted with permission. Photographer: Jill Greenberg.

Most mission statements also include a discussion of what the company would like to become in the future—its **strategic vision.** According to ex-GE CEO Jack Welch, "Good business leaders create a vision, articulate the vision, passionately own the vision, and relentlessly drive it to completion."[30] The vision of what the firm is capable of in the future and where it *wants* to go, as championed by its top leadership, sets the tone for everything that follows in the planning process. **Goals,** general statements of what the firm wishes to accomplish in support of the mission and vision, eventually become refined into specific, measurable, and (hopefully) attainable **objectives** for the firm.[31] Objectives at the corporate and SBU level provide the benchmarks by which organizational performance is assessed. Unfortunately, despite a formal mission, vision, goals, and objectives, it is all too easy for senior management and even the board of directors to become distracted and stray off course. Such action can create major problems both inside and outside the company, as demonstrated by the HP scandal featured in Ethical Dimension 2.

JetBlue Airways took to the air February 11, 2000, flying from John F. Kennedy International Airport in New York to Fort Lauderdale in Florida. Today, the upstart airline is rapidly becoming a major player, serving more than 50 cities (including several Caribbean locations) with well over 100 aircraft, and it has ambitious plans for continued growth. The company's vision is to offer great service with low fares—and make a profit—even when other air carriers are struggling to survive. Several important goals back up this vision:

- Start and remain well-capitalized.
- Fly new planes.
- Hire the best people.
- Focus on service.
- Practice responsible financial management.

To-date, JetBlue has mostly stayed true to course. While most of the major carriers continuously bleed red ink, JetBlue, though not perfect in bringing in every quarter's sales and profit goals, appears to be much more stable financially than the majority of other airlines. Much of the airline's success can be attributed to great market-driven strategic planning.

In terms of specific and measurable objectives, Neeleman established high performance expectations for financial results, operational processes, and customer satisfaction and loyalty. As mentioned earlier, JetBlue's Web site is very transparent in laying out company leaders' plans for the firm—Neeleman was always quite confident that the company had created a unique value offering that few (if any) competitors could readily duplicate. In the winter of 2007, JetBlue suffered

HP's Ethical Scandal Impacts Marketing Strategy

Developing a strategic marketing focus in an organization requires a commitment from senior management. As Jack Welch mentioned, good managers create, articulate, become passionate about, and focus the company on a vision. That requires a clear focus on what *is* and, critically, what *is not* important to the firm.

Many issues confront senior managers and it is easy to lose focus. For example, senior management is rightfully concerned about competitors or even the general public gaining access to sensitive company information (for example, financial data, cost figures, future marketing strategies, product plans, and pricing programs). To help protect sensitive data from getting into the wrong hands, companies implement sophisticated security measures. At the same time, the Sarbanes-Oxley Act of 2002 (commonly referred to as SOX) established specific procedures and processes to ensure ethical conduct at the highest levels of a company including the board of directors and senior management.

In the vast majority of companies the conflicting demands of securing sensitive information and open disclosure of business procedures exist relatively harmoniously. However, occasionally the system fails and the result is scandal and even criminal activity. Hewlett-Packard (HP), one of the leading global technology companies, recently found itself involved in a scandal that led to the dismissal of two members of its Board of Directors and the firing of several employees. The scandal was initiated when *The Wall Street Journal* reported sensitive information about future business plans that were meant to be communicated only inside the company and in internal discussions among the Board of Directors. HP Chairman Patricia Dunn was determined to find out who was leaking the information and started an investigation into the personal and business communications (phones calls, e-mail, etc.) of several board members without their knowledge.

Were the people involved in this mess simply unethical by nature? Evidence about some of the players' career tracks suggests just the opposite. Indeed, one of the fired HP officers was the ethics chief for the company and also a well-respected attorney. While stopping the leak of sensitive information was a valid goal, poor, even illegal, decisions were made about how to accomplish that goal. At critical decision moments, no one stepped back to reflect and asked important questions like: Does this make sense? Is this activity appropriate or ethical?

HP CEO Mike Hurd, while involved in the scandal, was not directly connected to the illegal activity. He admitted that mistakes were made during the process and the company subsequently instituted a number of changes to its ethics policies and business practices. While HP market performance remained strong, employees reported considerable conflict as the company dealt with changes to ethics procedures and policies. Hurd has admitted scandal has been a distraction for him and the company, and of course negative publicity about a company is never a good thing for customer confidence in its brands. When management gets distracted by ethics scandals, the company loses strategic focus and the company's brands could lose market share to competitors who take advantage of the scandalized firm's weakened state in the marketplace.[32]

Ethical Perspective

1. **Senior Management:** How should senior management incorporate ethical standards at all stages of the marketing planning process?

2. **Marketing Managers:** A company's brands can be quickly impacted by negative publicity surrounding ethical scandals. How might they be impacted and what might a marketing manager do to reestablish a brand damaged in this way?

3. **The Public:** Company image and trust can be regained by a CEO's quick public acknowledgment of an ethics problem accompanied by plans for changes in practice. What could HP's CEO have done better?

a highly publicized operational meltdown at its JFK airport home base due to a massive snow and ice storm, and Neeleman was right there on the Web site and in the public media. In addition to offering an apology, he also provided full refunds, free replacement tickets, and travel vouchers to stranded passengers and established the first passengers' bill of rights in the industry.

In developing a marketing plan, the marketing manager must proceed in the process with a strong understanding of and commitment to the firm's mission, vision, goals, and objectives. JetBlue's well-conceived and executed marketing plan is an integral element in its success.

HP does a great job of communicating the value proposition of its color Laserjet printers through strong price/feature advertising.

Organizational Strategies

At the firm level, a **strategy** is a comprehensive plan stating how the organization will achieve its mission and objectives. Put another way, strategy is like a road map to get the organization where it wants to go, based on good information gathered in advance. The choice of which direction a firm should go ultimately boils down to a *decision* by a firm and its managers. Strategy has two key phases: formulation (or development) and execution. And it occurs at multiple levels in the firm: corporate level, SBU (or business) level, and functional level (marketing, finance, operations, etc.). As we have discussed, the strategies developed and executed at each of these levels must be aligned and directed toward the overall organizational mission and goals.

A firm's **generic strategy** is its overall directional strategy at the business level.[33] Fundamentally, all firms must decide whether they wish to (or are able to) *grow,* and if not, how they can survive through *stability* or *retrenchment.* Exhibit 2.5 provides options for generic strategies for each of these three directions. The choice of generic strategy is usually driven by resource capabilities of the firm, as well as the competitive landscape. In the growth-oriented business culture in the United States, stockholders and financial analysts are constantly interested in knowing a firm's next growth strategy and can become quickly disenchanted, even with firms that are growing but at a slower than predicted rate. Yet, sometimes for reasons related to the competitive landscape or resource constraints, the best generic strategy for a firm may not actually be growth but be stability or retrenchment instead. Interestingly, the pressure to constantly achieve accelerated growth is much less intense in many business cultures outside the United States.

Competitor analysis is discussed in detail in Chapter 5. For now, it is worth noting that Michael Porter identifies three primary categories of **competitive strategy:** low cost, differentiation, and focus (or niche). Exhibit 2.6 describes each of these, and Exhibit 2.7 illustrates them further within a matrix format. Porter's overarching premise is that firms must first identify their **core competencies,**

EXHIBIT 2.5	Generic Business Strategies

Growth

- Organizations that do business in dynamic competitive environments generally experience pressure to grow in order to survive. Growth may be in the form of sales, market share, assets, profits, or some combination of these and other factors. Categories of growth strategies include:

Concentration–via vertical or horizontal integration.
Diversification–via concentric or conglomerate means.

Stability

- The strategy to continue current activities with little significant change in direction may be

appropriate for a successful organization operating in a reasonably predictable environment. It can be useful in the short term but potentially dangerous in the long term, especially if the competitive landscape changes.

Retrenchment

- An organization in a weak competitive position in some or all of its product lines, resulting in poor performance and pressure on management to quickly improve, may pursue retrenchment.

- Essentially, retrenchment involves pulling assets out of underperforming parts of the business and reinvesting in aspects of the business with greater future performance potential.

Source: J. David Hunger and Thomas H. Wheelen, *Essentials of Strategic Management,* 4th ed. (Upper Saddle River, NJ: Prentice Hall, 2007).

EXHIBIT 2.6 Competitive Strategy Options

Cost Leadership

- The organization strives to have the lowest costs in its industry and produces goods or services for a broad customer base. Note the emphasis on *costs* not *prices.*

Differentiation

- The organization competes on the basis of providing unique goods or services with features that customers value, perceive as different, and for which they are willing to pay a premium.

Focus (or Niche)

- The organization pursues either a cost or differentiation advantage, but in a limited (narrow) customer group. A focus strategy concentrates on serving a specific market niche.

Source: Reprinted with the permission of The Free Press, a Division of Simon & Schuster Adult Publishing Group, from *Competitive Advantage: Creating and Sustaining Superior Performance,* by Michael E. Porter. Copyright © 1985, 1988 by Michael E. Porter. All rights reserved.

EXHIBIT 2.7 Competitive Strategy Matrix

Competitive Scope	Competitive Advantage: Lower Cost	Competitive Advantage: Differentiation
Broad Target	Cost Leadership	Differentiation
Narrow Target	Cost Focus	Focused Differentiation

Source: Reprinted with the permission of The Free Press, a Division of Simon & Schuster Adult Publishing Group, from *Competitive Advantage: Creating and Sustaining Superior Performance,* by Michael E. Porter. Copyright © 1985, 1988 by Michael E. Porter. All rights reserved.

or the activities the firm can do exceedingly well. When these core competencies are superior to those of competitors, they are called **distinctive competencies.** Firms should invest in distinctive competencies, as they offer opportunity for **sustainable competitive advantage** in the marketplace, especially if the competencies cannot be easily duplicated or usurped by competitors. Sources of differential advantage will be developed further in Chapter 9.

As illustrated in Exhibit 2.8, Miles and Snow propose several categories of firms within any given industry based on **strategic type.** Firms of a particular strategic type have a common strategic orientation and a similar combination of structure, culture, and processes consistent with that strategy. Four strategic types are prospectors, analyzers, defenders, and reactors—depending on a firm's approach to the competitive marketplace.

JetBlue has historically followed an internal growth strategy. As some of its rivals continue to falter, it will be interesting to see how aggressive JetBlue might become in terms of growth through concentration via acquisitions. Like its much larger

EXHIBIT 2.8 | **Miles and Snow's Strategy Types**

- **Prospector:** Firm exhibits continual innovation by finding and exploiting new product and market opportunities.
- **Analyzer:** Firm heavily relies on analysis and imitation of the successes of other organizations, especially prospectors.
- **Defender:** Firm searches for market stability and production of only a limited product line

directed at a narrow market segment, focusing on protecting established turf.

- **Reactor:** Firm lacks any coherent strategic plan or apparent means of effectively competing; reactors do well to merely survive in the competitive marketplace.

Source: Adapted from Raymond E. Miles and Charles C. Snow, *Organizational Strategy, Structure, and Process* (New York: McGraw-Hill, 1978). Reprinted with permission of the authors.

competitor Southwest Airlines, JetBlue executes a low-cost strategy in the competitive marketplace. Because it has no unions, hedges on fuel prices, and standardizes the types of planes flown, JetBlue enjoys numerous cost advantages over the competition. However, JetBlue differs from Southwest in that its strategy (in the context of Exhibit 2.8) is cost focus, while Southwest's is cost leadership. The difference is that Southwest has defined the scope of its competitive marketplace much more broadly then has JetBlue; for instance, Southwest is basically a nationwide carrier, while JetBlue focuses on some specific geographic markets. In terms of strategic type, JetBlue can be labeled a prospector. It has enjoyed strong **first-mover advantages** by providing television, movies, and games in every seat along with comfy leather accoutrements and plenty of legroom—all at bargain prices! Exhibit 2.8 provides typical characteristics of firms that fall into each of the strategy types.

To summarize, for purposes of marketing planning, it is necessary to be mindful of the organizational strategies in play when developing marketing strategies. One could reasonably argue that a fine line exists between organization-level strategies and marketing strategies, and, in many firms, the market-driven strategies developed within the context of the marketing plan ultimately rise to the organizational level.[35] Fortunately, the distinction is moot so long as the strategies developed and implemented are fully supportive of the organization's mission, vision, and goals.

 FYI

Whirlpool takes its core competencies seriously. In fact, the company has a corporate vice president of core competencies. One of the company's most important competencies is innovation, so the VP of core competencies doubles as the global vice president of innovation as well. To instill innovation throughout the company, Whirlpool trained 22,000 employees to look for market and in-job innovations. Whirlpool encourages employees to suggest ideas and allows experiments, including those that might result in a failure. The result? New products such as the Duet washer/dryer system and the Gator Pak for tailgate parties have gained wide customer acceptance.[34]

Situation Analysis

The marketing manager must perform a complete **situation analysis** of the environment within which the marketing plan is being developed. The situation includes elements of the macro-level external environment within which the firm operates, its industry or competitive environment, and its internal environment.[36] Think of external environmental factors as those a firm must be mindful of and plan for, yet has little or no direct ability to impact or change. On the other hand, internal environmental factors include the firm's structure and systems, culture, leadership, and various resources, all of which are under the firm's control. Ironically, when undertaking a situation analysis, managers often have more difficulty assessing the internal environmental components than the external, perhaps because it is much more difficult to self-assess and potentially criticize that for which the managers are responsible.[37]

Macro-Level External Environmental Factors

Major categories for analysis within the external environment include:

- *Political, legal, and ethical.* All firms operate within certain rules, laws, and norms of operating behavior. For example, JetBlue has myriad regulations administered by the Federal Aviation Administration, the National Transportation Safety Board, and the Transportation Security Administration. In the airline industry, the regulatory environment is a particularly strong external influence on firms' marketing planning.

- *Sociocultural/demographic.* Trends among consumers and in society as a whole impact marketing planning greatly. Many such trends are demographic in nature, including changing generational preferences and the rising buying power of minority groups domestically and consumers in developing nations in the global marketplace.[38] Speaking of generational preferences, JetBlue jumped on the video game trend among children and teens by providing in-seat games, much to the delight of parents who no longer have to entertain the kids for the duration of the flight.

Demographic factors influence a company's marketing strategy. For example, Toyota's marketing strategy for its Yaris car model is completely different from its strategy for the Tundra truck. The Yaris is aimed at the 18 to 34 age group. As a result, marketing for Yaris emphasizes the car's "cheeky, irreverent, and mischievous" personality. Ads for the Yaris appear where younger buyers spend time, namely on video games, in social networking sites like MySpace, and at events like the South by Southwest Music festival in Austin, Texas.[39]

- *Technological.* Constantly emerging and evolving technologies impact business in many ways. The goal is to try to understand the future impact of technological change so a firm's products will continue to be fresh and viable. JetBlue ordered a number of new downsized "regional jets," planes that carry about 50 passengers and allow for entry into smaller, underserved markets. The airline is banking on these attractive, comfortable new aircraft to provide a market edge over the competition.

- *Economic.* The economy plays a role in all marketing planning. Part of a marketing plan is a forecast and accompanying budget, and forecasts are impacted by the degree to which predicted economic conditions actually materialize.[40] Fuel prices are a major economic cost element for any airline. JetBlue was a pioneer in hedging against rising fuel prices—that is, making speculative long-term purchase commitments betting on fuel prices going up.

- *Natural.* The natural environment also frequently affects marketing planning.[41] JetBlue's highly publicized winter weather fiasco at JFK airport in 2007 prompted immediate changes in the way the company communicates with its customers. And on a broader scope, the concept of environmentally friendly marketing, or *green marketing*, has been a growing trend in socially responsible companies. *Sustainability*, which refers to business practices that meet humanity's needs without harming future generations, has evolved into a part of the philosophical and strategic core of many firms.

Competitive Environmental Factors

The competitive environment is a particularly complex aspect of the external environment. Chapter 6 is devoted to providing a more complete grounding in competitor analysis. For now, let's identify several factors, or forces, that comprise a basis for assessing the level and strength of competition within an industry. The forces are portrayed in Exhibit 2.9 and summarized below:

Pepsi executes a strong differentiation strategy by making connections with young, hip, urban consumers.

- *Threat of new entrants.* How strong are entry barriers based on capital requirements or other factors? A cornerstone of JetBlue's initial market entry success was the fact that it was exceptionally well-capitalized. Not many new airlines are.

- *Rivalry among existing firms.* How much direct competition is there? How much indirect competition? How strong are the firms in both categories? JetBlue's industry contains a number of firms that are much larger, but based on JetBlue's unique value proposition few of them can deliver the same customer experience that JetBlue can.

- *Threat of substitute products.* Substitutes appear to be different but actually can satisfy much or all of the same customer need as another product. Will teleconferencing PC-to-PC (using products such as Skype) reach a point in the near future such that business travel is seriously threatened, thus impacting JetBlue and other airlines?

- *Bargaining power of buyers.* To what degree can customers affect prices or product offerings? So far, JetBlue has not been in much head-to-head competition with Southwest, AirTran Airways, Frontier Airlines, or other low-fare carriers in its primary markets. Should this change, passengers will have more power to demand even lower fares and/or additional services from JetBlue.

- *Bargaining power of suppliers.* Suppliers impact the competitive nature of an industry through their ability to raise prices or affect the quality of inbound goods and services. Jet fuel literally fires the airline industry's economic engine. Also, few manufacturers of commercial aircraft still exist. Both of these factors point to a competitive environment with strong supplier power.

One other competitive force not directly addressed by Porter is the *relative power of other stakeholders.* This force is becoming more and more relevant in assessing industry competitiveness. The level of activity by unions, trade associations, local communities, citizen's groups, and all sorts of other special-interest groups can strongly impact industry attractiveness.[42] Founder David Neeleman established JetBlue as a non-union shop with the goal of keeping it that way by hiring the very best people and treating the people right. The union environment in the airline industry adds multiple complexities to the ability to stay competitive.[43]

Internal Environmental Factors

Major categories for analysis in the internal environment include:

- *Firm structure and systems.* To what degree does the present organizational structure facilitate or impede successful market-driven strategic planning? Are the firm's internal systems set up and properly aligned to effectively serve customers? David Neeleman had his organizational chart right on the company Web site and talked openly about being a lean and mean

EXHIBIT 2.9	Forces Driving Industry Competition

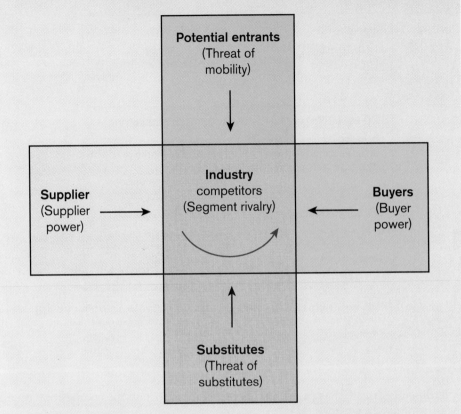

operation. It's hard to find much evidence that JetBlue's structure and systems offer impediments to its marketing planning.

- *Firm culture.* As discussed previously, successful marketing planning requires a culture that includes customer orientation as a core value. If a firm's culture does not value and support a customer orientation and customer-centric approach to the overall business, marketing planning will likely disappoint.[44] A close review of the communication with customers on JetBlue's Web site provides evidence that customer orientation is a core value at the company.

- *Firm leadership.* Of course, the CEO must believe in and continuously support (financially and otherwise) the structure, systems, and culture necessary for market-driven strategic planning.[45] JetBlue's employee-friendly—and customer-friendly—approach epitomizes such leadership and commitment.

- *Firm resources.* Finally, internal analysis involves taking an honest look at all aspects of a firm's functional/operational-level resources and capabilities and how they play into the ability to develop and execute market-driven strategies.[46] Key resources for study are:

  - Marketing capabilities.
  - Financial capabilities.
  - R&D and technological capabilities.
  - Operations and production capabilities.
  - Human capabilities.
  - Information system capabilities.

EXHIBIT 2.10 | SWOT Analysis Template

	Strengths (S) List 5–10 *internal* strengths here	Weaknesses (W) List 5–10 *internal* weaknesses here
INTERNAL FACTORS **EXTERNAL FACTORS**		
Opportunities (O) List 5–10 *external* opportunities here	**S/O Based Strategies** Generate strategies here that use **strengths** to take **advantage** of **opportunities**	**W/O Based Strategies** Generate strategies here that take **advantage** of **opportunities** by **overcoming weaknesses**
Threats (T) List 5–10 *external* threats here	**S/T Based Strategies** Generate strategies here that use **strengths** to **avoid threats**	**W/T Based Strategies** Generate strategies here that **minimize weaknesses** and **avoid threats**

Source: J. David Hunger and Thomas H. Wheelen, *Essentials of Strategic Management*, 4th ed. (Upper Saddle River, NJ: Prentice Hall, 2007). Reprinted from Long Range Planning 15, no.2 (1982), Weihrich "The TOWS Matrix–A Tool for Situational Analysis," p.60. Copyright 1982 with permission of Elsevier and Hans Weihrich.

JetBlue historically has performed better than almost all the competition on all these resource dimensions.

Summarize the Situation Analysis into a SWOT

Upon completion of the situation analysis, a convenient way to summarize key findings is into a matrix of strengths, weaknesses, opportunities, and threats—a **SWOT analysis.** Exhibit 2.10 provides a template for a SWOT analysis. Internal analysis reveals strengths and weaknesses, while external analysis points to potential opportunities and threats. Based on the situation analysis and SWOT, it is now possible to begin making decisions about the remainder of the marketing plan.

Besides helping a marketing manager organize the results of a situation analysis, the SWOT analysis template is also useful in beginning to brainstorm marketing strategies that might be appropriate depending on which of four possible combination scenarios predominate in a firm's situation: internal strengths/external opportunities, internal strengths/external threats, internal weaknesses/external opportunities, or internal weaknesses/external threats. During the situation analysis it is essential to begin to critically and realistically examine the degree to which a firm's external and internal environment will impact its ability to develop marketing strategy. The more honest and accurate the portrayal provided by the SWOT analysis, the more useful the remainder of the marketing planning process will be.

Additional Aspects of Marketing Planning

Additional elements of marketing planning are identified below. As they derive their content primarily from future chapter topics, reference is made where relevant to the chapters from which the content can be derived.

Perform Any Needed Market Research

Chapter 4 provides ideas on how a customer relationship management (CRM) system enhances marketing planning and decision making. Chapter 5 discusses collecting and analyzing market information. And Chapters 7 and 8 outline key aspects of understanding customers in consumer and business markets, respectively. JetBlue has an effective CRM system through its TrueBlue rewards program. It also engages in ongoing market and consumer research to pinpoint trends and opportunities.

The Four Seasons Hotel goes one step further with its CRM system. Not only does the company keep information on its guests, but each hotel also has an employee called a "guest historian" whose job it is to track guest preferences. If a guest wants two chocolates on the pillow rather than one, for example, Four Seasons will record and remember that fact for next time.[47]

Establish Marketing Goals and Objectives

What is expected to be accomplished by the marketing plan? Based on what is learned from the situation analysis, competitor analysis, and market research, goals and objectives can now be developed related to what the marketing manager intends to accomplish with the marketing plan. JetBlue's marketing goals focus on enhancing the safety, comfort, and fun of customers' travel experience, building high satisfaction and loyalty among JetBlue users, and attracting new users to the brand.

Develop Marketing Strategies

As we mentioned earlier, marketing strategies provide the road map for creating, communicating, and delivering value to customers. An overarching decision that must be made is which combinations of products and markets to invest in. A product-market combination may fall into one of four primary categories, as illustrated by Exhibit 2.11, Igor Ansoff's Product-Market Matrix:

- **Market penetration strategies** involve investing in existing customers to gain additional usage of existing products.
- **Product development strategies** recognize the opportunity to invest in new products that will increase usage from the current customer base.
- **Market development strategies** allow for expansion of the firm's product line into heretofore untapped markets, often internationally.
- **Diversification strategies** seize on opportunities to serve new markets with new products.

JetBlue began business with a primary focus on product development. The clean new planes, comfy leather seats, full spectrum entertainment console, and friendly staff were all welcomed by fliers as a long overdue change from other airlines' cattle-call mentality. However, more recently the company focused on taking its winning formula into a number of new geographic markets. This market development strategy dramatically increased the number of cities on JetBlue's route system and especially increased opportunities for customers from underserved smaller cities such as Sarasota, Florida; White Plains, New York; and Tucson, Arizona, to experience the airline. JetBlue has also added international destinations into the travel mix such as Cancun, Aruba, and Nassau.

Once the product-market combinations have been established, it is time to develop the value offering, which is the topic of Part 3. This involves market segmentation, target marketing, and positioning strategies. In addition, strategies for branding, service, and pricing must be worked out.

Finally, supply chain and integrated marketing communication strategies must be put in place to successfully communicate and deliver the value offering to customers. Chapters 15 to 18 in Part 4 provide the background necessary to complete this section of the marketing plan.

Evidence of JetBlue's success in creating, communicating, and delivering its value offering can be found on the airline's Web site. There one can view current

EXHIBIT 2.11 | Product-Market Combinations

Product Emphasis

		Existing Products	New Products
Market Emphasis	**Existing Markets**	**Strategy = Market penetration** Seek to increase sales of existing products to existing markets	**Strategy = Market development** Create growth by selling new products in existing markets
	New Markets	**Strategy = Market development** Introduce existing products to new markets	**Strategy = Diversification** Emphasize both new products and new markets to achieve growth

Source: From H. Igor Ansoff, *The New Corporate Strategy* (New York: John Wiley & Sons, 1988). Reprinted with permission of John Wiley & Sons, Inc.

television ads, take a virtual tour of the aircraft, peruse the list of available in-flight entertainment, and even send a virtual JetBlue postcard to a friend.

Create an Implementation Plan Including Forecast, Budget, and Appropriate Marketing Metrics

As pointed out earlier, strategy *development* is only part of marketing planning. The other part is strategy *implementation,* including measuring results. The process of measuring marketing results and adjusting the marketing plan as needed is called **marketing control.**

> Progressive and GEICO were the No. 3 and No. 4 players in the car insurance market when they decided to invest in an advertising offensive against the market leaders, State Farm and Allstate. The two upstarts spent a combined $500 million on advertising, which was $170 million more than the two top players combined. Was the investment effective? To see if the spending delivered results, the companies looked at whether they were gaining market share. Indeed, fourth-place GEICO increased its market share by 14.8 percent and Progressive gained 12 percent while leader State Farm lost .3 percent and Allstate's share rose a mere 4 percent.[48]

In a marketing plan, every strategy must include an implementation element. Sometimes these are called action plans or programs. Each must discuss timing, assign persons responsible for various aspects of implementation, and assign resources necessary to make the strategy happen.[37] Forecasts and their accompanying budgets must be provided. Then, appropriate metrics must be identified to assess along the way to what degree the plan is on track and the strategies are contributing to achievement of the stated marketing objectives. Chapter 19 provides the background necessary for selecting marketing metrics appropriate for various marketing objectives and strategies, as well as instruction on preparing action plans for implementation, developing forecasts and budgets, establishing controls and contingency plans, and conducting a marketing audit.

On the JetBlue Web site, the Investor Relations, Press Releases, and Online Annual Report sections provide compelling evidence that the company is highly oriented toward measurement of marketing results. And although the airline industry as a whole has suffered in recent years due to increased costs, JetBlue has generally received better reviews than most other airlines from Wall Street analysts in part because of the clarity of JetBlue's goals, metrics, and controls.

Develop Contingency Plans

A final step marketing managers should take is to develop contingency plans that can be implemented should something happen that negates the viability of the marketing plan.[49] As you've learned, in marketing planning, flexibility and adaptability by managers is critical because unexpected events and drastic changes in various aspects of the external environment are the norm rather than an exception. To address this eventuality, a firm should incorporate contingency plans into the process.

Contingency plans are often described in terms of a separate plan for a worst-case, best-case, and expected-case performance against the forecast. That is, the implementation of the marketing strategies would be different depending on how performance against the forecast actually materializes. If better, the firm could quickly shift to a best-case implementation scenario. If worse, then the shift would be to a worst-case scenario. Having these contingency plans in place avoids scrambling to decide how to adjust marketing strategies when performance against a forecast is higher or lower than expected.

When developing contingency plans, the firm should be realistic about the possibilities and creative in developing options for minimizing any disruption to the firm's operations should it become necessary to implement them. Some firms use contingency planning to reduce the chances they would make a public relations blunder when confronted with an unexpected challenge that generates negative publicity in the media such as product tampering or failure, ethical or legal misconduct of an officer, or some other aspect of their operation that garners bad press.[50]

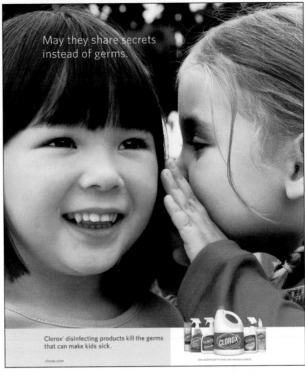

Well-executed marketing strategy can result in very powerful messages and branding.

CLOROX ® is a registered trademark of The Clorox Company. Used with permission. Clorox ® advertisement. © 2009 The Clorox Company. Reprinted with permission. Image © Sven Wiederholt.

Sometimes a marketing plan can be used to reinvent or reinvigorate a brand in order to align with a corporate growth strategy. For example, for years P&G emphasized the dryness and absorbency of its Pampers brand diapers. The strategy was working, but P&G wanted to boost sales even more. So, it created a new campaign that emphasized baby development, not dryness. P&G supported the campaign with its Pampers Web site, offering expert advice tailored to each stage of baby development with helpful tips, tools, and activities. The result? Double-digit growth for the Pampers brand.[51]

Recently, JetBlue has had to invoke a contingency plan for growth due to higher jet fuel costs (the entire industry has felt the impact). For all airlines, fuel costs have raised ticket prices and squeezed profit margins, drastically affecting achievement of forecasts. In reaction to a worst-case scenario, JetBlue has cut orders for new planes and postponed entry into some new market areas that it would like to develop. At best, in this environment JetBlue hopes to achieve stability in the short run at its current size and would also obviously benefit if other competitive carriers decide to stop operating.

TIPS FOR SUCCESSFUL MARKETING PLANNING

Developing a marketing plan is an essential process for firm success. In addition to its direct impact on a firm's ability to compete, ongoing marketing planning also has a strong internal organizational benefit of providing a rallying point for developing creative ideas and for gaining input from important stakeholders throughout the various areas within an organization.[52] Who should be involved in marketing planning? The answer is: anyone from any unit at any level whose contribution and participation in the process will enhance the likelihood of a successful outcome. Marketing planning provides a unique opportunity for organization members to contribute to the success of a firm in a very concrete and visible way.

Here are a few final tips for having a successful marketing planning experience.

1. *Stay flexible.* Don't forget that marketing plans are not set in stone. Markets and customers change, competitors do unexpected things, and the external environment has a nasty habit of creating unexpected surprises. Great marketing managers understand when to adjust a plan. Nimble organizations tend to be much more successful in their marketing strategies.

   In his provocative book, *The Rise and Fall of Strategic Planning,* strategy expert Henry Mintzberg builds the case that organizations sometimes spend so much time focused on planning for the long term that they miss the opportunities presented by the next customer who walks through the door.[53] Mintzberg's concern is valid and points to the need for viewing planning as an ongoing, organic process in which managers exhibit flexibility and adaptability to changing market conditions. Marketing plans are not written in stone—that is, after a plan is prepared myriad changes in the firm's external and internal environment may create a need for marketing managers to quickly alter their strategies in the marketplace.[54] The more nimble a company is in changing course to address new conditions as they arise, the more successful its marketing strategies will be.

2. *Utilize input, but don't become paralyzed by information and analysis.* Great marketing managers value research and analytics, but also know when to move forward with action.

3. *Don't underestimate the implementation part of the plan.* This is such a common mistake it is nearly synonymous with poor marketing planning. The quality of the action plans and metrics often make or break the success of the plan. Put another way, a good plan on paper is useless without effective implementation.

4. *Stay strategic, but also stay on top of the tactical.* Remember that marketing has these two levels of interrelated issues, and both the strategic and tactical elements have to be right for the plan to be successful.

5. *Give yourself and your people room to fail and try again.* Marketing planning is by no means a predictable science. It is more realistic to think of it as both science and art, and creativity and risk-taking are to be rewarded. All great marketing managers have experienced both success and failures in marketing planning. As in baseball, it's not one or two times at bat but rather the long-term batting average that separates the great from the average performer.

VISIT THE APPENDIX FOR A MARKETING PLAN EXAMPLE

Often the best way to learn is through example, so in the appendix to this chapter we have provided an abbreviated example marketing plan for the fictitious company CloudCab Small Jet Taxi Service. Take this opportunity early in the course to familiarize yourself with the flow and content, albeit abbreviated, of a typical marketing plan.

In addition, at the end of each chapter you will find a Marketing Plan Exercise that is designed to highlight aspects of that chapter as they pertain to a manager's ability to build an effective marketing plan. Use these activities to build your own knowledge and skill in the marketing planning process.

SUMMARY

Marketing planning is an ongoing process of developing and implementing market-driven strategies for an organization. Great marketing planning is essential for success in the marketplace. Once established, marketing plans are not set in stone. Instead, marketing managers must be flexible enough to constantly assess changes in the external and internal environment and adjust strategies and tactics accordingly. The chapter introduces the essential elements of marketing planning. The content elements for completing the various aspects of the template are covered in the chapters throughout the remaining three parts of the book.

KEY TERMS

benefit 30
utility 30
value proposition 30
customer satisfaction 31
customer loyalty 31
customer retention 31
customer switching 31
value chain 31
value-creating activities 31
marketing planning 33
marketing plan 33
market-driven strategic planning 35
corporate-level strategic plan 35

SBU-level strategic plan 35
portfolio analysis 35
Boston Consulting Group (BCG) Growth-Share Matrix 35
GE Business Screen 35
functional-level plans 37
mission statement 37
strategic vision 38
goals 38
objectives 38
strategy 40
generic strategy 40
competitive strategy 40

core competencies 40
distinctive competencies 41
sustainable competitive advantage 41
strategic type 41
first-mover advantages 42
situation analysis 42
SWOT analysis 46
market penetration strategies 47
product development strategies 47
market development strategies 47
diversification strategies 47
marketing control 48

APPLICATION QUESTIONS

1. What is a value proposition? For each of these brands, articulate your perception of their key value proposition:
   a. Caterpillar earth mover
   b. Apple iPod
   c. Wii home gaming system
   d. McDonald's hamburgers
   e. FedEx overnight delivery service

2. Consider the concept of the value chain. Identify a firm that you believe does an especially good job of investing in elements in the value chain to gain higher profit margins versus competition. Which two or three elements in the value

chain does that firm handle especially well? For each of those elements, what do they do that is better than their competition?

3. Why is it so important for marketing managers, when engaged in marketing planning, to successfully deal with both Marketing (Big M) and marketing (little m) elements? What would be the likely negative outcome if a marketing plan paid a lot of attention to strategies and little attention to tactics? What would be the likely negative outcome of the reverse?

4. Consider firms in any area of the retail business. Using Miles and Snow's strategy types, identify the following: (1) a firm that you believe is a prospector; (2) a firm that you believe is an analyzer; (3) a firm that you believe is a defender; and (4) a firm that you believe is a reactor. What characteristics of each led you to conclude they belong in their respective strategy type?

5. Historically, the theme park industry in Orlando is heavily affected by a large number of macro-level external environmental factors. From each of the five major categories of macro-level external factors, identify a specific example of how some element within that category might impact a theme park's marketing planning for the next couple of years. Be sure to explain *why* you believe each of your examples will be important for marketing managers to consider as they develop their marketing plans.

MANAGEMENT DECISION CASE: Dell's Marketing Strategy Woes

In January 2007 this banner headline appeared all over the business press: "HP Usurps Dell as Market Share Leader in PCs." To the countless believers in Dell's marketing strategy of mass customization, the news was nearly unbelievable. Yet there it was in print for all to see, complete with all the requisite facts, figures, and pundit analyses. What happened in the PC wars that left Dell's position vulnerable? The more accurate question might be: What happened (or didn't happen) within Dell itself that opened the door for HPs ascension to the top?

Dell may have transformed how consumers shop for technology, but what may actually need transforming now is Dell itself. The summer of 2006 was one of misfortune for the company. It began with a recall of expensive rechargeable battery packs that had the potential to self-ignite, was followed by a discouraging earnings report, and ended with the news that the Securities and Exchange Commission (SEC) is analyzing the way the company counts revenues. In fact, analysts estimated that Dell would end up reporting approximately $900 million less in net income versus the prior year.

So what's the root of Dell's newfound woes? A top technology industry watcher places the blame solidly on Dell's marketing strategy. "They're a one-trick pony. It was a great trick for over 10 years, but the rest of us have figured it out and Dell hasn't plowed any of its profits into creating a new trick." Over the past year or so, Dell's competitors—HP, Sony, Lenexa, Apple, and others—have stepped up their marketing game and, in the process, have moved various markets (both consumer and business customers) in their favor and away from Dell. During this time, Dell has steadfastly remained loyal to its core differentiation strategy (the pony's "one trick") of mass customization through ultra-efficient supply chain management and a direct sales channel. Critics say the company has failed to adapt to the changing world of technology, and instead of investing in new sources of differentiation has focused on cutting costs. The result: compromised customer service and lower perceived product quality. Not a good position to be in considering the hypercompetitive nature of the PC market.

Founder Michael Dell recently poured $115 million into a highly publicized effort to revive the company's reputation for product and service quality. But it may be too little, too late as competitors are far from resting on their laurels. Business customers have been switching in droves to Hewlett-Packard because of the mounting perception among company IT departments that Dell products have become too difficult to reliably manage and operate.

Former employees of Dell also have a lot to say on the company's cost/efficiency-fixated operations. Richard Snyder, formerly of Dell and now CEO of Asure Software, says many Dell employees have applied for jobs at his firm. He explains, "Dell is not a fun place to work, and it's less fun now than it used to be." Headhunters have become weary of working with the company. At this point, they'd rather recruit *from* Dell than for them.

Although the public story is that Dell is confident that the strategic choices being made are the right long-term decisions for the brand, former CEO Kevin Rollins may have inadvertently exposed the real restrictions of the Dell business model within its evolving marketplace: "There are some organizations where people think they're a hero if they invent a new thing," he said. "Being a hero at Dell means saving money." Former Dell managers can attest to this organizational culture/strategic core value as well. Within Dell, ideas that break from the norm are easily disapproved. One Dell alum notes, "You had to be very confident and thick-skinned to stay on an issue that wasn't popular. A lot of red flags got waved, but only once."

An unfortunate additional challenge is that it is becoming much more difficult for the company to attract customers to its Web site with low-priced models and then entice them into buying more than they planned, a bellwether Dell strategy. Now computers are so powerful in general that the prepackaged versions sold at retailers such as Best Buy are adequate for the vast majority of home and small-business users. Furthermore, as PC market share has shifted away from desktops and into notebooks, widespread publicity that the factories that make notebooks for Dell also make them for other companies didn't help Dell's image either—how can Dell claim a competitive advantage if other companies' products come off the same assembly line? Think of this as the commoditization of PCs. Sales of ancillary products have been spotty, as Dell has struggled to extend customer purchases to TVs with lower electromagnetic interference emissions, a DJ music player, and other products.

Investing in marketing strategies involving creativity and innovation always hold an element of risk, but, in the world of technology, big risks can be followed by even bigger rewards. As Dell remains true to its course of low-cost and mass-customization strategies, will a lack of real innovation and inspiration eventually doom Dell as a leader in the field?

Questions for Consideration

1. How would you describe Dell's current distinctive competencies? What other potential sources of distinctive competency might Dell work to develop?

2. Dell is currently engaged in a cost leadership strategy. If Dell decided to move more toward a differentiation strategy, what might be some sources of differentiation Dell could explore?

3. In terms of the Miles and Snow strategy types, in which category do you think Dell currently fits? What evidence leads you to this conclusion?

Source: Nanette Byrnes, Peter Burrows, and Louise Lee, "Dark Days at Dell," *BusinessWeek*, September 4, 2006, pp. 26–28.

MARKETING PLAN EXERCISES

ACTIVITY 1: Elements of a Marketing Plan

In the chapter, you learned that marketing planning drives the activities of the marketing manager and you were provided a framework for marketing planning. Before you move further through this course, it is important to be sure that you understand the flow and content of a typical marketing plan.

1. Read the annotated marketing plan example presented in the appendix to this chapter.

2. Make notes about any questions you may have about the example plan, and be prepared to bring those questions to class for clarification.

3. If you are going to be using Marketing Plan Pro Software to develop your marketing plan, take this opportunity to open your copy of the software and familiarize yourself with its functionality. An electronic template for your marketing plan that follows Exhibit 2.2 in the chapter (which is the same format used in the CloudCab Small Jet Taxi Service example in the Appendix) can be accessed at www.mhhe.com/marshall1e.

If you are using Marketing Plan Pro, a template for this assignment can be accessed at www.mhhe.com/marshall1e.

ACTIVITY 2: Situation Analysis

In the chapter you also learned about the key situation analysis areas of external macro-level environmental factors, competitive forces, and internal environmental factors that marketing managers must consider in marketing planning. You also saw how this information can be conveniently summarized and portrayed in a SWOT analysis.

1. Using the chapter discussion on situation analysis along with Exhibit 2.10 as a guide, develop a short list of internal strengths and weaknesses and external opportunities and threats. Focus on issues that you believe will be most important to your marketing planning over the next year or so.

2. Exhibit 2.10 suggests that you consider the four different scenario combinations of the SWOT to begin to brainstorm possible strategies. Based on what you know at present, develop one idea for a marketing strategy that might be appropriate for each of the four situational scenario combinations represented in the exhibit—that is, one strategy that uses internal strengths to take advantage of external opportunities you have identified; one strategy that uses internal strengths to avoid external threats you have identified; one strategy that takes advantage of opportunities by overcoming internal weaknesses you have identified; and one strategy that minimizes internal weaknesses and avoids external threats.

If you are using Marketing Plan Pro, a template for this assignment can be accessed at www.mhhe.com/marshall1e.

RECOMMENDED READINGS

1. W. Chan Kim and Renée Mauborgne, *Blue Ocean Strategy: How to Create Uncontested Market Space and Make Competition Irrelevant* (Cambridge, MA: Harvard Business School Press, 2005).

2. Bernard Marr, *Strategic Performance Management: Leveraging and Measuring Your Intangible Value Drivers* (Burlington, MA: Butterworth-Heinemann, 2006).

3. Frederick F. Reichheld, *Loyalty Rules! How Leaders Build Lasting Relationships in the Digital Age* (Cambridge, MA: Harvard Business School Press, 2001).

4. Roland Rust, Valarie Zeithaml, and Katherine Lemon, *Driving Customer Equity: How Customer Lifetime Value is Reshaping Corporate Strategy* (New York: Free Press, 2000).

5. Julia Sloan, *Learning to Think Strategically* (Burlington, MA: Butterworth-Heinemann, 2006).

APPENDIX

CLOUDCAB SMALL JET TAXI SERVICE Abbreviated Example Marketing Plan

NOTE TO READER

This is an *abbreviated version* of a marketing plan for a fictitious firm, CloudCab Small Jet Taxi Service. This appendix is designed to walk you through the main steps of marketing planning. The idea is to provide you with an example early in the course so you will have a better understanding throughout the chapters of how the pieces of a marketing plan come together. Chapter 2 is devoted to the topic of marketing planning, providing a marketing plan framework and explaining the parts. That framework is used to develop this abbreviated example. Note that in practice most marketing plans contain more depth of detail than is provided here. Also, remember that each chapter ends with a Marketing Plan Exercise designed to guide you in applying the concepts from that chapter to a marketing plan.

SITUATION ANALYSIS

CloudCab seeks to provide solutions for the time-conscious traveler using quick, luxurious jet transportation. The small company was founded in 2002 by former pilot Travis Camp and is now poised to be a first-mover into the California/Nevada/Arizona market. CloudCab will provide an alternative to frustrating waits at the airport and long car rides at a fair price for its customers.

CloudCab will use small, underutilized airports and a new class of Very Light Jet to quickly and comfortably transport customers from one city to another. Its customers will come primarily from businesses needing quick, on-demand transportation. Initially, CloudCab will not face much direct competition, so its biggest challenge will be to convince customers of its benefits over more traditional products.

Macro-Level External Environment

Political and Legal

Like all companies using the skies, CloudCab is subject to the rules set forth by the Federal Aviation Administration and other regulatory bodies. Fortunately, smaller jets have many of the same air privileges as their larger counterparts. This ensures access to needed airspace and air traffic control services.

The political and legal environment has the potential to become an even more positive factor for CloudCab as business expands. CloudCab uses smaller, underutilized airports, thereby drawing traffic away from congested major hubs and increasing the efficiency of the entire system. If CloudCab is successful, this may actually induce lawmakers to provide incentives for companies like CloudCab.

Furthermore, larger airports are already facing capacity strain. If CloudCab ties up the governmental resources needed by larger planes carrying more passengers, there may be pressure to limit the use of small jets at large airports.

Sociocultural

The macro-trend of consumers leading time-poor lives continues as both individuals and companies strive to be more efficient in their day-to-day operations. Coupled with a post-9/11 increase in waiting times at airports, this has led today's consumers to be even more conscious of the time spent in transit. Many are willing to spend extra money on faster, more convenient travel options.

Technological

Until recently, small jet service on a large scale was prohibitively expensive. The limited number of people willing to pay for such service could not compensate for the high cost of the jet itself. Due to changes in technology and the advent of the Very Light Jet (VLJ) this has begun to change. Several companies have been able to produce VLJs for the relatively low price range of $1 million to $3 million each. Using these efficient three-to-six-passenger jets, a taxi-like air service is now economically feasible.

Economic

The overall state of the economy will have a large impact on CloudCab's success, since business travel declines precipitously during economic downturns. Since some industries inherently require more travel than others (e.g., consulting, sales) and thus have a larger impact on demand for CloudCab services, CloudCab should particularly watch the health of these industries as predictors of demand for its own services.

CloudCab is also heavily dependent on the availability and price of oil. Higher oil prices will erode CloudCab's margins, while shortages may effectively stall the business. The risk involved in relying on a potentially price-volatile resource must be effectively managed to ensure success.

Competitive Environment

Threat of New Entrants

If CloudCab is successful it may entice others to enter the market. CloudCab's business is very capital intensive, though not as much so as a traditional airline due to smaller, lower-cost jets and a limited operating area. Still, the capital needs are sufficient to deter entry by many.

The biggest hurdle facing new entrants is the lead time necessary to procure the VLJs. This requires planning years in advance of actual operation due to backlogs in manufacturing and high demand. Thus, if a company is not in the business now, it would likely be at least a few years until it was able to enter. In the meantime, CloudCab would have some warning that a new competitor was coming.

Rivalry among Existing Firms

Fortunately, CloudCab will be one of the first to market, so initially there will not be many direct competitors. For a while, companies currently pursuing similar strategies should have ample market share to coexist peacefully, especially since most are geographically concentrated. However, it is just a matter of time before a few establish themselves as the dominate brands and expand nationally, increasing the rivalry and pushing some weaker players out of business.

CloudCab will face some indirect competition from the start from other private jet options. These include partial ownership plans and pay-by-the-hour membership cards. Until now, these have been the solutions of choice for speedy, luxurious travel.

Threat of Substitute Products

CloudCab's greatest threat will likely come from substitute products. Consumers have a variety of options when it comes to transportation. For regional travel, they can choose to fly on a traditional airline, drive their car, or in some cases take a bus or train. These options do not provide nearly the same level of comfort and speed as air taxis, but they do accomplish the task of getting a person from Point A to Point B at a significantly lower cost. Also, for business travelers, technology solutions such as videoconferencing and even PC-driven solutions such as Skype Internet phone service make physical travel to some types of meetings nonessential. If national security travel limitations develop or an economic downturn forces firms to cut business travel, these substitutes will predominate.

Bargaining Power of Buyers

CloudCab primarily competes in the business-to-business (B2B) market space, and it will be catering to only a few customers per flight on a limited number of flights. This means that any one customer's decision to use CloudCab has a large proportional impact, especially during CloudCab's early years. CloudCab will have to treat each customer well because it cannot afford to lose any. Still, a single traveler will not be able to demand, or bargain for, changes from CloudCab because the cost of making those changes will likely be larger than the revenue collected from that one buyer. On the other hand, a major corporate client—supplying many passengers over time—would wield considerable power.

Bargaining Power of Suppliers

CloudCab uses a single manufacturer for its jets, thus the level of dependency is high. If the jets are not ready in time or do not meet specifications, CloudCab could be put out of business. If CloudCab's manufacturer is not able to fulfill its contract, CloudCab might have to wait years to have an order filled with another supplier. Consequently, CloudCab's supplier is in a strong position to bargain for better terms.

At present, the supplier has relatively few buyers, one of them being CloudCab. So as a buyer, CloudCab also has some bargaining power. This makes the two interdependent, and reduces the incentive for the supplier to treat CloudCab unfairly.

Internal Environment

Firm Structure

CloudCab, being relatively new, is far smaller than most businesses in the airline industry. Having few employees makes communication easy and response to change quick to occur. Realizing that the company's success depends heavily on customer adoption of the new offering, CloudCab executives' actions are driven primarily by the needs of the market.

CloudCab is led by founder and CEO Travis Camp. Robert Fray, chief operating officer and close friend of Camp, has been crucial in developing cost-saving measures to ensure CloudCab's prices are as competitive as can be. Other officers include Thomas Puck, chief financial officer; Elizabeth Vars, chief marketing officer; and Jeffery Brown, chief technology officer. All have airline industry experience, and Camp and Fray are former commercial pilots. The firm is in the entrepreneurial stage of its corporate development.

CloudCab is privately held and funded primarily through the investment of Travis Camp and Robert Fray, who combined have a controlling interest in the company. The rest of the funding has been obtained mostly from venture capital firms seeking returns based on a five-year time horizon.

Firm Culture

CloudCab is built on seizing opportunities to better serve the customer. It epitomizes a "lean and mean" culture. New ideas for improvements in efficiency and service quality are encouraged in this customer-centric culture. CloudCab has formalized reward systems for outstanding performance and attitude to promote high morale and productivity among its employees.

Firm Resources

Marketing capabilities: CloudCab has a strong, close-knit marketing team with a combination of experienced hands and recent college graduates. Several employees have ties with local media in major cities that can be used upon product launch.

Financial capabilities: CloudCab is well-financed through equity investments. It has purchased outright the 15 VLJs it plans to use in its operations. Current cash reserves should easily cover initial marketing and ongoing operating expenses, though investors have pledged further funds if needed.

R&D and technological capabilities: Lacking R&D capabilities in-house, CloudCab has chosen to purchase all aircraft and related systems from qualified vendors, but outsource needed maintenance on those aircraft and systems. CloudCab values keeping its systems current and ensuring the firm is in a position to take advantage of any oncoming industry breakthroughs in jet technology.

Operations capabilities: CloudCab presently has the capacity to serve four city locations in California and Nevada (see the Market Research section of this document). Following success in these markets, CloudCab will be able to expand using its fully scalable communications and logistics tracking systems.

Human capabilities: CloudCab's employees are capable and committed. Many employees have received stock and stock options as part of their compensation, tying the interests of company and employee together. CloudCab is presently staffed with 45 people and has plans to employ a total of 80 people when fully operational. Many functions such as maintenance, security, and janitorial work will be outsourced.

Information systems capabilities: CEO Camp is a strong believer in customer relationship management (CRM). Every time a customer flies, he or she will be given the option to fill out a comment card, the contents of which will be entered into CloudCab's central database. Employees of CloudCab with customer contact will also be able to make notes on customer observations. Both of these data sources will be coded categorically and used to assist in customer development and planning. Popular flight times and routes will also be tracked to better assist in modification of product offerings.

SWOT SUMMARY/ANALYSIS

External / Internal	Key Strengths (S) Customer focus Speed to market Industry knowledge	Key Weaknesses (W) Untested product Unknown brand Limited geographic reach
Key Opportunities (O) Time-conscious travelers VLJ availability Small airports underutilized	**S/O Based Strategies** Use VLJs to provide quick transportation between small airports	**W/O Based Strategies** Focus on and invest in building the brand and offering in a small market first
Key Threats (T) Traditional flights and cars Larger airports overcrowded Possibility of new, better jets	**S/T Based Strategies** Demonstrate benefits over alternatives, avoid large airports, and stay tech aware	**W/T Based Strategies** Don't try to compete against bigger airlines for mainstream customers

MARKET RESEARCH

To determine which locations to serve, CloudCab first gathered secondary data on air traffic patterns, popular destinations among private jet owners, and travel frequency for business and leisure. This allowed CloudCab to see where similar services were already being used for comparison.

CloudCab then gathered primary data on travelers' aspirations for where they would like to see Cloud-Cab operate and what features they would want the service to have. This was done through a combination of focus groups and surveys. Focus groups were comprised of travel purchasers within businesses, business travelers themselves, and upper-income leisure travelers. Surveys were distributed via e-mail with a goal of gaining responses from both business and leisure travelers.

All of the data were analyzed to form a complete picture of what travel patterns are like now, what they may be in the future, and what factors (translated into customer benefits) would create demand for Cloud-Cab services. CloudCab used the data to select its first four cities for operation: San Francisco, Los Angeles, Reno, and Las Vegas.

Research also revealed the following findings:

- In general, there seems to be a greater demand for sky taxis from business than from leisure travelers.
- Leisure travelers plan further ahead and have less need of on-demand service.
- Both leisure and business travelers want luxurious accommodations.
- Business travelers have more need of one-way flights than do leisure travelers.
- Time is the biggest priority for business travelers, while comfort is the biggest for leisure travelers.
- Some businesses, such as consulting and sales have a greater need for on-demand travel than others.
- There is a "sweet spot" in income level among leisure travelers where they are wealthy enough to afford CloudCab services but not wealthy enough to own their own jet.

MARKETING GOALS AND OBJECTIVES

Goal

The goal of CloudCab is to be the preferred provider of on-demand short flight service.

Objectives

Within the first 12 months of operation, CloudCab will:

1. Sell 5,500 flight itineraries.
2. Attain a rating of "highly satisfied" customer satisfaction scored by 90 percent of customers.
3. Achieve repeat purchase by 50 percent of customers.

MARKETING STRATEGIES

Product-Market Combinations

CloudCab will use a product development strategy to introduce its new on-demand jet service into the California/Nevada/Arizona market. Based on CloudCab's market research, the product will first be made available in San Francisco, Los Angeles, Reno, and Las Vegas. If the product is successful there, then CloudCab will gradually add more service locations. Once a firm foothold in the region is established, CloudCab will expand into new markets in other regions.

Initially, CloudCab will depart only from the four selected cities. However, customers will be able to use the service to fly round-trip to *any airport* they choose within the region of operation. For one-way flights, CloudCab will provide service only between selected cities, making the plane instantly available at that location for the next flight.

Market Segmentation, Target Marketing, Positioning

Segmentation

The market for on-demand small jet service can be easily divided between business travelers and leisure travelers. Leisure travelers can be further divided based on income levels, and business travelers can be further divided based on industry and other variables such as firm size. Of all possible segments, CloudCab has identified three that have especially high potential to be CloudCab customers:

- Leisure travelers with annual incomes between $300,000 and $1 million.
- Business travelers making B2B sales calls.
- Business travelers on assignment for mid-to-large-size consulting firms.

Target Marketing

CloudCab evaluated each of these segments to determine its focus for initial investment. The first segment, leisure travelers, has the means to afford CloudCab's service and could be a highly profitable market if effectively reached. However, its preference for round-trips over one-way and its tendency to book travel arrangements in advance does not fit well with CloudCab's on-demand service. Leisure travelers are also far less concentrated and thus harder to reach with marketing communications.

The second segment, business travelers in sales, would be easier to reach and would need CloudCab's one-way flights between select cities. Sales calls are a combination of previously scheduled appointments and client requests, making the demand for on-demand service in this group mixed. Sales professionals are often under pressure to keep traveling costs down though, making the profitability of serving this segment questionable.

The third segment, business travelers in consulting, shares sales professionals' need for one-way flights and on-demand service. Yet compared to sales professionals, there is less pressure to keep travel costs down since time and level of service to the client take precedence, and travel and other expenses are often billable to the client. Additionally, these travelers are largely concentrated in fewer firms, making it easier for marketing communications to reach this segment. Also, there is a substantial submarket of independent consultants from which to draw. For these reasons, CloudCab has decided to concentrate on the business consulting traveler segment as its primary target market. CloudCab will make its services available to other segments if they desire to use CloudCab, but CloudCab will not make any concentrated efforts to invest marketing dollars toward them in the beginning. Thus, high-income leisure travelers and sales professionals may be viewed as secondary target markets at present. No tertiary target markets have been identified as of yet.

Positioning

On one end of the travel spectrum, there exists the low-price, low-benefits group. This includes such offerings as traditional airfare and car transportation. Both involve a great deal of hassle, wasted time, and discomfort. The one advantage of this group is that it is affordable to the masses.

On the opposite end of the spectrum, there exists the high-price, high-benefits group. This group consists of private sole jet ownership, partial jet ownership similar to a time-share, and on the lower side, pay-by-the-hour jet service. These options afford their customers a high degree of luxury and many time-saving features, but at a price well outside the range of most travelers, business or leisure.

In the middle of these two groups of travel options is a wide chasm. Until now, no company has been able to strike a happy medium between the two. Utilizing new technology and a unique business model, CloudCab seeks to position itself in this void with a focus on the B2B consulting market. Using its on-demand small-jet service, customers flying from select cities will be able to access many of the same benefits private jet owners enjoy, but without the exorbitant cost associated with it. CloudCab's service will be faster and more enjoyable than traditional airline flights or ground transportation, yet cost far less than private jet ownership. This appears to be a strong positioning with high upside potential for messaging to the primary target market.

Marketing Mix Strategies

Product/Branding Strategies

CloudCab's product benefits center on convenience, dependable service, and a quality image. CloudCab will primarily focus on service to small "executive airports" near the four start-up cities, with the exception of Las Vegas, for which travelers will have direct access to McCharren (the main Las Vegas airport) due to its proximity to the "strip."

To use CloudCab, customers will have two options. They will be able to either call a qualified customer service representative to book their flight or go online and enter their flight and payment information themselves.

Branding of CloudCab will evoke in customers the imagery of being quickly and comfortably transported "by a cloud" from one location to another. This will be communicated through the product name CloudCab as well as its logo, an airplane seat lightly resting in a fast-moving cloud.

Service Strategies

Customer service representatives and airport attendants will be noticeably a cut above the ordinary—polite and professional at all times, both on the phone and in person. Because of the firm's CRM capabilities to provide personalized service to its most valued customers, CloudCab employees will be able to easily enter information into an internal database under individual customer profiles. This will allow CloudCab to consistently meet the expectations of its customers without the customer having to express preferences every time CloudCab is used.

Pricing Strategies

The pricing decision for CloudCab is made more difficult due to the newness of its product offering and lack (so far) of strong competitors in its markets. In the early stages, penetration pricing can be effective to gain customer trial, expose customers to the excellent service quality, and build customer loyalty for the brand. Such an approach can also serve to keep planes in full service, making the most of a small fleet.

However, the penetration pricing strategy has to be tempered by attention to CloudCab's financial objectives for revenue, margins, and ROI. Chances are that, once a loyal customer base is developed, some incremental price increases can be taken without major disruption in the customer base.

CloudCab can communicate its positioning through price. Being first to market, CloudCab has the opportunity to set the value of its product in the mind of the customer. In setting a price, CloudCab must be careful to realistically assess the actual time savings and comfort customers can expect to receive, and what those benefits are worth to them. In this way, the price will work together with CloudCab's integrated marketing communications (IMC) strategies to effectively position the product and communicate value.

Supply Chain Strategies

CloudCab has purchased the needed operational systems to properly track its planes and ensure they are always where they need to be. Customer service representatives will use these systems to give customers information on flight availability and schedule new flights. CloudCab's outsource firms and supply chain partners will also have access to the system to ensure needed materials arrive where and when they are needed for everything from pillows to jet fuel.

Integrated Marketing Communications (IMC) Strategies

CloudCab will first use IMC to *create awareness* of CloudCab and *build interest* in the benefits of its service. All efforts will be focused on conveying a clear and consistent message. CloudCab's unique selling proposition will be that it is akin to a taxi service in the air, much quicker and more comfortable than other travel modes.

To convey this message, CloudCab will use targeted advertising, direct marketing, personal selling, and buzz marketing. Advertising will be limited to publications with high readership among the target market. Direct and interactive marketing—primarily via mail, e-mail, and the Web—will be used to provide sales promotion incentives to customers to try CloudCab's service. Personal selling efforts will be made at consulting firms to attempt to gain contracts to make CloudCab one of the firm's transportation methods of choice. Finally, to generate buzz through public relations (PR), CloudCab will pitch stories to the media about its official launch date and first flight as a revolutionary way to travel.

Although these strategies should get CloudCab off the ground, over the long run the company will rely heavily on buzz generated by positive customer experiences to grow the business. The more people CloudCab effectively serves, the more potential brand ambassadors there will be. This should translate into an exponential sales growth for CloudCab.

IMPLEMENTATION

CloudCab possesses the needed resources for a successful launch early next year. The action plan below details the marketing communication initiatives CloudCab will undertake to increase market share and reach its goal of 5,500 flights in its first year of operation.

Marketing Action Plan for Initial Launch

Action	Date	Duration	Cost	Responsibility
Targeted print ads	December 1	4 months	$265,000	CMO Vars
CloudCab direct marketing to identified targets	February 1	3 months	$170,000	CMO Vars
Personal sales calls on key target firms	March 1	2 months	$210,000	CEO Camp and others
First CloudCab flight	May 1			COO Fray
Media coverage of first CloudCab flight	May 1	1 week	$ 3,000	CMO Vars

Monthly Sales Forecast to End of First Year

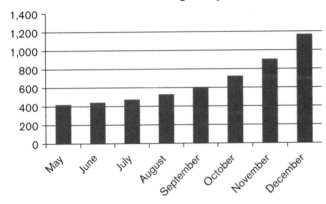

Number of Flights by Month

First-Year Budget

Using its forecasted sales volume, CloudCab can begin to establish a budget for its first year of operation. For now, CloudCab will use an estimated price of $1,200 per flight.

Revenue	5,287 x $1,200	$ 6,600,000
Fuel Costs		2,600,000
Promotional Activities		648,000
Salaries		1,200,000
Outsourced Systems		700,000
Operating Income		1,452,000
VLJ purchases		9,500,000
Net Income		$(8,048,000)

Marketing Control and Metrics

CloudCab must continually evaluate its marketing efforts to ensure its performance is on track against stated first-year objectives. The following metrics are associated with each objective.

Objective 1: Sell 5,500 Flight Itineraries

CloudCab will track sales to monitor if monthly targets are being met. If they are not, the market will have to be surveyed to determine awareness levels, and direct-mail response rates and personal selling closing ratios be examined. In doing this, problem areas should be identified and resolved. If the problem cannot be addressed via CloudCab's current IMC mix, other elements may be added to the mix to find better ways of reaching the target audience.

Objective 2: Attain a Rating of "Highly Satisfied" Customer Satisfaction Scored by 90 Percent of Customers

Progress will be monitored by ongoing customer satisfaction measurement.

Objective 3: Achieve Repeat Purchase by 50 Percent of Customers

The CRM system will be utilized to track frequency of usage by customers.

CONTINGENCY PLANNING

CloudCab's product requires significant capital investment to bring to market and cannot be easily modified. Consequently, if CloudCab's target market does not respond to the product as planned, it would likely be easier to change the market to fit the product than to change the product to fit the market. If consultants do not find sufficient value in CloudCab and purchase at the anticipated level, then investment will be made against the secondary target market of salespeople.

In addition, CloudCab needs to closely track usage by leisure travelers. If it happens that despite Cloud-Cab's intentions, a larger than anticipated number of customers are leisure travelers or represent some business segment besides consulting, then CloudCab would consider refocusing its marketing efforts on both of these targets. It will have a contingency IMC plan in place that anticipates this eventuality.

CHAPTER 03

UNDERSTANDING THE GLOBAL MARKETPLACE: MARKETING WITHOUT BORDERS

LEARNING OBJECTIVES

- Identify the various levels in the Global Marketing Experience Curve.

- Learn the essential information components for assessing a global market opportunity.

- Learn the stages of a classification system for evaluating and marketing in an emerging market.

- Define the key regional market zones and their marketing challenges.

- Describe the strategies for entering new global markets.

- Recognize key factors in creating a global product strategy.

EXECUTIVE PERSPECTIVE

Executive Ken Alloway, Global Product and Marketing Manager

Company ABB Inc.

Business Power products, power systems, automation products, process automation and robotics.

What kinds of challenges have you faced in getting the right market information needed to make global business decisions?

As our global reach expands, one challenge we face is getting reliable market intelligence about all parts of the world. To make business decisions about whether to invest in a new market or expand a product portfolio, we need the right market information. We find that we are introducing new products and services in countries and parts of the world that have limited experience with such technology. This lack of experience with such products and services means that the market intelligence is less accurate than we'd like. The less reliable the market intelligence, the greater the risk. One solution we've found is to use our local workforce in various countries to supplement local market information.

How has the Internet helped facilitate your success in global marketing?

The Internet has increased the productivity of the workplace substantially. It allows us to share information live among any number of countries. We can collaborate and receive instant feedback from anywhere around the world. This instant collaboration reduces the time required to collect the needed market intelligence. In turn, this allows us to make faster decisions and quickly confirm our strategy to move forward with projects.

In addition to using the Internet to gather market intelligence, we are now using it to train our global workforce through online presentations and tests. The interactive aspect of the Internet allows us to gauge the knowledge of our sales force and know where to focus our training efforts. As a result, we've achieved substantial improvements in our sales force, and we've achieved those improvements cost effectively.

When you enter a market outside the United States, how do you decide what market entry strategy is best?

We start by studying how the customer evaluates our products and services. Our goal is to determine if the market sees a value for the product or service. In some cases, we may learn that the product or service doesn't fit the new market. The product or service may be too sophisticated and thus too costly, or perhaps the customer does not value the technology. In those cases, we must determine if we can alter the product or service to the market need and still have a viable business case. In addition, many markets outside of the United States are extremely cost-focused. This means that we have to determine if we are willing to participate in a market that is strictly price-driven rather than value-driven.

MARKETING IS NOT LIMITED BY BORDERS

From large multinationals to small start-up companies, business is no longer confined to a company's local market. Worldwide distribution networks, sophisticated communication tools, greater product standardization, and the Internet have opened world markets. Large companies such as Nestlé, Procter & Gamble, IBM, and General Electric leverage their considerable assets to build global companies that do business anywhere in the world (see Exhibit 3.1). At the same time, with relatively minimal investment, small companies access international markets with only a Web site and an international shipping company.[1]

While the opportunities have never been greater, the risks have also never been higher. Global marketing mistakes are expensive. The international competitive landscape includes sophisticated global companies as well as successful local organizations. The operating environment varies dramatically around the world creating real challenges for companies moving into new markets. Global customers demand different products, which means that successful products in a company's local market frequently have to be adapted to new markets.[2] All these factors establish global marketing as one of the most demanding but rewarding areas in marketing.

As you study topics like marketing communications, product development, or consumer decision making, consider how each is affected by global markets. Our goal in this chapter is to identify very early in your study of marketing management the challenges marketers face in global markets today. While it is certainly true that the global marketing manager for Huggies has different challenges than the marketing manager for a small software company, it is equally true that both need to know how marketing internationally is similar and different to marketing in their home market. Because marketing has no borders we put this discussion at the beginning of the book.

With sales slowing in the United States, Kentucky Fried Chicken has moved successfully into global markets, most notably China. There are currently 1,700 KFC stores across China with sales of almost $500 million and growing at a double-digit rate annually. Its mascot, Chicky, is reportedly more popular than Ronald McDonald. KFC has adapted its menu to local tastes by creating such favorites as Dragon Twister (a chicken sandwich with Peking duck sauce, cucumbers, and scallions).[3]

EXHIBIT 3.1	World's Largest International Companies in 2008

Company	Revenue ($ Millions)
Wal-Mart Stores	$378,799
ExxonMobil	372,824
Royal Dutch Shell	355,782
BP	291,438
Toyota Motor	230,201
Chevron	210,783
ING Group	201,516
Total	187,280
General Motors	182,347
Conoco Phillips	$178,558

Source: From Fortune Global 600, July 23, 2007. Copyright © 2007 Time, Inc. All rights reserved.

THE GLOBAL EXPERIENCE LEARNING CURVE

An understanding of marketing beyond home markets develops over time as a company gets more international business experience. This process is referred to as *the global experience learning curve*. In some cases this happens quickly. General Motors moved into Canada in 1918, only two years after being incorporated, and eBay opened in the United Kingdom during its first year of operation. However, other companies take much longer to push into global markets. Wal-Mart opened its first international store in Mexico City in 1991; nearly 30 years after Sam Walton opened the first store in Bentonville, Arkansas. Exhibit 3.2 lists the global expansion histories of a number of companies.

Bennetton takes a global perspective targeting the United States and other countries around the world with many different products.

EXHIBIT 3.2	Examples of Global Companies and Their Expansion into Global Markets

Years to Expansion	U. S. Company	First Expansion
29	Wal-Mart (est. 1962)	1991: Wal-Mart opens two units in Mexico City.
20	Hewlett-Packard (est. 1939)	1959: – HP sets up a European marketing organization in Geneva, Switzerland, and a manufacturing plant in Germany.
26	Tyson Foods (est. 1963)	1989: Tyson establishes a partnership with a Mexican poultry company, to create an international partnership, http://www.tyson.com/Corporate/AboutTyson/History/1970s.aspx.
25	Caterpillar (est. 1925)	1950: Caterpillar Tractor Co. Ltd. in Great Britain is founded.
19	Home Depot (est. 1979)	1998: Home Depot enters the Puerto Rican market followed by entry into Argentina.
18	Gap (est. 1969)	1987: The first Gap store outside the United States opens in London on George Street.
12	Goodyear (est. 1898)	1910: Goodyear's Canadian plant opens.
10	FedEx (est. 1971)	1981: International delivery begins with service to Canada.
1	PepsiCo (est. 1965)	1966: Pepsi enters Japan and Eastern Europe.

The global experience learning curve moves a company through four distinct stages: no foreign marketing, foreign marketing, international marketing, and global marketing. The process is not always linear; companies may, for example, move directly from no foreign marketing to international marketing without necessarily engaging in foreign marketing. In addition, the amount of time spent in any stage can vary; some companies remain in a stage for many years.

Companies with No Foreign Marketing

Many companies with *no direct foreign marketing* still do business with international customers through intermediaries or limited direct contact. In these cases, however, there is no formal international channel relationship or global marketing strategy targeted at international customers. Of course, any company with a Web site is now a global company as someone can visit the site from anywhere in the world, but companies with no foreign marketing consider any sales to an international customer as incidental.

The typical company with no foreign marketing is usually small with a limited range of products. Increasingly though, small companies move into international markets much faster than even a decade ago. This is due, in part, to domestic distributor relationships, local customers with global operations, and effective Web sites, which have all created international opportunities for many small companies with limited resources.

Companies with Foreign Marketing

Companies often develop a more formal international strategy by following their existing customers into foreign markets. Domestic customers with global operations may demand more service or place additional orders that require the company to work with their foreign subsidiaries. This stage of the global experience learning curve is called *foreign marketing* and involves developing local distribution and service representation in a foreign market in one of two ways. One method is to identify local intermediaries in appropriate international markets and create a formal relationship. The second approach is for the company to establish its own direct sales force in major markets, thereby expanding the company's direct market reach.

In either scenario, key activities (product planning and development, production) are still done in the company's home market, but products are modified to fit international requirements. Global markets are important enough for management to build international sales forecasts, and manufacturing allocates time specifically to international production. At this point, international markets are no longer an afterthought but, rather, an integral, albeit small, part of the company's growth model.[4]

International Marketing

When a firm makes the commitment to produce products outside its domestic market it is engaged in *international marketing*. While companies can be heavily involved in international markets with extensive selling organizations and distribution networks, the decision to produce outside its home market marks a significant shift toward an integrated international market strategy. Global markets become an essential component of the company's growth strategy, and resources are allocated to expand the business into those markets. The company incorporates an international division or business unit that has responsibility for growing the business in targeted foreign markets.

International marketing aligns the company's assets and resources with global markets, but, in the vast majority of companies, management still takes a "domestic first" approach to the business. As a result, the corporate structure still divides international and domestic markets.

Ryanair, sometimes referred to as "Wal-Mart on Wings," dominates the low-cost airfare market in Europe with a no-frills service that charges passengers for everything (assigned seats are extra as well as priority boarding). Also, the airline is a rolling billboard of advertisers with passengers even seeing ads on the back of seat-back trays. However, the company does offer very low prices.[5]

Global Marketing

A *global marketing* company realizes that all world markets (including the company's own domestic market) are, in reality, a single market with many different segments. This frequently happens when a company generates more than half its revenue in international markets. Exhibit 3.3 highlights companies considered traditional American companies but which generate more than half their revenue outside the United States.

The most significant difference between international and global marketing organizations is management philosophy and corporate planning. Global marketers treat the world as a single, unified market with many different segments that may or may not fall along country political boundaries. International marketers, on the other hand, define markets along traditional political boundaries and, most often, assign unique status to their domestic market.

Gruma is the world's leading producer of tortillas. Despite price controls in its home market, Mexico, the company continues to grow. Two-thirds of the company's $3 billion annual sales comes from global markets. Building on market dominance in Mexico, the company has bought brands and has built manufacturing plants around the world. The company currently operates 89 global plants with the most recent in Shanghai that was built specifically to supply KFC restaurants in China.[6]

EXHIBIT 3.3	Large U.S. Companies with Over 50% of Revenue from International Markets

Company	Percent of Sales from International Markets
Coca-Cola	71%
McDonald's	66
Hewlett-Packard	65
Dow Chemical	62
Nike	62
3M	61
Motorola	54
Caterpillar	52
Chevron	52

| EXHIBIT 3.4 | Top 5 Economies Based on GDP |

Top 5 Economies	GDP (purchasing power parity)
European Union	$ 14,380,000,000,000
United States	$ 13,840,000,000,000
China	$ 6,991,000,000,000
Japan	$ 4,290,000,000,000
India	$ 2,989,000,000,000

Source: *2008 CIA World Fact Book*

The first step in moving into global markets is to evaluate the market opportunities. Since a company's management team is usually less familiar with foreign markets, research helps fill in the blanks, providing critical information for decision makers.

Essential Information

Global market research focuses on five basic types of information.

Economic

An accurate understanding of the current economic environment, such as gross domestic product (GDP) growth, inflation, strength of the currency, and business cycle trends, is essential. Also, depending on the company's target markets (consumer or business), additional economic data on consumer spending per capita (consumer products) or industrial purchasing trends (business products) are also needed to facilitate decision making. Exhibit 3.4 identifies the five largest economies in the world based on GDP, which is the total market value of all final goods and services produced in a country in a given year and one of the most widely used measures of economic growth.

Culture, Societal Trends

Understanding a global market's culture and social trends is fundamental for consumer products and helpful for business-to-business marketers. Cultural values, symbols and rituals, and cultural differences affect people's perception of products while B2B companies must learn local cultural practices to recruit employees and establish good business relationships.[7]

Business Environment

Knowledge of the business environment is essential for companies moving into foreign markets where they will invest significant resources. Ethical standards, management styles, degree of formality, and gender or other biases are all critical factors that management needs to know before entering a new market. Failure to understand the business environment can lead to misunderstanding and lost relationships as the company enters a new market. (See Exhibit 3.5 for examples.)

Political and Legal

Local political changes can create significant uncertainties for a business. As witnessed in Bolivia and other countries, new governments sometimes alter the relationship of government to industry by exerting greater control and even nationalizing some industries.

EXHIBIT 3.5	Business Customs in Five Selected Countries

When you are doing business in. . .	Remember. . .
The Czech Republic	Relationship building is important. Start with small talk and get to know the individual you are working with.
France	You should address the French as Monsieur or Madame followed by their last name. Use first names only after you are encouraged to do so.
Japan	Exchanging business cards is like a little ceremony. Use both hands to accept the card and look over each side before you slip it into your jacket pocket or briefcase.
Germany	Punctuality is extremely important. Be on time or you may seem disrespectful.
Colombia	Colombians stand closer to each other than do Americans. Do not step back if you feel they are too close; you may seem rude.

Source: www.kwintessential.co.uk/etiquette/doing-business-in.html.

Learning the legal landscape is fundamental before committing resources in a foreign market. Developing countries frequently limit the flow of money out of a country, making it harder for a foreign company to transfer money back home. Labor laws also vary widely around the world. Germany and France, for example, make it difficult to terminate someone once that person has been hired, while Great Britain's termination policies are more consistent with those of the United States.

Coca-Cola and PepsiCo are both selling their soft drinks in Iran, one of the Middle East's biggest beverage markets and a country that American companies are banned from doing business in. However, some American food products companies have obtained permission from the U.S. Treasury and are marketing their products through local subsidiaries. The two soft drink giants currently control 50 percent of the Iranian soft drink market, making Iran the latest battleground in the cola wars.[8]

Specific Market Conditions

Before entering a foreign market, a company has some understanding of the specific market conditions for its own products as a result of business knowledge. However, it is unlikely a company has in-depth knowledge about market trends, competitors, and unique market characteristics. Unfortunately, many companies that follow customers into a particular market believe it is unnecessary to know a lot about local market conditions. This lack of understanding can limit growth opportunities. The more a company knows about the local market environment, the better they will be able to leverage their investment in that market. The accompanying FYI examines how Toyota is learning to attack the big pickup truck market in the United States.

Toyota made a significant investment to the U.S. truck market by building a plant near San Antonio to produce the Toyota Tundra.

Toyota introduced a new version of its Tundra truck aimed directly at the last big market dominated by U.S. auto manufacturers—the full-size pickup truck market. A worldwide leader in automobiles, Toyota enjoys market leadership in its home market (Japan) and strong positions in other markets around the world such as the United States. Given the success of full-size pickups (three of the top five selling vehicles in the United States are full-size pickup trucks: the Ford F-150, Chevrolet Silverado, and Dodge Ram), Toyota wanted to build a full-size pickup truck to compete with Ford, Chevy, and Dodge.

Toyota introduced the Tundra in May 1999 and, while it sold well, critics called it too small and "car like" to compete with the big American trucks and referred to the Tundra as a "7/8" scale pickup truck. The company decided that a more aggressive strategy was needed and redesigned the Tundra to be bigger and more powerful. To support the redesigned Tundra, Toyota built a new $1.3 billion plant in San Antonio, Texas, and allocated more than $100 million for marketing communications during the product's rollout.

Pricing for the new product was a challenge as dealers wanted competitive pricing (low prices) to target Ford and Chevy buyers. Toyota, however, chose an interesting strategy of maintaining a higher base price relative to the market leaders but including more features such as traction control and side air bags. The company knows buyers focused primarily on price will probably not purchase the new Tundra. However, Toyota believes the Tundra competes well in the most profitable segment of the pickup market, option-loaded trucks with a long list of standard features. Here, Toyota's strategy of including many features that are considered extra on competing trucks makes the Tundra a better value.[9]

Emerging Markets

World economic growth for much of the 20th century was fueled by the **developed economies** of Western Europe, the United States, and Japan. Over the past 25 years, however, while developed economies continue to grow, the most significant economic growth is found in **emerging markets.** Indeed, 75 percent of world economic growth over the next 20 years is projected to come from emerging economies, most notably China and India. These economic growth engines create market opportunities for companies, which, in turn, means marketers need to understand the unique challenges and opportunities of emerging markets.[10] Exhibit 3.6 highlights the fastest-growing economies in the world. Notice that the fastest-growing economies are small and their significant percentage growth is due in large part to the fact that the country's economy is starting from a much smaller economic base. Azerbaijan, for example, grew an amazing 23.40 percent in 2007, but that does not mean it represents a good market opportunity.

It is a cliché but still true that not all markets are created equal, and part of assessing a country's global opportunity involves understanding its stage of economic development. Economic historian Walt W. Rostow developed a classification system for evaluating markets that has been widely adopted. This classification system includes five stages of development and works best as a general guide rather than a model of specific global markets' economic development. It does not account for unique historical or current events affecting the country of interest. The final stage represents the economies of the United States, Germany, Great Britain, Japan, and other developed, industrialized countries.

EXHIBIT 3.6 Fastest-Growing World Economies

Country	2007 GDP Real Growth Rate (%)
Azerbaijan	23.40%
Bhutan	22.40
Angola	21.10
Timor-Leste	19.80
Macau	16.40
Qatar	14.20
Armenia	13.80
Afghanistan	12.40
Equatorial Guinea	12.40
Georgia	12.40

Source: *2008 CIA World Fact Book.*

Stage 1: The Traditional Society (for example, Sudan). Dependent on agriculture as the primary driver of the economy, these economies lack the capabilities to industrialize. Illiteracy is high, which hinders advances in technology.

Stage 2: Preconditions for Take-Off (for example, Romania). In these economies, new investments in infrastructure (transportation, communication, education, and health care) create the foundation for growth and encourage industrial expansion. Often these changes are driven by investments from private organizations (foreign companies looking to expand operations). Global companies target countries at this stage for production and other facilities because the cost of entry is very low. Moreover, it is possible to build a strong market position before the economy enters the next stage. In addition, countries at this stage often receive government assistance (from industrialized economies such as the United States or European Union or nongovernmental agencies such as the United Nations).

Stage 3: Take-Off (for example, The Czech Republic). The investments in infrastructure yield sustainable economic growth, which makes an economy look much more attractive to foreign investors. The economy transitions from agricultural to industrial. Banking systems, technology industries, and other "skilled" industries come into the market as business opportunities increase.

Stage 4: Maturity (for example, China). The economy, through private and public investments, seeks to maintain growth rates. As the economy grows, investments focus on expanding the infrastructure (technology and communications networks) to attract additional industrial investment. At this point, local companies begin to look outward and enter the global marketplace. Governments through legislation and public policy or investors through private development will target certain key industries to create a core global competency. Ireland, for example, identified technology and banking as key industries in the 1980s and created special incentives to attract companies in those industries. As a result Ireland is now a world leader in both technology and banking.

Stage 5: High Mass Consumption (for example, Germany). Consumption patterns shift as consumers demand higher levels of service and more durable goods.

Income levels rise, creating a large population with discretionary income. Put another way, people are no longer concerned with simply surviving (food, shelter) but, rather, seek products and services that enhance the quality of their life. In other words, products are not needed but wanted.

> Silverjet was one of several start-up airlines targeting the business traveler. Competing against established carriers such as British Airways, it offered business-class service between New York and London for $1,000 to $3,500 round-trip compared to $8,000 on other airlines. Early success led the major airlines to upgrade their business class but not match the new competitors on price. Luxury airlines like Silverjet do not have a history of success; rising fuel costs and a economic downturn forced the company into bankruptcy, however, demand for business class travel remains strong.[11]

Marketing in Emerging Markets

The nature of emerging markets means traditional marketing methods will not be effective. For example, if the majority of a country lacks a television or radio and cannot read, traditional advertising campaigns will not work, or if a country lacks a distribution network, it will not be possible to deliver products to customers.

The challenge for marketers, particularly consumer products companies, is that demand for their products may be strong but there is insufficient income to purchase the product and inadequate infrastructure to support sophisticated market programs. Soon after the Velvet Revolution in the Czech Republic, Estee Lauder opened a store in Prague targeted at Czech women living in the capital.[12] At first the company experienced problems because products that sold well in Western Europe and the United States simply were not being purchased. The company came to realize the products were sized and priced according to Western European standards and too expensive for the local Czech businesswoman. The solution was to sell sample sizes (which are often offered as premiums in promotional packages sold in the United States) for a fraction of the large product sizes. Czech women wanted to purchase Estee Lauder cosmetics, but at a size and price consistent with the local market.

Multinational Regional Market Zones

The single most significant global economic trend over the past 15 years is the emergence of regional market zones around the world. **Regional market zones** consist of a group of countries that create formal relationships for mutual economic benefit through lower tariffs and reduced trade barriers. In some cases, such as the European Union, their influence extends beyond economic concerns to political and social issues. Many countries believe membership in an economic alliance will be essential for access to markets in the future. As the world divides itself into a handful of powerful economic alliances, countries feel pressure to align with a regional market zone. Exhibit 3.7 identifies four of the largest regional market zones.

Regional market zones generally form as a result of four forces. The first and most fundamental factor is *economic*. Many small and medium-sized countries believe growth in their own country will be enhanced by forming alliances with other countries. By enlarging the trading area and creating a market zone, each country benefits economically and the market zone has more power in the global marketplace. Second, research suggests *geographic proximity* to other alliance partners is advantageous in the development of a market zone. Transportation and communication networks are more likely to connect countries close to one

EXHIBIT 3.7 | **Top Four Regional Market Zones**

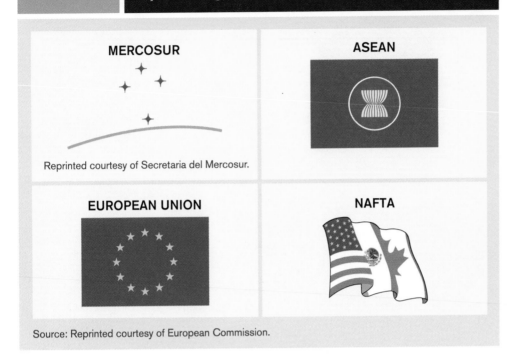

MERCOSUR

Reprinted courtesy of Secretaria del Mercosur.

ASEAN

EUROPEAN UNION

NAFTA

Source: Reprinted courtesy of European Commission.

another, making it easier to facilitate market zone activities. Other issues such as immigration also tend to be handled more effectively when the distance between partners is minimized. The third factor is *political.* Closely related to increased economic power is increased political clout, particularly as smaller countries form broad political alliances. A prerequisite for effective political alliances among countries is general agreement on government policies. Countries with widely disparate political structures find it difficult to accommodate those differences in a political alliance. *Culture similarities,* such as having a shared language, among alliance partners also facilitate markets zones as shared cultural experiences encourage greater cooperation and minimize possible conflicts from cultural disparities.

Europe

The **European Union** is the most successful regional market zone and it is also one of the oldest. Founded more than 50 years ago by six countries (Belgium, France, Italy, Luxembourg, the Netherlands, and West Germany) with the Treaty of Rome, the EU now includes 25 countries spanning all of Europe (see Exhibit 3.8). In addition, two countries, Croatia and Turkey—are seeking membership in the European Union. The process of becoming a member of the EU takes many years, and applicants must meet a wide range of economic, social, and legal criteria. One of the most difficult challenges for many member states is meeting targeted government spending and total debt limits. France and Germany (the two largest members of the EU) have both failed to meet government spending limits in recent years, and the debt limits of countries like Italy exceed the EU guidelines. With few consequences for missing EU targets, many governments focus more on local country priorities than EU directives.[13]

The EU has become one of the most dominant economic entities in the world, its economic output is the largest in the world, and its currency, the euro, is one of the leading world currencies. The European Union's influence extends far beyond economics because member countries grant the EU significant political and social power to enact laws, create taxes, and exert tremendous social

EXHIBIT 3.8 **Composition of the EU since its creation**

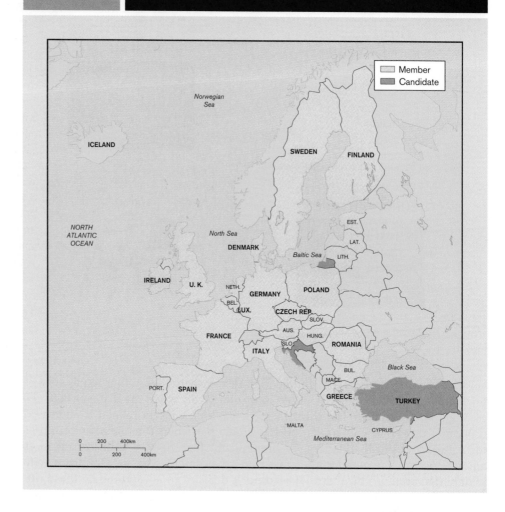

influence in the lives of citizens. For example, the EU has adopted strong socially responsible policies for companies doing business in member countries. Ethical Dimensions 3 examines McDonald's strategy for dealing with increased environmental and social concerns in Europe

Americas

The most significant market zone in the Americas is the alliance of the United States, Canada, and Mexico, which is commonly referred to by the treaty that created the alliance, **NAFTA (North American Free Trade Agreement).** NAFTA created the single largest economic alliance and has eliminated tariffs between the member countries for more than 15 years. Exhibit 3.9 lists NAFTA's main provisions. Many industries, such as automaking, have manufacturing plants in Mexico to supply the U.S. market. Retailers have also benefited; Gigante, a large Mexican supermarket chain, operates in the United States while Wal-Mart, a U.S. company, has over 800 stores in Mexico.[14]

NAFTA is not the only market zone in the Americas. **MERCOSUR,** the most powerful market zone in South America, was inaugurated in 1995 and includes the major economies of South America: Argentina, Bolivia, Brazil, Chile, Paraguay, and Uruguay. With over 200 million people and a combined GDP of more than $1 trillion, it is currently the third-largest free trade area in the world.[15] One of the drawbacks has been a limited transnational transportation network, which restricts the movement of goods between member countries. However, MERCO-SUR has overcome this problem by successfully leveraging the combined economic

When Ethics Meets Good Business in Europe

Companies no longer consider ethical decisions and good business decisions to be mutually exclusive. For example, McDonald's takes a comprehensive environmental approach to its European operations with a variety of strategies targeted at increasing the environmental footprint of the company. Among the many product changes instituted by McDonald's is the sale of coffee certified by the Rainforest Alliance, a global nonprofit based in New York, at its more than 7,000 European outlets. McDonald's seeks to differentiate itself from other upscale food chains and other coffeehouses by selling a new brand of socially responsible coffee, Kenco. Steve Easterbrook, president and COO of McDonald's U.K., states, "We can offer our customers great tasting coffee that doesn't cost the earth and benefits coffee growers, their communities, and the environment."

The change to environmentally friendly coffee is the latest in a series of strategic moves designed to position McDonald's as a leader in the environmental movement. Whenever possible, the company purchases from local producers who meet established standards for animal welfare and safe environmental practices. It also bans the use of certain growth-promoting antibiotics in its poultry (a significant concern in Europe).

Increasingly, consumers consider a product's environmental impact in making their purchase decision. Is the product safe? Is the product healthy? What is the effect of the product on the environment? McDonald's research suggests consumers are willing to pay for "green" products. "Consumers more than ever want to do business with those companies that share their values, and because of our track record on environmental issues, we see lots of opportunity to close the gap between misconceptions and reality," says Bob Langert, McDonald's vice president of corporate social responsibility.

The challenge McDonald's faces is balancing environmental responsibility with consumer expectations about product quality and, in this case, tastes and value. Before making a change, McDonald's must know whether the market will accept it, which means significant product testing as well as sourcing of quality products.

McDonald's realizes that being sensitive to the health of its customers and the environment as a whole makes sense for its customers, the environment, and the company. Rita Clifton, chairman of Interbrand, U.K., notes, "Companies are increasingly trying to boost social responsibility programs because they know that not to do so is a major corporate risk."[16]

Ethical Perspective

1. **McDonald's:** Should McDonald's support the additional costs of carrying environmentally friendly coffee if it becomes unprofitable? Do you see any challenges for McDonald's in selling Kenco coffee?

2. **Consumers:** What is the price differential you would be willing to pay for McDonald's environmentally friendly gourmet coffee?

3. **Competitors:** How should Starbucks respond to this challenge by McDonald's?

EXHIBIT 3.9	Key Provisions of NAFTA

NAFTA aims to:

- Eliminate barriers to trade in, and facilitate the cross-border movement of, goods and services between the territories of the Parties.
- Promote conditions of fair competition in the free trade area.
- Increase substantially investment opportunities in the territories of the Parties.
- Provide adequate and effective protection and enforcement of intellectual property rights in each Party's territory.
- Create effective procedures for the implementation and application of this Agreement, for its joint administration and for the resolution of disputes; and
- Establish a framework for further trilateral, regional, and multilateral cooperation to expand and enhance the benefits of this Agreement.

Source: www.mac.doc.gov/nafta/chapter1.html.

Many countries, including the United States, and even some cities promote their strengths to attract companies to locate there. The state of Ohio presents a "balanced" approach to life and work

power of the individual member countries and creating additional economic benefits for its members.

Asia

The most important Asian market zone is **ASEAN,** which was founded in 1967 and comprises 10 countries in the Pacific Rim (Brunei Darussalam, Indonesia, Malaysia, Philippines, Cambodia, Laos, Myanmar, Singapore, Thailand, and Vietnam). After the 1997–1998 Asian financial crisis, the group added China, Japan, and South Korea. While the relationships with these "plus 3" countries are less developed than the full member countries, the combined economic activity of all participants makes ASEAN a powerful global economic force.[17] The GDP of the 10 full members is over $600 billion, and if the "plus 3" countries are included the combined total is over $7 trillion.

Marketing in Regional Market Zones

The formation of regional market zones presents marketing managers with a number of challenges and opportunities. As market zones lower tariffs and reduce trade barriers, companies view zone members more holistically. Rather than looking at Brazil and Argentina as separate markets, companies can develop regional marketing plans that facilitate greater cost efficiencies (e.g., lowering distribution costs) and increase effectiveness of the marketing effort (e.g., creating regional advertising campaigns based on the free flow of products throughout the zone). In addition, greater market zone coordination dramatically reduces transaction costs and makes it easier for companies to determine appropriate product cost models and subsequent pricing strategies.

At the same time, however, each of these market zones suffers from internal conflicts. Lowering trade barriers, reducing tariffs, and harmonizing government spending and taxation rates among members requires difficult choices that all too often governments are not willing to make. When internal conflicts (high trade barriers and tariffs or increased government spending and taxation) remain between market zone members, marketers must deal with greater marketing complexity and higher costs. In addition, while members open markets between themselves, they frequently raise barriers to other market zones and individual countries. The results are bilateral agreements with individual countries that negate the advantages of operating in a market zone.

SELECT THE GLOBAL MARKET

Conducting a thorough assessment of potential global market opportunities is an essential first step in entering the global market. Once the analysis is completed, it is time to select specific countries for future investment. Deciding which countries to enter is difficult because the risk of failure is very high. Targeting the wrong country can lead to very high costs and unprofitable long-term investments. Wal-Mart pulled out of the German market at an estimated cost of $400 million. On the other hand, moving too slowly into a market can hamper growth and limit profit potential in the future. EBay's decision to move slowly into China cost the company a dominant position in the market.

Bollywood, India's film industry, has been overshadowed by its U.S. counterpart, Hollywood. Despite making more than 1,000 movies a year, total sales are less than $2 billion compared with slightly more than 500 Hollywood films grossing more than $18 billion worldwide. Using the Hollywood business model, companies such as UTV Software Communications are creating movies using tighter budgets, and then exporting them to new markets like the United States, while merging with former competitors to create economies of scale.[18]

Identify Selection Criteria

Companies usually have a variety of different criteria for evaluating and selecting global markets. The criteria should reflect the company's commitment to ongoing corporate objectives and incorporate both market and financial targets designed to help marketing managers consider not only the marketing implications of choosing a particular country but also the financial consequences of the decision.

Market selection criteria incorporate the nature of the competitive environment, including both local and global competitors, as well as target market size and future growth rates. Marketing managers need to know which markets will be the easiest and which will be the most difficult to enter. In addition, the size and future growth potential of international markets is critical in making the long-term commitment to produce in an international market. On the other hand, financial criteria focus on the cost of market entry and profitability estimates over given time periods. Decision makers are particularly interested in knowing the size of the investment and the length of time it will take before the company can expect to be profitable in a new market.[19]

Company Review

As a marketing manager you will need to evaluate global market opportunities against key company characteristics to look for markets that maximize the company's strengths while minimizing weaknesses. Moving into new foreign markets brings greater risk to the company. As a result, decision makers must consider whether their company philosophy, personnel skill sets (principally in critical areas such as marketing and logistics), organizational structure, management expertise, and financial resources support the move into new countries (see Exhibit 3.10). Comparing the analysis of market opportunities with company characteristics drives the final selection as management looks for the best fit between each country's mix of opportunities/threats and the company's strengths/weaknesses.

DEVELOP GLOBAL MARKET STRATEGIES

After selecting a country, you must develop a comprehensive marketing strategy. International expansion requires a reassessment of existing marketing strategies. Companies often mistakenly believe they can adapt existing market strategies to new international markets. Unfortunately, successful market tactics in the company's home market often fail to translate well into foreign markets. As a result, it is necessary to construct a marketing plan specifically designed for entering global markets.

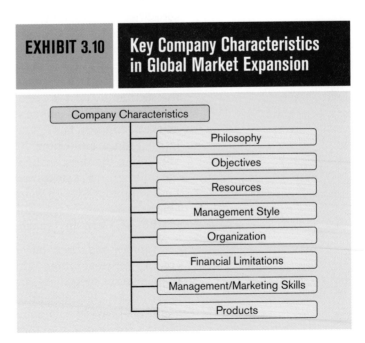

EXHIBIT 3.10 | **Key Company Characteristics in Global Market Expansion**

Company Characteristics
- Philosophy
- Objectives
- Resources
- Management Style
- Organization
- Financial Limitations
- Management/Marketing Skills
- Products

Market Entry Strategies

The first decision is how to enter the market. An entry strategy is the framework for entering a new global market, so choosing the right strategy is critical. This decision affects all other marketing decisions. In addition, deciding on a market entry strategy has long-term implications because once the strategy is selected it is difficult and expensive to change.

Entry into new global markets follows one of four basic strategies: exporting, contractual agreements, strategic alliances, and ownership. Within these basic strategies are various options. Generally, companies enter new markets by exporting because it offers minimal investment and lower risk. At the same time, potential return on investment and profitability are lower and the company has very little control over the process. As a company strengthens its international involvement there is the potential for greater financial returns and control over the process; however, risk and company investments increase.

Exporting

Exporting is the most common method for entering foreign markets and accounts for 10 percent of all global economic activity. Primary advantages include the ability to penetrate foreign markets with minimal investment and very little risk. Frequently, companies lack a coherent exporting strategy and take an opportunistic approach that simply fills orders without regard to any specific analysis or targeting.

Most people consider exporting an initial entry strategy and not a long-term approach to global marketing. However, some very large companies find exporting a viable strategy despite a global market presence. Boeing and Airbus, the two manufacturers of large jet airliners, both follow an exporting strategy, manufacturing the jets in their home markets (Boeing in the United States, Airbus in Europe) and then using a direct sales force to market their planes around the world.[20]

Internet. Without question, the Internet has expanded the global reach of every company with a Web site. Initially, the Internet was considered a tool for increasing domestic sales, but that has changed as Internet access has expanded worldwide. Exhibit 3.11 highlights the growth of the Internet since 1990. Critical to the success of the Internet market entry strategy is easy payment and credit terms offered by global credit companies such as MasterCard, Visa, and American Express. Credit cards and other financial payment systems have greatly simplified transactions, making it easier for the customer to purchase and more secure for the company to sell products anywhere in the world. Another key is the ability to deliver products anywhere in the world on time and in good working order using global delivery companies such as UPS, FedEx, and DHL. This greatly enhances customer and company confidence in a successful transaction.

Internet retailers such as Amazon.com have moved aggressively into global markets. Amazon has opened sites for Germany, the United Kingdom, Canada, Japan, France, and China. In the United Kingdom and Germany, Amazon's sites are among the most visited commercial sites. The Internet has also expanded the international market reach of catalog retailers such as L.L. Bean and Lands' End. People in foreign markets who never have seen an L.L. Bean catalog are able to make purchases online because the company Web site offers instructions in Chinese, German, French, and Spanish.[21]

Exporter and Distributor. The next of level of exporting involves having country representation, which can take several forms. **Exporters** are international market specialists that help companies by acting as the export marketing department. They generally do not have much contact with the company, but exporters provide a valuable service with their knowledge of policies and procedures for shipping to foreign markets. For small companies with little or no

EXHIBIT 3.11

Internet Access around the World

Country	Number of Users in 1990	Current Number of Users
Australia	100,000	11,240,000
Austria	10,000	4,277,000
Belgium	100	5,220,000
Canada	100,000	28,000,000
Denmark	5,000	3,500,000
Finland	20,000	3,600,000
France	30,000	31,295,000
Germany	100,000	42,500,000
Israel	5,000	2,000,000
Italy	10,000	32,000,000
Japan	25,000	88,110,000
Korea, Rep	10,000	35,590,000
Netherlands	50,000	15,000,000
Norway	30,000	3,800,000
Spain	5,000	19,690,000
United Kingdom	50,000	40,200,000
United States	2,000,000	247,000,000

Source: http://earthtrends.wri.org/. and *2008 CIA World Fact Book*, October, 2008.

international experience, exporters expedite the process of getting the product to a foreign customer.

Distributors represent the company and often many others in foreign markets. These organizations become the face of the company in that country, servicing customers, selling products, and receiving payments. In many cases, they take title to the goods and then resell them. The primary advantages are that distributors know their own local markets and offer a company physical representation in a global market, saving the company from committing major resources to hire and staff its own operations. The disadvantages are lack of control since distributors do not work directly for the company and lower profitability resulting from the distributor's markup.

Direct Sales Force. Staffing a direct sales force in foreign markets is a significant step for a company moving into global markets. It is expensive to staff and maintain a local sales team in a foreign market; however, companies will often make the commitment because of the level of control and expertise offered by company-trained salespeople. For some industries, creating a direct sales force is required because customers will demand that company salespeople be in the country. This is often the case in the technology and high-end industrial product industries.

Contractual Agreements

Contractual agreements allow a company to expand participation in a market by creating enduring, non-equity relationships with another company, often a local company in that market. Most often these agreements transmit something of value such as technology, a trademark, a patent, or a unique manufacturing process in return for financial compensation in the form of a licensing fee or percentage of sales.

> Sony, unable to perfect blue laser technology in its own labs, licensed the technology from a small Japanese company, Nichia Corporation. Sony spent five years and hundreds of millions of dollars on development but, in the end, turned to Nichia, which held more than 800 patents on blue laser video technology. At the same time, competitors such as Toshiba came to market with competing formats (HD DVD). However, with acceptance of the Blu-Ray format by large movie studios, it appears Sony's investment has paid off.[22]

Licensing. Companies choose **licensing** when local partnerships are required by law, legal restrictions prohibit direct importing of the product, or the company's limited financial resources limit more active foreign participation. Companies seeking to establish greater presence in a market without committing significant resources can choose to license their key asset (patent, trademark) to another company, effectively giving the company the right to use that asset in that market. Small and medium-sized companies with a specific product competence that lack the willingness or expertise to invest heavily in foreign operations can identify a license partner in a particular foreign market to manufacture products or provide critical services such as local distribution. In addition, larger companies use this approach to help in exporting and even manufacturing products where more extensive investments are not justified. Pharmaceutical companies are global manufacturers but also license their products in a number of foreign markets. For example, Helsinn Healthcare SA and PT Kalbe Farma Tbk. signed an agreement giving Kalbe Farma the exclusive license and distribution rights in Indonesia for Aloxi, a drug that prevents nausea and vomiting after chemotherapy.[23] In these situations, there is limited direct risk to the company, though selecting the wrong licensing partner can be a major problem. On the other hand, licensing does not offer high profit potential and can limit long-term opportunities if a company awards an extended licensing contract.

Franchising. This market entry method has been growing over the last decade and enables companies to gain access to a foreign market with local ownership. The franchiser, usually a company seeking to enter a foreign market, agrees to supply a bundle of products, systems, services, and management expertise to the franchisee in return for local market knowledge, financial consideration (franchisee fee, percentage of sales, required purchasing of certain products from franchiser), and local management experience. Franchisers exert a great deal of control with extensive franchise agreements that dictate how the franchisee will operate the business.[24] In this way, the franchiser is able to maintain some level of quality control at the point of customer contact. As Exhibit 3.12 shows, with more than 27,000 franchises, 7-Eleven leads the list of franchising companies although Subway and McDonald's are not far behind

Franchising, as a global market entry strategy, really took off in the 1990s and has been the first point of entry for many retailers looking to expand international operations. McDonald's, Burger King, KFC, and others have created large franchising networks around the world. Nearly two-thirds of McDonald's restaurants are outside the United States. Combining low capital investments, rapid expansion opportunities, and local market expertise, franchising offers many advantages as a market entry strategy. However, there are also challenges. Worldwide,

EXHIBIT 3.12	Major Franchising Companies and Number of Franchises

Company	Approximate Number of Franchises
7-Eleven, Inc.	27,161
Subway	26,197
McDonald's	22,554
Curves	9,583
Domino's Pizza	7,652
Dunkin' Donuts	6,892
RE/MAX International Inc.	6,538
Super 8 Motels	2,034
GNC	2,019
Jiffy Lube International Inc.	1,946

consumer tastes vary significantly and franchisers need sufficient resources to create products that will meet demands of global customers while maintaining quality control.

Strategic Alliances

As a market entry strategy, **strategic alliances** have grown in importance over the past 20 years in an effort to spread risk to other partners. In some industries, strategic alliances now dominate the competitive landscape. Nowhere is this more noticeable than in the airline industry. **one**world Alliance (American Airlines, British Airways, Qantas, Cathay Pacific), Sky Team (Air France, KLM, Delta, Continental, Korean Air, AeroMexico), and Star (United, Lufthansa) have created a worldwide network of airline partnerships that include code-sharing, frequent flyer mileage partnerships, and some logistical support. All these alliances are designed to make each airline stronger at its weakest point. Building a global airline is extremely expensive and it is much more cost-effective for Delta to partner with Air France to reach cities inside Europe than it is to build its own network. In reality, it would not even be possible with local legal restrictions favoring local airlines.[25] As a result, creating strategic alliances is a necessity, and airlines create broad global partnerships to extend their reach (see Exhibit 3.13).

International Joint Venture. A specific type of strategic alliance called joint venture enables many companies to enter a market that would otherwise be closed because of legal restrictions or cultural barriers.[26] Additionally, like all strategic alliances, it reduces risk by spreading risk to other partners. **Joint ventures** are a partnership of two or more participating companies and differ from other strategic alliances in that (1) management duties are shared and a management structure is defined, (2) other corporations or legally entities, not individuals, formed the venture, and (3) every partner holds an equity position. Since both partners have equity in the joint venture and share in management duties, it is essential to choose the right partner. To avoid problems, each partner must define what it brings to the joint venture in terms of reputation, resources, and management expertise. Additional critical topics include management structure, cost sharing, and control.

EXHIBIT 3.13 | **Airline Strategic Alliances**

STAR ALLIANCE

Air Canada, Air China, Air New Zealand, ANA, Asiana Airlines, Austrian, bmi, Egyptair, LOT Polish Airlines, Lufthansa, Scandinavian Airlines, Singapore Airlines, South African Airways, Spanair, Swiss International Air Lines, TAP Portugal, Thai Airways International, Turkish Airlines, United, and US Airways

Aeroflot, AeroMexico, Air France, Alitalia, China Southern, Continental Airlines, CSA Czech Airlines, Delta Air Lines, KLM Airlines, Korean Air, and Northwest Airlines

American Airlines, British Airways, Cathay Pacific Airways, Finnair, Iberia, Japan Airlines, LAN Airlines, Malev Hunganian Airlines, Qantas, and Royal Jordanian

SABMiller is battling Anheuser-Busch and other brewers for market presence in China. After losing opportunities to partner with other local Chinese brewers, SABMiller focused on a 12-year-old joint venture with China Resources Snow Brewing Ltd. The joint venture has been a success with CR Snow overtaking Tsingtao (Anheuser-Busch's joint venture partner) as the leading beer company in China. SABMiller positions Snow as the freshest beer and supports the compaign with heavy advertising.[27]

Direct Foreign Investment

The market entry strategy with the greatest long-term implications is **direct foreign investment.** Risks go up substantially when a company moves manufacturing into a foreign market. Although this is the riskiest market entry strategy, future market potential can position it for long-term growth. A company must consider a number of factors including:

- *Timing*—unknown political or social events, competitor activity.
- *Legal issues*—growing complexity of international contracts, asset protection.

- *Transaction costs*—production and other costs stated in various currencies.
- *Technology transfer*—key technologies are more easily copied in foreign markets.
- *Product differentiation*—differentiating a product without increasing cost.
- *Marketing communication barriers*—local market practices vary a great deal.

The size of the investment and risk to the company means a company should consider a wide range of costs and potential problems as well as the market opportunity. Issues like loss of product technologies can be overlooked as the company considers the opportunity to expand into new markets.[28] All too often companies have committed significant resources before they realize that a critical issue has substantially raised the investment and risk.

Organizational Structure

Once marketing managers decide on a specific market entry strategy, they must create an efficient and effective global market organizational structure. This challenge requires constant monitoring and adaptation. No one ideal structure exists. A recent study of 43 multinational U.S. companies reported they planned to make a total of 137 organizational changes to their international operations over the next five years. This suggests that the best organizational structure is, at best, a moving target that evolves over time (see Exhibit 3.14).

Before a company decides on its organizational structure, it must make two critical decisions. The first involves **decision-making authority.** As companies grow, lines of authority become longer and more complicated, so clearly defined

| EXHIBIT 3.14 | The Most Common International Organizational Structure |

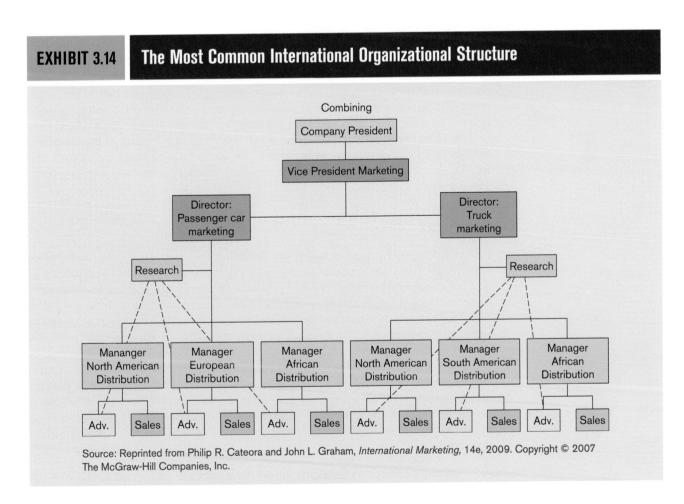

Source: Reprinted from Philip R. Cateora and John L. Graham, *International Marketing*, 14e, 2009. Copyright © 2007 The McGraw-Hill Companies, Inc.

protocols regarding which decisions are made at each level of the organization are important. A decision normally made by senior management becomes more difficult when executives are eight time zones away.[29]

The **degree of centralization** is a second critical decision since it affects resource allocation and personnel. Three primary organizational patterns employed by organizations around the world are centralized, decentralized, and regionalized. The primary advantages of a more centralized structure include greater control and, as a result, more consistency across the organization. It is also more efficient in creating centers of expertise that bring together knowledgeable people to address key organizational issues (for example, R&D, legal, and IT). Decentralized organizations, on the other hand, offer a hands-on management approach that facilitates rapid response to changing market conditions. The regional organization seeks to combine advantages of both approaches by centralizing key functions while pushing decision making closer to the global market.[30]

Once decision-making authority has been established and degree of centralization defined, companies usually adopt one of three organizational structures in building their international operations. First, **global product lines** work well for companies with a broad, diverse range of products. This model is based on the global functionality and appeal of the products and enables companies to target similar products to customers around the world. A product line structure can also be divided by customer, providing an even closer link between product usage and customer need. The disadvantage is that some organizational functions such as the direct sales force may be duplicated in markets where the company believes there is significant market opportunity. Siemens, the large German conglomerate, maintains specialized direct sales forces by product and customer. This approach works for Siemens because its diversified product portfolio includes everything from large power generators to sophisticated medical equipment. A second structure, **geographic regions,** divides international markets by geography, building autonomous regional organizations that perform business functions in the geographic area. This model works particularly well when local government relationships are critical to the success of international operations as it affords company management a closer connection to local customers. Large construction and engineering companies such as Halliburton maintain operations geographically with specific operations in each area that are suited to the environments in which they operate. The **matrix structure** is the third form and is a hybrid of the first two. Not surprisingly, most companies today use some form of matrix structure that encourages regional autonomy while building product competence in key areas around world.

Product

Global market expansion is based on the belief that people or other businesses outside the company's home market will purchase its products. Acceptance of that belief depends largely on what products the company will sell in those new markets. Does it, for example, simply take its existing product with no modifications? Does it create a new product developed specifically for foreign markets, or something in between? The answers to these questions are fundamental to global market expansion.

Some products are more easily accepted than others in new markets around the world. Several consumer electronics products such as digital music players and digital cameras are essentially the same product around the world. But many products, like food, do not travel well across borders. Those products usually need to be adapted to fit local tastes. A company may select from three basic product options:[31]

- **Direct product extension:** Introduce a product produced in the company's home market into an international market with no product changes.

| EXHIBIT 3.15 | Example of Product Adaptation Strategy |

The all new Hot Dog £1.39

McDonald's Product Adaptation
Adaptation of the classic American Hot Dog for the British market.

Advantages include no additional R&D or manufacturing costs. Disadvantages are that the product may not fit local needs or tastes.

- **Product adaptation:** Alter an existing product to fit local needs and legal requirements. Adaptation can range from regional levels all the way down to city-level differences. (Exhibit 3.15 offers an example of a McDonald's Hot Dog product adaptation.)
- **Product invention:** Create a new product specifically for an international market. Sometimes old products discontinued in one market can be reintroduced in a new market, a process known as backward invention. Cell phone manufacturers have adopted this strategy, taking phones that have been replaced in European or Asian markets and introducing them in Latin America. Another strategy is forward invention or creating new products to meet demand in a specific country or region.

Consumers

Moving into global consumer markets creates significant challenges because companies with little international experience find it difficult to assess, develop, and market products targeted at consumers with widely different needs, preferences, and product usage demands. Even experienced global marketers sometimes fail to identify specific consumer trends in foreign markets. Four specific product issues face international consumer marketers—quality, fitting the product to the culture, brand strategy, and country of origin.

Quality

The perception of quality varies drastically around the world, which makes it hard for a company developing or adapting a product for a global market. What works in one market may fail in another, as cell phone manufacturers have learned. In Europe, Japan, and the United Sates, cell phones must have a roaming capability to be successful, but Chinese consumers do not consider it an important feature.

Global consumers are knowledgeable about product quality and have a clear understanding of what they are willing to pay for at a given quality level. Research suggests the relationship of price and quality, or the value proposition that we focus on in this book, remains a key factor in consumer decision making. The test

Panasonic and Verizon Wireless join forces to create a product for difficult work conditions found in many parts of the world

© Matthias Clamer. Courtesy Verizon Wireless and Panasonic.

for many organizations is providing quality when they lack control over the delivery of key quality dimensions such as service. As we discussed earlier, in many situations companies do not provide key elements of the product experience, which is one reason good international partners are so important.

Fitting the Product to the Culture

Culture differences exert tremendous influence on consumer product choices and are critical in international markets. Brand names as well as product colors and features are heavily influenced by the culture in local foreign markets. Exhibit 3.16 shows one example of how companies often fail to consider cultural characteristics in their marketing decisions.

Language differences have created unique and occasionally humorous examples of marketing mistakes. When Coca-Cola introduced Diet Coke in Japan, initial sales were disappointing until the company realized that Japanese women do not like the concept of dieting and the Japanese culture relates dieting to sickness (not a desired connection with a product). The company changed the name to Coke Light, which has been much more effective around the world. Companies also have to adapt their products to fit local markets. Manufacturers of kitchen products have found the Japanese market difficult to penetrate. Mr. Coffee and Philips Electronics NV found their coffeemakers did not sell well in Japan because Asian kitchens in general are much smaller than Western kitchens. The larger coffeemakers sold in the United States did not fit on Japanese kitchen counters.

Brand Strategy

As we will explore in Chapter 11, companies often seek to create a unified branding strategy around the world. In some cases this is effective. Coca-Cola, Caterpillar, Apple, Kellogg, BMW, and others have created powerful global brands. As companies acquire local brands one of the first decisions is whether to fold a local brand into a global brand. Companies have to consider local conditions, but, when possible, companies are harmonizing brands to build brand awareness and extend marketing communication dollars.

Local brands, on the other hand, offer companies distinct awareness and built-in market loyalty. Nestlé, for example, follows a local branding strategy for

EXHIBIT 3.16	Cultural Mistakes in Marketing

Pepsi's "Come Alive with the Pepsi Generation" campaign didn't go over well in China. It translated into "Pepsi Brings Your Ancestors Back from the Grave."

individual products (the company carries more than 7,000 brands) but also promotes the Nestlé corporate brand globally. It believes that local branding helps differentiate its products.

Samsonite, the iconic American luggage company, has moved its headquarters to London in an effort to get close to 60 percent of its sales. While the company's image fell in the United States during the 1990s, Europe and Asia continued to view Samsonite as a premium brand. The company has upgraded its design staff and introduced new, higher-quality products. In addition, the company sells signature leather products (shoes, wallets, and more) to build the brand.[32]

Country of Origin

Increasingly, customers apply what is known as the country-of-origin effect in their purchase decisions. The **country-of-origin effect** is the influence of the country of manufacture, assembly, or design on a customer's positive or negative perception of a product.[33] "Made in Japan," "Made in Italy," "Made in the United States" has meaning to customers, and they infer that a product has certain qualities based on its country of origin. Such perceptions can change over time. Immediately after World War II, products made in Japan were considered of poor quality and inexpensive, which may seem hard to believe in light of the preeminent view of Japanese quality in the 21st century. Budweiser is a product with a very strong country-of-origin effect. Consumers around the world identify the product as American. With the purchase of Anheuser-Busch by InBev, based in Belgium, the widely held American identity of Budweiser may be challenged.

Companies use ethnocentric messages to differentiate their products from foreign brands. Ford and General Motors have both used their American heritage in advertising to foster a "buy American" feeling among consumers. Interestingly, Japanese automobiles manufactured in the United States frequently carry a higher percentage of U.S. parts than cars assembled in Mexico for American automobile manufacturers.[34] Research reports the following regarding country of origin:

- People in developed countries prefer products manufactured in their own country.
- Manufacturers from countries viewed favorably in the world tend to highlight their country of origin more than those from less developed countries.
- Countries have developed certain areas of influence in which the country of origin makes a difference, such as Japan and Germany for cars, the United States for technology, and France for wine and luxury goods.

Market Channels

One of the thorniest issues facing global marketers is getting their product to the customer.[35] American and European companies, in particular, are used to sophisticated channels of distribution that seamlessly move products from manufacturing sites to the customer at relatively low cost. Well-coordinated transportation and logistics systems lower distribution costs and increase customer choices at the point of sale.

Many companies have to rethink their distribution strategy when they enter global markets and find inadequate transportation networks, poorly organized or not easily accessible distribution systems, as well as an almost unlimited number of fundamentally different channel structures. Companies are frequently unprepared for the complexity of penetrating a foreign distribution system. The stakes are high because channel decisions are, at least in the short run, difficult and expensive to adjust. Companies able to develop successful channel strategies gain a competitive advantage in that market and effectively limit the options of other competitors.

Channel Structures

Unless the product is produced in the country where it is sold, all products pass through a global channel of distribution (see Exhibit 3.17). The product must move from the country of manufacture through an international channel between countries to the local international market distribution channel. Obviously the producer is most familiar with the distribution network in its home country. However, goods going to international markets use different intermediaries such as trading companies or international agents that require modifications to existing channels. Coordinating the movement of products between countries usually means hiring specialists familiar with legal issues as well as the most effective and efficient means of transportation. Companies have a number of transportation choices and, in addition to cost, should consider risk and length of time in transit. The producer faces the greatest challenge in the last stage, getting the product into the local channel and ultimately to the customer. International shipping specialists can help identify local distribution partners, but the company is more likely to look for channel alliances that fit overall business objectives and not simply distribution channels.

Channel Factors

In selecting a channel partner, companies should consider six strategic objectives known as the Six Cs of channel strategy: Cost, capital, control, coverage, character, and continuity offer a checklist for evaluating channel options.

Cost Estimating channel costs includes: (1) the initial investment in creating the channel and (2) the cost of maintaining the channel. As companies expand into new markets, many search for ways to increase the efficiency of local distribution systems by eliminating unnecessary middlemen, thereby shortening the channel to the customer.[36]

Capital An inadequate global market distribution system is expensive both in terms of adding cost to the product and creating long-term damage to the

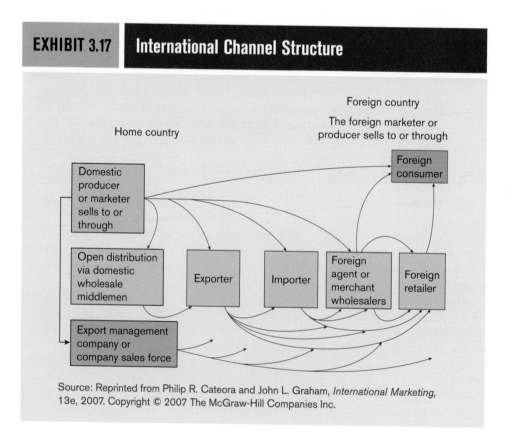

EXHIBIT 3.17 International Channel Structure

Source: Reprinted from Philip R. Cateora and John L. Graham, *International Marketing*, 13e, 2007. Copyright © 2007 The McGraw-Hill Companies Inc.

brand and the company's reputation. If a channel network is already in place, the investment is low; however, if the company needs to develop or greatly improve an existing system, the cost can be very high.

Control The more control the company wants in the channel the more expensive it is to maintain. As a result, companies generally look for a balance between channel control and cost. The complexity of global supply chains coupled with lack of local market knowledge make the task of creating a distribution system so expensive that all but the most accomplished global marketers rely on local distribution networks in foreign markets.

Coverage Local distribution networks around the world may lack full exposure to a given market. Even in the United States, for example, complete coverage of a consumer market necessitates multiple distribution channels. As a result, it is necessary to evaluate which distribution network best reaches the target customers, which may not necessarily be the network with the widest distribution. Targeting upper- and middle-class consumers in China requires extensive distribution in cities along the coast (Beijing, Shanghai, and Guangzhou) but minimal distribution in the rest of the country.

Character The long-term nature of channel decisions makes character an issue in selecting the best channel partner.[37] The capabilities, reputation, and skills of the local channel partner should match the company's characteristics. A service-oriented company should look for local channel partners with a reputation for excellent service and high customer satisfaction.

Continuity Changing a distribution system creates anxiety among customers and gives competitors an opportunity to take advantage of inevitable inefficiencies and disruption of service. Identifying channel partners with a long-standing presence in the market provides some security; however, the best local partners are also the most difficult to establish a relationship with as they frequently already have established involvement with competitors.

Marketing Communications

Another factor to consider is global marketing communications, which place additional demands on an organization's communication strategy. The core elements of communicating to a customer in a home market (language, images, color, cultural contextual cues) can be vastly different in foreign markets.[38] In addition, media are different and companies that rely on one form of media in their home market will have to adapt to other media.

Advertising

Global market advertising follows one of four basic approaches that vary by degree of adaptation. The first strategy creates **global marketing themes** adjusting only the color and language to local market conditions. The basic ad template remains unchanged throughout the world. A second strategy, **global marketing with local content,** keeps the same global marketing theme as the home market but adapts it with local content. Local content is incorporated in a standardized template to encourage a local look and feel to the ad. This includes images as well as written copy, but the ad still relates to the same global marketing message. A third approach is a **basket of global advertising themes.** Here related but distinct ads built around several marketing messages are generated, often by the company's lead advertising agency, and local marketers select the ads that best fit their specific market situation. Finally, some companies allow **local market ad generation.** Marketers have the authorization to create local ads that do not necessarily coordinate with global marketing messages. However, this strategy still requires coordination at higher levels in the company to ensure consistent quality. It takes considerable resources to market products globally and the leading global

EXHIBIT 3.18 — World's Largest Advertisers

Top 5 Global Marketers	
1. $8.5 billion	Procter & Gamble Co.
2. $4.5 billion	Unilever
3. $3.4 billion	General Motors
4. $3.1 billion	L'Oreal
5. $3.0 billion	Toyota

Source: http://adage.com/images/random/datacenter/2007/globalmarketing2007.pdf.

advertisers identified in Exhibit 3.18 all spend well in excess of $2 billion advertising globally every year.

Personal Selling

The salesperson–customer relationship is dramatically different around the world. In the United States, the relationship is very business-focused and less personal. In Latin America and Asia, the relationship is much more personal. Actual business negotiations often do not begin until a personal relationship has been established. Companies need sensitivity in selecting, hiring, and training their global sales force to accommodate local business cultures.

Sales Promotion

A relatively small part of U.S. marketing communication budgets is allocated to sales promotion; however, this can be a significant component of marketing communication strategy in global markets. The need to stimulate consumer trial and purchase can be greater. Both PepsiCo and Coca-Cola sponsor traveling carnivals to outlying villages in Latin America with the purpose of encouraging product trial.[39]

Public Relations

The expansion of global communications has greatly increased the importance of international public relations. Companies realize that dealing with crises must be done quickly and effectively as global news organizations move instantly on stories around the world. Getting the company's perspective on a story requires coordination by the company and public relations consultants before release to the public. Public relations can also enhance other elements of a marketing communications strategy.[40] When companies introduce new products, they frequently schedule them to coincide with press conferences and news cycles in other countries.

Pricing

There are three main pricing strategies. No single pricing strategy accommodates every local foreign market, so most companies follow a combination of cost-based and market-conditions-based pricing in setting a final price to market.[41]

One World Price

The company assigns one price for its products in every global market. In theory, this approach enables a company to standardize other elements in the marketing mix and simplifies financial forecasting. In reality, this strategy is not followed very often. While price is constant, the cost to produce, distribute, and market the product varies dramatically, creating wide fluctuations in profit margins. Furthermore, local conditions such as competitive pressures, economic circumstances, and other local market factors can have a significant effect on the final product price.

Local Market Conditions Price

The company assigns a price based on local market conditions with minimal consideration for the actual cost of putting the product into the market. Responding to the market is certainly vital in assigning the final price, but local conditions may not reflect the reality of bringing the product to market for an international company. Local competitors do not incur the transportation costs, potential tariffs, and other related expenses of bringing a product in a foreign market. As a result, companies must be particularly sensitive to local market pricing when setting their price. Strong local or even global competitors that dictate local market prices should be considered in assessing the attractiveness of a global market opportunity. One solution is to identify valued-added product features that allow a higher final price to customer.

Cost-Based Price

This strategy considers cost plus markup to arrive at a final price. While the focus on costs precludes charging an unprofitable price, it does not consider actual market conditions. If costs are high as a result of tariffs or transportation, the final price may be too high for the market.

Hyundai has successfully expanded in the global car market. However, strength in the Korean currency, the Won, has put the company at a competitive disadvantage in the United States. The company is constrained by Japanese and U.S. manufacturers because their products have a price advantage relative to Hyundai models even with the additional features offered on Hyundai cars. Without the price advantage, buyers are less willing to buy a Hyundai.[42]

Price Escalation

A considerable quandary for companies in global marketing is that the costs of doing business globally are often higher than in their home market. Many people are surprised that products sold in their home country are frequently twice as much in foreign markets. Four primary forces drive higher costs and create price escalation.

- **Product export costs:** Differences in the product configuration, packaging, and documentation raise the cost of many products for international markets. A key internal cost issue is **transfer pricing** or the cost companies charge internally to move products between subsidiaries or divisions. If companies charge too high a price internally, it can make the final product price uncompetitive because the local subsidiary must add a markup to arrive at a final price.

- **Tariffs, import fees, taxes:** Governments all around the world impose tariffs, fees, and taxes on imported products to protect industries in their home market and increase their revenue.

- **Exchange rate fluctuations:** For many years, the U.S. dollar was the standard for all international contracts, which tended to minimize currency fluctuations as everything was priced in dollars. Now, currencies float and products are priced using a market basket of currencies. Since currencies can easily float 15 to 20 percent against each other, the assigning of currency values in international contracts is critical. Increasingly, companies want contracts written in their home currency to protect their risk of loss due to currency fluctuations.[43]

- **Middlemen and transportation costs:** Creating a channel for global markets extends the number of channel members and increases costs. Each channel partner requires compensation, which raises the final price to the customer. Moreover, transportation costs increase as the distance to a local market increases.

Global Pricing Issues

In addition to price escalation, there are two other global pricing issues. The first, **dumping,** refers to the practice of charging less than actual costs or less than the product price in the company's home markets.[44] The World Trade Organization and most national governments have outlawed this practice and, if dumping is proven, a government can impose a tax on those products. Dumping is generally not a problem when global markets are strong; however, the willingness to price export goods based on marginal costs rather than full costs increases when markets weaken. The second major issue is the **gray market,** which involves the unauthorized diversion of branded products into global markets. Gray markets distributors (who are often authorized distributors) divert products from low-price to high-price markets. Companies should carefully watch unusual order patterns among their distributors because that can signal a gray market problem.[45]

SUMMARY

Global marketing has become synonymous with marketing. Companies cannot rely solely on their domestic markets for long-term growth. Technology and sophisticated distribution systems make it easy for a company anywhere in the world to become an international marketer. However, companies generally go through a global experience learning curve as their international business expands.

As companies consider new international markets, their first task is to assess the market opportunity. Unlike domestic markets, companies find they often lack in-depth knowledge of international markets, which presents significant challenges.

The growth of international markets has led to the development of regional market zones that bring countries together into trade alliances and sometimes political alliances.

Developing global market strategies involves the highest levels of the company. From organizational structure, product development, distribution, communications, to pricing, companies seek to maximize the efficiencies of global market opportunities while creating effective local market strategies to satisfy local market demands.

KEY TERMS

developed economies 70

emerging markets 70

regional marketing zones 72

European Union 73

NAFTA (North American Free Trade Agreement) 74

MERCOSUR 74

ASEAN 76

exporting 78

exporters 78

distributors 79

contractual agreements 80

licensing 80

franchising 80

strategic alliances 81

joint ventures 81

direct foreign investment 82

decision-making authority 83

degree of centralization 84

global product lines 84

geographic regions 84

matrix structure 84

country-of-origin effect 87

global marketing themes 89

APPLICATION QUESTIONS

1. You are the marketing manager for a small company located in the United States that manufactures specialized parts for high-end ink-jet printers. The company's largest customer (Hewlett-Packard) has asked your company to supply parts to 10 of its distribution and repair sites around the world. The company has never sold products outside the United States so this represents a significant step for the company. What stage in the global experience learning curve is the company likely entering and why? Identify the activities the company should undertake at this stage.

2. You are the market research director for a consumer product company. You have been asked to evaluate China as a potential market for your company's products and begin a search of secondary data. What are types of information you would consider in assessing China? How would you find information on these issues?

3. You are the marketing manager for Oxymoron detergent and have been instructed to introduce this product into Argentina. What six factors would you need to consider in determining the proper channel of distribution for the introduction of Oxymoron detergent?

4. Compare and contrast the pricing strategy of Apple's iPods around the world to Microsoft's Zune. Then, as marketing manager for SanDisk, how would you price a new MP3 player that will be introduced in 35 countries in the very near future? What pricing strategy would you choose and why?

5. You are the chief marketing officer for Digital Distributed Products (DDP), manufacturer of Wi-Fi hardware found on laptop computers. The company's No. 1 distributor in Germany just called and said it is experiencing significant "gray market" products coming in from Russia. Customers are saying DDP products are available at a significant discount from the distributor's legitimate price. As the CMO how would you address this problem?

MANAGEMENT DECISION CASE: A Newcomer Competes in the Global Computer Business

Yang Yuanqing was not content to be chairman of Lenovo, the largest computer company in China with over 35 percent of the PC market. He envisioned being a worldwide leader in computers and, almost overnight, Yuanqing transformed Lenovo from a $3 billion Chinese computer company to a $13 billion global technology giant with the acquisition of IBM's personal computing business in 2005. Now with headquarters in Beijing and Raleigh, North Carolina, he is chairman of the world's third-largest computer company behind Dell and HP.

Blending an upstart Chinese company that is much smaller than the American business icon (IBM) it acquired has been a challenge. Yang realized the need for Western management skills to help run the company and hired William Amelio, former head of Dell's Asian markets, as president and CEO. The two have a complex managing relationship with Yang focusing on marketing and distribution while Amelio concentrates on supply chain, a critical area as it targets new markets, including the United States.

The company believes its success in China can be replicated around the world. As Yang states, "We want to extend the business model that was so successful in China out across the world." Its home market represents its most profitable market, not unlike many other companies with worldwide operations.

However, Lenovo's strong position in China is under attack by competitors. Over the past several years, Dell has invested $16 billion in China, building factories and creating an efficient supplier network. Dell's investment in China has been more than Lenovo's entire revenue over the same period. At the same time, Acer, the No. 4 global computer company based in Taiwan, is aggressively closing in on Lenovo. It has developed an aggressive strategy in emerging markets such as China and India while also targeting the U. S. market using agreements with Wal-Mart, CompUSA, and Circuit City to market its products in the United States.

Lenovo struggles to generate significant profits outside China and, despite the rights to use the IBM brand and "Thinkpad" for five years, sales have actually declined in the U.S. market. Building a global brand takes time, so Lenovo is leveraging the IBM brand while it builds up its own brand and product line. Three years after the IBM purchase, the company is transitioning away from the IBM brand in its advertising. Also, the company has introduced its two lines of notebook computers in the United States, the 3000 and Ideapad series. Targeting business users, the core IBM market for many years, the company is going head-to-head with Dell and HP in the United States. Lenovo believes that a strong global brand is the result of a customer-focused product mix and good customer service. The company's focus on expanding beyond its home market puts it at the forefront of Chinese companies seeking to turn their local success into a global brand.

Another weakness in the U.S. market is the supply chain. Lenovo's success with Chinese suppliers has not translated easily in the United States. Amelio wants to make the U.S. supply chain more efficient while maintaining the quality level associated with IBM products. In retail, Lenovo partners with Best Buy (in its Best Buy for Business centers).[46]

Questions for Consideration

1. Lenovo has adopted a gradual phaseout of the IBM and ThinkPad brands. Do you think Lenovo should continue to use the IBM and ThinkPad brands or focus more on establishing its own brand identity?

2. Lenovo is moving aggressively into new global markets. How would you assess this strategy of global expansion in light of the increased competitive pressures in its home market, China?

3. What challenge does a Chinese company like Lenovo face as it moves into the global marketplace?

MARKETING PLAN EXERCISE

ACTIVITY 1: Thinking Globally; Marketing Plan Tasks

For any company doing business in a global market it is essential to consider the unique elements of that market in developing the marketing plan. Consider the discussion in Chapter 2 as you:

- Identify possible global markets for a new product.
- Determine essential information needed to assess the market opportunity.

Keep in mind that specific marketing strategies will be presented throughout the book. However, it will be important to keep the global marketing discussion in mind as you develop your marketing plan.

If you are using Marketing Plan Pro, a template for this assignment can be accessed at www.mhhe.com/marshall1e.

RECOMMENDED READINGS

1. Thomas L. Friedman, *The World Is Flat* (New York: Farrar, Strauss and Giroux, 2005).

2. Jagdish Bhagwati, *In Defense of Globalization* (Oxford: Oxford University Press, 2004).

3. Pietra Rivoli, *The Travels of a T-Shirt in a Global Economy* (New York: Wiley, 2005).

4. Martin Wolf, *Why Globalization Works* (New York: Yale University Press, 2005).

part TWO

Information Drives Marketing Decision Making

CHAPTER 04

PERSPECTIVES ON CUSTOMER RELATIONSHIP MANAGEMENT

LEARNING OBJECTIVES

- Define CRM and articulate its objectives and capabilities.

- Describe the CRM process cycle.

- Understand the concept of customer touchpoints and why touchpoints are critical in CRM.

- Distinguish customer marketing from consumer marketing, and understand why the distinction is important.

- Discuss what happens when CRM fails and how to avoid potential failure.

EXECUTIVE PERSPECTIVE

Executive Jay File, Marketing Director

Company Chick-fil-A

Business Restaurant chain

How do you identify loyal, repeat customers and provide them with reasons to come back?

We conduct quarterly evaluations on customer loyalty called the Customer Loyalty Monitor program, which gives us a quantitative determination of the percentage of customers at each location that visit a certain number of times per month and their rating of us. These evaluations allow our operators (franchisees) to determine areas of improvement from an operations standpoint. We want to make sure that every customer, on every visit, has an operationally excellent experience every time. The evaluation looks at four areas: taste of food, speed of service, attentive and courteous team members, and restaurant cleanliness. We have determined that when we hit the mark in these areas, customers' expectations are being met and often exceed our industry standards. We try to get customers to come back more often by introducing new day parts (breakfast or dinner) or new menu items. Ideally, customers come back because they have faith and trust that Chick-fil-A will go beyond their usual expectation of fast food by delivering a "wow" experience.

A customer-centric culture places the customer at the center of everything that happens, both inside and outside the firm. How does your company ensure such a culture exists?

We listen to customers daily through extensive customer-focused research, listening posts, and ongoing conversations. We are always talking with customers at our restaurants and asking questions about their experience and what we can do to improve. We also receive feedback from our CARES program that provides an open forum of communication (written, verbal, e-mail) about customers' experiences—both when excellent and when opportunities for improvement exist. We are always conducting customer focus groups and panels to better understand our target customer and how to best reach them with advertising, product offerings, and the overall Chick-fil-A experience. Our role in marketing is to ensure the company is listening and talking with customers on an ongoing basis and staying customer focused.

All 500 Chick-fil-A staff members work one day a year in a restaurant location to experience the daily operations of the business and be able to talk with customers at our counters and dining rooms. This in-unit experience keeps all staff better connected with our customers.

How do you know when you have developed a *relationship* with your customers?

We are trying to emotionally connect with our customers by leveraging the four assets of Chick-fil-A: our food, people, cows, and influence. When we're leveraging these marketing assets, we feel we are able to emotionally connect with customers in a way that creates a long-term relationship, not just a transaction for food today. We know we have developed a relationship when they become a Chick-fil-A "Raving Fan." We define a raving fan as a customer that demonstrates three characteristics: They come more often, willingly pay full price, and tell others about us—essentially being an ambassador for us in the community.

WHAT IS CUSTOMER RELATIONSHIP MANAGEMENT?

Defining customer relationship management (CRM) is a great place to begin. CustomerThink.com, formerly CRMGuru.com, bills itself as "the global thought leader in customer-centric business strategy." CRMGuru.com founder Bob Thompson has offered the following definition of CRM:

> CRM is a business strategy to select and manage the most valuable customer relationships. CRM requires a customer-centric business philosophy and culture to support effective marketing, sales, and service processes. CRM applications can enable effective customer relationship management, provided that an enterprise has the right leadership, strategy, and culture.[1]

You should quickly recognize that the above concept is consistent with much of the learning from Chapter 1, which emphasized that value and customer relationships are two of the core concepts in marketing. Chapter 2 discussed marketing planning as the means by which firms create, communicate, and deliver value to customers. You have seen how concepts of customer orientation and a customer-centric philosophy of business are essential ingredients of organizational success. CRM enables and supports the implementation of a customer orientation.[2]

Up front, it is important to state that some people have already (mistakenly) dismissed CRM as just another business fad that has passed its prime. Remember the various marketing buzzwords introduced in Chapter 1? Some might say that CRM is just another consultant-hyped repackaging of business principles everyone already knows. However, thoughtful managers understand and view CRM differently. Let's consider other definitions of CRM offered by several highly regarded sources:

From Professor George Day of the Wharton Business School:

> CRM is a cross-functional process for achieving a continuing dialogue with customers, across all of their contact and access points, with personalized treatment of the most valuable customers, to increase customer retention and the effectiveness of marketing initiatives.[3]

> In banking, when a customer makes a huge deposit or withdrawal, it's a signal that the customer may be preparing to make an even bigger financial move. Banks such as Barclays want to know about these event-trigger transactions so that they can contact the customer with the right marketing pitch, such as to offer them a new product or to ensure that they don't leave the bank. CRM software now tracks all customer transactions across all touchpoints, including the Internet, ATMs, telephones, letters, e-mail, or face-to-face and lets banks respond quickly to these events, before an opportunity is lost.[4]

From Ron Swift, author of *Accelerating Customer Relationships* and vice president at leading CRM firm Teradata, a division of NCR:

> CRM is an enterprise approach to understanding and influencing customer behavior through meaningful communications in order to improve customer acquisition, customer retention, customer loyalty, and customer profitability.[5]

From Don Peppers and Martha Rogers, founding partners of the Peppers and Rogers group and coauthors of several books on one-to-one customer relationships:

> CRM is an enterprisewide business strategy for achieving customer-specific objectives by taking customer-specific actions.[6]

The core message of how CRM contributes to firm success provides compelling evidence that CRM is not merely a fad. Careful perusal across these definitions yields strong commonalities, synthesized within the following key points. CRM:

- Cuts across the whole business enterprise.
- Is a business strategy, set of operational processes, and analytic tools.
- Is enabled by technology but is not just "the software."
- Has the ultimate goal of maximizing performance of the customer side of the enterprise.
- To be successful, requires a customer-centric philosophy and culture, as well as leadership and commitment to CRM from the top.

CRM enables great marketing in part because of its ability to facilitate two-way interactions with customers through Smart Phones and other convenient communication modes.

Why an entire chapter devoted to CRM in a marketing management textbook? Two simple reasons: (1) CRM is a timely and relevant topic that ties together a number of important concepts of modern marketing management; and (2) CRM is an important *enabler* of great marketing. From a managerial perspective, gaining an understanding of CRM *now* will set the stage for much of what follows in this book. Any competent marketing manager must understand CRM. The goal of this chapter is not to transform you into an instant CRM guru. Rather, it is to provide perspectives on CRM that will assist you as a current or future manager in developing and implementing a customer-centric approach to your business, an activity that is central to maximizing firm success and far from a fad.[7]

In fact, you will find that the overview of CRM in this chapter builds directly on what you learned in Part 1 about value and customer relationships at the core of marketing and then later connects directly to many of the elements of marketing management to be developed in future chapters, including market research, marketing communication, and marketing metrics. Let's begin by connecting CRM to what we've learned so far.

OBJECTIVES AND CAPABILITIES OF CRM

To begin, we can now offer our own preferred definition of **customer relationship management (CRM):** a comprehensive business model for increasing revenues and profits by focusing on customers. Significantly, this definition does not speak to who should "own CRM" within the organization. In the mid-1990s, the introductory days of CRM systems by Siebel and others, CEOs tended to relegate the operation of a firm's CRM system to the information technology group. After all, CRM is technology-based, isn't it? But legendary horror stories abound about CEOs who purchased multimillion-dollar CRM installations purely on the recommendation of the IT department, without any significant consultation with those in the firm who would be the system's primary *users,* such as salespeople, marketing managers, and customer service representatives. In the end, through the school of hard knocks, firms learned that no one group should have "ownership" of the CRM system. Positioning CRM as a comprehensive business model provides the impetus for top management to properly support it over the long run and for various internal stakeholder groups to have the opportunity to both use it and impact how it is used.[8]

Fortunately, with many of the initial CRM adoption misfires relegated to the past, most companies are now adopting CRM as a mission-critical business strategy. It is considered mission-critical largely because of competitive pressures in the marketplace; nobody can afford to be the lone wolf that does not have a handle on the customer side of an enterprise in a competitive space.

To optimize CRM's potential for contribution to the bottom line companies are redesigning internal structures, as well as internal and external business processes and systems, to make it easier for customers to do business with them. Although marketing does not "own" CRM, because of CRM's focus on aligning the organization's internal and external processes and systems to be more customer-centric, marketing managers are a core contributor to the success of CRM by virtue of their expertise on customers and relationships.[9] And in particular, as Chapter 18 will discuss in detail, the sales force in CRM-driven organizations has taken center stage in executing a firm's customer management strategies, complete with new titles befitting the new sales roles such as "client manager," "relationship manager," and "business solution consultant."

Ultimately, CRM has three major objectives:

1. *Customer acquisition*–acquisition of the *right* customers based on known or learned characteristics that will drive growth and increase margins.
2. *Customer retention*–retention of satisfied and loyal profitable customers and channels, and thus to grow the business profitably over the long run.
3. *Customer profitability*–increased individual customer margins, while offering the right products at the right time.[10]

Masterfoods' dog-food brand Pedigree operates a CRM program that helps dog owners raise puppies. The CRM program combines information on every pedigreed dog born in the United Kingdom, including its birthday and breed, with customer information to issue Pedigree Puppy Club mailings and e-mails. These mailings include a month-by-month care guide on behavior, health, and nutrition. The program has helped Pedigree capture about 50 percent of the puppy market.[11]

EVERYONE LIKES MUSHROOMS IN THEIR OMELETTES, EXCEPT PEOPLE WHO DON'T.

Complimentary, cooked-to-order breakfast, two-room suites, open-air atriums and evening Manager's Reception.° These are just some of the ways Embassy Suites Hotels® puts extra thought into everything we do.

EVERYTHING FOR A REASON®

EMBASSY SUITES HOTELS°

TheHiltonFamily   For locations and reservations, please call 800-Embassy or visit embassysuites.com for Our Best Rates, Guaranteed.

Hoteliers such as Embassy suites can customize offerings to loyal users by maintaining customer preference profiles.

To accomplish these objectives requires a clear focus on the product and service attributes that represent value to the customer and that create customer satisfaction and loyalty. **Customer satisfaction** means the level of liking an individual harbors for an offering—that is, to what level is the offering meeting or exceeding the customer's expectations? **Customer loyalty** means the degree to which an individual will resist switching, or defecting, from one offering to another. Loyalty is usually based on high satisfaction coupled with a high level of perceived value derived from the offering and a strong relationship with the provider and its brand(s). Customer satisfaction and loyalty are two extremely popular metrics used by marketing managers to gauge the health of their business and brands.[12]

All of this implies strong integration of CRM into the overall marketing planning process of a firm. Perusal of the elements of marketing planning presented in Chapter 2 reveals numerous points at which information derived from a CRM system can assist in the strategy development and execution process. Key parts of a marketing plan that rely on CRM-generated information include the situation analysis, market research, strategy development, implementation, and measurement phases of marketing planning. In fact, many of the metrics that marketing managers use to assess their success are derived directly from the firm's CRM system.[13]

One of the most important metrics in CRM is that of the **lifetime value of a customer.** Fredrick Reichheld in his books on customer loyalty has demonstrated time and again that investment in CRM yields more successful long-term relationships with customers, and that these relationships pay handsomely in terms of cost savings, revenue growth, profits, referrals, and other important business success factors. It is possible to actually calculate an estimate of the projected financial returns from a customer, or **return on customer investment (ROCI),** over the long run. This analysis provides a very useful strategic tool for deciding which customers deserve what levels of investment of various resources (money, people, time, information, etc.). Chapter 19 is devoted to identifying and exemplifying the use of marketing metrics. Many of the most useful marketing metrics derive their power and functionality from CRM.

Proliferation of ROCI analysis has raised the prospects of **firing a customer** who exhibits a low predicted lifetime value, and instead investing resources in other more profitable customers. Of course, such action assumes other more attractive customers exist.[14]

> A loyal customer spends a lot of money with a company over time. For example, the average Cadillac customer spends more than $300,000 on Cadillacs during his or her lifetime. A CRM system can help a company track how much a given customer spends with the company over time. Knowing the value that a particular customer brings to a company can also help encourage employees to treat that customer well.[15]

THE CRM PROCESS CYCLE

The process cycle for CRM may be divided into the following four elements: (1) knowledge discovery, (2) market planning, (3) customer interaction, and (4) analysis and refinement. Elements of the process cycle are portrayed in Exhibit 4.1 and discussed below.

EXHIBIT 4.1	Process Cycle for CRM

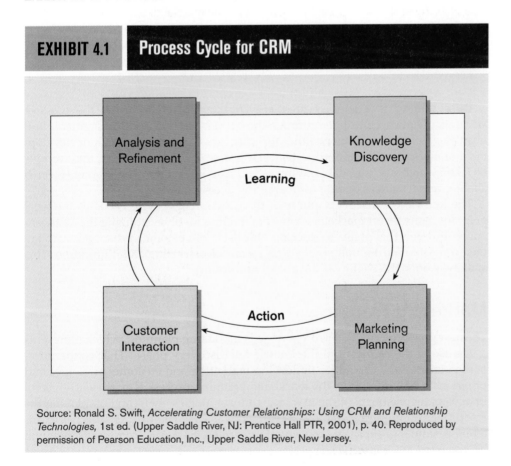

Source: Ronald S. Swift, *Accelerating Customer Relationships: Using CRM and Relationship Technologies*, 1st ed. (Upper Saddle River, NJ: Prentice Hall PTR, 2001), p. 40. Reproduced by permission of Pearson Education, Inc., Upper Saddle River, New Jersey.

Knowledge Discovery

Knowledge discovery is the process of analyzing the customer information acquired through various customer touchpoints, or customer "contact and access points" in the terminology of George Day's definition of CRM.[16] At their essence, **touchpoints** are where the selling firm touches the customer in some way, thus allowing for information about him or her to be collected. These might include point-of-sale systems, call-center files, Internet accesses, records from direct selling or customer service encounters, or any other customer contact experiences. Touchpoints occur at the intersection of a business event that takes place via a channel using some media, such as online inquiry from a prospect, telephone follow-up with a purchaser on a service issue, face-to-face encounter with a salesperson, and so on.[17]

A **data warehouse** environment is the optimal approach to handling all the customer data generated through the touchpoints and transforming it into useful information for marketing management decision making and marketing planning. A data warehouse affords the opportunity to combine large amounts of information and then use data mining techniques to learn more about current and potential customers.[18]

FYI

Insurance company Corona Direct gets new customers through direct mail. But mailing out 4 million letters at a cost of 65 cents each was getting expensive. Corona Direct decided it would use its data to better target clients on its prospect direct-mail list. "We had a lot of client history in the data warehouse, and the software could take all of the fields together to tell us our best prospects to mail to depending on gender, age, type of client, and location," said Philippe Neyt, commercial director for the company. By using data from its customer warehouse, Corona Direct identified better prospects and sent out fewer letters, but received the same number of new customers.[19]

Data mining is a sophisticated analytical approach to using the massive amounts of data accumulated through the CRM system to develop segments and micro-segments of customers either for purposes of market research or development of market segmentation strategies. It is important to remember the concepts of a data warehouse and data mining as you read in Chapter 5 on market research about internal sources of data for marketing decision making.[20]

The knowledge discovery phase of the CRM process cycle becomes the focal point for many direct marketers. Direct marketing involves utilizing the data generated through this phase to develop "hit lists" of customer prospects, who are then contacted individually by various means of marketing communication. This activity is often referred to as **database marketing.**[21]

Marketing Planning

The next phase in the CRM process cycle is marketing planning, which represents a key use of the *output* from the knowledge discovery phase. That is, the information enables the capability to develop marketing and customer strategies and programs. CRM input into the marketing planning process is particularly useful in developing elements of the marketing mix strategies, including employing the marketing communication mix in integrated ways to customize approaches to different customer groups (this concept of integrated marketing communication will be discussed in Chapter 17).[22]

Customer Interaction

The customer interaction phase represents the actual implementation of the customer strategies and programs. This includes the personal selling effort, as well as all other customer-directed interactions. These must be aimed at all the customer touchpoints, or channels of customer contact, both in person and electronically.[23]

Analysis and Refinement

Finally, the analysis and refinement phase of the CRM process is where **organizational learning** occurs based on customer response to the implemented strategies and programs. Think of it as market research in the form of a continuous dialogue with customers, facilitated by effective use of CRM tools. With such an ongoing commitment and capability related to customer research, continuous adjustments made to the firm's overall customer initiatives should result in more efficient investment of resources and increasing ROCI.[24]

MORE ON CUSTOMER TOUCHPOINTS

You have read that CRM initiatives depend heavily on interactions with customers, suppliers, or prospects via one or more touchpoints—such as a call center, salesperson, distributor, store, branch office, Web site, or e-mail. CRM entails both acquiring knowledge about

Even a manufacturer like Campbell's Soup can utilize touchpoints to communicate highly usable information to customers, in this case via a recipe for a new meal idea using soup and risotto.

customers and (where feasible) deploying information to customers at the touchpoint. Some touchpoints are *interactive* and allow for such two-way information exchange. That is, they involve *direct interface* between a customer and a firm's customer contact person in the form of a salesperson, telemarketer, customer service representative, interactive Web site, and so on. Other touchpoints are *noninteractive*; that is, the customer may simply provide information on a static Web site's data entry form or by mail, without the capability of simultaneous direct interface with a company representative. To maximize a firm's ability to successfully use touchpoints, an ongoing concerted effort must be undertaken to: (1) identify *all* potential touchpoints, (2) develop specific objectives for what kind of information can be collected at each touchpoint, (3) determine how that information will be collected and ultimately integrated into the firm's overall customer database, and (4) develop policies on how the information will be accessed and used.

Retailer Brookstone is using customer data from multiple touchpoints, including in-store visits, phone calls, or visits to its Web site. Brookstone records and remembers each customer in multiple ways: by their e-mail address, by their phone number, or by their membership number in Brookstone's loyalty program. Brookstone records all purchases that a customer makes through any of these touchpoints. Those purchases then earn a reward, which the customer can apply toward future purchases.[25]

The aspect of CRM involving customer information collected through touchpoints raises substantial ethical and legal issues for the firm regarding privacy, particularly in the consumer marketplace. Clearly, a key component of a strong

CRM's Dark Side: The Cost of Protecting Customer Data

A critical success factor of CRM is the ability to collect, analyze, and act on customer data. This often means gathering *confidential* customer data. An inherent problem with collecting this information, making it available to individuals inside the organization, and then empowering them to deal with the customer is the resulting opportunity for theft of confidential customer records.

One industry particularly vulnerable to data theft is financial services, which collects and uses sensitive customer information such as specific purchase patterns (what, where, when, and how much customers spend) then links the information to account numbers and other private information. Securing information and making it available only to those who really need to know it is a vital part of keeping customers' trust.

Both customers and firms are increasingly concerned about securing critical customer data. The size of the company and level of security doesn't always protect against theft, as security breaches have occurred at Bank of America, Wachovia Bank, FedEx, Blue Cross, and TJ Maxx, for example. Any company is vulnerable either from external hackers who gain access to data or internal sources (employees) who violate company policies to steal sensitive data from the inside.

The costs of data theft are high and extend well beyond the direct cost/value of the data itself. Checkpoint, a leader in identification and verification services, was hacked by thieves who stole confidential data for 145,000 customers. The result was the identity theft of more than 700 individuals, resulting in over $26 million in legal fees and fines and a major public relations meltdown for the company. A firm's company image, reputation, and brands can be severely damaged when customer trust is breached in this way, and once customer trust is lost it is difficult—maybe impossible—to regain. One study suggests that companies can expect 20 percent of their customers to defect after such an event and another 40 percent to take steps toward defecting, including checking out alternative vendors.

For firms, the cost of data protection is high with encryption, back-up data files, and other security measures running in the millions of dollars. As a result, companies often take a wait-and-see attitude on investing in such measures, as noted in a recent study where only one-third of financial service companies reported encrypting data in storage. Of course, the cost of customer defection based on lost trust is also very high. The challenge for many companies is finding the right balance between securing customer data and incurring unnecessary levels of data security costs. Unfortunately, many companies end up copping an attitude of "it won't happen to us."[26]

Ethical Perspective

1. **Companies:** What priority would you place on securing customer data? For example, would you invest $10 million in greater security for customer data or an upgrade for a four-year-old network?

2. **Customers:** How would you respond if your bank told you that your data had been compromised? Would you consider changing banks?

customer relationship with a firm is a high level of *trust*.[27] Customers must be absolutely certain that the information a firm collects and stores about them will not be used for unintended purposes. Often referred to as the "dark side of CRM," this issue has become so prominent in some industries that firms are beginning to publicly promote guarantees of nonabuse of stored customer information as a means of attracting customers.[28] It is a feature that resonates well with customers and likely provides a strong point of differentiation over competitors. Ethical Dimension 4 looks at customer trust and what can happen when that trust is violated by theft of personal information.

Subway has created a loyalty program that protects people's privacy. Customers receive a card that gives them coupons and promotions. Customers can stay anonymous, if they choose, and use only the card's number when making purchases. "We don't need to know who you are specifically to target you. We can target you by the unique identifier of the card," said Marina O'Rourke, Subway's director of retail technology. "We may or may not know that you're Joe Smith of 123 York St., Brooklyn, N.Y., but we know that there is a unique identifier and you are a customer who does this behavior."[29]

Touchpoints: The USAA Experience

For an example of how information collected through touchpoints works to the benefit of both a firm and its customers, consider the case of USAA Insurance, based in San Antonio, Texas. USAA's core market began with military officers and their families; the firm was established because many years ago officers had difficulty getting insurance at reasonable rates due to the extreme mobility associated with their career paths. USAA has grown to become a broad-based insurance and financial services provider with a bank, virtual retail store, and one of the largest volume credit-card operations worldwide. Ninety-nine percent of USAA's business is conducted over the phone or online. The company also has one of the most sophisticated, and best-managed, CRM systems in the world. USAA was rated the No. 1 customer service champ in *BusinessWeek*'s first-ever ranking of companies where the customer is king.[30]

USAA takes great care to protect the information stored about its customers, who are called members. The company is very transparent in asking members for permission before information is shared even between USAA's own internal divisions (insurance, bank, retail, credit card, etc.), let alone with any outside companies. Whenever a member makes contact with USAA, the level of security becomes very apparent through access codes and verifications of identity. USAA is diligent about collecting and continually updating information on members yet is not obtrusive either in how it collects the information or in how it uses the information for outbound communication.

Firms typically use customer information collected for purposes of up-selling and cross-selling current customers on other available products and services they might want and need—and USAA is no different. One way CRM facilitates customer relationships is through a firm's capability to better customize its product line to individual customers, a process known as one-to-one marketing. However, unlike some other firms, USAA has very strict policies on the voracity with which such selling can be executed. USAA will not risk damaging a long-term member relationship through overly aggressive selling approaches.

Even though a USAA member is likely to never meet a USAA employee face-to-face, USAA continually scores among the highest of any financial services firm on customer satisfaction and loyalty; USAA members simply do not leave. One of the key results of USAA's commitment to CRM is the capability for any one of the thousands of USAA customer representatives a member may reach on a given call to pull up that member's record and carry on a conversation as though they have been doing business for years. Customer representatives undergo extensive training not just on the technical aspects of the CRM system, but also on the strategic aspects of using CRM to operationalize a customer-centric culture and build long-term relationships with members. Ask USAA members how they like doing business with the company, and they are likely to respond very favorably and with conviction. USAA executives, and USAA members, attribute much of the success of the firm to its customer-centric culture, operationalized through well-executed CRM.[31]

CUSTOMER MARKETING VERSUS CONSUMER MARKETING

An important distinction in organizational philosophy and focus can be spotted by observing whether a firm's marketing managers tend to talk about customers or consumers. The following description of consumers is only partially facetious. In marketing, consumers tend to be thought of in the role of faceless reactors to a firm's marketing strategies to the masses. In fact, the term **mass marketing** was coined to connote this classic style of consumer marketing. In this context, consumers are the perennial subjects of sophisticated marketing research in the

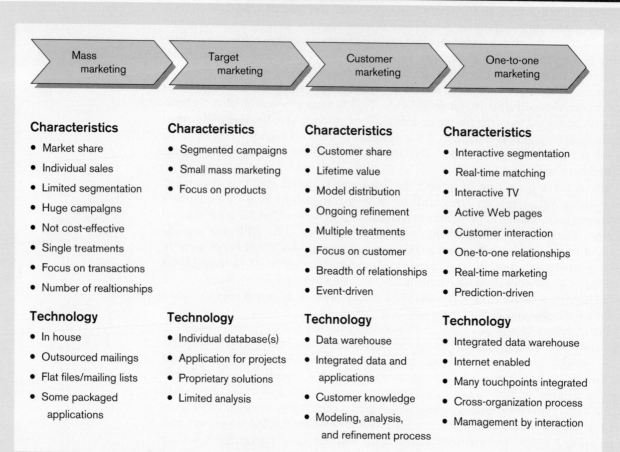

Source: Ronald S. Swift, *Accelerating Customer Relationships: Using CRM and Relationship Technologies,* 1st ed. (Upper Saddle River, NJ: Prentice Hall PTR, 2001), p. 38. Reproduced by permission of Pearson Education, Inc., Upper Saddle River, New Jersey.

form of surveys, focus groups, and purchase diaries. But to actually get to know a consumer individually—to make a concerted effort to respond to his or her unique needs and wants—is a very different way of thinking from that of traditional mass marketing approaches.[32]

Mass marketing is still alive and well today, but many firms are evolving away from it as their primary approach to marketing. In the 1960s, many firms began to apply principles of segmentation, target marketing, and positioning to mass markets to create different strategies and marketing programs for different consumer groups within those markets. A major change in mind-set precipitates a shift from targeted **consumer marketing** (i.e., marketing to big groups of like-minded buyers) to **customer marketing,** or a focus on developing relationships with individuals. Ultimately, it is the sophistication and multiplicity of available technology today—and especially CRM—that enables the shift to mass customization and one-to-one marketing as introduced in Chapter 1.[33] Firms which choose to make the investment are now able to better customize offerings to the wants and needs of individual users. Phases of this evolutionary process in marketing, with characteristics and technology attributes of each, are shown in Exhibit 4.2.

Kristin Micalizio, vice president–direct marketing at the office supply company Office Depot, talked about her company's one-to-one marketing efforts: "E-mail is our largest online driver of one-to-one marketing. Search, display advertising, and contextual advertising have opened up new opportunities, allowing Office Depot to market in a more one-to-one fashion through behavioral, geographic, and demographic targeting." Going forward, "We will continue to contact our customers in the ways that they want with creative formats and exciting marketing pieces," Micalizio said.[34]

Advantages of Customer Marketing

CRM-driven one-to-one marketing has several advantages over traditional mass marketing including the following:

- Reduced promotional costs due to decreased reliance on expensive mass media and redirection of promotional investment to more targeted promotional vehicles such as targeted advertising and direct marketing.

- Improved targeting of specific customers by focusing on their needs and wants.

- Improved capability to track the effectiveness of a given promotional campaign.

- Increased effectiveness in competing on value-adding properties such as customization and service, thus reducing reliance on price competition.

- Increased sensitivity to the differing levels of potential across customers, thus reducing overspending on low-ROI customers or underspending on high-ROI customers.

- Increased speed in the time it takes to develop and market a product (product development cycle).

- Improved use of the customer channel, enabling customers to interact more directly and efficiently with the firm, thus making the most of each contact with a customer.[35]

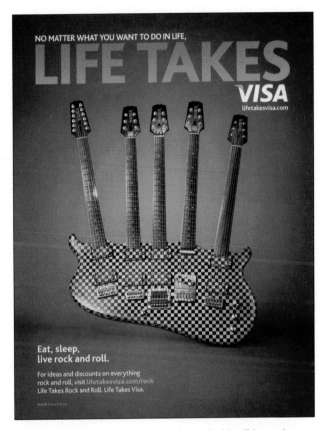

Visa does a great job of customer marketing by identifying and connecting with different groups based on lifestyle. Clicking on the URL in this ad opens the door to joining a community with similar interests (and bonding with the Visa brand!).

HAMER is a registered trademark of Kaman Music Corporation, and is used herein with express written permission. All rights reserved. Photo: Staudinger+Franke/Marge Casey + Associates.

The company 1-800-Flowers sells the product its name suggests—flowers. But it also owns other gift product lines, including food (the Popcorn Factory) and toys (HearthSong). As a result, cross-functional CRM at 1-800-Flowers means knowing that a customer who is calling 1-800-Flowers for the first time might also be a frequent, highly valued customer of HearthSong. The company wants its call centers and online sales engines to know if a first-time caller to one store is a frequent customer of a sister store so the company can approach them with an appropriate level of familiarity.[36]

CRM CORE CONCEPTS ARE NOT NEW

The fact is, many of the underlying concepts of CRM are not all that new. You could open a marketing management textbook from 25 years ago and find a discussion of many of the tenets of what we now refer to as CRM. What has changed in the environment to allow for the more integrated approach to managing customers represented by modern CRM is today's technology; the development of more sophisticated approaches to data management became the spark that allowed CRM to flourish. Yet, it is a serious mistake to consider CRM as merely a software program. In fact, many firms that adopted CRM in its early days struggled with their CRM initiatives precisely because they bought the sophisticated software but did not have the culture, structure, systems, leadership, or internal technical expertise to make the initiative successful.[37]

The next sections highlight two characteristics of CRM—its ability to facilitate a customer-centric culture and its ability to enable the transformation of a firm into a relationship-based enterprise.

CRM Facilitates a Customer-Centric Culture

As you know, a firm that is customer-centric places the customer at the core of the enterprise including everything that happens, both inside and outside the firm. Customers are the lifeblood of any business—without them a firm has no sales, no profits, and ultimately no business. As such, marketing managers must approach their role with the attitude that customers are worth investing considerable resources against so long as an acceptable return on that investment can be anticipated.

At the strategic marketing level, a customer-centric culture includes, but is not limited to, the following major components:

1. Adopting a relationship or partnership business model overall, with mutually shared rewards and risk management.
2. Redefining the selling role within the firm to focus on customer business consultation and solutions.
3. Increasing formalization of customer analysis processes.
4. Taking a proactive leadership role in educating customers about value chain opportunities available by developing a business relationship.
5. Focusing on continuous improvement principles stressing customer satisfaction and loyalty.[38]

Borgata, a casino destination resort that opened in Atlantic City, New Jersey, in 2003, has become one of the most customer-centric casinos on the strip. Information on visitors' habits from the facility's 3,600 slots, 163 table games, and 2,000 guest rooms and suites is fed into a database. To help capitalize on that information, the company has a sophisticated CRM program that fosters loyalty and encourages repeat customer visits to Borgata by creating a sense of personalization in the relationship Borgata has with its customers.[39]

The effort a firm makes toward cultivating a customer-centric culture requires a high degree of formalization within the firm. **Formalization** means that structure, processes and tools, and managerial knowledge and commitment are formally established in support of the culture. With these elements in place, strategies and programs can be successfully developed and executed toward the goals related to customers, accompanied by a high degree of confidence they will yield the desired results. Today, the most prevalent formalization mechanism of a customer-centric culture is CRM.

As mentioned in Chapter 1, firms that are customer-centric have a high level of customer orientation. Organizations practicing a customer orientation place the customer at the core of all aspects of the enterprise and:

1. Instill an organization-wide focus on understanding the requirements of customers.
2. Generate an understanding of the customer marketplace and disseminate that knowledge to everyone in the firm.
3. Align system capabilities internally so that the organization responds effectively to customers with innovative, competitively differentiated, satisfaction-generating products and services.[40]

How do the concepts of customer centricity and customer orientation connect to the actions required by individual members of a firm? One way to think about how an organization member might exhibit a customer orientation is through a **customer mind-set,** which is a person's belief that understanding and satisfying customers, whether internal or external to the organization, is central to the proper execution of his or her job.[41] It is through organization members' customer mind-set that a customer orientation "comes alive" within a firm. Exhibit 4.3 provides example descriptors of customer mind-set both in the context of customers outside the firm as well as people inside the firm with whom one must interact to get the job done (internal customers). Concepts of internal customers and internal marketing are developed further in Chapter 13 on service as the core product.

Wal-Mart has been working hard to solidify its community connectedness, organizational culture, and business model to allow the "world's largest retailer" to become an enabler of customer relationships.

FYI

Ernie Coutermarsh is senior vice president of F.W. Webb, a plumbing and heating distributorship. He describes the customer mind-set at his company: "Here, the employees are empowered to take action on any customer issues. They have the authority to solve any problem and initiate solutions. We encourage employees to not look the other way when they see something that can be done better." It's all in the culture, Coutermarsh says. "When the customer wins, the company wins and everyone within the company wins. The employees share in the rewards of doing it right." Coutermarsh adds that employees who excel at "doing it right" are trumpeted to the company as a whole, and pointed to as examples of good customer service.[42]

External Customer Mind-Set

I believe that. . .

- I must understand the needs of my company's customers.
- It is critical to provide value to my company's customers.
- I am primarily interested in satisfying my company's customers.
- I must understand who buys my company's products/services.
- I can perform my job better if I understand the needs of my company's customers.
- Understanding my company's customers will help me do my job better.

Internal Customer Mind-Set

I believe that. . .

- Employees who receive my work are my customers.
- Meeting the needs of employees who receive my work is critical to doing a good job.
- It is important to receive feedback from employees who receive my work.
- I focus on the requirements of the person who receives my work.

Score yourself from 1–6 on each item such that 1 = strongly disagree and 6 = strongly agree. Total up your score; a higher total score equates to more of a customer mind-set.

Source: Karen Norman Kennedy, Felicia G. Lassk, and Jerry R. Goolsby. Reprinted with kind permission from Springer Science + Business Media: *Journal of the Academy of Marketing Science,* "Customer Mind-Set of Employees Throughout the Organization," Vol. 30, 2002, pp.159–171, by Koren Norman Kennedy, et al. Copyright©2002.

CRM Enables Transformation into a Relationship-Based Enterprise

As we surmised from the various experts' definitions of CRM earlier in the chapter, CRM represents a business strategy, a set of operational processes, and analytic tools to enable or facilitate a truly customer-driven enterprise. Facilitating long-term, win-win relationships between buyer and seller firms—a **relationship-based enterprise**—is a central goal of CRM. To move toward being such a firm, and to improve the effectiveness of CRM's role in this process, several critical questions must be answered by marketing managers.[43] These questions are grouped by categories: customers, the relationship, and managerial decision making.

Customers

1. Who are our customers?
2. What do our customers want and expect?
3. What is the value proposition of our customers?

The Relationship

4. What kind of relationship do we want to build with our customers?
5. How do we foster exchange of value between us and our customers?
6. How do we work together and *share* control?

Managerial Decision Making

7. Who are we and what is our value proposition?
8. What do our products and brands represent to customers?
9. How do we organize to move value closer to our customers?

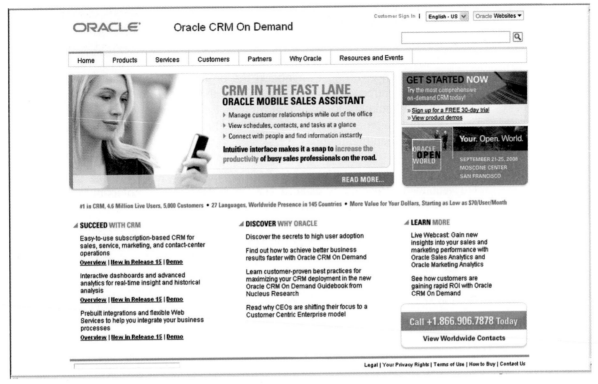

Oracle CRM On Demand has been successful providing subscription-based CRM applications that allow salespeople, marketers, service personnel, and customer contact people to access customer data easily. Moreover, its customizable applications encourage users to easily input customer data into the company's customer information system. Reprinted courtesy of Oracle Corporation.

10. How do we measure and manage our performance?

11. How do we increase our capacity for change?

Clearly, these questions are not trivial. The amount of time and other resources invested toward gaining satisfactory answers to these questions is directly related to the capability of CRM to enable a relationship-based enterprise. The answers guide (1) the evolution of the firm's relationships with customers, (2) the creation of a companywide relationship management strategy, and (3) the selection of CRM solutions with the most appropriate combination and application of supporting technologies.[44]

WHAT HAPPENS WHEN CRM FAILS?

Not surprisingly, when CRM fails it is usually not because of the *software* part of CRM. Rather, CRM failures are usually attributable to something related to the *people* part—a firm's culture, structure, and strategy. Specifically, issues related to leadership and management are the most commonly cited reasons CRM does not live up to its potential in a firm.

Consider the following problems that are not at all uncommon in firms adopting CRM. Each problem is coupled with an appropriate "fix."

- *Flavor of the month club*—Trying one CRM software package after another, usually through upgrading, occurs under the pretense that no system has been a good fit. To correct this, the process must be reversed. Involve *every user* in determining *in advance* what the key desired deliverables are from the CRM system, then purchase the system that meets those goals.

- *No allowances for organizational change*—Successful adoption of CRM can't be a "technology first, change later" process. Instead, organization-wide discussions and formal plans for organizational change must be in place *before* implementing the CRM program. This includes changes in culture, structure, processes, systems, and leadership and management.

- *Low level of employee buy-in*—Because CRM is an enterprisewide initiative, it will touch nearly everyone in a firm in some way over time. The time spent up front in involving everyone in the organization with the CRM selection/design process will pay dividends later through better utilization and results. It is particularly important that the firm realign its performance management system, such as incentives and rewards, to motivate utilization of CRM by organization members.

Nationwide Building Society, a U.K. financial services company, wanted to deliver more sensitive, satisfying experiences to its customers through the channels they prefer. The company hoped to do this via CRM technology. But first, Nationwide set up a companywide training program. Nationwide knew that each customer contact is a potential sales or service opportunity, and its employees would be using CRM software to support 25,000 customer interactions each day. A company that doesn't train all users on the system could experience complete disaster because without employee education and buy-in, the system won't work.[45]

- *Business units silos*—CRM needs cross-functional integration of information gathering, analysis, and dissemination inside a firm to work. Lack of cross-functional planning and poor communication among departments within a firm cause difficulties in CRM. The biggest mistake is thinking CRM is "owned" by the IT people in a firm simply because the process is technology-driven. No one functional group should control CRM. Instead, with strong leadership support from the top, cross-disciplinary teams should be established from the very initiation of the planning stages for CRM that require IT, marketing, operations, and the other functional areas to work together to maximize the opportunity CRM affords.

- *Poor training*—CRM doesn't work on autopilot, and even the best CRM system in the hands of a poorly trained user will add little value to a firm's customer initiatives. When a firm makes a commitment to invest in CRM, it is also making an implicit commitment to make initial and ongoing training *priority one* in implementing CRM. Firms should develop a system for employee feedback to management on CRM successes and failures and should foster a climate for employee input on ideas for system improvements. The best firms institutionalize these processes through reward systems with payoffs to employees whose ideas help increase the effectiveness of the CRM initiative.[46]

The truth is, implementing a CRM system and then having it disappoint or fail is much worse for a firm than if it had never attempted CRM. It is much harder to go back after the fact and correct fundamental mistakes in CRM implementation. Not only can a CRM failure represent a substantial financial hit for the company, but it also is demoralizing to the organizational culture, particularly when competitive firms may be visibly successful in using a similar system. The bottom line is, when considering CRM, the likelihood of a successful implementation increases dramatically when the firm can demonstrate the following characteristics:

- Strong internal partnerships exist throughout the firm around the CRM strategy.

- Organization members at all levels and in all areas are actively involved in collecting information using the CRM system.

- CRM tools are employee- and customer-friendly.

- Reporting consists only of data the firm can actually use.

- The CRM system is only as high-tech as necessary; if a lower tech solution is sufficient, it should be used.

In the end, the software part of CRM will work, and can probably do far more for any firm than expected. CRM's real strengths, as well as its fragilities, rest with how the organization chooses to use CRM as a means of enabling a customer-centric culture and operationalizing a customer orientation as an ongoing driver of the enterprise. CRM across all dimensions—as a business strategy, set of processes, and analytic tools—has amazing potential to facilitate great marketing planning and management.

SUMMARY

Customer relationship management (CRM) is a comprehensive business model for increasing revenues and profits by focusing on customers. CRM works effectively by focusing on acquisition and retention of profitable customers, thus enhancing customer satisfaction and loyalty. Successful CRM runs on information acquired through various customer touchpoints such as a salesperson, customer care representative, or Web site. After this information is collected it must be protected to avoid breaching customer trust and privacy. CRM enables *customer marketing*—a focus on developing relationships with *individuals*—instead of consumer or mass marketing, which is marketing to big groups of like-minded buyers.

KEY TERMS

customer relationship
   management (CRM) 99
customer satisfaction 100
customer loyalty 100
lifetime value of a customer 100
return on customer
   investment (ROCI) 101

firing a customer 101
touchpoints 102
data warehouse 102
data mining 102
database marketing 102
organizational learning 103

mass marketing 105
consumer marketing 106
customer marketing 106
formalization 108
customer mind-set 109
relationship-based enterprise 110

APPLICATION QUESTIONS

1. This chapter talks about CRM as an "enabler of great marketing." In what specific ways does CRM enable great marketing? That is, what can a marketing manager do better because his or her firm effectively practices CRM?

2. Consider each of the brands below. Assuming that a strong CRM system is in place in each brand's parent firm, what specific actions can marketing managers take in each case to ensure high satisfaction and loyalty among the most profitable customers?

   a. Chick-fil-A

   b. State Farm Insurance

   c. Amazon.com

   d. Dell computer

   e. GE home appliances

3. Consider the CRM process cycle of knowledge discovery, market planning, customer interaction, and analysis and refinement. Pick a company of interest to you and identify one of its important brands or product lines (it can be a good or a service). Chart what you believe the CRM process cycle should be for that firm, paying particular attention to identifying the relevant customer touchpoints. Be as specific as you can in describing each of the cycle elements.

4. The "dark side of CRM" involves the mishandling or unintended use of confidential customer information. Do some research online and find an example of a firm that misused or lost such information. What happened? After the problem came to light, what did the firm do to attempt to regain customer trust and confidence?

5. Assume for a moment that you are engaged in the start-up of an entrepreneurial venture. You are a strong believer in CRM as a comprehensive business model for increasing revenues and profits by focusing on customers, and you want to start your firm off with a strong customer-centric culture. Consider the five components of a customer-centric culture identified in the chapter. What steps will you take to ensure that each of the elements of a customer-centric culture is an integral part of your business model from day one?

MANAGEMENT DECISION CASE: Amazon Markets Its "Backroom" Capabilities

Amazon.com has spent 12 years and $2 billion perfecting many of the pieces behind its online store. By most accounts, those operations are now among the biggest and most reliable in the world and represent unique competencies for Amazon that carry high potential value for customers. Now, Amazon is starting to rent out almost everything it uses to run its own business, from rack space in its 10 million square feet of warehouses worldwide to spare computing capacity on its thousands of servers, data storage on its disk drives, and even some of the millions of lines of software code it has written to coordinate all that.

"All the kinds of things you need to build great Web-scale applications are already in the guts of Amazon," says founder Jeff Bezos. "The only difference is, we're now exposing the guts, making [them] available to others."

For example, with its Simple Storage Service (S3) Amazon charges 15 cents per gigabyte per month for businesses to store data and programs on Amazon's vast array of disk drives. It charges other merchants about 45 cents a square foot per month for real space in its warehouses. Through its Elastic Compute Cloud service, or EC2, it rents out computing power, starting at 10 cents an hour for the equivalent of a basic server computer.

Bezos is initially aiming these services at start-ups and other small companies with a little tech savvy. But businesses of all kinds are the ultimate target market. Already, Amazon has attracted some high-powered customers. Microsoft is using the storage service to help speed software downloads, for instance, and the service is helping Linden Lab handle the crush of software downloads for its fast-growing Second Life online virtual world.

How did the idea to sell its internal unique competencies come about? Initially, Amazon invested to modernize its own massive collection of data centers and the software running on them. The result was that Amazon made it much faster and easier to add new Web site features. With improved speed and software, small teams at Amazon could go hog wild with new ideas, such as building customer discussion boards on each product page and using software to play music and videos on the site.

Next came an epiphany: If the new computer setup allowed folks *inside* Amazon to be more creative and independent, why not open it up to *outsiders* too? So in 2002, Amazon began offering outside software and access for Web site developers to selected Amazon data such as pricing trends, gradually adding more and more services. These developers are now building new services on top of Amazon technology, further feeding back into Amazon's core retail business. One service, Scanbuy, lets people check Amazon prices on their cell phones to see if they're better than prices in a retail store. Bezos envisions embedding the tasks of product distribution and knowledge work right into the flow of more automated business processes such as order taking and payment processing. For instance, a new service called Fulfillment by Amazon lets small and midsize businesses send their inventory to Amazon warehouses. Then when a customer places an order, Amazon gets an automated signal to ship it—no fuss, no servers or software or garages full of stuff.

Don MacAskill, SmugMug's co-founder and CEO, upon seeing how easily and cheaply SmugMug could back up its photos on S3, said, "My eyes got all big." Now, by zapping customers' photos to Amazon to store on its servers, he avoids the need to buy more storage devices of his own—and saves $500,000 a year. "Everything we can get Amazon to do, we will get Amazon to do," added Chris MacAskill, SmugMug's co-founder. "You're going to see all kinds of start-ups get a much better and faster start" by using Amazon's services.

Questions for Consideration

1. What value proposition is Amazon offering its customers with this new service?

2. Amazon has pioneered many technologies that enhance customer relationship management, such as its recommendation service that suggests books to customers based on their previous purchases as well as the purchases of other customers who have bought similar items. How could other organizations use Amazon's CRM technologies?

3. How might a company use Amazon's back-end technology to integrate all of its customer touchpoints?

Source: Robert D. Hof, "Jeff Bezos' Risky Bet," *BusinessWeek Online*, November 13, 2006, www.businessweek.com/magazine/content/06_46/b4009001.htm.

MARKETING PLAN EXERCISE

ACTIVITY 4: Plan for a CRM System

In this chapter, you learned about the value of CRM in fostering a customer-centric culture and establishing a relationship-based enterprise. At this point in the development of your marketing plan, the following steps are needed:

1. Establish the objectives of your CRM system with regard to customer acquisition, customer retention, and customer profitability. Pay particular attention to driving high customer satisfaction and loyalty among profitable customers.

2. Map out the CRM process cycle you will employ in your business. Identify all the relevant touchpoints you plan to utilize—both interactive and noninteractive.

3. Prepare a set of guidelines on the ethical handling of customer data, with a focus on avoiding misuse and theft.

4. Consider the reasons for CRM failure identified in the chapter. Develop an approach to ensure that each can be avoided in your firm.

If you are using Marketing Plan Pro, a template for this assignment can be accessed at www.mhhe.com/marshall1e

RECOMMENDED READINGS

1. Kristin Anderson and Carol Kerr, *Customer Relationship Management* (New York: McGraw-Hill, 2002).

2. Stanley A. Brown, Moosha Gulycz, and Stanley Brown, *Performance-Driven CRM: How to Make Your Customer Relationship Management Vision a Reality* (Toronto: John Wiley & Sons Canada, 2002).

3. Karl Hellman and Ardis Burst, *The Customer Learning Curve: Creating Profits from Marketing Chaos* (Cincinnati, OH: Thomson/South-Western, 2004).

4. Mark Hurd and Lars Nyberg, *The Value Factor: How Global Leaders Use Information for Growth and Competitive Advantage* (Princeton, NJ: Bloomberg Press, 2004).

5. Kaj Storbacka and Jarmo R. Lehtinen, *Customer Relationship Management: Creating Competitive Advantage through Win-Win Relationship Strategies* (New York: McGraw-Hill, 2001).

CHAPTER 05

MANAGING MARKETING INFORMATION

LEARNING OBJECTIVES

- Describe the difference between market information systems and market research systems.

- Identify how critical internal (inside the firm) information is collected and used in making marketing decisions.

- Explain essential external (outside the firm) information collection methods.

- Recognize the value of market research and its role in marketing.

- Define the market research process.

- Illustrate current research technologies and how they are used in market research.

EXECUTIVE PERSPECTIVE

Executive Joe Rand, Director of Marketing

Company Disney Cruise Line

Business Travel

What data from your firm's internal information system is the most useful in making marketing decisions and why?

Disney Cruise Line has numerous recurring research projects that provide us critical insights on our various guest segments. Although each piece of research contributes to the overall understanding of our guest, the most valuable is an annual study that we've named *Passenger Profile*. The passenger profile pulls together three central consumer insights—demographics, psychographics, and behavior—and provides multiyear trending for each. This guides many of the decisions that we make both from an operations and a marketing point of view. Specific to marketing, we mine this information to understand any changes to our primary guest segment, which are families with young children. For example, we look for any changes in their demographics (both at-home and onboard), how they learned about us, which other brands they considered, and their attitudes/perceptions of our brand.

How do you use qualitative research approaches such as focus groups and depth interviews to assist in marketing planning?

Virtually all of our research efforts include some qualitative element. I believe that is the way to capture the most powerful insights. We supplement our ongoing quantitative research, which includes surveys, etc., with a variety of qualitative studies to probe further on specific topics. For example, if we're considering a change to a marketing program or an onboard experience, we often test it using qualitative research. We recently did just that when we wanted to learn more about our past guest program, Castaway Club. This program is designed to continue communicating with guests who have sailed with Disney Cruise Line once they get home and, when they come back to sail with us again, to recognize them and treat them as special guests once they're onboard. We wanted to understand which elements of the program are most valuable to our past guests and what else we could do to take the program to an even higher level.

When you think about your overall market research initiatives, what are some key success factors that come to mind?

We have the ability to leverage the best secondary research from our industry and an incredible research staff that leads all of our primary research efforts and includes Disney Cruise Line in relevant studies being conducted for the Disney Parks & Resorts segment. Being affiliated with The Walt Disney Company also affords us the ability to harness consumer insights from other areas of the company and to internally benchmark our marketing efforts to determine what's working and why.

MAKING GOOD MARKETING DECISIONS—THE NEED TO KNOW

Information is power speaks to the importance of good information in decision making. Companies realize the right information at the right time and in the right format (a critical but often neglected part of the process) is essential for decision makers. Marketers are usually the ones entrusted with scanning the environment for changes that might affect the organization. As a result, creating procedures that collect, analyze, and access relevant information is a critical part of marketing management.[1]

A significant problem for most managers today is not having too little information but having too much. They frequently see interesting information that has no relevance to the immediate problem. As a result, companies need information systems that can collect and analyze huge amounts of information and then keep it for the right time and circumstance. Pulte Homes is one of the largest home builders in the United States. The company conducts research to learn how people move around in a home (the design flow), what features consumers want (for example large master bedrooms and bathrooms), and what extras they want (upgraded countertops and wood trim). Also, Pulte studies demographic changes. For example, a large segment of the population, baby boomers (ages 45–60), is moving toward retirement; this may lead the company to design and build smaller homes with more special features. Also, the downturn in the real estate market has led the federal government to adopt changes in real estate financing, and many states have followed suit with additional legislation. Finally, Pulte also needs to study changes in federal and state laws that affect home construction, such as the modifications to home building codes in Louisiana after Hurricane Katrina. These changes affect the homes people buy and, as a result, Pulte needs to be knowledgeable in all these areas.[2]

In addition to storing large amounts of data, marketing managers need a system to design and execute research that generates precise information. Consider the Apple iPhone. Before introducing the product, Apple conducted tests with actual users to be sure the product fit their needs and performed as promised. The company also studied a wide range of other issues including which markets offered the greatest growth potential, competitors such as Nokia, and long-term technology trends to identify key technologies for iPhone now and in the future such as the touch-screen interface. Marketing managers needed this information to make critical decisions as iPhone was being developed and the marketing plan

Porsche studied SUV buyers to develop an SUV that embodied what SUV and Porsche buyers want in an SUV. The result was the Cayenne, which reflected the core elements of Porsche and the practicality of an SUV.

The PORSCHE CREST, PORSCHE, BOXSTER, CARRERA, CAYENNE, and the distinctive shape of the PORSCHE 911 and BOXSTER automobiles are registered trademarks in the United States of Dr. Ing. h. c. F. Porsche AG and Porsche Cars north america, Inc. Copyrighted by Dr. Ing. h.c. F. Porsche AG. Porsche Cayenne print ad published Spring 2007 in the U.S.

When do you tell it that it's not a sports car?

The new Cayenne. Starting at $43,400.

PORSCHE

put together. With the success of iPhone, competitors study it to learn how key features can be duplicated in their own products.[3]

These examples highlight the two fundamental types of market information decision makers need today. The first is data related to broad areas of interest such as demographic and economic trends, or the customer order fulfillment process inside the company. These data are used in strategic planning to help forecast potential new opportunities for company investment or deal with possible problems before they become a major issue for the company.[4] The second type of information needed addresses a specific question, for example, what is the best kitchen design for a retired baby boomer couple? Or, what features would a young urban professional want on an iPhone? Questions like this require unique research designed to answer specific questions.[5] This chapter will examine both types of information needs. We'll start by discussing the market information system that is designed to bring together many different kinds information useful to the marketing decision maker. Then we'll look at marketing research, which is the process marketers use to conduct research on specific market questions.

> Plantronics watched cities and states pass laws mandating the use of hands-free devices with cell phones while driving, then it invested in specific research to design and build Bluetooth headsets to fit the human ear. Bluetooth headsets experienced sales growth of more than 60 percent and are projected to more than double by 2010.[6]

MARKET INFORMATION SYSTEM
The Nature of a Market Information System

As noted earlier, marketing decision makers need limited amounts of the right data at any given time. Put simply, managers need what they need when they need it. When there is too much information, managers tend to either spend an excessive amount of time analyzing or get overwhelmed and ignore all the data. If they have too little information, managers are more likely to make poor decisions because they don't have all the facts. In either case, incorrect decisions are often the result. Exhibit 5.1 summarizes the various ways marketing research is used in making marketing decisions. As you can tell from Exhibit 5.1, market research takes many forms both inside and outside an organization.

A **market information system (MIS)** is not a software package but a continuing process of identifying, collecting, analyzing, accumulating, and dispensing critical information to marketing decision makers. The MIS is really an "information bank" where data relevant to the company's marketing efforts are collected and stored until such time as management needs to "withdraw" it. Generally, this information is not specific to a particular problem or question; rather, it is important information that the marketing decision maker will need at the appropriate time.[7] A company needs to consider three factors in creating an MIS.

First, what information should the system collect? In evaluating internal and external information sources, companies need to consider not only what information is important but also the source of the data. Think about all the ways a company gets competitor data—salespeople and customers in the field, competitor materials and Web sites, business-related Web sites such as Hoover's, and many others. Because there are so many sources of information, decisions must be made about what information will be collected and where it will come from.

Second, what are the information needs of each decision maker? Not all managers need the same information. The CEO probably doesn't want or need daily sales figures across individual product lines, but the local sales manager does. A good MIS is flexible enough for managers to customize the information they receive and, in some cases, the format they receive it in.

EXHIBIT 5.1 | Marketing Research Is Critical to Marketing Decisions

Stages or Processes within Marketing Planning	Appropriate Marketing Research
Situation Analysis • Identification of competitive strengths and weaknesses • Identification of trends (opportunities and threats)	• Competitive barrier analysis • Analysis of sources of competitive advantage • Trend analysis • Positioning analysis • Identification of public and key issues concerns • Measure of market share
Selection of a Target Market • Analysis of the market • Selection of a target market	• Identification of segmentation bases • Market segmentation study • Needs assessment • Determination of purchase criteria • Buyer behavior analysis • Market demand estimation
Plan of the Marketing Mix • Product	• Product design assessment • Competitive product analysis • Competitive packaging assessment • Packaging trends assessment • Definition of brand image descriptors • Identification of brand name/symbol • New product ideation (concept development) • Package development or redesign
• Price	• Measure of price elasticity • Industry pricing patterns • Price-value perception analysis • Analysis of the effects of various price incentives
• Distribution	• Merchandising display assessment • Inventory management assessment • Location analysis (site analysis) • Market exposure assessment
• Promotion	• Message assessment • Content analysis • Copy testing • Media assessment • Media buy assessment
Marketing Control • Marketing audit	• Promotion effectiveness study • Assessment of effectiveness of marketing mix

Source: Reprinted from Donald R. Cooper and Pamela S. Schindler, *Marketing Research*, 2006. Copyright © 2006 The McGraw-Hill Companies, Inc.

Third, how does the system maintain the privacy and confidentiality of sensitive information? Company databases hold a great deal of confidential data on customers, suppliers, and employees. By limiting access to the data to those with a need to know, companies protect relationships and build trust.

Internal Sources—Collecting Information inside the Company

At the heart of marketing is the relationship among the company, its products, and customers. Critical to that relationship is a clear understanding of what is, and is not, working in the customer interface. Think about the senior manager at

Microsoft who is concerned about rising dissatisfaction with customer support among its Office suite users. While there could be a number of reasons for this increase, the manager will first want to look at internal customer service metrics that include call wait times, ability of customer service representatives to handle the problems efficiently and effectively, number of customers who call back to address a problem, and a host of other metrics. These are all internal sources of data. By looking at such critical internal metrics collected as part of the market information system, management is able to do two things. First, in our example, management might see that an increase in call wait times has led to higher customer dissatisfaction. Here information is used to identify the problem. A second and more effective use of market information systems is to proactively address issues before they become a problem.[8] For example, management can set a benchmark stating that call wait times will not exceed two minutes. In this way, management can deal with a problem before it becomes a significant concern for the company. Of course, the investment in time and money needed to create and monitor such a system is significant.

A market information system can be as complicated as the company wants or can afford. It is expensive to collect and analyze data, and most companies don't maximize their existing information. Often, simply checking secondary sources such as legitimate Web sites will provide sufficient information for the marketing manager to make a decision in a particular situation. More formal information systems, however, provide a great deal more information that can help guide strategic decisions (changes in demographics can lead to new market opportunities) or address critical tactical issues (shorten call wait times for customer service).[9] Exhibit 5.2 identifies five common internal sources of data collected as a regular

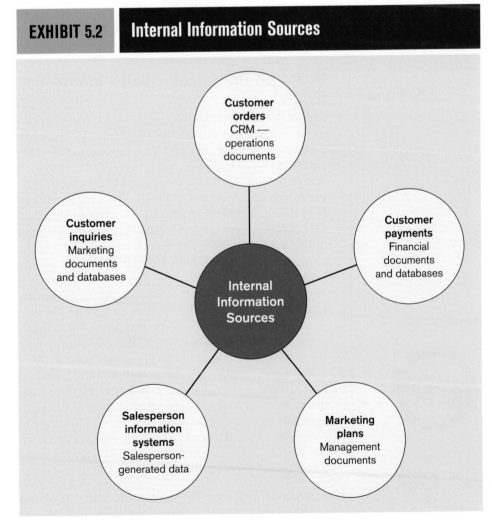

EXHIBIT 5.2   Internal Information Sources

part of doing business. Unfortunately, managers are often not aware of all the information in their own company.

From the Customer's Order to Order Fulfillment

Tracking a customer's initial inquiry through to order placement, delivery, payment, and follow-up after the purchase offers insight about the customer as well as insight about how well the company is working. CRM systems use customer data collected through market information systems to help drive customer-centric strategies as discussed in Chapter 4. More specifically, the data collected and analyzed in a CRM system enable companies to:

- **Identify the frequency and size of customer orders.** By charting the frequency, size, and specific items included in an order, it's possible to assess customer satisfaction

- **Determine the actual cost of a customer order.** Tools such as activity-based cost accounting can allocate time and overhead costs to specific customers. By combining that with information from each customer order, it is possible to get accurate cost and profitability measures of individual customers.

- **Rank customers based on established criteria like profitability.** Not all customers are equal, and the customer mix changes over time. Companies need to understand how each customer rates on a defined set of criteria to better allocate current resources and develop strategies for future growth.

- **Calculate the efficiency of the company's production and distribution system.** Tracking customer orders makes it possible to assess many of the company's critical functions.

Heard on the Street – Sales Information System

One of the best internal information sources is the sales force. Salespeople are on the front lines of the company-customer interface and have unique access to the customer. As a result, they are an excellent information source not only about the customer but also about market trends and even the competition.[10] This is particularly true in a business-to-business environment where salespeople are often the primary method for communicating with customers. Salespeople are usually the first to hear about changes with the customer, such as new personnel or the need for new products. What's more, as they interact with customers, salespeople frequently learn a great deal about competitor tactics and plans.

Regrettably, companies time and again fail to maximize this information source. While salespeople may share what they learn with local management or other salespeople, companies have traditionally not had formal systems of collecting and analyzing data from the sales force.[11] This is changing, however, as management creates formal sales information systems to collect, analyze, store, and distribute information from the field to appropriate decision makers in the company.[12] A sales information system includes:

- **Formal systems for collecting data (getting the data).** Many salespeople write call reports

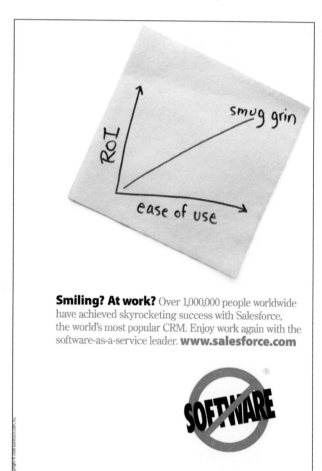

Salesforce.com has been successful providing online CRM applications that allow salespeople to access customer data easily. Moreover, its customizable applications encourage salespeople to input customer data into the company sales information system.

summarizing each sales call. Much of the information on a call report is relevant in a sales information system. This includes products discussed with the customer, customer concerns, and changes in personnel.

- **Interpretation of data (analysis).** This may be done at the local level by sales managers who add additional insight to the "raw" data from the salesperson. In more sophisticated sales information systems, people at regional or national offices will analyze data from many salespeople looking for broad trends.

- **Distribution of data (getting the analysis to decision makers and back into the field).** A sales information system needs to distribute the information to management as part of a larger market information system. At the same time, it is important to get the information back out to the sales force. When trends, problems or solutions to problems, and opportunities are identified, salespeople benefit from learning quickly so they can respond in the field. Much of this information has a time value. If salespeople do not get the analysis in a timely manner, much of the benefit will be lost. For example, suppose a company learns from several salespeople that a major competitor is contacting customers about a new product. Getting this information to the entire sales force quickly will enable them to develop responses for their own customers.

Balancing research with management insight is a challenge. The Gap had its own internal research group, Consumer Insights, conduct focus groups and survey consumers and employees to develop a line of clothes. The results were not impressive: Critics charged that consumers often don't know what clothes they will want to buy in the future so asking does not necessarily yield successful clothing designs.[13]

External Sources—Collecting Information Outside the Company

Staying connected to the business environment is no longer optional. Success is based, in part, on both the quality and quantity of information available to management. As a result, most companies engage in collecting, analyzing, and storing data from the macro environment on a continuous basis known as **marketing intelligence.** The ability to do this well is a competitive advantage; successful companies accurately analyze and interpret environmental information then develop strategies to take advantage of opportunities and deal with threats before they become a problem (see Exhibit 5.3).

Demographics

Populations change over time, and companies must be aware of those changes. Not tracking and responding to demographic changes is a management failure because the data are easy to obtain and major changes occur slowly. Surprisingly, many companies do not do a good job of either learning about demographic trends or responding to them.

Demographics can be defined as the statistical characteristics of human populations, such as age or income, used to identify markets. They provide a statistical description of a group of people and are extremely useful in marketing for two reasons. First, *demographics help define a market.* How old is a typical customer? How educated? What is the typical customer's income? These are all demographic characteristics that help describe a market. For example, a typical Mercedes-Benz automobile owner in the United States is a male, successful, and over 50 years old. By analyzing demographics, a company can define not only the "typical" customer but also its market at large. Second, *studying demographics helps identify new opportunities.* As baby boomers age, they will need, among other things, retirement communities. This represents an opportunity for companies to build unique retirement properties specifically for baby boomers.

EXHIBIT 5.3 | **External Forces Affect Marketing Decisions**

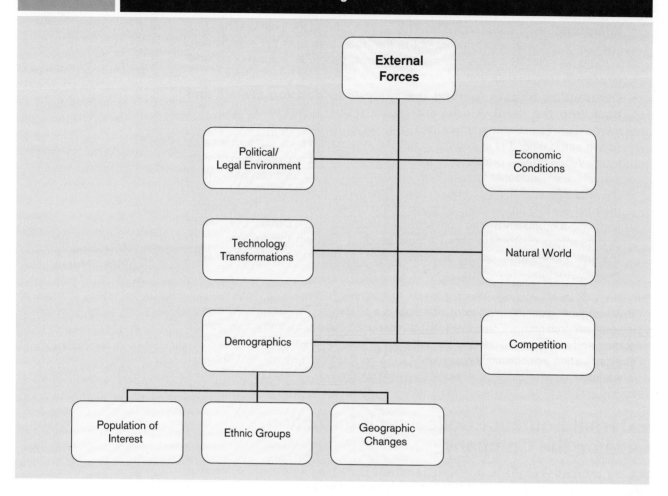

Companies that deal directly with consumers develop customer profiles based on demographic information and compare their profiles against those of competitors. For example, the typical Mercedes-Benz owner tends to be older than a BMW owner. Companies even create pictures of their "average" customer, highlighting key demographic data (age, gender, and ethnicity).

Populations of Interest Marketers are not interested in all groups, only populations of interest. The difficult part for many marketers is separating relevant demographic data from irrelevant. For example, does cell phone maker Nokia need to know that world population growth is faster in less developed countries (among less developed countries the population is growing at 2 percent per year while developed countries are growing at less than 1 percent)? Your first response might be no as Nokia is likely interested in more developed countries with established cellular networks and people who can afford the technology. However, while less developed countries do not need the new, expensive Nokia phones, they could use older, less expensive technology to encourage economic development and build a communication network. Targeting less developed countries may offer Nokia an opportunity to establish a market presence in these countries even as they develop economically.

Ethnic Groups Many countries are becoming more ethnically diverse as individuals increase their mobility. While some countries, such as the United Arab Emirates in the Middle East, have populations composed of a single ethnic group, others like the United States are much more ethnically diverse. Nearly three-quarters of the U.S. population is white, but trends project that whites will be less than

50 percent of the population in less than 30 years. Hispanics have shown the greatest increase among ethnic groups in the United States over the past 10 years. They are currently the second-largest minority group (recently passing African Americans) and are expected to continue growing as a percentage of the U.S. population.

The European Union has made it possible for individuals to move freely around member countries. While many of the member countries are still dominated by local ethnic groups, the European continent is becoming more ethnically diverse. For the most part, this leads to greater opportunities; however, some countries such as France find it difficult to assimilate certain groups into their culture. The market challenge then becomes developing effective marketing strategies across different ethnicities living in the same area.

Geographic Changes People are moving not only in the United States but around the world. As we just noted, the opening of borders in the European Union has increased the mobility of those living in the EU. A decades-old trend—people moving from the countryside to the city—continues around the globe and some cities, such as Mexico City, Sao Paulo, and others, find it difficult to cope with the influx of people that stretches their ability to provide social services (see Exhibit 5.4).

The changes present opportunities but also challenges. The growth of Asian cultures means many companies must adjust their marketing strategies to fit the unique needs of Asian consumers. Appliance companies such as

The Hispanic market represents one of the fastest growing demographic groups in the United States. Extended Hispanic families can be comprised of several generations.

EXHIBIT 5.4	Top 10 Cities in Population with Projected Growth Rates

Agglomeration	Country	Population (millions)			Rank			% of Average Annual Change	
		1975	2003	2015	1975	2003	2015	2000–2005	2010–2015
Tokyo	Japan	26.6	35.0	36.2	1	1	1	0.5	0.2
Mexico City	Mexico	10.7	18.7	20.6	4	2	4	1.0	0.8
New York	USA	15.9	18.3	19.7	2	3	6	0.7	0.6
São Paulo	Brazil	9.6	17.9	20.0	6	4	5	1.4	0.7
Mumbai (Bombay)	India	7.3	17.4	22.6	15	5	2	2.6	2.0
Delhi	India	4.4	14.1	20.9	25	6	3	4.2	2.8
Calcutta	India	7.9	13.8	16.8	11	7	10	1.8	1.7
Buenos Aires	Argentina	9.1	13.0	14.6	7	8	12	1.2	0.8
Shanghai	China	11.4	12.8	12.7	3	9	15	−0.3	0.3
Jakarta	Indonesia	4.8	12.3	17.5	23	10	8	3.6	2.5

Source: *United Nations World Urbanization Prospects, The 2003 Revision* (Geneva and New York: United Nations, 2003).

Whirlpool have redesigned their products to fit in smaller Asian kitchens. Coincidentally, downsizing products is a strategy consistent with the migration of people to urban centers. Mr. Coffee, Braun, and others have created coffeemakers designed for single households in the smaller living environments often found in large cities.

Economic Conditions

Companies are keenly interested in the ability of their customers to purchase products and services. It is not surprising then that a good understanding of current and future economic trends is important in an effective market information system. There are two principal types of economic knowledge. The study of individual economic activity (firm, household, or prices) is known as **microeconomics.** At the other end of the spectrum, **macroeconomics** refers to the study of economic activity in terms of broad measures of output (Gross national product or GNP) and input as well as the interaction among various sectors of an entire economy. Both are important for marketing managers. Microeconomics helps marketing managers understand how individuals set priorities and make buying decisions. Macroeconomics, on the other hand, gives a 'big picture" perspective for an economy and can be helpful at looking for broad economic trends.

EXHIBIT 5.5	Common Economic Terms Defined

Comparative Advantage

The ability of a producer to produce a good at a lower marginal cost than other producers; marginal cost in the sacrifice of some other good compared to the amount of a good obtained.

Consumer Price Index (CPI)

A measure of the average amount (price) paid for a market basket of goods and services by a typical U.S. consumer in comparison to the average paid for the same basket in an earlier base year.

Discount Rate

The interest a private bank pays for a loan from the U.S. Federal Reserve System.

Federal Reserve System

The U.S. central bank consisting of 12 regional banks run by a board of governors appointed by the president for overlapping 14-year terms; formally independent of the executive and congressional branches of government; private bank members of the system own their assets.

Foreign Currency Reserve

The foreign currencies that a central bank keeps on hand for intervention.

Gross National Product (GNP)

Value of all the goods and services produced in an economy, plus the value of the goods and services imported, less the goods and services exported.

Inflation

Increase in the overall level of prices over an extended time period.

Interest

The annual earnings that are sacrificed when wealth is invested in a given asset or business. The interest sacrificed by investing in a given business is often called the cost of capital.

International Monetary Fund (IMF)

The overseer for the exchange rate system and international monetary relations.

Nominal GNP

GNP measured in current prices.

Nominal Interest Rate

The cost inflicted by inflation eroding the value of stored dollars plus the forgone real interest rate; the opportunity cost of holding money.

Price Elasticity of Demand

A measure of the responsiveness of the quantity demanded of a good to changes in that good's price.

Real GNP

The GNP of any year measured in the prices of a base year. Real GNP is nominal GNP adjusted for inflation.

Source: FACSNET, www.facsnet.org/tools/ref_tutor/econo_term/glossary.html), accessed November, 2008.

Indicators such as the GNP measure the health of an economy and are helpful in spotting trends. For example, if the GNP goes up, it is generally viewed as a sign the economy is doing well. As an economy slows, the GNP will slow. Exhibit 5.5 defines key economic terms used by marketing managers to assess the economic conditions of a market.

Technology Transformations

Few areas in business have been more affected by technology than marketing. Technology has been one of the major catalysts for change in the marketplace. Faster, smaller, and easier-to-use computers and powerful software facilitate sophisticated analyses right on the desks of front-line managers from anywhere in the world. Complex supply chain and manufacturing processes coupled with Internet connectivity allow customers real-time access to the entire manufacturing process. Consider the online order process for HP. A consumer places the order online, gets a final price and expected delivery date, then follows it from the assembly plant literally to their front door with a tracking number from the shipping company.

Even technology companies find it difficult to evaluate the effect of technology in the marketplace. Microsoft, for example, underestimated the power of Apple's decision to link hardware (iPod) and software (iTunes) in online music. In an effort to build a seamless product, Microsoft abandoned its own proprietary music software to create Zune's look and feel. The ability of iPod to sync easily with iTunes provided a much simpler interface for the customer.[14]

Marketing managers need to know the role of technology in their business today and also, perhaps even more importantly, its role in the future. Successfully assimilating technology into a business takes time and money. Almost every organization has had at least one negative experience with technology. Hershey Foods, for example, tried to bring a new CRM system online at the busiest selling season of the year for candy, Halloween, only to find problems implementing the system. The company estimated it was unable to fill $100 million worth of candy orders as a result of issues related to integrating the new software.[15] Read Ethical Dimension 5 to see a growing concern in collecting accurate information over the Internet.

Natural World

Everyone lives on planet Earth, and business operates within the constraints of available natural resources. Two key issues drive marketers' need to know about the natural world. First, individuals, governments, and business all recognize the need to manage the available resources well. It took the world roughly 150 years to use 1 trillion barrels of oil; however, it is predicted the world will use the next trillion barrels by 2030 and, while there may be a lot of oil left, it will be harder to get and more expensive. Governments and businesses are concerned about the effect of increasing energy costs on economic growth. Other resources such as water are also becoming increasingly scarce in parts of the world. In the Western United States, for example, growth in communities such as Phoenix is considered in the context of water access, which limits future development as water becomes scarcer.

A second concern regarding the natural world is pollution. In some parts of the world, pollution takes a significant toll on the quality of life and economic growth in a community. In Mexico City, driving is limited for everyone to certain days during the week as congestion and smog create huge clouds of pollution that hang over the city. Concern about water pollution has led Chinese government officials to declare "more than 70 percent of the rivers and lakes have been polluted to some extent" and count losses in the billions of dollars. These concerns influence marketers as they make decisions about how and where products are manufactured. For example, energy companies such as Chevron are investing billions to identify and develop more environmentally safe energy.

The Source of the Click

Internet ad spending is projected to double in five years to more than $30 billion. The pay structure has evolved along two distinct lines. About half of all Internet ads are priced based on the number of people viewing the ad, similar to traditional television advertising. The other model for Internet advertising charges by the click. If someone views an ad and then chooses to click on the ad through to the advertiser, the advertiser pays a fee ranging from a few pennies to $20. A critical assumption is the click's legitimacy; it is supposed to represent someone actively seeking information from the advertiser's site.

Two companies control the vast majority of Internet ad placements—Yahoo and Google. While Google and Yahoo generate most of their revenue on legitimate Web sites, they also send ads to affiliated sites, known as "domain parking Web sites," which are basically advertising sites with very little content. Publicly they state these sites provide a useful service by directing Internet surfers to relevant information. However, companies are starting to express concern that some of these sites may actually be generating illegitimate clicks, clicks by individuals (or other computers) who are not legitimate potential customers.

Click fraud, estimated at $1 billion, has become a big issue for many Internet advertisers. Web sites with names such as "insurance1472.com" are dummy sites located primarily in Asia and Eastern Europe that generate false clicks. The process works like this. First, ABC Company contracts with Google or Yahoo to advertise on the Internet and negotiates the fee ABC will pay for each click from an ABC ad to the company Web site. Second, Google or Yahoo displays the ad on legitimate Web sites but also sends the ad to domain parking Web sites. Third, these sites distribute the ads to parked Web sites that are often just lists of ads. Fourth, the owner of the parked Web site sends out a list of sites to individuals known collectively as "paid-to-read groups." These individuals' role is to click on ads for which they receive a small payment. Finally, Google or Yahoo charges ABC Company for the click, then shares part of the revenue with the domain parking Web site, which shares it with the other participants in the fraud.

Adding to the challenge for advertisers is the difficult position of Google and Yahoo, who make more money when click fraud occurs. Both companies strongly deny any wrongdoing and actively police their ad placements. However, both have settled click fraud class action suits with advertisers and instituted a number of changes to their business model to curb the problem.[16]

Ethical Perspective

1. **Advertisers:** How would your view of Internet advertising change if the statistics related to the number of people who "click through" an ad were not accurate?

2. **Google and Yahoo:** While you are concerned with click fraud, the process actually generates significant revenue, what do you do?

Political/Legal Environment

Political judgments and, more broadly, the legal environment significantly affect company decisions and sometimes an entire industry. In 2003, the National Do Not Call Registry was created to minimize intrusive telemarketing calls. By registering, individuals protect themselves from telemarketing calls. Telemarketing companies are subject to significant fines if they call someone listed on the register. Millions of people signed up, and many companies were forced to reconfigure their marketing communications strategy.[17]

Local, state, and federal legislatures pass more business-related legislation than ever before. In addition, government agencies are more active in monitoring business activity. During the 1990s the Securities and Exchange Commission actively pursued several antitrust actions, the largest against Microsoft for illegal monopoly activity. As a result, Microsoft made changes to Windows Vista that opened it up to outside software vendors.

Information is important to all organizations not just companies. As a result of September 11, 2001, the Department of Homeland Security has worked to coordinate information among many different law enforcement agencies. While much work still needs to be done, the first step in the process was to survey law enforcement experts to identify their needs, and the result was a better, more user-friendly system that was implemented sooner than expected.[18]

Competition

One of the most important external environmental factors to consider is the competition. Companies want to know as much as possible about competitors' products and strategies. In highly competitive markets, companies are constantly adjusting their strategies to the competition. Airlines, for example, track competitor pricing and adjust their pricing almost immediately to changes in the marketplace. When one airline offers a sale in a specific market, competitors will soon follow with sales in the same market. Identifying, analyzing, and effectively dealing with competitors is the focus in Chapter 6.

MARKETING RESEARCH SYSTEMS

Marketing managers are confronted with an unlimited number of problems, opportunities, and issues that require specific answers. Sometimes the information needed is not available from other sources or even from the company's own market information system. To get specific answers to important management questions, marketing research is necessary.

The Importance of Market Research to Managers

Consider the following:

- You are a marketing manager for Harley-Davidson Motorcycles, and 90 percent of your bikes are sold to men. You believe women are a great potential target market but have had little success selling Harleys to them. What do you do?

- You are the director of advertising for McDonald's, and the company is getting ready to roll out a new advertising campaign designed to increase sales of a new sandwich. However, senior management wants to know if it will work. What do you do?

The answers to situations like these lies in market research. **Market research** is the methodical identification, collection, analysis, and distribution of data related to discovering then solving marketing problems or opportunities and enhancing good decision making. Several things come out of this definition. Good marketing research:

- **Follows a well-defined set of activities and does not happen by accident.** Rather, it comes as a result of the methodical identification, collection, analysis, and distribution of data.

- **Enhances the validity of the information.** Anyone can "Google" a topic and come up with a lot of information. However, following the market research process enhances the confidence that the research will discover then solve marketing problems and opportunities.

- **Is impartial and objective.** It does not prejudge the information or develop answers to fit an already decided outcome; rather, it enhances good decision making.

Marketing research is also big business. In 2007, nearly $8.6 billion was spent on marketing research in the United States and even more was spent in the rest of the world. This does not include the research conducted in-house by internal market research departments.[19] Some of these departments, such as McDonald's internal research group, are larger than many research companies and spend hundreds of millions of dollars a year conducting market research for their own organizations. Exhibit 5.6 lists the top market research companies in the world.

The Marketing Research Process

At the heart of the marketing research process is a search for understanding. Sometimes management seeks answers to a particular problem. In other situations, an

EXHIBIT 5.6 — Top Five Market Research Companies in the World

Organization	Headquarters	Total Revenue
The Nielsen Co.	New York	$4.220 billion
IMS Health Inc.	Norwalk, Conn.	$2.192 billion
TNS	New York	$2.137 billion
GfK AG	Nuremberg, Germany	$1.603 billion
Kantar Group	Fairfield, Conn.	$1.551 billion

opportunity needs to be evaluated before committing resources. By following the marketing research process, marketing managers can have greater confidence in the information they are receiving and, hopefully, make better informed decisions. As shown in Exhibit 5.7 the process consists of six steps.

Define the Research Problem

One of the biggest challenges facing a marketing researcher is accurately defining the problem. What exactly is the issue/opportunity/problem? Often managers are not clear about the problem and need help defining it. It is not uncommon for a market research professional to get a call that starts something like this, "I have a problem. Sales have been falling for six months and I am losing business to my competitors." The researcher knows that the real problem is not the company's declining sales; falling sales are the result, a symptom, of the real issue. Market research can be a useful tool helping senior managers identify and deal with the real issue.[20]

Given that management often does not have a clear understanding of the problem, defining the research problem involves two distinct steps. First, management, working with researchers and marketing decision makers, defines the **management research deliverable.** Exactly what does management want to do with this research? Keep in mind that decision makers are looking for information to help them make better, more informed decisions. For example, if you are the director of advertising for McDonald's, you want to increase sales of a new sandwich, and a new advertising campaign can help accomplish that goal. However, before you decide to spend a lot of money on the campaign, you want to know if it is going to be successful.

Once the management research deliverable has been identified, the next step is to define the **research problem.** Exactly what information is needed to help management in this situation? In our example that means assessing the target market's response to the new advertising campaign.

In the McDonald's example, the research problem is fairly straightforward. However, there are often multiple research problems and researchers will have to prioritize which problems to study first. Consider the example of Harley-Davidson motorcycles and targeting more female riders. Management may want to know:

EXHIBIT 5.7 — The Marketing Research Process

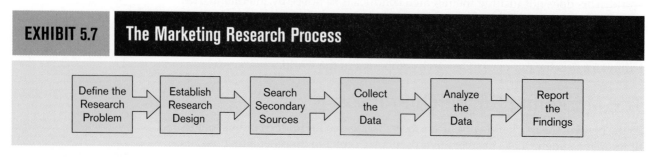

Define the Research Problem → Establish Research Design → Search Secondary Sources → Collect the Data → Analyze the Data → Report the Findings

EXHIBIT 5.8 — Research Design Activities

Activity	Question to Be Answered
Type of research	What kind of research needs to be done?
Nature of data	What kind of data do we need?
Nature of data collection	How should we collect the data?
Information content	What do we need to know?
Sampling plan	Who should be included in the research?

(1) How many women would be in the market for a motorcycle and, more specifically, how many women would be in the market for a large bike like a Harley? (2) What kind of motorcycle would they want to buy? (3) If Harley-Davidson were to create a new bike, how would loyal, dedicated Harley-Davidson owners react to it? You can begin to see why it is necessary for management and researchers to prioritize the problems and identify which research issues to address first.[21]

Establish the Research Design

Following problem definition, companies must establish a research design, or a plan of action for attacking the research problem. Research designs consist of five activities, each of which is designed to address a specific question about the research process as shown in Exhibit 5.8. It is critical that researchers develop and execute a research design so that decision makers can have confidence in the research findings. Effective market research is dependent on creating a research design and then executing it.[22] Conversely, and this is a problem for decision makers, bad market research cannot yield good information. When this happens, it severely limits management's confidence in the results.

While multiple designs often could work in any research situation, it is important to specify one design and follow it throughout the research. Decisions made at the research design stage affect the rest of the project, and it is not appropriate to start over once a project has begun. Let's examine each of these activities.

M. D. Anderson Cancer Center in Houston wanted to improve the efficiency and effectiveness of the doctors working in the hospital. The hospital engaged market researchers to design the right research to get the right information. Using techniques such as experience mapping, the hospital was able to increase the efficiency of doctors and enhance patient satisfaction by adopting mobile technology.[23]

Type of Research: What Kind of Research Needs to Be Done? Not all marketing research involves complex, costly studies. People do marketing research all the time and don't think of it that way. For example, a salesperson who visits a Web site to learn more about a customer before a sales call is engaged in marketing research. The key is to fit the research to the unique requirements of the situation.

There are three basic types of research: exploratory, descriptive, and causal. While the complexity and methodology changes for each type of research it is not necessarily true that causal research is better than exploratory. Let's look at each research type more closely.

As the name implies, **exploratory research** is really about discovery. Reasons for conducting exploratory research include:

- Clarify the research problem.

Exploratory research is often good enough. With wireless access it is possible to do research almost anywhere.

- Develop hypotheses for testing in descriptive or causal research.
- Gain additional insight to help in survey development or to identify other research variables for study.
- Answer the research question.

Many times conducting exploratory research will provide sufficient information to answer the research question. Even if more sophisticated research is needed, exploratory research is usually the first step.

Descriptive research seeks to describe or explain some phenomenon. Often this involves something going on in the marketplace and can include issues such as:

- Identify the characteristics of our target market.
- Assess competitor actions in the marketplace.
- Determine how customers use our product.
- Discover differences across demographic characteristics (age, education, income) with respect to the use of our product or our competitors.

Descriptive research uses many different methods including secondary data, surveys, and observation. Some of these methods are also used in exploratory research. The difference is how you use the information. Descriptive research uses a different, more restrictive and rigorous methodology than exploratory research.

Descriptive research identifies associations between variables; for example, the customers for Harley-Davidson motorcycles tend to be middle-aged, successful men. **Causal research** tries to discover the cause and effect between variables.

For example, in our Harley-Davidson example, does an increase in Harley-Davidson advertising directed toward men lead to increased sales of Harley-Davidson motorcycles? This can be particularly useful in making important marketing decisions. Consider a critical decision faced by all marketing managers: What effect will a price increase have on sales? Causal research can determine the change in the number of sales for different price levels. The types of research vary a great deal, so the question becomes what kind of research is appropriate in a given circumstance? The following factors help make that determination.

Benefit versus cost: Before making any other decisions about the type of marketing research to use, it is essential to assess the benefits versus the costs. Put simply, if the benefits of doing the research do not exceed the cost, don't do the research.

Time until decision: Decision makers sometimes have very little time between realizing a need for additional information and making the decision. When time is very short (a matter of days) it is simply not possible to conduct in-depth marketing research. The Internet can cut the time needed for a study from months to weeks, but when time is short researchers may have to rely on more exploratory research and the use of secondary data.

Nature of the decision: The more strategic the decision the more important the information and the greater the need for primary data. Conversely, if the decision is primarily tactical (for example, decisions about where to place advertising) secondary data, like reviewing a media's demographics and rate card, will likely be sufficient to make the decision.

Availability of data: As we saw in Chapter 4, companies already have a lot of data as a result of CRM and other internal information systems. Consequently, it may not always be necessary to collect primary data when existing or secondary data will provide the necessary answers to the research problems.

Nature of Data: What Kind of Data Do We Need? Once the type of research has been determined, the next step is to evaluate what kind of data is needed for the research. The nature of the data will determine how the data are collected and is driven by the kind of research the company is undertaking.[24] The basic question is, does the research require **primary data**—data collected specifically for this research question—or will **secondary data**—data collected for some other purpose than the problem currently being considered—be sufficient? Even if primary data are collected, almost all research involves some secondary data collection, which we will talk about in the next section.

Primary data are collected using one of two approaches: qualitative and quantitative. **Qualitative research** is less structured and can employ methods such as surveys and interviews to collect the data, qualitative research employs small samples and is not meant to be used for statistical analyses. **Quantitative research** is used to develop a more measured understanding using statistical analysis to assess and quantify the results.[25] Now let's look at the nature of data collection.

Nature of Data Collection: How Should the Data Be Collected? No one technique is better than another, but it is important to use the right technique based on an assessment of the research problem and research type. Let's evaluate the various approaches to collecting primary data. Exploratory research techniques include focus groups and in-depth interviews.

Without question, the most widely used qualitative research technique is focus groups. Perhaps for this reason, it is also one of the most misused.[26] A **focus group** is a meeting (either in person or increasingly online) of 6 to 10 people that is moderated by a professional who carefully moves the conversation through a defined agenda in an unstructured, open format. Generally, the participants are selected on the basis of some criteria.[27] For example, they may be current customers or possess certain demographic characteristics (age, income, education) but they will all have at least one shared attribute.

The value of focus groups lies in the richness of the discussion. A good moderator can draw out a lot of information from the participants. For example, the marketing manager for Harley-Davidson might use focus groups to learn how women relate to motorcycles. The trade-off is a deeper understanding of each participant versus a more superficial knowledge of additional people. Herein lies the mistake many people make with focus groups. They assume that the results of a focus group are generalizable to a population of interest. This is not the case. Focus groups are not a representative sample and care should be taken to interpret the results properly. However, focus groups do provide insights on an issue that are useful to researchers as they develop quantitative research techniques. Focus group data provide a good starting point from which researchers can develop specific questions used in survey instruments.[28]

Another common qualitative technique is the in-depth interview. An **in-depth interview** is an unstructured (or loosely structured) interview with an individual who has been chosen based on some characteristic of interest, often a demographic attribute. This technique differs from focus groups in that the interview is done one on one rather than in a small group. The same advantages and disadvantages are present here as with focus groups so researchers most often use this technique to help formulate other types of research (surveys, observational research).

Descriptive research techniques include surveys, behavioral data, and observational data.

Of the quantitative research techniques used to collect primary data, surveys, in their various forms, are the most prevalent. While they can be used informally in exploratory research, their most common purpose is in descriptive research. **Surveys** are structured questionnaires given to a sample group of individuals representing the population of interest and are intended to solicit specific responses to explicit questions.[29]

Harley-Davidson does market research to learn more about developing products that appeal to women.

There are a number of survey methods. Historically, mail and telephone surveys were most common. Today, electronic surveys have become widely adopted for their speed, ease of use, and relatively low cost. E-surveys can easily be done over the Internet using services such as Zoomerang or Survey Monkey.[30]

Behavioral data include information about when, what, and how often customers purchase products and services as well as other customer "touches" (for example, when they contact the organization with a complaint or question). When companies match this kind of information with demographic and psychographic information they can see differences in purchase patterns. Behavior is usually more reliable than surveys because it is based on what the respondents actually do rather than what they say they are going to do.

Harrah's Entertainment uses data mining techniques to develop sophisticated models of its customers. These models include the guests' gambling habits, how much they win or lose, how much time they spend gambling each time they visit, as well as basic demographics such as age and gender. Harrah's then designs specific packages that include gourmet dining and getaway weekends. Results have been positive with 20 percent annual growth over the last five years.[31]

It is possible to get a lot of insight about people by simply watching what they do in various situations. **Observational data** are the behavioral patterns among the population of interest. One of the most common uses of this type of research is in retailing. Retailers' watch how people move through a store, noting what aisles they go down and where they spend their time. In recent years a more intrusive approach to observational data has been used to actually examine people in a personal setting (for example, their homes). In this approach the observer enters into the world of the individual rather than standing back and simply watching activities. Researchers see people in a very personal environment to better understand how people use and interact with products.

A variation of observational data is mechanical observation. **Mechanical observation** uses a device to chronicle activity. Some forms of mechanical observations are benign and not intrusive on the individual. Turnstiles, for example, record people coming or going out of an area. Traffic counters record the number of cars on a given street for a set time period.

There are, however, mechanical devices that are more invasive. *Mechanical devices* can be very useful for researchers but are often used sparingly because of the cost and also the bias associated with the respondent's awareness of the device. Eye cameras can track the movement of an eye as the individual watches an ad. From this researchers can determine what the person sees first, what he is focusing on in the ad and how his eyes move around the ad. Another device, the galvanometer, is attached to the skin and measures subtle changes in skin temperature. Researchers can then determine if the respondent found the ad interesting.

Information Content: What Do We Need to Know? A critical part of research design involves determining exactly what information is needed and how to frame the questions to get that information. From the questions used in focus groups to long questionnaires, it is important to consider the structure and wording as well as the response choices. Most often this issue comes up in designing questionnaires. As the most commonly used primary research technique, the survey questionnaire allows a lot of variability in its design and structure. Some surveys, such as the comment cards, are short and ask only a few questions. Others, such as new car satisfaction surveys, can be much longer and ask dozens of questions. No matter what the situation, careful attention must be paid to the design, structure, and format of each question. For years marketers have been interested in building and measuring customer loyalty. The FYI discusses a controversial new approach to measuring customer loyalty in a single question.

FYI

Measuring customer loyalty is an elusive but important goal in marketing research because loyal customers are better customers. However, the linkage of customer loyalty to specific corporate marketing objectives is difficult to establish. Many managers believe an accurate measure of loyalty does not exist.

Developed by Satmetrix, Bain & Company, and Frederick Reichfield, the Net Promoter Score (NPS) provides a simple measure of loyalty by asking one question: Would the customer recommend a brand to a friend or colleague? Many companies have measured a customer's willingness to recommend a product for many years, but the current approach suggests one question will measure loyalty accurately. Not everyone agrees, and critics point out the measure is not appropriate in all situations. For example, important capital expenditures, such as large IT purchases, are often directed by senior management irrespective of current user preferences.[32]

Today, researchers must also consider the method of survey delivery. For example, mail surveys differ significantly from telephone surveys because respondents interact with the questions differently. Electronic surveys present a different challenge, although their structure is more easily adapted from a mail questionnaire.

Researchers must consider which of the many types of question formats is most appropriate for the situation. One of the most basic decisions is whether to use open-ended or closed-ended questions. **Open-ended questions** encourage respondents to be expressive and offer the opportunity to provide more detailed, qualitative responses. As a result, these kinds of questions are often used in exploratory research. **Closed-ended questions,** on the other hand, are more precise and provide specific responses. As a result, they allow for more quantitative analysis and are most often used in descriptive research. Frequently, questionnaires will contain a mix of open-ended and closed-ended questions to get both qualitative and quantitative information in a single survey.

Sampling Plan: Who Should Be Included in the Research? Once the other elements of the research design have been developed, it is time to consider who will be selected for the research. The most basic decision is whether to conduct a census or to sample a group of individuals from the population. A **census** is a comprehensive record of each individual in the population of interest, while a **sample** is a subgroup of the population selected for participation in the research. A census may seem like the better approach because everyone in the population is included in the study. Unfortunately, most of the time the number and diversity of the population is so large that it is simply not physically or financially possible to communicate with everyone. As a result, sampling is by far the preferred method of selecting people for marketing research.[33]

There are two basic approaches to sampling: probability and nonprobability sampling. It is important to keep in mind that one is not necessarily better than the other; rather, the key to making the right choice is to match the sampling approach with the research. Budgetary constraints will also likely influence the decision. **Probability sampling** uses a specific set of procedures to identify individuals from the population to be included in the research. From here, a specific protocol is identified to select a number of individuals for the research. As an example, suppose Bank of America is interested in finding out more about a group of its customers holding a certain kind of credit card. Let's assume there are 10 million customers holding this particular card. The bank wants to randomly choose 5,000

individuals for the survey. That means that everyone has a 5,000/10,000,000=
.0005 chance of being selected. Next, Bank of America will create an algorithm
to randomly identify 5,000 individuals from the list of 10 million. The algorithm
ensures that, while everyone has a .0005 chance of being selected, only 5,000 will
be sampled from the entire group.

A second approach is called **nonprobability sampling** and, as the name implies,
the probability of everyone in the population being included in the sample is not
identified. The chance of selection may be zero or not known. This type of sampling is often done when time and/or financial constraints limit the opportunity
to conduct probability sampling. The most significant problem with nonprobability sampling is that it significantly limits the ability to perform statistical analyses
and generalize conclusions beyond the sample itself.

Search Secondary Sources

Secondary data are almost always part of marketing research. Searching a wide
variety of sources and compiling additional information provide greater insight
to the research problem and supplement the primary data collected for a specific
study. We have already discussed the availability of information inside the company, so let's turn our attention to external sources of secondary data.

Government Sources Federal, state, and local governments are an important
resource in collecting information on a variety of topics. For example, the U.S.
Census Bureau publishes a library full of reports on business and consumer demographic trends. In 2002, the Census Bureau released the Economic Census providing an in-depth analysis of business activity in the United States. Often, data
are available by zip code, which can be useful for marketers in targeting specific
groups of people. States also publish additional data on economic activity. Finally,
local governments publish records such as business licenses as well as general
economic activity in that area. Governments provide a great deal of information
on a variety of activities. From here marketers can identify areas, even down to
specific streets, and get detailed demographic information, which is very useful in
a number of ways including targeted marketing communications campaigns.

Market Research Organizations A number of market research organizations
publish data helpful to marketers. One resource many people are familiar with
is Nielsen Media Research's TV ratings. The ratings are the basis for establishing
national, cable, and local advertising rates. Another service well known to automobile enthusiasts is the J. D. Power automobile quality and customer satisfaction
rankings. While automobile manufacturers pay a fee for more detailed information, the public has access to the overall rankings.

Other organizations publish data that can be useful to marketers in particular industries. For example, YPB&R advertising agency, in partnership with the
Yankelovich research firm, publishes the National Travel Monitor for both leisure
and business markets every year. The monitor profiles travel patterns and market
segments in the travel industry. This research is very useful for any business connected to the travel industry such as airlines, hotels, and cruise lines (Exhibit 5.9).

There are also information data services such as Information Resources,
InfoScan, and Nielsen's ScanTrack that track scanner data from thousands of
retailers. These organizations match sales data with demographic records to give a
detailed picture of how well a product is doing in a particular area or within a certain target market. This information is useful for consumer products companies
that want to assess the success of specific marketing activities (for example, how
well is an advertising campaign working with a target market).

The Internet It is now possible to access a huge amount of information using
search engines to identify hundreds, even thousands, of information sources. Care
should be taken, however, to evaluate the validity of the data and the reliability of
the source. Generally two kinds of data sources can be found on the Internet. The
first are market research organizations (such as the ones we just discussed) willing
to share or sell market data. A second source is "general knowledge" sites such as

| EXHIBIT 5.9 | Yankelovich Cruise Line Example |

Luxury Cruise Line
CASE STUDY

Yankelovich®
Insights Integration℠

Luxury Cruise Line Identifies Next Generation of Cruisers

PUTTING ATTITUDES TO WORK

The passenger database was profiled using attitudinal data elements from Yankelovich's MindBase® and Lists with Attitude℠. The proportions of cruise line passengers for each of these attitudinal data elements were compared to the total population, identifying groups most apt to be passengers. The attitudinal data helped the cruise line understand their passengers—what interests them, and what their travel style is—creating a more robust profile than demographics alone. New list rentals by attitudinal data were recommended to expand the customer acquisition universe.

ANALYSIS RESULTS

- The cruise line identified the best current passengers using MindBase. By both sheer numbers and when compared to the rest of the US population, best passengers comprised between 35%-70% of the customer base depending on product category.

- Based on the new customer profile, the business was able to identify potential future passengers through MindBase and Lists with Attitude for targeted prospect list rentals.

BUSINESS OBJECTIVE

A luxury cruise line was searching for new list rental sources of prospective cruisers. The cruise line understood its current passengers mainly from a demographic perspective, limiting the company's prospecting capabilities.

CLIENT NEEDS

- **Find new sources of targeted prospect names**
- **Find tools to help prioritize marketing efforts more effectively**

© Yankelovich, Inc. 2007   For more information call 919.932.8858 or visit www.yankelovich.com

Courtesy of Yankelovich. Inc.

business publications, academic research sites, or other independent sources that have data applicable to the research problem.[34]

Advantages and Disadvantages of Secondary Data Sources As we discussed earlier, secondary data are almost always the first place to go in conducting a market research project. Even if primary data are collected, it is a good idea to see what has been done already that may be applicable now. Secondary data come with two primary advantages. First, it's a fast way to get information. Just a few minutes on a search engine can yield a lot of information. Of course, it takes much longer than that to look through it all. A second, and related advantage, is cost. Secondary data are relatively less expensive. Even if a company chooses to subscribe to organizations such as J. D. Power and Associates, thereby getting access to more detailed data, it is still more cost effective than conducting a primary research study.

Of course, there are very distinct disadvantages. First and most important, secondary data will, almost by definition, not fit the research problem exactly. As a result, a specific answer to the research problem will not be possible using secondary data alone. Second, secondary data are not current. Sometimes the information may be only a few weeks or months old or it may be dated to the point where it is no longer useful for the current project. Third, without a clear understanding of the methodology used to collect and interpret the secondary data one should be a little skeptical about its validity.[35]

> Chili's uses a wide variety of primary and secondary data sources to help decision makers, including Site Analytics, a research company that provides site location analysis to restaurants and stores. The research is combined with other data from Chili's and is used to evaluate individual store sites. Use of the tools has led to more accurate store placement and planning.[36]

Collect the Data

Now, it is time to find and engage the respondent to collect the data. **Data collection** involves access and distribution of the survey to the respondent then recording the respondent's responses and making the data available for analysis. A company can choose to collect the data using its own resources or hire a market research firm to administer the data collection. The choice often depends on the company's internal expertise in market research as well as the resources required to complete the job.

This stage in the market research process presents several unique challenges. First, data collection is often the most costly element in the market research process. Second, the greatest potential for error exists as data are collected.[37] For example, respondents may not respond to certain questions or fill out the survey incorrectly. Finally, the people collecting the survey may be biased or make mistakes.

Technology, in the form of online surveys, can help to mitigate some of the issues with data collection. For example, electronic survey methods are often more cost effective than other survey methodologies. In addition, there is less chance of transcription error as no one has to input the data into a computer. Unfortunately, not everyone has access to a computer. As a result, certain target markets may be underrepresented if a survey requires completion of an online survey. Additionally, people may still input inaccurate responses.[38] We will talk about online research tools in the next section.

Photodex ProShow Gold is one of many software packages designed to enhance presentations. The presentation of a research report often includes sophisticated software designed to clearly present research findings and recommendations.

Analyze the Data

Once the data are collected, coded, and verified, the next step is to analyze the information. The appropriate analysis is performed based on the research questions developed at the beginning of the research. A common mistake is using unsuitable analyses that are not supported by the data.

Analysis of the data will lead to findings that address the research questions. These findings are, in a sense, the "product" of the research. In most cases, researchers will also interpret the findings for decision makers.

Report the Findings

The best research projects are only as good as the final report and presentation. If the research is done well but the report is poorly written and presented, managers will not benefit from the research. Exhibit 5.10 provides a basic framework for a research report. Note that, for managers, the key section of the report is the Executive Summary as it presents a summation of the analysis and essential findings. Keep in mind that managers are not really interested in the number of secondary data sources, questionnaire design, or sampling plan; rather, they want to see the findings.

Market Research Technology

Market research has benefited from better, more cost-effective technology. The use of powerful software tools and online technologies brings research to any level in the organization. Sales managers can survey customers, analyze the results, and make decisions without costly, time-consuming external studies. Sophisticated software incorporating CRM and marketing decision support systems can do in-depth analyses that offer unique insights about customers or market trends not

| EXHIBIT 5.10 | Outline of a Research Report |

	Short Report		Long Report	
Report Modules	**Memo or Letter**	**Short Technical**	**Management**	**Technical**
Prefatory Information		1	1	1
Letter of transmittal		✓	✓	✓
Title page		✓	✓	✓
Authorization statement		✓	✓	✓
Executive summary		✓	✓	✓
Table of contents			✓	✓
Introduction	1	2	2	2
Problem statement	✓	✓	✓	✓
Research objectives	✓	✓	✓	✓
Background	✓	✓	✓	✓
Methodology		✓ (briefly)	✓ (briefly)	3
Sampling design				✓
Research design				✓
Data collection				✓
Data analysis				✓
Limitations		✓	✓	✓
Findings		3	4	4
Conclusions	2	4	3	5
Summary and conclusions	✓	✓	✓	✓
Recommendations	✓	✓	✓	✓
Appendices		5	5	6
Bibliography				7

Source: Reprinted from Donald R. Cooper and Pamela S. Schindler, *Marketing Research, 2006.* Copyright © 2006 The McGraw-Hill Companies, Inc.

possible just a few years ago. In most respects, making market research tools available throughout the company has been a big success. Unfortunately, as the access to market research technology has increased, so has the misapplication of the technology. Without implementing the market research process presented earlier, no amount of technology can create worthwhile results.

Online Research Tools

Online research tools fall into three categories: databases, focus groups, and sampling. Each of these three categories offers unique opportunities to expand the reach and usefulness of market research. Let's examine each more closely.

Online Databases An **online database** is data stored on a server that is accessed remotely over the Internet or some other telecommunications network. Many, if not most, companies now have databases available to employees, suppliers, even customers. Information on orders, shipments, pricing, and other relevant information is available to salespeople and customer service personnel who need to access it.[39]

Independent online databases available from government and other sources are extremely useful tools in market research. Organizations such as the World Bank offer a wide range of databases with country-specific economic data, most of which is free. Fee-based services, while expensive, offer access to a wide range of information. Lexis/Nexis, for example, enables market researchers to access thousands of business and trade publications and market studies. These services make it possible to review market research reports, industry and company analyses, even market share information.[40]

Online Focus Groups The virtual focus group is becoming a viable alternative to the traditional focus group format (6 to 10 people in a room). Offering distinct advantages in terms of convenience and cost-efficiency, online focus groups provide data quickly and in a format that is usually easier to read and analyze. Traditional focus groups require someone to transcribe the spoken words into a transcript. With online focus groups, everything is already recorded by computer.

The primary disadvantage of online focus groups is that participants are limited to those with access to a computer or workstation. In addition, as people often participate remotely, it is not possible to verify who is actually responding to the questions. Measures can be employed to verify participation (for example, passwords), but the reality is that, in most cases, you must rely on the individual to be honest. One final problem is the lack of control over the environment. Traditional focus groups create an environment where participants are required to focus on the questions. Online focus groups enable participants to be at home, work, or even a remote location with wireless access. As a result, participants can become distracted and environmental factors can affect their concentration and responses.

Online Sampling If someone has access to a computer with an Internet connection, that person can complete a questionnaire. Online sampling has become increasingly popular as a data collection methodology. As with online focus groups, the primary advantages are convenience and cost-efficiency. Respondents are free to complete the survey when it is best for them, and sending a survey online is essentially free. Online survey companies such as QuestionPro offer a complete service from survey design and a variety of delivery methods (traditional e-mail, popup surveys, company newsletter integration, and others) to data analysis and presentation of findings.[41]

SAS offers powerful analysis tools to help managers more clearly understand market data.

Statistical Software

One of the real benefits of market research technology today is the ability to put powerful statistical software in the hands of front-line managers. With the proper training and data, it is now possible for managers to conduct analyses that were not possible even five years ago. Two software packages dominate desktop statistical analysis—SPSS and SAS. SPSS offers a range of marketing analytical tools. Its statistical software combines an easy-to-use interface with powerful statistical tools in a format that managers at all levels can use. The other widely used package is called SAS and it offers many of the same features. One of the real advantages of these packages is their ability to take the findings of the data analysis and create tables and reports.[42]

> Efficient Frontier, a technology start-up in California, employs complex mathematics to optimize online advertising campaigns. The company's proprietary algorithms calculate a return on investment and rate of response for every ad placed by an advertiser. The goal is to eliminate guessing from ad placement and base it solely on statistical analysis based on data provided from the Internet.[43]

Interestingly, while dedicated statistical packages offer powerful analytical tools and outstanding reporting capabilities, probably the most widely used tool for analyzing business data is one almost everyone already has on their computer—Excel spreadsheets. Part of the Microsoft Office suite of products, Excel offers the ability to analyze data using formulas created by the user or statistical functions already embedded in the software. While not a dedicated statistical package, it is certainly a useful tool in basic data analysis. Access to powerful statistical tools coupled with management's concern for quality has led to sophisticated analytical systems as highlighted in the FYI.

FYI

DMAIC (**D**efine **M**easure **A**nalyze **I**mprove and **C**ontrol) is an acronym used in the quality improvement process called Six Sigma. The process applies sophisticated research and analysis techniques using specific data on internal company processes to drive more effective business strategies with a focus on customer satisfaction.

The diagnostic precision of Six Sigma runs counter to business processes, which are less structured and difficult to measure because the ambiguity and lack of specific success metrics puts truly innovative products and strategies at a disadvantage. The problem is that "Innovation is, by its very definition, based on the idea that the value resides in the introduction of something unexpected," states Dev Patnaik, principal at Jump Associates, a design strategy firm in San Mateo, California.

Motorola reports over $17 billion in savings from Six Sigma implementation and used it to assist product development engineers with the RAZR. Notes Michael S. Potosky, Motorola's corporate director of Six Sigma, "Six Sigma's stamp is all over the RAZR." The Six Sigma process was credited with improving the design of the antenna to maintain call clarity but remain hidden. Unfortunately, Motorola was not able to keep its advantage in innovative cell phone design and is selling its mobile device division, creator of the RAZR. Statistical processes, while important in product design, cannot take the place of the products that add value to the customer.[44]

Market Research Challenges in Global Markets

The primary difference between domestic and international research is that international market data are more difficult to get and understand than domestic data. In most Western European countries and the United States, it is much easier to access quality data than in the rest of the world. Let's examine some of the challenges market researchers face in finding, collecting, and then analyzing market data in foreign markets.

> Because language, symbols, and colors are culture-specific, marketers seek common product elements that translate across global markets. Research suggests the sense of touch or tactile sensation could be a unifying product characteristic. The classic contoured Coke bottle is universally recognized as a Coke. At the same time, cologne manufacturers such as Calvin Klein design their bottles to convey a unique tactile sensation such as the recently released Euphoria.[45]

Secondary Data

Exhibit 5.11 identifies the top 20 countries in marketing research spending. The United States, and to a lesser extent, Japan and the European Union are data-rich market environments. Unfortunately, that level of information is not found anywhere else in world. In certain areas, such as Central Europe, this is because they have only recently moved to open market economies. In other parts of the world, such as China and India, the culture does not encourage the free flow of information. This makes it difficult for any organization, even governments, to collect good information. Let's consider three major challenges researchers face as they collect data around the world.

Data Accessibility In the United States, businesspeople are accustomed to easily accessing information that simply does not exist in much of the world. The U.S. Census Bureau provides detailed information across a wide range of business sectors, including retailing and distribution, as well as specific data on many different economic and personal criteria such as income per capita, population by county, and zip code (broken down by gender, age, ethnic mix, and many other characteristics). From government sources (U.S. Census Bureau; Department of Commerce; EU Business Development Center), nongovernment business organizations (U.S. Chamber of Commerce, OECD), and private research organizations, a great deal of information is available to managers. The quantity and quality of data found in the United States is not available in most of the world.

Data Dependability A second major issue is the reliability of the data. Can the information be considered accurate? Regrettably, in many cases it cannot. Government agencies, particularly in developing countries, will distort data to present a more favorable analysis. The data are often reported incorrectly because people do not want the government to know the true figures, usually because of higher tax concerns. In other cases, governments want to present optimistic results that enforce government policies so they alter the data to reflect government accomplishments.

Data Comparability Comparing secondary data from foreign markets risks three other problems. First, developing countries often lack historical data, making it much harder to assess long-term economic or business trends. Second, the available data are outdated so they are ineffective for making decisions in the current economic environment. Finally, terms used in reporting information are not consistent. Standardized business terminology used in industrialized countries has not been adopted by many developing regions, making it difficult for researchers to interpret data.

Primary Data

Essential information about economic and general business trends can be gathered from secondary sources, but to get specific market data such as customer preferences, primary data are necessary. Collecting primary data presents many challenges for marketers that are almost always compounded in global markets. Some of the specific problems of international primary data collection include the following issues.

Unwillingness to Respond Cultural, gender, and individual differences create wide disparities in the willingness to provide personal information. The United States has an open information culture and people are much more willing to respond, but this openness is not shared around the world. In addition, government agencies such as the Securities and Exchange Commission require publicly traded companies to provide accurate business information including valid financial results. Nongovernment agencies such as trade associations report studies widely used in business. The National Realtors Association, for example, publishes quarterly data on the housing industry that is considered an accurate assessment of the real estate market in the United States.

As we discussed earlier, many people don't respond because they are concerned about government interference or additional taxes. However, concerns about privacy and how personal data are used generate a broad distrust of surveys among consumers and businesses. It is not difficult to understand these concerns. In countries formerly under the control of the Soviet Union (Czech Republic, Poland, Hungary, and others), for example, people were concerned that personal information provided to authorities could be used against them. After the fall of the Soviet Union, the historical problems created by decades of living in a closed society made it very difficult for companies such as A. C. Nielsen to collect valid consumer opinions and business data.

EXHIBIT 5.11	Top 20 Countries for Market Research Expenditures
United States	$6,660
United Kingdom	1,997
Germany	1,805
France	1,580
Japan	1,164
Italy	581
Canada	477
Spain	395
China	387
Australia	383
Netherlands	305
Sweden	273
Mexico	267
Brazil	195
Belgium	164
S. Korea	161
Switzerland	133
Finland	113
Denmark	106
Taiwan	81

Source: Reprinted from Philip R. Cateora and John L. Graham, *International Marketing*, 13th ed, 2007. Copyright © 2007 The McGraw-Hill Companies, Inc.

Unreliable Sampling Procedures Related to the quality of data noted earlier is the problem of unreliable or inadequate demographic information to conduct primary research. In many countries, there is no way to locate or identify who lives where or even how many people live in a given location, something businesspeople in the United States take for granted. In the United States, sophisticated global positioning system (GPS) devices can direct people to specific locations based on maps and other data stored on a hard drive. Consider the problem then, if you are in a medium or small South American or Asian city where maps do not exist and street names are not even posted. The lack of reliable census information coupled with an inadequate infrastructure leave market researchers in many countries with no accurate sampling frame from which to draw respondents.

Japanese consumers are radically changing the way they interact with the Internet. As recently as 2003, fewer than 2 out of 10 Japanese accessed the Internet over cell phones. Today that number is nearly 6 out of 10. These changes in consumer behavior dramatically affect Internet research as respondents will not have the time, interest, or ability to complete long surveys. Market researchers who do not consider this change in creating their surveys miss a large part of the sample population.[46]

Inaccurate Language Translation and Insufficient Comprehension Getting people in global markets to actually complete a survey presents three challenges. First, simply translating surveys can be a challenge. For example, Chinese is written with characters known as hànzi with each character representing a syllable of spoken Chinese with its own meaning. To read fluently in Chinese requires knowledge of more than 3,000 symbols. Second, word usage changes dramatically around the world. In the United States and Western Europe, "family" generally refers to the immediate family unit, including a father, mother, and their children, while in many Latin and Asian cultures "family" almost always includes the extended family, including all aunts, uncles, cousins, and grandparents. When a survey asks about family members, then, the responses could vary dramatically.

A final problem is insufficient language comprehension. In many parts of the world illiteracy rates are high, which rules out most survey methodology (see Exhibit 5.12). In addition, some countries use multiple languages, making translation costly and increasing the likelihood of mistranslation. India, for example, recognizes 14 official languages with many additional nonofficial languages. Imagine writing a survey that would translate well into over a dozen languages.

EXHIBIT 5.12	World Literacy Rates

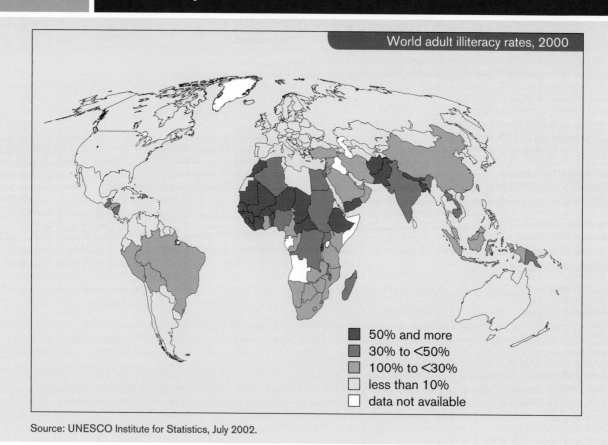

World adult illiteracy rates, 2000

- 50% and more
- 30% to <50%
- 100% to <30%
- less than 10%
- data not available

Source: UNESCO Institute for Statistics, July 2002.

SUMMARY

Marketers know that accurate, relevant, and timely information is an essential element in marketing management. There are two sources of information: that which comes from outside the company and that which can be found internally. Being aware of environmental forces such as demographic profiles and changes, economic conditions, emerging technologies, changes in the natural world, and the political and legal environment enables marketers to create more effective short- and long-term marketing strategies.

Critical to assessing marketing information is a thorough understanding of the market research process. The process involves six specific steps: define the problem, establish the research design, search secondary sources, collect the data, analyze the data, and present the research findings. Researchers must follow the market research process to ensure the data are valid and useful for decision makers.

KEY TERMS

market information system (MIS) 119
marketing intelligence 123
demographics 123
microeconomics 126
macroeconomics 126
market research 129
management research
  deliverable 130
research problem 130
exploratory research 131

descriptive research 132
causal research 132
primary data 133
secondary data 133
qualitative research 133
quantitative research 133
focus group 133
in-depth interview 133
surveys 133
behavioral data 134

observational data 134
mechanical observation 134
open-ended questions 135
closed-ended questions 135
census 135
sample 135
probability sampling 135
nonprobability sampling 136
data collection 138
online database 140

APPLICATION QUESTIONS

1. Imagine you are the vice president of sales for a large security company and you have been asked to put together a sales information system that collects, analyzes, interprets, and distributes information from the sales force. How would you do it? What information would you ask salespeople to collect?

2. As a market manager at Lenovo, what key information from outside the company would be important to help in the design of a new laptop for small- and medium-sized businesses?

3. The marketing manager for Disney Cruise Line wants to know what demographic trends will affect the cruise line business over the next five years. What kind of research is needed to address this question? Conduct some secondary research and try to you identify two or three important demographic trends that might affect the cruise line business.

4. The market research director for John Deere has just received a call from the marketing manager in the company's lawn tractor division. The manager wants to know how the new advertising campaign is being received by current customers. Design a research study for this research. Be sure to include a problem definition and research design.

5. The alumni director at your institution wants to know how to serve the alumni better. Design a survey of no more than 10 questions that the alumni director can use to ask alumni about their interest in getting more involved with their school.

MANAGEMENT DECISION CASE: The Cost of Building an Eco-Friendly Home

With energy costs rising and heightened awareness about the long-term effects of manufactured products on the environment, the decision by KB Homes (one of the largest home builders in the United States) to use wood harvested in an environmentally friendly way, using guidelines from the Forest Stewardship Council, seems like a good idea. The company wanted to be a good corporate citizen by offering the more eco-sensitive wood as well as meeting the expected consumer demand for products that are less damaging to the environment. On a $700,000 home being built in Northern California, however, the company was unable to get the $3,500 premium for the environmentally friendly wood. Other KB eco-friendly home options included bamboo flooring (significantly less than 1 percent of homeowners purchased bamboo) and Whirlpool front-loading washing machines that use less water and electricity (only 3 percent of homeowners purchased the Whirlpool machines). Jeffrey T. Mezger, CEO of KB Homes, summarized the problem, "We're trying to understand the balance between our social obligations and our obligation to shareholders. You can't just give away margin."

While interest in "green" homes is growing with 10 percent of new homes in 2010 expected to be eco-friendly (up from 2 percent in 2005), home builders have been unable to get large numbers of buyers to pay the cost. Even with established products that provide clear advantages to the homeowner, market acceptance has been difficult. Solar panels, for example, have a high initial cost but can pay for themselves in utility savings in just a few years. In 2006, the Solar Energy Industry Association reported a 75 percent increase in the installation of solar electric panels to 8,512 units, and while the percentage increase is impressive it is tempered by the fact that 1 million homes were built in the United States during the same period, which means that less than 1 percent of new homes built during that time installed solar electric panels. McStain Neighborhoods, a builder of green homes in Colorado, offers a $25,000 solar panel option, but in six years it has installed the panels on only three homes out of the 300 homes it builds each year.

Many home builders cite the need for legislation that supports eco-friendly products through tax breaks and subsidies. The federal government and many state governments are looking at various tax incentives to encourage consumers to incorporate more environmentally responsible products into their homes. Additionally, local building codes are encouraging and in some cases requiring builders to provide eco-friendly options. Environmental product suppliers have also worked to reduce the cost of many products and, as volume increases, the costs are expected to go even lower.

Another strategy is for home builders to add eco-friendly products to the price of the home rather than include them in the options list. One builder, Clarum Homes in California, includes an array of green products such as satellite-controlled sprinkler systems and recycled wood decks that add about $22,000 to the cost of a $700,000 home. The company believes adding the features helps its homes stand out in a very competitive market.

KB Homes has a marketing initiative called "myEarth," which cues home buyers to the environmentally sensitive options as they work through the home buying process at each of the 30 design studios around the country. One example of the process is to cue home buyers to purchase tankless water heaters, which save water and energy, when they are selecting appliance options. The company concedes it is a challenge getting customers to take a long-term view as they sort through hundreds of home buying decisions that cost thousands of dollars.[47]

Questions for Consideration

1. As the vice president of product strategy at KB Homes, what eco-friendly strategy would you follow in designing new homes?

2. The vice president of marketing for a home builder has asked you to develop a strategy for increasing sales of environmentally sensitive features in the company's homes that sell for $500,000 to $750,000. How would you seek customer feedback on the following eco-friendly features in a new home?

   a. Solar panels.

   b. Tankless water heater.

   c. Wood harvested in an eco-friendly manner.

3. Consider what green features you would want in a home and assign dollar values to those features based on the overall value you believe they add to the home. Then go online and check out the real cost of those features.

MARKETING PLAN EXERCISE

ACTIVITY 5: Identify Critical Information

This exercise asks you to identify the critical information needed to create the marketing plan. In that regard it is important to evaluate existing information (internal inside and secondary data) as well as new information gathered through primary research. This assignment includes:

1. Catalog internal sources of information available to you inside the organization and what information you will receive from each source.

2. Identify secondary data sources and the specific information you need from each source.
   a. List sources.
   b. Date.
   c. Assess the relevance of the data to the project.

3. List primary data needs to create the marketing plan. Then develop the specific instruments (focus group questions, surveys) that you will use later in the marketing plan.

If you are using Marketing Plan Pro, a template for this assignment can be accessed at www.mhhe.com/marshall1e.

RECOMMENDED READINGS

1. Robert J. Kaden and Jay Conrad Levinson, *Guerilla Marketing Research: Marketing Research Techniques That Can Help Any Business Make More Money* (London: Kogan Page, 2006).

2. Edward F. McQuarrie, *The Market Research Toolbox: A Concise Guide for Beginners,* 2nd ed. (Thousand Oaks, CA: Sage Publications, 2005).

3. D. V. L. Smith and J. H. Fletcher, *The Art and Science of Interpreting Market Research Evidence* (New York: Wiley, 2004).

4. Gerald Zaltman, *How Customers Think: Essential Insights into the Mind of the Market* (Boston: Harvard Business School Press, 2003).

CHAPTER 06

UNDERSTANDING COMPETITORS: ANALYSIS TO ACTION

LEARNING OBJECTIVES

- Recognize the importance of the competitive environment in shaping marketing decisions.

- Understand how environmental forces shape the competitive environment.

- Differentiate between competitors as defined by the company and competitors defined from the customer's perspective.

- Consider how the competitor mix changes as companies evaluate strategic factors.

- Identify future competitors before they become a threat and recognize key elements in a competitor analysis.

- Apply competitor analysis to marketing strategy and develop a competitive intelligence system.

EXECUTIVE PERSPECTIVE

Executive Samantha Wilson, Manager, Marketing

Company CHEP U.S.A.

Business Pallet and container pooling services

How do you view the direct competitor landscape for CHEP?

CHEP is the global leader in pallet pooling and related logistical solutions. Combining superior technology and over four decades of experience, CHEP handles pallet and container supply chain logistics for customers in the consumer goods, produce, home improvement, raw materials, and automotive industries. CHEP identifies direct competitors as other firms possessing these resources, but no other company matches CHEP's global product range or geographic reach.

Our direct competitors specialize in the renting or leasing of distribution platforms. But for new firms to enter this market, a sizeable capital investment and a significant logistical infrastructure are required—major market entry barriers. With assets totaling over 265 million pallets and containers moving through thousands of supply chains around the world, CHEP has a strong competitive advantage.

Given CHEP's dominant position, in what ways are indirect competitors important for you to consider?

Indirect competitors are a very important consideration for CHEP in the context of firms that create logistical solutions that standardize and improve the supply chain. Interestingly, our indirect competitors are often our own potential customers who use supply chain strategies built on the purchase and management of an *internal* pallet source. Through this process, pallets are purchased, used, and then destroyed or sold to pallet recyclers. Some revenue is generated for the firm as a result of this process, but that revenue is easily offset by decreased overall supply chain efficiencies and by the indirect costs of sourcing.

To illustrate this point, consider a firm I'll call "Company W," a manufacturer of bottled water. Part of Company W's distribution strategy includes the purchase and use of midgrade white wood pallets. Each year, a portion of the company's resources are used to purchase, manage, repair, and dispose of these internal pallet assets. This practice reduces the focus on their core competency, which is producing bottled water. The CHEP solution is designed to manage Company W's supply chain quality by providing access to a high-quality platform that is managed, tracked, and maintained through an infrastructure that includes over 130 service centers across the country. By partnering with CHEP, Company W can instead focus on its own value proposition while gaining cost savings and efficiencies based on our core competencies.

What role does competitive intelligence play in CHEP's marketing planning?

CHEP gathers competitive data through many different means such as trade shows, industry publications, and tracking competitor press releases, among others. Assembling data from these sources is valuable and provides a better understanding of industry trends. But we don't overfocus on what competitors are doing. Rather, our greater focus is providing thought leadership in sustainability and product damage reduction—things we know are value-adding to our customers and drive business our way.

CHEP is more than just a distribution platform. In fact, our CHEP Innovation Center is the epicenter of next-generation distribution platforms and supply chain advances. Using Six Sigma methodologies, the CHEP Innovation Center lets customers test load configurations (how products are stacked on pallets) or simulate the rigors of transportation and its effects on products.

KEY SUCCESS FACTOR–KNOW YOUR COMPETITOR

As we discussed with JetBlue in a previous chapter few industries are more competitive than the airline industry. Consolidation, bankruptcy, and fierce competition have characterized the industry over the past decade. All the traditional "major" U.S. carriers have either filed for bankruptcy or come very close. Collectively they have lost over $20 billion since September 11, 2001. Fluctuating environmental factors such as high fuel prices, strong global competitors, large capital costs (the price of a single Boeing 777 ranges from $171 million to $250 million), and other issues create a challenging operating environment.[1]

One airline, however, has an amazing record of success despite the environmental and competitive turbulence. Southwest Airlines has grown from a start-up airline in 1971 to the largest carrier of domestic passengers in the United States. Today, Southwest controls 90 percent of the low-fare market. Herb Kelleher, executive chairman and cofounder, credits learning from the established major airlines as a critical element in the company's success. First, Southwest rejected the hub-and-spoke system adopted by all the major airlines in favor of a short-haul point-to-point system. Second, while the major airlines fly many different kinds of aircraft, Southwest has created efficiencies in turnaround-time, parts inventory, and other cost savings by flying only Boeing 737s.[2]

By studying and learning from competitors, then developing and implementing its own strategies, Southwest has become a dominant U.S. carrier (see Exhibit 6.1). The company created a new market by understanding its competitors and listening to the market. This is called a **customer orientation.** At the same time, other companies follow a more reactive strategy and use competitor analysis as the primary driver for their strategies, in essence a "follow the competitor" approach that is known as a **competitor orientation.**

How important is it to be able to learn from and effectively manage competitors? Noted Dutch business strategist and former head of planning at Royal Dutch

EXHIBIT 6.1	U.S. Airlines and Their Domestic Market Share

Airline	Market Share (%)
American	14.6%
Southwest	12.6
United	11.1
Delta	10.7
Continental	7.7
US Airways	7.2
Northwest	6.6
JetBlue	4.2
AirTran	3.1
Alaska	2.7
All other airlines	19.5

Source: *Bureau of Transportation Statistics*, October 2008, www.transtats.bts.gov.

Shell Arie De Gues puts it this way, "The ability to learn faster than your competitors may be the only sustainable competitive advantage."[3] As we saw in Chapter 5, the difference between success and failure is defined, in part, by a company's ability to get the right information to decision makers at the right time. An essential piece of the knowledge puzzle is identifying and understanding your competitors, then developing and implementing strategies to defeat them.

This chapter will focus on identifying, analyzing, and taking action against the competition. First, we will identify strategic forces that help define competitors from the company's point of view. Then the focus shifts to identifying competitors from the customer's point of view. From there we will discuss competitor analysis using relevant criteria that results in an assessment of the company's strengths and weaknesses. Finally, we will discuss specific marketing strategies to dominate competitors. Understanding competitors and developing strategies to deal with them is an essential component of a marketing plan because customers relate to a product in the context of the available options, which includes competitor products.[4] Without knowledge of competitors, a marketing plan does not accurately reflect what is happening in the marketplace.

> While high-end watches such as Cartier and Rolex continue to sell well, the sub $50 watch market is experiencing significant sales declines as young people (the primary target market) move to other devices such as cell phones, MP3 players, and PDAs. Seiko, Timex, and others are now developing new watches that do much more than tell time in response to competitors that didn't even exist 10 years ago.[5]

DISCOVERING COMPETITORS– STRATEGIC FORCES

Companies in any given industry operate in a unique set of circumstances. All competitors in an industry face environmental, process, managerial, and financial challenges. As a result, companies seek to identify competitors based on strategic forces—forces that affect an industry—to discover sources of competitive advantage.[6]

Industry Structure

One of the most basic strategic forces is the structure of the industry, which is defined by two characteristics: (1) the number of companies selling products, and (2) the degree of differentiation among the products. Industries with many companies selling undifferentiated (most farm produce such as corn) or differentiated (clothes, for example) products behave much differently from an industry with a single company (the electric utility in your area). Let's examine industry structure more closely. Exhibit 6.2 provides a summary and example of each market structure.

Monopoly

A **monopoly** exists when a market is controlled by a single company offering one set of products. In this structure, the monopoly company sets the price and controls product development. There is little need to advertise a particular brand's benefits as the company has no direct competitors, at least in the short run.

Many governments watch monopolistic companies closely because their powerful market positions can potentially harm consumers. As a result, many monopolies are allowed to exist, in part, because of government oversight. For example, utilities (electric, water) in the United States must seek approval from local or state regulatory agencies before increasing the price of their services.[7]

EXHIBIT 6.2 | **Examples of Industry Structures**

Different Industry Structures

Industry Structure	Number of Competitors	Degree of Competition	Company	Industry
Monopoly	None	No direct substitutes possible	Systembolaget	Swedish liquor store industry
Oligopoly	2–3	Very high	Coca-Cola	Carbonated soft drinks
Monopolistic competition	Some	Very high among major competitors	McDonald's	Restaurant
Pure competition	Many	Very high among all competitors	Kaiser Aluminum	Aluminum

FYI

With certain exceptions, monopolies are not allowed in the United States. As a result, one of the hurdles for companies seeking to merge is approval from the Justice Department. A key question in any merger of two companies operating in the same basic market space is the definition of the market. In other words, what is the market and how is it defined.

The merger of XM and Sirius Satellite radio deals with this question directly. As the only two satellite radio providers in the country, it can be argued that a merger would create a monopoly (one company with 100 percent of the satellite radio market); however, XM and Sirius argue that the market is all audio entertainment (AM, FM radio). If that definition is used, then the combined market share of their merged company would be less than 5 percent and therefore not a monopoly. The Justice Department has allowed the merger, and the Federal Communications Commission gave final approval in 2008.[8]

Oligopoly

An **oligopoly** differs from a monopoly in that there are more companies in the industry manufacturing products that are either standardized (steel) or differentiated (automobiles). When the products are standardized, it becomes difficult for any one company to break out and charge a premium price. The products are considered a commodity, and price is set, for the most part, by market forces.

When products are different, however, it is possible to have greater price variability. For example, luxury carmakers can charge a premium for their cars because they are perceived as different from other products in the market. Exhibit 6.3 lists the luxury automakers and their model lines. The perceived difference between these and other cars can be based on a variety of factors such as quality, features, or service and creates competitive space in the marketplace. Companies seek leadership in a given market space. Porsche, for example, is a leader in high-performance, high-quality sports cars, and that leadership enables them to charge a significant premium over other automobile manufacturers.[9]

EXHIBIT 6.3 | Luxury Carmakers

Maker	Sedan/Coupe	Sports Car	SUV
Acura	RL, TL, TSX, RSX	NSX	MDX
Audi	A3, A4, A6, A8, R8, S4	TT	Q7
BMW	3,5,6, 7 Series and M models	Z4	X3 SAV, X5 SAV
Infiniti	Q, M, G Sedan	G Coupe	QX, FX
Lexus	LS, GS, ES, IS	SC	RX, GX, LX
Mercedes-Benz	C, E, S, CLS, CLK, CL Series	SLK, SL Roadster	M, G, R class

Monopolistic Competition

Monopolistic competition exists when many companies offer unique products in different market segments. The difference between an oligopoly and monopolistic competition is in the number of companies operating in the industry. Companies in both market structures seek to identify opportunities and create unique products that allow a price premium, but monopolistic competition has more competitors in the marketplace.

Restaurants are frequently cited as an example of monopolistic competition. While there are obvious differences between Chinese and Italian restaurants, they still compete for the "dining out dollar." Competition is fierce; 60 to 90 percent of all restaurants go out of business in three years. Exhibit 6.4 identifies some major U.S. restaurant chains in the casual dining segment. Even though six major companies dominate in the casual dining market, there are 10 major competitors because some companies have multiple restaurant chains.[10]

More specifically, in a given geographic area, all restaurants of a particular theme (for example, Italian) compete against one another. If diners want Italian, they will consider only restaurants serving that kind of food. This adds another layer of competition.

A restaurant that is able to establish a favorable reputation with respect to particular attributes such as good food or great service will be able to charge more. In addition to the price premium, restaurants with a strong reputation often have high demand for their product. The end result is that, while there are many competitors, individual companies able to create a unique product experience benefit from higher prices and strong demand for their products.[11]

Pure Competition

In **pure competition,** many companies offer essentially the same product. Because there is little, if any,

Mercedes Benz positions itself as an industry leader in luxury cars and its advertising reflects that position.

© Courtesy of Daimler AG

EXHIBIT 6.4 **Major Restaurant Chains in the U.S. Casual Dining Segment**

Outback Steakhouse, Inc.	Reprinted courtesy of Outback Steakhouse, Inc.
Darden Restaurants, Inc.	Reprinted Courtesy of Red Lobster / Reprinted Courtesy of Bahama Breeze/Darden Restaurants, Inc.
P.F. Chang's China Bistro, Inc.	
The Cheesecake Factory Inc.	Reprinted Courtesy of The Cheesecake Factory, Inc.
Applebee's International, Inc.	

Source: Hoover's, www. hoovers.com/free/, accessed November 2008.

differentiation, sellers lack the ability to create a price premium. An example is the market for commodities such as corn and soybeans. Many sellers all provide the same product in an open market. There is no differentiation in the product and, as a result, sellers must take the market price. In this situation, marketing communication costs are low because sellers cannot generate any perceived differences between their products. Profit margins are generally lower, and sellers focus on creating cost efficiencies to increase profitability.

Supply Chain

The movement of raw materials into the manufacturing process and on to the final consumer links many companies through a complex logistics network and is known as the **supply chain.** In contrast to the old model of marketing channels, the supply chain is characterized by high levels of coordination and integration among the members. Relationships among supply chain companies are often strategic with sensitive information passed between organizations to help facilitate the value offering. Chapter 15 provides a detailed discussion on this important concept and its role in delivering value to the customer.

Most often companies view competitors as those existing at the same level in the supply chain. Wal-Mart competes against Target, Kmart, and other retailers. Sony competes against Panasonic, Samsung, and other electronics manufacturers. However, competitors can also be vertical, coming from other levels in the supply chain. Companies sometimes integrate backward (away from the consumer) or forward (toward the consumer) in the supply chain. New competitors are created when companies expand vertically in these ways and supply chain partners become competitors.

Manufacturers may move toward the customer and open stores that reach them directly. Ralph Lauren has hundreds of stores around the world selling directly to the customer. The company also sells products through department and specialty retailers such as Macy's, Nordstrom, Saks Fifth Avenue, and Nieman-Marcus. These retailers face direct competition from Ralph Lauren outlet stores.[12]

In other situations, retailers move into the supply chain by creating their own brands and contracting with manufacturers to make the products. Costco sells a line of diapers, made by Kimberly-Clark, under its Kirkland brand. Since Kimberly-Clark has its own market-leading brand of diapers (Huggies), the Kirkland brand competes directly with Huggies.

> Huggies' primary competitor is not Kirkland diapers but Procter & Gamble's Pampers brand. Kimberly-Clark has announced plans to boost its marketing dollars to $200 million in an effort to offset a push from Pampers. Pampers has aggressively used communication tools such as the Internet to boost sales and also product enhancements such as the introduction of training pants.[13]

Product Capabilities

As discussed in Chapter 2, companies develop product market combinations based on capabilities in a particular product area, such as brand recognition, that it believes are transferable to new markets. Apple, for example, was a computer company until it introduced the iPod as a personal MP3 music player (see Exhibit 6.5). Before the introduction of iPod, the portable MP3 music player market was dominated by products from Rio and Creative Design. However, Apple's strong brand recognition, coupled with an innovative and simple product design, made iPod the market leader.[14] The company continues to define the MP3 player market with new iterations of existing products, such as the Nano, and new products like the iPod Touch. Apple transferred its knowledge of digital media, software, and product design into new markets, the personal MP3 player with the iPod and cell phones with iPhone. Its products are now the benchmark by which competitors are judged.

> Creative Design introduced its Nomad MP3 players in 1999, two years before Apple brought out iPod. The company still sells MP3 players under the Zen and MuVo brands but is a minor player in the market. Leveraging its understanding of consumer electronics, however, Creative Design joined the Apple iPod marketplace and now sells a line of iPod portable speakers.[15]

Company Culture

Culture plays a critical role in defining a company's view of its own competitive environment. A company's tolerance for risk, attitude toward innovation, and willingness to invest in research and development are among the characteristics that play a part in decisions to enter new markets and create new products.

EXHIBIT 6.5   The Apple iPod Line

Apple continues to define the MP3 player market with new innovations of its popular iPod line.

Studying a competitor's culture often provides clues about its future strategies. A company like Google, with a history of innovation, aggressively looks for new market opportunities, while more conservative companies such as Sony take a more deliberate approach to new products and markets. For example, Sony was slow to make the move to flat panel TVs while it focused on its own Trinitron models.

A classic example of corporate culture is the railroads' definition of their business in the early 20th century. Senior managers at the Union Pacific railroad thought they were in the railroad business. They did not look beyond their immediate business (railroads) and consider that they were really in the broader business of transportation. As a result, automobile manufacturers and airlines overtook railroads as leading transportation companies. Companies willing to encourage risk and innovation can overcome failure. Sony was a small Japanese company that failed in its first product introduction, an electric rice cooker, but went on to become a global leader in electronics. The difference was due, in part, to a corporate history of risk taking that resulted in product innovations such as the world's first direct view television, Walkman cassette players, and Discman CD players.[16]

A study identified the following as the most innovative companies in the world: (1) Apple, (2) Google, (3) Toyota Motor, (4) General Electric, and (5) Microsoft. It is not surprising that each of these companies is the market leader in its industry.[17]

Global Issues

Companies look for any competitive advantage and that often includes moving into global markets. At the same time, governments have an interest in protecting local companies and their employees from foreign competition. The result is often the use of government quotas, import fees, and a host of other regulations designed to limit foreign competitors in a country. For many years, U.S. farmers have argued that government regulations severely limited access to the Japanese market despite the ability of U.S. farmers to delivery high-quality products at lower prices. The World Trade Organization (WTO) seeks to expand trade bilaterally between nations and globally among all nations. Despite its best efforts, however, the vast majority of governments around the world engage in some protection of local industries.[18]

HP Printers increasingly complete against Wal-Mart and other online photo services.

DISCOVERING COMPETITORS—THROUGH THE CUSTOMERS' EYES

Imagine that you are a marketing manager at Hewlett-Packard responsible for the sale of HP photo printers. Who are your competitors? Certainly they would include similar products from Canon, Epson, and other printer manufacturers. However, think about the question from the customer's perspective. They might respond with an entirely different set of competitors that included Wal-Mart or even a Sony digital video recorder. The customer, for example, may not want to print digital pictures at home and would choose online printers such as Shutterfly or Wal-Mart's photo center instead. They may believe this is an easier option than printing the pictures at home with the hassle and cost of paper and ink. Or perhaps they do not want digital pictures at all but focus on digital video that can be shown in many formats. These customers may view their pictures on a computer screen or television and do not see the need for a printer. In either case, the customer has not chosen an HP color photo printer.[19]

Discovering the competition through the customer's eyes expands a company's knowledge and understanding of the customers and the competition. Management often focuses on immediate, direct competitors. This leads to a competitor orientation in which companies become fixated on the competition and not the market. Customers, on the other hand, identify competitors based on a host of factors including product substitutability, usage, and the options open to them in the buying decision process. In essence, they want to find the product that will best meet their needs. A company that uses customers to define the competition can develop a competitive strategy that is responsive to the market. There are three customer perspectives, and each creates a unique set of competitors.

Direct Competitors

Dasani versus Evian, Crest versus Colgate, Shell versus Exxon, these are natural, head-to-head competitors, and most consumers include them together when making decisions about bottled water, toothpaste, or gasoline.

Crest and Colgate battle for the No. 1 toothpaste brand. Currently, Procter & Gamble's Crest claims the top spot with 35 percent of the toothpaste market, two percentage points ahead of Colgate. P&G introduced its Pro-Health line of toothpaste to compete directly with Colgate's Total brand. Together the two brands and all their brand extensions account for more than 65 percent of all toothpaste sold.[20]

Direct competitors offer products considered very close substitutes for a company's current products and services. They operate in the same industry and are already known and part of a competitor analysis.

Marketing managers generally have no trouble identifying direct competitors. The challenge, however, is defining them from the customer's perspective. For example, Dasani and Evian are both global brands and direct competitors. However, a shopper at Wegmans (a regional grocer popular in the Northeast United States) may prefer Wegmans Spring Water. As a marketing manager you must know not only the large national or global competitors but also regional and even local competitors that may be successful in particular markets.

While not a global brand, Wegmans Spring Water does compete with Dasani and Evian from the customer's perspective. As the customer stands in the aisle at Wegmans, she is faced with several bottled water options, including local bottled waters as well as Dasani and Evian. Consequently, at the point of purchase, Dasani and Evian face a host of local direct competitors. As you can see in Exhibit 6.6, some of these brands are limited to one or two regions of the country, but, at the point of sale, they can still represent a competitive threat to Dasani or Evian.[21]

Indirect Competitors

Looking at the competition from the options available to customers often expands the number of competitors. Customers consider products that solve a problem or

EXHIBIT 6.6

Local and Regional Bottled Water Companies

Company	Headquarters	Distributed
Arrowhead	Brea, California	Nationwide and Canada
Good Hydration	Hampstead, Maryland	Nationwide and the Caribbean
Ozarka	Greenwich, Colorado	Arkansas, Texas, Louisiana, Mississippi, and portions of Tennessee, Missouri, and Kansas
Deep Rock	Telogia, Florida	National and internationally
Snow Valley	Upper Marlboro, Maryland	Maryland, Delaware, Washington, D.C., Virginia, and Pennsylvania

Source: *Bottled Water Web*, www.bottledwaterweb.com/, accessed November 2008.

meet a need. This means they do not define competitors in terms of the companies in a particular industry. Instead, they contemplate options beyond direct competitors.[22] As the options expand, the substitutability of the product also increases. What may be considered a one-of-a-kind product such as a trip to Disney World becomes one of many options when you define the competitors as any possible vacation a family may consider in the upcoming year. A company that fails to understand customer options can miss key competitors.

By expanding the numbers of potential competitors based on customer options, companies identify **indirect competitors.** These competitors offer products that may be substituted based on the customer's need and choice options. McDonald's, the largest fast-food company in the world, did not respond quickly when grocery chains started offering prepared meals (soup and salad bars, deli sandwiches) and, as a result, did not recognize that people were choosing to expand their dining out options.

Consider bottled-water consumers' decision-making process and overall view of the product. Take, for example, a family of four that uses enough bottled water to justify the installation of a home water-filtration system. While the initial cost is high, the family may find the cost per gallon lower than bottled water. By choosing the water-filtration system, the customer decides to substitute filtered water for Dasani bottled water. As a marketing manager you must understand all the options to develop effective marketing strategies to deal with the threat.

Product Use

Product usage is a third way of defining competitors. Customers often find new uses that alter the original intent or design of a product. As a product manager for Folgers coffee, you might consider your competitors to be Maxwell House, Eight O'Clock, and Hills Bros. and you would be right, but Exhibit 6.7 shows even more competition for the coffee drinker's business. The growth of Starbucks and a host of regional coffee shops has changed the coffee-drinking habits of millions of consumers.[23] As a result, millions of coffee drinkers now consume more coffee outside the home than ever before, consumers drink more specialty coffees, and coffee is seen as more of a social drink. Folgers has responded with different coffee blends and flavors designed to encourage people to consume more coffee in the home.

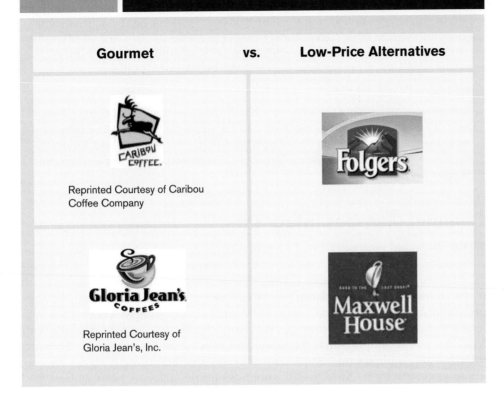

EXHIBIT 6.7 | **Options for Coffee Drinkers**

Gourmet	vs.	Low-Price Alternatives
Reprinted Courtesy of Caribou Coffee Company		Folgers
Reprinted Courtesy of Gloria Jean's, Inc.		Maxwell House

DISCOVERING FUTURE COMPETITORS– LIKELY CANDIDATES

In today's dynamic environment, new competitors appear quickly. Also, constantly evolving business relationships turn strategic partners into competitors in many industries. Microsoft worked as a strategic partner with IBM in the early 1980s licensing the MS-DOS operating system in IBM personal computers. However, by the early 1990s the partnership had changed and the partners become more like competitors. Today, IBM does not even compete in the personal computer market, while Microsoft continues to extend its dominance in operating systems with the release of Vista.[24]

As a result, scanning the environment is critical to staying ahead of future competitors. Anticipating strategic moves by potential competitors enables a company to respond proactively rather than reacting to a situation. Indeed, an important reason for maintaining a marketing intelligence system is to anticipate potential competitors *before* they become real competitors.[25]

Strategic Expansion

New competitors often come from companies that operate in similar market spaces but have traditionally chosen not to compete directly. In **market expansion,** competitors operating in closely related markets expand into new markets to compete more directly. Tesco, a large British food retailer, has expanded into the United States with a new store concept called Free and Easy Neighborhood markets. These stores will be smaller than traditional grocery stores and carry fewer items.

The concept is being watched by convenience stores such as 7-Eleven as well as larger grocery chains like Safeway and Kroger.[26] **Product expansion** occurs when a company leverages its existing expertise (technical product experience or supply chain) to create new products for existing or new markets. SanDisk, for example, used its knowledge of portable storage media to create its own line of MP3 players. In both market and product expansion, new competitors are generally known, but their expansion strategy creates a more direct competitive threat.

Carrefour, a major global retailer, is not well-known in the United States. However, it has been one of the most successful global retailers in expanding into new markets. Recently, its five fastest-growing markets included countries from Asia (China), Latin America (Argentina, Colombia), and Europe (Romania, Poland, and Greece).[27]

Channel Member Integration

As we discussed earlier, channel members, even channel partners, can become competitors when they choose to take on operations historically performed by other supply chain members. This type of integration occurs in one of two ways. In **backward integration,** companies merge operations back up the supply chain away from the consumer. McDonald's, for example, created its own farms in Russia to supply that market. Now the farms compete directly with local farmers. A company that moves toward the end user is engaged in **forward integration.** Apple created Apple Stores to sell products directly to consumers. These stores compete directly with other electronics retailers such as Best Buy and Circuit City.

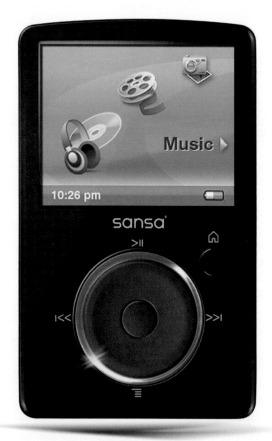

Sansa's line of MP3 players are positioned against Apple's iPod players. The company's Sansa Fuze Mp3 player competes directly against Apple's iPod Nano players.

Merger and Acquisition

In recent years, merger activity in a number of industries has brought new competitors into markets. News Corp.'s purchase of MySpace, for example, instantly introduced a major media company into a market dominated by small start-ups and social connection Web sites, thus changing the competitive environment.[28] While it is difficult to predict future competitors that will enter a market through acquisition or merger, it is possible to look for small, successful competitors with good growth opportunities as they often represent the best candidates for acquisition. A small company can become a major competitive threat relatively quickly once it is acquired by a larger, well-funded company willing to invest resources.

Defending Market Space

To defend existing markets, companies that were direct competitors before may join forces to proactively deal with threats in the marketplace. NBC Universal and News Corp. formed a video online Web site to compete directly with Google's YouTube. They were concerned that YouTube could dominate the online video market, making it more difficult for them to offer their video content online. Another approach companies might consider involves working with competitors, as highlighted in the FYI.

Increasingly, customers look for sophisticated solutions that involve products from many vendors including direct competitors. This pressures competitors to work together instead of against each other. By partnering, competitors often stand a better chance of increasing the overall size of the market as customers will be more willing to consider bundled options when competitors present a unified solution. When competitors don't cooperate, customers can get confused and decide not to purchase or choose a different product. For several years, competing high-definition DVD formats from Toshiba and Sony created confusion for consumers who were slow to purchase players for fear of choosing the "losing" format. With the decision by the major film studios to focus on Sony's Blu-ray format, Toshiba announced it would stop making the HD-DVD format, leaving the "winning" format in a strong competitive position. However, as the battle was being fought, the market may have changed. Amazon, Apple, and others now offer a wide range of video entertainment online and it is not clear whether the Blu-ray format will meet with wide market acceptance.[29]

ANALYZING COMPETITORS

Identifying competitors, while crucial, is only the first step in understanding the competition. It is important to remember the goal in this process is to deal more effectively with competitive threats. As a result, a company must not only identify but also assess each competitor and then develop an action plan for competitive success.

Competitor analysis yields two primary benefits. First, companies can evaluate their own strategies against competitors and make adjustments. For example, many retailers have adjusted their pricing strategies to accommodate Wal-Mart's low-cost strategy. It is also valuable to evaluate new strategies against the competition to assess their reaction. **Competitive scenario analysis** enables companies to test competitor reaction to possible strategic scenarios such as product modifications or new advertising campaigns. Second, competitor analysis can identify new opportunities and/or threats. It is always possible to learn from competitors. While automobile manufacturers already had hybrid technology in development, the success of Toyota's Prius spurred Ford, General Motors, and others to accelerate the introduction of their own hybrid vehicles. There are more than 17 different hybrid models available in the United States, up from 11 in 2006 and at least 5 new models are scheduled to be introduced by 2010. The five specific areas of focus in a competitor analysis are: strategies, resources, culture, objectives, and finally strengths/weaknesses.[30]

Strategies

Companies, even industries, frequently follow an established strategic model. Product introductions (new car models frequently debut in the fall), price increases (price changes in the theme park industry are often announced in the spring), and new advertising campaigns (soft drink companies introduce new campaigns at the beginning of the year) often track historical patterns. Studying these trends, particularly with respect to specific competitors, can be a source of insight into their future behavior. Mistakes can sometimes be avoided by learning from the competition. As we saw at the beginning of the chapter, Herb Kelleher, cofounder of Southwest Airlines, studied the major airlines and learned from their mistakes. As a result, Southwest implemented a strategy that differed dramatically from that of the major airlines and included such changes as a point-to-point system to minimize large overheard costs and congestion and flying a single type of aircraft to minimize inventory and turnaround costs. Southwest created a new category of airline, the low-cost carrier, that now includes JetBlue and AirTran among others and dominates consumer travel.[31]

Resources

The ability to access financial resources and a quality workforce represents a significant advantage for a competitor. The competitive landscape can change dramatically very quickly as a result of resource constraints or an infusion of money from an outside source. It is important to know the competitor's resources in order to plan accordingly. To evaluate a competitor's financial resources consider the following questions:

- What is the company's bond rating? Bond rating is an indicator of the cost of capital.
- What are the company's operating costs (does it have a cost advantage)?
- What is the company's investment in plant and equipment (future commitments)?
- How easily can it access the equity market (stock)? What has been the company's stock performance over the past 12 months?
- Does the company have a lot of cash on hand?

Employees are another critical resource that should be evaluated.

- How many employees currently work at the company?
- Is the company actively recruiting for certain positions (recruiting for new engineers or product development employees may indicate a strategy focused on new products)?
- What are the salary ranges of major job positions at the company?
- What is the ratio of employees to sales (for example, how many employees does it take to generate a million dollars in sales)? Compare that with other companies in the industry.
- What is the hiring policy of the company? Does it hire experienced people from other companies in the industry or younger, less-experienced individuals and train them internally?
- Does the company pay below, equal to, or above the industry average at key positions?

Laidlaw, one of only two American hanger manufacturers, found it difficult to compete against foreign competitors. It needed additional financial resources and was acquired by several private equity firms. The new owners wanted to leverage the company's brand name while outsourcing the manufacturing process to China. Chinese hanger imports are up more than 800 percent in the last five years, forcing many American hanger companies out of business. Laidlaw will remain a dominant hanger company although its hangers are now manufactured overseas.[32]

Culture

A company's culture is a critical element in competitor analysis. A good place to begin evaluating a competitor's culture is the senior management team. Senior management sets the tone in an organization, and studying the backgrounds of key senior people (particularly the CEO) can offer insights into a company's tolerance for risk and overall corporate focus. Larry Ellison, CEO of Oracle, has a reputation as an aggressive executive. One of his favorite books, *The Art of War* written by Sun Tzu in the sixth century, inspires his overall approach to Oracle's business strategy.

ETHICAL DIMENSION 6

Ethics as a Strategy

Two companies dominate the enterprise software (suite of software applications encompassing an entire company and designed to solve business problems) market, Oracle and SAP. Fierce competitors, both companies compete directly for almost every customer in the high-ticket enterprise software market. As a result, they know each other well and never miss a chance to gain a competitive edge. Oracle, led by CEO Larry Ellison, has a reputation for being aggressive and consistently demonstrates a willingness to play hardball with competitors. When Oracle was competing against PeopleSoft, the company announced a hostile takeover, which caused potential customers to question PeopleSoft's long-term viability, thereby weakening its market position and eventually making it easier for Oracle to purchase the company.

SAP pursues Oracle customers through a variety of competitive strategies. It acquired Tomorrow Now, a low-cost support provider for PeopleSoft, J.D. Edwards, and Seibel Systems software (all companies owned by Oracle). Through its SAP TN, the TomorrowNow subsidiary based in Texas, the company services 300 Oracle customers with low-cost phone support and upgraded software. This cuts directly into Oracle's highly profitable service agreement business. SAP makes it clear that it is targeting Oracle customers as part of an extensive coordinated plan to gain market share against its primary competitor. SAP has also announced that nearly 500 customers have signed up for the company's "safe passage" program that significantly lowers SAP product prices for Oracle customers willing to switch to SAP.

The nature of the competitive battle took a different turn when Oracle charged in court that SAP TN had engaged in illegal data theft of key proprietary information from Oracle computers. Oracle reports in the lawsuit that it noticed a spike in customer access to sensitive software and support materials and traced it back to SAP TN. While SAP TN was a legitimate provider of support services to existing Oracle customers, the complaint states that SAP employees unlawfully used legitimate customer access codes to gain unauthorized access to the confidential data. Oracle references the company's software agreements, which state that customer support material is confidential and limited to the use of Oracle's customers. Not surprisingly SAP states the charges are unfounded and represent an attempt by Oracle to distract SAP as it successfully competes against Oracle.

While the charges are serious, some believe Oracle and Larry Ellison have already accomplished a great deal simply by bringing the charges. The negative PR has created concern among customers and put SAP on the defensive. The overall effect, whether by design or random chance, has strengthened Oracle.[33]

Ethical Perspective

1. **Oracle:** Is it appropriate to use ethical issues as part of a coordinated competitive strategy? Should Oracle talk about this issue with potential customers when making a sales presentation?

2. **SAP:** How would you address this issue with customers? How would you respond to Oracle as it seeks to gain competitive advantage from SAP's alleged unethical and perhaps illegal access to confidential data?

Executives will sometimes use ethical issues as part of a strategy to deal with competitors. Read Ethical Dimension 6 to see how Ellison and Oracle are raising ethical concerns about their most formidable competitor, SAP.

When there is a change at the top, a new CEO will often seek to put his or her 'stamp" on the organization. By studying the individual's background, it is possible to understand the strategies they have used in the past. Mark Hurd, HP CEO, was brought in from NCR to help turn around Hewlett-Packard, and his experience in turning around NCR was cited as a reason for his selection. At NCR, Hurd had aggressively cut costs and redirected the company to focus on core businesses; he has followed a similar strategy at HP with successful results.

It is also helpful to know the overall reputation of the company. Over time, most companies develop a reputation. The reputation is affected by and, in turn, influences the company culture. For example, 3M has a history of innovation. The company's success is based, in part, on a culture that encourages research and development leading to new products. Knowing the company's corporate culture is an indicator of potential future strategy. Of course, companies do go "outside the box" and make significant and dramatic strategic shifts, but, even in those situations, the company will rely on the existing culture to implement the strategy. Consider Jeffrey Immelt, CEO at General Electric, and his quest to create a stronger culture of innovation at GE (see Exhibit 6.8). Immelt has initiated dramatic change in GE's culture. Under Jack Welch, GE's former CEO, the company focused on growth, but Immelt is changing the company's focus toward innovation. Dramatic changes in corporate culture create opportunities and threats for competitors.[34]

Corporate Objectives and Goals

When you know the goals and objectives of a competitor, you have a pretty good idea of the company's strategy. One benefit of search engines such as Google or Lexis/Nexis is the ability to examine a vast amount of information; if it is in the public domain a good search engine can find it. That means when management at a competitor discusses goals and objectives this information is often accessible. For example, if a company newsletter states: "Our goal is to improve customer satisfaction," or "We expect to see significant growth in this market," you can usually translate that information into specific strategies. Tracking public statements is certainly one way of identifying a competitor's goals and objectives.

Bass Pro Shops and Cabela's have surpassed L.L. Bean, the historical leader in outdoor gear. Now third behind its fast-growing competitors, L.L. Bean chose a different retail strategy to compete against the giant retail experience created by Bass Pro Shops and Cabela's. L.L. Bean is building smaller stores with a focus on apparel with no fishing ponds or climbing walls (notable features in its larger competitors).[35]

EXHIBIT 6.8	GE's Quest to Become More Innovative

Product Portfolio	Organiztional Culture
Bio Sciences With Amersham, GE can bring diagnostics down to the cellular level and be a leader in personalized medicine	**Pay** Link bonuses to new ideas, customer satisfaction, and sales growth with less emphasis on bottom-line results
Renewable Energy BE moved into solar and wind power and biogas acquistions such as Enron Wind	**Risk** Spend billion to fund "imagination breakthrough" projects that extend the boundaries of GE
Security BE bought its way into fire safety and industrial security with Edwards Systems. Icon Track and InVision gave it entrèe into homeland security, from bomb detection to screening for narcotics	**Experts** Rotate executives less often, and bring in more outsiders to create industry experts instead of professional managers

G.E. is redefining itself into a innovation company. Change in company culture is always a challenge.

Source: *BusinessWeek*, March 28, 2005. p. 64.

Additional information can be learned from a company's annual report as well as mandatory documents filed with the Securities and Exchange Commission (SEC) such as the 10-K. Available at the SEC government Web site, 10-K reports present a great deal of information about the company's operations and strategies (see Exhibit 6.9). In particular, Part 1, Item 1–Business and Part 2, Item 7 and 7a–Management Discussion on Operations and Market Risk, include specific discussions of current business activities and ongoing operations. While these data may be available from other sources such as trade publications, the 10-K does offer unique insights on management's current view of business operations. When coupled with a company's annual report, the 10-K provides significant insights about a competitor.

Starbucks provides data about itself in a variety of ways. Visit a Starbucks and you can find information on the company's products, business philosophy, and social responsibility initiatives. Each store also has a bulletin board that posts local community events.

Strengths and Weaknesses

A competitor analysis also includes a summary of competitor strengths and weaknesses. A competitor's strength is regarded as a threat while a competitor's weakness is an opportunity to attack. Depending on their magnitude, threats (competitor strength) and opportunities (competitor weakness) can lead a company to

EXHIBIT 6.9	Example of a Form 10-K

UNITED STATES SECURITIES AND EXCHANGE COMMISSION
Washington, DC 20549

Form 10-K

☑ **ANNUAL REPORT PURSUANT TO SECTION 13 OR 15(d) OF THE SECURITIES EXCHANGE ACT OF 1934**
For the fiscal year ended September 30, 2007
or

☐ **TRANSITION REPORT PURSUANT TO SECTION 13 OR 15(d) OF THE SECURITIES EXCHANGE ACT OF 1934**
For the transition period from   to   .
Commission File Number: 0-20322

Starbucks Corporation

(Exact name of registrant as specified in its charter)

Washington	**91-1325671**
(State or other jurisdiction of incorporation or organization)	*(IRS Employer Identification No.)*

2401 Utah Avenue South
Seattle, Washington 98134
(Address of principal executive offices, zip code)

(Registrant's telephone number, including area code):
(206) 447-1575

Securities Registered Pursuant to Section 12(b) of the Act:
Common Stock, $0.001 Par Value Per Share

Securities Registered Pursuant to Section 12(g) of the Act:
None

Source: www.starbucks.com.

develop specific strategies that effectively minimize or neutralize strengths while exploiting weaknesses.

Benchmarking

An important management tool called benchmarking enables a company to evaluate its business processes against other companies to determine what it does well and what it can improve. After assessing the company's business processes, managers look for industries and, more specifically, companies with similar characteristics. Companies targeted as leaders in critical areas are identified, and the company learns through interviews or research as much as possible about that "best practice," or benchmarks, with the express purpose of incorporating the benchmark company's success into its own business practices. This process is particularly useful in competitor analysis because the company can evaluate competitor business processes in an effort to learn how to do things better or to exploit competitor weakness if the company identifies areas where it outperforms the competitor.[36]

COLLECTING COMPETITIVE INTELLIGENCE

As discussed in Chapter 5, today the primary issue in collecting competitive information is not too little but too much. The Internet provides an almost unlimited number of resources. As a result, it is important to discern which sources provide the most reliable, current, and cost-effective information. Let's examine the primary sources of competitive information.

Company Web Site

The single best source for competitive information is the company's own Web site. Publicly traded companies will post their annual report and other data, often in the "investor relations" area. Many companies have press kits available online that include current company news and biographies of senior management. For example, the ExxonMobil Web site posts streaming video of senior executives talking about various issues related to the company.

New product introductions, detailed explanations of existing products, changes in personnel, even new programs and strategies are frequently located on the company Web site. Accordingly, it is a good idea to visit competitors' Web sites on a regular basis. While competitors are not likely to divulge company secrets on their Web sites, they should be among the first places to go in conducting a competitor analysis.

Government Sources

As we mentioned, the Securities and Exchange Commission is a great source for company information, but other government sites also provide helpful information. The United States Trademark and Patent Office provides details about patent applications and is an excellent source of information about competitor's new-product developments. Detailed descriptions of product ideas as well as developments in basic research as filed in a patent application are posted to the agency's Web site. This kind of information is valuable to large companies and small entrepreneurs who want to keep track of competitors or check the viability of a product idea. New-product developers spend a great deal of time investigating possible patents that may conflict with a new product or seeking product opportunities.

Local governments are a good source of information about competitor operations in that area. For example, if a competitor is seeking to expand manufacturing capacity, any legal notices will be filed with the appropriate local or state agencies. Keeping track of all these information sources becomes a real challenge when the competitor is a large company. This is one reason an established information system is so important.

Business Publications

There is no shortage of business publications and Web sites. *The Wall Street Journal, BusinessWeek, Fortune, Forbes,* and many others feature articles in every issue on industry trends as well as analyses of individual companies. Exhibit 6.10 lists the top publications. In addition, online sites such as Hoover's provide detailed information on thousands of companies, much of it at little or no cost. While the Internet is a great tool offering incredible access to information about competitors, it is important to evaluate all information. All sources of competitive data should be reviewed with a critical eye to the reliability of the information.

BusinessWeek offers articles related to new, innovative companies and products. Metrokane, a manufacturer of kitchen utensils and products, was featured in an issue. The company's popular corkscrew, The Rabbit, has been instrumental in taking the company from $2.5 million in sales in 1999 to over $18 million. Part of the article detailed the history of the Rabbit and provided insights on the company's overall approach to business. Articles like this are very helpful in understanding company strategic thinking and new product ideas.

Search Engines

Popular search engines tap an unlimited supply of information. In a matter of minutes it is possible to get hundreds, even thousands, of links. As we mentioned previously, the problem then is sorting through all the available data to find the most relevant information. One way to sort is to use fee-based search engines such as ProQuest and Lexis/Nexis. These search engines can access more data with sophisticated filters that will target specific information more easily.[37]

Salespeople

In the business-to-business environment, salespeople are frequently the most important link between the company and external marketing information. Their access to customers and suppliers is a vital source of competitor information. At trade conferences, at supplier meetings, and in customer offices, salespeople often hear information about competitor strategies including new-product launches and marketing communication campaigns. Unfortunately, many companies fail to capitalize on this valuable information source. Formal systems for collecting data from salespeople frequently do not exist and, when information is collected, it is not made available to everyone.

Customers

Another underutilized source of competitor information is the company's own customers. Through appropriate market research, it is possible to get a great deal of information about the competition by simply asking customers specific and relevant questions. In retailing, for example, consumers are frequently asked about their shopping habits. Where do you purchase this product? Which company has the best customer service? Who has the lowest price? This information is all part of the competitive analysis.

CHALLENGE COMPETITORS: VALUE DELIVERY STRATEGIES IN A COMPETITIVE ENVIRONMENT

Competitor analysis is an essential tool in creating customer value. Indeed, turning the results of the competitive analysis into action items is the primary reason for conducting the analysis in the first place. Too often companies fail to maximize their competitive information. Depending on the companies' position in the market, product mix, available resources, and competencies, there are a number of specific competitive strategies

As discussed in Chapter 2, evaluating the competition often occurs as part of a broader strategic environmental analysis. In that context, competitor analysis focuses on the big picture and identifies overall competitor strategy. At the tactical level, competitor analysis is much more specific, such as "what are the advantages and disadvantages of our competitor's product."

Depending on the company's position in the market and the life cycle stage of the product (new, growth, mature, decline), strategies are developed to deal with competitive threats. The challenge is to balance company marketing objectives and strategy against competitive threats that dictate changes. A thorough knowledge of competitors is essential to marketing managers as they create an effective marketing strategy and implement a marketing plan.

EXHIBIT 6.10	Top Business and Finance Publications

BusinessWeek

THE WALL STREET JOURNAL
Reprinted by permission of The Wall Street Journal. Copyright © Dow Jones & Company, Inc. All Rights Reserved Worldwide.

Entrepreneur.com

FINANCIAL TIMES
Reprinted Courtesy of Financial Times Limited.

Reprinted by permission of Barron's Online. Copyright © Dow Jones & Company, Inc. All Rights Reserved Worldwide.

Reprinted by permission of Forbes Magazine © 2008 Forbes LLC.

Kiplinger

eBay dominates the online auction market accounting for 90 percent of all online auctions and has posted annual growth of 40 percent since 1999. Now, Google and Microsoft have announced plans for online classified services which are projected to become a far bigger format for connecting buyers and sellers ($1.7 billion in online auction revenue versus a projected $27 billion in online classifieds). Both Google and Microsoft believe their new approach will be the more effective strategy in the long term.[38]

SUMMARY

Companies operate in a highly competitive environment and a key success factor is the ability to discover, analyze, and then confront competitors. A good understanding of the competitive environment is critical in developing effective marketing strategies. Three methods are used to identify competitors: application of strategic forces, customer perspective, and potential new competitors. An analysis of competitor strategies, resources, culture, and objectives is necessary to fully understand their strengths and weaknesses. From this analysis it is possible to develop effective marketing strategies directed against the competition.

KEY TERMS

customer orientation 150
competitor orientation 150
monopoly 151
oligopoly 152
monopolistic competition 153

pure competition 153
supply chain 154
direct competitors 157
indirect competitors 158
market expansion 159

product expansion 160
backward integration 160
forward integration 160
competitive scenario analysis 161

APPLICATION QUESTIONS

1. Consider the challenge for Eclipse Aviation as it creates a market for its ultra-efficient Eclipse 500 mini jet. Seating up to four people and costing $1 million to $2 million, it is substantially cheaper and smaller than today's corporate jet. Who are the competitors for Eclipse as it enters the small-jet market? What criteria would you use to define the competitive set for Eclipse?

2. The owner of a successful, family-owned Italian restaurant in your city has called and asked if you would help with the marketing of the restaurant. The average meal price is about $30 per person including a bottle of wine. The owner takes great pride in the family restaurant and tells you the restaurant has no competitors. How would you respond? How would you define the competitors for the restaurant?

3. You are the owner of a successful chain of tea shops called Grace's Teas located in the Northeast. With 15 shops in Boston and 20 in New York, the company has developed a strong local following of devoted tea aficionados. The company's target market tends to be wealthy professional women who enjoy a social experience with friends as well as moms and daughters who book birthday parties and small social events. This follows a trend nationally of growing interest in local tea shops. Who might be considered potential

new competitors to this and why? What strategic options might the owner of Grace's Teas consider to deal with potential new competitors?

4. The marketing manager for Aeropostale clothing stores wants to know about the competitors for high-fashion jeans. Identify and briefly discuss all the various competitors (direct and indirect) for Aeropostale fashion jeans. Be sure to include an explanation for why each needs to be considered a competitor.

5. Before entering your current college or university, what other educational options did you consider? Why? Did you consider other learning environments (online versus on campus)? What made you choose the school you are attending now?

MANAGEMENT DECISION CASE: The Search for Microsoft

Microsoft has dominated the computer operating system market for decades. More than 90 percent of the world's personal computers use its Windows or Vista operating systems. Likewise, its server software, after several failed attempts, drives many of the servers in the world. However, one notable technology area has eluded Microsoft, the Internet. Company history suggests that Microsoft often stumbles when creating new products, frequently taking a couple of product iterations to reach market acceptance. Unfortunately, in this case, Microsoft is losing rather than gaining ground as it moves through new product offerings.

The highly competitive search engine industry has created a huge business in Internet search advertising for market leaders Google and Yahoo. Microsoft, despite repeated new-product enhancements, has failed to break the dominance of the two leaders. Consider that in 2005 MSN Search accounted for 14 percent of all Web searches compared to Google's 46 percent. Fast-forward to 2008 and Microsoft's new search engine, MSN Live Search, now accounts for less than 10 percent while Google's handles more than 56 percent of all Web searches. This translates into billions of dollars of lost Internet advertising revenue for Microsoft. Piper Jaffray & Co. estimates that Internet search advertising revenue will reach nearly $45 billion in 2011. Google and, to a lesser extent Yahoo, are currently positioned to take most of that new revenue.

Beyond the loss of revenue in fast-growing Internet ad sales, Microsoft understands there is more at risk. Increasingly, the Internet is able to handle functions that historically resided on the computer, including essential office tools such as word processing and spreadsheets. Both Google and Yahoo have introduced Web-based word-processing applications. If Microsoft is not a major online player, it risks losing core business to Internet companies capable of providing the same functions at lower cost. At the same time,

Microsoft faces the challenge of identifying large markets from which it can drive large revenue streams. Small, niche markets that need specific applications do not offer the company sufficient growth potential and are, in fact, better served by Internet solutions providers who deliver more targeted solutions.

The market leader, Google, keeps improving its business model. It is estimated that, as a result of its huge and growing database of information, the company is able to get 50 percent more revenue per search than competitors because it can better target its Internet ads. With higher profit margins and revenue, the company has invested heavily in introducing new products. For example, Google recently announced a feature that allows advertisers to pay for an ad only when a product is actually ordered, which provides a higher level of confidence and security for advertisers. Microsoft's search engine strategy, on the other hand, has been confusing for consumers. The company took a reasonably successful online service (MSN) from the 1990s and attempted to introduce a new brand—Live—incorporating both the old MSN franchise and the new brand, which only confused consumers. Was MSN Live a search engine or a content provider like AOL? In the end, many consumers simply moved to Google or Yahoo.

As Microsoft struggles to regain momentum in the critical search engine business, it still has significant resources and the ability to recover. The company has introduced a new feature for advertisers that incorporates demographic data (provided by users who sign up for MSN and Live services) to help direct more targeted advertising. It is also working to get the Live toolbar preloaded on new computers in the same way Google has done with Dell and other computer companies. Lenovo has agreed to load the Live toolbar on its machines. Microsoft finds itself in the unusual position of trying to catch market leaders instead of being the market leader.[39]

Questions for Consideration

1. Identify potential competitors for Microsoft's Internet search engine product Live. Are there any new competitors that could threaten Microsoft's market follower position?

2. You are an executive at Microsoft. Analyze Google as a competitor using the analysis tools provided in the chapter (strategies, resources, culture, and objectives).

3. Develop two or three strategies Microsoft could use to confront Google's Internet search engine market dominance.

MARKETING PLAN EXERCISE

ACTIVITY 6: Determine Competitive Landscape

This chapter focused on identifying and analyzing competitors to develop an essential understanding of the competitive forces that shape the company's value offering. This exercise consists of two elements.

1. Identify all competitors (direct and indirect) of your company using

   a. Strategic forces

   b. Customers' perspectives.

   Keep in mind that local or regional companies can also be considered competitors by the customer. Also, scan the competitive environment for potential competitors including global competitors that could move into your markets.

2. Once you have identified a list of competitors, including potential competitors, conduct a competitive scenario analysis on those competitors judged to be the biggest challenge in the current environment.

If you are using Marketing Plan Pro, a template for this assignment can be accessed at www.mhhe.com/marshall1e.

RECOMMENDED READINGS

1. Clayton M. Christensen and Michael E. Raynor, *The Innovator's Solution* (Boston: Harvard Business School Press, 2003).

2. Benjamin Gilad, *Early Warning: Using Competitive Intelligence to Anticipate Market Shifts, Control Risk, and Create Powerful Strategies* (New York: American Management Association, 2003).

3. John E. Prescott, *Proven Strategies in Competitive Intelligence: Lessons from the Trenches* (New York: Wiley, 2001).

4. Chris West, *Competitive Intelligence* (New York: Palgrave Mcmillan, 2003).

5. Craig S. Fischer and David L. Blenkhorn, *Controversies in Competitive Intelligence: The Enduring Issues* (New York: Praeger, 2003).

CHAPTER 07

UNDERSTANDING CUSTOMERS: BUSINESS-TO-CONSUMER MARKETS

LEARNING OBJECTIVES

- Understand the value of knowing the consumer.

- Recognize how internal factors affect consumer choices.

- Consider the role of personal and psychological factors in consumer decision making.

- Identify significant factors outside the consumer that have an effect on consumer choices.

- Appreciate the critical and complex role of cultural, situational, and social factors in a consumer purchase decision.

- Understand the consumer decision-making process.

EXECUTIVE PERSPECTIVE

Executive Mary Cavanaugh Knapp, Director, Brand Marketing

Company NBC Universal, Universal Orlando Resort

Business Vacation destination with two theme parks, a night-time entertainment complex, and three onsite luxury hotels

What motivates a consumer to choose to purchase your brand over those of your competitors?

The success of Universal Orlando Resort is directly attributed to product differentiation. In the very competitive Orlando theme park market, it is absolutely essential for Universal to clearly make a distinction between its brand and product offerings and those of the competition. To do so, we must focus on the specific attributes that make us different—and be perceived as more attractive to certain audiences than our primary competitors. Providing an array of products that are appealing and relevant to today's families gives us the ability to clearly differentiate our product from the competition.

Universal Orlando Resort's target audience is families with children ages 8 to 17. The rides and attractions are based on blockbuster movies and cutting-edge, family entertainment that children of this specific age group are immediately drawn to through all of our marketing efforts.

Describe the "personality" of your brand? How do you make this come through for consumers considering purchase?

Universal Orlando Resort is a brand that has "edginess" about it. We position the experience of our products with images, messaging, and music that are cool, hip, relevant, and thrilling. Other key descriptive words and phrases about our brand are: experimental, immersive, technological, behind-the-scenes, on-the-cutting-edge, and edge-of-your-seat.

Theme park entertainment is powerful. It delivers emotion and relevance. Throughout all of the mediums of communication, these elements shine through. Our Web site and advertisements include action shots of families having fun together. They include people laughing, screaming, and generally greatly enjoying themselves. It shows Mom at the spa and Dad playing golf—with great food, dancing, and having the time of their lives. The Universal Orlando Resort personality is clear in everything we do.

What do you do to make it easy for prospective consumers to gather information about your brand for use in making a purchase decision?

Universal Orlando Resort has an interactive Web site that is packed full of information for our prospective consumers. It contains everything about the resort for Florida residents and for tourists visiting the Orlando area. The Web site is designed for ease of use for people who are completely new to our products and for those who want to quickly search an upcoming event or new attraction.

We are also included in Orlando and family vacation Internet search engines and throughout all their relevant partner Web sites and brochures. Universal Orlando Resort partners with key groups in the travel industry to promote our products throughout the country and the world. For example, we work closely with the American Automobile Association (AAA) in both its travel and "Show Your Card & Save" programs. With millions of Americans in AAA's membership base, this provides an additional means of distribution for information about our vacation destination.

Regal Cinemas is investing millions of dollars to atract movie-goers to their theaters.

THE POWER OF THE CONSUMER

It's a Friday night and a group of people are considering how to spend the evening. A consensus forms around watching a movie. The discussion focuses on two choices: visit the local multiplex theater to see a first-run showing of the latest hit movie, or go to a friend's house and watch a classic on the 50-inch plasma television with surround sound. Ultimately, they decide to watch *Spider-Man 3* at the friend's house. This interaction is repeated thousands of time each weekend and represents just one example of consumer decision making.

Marketers are fundamentally interested in learning about the process people use to make purchase decisions. In our example, the implications of the seemingly innocuous decision to watch a movie at home are very significant. Movie theaters are concerned because attendance has been falling for a decade while sales of DVDs and video on demand have been growing at double-digit rates. Theater owners are investing millions of dollars to get people to choose a night out at the movies instead of going home. At the same time, movie studios such as Paramount, Sony, Time Warner, and Disney are paying attention. Because they want to maximize revenue, they have shortened the time between theatrical release and DVD sales, in addition to making first-run movies available via video on demand.[1] Finally, theme parks such as Universal Orlando Resort are interested because they invest millions to combine successful movies with live-action shows and rides to extend the movie's experience.

Delivering value to the customer is the core of marketing, and a company can only do that with a thorough accurate and timely understanding of the customer. Complex forces influence consumer choices, and these forces change over time, which adds to the challenges marketers face. Exhibit 7.1 displays a model of the consumer decision process, which is a complex interaction of internal (personal and psychological characteristics) and external (cultural, situational, and social stimuli) forces that, joined with a company's marketing activities and environmental forces, affect the purchase decision process. This chapter will identify the internal and external forces affecting the process, then focus on the consumer decision process itself.

INTERNAL FORCES AFFECT CONSUMER CHOICES

Among the most difficult factors to understand are those internal to the consumer. Often, consumers themselves are not fully aware of the role these important traits play in their decision making. Compounding the challenge is the fact that these characteristics vary by individual, change over time, and affect decisions in complex ways that are difficult to know. Exhibit 7.2 identifies examples of internal forces.

Personal Characteristics

Personal attributes are frequently used to define an individual. Age, education, occupation, income, lifestyle, and gender are all ways to identify and classify someone. The *American Heritage Online Dictionary* defines **demographics** as, "The characteristics of human populations and population segments, especially when used to identify consumer markets." It is helpful to understand the demographics of a target market for two reasons. First, knowing the personal characteristics of a target market enables marketers to evaluate relevant statistics against competitors

EXHIBIT 7.1   **Model of the Consumer Decision Process**

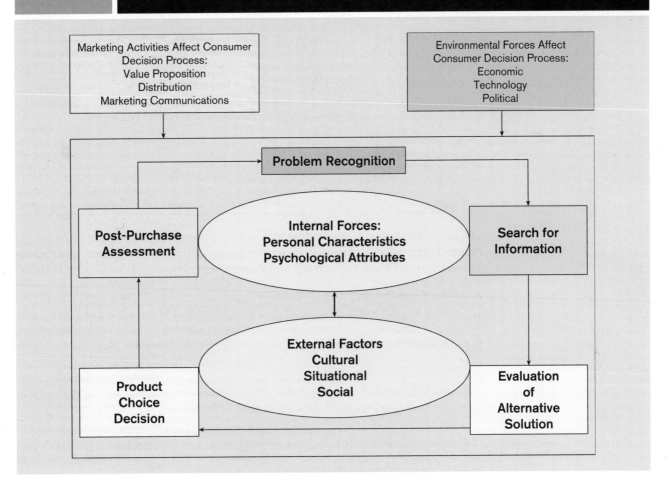

and the overall population using broad demographic studies like the U.S. Census reports. Comparing demographic data such as age and income to competitor data enables you to assess how your target markets match up with competitors. Second, personal characteristics like age, income, and education play a critical role in consumer decision making, affecting information search, possible product choices, and the product decision itself.[2] Demographics are also an important tool

EXHIBIT 7.2   **Internal Forces Affecting Consumer Choices**

Personal Characteristics	*Psychological Attributes*
Age	Motivation
Education	Attitude
Occupation	Perception
Income	Learning
Lifestyle	Personality
Gender	

in market segmentation, and Chapter 9 will explore how demographics are used to make decisions about targeting customer groups.

Companies sometimes create personas to summarize demographic characteristics. Best Buy identified five potential users of the Geek Squad (the in-house computer support service) — Jill, a suburban mom; Charlie, a 50-year-old curious about new technologies; Daryl, a technology "hot dog"; Luis, a small-business owner; and Nick, a prospective Geek Squad agent. Best Buy designed Geeksquad.com to fit these five personalities identified by research[3].

FYI

Demographic changes often create new markets or expand existing ones. The United States is currently experiencing three key demographic transformations that include Hispanics, baby boomers, and the remote workforce.

- Hispanics are among the fastest-growing subcultures in the United States and currently represent 12.5 percent of the population. Many are recent immigrants that would like to communicate with family and friends outside the United States. **Marketing opportunity:** Develop easy-to-use, low-cost, VoIP technologies and online discussion groups to encourage communication between family and friends. **Implementation strategy:** Increase personalization of services such as GPS location mapping and technology platforms such as mobile Web browsers to deliver individual content targeting Hispanics.

- The U.S. population is aging with the first of the baby boomers (people born between 1946 and 1964) considering retirement options, health care planning, and lifestyle changes that offer companies in a number of industries growth opportunities. **Marketing opportunity:** Develop Web portals to help retirees manage finances, health care, and other lifestyle issue for baby boomers. **Implementation strategy:** Increase the portability of services enabling users to conduct transactions with their cell phones and enhanced international cell phone coverage.

- Increasingly people work outside the office. Recent statistics suggest nearly 10 percent of the population has a residence-based business and another 10 percent telecommute at least part time. **Marketing opportunity:** Create technologies that enhance communication and remote work productivity[4]. **Implementation strategy:** Converge voice, video, and data to create a single platform to enable employers to speak to remote employees.

Life Cycle Stage (Age)

As individuals age, their lives change dramatically, and as a result, so do their purchase patterns. From childhood to retirement, purchase behavior is shaped by a person's stage of life, and while specific aspects of the marketing mix change from one generation to the next, children still want to play, families still need homes and everything that goes in them, and seniors still focus on retirement. Marketers realize that changes in life stage (for example, graduating from college, getting married, or having a child) transform an individual's buying habits and are referred to as the **family life cycle.** These life changes mirror the individual's family environment and include the number, age, and gender of the people in the immediate family.

Beauty companies have focused on the aging process for women, particularly baby boomers. Unilever's Dove product strategy and marketing communications speak to "Real Beauty" and reinforce that the beauty of a woman comes from inside and outside, where of course, Dove products can help. The product and message are working with double-digit sales increases over the last several years, reaching almost $600 million a year[5].

Historically, age has been a primary construct for identifying a person's life cycle. A new trend is emerging, however, as people move beyond traditional roles. Young adults are marrying and having kids later in life, altering the traditional view of 30-somethings as family builders. Concurrently, American couples are having children far into their 40s, significantly changing the buying behavior of individuals who might normally be planning retirement. Let's consider U.S. population trends by age (see Exhibit 7.3). For example, one important marketing insight from examining these population trends is that while the population is growing, it is also getting older. As we have discussed, the aging population leads to market opportunities for products, such as Dove, which have surged in the past 10 years.

Occupation

People are influenced by their work environment. From the executive suite to the plant floor, people who work together tend to buy and wear similar clothes, shop at the same stores, and vacation at the same places.[6] As a result, marketers identify target groups based on an individual's position in an organization.

In addition to broad occupational categories (union worker, management) marketers also target specific occupations. Physicians, for example, have a host of products, from PDAs to vacations, designed specifically for them. Given the amount of time spent working, it is not surprising that individuals develop similar interests and purchase behaviors.

| EXHIBIT 7.3 | U.S. Population Trends by Age |

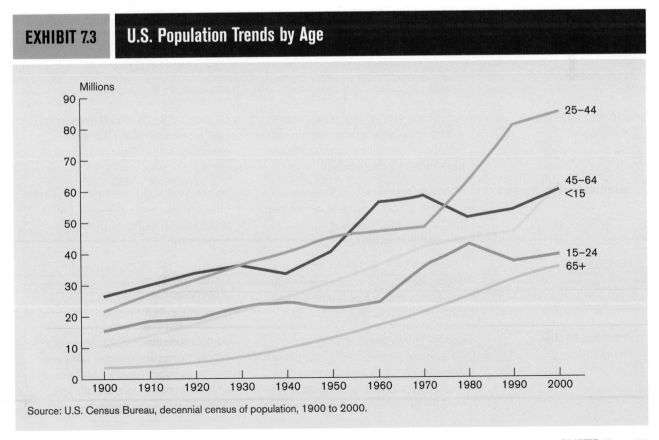

Source: U.S. Census Bureau, decennial census of population, 1900 to 2000.

VARIABLE FLOW TURBO. INSTANT RESPONSE FOR THE INSTANT-MESSAGING CROWD.

The Acura RDX. Everything about it delivers instant gratification. Its i-VTEC® engine features a turbocharger so advanced it greatly minimizes lag. While innovative luxuries like its available voice-activated navigation with real-time traffic® and Zagat® restaurant reviews deliver information the way you'd expect. On demand. See it at acura.com or call 1-800-To-Acura. **Advancing acceleration.**

ACURA
ADVANCE.

Acura links its products to specific target markets using lifestyle activities like instant messaging

Lifestyle

Even though people share the same life cycle stage or occupation, their lifestyles may be dramatically different. **Lifestyle** references an individual's perspective on life and manifests itself in that person's activities, interests, and opinions (AIO). By learning about what the person likes to do, his or her hobbies, and views about the world, marketing managers develop a holistic view of the individual. As the name implies, lifestyle is how people choose to live and how a person lives dictates what she or he buys. By choosing particular activities, developing unique interests, and holding on to specific opinions, an individual identifies what is really important. Marketers seek to match their products and services with the consumer's lifestyle.[7] New technologies enable marketers to not only know a great deal about their customers but also to direct targeted marketing messages. However, privacy issues and the intrusive nature of these technologies can increase ethical concerns (see Ethical Dimension 7). Exhibit 7.4 summarizes important lifestyle trends in the United States.

Just as women's roles in the workforce have changed over the past several decades, so has their purchasing behavior. Increased purchasing power and wealth for women have led to new purchasing roles. Auto purchases, for example, were historically dominated by men; however, women now influence 80 percent of vehicle purchases and 40 percent of SUV sales. The cosmetics industry, while offering some products to men, focuses primarily on women.

Gender roles are behaviors regarded as proper for men and women in a particular society. These roles change over time and across cultures. In general, women

EXHIBIT 7.4	Lifestyle Trends in the United States

	Trend	Marketing Example
Health-conscious eating	Americans are turning to healthier eating styles, which can be seen in most restaurants with new low-calorie and low-carbohydrate menus.	Season's 52–Darden Restaurants new restaurant chain features a changing menu of healthy foods.
Single-parent homes	Although the majority of families in the United States consist of two-parent homes, single-parent homes are increasing steadily.	Target, Wal-Mart, and other retailers offer a wide range of books, DVDs, and other products targeted at single parents.
Online era	There has been a steady increase in online shopping and information gathering. This is only expected to increase as technology increases.	Amazon—One of the first and largest online shopping Web sites, Amazon continues to experience double-digit growth every year.
Women in the workforce	In 2007, 46% of the workforce was made up of women and is continuously growing. As more and more women begin their careers, we have seen more and more men help in raising the kids.	Day care centers—Companies are including on-premise day care centers as part of their benefits packages; in addition, private centers continue to see significant growth.

ETHICAL DIMENSION 7

Hello, Who Are You?

You probably thought your cell phone was just for phone conversations, right? Well, not anymore. Meet the new "sell phone," which combines Internet tracking data with your location to target very personal, specific ads right to your cell phone. Marketers are now testing technology tools that will deliver a message right to you about a store or promotion just as you pass that store. You will be able to see a Starbucks coupon pop up on your cell phone with a note that tells you the nearest Starbucks is one block away on your right.

Presently, the limiting factor is not the technology but the cellular service providers who are not sure how best to move forward. Many advertisers are also taking a wait-and-see approach as everyone works through Federal Communications Commission (FCC) rules regarding use of private customer data such as location information. At this point, the FCC is requiring mobile advertisers to get an individual's permission to release sensitive customer data before the cellular service can release the information to the advertiser. Similar rules apply to e-mail but spammers do not get the necessary permission before filling your mailbox.

Medio Systems and other companies are moving ahead and delivering targeted advertising to phones serviced by Verizon, T-Mobile, and others. Sprint Nextel is also implementing location-based targeted advertising. Advertisers see the potential to bypass much of the communications clutter that people disregard every day. By some estimates, people are exposed to as many as 3,000 ads each day, with the vast majority of the messages being ignored.

Cellular companies can locate a user within 50 to 300 meters and offer advertisers a captive audience. The marketing company collects Internet tracking data then matches where the consumer has been on the Internet with his or her actual location. If someone has visited the Barnes & Noble Web site recently and her location shows her close to a Barnes & Noble, a specific message that could include a coupon or other promotion can be sent directly to the cell phone. In 2008 advertisers spent in excess of $3 billion on mobile advertising, a minuscule sum compared to traditional advertising channels, but that number is expected to grow dramatically over the next few years to $19 billion in 2011.

A number of individuals and advocacy groups, however, are concerned about the potential invasion of consumer privacy. At minimum, advertisers will learn customer cell numbers, and many cell phone users are not happy about that prospect[8].

Ethical Perspective

1. **Advertisers:** The ability to reach targeted customers at the right moment has been the goal of advertising for decades. This new technology enables "just-in-time" advertising. As an advertiser, would you consider mobile advertising? How would you address customer concerns about privacy?

2. **Cellular service providers:** A potential source of revenue, the ability to target cell phone users, is available today and represents very little incremental cost to the service provider. Just because it is possible, should marketing companies be allowed to send mobile ads? How do you safeguard the privacy of your customer?

3. **Consumers:** Ensuring customer confidentiality is an essential element of the contract between cell service provider and consumers. Would you want to receive mobile ads?

have been adding new roles as they move into the workforce and positions of political power. In the United States, this means that men and women are more likely to share responsibilities than live in a traditional household where the men work and women stay at home to raise the children.

Differences in women's roles have created vastly different market segments. At one end are traditional homemakers who derive satisfaction primarily from maintaining the household and nurturing the family. At the other extreme is the career woman who is either single or married and who makes a conscious choice to work and derives personal satisfaction from her employment. Other segments include trapped housewives that are married but prefer to work and trapped working women who would prefer to be at home but must work because of financial necessity or family pressure.

Marketing managers understand that men and women vary not only in the products they require but also in the marketing communications they are receptive to. For example, women constitute the majority of Internet users in the United

States and have for several years.[9] In addition, women and men both read magazines but the kinds of magazines they read vary greatly so marketers place ads in different magazines to reach both groups. Men prefer automotive and sports magazines while women choose health and epicurean magazines. In addition, the message itself varies by gender with men preferring a "self-help" message and women responding to a "help others" communication. All this suggests that gender roles are a critical personal characteristic affecting consumer choices.[10]

Psychological Attributes

The consumer decision process involves a number of psychological forces that profoundly affect the consumer choice process. These forces drive the need, shape the content and format of information stored in memory, and have an effect on point of view about products and brands.

Motivation

At any given time people experience many different needs. Most are not acted upon; however, when need reaches a particular strength or intensity, it becomes a motive that drives behavior. People prioritize needs, making sure that stronger, more urgent needs get met first. **Motivation** is the stimulating power that induces and then directs behavior. It is the force by which powerful unmet needs, or motives, prompt someone to action.

Many theories have been developed over the years to explain human motivation. Exhibit 7.5 provides a summary of four popular theories of motivation and how they are used in marketing. The best known and most popular of these theories is the Hierarchy of Needs, which was developed by psychologist Abraham Maslow. Maslow's theory proposes a series of needs that flow from lower order (physiological) to higher order (self-actualization). The theory suggests that people meet physiological needs such as hunger and sleep before they satisfy other needs. Once those needs are satiated, other needs become more important. At the highest level in the hierarchy, people seek human ideals related to justice, wisdom, and the meaning of life.[11] Maslow asserts that people never fully meet this need, and higher order needs continue through an individual's life.

As is the case with any theory on motivation, the Maslow's Hierarchy of Needs theory is a good summary of human needs but should not be considered a comprehensive model. The model does not explain the level of intensity needed to move people from one need to the next. For example, how much financial security (a safety need) does someone need before social needs become a priority. In addition, research suggests that Maslow's hierarchy works better in Western cultures than in Eastern ones where social needs take on a higher value than personal needs.

Marketing managers find Maslow's theory beneficial in identifying where products fit into an individual's overall needs. Products are often targeted at more than one set of needs. For example, dining at an upscale restaurant is certainly designed to satisfy the basic physiological need for food. However, the atmosphere and interior design encourages conversation with friends and a sense of belonging, thus meeting customers' social needs. Finally, if the restaurant is popular it may address an individual's need for status, respect, and prestige, thus fulfilling a self-esteem need.

Waiting in line at the local McDonald's or Burger King is quite common in McAllen, Texas, where fast-food customers choose the quick alternative 25 times a month, more than anywhere else in the country. The national average for eating fast food is 17 times a month, with Southern cities dominating the list (Greenville, North Carolina, was No. 2). The Northeast and West have the lowest number of fast-food fanatics, with residents of Portland, Maine, stopping by their favorite fast-food restaurant just 11 times per month.[12]

EXHIBIT 7.5 | Contemporary Theories of Motivation

	Theory	Key Elements	Marketing Implications
Maslow's Hierarchy of Needs Theory	Humans have wants and needs that influence their behavior. People advance only to the next level if the lower needs are meet.	1. **Physiological** 2. **Safety** 3. **Love/Social** 4. **Self-Esteem** 5. **Self-Actualization**	Individuals are not interested in luxuries until they have had basic needs (food, shelter) met.
Herzberg's Two-Factor Theory	Certain factors in the workplace result in job satisfaction.	1. **Motivators:** challenging work, recognition, and responsibility 2. **Hygiene factors:** status, job security, salary, and benefits	Satisfying hygiene factors does not create a loyal employee or customer. For a company to really create satisfied employees it is important to focus on motivators.
Aldelfer's ERG Theory	Expansion on Maslow's hierarchy placing needs in three categories.	1. **Existence** 2. **Relatedness** 3. **Growth**	People need a sense of belonging and social interaction. Creating a relationship with the customers extends the customers' satisfaction with the product.
McClelland's Achievement Motivation Theory	There are three categories of needs and people differ in the degree in which the various needs influence their behavior	1. **Need for Achievement** 2. **Need for Power** 3. **Need for Affiliation**	Companies can be successful targeting one of three basic needs.

Attitude

From religion to politics, sports to tomorrow's weather, people have an attitude about everything. An **attitude** is defined as a "learned predisposition to respond to an object or class of objects in a consistently favorable or unfavorable way."[13] Several key points come from this definition. First, attitudes are learned or at least influenced by new information. This is important for marketers because they seek to affect a person's attitude about a product. Second, attitudes are favorable or unfavorable, positive or negative. In other words, attitudes are seldom, if ever, neutral. As a result, marketers play close attention to people's attitudes about their products because they play an important role in shaping a person's purchase decision.

Initially, a person's attitudes are formed by their values and beliefs. There are two categories of values. The first refers to cultural values based on national conscience. Americans, for example, value hard work and freedom among other things. In Japan, national values include reciprocity, loyalty, and obedience. The second category is personal values held by the individual. Products possessing characteristics consistent with a person's value system are viewed more favorably.

While values may be based, in part, on fact, beliefs are a subjective opinion about something. Since they are subjective (emotional and not necessarily based on fact) marketers become concerned that a negative product belief will create a negative attitude about that product, making the attitude more difficult to

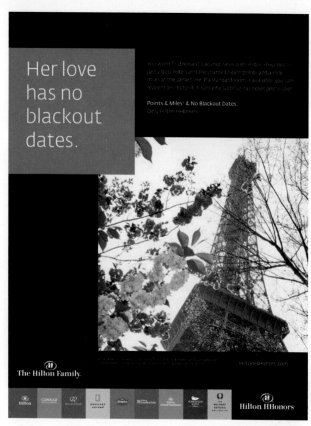

Her love has no blackout dates.

Points & Miles® & No Blackout Dates.
Only Hilton HHonors

The Hilton Family.

Hilton HHonors®

HiltonHHonors.com

There is a common belief among many in loyalty reward programs that they will not be able to use their points for rewards. Hilton attempts to deal with that belief by delivering a message about the availability of rooms using points without blackout dates.

overcome.[14] It is also important to note that beliefs, once formed, are resistant to change. Personal experiences, marketing communication, and information from trusted sources, such as family members or friends, all shape a person's belief system.

Values and beliefs come together to shape attitudes about an object whether it is Coke, the environment, or your favorite sports team. This overall predisposition is the result, generally, of an individual's assessment of that object on several attributes. For example, an attitude about Coke could be based on attributes such as health, which could be a positive belief—Coke's caffeine give you energy—or a negative belief—Coke has a lot of sugar and calories. Coke is presented as a fun, youthful drink and youth is an American value.[15]

Because people's beliefs/values impact their purchase decisions, marketing managers try to learn about those beliefs/values. They do that by having customers check off rating scales that evaluate a product's performance on a list of attributes. This is important information because most attitudes result from an individual's assessment of an object using a **multiattribute model** that evaluates the object on several important attributes. Learning which attributes are used and how individuals rank those attributes is particularly helpful to marketers in creating specific marketing messages as well as the overall value proposition.[16] For instance, individuals who value the environment and ecology will place a higher priority on fuel economy and other environmentally friendly characteristics in the purchase of a car.

Perception

People are inundated with information. Indeed, there is so much information that it is not possible to make sense of everything so people use a process called perception to help manage the flow of environmental stimuli. **Perception** is a system to select, organize, and interpret information to create a useful, informed picture of the world.

In marketing, perception of a product is even more important than the reality of that product because, in a very real sense, an individual's perception is his or her reality. Perception drives attitudes, beliefs, motivation, and, eventually, behavior. Since each individual's perception is unique, everyone's perceptual response to the same reality will vary. Two people will see an ad for a new Sony LCD flat-panel television, but their perception of the ad will be very different. One may see a high-quality television worth the money, while the other sees an overpriced television that does not warrant a premium price. Their attitude toward the ad and the product are affected by their perceptions.

Perception is shaped by three psychological tools: selective awareness, selective distortion, and selective retention.

Selective Awareness An individual is exposed, on average, to between 2,000 and 5,000 messages daily.[17] People cannot process, let alone retain, all those messages, so they employ a psychological tool known as **selective awareness** to help them focus on what is relevant and eliminate what is not. The challenge for marketers is breaking through people's decision rules, which are designed to reject the vast majority of stimuli they see every day.

Research provides several insights about these decision rules. First, not surprisingly, people are more likely to be aware of information that relates to a current

182   **part TWO**   Information Drives Marketing Decision Making unmet need. Someone looking to change cellular providers will pay more attention to ads from cellular companies than someone who is happy with her current service. Second, people are more receptive to marketing stimuli when they expect them. Customers entering a Best Buy or Circuit City anticipate seeing audio equipment and, as a result, pay more attention to it. Finally, people are also more likely to become aware of marketing stimuli when it deviates widely from what is expected. For several years, GEICO used a caveman as its primary "spokesperson." In addition to the creativity behind this approach, one of the reasons the campaign did well was because it deviated from normal insurance ads. People didn't expect to see a caveman talking about insurance.[18]

Selective Distortion Breaking through the customer's selective awareness is an important first step. However, even if a stimulus is noticed, there is no guarantee it will be interpreted accurately. Information can be misunderstood or made to fit existing beliefs, a process known as **selective distortion.**

The issue for marketers is that selective distortion can work for or against a product. If an individual has a positive belief about a powerful brand or product, information that is ambiguous or neutral will likely be interpreted positively. Even negative data can be adjusted to align with an individual's existing beliefs. For example, despite the negative implications of the information, a recall of Toyota Prius cars did not slow sales, in part, because people's perception of Toyota's overall quality offset the negatives associated with a product recall. On the other hand, a negative belief can lead to negative interpretation. In the 1990s General Motors worked hard to improve the quality of its cars. This came after several decades of being rated below Japanese cars from Toyota and Honda in terms of quality. Despite significant quality improvements validated by independent researchers like J.D. Power and Associates, people continue to believe GM car quality is inferior to Japanese cars. Sometimes a positive belief can work against a marketer, particularly when the belief leads to an incorrect interpretation.[19] When Eveready introduced the Energizer Bunny advertising campaign, it found people liked the commercials, but also found people believed the commercials were referencing Duracell batteries (Eveready's primary competitor). Part of the reason was that people strongly identified with Duracell (the brand had high brand recognition and market share) and distorted the information in the ads to fit their perception of Duracell.

Selective Retention Even if a stimulus is noticed and interpreted correctly, there is no guarantee it will be remembered. While selective awareness significantly controls the amount of information available to the individual's consciousness, selective retention acts as an additional filter. **Selective retention** is the process of placing in one's memory only those stimuli that support existing beliefs and attitudes about a product or brand. This is significant because **memory** is where people store all past learning events; in essence it is the "bank" where people keep their knowledge, attitudes, feelings, and beliefs.[20] There are two types of memory—short and long term. **Short-term memory** is what is being recalled at the present time and is sometimes referred to as working memory, while **long-term memory** is enduring storage, which can remain with the individual for years and years. Marketing managers are particularly interested in understanding an individual's long-term memory recall about their brand.

Selective retention tends to reinforce existing attitudes and creates a real challenge for marketers trying to overcome negative beliefs and attitudes since people are less likely to be aware of or retain information to the contrary. Audi, despite strong products and sales, still suffers from negative perceptions because of product problems related to the Audi 5000. Some people still remember a problem with sudden acceleration in the car that led to several accidents. While later research suggested the problem was not as severe as originally reported, Audi has had trouble overcoming persistent consumer attitudes over the past 20 years.

In 2001 Staples complaints-to-kudos ratio was 8 to 1, and the company knew it had to change. Research showed that customers wanted an easier shopping experience and were less concerned about price. The result was the iconic "easy" button made famous in commercials and on office desks all over the country. The "easy" message reinforced customer attitudes about the shopping experience and has helped vault Staples to No. 1 in the office supply market, ahead of Office Depot, the previous leader.[21]

One last point about perception regards a controversial issue—the affect of subliminal stimuli on perception. While people are aware of most stimuli around them, a number of other stimuli go unnoticed. In most cases, the stimuli are either presented so fast they are not recognized or they overload the individual and are "lost" in the person's consciousness. These stimuli are termed subliminal, and many critics of advertising suggest the stimuli can affect consumer behavior. Despite many claims to the contrary, however, research has uncovered no evidence that a subliminal message, whether sent deliberately or accidentally, has any effect on product attitudes or choice behavior.

Given the psychological processes people use to limit their awareness of marketing stimuli and control retention of any remaining information, it is easy to see why marketers must deliver a message over and over. Without repetition, the message is not likely to break through selective awareness and even less likely to be retained by the individual.[22]

Learning

How does an individual become a consumer of a particular product? Most consumer behavior is learned through a person's life experiences, personal characteristics, and relationships.

Learning is any change in the content or organization of long-term memory or behavior. Learning occurs when information is processed and added to long-term memory. Marketers can therefore affect learning by providing information using a message, format, and delivery that will encourage customers to retain the information in memory.

There are two fundamental approaches to learning. The first, **conditioning,** involves creating an association between two stimuli. There are two types of conditioning: classical and operant. Classical conditioning seeks to have people learn by associating a stimulus (marketing information, brand experience) and response (attitude, feeling, behavior).[23] Recently, many companies have started using popular songs from the 1960s and 1970s in their advertising. When individuals, particularly baby boomers, hear that music it connects them with positive memories and, not coincidentally, the product and brand being advertised. This is conditioned learning, by connecting the stimulus such as music with a response such as a positive association with a particular brand.

The other type of conditioning, operant conditioning, entails rewarding a desirable behavior, for example a product trial or purchase, with a positive outcome that reinforces that behavior.[24] For example, many different types of food retailers offer product samples in their stores. Frito-Lay, for instance, offers free in-store samples of Doritos for the express purpose of getting people to try the product, enjoy the product, and finally purchase a bag of Doritos. Enjoying the Doritos reinforces the positive attributes of the product and increases the probability of a purchase. Since the consumer must choose to try the product for operant conditioning to occur, Frito-Lay wants to make the trial as easy as possible.

While conditioning requires very little effort on the part of the learner, **cognitive learning** is more active and involves mental processes that acquire information to work through problems and manage life situations.[25] Someone suffering from the flu and seeking information from their friends, doctors, or medical Web sites about the best over-the-counter remedy for their specific symptoms is engaged in cognitive learning. They are looking for information to help solve a problem. Marketers must understand consumers sometimes engage in this type of activity and be proactive in providing the information sought by the consumer. Consider a box of Theraflu caplets, Theraflu Daytime cold lists six symptoms right on the front of the box that the product will help relieve. This kind of information is critical at the point of purchase as an individual considers which product will help him feel better faster.

Personality

When people are asked to describe someone, most of us do not talk about the person's age or education. Rather, our response generally reflects the individual's personality and is based on our interactions with that person in different situations. Our descriptions usually include various personality dimensions such as kind, outgoing, or gentle. **Personality** is a set of unique personal qualities that produce distinctive responses across similar situations.

Many theories of personality have been developed, but marketers tend to focus on personality trait theories because they offer the greatest insights on consumers. Personality trait theories all have two basic assumptions: (1) each person has a set of consistent, enduring personal characteristics, and (2) those characteristics can be measured to identify differences between individuals. Most believe personality characteristics

Verizon Wireless wants small business owners to consider them the best option in dealing with mobile e-mail solutions.

Courtesy Verizon Wireless

are formed at a relatively early age and can be defined in terms of traits such as extroversion, instability, agreeableness, openness to new experiences, and conscientiousness. These core traits then lead to outward characteristics, which are what people notice. For example, an extrovert would favor the company of others and be comfortable meeting new people. A conscientious person would exhibit behaviors that are considered careful, precise, and organized. Knowing the personality tendencies of a target audience can help marketers in developing product features such as mobile devices with Wi-Fi for extroverts so they can communicate easily with others or marketing communications that incorporate images consistent with the individual's personality.

While it is certainly beneficial for marketers to know the personality characteristics of their target audience, another application is the association between a brand and specific personality characteristics. This association is known as a **brand personality.** Research suggests that consumers purchase brands that have a personality consistent with their own.[26] Research on brand personality identified five traits:

- Sincerity (down-to-earth, honest, wholesome, cheerful).
- Excitement (daring, spirited, imaginative, and current).
- Competence (reliable, intelligence, and successful).
- Sophistication (upper class and charming).
- Ruggedness (outdoorsy and tough).

Knowing a brand's personality helps marketers connect their brand to a customer. For example, MetLife insurance has carefully considered its brand personality and arrived at the following characteristics: sincere and competent. Not coincidentally, these are characteristics that people in the market for insurance might find beneficial in an insurance company.

Crocs are cool. Growing from sales of $1 million in 2003 to over $847 million in 2007, Crocs footwear has become a global phenomenon. The company's success, in part, has been the result of a strong brand personality with bright colors, ease of use, and odor-preventing materials. However, in the unpredictable world of shoe fashion, the company realizes it must keep creating new products that appeal to its most important market, youth. Consequently it brought out new products including Disney-themed shoes (shoes with holes shaped like Mickey Mouse's silhouette)[27].

EXTERNAL FACTORS SHAPE CONSUMER CHOICES

While internal factors are fundamental in consumer decision making, forces external to the consumer also have a direct and profound effect on the consumer decision process. These factors shape individual wants and behavior, define the products under consideration, target the selection of information sources, and shape the purchase decision. Three wide-ranging external factors that have the most significant impact on consumer choices are: cultural, situational, and social.

Cultural Factors

Culture is a primary driver of consumer behavior because it teaches values and product preferences and, in turn, affects perceptions and attitudes. Beginning in childhood and continuing on throughout life, people respond to the culture in which they live. In recent years, despite the globalization of communications and universal nature of the Internet, people have developed a heightened awareness of their own culture and subculture.

Marketers need to be aware of culture for two reasons. First, learning a target market's culture is essential to an effective marketing strategy. Creating a value proposition that incorporates cultural cues is a prerequisite to success. Second, failing to understand cultural norms has a significant negative effect on product acceptance.

Culture

Culture assimilates shared artifacts such as values, morals, beliefs, art, law, and customs into an organized system that enables people to function as members of society. In school, children learn basic cultural values through interaction with classmates and formal classroom learning. At a very early age, young people learn values and concepts about their culture. Among the values shared by Americans, for example, are achievement, hard work, and freedom while Japanese value social harmony, hierarchy, and devotion.

While culture affects people in many ways, three factors are particularly relevant in consumer behavior: language, values, and nonverbal communications. **Language** is an essential cultural building block and the primary communication tool in society. At the most basic level it is important to understand the language, making sure that words are understood correctly.[28] However, language conveys much more about a society and its values. Scandinavian cultures, for example, place a high value on spending time together. They have more words to express "being together" than English does, and their meaning implies a more intimate sharing of thoughts and ideas. These concepts do not translate into the Anglo-American language and are not easily understood. In addition, language is such an important cultural element that frequently a culture will seek to protect its language. France, for example, has passed a number of laws to prohibit

English words from being used in advertising, banning terms such as *crossover* and *showroom*.[29]

Cultural values are principles shared by a society that assert positive ideals. These principles are often viewed on a continuum. Consider the value of limited versus extended family. In the United States, the obligation and commitment to family is often limited to an individual's immediate family, including their parents, children, and siblings. Most Latin American cultures, on the other hand, have a more wide-ranging definition of family that includes extended family members such as cousins and grandparents and also more inclusive with extended family members living together.

The last cultural factor is **nonverbal communication.** While a number of factors fall into this category (refer to Exhibit 7.6 for a more complete discussion), let's focus on two: time and personal space. The perception of time varies across cultures. Americans and Western Europeans place a high value on time and view it in discrete blocks of hours, days, and weeks. As a result, they focus on scheduling and getting as much done in a given period as possible. Latin Americans and Asians, on the other hand, view time as much more flexible and less discrete. They are not as concerned with the amount of work that gets done in a given time block. How does this affect marketing? Salespeople who have been trained in an American sales environment are often frustrated to find their Asian and Latin American customers less concerned about specific meeting times and more concerned about spending time building a personal relationship.

Personal space is another example of nonverbal communication that varies across cultures. In the United States, for example, most business conversations occur between three and five feet, which is a greater distance than in Latin American cultures. Salespeople used to a three-to-five-foot distance can find it a little disconcerting when the space shrinks to 18 inches to three feet. Not understanding these differences can lead to confusion and embarrassment and even create a problem in the business relationship.[30]

Subculture

As consumer behavior research has discovered more about the role of culture in consumer choices, it has become evident that beyond culture, people are

EXHIBIT 7.6	Nonverbal Communication

Nonverbal Communication: the means of communicating through facial expressions, eye behavior, gestures, posture, and any other body language

Positive nonverbal communication during a presentation	• Eye contact • Smiling • Steady breathing • Tone of voice • Moving closer to the person
Negative nonverbal communication during a presentation	• Swaying • Stuttering • Hands in pockets • Fidgeting • Looking at watch or clock

Caution: Nonverbal communication can contradict what is spoken if not used correctly.

influenced even more significantly by membership in various subcultures. A **subculture** is a group within the culture that shares similar cultural artifacts created by differences in ethnicity, religion, race, or geography. While part of the larger culture, subcultures are also different from each other. The United States is perhaps the best example of a country with a strong national culture that also has a number of distinct subcultures (see Exhibit 7.7).

Several subcultures in the United States have become such powerful forces that companies now develop specific marketing strategies targeted at those groups. Large companies such as Procter & Gamble and General Motors have begun targeting the Hispanic and African-American markets with specific products, distribution channels, and marketing communications. For example, Procter & Gamble created a line of beauty care products called Textures and Tones that includes new products, packaging, and promotional campaigns targeted specifically for African-American women in the United States and Latin America. L'Oreal, the cosmetics company, has a research center outside Chicago that focuses exclusively on the African-American market and has resulted in a number of products in its Soft-Sheen Carson and Mizani brands.[31]

Situational Factors

At various points in the consumer decision process, situational factors play a significant part. Situational factors are time-sensitive and interact with both internal and external factors to affect change in the consumer. Because they are situational, they are difficult, if not impossible, for the marketer to control. However, it is possible to mitigate their effects with a good marketing strategy.

Physical Surroundings

People are profoundly affected by their physical surroundings. An individual viewing an ad on *American Idol* will react differently whether watching the show alone or at a party with friends. Same show, same ad, but a different reaction as a result of the physical surroundings at the time the marketing message is being delivered. As we will see in Chapter 16, retailers devote a lot of time and resources to creating the right physical surrounding to maximize the customer's shopping experience. They know people respond differently to changes in color, lighting, location of the product within the store; indeed, almost every element of the customer's experience is considered important in the consumer choice process.

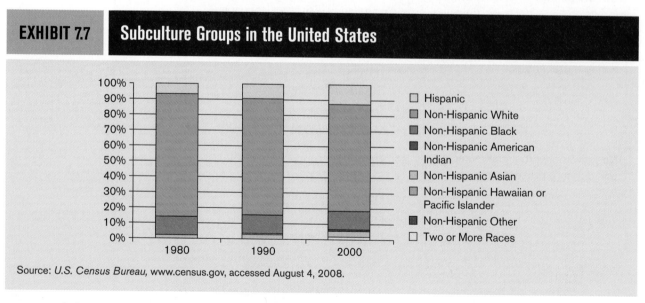

EXHIBIT 7.7 — Subculture Groups in the United States

Source: *U.S. Census Bureau*, www.census.gov, accessed August 4, 2008.

Hospitals have generally not been known for their friendly, warm surroundings but that is changing. Arkansas Children's Hospital recently spent $8 million to create more family space near the patients, adding lockers and laundry facilities and increasing the size of the waiting rooms. The result is higher patient satisfaction, less stress on nurses, and lower overall costs because of lower levels of nurse turnover and more efficient time management. All over the country, hospitals are upgrading their facilities to increase employee and patient satisfaction while lowering costs.[32]

Personal Circumstances

An individual's behavior is always filtered through their immediate personal circumstances. Parents with crying children shop differently than parents with small kids enjoying the experience, and parents without the kids along shop differently than parents with their children present. At the point of consumer choice, many things can influence the final purchase. If the line at the checkout is too long, people may eliminate certain discretionary items or forgo the entire purchase.

While it is not possible for marketers to control personal circumstances, it is important to understand how personal situations influence the choice process. Consider cold medicine such as Tylenol Cold Relief. Johnson & Johnson, maker of Tylenol Cold medicine, knows that people frequently purchase the product when they are not feeling well. As a result, the company makes the product readily available using a wide distribution channel.

Time

Time is a critical situational factor that affects individuals throughout the consumer choice process. An emerging consumer trend in many industrialized countries is the willingness to trade time for money. This is evidenced in a study that reported a majority of Americans would like to have more time for family and are seeking ways to simplify their lives.[33] For many people, time is a resource to be used, spent, or wasted and, for these people the issue is not always the best price but, rather, the best service. Increasingly, customers are asking if the purchase of this product will give them more time or be less of a hassle than another product. Automobile manufacturers and dealers have responded by creating more "hassle-free" shopping experiences. Instead of going through a difficult negotiation process to get the lowest price, dealers are offering low, fixed prices that reduce some of the hassle.

Social Factors

Humans are social beings. Everyone seeks social interaction and acceptance on some level. As people move through life, they affect and, in turn, are affected by various social factors. These factors include groups like their family, social class, reference groups, as well as individual opinion leaders.

Family

The first group any individual belongs to is the family. Families are the single most important buying group and they influence the consumer choice process in two ways. First, the family unit is the most influential teacher of cultural values. Children are socialized into a community and its values primarily through the family unit as they interact with parents, siblings, and extended family members. Second, children learn consumer behavior from their parents. As adults and later parents, they model the behavior first learned as a child.

The most basic definition of a **family** is a group of two or more people living together and related by birth, marriage, or adoption. Historically, in the United States and much of the world, the traditional family included a married couple with children of their own or adopted children. However, the last 40 years have witnessed changes in the family structure. In the 1970s the traditional family comprised 70 percent of all households. Today that number has dropped to a little over half of all households (53 percent).

New family structures are now much more prevalent. These emerging family structures create a number of challenges for marketers.[34] Single-parent households, for example, often report discretionary time is in short supply. Grocery stores have seized on this opportunity by creating deli bars that cater to working fathers and mothers who pick up dinner on their way home from work. Exhibit 7.8 provides a summary of family households in the United States.

The **Household Life Cycle (HLC)** is fundamental to understanding the role of family in the consumer choice process (see Exhibit 7.9). The traditional family life cycle consists of a fairly structured set of activities that begins when single people get married (20s), start a family (30s), raise kids (40s to 50s), watch as the kids grow up and leave home (50s to 60s), and finally enter into retirement (60s and beyond). However, while this model is still relevant in many cases, several new models have emerged to reflect changes in the Household Life Cycle. People are marrying later and putting off the start of a family. Women are having children later in life for a variety of reasons (marry later, focus on career). Couples raise kids then divorce and remarry, creating blended families, or they start new families of their own.

Each group in Exhibit 7.9 offers opportunities and challenges for marketing managers. From basic needs that motivate individuals to engage in the process through information search and then on to final purchase decision, each group thinks and behaves differently. It is essential to identify and understand the HLC group for each target market. Each group makes completely different choices based on their stage in the life cycle.[35] For example, two couples (35 years old, married, professionals) one with two children the other without have very different lifestyles, values, and purchase priorities.

Individual responsibility in family decision making references the way individuals inside the family make decisions. There has been a great deal of research on the roles of various family members in the decision-making process. Across all the purchases in a household, research suggests, not surprisingly, that husbands and wives each dominate decision making in certain categories and jointly participate in others. For example, husbands tend to dominate insurance purchase decisions while wives are primary decision makers in grocery shopping.[36] Children, even at an early age, exert influence and dominate decisions for products such as cereal and indirectly influence decisions on things like vacations. However, traditional family responsibilities are changing as family units change. Single-parent households have shifted traditional purchase decisions. For example, single fathers must take on the responsibility for selecting their child's school.

Social Class

In every society, people are aware of their social status; however, explaining the social class system to someone from outside the culture is often a challenge. People learn about social class and their social status at a very early age from their parents, school, friends, and the media. **Social class** is a ranking of individuals into harmonized groups based on demographic characteristics such as age, education, income, and occupation.

Most Western cultures have no formal social class system; however, there is an informal social ranking. These informal systems exert influence over an individual's attitudes and behavior. Two factors drive social status. Success-driven factors have the greatest effect on social status and include education, income, and occupation. Innate factors, the second category, do not result from anything the individual has done but, rather, are characteristics the individual has inherited from birth. Gender, race, and parents are the primary innate factors determining social status.

Social class is not the result of a single factor, such as income, but rather a complex interaction among many characteristics. While some social class drivers are not in the individual's control, people do make choices about their education and occupation. Therefore, it is possible for people, particularly in societies providing

EXHIBIT 7.8 Breakdown of U.S. Households

Subject	1950	1960	1970	1980	1990	2000
HOUSEHOLDS BY TYPE						
Total households	100.0	100.0	100.0	100.0	100.0	100.0
Family households	89.4	84.9	80.3	73.2	70.2	68.1
Nonfamily households	10.6	15.1	19.7	26.8	29.8	31.9
1 member	9.5	13.3	17.6	22.7	24.6	25.8
2 or more members	1.1	1.7	2.1	4.1	5.3	6.1
FAMILY TYPE BY PRESENCE OF OWN CHILDREN UNDER 18 YEARS						
Total families	100.0	100.0	100.0	100.0	100.0	100.0
No own children under 18 years	48.1	43.1	45.1	48.8	52.1	51.8
With own children 18 years	51.9	56.9	54.9	51.2	47.9	48.2
Under 6 years only	(NA)	13.9	12.7	12.4	12.2	11.2
Under 6 years and 6 to 17 years	(NA)	16.9	13.4	9.7	9.9	9.6
6 to 17 years only	(NA)	26.1	28.7	29.0	25.7	27.4
Married-couple families	100.0	100.0	100.0	100.0	100.0	100.0
No own children under 18 years	44.9	40.7	44.3	49.8	53.7	54.4
With own children under 18 years	55.1	59.3	55.7	50.2	46.3	45.6
Under 6 years only	(NA)	15.1	13.5	12.8	12.3	10.8
Under 6 years and 6 to 17 years	(NA)	18.1	13.9	10.0	10.1	9.8
6 to 17 years only	(NA)	26.1	28.3	27.3	23.9	25.0
Female householder, no husband present	100.0	100.0	100.0	100.0	100.0	100.0
No own children under 18 years	66.0	54.9	45.4	39.8	43.5	41.4
With own children under 18 years	34.0	45.1	54.6	60.2	56.5	58.6
Under 6 years only	(NA)	6.4	8.9	11.3	11.9	11.9
Under 6 years and 6 to 17 years	(NA)	10.2	11.8	9.7	10.2	9.9
6 to 17 years only	(NA)	28.5	33.9	39.3	34.4	36.9
Male householder, no wife present	100.0	100.0	100.0	100.0	100.0	100.0
No own children under 18 years	80.7	76.7	70.0	61.5	56.9	50.1
With own children under 18 years	19.3	23.3	30.0	38.5	43.1	49.9
Under 6 years only	(NA)	3.2	3.9	8.7	12.3	13.5
Under 6 years and 6 to 17 years	(NA)	3.7	4.3	3.8	5.6	6.5
6 to 17 years only	(NA)	16.3	21.9	25.9	25.2	29.8
HOUSEHOLDS BY AGE OF HOUSEHOLDER						
Total households	100.0	100.0	100.0	100.0	100.0	100.0
Under 65 years	84.8	82.5	80.7	79.9	78.3	79.0
Under 25 years	4.8	5.1	7.3	8.3	5.5	5.2
25 to 34 years	20.5	18.4	18.3	22.8	21.6	17.3
35 to 44 years	22.7	22.1	18.6	17.4	22.2	22.7
45 to 54 years	20.2	20.4	36.5	15.7	15.6	20.2
55 to 64 years	16.5	16.5	(NA)	15.7	13.5	13.5
65 years and over	15.2	17.5	19.3	20.1	21.7	21.0
65 to 74 years	10.8	12.1	(NA)	12.4	12.5	10.9
75 to 84 years	4.4	4.7	(NA)	7.7	7.4	7.8
85 years and over	(NA)	0.7	(NA)	(NA)	1.8	2.3
ONE-PERSON HOUSEHOLDS BY SEX AND AGE OF HOUSEHOLDER						
Total	(NA)	100.0	100.0	100.0	100.0	100.0
Male	(NA)	37.2	35.7	38.9	40.8	43.3
Female	(NA)	62.8	64.3	61.1	59.2	56.7
Under 65 years	(NA)	59.0	55.6	61.2	60.9	64.3
Male	(NA)	25.1	24.7	30.9	32.3	34.5
Female	(NA)	33.8	31.0	30.3	28.6	29.8
65 Years and over	(NA)	41.0	44.4	38.8	39.1	35.7
Male	(NA)	12.1	11.0	7.9	8.4	8.8
Female	(NA)	29.0	33.3	30.9	30.7	26.9

Source: U.S. Census Bureau, decennial census of population, 1940 to 2000; decennial census of housing, 1940 to 2000, www.census.gov.

EXHIBIT 7.9 | Stages in the Household Life Cycle

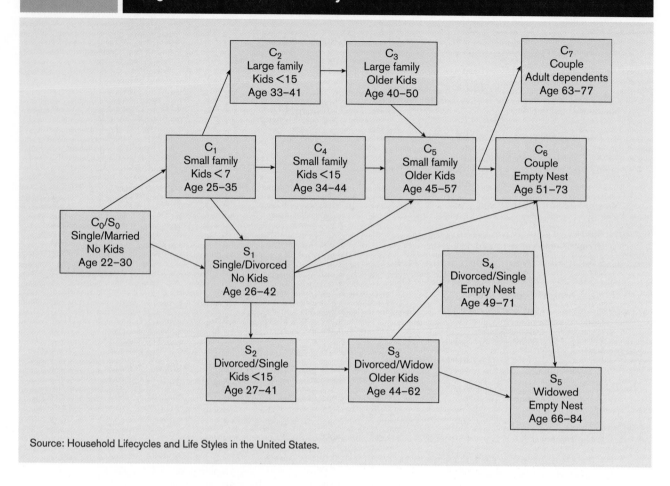

Source: Household Lifecycles and Life Styles in the United States.

educational opportunities, to move into new social classes based on their achievements. In addition, the availability of easy credit, creative pricing, and new financing arrangements enable and even encourage people to engage in aspirational purchases. **Aspirational purchases** are products bought outside the individual's social standing. Over 50 percent of the luxury cars sold in the United States are leased. By offering special financing terms, individuals with lower income levels now drive a BMW, Mercedes-Benz, or Lexus. This enables people to drive a car they normally could not afford, an aspirational purchase.

From a marketing perspective, the impact of social status on consumption behavior is profound, affecting everything from the media people choose to view (lower classes watch more TV while upper classes tend to read more) to the products they buy (lower classes tend to buy more generics while the upper classes select more branded products).

Retail stores create different products mixes based on the social status of the shoppers at that store. Target, for example, maintains the same basic product mix across all its stores. However, it does add higher-priced brand names in stores serving primarily upper-class neighborhoods while stores with a middle-class demographic get a slightly different product mix.

Opinion Leaders

The previous discussion on external factors focused primarily on group influences such as social and cultural factors; however, external factors also include personal influences. Consider, for example, Walter Mossberg, technology writer for *The Wall Street Journal.* His columns reviewing and commenting on new technologies are widely read and highly regarded. Jerry Yang, co-founder of Yahoo, says Mossberg is "one of the most trusted and influential voices in technology."[37] People listen and then respond to his columns. The day after he gave a positive review to Mailblocks, a spam blocker, sales tripled. Mossberg is an example of an influential opinion leader. His expertise in technology products and services makes him an information source for many people and an opinion leader.

Opinion leaders fulfill an important role by classifying, explaining, and then bestowing information, most often to family and friends but occasionally to a broader audience, as is the case with Walter Mossberg. People seek out opinion leaders for a variety of reasons, including unfamiliarity with a product, reassurance about a product selection before purchasing, and anxiety resulting from high involvement with the purchase of a particular product. Anyone whose opinions are valued by the individual can be an opinion leader. For instance, the friend who enjoys cars could be an opinion leader about automobiles; the relative with a background in information technology might be the expert on technology.

Burberry has historically targeted wealthy individuals with their expensive clothes and accessories. However, more recently the company has introduced less expensive items to appeal to a broader target audience.

While opinion leaders are often defined by product class, such as Mossberg's expertise in technology, another influential group has emerged. This new group, whose members are called **market mavens,** has information about many kinds of products, places to shop, and other facets of markets, and the members initiate discussions with consumers and respond to requests from consumers for market information.[38] The key difference between opinion leaders and market mavens is the focus on their market knowledge. Market mavens have a broader understanding and expertise that goes beyond product to include other elements of the purchase decision such as shopping experience and price.

In their role as information gatekeepers, opinion leaders and market mavens exert influence over an individual's product and brand choice. As a result, marketers seek to understand the roles of these two groups so they can identify the members and, in turn, encourage them to try a particular product. Marketers encourage these individuals using these activities:

- Market research. As a primary source of information for interested individuals, it is critical that opinion leaders and market mavens are familiar with a product and understand its advertising so they can convey the information accurately. Many market researchers focus on the way these individuals interpret messages to ensure the marketing mix is working correctly.

- Product sampling. Testing a product is an essential part of any gatekeeper's acceptance. As a result, the leaders are prime targets for product sampling.

- Advertising. Companies use opinion leaders and market mavens to influence decision makers whether it is a business leader or an individual consumer. Accenture Consulting hired Tiger Woods as its spokesperson because he is an opinion leader. The company hopes Tiger's qualities—successful, focused, and a winner—influence business leaders looking for a consulting firm.

References Groups

Everyone identifies with and is influenced by groups. In most cases, the individual may belong to the group or seek membership, while in other situations the group is perceived negatively and the individual works to disassociate himself. A **reference group** is group of individuals whose beliefs, attitudes, and behavior influence (positively or negatively) the beliefs, attitudes, and behavior of an individual.[39] Three characteristics are used to categorize reference groups: association, desirability, and degree of affiliation.

The association with reference groups can be formal or informal. Students, for example, have a formal relationship with their college or university and, as a result, respond to and connect with other students at the school. At the same time, a student has a number of informal relationships with other groups. Circles of friends and classmates, while not a formal group, can exert a lot of influence over an individual.

A key characteristic impacting the degree a group affects the individual is the extent to which an individual desires to be associated with the group. **Desirability** is the extent and direction of the emotional connection an individual wishes to have with a particular group. Individuals can really want to belong to a group or not, and the linkage can be either positive or negative. Sports teams encourage participation at many levels. Like many cities, Boston has a number of established sports teams, including the Red Sox, Patriots, Celtics, and Bruins, each with thousands of supporters, though the level of support varies widely. Dedicated fans with the available resources become season-ticket holders, spending thousands of dollars to attend every game. Many Boston residents are not actively involved with any team or are ardent fans of one team but show less interest in the others. Some Boston residents may even support teams from other cities, perhaps the New York Yankees, and hold negative perceptions of the local team. As a result, the desirability of belonging to the reference group known as a "Boston sports fan" is person- and even team-specific.

The **degree of affiliation** indicates the amount of interpersonal contact an individual has with the reference group. **Primary groups** are marked by frequent contact, while less frequent or limited dealings are known as **secondary groups.** Individuals come in frequent contact with co-workers, close friends, and other groups such as religious, special-interest, or hobby groups that may be primary or secondary depending on the level of contact. Over time, the degree of affiliation will likely change; for example, when someone changes jobs the primary group of co-workers will also change.

> Kids have found a new place to socialize in online virtual worlds produced especially for them. WebKinz, created by Canadian toymaker Ganz, sells plush toys with passwords that allow kids ages 8 to 12 free access to the site. Online, the puppy or monkey plush toy comes alive. Kids adopt the pet, give it a name and gender, then get "jobs" to support it, play games, enter trivia contests, and have chat sessions. Internet marketers are interested in this platform because children spend more than two hours per visit on WebKinz compared to 31 minutes on YouTube.[40]

THE LEVEL OF INVOLVEMENT INFLUENCES THE PROCESS

One significant outcome of motivation, discussed earlier, is **involvement** with the product because it mediates the product choice decision. Involvement is activated by three elements: the individual's background and psychological profile, the aspirational focus, and the environment at the time of the purchase decision. As we noted, motivation is unique to each individual and drives purchase decisions. Aspirational focus is anything of interest to the buyer and is not limited to the product itself. It is possible to be involved with a brand, advertising, or activities that occur with product use.

Many people ride motorcycles but far fewer ride Harley-Davidson motorcycles and, among Harley riders, some get tattoos of the Harley-Davidson logo. Clearly these people are highly involved beyond the product and associate strongly with the Harley lifestyle. Finally, the environment changes the level of involvement. Time, for example, can limit involvement if there is pressure to make a decision quickly but can enhance involvement if there is sufficient time to fully engage in the decision process. Involvement influences every step in the choice decision process, and as a result, marketers create strategies based on high and low levels of involvement. For example, high-involvement purchases drive buyers to more cognitive learning such as the new car buyer who visits car dealers, checks out automotive Web sites, and seeks out the advice of automotive experts for information on cars in an effort to make an informed purchase decision. On the other hand, conditioning works well with low-involvement purchases such as the purchase of gasoline where people frequently purchase from the same station because of various factors such as price and location.[41]

Decision Making with High Involvement

Greater motivation that leads to greater involvement results in a more active and committed choice decision process. When someone is concerned with the outcome of the process, they will spend more time learning about product options and become more emotionally connected to the process and the decision. Someone stimulated to acquire new information is engaged in **high-involvement learning.** For example, someone interested in purchasing a new digital camera will seek out product reviews in *Consumer Reports* and online sources to discover information that will assist in the choice decision. Some, despite a brand preference, may be willing to experiment with other brands and seek out additional information looking for a new alternative. A high level of involvement usually means the entire process takes longer. High-involvement consumers report high levels of satisfaction in their purchase decision. This is not surprising since these consumers spend more time engaged in the decision process and, therefore, are more comfortable in their decision.

Many companies look to high-involvement customers for insights on product development and strategy. Starwood Hotels and Resorts asked hundreds of its most traveled customers to participate in an online community for the purpose of developing a new hotel concept—Aloft. The managers wanted to know how best to improve the hotel experience, how to brand the product, what services to include, and even the design of furniture in the rooms. Starwood then invited these customers to test the Aloft prototype in Second Life's virtual world[42].

Decision Making with Limited Involvement

While high-involvement purchases are more significant to the consumer, the vast majority of purchases involve limited or low involvement. From the purchase of gasoline to the choice of restaurants, decisions are often made almost automatically, often out of habit, with little involvement in the purchase decision. The reality is that consumers tend to focus their time and energy on high-involvement purchases while making many purchases with little or no thought at all.

Low-involvement learning happens when people are not prompted to value new information. This is more prevalent than high-involvement learning because the vast majority of marketing stimuli occur when there is little or no interest in the information. People do not watch TV for the commercials, they watch for the programming; advertising is just part of the viewing experience. Likewise, print advertising exists alongside articles and is often ignored. While people are not actively seeking the information, they are exposed to advertising and this, in turn, affects their attitudes about a brand. Research suggests that people shown ads in a low-involvement setting are more likely to include those brands in the choice decision process. Low-involvement consumers spend little time comparing product attributes and frequently identify very few differences across brands. Because the decision is relatively unimportant, they will often purchase the product with the best shelf position or lowest price with no evaluation of salient product characteristics.[43]

Marketers consider several strategies in targeting low-involvement consumers. The objective of these strategies is to raise consumer involvement with the product. Generally, time is the defining characteristic for these strategies. Short-term strategies involve using sales promotions such as coupons, rebates, or discounts to encourage trying the product and then hoping the consumers will raise their product involvement. Long-term strategies are more difficult to implement. Marketers seek to focus on the product's value proposition, creating products with additional product features, better reliability, or more responsive service to increase customer satisfaction. Additionally, strong marketing communications campaigns that speak to consumer issues or concerns can raise involvement with the product. A classic example of this tactic is Michelin's highly effective and long-running advertising campaign that links a relatively low-involvement product, tires, with a significant consumer concern, family safety. Tires are not typically a high-involvement product, however, when the voiceover on the commercial says, "Because so much is riding on your tires" while showing a baby riding in the car, consumer involvement in the product and more specifically the brand increases.

While a low-involvement consumer demonstrates little or no brand loyalty, they are also, by definition, open to brand switching. As a result, brands can experience significant gains in consumer acceptance with an effective, comprehensive marketing strategy.

THE CONSUMER DECISION-MAKING PROCESS

Every day, people make a number of consumer decisions. From breakfast through the last television show watched before going to bed, people are choosing products as a result of a decision-making process. Learning about that process is a vital step for marketers trying to create an effective marketing strategy.

Years of consumer research have resulted in a five-stage model of consumer decision making. While not everyone passes through all five stages for every purchase, all consumers apply the same fundamental sequence beginning with problem recognition, followed by search for information, evaluation of alternatives, product choice decision, and finally post-purchase evaluation. Each time a purchase decision is made, the individual begins to evaluate the product in preparation for the next decision (see Exhibit 7.10)

However, as noted earlier, someone driving home from work does not go through an extensive search for information or evaluate a number of alternatives in purchasing gasoline for the car. In all likelihood, the consumer buys from a station he or she knows well and shops at regularly. Nevertheless, this model is helpful because it illustrates what can be called the "complete decision-making process," which occurs when people are fully involved in the purchase.

Problem Recognition

Every purchase decision made by an individual is initiated by a problem or need that drives the consumer decision-making process. Problems or needs are the result of differences between a person's real and preferred state.

People live in the perceived reality of present time or **real state.** At the same time, people also have desires that reflect how they would like to feel or live in the present time and this is known as a **preferred state.** When the two states are in

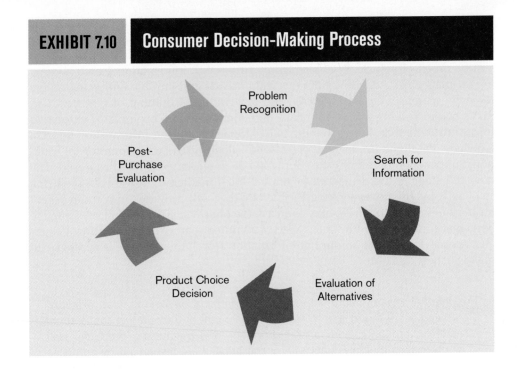

| EXHIBIT 7.10 | Consumer Decision-Making Process |

Problem Recognition

Search for Information

Evaluation of Alternatives

Product Choice Decision

Post-Purchase Evaluation

balance, the individual does not require anything and no purchase occurs. However, where there is a discrepancy in the two states, a problem is created and the consumer decision-making process begins.

The discrepancy, or gap, can be created by internal or external drivers. Internal drivers are basic human needs such as hunger and security. Someone is hungry (real state) and wants to eat (preferred state). This will lead to a number of choices: eat at home, dine out, or go to the grocery store. It may even trigger other options such as calling a friend, which addresses a need for social interaction. External drivers happen as people interact with the world. Some of these triggers result from a company's marketing efforts but most arise when an individual experiences something that creates a desire, like seeing a friend driving a new car or hearing about a good new restaurant.

Despite internal or external stimuli, people do not respond to every gap between a real and preferred state. Sometimes the disparity is not sufficient to drive the person to action. A person may want a new car but does not act on that feeling because he or she lacks the financial resources or simply cannot justify the purchase. When the conflict between real and preferred states reaches a certain level, the decision-making process begins.

Marketers need to understand problem recognition for several reasons. First, it is essential to learn about the problems and needs of the target market to create value-added products. Second, key elements of an effective marketing strategy, particularly communication, are predicated on a good knowledge of problem recognition triggers. For example, the classic advertising campaign by the California Milk Processor Board, "Got Milk," spoke directly to the recognition of the problem—do you have milk in your refrigerator. The success of the campaign has been credited with reinvigorating the sale of cow's milk since the ads started running in the early 1990s.

Search for Information

Once a problem is recognized and action is required, people seek information to facilitate the best decision. The search for information is not categorical; rather, it operates on a continuum from limited to extensive. Consider the following examples. A couple notices the low-fuel light comes on as they are driving home from a party. The driver recalls their "local" station is on the way home and, without any additional information, stops at the station and fills up the car. This is an example of **minimal information search.** The same couple now finds out they are going to have a baby and realize their Infiniti G35 coupe has to be replaced with a more practical vehicle. They engage in a thorough information search reviewing car magazines, soliciting opinions from friends and family, conducting online research, reading *Consumer Reports,* and test-driving a number of new cars and SUVs before making a final purchase decision. This is an example of **extensive information search.** Between these two extremes is **limited information search,** which, as the name implies, involves some, albeit restricted, search for information. Suppose the wife from the couple in our previous examples has a cold. The husband stops at the drugstore to get her some medicine. At the cold medicine aisle he scans the boxes looking for the one that will provide "maximum relief" for his wife's symptoms. He may even ask the pharmacist for help in selecting the best choice. At this point he is engaged in a limited search for information. Generally, people do only the amount of information search they believe is necessary to make the best decision.

> The Internet makes more information available to everyone. For example, broadband users report that more than 10 percent of their time online is spent researching products, comparison shopping, and purchasing products. Half of all purchases by individuals with online access are influenced by an online information source. Finally, the amount of time spent online researching a product category suggests consumers are seeking more information to help them become better, more informed buyers[44].

Tylenol Cold provides a great deal of information on the package to help consumers make a decision in the store at the point of purchase.

Information Sources

There are two basic sources of information: internal and external. **Internal information search,** as the name implies, is all information stored in memory and accessed by the individual. This is always the first place people consider for information. Past experiences, conversations, research, preexisting beliefs and attitudes create an extensive internal database that is tapped by the individual once the problem is recognized. In our example of the car low on gas, the driver searched internal information and found past experiences provided sufficient information to make a decision.

Even when additional information is needed, internal information is used to frame the external search. Price limits and key performance metrics, criteria often used in the evaluation of alternatives, are frequently derived from information stored in memory. People gather and process information even if they are not actively involved in the purchase decision process. Consequently, an individual's internal information is changing all the time. As people get older, gain more experience with a product or brand, and gather more information, they often rely more on internal information and conduct a less external information search.

The second fundamental source of information is external. Once people have determined internal information is not sufficient to make the purchase decision, they seek information from outside sources. **External information sources** include independent groups (sources), personal associations (friend and family), marketer-created information (sales brochures, advertising), and experiences (product trial and demonstrations).

An organization's marketing communications represent only one source, albeit an important one, among several external information source options. However, company marketing communications can play an important role in influencing other sources of information such as personal contacts. For example, when Johnson & Johnson introduces new baby care products, it spends a lot of money providing product samples and information for pediatricians and nurses in an effort to support the company's direct marketing communications to young mothers. So even though consumers indicate company-sponsored marketing information is of limited value in making purchase decisions, the company's marketing efforts can play a more significant role when considered in light of their effect on other external information sources. Exhibit 7.11 is a summary of external information sources and highlights the diversity of available information resources.

Defining the Set of Alternatives

At some point in the search for information, often during the internal information search, people begin to limit the number of alternatives under consideration. From a practical perspective, it is simply not possible to gather and process information on many different options. This is known as bounded rationality and defines people's limited capacity to process information.

People begin with a very large set of possible alternatives known as the **complete set.** This set includes a variety of options across different brands and perhaps even products. Consider a person looking for mobile, wireless Internet access. The complete set could include different product options (PDA, cell phone, laptop computer) and brands (Apple, Dell, Sony, Toshiba, Hewlett-Packard, Nokia,

| EXHIBIT 7.11 | Sources of External Information |

External Information Sources	Example	Marketing Implications
Independent groups	*Consumer Reports* *Consumer's Union*	Favorable reviews from independent sources are an important source of external information. Marketers need a strategy to reach independent sources with relevant information.
Personal associations	Family Friends	These associations can be an important external source of information in certain decisions. Marketers seek to influence reference groups and opinion leaders through favorable product reviews and effective marketing communications.
Marketer information	Advertising	Effective marketing communications reinforce messages to other external information sources such as independent groups.
Experiential	Product trials	Product samples for certain categories such as food are easy to provide. Encourage people to seek out product trials and demonstrations when a sample is not appropriate (electronics, automobiles).

and Motorola). Based on the individual's choice criteria, however, this large set of possible options will be reduced. Keep in mind that the complete set is not *all* options available to the buyer; rather, the set is the options that the buyer is aware of when the search process begins. The extent of the buyer's knowledge about the problem and available options determines the set of possible alternatives in the complete set.

As consumers move through the search for information, certain products (PDAs) may be eliminated in favor of others (cell phones) and brands will be evaluated and discarded. The **awareness set** reduces the number of options. At a minimum, the number of different product categories, if considered, will be reduced and some brands discarded. Interestingly, the awareness set can include choices across product categories. In our example, it is still possible for a particular brand of PDA and cell phone to remain in the awareness set despite the fact they are different product categories. From the awareness set, individuals conduct an additional information search. Based on additional information and evaluation, a **consideration (evoked) set** is created, which encompasses the strongest options. It is from the consideration set that the product decision is made.

Marketers are vitally interested in learning about the information search process for two reasons. First, marketers must identify important external information sources so they can direct their resources to the most effective external sources. Second, they must learn how consumers choose products for inclusion in their awareness and consideration sets to create marketing strategies that increase the probability of being in the consideration set.

Evaluation of Alternatives

Concurrent with the search for information are the analysis and evaluation of possible product choices. As we discussed previously, consumers move, sometimes quickly, from many options to a more restricted awareness set and from there to a final consideration set from which a decision is made. During this process, the individual is constantly evaluating the alternatives based on internal and external information.

The consumer choice process is complex and ever changing. Environmental and personal factors at the moment of decision dramatically affect the purchase decision. As a result, it is impossible to develop a consumer choice model for every purchase. However, years of research suggest consumers make product choices primarily from three perspectives: emotional, attitude based, and attribute based.

Emotional Choice

Not all purchases are made strictly for rational reasons. Indeed, product choices can be **emotional choices,** based on attitudes about a product, or based on attributes of the product depending on the situation. Frequently, the product choice encompasses a mix of all three. An individual goes to Starbucks for the personal pleasure of enjoying a cappuccino (emotional). That same person also considers Starbucks the best choice for getting together with friends after evaluating other choices (attitude based). Finally, the individual finds Starbucks' cappuccinos simply taste better than other competitors (attribute based).

While emotions have been considered an important factor in decision making for many years, it is only recently that marketers began to develop specific marketing strategies targeting emotion-based decisions. Product design and execution even focus on creating an emotional response to the product. From there, marketing communications connect the product to the target audience using images and words that convey an emotional connection. Exhibit 7.12 shows an ad that communicates emotion to the reader.

Attitude-Based Choice

Early in the evaluation of alternatives, people regularly use beliefs and values to direct their assessment. As consumers create the awareness set, they discard or include products and brands using existing attitudes. **Attitude-based choices** tend to be more holistic, using summary impressions rather than specific attributes to evaluate the options and affect even important purchases such as a car or house. It is not uncommon for beliefs to affect the actual product decision. For example, "it is important to buy cars made in America" or the opposite, "foreign cars are better than American products." When two brands are judged to be relatively the same, people frequently look to existing attitudes to guide their decision. When someone responds to a question about why he bought a particular product with, "I always buy . . ." or "this is the only brand I use . . ." they are likely making an attitude-based choice decision.

Attribute-Based Choice

By far the most prevalent approach to product decisions is **attribute-based choice** based on the premise that product choices are made by comparing brands across a defined set of attributes. These evaluative attributes are the product features or benefits considered relevant to

| EXHIBIT 7.12 | Ketel One Offers an Emotional Choice |

Ketel One is connecting to their customers on an emotional level reinforcing the old adage - "One picture is worth a thousand words."

the specific problem addressed in the purchase decision. Antilock brakes are a product feature that translates into a consumer benefit—better control in a hazardous situation. Most consumers could not describe how antilock brakes actually work but are quite aware of the benefits and would eliminate a car from the choice process if it failed to have that product feature. Not all evaluative attributes are tangible. Brand image, prestige, attitudes about a brand or product can also be used as evaluative criteria.

> Kohl's Department Stores has been successful targeting family-oriented "middle-class soccer moms." Recently, the company has targeted younger, professional women by bringing in designer labels such as Candies (shoes) and Elle. With a focus on value and convenience, Kohl's connects with customers on two key attributes critical to their purchase decisions.[45]

Product Choice Decision

The end result of evaluating product alternatives is an intended purchase option. Until the actual purchase, it is still only an "intended" option because any number of events or interactions can happen to dissuade or alter the final purchase decision. Four purchase event characteristics affect the actual choice decision:

Physical surroundings–the environment for the purchase. From store colors to the employees, consumers respond to their physical environment. For example, while the color red creates awareness and interest, it also creates feelings of anxiety and negativity. Blue is calmer and considered the most conducive in creating positive feeling with the customer. Crowding can have a negative effect on purchase decisions because, if the store becomes too crowded, people will forgo the purchase, perhaps going somewhere else.

Social circumstances–the social interaction at the time of purchase. Shopping is a social activity and people are influenced by the social interaction at the time of purchase. Trying on an outfit alone may lead to the purchase; however, when putting on the outfit while shopping with a friend, it is unlikely the clothing will be purchased if the friend does not like it.

Time–the amount of time an individual has to make the purchase. The product choice decision can be affected by time pressure. The consumer will be less willing to wait for the best solution and more likely to purchase an acceptable alternative.

State of mind–individual's state of mind at time of purchase. An individual's mood influences the purchase decision. People in a positive state of mind are more likely to browse. Negative mood states are less tolerant and lead to increased impulse and compulsive purchases.

As a result of these purchase event characteristics, the intended purchase can be altered despite the information search and evaluation process. Some of these characteristics are at least nominally in the marketer's control. Other characteristics, such as an individual's state of mind, are uncontrollable and must be dealt with at the moment of purchase by employees who, it is hoped, have the skills and training needed to handle difficult situations.[46]

The final purchase decision is not a single decision, but rather, the consumer confronts five important decisions:

What: select the product and, more specifically, the brand. Included as part of the product choice are decisions about product features, service options, and other characteristics of the product experience

Where: select the point of purchase. Select the retailer and, increasingly, the channel–retail store (bricks) or online (clicks)–through which the product is to be purchased.

How much: choose the specific quantity to be purchased. For example, warehouse clubs, such as Sam's Club and Costco, offer consumer options on purchase quantity. If you have the ability to store products, it is possible to save money by purchasing in larger quantities.

When: select the timing of the purchase. The timing of the purchase can make a difference in the final purchase price. Car dealers traditional offer better deals at the end of the month as they try to meet monthly sales quotas. Through sales and other marketing communications, marketers encourage consumers to purchase sooner rather than later.

Payment: choose the method of payment. The selection of a payment method makes a big difference to the consumer and marketer. Marketers want to make it easy for the consumer to purchase; however, not all payment methods are equal. Credit cards charge the retailer a fee that, in turn, is passed back to the consumer. One payment method, the debit card, is becoming popular with younger adults and combines the convenience of a credit card with the fiscal responsibility of using cash. Indeed, the consumer can often choose to not purchase the product at all, as other choices are available besides purchase. They can rent or lease products such as automobiles, making it possible to use products they could not normally afford.

Consumers make a number of decisions at the point of purchase. Often, the selection of where the product will be purchased is done in conjunction with the product evaluation.

Post-Purchase Assessment

Once the purchase is complete, consumers begin to evaluate their decision. Attitudes change as they experience and interact with the product. These attitudinal changes include the way the consumer looks at competitors as well as the product itself. At the same time, marketers want to foster and encourage the relationship and, as we discussed in Chapter 4, increasingly focus resources to build the customer relationship. Most of a CRM program is built around the customer's experience after the purchase. The four critical characteristics of post-purchase assessment are: dissonance, use/nonuse, disposition, and satisfaction/dissatisfaction.

Dissonance

High-involvement, large purchases often lead to a level of doubt or anxiety known as **post-purchase dissonance.** Most purchases occur with little or no dissonance.[47] The likelihood of dissonance increases if one or more of the following purchase decision attributes are present: (1) a high degree of commitment that is not easily revoked; (2) a high degree of importance for the customer; (3) alternatives are rated equally and the purchase decision is not clear. Also, the individual's own predisposition for anxiety can create additional dissonance. Big-ticket purchases frequently include several of those characteristics. For example, buying a house, the single biggest purchase most people will ever make, is a big commitment that can be complicated when two or three homes are evaluated as more or less equal by the consumer.

How do consumers reduce dissonance? The single most effective method is a thorough information search and evaluation of alternatives. When consumers are confident that due diligence has been done, they have less anxiety after the purchase. If dissonance remains a problem, additional information can be sought to reduce anxiety and reinforce the decision. Marketers can direct marketing communications to reduce dissonance particularly with large purchases such as automobiles. As part of a CRM program, many companies follow up with customers after the purchase to assess their satisfaction.

Use/Nonuse

Consumers buy a product to use. Marketers are acutely interested in learning how customers use the product for several reasons. First, it is important the customer knows how to use the product correctly. Buying a new television can quickly become a negative experience if it is not set up properly. As a result, marketers want to be sure the customer understands how the product is to be used and any setup procedures that may be needed to ensure proper function. Second, a satisfied customer means a greater likelihood of additional purchases. Buying and riding a bicycle means the consumer is more likely to buy a helmet, light, bike rack, and other accessories.

Many products are purchased but not used or at least not consumed immediately. Some products are returned because the consumer has a negative experience such as a defective product. Marketers, of course, work to avoid a negative experience. Building customer relationships and making sure the customer understands the product and how it is to be used reduce the probability of consumers returning the product. Another potential post-purchase problem can be that the product is purchased and not used. In these situations, marketers seek to stimulate product usage. Campbell Soup Co. found customers frequently had several

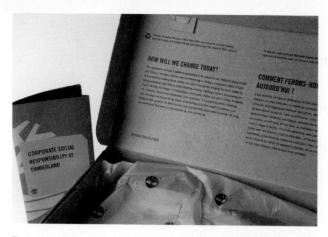

Timberland is one of many companies that uses recycled materials in its packaging.

cans of soup on their shelf for long periods of time. The company developed a marketing communications program to encourage faster consumption of the product. Many packaged foods include expiration dates encouraging consumers to use the product quickly and repurchase.

Disposal

Increasingly, marketers are concerned about how products are disposed of once they are no longer in use. Environmental concerns consistently rank as a major issue for consumers in many parts of the world. People living in the United States, for example, produce nearly 2,000 pounds (1 ton) of garbage per person every year. Once a product is consumed, in most cases, a physical object remains and needs to be disposed of. New technologies such as computer CPUs and monitors are particularly difficult to discard because they contain dangerous chemicals.

Environmentally friendly products encourage proper use and disposal. Companies including Coca-Cola use recycled materials in their manufacturing and packaging. At the same time, companies are encouraging consumers to recycle on their own. Dell and other computer companies have a program that encourages consumers to recycle their old computers.[48]

Satisfaction/Dissatisfaction

Consumers evaluate every aspect of the product. As previously noted, this includes any dissonance present at the time of purchase, use or nonuse of the product, the product disposition, the purchase experience, and even the value equation. This results in the consumer's satisfaction or dissatisfaction with the product and purchase decision. In addition, various dimensions of the overall experience will be satisfactory or unsatisfactory. A customer may love the product, but dislike the dealer or retailer.

Most products are evaluated on two dimensions—instrumental performance and symbolic performance. **Instrumental performance** relates to the actual performance features of the product and answers the question: Did the product do what is what supposed to do? **Symbolic performance** refers to the image-building aspects of the product and answers the question: Did the product make me feel better about myself? A product that performs poorly on instrumental dimensions will ultimately lead to dissatisfaction. However, for a consumer to be fully satisfied with the product, it must perform well both instrumentally and symbolically. A new Hyundai automobile may have scored high on instrumental performance but low on symbolic performance. Is the customer dissatisfied? No, but it is not certain that person will purchase another Hyundai.

There are two primary outcomes of consumer dissatisfaction with a product: a customer will either change his or her behavior or do nothing. When a customer has an unfavorable experience at the bank, she may not leave but her opinion of the bank diminishes. Over time, this will erode the consumer's evaluation of the bank. The second result of consumer dissatisfaction is a change in behavior. The consumer may simply choose to stop shopping at that store or purchasing a particular product. Another option is to complain to management. Marketers are aware that for every complaint, there are eight "quiet" but dissatisfied consumers who chose to walk away. An even greater concern is consumers telling friends about a bad experience or complaining to government agencies. Finally, dissatisfied consumers who believe their legal rights have been violated may take legal action for damages related to the purchase experience.

SUMMARY

A thorough knowledge and understanding of customers is an essential element in developing an effective value proposition. For business-to-consumer companies this means learning about how and why consumers buy products and services. This chapter talks about the consumer buying decision process. We discuss the two complex, critical forces (internal and external) that shape the consumer decision-making process. We offer an in-depth analysis of the process a consumer uses in making a purchase decision. The distinction is made between high- and low-involvement decisions, which dramatically affects the degree to which the consumer engages in the entire buying decision process.

KEY TERMS

demographics 174
family life cycle 176
lifestyle 178
gender roles 178
motivation 180
attitude 181
multiattribute model 182
perception 182
selective awareness 182
selective distortion 183
selective retention 183
memory 183
short-term memory 183
long-term memory 183
learning 184
conditioning 184
cognitive learning 184
personality 185

brand personality 185
culture 186
language 186
cultural values 187
nonverbal communication 187
subculture 188
family 189
Household Life Cycle (HLC) 190
social class 190
aspirational purchases 192
opinion leaders 193
market mavens 193
reference group 194
desirability 194
degree of affiliation 194
primary group 194
secondary group 194
involvement 194

high-involvement learning 195
low-involvement learning 195
real state 196
preferred state 196
minimal information search 198
extensive information search 198
limited information search 198
internal information search 198
external information sources 199
complete set 199
awareness set 200
consideration (evoked) set 200
emotional choice 200
attitude-based choice 201
attribute-based choice 201
post-purchase dissonance 203
instrumental performance 204
symbolic performance 204

APPLICATION QUESTIONS

1. As we have discussed, understanding the consumers in a target market is critical to creating an effective value proposition. Assume you are the vice president of marketing for Regal Cinemas. What do you think is the demographic profile (including the age, income, and life cycle stage) of your largest target market? As part of a mini-market research project, visit a movie theater on a weekend and track the people entering. How old are they? Are they families or people meeting friends?

2. You are the marketing manager for the Bowflex Series 7 treadmills. You believe the product appeals to both men and women. As you develop the marketing strategy, what differences might you consider in the product based on whether a man or woman is buying? What about the marketing communications (message, choice of media)?

3. Disneyland has traditionally marketed to families; recently, however, new household life cycle patterns have led to changes in the marketing strategy. Identify three household life cycle stages that Disney may want to consider in the future.

4. The consumer decision process varies by purchase for each individual. Compare and contrast the consumer decision-making process you go through in buying gas for your car with the purchase of a new home entertainment system. How are the processes similar and how are the two purchase decisions different? Why do you think they are different?

MANAGEMENT DECISION CASE: Zillow Changes the Rules in Real Estate

If you own a home or are thinking of purchasing one, you may have spent considerable time searching Zillow's database of 80 million homes and counting. Started by two former Microsoft employees, Richard Barton and Lloyd Frink, Zillow is revolutionizing the $2.2 trillion real estate market despite the fact the Web site debuted in early 2005. Barton has some experience shaking up industries; he convinced Bill Gates to start Expedia, which began a transformation of the travel industry that continues today. One of Barton's first hires at Expedia was Lloyd Frink.

After cashing out of Expedia in 2003 (Barry Diller bought Expedia for $1.5 billion), Barton and Frink set their sights on the real estate market. While a huge economic engine, the real estate industry had not experienced significant change in its business model for many years. The two entrepreneurs were well aware that real estate professionals leveraged their access to information through online MLS databases to maintain a powerful position with consumers. They believed a Web site that "unlocked" much of the information available through public sources would be a winner with consumers wanting to know more about real estate. Zillow generates more than 4 million visitors a month and has empowered many consumers by providing useful information about their local real estate market. Zillow also satisfies a voyeuristic tendency among many visitors to check out prices for their bosses' homes as well as friends, family, and even celebrities.

Zillow works by first accessing government data generally from local tax assessors and other public sources. However, it also encourages homeowners to add information to their home's database. Tax records often do not reflect new renovations such as a remodeled kitchen or bedroom, so home owners are asked to update their home's information. Once users have typed in an address, a wealth of information is displayed. Using mapping and satellite photographs from Microsoft's Virtual Earth, the company shows an aerial view of the home and surrounding properties. Charts also display the value of the home over 1, 5,

and 10 years and compares it with home sales in the local zip code, state, and nation. Also, square footage, date and price of last sale, and other tax-related information is available. Zillow also flags nearby properties that have sold recently. Another option for home owners is called "Make Me Move," which allows home owners to input a price for their property that, if a matching offer is made, will make them move. Zillow says this feature has surprised some owners who have been contacted by people looking to purchase their home at the "Make Me Move" price. Zillow is moving to a model that not only provides information but also brings buyers and sellers together.

Not surprisingly, real estate agents are not as enthusiastic about Zillow. They argue that Zillow does a poor job of putting the numbers in context and is not accurate much of the time. Indeed, Zillow admits that the accuracy of its home values (called Zestimates) varies widely. Many real estate professionals are concerned that Zillow will develop the primary relationship with consumers, taking over the real estate pros' traditional role as middlemen. Barton disagrees and suggests there is room for both real estate agents and Zillow, which is perhaps not surprising since much of Zillow's current revenue stream comes from real estate advertising.

The real estate market is undergoing dramatic change as information becomes accessible and buyers and sellers interact more directly. Despite the ups and downs of the real estate market, interest continues to increase for information-hungry buyers and sellers[49].

Questions for Consideration

1. As a real estate agent, how would you address customer questions about Zillow and its value in the home buying/selling process?

2. Zillow has the potential to significantly change the real estate market. What effect might this have on consumers looking to purchase a home? What effect would this have on a home seller?

MARKETING PLAN EXERCISE

ACTIVITY 7: Define Consumer Markets

For those marketing products to consumers (or through a channel that sells directly to consumers), understanding the purchase decision process of the target market is an essential element of the marketing plan. This exercise includes the following activities:

1. Develop a demographic profile of the customer to include

   a. Age

   b. Income

   c. Occupation

   d. Education

   e. Lifestyle (activities, interests, opinions)

2. Describe the motivation of the target consumer. Why is the consumer buying the product?

3. What external forces will influence the target consumer as he or she considers the purchase? For example, will the consumer's culture or subculture affect the purchase decision? How?

4. Describe the consumer's typical consumer purchase decision process? What is the likely process a consumer will go through in making the decision to purchase the product?

If you are using Marketing Plan Pro, a template for this assignment can be accessed at www.mhhe.com/marshall1e.

RECOMMENDED READINGS

1. Arjun Chaudhuri, *Emotion and Reason in Consumer Behavior* (New York: Butterworth-Heineman, 2006).

2. S. Ratneshwar, *Inside Consumption Perspectives on Consumer Motives, Goals, and Desires* (Florence, Kentucky: Routledge, 2005.)

3. William J. McEwen, *Married to the Brand: Why Consumers Bond with Some Brands for Life* (New York: Gallup Press, 2005).

4. Gerald Zaltman, *How Customers Think: Essential Insights into the Mind of the Market* (Boston: Harvard Business School Press, 2003).

5. Paco Underhill, *Why People Buy: The Science of Shopping* (New York: Simon & Schuster, 2000).

CHAPTER 08

UNDERSTANDING CUSTOMERS: BUSINESS-TO-BUSINESS MARKETS

LEARNING OBJECTIVES

- Recognize the importance of B2B marketing.

- Understand the differences between B2C and B2B markets.

- Understand the critical role of the buying center and each participant in the B2B process.

- Learn the B2B purchase decision process and different buying situations.

- Comprehend the role of technology in business markets.

EXECUTIVE PERSPECTIVE

Executive Steve Stiger, Group Vice President, Marketing and Business Development

Company Bright House Networks

Business Broad-based communications including cable television, high-speed Internet, local and long-distance phone service

How important is the B2B portion of your business in the context of your overall market?

The B2B portion of our market is vital from several perspectives.

1. It's a natural extension of our fiber network capability. Our network passes businesses as it passes residential homes.

2. It's strategically important because it offers a large revenue potential. Though there are more residential homes versus businesses in our footprint, the B2B segment typically presents significantly higher average revenue per user opportunity on a per-account basis.

3. From a brand and positioning perspective, it is important to be viewed by all business segments as a provider of a robust portfolio of video, voice, and high-speed data products.

4. As a market leader, we want to maximize share and preempt competitors from gaining a foothold in one business segment and exploiting that presence through excursions into new segments.

What are some of the important differences you find in marketing in the B2B space versus the B2C space?

The value propositions required to compete and market in B2B versus B2C are often quite different. Because the utility derived from our products is so diverse, it is important to understand the differential needs within each of these broad market groups. From this stems the benefits-based messaging and approaches that must be developed to present our products that best meet these needs.

An example would be network redundancy, which is a nonnegotiable, top priority for many B2B customers. Conversely, B2C customers typically view our products more from an entertainment and information perspective.

We also deploy push and pull marketing tactics differently in the respective segments. Our B2C strategy focuses more heavily on pull tactics such as advertising. Our B2B approach focuses more on push tactics such as dedicated account executives who manage the relationships with these business customers.

What type of follow-up strategies after the sale do you have in place for major organizational customers?

We rely on our account executives to provide a more personal level of service. Due to the importance of our products to the performance of their own businesses, major organizational customers don't want to call a 1-800 number—they want to talk with an individual who's always available to them, understands their problem, and can handle it with great speed and accuracy. We provide this with our dedicated account teams who deliver the service that is so important to meeting the business needs of each account. Large business accounts need things done in real time—it has to work or it isn't of value to them.

ORGANIZATIONAL BUYING: MARKETING TO A BUSINESS

Many people believe marketing is focused primarily on consumers—the ultimate users of the product. This is due at least in part to the fact that most people experience marketing as a consumer. The reality, however, is that large consumer products companies purchase hundreds of billions of dollars of products and services every year (Exhibit 8.1 shows the largest national business-to-business markets). General Motors, for example, spends over $60 billion a year on products and services. Everyone knows Hewlett-Packard (HP) and General Electric (GE) because of the products they sell to consumers, but these companies derive most of their revenue from selling to other businesses. Many companies that are primarily consumer oriented, such as Sharp Electronics Corp., sell in the business-to-business (B2B) market as well.

> Sharp Electronics invested nearly $3 billion in its Kameyama factory in Japan to build LCD televisions. While the company designed the plant for its own production requirements, the economics of plant design dictated that Sharp build excess capacity for the future. As a result, Sharp, the market leader in LCD technology, and its Aquos brand of LCDs account for 90 percent of the plant's production. However, the remaining 10 percent is sold to LG Philips, Toshiba, JVC, and Mitsubishi.[1]

In many cases, companies are selling products that end up as components in a finished product. General Electric is a world manufacturing leader in commercial

| EXHIBIT 8.1 | The Largest Business-to-Business Markets |

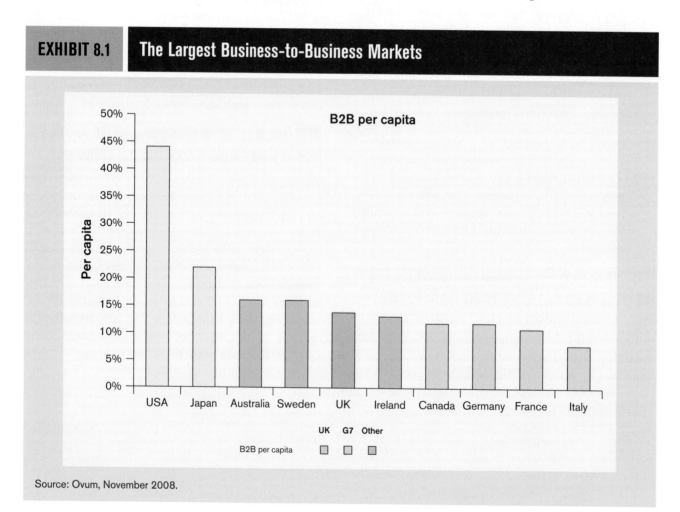

Source: Ovum, November 2008.

jet engines that power half of the jets flying today. Also, companies must purchase products to help them maintain their business. HP is a global company providing IT solutions to companies worldwide. Its products are not a component of another product but, rather, help a business run better. While many companies serve business-to-consumer markets, all companies operate in a business-to-business market as we will see in this chapter. From General Electric to Wal-Mart, companies must understand and work with other companies as part of their business operations.[2]

In this chapter, we explore **B2B markets.** The first part of the chapter defines business-to-business markets and delineates the differences between B2B markets and consumer markets. Next, we discuss the business market purchase decision process, which is different from the process consumers use in making a purchase decision. Finally, the significant role of technology in business-to-business markets relationships will be presented.

HP derives most of its revenue selling business to business. Here HP highlights its business services and how they can help a company succeed against competitors.

DIFFERENCES BETWEEN BUSINESS AND CONSUMER MARKETS

Business markets and consumer markets are not the same. Five distinct differences dramatically affect marketing strategy and tactics (see Exhibit 8.2). These differences create unique opportunities and challenges for marketing managers because success in consumer marketing does not translate directly to business markets and vice versa.

Relationship with Customers

As we discussed in Chapter 4, many consumer product companies now focus on building strong relationships with their customers. However, even when a relationship is cultivated with the customer, it is impersonal and exists primarily through electronic communication or direct mail.

The opposite is true in business markets. The nature of business markets requires a more personal relationship between buyer and seller. Every relationship takes on additional significance as the sales potential of each customer increases. A strong personal relationship is critical because business customers demand fast answers, good service, and, in general, want a close relationship with suppliers.[3] As a result, companies selling in a B2B market invest more resources to foster and maintain personal contact with their customers than in a consumer market. In some cases, companies even invest in their suppliers to strengthen the relationship.

Northwest Tool & Die in Michigan was headed for bankruptcy as low-cost competitors from Japan, Korea, and China captured much of its market. Honda Motor Co., however, invested in the company, upgrading facilities and demonstrating more efficient manufacturing processes. In addition, Honda directed millions of dollars in contracts to the company. Honda believes it has made a good investment supporting local businesses in the United States and ensuring a quality supplier for the future.[4]

EXHIBIT 8.2 | **Differences between Business and Consumer Markets**

	B2B Market (Business)	B2C Market (Consumer)
Relationship with customers	Invest more in maintaining personal relationships	Impersonal; exist through electronic communication
Number and size of customers	Fewer but larger customers	More customers but buy in smaller, less frequent quantities
Geographic concentration	Suppliers located strategically by the buyers	Could be anywhere in the world
Complexity of buying process	Complex process that can take a long time (years in some cases) and involve more people	Fewer people, often just one, directly involved in the purchase decision and the purchase decision is often based on personal and psychological benefits
Complexity of supply chain	Direct from supplier to manufacturer	Complex with products moving through the channel to reach the consumer
Demand for products	Derived from consumer demand, fluctuates with changes to consumer demand, and more inelastic (less price sensitive)	Consumer perceptions about their own needs mitigated by environmental factors and marketing stimuli

A more personal relationship most often connotes a greater emphasis on personal selling and, increasingly, technology. Customers want direct communication with company representatives and prefer someone they know and trust. The individual most responsible for maintaining a relationship is the salesperson. Personal selling also offers companies the most effective method for direct communication with the customer. Technology has greatly improved the quality and quantity of communications between buyer and seller. However, one-on-one personal communication is still the most important tool in developing and maintaining a strong customer relationship in business markets.

At the same time, technology plays a critical role in connecting buyer and seller. Integrating IT systems that enhance sales response times, provide better customer service, and increase information flow is now an accepted element in a successful B2B customer relationship. Customers demand not only a personal relationship with their vendors but also an efficient one. Most companies now require vendor Internet connectivity to increase efficiency.

Number and Size of Customers

Business markets are characterized by fewer but larger customers. Goodyear, for example, may sell one set of tires to a consumer over the course of three years, but every year the company sells millions of tires to Ford Motor Company. Add up all the major automobile companies, and there are fewer than 25 business customers for Goodyear. Not surprisingly, the company maintains a dedicated sales force just for the automobile manufacturers.

The large size and small number of customers places a higher value on each customer. Although consumer products companies value customer relationships, it is not possible to satisfy every customer every time nor is it economically feasible. However, in a business market setting, losing even one large customer has striking implications for a company.[5] Wal-Mart is Procter & Gamble's single

| EXHIBIT 8.3 | The 20 Most "Wired" Cities in the United States |

1. Atlanta, Georgia	11. Washington, D.C.
2. Seattle, Washington	12. Minneapolis, Minnesota
3. Raleigh, North Carolina	13. Boston, Masschusetts
4. San Francisco, California	14. Miami, Florida
5. Baltimore, Maryland	15. Tampa, Florida
6. Orlando, Florida	16. Cincinnati, Ohio
7. Charlotte, North Carolina	17. Denver, Colorado
8. Chicago, Illinois	18. Phoenix, Arizona
9. New York, New York	19. Dallas, Texas
10. Portland, Oregon	20. San Diego, California

Source: *Forbes*, "Most 'Wired' Cities," www.forbes.com/wireless/2008/01/09/wired-cities-wifi-tech-wireless-cx_ewo110wired.html. November 2008.

biggest customer accounting for 17 percent of company sales (roughly equivalent to $9 billion). At its Arkansas office, P&G has a 300-member staff dedicated to one customer—Wal-Mart.

Geographic Concentration

Business markets tend to concentrate in certain locations.[6] Historically, the automobile industry concentrated in the Midwest, particularly Detroit, and technology firms dominated Silicon Valley in California. As a result, their suppliers congregated nearby. A software developer, for example, that wants to be close to its primary customers should set up an office in San Jose, California. While the Internet allows people to live anywhere, the nature of business relationships means companies want to have a strong presence near their best customers. Exhibit 8.3 highlights the Internet connectivity of cities around the United States measuring broadband adoption, number of companies providing broadband access, and public access wi-fi hotspots per capita to determine the "most wired" cities.

Complexity of the Buying Process

The B2B customer buying process, discussed later in the chapter, is more complex than the consumer purchase decision process. It takes longer and involves more people, making the seller's job more challenging. In addition, as companies connect with customers, the number of relationships increases and it is difficult for one individual, the salesperson, to keep up with the complexity of the relationships.[7] Companies also face competing forces in critical decisions about their products (See Ethical Dimension 8).

Complexity of the Supply Chain

The movement of goods through a channel to the ultimate consumer requires a high level of coordination among the participants. A **supply chain** is the synchronized movement of goods through the channel. It is far more integrated than ever before as companies seek to keep production costs low, provide maximum customer input and flexibility in the design of products, and create competitive

ETHICAL DIMENSION 8

Implications of Biofuels

As the United States and many other industrialized countries wrestle with the high cost of energy, few energy options offer a dual win for consumers—environmentally sensitive and fuel efficient. Coal, for example, is prevalent in some parts of the world, including the United States, but is harmful to the environment. Solar and wind power generation are clean energy sources but are difficult to harness in sufficient quantities to make a significant impact on the use of fossil fuel. One source of energy that both reduces the dependence on oil and offers a cleaner burning, is ethanol. Produced from corn, ethanol lowers the use of fossil fuel and has been a critical piece of the federal government's plan to lessen U.S. dependence on foreign oil. Current plans call for renewable fuels such as ethanol to account for 15 percent of gasoline burned in the United States by 2017. The move to biofuels is also happening in other parts of the world. Europe is requiring that nearly 6 percent of its diesel fuel come from plants by 2010.

The benefits of biofuels do not come without a cost. Livestock farmers have experienced a dramatic increase in the price of corn, doubling from $2 a bushel to over $4 a bushel. This price increase is due primarily to huge increases in demand for corn to make ethanol. The 2006 crop of 10.5 billion bushels of corn was the third largest ever recorded; nearly 20 percent of the corn was used in the production of ethanol, and 24 percent of the 2008 crop went into ethanol.

This focus on greater energy independence and more environmentally friendly fuel is creating difficult choices for companies, government officials, and farmers. Ethanol is becoming more readily available, but higher feed corn prices have led to higher prices for meat and poultry at the grocery store. Chicken feed costs, for example, are increasing an estimated $1.5 billion per year. Ultimately, some predict competition for bio products as producers choose between using corn and other plants for fuel or food.

Around the world, difficult choices are being made. In Germany, increased demand for rapeseed, used as a biofuel in Europe, has led to steep price increases for other uses of the product, such as cooking oil and protein meal. Indonesia and Malaysia suffered significant air pollution recently as millions of acres of forests were cleared to plant oil palms used in biofuels in Asia.

The use of corn as a biofuel is not particularly efficient as it takes 7 gallons of fossil fuel to produce 10 gallons of ethanol. Additionally, while it does produce lower greenhouse gases, the comparison with fossil fuels is not dramatic. Researchers are looking for more efficient biofuels. Pine groves, prairie grass, and other plants have even greater potential than corn, producing cleaner fuel with less energy.

From consumers to energy companies and farmers, the increased use of biofuels means choosing, at least in some cases, between greater energy dependence and higher food prices as limited quantities of critical plants raise prices for a variety of products.[8]

Ethical Perspective

1. **Oil companies:** Should they invest in alternative fuel technologies such as ethanol to reduce fossil fuel consumption?

2. **Consumers:** Should they be willing to pay higher food prices to achieve greater energy independence and cleaner burning fuel?

3. **Farmers:** Should they be required to invest in greater production of critical biofuel plants such as corn?

---

advantage. At the same time, the supply chain in B2B markets is generally more direct with suppliers and manufacturers working closely together to ensure efficient movement of products and services.

Demand for Products and Services Is Different in a Business Market

Product demand in business markets is different from consumer demand on three critical dimensions: derived demand, fluctuating demand, and inelastic demand. All three offer unique challenges and opportunities for marketers. For example, two of the three differences (derived and fluctuating demand) deal with the relationship between B2B and B2C demand and suggest B2B marketing managers must first understand their customer's markets before they can sell to the customer. The final dimension (inelastic demand) is an opportunity for a seller but must be managed carefully to maintain a successful relationship.

Derived Demand

Demand for B2B products originates from the demand for consumer products, or, put another way, demand for B2B products is **derived demand.** If consumers are not buying Ford cars and trucks, then there is no need for Ford to purchase Goodyear tires. Therefore, it is important for Goodyear to understand the consumer market for automobiles for two reasons. First, knowing what consumers are looking for in a car is critical to designing tires for those cars. Second, knowing the consumer automobile market is essential to create a value proposition that speaks to Ford's need to sell more cars and trucks to consumers.

XL Capital positions itself as one of the leading global insurance/reinsurance companies with the ability and resources to handle large industrial risks anywhere in the world.

Courtesy XL Capital Group Insurance

In addition to the demand for specific Ford products, such as the Flex or Mustang, Goodyear scans the environment for anything that might affect consumer demand. Environmental factors have long-term and short-term effects on consumer product choices. For example, long-term economic factors such as the rapid rise in the price of gasoline have had a significant negative effect on the sales of SUVs, and short-term factors like a hurricane in Florida or the Southeast can limit distribution and sale of products in those areas for a while. B2B sellers understand that business customer success frequently means finding ways to assist them in their consumer markets. This is a challenge for business marketers because, despite having a great product and providing great service at a competitive price, they may still not get the business because consumer demand for their business customer's product is weak.

> Boeing realizes that airlines will not purchase the 787 Dreamliner unless passengers want to fly it. As a result, the company must not only create a value proposition for primary customers—the airlines—but Boeing must also build interest among the flying public. The company has spent millions marketing the new plane to consumers as well as building a showroom for airline executives to highlight passenger amenities and demonstrate the passenger friendly attributes of the 787.[9]

Fluctuating Demand

The relationship between consumer demand and demand for business products presents a real challenge for business-to-business marketers. Small changes in consumer demand can lead to considerable shifts in business product demand and is referred to as the **acceleration effect.** This makes forecasting the sale of consumer products important because making even a small mistake in estimating consumer demand can lead to significant errors in product production.

Inelastic Demand

Business products experience fairly **inelastic demand,** meaning changes in demand are not significantly affected by changes in price. Apple, for example, will not buy more processors from Intel if Intel lowers the price nor will it buy fewer chips if Intel raises the price until the price increase becomes so high that Apple considers alternative vendors. Apple designs some of its computers around Intel processors and to change vendors creates disruption and costs in other areas of the manufacturing process. Price increases, particularly incremental changes, are often accepted because manufacturers are hesitant to disrupt manufacturing processes, which, in turn, creates inelastic demand in the short run. Exhibit 8.4

EXHIBIT 8.4 | Examples of Elastic and Inelastic Demand

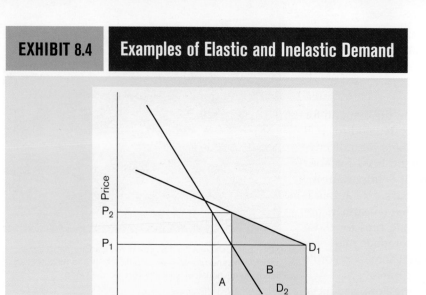

Reprinted from Stephen Slavin, *Economics,* 9th ed., 2009. Copyright © 2009 The McGraw-Hill Companies, Inc.

has two demand curves, D1 and D2. As price rises from P1 to P2 the demand changes. The more elastic demand curve is the one with the largest shaded area—B. Demand in business-to-business markets is generally more inelastic than consumer markets, which means changes in price have less effect on demand—the smaller shaded area A. This makes D2 an example of inelastic demand.

BUYING SITUATIONS

People involved in making business **buying decisions** face many choices as they move through the purchase decision process. Business buying decisions vary widely based on the:

- Nature of the purchase (large capital outlay like that needed for a new manufacturing plant versus simply ordering office supplies).
- Number of people involved in the decision (one or many).
- Understanding of the product being purchased (new to the firm or a familiar product purchased many times before).
- Time frame for the decision (short time requiring an immediate purchase decision or a longer lead time).

Some decisions require little or no analysis before the purchase decision. Others require updating information or changing existing purchase orders before the purchase decision can be made. Finally, some decisions require an in-depth analysis of the product. These three scenarios are referred to as straight rebuys, modified rebuys, and new purchases (see Exhibit 8.5).

Straight Rebuy

Many products are purchased so often that it is not necessary to evaluate every purchase decision. Companies use a wide range of products on a consistent basis (office supplies, raw materials) and simply reorder when needed. This type of purchase is called a **straight rebuy.** Increasingly, this is done automatically via secure

EXHIBIT 8.5	Types of Buying Situations
Straight rebuy	Reorder products that are used on a consistent basis
Modified rebuy	Familiar with product and supplier, but still seek additional information
New purchase	First-time purchase of product or service

Internet connections with approved or preferred suppliers. Far fewer people are involved with the purchase decision; often it is handled by one person in the purchasing department.

The goal of business sellers in straight rebuy situations is to become the preferred supplier. A company given approved status must be diligent and mindful of competitors seeking to displace it. Companies not on the approved list are called **out suppliers.** Their primary task is to obtain a small order, an opening, then leverage that opportunity to gain additional business. This is a challenge, however, if the approved supplier is doing a good job of meeting the customer's needs. From time to time, many companies order small quantities from nonapproved suppliers just to keep the approved supplier from becoming too complacent or to evaluate a potential new vendor.[10]

Modified Rebuy

A **modified rebuy** occurs when the customer is familiar with the product and supplier but is looking for additional information. Most often this need for change has resulted from one or more of three circumstances. First, the approved supplier has performed poorly or has not lived up to the customer's expectations. Second, new products have come into the market triggering a reappraisal of the current purchase protocols. Third, the customer believes it is time for a change and wants to consider other suppliers.

All three situations create opportunities for out suppliers to gain new business. When a purchase contract is opened up for a modified rebuy it represents the best opportunity for a new supplier. At the same time, however, the current approved supplier seeks to maintain the relationship. The approved supplier almost always has the advantage, particularly if it has a close relationship with the customer, because it knows the people involved and usually gets access to critical information first.

New Purchase

The most complex and difficult buying situation is the new purchase. A **new purchase** is the purchase of a product or service by a customer for the first time. The more expensive, higher risk, and greater the resource commitment, the more likely the company will engage in a full purchase decision process (outlined later in the chapter).

This process almost certainly involves a group throughout the entire decision process, even though the final decision may rest with a single individual. Because the company's purchasing personnel have had very little experience with the product, they seek information from a variety of sources. First and foremost, vendor salespeople are a key source of information about the product's capabilities. If they do their job well, they help the customer define its needs and how best to address them. Another avenue of information for companies is to hire consultants who, as unbiased experts, can assess and educate customers on their needs and possible solutions. Finally, the company must scan its own resources, including past purchase records, for relevant information.

Italian designer clothing may no longer be "made in Italy." As the euro strengthens, low-cost rivals proliferate, and labor costs rise, Italian luxury goods such as Armani, Gucci, and Prada have moved production out of Italy to locations in Eastern Europe, China, and Turkey. This a significant strategic shift for these companies as they move away from a decades-old tradition of marketing the mystique and exclusive quality of products made in Italy. Executives say they only made the decision after carefully guaranteeing the quality of their products no matter where they are produced.[11]

BUYING CENTERS

As we discussed, business purchases are seldom made by just one person, particularly in modified rebuy and new purchase situations. A number of individuals with a stake in the purchase decision come together to form a **buying center** that manages the purchase decision process and ultimately makes the decision. The individuals included in the buying center may have direct responsibility over the decision (purchasing department) or financial control of the company (senior management). In other cases, the individuals might have a specific expertise helpful to the decision (engineer, consultant).[12]

Buying centers usually are not permanent groups but are convened to make the decision and then disband. Also, individuals may participate in more than one buying center at any given time. Purchasing agents are apt to be members of several buying centers. In addition, while the vast majority of buying center participants work for the customer, others, such as outside consultants, are invited into the group because of their expertise. This happens, for example, in new purchases when a company believes it lacks sufficient internal knowledge and experience to make an informed decision. Most buying centers include a minimum of five people; however, they can be much larger. In larger multinational corporations, buying centers for companywide purchase decisions, such as a new corporate CRM system, can include dozens of people from all over the world.

Members of the Buying Center

Every participant in a buying center plays a certain role and some may play multiple roles (see Exhibit 8.6). In addition, an individual's role may change. As people move up in an organization, they can move from user to influencer and finally a

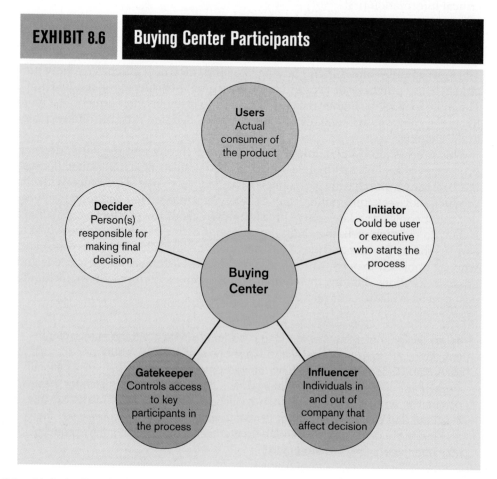

EXHIBIT 8.6	Buying Center Participants

Users — Actual consumer of the product

Initiator — Could be user or executive who starts the process

Influencer — Individuals in and out of company that affect decision

Gatekeeper — Controls access to key participants in the process

Decider — Person(s) responsible for making final decision

Buying Center

decider. These functions can be defined formally by the company or informally as a result of an individual's expertise or influence. Let's examine each of the five major roles.

User

Users are the actual consumer of the product and play a critical role. While typically not the decision makers, they do have a lot of input at various stages of the process. They are the first to recognize the problem based on a need, and they help define the product specifications. Finally, they provide critical feedback after the product purchase. As a result, their responsibility is enhanced in new purchase and modified rebuy situations when product specifications are being set for the purchase decision.

Initiators

The **initiator** starts the buying decision process usually in one of two ways. In one scenario the initiator is also the user of the product as in the secretary who reorders when office supplies run low. A second scenario occurs when senior executives make decisions that require new resources (manufacturing sites, product development, and information technology). In these situations the executives act as initiators to the purchase decision process.

Influencers

Individuals, both inside and outside the organization, with relevant expertise in a particular area act as **influencers,** providing information that is used by the buying center in making the final decision. Engineers are frequently called on to detail product requirements and specifications. Purchasing agents, based on their experience, are helpful in evaluating sales proposals. Marketing personnel can provide customer feedback. In all of these cases, the influencer's knowledge on a given topic relevant to the purchase decision can affect the purchase decision.

Gatekeepers

Access to information and relevant individuals in the buying center is controlled by **gatekeepers.** Purchasing departments act as gatekeepers by limiting possible vendors to those approved by the company. Similarly, engineering, quality control, and service department personnel create product specifications that, in essence, limit the number of vendors. At the same time, basic access to key people is controlled by secretaries and administrative assistants. One of the toughest challenges facing salespeople in a new purchase or modified rebuy situation is getting access to the right people.

Deciders

Ultimately, the purchase decision rests with one or more individuals, **deciders,** in the buying center. Often it will be the most senior member of the team; however, it can also include other individuals (users, influencers), in which case the decision is reached by consensus. The more expensive and strategic the purchase, the higher in the organization the decision must go for final authority.[13] It is not uncommon for the CEO to sign off on major strategic decisions about technology, new manufacturing plants, and other key decisions that affect fundamental business processes.

surprises? i don't like surprises. do i look like i like surprises?

we don't shock you with hidden shipping surcharges. see how you can save by shipping with us. just return this card or visit usps.com/save

TODAY'S MAIL

The USPS targets a concern among many decision makers: hidden fees that arise after a purchase. In this message the USPS seeks to minimize that issue suggesting the USPS does not apply charges after the package delivery.

Who is part of the buying center? → Who are the most significant influencers? → What are the decision criteria for evaluating the various product options? → Buying Center Target Market

Costly capital equipment purchases often include the chief financial officer (CFO) who will most likely be a key decider. CFOs will employ a wide range of financial tools, including discounted cash flow analysis of the proposed investment, as they determine the most appropriate purchase decision.

Pursuing the Buying Center

Buying centers present marketers with three distinct challenges as presented in Exhibit 8.7. First, who is part of the buying center? Simply identifying the members of a buying center can be difficult and is made more challenging by gatekeepers whose role, in part, is to act as a buffer between buying center members and outside vendor representatives. The job of identifying membership in the buying center is made even more complex as participants come and go over time. Second, who are the most significant influencers in the buying center? This is critical in both preparing a sales presentation and following up. Targeting influencers is important in persuading the buying center to purchase the salesperson's product. Finally, what are the decision criteria for evaluating the various product options? A very real concern for salespeople is making sure their products perform well on critical evaluation criteria; however, without a good understanding of evaluation criteria it is not possible to assess the probability of the product's success.

THE PLAYERS IN BUSINESS-TO-BUSINESS MARKETS

B2B markets are not homogenous. The complexity of business markets rivals that of consumer markets with more than 20 million small businesses in the United States alone. The number grows dramatically when you include large corporations, nonprofit institutions, and government entities. The diversity of businesses coupled with the unique characteristics of business-to-business markets means companies selling in B2B markets need to know their markets very well. Let's explore each of the major categories of business markets to better understand their similarities and differences.

The North American Industrial Classification System (NAICS)

Historically, the basic tool for defining and segmenting business markets was a classification system known as the Standard Industrial Classification (SIC) codes developed by the U.S. government in the 1930s. The SIC system organized businesses into 10 groups that further broke down business categories based on their output (what they produced or their primary business activity). For many years, it was the foundation for business segmentation in the United States.

The SIC codes were updated in the 1990s and are now called the **North American Industrial Classification System (NAICS).** The system has been expanded to include businesses in Mexico and Canada. NAICS defines 20 major business

EXHIBIT 8.8 | **NAICS Example**

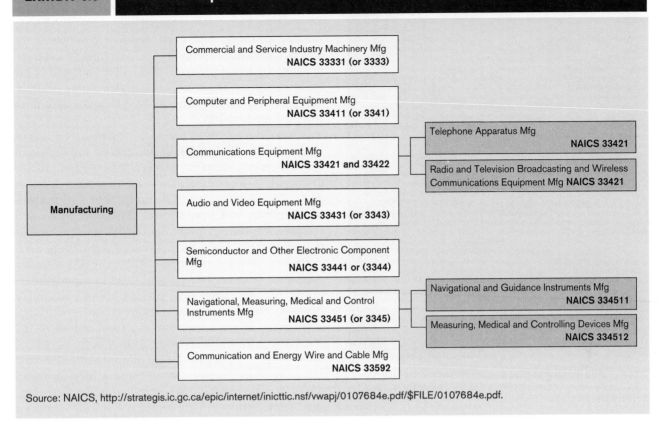

Source: NAICS, http://strategis.ic.gc.ca/epic/internet/inicttic.nsf/vwapj/0107684e.pdf/$FILE/0107684e.pdf.

sectors based on a six-digit hierarchical code. The first five digits are standardized across Mexico, Canada, and the United States while the sixth digit enables countries to adjust the code to fit the country's own unique economic structure.[14]

The NAICS is not perfect; companies are classified on the basis of their primary output, which means that large companies with multiple businesses across different sectors are not accurately represented as they receive only one NAICS code. However, the system does offer a great starting point for researching a particular business market. It is possible to purchase detailed information on each of the codes in the system. This information includes data on companies listed in each code, number of employees, sales revenue, their location, and contact information. Exhibit 8.8 provides an example.

Manufacturers

One of the largest groups of business customers are manufacturers, which consume two types of products. First, components used in the manufacturing process are called **original equipment manufacturer (OEM)** purchases. Companies selling OEM products work to convince the OEM customer their products offer the best value (price and quality) to the OEM's customers. Intel's reputation for overall value among consumers has enabled the company to build a strong business with OEM computer manufacturers such as HP to the point that HP, and others, promote "Intel Inside."

OEM customers purchase in large quantities to support their own product demand. Two important outcomes result from this purchase power. First, OEM customers seek the very "best" prices from sellers. *Best* does not always mean lowest; other factors play an important role.[15] The assurance of product quality, ability to meet demand, just-in-time product delivery schedules, and other factors

Demonstrating the value of a major purchase is critical to the final purchase decision. Cirrus Airplanes indicates their airplanes should be considered a member of the "staff" and will make executives more productive.

frequently figure into the final selection of product and vendor. The second result of large purchase quantities is the ability to dictate specific product specifications. OEM customers often compel suppliers to modify existing products and even develop new products. Sellers work closely with the OEM engineers and technicians to develop products that will fit the need of the OEM customer. The benefit is a high volume of product sales and the opportunity to develop a long-term strategic relationship.[16]

A second category of products purchased by manufacturers are called **end user purchases** and represent the equipment, supplies, and services needed to keep the business operational. There are two major types of end user purchases: **capital equipment** and **materials, repairs, and operational (MRO)** supplies and services. Capital equipment purchases involve significant investments and include major technology decisions (mainframe computers, ERP and CRM software packages) or critical equipment need in the manufacturing process (large drill presses, robotic assembly systems). Since these purchases are considered a long-term investment, customers evaluate not only the purchase price but also other factors such as cost of ownership, reliability, and ease of upgrading. The cost and long-term commitment of these purchases mean senior management is often involved in the final decision. Frequently a buying center will evaluate options and make a recommendation to senior management.

MRO supplies, on the other hand, are products used in everyday business operations and are typically not considered a significant expense. Purchasing agents or individuals close to the purchase decision, such as an office manager, are responsible for MRO purchases. Many of these purchases are straight rebuys; the individuals involved do not want to spend a lot of time making the purchase. Vendors in these industries are well aware that once they have a customer, the business is assured until the company does not perform up to customer expectations. Put another way, the business is theirs to lose.

Increasingly, airlines are trying to maximize the efficient use of aircraft and minimize fuel costs. Sophisticated software from companies such as EDS, Deutsche Lufthansa, Boeing, and others incorporates meteorological data and onboard navigation technologies to develop route plans that dramatically lower airline costs. For example, using such software, United Airlines was able to save more than $1,600 on a single flight from San Francisco to Frankfurt by minimizing overfly charges (a charge by countries for flying in the airspace) and lowering fuel costs.[17]

Resellers

Companies that buy products and then resell them to other businesses or consumers are called **resellers.** Home Depot, for example, buys home products and then resells them to consumers, building contractors, and other professionals in the construction industry. Chapter 16 provides an in-depth discussion of consumer resellers, but it is important to note that resellers have unique needs when it comes to purchase decisions. Just as manufacturers need end user products, resellers also need equipment and supplies to run their businesses. Retailers need technology such as computers and checkout counters to keep track of sales and inventory.

Distributors need stocking and inventory management systems to maintain their distributions centers and also have the same MRO needs.

Government

The single largest buyer of goods and services in the world is the U.S. government. Combined with state and local governments, the value of purchases is over $2 trillion. Local, state, and particularly federal **government** entities have unique and frequently challenging purchase practices. Detailed product specifications must be followed precisely, and the purchase process is often long. The purchase decision by the Department of Defense on the F-22A Raptor fighter took four and a half years and involved thousands of product specifications.[18] While the government is theoretically open to all vendors, the reality is that experience with the government purchase process is usually a prerequisite to success.

Federal and state governments make a number of resources available to potential vendors; it is possible to obtain guidelines from the federal government. Furthermore, some private companies exist to offer assistance in learning about the process. The National Association of State Purchasing Officials publishes information on selling products and services to each of the 50 states. In addition, small-business organizations, such as the Small Business Administration, provide information on federal government contracts and contact personnel at government agencies.

Institutions

Institutions such as nonprofits, hospitals, and other nongovernment organizations (NGOs) represent a large and important market that has some unique characteristics. First, profitability does not play as significant a role in many of these organizations; rather, the delivery of service to the targeted constituency is the primary objective. Profit, or surplus as it is often called in the nonprofit community, is important but is not the fundamental driver in decision making. For example, Adventist Health System, which owns and operates health care facilities in 12 states, is a large nonprofit health care provider that considers a range of priorities in making important strategic decisions.[19] A second unique characteristic is a limited number of resources. Even the largest NGOs, including the Red Cross, do not have access to the capital and resources of most large for-profit organizations.

THE BUSINESS MARKET PURCHASE DECISION PROCESS

In some respects business market purchase decisions follow the same basic process as consumer decisions. As presented in Exhibit 8.9, a problem is recognized, information is collected and evaluated, a decision is made, and the product experience is then evaluated for future decisions. However, there are also significant differences between business market purchase decisions and consumer purchase

EXHIBIT 8.9 | **Model of Business Market Decision Process**

Problem Recognition → Define the Need and Product Specifications → Search for Suppliers → Seek Sales Proposals—Response to RFP → Making the Purchase Decision → Post-Purchase Evaluation of Product and Vendor

decisions. These differences make the process more complex and require the involvement of more people. One key difference is that, while consumer decisions often include an emotional component, business goals and performance specifications drive organizations toward a more rational decision process.

As we discussed, the process is not used for every purchase decision. In straight rebuy situations, the problem is recognized and the order is made. Defining product specifications, searching for suppliers, and other steps in the process were probably done at one time but, once a supplier is selected, the purchase decision process becomes more or less automatic. A selected or approved list of suppliers shortens the decision process dramatically. Buyers go to the targeted vendor or choose from a list of suppliers and make the purchase. This process is consistent across organizations. Modified rebuys, on the other hand, are much more organization and situation specific. In some situations, the process may be more like a straight rebuy with some changes to product specifications or contract terms. In other situations, it may resemble a new purchase with an evaluation of new suppliers and proposals. New purchases will include all the steps in the process. As a rule, a new purchase takes longer because going through each of the steps takes time. In some cases, the process may take years as in the building of a new oil refinery or automobile assembly plant.

Problem Recognition

The business market purchase decision process is triggered when someone inside or outside the company identifies a need. In many cases, the need is a problem that requires a solution. The paper supply is running low and the office manager reorders more. A company's manufacturing facilities are at full capacity and it must consider options to increase production. In other situations, the need may be an opportunity that requires a new purchase. New technology can increase order efficiency or a new design of a critical component can improve the effectiveness of a company's own products, giving it an edge with consumers. As companies struggle to deal with higher energy prices, new alternative solutions, sometimes using older technologies, are being adopted for use in interesting ways; the FYI provides an example.

FYI

The world's shipping fleets have been particularly hard hit by the higher energy prices and are seeking cleaner, more environmentally sensitive ways to power ships. Beluga, one of Germany's leading shipping companies, is employing a greener power source designed to save $1,200 a day in fuel costs. The source? A kite. SkySails, based in Hamburg, has created the first 21st century application of a centuries-old concept. Currently the company focuses on cargo vessels, oil tankers, fishing trawlers, and big yachts as its primary markets. The kites have a surface area of 1,100 square feet and extend up to 1,000 feet up and away from the ship. Each costs $400,000 to $800,000 per vessel. The payoff for the investment is fuel cost savings as high as 30 percent.[20]

Employees frequently activate the purchase process as part of their job. The office manager is responsible for keeping the office stocked with enough supplies. The vice president of strategic planning is tasked with planning for future manufacturing needs. However, salespeople from either the buying or selling company's sales force or channel partners also initiate the purchase process by helping identify a need or presenting an opportunity to increase efficiency or effectiveness. This is most likely to happen when the salesperson has established a trusted relationship with the company. Trade shows are also a source of new ideas; attendees often go to see what is new in the marketplace. Traditional marketing communications such as advertising and direct mail are less effective in business markets but are important in supporting the more personal communication efforts of salespeople.

Define the Need and Product Specifications

Once a problem has been identified, the next step is to clearly define the need. Individuals from across the organization clarify the problem and develop solutions. Not all problems lead to a new purchase. A vice president of information technology may notice an increase in call waiting times, but the issue could be a lack of training or a shortage of employees. The solution might include a new, expanded phone and call management system, but it will be up to management, working with other employees, to determine what is needed.

As part of describing the need, product specifications should be defined so that everyone inside and outside of the company knows exactly what is needed to solve the problem. This serves two important purposes. First, individuals inside the organization can plan for the future. Purchasing agents identify possible vendors while managers estimate costs and build budgets based on the specifications. Users plan how to assimilate the new purchase into existing work processes. The buying center will use the product specifications to help evaluate vendor proposals. Putting product specifications into a document for distribution is known as a **request for proposal (RFP).** The second purpose of outlining product specifications is to guide potential suppliers. Product specifications as contained in the RFP become the starting point from which vendors put together their product solution. In the best-case scenario, there is a good fit between what the customer is asking for and the supplier's existing products.[21] Much more often, however, there are some specifications in which the potential products compare favorably and others where competitors excel. Exhibit 8.10 identifies the key sections of a request for proposal. RFPs generally require a great deal of information, and it takes a significant amount of time for a company to prepare a successful sales proposal.

The challenge for salespeople is to get involved in the purchase decision process as early as possible. If the salesperson, for example, has a strategic relationship with the customer, it may be possible to help define the product specifications. This is a real advantage because the vendor's salespeople can work to create specifications that present their products in the most favorable way. Product specifications are often written in such a way as to limit the number of vendors. Companies realize that not knowing the product specifications puts them at a disadvantage over other vendors. It is still possible to win the order, but the job becomes more difficult.

Search for Suppliers

Once the company's needs have been identified and production specifications have been outlined, business customers can identify potential suppliers. Two methods are commonly used to determine the list of vendors. First, companies create a list of preferred or approved suppliers and go to that list whenever a new purchase is being considered. The list can result from the company's cumulative experience. In this situation it is important to keep the list current with respect to existing vendors and also any new vendors.

A second, more complex method is to search for and identify potential suppliers. The Internet has become a valuable tool for companies in identifying potential suppliers. General search engines and even dedicated supplier search Web sites, such as Thomas Global Register, are easy to use and enable customers to identify specific potential vendors. Of course, companies still need to perform due diligence by checking vendor customer references, and in critical purchases it is advisable to research the vendor's financial stability and management capabilities.

EXHIBIT 8.10 | **Sections of a Request for Proposal**

1. **Statement of Purpose:** Describe the extent of products and services your organization is looking for, as well as the overall objectives of the contract.

2. **Background Information:** Present a brief overview of your organization and its operations, using statistics, customer demographics, and psychographics. State your strengths and weaknesses honestly. Don't forget to include comprehensive information on the people who will handle future correspondence.

3. **Scope of Work:** Enumerate the specific duties to be performed by the provider and the expected outcomes. Include a detailed listing of responsibilities, particularly when subcontractors are involved.

4. **Outcome and Performance Standards:** Specify the outcome targets, minimal performance standards expected from the contractor, and methods for monitoring performance and process for implementing corrective actions.

5. **Deliverables:** Provide a list of all products, reports, and plans that will be delivered to your organization and propose a delivery schedule.

6. **Term of Contract:** Specify length, start and end dates of the contract, and the options for renewal.

7. **Payments, Incentives, and Penalties:** List all the terms of payment for adequate performance. Highlight the basis for incentives for superior performance and penalties for inadequate performance or lack of compliance.

8. **Contractual Terms and Conditions:** Attach standard contracting forms, certifications, and assurances. You may include requirements specific to this particular contract.

9. **Requirements for Proposal Preparation:** A consistent structure in terms of content, information, and document types simplifies things for the people evaluating the proposals. Therefore, you should request a particular structure for the proposal and provide an exhaustive list of documents you want to receive.

10. **Evaluation and Award Process:** Lay down the procedures and criteria used for evaluating proposals and for making the final contract award.

11. **Process Schedule:** Clearly and concisely present the time line for the steps leading to the final decision, such as the dates for submitting the letter of intent, sending questions, attending the preproposal conference, submitting the proposal.

12. **Contacts:** Include a complete list of people to contact for information on the RFP, or with any other questions. Incorporate their name, title, responsibilities, and the various ways of contacting them into this list.

Source: *RFP Evaluation Centers*, www.rfp-templates.com.

Potential suppliers employ sophisticated SEO (search engine optimization) tools to get listed on the critical "first page"—the most desired location on any search results page. For example, suppliers link to trade groups that drive traffic to their Web site and increase the probability of rising on the organic list. In addition, companies target keywords that minimize competitor access to first-page search results. Finally, it is possible to purchase keyword ads that test which phrases will drive the most Web traffic.[22]

Seek Sales Proposals in Response to RFP

Companies frequently solicit proposals from a number of vendors for two reasons. First, even if there is a preferred vendor, getting more information about available options from other suppliers is a good idea. If it is an open vendor search, then the proposal becomes a valuable source of information as well as the primary evaluation tool. Second, getting additional proposals helps in negotiating with the preferred vendor. When a vendor is aware that other proposals are under consideration, that vendor works harder to meet the expectations of the customer.

Sales proposals, particularly those submitted in response to an RFP, are written so they can be studied and sent to various individuals inside the company. At this stage, vendors may or may not be invited to make a presentation. If they are, a copy of the presentation will usually be submitted as part of the proposal. Numerous software packages can help create sophisticated sales proposal packages. Oracle, for example, includes a sales proposal module in its CRM solutions software. In addition, many companies have created their own proprietary software to aid salespeople in creating a sales proposal. Putting together a template that is used throughout the company helps unify the content and look of a sales proposal.

Communicating with business customers usually involves salespeople working directly with the individuals in the buying center to develop best solution.

However, this step is usually characterized by limited vendor contact. Again, many companies are asked to submit proposals from which a smaller set of potential vendors will be selected. As a result, the sales proposal plays a critical role in marketing to businesses. Most of the time it is the first and best chance to impress the customer. In general, proposals accomplish two objectives. First, the proposal clearly specifies how the company's products will meet the product specifications detailed in the RFP. Second, the proposal makes the case for selecting the company by presenting any additional information such as unique product features, service programs, or competitive pricing to help persuade the customer.

Make the Purchase Decision

Once the proposals are submitted, the next step is the purchase decision. Given the time and analysis companies put into the decision process one might think the decision is straightforward. The reality, however, is more complex, as detailed in Exhibit 8.11. Often the final decision involves trade-offs between equally important evaluation criteria and equally qualified vendors.

Product Selection

The first purchase decision is the **product choice.** In many cases the product decision is based on a single criterion, for example product cost (the office manager purchasing printer paper at the lowest price). Single-criterion decisions usually fall into a straight rebuy or very limited modified rebuy situation and do not require a buying center to assist in the new purchase decision. Much of the time, however, no one product fits all the product specifications exactly. As a result, the final decision assesses the product against the product evaluation criteria and determines the optimal solution.[23] Consider a company purchasing a new office copier. The first response might be, "pick the best copier" but what is the definition of "best"? One person might define best as most copies per minute, another as lowest cost per copy, a third may consider the lowest maintenance costs to be the best. As a result, it is important to define the evaluation criteria and then follow a consistent and fair methodology

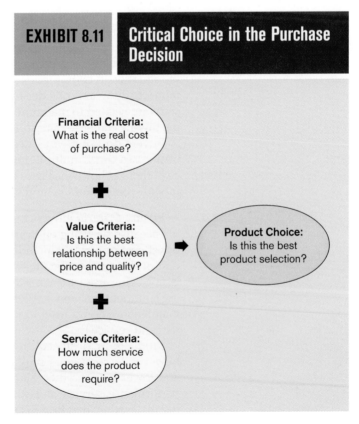

EXHIBIT 8.11	Critical Choice in the Purchase Decision

Financial Criteria:
What is the real cost of purchase?

+

Value Criteria:
Is this the best relationship between price and quality?

Product Choice:
Is this the best product selection?

+

Service Criteria:
How much service does the product require?

in evaluating the sales proposals. Three primary criteria are used to evaluate the product choice.

Financial Criteria Financial criteria are a set of analyses and metrics grouped together to assess the cost of ownership. The actual purchase price is just one consideration in determining the real cost of a purchase. Maintenance and operating costs, repair charges, and supplies are all costs associated with ownership that can vary across product choices. These costs are then evaluated against the stated life of the product. This is important as some products with a higher initial price actually cost less over time because of the product's longer life. Financial analysis also evaluates the time it takes to break even on the investment. A company considering new equipment designed to lower manufacturing costs will want to know how long it will take to recoup the investment given the projected savings.

Business-to-business marketers understand that presenting a strong financial case for their products is an essential part of selling the product. As a result, many of these financial analyses are performed by the supplier and included in the sales proposal. Buyers then compare, and verify, the analyses across vendors.

With sales of automobiles in Japan at their lowest level in more than two decades, a shrinking population, and wages among the highest in Asia, it seems an odd time for Toyota, Nissan, and Honda to be investing in new auto plants in their home country. However, all three manufacturers have made significant investments in new car plants in Japan. The companies believe that while the investments are large (each company is investing more than $1 billion), the new plants provide needed manufacturing flexibility to build multiple models in the future. In addition, the companies argue that these new plants give them the ability to test new manufacturing technologies that can be introduced at facilities around the world.[24]

Value Criteria Value is the relationship between price and quality and it is a significant facet of the purchase decision. B2B buyers are aware that the lowest-cost product may not be the right product, especially in critical OEM equipment where failure can mean customer dissatisfaction or in strategic purchases such as a new IT system where failure can cause serious business disruption. On the other hand, it is costly to overengineer a product and purchase more than is needed for the situation. A computer network that must work 100 percent of the time is much more costly when considering the backup systems and redundant hardware and software needed to maintain it than a system with 95 percent run time. It is up to the buying center to determine the specifications needed to do the job.[25]

Buyers do not always need the highest-quality product, which is why most businesses carry multiple lines with different quality and price levels. Offering customers a choice increases the likelihood of success and minimizes the opportunity for competitors to target gaps in a company's overall product line.[26]

Service Criteria Buyers are concerned with the service requirements of a product because servicing equipment costs a company in two ways. First, there is the direct cost of service, including labor and supplies. Second, there is the indirect cost of downtime when a system is out of service, which means the equipment is not being used for its intended purpose.[27] As we discussed in "Understanding Competitors," in Chapter 6, Southwest flies only Boeing 737s in part because maintenance crews need to know only one plane, which makes it easier to maintain and service the 737.

Products are designed, in part, to minimize service costs. There are trade-offs, however, as companies seek the best compromise between product performance and lower service costs. Knowing the buyer's specific priorities with regard to performance, service, and other critical criteria is essential to designing and building the product that best fits the product specifications.

Companies like IBM work with industries like the Chemical and Petroleum Industry to develop comprehensive "one stop" solutions.

Reprinted courtesy of International Business Machines Corporation, Copyright 2008 © International Machines Corporation.

Supplier Choice

Businesses buy not just a product; they also make a **supplier choice.** Often, multiple sellers will be offering the same product or very similar product configurations. As a result, supplier qualifications become part of the purchase decision. Decision makers know a purchase decision can turn out badly if the wrong vendor is selected, even if the product choice is correct.[28]

The most fundamental criterion in vendor selection is **reliability,** which is the vendor's ability to meet contractual obligations including delivery times and service schedules. Strategic business-to-business relationships are based, in part, on a high level of trust between organizations. In those situations, the supplier's reliability becomes an essential factor in the final selection. Furthermore, a judgment is often made about the seller's willingness to go above and beyond what is specified in the contract. All things being equal, the seller with the best reliability and intangibles, like a willingness to do a little more than required, usually gets the order.[29] Complex factors often go into the selection of a supplier; in the FYI consider Intel's strategy of opening a chip fabrication plant in China.

FYI

Intel, the world's largest maker of computer chips, built a chip fabrication plant in China. The $2.5 billion investment follows earlier Intel investments in chip packaging and testing facilities. This new plant represents a significant commitment by the company, employing nearly 1,500 workers in 1.7 million square foot of space. The plant builds chip sets (dedicated chips used in a wide range of products that do not require cutting-edge fabricating technology) and represents the first time the company constructed a new facility to build lower-level technology products.

(continued)

FYI [continued]

This facility bolsters Intel's presence in the fastest-growing technology market in the world, a fact not lost on Intel executives. While the primary objective of the plant is to manufacture chip sets, Intel believes it will also serve an important purpose by demonstrating Intel's commitment to China, which can help in getting new business. In addition, the plant gives the company an advantage over competitor Advanced Micro Devices (AMD), which does not manufacture in China.[30]

Personal and Organizational Factors

Several additional factors affect product and supplier choices. Suppliers often find it difficult to understand the role these factors play in the final decision, but their influence can be profound. The first, **personal factors,** refers to the needs, desires, and objectives of those involved in the purchase decision. Everyone in the buying center comes with their own needs and goals. Someone might see this as an opportunity for promotion, another believes he will receive a raise if he can be successful, a third may want to impress management. It is not possible to separate the individual agendas people bring to the buying center from the purchase decision. In addition, individuals in the buying center come to the group with their own perspective of the decision. Engineers, for example, tend to focus on product performance and specifications. Accountants often concentrate on the cost and other financial considerations. Purchasing agents give attention to vendor quality and ease of ordering. One reason buying centers are effective is their ability to bring individuals with different perspectives together to evaluate possible product options.

Another influence on the product and supplier choice is organizational factors. The primary **organizational factor** is risk tolerance. Individuals and companies all have a certain tolerance for risk. Their product decisions will be influenced by their aversion to or acceptance of risk.[31] Consider the IT manager looking to purchase a new network for his company. Two suppliers have submitted proposals that meet the product specification. One is a local vendor with an excellent reputation. This vendor has quoted a lower price and guaranteed better service. The other is Cisco Systems, the world leader in network equipment and software. The manager for the company with a low risk tolerance will probably choose Cisco Systems. It represents the "safe" choice. His superiors would never question purchasing from the market leader. If the same individual works for a risk-tolerant organization, the decision might be to go with the vendor offering better price and service. The cost of a mistake is high. If the network goes down and the company suffers a business disruption because the supplier has performed poorly, questions about the supplier selection arise. Risk tolerance does play a role as the buying center moves closer to a final decision.

Post-Purchase Evaluation of Product and Supplier

Once the purchase decision is made, buyers begin the process of evaluation (see Exhibit 8.12). Initially, they assess product performance and the seller's response to any problems or issues. A key for business marketers is to make sure the customer understands the proper operation and maintenance of the product. At the same time, buyers consider the level of support provided by the seller and expect follow-up after the sale to be sure there are no problems. Dealing with complaints, resolving customer problems, and making sure the company is meeting customer expectations are critical to ensuring customer satisfaction.

The evaluation process is designed, in part, to help customers make better purchase decisions in the future. Being the current seller is a distinct advantage because, if the customer evaluates the purchase decision positively, there is no need to change the decision next time. In essence, the evaluation process, if handled properly, can be the best sales tool for the seller when it comes time for the next purchase decision.

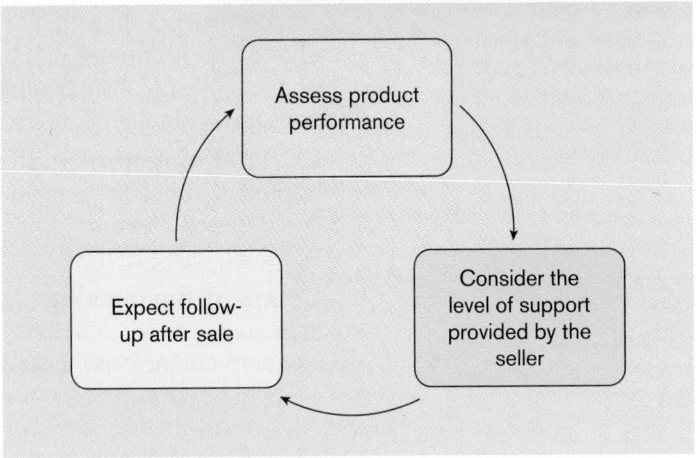

Naturally, the opposite is also true. If the product performs poorly or the seller does not meet customer expectations, competitors can use those mistakes to trigger a modified rebuy or even a new purchase decision process that increases their probability of success. Losing a customer is disappointing; however, it also represents an opportunity. By using well-developed service recovery strategies, companies can reacquire customers (Chapter 13 discusses service recovery strategies).

EXHIBIT 8.12 **Post-Purchase Evaluation Criteria**

Navteq is a market leader in creating maps used in the navigation systems found on many luxury cars such as the Cadillac Escalade and BMW 7 series. However, the company found automakers were considering fewer options as consumers resisted the high price of onboard navigation systems. As a result, Navteq moved into new markets. In 2000, onboard mapping was 100 percent of Navteq's revenue, but that number has dropped to less than 50 percent. The company realizes it is important to always be positioned for new market opportunities. Nokia realized the potential for growth and acquired Navteq to expand its reach in wireless mapping.[32]

THE ROLE OF TECHNOLOGY IN BUSINESS MARKETS

Technology has transformed the business purchase decision process. From the Internet to portable handheld optical scanning devices, technology has made the purchase decision process more efficient and effective. Technology has also pushed the purchase decision process closer to the product user because front-line managers can now make purchases directly.[33]

Sophisticated programs manage inventories and automatically replenish supplies. By linking directly with **electronic data interchange (EDI),** customer computers communicate directly with supplier computers to reorder as needed. Late deliveries, defective products, and other issues related to supplier performance can be identified and dealt with before they become a major problem. Collaboration between business buyers and sellers has increased significantly as a result of technology linkages.[34]

E-Procurement

B2B transactions have been growing at a phenomenal rate with online B2B commerce worldwide in excess of $1 trillion, a much larger amount than that generated by B2C online sales. The process of business purchasing online is referred to as **e-procurement.**[35] Let's examine the various e-procurement methods:

Industry purchasing sites: Industries have formed Web sites to streamline and standardize the e-procurement process. Steel, chemicals, paper, and automobile manufacturers have created integrated Web sites to assist their own purchasing departments in online purchasing and supplier selection.

Business function sites: Certain business functions have Web sites to standardize purchasing. For example, individual utilities used to negotiate by phone to buy and sell electricity with each other; however, today the purchase of electricity by utility companies is now done over a Web site dedicated to energy management

Extranet to major suppliers: Many companies have set up direct links to approved suppliers to make the purchase easier and move it closer to front-line decision makers.[36] Office Depot, for example, has a number of direct relationships using EDI with thousands of companies.

Company buying sites: Many large companies have created their own Web sites to assist vendors. RFPs and other relevant supplier information as well as some contact information are accessible for review.

SUMMARY

Several significant characteristics differentiate business and consumer markets including the concentration and number of customers found in business markets. In addition, the buying process itself is often longer and more complex. The demand for products in B2B markets is also different, creating both a challenge and an opportunity for business sellers.

Different types of selling situations lead to very different types of customer decision processes. Business customers interact with their suppliers in very different situations from a straight rebuy to new purchases. The greatest opportunity for a business seller to win new business comes in modified rebuy and new purchase situations.

The buying center is a team of individuals, from inside and outside the organization, that engages in the purchase decision process and either makes or recommends to the decision maker the final product selection. It is essential for business sellers to identify and become familiar with the buying center involved in any purchase decision.

The purchase decision process includes six steps from problem identification through to purchase decision and post-purchase evaluation of the product and supplier. In a new purchase decision, the process can take months or even years and may involve dozens of individual customers inside the organization. The actual purchase decision involves two distinct decisions. Initially, based on an evaluation of product options against product specifications the product choice decision is made. Often a second decision about the supplier is also required.

Technology is playing a major role in business-to-business marketing. The growth of online purchasing, also known as e-procurement, has transformed B2B alliances and made the process faster and more accurate.

KEY TERMS

B2B (business-to-business) markets 211
supply chain 213
product demand 214
derived demand 215
acceleration effect 215
inelastic demand 215
buying decision 216

straight rebuy 216
out supplier 217
modified rebuy 217
new purchase 217
buying center 218
users 219
initiator 219
influencers 219

gatekeepers 219
deciders 219
North American Industrial Classification System (NAICS) 220
original equipment manufacturer (OEM) 221
end user purchases 222
capital equipment 222

APPLICATION QUESTIONS

1. You are the marketing manager for HP laptop computers. Identify and briefly discuss the differences between the consumer market for laptops and the business market. Then give an example of each difference using college students as the consumer market and defense-related companies as the business market.

2. You work for Siemens Power Generations Systems and are responsible for the sale of large, expensive ($2 million to $5 million) turbine generators to power utility companies. You have been contacted by the Ever-sure Utility Corporation in Anytown, USA. Identify the buying center you are likely to find inside the company and how you would market the generators to the buying center group.

3. You are vice president for information technology at your university. Recently you have been authorized to upgrade the network servers on campus. Draft an RFP that will be given to prospective vendors to help guide them in their sales process.

4. You are the primary sales representative for IBM calling on your university and are responsible for finalizing the sale of 20 new network servers. What is the most important factor you would focus on in making the sales presentation to the vice president of information technology and why? What other characteristics would you discuss and why?

MANAGEMENT DECISION CASE: Cisco's Brave New World

The power of the Internet is driven in no small measure by routers spread around the world that direct the flow of digital information. Most of those routers were made by Cisco. Started by computer scientists from Stanford in 1984, the company envisioned a digital world connected by the Internet and managed by thousands of network servers and routers. As it turns out, the company's vision was correct, and Cisco now controls over 80 percent of the router market that makes up the foundation of the Internet. With sales in excess of $30 billion a year and projections of double-digit growth, the company is an acknowledged world technology leader.

At the same time, John Chambers, CEO, is positioning the company to take advantage of new opportunities and deal with potential threats. Cisco is widely regarded as a business-to-business company that builds great hardware. Its core business is selling expensive hardware to network administrators in telecom and other industries. However, while that remains the company's core business, it also realizes fundamental changes in the way people use the Internet, coupled with emerging wireless technologies, are creating new opportunities. Put simply, the world is moving to a network computing model in which applications and information will be networked rather than residing in a box on the individual's desk. Cisco believes that managing the services and applications needed to run a network computing model is the next big growth opportunity in technology.

Cisco is not alone in that vision. Most notably, Microsoft also believes network computing is the future. Both agree that the day is coming soon when wireless devices will receive information from anywhere and send information to a variety of devices including other wireless products such as cell phones, PCs, or any other device on the network (for example, a TV). However, at this point, the shared vision of Cisco and Microsoft takes two distinct directions. Microsoft believes the power to control access and direct information should reside in the programs on the device, which is, not surprisingly, Microsoft's strength. As a result, the company focuses on the integration and connectivity of its core applications such as Office 2007. Cisco, on the other hand, contends the network itself is the most logical place to manage the flow of data. If correct, Cisco would be positioned to control the network platform much like Microsoft does with Windows and the PC environment.

The current battleground is office phone systems. Web conferencing has created significant growth opportunities in office phone systems. Currently, Cisco has nearly 25 percent of the office phone system market (roughly 12 million phones) using its Unified Communications software. The company has also offered new products such as TelePresence, a high-end $300,000 videoconferencing room with sophisticated video screens and systems. In addition, it purchased WebEx Communications, the web conferencing leader, which competes directly with Microsoft's Live Meeting service (the No. 2 in Web conferencing).

Cisco does face challenges. It has not been able to demonstrate success in selling directly to businesses. The company's historical success selling to network administrators does not automatically translate to winning over a company's IT executives. At the same time, it must find ways to cooperate with other key players, such as Microsoft, that control key parts of the technology platform. In addition, other competitors such as Apple offer different visions of the future that, if successful, will limit Cisco's growth opportunities.[37]

Questions for Consideration

1. Evaluate Cisco's strategy of moving away from its core business, routers and network hardware, to software and services that support network computing.

2. Identify two or three new growth opportunities for Cisco that focus on network computing (for example, moving into consumer products that help network a home).

3. Identify challenges and opportunities for Cisco as it moves more aggressively into the business market, selling office phones systems, Web conferencing devices, and other products and services directly to company IT executives.

MARKETING PLAN EXERCISE

ACTIVITY 8: Determine Business Market Relationships

This exercise has four primary activities:

1. Conduct an analysis of your key market opportunities to assess the fundamental nature of these markets. This analysis should include a description of:

   a. Who are the key companies in this market? How much business do you do with the industry leaders? What share of their total business do you have?

   b. Where are these companies located?

2. Identify the probable company structure and business center participants you would encounter in selling to your key business-to-business customer.

3. Put together a probable buying decision process for key B2B customers and discuss your internal process in selling to these customers in this process.

4. Develop a list of second-tier customers in key B2B markets that represent future potential customers.

If you are using Marketing Plan Pro, a template for this assignment can be accessed at www.mhhe.com/marshall1e.

RECOMMENDED READINGS

1. John Coe, *The Fundamentals of Business-to-Business Sales & Marketing* (New York: McGraw-Hill, 2003).

2. Jill Konrath, *Selling to Big Companies* (New York: Kaplan Business, 2005).

3. Jeff Thull, *Mastering the Complex Sale: How to Compete and Win When the Stakes Are High* (Hoboken, New Jersey: Wiley, 2003).

4. *Harvard Business Review on Marketing* (Boston: Harvard Business School Press, 2002).

5. *Harvard Business Review on Teams That Succeed* (Boston: Harvard Business School Press, 2004).

part THREE

Developing the Value Offering

CHAPTER 09

SEGMENTATION, TARGET MARKETING, AND POSITIONING

LEARNING OBJECTIVES

- Explain the criteria for effective segmentation.

- Identify the various approaches to market segmentation.

- Describe the steps in target marketing.

- Understand the continuum of approaches to target marketing strategy.

- Define positioning and link it to the use of the marketing mix.

- Use and interpret perceptual maps.

- Identify sources of differentiation.

- Avoid potential positioning errors.

EXECUTIVE PERSPECTIVE

Executive Steve Stiger, Group Vice President, Marketing and Business Development

Company Bright House Networks

Business Broad-based communications including cable television, high-speed Internet, local and long-distance phone service

What are some key ways you go about segmenting the consumer (end user) marketplace?

Marketing is rarely about approaching just one group. The better we can understand our customers and non-customers, the more effectively we can tailor messages and approaches to best serve each segment.

We evaluate many factors. We start by segmenting customers and noncustomers within respective video, voice, and high-speed data segments. Similarly, non-customers are segmented into "never" and "formers." Formers are then evaluated by disconnect reason.

We segment by level of service—single play, double play, or triple play—which provides insights on customers who subscribe to single versus multiple products. We segment customers by the technology they subscribe to from us—do they have a set-top box or not? Multiple set-top boxes? High-definition or not? DVR?

We also segment by ARPU (average revenue per user). Finally, we segment by behavior—high churn versus low churn. Payment history and demographics are other factors.

What are some key ways you segment the business marketplace?

We evaluate customers and noncustomers from the perspective of delivering video and high-speed data to each segment. Size is a crucial factor, as are the needs of each respective business. Small, home-based businesses are on one end of the spectrum and large enterprise businesses are on the other.

There are significant differences between these segments. Often, we find that our small, home-based business customers behave in many ways like our residential customers. For example, small business customers will have high-speed Internet service with us, and they may also have video service with us.

What is your general positioning strategy for the consumer marketplace?

Our brand position revolves around "easy." That is, we make it easier for our customers to do business with us. We are constantly striving to make it easy for customers to get what they want, when they want it, and where they want it—with one phone call and one appointment.

The technology utilized by many of our competitors means they must cobble together alliances with other companies in order to deliver products our fiber network enables us to provide. Often, this strains their ability to fulfill and diminishes the customer experience.

In addition, we focus our messaging on the fact we are a local company with local service people who live in the same community as our customers, unlike many of our competitors.

EXHIBIT 9.1

EXHIBIT 9.1 — Market Segmentation, Target Marketing, and Positioning

Market Segmentation
Dividing a market into meaningful smaller markets or submarkets based on common characteristics.

↓

Target Marketing
Evaluating the market segments, then making decisions about which among them is most worthy of investment for development.

↓

Positioning
Communicating one or more sources of value to customers in ways that connect needs and wants to what the product has to offer. Positioning strategies are executed through the development of unique combinations of the marketing mix variables.

FULFILLING CONSUMER NEEDS AND WANTS

In one of the band's most famous anthems, Rolling Stones front man Mick Jagger proclaims:

> You can't always get what you want.
> But if you try sometimes you just might find
> You get what you need.

Now, it's a safe bet that Mick Jagger wasn't thinking about needs and wants in the context of marketing and consumers when he and Keith Richards wrote that song in 1968, but the message resonates for marketing managers nonetheless. In fact, the triad of activities illustrated in Exhibit 9.1—market segmentation, targeting, and positioning—get at the heart of marketing's ability to successfully create, communicate, and deliver value to customers and thus successfully fulfill their needs and wants.

In Chapter 1, you read about the evolution of marketing through a series of stages including pre-industrial revolution, focus on production and products, focus on selling, marketing concept, and post-marketing concept approaches. The last stage, which is really a more sophisticated extension of the original marketing concept, includes attention to multiple sources of differentiation, customer orientation, relationships, and mass customization and one-to-one marketing by which firms (enabled by modern technology such as CRM systems) are capable of adding unique value to meet individual customer needs. What distinguishes much of marketing today from that of the past is this capability to more precisely home in on specific customers and customer groups and offer products or services that have a clear and compelling value proposition for those specific customers.[1]

Accomplishing this first requires the use of **market segmentation** to divide a market into meaningful smaller markets or submarkets based on common characteristics. Once a segmentation approach is developed, marketing managers engage in **target marketing,** which involves evaluating the segments and deciding which shows the most promise for development. In most ways, selecting target markets (also called market targets) is truly an *investment* decision. That is, a company must decide where to best invest its limited resources in developing markets for future growth. Everything else being equal, it should invest in the target markets that promise the best overall return on that investment over the long run.[2]

Finally, the way the firm ultimately connects its value proposition to a target market is through its positioning. **Positioning** relies on the communication of one or more sources of value to customers in a way that the customer can easily make the connection between his or her needs and wants and what the product has to offer. Positioning strategies are executed through the development of unique combinations of the marketing mix variables, introduced in Chapter 1 as the 4Ps: product (or more broadly—the offering), price, place (distribution/supply chain), and promotion.[3]

The process of effective market segmentation, target marketing, and positioning is one of the most complex and strategically important aspects of marketing management. It bridges the overall process of creating, communicating, and delivering value to customers in that if the segmentation is flawed, target selection is incorrect, or positioning is unclear, there is no *value* because the customer doesn't connect with the product. Having a product whose value proposition is a well-kept secret is not a good thing in marketing—marketing managers want the right customers to clearly recognize their products' value-adding capabilities.[4]

Let's first take a closer look at segmentation. Then we will go on to gain an understanding of target marketing. Finally, we will introduce positioning as a lead-in to the marketing mix chapters that follow. These three concepts are equally relevant in both the consumer and business marketplaces. The criteria used for developing segments are somewhat different between the two markets, but the general concepts and importance of the process are similar.

WHAT IS SEGMENTATION?

From a marketing manager's perspective, one way to think about markets is on a continuum that ranges from *undifferentiated*, where everybody essentially needs and wants the same thing, to *singular*, where each person has unique needs and wants. The territory between these two extremes is where segmentation approaches come into play.

Segmentation seeks to find one or more factors about members of a heterogeneous market that allow for dividing the market into smaller, more homogeneous subgroups for the purposes of developing different marketing strategies to best meet the segments' distinct needs and wants.[5] The operative word is *different*, as in **differentiation**, which means communicating and delivering value in different ways to different customer groups.[6] It is important to note that the basic logic and principles behind segmentation are sound, regardless of the basis on which a market is segmented:

- Not all customers are alike.
- Subgroups of customers can be identified on some basis of similarity.
- The subgroups will be smaller and more homogeneous than the overall market.
- Needs and wants of a subgroup are more efficiently and effectively addressed than would be possible within the heterogeneous full market.

Criteria for Effective Segmentation

Before developing and executing a segmentation approach, the marketing manager must be assured that several criteria for successful segmentation are met, as listed in Exhibit 9.2. The manager must satisfactorily answer these questions:

1. *Is the segment of sufficient size to warrant investing in a unique value-creating strategy for that segment as a target market?* Ultimately, there is no point doing market segmentation unless a positive return on investment is

EXHIBIT 9.2	Criteria for Effective Segmentation

1. Segment is of sufficient size to warrant investing in a unique value-creating strategy for that segment as a target market.

2. Segment is readily identifiable and can be measured.

3. Segment is clearly differentiated on one or more important dimensions when communicating the value of the product.

4. Segment can be reached (both in terms of communication and physical product) to deliver the value of the product, and subsequently can be effectively and efficiently managed.

Jill's
BOHEMIAN RHAPSODY

"I love the earthy vibe of a
peasant top
worn with
colorful beads."

WAL★MART

Even venerable brands like Wal-Mart have to constantly be looking for new target markets and rejuvenated positioning strategies—in this case through fresh new looks in young fashion.

expected. Size of a segment doesn't necessarily mean number of customers—when Bombardier markets its small Learjets, it knows the number of potential buyers is limited. Yet, segmentation is still a valid approach because of differences in needs and wants among customers and the financial size of the transaction.

2. *Is the segment readily identifiable and can it be measured?* Effective segmentation relies on the marketing manager's ability to isolate members of a submarket to create a unique appeal. Segmentation most often requires data and if secondary data on the markets of interest aren't available or if primary data can't be easily collected, it may not be possible to do segmentation.

3. *Is the segment clearly differentiated on one or more important dimensions when communicating the value of the product?* For segmentation to work properly, it must allow for the creation and execution of different marketing strategies to the different submarkets identified. Segments should be expected to respond differently to different marketing strategies and programs. Otherwise, there is no reason to differentiate.

4. *Can the segment be reached (both in terms of communication and physical product) in order to deliver the value of the product, and subsequently can it be effectively and efficiently managed?* Barriers to reaching a segment might include language, physical distance, or as in the case of some developing markets, transportation, technology, and infrastructure challenges. Firms have to be able to sustain their management of a target segment over time—if this activity becomes problematic it can be a drain on resources and result in poor ROI.

When considering segmentation, it is important to remember that an essential part of Marketing (Big M)—strategic marketing—is not just *identifying* existing segments but also *creating* new ones through product development strategies. The introduction of Apple's iPhone stimulated needs and wants on the part of consumers in uncharted areas in terms of a single product's capabilities to fulfill, thus creating a new market by opening up new avenues of value-enhancing possibilities.[7]

SEGMENTING CONSUMER MARKETS

In the consumer marketplace, the categories of variables used by marketing managers to develop segments can be conveniently grouped into four broad categories as illustrated by Exhibit 9.3: geographic, demographic, psychographic, and behavioral. Let's consider each of these segmentation approaches in turn.

Geographic Segmentation

One of the most straightforward approaches to segmentation is when evidence exists that consumers respond differently to marketing strategies and programs based on where they live. Thus, **geographic segmentation** divides consumer groups based on physical location. The key question is, do consumption patterns vary among the geographic submarkets identified? If so, firms can make tailored adjustments in their products to satisfy those regional differences in needs and wants.[8]

Within the United States, some of the more popular approaches to geographic segmentation include:

- *By region*—Northeast, Southeast, Midwest, and West, for example.
- *By density of population*—urban, suburban, exurban, and rural, for example.
- *By size of population*—Exhibit 9.4 shows the top 20 standard metropolitan statistical areas (SMSAs) in the United States.
- *By growth in population*—Exhibit 9.5 highlights the top 10 fastest-growing markets from 2000 to 2006, by number of people and percentage growth.
- *By climate*—colder Northern states versus warmer Southern states.

EXHIBIT 9.3

Consumer Market Segmentation Approaches

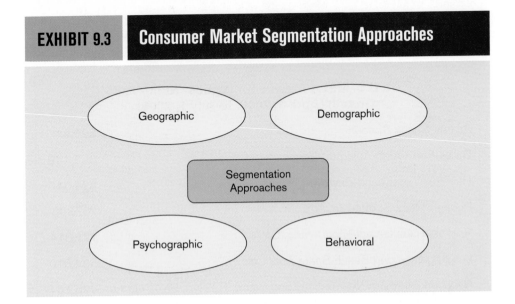

EXHIBIT 9.4

Top 20 U.S. SMSAs

Rank	SMSA	Pop. Millions	Rank	SMSA	Pop. Millions
1.	New York	18.3	11.	Atlanta	4.2
2.	Los Angeles	12.4	12.	San Francisco	4.1
3.	Chicago	9.1	13.	Riverside, Calif.	3.3
4.	Philadelphia	5.7	14.	Phoenix	3.2
5.	Dallas	5.2	15.	Seattle	3.0
6.	Miami	5.0	16.	Minneapolis	3.0
7.	Washington, D.C.	3.7	17.	San Diego	2.8
8.	Houston	4.7	18.	St. Louis	2.7
9.	Detroit	4.5	19.	Baltimore	2.6
10.	Boston	4.4	20.	Pittsburgh	2.4

Source: U.S. Census Bureau, 2000 census statistics posted December 2003. Largest city in each SMSA is listed.

Again, the key questions are whether segmenting by one or more of these geographic qualities means satisfying the criteria for effective segmentation and will it ultimately facilitate better communication and delivery of value to the submarkets than could be accomplished within the aggregate market? JCPenney, for example, segments its target market by geographic climate. Starting in early September, JCPenney begins marketing winter coats in its Chicago-area stores, an activity that won't begin until much later in Dallas, where customers are still expecting several more months of 80 to 90 degrees. The chain's Miami stores might never even stock traditional cold-weather apparel except in small quantities for travelers. JCPenney wisely recognizes different customer needs across different climates and builds its marketing plans accordingly.

EXHIBIT 9.5 | Growth in U.S. Cities

10 U.S. Metro Areas with Highest Numerical Growth (April 1, 2000, to July 1, 2006)	
Atlanta-Sandy Springs-Marietta, Ga.	890,211
Dallas-Fort Worth-Arlington, Texas	842,449
Houston-Sugar Land-Baytown, Texas	824,547
Phoenix-Mesa-Scottsdale, Ariz.	787,306
Riverside-San Bernardino-Ontario, Calif.	771,314
Los Angeles-Long Beach-Santa Ana, Calif.	584,510
New York-Northern New Jersey-Long Island, N.Y.-N.J.-Pa.	495,154
Washington-Arlington-Alexandria, D.C.-Va.-Md.-W.Va.	494,220
Miami-Fort Lauderdale-Miami Beach, Fla.	455,869
Chicago-Naperville-Joliet, Ill.-Ind.-Wis.	407,133

10 Fastest-Growing U.S. Metro Areas (April 1, 2000, to July 1, 2006)	
St. George, Utah	39.8%
Greeley, Colo.	31.0
Cape Coral-Fort Myers, Fla.	29.6
Bend, Ore.	29.3
Las Vegas-Paradise, Nev.	29.2
Provo-Orem, Utah	25.9
Naples-Marco Island, Fla.	25.2
Raleigh-Cary, N.C.	24.8
Gainesville, Ga.	24.4
Phoenix-Mesa-Scottsdale, Ariz.	24.2

Source: U.S. Census Bureau.

Geographic segmentation is useful but, in most instances, is an insufficient segmentation criterion in and of itself. Because people in the United States are extremely mobile and because the demand for many products is not determined by where a person lives, additional types of segmentation are needed to successfully target customers.

Demographic Segmentation

Another straightforward approach to segmentation is via demographic variables. In Chapter 7 you learned that demographics are the statistical characteristics of human populations such as age or income that are used to identify markets. **Demographic segmentation** divides consumer groups based on a variety of readily measurable descriptive factors about the group. Many different demographic variables are available for measurement including age, generational group, gender, family, race and ethnicity, income, occupation, education, social class, and geodemographic group. Demographic segmentation is one of the most popular segmentation approaches because customer needs and wants tend to vary with some degree of regularity based on demographic differences and because of the relative ease of measurement of the variables.[9] Let's look at the major demographic variables more closely (see Exhibit 9.6).

Age

Age segmentation presumes some regularity of consumer needs and wants by chronological age.[10] It is important to make the distinction between chronological age, actual age in years, and psychological or attitudinal age, which reflects how people see themselves.

McDonald's employs age segmentation to execute different marketing strategies to attract young children for a Happy Meal and older consumers for an early morning Egg McMuffin and coffee with friends. But marketers must take care to understand that age alone often is not sufficient for successful segmentation. Older consumers exhibit great differences from person to person on such things as income, mobility, and work status. In fact, marketing managers in companies ranging from travel to insurance to health care have come to realize that lumping older consumers into one group is not an effective segmentation approach because of the vast differences in other important variables.

Some very relevant issues related to age segmentation in home gaming are addressed in Ethical Dimension 9.

EXHIBIT 9.6 **Demographic Segmentation Variables**

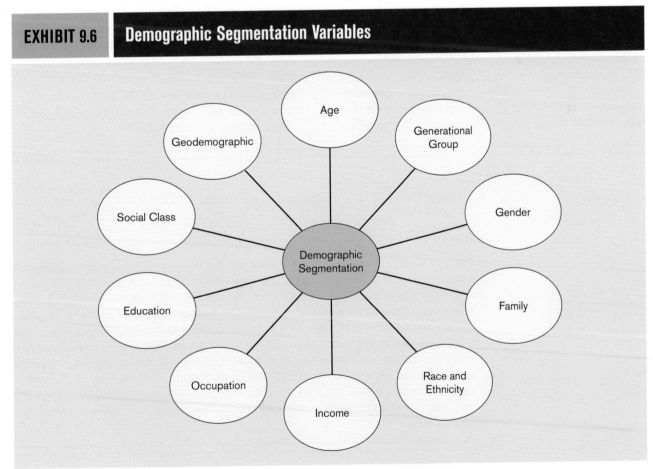

Game On

Ask someone who is the typical video gamer and most people would describe a teenage boy locked in his room for hours with his eyes glued to a monitor that depicts him chasing, and being chased by, bad guys causing all kinds of mayhem. Although millions of young men fit this description, video gaming has also brought in new players creating unique and vastly different market segments. The hard-core gamers are still predominantly men, but research suggests that more than 75 percent of *casual* gamers worldwide are women. Gamers still tend to be younger; nearly a third of the gamers in the United States are under 18 and three-quarters of all gamers are under 50 years old.

The most popular video game genres are action (30 percent) and sports (17 percent). Popular video games include "Madden Football" and online, first-person shooter games such as "Halo." PC games are dominated by strategy and have titles like "World of Warcraft" and "The Sims" (in several versions). The largest titles, like the annual "Madden Football," are billion-dollar brands and generate unit sales in the hundreds of thousands.

As the market continues to expand, video and online gaming companies are seeking new business opportunities. With the broader demographic appeal, advertisers now consider video games a legitimate advertising channel, spending more than $500 million annually. Most of that money goes to put advertisers into the games. However, advertisers will spend $200 million to create "advergames," games designed specifically to promote a brand. Coca-Cola and other companies have created games to get young people connected to the brand. In addition, many of these companies have created virtual stores as part of Second Life and other virtual worlds.

Several key questions remain for the video gaming companies. Critics of violent video games suggest a harmful net effect on teenagers, primarily boys, acting out the violence. They reference the highly interactive, participative nature of the games that draws players into the violence. In addition, critics suggest the games reward the violent behaviors that players repeat over and over as they continue to play the game. Psychologists report that all these activities: (1) thwart interactivity, (2) reward violent behavior, and (3) through repetition, lead to learned acceptance of violence as appropriate behavior. An example of this violence/reward mentality in gaming is the "Grand Theft Auto" game franchise. In 2008, "Grand Theft Auto 4" broke the Guinness world record for the highest revenue generated in the first 24 hours of release of any form of entertainment media, *ever!*[11]

A second issue for video game critics is the length of time children play the games. In a recent study, researchers reported teenage boys play video games on average 13 hours per week. When this much exposure is coupled with the dominance of violent games among this age group, psychologists and many parents get more and more concerned about the long-term effects.[12]

Ethical Perspective

1. **Video Game Developers:** They are meeting the needs of a target market by developing video games that appeal to that market. Is that a problem? What responsibility do they bear for the potential negative effects on young people?

2. **Parents:** If parents are aware of the violence, how should they handle the purchase and use of video games by their children?

FYI

The typical eBay users are 35 to 44 years old, but the peer-to-peer e-commerce giant wants to reach the next generation. To do so, eBay arranged a deal with Facebook, which is a site popular with college students. Through its Half.com subsidiary, eBay sells used textbooks on a special "Student Superstore" page on Facebook. The auction site also is looking at deals to reach even younger audiences found at MySpace, Bebo, and others. Along the way, eBay is learning that partnerships with social networking sites are less controlled than those with normal companies, as the young users of these sites have no qualms about expressing both positive and negative experiences with eBay. This loss of control by marketers is not going to change any time soon when it comes to dealing with consumer-generated content on Web sites such as these.[13]

Generational Group

One approach to age segmentation that helps get at the heart of differences in needs and wants is *generational segmentation*. Much research has been done on understanding differences in groups of people by generation. What defines a generational group and how does one know when a new generational group is emerging? Sociologists look for defining events such as wars, major economic upheaval, or sociocultural revolution as triggers for generational change. As with other segmentation approaches, the notion that different marketing strategies and programs can be developed and executed for different generational groups assumes some degree of homogeneity among the generational cohort.[14] The most recent generational groups, from oldest to youngest, along with their birth years are: the GI Generation (1901–1924), Silent Generation (1925–1945), baby boomers (1946–1964), Generation X (1965–1977), Generation Y (1978–1994), and Millennials (1994 to present). Exhibit 9.7 describes each of these generational cohorts including the core representative values of each.

Match.com realized it could be a good match for an underserved market in the dating game—divorcees and singles over 50 who wanted serious relationships. The company redesigned its site to make it easy to use and more relevant for baby boomers and single parents. Rather than run ads with young, attractive men and women, Match.com featured a 71-year-old with the user name DanishBeauty22. Match.com's focus on the boomer generation let it beat out racier, youth-obsessed rivals to become the largest online dating site in the United States.[15]

The generational group that has traditionally been the apple of the marketing manager's eye is the baby boomers. This is because there are so many of them and because they personify conspicuous consumption—acquiring products for the pure enjoyment of the purchase. An interesting aspect of boomers is that the oldest among the group have just entered their early 60s in age, and the majority of them will soon be facing decisions about retirement and beyond. Much of the research on baby boomers indicates that—at least in their minds—they don't age.[16] Recall that a marketer must be cognizant of the difference between chronological age and attitudinal age. It is anticipated that this forever-young generation will enter the segment we would traditionally label as "older consumer" without an old outlook on life and the future. This has profound implications for marketers in that it turns on end the stereotypical approaches to what products are marketed to them and how they are marketed.[17] Many boomers will become more active, spend more money, and want to experience more new things after retirement than they ever did while they were employed— that is, if you can get them to retire. Many smart marketers who happen to be of Generation X or Y would do well to rethink the potential impact of successful strategies aimed at these ageless boomers.

Generation X is often thought of as a transitional generation. Its members are comfortable with much of the new-age technology but, unlike Gen Y, they didn't grow up with it, they had to learn it. Gen X is pegged as being a very entrepreneurial group, partly because many advancement opportunities in traditional firms have been thwarted by the overabundance of boomers who occupy those positions. It has been estimated that

"I can eat most men under the table."

The sweetener for the real world.

Gen Xers appreciate products like Sweet'n Low that allow them to eat more of what they like.

EXHIBIT 9.7 | **Generational Groups and Representative Values**

GI (16 million born 1901–1924)

- Financial security and conservative spending (shaped by hard times and the economic depression of the 1930s)
- No such thing as problems—only challenges and opportunities
- Civic minded
- Duty to family, community, and country
- Unified and team oriented

Silent (35 million born 1925–1945)

- Strength in human relation skills
- Respectful of others' opinions
- Trusting conformists
- Health, stability, and wisdom
- Civic life and extended families

Baby boomer (78 million born 1946–1964)

- Forever young
- Individualistic
- Conspicuous consumption—great acquirers of goods and services
- Idealistic: value- and cause-driven despite indulgences and hedonism
- The end justifies the means

Generation X (57 million born 1965–1977)

- Lack of trust in society
- Cynical and media-savvy
- Entrepreneurial
- Accept diversity
- Environmentally conscious
- Work to live, not live to work

Generation Y (60 million born 1978–1994)

- Pragmatic
- Optimistic
- Team players
- Savvy consumers
- Edgy
- Focused on urban style
- More idealistic than Gen X
- Technology comes naturally

Millennial (42+ million born 1994 to present)

- Multicultural
- Highly tech-savvy
- Educated
- Grown up in affluence
- Big spending power

Gen X entrepreneurs are responsible for more than 70 percent of the new business start-ups in the United States. Gen X is not as consumption-crazed as the boomers, preferring more of a work-family life balance. For the marketing manager, this knowledge about the Gen X segment offers the opportunity to develop appeals to their independent spirit and practical nature.

Gen X is often referred to as the "baby bust" because it represents a natural cyclical downturn in birthrate. Because Gen X is such a small segment of the consumer market, many marketers have their eye squarely on the Gen Y and Millennial cohorts as the next great consumer frontier. Both of these groups are highly technology-savvy and don't balk at using any and every sort of communication medium to enhance their lives.[18]

Gender

Target Corporation claims that about 80 percent of the dollar sales in its stores are made to women. Many firms note that men account for the majority of online purchases. Such knowledge provides evidence of the power of *gender segmentation*, which recognizes differences in needs and wants of men versus women. Certainly, a wide variety of products are clearly marketed for the primary consumption of either men or women, but not both—think Rogaine, cigars, and athletic supporters versus pregnancy tests, lipstick, and bras, for example. In such cases, marketers can concentrate on linking the product's value-adding properties to its corresponding gender segment. What about cases in which a product appeals to both men and women, but on the basis of satisfying different—maybe subtly different—needs and wants?[19]

Take for example razors. Gillette learned some years ago that generally, women don't like to use a man's razor, which they had to do for decades because no thought was given to differences in gender usage preference. Research in the 1980s revealed that most women viewed men's razors as too bulky, with too many bells and whistles, and not feminine in color or design. Suddenly, Gillette found an underserved new submarket for segmenting its razor line: the female shaver! The result was a completely new brand and product line called Gillette Venus, whose tagline is "Reveal the Goddess in You." Venus comes in six models: Original Venus; Venus Embrace, which "embraces a whole new level of smoothness"; Venus Breeze, the only razor with built-in shave gel bars; Venus Vibrance, which gently exfoliates to reveal more radiant skin; Venus Divine, which contains "Intensive Moisture Strips" enriched with oils; and Venus Disposable, for the "Goddess on the Go."[20]

Family and Household

In years past, the concepts of family and household were fairly easy for marketers to define—a married man and woman, likely with children, and sometimes with other relatives such as a grandparent who had moved back in. Now, *family and household segmentation* can be more complex. Marketing managers are cognizant of all kinds of different family arrangements including singles, unmarried cohabitating couples, gay and lesbian couples, parents with 30-something offspring who boomeranged back home, very large extended families living in one household, and so forth. Many of these changes in the concept of family have evolved based on changing economic realities, social norms, and cultural/subcultural mores.

Marketers who want to use family and household in segmentation need to understand the overall picture. One way to portray this variable is through the **family life cycle,** which was introduced in Chapter 7 and represents a series of life stages defined by age, marital status, number of children, and other factors.[21]

When Amana introduced the microwave oven in the 1960s, it started out as a product that was marketed to the busy homemaker as a way to supplement her food preparation and make her day at home more efficient. Now, most new microwaves are sold to singles, both men and women, who, in many instances, don't use or even own a traditional oven.

Race and Ethnicity

Race and ethnicity segmentation has become of prime importance in the United States as the number of natural-born citizens of ethnic minorities grows and the number of immigrants has increased.[22] Exhibit 9.8 provides some important summary facts about the U.S. minority population.

In recent years, most firms have jumped on the bandwagon of segmenting by race and ethnicity, partly because many of these submarkets are growing quite rapidly in terms of both size and buying power and partly because they have historically been ignored by mainstream marketers.[23] African-Americans account for slightly more than 12 percent of the U.S. population, a figure that has not been growing. In years past, very few products were marketed specifically to the African-American segment other than by firms specializing only in that segment. Hair and beauty product pioneer Johnson Products, founded in 1954, was an early believer in the power of developing products such as Ultra Sheen, Afro Sheen, Classy Curl, and others that brought the company consistently double-digit sales increases throughout the 1970s and 1980s. Ultimately, the product line became so attractive that it was acquired by mainstream beauty care manufacturer L'Oreal and eventually by Wella Corporation, another broad-line marketer of beauty care products. Today, almost all major cosmetic and beauty aid firms, from Avon to Procter & Gamble, market products specifically designed to appeal to this vital market segment.

In contrast to the stability of the African-American segment, the Hispanic and Asian-American segments are both growing at a rapid rate. As Exhibit 9.8

EXHIBIT 9.8 **U.S. Minority Population Tops 100 Million**

General Update

- In June 2007, the nation's minority population reached 100.7 million, according to the national and state estimates by race, Hispanic origin, sex, and age released by the U.S. Census Bureau. A year earlier, the minority population totaled 98.3 million. California had a minority population of 20.7 million—21 percent of the nation's total. Texas had a minority population of 12.2 million—12 percent of the U.S. total.

- Hispanic remained the largest minority group, with 44.3 million on July 1, 2006—14.8 percent of the total population. Black was the second-largest minority group, totaling 40.2 million in 2006. They were followed by Asian (14.9 million), American Indian and Alaska Native (4.5 million), and Native Hawaiian and Other Pacific Islander (1 million). The population of non-Hispanic whites who indicated no other race totaled 198.7 million in 2006.

- With a 3.4 percent increase between July 1, 2005, and July 1, 2006, Hispanic was the fastest-growing minority group. Asian was the second fastest-growing minority group, with a 3.2 percent population increase during the period of 2005–2006. The population of non-Hispanic whites who indicated no other race grew by 0.3 percent during the one-year period.

- Four states and the District of Columbia are "majority-minority." Hawaii led the nation with a population that was 75 percent minority in 2006, followed by the District of Columbia (68 percent), New Mexico (57 percent), California (57 percent), and Texas (52 percent). No other state had a minority population exceeding 42 percent of the total.

Hispanic Highlights

- Hispanics accounted for almost half (1.4 million) of the national population growth of 2.9 million between July 1, 2005, and July 1, 2006.

- California had the largest Hispanic population of any state as of July 1, 2006 (13.1 million), followed by Texas (8.4 million) and Florida (3.6 million). Texas had the largest numerical increase between 2005 and 2006 (305,000), with California (283,000) and Florida (161,000) following. In New Mexico, Hispanics

comprised the highest proportion of the total population (44 percent), with California and Texas (36 percent each) next in line.

- The Hispanic population in 2006 was much younger, with a median age of 27.4 compared with the population as a whole at 36.4. About a third of the Hispanic population was younger than 18, compared with one-fourth of the total population.

African-American Highlights

- The African-American population increased by 1.3 percent, or 522,000, between 2005 and 2006.

- New York had the largest African-American population in 2006 (3.5 million), followed by Florida (3 million) and Texas (2.9 million). Texas had the largest numerical increase between 2005 and 2006 (135,000), with Georgia (101,000) and Florida (86,000) next. In the District of Columbia, the black population comprised the highest percentage (57 percent); Mississippi (37 percent) and Louisiana (32 percent) were next.

- The African-American population in 2006 was younger, with a median age of 30.1, compared with the population as a whole at 36.4. About 31 percent of the black population was younger than 18, compared with 25 percent of the total population.

Asian Highlights

- The Asian population rose by 3.2 percent, or 460,000, between 2005 and 2006.

- California had the largest Asian population on July 1, 2006 (5 million), as well as the largest numerical increase during the 2005–2006 period (114,000). New York (1.4 million) and Texas (882,000) followed in population; Texas (43,000) and New York (34,000) followed in numerical increase. In Hawaii, Asians made up the highest proportion of the total population (56 percent), with California (14 percent) and New Jersey and Washington (8 percent each) next.

- The Asian population in 2006 was younger with a median age of 33.5, compared with the population as a whole at 36.4.

demonstrates, Hispanics have overtaken African-Americans as a percentage of the U.S. population. An obvious challenge with the Hispanic segment, at least from the perspective of recent immigrants, has been the language barrier.[24] In the past, marketers' use of the Spanish language and symbolism in communicating with customers has mostly been through attempts at humor. Consider Taco Bell's "Yo quiero Taco Bell"-uttering Chihuahua dog or the Frito Bandito, for example. But today, marketers are taking Spanish-speaking Americans very seriously.[25] Compared to other groups, these segments are younger, more oriented toward developing long-term relationships with people and brands, have more people per family and household, and have experienced a tantalizingly strong increase in disposable income.

Income

Income segmentation is based on a very quantifiable demographic variable, and it is usually analyzed in incremental ranges. The average income of U.S. families has been rising recently, but at a declining rate of increase compared to prior decades.[26] Marketers use income as a segmenting approach very frequently. Examples on the lower-income side include deep-discount retailers and dollar menus at fast-food restaurants. Examples at the higher end include luxury automobiles, gourmet restaurants, and exotic travel experiences. Interestingly though, there is not necessarily a direct correlation between income and price preferences. Southwest Airlines, for example, is a low-priced carrier yet maintains a certain cache with many high-income customers largely because of its fun style and spirit.[27]

Using income alone as a segmentation approach has some problems. First, many people either purposely misstate or refuse to reveal their income on questionnaires and in interviews used in collecting data for identifying segments. Second, with the readily available credit that is pervasive in the U.S. consumer marketplace, actual income may not necessarily drive one's ability to purchase products that in prior days were reserved for those with more income.[28] Cars costing tens of thousands of dollars can be had by nearly anyone nowadays by extending payments out six or more years. Even the old standby of income segmentation, home ownership, has fallen victim to wild mortgage schemes during many years of low initial interest, no-interest, and 40- and 50-year terms to entice buyers to go ahead and sign their financial lives away (which we now know had the unintended consequence of facilitating a meltdown of the mortgage banking industry).

Marketing upscale liquor to upper-crust customers is a unique art form. TV ads don't work well because they are so costly and miss the mark with selective society sophisticates. Instead, to introduce its $200-a-bottle Johnny Walker Blue Label, the company sponsored art gallery openings. Artsy ads and private gallery parties boosted sales of Blue Label by 25 to 30 percent.[29]

Occupation

Occupational segmentation recognizes that there may be a number of consistent needs and wants demonstrated by consumers based on what type of job they have. The U.S. Bureau of Census lists numerous standardized categories of occupations including Professional/Managerial, Technical, Government, Trades, Agricultural, Educator, Student, and Unemployed.[30] In the United States, the workplace and our peer group of fellow workers is one of the strongest reference groups, and as you learned in Chapter 7, reference groups can be very powerful influencers on consumer behavior. All sorts of product lines are directly affected by occupation, including the clothing, equipment, and other personal support materials needed to fit in with the occupational peer group. Sometimes the employer influences purchase choice by offering tuition reimbursement, health care preferred provider networks, or discounts on products and services for employees. As a segmentation variable, occupation is very closely related to income although the two are not perfectly correlated.[31] That is, many traditionally blue-collar jobs may pay higher wages than white-collar positions depending in part on the strength of the union within the firm and industry. Obviously, occupation is also related to education in that the latter usually enables the former.

Education

In U.S. society, research consistently shows that education is one of the strongest predictors of success in terms of type of occupation, upward mobility, and long-term income potential. Everything else being equal, *educational segmentation* might lead a firm to offer its products based on some anticipated future payoff from the consumer. Take credit cards, for example. Why are credit card providers so eager to market themselves to college-bound high school seniors? Because they know that, even with low beginning credit limits, gaining usage early increases the chances of loyalty to the card over the long run—after the student finishes college, gains professional employment, and starts making a bigger salary. Unfortunately, educational segmentation works the other direction as well, which is a potential dark side of segmentation in general. Unscrupulous marketers have been accused of using educational segmentation (often combined with a language barrier) to intentionally take advantage of uneducated consumers in a host of ways including pushing unhealthy or untested products, encouraging bad financial investments, and promoting various illegal sales approaches such as taking the money for household or automobile repairs up front and employing illegal pyramid schemes.[32]

> Whole Foods Markets doesn't try to sell groceries to everyone. Rather, it's trying to meet the needs of a certain set of customers. Those customers are older, more focused on health and wellness, and concerned about issues such as global warming. They see Whole Foods as a symbol of an eco-friendly, healthy, socially responsible lifestyle with which they identify.[33]

Social Class

Social class segmentation involves grouping consumers by a standardized set of social strata around the familiar lower class, middle class, and upper class, and each of these contains several substrata. Exhibit 9.9 shows a traditional approach to segmentation by social class in the United States.

The composition of social classes takes into account several important demographic variables including income, occupation, and education.[34] However, nowadays many mitigating factors might affect one's inclusion in one or the other of the class strata. Readily available credit has flattened the classes and made many luxury products affordable to a broad spectrum of consumers who in the past would not have been able to purchase them. And who doesn't know someone who is quite wealthy that also shops at Target for staple goods? Although the very upper and very lower strata are still potentially useful for segmentation, it has become increasingly difficult to segment among the groups within the big middle stratum. Because of this, most marketing managers today prefer to either defer to other demographic variables for segmentation or, more likely, to look at psychographics and behavioral segmentation approaches that capture much of what used to be evidenced by social class.[35]

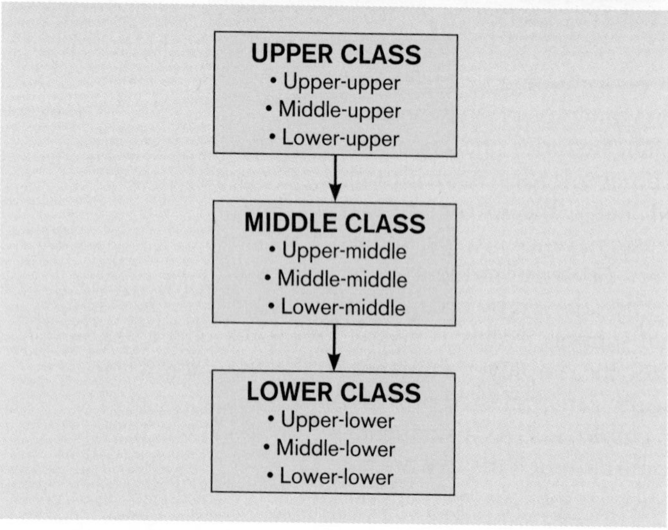

Geodemographics

A hybrid form of segmentation that considers both geographic and demographic factors is

EXHIBIT 9.9 Traditional Social Class Strata in the United States

UPPER CLASS
- Upper-upper
- Middle-upper
- Lower-upper

MIDDLE CLASS
- Upper-middle
- Middle-middle
- Lower-middle

LOWER CLASS
- Upper-lower
- Middle-lower
- Lower-lower

called *geodemographic segmentation*. Typically, marketers turn to firms that specialize in collecting such data on an ongoing basis to purchase data relevant to their geographic area of focus.[36] Let's say for example that you are interested in coming into the Orlando metropolitan area with a new upscale type of convenience store and gas station to compete for customers, especially females, who don't like the ambience at a typical convenience store. Your research shows that it will be important to place your stores in neighborhoods trafficked by consumers who are more likely to be attracted to your upscale merchandise and more pleasant surroundings. Where do you turn for data on segments that might be a good match for your product?

Segmentation approaches fulfill different roles. "For example, a geodemographic classification of the simplest kind means your company is probably at the early stages of using direct marketing," says John Wallinger, database director at Craik Jones Watson Mitchell Voelkel, a communications agency. "As a company matures, the more segmentation approaches it tends to get involved with." Many companies have psychographic or behavioral based classification systems that are very useful ways of describing their typical customer.[37]

One source is Nielsen's Claritas, which continually updates a large database called PRIZM-NE that is zip-code driven. PRIZM profiles every zip code in the United States by both demographic and lifestyle (psychographic) variables. Over time, PRIZM has discovered 62 "neighborhood types" into which all zip codes fall. Exhibit 9.10 describes several PRIZM clusters that might be potential customers for your new upscale convenience and gas store.

Judging from the description of the product, these PRIZM clusters seem to be likely segments of interest: Winner's Circle, Money and Brains, and Executive Suites. Certainly, other clusters not shown in Exhibit 9.10 might also fit your profile of assumed consumer needs and wants. The next step would be to seek zip codes whose location involves traffic patterns that will feed these consumer clusters into your convenience stores. These locations might involve being either close to housing additions or on key routes that members of these clusters take between home and work.

EXHIBIT 9.10	Sample PRIZM Clusters

Winner's Circle

Among the wealthy suburban lifestyles, Winner's Circle is the youngest, a collection of mostly 25- to 34-year-old couples with large families in new-money subdivisions. Surrounding their homes are the signs of upscale living: recreational parks, golf courses, and upscale malls. With a median income of nearly $90,000, Winner's Circle residents are big spenders who like to travel, ski, eat out, shop at clothing boutiques, and take in a show.

Money and Brains

The residents of Money and Brains seem to have it all: high incomes, advanced degrees, and sophisticated tastes to match their credentials. Many of these city dwellers, who are predominantly white with a high concentration of Asian-Americans, are married couples with few children who live in fashionable homes on small, manicured lots.

Executive Suites

Executive Suites consists of upper-middle-class singles and couples typically living just beyond the nation's beltways. Filled with significant numbers of Asian-Americans and college graduates—both groups are represented at more than twice the national average—this segment is a haven for white-collar professionals drawn to comfortable homes and apartments within a manageable commute to downtown jobs, restaurants, and entertainment.

Source: www.claritas.com.

Psychographic Segmentation

make the call

Music and fashion complete each other—just try to imagine one without the other. Together they give you the power to shed inhibitions, assume a new identity, express yourself. Supermodel Niki Taylor calls up the many sides of her personality with help from Nokia, the world's largest manufacturer of wireless phones.

NOKIA
CONNECTING PEOPLE

www.NokiaUSA.com

Nokia is clearly messaging about a lifestyle in this ad—connecting a hip fashion image around their phones.

Another approach to segmenting consumer markets is through **psychographic segmentation,** which relies on consumer variables such as personality and *AIOs* (activities, interests, and opinions) to segment a market. Psychographic segmentation is sometimes also referred to as segmentation by lifestyle or values. Psychographic segmentation builds on a purely demographic approach in that it helps flesh out the profile of the consumer as a human being and not just a location or demographic descriptor.[38] Psychographic segmentation brings individual differences into the profile along with the more readily measurable descriptive variables we have discussed so far.

An important challenge of using psychographic segmentation involves the reliability and validity of its measurement. Unlike geographic and demographic measures, which are relatively objective in nature, psychographic measures attempt to "get into the head" of the consumer. One way to better assure that such measures are reliable and valid is through the use of standardized questionnaires that reflect the experiences of a large number of users over an extended period. One popular psychographic instrument is **VALS™ (**formerly known as **Values and Lifestyles),** a product of SRI Consulting Business Intelligence (SRIC-BI). Want to know your own VALS™ type? Just go to www.sric-bi.com/VALS, click on "VALS™ Survey," and complete a questionnaire.

When Levi Strauss saw Dockers sales declining due to changing fashion tastes and a flood of khaki competitors, the company refocused Dockers as a lifestyle brand. The company designed and marketed a wider range of apparel tailored for four different occasions—work, weekend wear, dressing up, and golf. The new brand name, Dockers San Francisco, emphasizes the lifestyle image and the brand's roots. The changes reversed declining sales and put Dockers back on the path of growth.[39]

VALS™ divides U.S. adults into eight groups that are determined both by primary motivation and by resources. Exhibit 9.11 portrays the basic VALS™ framework. Note that the key drivers in the system are the person's level of resources (high/low), innovation (high/low), and primary motivation (ideals, achievement, and self-expression). According to SRIC-BI, "Each of us is an individual. Yet each of us also has personality traits, attitudes, or needs that are similar to those of other people. VALS™ measures the underlying psychological motivations and resources that groups of consumers share that predict each group's typical choices as consumers." VALS™ has shown consistently strong evidence of reliability and validity.[40]

Again quoting SRIC-BI, "Consumers who are motivated primarily by ideals are guided by knowledge and principles. Consumers who are motivated primarily by achievement look for products and services that demonstrate success to their peers. And consumers who are motivated primarily by self-expression desire social or physical activity, variety, and risk." Notice the psychographics—the strong grounding of content in individual lifestyles and values. VALS™, or any similar psychographic instrument, works to help marketing managers successfully match people to products and helps focus the communication of value in ways that a particular VALS™ group is most likely to connect with. Product

EXHIBIT 9.11 | VALS™ Framework

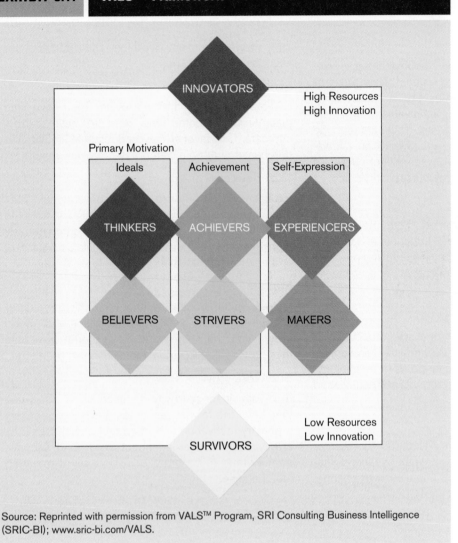

Source: Reprinted with permission from VALS™ Program, SRI Consulting Business Intelligence (SRIC-BI); www.sric-bi.com/VALS.

ownership, preferred media, hobbies, and so on are determined by integrating the VALS™ questionnaire into larger surveys such as MediaMark Research, Inc. (MRI) or client private studies. Geographic concentrations of the VALS™ types are found using GeoVALS™.

Urban Outfitters, Inc., created hybrid concepts based on distinct demographics and psychographics with its Urban Outfitters, Free People, and Anthropologie brands, thereby reducing cannibalization among the brands. Clothing retailer Chico's zeros in on an ignored segment of the population: older and larger-sized females. It caters to these customers via dressing rooms without mirrors, friendly sales associates, and a "0, 1, 2, 3" sizing system.[41]

Exhibit 9.12 describes each of the eight VALS™ types.

Assume that you take the survey and discover you are an Achiever. Lots of hard-driving MBA students and undergraduate business majors are Achievers. The profile of Achievers shown in Exhibit 9.12 provides evidence of how a marketing manager might appeal to Achiever consumers through products that reflect status, prestige, and success. Brands that would seem to connect well with this type include Ritz-Carlton, BMW, and Bose.

EXHIBIT 9.12 | Description of the VALS™ Types

Innovators

Innovators are successful, sophisticated, take-charge people with high self-esteem. Because they have such abundant resources, they exhibit all three primary motivations (ideals, achievement, and self-expression) in varying degrees. They are change leaders and are the most receptive to new ideas and technologies. Their purchases reflect cultivated tastes for upscale, niche products and services.

Thinkers

Thinkers are mature, satisfied, comfortable, and reflective. They tend to be well-educated and actively seek out information in the decision-making process. They favor durability, functionality, and value in products.

Believers

Believers are strongly traditional and respect rules and authority. Because they are fundamentally conservative, they are slow to change and technology-averse. They choose familiar products and established brands.

Achievers

Achievers have goal-oriented lifestyles that center on family and career. They avoid situations that encourage a high degree of stimulation or change.

They prefer premium products that demonstrate success to their peers.

Strivers

Strivers are trendy and fun loving. They have little discretionary income and tend to have narrow interests. They favor stylish products that emulate the purchases of people with greater material wealth.

Experiencers

Experiencers appreciate the unconventional. They are active and impulsive, seeking stimulation from the new, offbeat, and risky. They spend a comparatively high proportion of their income on fashion, socializing, and entertainment.

Makers

Makers value practicality and self-sufficiency. They choose hands-on constructive activities and spend leisure time with family and close friends. Because they prefer value to luxury, they buy basic products.

Survivors

Survivors lead narrowly focused lives. Because they have the fewest resources, they do not exhibit a primary motivation and often feel powerless. They are primarily concerned about safety and security, so they tend to be brand loyal and buy discounted merchandise.

Source: Reprinted with permission from VALS ™ Program. SRI Consulting Business Intelligence (SRIC-BI); www.sric-bc.com/VALS.

Behavioral Segmentation

Behavioral segmentation divides customers into groups according to similarities in benefits sought or product usage patterns.

Benefits Sought

Why do people buy? That is, what are the crucial value-adding properties of an offering? For many people, a Wal-Mart Supercenter offers the ultimate in one-stop shopping. The idea of going to one store and getting everything from groceries to CDs to kitty litter has a lot of appeal, if the critical benefit sought is broad selection, low prices, and infrequent, extended trips to the store. On the other hand, in recent years Walgreens drugstores have been cropping up on corner after corner of high-traffic streets. Walgreens has been extremely successful in appealing to a shopper seeking a different set of benefits, namely less time in the store and a lower level of hassle. The chain caters to consumers for whom the convenience of having a store that is close to home or en route to work trumps other potential benefits such as selection and price.[42]

For many marketing managers, segmentation by benefits sought is the best place to start the process of market segmentation. You might begin by identifying groups interested in the specific bundle of benefits afforded by your offering and then move toward utilizing the other segmentation variables to further hone the profile of the core group that is attracted to your product's benefits.

Usage Patterns

Segmentation by usage patterns includes usage occasions, usage rate, and user status. Occasions means specifically when the product is used. Why do you buy greeting cards? What causes you to take your significant other out for that special dinner? What makes you break down and rent that tux or buy that formal? Each of these purchases is driven by an occasion, and marketers are very savvy at playing to consumers' desires to use occasions as a reason to buy.[43]

Listerine in an example of usage-based segmentation. Back when Listerine was marketed as just a mouthwash, it tended to be used sporadically or in the morning as part of the day's hygiene routine. But now that the product also addresses such oral concerns as gingivitis and gum disease, the usage rate is way up with many people developing a regular, twice-a-day regimen. This greatly enhanced the usage rate for the product.[44] Marketers often segment based on whether a consumer is a light, medium, or heavy user. Many firms subscribe to the concept of the *80/20 rule*—that 80 percent of the business is done by 20 percent of the users.

Degree of customer loyalty is another important focus for segmentation. In Chapter 4 we commented on the capability of CRM to aid marketing managers in identifying, tracking, and communicating with especially loyal patrons so marketers can implement strategies to keep those patrons loyal and reduce temptation to switch. In practice, loyalty programs for airlines and hotels, as well as frequent shopper cards for supermarkets and other retailers, all play on the notion of keeping the segment of heaviest users satisfied and using the product and of building a relationship between the customer and the brand and company.[45]

Finally, as you read in the chapter opening Executive Perspective by Steve Stiger at Bright House Networks, segmenting users into groups such as former users, current users, potential users, first-time users, and regular users can be very advantageous. Often, firms will come up with extra incentives for former users to retry a product or for potential users to make that initial purchase. It is critical to influence the segment of first-time users to take the plunge and purchase. CRM programs enable marketing managers to customize the value offering, thus maximizing the appeal to each of these user status segments.

EXHIBIT 9.13	Examples of Segmentation Approaches

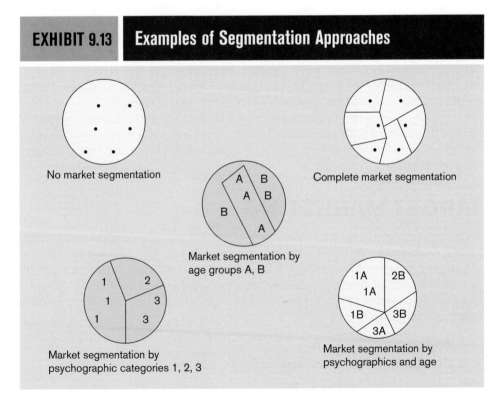

No market segmentation

Complete market segmentation

Market segmentation by age groups A, B

Market segmentation by psychographic categories 1, 2, 3

Market segmentation by psychographics and age

Firms Use Multiple Segmentation Approaches Simultaneously

We have seen that geographic, demographic, psychographic, and behavioral approaches to segmenting consumer markets all have strong potential. In practice, these approaches are not applied one at a time. Firms develop a profile of a segment that might include aspects of any or all of the segmentation approaches we have discussed. Exhibit 9.13 on page 255 provides visual examples of a range of segmentation approaches, including combinations of several types of segmentation.

Developing the right segmentation strategy is one of the most important aspects of the marketing manager's role. Expertise in market segmentation is highly valued by companies across many industries because of the process's complexity and the potential for effective segmentation to have a major impact on a firm's success in the marketplace.[46]

Best Buy, a consumer electronics retailer, has successfully adopted a customer-centric marketing approach. The company identified multiple customer segments, each of which is differentiated based on clear needs/wants. Best Buy is delivering value propositions to those segments. The overall corporate message is "Thousands of possibilities—get yours." The message is all about providing customers with the breadth of choice of a mass merchandiser but with the clear promise of a tailored, total experience of a boutique catering to a specific customer segment.[47]

Segmenting Business Markets

Chapter 8 provided an extensive treatment of the many important properties unique to business markets. The variables relevant to segmentation of business markets share some overlap with those in consumer markets, but it is worth highlighting several unique segmentation approaches here as well. Exhibit 9.14 summarizes several key approaches to business market segmentation.

In some ways, business market segmentation is more straightforward than that of consumer markets. This is partly because there is often a more defined universe of potential customers.[48] For example, using one variable from each set in Exhibit 9.14, a firm might create a profile segment for focus that includes one industry, current nonusers, price-focused, large quantity, and strong loyalty. In any given industry in the business-to-business market, this segmentation profile would probably narrow the segment to include just a few firms. This would allow for a focused approach to communicating and delivering value to this profile of firms. Of course, as with consumer markets, segments must meet the criteria for effective segmentation and if the profile above appears too narrow, one or more of the variables can be removed.

TARGET MARKETING

Target marketing is the process of evaluating market segments and deciding which among them shows the most promise for development. The decision to invest in developing a segment into a target market represents an important turning point in the marketing planning process because, from this point forward, the direction of a firm's marketing strategies and related programs are set.[49] The three steps in target marketing are:

1. Analyze market segments.
2. Develop profiles of each potential target market.
3. Select a target marketing approach.

EXHIBIT 9.14 | **Business Market Segmentation Variables**

- Demographic
  - Industry
  - Company size
  - Location
- Operating Variables
  - Technology
  - User status
  - Customer capabilities
- Purchasing Approaches
  - Purchasing function organization
  - Power structure

- Nature of existing relationship
- General purchasing policies
- Purchasing criteria
- Situational Factors
  - Urgency
  - Specific application
  - Size of the order
- Personal Characteristics
  - Buyer-seller similarity
  - Attitudes toward risk
  - Loyalty

Source: This listing is derived from an influential early book on business markets—Thomas V. Bonoma and Benson P. Shapiro, *Segmenting the Industrial Market* (Lexington, MA: Lexington Books, 1983).

Analyze Market Segments

A number of strategic factors come into play when analyzing whether a segment is a good candidate for investment as a target market. Many different factors should be considered in the analysis. The goal is to determine the relative attractiveness of the various segments using an ROI (return on investment) approach. Everything else being equal, it is prudent to assign a high level of attractiveness to segments that provide the quickest, highest-level, and longest-sustaining anticipated ROI.[50]

Several factors should be considered when analyzing segment attractiveness. The following are among the most important: segment size and growth potential, competitive forces related to the segment, and overall *strategic fit* of the segment to the company's goals and value-adding capabilities.

Segment Size and Growth Potential

When Procter & Gamble was considering acquiring Gillette in 2005, one strong attraction was entry into the lucrative shaving market, which would place P&G solidly into the men's toiletries market—a market space in which the company had little product representation. By 2008, the U.S. men's toiletries market was expected to hit $1 billion in sales, with an annual growth rate of 4 to 5 percent per year. The opportunity for P&G to gain a substantial chunk of those sales by acquiring Gillette (which has about 70 percent of the razor and blade business) was too tempting to pass up—even at the price of $57 billion. P&G sees its strategic investment in this new target market as an opening to developing more new products for men.

Segment Competitive Forces

In Chapter 2 we identified Michael Porter's six competitive forces that firms must be cognizant of when considering investment in new target markets. For P&G's Gillette razor and blade business, several of these predominate. First, rivalry among existing firms is fierce. Schick, a distant No. 2 to Gillette in market share, is nonetheless a scrappy competitor willing to match Gillette's penchant for grandiose innovation (think six-bladed Fusion) with some product bravado of its own (Quattro Chrome, Midnight, and Power versions). Second, a strong threat of substitute products is present in the form of convenient, heavily promoted electric shavers as well as an emerging product category of depilatories for men. Finally, bargaining power of suppliers has become more of an issue in the razor and blade industry primarily due to the rising cost of the metals required for production of today's finely honed blades. If the base price of steel and its transportation were to take a major spike upward, more consumers might become disenchanted with the constant replacement routine for blades and switch to electric shavers. Still, even with these competitive forces at play, P&G's analysis indicated a highly positive ROI for its entry into the market.

Strategic Fit of the Segment

Strategic fit means there is a good match of a target market to the firm's internal structure, culture, goals, and resource capabilities. In the case of the P&G acquisition of Gillette, P&G executives have been widely quoted as saying that one of the primary areas of attractiveness of entering the razor and blade segment was its natural fit within P&G's sophisticated supply chain system, especially in international markets. P&G has already dramatically increased the level of distribution of Gillette products in many countries, simply by plugging the existing products into P&G's vast network of customer relationships. The nature of Gillette's products was a great strategic fit for much of what P&G already does in the market.

FYI

Sometimes, a company will acquire another company to improve its strategic fit to a particular business segment. Johnson Controls, which provides power control systems, made a major change to its marketing strategy after it acquired York International, a global supplier of heating, ventilating, and air-conditioning (HVAC) equipment and services. Previously, Johnson Controls and York each had relatively small service businesses in the HVAC space. After the acquisition, Johnson Controls has been able to expand its HVAC service business to retail stores and businesses with many buildings. "Now when customers are building a building, rather than going to multiple vendors for chillers, air handlers, control systems, and other mechanical equipment, they can go to a one-stop shop. It's attractive to more types of customers," said Andrew DeGuire, vice president-strategy at Johnson Controls.[51]

Develop Profiles of Each Potential Target Market

Once the market segments have been analyzed, marketing managers need to develop profiles of each segment under consideration for investment as a target market. Especially within the context of marketing planning, specifying the attributes of each segment and describing the characteristics of a "typical" consumer within that segment—from a geographic, demographic, psychographic, and behavioral perspective—are invaluable to gaining a better understanding of the degree to which each segment meets the criteria set out by a firm for segment attractiveness and target market ROI. Subsequently, a decision can now be made on prioritizing the segments for investment to develop them as target markets.[52]

Usually, this analysis results in segments that fall within four basic levels of priority for development:

1. **Primary target markets**–those segments that clearly have the best chance of meeting ROI goals and the other attractiveness factors.
2. **Secondary target markets**–those segments that have reasonable potential but for one reason or another are not best suited for development immediately.
3. **Tertiary target markets**–those segments that may develop emerging attractiveness for investment in the future but that do not appear attractive at present.
4. **Target markets to abandon for future development.**

EXHIBIT 9.15 | **Continuum of Target Marketing Approaches**

Very Broad			Very Narrow
Undifferentiated target marketing	Differentiated target marketing	Concentrated target marketing	Customized target marketing

Select a Target Marketing Approach

The final step in target marketing is to select the approach. Exhibit 9.15 portrays a continuum of approaches to target marketing from very broad to very narrow. Four basic options in target marketing strategy are undifferentiated, differentiated, concentrated (also called focus or niche), and customized (or one-to-one).

Leap Wireless International Inc., under the brand name Cricket, targets niche markets overlooked by larger carriers: young, low-income, and ethnic customers. The company doesn't require credit checks or contracts and it offers flat-rate service rather than charging for minutes. That formula has paid off. The San Diego-based company has attracted 2 million subscribers at a time when more than three-quarters of Americans already have cell phones.[53]

Undifferentiated Target Marketing

The broadest possible approach is **undifferentiated target marketing**—which is essentially a one-market strategy, sometimes referred to as an unsegmented *mass market*. Firms whose market approach is grounded in Porter's competitive strategy of low cost may use a relatively undifferentiated target marketing strategy based primarily on the resulting price advantage.[54] Southwest Airlines and Wal-Mart are two firms that have built their businesses on their inherent internal cost advantages, passing along a price advantage to the mass market. But most firms don't have the kind of cost efficiencies it takes to operate such a target marketing approach and instead have to rely on developing sources of differentiation other than price.

Differentiated Target Marketing

Differentiated target marketing, often referred to as simply *differentiation*, means developing different value offerings for different targeted segments. Possible sources of differentiation are many and include innovation/R&D, product quality, service leadership, employees, convenience, brand image, technology, corporate social responsibility, and many others. A significant challenge with differentiation as a core market strategy is that competitors are constantly coming to market with new differentiators that trump the efficacy of the current ones. Overnight a new technological innovation or other strategic shift by a competitor can doom a firm's current source of differentiation to the junk heap.[55]

Breitling markets "Instruments for professionals"—not just ordinary watches—to its higher income target market.

FedEx famously differentiates based on speed of delivery and dependability of overall service to appeal to a target market willing to pay a price premium for these attributes. When UPS moved full force into the overnight package segment, its differentiating message was about full integration of services for the user through a smorgasbord of services including ground, overnight, and integrated supply chain solutions even for small-to-medium size businesses. About the same time, FedEx entered UPS's lucrative over-the-road transport space with FedEx Ground. Initially, because of UPS's domination FedEx had a difficult time differentiating itself in a meaningful way and only recently has FedEx Ground begun to gain widespread usage at a level that would even come close to affecting UPS's domination of that market.

Concentrated Target Marketing

A **concentrated target marketing** approach, which Michael Porter refers to as a *focus strategy* and is also popularly called a *niche strategy,* involves targeting a large portion of a small market. Many start-up firms enter a marketplace as a focus player. Because they are not saddled with keeping up with competitive demands in the broader market, firms using concentrated target marketing can realize cost and operational efficiencies and better margins than many first positioned as differentiators.[56] The danger of being a focus player is that sometimes these firms get too successful and are no longer able to fly under the radar of the differentiators, especially if the niche they occupy is a growing niche within the larger market.

Customized (One-to-One) Marketing

With the proliferation of CRM, firms are able to develop more customized approaches to target marketing. In Chapter 1 we said that **customized (one-to-one) marketing,** as conceived by leading proponents Don Peppers and Martha Rogers, advocates that firms should direct energy and resources into establishing a learning relationship with each customer and then connect that knowledge with the firm's production and service capabilities to fulfill that customer's needs in as custom a manner as possible.[57] The related approach of mass customization allows flexible manufacturing, augmented by highly efficient ordering and supply chain systems, to drive the capability for a consumer to build a product from the ground up as is the case when you order a computer from Dell. In the context of target marketing, customization represents a target of one individual for whom a unique value offering is developed.

Lands' End sells clothing by mail order and the Internet. In the late 1990s, it began offering customers the ability to order jeans, men's dress shirts, and other items to their exact measurements. This one-to-one customization has paid off. Not only do customers pay more for this service, but 25 percent of the people who choose this option are new customers of Lands' End and 33 percent purchase made-to-measure items more than once.[58]

POSITIONING

Once market segments have been defined and analyzed and target markets have been selected for development, the firm must turn its attention to creating, communicating, and delivering the value offering to the target markets—that is, positioning the product so that consumers understand its ability to fulfill their needs and wants. The marketing mix of product, supply chain, price, and promotion is at the heart of positioning, and positioning strategies for a target market are executed through the development of unique combinations of these marketing mix variables.[59] Effective positioning is so important that the remaining chapters in this book are devoted to the various marketing mix elements.

Positioning doesn't occur in a vacuum; firms must position their offerings against competitors' offerings. Although McDonald's might love to think that for the hamburger lover "it's all about McDonald's," the truth is that consumers of fast-food burgers are constantly bombarded with the output of positioning strategies not just by McDonald's but by Burger King and Wendy's as well.

In practice, much of the consumer research described in Chapter 5 is designed to facilitate successful positioning. Many positioning studies start with focus groups that allow participants to talk about aspects of their experiences with a product. From the focus groups, a set of attributes is developed for further analysis. Attributes of a product represent salient issues that consumers consider when evaluating the product. For fast-food restaurants like McDonald's, the set of relevant attributes includes items such as cleanliness of the restaurant, speed of service, breadth of menu offerings, healthy food options, prices, employee courtesy, and numerous others.

> Fabric-dye manufacturer Dylon International positions itself as "experts in color." Dylon is launching Color Protect detergent, which it claims is the first detergent that fixes color (meaning that darks, lights, and stripes can all be washed together). The product is packaged in black, which is different from the traditional colors used in the laundry sector, and it features pinwheel imagery. The Dylon logo has been updated to include a wheel of color that reflects the new positioning.[60]

Typically, after a series of focus groups to develop or confirm the relevant attributes, the positioning research moves to a survey methodology in which respondents rate the importance of each attribute, as well as the degree to which each of several competitors' products exhibit the attributes of interest.[61] For example, McDonald's might survey consumers about how important cleanliness of the restaurant, speed of service, breadth of menu offerings, healthy food options, prices, and employee courtesy are, and then ask them to provide their perceptions of how well McDonald's, Burger King, and Wendy's stack up in actually delivering these desired attributes.

The results of such a survey can be analyzed through a gap analysis that shows not only gaps by attribute in importance versus delivery, but also gaps among the competitors in delivery. Perhaps the analysis would reveal that McDonald's excels at healthy food options and cleanliness of the restaurant, but Burger King excels at breadth of menu offerings and prices. If that's the case, each firm has to decide if it is comfortable continuing to invest in these elements of positioning or if investment in other elements is warranted. Recently, Burger King has deliberately invested in positioning itself as the "non-healthy menu" choice, blatantly featuring in ads its bigger and much more decadent food items in terms of fat and calorie content than either McDonald's or Wendy's advertises (although each certainly offers a fair share of unhealthy items).[62]

Perceptual Maps

The data generated from the above analysis can be used to develop a useful visual tool for positioning called a **perceptual map,** which displays paired attributes in order to compare consumer perceptions of each competitor's delivery against those attributes.[63] Today this is usually accomplished by computer statistical software applications that plot each competitor's relative positioning on the attributes.

Exhibit 9.16 provides three different examples of paired attributes on a perceptual map. The first map shows a generic pairing of price and quality and identifies several quadrants of feasible positions based on price-quality pairings that result in positive perceived value by the customer. The logic is compelling as to why the

EXHIBIT 9.16 **Examples of Perceptual Maps Used in Positioning Decisions**

Generic Price-Quality Perceptual Map

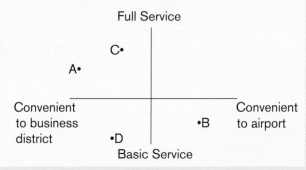

Perceptual Map for Hotel

Positioning involves trade-offs among relevant attributes, not just price and quality.

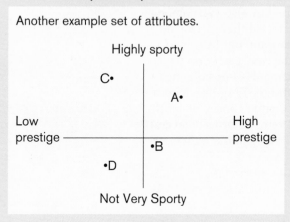

Perceptual Map for Automobile

Another example set of attributes.

other two quadrants are not feasible positioning. In the upper-left quadrant, marketing an inferior offering at a high price is the antithesis of good marketing management. It may seem that in the short run an opportunity exists to make a quick buck, but the approach runs counter to everything we've learned so far about value and building customer relationships as the core of successful marketing over the long run. The bottom-right quadrant's positioning of high quality at a low price seems attractive, but only firms that can legitimately sustain Porter's notion of low-cost strategy can reasonably consider such positioning. And even for those players, the idea of nurturing cost and efficiency savings in operations is not that you will take the entire savings to price; rather, Porter advocates that a low-cost strategy should afford the opportunity to take much of the savings to improved margins and increased reinvestment in product development, only reflecting perhaps a small price differential. Chapter 14 reveals the inherent dangers in positioning primarily based on low price.

The other two perceptual maps in Exhibit 9.16 show where existing competitors are in the market based on the attributes reported. Such perceptual maps can be very useful in helping visualize where to make strategic changes to either move your product closer to the main market (clusters of competition) or further differentiate your product away from the competitive cluster and into more unique market space. In this way, perceptual maps aid in **repositioning** a product, which involves understanding the marketing mix approach necessary to change present consumer perceptions of the product. McDonald's has recently been engaged in a repositioning strategy into more healthy food options to appeal to a primary target market of health-conscious baby boomers.

In actual practice, pairing just two attributes for consideration in making positioning decisions is overly simplistic. Data such as we described above are actually analyzed through a technique called multidimensional scaling that allows for interpretation of multiple attribute perceptions at the same time.

Sources of Differential Competitive Advantage

Effective differentiation is absolutely central to successful positioning strategies. Michael Porter, in his classic book *Competitive Advantage,* explains differentiation as follows:

> When employing a differentiation strategy, the organization competes on the basis of providing unique goods or services with features that customers value, perceive as different, and for which they are willing to pay a premium.[64]

Marketing managers can seek to create differentiation for their offerings in a variety of ways. The following are some of the most often used sources of differentiation.

Price leadership: Efficiencies in cost of labor, materials, supply chain, or other operational elements enabling the price leader to charge less. Example: Wal-Mart.

Innovative leadership: constantly developing the "next new thing." Example: Apple.

Service leadership: having an unusual and notable commitment to providing service to customers. Example: Ritz-Carlton, BMW.

Product leadership: performance, features, durability, reliability, style, and so on. Example: BMW.

Personnel leadership: hiring employees who are competent, reliable, courteous, credible, responsive, and able to communicate clearly. Example: Southwest Airlines.

Convenience leadership: making the product or service significantly easier to obtain. Example: Amazon.com.

Image leadership: symbols, atmosphere, and creative media. Example: BMW.

It is important to note that firms and brands often rely on multiple sources of differentiation simultaneously. Note above that BMW stakes a claim to differentiation by leadership in product, service, and image—a great position to be in.

Vittel + Energy strongly differentiates itself with the message that it "helps keep you hydrated and energized throughout the day, no matter what you're doing."

Positioning Errors

Sometimes, positioning strategies don't work out as planned. The following positioning errors can undermine a firm's overall marketing strategy:[65]

- *Underpositioning:* when consumers have only a vague idea about the company and its products, and do not perceive any real differentiation. Until recently, both Audi and Volkswagen suffered from underpositioning as many consumers struggled to identify salient points of differentiation between those brands and their competitors. However, both brands have beefed up their marketing communication to better clarify exactly what each stands for in the marketplace.

- *Overpositioning:* when consumers have too narrow an understanding of the company, product, or brand. Dell became so entrenched as a brand of PCs that it has been a bit of a struggle to extend the brand into other lucrative product lines. Neither HP nor Apple suffers from overpositioning; both have engaged in great positioning strategies over the long run.

- *Confused positioning:* when frequent changes and contradictory messages confuse consumers regarding the positioning of the brand. McDonald's found itself the victim of confused positioning as it moved out of the 1990s. It had tried (and failed) at so many diverse new product launches in the restaurants that many customers lost track of what the core of the brand was. Since then, under new top leadership, McDonald's has embraced its core differentiators of consistency of products and dependability of service, while growing new products at a much more conservative rate.

- *Doubtful positioning:* when the claims made for the product or brand are not regarded as credible by consumers. Sadly, firms that engage in unethical business practices often do not realize the magnitude of damage being done to their brand. Also, you will learn in the chapters on products and branding that trial is only the initial goal of marketing communication. After initial trial, firms need to ensure that the offering consistently meets or exceeds customer expectations so that repurchase—and loyalty—will occur, which is a process of customer expectations management. When FedEx promises 8 a.m. next-day delivery, it has to be sure its systems can actually produce such a level of performance all the time.

SUMMARY

Effective segmentation, target marketing, and positioning are central to marketing management because these decisions set the direction for the execution of the marketing plan. First, potential appropriate segmentation approaches must be identified. Second, the segments must be evaluated and decisions made about which to invest in for the most favorable ROI—these become your target markets. Finally, sources of differentiation must be identified that will result in customers perceiving fulfillment of needs and wants based on the value proposition of the offering.

KEY TERMS

market segmentation 238
target marketing 238
positioning 238
differentiation 239
geographic segmentation 240
demographic segmentation 243
family life cycle 247
psychographic segmentation 252

VALS™ (Values and Lifestyles) 252
behavioral segmentation 254
primary target markets 258
secondary target markets 258
tertiary target markets 258
undifferentiated target marketing 259

differentiated target marketing 259
concentrated target marketing 260
customized (one-to-one) marketing 260
perceptual map 261
repositioning 262

APPLICATION QUESTIONS

1. Go to the Nielsen/Claritas Web site (www.mybestsegments.com) and click on "ZIP Code Look-Up". There you will find a demo that allows you to type in a zip code of your choice and find out what PRIZM clusters predominate in that geographic area.

   a. What do the findings tell you about the overall composition of potential customers within that zip code?

   b. Based on the array of clusters represented, what kinds of start-up businesses might flourish within the geographic area? Why do you believe those businesses in particular would be successful?

2. Go to the SRI Consulting Business Intelligence Web site (www.sric-bi.com) and click through to the section on VALS™. Find the VALS™ survey and complete the questionnaire.

   a. Are the results surprising? Why or why not? Do you see yourself as part of the identified VALS™ segment?

b. If you are comfortable doing so, share your results with a few other people in the class and ask if they mind sharing their results with you. What is the consensus among the group about whether the survey actually captured a relevant profile about yourself and your classmates?

c. How might each of these brands benefit from the use of VALS™ as a psychographic segmentation tool:

  i. Ruth's Chris Steak House.

  ii. Walt Disney World Theme Park.

  iii. Target Inc.

  iv. Samsung.

  v. Porsche.

3. Assume for a moment that you are in marketing for Staples (the office supply company) and that the clients you are responsible for are business users (not end-user consumers). What five business market segmentation variables do you think will be most useful to consider as you move toward homing in on the Staples business target markets with the best ROI? Justify your choice of each.

4. Consider each of the brands below. Review the list of potential sources of differential competitive advantage (differentiation) highlighted in the chapter. For each: (a) indicate which one differentiation source you believe is most important to them currently and (b) indicate which other differentiation sources you believe might hold promise for development for them in the near future and *why*.

a. Carnival Cruise Lines.

b. Sears Craftsman Tools.

c. Avon.

d. Lowe's Home Improvement Stores.

e. The Salvation Army.

5. McDonald's is interested in your opinion of how it would stack up on a perceptual map against Burger King, Wendy's, Taco Bell, and Chick-fil-A on the attributes of convenience and product quality. Create the map by putting convenience as the vertical axis (high at the top and low at the bottom) and product quality as the horizontal axis (low on the left and high on the right). Then, indicate your perceptions of the five brands on these attributes by placing a dot for each in the spot that indicates your view (see chapter Exhibit 9.16 for examples).

a. What does the result reveal about McDonald's current positioning on these attributes, based strictly from your perception?

b. If possible, compare notes with others in your class. Do you find consistency?

c. In general, what opportunities for repositioning do you see for any of the brands to take advantage of current perceptions revealed on the perceptual map? What would they have to do to accomplish this repositioning?

MANAGEMENT DECISION CASE: New Targets and New Positioning at McDonald's

When McDonald's opened in 1955, it served two meals: lunch and dinner. Since then, Americans' days have gotten busier and longer—more night-shift workers, dual-earners, dispersed families. As demographics and eating habits have changed, McDonald's has had to reinvent itself to keep growing.

McDonald's now faces competition not just from hamburger joints such as Wendy's and Burger King but from Dunkin' Donuts for breakfast, Starbucks for breakfast and afternoon snacks, and convenience stores for late-night munchers. How has the company positioned itself to compete?

Take breakfast: customer Julie Brown goes to McDonald's to get breakfast for her daughter and the rest of the high school swim team while they practice. Brown's order includes more than $30 worth of Egg McMuffins, sausage breakfast biscuits, egg-and-sausage bagels, hash browns, orange juice—and a peach-mango smoothie for herself. Brown, 37, loves the wider variety of foods and drinks available at McDonald's today. "I used to have to go to five different places for everyone. I'd have to go to one place to get bagels. Smoothies at another. Coffee at another," she says. "Now I can get everything here, all at once."

McDonald's has also improved its coffee. After McDonald's rolled out a darker and stronger coffee same-store sales at breakfast increased 7.5 percent. To build on this momentum, the company is testing two more breakfast items: a Southern-style fried chicken biscuit and Newman's Own iced coffee.

To capture midday snackers, McDonald's entices them with its $1.29 Snack Wrap. Because so many consumers are on the go, the company designed a food that people could hold easily in one hand while gripping a steering wheel with the other. In the wee morning hours, workers like D.C. Chavis, 24, are finishing 12-hour shifts. Chavis used to pick up an after-work snack at an all-night convenience store or diner. Now he swings by McDonald's at least five times a week for the premium sandwich combo meal. The food is a lot better at McDonald's, he says, adding that the prices are cheaper and the brand is one he trusts. Says Chavis: "I was raised on McDonald's." By catering to the area's night owls and early birds, the location has increased revenue by 4.5 percent, or $90,000, over a year.

McDonald's used to be a place where you'd rush in, grab food, and rush out. Now, the company is redesigning its restaurants to be a place where customers can hang out. The new stores feature dark wood, flat-screen TVs, live plants, and even some leather lounge chairs. The place set is up to make customers comfortable. Retirees come in for morning coffee;—McDonald's has become their social center, and they're there every morning. Later in the day, young mothers go to McDonald's for a breather while their preschoolers scamper in the Play Place.

Increasingly, McDonald's is becoming a place for families to meet. Kim Borum, for example, is impressed by the restaurant's new design touches. It is 12:45 p.m., and she is leaving after joining her husband, Bennie, for lunch. The restaurant had always been conveniently located for the Borums, but she says they now eat at McDonald's two or three times a week. "The ambience of a place makes a big difference in how people feel about it," she says.

Like the Borums, the Stallings make McDonald's a rendezvous point. Angie Stallings is busy, busy, busy. When she is not working at Smith Elementary School, she's driving her 13-year-old daughter, Sarah, to and from cheerleading and basketball practice, or shuttling back and forth for evening meetings at the Capital Church. Constantly pressed for time, Stallings says, she brings Sarah to McDonald's at least three times a week for a quick meal.

In restaurant parlance, Stallings is a "heavy user." At McDonald's, the average customer comes in once every week, and 95 percent of the nation stops in over the course of a year. But it is the heavy user—someone who frequents the same fast-food chain twice a week or more—who really accounts for the steady rise in sales and profit for McDonald's.

Questions for Consideration

1. How is McDonald's using segmentation to attract new customers?

2. Discuss McDonald's target marketing to build more business with its existing customers.

3. How is McDonald's positioning itself relative to competitors like Starbucks or 7-Eleven?

Source: Michael Arndt, "McDonald's 24/7," *BusinessWeek*, February 5, 2007, p. 64–72.

MARKETING PLAN EXERCISE

ACTIVITY 9: Identifying Target Markets

In this chapter you learned that effective segmentation, target marketing, and positioning favorably impact marketing management. For purposes of your marketing plan, we'll leave the specifics of developing your overall positioning strategies to the upcoming chapters on the marketing mix. At this point, the following steps are needed.

1. Consider the various approaches to segmenting your market(s). What segmentation approaches do you recommend? Why do you recommend those approaches over other available approaches?

2. Evaluate your proposed segments against the criteria for effective segmentation. What does this evaluation lead you to conclude about the best way to proceed?

3. Systematically analyze each potential segment on your list using the three steps you learned in the chapter: (1) assess each in terms of segment size and growth potential, segment competitive forces, and strategic fit of the segment; (2) for the short set that emerges, develop profiles of each potential target market, then identify each of your final set as primary, secondary, tertiary, or abandoned; (3) select the target marketing approach for each of your primary targets.

4. Identify the likely sources of differential advantage on which you will focus later in developing your positioning strategies.

If you are using Marketing Plan Pro, a template for this assignment can be accessed at www.mhhe.com/marshall1e.

RECOMMENDED READINGS

1. David A. Aaker, *Strategic Market Management* (Hoboken, NJ: John Wiley & Sons, 2008).

2. George S. Day, *Market Driven Strategy: Processes for Creating Value* (New York: The Free Press, 1999).

3. George S. Day, *The Market Driven Organization: Understanding, Attracting, and Keeping Valuable Customers* (New York: The Free Press, 1999).

4. Louis V. Gerstner, Jr., *Who Says Elephants Can't Dance?* (New York: Harper Business, 2002).

5. Fredrick E. Webster, *Market-Driven Management: How to Define, Develop, and Deliver Customer Value* (Hoboken, NJ: John Wiley & Sons, 2002).

CHAPTER 10

THE PRODUCT EXPERIENCE: PRODUCT STRATEGY

LEARNING OBJECTIVES

- Understand the essential role of the product experience in marketing.

- Define the characteristics of a product.

- Recognize how product strategies evolve from one product to many products.

- Understand the life of a product and how product strategies change over time.

EXECUTIVE PERSPECTIVE

Executive Jay File

Company Chick-fil-A

Business Fast-food company

How does Chick-fil-A define its "product?" What is the essential benefit delivered and fundamental need met by your product?

When customers enter a Chick-fil-A, they expect great tasting food and a clean and pleasant dining environment, accompanied by exceptional service. That's it! Our brand strives to deliver not just the food but an overall dining *experience* that creates more "Raving Fans," who are our most loyal customers. We fulfill a basic daily need of food, but our brand delivers so much more. We want to emotionally connect with customers so they feel they are coming for not just a "transaction," but rather a truly memorable experience.

Speak about the quality of Chick-fil-A's products. You are well-known for high quality; how does your firm achieve consistency of product quality

We believe because we are in the restaurant business, at the foundation we must deliver great tasting food to all customers. Our focus begins with ensuring we deliver *Operational Excellence All Day, Every Day.* With a high-caliber operator running the business and selecting above-average team members, we already have an advantage over many quick-service restaurant

competitors. We then measure and track performance standards on food quality, speed of service, appearance standards, and cleanliness throughout the day to ensure the customer experience is the very best we can deliver. We believe in the golden rule; treat others as you would like to be treated, and when we do this we deliver a memorable experience.

What are some of the important decisions Chick-fil-A undertakes before deciding to add a new item?

Since we are a chicken chain, we focus exclusively on chicken products for breakfast, lunch, and dinner. Before we consider new items, we always ask the question "What needs improvement?" One of the best ways to get better is always working to keep the menu current and up to date with current trends. First and foremost, before we add anything we ask our current and potential customers what they desire. What do they expect from our brand? Second, we determine if the new product is a "fit" within our brand environment and overall menu. Third, we evaluate operational effectiveness of introducing a new product. Finally, we test the item in multiple markets to get a true day-to-day experience and evaluation of its sales and profit potential.

PRODUCT: THE HEART OF MARKETING

As we discussed in Chapter 1, the primary function of marketing and, more broadly speaking, the entire organization is to deliver value to the customer. The essential component in delivering value is the product experience, which is why it is considered the heart of marketing. Consider the problems at General Motors that led to plant closings and the elimination of the unprofitable Oldsmobile brand. Despite those decisions, CEO Richard Wagoner admits the key to GM's future success is developing cars that people want to buy. He understands the company's future is about the product, automobiles.[1]

Instead of focusing solely on its product, Starbucks has been successful selling "the Starbucks experience" that extends beyond drinking coffee to social interaction and lifestyle. The company defines the "product" (coffee) and the coffee drinking experience in a way that delivers value to millions of customers around the world every day. Given the importance of the product experience in delivering customer value, it is not surprising that companies place a great deal of significance on getting the product experience right.

When the product is wrong, no amount of marketing communications, no degree of logistical expertise or pricing sophistication will make it successful. Apple is widely regarded as a product innovator with the iPod, iPhone, iMac, and other products. However, the company has also experienced some product missteps. One of the most notable was Newton, the first PDA, introduced in the early 1990s but discontinued after Palm brought out its line of smaller, more user-friendly products. While technically superior to Palm, Apple did not understand the key value drivers in the product. People wanted PDAs with connectivity to other computers, a reasonable combination of features, and a realistic price (early Newtons cost over $1,000).[2] Newton's failure highlights an interesting fact; the best product technically is not always the most successful product. People look for the product that delivers the best overall product experience.

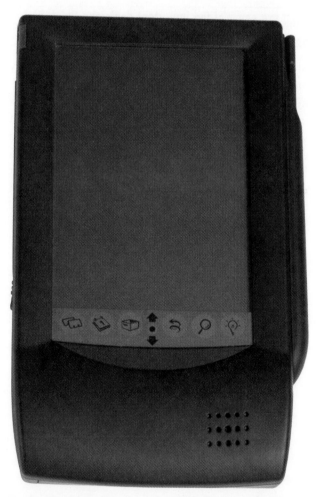

The Apple Newton, while technically better than similar PDAs, failed in the marketplace because it did not deliver a better product experience than competitors such as Palm.

Product Characteristics

Define the Product

What does the term *product* mean? Most people define a product as a tangible object; however, that is not accurate. The product experience encompasses a great deal more as we will learn over the next several chapters. Consider the customer walking into Starbucks; is he or she just buying a cup of coffee? Did the owner of a new Toyota Prius buy just a new car? Is a pair of Aeropostale jeans just a pair of jeans? The answer is that, while customers are buying a cup of coffee, a new car, and a pair of jeans, they are also buying a product experience. It is important for the marketer to understand exactly what the customer includes in that experience. This is a particularly difficult challenge because different target markets will view the same product in completely different ways. Parents buying their daughter a pair of jeans would probably consider Aeropostale jeans to be just another pair of jeans; however, to the teenager, the same purchase makes an important statement about herself and her choice of clothes.[3]

Product can be defined as anything that delivers value to satisfy a need or want and includes physical merchandise, services, events, people, places, organizations, information, even ideas. Most people have no problem considering a computer or car a product, but would these same individuals consider a get-away weekend at the Amelia Island Ritz Carlton in Florida a product? The Ritz-Carlton does and it develops a specific marketing strategy around the resort.

It is important to differentiate between a product and a product item. A product is a brand such as Post-It notes or Tide detergent. Within each product a company may develop a number of product items, each of which represents a unique size, feature, or price. Tide powder detergent offers five "scents," including fragrance free, in a variety of sizes designed to reach a variety of target markets.[4] Each combination of scent and size represents a unique product item in the Tide product line and is known by a **stock keeping unit (SKU).** An SKU is a unique identification number used to track a product through a distribution system, inventory management, and pricing.

Essential Benefit

Why does someone purchase a plane ticket? The answer quite obviously is it to get from one place to another. Simply stated, the essential benefit of purchasing a plane ticket is getting somewhere else; therefore, the essence of the airline product experience is transporting people. Successful airlines, indeed all companies, understand that before anything else they must deliver on the essential benefit.

The **essential benefit** is the fundamental need met by the product. No matter what other value-added product experiences are provided to the customer, the essential benefit must be part of the encounter. For example, an airline can offer low fares, an easy-to-navigate Web site, or in-seat video entertainment, but unless the customer receives the essential benefit (getting from Point A to Point B) the other items have very little meaning to the customer. Without the essential benefit, other benefits may actually increase the customer's dissatisfaction with the experience. What good are low fares if the customer doesn't arrive at the destination? Exhibit 10.1 illustrates four products and their essential benefits.

Core Product

Aircraft, pilots, flights attendants, baggage handlers, reservation agents, managers, and an IT system are a few of the elements needed to get people and their luggage from one place to another. An airline brings all those pieces together to create a product that efficiently and effectively delivers the essential benefit, transporting someone from Point A to Point B.

Companies translate the essential benefit into physical, tangible elements known as the **core product.** Some companies do it better than others, making this critical challenge an important differentiator separating successful companies from their competitors.[5] Southwest Airlines, for example, has done a very good job of translating the essential benefits of air travel. By using one kind of airplane, identifying efficiencies in everything from reservations to flight routes, and taking care of employees, the company is the industry leader in low-cost air travel and, in the process, revolutionized the entire airline industry. Contrast Southwest with the long list of carriers over the past 15 years that defined the core product experience in ways many customers found unsatisfying. Many of the "legacy" carriers such as United, U.S. Airways, and Delta, have experienced serious financial problems even bankruptcy, in part, because they have not adequately delivered a positive core product experience to the customer.

As a company creates the core product experience, it is vital to clearly understand customer expectations. Every aspect of the product experience is evaluated by the customer and then considered against a set of expectations. When an airline creates a flight there is an expectation that the flight will arrive at its stated

EXHIBIT 10.1 **Four Products and Their Essential Benefits**

Motorola RAZR – making and receiving telephone calls

BMW 3 Series convertible – providing reliable transportation

Evian bottled water – quenching thirst

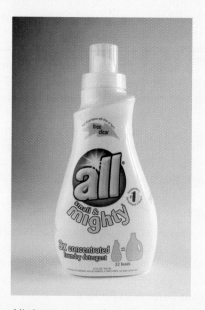

All detergent – cleaning laundry

time. If the flight does not arrive on time, the passenger assesses the reasons. Was it the airline's fault, the weather, or something else? Airlines are sensitive about their on-time arrival percentage and where they rank relative to the competition because they know customers believe this is an important characteristic of the core product experience. The customer's evaluation of a product experience against a set of defined expectations is a critical element contributing to overall satisfaction or dissatisfaction with the product.[6]

Enhanced Product

The core product is the starting point for the product experience. All cell phones deliver on the essential benefit of mobile communication, but there is a vast difference between the introductory "free" phone offered by many service providers and the latest Treo or Blackberry. Features, cutting-edge designs and colors, connectivity to other digital devices, and new functionality (such as MP3 capabilities) differentiate one product from another. As consumers around the world become more sophisticated, companies are required to look beyond delivering great core products to creating products that enhance, extend, and encourage the customer.

LG Electronics makes over 40 GSM cell phone models with a wide range of features and benefits that compete against phones from Nokia, Motorola, Samsung, and others. In an effort to offer consumer enhanced benefits, the company introduced a model, The Secret, made of carbon fiber and tempered glass and designed to be sturdy as well as operate as a fashion accessory. The company's overall cell phone strategy is to consider basic cell phone features secondary to the fashion.[7]

The **enhanced product** extends the core product to include additional features, designs, and innovation that exceed customer expectations. In this way, companies build on the core product, creating opportunities to strengthen the brand. Consider Southwest Airlines once again, which has done a good job of delivering people on time and meeting customer expectations regarding low-cost air travel. Southwest added features such as frequent flyer opportunities and reserved seating to further augment the customer's air travel experience. Exhibit 10.2 shows how the essential benefit, core product, and enhanced product are created for Southwest Airlines.

Consider Sharp Electronics, which has developed a strong market position for its Aquos line of LCD televisions. The company followed a strategy of developing and introducing enhanced versions of a successful core product. From its line of LCD display computer monitors, the company developed a new line of LCD televisions (Aquos) ranging from 13 inches to more than 100 inches and costing as much as $20,000 (see Exhibit 10.3).[8]

Product Classifications

Products can be classified in four ways. Two of the four classifications define the nature of the product: tangibility and durability. The other two classification

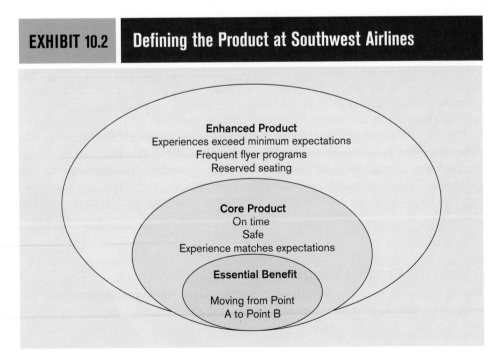

EXHIBIT 10.2   Defining the Product at Southwest Airlines

Enhanced Product
Experiences exceed minimum expectations
Frequent flyer programs
Reserved seating

Core Product
On time
Safe
Experience matches expectations

Essential Benefit

Moving from Point
A to Point B

EXHIBIT 10.3 | Sharp Aquos LCD Televisions

Specifications

Model Number	LC-65SE94U	LC-52SE94U	LC-46SE94U	LC-108D1U
Screen Size	65" Class (64 33/64" Diagonal)	52" Class (52 1/32" Diagonal)	46" Class (45 63/64" Diagonal)	108" Class (107 17/32" Diagonal)
Aspect Ratio	16:9	16:9	16:9	16:9
DTV Capability	HDTV	HDTV	HDTV	HDTV Monitor
LCD Panel	Advanced Super View/Black TFT	Advanced Super View/Black TFT	Advanced Super View/Black TFT	Advanced Super View/Black TFT
Number of Pixels (dots)	1920 x 1080	1920 x 1080	1920 x 1080	1920 x 1080
Built-in DVD Slot	—	—	—	—
AQUOS Net	X	X	X	—
Luminance (cd/m²)	450	450	450	400
Fine Motion Advanced (120Hz)	X	X	X	—
Dynamic Contrast Ratio*1	27,000:1	27,000:1	27,000:1	6000:1
Native Contrast Ratio	3000:1	3000:1	2700:1	1200:1
Viewing Angles (H x V)	176° x 176°	176° x 176°	176° x 176°	176° x 176°
Lamp Life*2 (Hours)	60,000	60,000	60,000	53,000
Backlight	5-Wavelength	5-Wavelength	5-Wavelength	HCFL
Tuner Type	ATSC / QAM / NTSC	ATSC / QAM / NTSC	ATSC / QAM / NTSC	—
Multi-pixel Technology	X	X	X	X
Response Time	4ms	4ms	4ms	8ms
Audio Output	15W + 15W	15W + 15W	15W + 15W	15W + 15W
Speakers Location/Type	Bottom/Detachable	Bottom/Detachable	Bottom/Detachable	
OPC (Optical Picture Control)	X	X	X	X
Terminals				
HDMI Input	3 (1080p compatible) - 1 side, 2 rear	3 (1080p compatible) - 1 side, 2 rear	3 (1080p compatible) - 1 side, 2 rear	3
DVI-I with Audio In	—	—	—	1
RGB 15-Pin Input	1	1	1	—
HD Component In	2 (1080p compatible) – 1 side, 1 rear	2 (1080p compatible) – 1 side, 1 rear	2 (1080p compatible) – 1 side, 1 rear	2 (1080p compatible) – 1 side, 1 rear
S-Video In	1	1	1	1
Composite Video In	3 (1 side, 2 rear)	3 (1 side, 2 rear)	3 (1 side, 2 rear)	2 (1 side, 1 rear)
Audio L/R In	4	4	4	4 (1 side, 3 rear)
RF	1	1	1	—
RS-232C 9-Pin In	1	1	1	1
Digital Audio Out	X	X	X	X
Power Source AC Input	120V	120V	120V	200-240V, 50/60Hz
Power Consumption	525W	302W	270W	1130W
Cabinet Color	Textured Black	Textured Black	Textured Black	High Gloss Black
Dimensions (W x H x D) with stand/with speakers	60 25/64" x 40 3/32" x 16 7/64"	48 29/64" x 33 25/64" x 13 1/2"	43 43/64" x 30 25/64" x 13 1/2"	N/A
with stand/without speakers	60 25/64" x 40 3/32" x 16 7/64"	48 29/32" x 33 25/64" x 13 1/2"	43 43/64" x 30 25/64" x 13 1/2"	101 17/64" x 71 15/32" x 23 5/8"
without stand/with speakers	60 25/64" x 37 49/64" x 3 61/64"	48 29/32" x 31 5/16" x 3 1/2"	43 43/64" x 28 5/16" x 3 1/2"	N/A
without stand/without speakers	60 25/64" x 35 3/4" x 3 61/64"	48 29/32" x 29 1/4" x 3 1/2"	43 43/64" x 26 17/64" x 3 1/2"	101 17/64" x 82 41/64" x 8 1/8"
Net Weight (lb.) with stand/with speakers	129.0	78.3	67.2	N/A
with stand/without speakers	123.5	73.9	62.8	551.2
without stand/with speakers	117.9	69.4	58.4	N/A
without stand/without speakers	112.4	65.0	54.0	429.9

*1 With Enhanced Picture Contrast Technology
*2 Typical time for power output decrease of about one half, assuming continuous use with brightness or dimming in standard mode and with a room temperature of 77°F
*3 With Fine Motion Mode on

Screen images in this brochure are simulated.
Design and specifications subject to change without notice.

Source: Sharpusa.com, Aquos G-Series pdf brochure, October 2008.

criteria deal with who uses the product: consumers or businesses. It is important to understand the nature and use of a product because marketing strategies differ among the various product classifications.

Tangibility: Physical Aspects of the Product Experience

Products, as opposed to services, have a physical aspect referred to as **tangibility.** Tangible products present opportunities (customers can see, touch, and experience the product) and also some challenges (customers may find the product does not match their personal tastes and preferences). Services, which we will explore in Chapter 13, are intangible. A significant challenge for marketers today is that many tangible products have intangible characteristics.[9] For example a significant element in an individual's satisfaction with a new car is the customer service before and after the purchase. Intangible products, on the other hand, such as services have tangible characteristics. For example, airlines introduce new airline seats to create a competitive advantage. Exhibit 10.4 identifies the tangible and intangible characteristics of a John Deere riding lawn mower.

Durability: Product Usage

Durability references the length of product usage. **Nondurable products** are usually consumed in a few uses and, in general, cost less than durable products.

Tangible Characteristic	Product Characteristic	Intangible Characteristic	Product Characteristic
Power	18.5 hp Briggs and Stratton engine	Comfort	Medium backseat without armrests with 3" range
Performance	Hydro-gear transmission 42" mower deck 7 mph ground speed	Ease of use	Two cup holders Large caster wheels for smoother ride Commercial style footrest flips up for easy access to mower deck

Sources: http://shopproducts.howstuffworks.com/26HP-54-Garden-Tractor/SF-I/PID-38869959, and http://www.deere.com/en_US/ProductCatalog/HO/servlet/ProdCatProduct?pNbr=SKU21896&tM=HO.

Examples of consumer nondurables include personal grooming products such as toothpaste, soap, and shampoo, while business nondurables include office supplies such as printer ink, paper, and other less expensive, frequently purchased items. Because these products are purchased frequently and are not expensive, companies seek a wide distribution to make them as readily available as possible, create attractive price points to motivate purchase, and heavily advertise these products. **Durable products** have a longer product life and are often more expensive. Consumer durables include microwave ovens, washers/dryers, and certain electronics such as televisions. Business durables include products that may be used in the manufacturing process such as machine presses or IT networks, as well as equipment such as office furniture and computers to facilitate the running of the business.[10]

Consumer Goods

Consumers purchase thousands of products from an assortment of millions of choices. On the surface it may seem difficult to develop a classification system for the variety of products consumer purchase, but the reality is that consumer purchase habits fall into four broad categories: convenience, shopping, specialty, and unsought.

Frequently purchased, relatively low-cost products for which customers have little interest in seeking new information or considering other options and rely heavily on prior brand experience and purchase behavior are called **convenience goods.** These products include most items people buy regularly such as toiletries, gasoline, and paper products and fall into four categories. Staples are usually food products people buy weekly or at least once a month such as Folgers coffee or Dannon yogurt. Impulse products, as the name implies, are purchased without planning. If you think about the products available in vending machines, you will have a good idea of an impulse product. Finally, there are a host of products people only purchase in times of emergency. For example, as hurricanes approach communities, people rush out to purchase extra supplies of food, gas, batteries, and other products. It is not uncommon to see occasional shortages of some products as distribution systems are strained to meet unplanned spikes in demands for these everyday products.

FYI

Johnson's Baby Shampoo, Band-Aids, Listerine, Sudafed, Bengay, Rolaids, Neutrogena, and many other brands belong to Johnson & Johnson (J&J), a global leader in health care products. While J&J's other primary businesses including pharmaceutical drugs, such as Risperdal and Procrit, and medical devices such as stents (metal tubes that help clear arteries) are bigger, the consumer products division is the fastest-growing business unit and accounts for 25 percent of sales. J&J consumer products hold the market-leading position in 22 consumer categories.

Interestingly, some of J&J's oldest brands have been experiencing the greatest growth. For example, sales of Listerine, the 112-year-old mouthwash, have grown 61 percent in five years to top $850 million. "The Pink Line," the phrase used at J&J to reference the extensive line of baby products that come in pink bottles, has shown double-digit sales increases. Finally, Neutrogena skin care products recently reported sales of $1.6 billion, an increase of 56 percent in five years. While almost all these products are considered convenience goods, they represent a substantial business globally.[11]

Products that require consumers to do more research and compare across product dimensions such as color, size, features, and price are called **shopping goods.** Consumer products that fall into this category include clothes, furniture, and major appliances such as refrigerators and dishwashers. These products are purchased less frequently and are more costly than convenience goods. Price concerns, a variety of choices at various price levels, many different features, and a fear of making the wrong decision are among the factors that drive consumers to research these purchases. As a result, companies often develop product strategies that target product price points with particular features to appeal to the broadest range of consumers. For example, Whirlpool brand makes over 30 different electric dryers ranging in price from $329 to $1,469 (see Exhibit 10.5).

Specialty goods are a unique purchase made based on a defining characteristic for the consumer. The characteristic might be a real or perceived product feature such as Apple iPod's easy user interface or brand identification like Porsche's reputation for building sports cars. Whatever the attribute(s), consumers apply decision rules that frequently minimize the number of different product choices and focus less on price. They are also more willing to seek out the product; however, expectations about product service, salesperson expertise, and customer service are higher. Bang and Olufsen's line of high-end electronic equipment is not available in regular retail outlets. Rather the company has a limited number of retail stores in major cities. Consumers wanting to purchase Bang & Olufsen equipment must seek out those stores.

The final categories of goods, **unsought goods,** are products that consumers do not seek out and, indeed, often would rather not purchase at all. Insurance, particularly life insurance, is not a product people want to purchase. In general, customers do not want to purchase products or services related to sickness, death, or emergencies because, in part, the circumstances surrounding the purchase are not pleasant. As a result, companies have well-trained salespeople skilled in helping customers through the purchase process. These salespeople often must be supported by extensive marketing communications.

| EXHIBIT 10.5 | Whirlpool Brand's Line of Full-Size Electric Dryers |

Source: Whirlpool.com, November 2008.

Reprinted Courtesy of Whirlpool Corporation.

In Chapter 4 we discussed USAA Insurance in the context of CRM, here we consider the company's broad range of insurance and banking services products to military personnel and their families. USAA's success is due in large part to its understanding of the unique challenges of its military customers. For example, the company created a mobile Web site for military personnel in remote locations with access to the Internet. The focus on customer service has enabled this company to be consistently rated one of the best customer-focused companies in the world.[12]

Business Goods

Businesses buy a vast array of products that can be classified into three broad areas based on two dimensions: (1) whether or not they are used in the manufacturing process and (2) cost. Goods incorporated into the company's finished product as a result of the manufacturing process are either materials or parts. **Materials** are natural (lumber, minerals such as copper) or farm products (corn, soybeans) that become part of the final product. **Parts** consist of equipment either fully assembled or in smaller pieces that will be assembled into larger components and, again, used in the production process.

In addition to the products that are used directly in the production process, companies purchase a number of products and services to support business operations. These can generally be placed on a continuum from low-cost/frequent purchases to very high-cost/infrequent purchases. **MRO** (maintenance, repair, operating) **supplies** are the everyday items that a company needs to keep running. While per unit cost is low, their total cost over a year can be high.

At the other end of the cost/purchase frequency continuum are **capital goods,** which are major purchases in support of a significant business function. Building a new plant, or a new IT network can require large equipment purchases that cost millions of dollars and require significant customization. These purchases are negotiated over a period of months, sometimes years. Consider that it takes 8 to 10 years to get a new large-scale oil refinery built and costs between $4 billion and $6 billion. Companies selling capital goods to businesses focus on personal selling and a high level of customer service with significant product customization.

Railroads need to constantly replace older engines and cars with more reliable equipment incorporating the latest technologies. Long-term (standardizing maintenance programs) and short-term (quantity discounts) efficiencies dictate the purchase decision, which can involve billions of dollars. Bombardier, a world leader in railcar manufacturing, has invested heavily in upgrading rail technology over the past 10 years. The result has been a string of major sales to world customers including the French National Railway ($1.8 billion), Deustche Bahn (German national railway) ($1.6 billion), and the Chicago Transit Authority ($577 million).[13]

Product Discrimination: Create a Point of Differentiation

A fundamental question in the product purchase decision making process is what makes this product different? As a result, marketing managers must identify important characteristics that successfully differentiate their product from others in the customer's mind. Then they must produce those elements in the product itself, balancing a number of factors including customer preferences, costs, and company resources. Exhibit 10.6 identifies product discriminators and gives an example.

Form

The most elemental method of differentiating a product is to change its **form**—size, shape, color, and other physical elements. Many products considered very similar in functionality can be differentiated by variations in packaging or product delivery. Among the reasons cited for the growth in milk consumption over the past several years has been new packaging that delivers the product in smaller, more

Bombardier builds a wide range of rail cars and locomotives to meet transportation needs around the world. This train was designed for a transportation system in Nottingham, England.

EXHIBIT 10.6 | **Product Discriminators**

Form		With 54-nozzle spray heads, WaterTile Ambient Rain overhead showering panels provide luxurious water delivery.
Features		The wealth of improvements and refinements in a TX4 sets it apart from any other taxi. New features include a Euro IV compliant engine, greener, cleaner, and delivering big torque at low speed and an improved in-car entertainment system, with superior sound and MP3 compatibility.
Performance Quality		Oil companies produce several grades of gasoline to meet the demands of consumers.
Conformance Quality		Crest Whitestrips are a good low-priced teeth whitener. The system also comes with a standard 60-day money back guarantee, should you not care for the results.
Durability		Timberland has a reputation for building high quality, durable products like these boots that come with a commitment to customer satisfaction.

(continued)

EXHIBIT 10.6 **Product Discriminators [continued]**

Reliability		Carrier promotes the fact that its air conditioners are reliable. In addition, it provides different quality levels with varying warranties.
Repairability		Many bicycle manufacturers highlight the easy repair of the bikes. A key point is that anyone can fix most of the problems that may occur.
Style		*Style* magazine is all about promoting style in a person's life.

portable plastic containers that preserve freshness so the milk tastes better longer and is easier to use in more situations (see Exhibit 10.7). Additionally, dairies have developed methods to extend shelf life, improving freshness and accessibility.

EXHIBIT 10.7 **Form Variations for T.G. Lee Milk Products**

Features

When asked what makes a product different, many people will respond by talking about features. A **feature** is any product attribute or performance characteristic and is often added or subtracted from a product to differentiate it from competitors. However, while delivering consumer value is the primary driver in making product decisions, a company must balance the features customers want with what they will pay at a given quality level.[14]

Interestingly, based on their research, competitors often create products with very different feature configurations. Cell phone manufacturers, for example, are constantly assessing the feature mix across their product line. When comparing similar Samsung versus Nokia models, a number of feature differences will be easily identified. One of the great challenges for marketers is determining the feature mix that best satisfies the needs and wants of the target audience and at what price? No competitors ever arrive at the same feature mix, which means decisions about which features to include and exclude are critical to a product's success.

> Commercial jet aircraft are among the most complex and challenging products to design and build. Two companies, Boeing and Airbus, control the market. Each company, however, had a dramatically different view of the market. Airbus believed the future of commercial jets was in making a huge aircraft capable of carrying 600 people or more to large hubs around the world and so it created the A380. Boeing, on the other hand, believed airlines (and the passengers who fly) wanted jets that were more efficient and smaller, yet provided more room for passengers.[15]

Performance Quality

Should a company always build the highest-quality product? Some people would say the answer is yes. However, the answer is more complex than that. Essentially, companies should build products to the performance quality level that their target audience is willing to pay for. Often this means a company will build products at multiple performance levels to meet demand at various price points. Keep in mind that the key is to deliver value to the customer. For many years, Pioneer Electronics has offered an extensive line of plasma televisions that can be purchased at stores such as Best Buy and Circuit City. At the same time, the company also carries a more expensive line, Elite, that uses higher quality materials and components. The Elite models are available only at high-end stereo specialty stores.[16]

The market's perception of the company's performance quality is critical in defining its market space. Companies generally try to match product performance quality with the market's perception of the brand. Timex will not develop a $25,000 watch because the market would not expect, and may not accept, a watch with production quality at that level from Timex, although they do expect it from Rolex.[17] At the same time, companies need to be careful not to lower performance quality too dramatically in an effort to cut costs or reach new markets. Losing control of a quality image can do significant harm to a brand's image. For example, product safety remains a critical concern for consumers. Products that fail to meet quality standards can lead to a loss of consumer confidence. Ethical Dimension 10 discusses a growing concern about products shipped from China.

Conformance Quality

An important issue for consumers is **conformance,** which is the product's ability to deliver on features and performance characteristics promised in marketing communications. The challenge for marketers and manufacturing is that every product must deliver on those promises. A product is said to have high conformance quality when a high percentage of the manufactured products fulfill the stated performance criteria.[18] If someone opened a Coke and there was no "fizz" it wouldn't be a Coke. The challenge for Coca-Cola and its bottlers is to ensure that every Coke has just the right carbonation when the consumer opens the can or bottle anywhere in the world.

Durability

Consumer research and purchase patterns affirm that people find **durability,** the projected lifetime of the product under specific operating conditions, an important discriminating product characteristic and are willing to pay a premium for products that can demonstrate greater durability.[19] KitchenAid appliances have a reputation for durability that has translated into a price premium for their products.

That Strawberry Came from Where?

Americans like fruits and vegetables; unfortunately, it is difficult to grow enough produce in the United States to meet the demand. This is particularly true for food manufacturers such as Kellogg, General Mills, and Kraft, which rely on imported produce from around the world to meet the demand. In addition, large retailers like Wal-Mart are looking to stock fresh fruits and vegetables 365 days a year instead of having only a limited availability of the fresh produce that happens to be in season.

A small but rapidly growing source of fresh produce for American consumers is China. While total exports are a fraction of the total U.S. produce market, growth has been exponential. For example, in 2000, Chinese exports of fresh garlic amounted to 1 million pounds or less than 1 percent of U.S. demand; however, in 2005 China exported 73 percent of U.S market demand and 83 percent in 2007. Strawberries are another example, with Chinese exports increasing from 1.5 million pounds in 2000 to 33 million pounds in 2007. Overall, Chinese exports of fresh produce are more than doubling every year.

As a consumer it is great to enjoy a strawberry in January, especially since prices have not gone up dramatically despite the need to transport the produce long distances. Food experts, however, are becoming increasingly concerned about the quality of the produce coming out China. The FDA recently reported that 107 food imports from China were detained in one month because the products were preserved with harmful chemicals and pesticides. This comes after the tainted pet food scandal in 2007 where pet food from China was laced with a harmful chemical that killed a number of cats and dogs as well as milk with the dangerous chemical melamine in 2008.

Another issue driving the import of food products from China is the growth of organic foods. Dean Foods, Kellogg, and Wal-Mart are importing organic strawberries, soybeans, mushrooms, and broccoli from China, and the same concerns about product quality exist, particularly since China didn't institute any organic food standards until 2005.

China is becoming a major exporter of food products worldwide, producing nearly half of the world's vegetables and 16 percent of the world's fruits. In addition, the nation is expanding the amount of land dedicated to vegetable and fruit farming. Currently, however, the quality-control standards established in the United States and other parts of the world to ensure product safety are not enforced. At the same time, consumers benefit from easy access to low-priced fruits and vegetables, and companies benefit from having product available for sale year-round. Yet the question still remains, is the strawberry safe?[20]

Ethical Perspective

1. **American companies importing Chinese produce:** Should they stop importing fresh produce from China until product quality and safety standards match those in the United States? If consumers want fresh produce year-round, shouldn't companies seek out the lowest-cost provider?

2. **U.S. federal government:** Should it ban fresh produce from China until product quality and safety is assured? What responsibility does the government have in ensuring the quality and safety of Chinese produce?

3. **Consumers:** What role do consumers have in making sure the food products they consume are safe?[19]

Reliability

A similar discriminator references the dependability of a product. **Reliability** is the percentage of time the product works without failure or stoppage. Businesses and consumers consistently report this is an important discriminator in their purchase decision; however, a product can be too reliable. While it is possible to build computers that will last for years and cost a premium, most computer manufacturers do not build them because computer technology changes so quickly and product improvements happen so fast that people will not pay the premium for a computer that will last for many years.[21] They know that better, cheaper technology will be available before the computer actually malfunctions.

Repairability

Increasingly, consumers and businesses evaluate the **repairability,** ease of fixing a problem with the product, as part of the product evaluation process. As a result, companies have built better diagnostics into their products to help isolate, identify, and repair products without the need for the costly repairs of a professional service.[22] Luxury cars such as the Chevy Corvette are available with tires that enable the driver to continue driving even after the tire has been damaged. At the same time and where appropriate, products are designed to "call in" to repair services online or on the phone. Cell phone manufacturers and service providers work together to build self-diagnostic phones that can be accessed in the field by service technicians. The technician can look at the phone's functionality and actually do minor software upgrades or repairs during a phone call.

Style

One of the most difficult discriminators to accurately assess and build into a product is the look and feel of the product, or **style.** It is easy for someone to say a particular product has style, but designing it into a product can be a challenge. More than any other discriminator, style offers the advantage of being difficult to copy. While many companies from Sony to Samsung have tried to copy the iPod, no one has created a product that combines the functionality and elegance of Apple's product. Apple has a history of creating stylish products.

The real challenge is that style can be difficult to create consistently. Consumer tastes change over time, and what is considered stylish can quickly lose it appeal. Companies invest in information systems that help them spot trends. Once a trend is identified, product development teams must be able to translate it into design elements that can be incorporated into the product.[24] In some industries this is critical; for example, clothing manufacturers anticipate future trends, then use efficient production processes to design, build, and distribute their clothes while a particular style is still popular (see Exhibit 10.8).

In creating the "Palace bottle" Evian is taking a bottle of water and adding an element of style.

Evian, a world leader in bottled water, added style to its basic product by introducing a new product, the Palace bottle, that is sold only in high-end restaurants and hotels. The 25-ounce bottle made of high-quality PVC resembling glass sells for $5 to $8, rests in a metal base, and is served at the table with a stainless-steel spout. A more slender shape than the bottles found in other venues, it is designed to create a unique drinking experience for those willing to pay a premium.[23]

Product Plan: Moving from One Product to Many Products

Our discussion thus far has focused on a single product; however, companies generally create a range of products. These products can be variations or extensions of one basic product or completely different products. Most people would consider Post-it Notes, 3M's iconic brand of self-adhesive notes, a single product but over 600 Post-It products are sold in more than 100 countries.[25] When you couple the extensive range of Post-it products with the thousands of products offered by 3M across more than 40 core product lines, it becomes apparent why management must understand how a product fits into the company's product strategy.

| EXHIBIT 10.8 | Clothing Retailer Gap |

Developing a plan sets strategy not only for a single product, but also for all the products in the company's catalog.

Product Line

A **product line** is group of products linked through usage, customer profile, price points, and distribution channels or needs satisfaction. Within a product line, strategies are developed for a single product, but also for all the products in the line. For example, 3M develops a strategy for each Post-it product, such as Post-it cards, that identifies possible product uses, different target markets, and marketing messages. At the same time, the company combines individual products for specific markets to create consumer-based solution catalogs. Students can find Post-it products targeted for them and teachers can find a separate listing of products.

Campbell Soup recently garnered an unexpected award, the hottest new product in the grocery business with a line extension of the 136-year-old Campbell's Red and White soups. Its "Reduced Sodium" soup line generated more than $100 million in sales in its first year. Introducing carefully targeted line extensions has helped Campbell's entire soup line, which accounts for nearly 50 percent of Campbell's revenue.[26]

Companies must balance the number of items in a product line. Too many items and customers find it difficult to differentiate between individual products. In addition, cost inefficiencies involved in producing multiple products lower margins for the entire product line. Too few products and the company runs the risk of missing important market opportunities. Nike dealt with this problem as highlighted in the FYI.

A T-shirt is a T-shirt, right? Not if you are Nike. The company has 30 different designs, many with minimal differences such as curved or straight hems. When the company announced a new line of clothing, Sports Essentials, it decided to create the perfect T-shirt and standardize all future designs around the new template. The process included using new fabrics and stitching, resulting in a product that Nike retails for $25.

The T-shirt redesign is part of Nike's corporate strategy to simplify its product offerings. Ninety-five percent of apparel sales are generated by 40 percent of the product items. Compounding the problem is that while Nike has some of the most popular shoe brands on the planet in Air Jordan and Air Force1, the company's apparel sales have not matched shoe sales. The T-shirt is an essential element of Nike's product line strategy to increase sales of apparel.[27]

Product Mix

Combining all the products offered by a company is called the **product mix.** Small, start-up companies frequently have a relatively limited product mix but, as companies grow, their list of products grows as well. Developing strategies for the entire product mix is done at the highest levels of the organization.[28] Large companies, like 3M or GE, have widely disparate product lines that encompass hundreds of products and thousands of product items. Exhibit 10.9 lists some of the more than 55,000 products in 3M's product mix that range from Post-it Notes to communication technology systems and a host of industrial applications.

Product Decisions Affect Other Marketing Mix Elements

Decisions about the product affect other elements of the marketing mix. Let's look at how two key marketing mix elements, pricing and marketing communications, are influenced by product decisions.

Pricing

Pricing is one of the key marketing mix components and will be covered in detail in Chapter 13; however, several key issues related to product line pricing are appropriately covered here. Individual product pricing within the context of a broader product line requires a clear understanding of the price points for all the products in the line. Often multiple price points are targeted at specific markets with unique features following a "good, better, best" product line strategy. This strategy develops multiple product lines that include products with distinct features at each particular price point to attract multiple target markets. When new products are introduced, marketers carefully consider customer perceptions of the product's feature mix and price point to avoid customer confusion.

Anheuser-Busch, now owned by InBev, continues to create new market opportunities for the company's high-end Michelob product line. Recently, AB introduced Celebrate by Michelob, which retails at $10 per bottle. The premium-priced beer is not sold in six-packs and is meant to be drunk from a snifter instead of a glass. The company carefully considered its pricing strategy with Celebrate to be sure it was consistent with its other Michelob products.[29]

EXHIBIT 10.9   **3M's Product Mix of 55,000 Products**

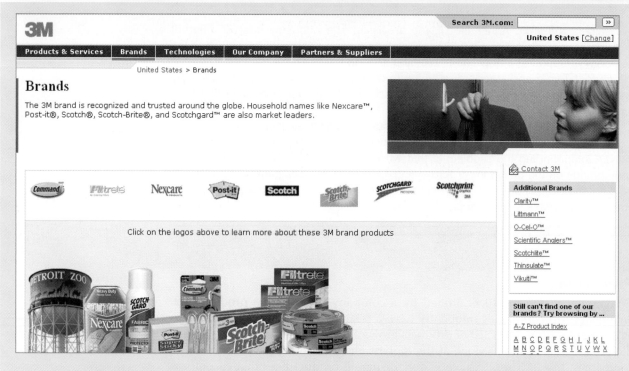

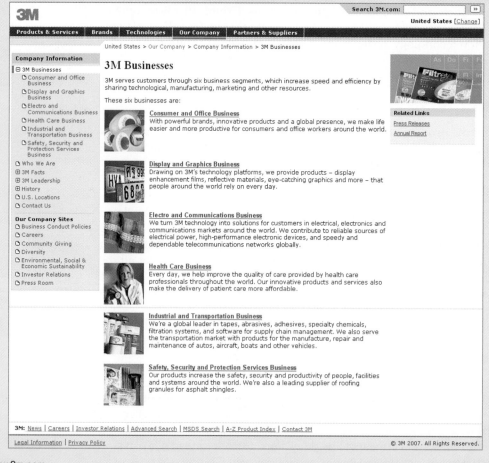

Source: www.3m.com.

Reprinted courtesy of 3M Corporation.

Technology companies, for many years, have faced the challenge of pricing new products that are less expensive but with more features than previous models. Dell and HP are sensitive to pricing new products because as new, more powerful, less-expensive products come into the product mix, demand often drops for existing products. Dell prices new computer models to minimize disrupting demand for its existing products while, at the same time, lowering prices of existing products to create greater separation between the new product and current products (see Exhibit 10.10).

Marketing Communications

A key strategic decision for marketers is the degree to which marketing communications focuses on a single product item versus a product brand. Usually, companies do both, but the emphasis on one approach versus the other makes

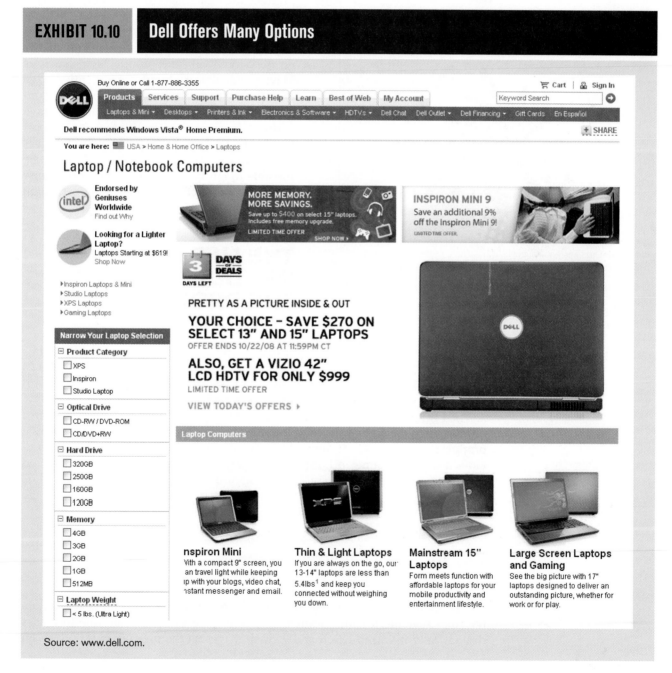

EXHIBIT 10.10 **Dell Offers Many Options**

Source: www.dell.com.

Häagen-Dazs

made like no other™

even more de lechable

Eager to surpass perfection, we took our original Latin-inspired blend of caramel and sweet cream and added a touch of the world's finest cinnamon. Surely your sweet tooth will dance the rumba with delight.

New Häagen-Dazs® Cinnamon Dulce de Leche Ice Cream

Haagen Dazs has been successful building a product line that features old favorites but also frequently introduces new product flavors.

Courtesy of Dreyer's Grand Ice Cream, Inc.

a big difference in the communications strategy. For example, 3M focuses much of its Post-it marketing communications on the Post-it product line, emphasizing the brand. Contrast that with Haagen-Dazs, which focuses on specific products (ice cream, sorbet, and yogurt) and specific product items within each product (chocolate, almond hazelnut swirl, pineapple coconut).

A second communications issue is the allocation of communications budget dollars across product items in a product line. Haagen-Dazs has more than 30 specific kinds of ice cream and dozens of other products across its entire product line. The company must make decisions about the allocation of budget dollars to each product then each specific product item. This raises several challenges for marketing managers. Do they allocate dollars based on the most popular flavors like chocolate and vanilla? Or do they focus on new product items such as Mayan chocolate to build a competitive edge with products that are not offered by the competition? New products almost always have additional communication budgets to support the product's introduction. The assumption is that, once the product is established, it will be possible to cut back on the heavy expenditure of a new product communications campaign (see Exhibit 10.11).

THE LIFE OF THE PRODUCT: BUILDING THE PRODUCT EXPERIENCE

Companies create, launch, and transform products as market conditions change over time. This product evolution is referred to as the **product life cycle (PLC)** and defines the life of a product in four basic stages: introduction, growth, maturity, and decline (see Exhibit 10.12).[30]

The PLC generally refers to a product category (touring bicycles) rather than a product item (Giant Sedona bicycles) although companies often track their own product items against an industry PLC. The PLC is a useful tool because it: (1) provides a strategic framework for market analysis, (2) tracks historical trends, and (3) identifies future market conditions. Giant Bicycles, for example, can evaluate the current touring bike market and then consider growth opportunities for the Sedona brand based on that product's position in the PLC.

Product Life Cycle Sales Revenue and Profitability

Notice there are two lines on the PLC graph. The top line charts the industry sales revenue for the product over time. The sales revenue line increases dramatically in introduction and growth stages as the product moves through

EXHIBIT 10.12 **The Product Life Cycle**

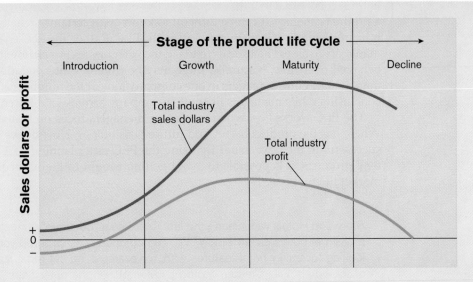

Reprinted from Roger Kerin, Steven Hartley, and William Rudelius, *Marketing*, 9th ed., 2009. Copyright © 2009 The McGraw-Hill Companies, Inc.

the consumer adoption process. At some point, sales begin to decline. However, a sales decline does not necessarily mean the death of the product. Companies may create new products or market conditions may change, which can reinvigorate the product and start a new growth phase. Bottled water was long considered a product in decline until Evian, Dasani, Zephyrhills, and others developed new packaging, added new flavors, and emphasized the healthy aspects of water. Now the product category is experiencing a period of significant growth around the world.

The second line on the PLC graph is the total profits from the companies that compete in that industry. When the product is introduced, the category pioneer, the company introducing the product, has incurred product development costs. At the same time, new companies entering the market also sustain product development and initial marketing costs associated with the product launch. As a result, the industry starts the PLC "in the red" (no profits). As the product category grows, successful companies recoup their initial costs and begin to realize a return on their investments.

Product Life Cycle Timeline

The speed at which products within a category move through the PLC is not consistent, and there is a great deal of variability across product categories. In some cases, a product moves through an entire cycle in a period of months and is replaced with the next product design. **Fads** come and go quickly, often reaching only a limited number of individuals but creating a lot of buzz in the marketplace.[31] Often, women's fashion is seasonal with a product line being introduced in the spring, moving through its growth cycle in the summer and fall, then finally into decline by winter. The cycle takes one selling season, in this case, one year. With other products such as men's suits, it may take decades from introduction to decline. Men's classic two-piece suits experience incremental changes every season, but the same basic design has been around for many years. The functionality of the product has made it an enduring style for men.

Product Life Cycle Caveats

It is important to note several caveats about the product life cycle. The PLC is a helpful conceptual tool that works best when viewed as a framework for studying a product category. It can be difficult to know with certainty what stage a product is in, particularly at transition points in the PLC. Rather, the PLC enables marketing managers to assess historical trends in the category and track how the product has behaved over time. Naturally, there may be different interpretations of the same data as marketing managers in one company look at the numbers and arrive at one conclusion while managers in another company arrive at a different conclusion.

The PLC works best when marketing managers focus on historical precedent. Where has the product been? And future possibilities. How do we plan now to be successful in the next stage? By using the PLC as a planning tool for developing new products, it is possible to avoid getting caught in the immediacy of volatile market fluctuations.

Starwood Hotels was among the first to create a "boutique" concept and create a chain of hotels called simply "W." The company has targeted young travelers looking for quirky hotel features with, for example, no set room layouts for any of the hotels. Ritz-Carlton, owned by Marriott, on the other hand, continues to focus on elegant, more traditional hotels. While significantly upgrading its properties, the tradition of referring to guests and staff as "ladies and gentlemen" continues.[32]

Introduction Phase

The beginning of the product life cycle, the introduction phase, is the launch of the first product in the category. It is a challenging time for the product pioneer and competitors as sales are low, profits are nonexistent, and it is unclear if the market will accept the product.

Market Conditions

The company that takes the risk and introduces a new product, creating a new product category, is called the Pioneer. Conventional wisdom holds that pioneers enjoy an advantage because they have the opportunity to establish themselves in the market before competitors. They can define the market space with their product characteristics, features, and brand.[33] In some cases, it is possible to identify the brand so closely with the market that it defines it. Google is so well-known that it has become the verb used to conduct an Internet search; "to Google something" means to do an Internet search. If the consumer adoption process is relatively fast, the product pioneer will become widely adopted in the market mainstream before competitors have an opportunity.

Note, however, that being first to market does not guarantee market dominance in the future. Apple was first to market with a PDA, Newton, but was unable to capitalize and eventually discontinued the product. Do you remember Microsoft's Bob operating system? Did you ever shop at Kmart's Builders Square, a direct competitor to Home Depot and Lowe's, or fly on a Boeing 717, a 100-seat passenger jet? Your answer to these questions is most likely no because these companies were not able to sustain their market advantage with these products (see Exhibit 10.13).

Market followers, those coming in immediately after the market pioneer, also have a history of success. Sperry was actually the first computer manufacturer but was over taken by IBM, GE became the eventual market leader over EMI in CAT scan equipment, and Apple overtook Rio in portable digital music players. Market followers have the opportunity to learn from market leader mistakes, benefit from missing or poorly designed product characteristics and features, and focus on bigger target markets.

EXHIBIT 10.13 | **Market Leaders with Product Failures**

Lockheed L-1011	The aircraft was a technically sound design (indeed, more advanced than the competing McDonnell Douglas DC-10). However, the cost of the development of the Rolls-Royce RB211 engine caused Rolls-Royce to go bankrupt and delayed the program. In the end, with only 250 frames sold, and 500 needed for the project to break even, the L-1011 resulted in a loss to Lockheed of $2.5 billion, or $10 million per aircraft. Lockheed left the civil airliner market after the failure of the L-1011.	
New Coke	Coca-Cola changed the formula and taste of its flagship product, a universally successful drink whose name was almost synonymous with soft drinks. Introduced in the United States on April 23, 1985, it was a marketing and public relations debacle, and the company had to backtrack and return to the older formula. Though there had been plans to roll out New Coke internationally, its prompt failure prevented this, so New Coke was only ever sold in the United States. When the company went back to the original formula, demand for the classic taste grew to a greater extent than before New Coke, propelling Coca-Cola to a market lead over archrival Pepsi, making the situation an unintentional success for Coca-Cola. Many maintain that the flub was intentional and that the heads of Coca-Cola planned the whole thing.	
Betamax VCR System	Sony's proprietary recording technology produced a sharper picture than VHS, but initially could only record for one hour. Also by not licensing the Betamax format, Sony was overwhelmed in the marketplace by the many competing, licensed VHS manufacturers.	

This stage is marked by relatively few competitors able to get developed products to market quickly. At this point, competitors are benchmarking off a single product or, at most, very few products. Increasingly, however, competitors are able to shorten the period between new product category introduction and the introduction of their own competitive product. This places a great deal of pressure on the product pioneer to develop a strong market position quickly.

When market followers are preparing to enter the market, consumers are learning about the product, evaluating its applicability to their current situation, and determining their level of interest and involvement. Innovators and early adopters will be the primary target markets at this stage. Companies need to begin communicating with these groups before product launch through directed marketing communications and viral marketing campaigns.[34]

The essential marketing objective during the introduction phase is to build market awareness for the product leading to trial purchase. Companies large and small face a challenge in creating awareness because the majority of the market is unaware of the product at introduction. Awareness, however, is only one of the objectives; the company also wants the customer to try the product.

Strategy

Product Products at introduction often lack sophisticated features found on later models as the market expands in the growth stage. The product pioneer faces a challenge because if a product is poorly designed or lacking in important features, the market may not accept it. Furthermore, competitors can target weak products with additional features, better design, or quality and overtake market leaders.[35]

Price Companies choose one of two different pricing strategies at product introduction: market penetration or market skimming. A company that wants to take a large percentage of the market quickly, perhaps to discourage competitors from entering or to encourage customers to make a trial purchase, will follow a **market penetration** pricing strategy. This involves introducing the product into the market at an attractive price and is designed to build market share. Market penetration requires sophisticated cost controls and a real understanding of market dynamics since margins are lower. The second, and more widely adopted, pricing strategy used during introduction is **market skimming,** which adopts a high initial price to market. Innovators and early adopters are not as price-sensitive as the rest of the market, which gives the company the chance to recoup developmental costs before competitors enter the market and prices begin to fall.[36]

Marketing Communications Two key objectives dominate marketing communications during introduction. First, because the product is new and people are not aware of it, the first objective is to inform and educate the target audience about the product's benefits, characteristics, and features. As part of this educational process, it may be necessary to reduce customer anxiety and help consumers understand the potential of the product for them personally. One major concern of online buyers, even today, is the security of making an Internet purchase. Amazon, eBay, and others educated consumers about the security of their online services and adopted sophisticated encryption software to protect sensitive customer data.[37]

A second objective of marketing communications during the introductory stage is motivating the customer to try the product. Marketers employ a variety of tools consistent with the overall marketing strategy to move first-time buyers to action. As we will discuss in Chapters 17 and 18, many options are open to the marketing manager. Often, consumer goods companies use sales promotion methods such as coupons and contests that encourage trial purchase as well as targeted direct-mail campaigns to support national advertising. Market pioneers stimulate primary demand, or demand for the product category rather than a specific brand.

Distribution At the time of product launch and into the introduction stage, there are generally two distribution strategies. One strategy is to adopt a fairly wide distribution network at product release but limit product availability. Microsoft followed this approach with the introduction of its Xbox video game system, making it available at a wide range of retail outlets but dramatically limiting the number of products at any one store. Market anticipation created long lines, which added to the excitement at product launch. The other strategy is to limit distribution but increase product availability. Consumer products companies such as Procter & Gamble and Frito-Lay introduce new products in limited markets to increase product availability in those markets. As production makes more products, and based on the product's success, the company will move into new markets over time.[38]

Growth Phase

The most dramatic increase in sales revenue occurs during the **growth phase.** It is a stage marked by rapid expansion as competitors come into the market and customers learn, understand, and begin to adopt the product. For the product pioneer, these market changes trigger strategic adjustments. Some pioneers are able to maintain market share, while others find the new competitors overtake them. Apple's iPod dominates the portable music player market but that was not always the case. The Diamond Rio, introduced in 1998 (three years before iPod) is credited with being the first mass-market digital audio player. Despite some significant drawbacks (it cost $200 and held less than 20 songs) it was a success in its first year.

Market Conditions

This stage is characterized by new competitors entering the market to capitalize on market growth. Some companies, often large, established competitors, develop long-term market strategies aimed at a broad range of market segments. Small and medium entrepreneurs identify market niches and develop specialized products targeted at specific customer needs.[39]

Customers are entering the market in big numbers as the product becomes more mainstream. Early majority adopters seek out the midmarket products while innovators and early adopters purchase next-generation models or new products with additional features. [40]

Strategy

Product Having learned from first-generation products, new products introduced in the growth stage generally have more features and better design. Market pioneers introduce next-generation products in an effort to maintain market leadership. Product models begin to diverge as market segmentation drives product strategy. [41]

Diamond Rio, Compaq, and later iRiver created the digital audio music player product category and experienced steady growth from 1998 to 2000. However, significant growth did not occur in that market until Apple introduced the iPod. Apple made several significant improvements over existing models at the time. The iPod used a hard drive to store music (many players at the time used flash drives), and the user interface was easier to use. In addition, Apple created iTunes, a digital music download service, which is now the industry standard that worked seamlessly with iPod.

Even after the iPod was introduced, it took 18 months from iPod's introduction in 2001 for it to reach $1 million in sales. Not until the introduction of the third-generation iPod did sales began to accelerate. First-generation iPod's had monochrome screens, had limited storage capacity (the first iPod had 5 GB storage while the iPod classic has 80 or 160 GB), and lacked the sophisticated software applications found on current models. More recently, the iPod Touch offers Internet connectivity, touch-screen technology, and larger screens.

Price As the number of models expands, prices move in two directions. New competitors and market pioneers all create new models with the latest features at high price points. At the same time, existing models or earlier generations move down in price.[42] The product line is designed to offer a wide range of product options at various price points to many target markets. Apple maintains a range of iPod products priced from $49 to $499.

Marketing Communications At this stage, marketing communications link the brand with key product features and highlight the points of differentiation between the company's products and competitors'. The focus shifts to stimulating greater selective demand (demand for a specific brand) and less primary demand (product category demand). Sony, Creative Labs, and Apple's marketing communications now concentrate exclusively on individual models and branding. The product category has moved well into the growth stage.

Distribution As models proliferate and market segmentation becomes more pronounced, companies seek broader distribution for their products. Companies face a challenge in expanding the market while maintaining expected levels of product quality and customer service. As the product moves into new distribution channels, it is not always possible to control product display, train the salespeople adequately on the product, or ensure a positive customer experience. At the same time, customers are more knowledgeable about the product and may not require the same experience as they did during the introduction stage. The challenge becomes knowing the target markets well enough to identify the most appropriate distribution channels. Apple iPods are now available at Costco and other discounted locations as many shoppers are already familiar with iPod and do not require the hands-on experience of the Apple store or other electronics retailers to make the purchase decision.

Maturity Phase

Most established products are in the **maturity stage** of the product life cycle. Because the stage is the transition from high growth to relative sales stability or decline, products can reside here for a long time.[43] The three phases to maturity are defined by the sales growth of the product category. In the first phase, **relative market expansion,** product category sales continue to grow but at a rate significantly less than the growth stage. Cell phone sales continue to grow but not at the 15 to 20 percent growth rate experienced in the late 1990s. This suggests that cell phones are entering maturity in the United States although their growth in Asia and other global markets continues to expand at a higher rate.

The second phase of maturity, called **market stability,** is the period of no growth as the market reaches saturation. Everyone who is part of the target market has tried the product and there are few, if any, untapped markets left to attack. Any product category growth reflects population growth and product replacement sales (especially for consumer products). In the final phase, **market deterioration,** the market starts to lose customers and competitors begin to feel the pressure of overcapacity in the market. From here the product moves into the decline stage of the PLC.

Market Conditions

Early in maturity many competitors remain in the market. Some late entrants will come in while the market is still growing despite the fact that growth rates have declined. Audi entered the SUV market in 2006 despite slowing product category sales. Many late entrants into a mature market want to recoup their development costs, even though the market is declining, because the investment is too high to withdraw. Additionally, companies are willing to risk a product launch because they know that if the product is well-received there is still an opportunity for success albeit as a niche product.

As the product moves deeper in the maturity stage, competitors begin to withdraw as growth rates decline. The first companies to exit the market are usually marginal players who were successful only as long as new customers were coming into the market. Once the market growth begins to slow, their problems (poor product design or quality, ineffective marketing campaigns, lack of cost control) overwhelm them.

Those companies that remain fall into two broad categories. A few large players dominate the market followed by a number of smaller companies with specific products meeting specialized market needs. Market leaders carve out particular market spaces (high quality or low price) and drive profitability by capturing dominant market share coupled with reduced costs.[44]

As market growth slows, companies aggressively seek potential new target markets. There are two sources of new customers at this stage in the product life cycle. First, product nonusers are individuals who have not yet tried the product. A company capable of converting nonusers to the product can create a competitive advantage as the market slows. A second strategy is to convert users of competitive products. One challenge is that maintaining market share can be expensive as market followers aggressively attack to gain market share. Colgate, a world market leader in toothpaste, is constantly challenged by Crest, Aqua-Fresh, and others who use sales promotions to drive sales growth.

Strategy

Product As mentioned, companies follow different strategies in maturity depending on their market (leader, follower) and product (high quality, low price, niche) position. Quality improvements and additional features are appropriate for products positioned at the high-quality end of the market. "Bigger, better, stronger" creates a powerful incentive for customers to try the product.[45]

In the low-price market space, companies focus on cost management and ease of purchase. As the product moves into market deterioration and decline, all companies left in the market focus on cost management.

Price Early in the maturity stage, market leaders begin to notice price pressure as smaller competitors' lower prices to increase sales. This is usually one sign the product has moved into a mature phase. With time and slower market growth rates, price pressure becomes more pronounced. Price pressure will vary depending on where the company chooses to compete, but across the product category customers are more price sensitive and feature focused. The company's response to increased price sensitivity will depend, in large measure, on the product strategy. A new product strategy with additional features affords higher price stability and less pressure to lower prices. However, as growth slows, management will feel pressure to reduce new-product investment, which puts additional pressure on lowering price to remain competitive.

Marketing Communications As the market slows, one area that comes under scrutiny is marketing communications. Increasingly, companies in the consumer products sector spend a high percentage of the marketing communications budget on mature products (some estimate 60 percent of the entire communications budget) because of the need to support the brand and reinforce key product differentiators.

Gap Jeans demonstrates product features through its "Favorite Fits" product line.

It is important to separate true brand communications from sales promotion at this stage. Marketing managers, in an effort to drive sales, often resort to sales promotion to induce short-term sales with coupons. However, marketing communications that support the brand create long-term brand value. When you consider the true value of a brand, the investment in long-term brand building communications at this stage of the PLC is probably worth it.

Distribution Early in the maturity phase, the product reaches its maximum distribution with a variety of outlets targeted at a wide range of target markets. At this point, however, manufacturers ask for additional channel support (cross and joint promotions) while channel members begin to identify weak products in the market. By late in the maturity phase, channel members start dropping poor market performers or products that lack sufficient sponsor support. Often distribution channels settle on fewer, larger market players to maximize the brand presence of a few brands as the market slows.

> Procter & Gamble continues to expand in the rapidly growing Chinese market. The company has enjoyed great success localizing its global brands such as Crest and Pampers. However, as growth in urban areas begins to stabilize, P&G looks to expand into rural areas, home to 700 million Chinese. Critical to success is P&G's ability to manage a distribution channel that is far different from that in the larger cities. P&G trained local shop owners (10,000 in all) about the products as they represent the most trusted source of information among rural Chinese consumers.[46]

Decline Phase

At some point products enter a period of sales decline. In some cases, the decline may be slow as it was with typewriters, or rapid as with 3.5-inch floppy disks. Consumer preferences change or technology evolves, creating new opportunities and leaving old products chasing a much smaller market or even a nonexistent market.

Marketing managers face difficult decisions with products in sales decline. Often managers spend disproportionate time and resources in an attempt to rescue the product, sometimes it works but often it doesn't. IBM spent millions of dollars creating new, better versions of its classic Selectric typewriter but eventually realized that the Selectric could not transition to the computerized word-processing age and discontinued the product in the mid-1990s.

Market Conditions

At this point in the product's life cycle, profit margins have been dramatically reduced, particularly compared to growth and early maturity. Customers have moved on, and competitors are fighting for a piece of a smaller market, which may or may not continue to shrink. As a result, some competitors choose or are forced to leave the market, and those that remain focus on maintaining profit margins. Further compounding the challenge for many marketing managers is the timing of the market decline. Managers seek to understand if the sales decline is a short-term problem, resulting from outside forces (home sales dropping as a result of interest rate increase), or a fundamental shift in the market with long-term implications (computers replacing the typewriter).[47]

Strategy

Product The most important strategic decision in the decline stage is the future of the product. Carrying a product with low market share, modest customer support, and little or no chance of growth is expensive. Not only are direct expenses (marketing communication, manufacturing, distribution) high relative to the return on investment, but also indirect expenses (management time, allocation of resources away from projects with a higher probability of success) become an additional burden.

Planning for **product deletion** is always a challenge inside and outside the company. Internally, people assigned to the product need to be reassigned or terminated, creating anxiety and uncertainty. Additionally, once the decision is made it becomes more difficult to motivate people to continue working hard during the deletion process. Externally, customers are often not willing to purchase products they know are going to be discontinued. When General Motors announced it was going to abolish the Oldsmobile line, sales dropped even though GM said it would support the brand after it had been eliminated and honor all warranties. All of these issues present a problem of timing. When and how products are deleted has far-reaching effects not only on employees and customers but on future products as well. If a company is perceived as doing a poor job of deleting unsuccessful products, customers may choose not to support new products in the future. When the Audi 5000 had problems with its transmission in the mid-1980s, the company was not able to respond quickly to criticism and was eventually forced to take the car off the market. It took over a decade for Audi to bring customers back to the brand in the United States.[48]

George Eastman changed photography over 100 years ago but creating a simple way for everyone to take a picture. His revolutionary film processing methodology transformed photography from a difficult, expensive process into something as easy as "you press the button, we do the rest." However, technology changed the face of photography and Kodak recently announced it would leave the film business. Despite its success in dominating the film business it was not prepared for digital photography.[49]

A second possible product strategy is called **harvesting.** This strategy involves a measured but consistent investment reduction in the product. While harvesting also means decreasing other marketing elements (reducing marketing communications, cutting distribution support), the core of the strategy involves eliminating future investment in the product, essentially letting the existing product gradually lose market share until the point at which it is deleted. By lowering costs to the absolute minimum, the company can extract whatever profit remains in the market. A company may also adopt this strategy with the intention of assessing the long-term prospects for the product. As we discussed, when sales declines are due to external forces, it is possible for the product to rebound. In those circumstances, a company may take a "wait-and-see" approach to the market and reduce expenditures until managers can identify the long-term prospects for the market.

A third, more risky, product strategy is to consider additional product investment. Once the marginal competitors have left the market, remaining players often find the market more attractive. Fewer competitors translate to more customers for those remaining in the market. As a result, an appealing product choice is investing in modest product improvements to expand the market share of the existing product. The goal is to develop a dominant market position without expending too many resources.

Price There is significant price pressure from two sides. First, competitors engage in price competition to acquire additional market share and keep inventories low. Since new customers are not entering the market, remaining customers become price sensitive, which creates additional pressure to offer sales and reduce product price. Second, costs remain high as overhead costs are spread over few products. In addition, direct costs (materials, labor) are also higher as suppliers raise prices due to lower sales volume. The pressure to lower price, while costs remain high, is a primary reason companies need specific strategies to deal with products in decline. Unfortunately, many companies have not developed successful decline strategies.

Marketing Communications One of the first items cut when a product enters the decline stage is marketing communications. While a difficult decision, marketing managers are faced with a trade-off. They know it is important to continue to support the product with marketing communications but the cost is not justified by the sales revenue. Keep in mind the market is getting smaller and most of the target audience is already brand loyal; it is not easy to induce brand switching at this point. Depending on the product strategy, communication focuses on product improvements to capture market share or, more likely, on price and availability of the product.

Distribution As sales decline, product investment and support is cut back, which often leads to reduced distribution channels. Many channel partners will not carry products in sales decline. In addition, if a distribution outlet experiences a lack of product support, it will cease to support the product as well. Products in sales decline find it harder to stay in the marketplace, which exacerbates the sales decline.

SUMMARY

The product experience is the essential element in delivering value to the customer. Organizations understand that, no matter what else happens in the customer experience, the product must deliver on its value proposition to the customer. Products have a detailed set of characteristics that include defined customer benefits as well as core and enhanced product attributes. Companies develop individual product strategies consistent with broader product line and category strategies that, in turn, achieve corporate goals and objectives. Products follow a product life cycle that includes introduction, growth, maturity, and decline. As a product moves through the cycle, marketing strategies change to meet new market conditions.

KEY TERMS

product 271
SKU (stock keeping unit) 271
essential benefit 271
core product 271
enhanced product 273
tangibility 274
durability 274
nondurable product 274
durable product 275
convenience goods 275
shopping goods 276
specialty goods 276
unsought goods 276

materials 278
parts 278
MRO supplies (maintenance, repair, operating) 278
capital goods 278
form 278
features 280
conformance 281
reliability 282
repairability 282
style 283
product line 284
product mix 285

product life cycle (PLC) 288
fads 289
market penetration 292
market skimming 292
growth phase 293
maturity stage 294
relative market expansion 294
market stability 294
market deterioration 294
product deletion 297
harvesting 297

APPLICATION QUESTIONS

1. You are a marketing manager for Starbucks. Describe the following as it relates to the product experience at Starbucks: essential benefit, core product, and enhanced product. Now imagine you are the marketing manager for Aquafresh Extreme toothpaste. Describe the product experience in terms of essential benefit, core product, and enhanced product.

2. Choose two comparable phones from Motorola and Nokia and examine each product. How does the product form differ between the two products? How are they the same? Now consider the features of the two products. What features are unique to each phone? Which phone, overall, appeals to you most and why?

3. One of the most difficult characteristics of a product to define is style. You are the marketing manager for Cadillac; define the product style for an Escalade. Compare and contrast that with product style for a Chevrolet Tahoe (another large SUV built on the same platform as the Escalade).

4. You are the marketing manager for Coca-Cola products in the United States. Describe the product line for Coke branded products and briefly describe how each product differs from the other products in the Coke brand product line.

5. Motorola is introducing a new phone that incorporates an MP3 music player, Internet surfing capability using new 3G technology, a GPS program, and other new features that will greatly expand the features available on a cell phone. Develop a marketing strategy for the introduction of the product.

MANAGEMENT DECISION CASE: It's Not Your Dad's Malibu

A popular car brand from the 1970s is getting a significant face-lift in hopes of reinvigorating sales. The stakes for General Motors and Chevy could not be higher. GM is under tremendous pressure to produce cars that people want to buy. As the market for big SUVs and trucks slows, GM is looking for success among its car brands. The company wants to reproduce the success of Cadillac, which was able to redefine itself with new models and reinvigorate sales with renewed consumer excitement.

Expectations for Chevrolet and, more specifically, the Malibu, are high. Management targets 20 percent sales growth for the new Malibu over its previous model. At the same time, it has the unenviable task of competing directly against two of the most popular cars in the country, Toyota Camry and Honda Accord. If that were not enough, the push for quality in the last decade has raised the bar for new cars so consumers no longer tolerate poor quality. Finally, automakers will introduce nearly 60 new cars in the next year, flooding the market with new models and designs. It's no wonder that Malibu faces a significant challenge meeting sales targets and consumer expectations.

The old product design process at Chevrolet and across all of GM was often regarded as inefficient and ineffective as witnessed by Chevrolet's declining market share. Practically speaking, cars were designed by committee (engineers, marketers, and finance) and resulted in compromises that often made everyone unhappy. Today, under the direction of Vice Chairman Robert Lutz, the product development process has been dramatically changed to focus on designing cars that appeal to consumers. Every car design begins with a vision for the car. From there marketing and finance departments can make suggestions. Adding to the process is a realization that the company must design products without the significant resources available

to Toyota. With the exception of Cadillac, GM cars are not able to maintain a price premium in the market so design changes and product development must be done inexpensively.

The next-generation Malibu is a good example of Chevrolet's new design strategy. Working within tight budget constraints, designers looked for inexpensive ways to make the car look more expensive. A number of design cues are used to give the look and feel of an expensive car. For example, headlights are wrapped around the front edge of the care giving it a more classic look and the impression that the wheels were further forward on the car. This was done because designers could not justify the millions needed to redesign and manufacture the wheels further forward (a design favored by consumers) but through lower-cost visual cues they accomplished much of the desired effect for consumers.

Given GM's recent history with new-car introductions (except for Cadillac) there is room for doubt. However, the company is confident and has high expectations for the new Malibu[50].

Questions for Consideration

1. Go to the Chevrolet Web site and view the new Malibu. In your opinion, have the designers successfully redesigned the Malibu to appeal to Gen X and Gen Y buyers?

2. Assess Chevrolet's product mix. How does it compare in terms of product line depth and width with Toyota and Honda?

3. You are a product designer at Chevrolet responsible for the next Malibu, What process would you follow in coming to the next design?

MARKETING PLAN EXERCISE

ACTIVITY 10: Define the Product Strategy

In this chapter we looked at the essential element in the marketing mix—the product. Developing an effective marketing plan begins with an understanding of your product, its role in the company's overall business strategy, and, more specifically, where it fits in the company's product mix. Additionally, it is important to establish a new-product development process that ensures a new product pipeline of potentially successful new products. Your assignment in this chapter includes the following activities:

1. Define the product to include:
   a. Value proposition.
   b. Characteristics.
   c. Nature of product (consumer versus business product, and what type of product it represents).

2. Identify the product's position in the product line (if offered with other similar products) and, more broadly, the company's overall product mix. Address the following:
   a. How would this product differ from other products in the product line (if appropriate)?
   b. What price point would this product target and is there any conflict with existing products?
   c. How does the marketing message differ for this product from other products in the product line?

3. Define a new-product development process for next-generation products. While the product may be new, it is important to have a plan in process for next-generation models.

If you are using Marketing Plan Pro, a template for this assignment can be accessed at www.mhhe.com/marshall1e.

RECOMMENDED READINGS

1. Mark Levin and Ted Kalal, *Improving Product Reliability: Strategies and Implementation* (New York: Wiley, 2003).

2. Michael McGrath, *Next Generation Product Development: How to Increase Productivity, Cut Costs, Reduce Cycle Times* (New York: McGraw-Hill, 2004).

3. Linda Gorchels, *The Product Manager's Handbook,* 3rd ed. (New York: McGraw-Hill, 2005).

4. Kenneth B. Kahn, *The PDMA Handbook of New Product Development,* 2nd ed. (New York: Wiley, 2004).

5. Clifford Fiore, *Lean Strategies for Product Development: Achieving Breakthrough Performance in Bringing Products to Market* (Milwaukee, WI: ASQ Quality Press, 2003).

CHAPTER 11

THE PRODUCT EXPERIENCE: BUILDING THE BRAND

LEARNING OBJECTIVES

- Recognize the essential elements in a brand.

- Learn the importance of brand equity in product strategy.

- Explain the role of packaging and labeling as critical brand elements.

- Define the responsibility of warranties and service agreements in building consumer confidence.

EXECUTIVE PERSPECTIVE

Executive Pete Barr, President/CEO

Company Fry-Hammond-Barr

Business Full-service marketing communication agency

How do you see the role of branding as it pertains to successful marketing management today?

Branding is a long, slow journey for which not all marketers have sufficient patience and focus at times. Because branding outreach and messaging usually cannot be related to ROI, it is often relegated to a "below-the-line" expense that many times becomes endangered in terms of financial support. Branding plays a critical role in marketing because it acts as a backdrop or foundation from which all product messages derive. Your brand is your company's essence, its personality, and the glue that holds the entire marketing plan together. Over time, brand equity can build into brand energy and can propel products and services into new markets, fueling sales and growth. Branding should be at the top of all marketing managers' lists in order for their products or services to remain top-of-mind with consumers.

Why is it so important that packaging and advertising work together to communicate a brand image?

Packaging is perhaps the most important link in the brand experience chain because it is the *physical embodiment* of the brand and the visual imprint that consumers file away in their subconscious. When consumers make purchase choices they rely on habits and recall of familiar experiences and images. Advertising messages bring the brand to life, many times through words and music. Advertising extends the name, logo, and product benefits to consumers so that brand recognition occurs when the consumer engages in making a purchase choice among competing brands. A brand's advertising and packaging must be consistent in terms of color, look, feel, and personality, to minimize consumer confusion.

As a brand moves through its natural life cycle of introduction, growth, maturity, and decline, how does the marketing communication approach need to change?

Consumer research and feedback should be monitored throughout a brand's life cycle, giving the marketing manager valuable consumer insight to drive marketing planning and strategy. Brands that are growing can ride the wave of brand buzz and acceptance with brand extensions into new markets—touting specific benefits to specific markets. Thus, in the growth stage, marketing stays fresh and new as it leverages the surge and gains valuable market share. As the brand matures, its market share must be defended with efforts that support the most valuable and unique features of the brand. When a brand moves from maturity to decline, the marketing messaging should target the most loyal of consumers to slow the decline and continue to fend off any remaining competition.

BRAND: THE FUNDAMENTAL CHARACTER OF A PRODUCT

Why does someone purchase a $65 Ralph Lauren Polo shirt instead of a $10 Wal-Mart pullover polo shirt? In part, the quality is better, but something else is also driving the purchase—a complex relationship between the individual purchasing the shirt and the brand Polo. Why do Ralph Lauren and other manufacturers such as Lacoste and Tommy Hilfiger prominently display their logo on merchandise? Because people who buy those products want others to know who manufactured the shirt, jacket, or pants. Equally important, the manufacturers want everyone to see the logo. Both customers and manufacturers realize the importance of the brand.

If asked, you could probably identify the logo for Ralph Lauren Polo but how would you define the Polo brand? Exhibit 11.1 highlights some of the different ways Ralph Lauren translates his brand into products and services. A **brand,** as defined by the American Marketing Association, is "a name, term, sign, symbol, or design, or a combination of them, intended to identify the goods or services of one seller or groups of sellers and to differentiate them from those of competitors." While the "Polo Pony" is a recognizable symbol of Polo products, customers and noncustomers assign a much deeper meaning to the brand.[1] In this chapter we'll focus on branding and critical elements in the branding process to learn more about this essential product building block. First we will discuss the many roles of a brand, including those assigned by customer, company, and competition as well as potential problems for a brand. Next, we'll examine an important concept—brand equity—which is used to frame the relationship of the brand to the customer. In addition, we examine four branding strategies. Finally, two other key elements of a customers' overall perception of a brand are examined: packaging and labeling as well as warranties and service agreements.

The importance of branding is not limited to consumer products. Business-to-business customers also consider brands when making purchase decisions. As we will see in this chapter, brands are important for customers and companies, which is why marketing managers are vitally interested in learning as much as possible about their customers' brand perceptions then developing effective branding strategies.

Brands Play Many Roles

Brands take on different roles for customers, manufacturers, even competitors. No other single product element conveys more information about the company. **Branding strategy** is an integral part of the product development process because companies know that successful new products result from a well-conceived branding strategy. At the same time, established products are defined, in large measure, by their brand, and companies work very hard to protect this critical asset. Let's examine brand roles.

Customer Brand Roles

Whether the customer is a consumer or another business, brands have three primary roles. First, the brand conveys information about the product. Without any additional data, customers construct expectations about quality, service, even features based on the brand. Years after ending the marketing communications campaign, many customers see the FedEx logo and still think, "Absolutely, positively, overnight." The logo itself creates an expectation of service though FedEx now offers many delivery options and products.

Scent-Air Technology is one of several companies that will custom-design a fragrance to help consumers connect with a brand. For example, Sony pumps a vanilla and mandarin aroma in 36 Sony Style stores, while Doubletree Hotels uses a chocolate chip cookie scent in its lobby. These companies and others understand that scent plays a significant role in the overall brand experience. Products that smell good sell better.[2]

EXHIBIT 11.1 **The Polo Brand**

Brands also educate the customer about the product. People assign meaning to their product experiences by brand and, over time, make judgments about which brands are best at meeting their needs and which are not. As a result, product evaluations and purchase decisions become less formidable as the customer relies on the cumulative brand experience to simplify the purchase process.[3] The thought process works something like this, "I have had great product experiences with Brand X in the past. I will purchase Brand X again making this purchase decision easier and faster." In essence the customer's "brand education" helps make the purchase decision with less effort. For many, home repair is daunting so hardware retailers like Lowe's provide as much information as possible to reduce anxiety about the process. Indeed, Lowe's has worked hard to develop a reputation for making the home repair process easy for everyone.

A third brand role is to help reassure the customer in the purchase decision.[4] For many years there was a phrase in IT, "No one ever got fired for buying IBM." IBM's reputation and market dominance in the large computer and network server market meant that even if the product did not meet performance expectations, the customer felt more secure and less anxious about choosing IBM equipment. Older, established brands like Lysol provide a sense of security and reduce concerns about product quality (see Exhibit 11.2).

Company Brand Roles

Brands also perform important roles for the brand's sponsor (manufacturer, distributor, or retailer). They offer legal protection for the product through a trademark (see Exhibit 11.3). By protecting the brand, the company is able to defend essential product elements such as its features, patentable ideas in manufacturing or product

EXHIBIT 11.2	Consumer Brand Roles

Convey information: FedEx

Educate the customer: Lowe's

Help reassure the customer

EXHIBIT 11.3 **Selected Guidelines for Use of Apple Trademarks**

GUIDELINES FOR USING APPLE TRADEMARKS AND COPYRIGHTS (FORMERLY ENTITLED GUIDELINES FOR THIRD PARTIES USING APPLE TRADEMARKS AND COPYRIGHTS)

These guidelines are for Apple licensees, authorized resellers, developers, customers, and other parties wishing to use Apple's trademarks, service marks or images in promotional, advertising, instructional, or reference materials, or on their Web sites, products, labels, or packaging. Use of the "keyboard" Apple Logo (Option-Shift-K) for commercial purposes without the prior written consent of Apple may constitute trademark infringement and unfair competition in violation of federal and state laws. Use of Apple trademarks may be prohibited, unless expressly authorized.

If you are a licensee of an Apple trademark or logo and have been provided with special trademark usage guidelines with your license agreement, please follow those guidelines. If your license agreement does not provide usage guidelines, then follow these guidelines. If you are an Apple Authorized Reseller, you need to refer not only to these guidelines but also to the Apple Corporate Identity Guidelines for Resellers and the AppleFund Guidelines which are posted to the Apple Sales Web site.

Apple's trademarks, service marks, trade names, and trade dress are valuable assets. In following these guidelines, you help us protect our valuable trademark rights and strengthen our corporate and brand identities. By using an Apple trademark, in whole or in part, you are acknowledging that Apple is the sole owner of the trademark and promising that you will not interfere with Apple's rights in the trademark, including challenging Apple's use, registration of, or application to register such trademark, alone or in combination with other words, anywhere in the world, and that you will not harm, misuse, or bring into disrepute any Apple trademark. The goodwill derived from using any part of an Apple trademark exclusively inures to the benefit of and belongs to Apple. Except for the limited right to use as expressly permitted under these Guidelines, no other rights of any kind are granted hereunder, by implication or otherwise. If you have any questions regarding these guidelines, please talk to your Apple representative or send an e-mail to Apple's Trademark Department at appletm@apple.com.

Authorized Use of Apple Trademarks

2. **Compatibility:** Developers may use Apple, Macintosh, iMac, or any other Apple word mark (but not the Apple Logo or other Apple-owned graphic symbol/ logo) in a **referential phrase** on packaging or promotional/advertising materials to describe that the third party product is compatible with the referenced Apple product or technology, provided they comply with the following requirements.

    a. The Apple word mark is not part of the product name.

    b. The Apple word mark is used in a referential phrase such as "runs on," "for use with," "for," or "compatible with."

    c. The Apple word mark appears less prominent than the product name.

    d. The product is in fact compatible with, or otherwise works with, the referenced Apple product.

    e. The reference to Apple does not create a sense of endorsement, sponsorship, or false association with Apple or Apple products or services.

    f. The use does not show Apple or its products in a false or derogatory light.

Unauthorized Use of Apple Trademarks

1. **Company, Product, or Service Name:** You may not use or register, in whole or in part, Apple, iPod, iTunes, Macintosh, iMac, or any other Apple trademark, including Apple-owned graphic symbols, logos, icons, or an alteration thereof, as or as part of a company name, trade name, product name, or service name except as specifically noted in these guidelines.

2. **Apple Logo and Apple-owned Graphic Symbols:** You may not use the Apple Logo or any other Apple-owned graphic symbol, logo, or icon on or in connection with Web sites, products, packaging, manuals, promotional/advertising materials, or for any other purpose except pursuant to an express written trademark license from Apple, such as a reseller agreement.

3. **Variations, Takeoffs or Abbreviations:** You may not use an image of a real apple or other variation of the Apple logo for any purpose. Third parties cannot use a variation, phonetic equivalent, foreign language equivalent, takeoff, or abbreviation of an Apple trademark for any purpose. For example:
   Not acceptable: Appletree Jackintosh Apple Cart PodMart

4. **Disparaging Manner:** You may not use an Apple trademark or any other Apple-owned graphic symbol, logo, or icon in a disparaging manner.

5. **Endorsement or Sponsorship:** You may not use Apple, Macintosh, iMac, or any other Apple trademark, including Apple-owned graphic symbols/logos, or icons, in a manner that would imply Apple's affiliation with or endorsement, sponsorship, or support of a third party product or service.

6. **Merchandise Items:** You may not manufacture, sell or give-away merchandise items, such as T-shirts and mugs, bearing Apple, Macintosh, iMac or any other Apple trademark, including symbols, logos, or icons, except pursuant to an express written trademark license from Apple.

7. **Apple's Trade Dress:** You may not imitate the distinctive Apple packaging, Web site design, logos, or typefaces.

8. **Slogans and Taglines:** You may not use or imitate an Apple slogan or tagline.
   For example: "Think different."

9. **Domain Names:** You may not use an identical or virtually identical Apple trademark as a second level domain name.
   Not acceptable: "imac.com" "imacapple.com" "imac-apple.com" "podmart.com."

design, and packaging.[5] A second critical role is that brands offer an effective and efficient methodology for categorizing products.[6] Sony has thousands of products across many product categories and branding helps keep track of those products.

Apple dominates the MP3 player market with iPod, and the iPhone has been a big hit with consumers; however, one market for Apple's products has been elusive—the corporate market. The company is seeking to change that by updating software and incorporating new features into the iPhone that target the corporate mobile user. But in this market space, the leader is RIM's (Research in Motion) popular line of Blackberry products. Apple must compare itself to an established market leader.[7]

Competitor Brand Roles

Market-leading brands provide competitors with a benchmark against which to compete. In industries with strong market-leading brands, competitors design and build products targeted specifically at the market leader. In these situations, the competitor leverages its product strength against the market-leading brand's perceived weakness. For years, pleasure motorboat manufacturers would frame their sales message with, "we are just as good as Sea Ray (the market leader) but less expensive." Sea Ray enjoyed a price premium in the market and competitors such as Regal, Chaparral, Rinker, and others would target their price points and feature mix against Sea Ray boats.

The Boundaries of Branding

While branding can have a strong effect on the product experience, it is not all-powerful. A good branding strategy will not overcome a poorly designed product that fails to deliver on the value proposition.[8] Too frequently companies put a good brand on a bad product, which often leads to erosion of the brand's value. In 2001, Pontiac introduced the Aztec that, among other things, was noted for its distinct, though much maligned, shape. Sales never lived up to GM's expectations because the Pontiac brand was not able to overcome the inherent problems in the vehicle. Production was stopped after the 2005 model.

A brand must also be protected. Counterfeit products or illegal activities conducted under the name of another company's brand can do significant damage to the brand.[9] This is why companies aggressively protect their brands around the world. Read Ethical Dimension 11 to find out more about the challenge Diageo, a leading spirits manufacturer, confronts in using digital marketing strategies while it protects the company's brands by maintaining ethical guidelines on product usage and access to confidential company data.

Finally, there must be real, identifiable and meaningful differences among products. If all products are perceived to be equal then it is more difficult to create a **brand identity,** which is a summary of unique qualities attributed to the brand.[10] Commodities are difficult to brand because customers often fail to perceive a difference among products. Major oil companies such as Exxon, Shell, and BP want to differentiate their gasoline from competitors but find it difficult because most people do not perceive a difference. Despite all their efforts, companies still find it difficult to overcome perceptions about a brand as noted in the FYI.

FYI

Can you name the country of origin for the following brands: Nokia, Lego, Samsung, Ericsson, and adidas? A study of undergraduate students found that many cannot

(continued)

ETHICAL DIMENSION 11

Baileys' and the Digital Bar

While you may not be familiar with the company Diageo, you are almost certainly familiar with its brands, which hold dominant positions in their respective markets—Smirnoff (the No. 1 vodka in the world), Johnnie Walker (the No. 1 Scotch whisky in the world), Guinness (the No. 1 stout in the world), Captain Morgan (the No. 2 rum), Bailey's (the top liqueur), Jose Cuervo (the No. 1 tequila in the world), and Tanqueray (the No. 1 imported gin in the United States). The company's impressive list of brands is sold in more than 180 countries and dominates the premium spirit market with sales in excess of $15 billion.

Diageo, like many consumer product companies, is moving dramatically into digital marketing as it targets younger customers (Generations X and Y). However, unlike Procter & Gamble or Lever Brothers, Diageo and other alcohol companies must adhere to ethical standards on product usage. More specifically, the company is responsible for making sure it targets young people of legal drinking age. This creates a particular challenge in digital marketing as it is difficult, if not impossible, to know with certainty who is receiving the message. For example, a visit to a Diageo brand Web site will ask for the individual's birthday and location. If the visitor is from the United States, the individual must be over 21 to access the site; however, it is possible for someone to type in any date.

In an effort to more effectively target its younger customers, Diageo opened a virtual bar in Second Life virtual world. The company's marketing research suggests that it is one of the methods for reaching what it calls "digital natives," which are people who are most comfortable online and receive most of their information over the Internet. The company believes that more traditional marketing communications such as TV or print will not work with this group. However, the virtual bar has raised some significant concerns about corporate governance and reputation. Diageo is particularly concerned about underage avatars coming into the bar and uses employees to act as bouncers checking virtual identification.

Managers at Diageo are watching the virtual bar very carefully. While they acknowledge that reaching out to young people requires embracing new digital technologies, they are concerned about underage access to adult content and violating the ethical codes of conduct.[11]

Ethical Perspective

1. **Diageo:** The company faces a challenge—to find effective digital technologies that connect with younger customers while maintaining ethical standards regarding underage drinking. How should the company deal with this challenge? If you were CEO at Diageo would you sponsor a virtual bar in Second Life? Why or why not?

2. **Customers:** Do younger customers have a responsibility to voluntarily not participate in adult activities in virtual communities like Second Life?

3. **Government:** Given the growth of virtual communities, should the government create stricter guidelines for underage access to adult content?

FYI [continued]

successfully identify where those global brands originate. Less than 5 percent of 1,000 undergraduate students surveyed correctly identified Nokia's home. More than half put Japan as the country of origin because they believe Japan makes quality products, and Nokia was perceived as a quality product. At the same time, less than 10 percent of the respondents were able to correctly identify the homes of Lego, Samsung, and Ericsson.

The research suggests that many young people make assumptions about a product's country of origin based on perceived strengths about a country. So, because Japan is recognized as a leader in electronics it was believed by many that Nokia must be Japanese. The most frequently cited countries of origin were, perhaps not surprisingly, Japan, United States, and Germany. Now for the answers: Nokia is based in Finland; Lego, Denmark; Samsung, Korea; Ericsson, Sweden; and adidas, Germany.[12]

BRAND EQUITY–OWNING A BRAND

Equity is about ownership and value. For example, people often think of their homes when they consider the term *equity*. Home equity is the difference between the price of the home (asset) and the mortgage (liability). The larger the difference between the value of the property and the mortgage loan value, the more equity is accrued to the homeowner.

In a very real sense the same is true of brand equity. Every brand has positives—for example, Mercedes-Benz has a reputation for high-quality cars—and negatives—Mercedes also has a reputation for being expensive. The greater the perceived difference between the positives and negatives, the more a customer will develop equity in the brand. When customers take "ownership" of a brand, they make an "investment" that often extends beyond a financial obligation and includes emotional and psychological attachment. Then the company can realize a number of benefits, which we discuss in the next section; however, if the company does a poor job of managing the brand, such as lowering the product quality, those same customers may become negative. As a marketing manager, you want to learn about the brand equity of your products to better understand the relationship of your product to target markets and create more effective marketing strategies.[13]

Defining Brand Equity

Brand equity can be defined as "a set of assets (and liabilities) linked to a brand's name and symbol that adds to (or subtracts from) the value provided by a product or service to a firm or that firm's customers." This definition, developed by David Aaker, can be broken into five dimensions:[14]

- **Brand awareness:** The most basic form of brand equity is simply being aware of the brand. Awareness is the foundation of all other brand relationships. It signals a familiarity and *potential* commitment to the brand.

- **Brand loyalty:** This is the strongest form of brand equity and reflects a commitment to repeat purchases. Loyal customers are reassured by the brand and are often ambassadors to new customers. Loyal customers enable a company to reduce marketing costs, leverage trade relationships, and speak to competitive threats with greater success.

- **Perceived quality:** Brands convey a perception of quality that is either positive or negative. Companies use a positive perceived quality to differentiate the product and create higher price points. Rolex watches have been able to sustain a price premium long into their life cycle because of the perceived quality in design and performance of the product.

- **Brand association:** Customers develop a number of emotional, psychological, and performance associations with a brand. In many cases, these associations become a primary purchase driver, particularly with brand loyal users. Dell has a reputation as a mass-market computer company with reasonably good-quality products but poor customer service. As a result, competitors, such as Hewlett-Packard, have been able to create market opportunities by associating their brand with higher levels of product support and customer service.

- **Brand assets:** Brands possess other assets such as trademarks and patents that represent a significant competitive advantage. Google is very protective of its search algorithm intellectual property, which, in the view of the company, gives the company a significant advantage over other search engines.

Let's consider the implications of these dimensions for marketing managers. First, moving customers from brand awareness to loyalty requires a thorough understanding of the target market and a successful marketing strategy. This is accomplished by developing a strong value offering and then communicating that to the target market. This is an essential element of the marketing manager's job.[15] Second, as we discussed in Chapters 7 and 8, customers develop perceptions about a product and associate it with attitudes and even emotion that are encompassed in a product's brand equity. By learning how customers view competitors' as well as their own brand, managers seek to affect people's perceptions and attitudes about their product.[16] Finally, managers protect their brands because they represent a vital asset for the company. They are vigilant about how they are portrayed in the marketplace, particularly by competitors.

Coca-Cola has created one of the most powerful global brands and its logo, displayed on a Coke truck in India, is recognized around the world.

Both the customers and the company have a stake in the brand's success. People do not want to purchase a brand if there is a question about quality, performance, or some other dimension of the product experience. They seek to maximize the benefits of the purchase and minimize the disadvantages. At the same time, companies understand every brand has liabilities that must be overcome to enhance the customer's perceived equity in the product. As a result, marketing managers constantly battle to increase brand equity or the customer's perception that the product's positive elements are greater than the negative elements. Brands do have real value and represent a significant company asset.[17] Exhibit 11.4 lists the most valuable brands in the world as measured by *BusinessWeek*. Note the value of these brands runs into the billions of dollars and changes are based on a number of things including changes in company strategy, brand success or failure, competitive pressures, and consumer acceptance.

| EXHIBIT 11.4 | The Most Valuable Brands in the World |

2008 Rank	2007 Rank	Name	Country	2008 Value ($ mil)	2007 Value ($ mil)	Change in Value (%)
1	1	Coca-Cola	U.S.	66,667	65,324	2%
2	3	IBM	U.S.	59,031	57,091	3
3	2	Microsoft	U.S.	59,007	58,709	1
4	4	GE	U.S.	53,086	51,569	3
5	5	Nokia	Finland	35,942	33,696	7
6	6	Toyota	Japan	34,050	32,070	6
7	7	Intel	U.S.	31,261	30,954	1
8	8	McDonald's	U.S.	31,049	29,398	6
9	9	Disney	U.S.	29,251	29,210	0
10	20	Google	U.S.	25,590	17,837	43%

Source: *BusinessWeek*, September 29, 2008, p.56.

A study in Great Britain reported that 72 percent of the market value for the FTSE 350 (Britain's stock exchange) is based on intangible assets and, more specifically, the brands associated with the company. Yet, many companies continue to eliminate successful brands because of globalization and economies of scale. Consumers may not always care; however, Mars found that deleting a brand can matter. It changed the name of an existing candy bar, Marathon, to Snickers, and consumers stopped buying it. Mars relented and now offers the Snickers Marathon bar in Great Britain.[18]

Benefits of Brand Equity

Building brand equity takes time and money. Given the necessary commitment of resources required to build brand equity, it is reasonable to question whether it is worth the investment. High brand equity delivers a number of benefits to the customers and manufacturers, retailers, and distributors or brand sponsors who control the brand. Three benefits are perceived quality, brand connections, and brand loyalty. Let's consider each of these benefits from two perspectives, the customer and the company managing the brand or the brand sponsor. Many of these benefits are difficult to quantify but dramatically affect the success or failure of the brand.

Perceived Quality

Customers All things being equal (value proposition, product features) the *branded product gives customers a reason to buy.* This is a big advantage over unbranded products because customers will infer a level of quality from the branded product that facilitates their purchase decision.[19]

Brand sponsor The perceived quality of a brand provides three distinct benefits to the company. First, the perception of a brand's quality enables companies to extend the product range. Porsche introduced the Cayenne SUV as the first high-performance sporty SUV. As noted in Chapter 5, the company built on the market's existing perception of high quality and sporty automobiles to introduce a product into a category that, to that point, had not been considered a "sports vehicle." Second, the perception of quality can lead to a price premium opportunity.[20] P&G and other consumer products companies, for instance, enjoy consistently higher prices (and margins) than generic and other locally branded products in the same category. Finally, the perception of quality is an excellent differentiator in the market. For example, Ray-Ban was among the first to successfully brand sunglasses. Its branding strategy positions the sunglasses in the high-quality, premium-priced segment of the market and has been successful for more than 60 years.

Linking Benefit to Strategy Successful marketing strategy builds quality into the entire customer experience—product, service, and any interaction with the company. As companies extend their product lines, they must ensure the customer's brand experience remains positive; put simply, get it right before you introduce new products and services.[21] Quality can create a price premium, but managers understand that to validate that price premium they must constantly validate the value proposition for the customer and answer the customer question, "what makes this product different?"[22]

Brand Connections

Customers Two primary customer advantages result from brand associations. First, customers process, store, and retrieve product information by brand, which is a big advantage for strong brands. People are more likely to connect information with a brand they know rather than sort through information on unfamiliar brands. For example, consumers generally don't consider checking accounts from all banks; rather, they consider the branded product such as Bank of America's checking or another brand they know. A second benefit is that strong brands generate a more positive attitude toward the product.[23] Customers generally have more upbeat thoughts about a powerful brand than a weak brand or generic product. Cisco network servers are an industry leader with an excellent reputation supported by IT professionals who use a wide range of other manufacturers.

Brand Sponsor When customers identify with a brand and then transfer that loyalty to the product it creates an additional barrier to entry for new brands,[24] particularly for smaller firms that lack brand recognition. The default choice for network servers is Cisco in many corporate IT departments because executives have heard of Cisco even if they are not familiar with the product itself, thus making it harder for other servers to enter the market.

Linking Benefit to Strategy Because of customer brand connections, marketing managers generally want to extend the brand to new products. However, extending a brand needs to fit the target market's perception of the brand. When Toyota, Honda, and Nissan created luxury cars, they realized the need to create a new brand because the target markets would be less willing to accept their current brands in a luxury automobile. It is also important for strong brands to reinforce their market presence because it helps maintain a barrier to entry.

Brand Loyalty

Customers Brand loyal customers do not spend as much time searching for new information and, as a result, generally spend less time in the purchase decision process.[25] Motorcycles have experienced a high degree of brand loyalty among the major competitors such as BMW, Honda, and Harley-Davidson. It is not unusual to find owners across all three brands that are driving their third or fourth motorcycle. Read the FYI to find out more about Harley-Davidson.

FYI

One of the most celebrated brands in history is Harley-Davidson. Its heavyweight motorcycles are No. 1 worldwide with 26 percent of the market. Even in Japan, which is home to Honda and Suzuki, Harley is the market leader. The company is experiencing significant growth in China, and international sales now account for more than 20 percent of all Harleys sold. The average age of a Harley owner is 46, and more than half of current owners are previous Harley owners.

Its customers are so loyal that many have tattooed the logo on their body. The HOG (Harley Owners Group) boasts a large membership willing to spend a lot of money on all things Harley. Indeed, Harley-Davidson has come to symbolize more than a motorcycle, it is a lifestyle.

Given Harley-Davidson's growth internationally and its uncompromisingly loyal customers, the company's strategy would seem to be on track. However, Harley faces a challenge; its core market of baby boomers is getting older and there is a question whether the company will be as successful with Generation X and Millennials. Younger buyers favor speed and styling and don't necessarily want their dad's motorcycle.

Source: http://investor.harley-davidson.com/demographics.cfm?bmLocale=en_US, October, 2008.

Brand Sponsor Loyalty to the brand offers four distinct benefits that represent real market advantages to the brand sponsor. A well-executed branding strategy helps reduce long-term marketing costs giving the brand sponsor more flexibility in the marketing budgets. Starbucks has a relatively small advertising budget because it is so well-known that it doesn't need to spend much money raising brand awareness. Branded products give sponsors additional channel leverage.[26] Wal-Mart's ability to extract lower prices from suppliers is legendary, but companies understand the importance of having their products in the world's largest retailer. Brand-loyal customers are vocal and tell others about their experiences, which attracts new customers. Disney has a loyal base of guests who visit the parks every year and become excellent ambassadors for the company. The company offers loyal users specific benefits to cultivate continued loyalty and encourages them to bring new guests. Finally, brand-loyal customers are forgiving, which enables companies to respond to a negative experience. Frequent guests to the Disney parks are not shy about voicing their opinions about everything from rides to the cleanliness of the parks. This creates a sense of ownership (equity) and loyalty.

Linking Benefit to Strategy Because of customer loyalty, marketing managers with a strong brand have greater flexibility in their marketing budgets. For example, Starbucks spends very little on paid advertising because customers already have brand equity. At the same time, Intel, which makes a product most people never see, spends a great deal of money building its brand and now people ask for "Intel Inside." Marketing managers know that loyal customers are great advocates for a brand. As a result, blogs and other online communities have become excellent tools for marketers to reinforce the brands message.[28]

> Blogs are becoming an important communication channel. There are more than 9 million blogs with 40,000 being added each day. Most are not legitimate forums for businesses and customers, but satisfied and, equally important, unsatisfied customers are finding a voice on the Internet. Companies are taking notice. General Motors has developed a comprehensive blog strategy, with Bob Lutz, GM vice chairman, having his own blog (fastlane.blog).[27]

BRANDING DECISIONS

Branding is a complex concept that brings together all the elements of a product into a single, focused customer idea. As a result, the branding decision is among the most important in marketing. Four basic strategic decisions in defining a brand are (1) stand-alone or family branding, (2) national or store branding, (3) licensing, and (4) co-branding.

Stand-Alone or Family Branding

Does the brand stand alone or exist as part of a brand family? Each choice has advantages and disadvantages. **Stand-alone brands** separate the company from the brand, which insulates the company if there is a problem with the brand. But stand-alone brands are expensive to create and maintain as there is little or no synergy between company brands. **Family branding** advantages and disadvantages are just the opposite. There is synergy among members of a brand family, but a negative event with one product often leads to negative publicity for the entire brand family.[29]

Lever Brothers, a worldwide leader in consumer products, follows a stand-alone brand strategy in its personal care division with nine brands that operate independently of each other (AXE, Dove, Lifebuoy, Lux, Ponds, Rexona, Sunsilk, Signal, and Vaseline) (see Exhibit 11.5). Heinz, on the other hand, uses a family branding strategy with all products introduced under the Heinz brand (ketchup and other condiments).

Companies also use branding to extend a line. For example, White Wave Foods, manufacturer of International Delight coffee creamers, frequently adds new flavors to the line. Each new product extends the line of International Delight creamers. Increasingly, as companies seek new, creative ways to connect with customers, they are including them in the brand building process.[30] Also, a company can use

EXHIBIT 11.5 | **Sample of Branding Decisions**

its brand to expand into new product categories, known as a **category extension.**[31] Dell used its brand to expand into new product categories including printers and consumer electronics such as LCD and plasma televisions. Exhibit 11.6 illustrates product extensions through brand, line, and category.

Doritos took an unusual approach in naming its new brand extension. It allowed the customer to name the product. Using the code name X-13D, Doritos created a lot of buzz around the product by first offering on eBay then creating a Web site soliciting customer input on the product name. The Web site allows targeted customers (teenagers) to edit and create their own dialogue for two commercials created for the product. Over 100,000 name suggestions were received.[32]

Yet another option is combining family brands with a more distinct individual product brand. Many companies follow a variation of this strategy. American

EXHIBIT 11.6 **Brand, Line, and Category Extensions**

Brand Extension: AXE

Line Extension: International Delights

Category Extension: Dell

Express recently introduced the One card that incorporates the American Express brand as well as its own stand-alone brand One. Sony, for years, has followed a strategy of linking individual brands (Bean, Discman, Trinitron) with the corporate logo and brand.

National or Store Branding

Another decision is whether the product should adopt a national or store brand strategy. Large consumer products companies such as Procter & Gamble create **national brands** that are sold around the country under the same brand. Gillette Fusion, Crest toothpaste, and many others are national brands that can be found anywhere. National brands enable manufacturers to leverage marketing resources by creating efficiencies in marketing communications, and distribution.[33] In addition, national brands generally have a higher perceived quality and, as a result, enjoy a price premium. However, developing a national brand is costly and lower-priced store brands are strong competitors in many product categories.[34]

An alternative to creating a national brand is a **store brand.** Many large retailers create a store brand to market their own products. For example, Wal-Mart has a number of store brands including Equate, which includes a broad range of personal care product categories (skin care, hair care, toothpaste, and others), and Ol' Roy dog food. Often contracting with the large manufacturers such as Procter & Gamble, retailers are able to compete directly with national brands by offering lower prices.

Licensing

Companies can also choose to extend their brand by **licensing**—offering other manufacturers the right to use the brand in exchange for a set fee or percentage of sales. There is very little risk to the brand sponsor, and licensing can generate incremental revenue. In addition, it can extend the brand and build more brand associations among new users creating additional benefits.[35] The brand sponsor does need to monitor the licensees to assure product quality and proper use of the brand. Finally, license partners should fit the company's overall marketing strategy for the brand.[36] Among the best followers of the license strategy are movies, which license their brand (the movie) to a wide range of companies (restaurants, toy manufacturers, and others). The movie, *Iron Man*, grossed more than $500 million in worldwide box office sales, but its licensee sales are expected to exceed that amount. The creators of the movie, will add several hundred million dollars in revenue based on the licensing agreements with Audi, Burger King, LG Mobile Communications, 7-Eleven, and Sega.

Co-Branding

Frequently a company discovers advantages to linking its products with other products inside the company or externally with products from other companies, called **co-branding.** Co-branding joins two or more well-known brands in a common product or takes two brands and markets them in partnership. One advantage of co-branding is the opportunity to leverage the strengths of each brand to increase sales beyond what they could do independently. In addition, it may open each product up to new markets as well as lower costs by sharing marketing communications expenses.[37]

There are also several potential disadvantages. First, companies that co-brand externally give up some measure of control over their brand; by joining brands each company sacrifices some control to market the co-branded product. If one of the brands encounters a problem, for example a quality issue, it can have a negative effect on the co-branded product. Another potential disadvantage is overexposure; a successful product does not want too many co-branded relationships because it can dilute the brand's image.[38]

Successful co-branding relationships work best when both brands come together as equals that make sense in the marketplace. Costco and American Express joined together to offer a Costco-American Express card that allows users to get rebates on their purchases at Costco while expanding the reach of American Express to Costco members. Critical decisions in the process revolve around resource commitments, which company is spending what, and what other resources are asked of each company. In addition, it is important for each company in the relationship to understand the performance objectives and expected benefits of each partner.

Generally, co-branding involves one of four relationships. The first is a joint venture between two companies; for example, Nickelodeon and Marriott partnered to create a kid-friendly chain of vacation-oriented hotels.[39] A second type of co-branding affiliation happens when a company combines two of its own products. Procter & Gamble combined its Tide detergent and Downy fabric softener to create Tide Simple Pleasures and Downy Simple Pleasures in the U.S. market. In England, the company co-branded its Bold and Lenor detergents, creating a premium brand called Bold Infusions and Lenor Infusions.[40] A third type of co-branding relationship involves bringing multiple companies together to form a new branded product. For instance, Symbian, a joint venture that includes communications companies Nokia, Ericsson, Sony, Panasonic, Siemens, and Samsung, licenses its mobile operating system to a number of wireless manufacturers including LG and Fujitsu. The Symbian platform competes directly with Google's Android and Apple's mobile OS.[41] A final co-branding relationship involves retailers that share the same retail location. One example of this type of relationship in the United States is Yum Brands, which brings together its Taco Bell, Pizza Hut, and KFC brands under one roof in various locations, although the company is reconsidering that strategy and is looking to make each brand more distinct.[42]

PACKAGING AND LABELING: ESSENTIAL BRAND ELEMENTS

The product package and label must perform several critical roles in support of the brand. As a result, marketers, product developers, and package design specialists are involved in package design early in product development. Then, as product updates occur, the package is reconfigured to accommodate product modifications.

Colgate Palmolive reported fake Colgate toothpaste being shipped in phony packages in the United States. It was not clear where the fake toothpaste originated, but Colgate and other packaged goods companies took a number of steps to reduce counterfeit packaging. Document Security Systems works with manufacturers to make their packaging more secure. DSS has developed nine patented technologies to protect packages.[43]

Package Objectives

Protect

Above all, the package must protect the product. The challenge is defining how much protection is necessary and cost-effective. In some cases, as in a can of Coke, the package is a significant component of the product's overall cost so there is concern about any increases in package cost. However, the can of Coke must be strong enough to hold the carbonated beverage under variations in temperature and other use conditions. Additionally, Coca-Cola must consider a variety of package materials (plastic, metal), sizes, and shapes (regular can, Coke's classic "contour" design), and it must design each to operate more or less the same under a variety of situations (see Exhibit 11.7).

Protecting customers from unauthorized access to the product is also part of package design. Prescription bottles and most over-the-counter medicines are required to be tamper-proof and child-proof to protect customers. Package safety seals provide a layer of security and verification to the customer that the product has not been altered before purchase. Finally, a growing concern is product theft, particularly in the retail store.[44] As a result, the package design should include anti-theft methodology, such as bar coding or magnetic stripes, that discourages shoplifting.

IDEO, a leading design firm, is working with other design companies, SmartDesign and Continuum, as well as the two largest professional associations, AIGA and Industrial Designers Society of America, to create a greener, more environmentally sensitive approach to package design. The goal is to create packaging that not only protects the product but also minimizes the environmental effects of the packaging.[45]

Communicate

Packages communicate a great deal of information about the product. Some of that information is designed as marketing communications. At the point of sale, the package is the last marketing communication the customer will see before the purchase. Consequently, packaging plays a critical role in the company's overall marketing communications strategy, particularly for consumer products. Coke's distinctive contour bottle design (pictured in Exhibit 11.7) is so unique the package can be identified in the dark. Additionally, packaging offers the brand sponsor the opportunity to present the trademark, logo, and other relevant information in an appealing and persuasive manner. As the customer stands in front of a shelf full of products in a store, the marketer wants the brand to be clearly visible to the buyer. This means packaging must be designed to easily communicate critical brand messages quickly through color or design cues.[46] The familiar Coke swirl logo is among the most recognized brand symbols in the world and is easily identified on a store shelf or in a vending machine.

Unique package design can create a distinctive competitive advantage. Coke's contour bottle and L'eggs' egg-shape package for hosiery are important components of the overall brand image for those products. Their distinctive package design increases brand awareness at the point of sale where the customer makes the final purchase decision (see Exhibit 11.8).

Promote Usage

Package design also encourages product use. It does this in several ways. First, packages frequently show the product being used by a happy customer (Kashi Good Friends shows a couple enjoying a box of cereal), which supports the overall marketing message (see Exhibit 11.9). This connects the product to the target customer. Second, in many cases, packages visually demonstrate a product. Avery Paper shows each product clearly on the box; for example, a box of clear white mailing labels shows the label and how it can be used. Third, marketers and package designers make extensive use of blister packs (products encased in clear plastic) and other package designs to visibly present and protect the product. When buying a SanDisk Cruzer flash drive it is much easier to visualize using it when you can see the product and have key features highlighted on the package.

Effective Packaging

Effective packaging accomplishes the objectives noted above in a persuasive, interesting, and visually appealing manner consistent with the target market's expectations. Materials, shape, colors, graphics, indeed all the design elements are used to create an aesthetically appealing package for the customer.

| EXHIBIT 11.7 | Various Coke Package Designs, Shapes, and Sizes |

EXHIBIT 11.8 | Innovative Package Designs

Chewy Chips Ahoy bag
Goal: Improve freshness and convenience
Backstory: After months of in-home research, Kraft discovered that its customers often transferred Chips Ahoy cookies to jars for easy access and to avoid staleness. The company solved both problems by creating a patented resealable opening on the top of the bag.
Bottom line: Since launching in July 2005, sales have nearly doubled from the older packaging.

Kleenex Tissues oval box
Goal: Make a common household product unique
Backstory: Americans spend more on home decor during the holidays than at any other time, so Kimberly-Clark introduced an oval-shape Kleenex box that was a clear departure from its usual rectangular shapes. The goal was to position the product as a must-have accessory rather than a functional item.
Bottom line: It was the company's best-selling holiday line in history and Kimberly-Clark has followed it with designs for each season of the year.

Crest Vivid White toothpaste package
Goal: Stand out on store shelves
Backstory: When Procter & Gamble's Crest set out to develop a premium whitening product in 2003, designers avoided creating yet another horizontal, graphics-heavy toothpaste box. Instead, they turned to the beauty aisle for inspiration. "We drew upon the vertical packaging and the deep metallic blue used to convey 'premium,'" says design manager Greg Zimmer.
Bottom line: Crest toothpaste sales have risen while competitor Colgate's sales have fallen, according to IRI.

(continued)

EXHIBIT 11.9 | Kashi Good Friends Cereal Box

Aesthetics

Color plays a significant role in package design, indeed, in the entire branding strategy.[47] It is no accident that Coke's packaging has red as the dominant color (red connotes active and energetic) while Pepsi uses blue (fresh and relaxed). The colors reflect the brand and are carried through in the package design. Exhibit 11.10 relates the aesthetics of color to package design.

A visually appealing package, however, is not enough. It must be directed at the target audience to be successful. In most retail environments, a package has very little time to connect with the customer at the point of purchase. As a result, designs that are appropriate, interesting, and persuasive to the target market are critical.

EXHIBIT 11.8 Innovative Package Designs [continued]

Mazola Pure bottle
Goal: Communicate a brand identity
Backstory: Mazola shook up the 47-year-old pan-spray market with the debut of its alcohol-free oil, which aimed to profit from the growing trend in organic cooking. But the company knew that shoppers wouldn't discover the health-conscious brand if it encased the product in another steel cylinder. After considering hair spray and deodorant bottles, Mazola's designers settled on a curvy plastic container with an eye-catching iridescent finish.
Bottom line: The item overtook established brands to become the No. 2 spray.

Heinz Ketchup upside-down bottle
Goal: Increase functionality
Backstory: Heinz revolutionized the 170-year-old industry when it introduced its inverted bottle (consumers had complained for years about how hard it was to squeeze out that last bit of ketchup). The Pittsburgh-based company spent three years designing the convenient container, which is equipped with a vacuum cap that stops crustiness from forming around the lid.
Bottom line: A year after the bottle's debut, Heinz ketchup sales rose 6 percent, while the overall ketchup industry increased only 2 percent.

Domino Sugar four-pound canister
Goal: Create a more user-friendly package
Backstory: To boost flat sales, Domino replaced the ubiquitous paper packaging for sugar. The easy-to-store plastic canister enables the Yonkers, New York, company to charge a premium for a package that actually contains less sugar.
Bottom line: The canister has become one of Domino's best-selling retail items.

Zephyrhills Water created the Aquapod with a direct appeal to kids. Shaped like a rocket, the package drives the overall promotion of the product item. An Aquapod Web site created for kids is separate from the traditional Zephyrhills Web site and incorporates the rocket-shape Aquapod as part of the story line.[48]

Harmonizes with All Marketing Mix Elements

A successful product package coordinates with all other marketing mix elements and is an extension of the product's marketing strategy. At the point of purchase, the package reinforces marketing communications by connecting

EXHIBIT 11.10 — The Meaning of Color in Package Design

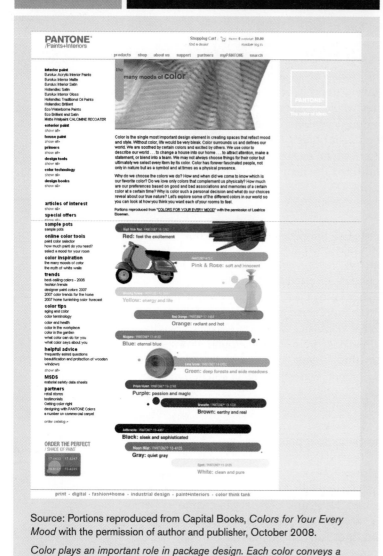

Source: Portions reproduced from Capital Books, *Colors for Your Every Mood* with the permission of author and publisher, October 2008.

Color plays an important role in package design. Each color conveys a different mood.

advertising images (logo, pictures on the package) to the customer. As a result, package designers frequently work closely with advertising and other marketing communications specialists to orchestrate an integrated message and look throughout the marketing communications process. Canon digital cameras are packaged in a small box dominated by a picture of the camera. The boxes stand alone as a promotional tool that includes the logo, camera model number, and picture. In addition, the package design and logo are coordinated with other collateral marketing literature as well as the Web site.

Labeling

The package label is an important and valuable location. Often there is not enough space to accommodate all the information relevant parties would like to include on the label. Consider, for example, that government agencies require certain information on almost every label while company attorneys want disclaimers to limit product liability. Also, marketing managers want promotional messages and brand information, while product managers would like product use instructions.

Legal Requirements

Labels must meet federal, state, even local rules and regulations. The Food and Drug Administration (FDA) requires all processed-food companies to provide detailed nutritional information clearly identifying calories, fats, carbohydrates, and other information. Other products must have warnings of a certain size that are easily read and understood by the customer.[49]

Hazardous materials such as cleaning products, pesticides, and many other items require 14 different pieces of information be included on the label. It is easy to understand why space on the label is at such a premium.

Consumer advocacy groups and government agencies evaluate labels to identify misleading or mislabeled products and there is a long history of legal prosecution for inappropriate, unethical, even illegal product labeling. In 1914, the federal government, through the Federal Trade Commission, first ruled misleading or blatantly phony labels were illegal and represented unfair competition. Since then, additional legislation has been passed by the federal government such as the Fair Packaging and Labeling Act (1967). States have also passed legislation, which, in most cases, supports federal legislation but also extends specific rules and policies (for example, the Michigan Food Label Law of 2000).

Consumer Requirements

Consumers want to use products out of the box and package labeling is the most convenient place for initial use instructions. Additionally, product precautions, simple assembly information, and appropriate age for product use may also be included on the package. Essentially, any information the consumer needs to make a product choice, particularly at the point of purchase, needs to be on the package.

> Robitussin redesigned its packaging to create a simpler look that provides specific product use information not only to help parents make a purchase decision but also to inform them about proper product usage. Using graphic design tools such as color coding and easier-to-read fonts, the package lists four key pieces of information: the product's formulation (the company makes four), whether it is drowsy or nondrowsy, the symptoms it treats, and the recommended age for usage. Results have been impressive, adding more than $50 million to the bottom line.[50]

Marketing Requirements

Since package labeling represents the last marketing opportunity before the purchase decision, as much label space as possible is allocated to marketing communications. Brand, logo, product image, and other relevant marketing messages take up the dominant space on the label. On a box of Procter & Gamble's Bounce fabric softener sheets, the brand name "Bounce" is approximately 50 percent of the space on the front panel and the rest of the space is a bright color (orange) with clean fresh images of a sun rising and a green field. P&G uses the entire front panel of the box to support the marketing efforts of the brand (see Exhibit 11.11).

WARRANTIES AND SERVICE AGREEMENTS: BUILDING CUSTOMER CONFIDENCE

Part of the customer's overall perception of a brand is the seller's commitment to the product. This commitment is most clearly articulated in the product's warranties and service agreements.[51] As part of the purchase contract with the customer, manufacturers are required by law to state the reasonable expectations for product performance. If the product does not meet those reasonable performance expectations, the customer has the legal right to return the product to the appropriate location for repair, replacement, or refund.

The two kinds of warranties are general and specific. **General warranties** make broad promises about product performance and customer satisfaction. These warranties are generally open to customers returning the product for a broad range of reasons beyond specific product performance problems. Many companies have adopted lenient policies that allow a product return without even asking the customer for a reason. Others require a reason, although there is often a great deal of latitude in what is an acceptable justification. **Specific warranties,** on the other hand, offer explicit product performance promises related to components of the product. Automobile warranties are specific warranties covering various components of the product with different warranties. The warranty for tires is by the

EXHIBIT 11.11	Bounce Fabric Softener Packaging

EXHIBIT 11.12 **Warranties for a 2008 Toyota Vehicle**

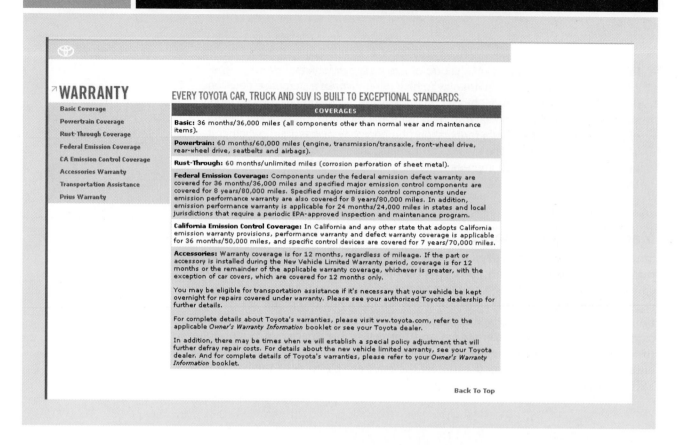

↗ WARRANTY

Basic Coverage
Powertrain Coverage
Rust-Through Coverage
Federal Emission Coverage
CA Emission Control Coverage
Accessories Warranty
Transportation Assistance
Prius Warranty

EVERY TOYOTA CAR, TRUCK AND SUV IS BUILT TO EXCEPTIONAL STANDARDS.

COVERAGES

Basic: 36 months/36,000 miles (all components other than normal wear and maintenance items).

Powertrain: 60 months/60,000 miles (engine, transmission/transaxle, front-wheel drive, rear-wheel drive, seatbelts and airbags).

Rust-Through: 60 months/unlimited miles (corrosion perforation of sheet metal).

Federal Emission Coverage: Components under the federal emission defect warranty are covered for 36 months/36,000 miles and specified major emission control components are covered for 8 years/80,000 miles. Specified major emission control components under emission performance warranty are also covered for 8 years/80,000 miles. In addition, emission performance warranty is applicable for 24 months/24,000 miles in states and local jurisdictions that require a periodic EPA-approved inspection and maintenance program.

California Emission Control Coverage: In California and any other state that adopts California emission warranty provisions, performance warranty and defect warranty coverage is applicable for 36 months/50,000 miles, and specific control devices are covered for 7 years/70,000 miles.

Accessories: Warranty coverage is for 12 months, regardless of mileage. If the part or accessory is installed during the New Vehicle Limited Warranty period, coverage is for 12 months or the remainder of the applicable warranty coverage, whichever is greater, with the exception of car covers, which are covered for 12 months only.

You may be eligible for transportation assistance if it's necessary that your vehicle be kept overnight for repairs covered under warranty. Please see your authorized Toyota dealership for further details.

For complete details about Toyota's warranties, please visit www.toyota.com, refer to the applicable *Owner's Warranty Information* booklet or see your Toyota dealer.

In addition, there may be times when we will establish a special policy adjustment that will further defray repair costs. For details about the new vehicle limited warranty, see your Toyota dealer. And for complete details of Toyota's warranties, please refer to your *Owner's Warranty Information* booklet.

Back To Top

tire manufacturer while warranties for the power train (engine, drive system) are generally different from the rest of the automobile (see Exhibit 11.12).

Warranties Help Define the Brand

The manufacturer's promise of performance helps define the brand for the customer. Victorinox, maker of the famous Swiss Army knife, states its warranty as follows: "Swiss Army Brands, Inc., warrants its Victorinox Original Swiss Army Knives to be free from defects in material and workmanship for the entire life of the knife." Swiss Army Knives have the reputation of being among the best knives in the world, and the company's warranty supports that perception. A company willing to stand behind its product for life provides a lot of reassurance to the customer. In addition, there is an implied quality perception about a product warranted for life.

Cost versus Benefit

Honoring a warranty incurs costs. At one level, the company must be competitive and offer warranties consistent with the industry. However, companies constantly evaluate their warranties (length of time, return/replacement/refund policies, nature of product performance) to consider whether the benefits of the warranty exceed the costs.[52] This is particularly true when companies offer warranties above the industry average. For years, luxury carmakers such as Lexus, Mercedes-Benz, BMW, Audi, and others offered warranties (four years or 50,000 miles bumper to bumper) beyond that provided by other manufacturers (GM, Ford, Chrysler, which offered three years or 36,000 miles). Offering longer warranties helped validate the perception of a luxury, quality automobile manufacturer. Recently, however, Mercedes-Benz has quietly reduced its warranty coverage by eliminating some free scheduled maintenance because the costs were too high. At the same time, Hyundai and others have expanded their warranties to build consumer confidence in their cars. They realize that extending the period of warranty coverage demonstrates they are making better cars in a very tangible way.

Convey a Message to the Customer

Warranties convey a powerful message to the customer about perceived product quality and manufacturer commitment to customer satisfaction. Particularly with expensive products or purchase decisions in which the customer has anxiety, the warranty can play a significant role in the final product choice. As a result, companies focus a lot of time not only creating the warranty but also considering how best to communicate it to the customer. In some cases, as in FedEx's classic tag line "absolutely, positively overnight," the warranty becomes part of the advertising campaign. With most products, however, companies take a lower profile and build warranty statements into the overall marketing communications strategy and product information.[53]

Nothing is more frustrating for a car owner than a problem soon after the car goes out of warranty. Lexus enjoys an advantage by making it much easier for local dealers to deal with out-of-warranty problems, thereby keeping the customer happy. Realizing that effectively handling out-of-warranty repairs was critical to long-term customer satisfaction, Cadillac now allows dealers to deal with customers' out-of-warranty issues immediately.[54]

SUMMARY

An essential element in any product is its brand. The brand conveys a great deal of information about the product and the customer experience. Powerful brands enjoy benefits in the market that other products do not. As a result, companies carefully consider a product's branding strategy in creating an overall marketing plan. Packaging and labeling are also critical brand elements that convey a lot about the product to the customer. Finally, customers attach great importance to the sellers' commitment to the products as conveyed in the product's warranties and service agreements.

KEY TERMS

1. You are the product manager for Ralph Lauren's Polo shirts. What specific information are you trying to convey in the brand's iconic polo pony logo? For example, what does the Polo brand say about quality, features, style relative to the Tommy Hilfiger or Lacoste brands?

2. Johnson & Johnson has been able to establish strong brand equity for its line of baby products. What benefits does J&J have because of its brand equity for these products?

3. You have been asked by Coca-Cola's product manager to present the arguments for and against extending the Coke brand to a new cola drink. What would be the arguments for and against extending the Coke brand to a new cola drink?

4. SanDisk is introducing a new MP3 player and you are responsible for creating the package design. What key information and other creative elements would you include on the package?

MANAGEMENT DECISION CASE: Apple's iPod Rules but Long Live the Record . . . Turntable

Sales of MP3 players and, more specifically, Apple's iPod have transformed the way people listen to music. People want their music mobile and available anywhere anytime. However, as music becomes more portable, there is one trade-off: music quality is lower on a MP3 player. Millions of people used to listening to music on their iPods are not aware or have forgotten that there is a format that provides much better sound quality—vinyl records.

Today, music is distributed in digital formats, but an interesting phenomenon has happened to turntables. Despite the lack of new releases on vinyl, demand for turntables is outpacing supply. The science of turntables did not stop despite the demise of vinyl records as a music format. Turntable manufacturers continued to create more stable suspension systems, better machined tone arms, and extremely quiet motors that, when coupled with the right audio equipment and speakers, are able to reproduce sound that is noticeably better than that from any MP3 player. For example, one high-end audio/video dealer in New York, Sound by Singer, sold one turntable in 2003 but is now selling more than 50 turntables a year priced at $18,500 to $30,000. At the same time, sales of low-and mid-priced models are also growing.

The market for turntables can be segmented into several target markets. First, baby boomers, the last group to purchase vinyl records in significant numbers, are rediscovering the sound quality of vinyl and have the financial resources to purchase higher-end quality turntables and audio equipment. Second, audiophiles unwilling to accept the sound quality of compressed MP3 music files are turning to state-of-the-art turntables capable of capturing the warmer, richer, and more dynamic range available on vinyl records. Finally, a small but growing number of Generation Xers and Millennials have learned, often from parents, about the better sound quality available on vinyl records.

Music labels are responding to the demand for records by reissuing classic albums from artists such as Joni Mitchell and Neil Young on higher-quality virgin vinyl as opposed to recycled plastic used in the past. In addition, they are also starting to issue new music from artists Norah Jones and Alison Kraus on vinyl. The hope is that making new music available on vinyl will encourage younger music enthusiasts to consider the advantages of vinyl over MP3.

Lower-priced turntables (under $1,000) from companies such as Pro-Ject, Rega, Avid, Linn, and Sota are extending high-quality vinyl sound reproduction into broader markets creating a mass-market appeal. They are still faced with significant market challenges as digital, portable music continues to dominate the music business. Many of the most popular turntable manufacturers lack significant brand recognition and operate in smaller, niche markets. Large electronics companies such as Sony offer limited, lower-end turntables designed primarily to digitize people's vinyl library for use on the MP3 player. Apple, for example, is invested in digital music and not interested in perpetuating the better sound quality of vinyl.[55]

Questions for Consideration

1. As a marketing manager for Pro-Ject (manufacturer of low-priced turntables based in the Czech Republic) what target market would you

consider most important over the next three to five years? Why?

2. How important is branding in the marketing of audio/video equipment?

3. As marketing manager for Sony, would you recommend the company develop a line of mid-to-high-quality turntables? Why or why not?

MARKETING PLAN EXERCISE

ACTIVITY 11: Define the Branding Strategy

As we have learned in this chapter, building a strong brand is critical to a product's long-term success. At the same time, it is important to understand how a product's position in its life cycle influences marketing mix decisions.

Specific activities include:

1. Create a package design for the product. Specifically, the design should include necessary legal statements, marketing communications, and other information considered important for the package.

2. Develop a warranty for the product. What elements are specifically covered in the warranty? Does the warranty meet, equal, or fail to meet market expectations and competitor warranties?

3. Create a branding strategy to include

  a. National/store.

  b. Stand-alone/family branding.

  c. Possible licensing considerations.

  d. Co-branding opportunities.

If you are using Marketing Plan Pro, a template for this assignment can be accessed at www.mhhe.com/marshall1e.

RECOMMENDED READINGS

1. Francis Kelly and Barry Silverstein, *The Breakaway Brand: How Great Brands Stand Out* (New York: McGraw-Hill, 2005).

2. Alina Wheeler, *Designing Brand Identity: A Complete Guide to Creating, Building and Maintaining Strong Brands* (Hoboken, NJ: Wiley, 2006).

3. Nicholas Ind and Rune Bjerke, *Branding Governance: A Participatory Approach to the Brand Building Process* (Hoboken, NJ: Wiley, 2007).

4. Rick Mathieson, *Branding Unbound: The Future of Advertising, Sales, and the Brand Experience in the Wireless Age* (New York: American Management Association, 2005).

5. Allen P. Adamson and Martin Sorrell, *Brand Simple: How the Best Brands Keep It Simple and Succeed* (New York: Palgrave McMillan, 2007).

CHAPTER 12

THE PRODUCT EXPERIENCE: NEW-PRODUCT DEVELOPMENT

LEARNING OBJECTIVES

- Recognize the importance of new-product development to long-term success.

- Understand the new-product development process.

- Comprehend the process consumers use in adopting a new product.

- Identify how new products become diffused in a market.

EXECUTIVE PERSPECTIVE

Executive Rick Rotondo, Chief Marketing Officer

Company Spectrum Bridge Inc.

Business Start-up high-tech telecom solutions

Why is defining and communicating what is the core product and its salient benefits so critical?

Frankly, if you can't define your product and benefits with crystal clarity and pinpoint precision, then you have no hope of your customers understanding your core value proposition. And if they can't understand the value proposition, they won't buy it. Or worse, they buy without really understanding it, which can lead to unfulfilled expectations and put a real burden on your engineering or customer support staff after purchase. In short, if you do a poor job defining your core product you will likely miss your true market potential, and if you misrepresent your product's benefits you will likely end up with disappointed customers who overwhelm your support staff.

What are some unique characteristics of the product development process in high-tech telecommunications?

In high-tech telecom, much of the time you are coming up with requirements for a product that may take two, three, or even four years to develop and launch into the market. This means you may have to *anticipate* a market need and a set of requirements that have yet to actually materialize in your customers' business or strategic plans. If this is the case, focus groups and guidance from existing customers might not help you much. A very real possibility is that this so-called "innovator's dilemma" can come back to bite you if you don't realize that you may be operating somewhat beyond the vision of your own customers.

Another reality is that technology is changing very fast; it may change to the point where you have to significantly alter your product or its main features or functionality during the development cycle. It's better to change course *during* product development than to spend all your time, money, and other resources developing a product that's obsolete before it even hits the market.

How do you see the role of disruptive innovation in the developmental process of technology products?

Having once had the title of "Director of Disruptive Technology," I believe that disruption is crucial for start-ups. It's crucial even for established companies that are looking to enter and dominate new market spaces. Of course, not *every* product has to be—or should be—disruptive. Disruptive innovation has to bring massive improvements in cost, functionality, and/or performance. For example, at Spectrum Bridge, our benchmark for a disruptive product is that the product must at a minimum show a tenfold improvement in at least one category to its intended customers.

You will have to spend a good amount of time and resources educating the market on your new disruptive innovation, because, by definition, the innovation will disrupt the status quo for the people and processes at your intended customers. So, with disruptive innovation expect to face resistance and even a little hostility sometimes. But if you are right, WOW, you can *dominate* the market and even actually change the world—I've seen it happen more than once!

NEW PRODUCTS–CREATING LONG-TERM SUCCESS

No matter how good a company's current products are, long-term growth depends on new products. This can be done in one of two basic ways: acquisition or internal development. Both approaches have their advantages and disadvantages.

"New" Defined

What does the term *new* mean? Everyday, consumers see or hear marketing communications that talk about "new and improved." At the same time, people speak about buying a new car (which may in fact be a used car) as well as a new TV (which may be last year's model). Let's look at how the term is defined by the product's manufacturer and customers.

> Marine energy, harnessing the natural wave action of the oceans to generate energy, is under development at several locations around the world. Most of the research is being done on the Scottish coast where the North Sea meets the Atlantic Ocean. There, companies such as General Electric, power companies like Canada's Emera, and smaller technology firms like Open-Hydro and Pelamis Wave Power are experimenting with new technologies. Brand-new technologies are what people often consider a "new product."[1]

Company Perspective

Most people would define *new* as a product that has not been available before or bears little resemblance to an existing product, and one type of new product is actually referred to as a **new-to-the-world product,** because it has not been available before. Sometimes new-to-the-world products are so innovative they create a fundamental change in the marketplace and are known as *disruptive innovation.* They are called disruptive because they shift people's perspective and frequently alter their behavior by offering dramatically simpler, more convenient, and usually less-expensive products than currently exist. In the process they frequently make existing products less desirable. Desktop computers, cell phones, and PDAs are examples of new-to-the-world products considered disruptive innovations.[2]

A second type of new-to-the-world product, *sustaining innovations,* are newer, better, faster versions of existing products that target, for the most part, existing customers. Sustaining innovations can be revolutionary by taking the market in a new direction. They can also be **upgrades or modifications to existing products** and represent incremental enhancements to current products.[3]

> Novartis Consumer Products has incorporated "edible film" to deliver its products in a new way. The company reports significant growth in two products, Thera-flu (up 28 percent) and Triaminic (up 26 percent), which it attributes to "Thin Strips." Triaminic now claims 20 percent of the pediatric cough and cold market for the first time. The market for edible film is growing very quickly as companies find new uses. Sales have grown from $100 million in 2005 to $350 million in 2008 and are projected to continue. New applications include pet medicine and sushi.[4]

Once a product has been developed and on the market, the company can extend the product by creating **additions to existing product lines.** For years, Coca-Cola has added new products to the Coke line, first with Diet Coke in the early 1980s and now many different Coke branded products including Coke Zero. These products are also available in various sizes and packaging, giving Coke many different product items. Exhibit 12.1 is another example of an addition to an existing product line.

Another "new" product approach is to **reposition existing products** to target new markets. The cell phone market used this strategy successfully to introduce cell phones in the mid-1990s. Originally cell phone service providers positioned the phones as a safety tool targeting individuals such as working women and moms. As the product become more widely adopted, the positioning of the product changed to become an important work tool. As the market for cell phones expands, the positioning has evolved to include younger users. Cell phones are the dominant communication device for teenagers, and phones have been created for kids as young as seven.

Cost reduction, as the name implies, is a specific method for introducing lower-cost products that frequently focus on value-oriented product price points in the product mix. Generally this approach involves eliminating or reducing features, using less-expensive materials, or altering the service or warranty to offer the product at a lower price point to the market.[5]

| EXHIBIT 12.1 | New Products Can Take the Form of Additions to an Existing Product Line |

Customer's Perspective

While the company follows a specific strategy in creating a new product, the customer is unaware and, in reality, often does not really care about how the product arrived in the marketplace. The customer's perspective is much more narrow and self-directed. The customer is most interested in an answer to the fundamental question—is this product new to me? From the company's perspective it is important to realize that every customer approaches a new product a little differently. For example, an individual going in to buy his or her first cell phone from a service provider can find the process intimidating. As a result, cellular providers handle those customers carefully to reduce anxiety, concentrating on things like ease of use and simple service packages. Experienced cell phone users are interested in talking about the latest phone capabilities, packages, and technology. One challenge companies face is dealing with historical customer perceptions. The FYI examines how Ford is looking to maximize a one world, one car, and one name approach while dealing with negative perceptions about a product more than 30 years old.

FYI

Ford is introducing a new edition of its successful European small car, Fiesta, to the rest of the world including the United States. A critical decision in the rollout of the car globally was the brand name; the decision was made to use the same name in every market around the world. For Ford, the decision was made more complicated by the fact that the name Fiesta already has a history in the United States. Specifically, the Fiesta was introduced in the late 1970s to the U.S. market but was so unpopular it was pulled after just two years. In addition, recent research suggests the name sounds "cheap" and does not compare well with other names such as the Honda Fit.

(continued)

Reasons for New-Product Success or Failure

Since new-product development is such a critical factor in the long-term success of an organization, you might think companies are good at the development process. Unfortunately, this is not the case; 70 to 80 percent of all new products worldwide fail. While it is true that many of those products are developed by small entrepreneurs, no company is immune to product failure. Have you ever heard of Levi's business wear or Mr. Coffee coffee or Dunkin' Donuts cereal? Probably not, because each of these new products failed despite the fact they were introduced by companies with a track record of marketing success. The reasons vary, but it is possible to identify the role of the company, customers, and competitors in the success or failure of a new product.[7]

Company

Success or failure of a new product is determined primarily by the actions of the company. Making bad decisions by not identifying the value proposition, designing and building a product that fails to meet customer expectations, poor marketing communications, inadequate distribution of the product, or incorrectly pricing the product are all factors that increase the likelihood of new-product failure.[8]

Other factors also contribute to a lack of success. Design and development of new products is expensive, and companies sometimes fail to adequately capitalize the process. This occurs in two ways. If new-product development does not follow a timeline, development costs will, all too frequently, exceed established budgets. Inadequate resource allocation forces companies to slow the development, redirect resources for one project to another, or even eliminate projects before product development has been completed. Companies with a strong commitment to new-product research and development have the flexibility to adjust; however, for many companies, the additional development costs mean difficult choices such as slowing the development process, reducing features, or even canceling a project. Start-up companies face another problem—lack of capital.[9] Access to capital markets is essential because many companies find it difficult to sustain new-product development using only the funds from ongoing operations. Large companies find it easier to access capital markets; however, small companies, particularly start-up organizations, find it difficult and expensive to generate outside funding.

Finally, competitive pressure, changes in target markets, and environmental conditions mandate shorter product development time. The Japanese auto manufacturers for years have enjoyed an advantage in product development, pushing U.S. automakers to develop cars at a much faster pace. U.S. manufacturers have reduced new-car development from nearly 5 years (in the 1980s) to 36 months; however, Toyota and Honda continued to shorten their time to market and now develop a new model in less than 30 months, which means cars more accurately reflect current consumer tastes and lower costs.[10]

Customers

Customers want products designed to meet their own specific needs, which connotes smaller, more focused target markets. One way companies manage specific customer needs is to create more specialized products that address the demands of smaller groups.

Consumers also change their purchase priorities abruptly, making product life cycles shorter. This is a particular problem for new products that lack a large base of brand-loyal customers. The product life cycle of a laptop computer in the 1990s was 12 months, now it is 9 months and it is expected to go even lower.

Kimberly-Clark's Huggies brand of disposable diapers has developed dozens of different diaper products for newborns, older babies, and toddlers, as well as specialized products for extra comfort, overnight, and swimming diapers. K-C even manufactures six different kinds of baby wipes.

Competitors

Companies react to competitor products in different ways. Some companies have a reputation for being aggressive in the marketplace and attack a new competitor quickly while others take a less-aggressive approach. Frito-Lay, the world's largest seller of snack foods, controls the snack aisle in grocery stores around the world and fights hard to maintain that dominance. When new competitors try to gain shelf space, Frito-Lay will introduce coupons and retailer incentives to keep its position on the shelf.[11]

For new products it is particularly important to consider how market leaders will react to an introduction. Frito-Lay, for example, has a great deal of leverage with retailers, which makes it difficult to get critical shelf space. Moreover, a loyal customer base is less likely to try new products.

Environment

Environmental concerns are among the biggest challenges facing the new-product development process today. Government regulations and new legislation, for example, can dramatically alter the development of a new product. As the government raises the corporate average fuel economy (CAFE) standards, gas mileage requirements for automakers, the auto companies are directed to develop and build smaller, more fuel-efficient cars. Despite looking a lot like a car, the PT Cruiser is designated, in terms of federal fleet mileage regulations, as a light truck to help Chrysler meet its CAFE federal requirements.[12]

Companies also must respond to societal demands. In many categories, new products today are more environmentally sensitive. Computer manufacturers now design their laptop batteries to be recyclable and encourage customers to dispose of batteries in an environmentally friendly manner. The challenge is to balance environmental concerns with product development costs. Research suggests that consumers prefer environmentally sensitive products, but are not willing to pay a significant price premium. If research development costs are too high, companies may price their product too high, increasing the probability of failure.

John Deere Credit, a subsidiary of John Deere, a world leader in farm and construction equipment, has initiated a new environmentally sensitive service—investing in wind energy. Working with farmers, it subsidizes the development of wind farms, buying wind turbines in India then helping farmers purchase and install the turbines. The company either buys the power from farmers or sells it directly to local utilities. To date, the company has put in more than 40 1.25 megawatt turbines primarily in Minnesota, Texas, and Iowa.[13]

NEW-PRODUCT DEVELOPMENT PROCESS

The new-product development process consists of three main activities and eight specific tasks. Failure at any step significantly lowers the probability of long-term success. The three major activities in new-product development are: (1) identify product opportunities, (2) define the product opportunity, and (3) develop the product opportunity.

There is a great deal of variability in the new-product development timeline. Products that are truly new to the world can take months or even years to develop. For example, Eclipse Aviation, makers of the first very-light jet, the Eclipse 500, took more than eight years to develop and test the product. Marketers must balance the product development process with the ever-changing demands of the marketplace. Take too long in product development and the market may have changed, rush the process and the product may be poorly designed or lack quality.[14]

Identify Product Opportunities

The first step in the new-product development process, identify potential product opportunities, has two specific tasks. First, companies must generate sufficient new-product ideas. Very few product ideas make it through the entire process and, as we have seen already, far fewer products actually become successful. As a result, it is important to have a steady flow of new ideas into the development process. Second, ideas need to be evaluated before resources are committed to development.

Generate New Ideas

Product ideas are generated in one of two ways: internal or external to the firm. While companies develop a preference for one approach over the other, the reality is both internal and external sources produce good new-product ideas. A number of factors, including the company's commitment to innovation, the reputation of competitors for new-product development, and customer expectations affect which approach a company prefers.[15]

Internal Sources include employees from R&D, marketing, and manufacturing. Key employees know both the capabilities of the company and the needs of the market. Therefore, it is not surprising that internal sources are the single best source for new-product ideas. Funding product research is expensive; companies spend billions of dollars every year to generate product ideas.

People who work directly with customers are another source of ideas. As salespeople, customer service representatives, and others interact directly with customers, it is possible to identify new-product ideas. Often these ideas are incremental changes to existing products that solve a particular problem; however, occasionally the customer challenge requires a truly innovative solution.

Working with academia helps support the research activities of many organizations. This is particularly useful when companies engage in pure research, which looks at cutting-edge ideas that often do not have immediate market applications. Dedicated research labs such as Bell Labs drive product ideas and testing. As part of the old AT&T, Bell Labs was responsible for many of the most significant technology products of the 20th century. In many cases, such as the development of the transistor, the research was years ahead of market need. Now, while AT&T Labs still employs more than 4,500 scientists, the focus is identifying new-product ideas that are more market-focused and customer-driven.

Pfizer boasts the largest R&D spending in the pharmaceutical industry—more than $7 billion in 2008—and employs more than five research scientists to help generate new products. The result of that research is over 400 chemical compounds in various stages of research across a number of therapeutic areas. While not all will be introduced, Pfizer does have an extensive product pipeline from which to draw new successful products.[16]

External An excellent source of ideas comes from individuals and organizations not directly connected with the company. In some industries, such as Internet applications, small entrepreneurs drive innovation. Myspace.com is a unique Internet destination owned by News Corp., one of the largest media companies in the world. Started in 2003 by two entrepreneurs who wanted a "place to hang out," the social networking Web site has more than 117 million unique users globally and continues to add over 200,000 new accounts per day. Its purchase by News Corp. in 2006 exemplifies how larger companies continue to grow by acquisition of smaller companies with innovative new products. Google, Yahoo, and Microsoft all maintain dedicated staff whose job it is to identify and acquire new start-up organizations with great product ideas.[17]

Customers Customers are also an excellent source of product ideas. Solving their problems can lead to innovative solutions that have market potential beyond the immediate customer. Many companies encourage customer input directly online through e-mail and online discussion groups. Ford, BMW, Mercedes-Benz, and others sponsor user group bulletin boards that discuss improvements to existing products. While this will not likely lead to "new-to-the-world" products, it can lead to incremental or even substantial enhancements to existing products.

The Future? What Future? I'm the Future! I'm ALWAYS ON!

Fifteen-year-old Olga is a Parisian high school student. She has five best friends she can't get enough of, and not enough time in a day to share and discuss everything they've got going on. In order to **stay connected to her peeps 24/7**, Olga is ALWAYS ON. She has created a blog where she sends tons of snapshots, videos, hip new URLs and info about the latest gadgets. Through her smart phone and laptop, she is linked to all her friends, their friends and their friends' friends. Her blog has grown and morphed into **a fascinating teenager's guide to Paris** which had over 40,000 visitors last month alone!

We at Alcatel-Lucent are thrilled that Olga and her friends are having so much fun. Our Bell Labs researchers in North America invented the technology that formed the foundation for the Internet. Nowadays, Bell Labs researchers around the world are making discoveries and working on future technologies that will transform the way the world communicates... again. And we can't wait to see how people like Olga will use these innovations to be ALWAYS ON.

Like Olga, millions of people are ALWAYS ON. Tell us your story at www.theworldisalwayson.com

Transforming communications for a world that's ALWAYS ON.

Alcatel-Lucent, the company that now owns Bell Labs, is applying its research resources to enhancing telecommunications around the world and, more specifically, the Internet.

When Cadbury-Schweppes wanted to expand beyond its core chocolate business one of the first things it did was survey 140,000 customers on their candy preferences. The result was Trident Splash, a new gum with three layers including a candy shell, a layer of sugarless gum, and a liquid center. The product has been a success and new flavors have been added since the product launch.[18]

Distributors Distributors are a good source for new-product ideas particularly when they are the primary link between the customer and the company. Small organizations generally do not have the resources for a national sales force and use distributors in many markets. Odyssey Software is a developer of wireless business applications for the Windows platform that uses a network of global distributors to market its products.[19] The distributor network is a key partner in the development of new products for the company. In actuality, almost anyone outside the organization can generate a new-product idea.

Companies understand that even though the majority of ideas from external sources will not pass the screening process they still want to encourage people to submit their product concepts. HP gets thousands of product ideas from a variety of individuals every year; however, very few are actually developed.

Screen and Evaluate Ideas

Ideas need to be screened and evaluated as quickly as possible. The screening process has two primary objectives. First, eliminate product ideas judged unworthy of

Just What the Doctor Ordered

Anyone who has ever sat in a pediatric doctor's waiting room will appreciate the challenge of keeping sick kids happy while waiting for an average of 26.5 minutes. From the doctor's staff, to the parents and kids, the minutes spent in a waiting room can be difficult. KidCare TV, based in Tampa, has developed a service using a broadband Internet connection to deliver three- to five-minute segments over 32-inch flat-screen TVs placed in pediatrician waiting rooms. The potential market for KidCare TV is big with over 60,000 pediatricians in the United States, and the company already has over 1,000 TVs installed.

The charge to the pediatrician—zero, which certainly has appeal to the doctor by making the waiting room a quieter, less-stressful environment for parents and kids. The segments feature content directed toward kids, such as cartoons and fun, interactive exercises, and child care tips directed to the parents. KidCare introduces several 30-second commercials in each segment from companies such as Capri Sun juice and Gerber Life Insurance. The company has also produced a "take home" DVD that doctors can send home with new parents offering a wide range of tips and suggestions on how to take care of a newborn. Seventeen segments have been produced on topics like "Early to Bed—Establishing a Daily Routine," "Parents 9-1-1—Finding a Babysitter," and "Which Came First—Introducing Your Pet to the New Baby." KidCare

TV notes that all video segments are produced in strict accordance with AAP (American Academy of Pediatrics) guidelines. The segments are available in English or Spanish.

Doctors who have KidCare TV currently installed in their offices generally support the service. They note the segments support medical concepts and good parenting concepts, and because the content is delivered digitally, any complaints about a specific ad or segment can cause it to be deleted quickly with no disruption of service.

However, critics argue that the service simply reinforces the already negative practice of kids spending too much time watching television. For example, the spokesperson for the American Academy of Pediatrics suggests that advertisers, not the kids, are the real beneficiaries of the service. Pediatricians have agued for a long time that kids need to spend more time exercising and less time watching TV, and critics question whether a TV in the waiting room conflicts with that message.[20]

Ethical Perspective

1. Parents: As a parent, how would you react to seeing a TV in your pediatrician's waiting room?

2. Pediatrician: Is there any inconsistency between arguing that children should spend more time exercising and having a TV in the waiting room?

3. KidCare TV: How would you respond to critics who argue that having children watching TV in a doctor's waiting room reinforces negative behavior to a child?

further consideration. New-product development is expensive and resources are scarce, so ideas are evaluated early to assess their viability. An idea is rejected for several reasons. Perhaps the proposal is just not very good or it may be reasonable but inconsistent with the company's overall business strategy. Evaluating ideas can sometimes create difficult choices for managers as they wrestle with broader societal issues.[21] Consider Ethical Dimension 12 regarding KidCare TV and what issues are raised by putting TVs in pediatric waiting rooms.

Two types of mistakes are associated with rejecting or moving forward with a new-product design, and both are potentially expensive for the company. The first is the **go-to-market mistake** made when a company fails to stop a bad product idea from moving into product development. This mistake runs on a continuum from very costly (the new product is not accepted and the company loses its initial investment) to not meeting targeted ROI projections (the product does not hit established benchmarks for profitability, or unit sales). Expensive mistakes often initiate a review of the screening process to figure out how the product made it through the development process. When the product fails to hit targeted benchmarks for success, the review may focus on errors in marketing strategy, target market adjustments, or competitive response to the product launch.

A **stop-to-market mistake** happens when a good idea is prematurely eliminated during the screening process. Almost every CEO can relate a story of the product success that got away. Most often companies are reluctant to talk about stop-to-market mistakes because it makes management uncomfortable and provides additional information about product development to competitors. For example, we have talked a lot about Apple, pointing out its wildly successful iPhone and iPod. But in addition to its failed Newton, which we discussed earlier, the company has also developed a number of other products that never made it to market. For example, the Macintosh PowerBook Duo Tablet was, arguably, the first tablet PC and was created in the early 1990s during the same period as Newton. Apple stopped development of the product, code-named PenLite, to avoid confusion with Newton. Among PenLite's many features was a wireless, full-function computer that connected with all PowerBook accessories.[22]

While revolutionary in design and function only 20 Concorde jets were manufactured. The high development costs and changing economic factors (rising energy prices) made the jet too expensive to buy and use. Only two airlines ever flew the Concorde—British Airways and Air France.

A second objective of the screening process is to help prioritize ideas that pass the initial screening and evaluation. All new-product concepts are not equal, and it is important to focus resources on those that best match the success criteria. The criteria used to prioritize the ideas vary by company but often include:

- Time to market (how long will it take to develop and get the product to market).
- ROI (what is the expected return for the dollars invested in the project).
- New product fit with overall company product portfolio.

This analysis includes an internal assessment by a team from specific areas across the company (finance, marketing, R&D, manufacturing, logistics).[23] Often these people are directly involved in new-product development and have a thorough understanding of the success criteria and the company's overall product portfolio. Additionally, a relevant member of senior management provides continuity with long-term strategic goals and leadership in the screening process. Members of the team are rotated to ensure fresh ideas as there is often a significant time commitment required and members of the assessment team have other responsibilities in the company.[24]

Define the Product Opportunity

Ideas that pass through the screening process move into a development phase to define the product potential and market opportunity. Three specific tasks in this stage are: (1) define and test the product idea, (2) create a marketing strategy for the product, and (3) analyze the product's business case.

Define and Test Product Concept

The product idea now needs to be clearly defined and tested. Ideas at this stage are frequently not fully developed or operational. At this point, depending on the concept, people and resources are allocated to move the product development forward and a budget is created to develop the product.

Product definition has three objectives. First, it defines the product's value proposition; what customer needs are being addressed and, in broad terms, at what price. Second, the definition briefly identifies the target market(s) and what is the purchase frequency. Third, the definition delineates the product's characteristics (look, feel, physical elements, and features of the product). As the product moves through development, the physical characteristics become more defined and particular features, often at different price points, are included in the prototypes.[25]

Target customers are useful in defining the product concept. Companies present models, limited prototypes, and verbal or written descriptions of the product concept to customers, individually or in focus groups. Computer graphics are also used to depict elements of the product and even functionality. For example, in the development of new jet airliners, Boeing and Airbus will develop sophisticated simulations that allow passengers to *virtually* sit in the airplane. In this way, customers get a more realistic perspective at a fraction of the cost to develop a full-scale working prototype.

During this phase, companies start getting market input to refine and develop the concept. Customers are asked about their attitudes toward the product idea and if they perceive the idea as different from other products on the market. Product developers want to know, Would you buy this product and how much are you willing to pay? The company needs to know if the product is appealing to the target audience. A second question is also essential in this testing, What would you like to change about the product concept? If customers suggest changes that are not feasible (too costly to implement, not technically possible), it dramatically reduces the viability of the project. Whenever possible, however, customer feedback is incorporated into the product's development. By making adjustments during this phase rather than waiting until after the launch, companies can increase the probability of success. Since the information is so critical, researchers use large samples of target customers to ensure confidence in the findings.

> In the early 1990s Philips developed a new technology called digital compact cassette (DCC) to compete directly with the more popular compact disc technology. While the DCC technology was more flexible than the CD and designed to work on standard magnetic tapes, DCC was never a success despite being good technically and easy to use.[26]

Create Marketing Strategy

The product development process leads to a distinct set of physical characteristics and a detailed feature mix. As the product becomes better defined, marketing specialists develop a tentative, but detailed, marketing strategy. Even though the product is still under development, there are several reasons for preparing a marketing strategy now. First, defining the target market is helpful to the product developers. In addition to the basic market information (size, geography, and demographics), product developers appreciate knowing how the product will be used (context, environment) and psychographics of the market (the market's activities, interests, and opinions). Marketers also assess the market share potential at critical points in time (how much market share can the new product get after one year). At this point, tentative pricing, distribution, and marketing communications strategies are created that will be adapted as the product gets closer to rollout.[27] Exhibit 12.2 discusses the rollout strategy for a new Cisco product. Often, as part of the initial marketing communications, appropriate publications will include articles about a new product. The FYI highlights how Nokia adjusted its distribution strategy in India based on market research. Finally, marketing managers begin to develop budgets for the product launch and estimates of the marketing communications budget, manufacturing capacity, and logistical needs.

In creating an effective new product marketing strategy it is important to clearly identify the product benefits to the target audience. Here the MINI is identifying a benefit: buy a MINI and you won't be bored. For someone in the MINI's target market, this benefit is attractive.

Nokia is focusing on emerging markets such as China and India for new growth opportunities. Among the challenges in these markets is the complex and vastly more diffused distribution channel. In both countries, Nokia found that the number of locations where technology, like cell phones, is available is much larger than in developed countries like the United States or France. For example, in China it is possible to purchase a phone at over 40,000 locations, and in India that number more than doubles to 90,000. From large stores to street vendors and kiosks, Nokia is developing new distribution models to reach customers where they work and live. Vendors are even mobile, riding rickshaws and bikes, so Nokia is developing distribution methods to get products in their hands.

The company is also looking at creative financing tools such as having families pool resources to purchase a cell phone. In India, Nokia observed that families were pooling money to buy a single handset then drawing lots to see who got to use it. They would continue this process until everyone had a handset.[28]

EXHIBIT 12.2 **A Market Strategy for a New Product: Cisco Product Rollout Targets Market Opportunities**

Cisco Systems rolled out several new products for the mobile workforce in vertical industries such as health care and retail. The networking giant said the products are a result of businesses' growing need for mobility.

"We've been working on this vision for a year by aligning our roadmaps and integrating our technologies across security, unified communications, wireless LANs, and wired networking," said Alan Cohen, Cisco's vice president of mobility solutions, in an interview. After conducting independent research and surveying business decision makers, Cisco came up with three key conclusions:

–Most businesses don't have a long-term mobile IT strategy.

–One out of four decision makers are out of compliance with industry regulations when it comes to security policies of their wired and wireless networks.

–Most businesses haven't planned for how to connect their assets to their network.

In response to those findings, Cisco created the Location Solution for the health care industry and the In-Store Mobility Solution for the retail industry.

With the Location Solution—a combination of Cisco's Unified Wireless Network software and Wi-Fi tags—businesses can track high-value assets and gather related information such as temperature, battery power, humidity levels, and usage status.

Cisco teamed up with AeroScout and WhereNet for chokepoint technology that wirelessly monitors passageways and associated tags. When a tagged asset moves through a chokepoint, an alarm can be triggered, which is particularly useful in health care for tracking expensive hospital equipment. "We've been doing location for years, but what people want is status, meaning knowing when something is in use at a hospital," Cohen said.

The In-Store Mobility Solution integrates unified communications—a term that refers to combining various forms of communication into one user interface—and Cisco's wireless technology so that retailers can consolidate multiple applications across a single wireless infrastructure and deliver them to employees, suppliers, and customers anywhere in a store. Shoppers get access to information and self-service shopping carts. For example, shoppers can receive notice of promotions, create shopping lists, and navigate a store directly from an interactive shopping cart for an improved customer experience, according to Cisco.

Source: By Elena Malykhina *InformationWeek,* May 22, 2007, http://www.informationweek.com/news/mobility/showArticle.jhtml?articleID=199700827, accessed November 2008.

Conduct Business Case Analysis

As the product definition is developed and a tentative marketing strategy created, a critical "go-no go" decision is made before the next product development stage. At this point, the costs have been small relative to the cost of moving to full product development, market testing, and launch. There is a lot of pressure to get the decision right because a mistake is expensive. The **business case analysis** is an overall evaluation of a product and usually assesses the product's probability of success. It is often done when there are changes to an existing marketing plan, such as an increase in the marketing communications budget. The business case would assess the feasibility of increasing the communications budget.[29] In new-product development, the business case focuses on two key issues. First, the total demand for the product over a specified period of time, usually five years, is determined. Second, a cash flow statement is developed that specifies cash flow, profitability, and investment requirements.

Total Demand Sales are defined in two ways: revenue (unit sales x price) and unit sales. Each provides important information. Revenue is the top line number in a profitability analysis and is affected by price variations common to global products with substantial price differences around the world. Because currencies fluctuate, which can lead to wide variations in revenue, and price increases can also dramatically affect total revenue, unit sales is often considered a more realistic picture of product growth and represents the number of units sold, in various product configurations, around the world.

Estimating total demand is a function of three separate purchase situations.

- **New purchases**—first-time sales. With new products, these sales are called trial purchases. This is also calculated as the trial rate (how many individuals in a particular target market have tried the product).

- **Repeat purchases**—the number of products purchased by the same customer. This can be important with frequently purchased products such as convenience goods that rely on frequent repeat purchases for success.

- **Replacement purchases**—the number of products purchased to replace existing products that have become obsolete or have malfunctioned. Estimates are made on the number of product failures in any given year based on the expected product life. As more products are sold into a market through first-time and repeat purchases, the number of replacement sales will increase.

Profitability Analysis To this point, costs have been primarily in R&D and market research. However, at the next step, the company will incur manufacturing, marketing, accounting, and the logistical costs of bringing the product to market. As a result, a thorough analysis is conducted of the short- and long-term product profitability. Exhibit 12.3 is an example of a five-year projected cash flow report.

Develop the Product Opportunity

If the result of the previous analysis is a "go" decision, then the number of people and the resources allocated to the product's development increases substantially. For much of the 20th century, companies would move a substantial number of new-product concepts through to this stage and use product development and market testing to screen and eliminate ideas. That changed in the 1990s as the cost of taking products to market increased dramatically while failure rates remained high. Companies now screen product ideas much earlier in the development process. As a result, far fewer product ideas make it to this stage, and those products targeted for further development and market testing have a much higher probability of actually being launched in the marketplace.[30]

Develop the Product

So far the product exists primarily as a concept, or at most, a working prototype, but if the product idea is to go forward it must move from viable product concept

Cold Mtn. Sports, Inc.

5 Year Monthly Financial Forecast
October 2006 to September 2011
Annual Summary

Condensed Operations	Sept 2007	%	Sept 2008	%	Sept 2009	%	Sept 2010	%	Sept 2011	%
Sales, net	11,832	100.0	13,620	100.0	15,639	100.0	17,206	100.0	18,928	100.0
Cost of Sales	9,142	77.3	10,524	77.3	12,084	77.3	13,295	77.3	14,625	77.3
Gross Margin	2,690	22.7	3,096	22.7	3,555	22.7	3,912	22.7	4,303	22.7
Departmental Expense	2,384	20.1	2,742	20.1	3,181	20.1	3,672	21.3	4,047	21.4
Income from Operations	306	2.6	354	2.6	374	2.4	240	1.4	256	1.4
Interest and Other net	(47)	−0.4	(47)	−0.3	(47)	−0.3	(47)	−0.3	(47)	−0.2
Income Taxes	(103)	−0.9	(123)	−0.9	(130)	−0.8	(78)	−0.5	(82)	−0.4
Net Income	156	1.3	184	1.4	197	1.3	115	0.7	126	0.7

Condensed Financial Condition	Sept 2007	Sept 2008	Sept 2009	Sept 2010	Sept 2011
Working Capital	1,335	1,548	1,759	1,880	2,011
Property and Equipment, Net	35	30	25	25	14
Other Assets	36	12	-	-	-
Other Liabilities	(500)	(500)	(500)	(500)	(500)
Equity	907	1,090	1,284	1,400	1,524

Condensed Cash Flow	Sept 2007	Sept 2008	Sept 2009	Sept 2010	Sept 2011
Total Cash Provided from Operations	118	(56)	14	(34)	(35)
Total Cash Used in Investing Activities	16	18	6	(6)	(4)
Total Cash Provided by Financing Activities	(134)	38	(20)	40	39
Total Cash Provided (Used)	-	(0)	(0)	0	(0)
Cash, at Beginning of Period	55	55	55	55	55
Cash, at End of Period	55	55	55	55	55

Regional Sales Margins	Sept 2007	%	Sept 2008	%	Sept 2009	%	Sept 2010	%	Sept 2011	%
North West	854	28.9	983	28.9	1,130	28.9	1,243	28.9	1,368	28.9
South West	419	14.2	483	14.2	555	14.2	611	14.2	672	14.2
Central	448	15.2	516	15.2	587	15.0	646	15.0	711	15.0
North East	640	21.7	737	21.7	848	21.7	933	21.7	1,026	21.7
South East	347	11.7	399	11.7	459	11.8	505	11.8	556	11.8
International	111	3.7	127	3.7	146	3.7	161	3.7	177	3.7
Internet Sales	136	4.6	157	4.6	180	4.6	198	4.6	218	4.6
Total	2,955	100.0	3,402	100.0	3,906	100.0	4,298	100.0	4,728	100.0

Source: www.alondon.com.

Reprinted courtesy of Allan P. London.

to a working product that meets customer needs profitably. The challenge for the development team is to design and build a product the customer wants to buy while hitting the company's success metrics—sales price, revenue, profit margins, unit sales, and cost to build.[31]

Motorola used very different approaches in creating the next generation of two major products. With RAZR[2] the challenge was to make the next generation of the most successful cell phone in history good enough so that 100 million-plus existing users would want to buy another. On the other hand, the ROKR was a relative failure and needed to be completely remade and rebranded. The ROKR, developed with Apple, failed to live up to its initial buzz because it had very limited song capabilities. The second-generation ROKR features greatly expanded music capabilities, a new logo, and a complete system of accessories from Motorola. Despite its best efforts however, Motorola has found it difficult to sustain the success of the RAZR.[32]

Previous research during concept testing provides substantial information about what customers are looking for in the product. Coupled with input from engineers, designers, and marketing specialists, the product definition developed earlier is operationalized. This process moves from a strategic understanding of the customer's basic needs to a specific operational definition of product's characteristics. Following this process, the product's physical characteristics are defined by targeting the essential benefits delivered to the customer.[33]

There are two product development models. The first incorporates more planning and follows a sequential timeline with key process metrics being met at each stage before moving on through the process. In this scenario, product development spends a lot of time creating a product that is considered close to the final product that will be rolled out to customers. Consequently, product testing is used primarily to affirm the extensive development done earlier in the process.

The next approach encourages more prototypes that incrementally move the product through the development process. Here the product does not need to be "perfect" before testing; rather, the idea is to continuously test the product and use the testing process to enhance the product and solicit customer feedback. Through this process, the market becomes aware of the product, and if properly managed, interest in the product is increased during development.

In this second method, the goal is to shorten the time spent in development, moving from development to testing as quickly as possible to minimize cost and get the product in the hands of potential users. The longer a company takes at this stage, the greater the likelihood that competitors learn of the product, customer preferences change, or external environment conditions dictate further product adjustments.

Product Testing Generally a product undergoes two types of testing. As the product's characteristics are being finalized, most of the testing is done internally by engineers, product specialists, and other employees. This type of testing, called alpha testing, helps clarify the basic operationalization of the product such as the physical characteristics and features.

At some point, the company will want potential customers to begin testing the product. Beta testing encourages customers to evaluate and provide feedback on the prototype. The product may be close to the final configuration but Beta tests allow for further product testing and refinement.[34]

> Google puts a lot of products into the market and encourages users to try them. From this input, the company is constantly updating the product. By following this strategy, it is able to take products live much faster. The company admits that this strategy creates product misses, but it also leads to product success (Google maps). Google calendar was in beta testing for several months and continues to test new features even as many people become regular users of the product.[35]

Test the Market

Once the product has reached the point where the product development team is satisfied with its performance, physical characteristics, and features, it is ready to be tested in the marketplace. To maintain security, minimize product information leaks, and disrupt competitor intelligence, products are often given code names. Once the product moves to the marketplace testing stage, a marketing strategy is created for the test using the product's market name. Some elements of the strategy such as brand name and packaging will have been tested with consumers during product development.[36] For example, engineers work with package design professionals to ensure that first, the product is protected, and second, the packaging maximizes marketing communications opportunities.

The amount of market testing is a function of several critical factors that are in conflict with one another. First, a company must evaluate the cost of being wrong.

While a great deal of money has been spent to this point, the cost of launching a product failure is much higher. The greater the risk of failure, the more market testing a company will want to do before a full product launch.

At the same time, market testing takes time, and competitors can take advantage to enhance their product mix or develop marketing strategies to counter a successful product launch. In addition, depending on the product, the selling season may dictate faster product rollout because waiting to long may cost the company significant sales. Ultimately, management must balance these factors and choose the optimum market testing strategy.[37]

Trader Joe's conducts a great deal of analysis before it introduces a new product in its stores. The company considers hundreds of new products every year but only a few make it onto store shelves.

Consumer Product Market Tests In creating the market test, management must make four key decisions:

- *Where:* The location of the market test is based on how well it reflects the potential target markets. Most market tests involve somewhere between two and five cities to mitigate regional differences in purchases patterns (if there are any).

- *How long:* Most test markets run less than a year. The test should be long enough to include several purchase cycles. With many consumer products, purchase cycles are relatively short (days or weeks) so there is less need for a long market test.

- *Data:* Critical information needed to make necessary decisions must be identified. Management frequently wants to know how long it takes for the product to move through the distribution system, tracking the product from manufacturing plant through to the point of sale (matching inventory as it leaves the plant with store sales). In addition, buyers are interviewed on their product experience.

- *Decision criteria:* Metrics for further action must be identified. At this stage it is difficult to pull a product, but if the product fails in the market test, management is faced with a difficult decision—drop the product or send it back for major redesign. If the product is a success, then the product launch decision is much easier. Exhibit 12.4 is a summary of the decision criteria used in market tests.

Consumer product market testing has two goals. First, provide specific numbers to the business case estimates including new (trial purchases), repeat, and, if appropriate, initial replacement purchases. Additionally, information about buyer demographics is evaluated against earlier target market scenarios and is compared against company business case models and historical data. The company takes data from the market test and projects the future.

The second objective of market testing is to get feedback on the tactics that can be used to adjust the marketing plan before product launch. While a company will often hold back implementing the entire marketing plan for security reasons, input from customers, distributors, and retailers is helpful in adjusting the final marketing plan.

Business Product Market Test Products designed for business markets are tested differently than their consumer product counterparts. Essentially, the tests are smaller in scope and involve fewer individuals and companies; however, they are no less important in the new-product development process. Because business markets are smaller, beta testing often includes only a few key customers with a long-standing company relationship. If, on the other hand, the company has independent distributors, it identifies a limited number for the market test and provides additional support to them as the product is being tested.[38]

EXHIBIT 12.4 | **Summary of Decision Criteria in Market Tests**

Category	Criteria
Financial	Gross margin
	Profit per unit shelf space
	Opportunity cost of capital needed to obtain the new item
Competition	Number of firms in the trading area
	Number of competing brands
Marketing strategy	Product uniqueness
	Vendor effort
	Marketing support
	Terms of trade: slotting allowances, off-invoice allowances, free cases, bill-back provisions
	Price
Other	Category growth
	Synergy with existing items

Source: www.emeraldinsight.com.

Often in parallel with beta testing, companies will use trade shows to solicit customer feedback. Trade shows are a cost-effective way to get customer input because they are an efficient and convenient location to introduce new products or test new product ideas.

Product Launch

At this point in the new-product process, it is time to implement the marketing plan. By now, considerable time, money, and human capital have been expended in the development of the product. Management has made the decision to launch the product. Now it is time to define the product's objectives (sales, target markets, success metrics), specify the value proposition, plan the marketing tactics, and implement the marketing plan. As we mentioned earlier, all of this will already have been done, but any necessary adjustments are made after the market test.

The product launch is critical to the long-term success of the product. Products that start poorly seldom recover from a poor launch. The pressure to create excitement, particularly for consumer products, leading to consumer trial purchase is a primary reason companies spend millions of dollars on a product launch.[39] Microsoft spent in excess of $500 million to introduce Vista in early 2007 and that does not include the hundreds of millions spent by Microsoft partners (Intel, Dell, and others) in support of Vista (see Exhibit 12.5). However, the product has met with mixed success, particularly among business users.[40]

Many marketing communication dollars are front-loaded at the product launch with the goal of creating sufficient product interest that will turn into repeat and replacement purchases later. If the product is not successful early, management is often unwilling to spend additional dollars as the product becomes widely distributed. The end result can be a downward spiral with low product interest generating fewer sales, which leads to more cutbacks in marketing support.[41]

EXHIBIT 12.5 | An Example of the Vista New-Product Launch Activities

**Microsoft Celebrates Worldwide Availability of Windows Vista and the
2007 Microsoft Office System: National Retail Activities**

January 29, 2007

"Wow" Moment (public)
The Terminal Building
11th Avenue at 27th Street
New York, NY
10:00 a.m. EST

Mike Sievert, corporate vice president, Windows Client Marketing, unveils a moment of "Wow," in New York, and kick starts the celebration for local, national and international audiences.

Luncheon with Microsoft CEO Steve Ballmer and Industry Partners (invite only–confirmed reservation required)

• 11:30 am EST: Doors open

• 12:00 pm EST: Buffet lunch is served

• 1:45 pm EST: Event ends

Live Webcast: Windows Vista and Microsoft Office 2007 Celebration with Microsoft Chairman Bill Gates
The Windows Vista Theatre–Times Square
3:45 p.m. EST

The celebration pays tribute to the millions of Microsoft customers, partners, and product testers around the world who provided input and feedback on these products– helping Microsoft transform the way people communicate, create and share content, and access information and entertainment in the new digital age.

January 30, 2007

Steve Ballmer Kicks Off Consumer Availability in New York (public)
Best Buy
529 5th Ave (44th & 5th Avenue)
New York
10:00 a.m. EST

Steve Ballmer visits Best Buy in New York to celebrate the official unveiling of Windows Vista and Microsoft Office 2007 to consumers. This activity includes product giveaways and an exciting opportunity for local schools to win a PC lab upgrade. Similar activities also occur in local markets around the country.

Source: www.microsoft.com, November 2008.

CONSUMER ADOPTION AND DIFFUSION PROCESS

A target market consists of many people with different predispositions to purchase a product. Some will want to adopt a product early; others will wait until much later. The rate at which products become accepted is known as the adoption process. Marketers are interested in knowing the rate at which a product will be adopted into a market as well as the timeline (how long will it take for the product to move through the process). Of particular interest in a new-product launch are the groups at the beginning of the process, innovators and early adopters.[42]

A.C. Nielsen, one of the world's leading market research firms, reports that early buyers are critical in the success of a new product because they provide critical insights on the degree to which consumers will accept the product. People in this group are more likely to communicate their preferences (and dislikes) to others. They are also likely to influence the decisions of people who come later in the adoption process. As a result, companies such as Procter & Gamble and Electronic Arts spend a great deal of time learning about early buyers of their products.[43]

Consumer Product Adoption Process

As we have discussed, new products come in various forms, from new-to-the-world products to incremental changes to existing products, but the consumer adoption process is less concerned with the product definition and more concerned with the individual consumer's perception of the product. A product can be in the market for a long time and still be considered an innovation to an individual consumer. The **innovation diffusion process** is how long it takes a product to move from first purchase to last purchase (the last set of users to adopt the product). An individual moves through five stages before adopting a product:

1. **Awareness**–know of the product, but insufficient information to move forward through the adoption process.
2. **Interest**–receive additional information (advertising, word of mouth) and motivated to seek out added information for further evaluation.
3. **Evaluation**–combine all information (word of mouth, reviews, advertising) and evaluate the product for trial purchase.
4. **Trial**–purchase the product for the purpose of making a value decision.
5. **Adoption**–purchase the product with the intent of becoming a dependable user.

Marketers, particularly those involved in a new-product launch, want to move consumers through the process as quickly as possible. One reason to spend heavily at the product launch phase is to move people through awareness, interest, and evaluation, getting them to try the product quickly. Sales promotion tools (coupons, product sampling), endorsements, third-party reviews, and other marketing communications methods are all part of a strategy to move people toward trial purchase. Trial purchase is the focus of a product launch marketing plan, because if you can get consumers to try the product, you can win them over with superior product design, features, and value.[44]

The Diffusion of Innovations

Everyone in a target market falls into one of five groups based on their willingness to try the innovation (see Exhibit 12.6). A person can be an innovator or early adopter in one product category and a laggard in another. However, marketers want to identify where individuals fall on the innovation curve for a particular product or product class. Interestingly, the process by which products become diffused in a market remains remarkably constant. Research into the adoption of the Internet in the United States found it very similar to the adoption of color television in the United States in the 1960s.

The process begins with a very small group who adopt the product perhaps through targeted marketing (they are given the product to try, for example) or high involvement with the product. From there, larger numbers in the different groups move through the adoption process. Two-thirds of all adopters for a given product fall in the early and late majority. The final group, laggards, may not move into the adoption process until late in the product's life cycle.[45]

EXHIBIT 12.6 | Consumer Product Adoption Chart

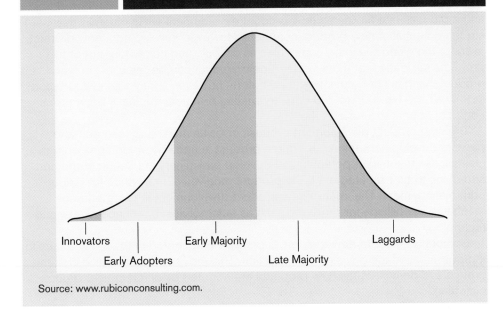

Innovators
Early Adopters
Early Majority
Late Majority
Laggards

Source: www.rubiconconsulting.com.

- **Innovators** (2.5 percent)—Product enthusiasts enjoy being the first to try and master a new product. Individuals in this group are prime candidates for beta testing and represent a good source of feedback late in the product development process or early in the product launch phase.

- **Early Adopters** (13.5 percent)—Product opinion leaders seek out new products consistent with the personal self-image. This group is not price-sensitive and is willing to pay the price premium for a product. At the same time, early adopters demand a high level of personalized service and product features.

- **Early Majority** (34.5 percent)—Product watchers want to be convinced of the product's claims and value proposition before making a commitment. This group is considered critical to long-term success as they take the product into the main stream.

- **Late Majority** (34 percent)—Product followers are price-sensitive and risk-averse. They purchase older generation or discontinued models with lower prices and fewer product features.

- **Laggards** (16 percent)—Product avoiders want to evade adoption as long as possible. Resistant to change, they will put off the purchase until there is no other option.

Today, microwave ovens come in all sizes and at least one is found in a high percentage of all homes. However, the product followed the diffusion process. At first, the product was slow to be accepted because of health concerns and the fact that many people simply did not know how to use it properly.

Ever heard of Akamai? Most likely you haven't, but if you've been to Yahoo, iTunes, or MySpace recently, you have used Akamai servers. Despite almost going bankrupt in the dot-com bust, the company has rebounded with sales approaching half a billion dollars. Forecasts suggest demand for bandwidth to download video will continue to explode. Company executives believe use of the Internet as a video delivery system is just getting started. As consumer acceptance of online video increases, so will the need for Akamai network products.[46]

SUMMARY

Critical to a company's long-term success is the development of new products and a process that facilitates new-product development while carefully assessing the potential of new-product concepts. However, developing a new product, even for the world's leading companies, is difficult, and nearly four out of five products fail in the first three years. A new product can be "new to the world," a product that has not been introduced before; however, it may also include products that have been upgraded or even existing products that have been repositioned to appeal to a new market.

The new-product development process involves marketing research and product development research. As the product is under development, companies assess the market potential and develop preliminary marketing strategies and plans to be executed once the product receives authorization for rollout from management. The cost of new-product development is rising and can reach into the billions for products such as automobiles, pharmaceuticals, and technology.

Companies want to how their products will be accepted in the marketplace in a process called the diffusion of innovation. This process identifies five customer groups and demonstrates how products are adopted by different user groups over time.

KEY TERMS

new-to-the-world product 330

modifications to existing products 330

additions to existing product lines 330

reposition existing products 331

cost reduction 331

go-to-market mistake 336

stop-to-market mistake 337

business case analysis 340

new purchase 340

repeat purchase 340

replacement purchase 340

innovation diffusion process 346

Innovator 347

Early adopter 347

Early majority 347

Late majority 347

Laggard 347

APPLICATION QUESTIONS

1. You are the marketing manager for McGraw-Hill responsible for new-product development. Recently, your technology development department created a new software application that enables students to learn marketing management more effectively. Take the product through the new-product development process. What would you need to know to make a launch decision for the product?

2. As a product manager for Nokia you are responsible for the introduction of a new line of mobile devices targeted at business users. The company's R&D team has presented you with a list of possible new features that can be added to the product in the next 18 months. When and how would these new features be added to the existing line of cell phones?

3. Assess the new-product launch of Microsoft Vista in 2007. Was the product a success initially? Why or why not? What has the company done since the product's launch to help support Vista?

4. The Pelamis marine energy project, discussed at the beginning of the chapter is researching the possibility of harnessing marine energy to generate electricity.

As a marketing manager for General Electric, how would you assess the progress of a project like Pelamis?

5. You are the marketing manager for a line of designer jeans from Levi Strauss and charged with defining the Innovator group of buyers. Who might be the innovators for Levi's designer jeans and why?

MANAGEMENT DECISION CASE: Keeping the Buzz at Burt's Bees

Branding is not just for big companies. Small companies find great success identifying a niche and creating a strong brand. One of the most successful in the high-end consumer personal care market is Burt's Bees. While not a household brand name like Oil of Olay or Axe, Burt's Bees has experienced tremendous growth in recent years by focusing on building an innovative, distinctive product line that appeals to consumers wanting higher-quality personal care products. Consumers express a high degree of loyalty and sign up at the company's Web site to be part of "the hive," a dedicated chat room. In addition, consumers can sign up for the company's newsletter. Much of the success is due to customer referrals—friends tell friends about Burt's Bees.

Started in 1984 by an unemployed waitress and an eccentric beekeeper, the company began by making candles and was incorporated in 1991 with sales of $1.5 million. At that point, the product line was expanded into personal care with the introduction of Burt's Bees lip balm. By 1998, sales exceeded $8 million and the product line had been expanded to over 100 items sold in 4,000 retail outlets. As the brand's reputation grew, sales began to take off, rising from $30 million in 2000 to over $250 million today. Burt's Bees now includes 150 products sold in 20,000 retail outlets including Walgreens and CVS. From the beginning, Burt's Bees developed natural, eco-friendly personal care products and its corporate philosophy still maintains a strong environmental focus.

Product expansion is driven by consumer feedback. Recently, the company introduced a complete line of body lotions as a result of consumer input. The company is also expanding its line of men's products to include shampoo and conditioner and baby care products including a baby body wash. The company realizes its core strengths and has no intention of developing products it perceives as damaging to the environment such as household cleaners. Following on the trends of improved personal health and wellness as well as increased environmental sensitivity, the company believes it has great growth potential.

The company operates in one of the most competitive market spaces globally, going up against Procter & Gamble and Unilever. In addition, as the company expands it distribution to more mainstream outlets, there is some concern core customers will perceive the products have lost their uniqueness. Finally, the growth in the number of Burt's Bees products can potentially lead to quality problems if not carefully managed. For example, a line of color cosmetics has not been as successful, in part, because the company was not able to compete effectively against larger, more established quality cosmetics from Estee Lauder and Clinique.[47]

Questions for Consideration

1. Define the brand equity of Burt's Bees. How would you assess the overall brand position for the company?

2. Keeping in mind the company's brand identity, develop a marketing strategy for the rollout of a new line of men's shampoo and conditioner products.

3. Create a long-term marketing strategy to continue to grow the company. Specifically, outline a three- to five-year strategy for new-product development.

MARKETING PLAN EXERCISE

ACTIVITY 12: New-Product Development

In this chapter we looked at the essential element in the marketing mix—the product. Developing an effective marketing plan begins with an understanding of your product, its role in the company's overall business strategy, and, more specifically, where it fits in the company's product mix. Additionally, it is important to establish a new-product development process that ensures a new product pipeline of potentially successful new products. Marketing plan activities in this chapter include the following:

1. Define a new-product development process for next-generation products. While the product may be new, it is important to have a plan in place for next-generation models.

   a. Do you want to expand existing products into new markets?

   b. Define expected features that will likely be added over the next 36 months and a timeline for introduction.

2. Does the company want to be known as innovative with regards to new-product development?

3. Chart the diffusion of the company's product into the market. Define each of the groups in the diffusion process.

If you are using Marketing Plan Pro, a template for this assignment can be accessed at www.mhhe.com/marshall1e.

RECOMMENDED READINGS

1. Michael McGrath, *Next Generation Product Development: How to Increase Productivity, Cut Costs, Reduce Cycle Times* (New York: McGraw-Hill, 2004).

2. Kenneth B. Kahn, *The PDMA Handbook of New Product Development,* 2nd ed. (New York: Wiley, 2004).

3. Clifford Fiore, *Lean Strategies for Product Development: Achieving Breakthrough Performance in Bringing Products to Market* (Milwaukee, WI: ASQ Quality Press, 2003).

4. Bruce T. Barkley, *Project Management in New Product Development* (New York: McGraw-Hill, 2008).

5. Karl Ulrich and Steven Eppinger, *Product Design and Development,* 4th ed. (New York: McGraw-Hill, 2008).

CHAPTER 13

SERVICE AS THE CORE OFFERING

LEARNING OBJECTIVES

- Understand why service is a key source of potential differentiation.

- Explain the characteristics that set services apart from physical goods.

- Explain the service-profit chain and how it guides marketing management decisions about service.

- Describe the continuum from pure goods to pure services.

- Discuss concepts of service quality and gap analysis.

- Measure service quality through use of SERVQUAL.

- Understand service blueprinting and how it aids marketing managers.

EXECUTIVE PERSPECTIVE

Executive Joe Rand, Director of Marketing

Company Disney Cruise Line

Business Travel

In what ways do you ensure that strong attention to service is at the core of your marketing strategy?

Over the last 50 years Disney theme parks have developed a reputation for offering excellent service. In fact, we consistently have high-profile companies study our guest service and try to incorporate our approach into their business models. As a division of the Disney Parks & Resorts segment, Disney Cruise Line extends that commitment to service excellence. Service is at the core of our brand and a key marketing strategy, with our cast members (employees) being the ultimate differentiator. We receive thousands of guest letters raving about the cruise experience, and virtually every one of them mentions cast members by name. When choosing between cruise lines, our guests value the service we provide, and it can be the ultimate deciding factor.

How do you measure perceived service quality from customers?

Disney Cruise Line measures satisfaction across the entire guest experience. The measurement begins with the onshore experience, beginning with the service quality in our reservations call center and on our Web site, through the transportation to/from the ship, and the actual check-in/boarding process. Onboard, we evaluate the guest experience by measuring their satisfaction with stateroom service, dining, entertainment, youth activities, shopping, shore excursions, spa/fitness center, and much more. Each of these areas provides our cast an opportunity to win our guests over,

or to damage the vacation experience. Disney Cruise Line senior leadership and front-line leaders across a variety of functional areas review the survey results from every voyage to ensure we have the ability to build on guest service "wins" and proactively address any "losses" while the experience is fresh in our cast's minds. This attention to detail is one of the cornerstones of our focus on excellence.

Even the best service firms may have that rare occasion when a customer's expectations for service aren't fully met. What is your view on service recovery?

We approach service recovery on a case-by-case basis. Often, service recovery is a proactive decision on the part of attentive, empowered cast members who notice that something has fallen short of expectations. In these cases, guests are "wowed" by someone noticing and taking the time to make it right. In other cases, however, we don't realize that there has been a "loss" and need to be made aware what fell short. The good news is our guests know we want them to have the vacation of a lifetime and are not shy about sharing wins and losses. That happens in two ways. First, our onboard guest service team records any incidents that are reported on the ship and provides appropriate service recovery. Secondly, we have a shoreside guest communications department that reviews all guest letters and determines if we've made a mistake that should be addressed via service recovery.

WHY SERVICE IS IMPORTANT

There's no debate that today we operate in an economy that is increasingly focused on intangible offerings—services—instead of just physical goods. A **service** is a product in the sense that it represents a bundle of benefits that can satisfy customer wants and needs, yet it does so without physical form. As such, the value a customer realizes from purchasing a service is not based on its physical attributes, but rather on some other effect the service has on him or her in fulfilling needs and wants. And differences in the quality of a service can be profound; just think for a moment about the best and worst experiences you've had with a server in a restaurant. Even if the food itself is good, it is the service aspect of a meal out that everyone remembers most. All the data suggest that we now live in a predominantly **service economy.** More than 80 percent of jobs in the United States are service-related. Compare that to 55 percent of jobs in 1970. The Bureau of Labor Statistics expects service jobs to account for *all* new domestic job growth for the foreseeable future, partly because the number of jobs outside the service sector is actually declining. Jobs represented in the **service sector** of the economy include such important categories as intellectual property, consulting, hospitality, travel, law, health care, education, technology, telecommunications, and entertainment—all high-growth job categories. In terms of U.S. gross domestic product, in 2006 services accounted for more than 75 percent and that number is growing. Impressively, services account for about 84 percent of all nonfarming-related jobs in the United States. The long-term shift from goods-producing to service-producing employment is expected to continue. Service-providing industries are expected to account for about 15.7 million new wage and salary jobs generated from 2006 to 2016, while goods-producing industries will see overall job loss. In today's workplace everyone is involved in service in some way; everyone has customers either outside or inside the firm, or both.

Changing U.S. demographics represent a major driver for why the service sector is thriving. For example, as baby boomers begin to retire and spend their discretionary income on travel and entertainment, firms in those industries will prosper. As the baby boomers continue to age, health services will begin to predominate their spending. In the meantime, the fixation of Generation Y and Millennials toward all things technological will continue to drive impressive growth in gaming, music, computing, cellular phone, and other technological industries.

Service as a Differentiator

In Chapter 9, we mentioned that service leadership and personnel leadership are two important sources of differentiation for a company. Recall that differentiation means communicating and delivering value in different ways to different customer groups. Presumably these groups are segments that show the most promise for return on marketing investment. As a marketing manager, a significant challenge with using differentiation as a core market strategy is that competitors are constantly coming to market with new differentiators that trump the efficacy of the current ones.

In his book *On Great Service,* Leonard Berry, a leading expert in the field of services marketing, advocates that a focus on service and on enabling employees to effectively deliver service can be one differentiator that is hard for the competition to replicate. Many firms are reluctant to invest in great service, largely because it takes time and patience before a return on the investment may be noticeable. But Berry's point is that although the payback might take time, once a firm is able to deliver great service as a core differentiator it is much more likely to provide a sustainable competitive advantage than are most other sources of differentiation.[1]

A New Dominant Logic for Marketing

That service is central to marketing management today is embodied in an important article that appeared in one of the field's leading journals, the *Journal of Marketing,* titled "Evolving to a New Dominant Logic for Marketing." The **new dominant**

logic for marketing implies a shift in worldview from the traditional goods versus services dichotomy to recognition of the following:

> Customers do not buy goods or services: [T]hey buy *offerings* which render services which create value . . . . The traditional division between goods and services is long outdated. The shift in focus to services is a shift from the means and the producer perspective to the utilization and the customer perspective.

In a service-centered view, tangible goods serve as "appliances" for service provision rather than ends in themselves such that in some ways the product becomes secondary or incidental to the service it propagates. This perspective has profound implications for how marketing managers approach their business in a world of increasingly commoditized physical goods. The most fundamental question is "Just *what is it* that we are marketing?" Or, put another way: What is the product and where does its value come from? A service-centered perspective is very consistent with a customer-centric approach in which people, processes, systems, and other resources are to be aligned to best serve customers. It disposes of the limitations of thinking about marketing in terms of goods taken to the marketplace and instead leads to opportunities for expanding the market by assisting the customer in the process of specialization and value creation.[2]

An overall service-centered view is fundamental to successful marketing management today. The remainder of this chapter is devoted to providing insights for effectively capitalizing on the service opportunities associated with an offering. First, unique characteristics of services are described that set services apart from physical goods for marketing managers. Second, the concept of the service-profit chain is introduced. Third, service attributes are discussed along with a continuum of products from pure goods to pure services. Fourth, the concept of service quality is introduced along with its measurement and uses by management. Finally, service blueprinting is introduced as a way for a marketing manager to map out the overall service delivery system for a business.

Korean Air shows the sumptuous nature of its 180-degree reclining seats to differentiate its premium class service from competitors.

CHARACTERISTICS OF SERVICES

Services possess several distinct characteristics different from physical goods. As illustrated in Exhibit 13.1, these are intangibility, inseparability, variability, and perishability. We'll discuss each one and its impact on customers and marketing.

Intangibility

A service cannot be experienced through the physical senses. It cannot be seen, heard, tasted, felt, or smelled by a customer. This property represents the **intangibility** of services versus goods; goods can easily be experienced through the senses. A State Farm Insurance agent issues a policy for an automobile. Yes, the customer will receive a written policy document. But the policy itself is not the product in the sense of a physical

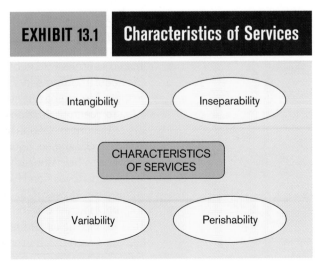

good such as a box of cereal or a bottle of shampoo. Instead, the product is the sense of financial security the insurance policy provides to the customer. It is the confidence that if something dire happens to the car, State Farm will fix it or replace it.

So how do customers draw conclusions about a brand such as State Farm if they can't actually try the product before purchase? This is one of the challenges of intangibles. Strong branding can be an important way to make a service seem more tangible. Service firms such as State Farm use strong imagery to send out signals about their products, increase trust, and ease customer uncertainty about what is being purchased. Ever see the ads saying "Like a good neighbor, State Farm is there"? This phrase and the accompanying visual images provide cues about the dependability of the service, replacing to an extent the ability customers have to try physical products in advance of purchase. When it comes to making purchase decisions about services, customers draw conclusions from what tangibles they can experience—things like the company's people, Web site, marketing communications, office ambience, and pricing. In a service setting, the importance and impact of marketing is heightened considerably because in many cases there's little else tangible for the customer to experience before purchase.[3]

One way that Intuit handles the intangibility of its Quicken and other financial software is through its Web site. The site helps potential customers and users understand the software. The site includes multiple forums to facilitate discussion between users, blogs, and a map feature that enables a business to search for local business service providers. The site also has a feedback button called "We Hear You" that enables Quickbooks users to submit product feedback. After comments are posted in the feedback area, Intuit responds publicly in that forum. Intuit also solicits customers for text and video content. "We're providing the infrastructure for users to create content and help each other," says Scott K. Wilder, group manager at Intuit Online Communities.[4]

Sometimes it is possible to enhance tangibility of a service through a bit of customer trial. For example, MBA programs often encourage prospective students to come to open houses or visit classes to gain a sense of how the school they are considering approaches teaching and learning. Vacation rentals such as Hilton Grand Vacation Club and Marriott Vacation Club actively solicit guests for tours of their facilities while prospects are visiting the area to allow them to experience a taste of what the location is like as a regular vacation destination. And advertising agencies make portfolios of past work available to prospective clients as a sampling of the firm's creative capabilities.[5]

FYI

Revolution Health is offering a free trial to help future customers determine if its fee-based services will be of value to them. The company has a mix of free and fee-based services. The free services include medical content and social networking for health issues. The fee-based services include a help phone line where consumers can connect to health professionals, such as registered nurses who can help explain a diagnosis or treatment options suggested by the patient's doctor. There also will be pros that can help consumers figure out their best insurance plan options, as well as scheduling services to help consumers set health care appointments. During the first 90 days of its launch, Revolution Health is providing a special offer of free membership till the end of the year. However, to have that $50 to $100 membership fee waived, people need to participate in some of the health portal's features, such as the health care rating system, during the site's preview period. This will help build the site's content credibility.[6]

Inseparability

Even with the best efforts at enhancing a service's tangibility, a customer still can't really experience it until it is actually consumed. This characteristic represents the **inseparability** of a service—it is produced and consumed at the same time and cannot be separated from its provider. With physical goods, the familiar process is production, storage, sale, and then consumption. But with services, first the service is sold and then it is produced and consumed at the same time. Perhaps it is more accurate to think of a service as being *performed* rather than produced.[7] In a theatrical play or an orchestral concert, many individuals have a part in the performance. Similarly, the quality of a service encounter is determined in part by the interaction of the players. Most elegant restaurants structure their customer encounters as elaborate productions involving servers, the wine steward, the maître d', the chef, and of course the table of diners. Benihana restaurants take the concept of service as drama to truly new heights of customer involvement and excitement—the company's tag line is "an experience at every table."

> Joe Maher, vice president for customer support for Foodbuy, describes all the services that accompany a meal at a restaurant. Music, he says, is a plus. "If it's ethnic cuisine, you want to have ethnically themed music. It adds another dimension. You want to create an atmosphere: it's the food, it's the way people look, it's the customer interaction and the music. So if you're preparing Cajun cuisine, you want to have some New Orleans jazz playing."[8]

The inseparability of performance and consumption of services heightens the role of the human service providers in the customer's experience. It also leads to opportunities for considerable customization in delivering the service. Finicky customers in the hair stylist's chair can coax just the right cut. Want two scoops of cinnamon ice cream instead of one on that apple tort? Just ask the server.

In the financial services industry, for example, customization of services is prominent. Bank tellers are empowered to take a quick look at your account record when you are at the window to make a deposit and might very likely suggest you do something different with your money if you're not currently optimizing your returns.[9] And cellular service providers know that if they don't proactively suggest updating rate plans, customers will be more likely to walk away once their contracted years are fulfilled.

Variability

An offshoot of the inseparability issue, **variability** of a service means that because it can't be separated from the provider, a service's quality can only be as good as that of the provider him-/herself.[10] Ritz Carlton, Nordstrom, Disney, and Southwest Airlines have become iconic firms in their industries largely by focusing on their people—hiring, training, keeping, and promoting the very best people they can get. Legendary Southwest Chairman Herb Kelleher built a business in part around ensuring that his people were *different* from typical airline employees— more engaged, fun, and fiercely loyal to the company.[11] The same can be said for the other firms above. Focusing on employees as a source of differentiation in marketing is usually a smart move, mainly because so many firms just can't seem to pull it off very well. The point is to remove much of the variability of customers' experiences with your service and instead provide a more dependable level of quality. Go into any Nordstrom and work with any of Nordstrom's sales associates and you will very likely experience the same high level of satisfaction with the service. The same is true for Ritz Carlton and any of the great service organizations.[12]

Goods, in general, tend to be much more standardized than services because, once a firm has invested in continuous process improvement and quality control in its manufacturing operations, products flow off the line with very little variation. With services, continual investment in training, retraining, and good management of people are required if variability is to be consistently low. It is in this area where the disciplines of marketing, operations, leadership, and human resource management probably have their closest intersection. What makes Ritz-Carlton great? A quick answer is: Its people. But what makes its people great? World-class operations, leadership, and HR practices. And the net effect for Ritz-Carlton is that its branding and market positioning are largely defined by its wonderful people and the way they handle each customer as a valued guest. For service firms, great marketing cannot take place without a strong overarching culture that values employees.

Perishability

If you schedule an appointment for a routine physical with your physician and then simply don't show up, the doctor loses the revenue from that time slot. That's **perishability**—the fact that a service can't be stored or saved up for future use.[13] Perishability is a major potential problem for service providers, and explains why, under the circumstances above, many physicians have a policy of charging the patient for the missed appointment. Ever wonder why an airline won't issue a refund or let you change your super-low-fare ticket after the door closes and the plane leaves without you? It's because the value of that empty seat—its ability to generate incremental revenue for the airline—dropped to zero when the door closed and the plane backed away from the gate.

Fluctuating demand is related to perishability of services.[14] Consider rental car firms such as Hertz, Avis, and the like in a city such as Orlando, which brings in both tourists and conventions. If demand were relatively constant, the rental car companies could keep the same basic inventory on the lot at all times. However, in the case of both individual vacationers and conventioneers, demand for cars varies considerably by season, and for the latter is driven by the size of the convention. The worst scenario is for the city to attract a huge convention and for the rental firms not to have sufficient cars available. No cars, no revenue for Hertz and Avis. Not to mention, the convention organizers would likely think twice before scheduling their event in Orlando again.

Because demand for most goods tends to be more stable and because they can generally be stored for use after purchase, this critical issue of synchronizing supply and demand is easier to deal with for goods than for services. Hertz and Avis don't want to maintain huge extra inventories of vehicles on off-peak periods; hence they might use price incentives to promote more rentals during those times. Or, they might literally move cars around—pulling in massive numbers of extra vehicles from other nearby markets such as Miami or Tampa to take care of high demand periods. One thing they know for sure is that if there are no cars on the lot, any opportunity for revenue perishes.

THE SERVICE-PROFIT CHAIN

In a now-famous *Harvard Business Review* article published in 1994, followed up by a book several years later, James Heskett and his colleagues proposed a formalization of linkages between employee and customer aspects of service delivery called the **service-profit chain.** Because of the inseparability and variability of services, employees play a critical role in their level of success. The service-profit chain, which is portrayed in Exhibit 13.2, is designed to help managers better understand the key linkages in a service delivery system that drive customer loyalty, revenue growth, and higher profits.

Internal Service Quality

This aspect of the service-profit chain includes elements of workplace design, job design, employee selection and development processes, employee rewards and

EXHIBIT 13.2 **The Service-Profit Chain**

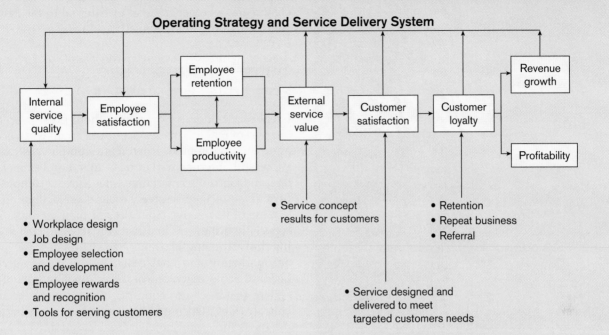

Operating Strategy and Service Delivery System

- Workplace design
- Job design
- Employee selection and development
- Employee rewards and recognition
- Tools for serving customers

- Service concept results for customers

- Service designed and delivered to meet targeted customers needs

- Retention
- Repeat business
- Referral

recognition approaches, and availability of effective tools for use by employees in serving customers. Considerable evidence exists that **internal marketing,** treating employees as customers and developing systems and benefits that satisfy their needs, is an essential element of internal service quality. Firms practicing internal service quality are **customer-centric**—they place the customer at the center of everything that takes place both inside and outside the firm. Firms that are customer-centric exhibit a high degree of customer orientation, which means they do the following:

1. Instill an organization-wide focus on understanding customers' requirements.
2. Generate an understanding of the marketplace and disseminate that knowledge to everyone in the firm.
3. Align system capabilities internally so that the organization can respond effectively with innovative, competitively differentiated, satisfaction-generating goods and services.

Elisa Scarletta, director of marketing communications at Applied Industrial Technologies, says that being customer-centric and continually improving customer satisfaction are a part of Applied's core values. "Talking to the customer regularly and interpreting that feedback is a fantastic tool for us," she says. "We take pride in improving our customer satisfaction, and the only way to know how we're doing is to ask the customer."[15]

In the context of internal service quality, it is assumed that a firm's culture, business philosophy, strategy, structure, and processes will be aligned in order to

We know what it takes to be a Tiger.

High performers distinguish themselves not only through the astuteness of their strategies, but also by their readiness to nimbly change course should circumstances dictate. That's one key finding from our extensive research on more than 500 of the world's most successful companies. For an in-depth look at our study of and experience with high performers, visit accenture.com/research

• Consulting • Technology • Outsourcing

accenture
High performance. Delivered.

Having Tiger Woods as a symbol for Accenture's consulting services has added a strong sense of pride to their organization, and of course, has also captured the attention of prospective customers.

create, communicate, and deliver value to customers. Finally, a focus on internal service quality implies that employees hold a **customer mind-set,** meaning that employees believe that understanding and satisfying customers, whether internal or external to the firm, is central to doing their job well.[16]

Satisfied, Productive, and Loyal Employees

Great service doesn't happen without great people. A big part of making the service-profit chain work is creating an environment in which all employees can be successful. Internal marketing is an integral element of this, and Harrah's Entertainment is a great example of a firm that almost obsessively focuses on facilitating the success of its people, regardless of their position, and especially if they are in direct contact with customers. It's not surprising Harrah's has such a zest for internal marketing and enablement of employee success. Leonard Schlesinger, one of the original authors of the service-profit chain concept, went on to become Harrah's CEO. During his tenure, the company became the most successful hotelier/casino in Las Vegas and continues to expand elsewhere as well. Harrah's stable of brands includes Caesars, Bally's, Paris, Rio, Flamingo, World Series of Poker, and others.[17]

To be executed effectively, internal marketing must include the following critical elements: competing for talent, offering an overall vision, training and developing people, stressing teamwork, modeling desired behaviors by managers, enabling employees to make their own decisions, measuring and rewarding great service performance, and knowing and reacting to employees' needs. Perhaps most important of all, employees must have a deep understanding of the brand and must be able to consistently articulate a clear, concise message to customers that reflects the firm's service strategy and branding.[18] At Harrah's, Schlesinger points with pride to the fact that everyone in the firm understands and can articulate its branding and values.

Jeanne Bliss, a former leader of customer service initiatives at Mazda Motor of America and now a managing partner at CustomerBLISS, cites the importance of articulating the brand values: "Be very clear about what you deliver to your customers—what is different and special about your product and service?" Rewarding employees for their customer service skills is also essential: "Develop and reward the skills for listening and understanding what the customer needs as the keys to good service," Bliss says.[19]

Greater Service Value for External Customers

There is strong evidence that attention to internal service quality and to employee satisfaction, productivity, and retention result in stronger value to external customers of a service. Remember that when the concept of value was introduced in Chapter 1 we discussed it as a ratio of what a customer gives versus what he or she gets in return from a purchase. Importantly, the customer inputs are not just financial—customers give up time, convenience, and other opportunities in making a purchase choice. Customers set their expectations for the value they hope to derive from a service based largely on the evidence provided by the marketer before the purchase. A fundamental rule in marketing is to not set customer expectations so high that they cannot be effectively met on a consistent basis.[20] This is because it is always better to underpromise and overdeliver than the reverse scenario. This concept is often called **customer expectations management.**

What does Southwest Airlines promise the flyer? The airline doesn't have traditional assigned seating, a first-class cabin, or even "real food" on flights. But it doesn't promise any of these things. In fact, it's built a business out of snubbing the other big airlines' approaches (and made a lot of money doing so). What Southwest *does* promise is a fun, on-time flight. So long as it can continue to deliver against that message, customers will likely continue to see Southwest as a great travel value.

Customer Satisfaction and Loyalty

In the service-profit chain, meeting or exceeding customer expectations leads to customer satisfaction, since the service was designed and delivered in a manner that added value. A strong correlation exists between satisfied and loyal customers. Loyalty sparks high **customer retention**—low propensity to consider switching to other providers—as well as repeat business, referrals, and **customer advocacy,** a willingness and ability on the part of a customer to participate in communicating the brand message to others within his or her sphere of influence.[21] Why do customers consider switching from one service provider to another? Reasons run the gamut from low utility to various forms of service failure to concerns about a firm's practices. A summary of causes of switching behavior is presented in Exhibit 13.3.

EXHIBIT 13.3	**Causes of Switching Behavior**

Pricing
- High price
- Price increases
- Unfair pricing
- Deceptive pricing

Inconvenience
- Location/hours
- Wait for appointment
- Wait for service

Core Service Failure
- Service mistakes
- Billing errors
- Service catastrophe

Service Encounter Failures
- Uncaring
- Impolite

- Unresponsive
- Unknowledgeable

Response to Service Failure
- Negative response
- No response
- Reluctant response

Competition
- Found better service

Ethical Problems
- Cheat
- Hard sell
- Unsafe
- Conflict of interest

Involuntary switching
- Customer moved
- Provider closed

Source: Susan M. Keaveney, "Customer Switching Behavior in Service Industries: An Exploratory Study," *Journal of Marketing,* April 1995, pp. 71–82. Reprinted with permission of the American Marketing Association.

Although it is strictly an online bank, ING Direct engages its customers in a way that encourages loyalty and advocacy. The bank's offerings are simple, straightforward, and easy to purchase. Beyond the basics, the company strives to position itself as an active ally to customers, offering specific, tangible payoffs that seem to resonate on an emotional level. The bank's formula for building loyalty has helped it generate over $47 billion of deposits in six years. ING Direct also explicitly encourages customers to promote the bank. It pays customers $10 for each referral and makes an initial deposit of $25 in the new account.[22]

Harrah's Entertainment understands the strong linkage between high customer satisfaction and loyalty and invests heavily in its most highly satisfied customers to ensure their loyalty and advocacy. Exhibit 13.4 portrays this relationship.

CRM and database marketing are key tools that allow Harrah's Entertainment, as well as any firm interested in increasing satisfaction and loyalty and improving retention, to use the concepts in Exhibit 13.4 to focus on serving the most profitable customers. For Harrah's, this approach manifests itself through the Total

EXHIBIT 13.4 | Focus on the Most Satisfied Customers

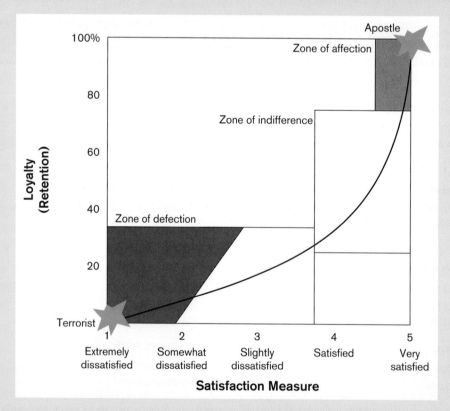

Source: Reprinted by permission of *Harvard Business Review,* from "Putting the Service-Profit Chain to Work", by James L. Heskett, Thomas O. Jones, Gary W. Loveman, W. Earl Sasser Jr., and Leonard A. Schlesinger, March/April 1994. Copyright © 1994 by the Harvard Business School Publishing Corporation, all rights reserved.

Rewards loyalty program. Harrah's has found that its ROI for customers in the "Zone of Affection" is considerably higher than in the other zones ("Indifference" and "Defection"). Very satisfied customer "apostles" are the ones that Harrah's wants to develop to the fullest extent to keep them coming back and spending money in its hotels and casinos. Research indicates that, although investing in indifferent customers to improve their satisfaction may yield some returns, only when customers reach the "Zone of Affection" do they truly maximize their profitability to the brand.

National Semiconductor Corp., a manufacturer of analog devices for electronics systems, has a sophisticated CRM system that tracks any kind of interest shown by a customer. "Once interest is shown, we check our database to determine whether that customer is an account holder," says Phil Gibson, vice president of corporate marketing at National Semiconductor. "If the account is known, the appropriate salesperson is notified. If the account is new, we begin a filtering process whereby that account is qualified. If the account is found to be of interest, it is delegated to a direct salesperson or delegated to distribution with guidelines on what to do with this customer."[23]

Revenue and Profit Growth

In the context of Exhibit 13.4, customers that are "satisfied" and "very satisfied" are identified through Harrah's Total Rewards loyalty program cards, which they use at hotel check-in, in slot machines, and at all gaming tables. They truly are the apple of the eye of Harrah's employees while they are on the property, and more broadly they represent the total focus of Harrah's marketing efforts—largely through direct marketing approaches with customized offers. Like slots? You'll get an invitation to a slot tournament. Poker's your thing? Look for an invitation to a poker tournament. It's not that Harrah's is disinterested in or doesn't want the money of the other customers, but it has learned from its research that customers in the "Zone of Affection" spend considerably more money and provide a substantially greater return on customer investment than others.[24]

Harrah's embraces customer satisfaction measurement; and it segments markets based on satisfaction score groups. The ultimate Harrah's customer is the "apostle"—highly satisfied, fiercely loyal, a frequent Harrah's guest who serves as a strong advocate for the Harrah's experience to friends and acquaintances. For the service-profit chain to provide insight for marketing managers into how to best develop and execute service strategies, a variety of metrics must be in place with measures taken continually. In fact, all aspects of the chain—from internal service quality to employee issues to value to satisfaction and loyalty to financial performance—must be quantified and used for marketing management decision making. Chapter 19 provides a detailed treatment of marketing metrics, and many of the measures developed and exemplified in that chapter relate directly to executing the service-profit chain.

Ohio Transmission & Pump Co., a distributor of pump, pneumatic, electrical, and mechanical devices, conducts surveys and interviews to gauge customer satisfaction. "Certainly, customer satisfaction is an important part of our strategy for all of the obvious reasons," says Philip Derrow, president and CEO of OTP. "However, the real challenge is converting the ambiguous emotion of 'satisfaction' into the concrete business value of earned customer loyalty." Too often, these terms are used interchangeably, though from an ROI point of view, they are very different. "Satisfaction is defined by what people say; loyalty is defined by what they do," Derrow says.[25]

SERVICE ATTRIBUTES

So far we've looked at why service is at the core of firm success, identified characteristics of services, and gained an understanding of the linkages in the service-profit chain. We're now ready to gain a better understanding of how services fit within the broader context of different types of offerings. A useful way to approach answering this question is through consideration of a continuum of goods and services that range from easy to evaluate to difficult to evaluate based on three major types of attributes relevant to any offering: search attributes, experience attributes, and credence attributes. Exhibit 13.5 illustrates exemplar goods and services across a continuum of these attributes.

Search Attributes

Depending on the type of offering, consumers may engage in a search for various alternative products to find the one that most closely meets their decision criteria for purchase. With physical goods, such comparison is usually relatively simple as there are many **search attributes,** which are aspects of an offering that are physically observable before consumption. For example, a shopper can compare the picture quality, price, and warranty of several high-definition televisions right on the Best Buy or Circuit City showroom floor. Because of the intangibility aspect of services, however, it is much more difficult to do such direct comparisons during a search process. Try comparing the performance of one mutual fund over another; the exercise gives new meaning to the old phrase "comparing apples and oranges." The bottom line is that services are low in search qualities because it is difficult to evaluate many aspects of them before purchase. Usually the customer doesn't truly know how the service performs until *after* the sale—that's the inseparability aspect of services.[26]

| **EXHIBIT 13.5** | **Continuum of Evaluation for Different Types of Offerings** |

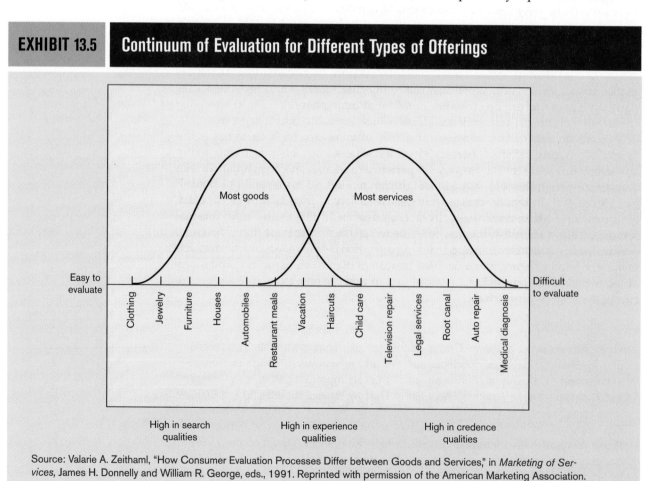

Source: Valarie A. Zeithaml, "How Consumer Evaluation Processes Differ between Goods and Services," in *Marketing of Services*, James H. Donnelly and William R. George, eds., 1991. Reprinted with permission of the American Marketing Association.

Experience Attributes

Experience attributes are aspects of an offering that can be evaluated only during or after consumption. Many services fit this category, including restaurants, vacations, hair cuts, and child care. They tend to have both tangible and intangible aspects; for example, a dining out experience includes a physical good, the meal, as well as the service portion. Based on the level to which customer expectations were met, a decision will be made about whether or not to repeat the purchase another time.[27]

Credence Attributes

In many cases, a customer cannot make a reasonable evaluation of the quality of a service even after use. Services such as television repair, legal services, dentistry, auto repair, and medical services require specialized training to deliver. The customer may only know the desired end state—a car that runs or a pretty new crown molar. To assess these **credence attributes** would require customers to have expertise not generally shared by the public. As such, many providers of services in this category rely on professional certifications or degrees to convey a level of trust to the purchaser. Thus, services at this end of the continuum are often referred to as **professional services**—providers such as doctors, lawyers, accountants, even plumbers. They typically have industry or trade groups that self-regulate the quality of their services and serve as a clearinghouse for information and referrals.

HELLO LUXURY. MEET CONVENIENCE.

GRAND HYATT DFW — TERMINAL D.

Luxury has never been this convenient. Step out of the terminal in to a world of first-class comforts at Dallas/Ft. Worth's "Best Luxury Hotel," as voted by TripAdvisor.com. Our guests enjoy countless amenities, including the Hyatt Grand Bed," 32" flat-panel TVs, soaking tubs, 24-hour fitness center, spa treatments and unique culinary experiences such as iTaste and Virtual Menu. Feel the Hyatt Touch." For reservations, call 972 973 1234. Visit grandhyattdfw.com.

The new Grand Hyatt DFW Airport portrays imagery that is very different from stereotypical airport hotels—such a service is heavy in experience attributes.

One interesting professional service for consideration is higher education. College business courses are high in credence attributes because of the difficulty in evaluating their real impact until much later, often after a student is able to apply knowledge and skills gained to a particular job situation. The perennial question in business education is, "Who is the customer?" One approach frames the companies that hire a business school's students as the primary customer, which would seem to imply the students are a product of the business school rather than its customer. Employing a marketing metaphor, this approach puts the professor in the role of product development and branding—positioning the student for success in the marketplace. This overall approach may be appropriate because business education is high in credence attributes. Understandably, however, all students want to be treated as "customers" too.

Like higher education, physicians and professional health care service providers in general exhibit some unique characteristics. Ethical Dimension 13 provides an example of one challenging issue in modern health care—patients who seek treatments outside the United States that are banned domestically.

Importance of Understanding Service Attributes

Because services tend to exhibit high experience and credence attributes, marketing strategies must be developed that consider the implications of these characteristics. As we've discussed, services customers tend to take their cues on what to purchase from whatever evidence they can gather to make up for the lack of ability to try the service beforehand. Word-of-mouth referrals, physical cues such as the ambience of the physical location, functionality of the Web site, and professionalism of the employees operate as a surrogate for trial. Because of the higher risk involved in purchasing a service versus a good, once a customer begins to have a positive experience with a service provider and build a relationship with

The Service of Medicine–Consumers' Global Search for a Cure

One of the most important global service industries is the delivery of health care. In the United States, for example, health care represents 16 percent of GDP, totaling nearly $2 trillion based on recent data. Despite the United States having an extensive health care system, the search for medical help by U.S. citizens in need has become a *global* effort. Each country has its own medical testing policies and protocols, which mean drugs and medical procedures not permitted in one country might be available in another country. For example, patients often purchase drugs in Canada and Mexico that are not available in the United States and travel to Europe for medical procedures that are not authorized to be performed here.

One medical issue, stem cell medicine, has generated serious political and social debate around the world. Medical researchers have reported significant benefits using stem cells across a wide range of medical problems. Although stem cells can be obtained from several sources, it is the use of embryonic stem cells taken from a fetus that causes significant moral concern for some. At present, stem cell research and the use of stem cells in therapy is more limited in the United States than other parts of the world such as Europe and Asia where it is much more widely accepted and available.

China has been especially aggressive in allowing stem cell medical therapy on humans, a procedure that is currently not available in the United States. Patients can seek treatment in Chinese clinics across a broad spectrum of medical problems such as severe spinal injuries, ataxia, cerebral palsy, and multiple sclerosis. In many cases, their U.S. doctors point out that the procedures have not been properly tested and discount the medical claims reported by the Chinese clinics. But patients who do make the trip to China feel they have exhausted their medical options in the United States, see little hope in continuing their current treatments, and are looking for other options. The extensive U.S. medical research and testing protocols mean that many of these procedures are probably years away from approval and will not benefit patients that are currently in need.

The average stem cell treatment in China costs $17,000, a fee obviously not covered by medical insurance. Further compounding the problem is the short-term beneficial nature of the treatments, which means therapy must likely be repeated for continued relief. In China, patients receive a variety of other treatment therapies including physical therapy, acupuncture, massage, and electrical stimulation in addition to the stem cell treatment. This makes isolating the benefits of the stem cell portion of the treatment very difficult.[28]

Ethical Perspective

1. **U.S. Physician:** Many doctors in the United States cite a lack of valid research and no evidence of long-term health benefits related to Chinese stem cell therapy. At the same time, patients who go to China often report benefits from the treatment. Once a patient has exhausted existing treatments in the United States, should a doctor recommend the patient consider Chinese stem cell treatment?

2. **U.S. Patient:** As a patient, would you consider traveling to China for stem cell therapy? If so, would you wait until all U.S. treatments had been exhausted?

the firm, customer loyalty to services tends to be greater than loyalty to goods. Of course, the flip side of that for the marketing manager is that if your competitor offers great service and people as a key differentiator, and you can't match it, it can be very difficult to get customers to switch to or even try a new provider.[29]

Working with a home builder can be a very scary experience. It's hard to know ahead of time if the builder will construct a good house. That's why potential customers rely on word-of-mouth recommendations from friends or relatives who have had first-hand experience. Pulte Homes is one of the top builders in the nation when it comes to customer satisfaction. That customer satisfaction brings in new customers. The average home builder has 7.4 percent of its prospects referred by family members or friends. Pulte, however, reported that more than 40 percent of its prospects come from referrals. A national study showed that the conversion rate for referred prospects nationally is double that of marketed prospects over a six-month period. Undoubtedly, a high rate of referrals is one of the most valuable assets a builder can have.[30]

SERVICE QUALITY

Earlier we mentioned the importance of managing customer expectations—the notion that underpromising and overdelivering is powerful because it contributes to a high level of customer satisfaction. Exceeding customer expectations is often referred to as **customer delight,** which has been shown to correlate highly with loyalty and high return on customer investment.[31] Firms practicing great service often build in **delightful surprises** for their customers as part of their service experience—the warm chocolate chip cookie you get at Doubletree on every stay was originally conceived as a delightful surprise, a fairly inexpensive way to make a memorable impact on weary travelers. Although Doubletree patrons have now come to expect their cookie, this little extra has become a part of the firm's branding and image, and customer surveys regularly indicate it is one of the most-loved aspects of the Doubletree experience.

Just what is service quality? In many respects, **service quality** represents a formalization of the measurement of customer expectations of a service compared to perceptions of actual service performance. The playing field for service quality is the **service encounter,** which is the period during which a customer interacts in any way with a service provider. This can be in person, by phone, or through other electronic means. While much of the actual service delivery might occur behind the curtain—consider the tax preparer who works on your IRS return or the travel agent who spends hours pulling together your extreme sport trip to Reykjavík—customer evaluations of a service tend to be based on the behaviors of the service provider and the accompanying physical surroundings during the service encounter itself. This is why the face-to-face time between customer and service provider is often called the **moment of truth.** Most customer judgments take place at that moment.[32]

More and more professional associations such as the American Academy of Dermatology are marketing themselves and their members' services directly to end user consumers.

Gap Analysis

Review the Gap Model of Service Quality, presented in Exhibit 13.6. The basis of the **gap model** is the identification and measurement of differences in five key areas of the service delivery process. Notice how the model is divided by a horizontal line, with the area below the line representing the provider side of the service encounter and the area above the line representing the customer side. For marketing managers, ongoing use of the gap model to identify emerging problems in service delivery is an important way to ensure service quality.

Let's take a closer look at each of the gaps. To illustrate the power of the analysis, we will develop a threaded example involving Outback Steakhouse. From a surface viewpoint, most people might assume that the founders of Outback—the original restaurant was in Tampa, Florida—built their differentiation primarily on the Australian theme and hearty portions at moderate prices. However, that is only part of their original success formula. From the beginning, Outback's founders relied heavily on its service delivery system to set it apart from other mid-priced, family-style restaurants. Their success is undeniable, with Outback units consistently leading their segment of the industry in customer turns per table, revenue and profit per square foot, and the all-important metrics of customer satisfaction. Using a service-profit chain approach to the business, Outback's

EXHIBIT 13.6 **Gap Model of Service Quality**

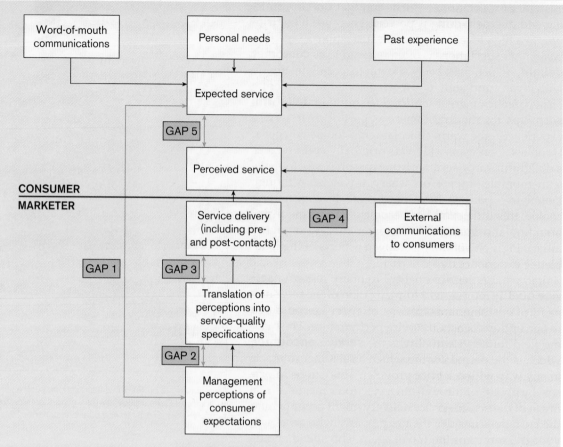

Source: A. Parasuraman, Valarie A. Zeithaml, and Leonard L. Berry, "A Conceptual Model of Service Quality and Its Implications for Future Research," *Journal of Marketing*, Fall 1985, pp. 41–50. Reprinted with permission of the American Marketing Association.

founders focused strongly on its people, assuring that every store manager is a proprietor/owner of the business. Servers, even college students, tend to stay much longer than the industry average due to higher tips generated by more rapid table turnover.[33]

Gap 1: Management's Perceptions of Customer Service Expectations versus Actual Customer Expectations of Service

In Chapter 5 you learned about the importance of ongoing, well-executed market research to provide input for marketing management decision making. Gap 1 is where a lack of the right customer data can wreck havoc on service delivery. Unfortunately, firms all too often make unfounded assumptions about customers' wants and needs and translate them into product offerings. Then management is surprised when new products fail or customers begin to switch to other providers.

Outback Steakhouse was an early leader in providing convenient phone-ahead curbside service for customer pickup. Although it varies by location, some stores do as much as 15 to 20 percent of their revenue in customer takeout. This is especially profitable because it requires little extra server labor to fill these pickup orders. How did Outback know to add this new service? Not surprisingly, it was through market research in the 1990s that showed customers were increasingly disappointed with traditional fast-food drive-throughs and were willing to pay more for a quality, convenient meal they could enjoy at home. Convenience and time utility are two major drivers of busy young professional families today, which just happens to be Outback's primary target market.[34]

Gap 2: Management's Perceptions of Customer Service Expectations versus the Actual Service Quality Specifications Developed

In Gap 2, management may or may not accurately perceive actual customer expectations of service, but regardless builds an aspect of the service delivery system that does not meet customer wants and needs. A perfect example of this would be if Outback had designed its curbside carryout system differently. Customers grabbing takeout after work do not want to park, get out of the car, and go into the restaurant to pick up the food. Almost all of Outback's competitors originally designed takeout that way. By designing the system as a curbside pickup in front of the store, Outback not only accurately met customer expectations of service but also designed service delivery specifications to match.

Gap 3: Actual Service Quality Specifications versus Actual Service Delivery

Interestingly, unlike the previous two gaps, this one has no element of perception—this gap strictly asks whether the service is provided in the manner intended. As such, when there is a negative gap at Gap 3, it nearly always points to management and employees simply not getting the job done. This could be due to vague performance standards, poor training, or ineffective monitoring by management.

Like many firms, Outback uses teamwork to enhance its service delivery system. Ever notice that more than one person makes contact with you at your table, asks how you are doing, brings food or drink, and so forth? To make the curbside pickup system work like clockwork, employees from the phone order-taker to the cooks to the car-runner must be in sync. If cars back up, employees are trained to go down the line to make contact, provide estimated remaining wait times, and even handle payment so that when the food does come out the customer can immediately depart. You may wait a while to get your table at an Outback restaurant on a peak evening (if it's a nice night you can sit outside and sip a beverage), but once you're seated the restaurant has aggressive standards for wait times for getting your meal at the table. When these wait times are significantly exceeded, the employees are trained to apologize, not offer lame excuses, and then offer something extra like a free dessert or a coupon for a free Bloomin' Onion next time.

This process is called **service recovery** and is actually a very strategic aspect of marketing management. Much research in services marketing has shown that **service failure,** when properly handled through service recovery, does not necessarily impact customer satisfaction, loyalty, or retention unless service failures become habitual.[35] All firms employing service as a marketing strategy must plan ahead for the eventuality of service failures and train employees to properly execute service recovery.

Sometimes a service failure can be quite severe, as was the case in February 2007 when JetBlue Airways found itself the victim of a major winter storm at New York's JFK airport. Word quickly spread via media stories, blogs, and word-of-mouth that many hundreds of JetBlue passengers were left stranded on airplanes that had pulled away from their gates but were not allowed to take off or return to the gate for up to 12 hours. By the next day, then-CEO David Neeleman had declared publicly that the airline had suffered an operational meltdown and that a series of bad decisions compounded with an already bad situation to make it even worse.[36]

Is service recovery even possible given the magnitude of the service failure that JetBlue's customers experienced at JFK? Neeleman certainly can't be faulted for lack of trying. Immediately after the incident he sent out an apology letter electronically to every customer in the company's database, backed up by a video message posted on the company Web site. This was followed by a new JetBlue Airways Customer Bill of Rights, which received press for being industry-leading. Neeleman's letter and the bill of rights are presented in Exhibits 13.7 and 13.8. Apparently

EXHIBIT 13.7 | **JetBlue Airways Service Recovery Letter**

jetBlue
AIRWAYS

An Apology from JetBlue Airways

Dear JetBlue Customers,

We are sorry and embarrassed. But most of all, we are deeply sorry.

Last week was the worst operational week in Jet Blue's seven year history. Following the severe winter ice storm in the Northeast, we subjected our customers to unacceptable delays, flight cancellations, lost baggage, and other major inconveniences. The storm disrupted the movement of aircraft, and, more importantly, disrupted the movement of JetBlue's pilot and inflight crewmembers who were depending on those planes to get them to the airports where they were scheduled to serve you. With the busy President's Day weekend upon us, rebooking opportunities were scarce and hold times at 1-800-JETBLUE were unacceptably long or not even available, further hindering our recovery efforts.

Words cannot express how truly sorry we are for the anxiety, furstration and inconvenience that we caused. This is especially saddening because JetBlue was founded on the promise of bringing humanity back to air travel and making the experience of flying happier and easier for everyone who chooses to fly with us. We know we failed to deliver on this promise last week.

We are committed to you, our valued customers, and are taking immediate corrective steps to regain your confidence in us. We have begun putting a comprehensive plan in place to provide better and more timely information to you, more tools and resources for our crewmembers and improved procedures for handling operational difficulties in the future. We are confident, as a result of these actions, that JetBlue will emerge as a more reliable and even more customer responsive airline than ever before.

Most importantly, we have published the JetBlue Airways Customer Bill of Rights—our official commitment to you of how we will handle operational interruptions going forward including details of compensation. I have a video message to share with you about this industry leading action.

You deserved better—a lot better—from us last week. Nothing is more important than regaining your trust and all of us here hope you will give us the opportunity to welcome you onboard again soon adn provide you the positive JetBlue Experience you have come to expect from us.

Sincerely,

David Neeleman
Founder and CEO
JetBlue Airways

JETBLUE AIRWAYS CUSTOMER BILL OF RIGHTS

Courtesy of JetBlue Airways.

JetBlue's customers believe this service recovery was appropriate and effective. JetBlue's customer ratings of quality have continued to be among the highest in the industry, ranking No. 2 overall in 2006 and 2007.[37]

Any airline will face service gaps, such as from a flight delay or lost luggage. What distinguishes a company is how it handles that service failure. To improve the speed of its service recovery, British Airways implemented a new way to compensate customers who experience a service failure. BA launched a "compensation card." BA employees can load that card with funds right at the counter, and the card is immediately usable at thousands of ATM or point-of-sale (POS) locations worldwide.[38]

| EXHIBIT 13.8 | JetBlue Airways Customer Bill of Rights |

JetBlue Airways Customer Bill of Rights

JetBlue Airways exists to provide superior service in every aspect of our customer's air travel experience. In order to reaffirm this commitment, we set forth this Bill of Rights for our customers. These Rights will always be subject to the highest level of safety and security for our customers and crewmembers.

INFORMATIONS

JetBlue will notify customers of the following:
- Delays prior to scheduled departure
- Cancellations and their cause
- Diversions and their cause

CANCELLATIONS

All customers whose flight is cancelled by JetBlue will, at the customer's option, receive a full refund or re-accommodation on a future JetBlue flight at no additional change or fare. If JetBlue cancels a flight within 12 hours of scheduled departure and the cancellation is due to a Controllable Irregularity, JetBlue will also provide the customer with a Voucher valid for future travel on JetBlue in the amount paid to JetBlue for the customer's roundtrip.

DEPARTURE DELAYS

1. Customers whose flight is delayed prior to scheduled departure for 1–2 hours due to a Controllable Irregularity are entitled to a $25 Voucher good for future travel on JetBlue.
2. Customers whose flight is delayed prior to scheduled departure for 2–4 hours due to a Controllable Irregularity are entitled to a $50 Voucher good for future travel on JetBlue.
3. Customers whose flight is delayed prior to scheduled departure for 4–6 hours due to a Controllable Irregularity are entitled to a Voucher good for future travel on JetBlue in the amount paid by the customer for the one-way trip.
4. Customers whose flight is delayed prior to scheduled departure for more than 6 hours due to a Controllable Irregularity are entitled to a Voucher good for future travel on JetBlue in the amount paid by the customer for the roundtrip.

OVERBOOKINGS

Customers who are involuntarily denied boarding shall receive $1,000.

GROUND DELAYS

For customers who experience a Ground Delay for more than 5 hours, JetBlue will take necessary action so that customers may deplane. JetBlue will also provide customers experiencing a Ground Delay with food and drink, access to restrooms and, as necessary, medical treatment.

Arrivals:

1. Customers who experience a Ground Delay of Arrival for 30–60 minutes are entitled to a $25 Voucher good for future travel on JetBlue.
2. Customers who experience a Ground Delay of Arrival for 1–2 hours are entitled to a $100 Voucher good for future travel on JetBlue.
3. Customers who experience a Ground Delay of Arrival for 2–3 hours are entitled to a Voucher good for future travel on JetBlue in the amount paid by the customer for the one-way trip.
4. Customers who experience a Ground Delay of Arrival for more than 3 hours are entitled to a Voucher good for future travel on JetBlue in the amount paid by th customer for the roundtrip.

Departures:

1. Customers who experience a Ground Delay on Departure for 3–4 hours are entitled to a $100 Voucher good for future travel on JetBlue.
2. Customers who experience a Ground Delay on Departure for more than 4 hours are entitled to a Voucher good for future travel on JetBlue in the amount paid by the customer for the roundtrip.

JetBlue Airways
Forest Hills Support Center
118-29 Queens Blvd
Forest Hills, NY 11375

1-800-JETBLUE   1-800-538-2583   jetblue.com

*These Rights are subject to JetBlue's Contract of Carriage and, as applicable, the operational control of the flight crew.
This document is representative of what JetBlue to incorporate into its Contract of Carriage, the legal binding document between JetBlue and its customers.

Courtesy of JetBlue Airways.

Gap 4: Actual Service Delivery versus What the Firm Communicates It Delivers

This gap fundamentally represents customer expectations management through marketing communications. Chapters 17 and 18 will familiarize you with the various forms of marketing communication including advertising, sales promotion, public relations, personal selling, and direct marketing. The messages the marketing manager puts out through these communication vehicles are in large measure what sets the expectations for the customer. Thus, deceptive advertising, overly zealous sales pitches, and coupon promotions backed by too little stock to handle demand all create a negative gap at Gap 4. In the case of Outback's curbside pickup, although it has done some advertising over the years, most of Outback's media ads focus more on special occasions and the fun theme of the restaurant. Because much of Outback's product is the experience provided the diner inside

EXHIBIT 13.9 | **Example Attributes**

1. Healthy food options.
2. Convenient locations.
3. Quick to-go pickup outside.
4. Clean restrooms.
5. Variety of menu items.
6. Friendly and courteous staff.
7. Children's food choices.
8. Fun ambience.
9. Accurate order fulfillment.
10. Speed of service.
11. Senior discounts.
12. Accommodating hours of operation.
13. Children's play area.
14. Innovative new menu items.

Customers would likely be surveyed on the attributes with questions such as the following, using an appropriate rating scale:

Rate the importance of each attribute to your decision to dine at _____ restaurant.
Rate how well _____ restaurant provides each attribute.

the restaurant, it has allowed the pickup business to grow more through word-of-mouth and in-store signage. Outback has not set any unrealistic expectations about its curbside takeout via its marketing communications.

Gap 5: Perceived Service by Customers versus Actual Customer Expectations of Service

Finally, Gap 5 represents the core issue of expectations versus perceptions and is the only gap that occurs exclusively in the customer's space. This is the gap between the service a customer expects to receive and the customer's perceptions of the level of service actually received. The score for this gap, which can be positive or negative, is the manifestation of a firm's customer expectations management strategy and the efficacy of its service delivery system.[39] For Outback Steakhouse, as well as most other firms, these scores are a direct flow-through into customer satisfaction measurement. Occasionally after eating at Outback, you might get a special receipt that has a toll-free number to call at Outback to answer a brief telephone questionnaire about your service encounter. Outback might offer some free food for completing the survey by providing you with an activation number. Almost always such survey research efforts are aimed at measuring importance scores (how important various aspects of a service are to the customer) versus actual performance scores (how well did we do on delivering against these service aspects during your last service encounter with us).

To provide an example of Gap 5 in practice, Exhibit 13.9 lists 14 hypothetical attributes that a restaurant like Outback might consider for analysis in terms of customer perceptions of their importance and Outback's performance. Then, Exhibit 13.10 portrays a matrix based on a hypothetical analysis of importance versus performance data for those 14 attributes, showing areas where the restaurant can invest in service improvement, areas where it needs to simply keep up the current service, areas of low priority

EXHIBIT 13.10 | **Importance–Performance Analysis Matrix**

for attention, and areas where too much emphasis is being placed on service aspects. One other analysis could be easily added—comparative matrices for several of Outback's closest competitors so the chain can easily see how well the competition is doing in delivering against the same attributes. Such analytical approaches are invaluable in allowing marketing managers to know how to best invest in service quality.

SERVQUAL: A Multiple Item Scale to Measure Service Quality

Marketers didn't separate out services for separate study from goods until the early 1980s. The movement toward a focus on service as a core differentiator was driven, in part, by a team of professors: Leonard Berry, Valarie Zeithaml, and A. Parasuraman. Much of their work resulted in the gap analysis approach described in the prior section.[40] But another important aspect of their research was determining what service quality really means from the perspective of customers. Their work uncovered five **dimensions of service quality,** illustrated by Exhibit 13.11 and described below.

Tangibles

Tangibles are the physical evidence of a service or the observable aspects that help customers form advance opinions about the service despite its general intangibility. Examples of tangibles include appearance of service providers, Web site, marketing communications materials, the ambience and look of the office or retail store. Such tangibles send cues to the customer about the quality of the service.

Reliability

Reliability is the ability to provide service dependably and accurately and thus to deliver what was promised. Reliability means performing the service right the first time and every time. Research has consistently demonstrated that reliability tends to be one of the most important aspects of service quality.

Responsiveness

Responsiveness is the willingness and ability to provide prompt service and to respond quickly to customer requests. Customers often complain about a lack of responsiveness on the part of service providers. Service providers exhibit poor responsiveness when they create difficulty making contact, exhibit poor follow-up, make excuses for poor service, and generally act as though they are doing the customer a favor.

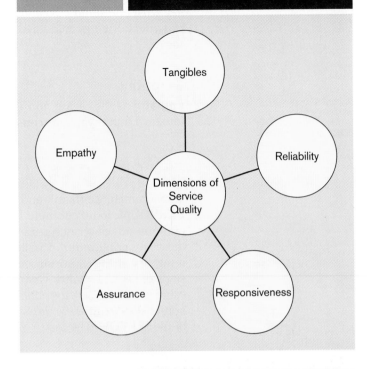

The effective use of SERVQUAL and gap analysis requires ongoing data collection from users. Firms such as MindField offer attractive online data collection options through Internet consumer panels.

Caterpillar sells heavy equipment. You've seen its familiar yellow bulldozers and trucks on construction sites. Caterpillar customers rely on the equipment to keep working—if a bulldozer breaks, all work comes to a halt. That's why Caterpillar differentiates itself through fast, responsive service. Caterpillar will ship spare parts to a customer anywhere in the world, from Alaska to Timbuktu, in just 24 hours.[41]

Assurance

Assurance is the knowledge and courtesy of employees, and the ability to convey trust and build a customer's confidence in the quality of the service. Service providers often provide assurance primarily through their own competence in the job.

Empathy

Empathy is the caring and individual attention a service provider gives to customers. Empathy means considering things from the customer's point of view.

The SERVQUAL Instrument

Parasuraman, Zeithaml, and Berry developed a measurement instrument called **SERVQUAL** to reflect these five dimensions.[42] The scale has been applied in tens of thousands of service settings across all types of industries. It can be adapted to most any application in which the marketing manager wishes to gain customer input about the importance and performance of a firm against the five dimensions of service quality. Companies track SERVQUAL scores over time to understand how their service quality is tracking so that marketing managers can create approaches to improve areas as needed.[43] Exhibit 13.12 provides a generic version of the SERVQUAL scale.

EXHIBIT 13.12	Generic SERVQUAL Instrument for XYZ Company

Please circle the number that best corresponds with your view related to XYZ.

1. XYZ has modern looking equipment.

Strongly disagree			Neither agree nor disagree			Strongly agree
1	2	3	4	5	6	7

2. The physical facilities at XYZ are visually appealing.

Strongly disagree			Neither agree nor disagree			Strongly agree
1	2	3	4	5	6	7

3. Employees at XYZ appear professionally dressed.

Strongly disagree			Neither agree nor disagree			Strongly agree
1	2	3	4	5	6	7

4. Materials associated with XYZ (Web site, promotional brochures, service tracking documents, invoices, etc.) are visually appealing.

Strongly disagree			Neither agree nor disagree			Strongly agree
1	2	3	4	5	6	7

(continued)

EXHIBIT 13.12 **Generic SERVQUAL Instrument for XYZ Company [continued]**

5. When employees at XYZ promise to do something by a certain time, they do so.

Strongly disagree			Neither agree nor disagree			Strongly agree
1	2	3	4	5	6	7

6. When a customer has a problem, employees at XYZ show a sincere interest in solving it.

Strongly disagree			Neither agree nor disagree			Strongly agree
1	2	3	4	5	6	7

7. XYZ employees perform the service right the first time.

Strongly disagree			Neither agree nor disagree			Strongly agree
1	2	3	4	5	6	7

8. XYZ employees provide their services at the time they promise to do so.

Strongly disagree			Neither agree nor disagree			Strongly agree
1	2	3	4	5	6	7

9. XYZ insists on error-free records.

Strongly disagree			Neither agree nor disagree			Strongly agree
1	2	3	4	5	6	7

10. Employees at XYZ tell you exactly when services will be performed.

Strongly disagree			Neither agree nor disagree			Strongly agree
1	2	3	4	5	6	7

11. Employees at XYZ give prompt service to you.

Strongly disagree			Neither agree nor disagree			Strongly agree
1	2	3	4	5	6	7

12. Employees at XYZ are always willing to help you.

Strongly disagree			Neither agree nor disagree			Strongly agree
1	2	3	4	5	6	7

13. Employees at XYZ are never too busy to respond to your requests.

Strongly disagree			Neither agree nor disagree			Strongly agree
1	2	3	4	5	6	7

(continued)

14. The behavior of employees at XYZ instills confidence from you.

Strongly disagree			Neither agree nor disagree			Strongly agree
1	2	3	4	5	6	7

15. You feel safe in your transactions with XYZ.

Strongly disagree			Neither agree nor disagree			Strongly agree
1	2	3	4	5	6	7

16. Employees at XYZ are consistently courteous to you.

Strongly disagree			Neither agree nor disagree			Strongly agree
1	2	3	4	5	6	7

17. Employees at XYZ have the knowledge to answer your questions.

Strongly disagree			Neither agree nor disagree			Strongly agree
1	2	3	4	5	6	7

18. XYZ employees give you individual attention.

Strongly disagree			Neither agree nor disagree			Strongly agree
1	2	3	4	5	6	7

19. XYZ has operating hours convenient to all its customers.

Strongly disagree			Neither agree nor disagree			Strongly agree
1	2	3	4	5	6	7

20. XYZ has employees who give you personal attention.

Strongly disagree			Neither agree nor disagree			Strongly agree
1	2	3	4	5	6	7

21. XYZ employees have your best interests at heart.

Strongly disagree			Neither agree nor disagree			Strongly agree
1	2	3	4	5	6	7

22. XYZ employees understand your needs.

Strongly disagree			Neither agree nor disagree			Strongly agree
1	2	3	4	5	6	7

Key to the instrument by SERVQUAL dimension: Tangibles = Questions 1–4; Reliability = Questions 5–9; Responsiveness = Questions 10–13; Assurance = Questions 14–17; Empathy = Questions 18–22.

SERVICE BLUEPRINTS

Earlier in the chapter, you read that from its inception Outback Steakhouse conceived of its service delivery system as an important source of differentiation in its positioning against other mid-priced family restaurants. How does a marketing manager conceive of such a system, lay it out, and then implement it so that everyone in the firm can follow it and play their part? The answer is through **service blueprints,** which borrows concepts from manufacturing and operations management to actually map out (likely through the use of computer software) a complete pictorial design and flow chart of all the activities from the first customer contact to the actual delivery of the service.

A simple example of a service blueprint for a floral delivery service is mapped out in Exhibit 13.13.

Note in tracking through the floral delivery service blueprint that activities are divided between those above the **line of visibility** (or those activities directly involving the customer that the customer sees) and those below the line of visibility to the customer (in this case, backstage operations and processing activities). The "moments of truth" we discussed earlier occur above the line of visibility.

> Kim Shacklett, vice president of call centers for J&L Industrial Supply, believes that good "invisible" services are essential because they impact the service the customer does experience. She advises that back-office operations be as efficient as possible. "Look hard at your internal processes," she says. "Many times there are wasted, non-value-added steps that delay outcomes." Customers will feel those delays directly, so having good procedures behind the scenes will help create a good service experience.[44]

A service blueprint is invaluable as a tool for marketing managers, especially for service encounters that are more complex than floral delivery, restaurants, and the like. First, the mere creation of the document serves to uncover potential bottlenecks in the service delivery system before it goes operational. Second, it represents a tremendous training device for employees involved in service delivery. Especially in a teamwork environment such as Outback Steakhouse where servers, cooks, and bartenders are so dependent on each other's performance to maximize the customer's positive experience overall, familiarizing each person involved in service delivery

---

EXHIBIT 13.13   Service Blueprint for Floral Delivery

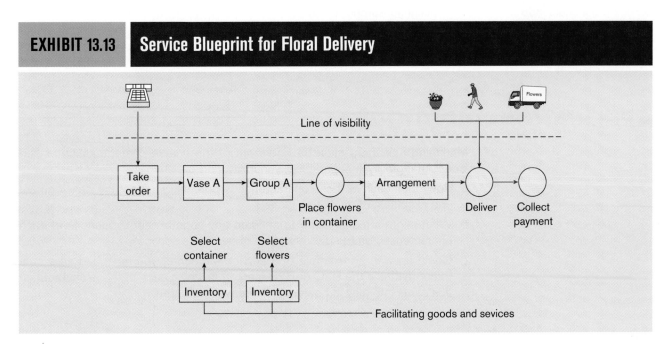

with exactly how his or her role fits into the entire system helps everyone take on a customer mind-set—even employees who ordinarily don't directly interface with the external customers such as the cooks.[45] Finally, using a service blueprint provides managers with an important way to integrate service topics into the performance evaluation process for all employees. Smart firms that rely on service for differentiation such as Outback, Ritz-Carlton, and Southwest Airlines provide incentives to their people who consistently contribute to the delivery of great service.

SUMMARY

In today's competitive marketplace, service is an important source of differentiation. But services have unique characteristics that must be understood as well as attributes that make services quite different from goods. An important concept for marketing managers to master is the service-profit chain, which provides a framework for linking elements of the service delivery system that drive customer loyalty, revenue growth, and higher profits. Key tools for establishing and measuring effective service include gap analysis, SERVQUAL, and service blueprints.

KEY TERMS

service 354
service economy 354
service sector 354
new dominant logic
  for marketing 354
intangibility 355
inseparability 357
variability 357
perishability 358
fluctuating demand 358
service-profit chain 358
internal marketing 359
customer-centric 359

customer mind-set 360
customer expectations
  management 361
customer retention 361
customer advocacy 361
search attributes 364
experience attributes 365
credence attributes 365
professional services 365
customer delight 367
delightful surprises 367
service quality 367
service encounter 367

moment of truth 367
gap model 367
service recovery 369
service failure 369
dimensions of service quality 373
tangibles 373
reliability 373
responsiveness 373
assurance 374
empathy 374
SERVQUAL 374
service blueprints 377
line of visibility 377

APPLICATION QUESTIONS

1. Marketing managers must be cognizant of the unique characteristics of services: intangibility, inseparability, variability, and perishability.
   a. How does each of these characteristics potentially impact the development and execution of marketing plans?
   b. What might a manager do to mitigate any negative consequences of each characteristic on the delivery of his or her firm's service?
   c. Come up with an example of a service encounter you have had as a customer (either in the B2C or B2B market) in which each of these characteristics came into play in how the service was delivered.

2. The service-profit chain guides managers toward understanding and facilitating successful linkages in the service delivery system to drive loyalty, revenue growth, and higher profits.

   a. What functional areas of a firm must a marketing manager effectively interface with to implement a service-profit chain approach?

   b. What potential impediments do you foresee in implementing the service-profit chain in an organization? How might these impediments best be overcome?

   c. What do you believe are the key advantages in implementing a service-profit chain approach?

3. Review Exhibit 13.5 and the accompanying discussion on search, experience, and credence attributes of offerings.

   a. Why are the types of offerings on the far right side of the continuum—professional services—difficult for customers to evaluate?

   b. What challenges does this difficulty create for marketing managers in professional services firms? Why?

4. Review the Gap Model of Service Quality (Exhibit 13.6). Consider each of the five gaps where customer expectations might not be met. Select a firm of your choice and for each potential gap list specific actions that the firm could take to improve the likelihood that customer expectations will be met on a regular basis.

5. Consider the five dimensions of service quality: tangibles, reliability, responsiveness, assurance, and empathy.

   a. Identify a recent service encounter you have experienced as a customer (either B2C or B2B) that you would classify as a generally bad experience. In what ways specifically did each of the five service quality dimensions contribute to your perceptions of poor service? Be as specific with your examples as you can. What could the service provider have done to improve each of the relevant dimensions and thus improve your experience?

   b. Repeat the above process but instead of a bad service experience this time identify a generally good service experience. For each relevant dimension, specifically what did the service provider do really well? Did you experience any delightful surprise? If so, what?

MANAGEMENT DECISION CASE: Customer Service Champ USAA

Insurance provider USAA has long been hailed as a company that excels in customer service. *BusinessWeek* ranked the company No. 1 in its 2007 ranking of the top 25 client-pleasing brands in its article, "Customer Service Champs."

Helping employees become more empathetic with customers was a common focus among the top brands on the *BusinessWeek* list. For example, USAA's home and auto insurance policies are only open to military members and their families. To help its employees—many of whom are not in the military—understand their customers better, the company does things like serving new employees MREs (meals ready to eat) during orientation so they can better identify with military life. Policy service manager Chin Cox, an

Air Force reservist, calls her team of call center reps "troops" and uses military time.

In another example, it was Stevie Salinas' second day of new-hire orientation when retired Lt. Col. David Sheets appeared in the doorway. "Atten-hut!" he commanded, bringing the room of 50 new employees to their feet. Surprised, the 23-year-old single mom watched as Sheets handed out manila envelopes. Inside each was a deployment letter identical to that received by the military. "Report to the personnel processing facility," the letter began, demanding recipients depart the next day.

Of course, Salinas, a fledgling member services representative, didn't actually have to ship off. Lt. Col. Sheets' appearance was part of an enhanced military awareness program begun last year by USAA. Earlier the same day, the five-foot-tall Salinas had strapped on a military helmet, 65-pound backpack, and flak vest. She'd eaten an MRE, the grub soldiers eat in the field. She'd joined others to read real letters from troops in Iraq. Hers was from a soldier who later died in the war and was addressed to his mother. "We were in tears," says Salinas.

Many companies give lip service to listening to the "voice of the customer." At USAA, that voice is transformed into what it calls "surround sound"— a comprehensive approach to training its employees to empathize with customers' unique needs. "We want to cover the light moments, the heart-wrenching moments, what it's like to be bored in the field," says Elizabeth D. Conklyn, USAA's executive vice president for people services.

"We try to develop empathy, not only for our members but also for the family side."

Such awareness efforts are helped by the fact that some 15 percent of USAA employees come from the military. For those that aren't military, managers like Cox give reminders. For example, when her 17 agents had to work on a recent Saturday, she gave out MREs as a reminder that, even though the cafeteria was open, soldiers in the field don't have options. "For one split second they're in the boots, so to speak, of our troops," says Cox. "The reason we have choices is because they're out there giving up theirs."

Providing excellent customer service is a way to turn loyal customers in to advocates. Consider this letter that a USAA customer wrote to *BusinessWeek* after reading the *BW* article about USAA:

> I have been a customer of USAA since 1962, when I was a brand new lieutenant and had no concept of what made an outstanding insurance company. This has been my only insurance company since, and I would never consider switching.
>
> As good as you made USAA's customer service sound, I think it's even better. The representatives are polite, knowledgeable, and extremely responsive. And if a customer has a valid claim, USAA is there to help, not impede. There is a strong bond of trust between the company and its customers, which is quite rare.
>
> It certainly has a lot to do with the integrity of the client base, which is current and ex-military personnel and their families. But it also reflects on a management that is strongly motivated to serve that client base and whose interests are above and beyond pure financial reward for themselves. You nailed this one.
>
> Todd L. Bergman, Honolulu

Questions for Consideration

1. How do you think USAA tackles variability of its service?

2. How would you design a SERVQUAL survey tailored to USAA?

3. Given USAA's success in serving its narrow niche of military customers, would you advise the company to expand to selling to other kinds of customers? Why or why not?

Source: Jena McGregor, "USAA: Soldiering on in Insurance," *BusinessWeek*, March 5, 2007, p. 56.

MARKETING PLAN EXERCISE

ACTIVITY 13: Differentiating via Service Quality

In your marketing plan, consider how you might effectively use service as a source of differentiation for your offering(s). As you learned in this chapter, to successfully accomplish this, you must be sensitive to nuances of services versus goods and also be able to ensure that the people and processes in your firm are able to properly support the service.

1. Evaluate the opportunity to utilize service as an important differentiator.

2. Employ a service-profit chain approach to identify people and operational aspects of your plan to support service differentiation.

3. Develop specific action plans and metrics in support of your service differentiation approach.

If you are using Marketing Plan Pro, a template for this assignment can be accessed at www.mhhe.com/marshall1e.

RECOMMENDED READINGS

1. Karl Albrecht and Ron Zemke, *Service America in the New Economy* (New York: McGraw-Hill, 2001).

2. Leonard L. Berry, *Marketing Services: Competing through Quality* (New York: The Free Press, 2004).

3. Leonard L. Berry, *Discovering the Soul of Service: The Nine Drivers of Sustainable Business Success* (New York: The Free Press, 1999).

4. Leonard L. Berry, *On Great Service* (New York: The Free Press, 1995).

5. Thomas K. Connellan and Ron Zemke, *Delivering Knock Your Socks Off Service* (New York: AMACOM, 2002).

CHAPTER 14

MANAGING PRICING DECISIONS

LEARNING OBJECTIVES

- Understand the integral role of price as a core component of value.

- Explore different pricing objectives and related strategies.

- Identify pricing tactics.

- Describe approaches to setting the exact price.

- Determine discounts and allowances to offer to channel members.

- Understand how to execute price changes.

- Examine legal considerations in pricing.

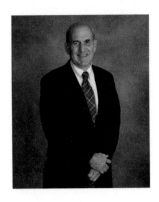

EXECUTIVE PERSPECTIVE

Executive Robert D. Finfrock, President

Company Finfrock Design-Manufacture-Construct

Business Designer/builder of commercial buildings and manufacturer of precast/prestressed concrete structures

When a firm allows its offerings to become commoditized, what happens to its ability to effectively price its goods and services?

If you let your offerings become commoditized, your ability to set prices is no longer under your company's control. The marketplace will dictate your price, and that will drive your price down.

How can a firm avoid being forced into a commodity-based pricing situation?

Your organization's offering becomes a commodity if customers see no meaningful difference between what you offer and what other competitors are offering, other than price. The way to avoid being in a commodity-based pricing situation is to differentiate your products. Differentiation of your products and services—which brings value to your customers in the form of benefits that your competitors cannot match—avoids commoditization. You must become the only company (or the clearly superior company) to offer benefits that are highly valued by customers.

For example, I came to realize that precast components, from the general contractors' perspective, had matured to the point where there was not much difference between competitors' offerings. But as a company, we knew that we had more knowledge about how to cost-effectively design, manufacture, and erect parking garages and other building structures than any of the architectural-engineering firms in the marketplace.

So, instead of selling just a product—precast concrete—we realized we could sell the product bundled with an integrated solution, a truly turnkey building solution. We'd be the only ones in the marketplace selling this integrated solution, rather than being one of many companies in a commodity business.

Offering a truly unique set of benefits increases your value relative to the competition, and customers will pay more for your offering.

Price is only one side of the value equation. In your view, what are some of the other key elements of perceived value by a customer?

Successful firms regularly evaluate the scope of their offerings in terms of maximizing customer value. One way to look at it is to look at what frustrates your customers and then eliminate those frustrations. In our industry, customers were most frustrated by risks. Our solution—to offer customers a single source of responsibility for the whole project—reduced much of that risk to customers.

In short, other perceived values in addition to price include:

- Lower risk.
- Improved competitive position.
- Lower investment.
- Improved productivity.

PRICE IS A CORE COMPONENT OF VALUE

You have learned that *value* is a ratio of the bundle of benefits a customer receives from an offering compared to the costs incurred by the customer in acquiring that bundle of benefits. From the customer's perspective, many but not all of those costs are reflected within the price paid for the offering. There are other types of costs, such as time invested in the purchase process or the opportunity costs of choosing one offering over another. But for most purchasers, regardless of whether the setting is B2C or B2B, the vast majority of costs are associated with the purchase price. As such, price—or more specifically the customer's *perception* of the offering's pricing—is a key determinant of perceived value. When customers exhibit strongly held beliefs that a firm's offerings provide high value, they are much more likely to remain loyal to the firm and its brands as well as actively tell others about their favorable experiences. Thus, marketing managers must take pricing decisions very seriously.[1]

From a marketing planning and strategy perspective, Michael Porter has consistently advocated that firms that are able to compete based on some extraordinary efficiency in one or more internal processes bring to the market a competitive advantage based on **cost leadership.** And although firms competing on cost leadership will likely also engage in one of Porter's other competitive strategies (differentiation or focus/niche), their core cost advantages translate directly to an edge over their competitors based on much more flexibility in their pricing strategies as well as their ability to translate some of the cost savings to the bottom line.[2]

For example, Southwest Airlines is widely regarded as a cost leader in its industry, which has become a critical factor in this era of high fuel costs. Southwest's internal process efficiencies stem from several important sources. First, it flies mostly the same type of plane—various series of the Boeing 737. This makes the maintenance process much more efficient than carriers whose fleet includes multiple types of aircraft. Second, Southwest has a very simple process of booking passengers and, until recently, had never even tested the idea of assigned seats. Finally, it avoids the delay-prone hub-and-spoke route system used by most of its competitors, instead often opting for smaller airports in major metropolitan areas (Midway in Chicago instead of O'Hare, for example). These and other internal efficiencies translate into a cost structure second to none in the industry.

But what does such cost leadership mean for Southwest's pricing decision making? A knee-jerk response might be to simply lower fares to match the level of cost advantage. That might increase sales volume, but it also might start a price war with other airlines that have cost advantages (AirTran and JetBlue, for instance). A more strategic approach—and the approach Southwest actually uses—is to translate part of its cost advantage into a more transparent, mileage-driven pricing structure for customers but at the same time take a portion of the cost advantage to increase the firm's profit margins, partly to reward shareholders and partly to reinvest for the firm's growth.

The United Kingdom's biggest electronics retailer, Currys, plays on the consumer's obsession with price checking by ensuring it comes in equal to or under the best price offered by competitors on big-ticket items such as printers or televisions. But the company makes up some margin through sales of accessories. For example, when consumers get to the checkout, the cashier points out that they haven't purchased a vital accessory. The accessory could be bought more cheaply elsewhere, but consumers rarely price-compare accessories. In selling the extra item, Currys has ensured its profitability while maintaining positive brand perception in the eyes of its customers.[3]

Is Goodwill Good or Just Good Business?

A small school 90 minutes from Mexico City is so poorly funded that it cannot afford toilet paper for the lavatories, but, thanks to Intel, an eighth-grade class is searching the Internet on new laptops. Intel, one of the largest technology companies in the world, is testing a program called "Classmate" that offers laptop computers for educational systems in poorer countries for around $300 each. While still expensive for the poorest nations, the company has pledged to lower costs even further and plans call for a $200 model.

At the same time, Dr. Nicholas Negroponte, professor at the Massachusetts Institute of Technology and co-founder of the MIT media lab, has been working on the XO computer through his One Laptop per Child (OLPC) foundation whose mission is to deliver computers to kids around the world for $100. OLPC has enlisted the help of Google, eBay, and Advanced Micro Devices (AMD)—AMD just happens to be Intel's major competitor in the chip market.

Although both organizations seek a similar goal—getting inexpensive laptops into the hands of poorer students—their approaches are very different. Negroponte is creating a new device with a specially designed interface that represents a dramatic departure from the world standard Microsoft Windows/Intel operating environment. Intel, on the other hand, is using its substantial leverage with suppliers to drive costs out of a standard laptop, preferring to work within existing hardware including its own chips and software products. Intel is testing its product in more than 35 countries while OLPC is still working on finalizing the product design.

Critics of Intel's approach suggest that, rather than goodwill, the company's focus on delivering low-cost computers to schoolchildren is designed to create a new market for its own products. As the world moves from desktop computers to laptops and, of more concern to Intel, mobile devices such as cell phones, the company has experienced slower growth and greater competition from AMD. Intel does not dominate the market for mobile-device computer chips in the same manner it does the computer market. Some experts believe that although the margins are low the market for very low-cost computers is huge and represents a growth opportunity for Intel.

Negroponte and OLPC have accused Intel of trying to drive the XO computer project out of business and suggest this is because OLPC buys it chips from AMD. Negroponte also argues that, although Intel's computers are inexpensive, the company views low-end computers as a market and not a human right.[4]

Ethical Perspective

1. **Intel:** Is it unethical for Intel to pursue the Classmate project if its primary purpose is to target a new market? Should the company be encouraged to develop the Classmate computer without a profit incentive; that is, should it offer the project only at cost?

2. **Governments:** Should governments support the OLPC project with its nonprofit perspective and low-cost computer over Intel's for-profit Classmate project?

Most importantly, Southwest's pricing model contributes not only to its financial performance but also is an integral part of its overall value proposition and provides a valuable lesson for the way a marketing manager should approach pricing decisions—that is, pricing decisions cannot be made in a vacuum but rather must consider the whole of the firm's offering, especially the concurrent decisions the firm is making about branding and products, service approaches, supply chain, and marketing communication. For the marketing manager, pricing is much more than an economic break-even point or a cost-plus accounting calculation. Price is a critical component that plays into a customer's assessment of the value afforded by a firm and its offerings. As such, managerial decisions about pricing should be undertaken methodically and always with a focus on how price impacts the all-important cost-versus-bundle-of-benefits assessment that equates to customer perceived value.[5] Ethical Dimension 14 evaluates some of these pricing concepts in terms of social responsibility.

The rest of this chapter details the important pricing decision-making process from a marketing manager's perspective: establish pricing objectives and related strategies; select pricing tactics; set the exact price; determine channel discounts and allowances; execute price changes; and understand legal considerations in pricing. Exhibit 14.1 protrays these elements of managing pricing decisions.

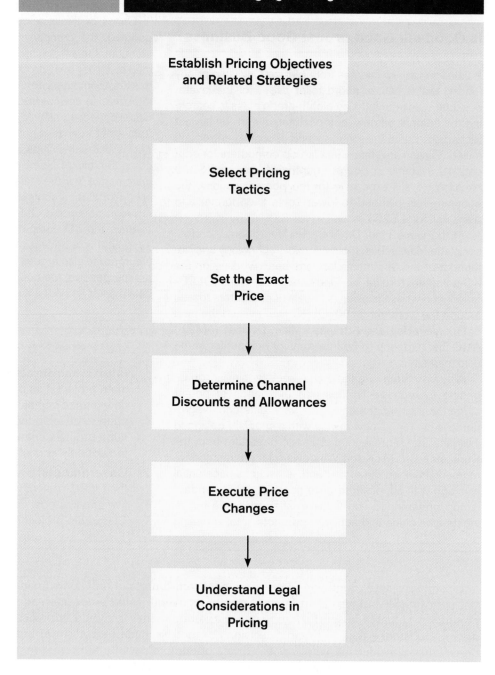

EXHIBIT 14.1 | **Elements of Managing Pricing Decisions**

Establish Pricing Objectives
and Related Strategies

↓

Select Pricing
Tactics

↓

Set the Exact
Price

↓

Determine Channel
Discounts and Allowances

↓

Execute Price
Changes

↓

Understand Legal
Considerations in
Pricing

ESTABLISH PRICING OBJECTIVES AND RELATED STRATEGIES

As illustrated in the Southwest Airlines example, pricing objectives are but one component leading to an overall value proposition. However, a product's price tends to be so visible and definitive that customers often have trouble moving past price to consider other critical benefits the product affords. This characteristic puts pressure on marketing managers to establish pricing objectives that best reflect and enhance the value proposition, while at the same time achieving the firm's financial objectives. Striking a balance between these two forces sometimes makes pricing an especially challenging part of marketing.[6]

Pricing objectives are the desired or expected result associated with a pricing strategy. Pricing objectives must be consistent with other marketing-related objectives (positioning, branding, etc.) as well as with the firm's overall objectives (including financial objectives) for doing business.[7] Exhibit 14.2 portrays several of the most common pricing objectives, along with their related strategies.

FYI

Dunkin' Donuts' pricing strategy is based on its positioning relative to rivals McDonald's and Starbucks in the breakfast market. Rather than engage in a price war with McDonald's, Dunkin' Donuts is trying to close the gap between itself and Starbucks. Although Dunkin' Donuts makes more money on breakfast sales overall than Starbucks, the average Dunkin' Donuts check is just $1.85, compared to $3.75 at Starbucks, notes food analyst Tom Miner of research firm Technomic. Dunkin' Donuts has positioned its new breakfast sandwiches as quick quality, at the same price as Starbucks at $2.99. "I think they're in a good position against their competitors," says Miner. "Their biggest challenge is to focus on a couple of very popular items and do them really well."[8]

The decision of which pricing objective or objectives to establish is driven by many interrelated factors. As you learn about each of the approaches, keep in mind that most firms attempt to balance a range of issues through their pricing objectives, including internal organization-level goals, internal capabilities, and a host of external market and competitive factors.

Penetration Pricing

Market share is the percentage of total category sales accounted for by a firm. When a firm's objective is to gain as much market share as possible, a likely pricing strategy is **penetration pricing,** sometimes also referred to as pricing for maximum marketing share. In markets where customers are sensitive to price and where internal efficiencies lead to cost advantages allowing for acceptable margins even with aggressive pricing, a penetration objective can create a powerful barrier to market entry for other firms, thus protecting market share.

Sometimes penetration pricing is used as part of a new-product introduction. In both the B2C and B2B markets, it is common for prices to be set low initially to ward off competition and then for prices to creep up over time.[9] Such pricing is built into the product's budget over the life cycle of the item. Recall from Chapter 10 that as a product progresses through the product life cycle, margins tend to be at their highest during the maturity stage. This is partly because weaker competitors tend to drop out due to penetration pricing earlier in the cycle (introduction and growth stages), which creates the potential for remaining firms to decrease spending and raise prices during the maturity stage.

Be careful with a penetration pricing strategy. Because price is a cue for developing customer perceptions of product quality, the value proposition may be reduced if a low price belies the product's

EXHIBIT 14.2	Pricing Objectives and Related Strategies

Objective: Market share maximization
Strategy: Penetration pricing

Objective: Market entry at the highest possible initial price
Strategy: Price skimming

Objective: Profit maximization
Strategy: Target ROI

Objective: Benchmark the competition
Strategy: Competitor-based pricing

Objective: Communicate positioning through price
Strategy: Value pricing

actual quality attributes.[10] An axiom in marketing is that customers always find it more palatable when a firm reduces a price than when it raises a price, and a corollary to the axiom is that once a price has been changed (one way or the other), changing it back creates confusion about positioning and brand image.

Price Skimming

A strategy of **price skimming** addresses the objective of entering a market at a relatively high price point. In proposing price skimming, the marketing manager usually is convinced that a strong price-quality relationship exists for the product. This might be done to lend prestige to a brand, or skimming is sometimes used in a new-product introduction by a firm with a first-mover advantage to skim early sales while the product has a high level of panache and exclusivity in the marketplace.[11]

Major developers of gaming consoles, including Nintendo, Microsoft, and Sony, always introduce a new platform with the objective of price skimming. Plasma televisions all started with very high price points and have gradually inched pricing downward as more and more customers began to purchase. Pharmaceutical companies justify very high introductory prices for new medications based on a necessity to recoup exorbitant R&D costs associated with their industry. Those same drugs steadily decline in price as more advanced competitive drugs come along, and, when patent protection runs out, the price drops precipitously as generic versions of the drug flood the market.

When Microsoft brings out a new edition of its Xbox 360, the new version contains upgrades and is sold at a higher price point. For example, the Xbox 360 Elite has a bigger hard drive, better high-definition video support, and a stylish black finish. The idea is to appeal to an elite class of hard-core game players who would like a little more of everything. When it hit stores in April 2007, the upgraded version had a list price of $479, $80 more than the Xbox 360 Pro and $180 more than the basic Xbox 360.[12]

Regardless of the motivation for a price skimming strategy, as with penetration pricing, when multiple-year budgets are developed, marketing managers must consider the likelihood of competitive entry and adjust pricing projections accordingly. An initial pricing objective of skimming will require modification over time based in part on the rate of adoption and diffusion by consumers.

In general, skimming can be an appropriate pricing objective within the context of a focus (niche) strategy. By definition, such an approach positions a product for appeal to a limited (narrow) customer group or submarket of a larger market. Because niche market players typically attract fewer and less-aggressive competitors than those employing differentiation strategies within the larger market, a focus strategy can usually support higher prices and the potential for skimming can be extended. The ability to use price skimming declines precipitously, however, if the product migrates from a niche positioning to that of a differentiated product within the larger market.[13]

Profit Maximization and Target ROI

Pricing objectives very frequently are designed for profit maximization, which necessitates a **target return on investment (ROI)** pricing strategy. Here, a bottom-line profit is established first and then pricing is set to achieve the target. Although this approach sounds straightforward, it actually brings up an important reason pricing is best cast within the purview of marketing instead of under the sole control of accountants or financial managers in a firm. When pricing decisions on a given product are made strictly to bolster gross margins, bottom-line profits, or

ROI without regard to the short- and long-term impact of the pricing strategy on other important market- and customer-related elements of success, the product becomes strategically vulnerable. Marketing managers are in the best position to take into account the competitor, customer, and brand image impact of pricing approaches.[14]

Still, in preparing product budgets and forecasts, marketing managers are expected to pay close attention to their organization's financial objectives. During the research that leads to a decision to introduce a new product or modify an existing one, one key variable of interest is whether the market will bear a price point that enhances the firm's overall financial performance. Often, **price elasticity of demand**—the measure of customers' price sensitivity estimated by dividing relative changes in quantity sold by relative changes in price—becomes central to whether a product can even be viably introduced within the context of a firm's financial objectives.[15] The basic price elasticity (e) equation is portrayed below:

$$e = \frac{\% \text{ change in quantity demanded}}{\% \text{ change in price}}$$

Unfortunately, price sensitivity is notoriously one of the most difficult issues to determine through market research. Sometimes, historical records or secondary data can provide evidence of pricing's impact on sales volume. When primary research methods are used to ask customers about pricing—whether through survey, focus group, experiments, or other methodology—they most often place the respondent into a hypothetical "what if" mode of thinking in which they are asked to predict how one price or the other might impact their decision to buy. This is a very difficult assertion for a person to make and can lead to bad data and ultimately poor pricing decisions. Importantly, in many instances, much of a customer's reaction to pricing is more psychological or emotional in nature than rational and logical.[16]

Finally, the idea of pricing based on purely economic models and solely for profit maximization raises important ethical concerns, especially in cases where essential products are in short supply. The latest wonder drugs, building materials after a major disaster, and new technologies needed for emerging markets are but three examples in which pricing for pure profit motive can damage both a firm's image and ultimately its relationships with customers. And as oil prices have soared over recent years, more and more consumer groups have been actively calling for investigation of the pricing practices of the big oil companies, and Congress has periodically called in the CEOs to testify about their profits. At the same time, independent distributors, gasoline retailers, and end-user consumers of gasoline have all struggled because of the high prices.[17]

Competitor-Based Pricing

Gaining a thorough understanding of competitors' marketing practices is a key element of successful marketing planning and execution. A competitor's price is one of the most visible elements of its marketing strategy, and you can often infer the pricing objective by carefully analyzing historical and current pricing patterns. Based on such analysis, a firm may develop **competitor-based pricing** strategies. This approach might lead the marketing manager to decide to price at some market average price, or perhaps above or below it in the context of penetration or skimming objectives.

The logic of competitor-based pricing is quite rational unless (a) it is the *only* approach considered when making the ultimate pricing decisions or (b) it leads to exaggerated extremes in pricing such that on the high end a firm's products do not project customer value or on the low end price wars ensue. A **price war** occurs when a company purposefully makes pricing decisions to undercut one or more competitors and gain sales and net market share.[18] Such was the case in the early

1990s when Sears embarked on a short-lived "low-price" strategy to compete with Wal-Mart on certain high-profile goods, sparking a major price war. Sears management, concerned at the time about losing the Gen X market to Wal-Mart and other discounters, fired the first salvo by publicly announcing a list of items on which it would not be undersold. One of these items, branded disposable diapers such as Pampers and Luvs, led the way in Sears' ads nationwide at prices well below cost.

Unfortunately for Sears, management grossly underestimated the power of Wal-Mart to thwart such competitive threats. First, Wal-Mart's chairman went public in the press by reiterating that Wal-Mart was the true low-price king in retailing (the company's tagline at the time was "Low Prices . . . Always") and assuring customers Wal-Mart would match any advertised Sears price. Then, within days and in market after market, Wal-Mart took to the newspapers with full-page ads discounting diapers to ridiculous levels never before seen, thus negating Sears' approach. This price war was short-lived and forced Sears to immediately rethink its pricing strategy.

Stability Pricing

A potentially more productive strategy related to competitor-based pricing is **stability pricing,** in which a firm attempts to find a neutral *set point* for price that is neither low enough to raise the ire of competition nor high enough to put the value proposition at risk with customers. Many factors go into selecting a specific product's stability price point. In markets where customers typically witness rapidly changing prices, stability pricing can provide a source of competitive advantage.[19] Southwest Airlines employs a stability pricing strategy by displaying only five or six fares to a particular destination, with price points based on when the ticket is purchased and the days of the week the customer will be traveling. Unlike most other domestic carriers, Southwest actually prices based on the distance of the trip and is less tied to load-maximization formulas in which a fare can change minute by minute depending on ticket sales. The airline's stability pricing approach has proved highly popular with customers, and it's been successful for the firm as its seat occupancy rate continues to be among the highest in the industry.

Value Pricing

Firms that have an objective of utilizing pricing to communicate positioning use a **value pricing** strategy. Value pricing overtly attempts to consider the role of price as it reflects the bundle of benefits sought by the customer. Because value is in the eyes of the beholder, affected by his or her perceptions of the offering coupled with the operative needs and wants, pricing decisions are strongly driven by the sources of differential advantage a product can realistically deliver. Effectively communicating a product's differential advantages is at the heart of positioning strategy, and exposure to these elements spurs the customer to develop perceptions of value and a subsequent understanding of the value proposition.[20]

Value pricing is complex and overarches the other pricing objectives discussed so far. Through value pricing, a marketing manager seeks to ensure that the offering meets or exceeds the customer's expectations—that is, when he or she does the mental arithmetic that calculates whether the investment in the offering is likely

The Butlins Hotel in the UK sends a strong value pricing signal by showing all the great extra activities you can engage in if you stay at their property.

to provide sufficient benefits to justify the cost. Put another way, value pricing considers the whole deliverable and its possible sources of differential advantage—image, service, product quality, personnel, innovation, and many others—the whole gamut of elements that create customer benefit. For instance, Toyotas and Hondas cost more to purchase initially than other comparable vehicles, but they last longer, require fewer repairs, are more fuel-efficient, and hold their resale value much better; overall, they have a lower lifetime cost of ownership.

From this assessment, the marketing manager makes a pricing decision that best reflects that product's capacity to be perceived as a good customer value. This high-impact decision helps frame customers' reactions and their relationship with the product and the company. Not surprisingly, Toyota and Honda drivers tend to be very brand loyal, with a very high repeat purchase rate, and many multiple-car families of one or the other.

FYI

Customers will accept a higher per-product cost if they understand the total value the product will deliver to them. For example, Richard Pedtke, president of the compact-vehicle division that makes Bobcat miniature loaders and excavators, buys hydraulic fittings made by Parker Hannifin for the Bobcats. Mr. Pedtke at first objected when one of Parker's new hydraulic fan motors cost much more than he expected. But when Bobcat's purchasing people sat down with Parker's sales team, Bobcat learned that the new motor replaced 11 separate parts in the company's existing machines. Moreover, the new design reduced leakage by eliminating hydraulic connections, was easier to install at Bobcat's factories, and opened up space inside the machines—all saving the company money.[21]

Would a firm ever benefit from pricing without regard to value? This is an intriguing question that can best be illustrated through the example of a positioning map like the one in Chapter 9. Exhibit 14.3 provides a positioning map with price on one axis and quality on the other. In this instance, we're using the term *quality* rather generically to simply connote a range of differential advantages that might comprise the perceived bundle of benefits for the offering.

Notice in Exhibit 14.3 that a diagonal range of feasible positioning options exists based on matching price to the benefits achieved. For most products, as long as the customer perceives the ratio of price and benefit to be at least at equilibrium, perceptions of value will likely be favorable. Thus, a poorer-quality product offset by a super-low price can be perceived as a good value just as a higher-quality product at a high price can be.

The key lesson marketing managers should draw about value pricing goes back to a key point about managing customer expectations in Chapter 13: Overpromising and underdelivering is one of the quickest ways to create poor value perceptions and thus alienate customers. Marketers will do well to not overpromise benefits, but rather should communicate and deliver a realistic level of benefits for a price.[22]

But what happens when one strays off the favorable diagonal of price/benefit harmony? In the lower right quadrant—high quality/low price—a penetration strategy might be in play. Or perhaps a firm is taking advantage of its cost leadership by offering a somewhat reduced price. However, over the long run, reducing price too much based on either of these pricing strategies can unnecessarily damage both margins and brand image. Penetration is usually intended to be a temporary strategy, giving the product a chance to gain a strong foothold in market share while warding off competition for a time. Michael Porter has long advocated

EXHIBIT 14.3   Generic Price-Quality Positioning Map

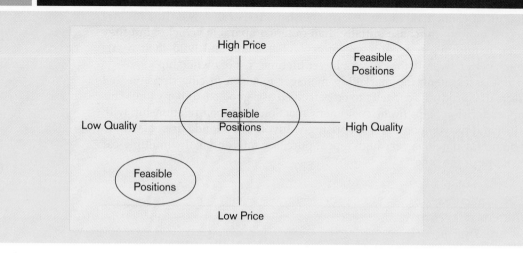

that cost leadership based on value chain efficiencies should not be wholesale translated to low prices—the reason the approach is called *cost* leadership, not *price* leadership. Successful cost leaders tend to offer a somewhat lower price in the marketplace, but they also translate a substantial portion of their efficiencies to margin, thus enhancing the long-term growth and performance of the firm. Bottom line, it may be all right to play in the bottom-right quadrant temporarily in the case of penetration or to creep slightly into that quadrant over the long haul with a properly executed cost leadership approach.

Clearly, operating in the upper-left (high price/low benefits) quadrant can be problematic. Some firms utilize price skimming strategies, especially on product introductions, even when all the bugs have yet to be worked out of the product. New technology products are notorious for having surprises in quality, functionality, and reliability crop up soon after introduction. When this happens, it can be extremely damaging to the value proposition and to the brand. In such cases, from an ethical perspective, one could question the firm's intent. Did the company rush a product to market to beat an impending entry by competition, pricing it high due to first-mover advantage, all the while knowing that serious quality problems existed? Firms and brands that continually attempt to operate in the high-price/low-benefits quadrant do not survive over the long run as customer trust is damaged. Unfortunately, some highly unscrupulous companies perpetuate their operations in this quadrant by constantly changing company name, location, and brand names. Stories of customer rip-offs are particularly prolific in the service sector (from construction to financial services to health care) because in this sector the offering is inextricably linked to the provider and it's difficult to assess quality until after the service is rendered.

Like many off-airport parking facilities, TheParkingSpot features much lower prices than on-airport parking but hopefully (because of their shuttles) without a concurrent loss of convenience.

SELECT PRICING TACTICS

Once management establishes the overall pricing objectives and strategies, it's time to develop and execute the pricing tactics in the marketplace that will operationalize the strategies. Exhibit 14.4 summarizes tactical pricing approaches.

As with establishing pricing strategies, for a variety of reasons firms frequently rely on combinations of pricing tactics in the marketplace rather than putting all their eggs in one basket. As you read about each approach, don't think of it as a stand-alone strategy but instead consider how it might work in tandem with other approaches that a marketing manager might decide to employ.

Product Line Pricing

As you have learned, firms rarely market single products. Most products are part of an overall product line of related offerings; and this is true whether the product is in the B2C or B2B marketplace, or in the realm of goods or service.
Product line pricing (or **price lining**) affords the marketing manager an opportunity to develop a rational pricing strategy across a complete line of related items. As a customer is evaluating the choices available within a firm's product line, the **price points** established for the various items in the line need to make sense and reflect the differences in benefits offered as the customer moves up and down the product line.

Consider the different types of rooms offered by a resort hotel on Maui. At top properties such as the Fairmont Kea Lani in Wailea, even a room on a lower floor with a limited view might easily run well over $400 per night during peak season. Exhibit 14.5 shows the array of room types and prices across the product line—the different grades of guest room.

EXHIBIT 14.4	Tactical Pricing Approaches

EXHIBIT 14.5	Product Line Pricing by Room Type at the Fairmont Kea Lani on Maui

Room Type	Description	Price
Moderate Suite	Limited view–parking facility or side street	$475
Fairmont Suite	Tropical garden or mountain view	$575
Partial Ocean View	Angled ocean view from lanai	$650
Ocean View	Partial ocean view	$725
Poolside	Direct walkout to upper lagoon pool	$725
Deluxe Ocean View	Spectacular full ocean view	$775
Signature Kilohana	Popular corner suite, panoramic ocean view, wrap-around lanai	$1,000

In price lining, the escalation of product prices up the product line has to consider factors such as real cost differences among the various features offered, customer assessments of the value added by the increasing level of benefits, and prices competitors are charging for similar products. Price lining can greatly simplify a customer's purchase decision making by clearly defining a smorgasbord of offerings based on different bundles of benefits at different prices. Regardless of the product category, customers often approach a purchase with some preconceived range of price acceptability in mind, and product line pricing helps guide them toward the best purchase match to their needs while facilitating easy comparison among offerings.[23]

Cedric Jungpeter, European spokesman for Levi Strauss, says his brand has used a pyramid price structure: "With three distinct brands—Levi's, Dockers, and Signature—we target different consumers and retail channels at a variety of price points." The latest addition to the company's stable of brands is Signature, designed for the value channel and traditionally sold in supermarkets. "We saw an opportunity for consumers who shopped at a different price points but who wanted a degree of what Levi's represented," reveals Jungpeter. Signature bears many of the hallmarks of the more upscale Levi's denim but, in line with its value position, has more limited detailing.[24]

Price lining can occur at a level much broader in scope than individual products. For example, Marriott has branded its entire family of accommodations based on different value propositions, supported by clearly delineated pricing strategies. Its offerings include Ritz-Carlton and JW Marriott for the most discriminating patron, Marriott and Renaissance at the next level of full service, and an array of differentially positioned brands such as Courtyard, Residence Inn, SpringHill Suites, Fairfield Inn, and TownPlace Suites. Marriott clearly communicates the differences and value in each of these brands, partly by how each is priced in relation to the others. By now you should have a strong sense of how strategically important price is within the marketing mix as a cue for customer's perceptions of value.[25]

Captive Pricing

Captive pricing, sometimes called **complementary pricing,** entails gaining a commitment from a customer to a basic product or system that requires continual purchase of peripherals to operate.[26] What is the most *profitable* part of Hewlett-Packard's office products business: printers or ink cartridges? It's the cartridges. And although other sources for replacement cartridges exist for HP machines, the company does a great job of convincing users that only genuine HP cartridges can be depended on for high-quality performance.

Like HP in printers, Gillette built its business in razors by hooking customers on the latest and greatest new multi-blade system through every type of promotion possible from Super Bowl ads to free samples. Gillette counts on the fact that we will go back time and again to repurchase the replacement blades that carry the real margins the company is after.

Captive pricing is just as common in the service sector, where it is sometimes called two-part pricing. Any firm that charges a monthly access fee, membership, retainer fee, or service charge and then bills by the specific service provided is using this pricing approach.

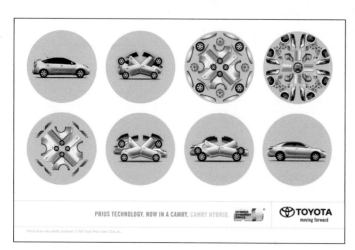

PRIUS TECHNOLOGY. NOW IN A CAMRY. CAMRY HYBRID. HYBRID SYNERGY DRIVE. TOYOTA moving forward

In this ad, Toyota strongly supports its product line pricing by clearly showing a Prius morphing into a more upscale vehicle—the new Hybrid Camry.

Price Bundling

When customers are given the opportunity to purchase a package deal at a reduced price compared to what the individual components of the package would cost separately, the firm is using a **price bundling** strategy.[27] Cable television providers want you to buy the full gamut of entertainment products from them, and the more you add to your bundle—digital television, premium channels, downloadable movies, local and long-distance phone service, cellular service, gaming, high-speed Internet—the better the deal becomes compared to the total of the individual prices of each piece of the bundle.

When Apple Inc. opened its iTunes Store, the company changed how consumers purchased music by letting them buy individual songs instead of full albums. Now Apple is giving its customers a new incentive to go back to their old album-buying ways. The company introduced a new offering on the iTunes Store, Complete My Album, that allows consumers to purchase at a reduced price the remaining songs from an album for which they've already bought single songs on iTunes. Apple typically prices full albums, most of which have 12 or so songs on them, at $9.99. "The idea here is that simple—once you bought singles from an album, we'll give you credit for it," says Eddy Cue, Apple's vice president for iTunes.[28]

A potential dark side to price bundling is that, in some industries, it can become unclear just what the regular, or unbundled, price is for a given component of a package. The cable/telecommunications industry is regulated to the point that this is less an issue, but in unregulated industries, unscrupulous firms sometimes set artificially high prices for the sake of pushing customers into buying a package. Later in the chapter we will review several of the most important legal considerations related to pricing.

Beyond legalities, ethical issues sometimes arise with regard to price bundling. For example, car shoppers often find every car on the lot within a given model has many of the same features automatically bundled as add-ons. How many of those features would you buy if you had a choice? The extra features being bundled typically carry much larger margins than the margin on the core vehicle itself. If you special order a car without the bundle, chances are you will be waiting months for it to be delivered to the lot—*if* the dealer will even order it for you.

Reference Pricing

As in price bundling, it can be useful for customers to have some type of comparative price when considering a product purchase. Such a comparison is referred to as **reference pricing** and, in the case of price bundling, the reference price is the total price of the components of the bundle if purchased separately versus the bundled price. The savings would be expected to stimulate purchase of the bundle so long as the perceived value realized is sufficient.

Reference pricing is implemented in a number of ways. Sometimes a product catalog might show a manufacturer's suggested list price next to the actual price the product is offered for in the catalog. In retail stores, in any given product category a private-label product (say, the Walgreens brand for instance) is often purposely displayed on a shelf right next to its national brand equivalent. The retailer hopes the savings realized by the direct price comparison of a bottle of Walgreens' mint mouthwash versus the bottle of Scope next to it will be enough to stimulate purchase. Reference pricing is very heavily used in B2B price lists, often reflecting price level differences depending on how many items are purchased or reflecting the amount saved by a firm's special "contract rate" with a vendor versus what a noncontract rate would be.

Clearly, reference pricing can create a powerful psychological impact on a customer by virtue of the savings (real or imagined) demonstrated by the comparison. Ever have a salesperson tell you that a price increase is imminent and if you don't purchase today you'll pay more tomorrow? Customer hedging behaviors against pricing uncertainty are driven by referencing projected prices in the future. And, of course, a sale or promotional price provides a strong reference point and, if the comparative difference is great enough, shoppers flock to the store as if going into battle to take advantage of temporary price reductions while they are in effect.[29]

Prestige Pricing

As mentioned earlier, one rationale for establishing a price skimming objective is **prestige pricing**—lending prestige to a product or brand by virtue of a price relatively higher than the competition. With prestige pricing, some of the traditional price/demand curves cannot properly predict sales or market response because it violates the common assumption that increasing price decreases volume. From the perspective of financial returns, prestige pricing is a phenomenal approach because, everything else being equal, commanding a premium price reflects directly on margins and bottom line.[30]

Prestige pricing plays on psychological principles that attach quality attributions to higher-priced goods—a typical response to some higher-priced products is that they must be better than their competitors otherwise the price would be lower. When the Norwegian glacier water Voss entered the U.S. market in 2002, it entered with a prestige pricing strategy that helped create a whole new category of ultra-premium bottled waters. Order Voss in a chic restaurant and you can expect to pay $12 to $15 per bottle. What's the value proposition that would support such a high price? The exclusivity of distribution, unique cylinder shape of the bottle, and exotic glacial imagery all combine so that a premium price actually enhances the customer's feelings of experiencing something really special (yes, water can be an experiential purchase). Promotion of Voss water has included numerous product placements showing celebrities and others among the rich and famous partaking of the brand. Had Voss entered the market without such a prestige pricing strategy it is highly unlikely it would have achieved the buzz and early cult status it did.

> Premium car brand Porsche understands the value of tight price control, which is vital in the luxury sector. Wayne Darley, head of brand communications and strategy at Porsche in the United Kingdom, states bluntly: "We have a policy not to discount our product—it would erode our premium positioning."[31]

Odd/Even Pricing

Odd pricing simply means that the price is not expressed in whole dollars, while **even pricing** is a whole dollar amount ($1.99 versus $2.00, for example). Odd pricing originally came about before the advent of sales taxes and widespread credit card use to bolster cash register security and reduce theft. That is, if a customer brings a $5.00 item to a clerk and presents a $5.00 bill for payment, it was believed that the temptation would be greater for the clerk to simply pocket the bill and not record the sale. It was reasoned that if the clerk had to make change—say a nickel if the item were priced at $4.95—the likelihood was higher that the sale would actually be rung into the cash register.[32]

Now, the rationale for odd pricing is very different and it is often regarded as a key element of **psychological pricing,** or creating a perception about price merely from the image the numbers provide the customer. Studies indicate that at certain important price breaks—$9.99 versus $10.00, $99.95 versus $100.00, and so on—customers mentally process the price as significantly lower because of the reduced digit count in the price point.[33] However, odd pricing can backfire if misapplied. For example, it seems acceptable for a bottle of Voss to be prestige priced at $12.95 instead of $13.00, but a physician, management consultant, or CPA wouldn't want to charge a client $195 instead of simply $200 for services rendered.

One-Price Strategy and Variable Pricing

An ethnocentric aspect of the U.S. marketplace is the nearly total reliance by marketers on a **one-price strategy** with end-user consumers. That is, except for temporary price reductions for promotional or clearance purposes, the price marked on a good is what it typically sells for. The Snicker bar at the convenience store is 99 cents regardless of whether you are a schoolchild or corporate CEO, and the clerk doesn't want to bargain with you about the price. A one-price strategy makes planning and forecasting infinitely easier than the alternative approach, **variable pricing,** which is found in many other countries and cultures but is relatively rare in the United States. With variable pricing, customers are allowed—even encouraged—to haggle about prices. Ultimately, *the* price is whatever the buyer and seller agree to—a marked price is nothing more than a starting point for negotiation. Variable pricing is traditional in the United States with a few consumer goods—cars, boats, houses, and the like. But it is the pervasive way of doing business with all sorts of products across large parts of the globe.

In the U.S. service sector, variable pricing is much more common. It is also more common in B2B in general versus B2C. When variable pricing is used in the United States, in some cases it carries legal limitations. Many pricing laws have been enacted specifically to protect both channel purchasers and end-user consumers from a variety of unfair pricing practices.

Target and Wal-Mart have historically used different pricing tactics—Target relies on high/low pricing with heavy promotion while Wal-Mart relies more heavily on everyday low pricing (EDLP).

Logo reprinted Courtesy of Target Brands, Inc. and Wal-Mart Stores, Inc.

Everyday Low Pricing (EDLP) and High/Low Pricing

The rise of Wal-Mart as the world's largest corporation has brought the concept of **everyday low pricing (EDLP)** to the forefront of global consumer consciousness. EDLP is not an option just for retailers; it's an important strategic choice for nearly any firm. The fundamental philosophy behind EDLP is to reduce investment in promotion and transfer part of the savings to lower price. Thus, firms practicing an EDLP strategy typically report substantially reduced promotional expenditures on their financial statements. They instead rely much more on generating buzz in the market about the EDLP to create and maintain customer traffic and sales volume. EDLP, when successfully implemented, has a strong advantage of reducing ups and downs in customer traffic, thus making forecasting more accurate.

The antithesis to EDLP is a **high/low pricing** strategy, in which firms rely on periodic heavy *promotional pricing,* primarily communicated through advertising and sales promotion, to build traffic and sales volume. The promotional investment is offset by somewhat higher everyday prices. Why would a firm elect high/low pricing instead of EDLP? Usually, the firm has little choice because of what competitors are doing. It takes a long time for any product or service provider to convince the market that it has EDLP. Most often, firms use various elements of promotion to build sales of new products, shore up sales of declining products, or combat competitors' promotional activity in the same marketplace. Some industries truly are over the top in employing high/low pricing strategies—airlines, auto dealerships, and personal computers are a few that run so many price promotions that customers are conditioned to wait and rarely purchase a product at full price. When high/low pricing reaches this fevered pitch in an industry, it almost always hurts the bottom line of all firms.[34]

> To entice customers into their stores, supermarkets turned to discounted fuel to attract customers. Grocers such as Food City recognize that fuel promotions build traffic because gasoline is so expensive these days. The basic premise of these programs is that by letting shoppers earn discounts toward gasoline purchases when they shop in the supermarket, retailers will gain more loyal shoppers and a broader customer base. "They cost something, but like any promotion you do to drive sales, fuel promotions position you favorably against the competition," explained Steve Smith, president and CEO of K-VA-T Food Stores, Inc., which operates Food City supermarkets. "Our first fuel promotion this summer was very successful. Now, we'd like to do it again and see how we can make it even more effective."[35]

Auction Pricing

Auctions have been around for centuries. In an auction, in which individuals competitively bid against each other and the purchase goes to the high bidder, the market truly sets the price (although some minimum bid amount is often established by the seller). As a strategy, **auction pricing** has gained in prominence as Internet commerce has come of age. The most famous example of auction pricing is eBay. Whereas in the past prices at auction were wholly dependent on the level of demand represented by a fairly small number of people either physically gathered at the auction location or connected through traditional telecommunication, today the Internet provides a vast electronic playing field for customers to participate in the auction on a real-time basis.

This phenomenon has resulted in a marketplace in which auction prices can be considerably more reflective of the real value of an offering versus other static price purchase environments. Besides standard auction approaches (buyers bid for a seller's offering), online **reverse auctions** are now very common in which sellers bid prices to capture a buyer's business. Priceline.com is a prominent example of a reverse auction firm that serves as a clearinghouse for extra capacity from airlines, hotels, and cruise lines.[36]

> DoubleClick is setting up an advertising exchange that will bring Web publishers and advertising buyers together on a Web site where they can participate in auctions for ad space. The service will let advertisers see information about what competitors bid for particular ads, in the same way that eBay shows visitors' past bids. And it will let publishers try to ensure that they sell their ad spots at the highest possible price, the way that airlines try to do with the seats they sell.[37]

SET THE EXACT PRICE

To set an exact price for an offering, be it a good or service, marketing managers should consider several calculations to arrive at the optimal price. We will discuss four methods here that are frequently used: cost-plus pricing/markup on cost, markup on sales price, average-cost pricing, and target return pricing.

Cost-Plus Pricing/Markup on Cost

Cost-plus pricing is really just a general heuristic that builds a price by adding a standardized markup on top of costs for an offering, hence the term **markup on cost.**[38] First an estimate of costs involved must be developed. In accounting courses, you learn that determining costs is no easy task. For example, many different types of costs can be considered, including fixed and variable costs, direct costs and indirect costs, and shared or overhead costs, which might be allocated to the offering on some prorated basis. Nevertheless, once a cost has been established, cost-plus pricing requires the predetermination of some standardized markup percentage that is to be applied based on company guidelines. Often, managers will receive a list of standard markup amounts by product line. Easy pricing decision making is the advantage of cost-plus pricing, but for most firms it is too simplistic.

Consider the following example. Assume the firm desires a standard markup of 50 percent over cost. Thus:

$$\begin{aligned}
\text{Cost} &= \$\ 7.00 \\
\text{Markup on cost } (.50 \times \$7.00) &= +\$\ 3.50 \\
\text{Price} &= \$10.50
\end{aligned}$$

Markup on Sales Price

In determining markup, one approach is to use the sales price as a basis. Consider the following example:

$$\begin{aligned}
\text{Sales price} &= \$12.00 \\
\text{Cost} &= \$\ 7.00 \\
\text{Markup} &= \$\ 5.00
\end{aligned}$$

The markup percentage is $\$5.00 \div \$12.00 = 41.7$ percent. That is, the $\$5.00$ markup is 41.7 percent of the sales price. In most applications, when a marketing manager simply refers to "markup," he or she is referring to this calculation—**markup on sales price,** which uses the sales price as a basis of calculating the markup percentage. This is because most important items on financial reports (gross sales, revenue, etc.) are sales, not cost, figures.[39]

All else being equal, calculating a markup on cost makes the markup appear higher than a markup on price even though the dollar figures are identical. For the above example, the markup on cost is $\$5.00 \div \$7.00 = 71.4$ percent, which seems more attractive than the 41.7 percent we calculated above. Sometimes marketers will refer to "100 percent markup," usually meaning they are simply doubling the cost to establish a price.

Average-Cost Pricing

Often pricing decisions are made by identifying all costs associated with an offering to come up with what the average cost of a single unit might be.[40] The basic formula for **average-cost pricing** is:

All costs ÷ Total number of units = Average cost of a single unit

To make this calculation requires predicting how much of the offering will be demanded. Assuming total costs of $100,000 and forecasted total number of units of 250, the average cost of a single unit is:

$$\$100,000 \div 250 = \$400$$

One can then add a profit margin to the total cost figures to calculate a likely price for a unit of the offering:

$$\$100,000 \text{ total cost} + \$25,000 \text{ profit margin} = \$125,000$$

Thus, the average price of a single unit based on the above profit margin is:

$$\$125,000 \div 250 \text{ unit} = \$500$$

Caution is warranted in employing average-cost pricing, as it is always possible that the quantity demanded will not match the marketing manager's forecast. Let's assume that instead of 250, the actual number of units in the above example turns out to be only 200. Revenue would drop to $100,000 but total costs would not drop proportionately because many of the costs are incurred regardless of sales volume. This example vividly illustrates the point made earlier in the chapter that it is unwise to base pricing decisions on costs alone. Market and customer factors must also be carefully considered in establishing a price.

Target Return Pricing

To better take into account the differential impact of fixed and variable costs, marketing managers can use **target return pricing.** First, a few definitions are in order. Fixed costs are incurred over time, regardless of volume. Variable costs fluctuate with volume. And total costs are simply a sum of the fixed and variable costs.[41] To use target return pricing, one must first calculate total fixed costs. Second, a target return must be established. Let's assume that total fixed costs are $250,000 and the target return is set at $50,000 for a total of $300,000.

Next, a demand forecast must be made. If demand is forecast at 1,500 units:

$$\text{(Fixed costs + Target return)} \div \text{Units} = (\$250,000 + \$50,000) \div 1,500$$
$$= \$200 \text{ per unit.}$$

Suppose the variable costs per unit are $50. This results in a price per unit of:

$$\$200 + \$50 = \$250$$

As with average-cost pricing, the effectiveness of target return pricing is highly dependent on the accuracy of the forecast. In the example above, if customer demand comes in at 1,000 units instead of 1,500, at a price of $250 the marketing manager will experience a $50 per unit loss!

Pricing doesn't get much better than "FREE," as in the case of this ad for Motorola Razr Smart Phone—plus your get a chance to meet David Beckham!

DETERMINE CHANNEL DISCOUNTS AND ALLOWANCES

Discounts are direct, immediate reductions in price provided to purchasers. **Allowances** remit monies to purchasers after the fact. In general, in B2B transactions marketing managers must be cognizant of several types of discount and allowance approaches that essentially amount to price adjustments for channel buyers. While the pricing discounts and purchasing allowances mentioned in this section primarily pertain to B2B, in some instances, end-user consumers may be offered some of the same price adjustments.

Sellers offer discounts and allowances for a variety of reasons. Paying a bill early, purchasing a certain quantity, purchasing seasonal products during the off-season, or experiencing an overstock on certain products are common rationale for offering various discounts and allowances. At its essence, the approach hopes to impact purchaser behavior in directions that benefit the selling firm by sweetening the buying organization's terms of sale.

Cash Discounts

Sellers offer **cash discounts** to elicit quicker payment of invoices. The rational purchaser weighs the discount offered for early payment versus the value of keeping the money until it is due. Ideally the cash discount results in financial advantage for both parties. Cash discounts are stated in a typical format such as 2%/10, Net/40, which translates to the buyer receiving 2 percent off the total bill if payment is received within 10 days of invoice date, but after that point there is no discount and the whole invoice is due within 40 days of the invoice date.

Trade Discounts

Trade discounts, also sometime called functional discounts, provide an incentive to a channel member for performing some function in the channel that benefits the seller. Examples include stocking a seller's product or performing a service related to that product, such as installation or repair, within the channel. Trade discounts are normally expressed as a percentage off the invoice price.

Cadbury Trebor Bassett, makers of the iconic Creme Egg that makes its appearance every spring, increased trade discounting when it needed to clear out high levels of stock. The company had built up inventory of Dairy Milk bars in case the company experienced any glitches while implementing a new IT system. The trade discounts and price promotions helped effectively clear that inventory of candy bars during the spring season.[42]

Quantity Discounts

Quantity discounts are taken off an invoice price based on different levels of product purchased. Quantity discounts may be offered on an order-by-order basis, in which case they are noncumulative, or they may be offered on a cumulative basis over time as an incentive to promote customer loyalty. From a legal standpoint, it is essential that quantity discounts are offered to all customers on an equally proportionate basis so that small buyers as well as large buyers follow the same rules for qualification. The later section on legal considerations in pricing extends the discussion about fairness in pricing practices.[43]

Seasonal Discounts

Firms often purchase seasonal products many months before the season begins. For example, a retailer might purchase a winter apparel line at a trade show a year before its season, accept delivery in August, begin displaying it in September, yet cold weather may not hit until November or December. To accommodate such lengthy sales processes, firms offer **seasonal discounts,** which reward the purchaser for shifting part of the inventory storage function away from the manufacturer.[44] Seasonal discounts are often expressed as greatly extended invoice due dates. In the winter clothes line example, terms of 2%/120, Net 145 would not be unusual.

Promotional Allowances

Within a given channel, sellers often want purchasers to help execute their promotional strategies. A consumer products marketer like P&G, for example, depends heavily on wholesalers, distributors, and retailers to promote its brands. When a retailer runs an ad for a P&G brand such as Crest toothpaste, it is nearly always in response to **promotional allowances** provided by the manufacturer. Ordinarily, upon proof of performance of the promotion, the retailer will receive a check back from the manufacturer to compensate for part of the promotional costs. The allowance might be calculated as a percentage of the invoice for Crest purchased from P&G or it might be a fixed dollar figure per dozen or per case.[45]

Geographic Aspects of Pricing

A variety of geographically driven pricing options are common within a channel. Among those most used are FOB pricing, uniform delivered pricing, and zone pricing.

FOB Pricing

FOB stands for free on board, meaning that title transfer and freight paid on the goods being shipped are based on the FOB location. For example, FOB-origin or FOB-factory pricing indicates that the purchaser pays freight charges and takes title the moment the goods are placed on the truck or other transportation vehicle. The greater the distance between shipper and customer, the higher the freight charges to the customer. In contrast, FOB-destination indicates that until the goods arrive at the purchaser's location, title doesn't change hands and freight charges are the responsibility of the seller.[46]

Uniform Delivered Pricing

Many direct-to-consumer marketers such as Amazon, Dell, and Lands' End practice **uniform delivered pricing,** in which the same delivery fee is charged to customers regardless of geographic location within the 48 contiguous states.[47] Pricing rates are quoted for other locations, and expedited delivery is generally available for a higher fee.

Zone Pricing

In a **zone pricing** approach, shippers set up geographic pricing zones based on the distance from the shipping location. The parcel post system of the U.S. Postal Service is set up this way.[48] Rates are calculated for the various combinations of sending and receiving zones.

Monsanto now uses zone pricing when selling some of its products, like Yield-Guard rootworm. "We want our pricing to fit as close as we can to local market conditions," says Jim Zimmer, vice president of marketing. Some geographic regions have less of a rootworm problem than other regions. Pricing the product less expensively in those regions leads to wider adoption there. Regions that face more problems with rootworms will pay a higher price because they face bigger problems with rootworms and therefore will derive more benefit from the product.[49]

EXECUTE PRICE CHANGES

Over time, price changes are inevitable. A marketing manager may want to raise or lower a price for competitive or other reasons, or competitors may make price changes that require a considered pricing response from your own firm. Among the marketing mix variables, price is the easiest and quickest to alter, so sometimes firms overrely on price changes to stimulate additional sales or gain market share. You've already seen that establishing pricing objectives and strategies and implementing pricing tactics is complex and entails important managerial decisions. It is important to also recall that in the overall scope of marketing planning and strategy, pricing does not take place in a vacuum. That is, a change in an offering's price—either up or down—can dramatically impact the effectiveness of the overall marketing mix variables in reflecting your offering's positioning in the eyes of customers.

It is important for marketing managers to conduct appropriate market research in advance of major price changes to try to determine the likely impact of a price change on customer perceptions of the offering and likelihood to purchase. Both qualitative research approaches, such as focus groups, and quantitative approaches, such as surveys and experiments, can be designed to determine the degree to which an anticipated price change might influence customer response. Ideally, price changes upward will reflect the **just noticeable difference (JND)** in a price, which is the amount of price increase that can be taken without affecting customer demand.

If a potential upward price change is being driven by pressure on margins, creative marketers often look for ways to save margin without increasing price. Over the years, candy manufacturers have been severely affected by swings in the price of sugar. As the sugar price has gone up, a good portion of the profit margin of a candy bar has been preserved by simply reducing the size of the bar. Today's chocolate lovers would be amazed at seeing how much larger a Snickers bar was in 1970 versus today; the basic bar has shrunk by more than one-third during that time. While the price of a bar has also risen dramatically during that period (an average of four times the 1970 price), the price increase would have been even more dramatic without the reduction in ounces.

In addition to reducing the offering in terms of size or quantity, other nonprice approaches to mitigating the pressure to maintain margins include altering or reducing discounts and allowances, unbundling some services or features from the original offering, increasing minimum order quantities, or simply reducing product quality. However, marketing managers should be cautious when they begin to consider altering the product itself to retain margins; customer response to such tinkering might be negative.

A worst-case scenario occurs when a firm takes a price decrease on an offering to stimulate volume and grow share, only to have one or more competitors immediately and aggressively jump in to meet or beat the price decrease, resulting in a price war. Price wars are the quickest way to destroy margins and bottom-line profit. The old marketing adage "We'll price our product lower but make it up on volume" doesn't work when competitive price pressure forces prices below cost!

Assume that you, as a marketing manager, just found out that a competitor has taken a price increase or decrease. You must evaluate the change and select the appropriate response for your product line. The basic principles and cautions about competing on price are the same, regardless of whether your firm or a competitor fires the first shot. If your firm is the market leader, you may find that competitors tend to create similar but somewhat inferior offerings at attractive prices in an attempt to knock you off as leader.

When formulating a response to a competitor's price reduction, remember to consider your offering from the perspective of its overall value proposition to customers and not be too quick to react in kind with a price decrease. In the case of a competitor's price increase, perhaps based on escalating costs or margin pressure, analysis may reveal the increase is an opportunity to both gain a price advantage and perhaps increase your volume and share, especially if you are a cost leader and can maintain desired margins at your current price. Or you may simply wish to take a concurrent price increase and enjoy the related margin enhancement. Remember, a cost leadership strategy does not necessarily imply price leadership; rather, the best cost leader firms take a portion of their cost leadership to margin and perhaps a portion to price advantage.

The trend in consumer products is toward bigger packs with more product inside—per piece, gum is cheaper in a 17-piece pack than in the 5-piece packs of yesteryear.

UNDERSTAND LEGAL CONSIDERATIONS IN PRICING

In the process of setting pricing objectives and developing and implementing pricing strategies and tactics, marketing managers must be aware that some aspects of pricing decision making can be very sensitive legally. Laws at the national, state, and local level are in place that impact a firm's pricing practices. Federal legislation includes the Sherman Antitrust Act (1890), Clayton Act (1914), Robinson-Patman Act (1936), and Consumer Goods Pricing Act (1975). The Federal Trade Commission (FTC) actively monitors and enforces federal pricing laws. Several of the more important legal considerations in pricing and their associated regulatory bases are discussed below.

Price Fixing

Companies that collude to set prices at a mutually beneficial high level are engaged in **price fixing.** When competitors are involved in the collusion, horizontal price fixing occurs.[50] The Sherman Act forbids horizontal price fixing, which could result in overall higher prices for consumers since various competitors are all pricing the same to maximize their profits.

When independent members of a channel (for example, manufacturers, distributors, and retailers) collude to establish a minimum retail price, referred to as retail price maintenance, vertical price fixing occurs. Vertical price fixing is illegal under the Consumer Goods Pricing Act, and for good reason. Vertical price fixing assures everybody in the channel is satisfied with their "cut" of the profits, but the profit boost is achieved by increased prices to consumers.

Price Discrimination

Price discrimination occurs when a seller offers different prices to different customers without a substantive basis, such that competition is reduced. The Robinson-Patman Act explicitly prohibits giving, inducing, or receiving discriminatory prices except under certain specific conditions such as situations where proof exists that the costs of selling to one customer are higher than to another (such as making distribution to remote locations) or when temporary, defensive price reductions are necessary to meet competition in a specific local area.[51]

Deceptive Pricing

Knowingly stating prices in a manner that gives a false impression to customers is **deceptive pricing.** Deceptive pricing practices are monitored and enforced by the FTC. Deceptive pricing may take several forms. Sometimes, firms will set artificially high reference prices for merchandise just before a promotion so that an advertised sale price will look much more attractive to customers.[52] Or a seller may advertise an item at an unbelievably low price to lure customers into a store, and once the customer arrives refuse to sell the advertised item and instead push a similar item with a much higher price and higher margin. When this occurs and it can be demonstrated that a seller had no true intent to actually make the lower-priced item available for sale, the practice is called **bait and switch** and is illegal. Finally, the ubiquitous reliance of retailers on scanner-based pricing has opened a plethora of stealth pricing fraud schemes, perpetrated by dishonest retailers who label an item on the shelf sign at a lower price than it is actually priced within the scanner database. For certain, some of the scanner errors result from mistakes and not fraud, but the nontransparent nature of scanner pricing puts a burden on the customer to return to the days of "buyer beware."

Predatory Pricing

A strategy to intentionally sell below cost to push a competitor out of a market, then raise prices to new highs is called predatory pricing. Predatory pricing is illegal but prosecuting it can be very tricky because intent must be proved. Other plausible explanations exist for drastic price reductions including inventory overstocks, so proving that predatory pricing has occurred is difficult.

Fair Trade and Minimum Markup Laws

Fair trade laws were popular in the past because they allowed manufacturers to establish artificially high prices by limiting the ability of wholesalers and retailers to offer reduced or discounted prices. Fair trade laws varied greatly from state to state, depending largely on how strong the independent retailer and wholesaler lobby was in a particular locale. These laws protected mom-and-pop operators from the price discounting by chain stores.[53]

Closely associated with fair trade laws are **minimum markup laws,** which require a certain percentage markup be applied to products. In one extreme case in the early 1970s, the State of Oklahoma took legal action against Target Corporation to force the discounter to obey Oklahoma's minimum markup law that prohibited advertising a wide variety of merchandise for less than a 6 percent profit. This effectively shut down Target's ability to advertise **loss leader products,** items (typically paper towels, toilet paper, toothpaste, and the like) sacrificed at prices below cost to attract shoppers to the store.[54] Target fought back by creating special versions of its famous full-color Sunday advertising inserts for Oklahoma shoppers that showed in very large type the nationally advertised sales price accompanied by a disclaimer clearly showing a much higher "in Oklahoma" price. In effect, the ads told Oklahomans they couldn't get the same prices as the rest of the country, and it didn't take long for Oklahoma consumers to come to their senses and realize that the state's fair pricing law might protect small retailers but it hurt everyday shoppers. In 1975, the federal Consumer Goods Pricing Act repealed all state fair trade laws and minimum markup laws.

SUMMARY

Clearly, price is a critical element in an offering's perceived value. Marketing managers must establish clear pricing objectives and related strategies, supported by well-executed pricing tactics. In setting the exact price, it is best to compare several approaches before making a decision. Several channel discounts and allowances are available that can impact purchaser behavior in ways that benefit the selling firm. Price changes are inevitable and marketing managers must anticipate customer and competitor responses. Finally, marketing managers must be sensitive to legal ramifications of certain pricing practices.

KEY TERMS

cost leadership 384
pricing objectives 387
market share 387
penetration pricing 387
price skimming 388
target return on investment (ROI) 388

price elasticity of demand 389
competitor-based pricing 389
price war 389
stability pricing 390
value pricing 390
product line pricing (price lining) 393

price points 393
captive pricing (complementary pricing) 394
price bundling 395
reference pricing 395
prestige pricing 396
odd pricing 396

APPLICATION QUESTIONS

1. Why might penetration pricing potentially negatively impact brand image and product positioning in the long run? Given this risk, why would a marketing manager use penetration pricing? Identify a brand (other than the examples in the chapter) that you believe is engaged in penetration pricing.

2. Pricing against competitors is common. Yet, the approach carries some significant problems.

   a. What are the advantages of competitor-based pricing?

   b. What are the risks of using competitor-based pricing exclusive of other approaches?

   c. Identify a few industries in which taking competitor-based pricing into account might be especially beneficial when developing an overall pricing strategy. What caused you to select the industries you did?

3. Review Exhibit 14.3 on price-quality positioning along with the accompanying discussion.

   a. Consider the low quality/high price quadrant. Identify a brand (other than the examples in the chapter) that you believe presently resides in this quadrant. How is it able to command a high price? Do you believe the pricing strategy is sustainable for that brand? Why or why not?

   b. Consider the high quality/low price quadrant. Identify a brand (other than the examples in the chapter) that you believe presently resides in this quadrant. In your opinion, why has the brand undertaken this pricing strategy? Do you believe there are risks to the brand in remaining too long in that quadrant? Why or why not?

4. Select any three of the pricing tactics identified in the chapter. For *each* tactic:

   a. Identify a brand (other than the examples in the chapter) that you believe is currently employing that tactic.

   b. Provide evidence to support the use of that tactic.

   c. Is the use of the tactic effective? Why or why not?

   d. What factors might cause a need to abandon this tactic in favor of another?

5. Assume that you are a marketing manager for Pantene shampoo and conditioner, two of Procter & Gamble's star products. Several competitors have recently begun to cut prices to retailers and also to offer more aggressive channel allowances to boost sales and market share.

   a. What options do you have as a response to the competitive price declines?

   b. What are the risks associated with each of the options?

   c. Assuming Pantene is the market leader in its category, what response to the price cuts do you recommend?

MANAGEMENT DECISION CASE:
Pricing Approaches in the Printer Industry

Eastman Kodak Co. designed a new line of Kodak printers that print high-quality photos. The ink is formulated so prints will stay vibrant for 100 years rather than 15. Most impressive of all, replacement ink cartridges will cost half of what consumers are used to paying. The new printers will be priced at $149 to $299. Black ink cartridges will cost $9.99, color ones will cost $14.99. If consumers buy Kodak's economical Photo Value Pack, which combines paper and ink, the cost per print is about 10 cents, compared with 24 cents for Hewlett-Packard's comparable package. "It's really a revolution of thought in how to bring the price of printing down and encourage people to print more," says David Morrish, senior vice president of merchandising for Best Buy Co., which has an exclusive on the product for three months.

If Kodak pulls this off, it could pose a huge challenge to the $50 billion printer industry. Those companies now rely on a razor-and-blades strategy, often discounting machines and making most of their profits on replacement cartridges. "We're very proud that we're coming to market 20 years late," Kodak CEO Antonio Perez says with a grin. "We think it will give us an opportunity to disrupt the industry's business model and address consumers' key dissatisfaction: the high cost of ink."

In particular, Kodak's strategy is an assault on the profit engine of industry leader HP. Printing supplied 60 percent of HP's $6.56 billion in operating earnings last year. Even before Kodak's new printer introduction, HP was facing strong competition from cheaper store-brand ink-jet printer cartridges. To fight back, HP has allegedly approached chain stores that sell store-brand cartridges compatible with its printers and offered them incentives if they end the practice. Because those replacement cartridges typically sell for 10 to 15 percent less than HP's, consumers could be the big losers if a lot of retailers take the printer giant up on its offer.

Staples Inc., the country's largest seller of replacement ink, confirmed to *BusinessWeek* it plans on phasing out sales of store-brand inks for HP printers. Industry analysts are watching the action closely. "The speculation is that [Staples] reached a deal with HP and got increased margin and soft money for marketing," says Charles Brewer, managing editor of *The Hard Copy Supplies Journal,* a trade publication that first wrote about Staples' move. "That line is selling very well for Staples. They wouldn't drop it without compensation."

Other retailers, including Best Buy Co. and Office Depot Inc., say they will continue to sell store-brand HP-compatible ink. "We carry what the customers ask for," says Scott Koerner, senior vice president for merchandising at Office Depot. "As long as the customers continue to ask for it, we intend to continue to carry it. This is about providing customer choice." Asked if industry behemoth HP approached Office Depot and asked it to stop carrying store-brand ink, Koerner said, "I can't comment on any conversations with HP one way or the other."

Executives in the ink cartridge remanufacturing industry say they are discussing whether to complain to regulators about the moves, which the executives say may harm consumers. Do these alleged tactics raise antitrust questions? "Antitrust law would only be violated if HP does something that significantly eliminates alternatives from the market and gives it enhanced market power as a result," according to Steven C. Salop, professor of economics and law at Georgetown University Law Center. "Right now, there are alternatives being sold at other office superstores, and other printer brands are being sold at Staples."

Questions for Consideration

1. What do you think of HP's move to offer retailers incentives not to sell their store-brand alternatives to HP cartridges?

2. HP recently sued two companies that sell refilled ink cartridges, arguing that the companies violate some of HP's patents. HP holds 9,000 patents related to imaging and printing, 4,000 of them for consumable supplies such as ink and cartridges. If companies are allowed to refill and resell HP cartridges, will this hurt HP's razor-and-blades strategy of selling its printers less expensively in hopes of making up profits in the cartridges? Is there something else that HP could do to sell printers at less than cost, but somehow make it up after the sale?

3. If you were Kodak, what kind of marketing campaign would you launch to compete against HP?

Source: Steve Hamm, "Kodak's Moment of Truth," *BusinessWeek,* February 19, 2007; and "Rivals Say HP is using Hardball Tactics," *BusinessWeek,* February 19, 2007. Reprinted with permission.

MARKETING PLAN EXERCISE

ACTIVITY 14: Pricing Your Offering

As you learned in this chapter, your approach to pricing is an integral aspect of positioning your offering. Price sends a signal to customers about the offering's quality and other characteristics. At the same time, effective pricing ensures margins and profits needed for continued success.

1. Review the options for pricing objectives and strategies and establish an appropriate set for your offering.

2. Review the various available pricing tactics and select a mix of tactics that you believe is most appropriate for your offering.

3. Consider the methods of establishing an exact price presented in the chapter. Use these approaches to develop a comparative set for review. Select a final price for the offering.

4. What channel discounts and allowances will you provide on your offering?

If you are using Marketing Plan Pro, a template for this assignment can be accessed at www.mhhe.com/marshall1e.

RECOMMENDED READINGS

1. Ronald J. Baker, *Pricing on Purpose: Creating and Capturing Value* (Hoboken, NJ: John Wiley & Sons, 2006).

2. Robert G. Docters, Michael Reopel, Jeanne-Mey Sun, and Stephen M. Tanny, *Winning the Profit Game: Smarter Pricing, Smarter Branding* (New York: McGraw-Hill, 2003).

3. Michael V. Marn, Eric V. Roegner, and Craig C. Zawada, *The Price Advantage* (Hoboken, NJ: John Wiley & Sons, 2004).

4. Rafi Mohammed, *The Art of Pricing: How to Find the Hidden Profits to Grow Your Business* (New York: Crown Business, 2005).

5. Kent B. Monroe, *Pricing: Making Profitable Decisions,* 3rd ed. (New York: McGraw-Hill, 2002).

6. Thomas T. Nagle and John Hogan, *The Strategy and Tactics of Pricing: A Guide to Growing More Profitably* (Upper Saddle River, NJ: Prentice Hall Business Publishing, 2005).

part FOUR

Communicating and Delivering the Value Offering

CHAPTER 15

MANAGING MARKETING CHANNELS AND THE SUPPLY CHAIN

LEARNING OBJECTIVES

- Define a value network and how organizations operate within this approach.

- Identify various types of intermediaries and distribution channels.

- Understand the impact of intermediary contributions via physical distribution functions, transaction and communication functions, and facilitating functions.

- Explain the different types of vertical marketing systems.

- Utilize suitable criteria to select appropriate channel approaches.

- Identify the logistics aspects of supply chain management.

EXECUTIVE PERSPECTIVE

Executive Samantha Wilson, Manager, Marketing

Company CHEP–U.S.

Business Pallet and container pooling services

How does your service fit into a client's value chain—that is, where do you add value to the client's operations?

CHEP understands the need for economical product distribution on all levels. CHEP equipment pooling facilitates a more efficient freight environment and helps decrease costs—an average savings of $1.50 for every pallet—by reducing product damage and pallet cost. Using the CHEP solution, manufacturers, distributors, and retailers of every size move products with confidence on CHEP pallets. Bottom line, from sturdy high-performance pallets to effective management systems, CHEP equipment pooling solutions simplify pallet administration and improve transportation efficiency, resulting in a more streamlined and profitable supply chain.

In what ways do customers use you as an outsourced supplier?

CHEP partners with suppliers, manufacturers, growers, transporters, distributors, and retailers to move their products through their supply chain. The CHEP solution improves efficiencies, reduces costs, and meets customer needs. Our services are based on a unique mix of customer-driven solutions, high-quality products, sophisticated control systems, a well-managed global service center network, and advanced logistics capabilities. These elements enable our customers to reduce the need for capital expenditures and concentrate on their core business competencies. Our customers can then focus on doing what *they* do best.

It is often said that an effective and efficient supply chain presents a major opportunity for competitive advantage to firms today. What is your view on this statement?

I agree. This is the value proposition of CHEP. By providing supply chain solutions designed to meet customer needs and allowing them to concentrate on their core competencies, CHEP is a direct driver of efficiency and innovation—we're proud of that. By using the CHEP solution, customers not only improve their supply chain and lower supply chain costs, but they also benefit from CHEP's environmentally friendly solutions. CHEP provides an efficient and sustainable supply chain platform due to its unique pooling model. With over 140 service centers across the country and over 75 million CHEP pallets flowing through the United States annually, the CHEP solution is built on providing sustainability throughout the supply chain.

For example, in 2006 alone CHEP USA reissued hundreds of millions of pallets worldwide, resulting in environmental savings of roughly 1.25 billion pounds of solid waste, 3.4 trillion BTUs of energy, and 596 million pounds of greenhouse gas emissions. The resulting savings could power every household in a city the size of Plano, Texas, for one year. Now, that's real pallet power.

THE VALUE CHAIN AND VALUE NETWORKS

The concept of the value chain, which was introduced in Chapter 2, is worth revisiting at this point. The value chain portrays a synthesis of primary and support activities utilized by an organization to design, produce, market, deliver, and support its products (see Exhibit 15.1).

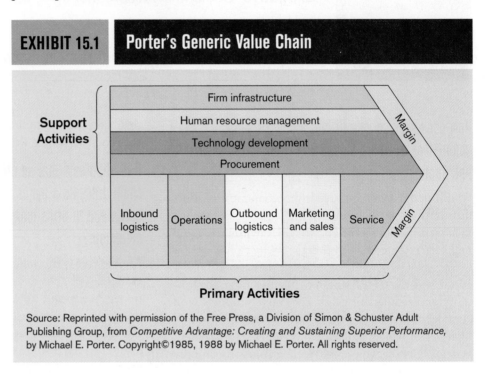

EXHIBIT 15.1	Porter's Generic Value Chain

Source: Reprinted with permission of the Free Press, a Division of Simon & Schuster Adult Publishing Group, from *Competitive Advantage: Creating and Sustaining Superior Performance*, by Michael E. Porter. Copyright©1985, 1988 by Michael E. Porter. All rights reserved.

Thinnovation.

The world's thinnest notebook. 13.3" widescreen display. Full-sized keyboard. MacBook Air

Apple adds value to customers in many ways through innovation, technology, and great marketing, service, and logistics.

Several of the value chain activities are directly relevant to what you will read about in this chapter, including inbound and outbound logistics, operations issues, and procurement. In fact, emblematic of the central role that channel and supply chain issues play in forming the value proposition of modern firms, it is telling that today more and more marketing managers are turning to elements of the "place P" within the 4Ps of the marketing mix for sources of differential competitive advantage.[1] How value is added by successfully managing a firm's channels and supply chain is the central topic of this chapter.

At the broadest level, a firm might view itself as integral part of a **value network,** which may be thought of as an overarching system of formal and informal relationships within which the firm participates to procure, transform and enhance, and ultimately supply its offerings in final form within a market space. Value networks are fluid and complex. They are composed of potentially numerous firms with which a company interacts vertically within its channel of distribution and horizontally across other firms whose contributions are essential to getting the right offering to the right customers. A value network perspective is a macro-level strategic approach that is being adopted by many firms in part because of the intense competition to cut costs and maximize process efficiencies every step of the way to market. The approach suggests opportunities for breaking outside of traditional thinking that marketing is encapsulated *within* an organization, and instead suggests looking for such opportunities as alliances, strategic partnerships, nontraditional channel approaches, and outsourcing opportunities to provide unique sources of competitive edge.[2]

At its core, a value network exists to co-create value. The aim is **value co-creation** by the participating suppliers, customers, and other stakeholders in which the members of the network combine capabilities according to their expertise and the competencies required from the situation.[3] The key elements of a value network are portrayed in Exhibit 15.2.

EXHIBIT 15.2	Elements of a Value Network

- The overarching process focus is on value co-creation.
- A shared vision exists within the network with a common aim of fostering value co-creation.
- Value co-creation is viewed as emanating from the expertise and competencies of all parties within the network.

- Network and team *relationships* are key elements in the co-creation of the value.
- This value is viewed as *network value.*
- Relationship conflicts are viewed as potential barriers to the creation of network value and a process for conflict co-management is essential.

Source: Derived from Stephen L. Vargo and Robert F. Lusch, "Evolving to a New Dominant Logic for Marketing," *Journal of Marketing* 68 (January 2004), pp. 1–17.

Based on the concept of value networks, a whole new breed of organization is arising called a **network organization,** or **virtual organization,** because it eliminates many in-house business functions and activities in favor of focusing only on those aspects for which it is best equipped to add value.[4] Such approaches are often pursued to provide quicker market response and to free resources to focus on the firm's core deliverables. Network firms usually formalize contracts with suppliers, distributors, and other important partners to contribute the aspects of the value chain those entities do best, then draw on their own internal capabilities to focus on core internal sources of value. Some network organizations operate much like a shell in which most or all of the actual manufacturing, distribution, operations, and maybe even R&D and marketing execution are outsourced to efficient experts.[5] Ethical Dimension 15 provides an interesting look at global outsourcing at Apple.

Scotts Miracle-Gro Company, which markets weed control and other lawn- and garden-care products, outsources the management of its warehouses. The warehouses are run by seven third-party logistics providers (3PLs). To oversee and evaluate how the warehouses are run, Scotts developed a 12-point performance management program for its 3PLs. Eight of the performance points emphasize improvements in staff behaviors, three focus on processes, and one spotlights technology. The warehouse management team developed specific expectations, procedures, and metrics that its 3PLs must meet to remain Scotts' partners.[6]

In the future, more firms, and especially start-ups, entrepreneurial organizations, and those whose core products are in the critical introduction and growth phases, will opt for a network organization approach to take advantage of the value network concept. This prediction is based on a competitive need for firms to be **nimble** in all aspects of their operation—that is, to be in a position to be

Outsourcing "Cool"

The Apple iPhone and iPhone 3G are an undeniable success. A "game changer," the iPhone has taken cell phones to a new level by offering a wide range of features (digital music player, Internet surfing, cell phone, PDA, e-mail) in an elegant touch-screen device with a huge display. The product incorporates a number of innovative designs that require sophisticated products from companies all over the world including Samsung chips and flash memory, Balda touch-screen, and Philips power management.

Of course, the unstoppable iPod dominates the digital music download market with a 70 percent market share. Over 100 million have been sold since its introduction in 2001 supported by an entire community of accessories from speakers to cases. As with iPhone, Apple did not invent the digital music player (i.e., MP3) but improved the product by creating innovative features in the iPod and changing the market perception. However, Apple does not assemble either iPod or iPhone because the challenges of handling the thousands of sensors, chips, and other parts is labor-intensive as well as technologically challenging. The company uses foreign manufacturers mostly in Asia because of their ability to handle complex technology manufacturing and their lower labor costs.

Apple chose Hon Hai Precision Industry in Taiwan to manufacture all iPod Nanos worldwide. Operating under the trade name Foxconn, the company is No. 4 on *BusinessWeek*'s IT 100 with sales exceeding $40 billion. The manufacture of Nanos is less than 5 percent of the company's total revenue. Hon Hai Precision Industry has been criticized for using sweatshop labor conditions in China to increase productivity. Hon Hai sued two Chinese reporters who had filed negative reports about the company's labor practices. Apple sent a team to China to investigate the allegations and reported that, while there were some abuses, overall the company was a good employer. Hon Hai has not experienced significant problems as a result of questions about its labor policies; however, the company has kept a very low profile and that is the way Apple prefers it. Negative publicity about events such as the working conditions in China can potentially damage Apple's carefully developed brand image.

Apple's brand image as a maker of cool, innovative products appeals to a broad range of people. Part of that image is based on the perception that Apple is a responsible corporation that is environmentally concerned and labor friendly.[7]

Ethical Perspective

1. **Apple:** How aggressive should Apple be in making sure its suppliers follow strict labor rules and policies? Should the company enforce U.S. labor standards or simply the standards of the local country?

2. **Consumers:** If you were aware that Apple was using a supplier that violated established labor practices, would you buy an Apple product? Do you research a company's policies about supplier labor practices or environmental policies before buying a product? If you don't, should you?

---

maximally flexible, adaptable, and speedy in response to the many key change drivers affecting business today such as rapidly shifting technology, discontinuous innovation, fickle consumer markets, and relentless market globalization.[8] Taking a value network approach frees up internal resources so a firm can be more nimble in addressing external uncontrollable opportunities and threats, thus yielding a potential competitive advantage over firms that have high costs associated with performing many of the value chain functions themselves. A network organization facilitates concentration on one's own distinctive competencies while efficiently gathering value from outside firms that are concentrating their efforts in their own areas of expertise within your value network.

Many organizations are beginning to consider their customers—both end users and within a channel—as important members of a value network. As you learned in Chapter 13, firms cultivate customer involvement in various aspects of product and market development to enable customer advocacy, which is a willingness and ability on the part of a customer to participate in communicating the brand message to others within his or her sphere of influence. There are several potential value-adding ways to involve customers, both in B2B and B2C settings, including participation in ongoing research, customer advisory panels, and providing recognition, rewards, and delightful surprises for customers that participate in the relationship at a high level.

Overall, managing marketing channels and the supply chain is a fruitful area of concentration for marketing managers because of its potential to enhance the value of the firm's goods and services in a variety of ways. As you read further about the various specific components of the "place P" in the marketing mix, keep in mind that in today's business environments the boundaries of just *how* these value-adding activities are delivered and *by whom* within the value network is a very open opportunity. As we have learned, these decisions are made with the knowledge that intelligent investment in the primary and support activities within the value chain should positively enhance profit margin through more efficient and effective firm performance.

CHANNELS AND INTERMEDIARIES

A **channel of distribution** consists of interdependent entities that are aligned for the purpose of transferring possession of a product from producer to consumer or business user. Put another way, a channel is a system of interdependent relationships among a set of organizations that facilitates the exchange process.[9] Most channels are not direct from producer to consumer. Instead, they contain a variety of **intermediaries,** formerly called middlemen, that play a role in the exchange process between producer and consumer.[10] A wide variety of types of intermediaries exists, and they usually fall within two principal categories: **merchant intermediaries,** who take title to the product, and **agent intermediaries,** who do not take title to the product.[11] Agent intermediaries perform a variety of physical distribution, transaction and communication, and facilitating functions that make exchange possible. Exhibit 15.3 provides further insight about major types of intermediaries.

EXHIBIT 15.3	Major Types of Intermediaries

MIDDLEMAN: Independent business entity that links producers and end-user consumers or organizational buyers.

MERCHANT MIDDLEMAN: Middleman that buys goods outright, taking title to them.

AGENT: Business entity that negotiates purchases, sales, or both but does not take title to the goods involved.

MANUFACTURERS' AGENT: Agent that usually operates on an extended contract, often sells within an exclusive territory, handles noncompeting but related lines of goods, and has limited authority to price and create terms of sale.

DISTRIBUTOR: Wholesale middleman, found especially when selective or exclusive distribution is common and strong promotional support is needed. Sometimes used synonymously for a wholesaler.

WHOLESALER: Entity primarily engaged in buying, taking title to, storing (usually), and physically handling goods in large quantities. Wholesalers resell the goods (usually in smaller quantities) to retailers or to organizational buyers.

JOBBER: Middleman that buys from manufacturers and sells to retailers. This intermediary is sometimes called a "rack jobber" to connote the service of stocking racks or shelves with merchandise.

FACILITATING AGENT: Entity that assists in the performance of distribution tasks other than buying, selling, and transferring title (examples include trucking companies, warehouses, importers, etc.).

RETAILER: Entity primarily engaged in selling to end-user consumers.

Source: *Dictionary of Marketing Terms*, 2nd ed., Peter D. Bennett, ed. (Chicago: American Marketing Association, 1995).

Frito-Lay uses a direct channel of distribution to retailers through which products are delivered by their own trucks, usually several times per week.

On the surface, intermediaries seem unnecessary. Wouldn't it be much more efficient for all channels to be direct from producer to consumer like Dell or Avon? The answer goes back to what we learned in Chapter 2 about the different types of utilities—form, time, place, and ownership. Sometimes you might hear a phrase such as, "We save you money by cutting out the middleman!" But in reality, cutting out intermediaries is not a guarantee of saving consumers' money. In the long run, channel intermediaries tend to continue to participate in a channel only as long as their value added to the channel supports their inclusion. If an intermediary of any of the types shown in Exhibit 15.3 doesn't carry its weight, the channel structure eventually will change accordingly to maximize efficiencies across the utilities. Thus, channel members add their value by bridging gaps in form, time, place, and ownership that naturally exist between producers and consumers.

Exhibits 15.4 and 15.5 illustrate examples within two distinct channel situations: one with end-user consumers as the final element in the channel and one ending with an organizational buyer in which the product is used within the business. The exhibits call attention to the fact that channels are distinguishable based on the number of intermediaries they contain—the more intermediaries that are involved, the longer the channel. A **direct channel,** portrayed as the first example in each exhibit, has no intermediaries and operates strictly from producer

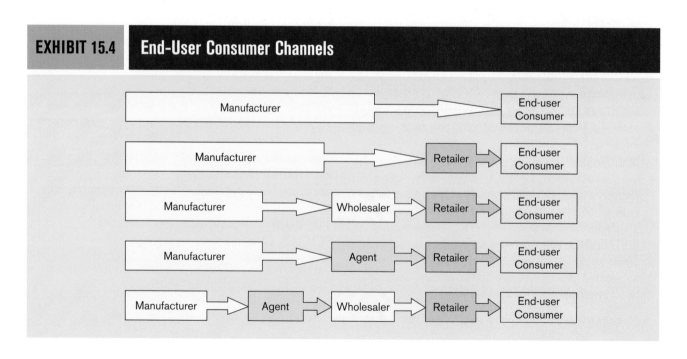

EXHIBIT 15.4   **End-User Consumer Channels**

Manufacturer → End-user Consumer

Manufacturer → Retailer → End-user Consumer

Manufacturer → Wholesaler → Retailer → End-user Consumer

Manufacturer → Agent → Retailer → End-user Consumer

Manufacturer → Agent → Wholesaler → Retailer → End-user Consumer

EXHIBIT 15.5   **Organizational Channels**

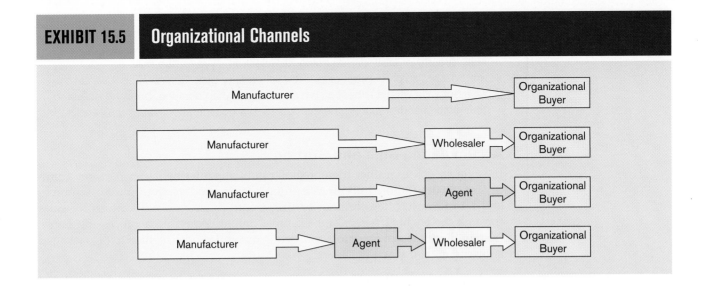

to end-user consumer or business user. An **indirect channel** contains one or more intermediary levels, as represented by all the other examples within each exhibit[12].

FUNCTIONS OF CHANNEL INTERMEDIARIES

Channel intermediaries enhance utilities by providing a wide array of specific functions. Their contributions can be classified into physical distribution functions, transaction and communication functions, and facilitating functions.

Physical Distribution Functions

One function of channel intermediaries is **physical distribution,** or **logistics,** which is the integrated process of moving input materials to the producer, in-process inventory through the firm, and finished goods out of the firm through the channel of distribution. A **supply chain** represents all organizations involved in supplying a firm, the members of its channels of distribution, and its end-user consumers and business users. The goal is coordination of these value-adding flows among the entities in a way that maximizes overall value delivered and profit realized.[13] The management of this process is called **supply chain management.** We will discuss more specific aspects of physical distribution and supply chain management later in the chapter. For now, let's examine how channel intermediaries contribute to the physical distribution function.

Breaking Bulk

In many industries, such as consumer health products, when finished goods come off a firm's production line, the manufacturer packages the individual pieces into large cartons for shipping into the channel of distribution. This is a convenient way for manufacturers to ship out the product. However, consumers shopping in a drugstore, whether a national chain such as Walgreens or an independent pharmacy in your hometown, don't need to see 144 units of a shampoo or deodorant on a store shelf. The function of **breaking bulk** occurs within a channel to better match quantities needed to space constraints and inventory turnover requirements.[14] Importantly, like most channel functions, breaking bulk could be performed by different types of intermediaries, in the case of Walgreens by the retailer's own warehouse and in the case of the local pharmacy by a drug wholesaler such as McKesson.

Raytheon Aircraft buys aluminum from a distributor rather than directly from a steel mill. Why? "The mills cannot support our lean product flow," says Michael Hull, director of strategic sourcing at Raytheon. "We let the mills do what they are best at, which is producing large volumes of bulk material. Then, we let the distributor do what it is best at, which is aggregating demand, breaking bulk, and then cutting and preparing the material for our consumption just as we need it."[15]

Accumulating Bulk and Sorting

In some industries, rather than breaking bulk, the intermediaries perform a process of **accumulating bulk**—that is, they take in product from multiple sources and transform it, often through **sorting** it into different classifications for sales through the channel.[16] Eggs, for example, might come into a processing house from individual farm operators for sorting by grade and size, then to be packaged and sent on their way to retailers.

Creating Assortments

Intermediaries engage in **creating assortments** when they accumulate products from several sources and then make those products available down the channel as a convenient assortment for consumers.[17] Assume for a moment you are looking for a new high-definition television (HDTV). With no channel intermediaries you would have to review the entire line of HDTVs from each manufacturer to truly understand the different product features offered across their product lines. But walk into Best Buy or go to the retailer's Web site and an assortment across those manufacturers is already waiting for your review, selected by Best Buy's expert buying staff based on features and value. Most consumers appreciate the convenience associated with having an assortment of choices available for review.

QVC expands the assortment available to its customers by offering a wide assortment on its Web site. A Web site must work in tandem with the on-air network and serve as the "anytime assortment," said Bob Myers, senior vice president for QVC.com. For instance, on any given day, QVC features about 280 items on-air, but 200,000 online, he said.[18]

Reducing Transactions

We've already seen how the introduction of even one intermediary into a channel can contribute to greatly **reducing transactions** necessary to complete an exchange. While it might seem counterintuitive to those who are not studying marketing management, channels with intermediaries actually tend to save end-user consumers money over what most direct producer to consumer distribution approaches would cost, given the same product.[19] Manufacturers' costs would skyrocket if they held the responsibility for interfacing with and delivering product to every one of their end users. Consider that conveniently located retailers save consumers a lot of money by reducing travel costs versus buying directly from a manufacturer. As mentioned earlier, in the long run, channel intermediaries remain in the channel only as long as they are adding efficiencies, reducing costs, and adding value within that channel.

Transportation and Storage

Relatively few producers operate their own transportation networks or provide warehousing facilities. Producers make money by pushing finished goods out the door and into the channel of distribution. As such, **transportation and storage** functions are among the most commonly provided channel intermediary activities. In the publishing industry, Amazon.com and other online booksellers play an invaluable role to both publishers and consumers by ensuring that sufficient inventories of the right books are available for shipping across a variety of transportation choices, from UPS ground to next-day air depending on the urgency of the order.

Transaction and Communication Functions

Another category of intermediary contribution within a channel is the performance of transaction and communication functions. These functions include:

- *Selling.* Often, intermediaries provide a sales force to represent a manufacturer's product line. This could take the form of manufacturers' representatives, or brokers, that represent a product line down the channel. Alternatively, the salespeople might work for a wholesaler or retailer.[20]

- *Buying.* Both wholesalers and retailers perform an important function by evaluating products and ultimately simplifying purchase decisions by creating assortments.[21]

- *Marketing communications.* Intermediaries frequently receive incentives from manufacturers to participate in helping promote products in the channel.[22] When a Target ad features Tide laundry detergent, it's a safe bet that Target has received a promotional allowance from P&G to feature the brand. Likewise, that shelf tag in your neighborhood pharmacy featuring a special price on Rolaids very likely was placed there by the pharmacy's wholesaler as part of a promotion by Pfizer.

Facilitating Functions

In a channel, **facilitating functions** performed by intermediaries include a variety of activities that help fulfill completed transactions and also maintain the viability of the channel relationships. These include:

- *Financing.* Without readily available credit at various stages in the distribution process many channels could not operate. In any given channel, when credit is required by one channel member it may be facilitated by another channel member such as a producer, wholesaler, or retailer, depending on the situation. Alternatively, credit may be facilitated by outside sources such as banks and credit card providers.[23]

- *Market research.* Because intermediaries are closer to end-user consumers and business users than manufacturers, they are in an ideal position to gather information about the market and consumer trends. Collecting and sharing market and competitive information helps members of the channel continue to offer the right product mix at the right prices.[24]

The H-E-B grocery store chain has a store in south Texas that focuses primarily on a Hispanic assortment of products. The store has a very different product mix compared to stores elsewhere in the country. The H-E-B store collects data at the store level on specific products and makes that available to manufacturers such as Procter & Gamble, which use the data to evaluate whether their products are selling well to Hispanic consumers.[25]

- *Risk-taking.* A big part of how an intermediary can add value is by reducing the risk of others in the channel. Any of the major physical distribution functions described above that are assumed by a channel member comes with potential risks and liabilities.[26] For example, accumulating bulk in perishable goods comes with a risk of spoilage if customer demand estimates are inaccurately high. Also, when product liability lawsuits are filed, the defendants named are nearly always anyone within the distribution channel that played a part in getting the product to market.

- *Other services.* Services performed by intermediaries run a gamut of activities such as training others in the channel on how to display or sell the products, repair and maintenance of products after a sale, and providing customized software for inventory management, accounting and billing, and other operational processes.

Genco provides product repair services for retailers and for consumer goods and electronics manufacturers such as Philips Consumer Electronics. Genco inspects all the returned goods at scanning stations in a central returns center to determine whether the products can be repaired. Products that can't be repaired may be reclaimed or sent to liquidators. Genco maintains a global network of liquidation channels that includes salvage buyers, online auction partners, B2B exchanges, fixed-price offerings, and category and bulk salvage.[27]

DISINTERMEDIATION AND E-CHANNELS

Driven largely by the advent of electronic commerce and online marketing, **disintermediation,** or the shortening or collapsing of marketing channels due to the elimination of one or more intermediaries, is common in the electronic channel. In the early days of e-commerce, many entrepreneurs rushed to market with a Web site to sell their favorite products. This dot-com boom quickly turned to a bust, however, in part because many of these new-age marketers didn't understand the basics of distribution channels. Simply opening a Web site that features a product is one thing, but it's another thing entirely to invest in the infrastructure and capabilities needed to consistently fulfill orders in a timely and accurate manner. Most postmortems on the cause of the dot-com bust point to poor channel and supply chain practices as the No. 1 reason so many of those initial e-marketers failed. That is, customer expectations were peaked by the novelty and convenience of buying online only to be dashed by delays and errors in product fulfillment after the sale.[28]

The Internet disintermediated thousands of travel agencies. Travel agents became unnecessary as people booked their own travel online. Other intermediaries, such as financial services and investment counselors, real estate agents, and insurance brokers, likewise began to worry about how to contend with customers accessing information on the Internet. Manuel and Maria Silva owned a Comer travel agency and saw their bookings dry up as people started using the Internet to book their travel. But the Silvas had an idea. They created a Web site loaded full of information about Portugal. People stumbling on this Web site thought they had discovered an official Portugal travel site and the mother lode of information about Portugal. By providing this value, the Silvas attracted potential customers from all over the world—not just those who could walk into their little travel agency store. In no time at all, the Silvas' profits soared.[29]

Today, electronic commerce has settled into a more rational position as one of several approaches within marketing management for distributing and promoting goods and services. E-marketers are much more savvy about how they set up and manage their channels and realize that disintermediation may not improve aggregate channel performance. The trend toward more stability in online shopping was facilitated in large measure by the entry of firms such as UPS and FedEx into the market of providing a broad range of integrated supply chain solutions.

Recently, many e-commerce (and other) firms are finding that handing over one or more of their core internal functions, such as most or all of their supply chain activities, to other (third-party) companies that are experts in those areas allows the firm to better focus on its core business. This approach, which is referred to as **insourcing** or **third-party logistics,** is attractive for many firms whose core competencies do not include elements of supply chain management. The trend has opened up opportunities for firms such as UPS and FedEx, as well as a host of other smaller firms, to change their business focus from mere shippers into broad-based logistics consultancies that handle all aspects of clients' supply chain functions.[30]

VERTICAL MARKETING SYSTEMS

Whereas standard marketing channels are comprised of independent entities, a **vertical marketing system (VMS)** consists of vertically aligned networks behaving and performing as a unified system.[31] A VMS can be set up in three different ways: corporate systems, contractual systems, and administered systems. At its essence, in a VMS a channel member *(a)* owns the others, *(b)* has contracts with them, or *(c)* simply forces cooperation through sheer clout within the channel.

Corporate Systems

In **corporate VMS,** a channel member has invested in backward or forward **vertical integration** by buying a controlling interest in other intermediaries. In the Midwest, what is now the Braum's Ice Cream and Dairy Store chain started in the 1930s as a family dairy farm in Kansas. Over time the Braum family acquired almost every aspect of its distribution channel—milk processing, other product manufacturing, transportation, warehousing, and the Braum's stores. An owned, or corporate, VMS such as that practiced by Braum's creates a powerful competitive advantage in the marketplace due to cost and process efficiencies realized when a channel is strictly controlled by one entity.

Contractual Systems

A **contractual VMS** consists of otherwise independent entities that are bound together legally through contractual agreement. The most famous example of this arrangement is a **franchise organization,** which is designed to create a contractual relationship between a franchisor that grants the franchise and the franchisee, or the independent entity entering into an agreement to perform at the standards required by the franchisor.[32] *Entrepreneur* magazine reports that franchising remains the highest-potential start-up and growth mechanism for small-business owners, and it's an effective way to expand a distribution channel quickly and efficiently. Subway, the world's largest franchise system, has over 27,000 outlets in 85 countries.

Another common contractual VMS is the **retailer cooperative,** or co-op. In this era of chain stores, independent retailers across a variety of product categories have banded together to gain cost and operating economies of scale in the channel. Associated Grocers is a retailer-owned co-op of more than 200 stores that, through enhanced buying and distribution power, can better compete with supermarket chains than if the stores were buying separately.[33] A variation on this concept is the **wholesaler cooperative,** such as Ace Hardware or Rexall Pharmacies, in which retailers contract for varying degrees of exclusive dealings with a particular wholesaler.[34]

Administered Systems

In an **administered VMS,** the sheer size and power of one of the channel members places it in a position of channel control. The lead player in such situations may be referred to as the **channel captain** or **channel leader,** signifying its ability to control many aspects of that channel's operations.[35] For years, P&G was the channel captain in every channel in which it was a member based on the clout of its extensive stable of No. 1 brands. It became notorious for dictating terms of sale, limiting quantities of promotional goods to intermediaries, and steamrolling uncooperative wholesalers and retailers into submission. But the rise of giant retailers—Wal-Mart, in particular—shifted the power in the channel and forced P&G to become more customer-compliant.

It is possible that an administered VMS can be more formally structured through strategic alliances and partnership agreements among channel members that agree to work in mutual cooperation. Today, P&G and Wal-Mart have developed a strategic alliance that includes connectivity of inventory, billing systems, and market research. The result is improved inventory management, more efficient invoice processing, and product development that better serves the consumer marketplace. Approaches such as this are often referred to as **partner relationship management (PRM) strategies.** The goal of PRM is to share resources, especially knowledge-based resources, to effect optimally profitable relationships between two channel members.[36]

CHANNEL BEHAVIOR: CONFLICT AND POWER

The very nature of channels, especially traditional channels composed of independent entities, fosters differences in channel power among members. **Channel power** is the degree to which any member of a marketing channel can exercise influence over the other members of the channel. As we saw with the administered VMS, power can directly influence the relationships within the channel. Ultimately, **channel conflict** can occur in which channel members experience disagreements and their relationship can become strained or fall apart. Unresolved channel conflict can result not only in an uncooperative and inefficient channel, but it can also ultimately impact end-user consumers through inferior products, spotty inventory, and higher prices.

Danskin sells activewear through 3,000 retail locations nationwide. When the company decided to launch its Web site, it was very mindful of the potential channel conflict. The company, therefore, initially offered only plus-sized products on the Web, so that it would not compete directly with the retail stores. When Danskin's retail customers did not show resistance to the Web site, Danskin slowly expanded its online presence, adding additional regular-sized apparel and more fashion styles. To avoid competing with its retail customers on price, Danskin's online merchandise was offered at the manufacturer's suggested retail price.[37]

French and Raven have identified five important sources of power that are relevant in a channel setting. Those power sources are illustrated in Exhibit 15.6 and explained below.

- *Coercive power.* **Coercive power** involves an explicit or implicit threat that a channel captain will invoke negative consequences on a channel member if it does not comply with the leader's request or expectations. Wal-Mart has exceedingly tight standards for how shippers must schedule delivery appointments at a Wal-Mart distribution center. If the truck misses the appointment by even a few minutes, the error results in punitive financial consequences for the vendor. If the problem becomes repetitive, a vendor will be placed on probation as an approved source.

EXHIBIT 15.6   Sources of Channel Power

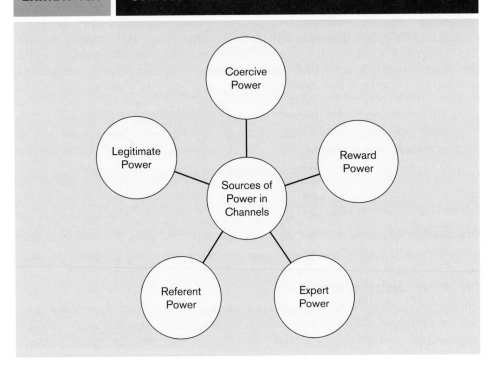

- *Reward power.* Despite Wal-Mart's ability to coerce, few vendors will turn up their nose at potential business from the retailing giant just because they can be difficult to work with. Naturally, the motivating force is Wal-Mart's huge **reward power** in the form of writing big orders.

- *Expert power.* Often, channel members adopt an approach of utilizing their unique competencies to influence others in the channel. **Expert power** might take the form of sharing important product knowledge, such as a representative from Clinique setting up a demonstration for cosmetic consultants in a Nordstrom store to stimulate sales expertise. Or, it might involve sharing of information such as Kroger Supermarkets providing consumer preference data to Frito-Lay to get it to produce a special flavor of chips for a specific geographic area that Kroger serves.

- *Referent power.* When a channel member is respected, admired, or revered based on one or more attributes, that member enjoys **referent power** within the channel. Only the best of the best brands can rely on this power source. In frozen foods, Stouffer's (a unit of Nestlé) commands a level of respect well above the competition because of its outstanding quality standards, successful marketing and branding strategies, and cooperativeness with retailers. When frozen-food sections of supermarkets are reset to accommodate new-product entries and remove discontinued items, Stouffer reps are often trusted to help store clerks reset the shelves and in many instances Stouffer's is given prime display space in the freezer case.

- *Legitimate power.* **Legitimate power** results from contracts such as franchise agreements or other formal agreements. When McDonald's requires franchisees that want to participate in the latest scratch-off game to sign an agreement as to how the game will be promoted and administered in the store, it is exercising legitimate power to control misuse of the promotional activity.[38]

SELECTING CHANNEL APPROACHES

Given the plethora of choices of channel intermediaries and channel structures that we've reviewed, marketing managers have a lot to consider when designing or selecting the channel approach that will best meet their needs. When marketing planning, a good channel decision can be one of the most important within the entire planning process and can lead to market advantage over competitors. Among the issues for consideration are:

1. What is the level of distribution intensity sought within the channel?
2. How much control and adaptability is required over the channel and its activities?
3. What are the priority channel functions that require investment?

Distribution Intensity

Distribution intensity refers to the number of intermediaries involved in distributing the product. Distribution strategies can be intensive, selective, or exclusive.

Intensive Distribution

When the objective is to obtain maximum product exposure throughout the channel, an **intensive distribution** strategy is designed to saturate every possible intermediary and especially retailers. Intensive distribution is typically associated with low-cost **convenience goods. Impulse goods** are also appropriate for intensive distribution, as their sales rely on the consumer seeing the product, feeling an immediate want, and being able to purchase now.

Selective Distribution

Shopping goods, goods for which a consumer may engage in a limited search, are candidates for **selective distribution.** Examples of goods that fit this approach include most appliances, mid-range fashion apparel, and home furnishings. A selective distribution strategy may require that intermediaries provide a modicum of customer service during the sale and, depending on the type of good, follow-up service after the sale. Intermediary reputation, especially of the retailers, can be an asset in selective distribution. For example, selecting a retailer whose brand connection enhances and is compatible with the product is essential. Distributing a Kenneth Cole watch or accessory at either Kmart or Tiffany & Company is not a good fit, but gaining distribution in Dillard's and Macy's makes a lot of sense.

Exclusive Distribution

When a manufacture opts for **exclusive distribution** in a channel, it is often part of an overall positioning strategy built on prestige, scarcity, and premium pricing. In Chapter 14 you read about Voss Water's highly successful entry into the ultra-premium bottled water market. Voss's

Avis selectively stocks varying quantities of Hummer H3s at its rental locations depending on the profile of rental customers in the different locales.

prestige was greatly enhanced by a distribution strategy that involved only one wholesale distributor per state, which had to be a liquor, wine, and spirits wholesaler with relationships already built among the exclusive restaurants and hotels that Voss was targeting. Exclusive distribution also often arises because a significant personal selling effort is required with the consumer before product purchase. Products that possess complex or unique properties that only a one-to-one in-person interaction with a customer can explain are often best served by intermediaries with specialized sales capabilities.[39]

Luxury brand Chanel keeps its exclusivity by selling its products only through upscale department stores such as Neiman Marcus and Saks Fifth Avenue and independent high-end boutiques like Jeffrey's in New York. When Global CEO Maureen Chiquet strategizes about the launch of a new perfume at Chanel, she tells her team, "Let's not be thinking about how big we can make this, but about how exclusive and special you can keep it."[40]

Channel Control and Adaptability

Review of the types of intermediaries in Exhibit 15.3 and channel examples in Exhibits 15.4 and 15.5 reveals a variety of options that can lead to more or less control and adaptability over the channel. Hiring an in-house sales force, investing in a fleet of trucks, building a warehouse facility, pursuing a corporate VMS through vertical integration, and engaging in a contractual VMS with other intermediaries each would increase a firm's control of the channel but at the same time limit its flexibility to change if the competition and other external forces require it. Other options, such as brokers, manufacturer's agents, and common carriers have the opposite effect in that a firm's influence and control in the channel is minimized but great flexibility is attained to dramatically and quickly alter aspects of the channel if needed.

In deciding on the right balance between control and flexibility in a channel, marketing managers must consider the type of products involved, cost issues among the various options, strength of belief in the accuracy of the sales forecast, and likelihood that major changes will occur in the customer or competitive marketplace that would necessitate restructuring the channel. Often, customers drive the ultimate choice a marketing manager makes about a channel, as flexibility or control differentially impact the value proposition from one customer to the next.

Prioritization of Channel Functions—Push versus Pull Strategy

The third aspect of channel decisions by marketing managers relates to what channel functions are most important to the success of the particular products. In large measure, this decision is framed by whether the general approach is a push strategy or a pull strategy. A **push strategy** means that much of the intensive promotional activities take place from the manufacturer downward through the channel of distribution. Think of this approach as an investment by the manufacturer in intermediaries so that they will have a maximal incentive to stock, promote, sell, and ship the firm's products. Push strategies usually are supported by heavy allowance payments to intermediaries for helping accomplish the manufacturer's goals. Examples include funding an extra incentive to a wholesale drug salesperson for pushing a particular medication to an independent pharmacy, or paying a **slotting allowance** or **shelf fee** to secure distribution in an intermediary's inventory listing and warehouse or onto a retail shelf.[41]

In contrast, a manufacturer employing a **pull straegy** focuses much of its promotional investment on the end-user consumer. In this case, heavy advertising in mass media, direct marketing, couponing, and other direct-to-consumer promotion are expected to create demand from intermediaries from the bottom of the channel upward. A pull strategy doesn't mean a manufacturer wouldn't engage in any channel incentives, but rather that the incentives would likely be greatly reduced versus a push strategy.[43]

Obviously, a number of important marketing management decisions about channel structure and types of intermediaries to best utilize are influenced by the degree to which the channel intermediaries are relied on to help create and support demand. The degree of push versus pull used is fundamental in framing the channel structure and relationships that are likely to optimize a product's success.

LOGISTICS ASPECTS OF SUPPLY CHAIN MANAGEMENT

Physical distribution, or logistics, is the integrated process of moving input materials to the producer, in-process inventory through the firm, and finished goods out of the firm through the channel of distribution. Traditionally, logistics was thought of as an internal flow going one direction—**outbound logistics.** That is, it was thought that logistics started with production and ended with receipt of finished good by the end-user consumer or business user. From a supply chain perspective, logistics professionals today tend to take a more holistic view of physical distribution. Thus, along with outbound logistics, it is important to consider **inbound logistics**—sourcing materials and knowledge inputs from external suppliers to the point at which production begins.

Today, the concept of reverse logistics must also be taken into account. **Reverse logistics** deals with how to get goods back to a manufacturer or intermediary after purchase. Product returns result for many reasons including spoilage and breakage, excess inventory, customer dissatisfaction, and overstocks.[44] In particular, online sellers in both the B2C and B2B space recognize that an inherent aspect of electronic commerce is the increased likelihood of product return. Returns are higher in this channel in large part because of the inability to physically examine the merchandise before purchase. Smart online sellers build return allowances—either free, with shipping charges, or with a restocking fee—into their pricing model. To do this, the seller must work out an efficient and customer-friendly procedure for how merchandise is to be returned. In many cases, the selling firm partners with one logistics company to handle the reverse logistics, in Dell's case UPS.

Several logistics aspects of supply chain management require close attention by marketing managers. These are order processing, warehousing and materials handling, inventory management, and transportation.

Fidelitone handles reverse logistics for companies including Best Buy. Consumer goods are returned for many reasons, and Fidelitone inspects the returns to determine if the shipment was wrong, or if it was the wrong color or wrong size, or if the returned item is defective. Returns have become a major aspect of customer service, but they have costs such as additional paperwork and distribution centers to handle the goods. That's why companies use intermediaries to provide these services.[45]

Order Processing

Receiving and properly processing customer orders is a critical step in getting product moving through the supply chain. It is also a point at which mistakes can easily occur, and when a mistake occurs in the order it usually carries through the whole fulfillment system. If the item ordered is in stock, outbound processing from inventory occurs. If the item is not in stock, referred to as a **stock-out,** then inbound replenishment processes are triggered.

Fortunately, in many modern organizations, order processing has become highly mechanized. Sophisticated and integrated **enterprise resource planning (ERP) systems** now manage much of the logistics process for many firms. ERP is a software application designed to integrate information related to logistics processes throughout the organization. Once data are entered, they are automatically linked through internal systems and become available for use with all relevant decisions that rely on the ERP information. ERP enables employees throughout the system, whether in sales, billing, customer service, or some other group, to take ownership of their piece of the supply chain and to accurately communicate order status both to the customer and among themselves.[46]

Warehousing and Materials Handling

In an ideal supply chain, materials of all kinds are handled as few times as possible. Any warehouse needs to be designed so that after goods are received and checked in, they move directly to their designated storage locations. Efficient, orderly, clean, and well-marked warehouses enhance the flow of goods.

Decisions must be made about the optimal size for a warehouse, how many warehouses to have, and where they should be located to minimize transportation costs. The last point is especially important if the warehouse serves as a distribution center in which functions such as breaking and accumulating bulk occur for ultimate reshipping to customers.

Inventory Management

To ensure that inventories of both raw materials and finished goods are sufficient to meet customer demand without undue delay, firms utilize sophisticated **just-in-time (JIT) inventory control systems.** A JIT system's goal is to balance the double-edge sword of potentially having too many goods on hand and creating unnecessary warehousing costs, with the chance of having so little inventory in stock that stock-outs occur requiring expensive rush production and express delivery situations.[47]

PRM arrangements often open up their collective IT systems for data sharing toward more reliable JIT inventory management. Wal-Mart's legendary capability of real-time analysis and data transmission to vendors about

Logistics issues are obviously critical in shipping food products such as chocolates. Exposure to too much heat or cold can ruin the inventory in transit.

EXHIBIT 15.7 Comparative Attributes across Different Transportation Modes

Low Cost	Speed	Reliability of Delivery	Ability to Deliver to Many Geographical Areas	Reputation for Delivering Undamaged Goods
1. Pipeline	1. Air	1. Pipeline	1. Motor	1. Pipeline
2. Water	2. Motor	2. Air	2. Rail	2. Water
3. Rail	3. Rail	3. Motor	3. Air	3. Air
4. Motor	4. Pipeline	4. Rail	4. Water	4. Motor
5. Air	5. Water	5. Water	5. Pipeline	5. Rail

Note: Numbers indicate relative ranking based on general trade-offs of cost versus other attributes of each mode.

inventories at any store or distribution center location has created a substantial competitive advantage over many other retailers. In any industry, customers expect product to be in stock and available, and when it's not they quickly become prone to switching to competitors. One component of ERP systems is usually **materials requirement planning (MRP).** MRP guides overall management of the inbound materials from suppliers to facilitate minimal production delays.[48]

Transportation

With the cost of fuel today, it is not unusual for transportation costs to run as much as 10 percent of cost of goods sold. Effective transportation management is one way that many firms keep a lid on costs while also optimizing delivery options for customers. Exhibit 15.7 provides a comparison of several transportation options on a variety of criteria such as dependability, cost, speed, and suitable products. The decision about which one or what mix of these transportation options to choose will have a major impact on a firm's bottom line.

FYI

Pendleton Woolen Mills has a sizable wholesale business that sells to independent retailers, outdoor specialty stores, and select department stores. The company has also grown a consumer-direct business, which includes more than 50 retail stores as well as a direct-mail catalog and e-commerce. To help manage the inventory across all of these channels, Pendleton created a single database. The database houses item information and gives a view of inventory across all of Pendleton's consumer-direct channels, including its own retail stores. With the new automated process, a virtual warehouse receives data daily on the aggregated inventory of Pendleton's stores. As a result, Pendleton is seeing improved order fill rates and fewer stock-outs or mistakes in customer service.[49]

Austria-based Niedermeyer is a retailer of photography equipment, electronics, and mobile phones. It has 150 sales outlets around Austria. In the past, Niedermeyer owned its own trucks, which would transport goods from the company's central warehouse to its stores. Now, the company outsources transportation to a core group of transportation providers. The transportation providers focus on transportation and can therefore provide transportation at lower cost than Niedermeyer could achieve on its own.[50]

LEGAL ISSUES IN SUPPLY CHAIN MANAGEMENT

As with pricing practices, a variety of laws impact the decision making about channels and logistics. Among others, the Sherman Antitrust Act (1890), Clayton Act (1914), and Federal Trade Commission Act (1914) provide much of the basis for legislation impacting supply chains. Three key legal issues related to distribution are exclusive dealing, exclusive territories, and tying agreements.

Exclusive Dealing

When a supplier creates a restrictive agreement that prohibits intermediaries that handle its product from selling competing firms' products, **exclusive dealing** has occurred. Whether a particular arrangement is legal depends on whether it interferes with the intermediary's right to act independently or the rights of competitors to succeed—that is, is competition lessened by the arrangement? Exclusive dealing lessens competition if it (1) accounts for substantial market share, (2) involves a substantial dollar amount, and (3) involves a big supplier and smaller intermediary, which sets up a case for coercion.

Exclusive dealing may be legal if the parties show exclusivity is essential for strategic reasons, such as to maintain product image. High-fashion brands often engage in exclusive dealing with retailers so that their image is not sullied by being merchandised in the store next to step-down labels. Also, if limited production capacity on the part of the supplier legitimately restricts its sales capabilities, exclusive dealing may also be legal. In this case, the point of the exclusive deal is to try to ensure the limited quantities of product have the best possible chance of being "sold through" to end users.[51]

Exclusive Territories

An **exclusive territory** protects an intermediary from having to compete with others selling a producer's goods. Can a producer always grant an intermediary an exclusive territory for sales purposes? Not necessarily. For this practice to be legal, it would have to be demonstrated that the exclusivity doesn't violate any statutes on restriction of competition. This issue often manifests itself in the context of suppliers limiting the number of retail outlets within a certain geographic area. One possible defense of exclusive territories might be that the costs of a new store (restaurant, retailer, dealer, etc.) entering the market are so great that the nature of the market and risks involved demand an opportunity for exclusivity.[52]

Tying Contracts

If a seller requires an intermediary to purchase a supplementary product to qualify to purchase the primary product the intermediary wishes to buy, a **tying contract** is in place. Example: "You can buy my printer, but to do so you *must* sign a contract to by my ink"—thus, the products are "tied together" as terms of sale. Tying contracts are illegal, but historically it has often been difficult to prove whether an agreement is or isn't a tying contract in a court of law.[53]

SUMMARY

Channel and supply chain decisions are central to creating a firm's value proposition. Competitive advantage can be gained through effective and efficient channel management, physical distribution, and logistics. Vertical marketing systems and partner relationship management strategies add attractive levels of integration among channel members. The aim of such value networks is value co-creation by the participating suppliers, customers, and other stakeholders in which the members of the network combine capabilities according to their expertise and the competencies required from the situation.

KEY TERMS

value network 412

value co-creation 413

network organization (virtual organization) 413

nimble 413

channel of distribution 415

intermediaries 415

merchant intermediaries 415

agent intermediaries 415

direct channel 416

indirect channel 417

physical distribution (logistics) 417

supply chain 417

supply chain management 417

breaking bulk 417

accumulating bulk 418

sorting 418

creating assortments 418

reducing transactions 418

transportation and storage 418

facilitating functions 419

disintermediation 420

insourcing (third-party logistics) 421

vertical marketing system (VMS) 421

corporate VMS 421

vertical integration 421

contractual VMS 421

franchise organization 421

retailer cooperative 421

wholesaler cooperative 421

administered VMS 421

channel captain (channel leader) 421

partner relationship management (PRM) strategies 422

channel power 422

channel conflict 422

coercive power 422

reward power 423

expert power 423

referent power 423

legitimate power 423

distribution intensity 424

intensive distribution 424

convenience goods 424

impulse goods 424

shopping goods 424

selective distribution 424

exclusive distribution 424

push strategy 425

slotting allowance (shelf fee) 425

pull strategy 426

outbound logistics 426

inbound logistics 426

reverse logistics 426

stock-out 427

enterprise resource planning (ERP) system 427

just-in-time (JIT) inventory control system 427

materials requirement planning (MRP) 428

exclusive dealing 429

exclusive territory 429

tying contract 429

APPLICATION QUESTIONS

1. Consider the concept of value co-creation.

   a. In your own words, explain the concept of value co-creation.

   b. What are some specific ways value can be co-created?

   c. Provide an example of a specific value network you believe results in a high level of value co-creation.

   d. Provide an example of a specific firm or firms that could benefit by establishing a value network and engaging in value co-creation. In what ways would this approach be an improvement over their existing business approach?

2. The chapter discusses the importance of being "nimble" in all aspects of a firm's operation—that is, to be in a position to be maximally flexible, adaptable, and speedy in response to change.

   a. Identify two firms in two different industries that you believe exhibit a nimble nature in their operations.

b. What specific evidence leads you to believe these firms are nimble, especially in their channel and supply chain activities?

3. Consider the issue of disintermediation in electronic channels.

   a. Do you believe that *all* channels will disintermediate down to simple direct channels over time? Why or why not?

   b. Does your opinion change if the question is asked only about B2C channels? Only for B2B channels? Why?

4. Consider this statement: "It's important in business today for all firms to work to cut out the middleman. Intermediaries represent costs that can be saved by finding ways to cut them out of the system. Down-channel buyers always benefit when this happens." Do you agree with this statement? Why or why not? Be specific in arguing your point based on what you learned in the chapter.

5. Exhorting firms to develop networks and alliances for purposes of value co-creation sounds like a good idea. However, is there a point at which such approaches can be taken too far *(a)* from a legal perspective, *(b)* from an ethical perspective, and *(c)* from a strategic perspective? Explain your viewpoint.

MANAGEMENT DECISION CASE: Avon's 5,000,000-Person Strong Distribution Network

Avon sells skin-care products as well as makeup and other items through a network of 5 million independent representatives. Its stock is rising. Investors are happy about, among other things, Avon's progress signing up 399,000 new salespeople in China, where a fast-growing middle class is compelling enough to outweigh the government's tight regulation of direct sellers. Renewed growth in Central Europe and the United States is helping, too. For the second quarter of 2008, revenue increased 28 percent over first quarter, to $2.7 billion, with net income of $235 million.

One of CEO Andrea Jung's most important moves in turning the company around has been forcing managers to make decisions based on fact rather than intuition. She has reorganized Avon's management structure, taking away much of the autonomy from country managers, in favor of globalized manufacturing and marketing. Previously, Avon managers from Poland to Mexico ran their own plants, developed new products, and created their own ads, but they often have tended to rely as much on instinct as numbers in decision making.

Now Jung has trimmed seven layers of management, bringing the total from 15 down to 8, and has finally launched the kind of numbers-heavy return-on-investment analysis that most large consumer products companies have been doing for decades. That analysis is directed from Avon's New York headquarters by an executive team. Recent recruits to the executive team have come from larger, more analytical consumer-products companies such as Gillette, Procter

& Gamble, PepsiCo, and Kraft. "When she speaks about what we have to do to achieve our goals, she is so much closer to the operations" now, says board member Paula Stern. "She has her hands directly on the levers that have to be moved."

Avon's new executives and their new data were on display at the conference of industry analysts. Traditionally, this show was heavy on product announcements and ad clips. But this year's edition contained nearly four hours' worth of PowerPoint slides. In them, the company provided a detailed explanation of what had gone wrong in many of its 114 worldwide markets.

One revelation: The roster of products for sale in Mexico had ballooned to 13,000. Another: Decreasing the payoffs for adding new representatives had stalled the U.S. business. At times, analysts seemed amazed that Avon could have been so out of touch with the basic forces that drove its own business. "Why," asked Deutsche Bank analyst Bill Schmitz, about 3½ hours into the meeting, "did it take a year and 8,000-plus [representative] surveys to figure out that people want to work less and earn more?" It was a rebuke, but one Schmitz made with good humor. Schmitz is one of five analysts (out of 15) who rate the stock a buy. Avon's appeal to them is that it gets 70 percent of its sales outside the United States, much of that from still-developing markets.

Avon's new data-centric approach is helping to change Avon's marketing and product development. The company sells many thousands of products, and

1,000 of those were introduced in 12 months. Savings from centralized manufacturing and other initiatives are being put into advertising and research and development, a strategy Jung hopes will get earnings climbing again.

Avon has been increasing its ad budget significantly in recent years (for example, $82 million in the first quarter of 2008, up 14 percent from the prior year), which seems to be helping drive sales growth. The company also invested heavily in is independent sales representatives through the Representative Value Proposition (RVP). Through the RVP, Avon has expanded its Sales Leadership program, increased sales campaign frequency, and improved commissions and incentives to representatives.

Avon is also doing more marketing to spark recruiting of new representatives including TV and newspaper ads supporting thousands of recruiting events in China. In Russia, the company sponsors a TV show featuring a character who sells Avon.

Questions for Consideration

1. What role do Avon's independent sales representatives play for the company?

2. Do you think it would be possible to disintermediate the reps if Avon sold directly over the Web or through catalogs?

3. What advantages do you think Avon achieves by selling through direct salespeople in emerging markets such as China?

Source: Nanette Byrnes, "Avon: More Than Cosmetic Changes," *BusinessWeek*, March 12, 2007, pp. 42–50; and "Avon Reports First-Quarter Total Revenue Up 14 percent," *PR Newswire*, April 29, 2008, http://findarticles.com/p/articles/mi_m4PRN/is_2008_April_29/ai_n25362759, accessed June 10, 2008.

MARKETING PLAN EXERCISE

ACTIVITY 15: Establishing Distribution Channels for Your Offering

Selecting the most appropriate channels of distribution for your offering and then working out the overall best approach to establishing and operating your supply chain is a critical element of your marketing plan.

1. Define and describe the value network within which you will operate. Develop an approach to ensure that your supply chain operation is a nimble as possible.

2. Decide what type of channel configuration is optimal for you and what intermediaries should be part of the channel.

3. Select what physical distribution functions you will accomplish in-house and how these will be set up. Then, select what physical distribution functions you will outsource and to whom.

4. Identify what aspects of e-channels you must address.

5. Decide:

   a. What level of distribution intensity you seek within each channel.

   b. How much control and adaptability is required over the channel and its activities.

   c. The priority channel functions that require investment.

6. Develop your plans for the following logistics functions:

   a. Order processing.

   b. Warehousing and materials handling.

   c. Inventory management.

   d. Transportation.

If you are using Marketing Plan Pro, a template for this assignment can be accessed at www.mhhe.com/marshall1e.

RECOMMENDED READINGS

1. David Blanchard, *Supply Chain Management Best Practices* (Hoboken, NJ: John Wiley & Sons, 2006).
2. *Harvard Business Review on Supply Chain Management* (Cambridge, MA: Harvard Business School Press, 2006).
3. *Harvard Business Review on Managing the Value Chain* (Cambridge, MA: Harvard Business School Press, 2000).
4. James William Martin, *Lean Six Sigma for Supply Chain Management* (New York: McGraw-Hill Professional, 2006).
5. V. Kasturi Rangan and Marie Bell, *Transforming Your Go-to-market Strategy: The Three Disciplines of Channel Management* (Cambridge, MA: Harvard Business School Press, 2006).

CHAPTER 16

POINTS OF CUSTOMER INTERFACE: BRICKS AND CLICKS

LEARNING OBJECTIVES

- Learn the significant drivers changing the customer interface.

- Understand the role of retailing in delivering customer value.

- Recognize the characteristics of retailing in order to differentiate among retailers.

- Assess the strengths and weaknesses of each of the major retail formats.

- Identify the evolving role of e-commerce in retail strategy.

- Create a retail strategy based on an understanding of key retail decisions.

EXECUTIVE PERSPECTIVE

Executive Mary Cavanaugh Knapp, Director, Brand Marketing

Company NBC Universal, Universal Orlando Resort

Business Vacation destination with two theme parks, a night-time entertainment complex, and three luxury on-site hotels

What are some of your most important customer touchpoints—that is, ways of collecting information from your customers and providing, where possible, information back?

The most important touchpoint with our guests is their first moment of contact with our company. Whether it's during their experience in our theme parks or hotels or when they first visit our Web site, this initial point of contact is critically important. As the experts say, "First impressions are everything."

When a guest arrives at one of our theme parks, we strive to collect demographic information such as e-mail addresses and zip codes so we can properly follow up (with the guest's permission, of course), or at the very minimum so we can determine the guest's travel point of origin (for research purposes). When a potential guest visits our Web site, we give that visitor an opportunity to register for our e-newsletters. We then e-mail special offers and important news about our upcoming events and attractions. We also survey our guests so that we can continue to provide the best possible products and services.

What types of retail store concepts do you find are working most successfully for you?

Universal Orlando Resort aligns itself with many of the most popular brands in our world today. By doing so, we position our destination, attractions, and products with the partners that are the most relevant and in tune with our audience.

Universal Studios theme park is the home to some of today's most popular movies—*Men in Black, Shrek, Revenge of the Mummy, Jaws, ET, Jimmy Neutron: Boy Genius*—and so many more! Each ride has a close affiliation with retail products that are sold in our theme parks and throughout all international markets.

Universal's Islands of Adventure is a theme park with five distinct islands—Marvel Super Hero Island, Toon Lagoon, Jurassic Park, The Lost Continent, and Seuss Landing. Together these "islands" encompass the most innovative and technologically advanced rides and attractions in the world. These highly popular themes and characters easily translate into merchandise that is sold throughout our resort and the world.

How do you effectively integrate electronic commerce with traditional at-the-park retailing approaches?

In this highly competitive Orlando market, it is very important for us to sell tickets to our theme parks *in advance* of a tourist's actual travel to the area. In all of our television and other mainstream advertising the primary call to action is to visit our Web site for tickets and information: www.universalorlando.com. We have very attractive ticket, hotel, and package offers that are *only* available on this Web site.

In the Florida resident market, the most valuable product is our annual pass. For it and other products, our goal is to market, sell, and communicate mainly through electronic media. This allows us to expand our reach by maximizing our marketing spending through the more cost-effective electronic distribution channels.

THE CHANGING RULES OF CUSTOMER INTERFACE

The way companies approach the customer interface has shifted dramatically as better technology, increased knowledge and growing sophistication of customers, and fierce competition have raised the stakes in relating to customers. The customer-company interface is a critical element in creating customer value. Companies seek better and more frequent interaction with their customers. At the same time, customers are more attached to their products. The result has been a concerted effort by both companies and their customers to redefine the customer interface.[1]

Customer Touchpoints

The Chapter 4 discussion about customer touchpoints focused on collecting information from and, where possible, providing information back to the customer. Certainly, that is a critical component of touchpoints, particularly as it relates to customer relationship management. Here, however, we are going to address the importance of the touchpoint in creating and reinforcing the company-customer connection.

Customer touchpoints occur in many ways—retail store, direct-mail piece, e-mail, company Web site, and even advertising. In some cases, there is two-way interaction (retail store visit, Web site bulletin board) while in other cases the interaction is one way as in advertising or direct mail. However, no matter the nature of the touchpoint, the customer is connecting with the company as part of a specific strategy to contact that person a certain number of times over a given period.[2]

> Most banks drive customers to the Internet using technology to make the customer experience more convenient and less personal. Commerce Bank, based in New Jersey, has taken a different strategy, focusing on nicer bank branches, longer operating hours, and more trained staff. In short, the bank's strategy involves more, not less, personal service. Results suggest customers appreciate the extra service as Commerce posts higher deposits per branch and better growth rates than the industry average.[3]

Go to the Customer

Customers are no longer satisfied interacting with a company or product based primarily on visiting a retail store. They want access to the company (information, customer service) immediately, whatever their location. As a result, customer service has revolutionized service delivery by improving telephone support, pushing more information through mobile communications, and, of course, creating effective, customer-oriented Web sites that address a wide range of customer requests from product information, purchase, and customer support.[4]

Customer Interface 24/7

Higher service expectations have created a demand for 24/7 service, support, and information. Customers want access to the company when it is convenient for them, and this means extending customer service and support beyond normal business hours. Increasingly, customers connect in the early morning, evening, or weekends and consider convenience and access to customer service in the decision-making process. In addition, the global nature of company operations coupled with worldwide access to the Internet means at least minimal customer support must go on 24/7/365 days a year. Specifically, Web sites generate customer contact

EXHIBIT 16.1 **Five Popular Offshore Call Center Destinations**

The Philippines

- Good English-language skills.
- Mushrooming call centers are putting pressure on labor supply.
- Call centers located primarily in Manila and nearby Makati.
- High infrastructure costs.
- People are in tune with U.S. culture.

India

- India has a huge reservoir of educated workforce comfortable with the English language.
- It has a 12-hour time difference with the United States and 6 to 7 hours with Europe.
- Low labor cost but high attrition rate.
- Low infrastructure cost.

South Africa

- It is in the same time zone as the European region.

- Shares cultural and historical affinity with Europe.
- People proficient in European and African languages.

Ireland

- Shares the same time zone as EU countries.
- Highly developed infrastructure.
- Well-educated workforce.
- Language advantage.

Singapore

- Has a free trade agreement with the United States.
- *Global Information Technology Report 2005–2006* ranks Singapore second in IT readiness after the United States.
- The country has a good and efficient regulatory environment.
- Politically stable.

Source: Sourcingmag.com, www.sourcingmag.com/content/c060619a.asp, accessed November 2008.

all the time and responding to the customer quickly, accurately, and persuasively increases the pressure to improve customer service and response infrastructure. Companies create call centers around the world to handle regional customer traffic over the course of a 24-hour business cycle. Additionally, companies create global call center strategies that enable 24-hour response despite the problems of multiple time zones.[5] For example, companies including Dell maintain call centers in India to handle calls in the evening and later time zones (West Coast) (see Exhibit 16.1).

RETAILING

Retailing is any business activity that creates value in the delivery of goods and services to consumers for their personal, nonbusiness consumption and is

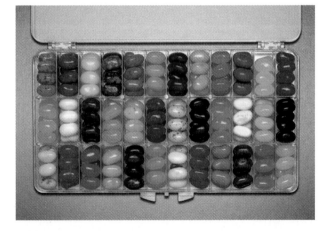

Jelly Bellys reaches out to consumers in a variety of ways beyond its product. The company's Web site offers visitors fun activities and lists of company-sponsored events.

an essential component of the supply chain. As we discussed in Chapter 14, an efficient, effective supply chain moves materials from manufacturer to consumer. Retailing, in whatever form, is the point of contact in the supply chain with the consumer of the product.

The retail sector plays a fundamental role in terms of employment and economic activity for any economy. In the United States, for example, retailing accounts for nearly 22 percent of all employment and generates 10 percent of the gross domestic product. More importantly, it provides a vital connection between

Most people know Wal-Mart is the world's largest retailer but the world's second largest retailer, Carrefour based in France, is a powerful retailer with thousands of different retail formats around the world.

companies and customers. Retailing, however, plays a critical in economies around the world and is growing in a number of emerging countries. (see Exhibit 16.2).

The Role of Retailing

In an increasingly interconnected world where consumers communicate directly with manufacturers, some question the long-term viability of retailing. Some suggest that retailing, at least traditional store-based retailing, will give way to Internet-based shopping experiences like Amazon. However, despite predictions about the demise of traditional retailing in the late 1990s, the retail sector continues to grow.[6] While the Internet has definitely altered the retail landscape retailers still perform four critical functions that add value for companies and consumers. Let's examine each of these functions.

Offer Variety for Consumers

Retailers create an assortment of products that fit the consumer's needs. Some retailers define their assortment of products very broadly and offer a wide variety of products to consumers. Wal-Mart and Target carries everything from food, clothing, hardware, garden, to automotive products. Grocery chains like

EXHIBIT 16.2	Top 10 Global Retail Market Opportunities

2007 rank	Country	Region	Country risk	Market attractiveness	Market saturation	Time pressure	GRDI score
		Weight	25%	25%	30%	20%	
1	India	Asia	67	42	80	74	92
2	Russia	Eastern Europe	62	52	53	90	89
3	China	Asia	75	46	46	84	88
4	Vietnam	Asia	57	34	76	59	74
5	Ukraine	Eastern Europe	41	43	44	88	69
6	Chile	Americas	80	51	42	43	69
7	Latvia	Eastern Europe	77	32	21	86	68
8	Malaysia	Asia	70	44	46	54	68
9	Mexico	Americas	83	58	33	33	64
10	Saudi Arabia	Mid. East/ N. Africa	65	40	66	35	64

Legend:
- 0 = high risk
- 100 = low risk
- 0 = low attractiveness
- 100 = high attractiveness
- 0 = saturated
- 100 = not saturated
- 0 = no time pressure
- 100 = urgency to enter

Source: Euromoney, World Bank, *Global Competitiveness Report 2005-2006*, A.T. Kearney analysis.

Wegmans, and Albertsons want to become "one-stop shops" offering consumers so many choices they will consider it their first choice when shopping.[7] Around the world, new retail concepts are developed that appeal to particular consumers needs. Read the FYI to find out more about a fast-growing retail operation in Japan that is looking to expand globally.

FYI

Does a minimalist retail setting, lots of products, and low prices sound familiar? Probably. That strategy, perfected by IKEA, is employed successfully in varying degrees by companies around the world. The strategy is also followed by Muji, the Japanese retailer of cool and functional products. More formally known as Mujirushi Ryohin (which translates to "No Brand, High Quality") the chain of 387 stores in over 15 countries posts annual sales in excess of a billion dollars and a loyal following of bargain-hungry, fashion-oriented consumers. Muji has announced plans to add more than a dozen stores a year over the next several years and just recently opened its first U.S. store in New York City.

Following the Japanese model, the company identifies high-traffic locations building modest stores (5,000 square feet or less) that accommodate more than 7,000 products. The product range is broad, with everything from socks to front-loading washers/dryers. It is even possible to purchase a prefab home in some stores. The company's unique positioning targets a wide range of established competitors such as IKEA and Crate & Barrel in furniture, GAP in apparel, and Target in housewares.[8]

A typical supermarket carries between 20,000 and 30,000 product items. While that may seem like a large number, it is only a small fraction of all the products available. As a result, it is critical to select the right variety of products based on the demographics of the store's shoppers. The single college student shopping at a supermarket close to campus does not likely require the large economy box of detergent that the homemaker across town needs. Keep in mind that manufacturers make dozens of sizes and formats of each product. Procter & Gamble makes over 45 different Tide products, not including the various box sizes. An individual store will likely carry three to five different Tide products in a couple of box sizes.[9]

Separate Large Product Volume into Consumer Purchase Quantities

Supply chains work most efficiently and effectively when producing large volumes of products and moving them through the distributions system in bulk. However, consumers don't need or want the quantities produced by manufacturers. Retailers play a vital role assimilating the large quantities produced by manufacturers and offering smaller, more consumer-friendly quantities for the consumer.[10] Panasonic, for example, produces hundreds of 42-inch flat-panel plasma TVs each day, but an individual consumer needs only one at any given time. Retailers such as Best Buy and Circuit City, as well as online retailers like Amazon, enable Panasonic to manufacture in efficient product volume then transport the televisions from plants in Asia to any retailer in the United States where it is possible to purchase a single TV at a competitive price.

Maintain Inventory Levels

One of the most important retailer functions is holding inventory in advance of a consumer purchase. Consumers around the world want to purchase when they are ready and expect the product to be available on demand. However, there is a cost of keeping products close to the customer. Products move through the supply chain in large quantities and are stored in warehouses that can be owned by manufacturers, distributors, or the retailer. It is from these warehouses that online retailers often ship directly to the consumer.

Many consumers, however, want to see the product in person before purchasing it. Additionally, in many cases, they want to take the product home for immediate consumption. As a result, retailers provide a valuable service to the consumer by keeping the product in inventory ready for purchase. At the same time, the retailers' inventory helps manufacturers because it stores the product close to consumers and makes it easier for them to purchase.[11]

> Topshop, the London-based fashion retailer with annual sales over a $1 billion, is so focused on delivering the latest fashions while maintaining inventories that it schedules new product deliveries three times a day as opposed to the normal once a day. The strategy is cited as one reason the chain experiences annual sales of more than $2,000 per square foot, which is dramatically higher than industry leaders like GAP, whose stores generate only $400 worth of sales per square foot.[12]

Make Additional Services Available to Consumers

Retailers offer additional services that facilitate the purchase for the consumer (see Exhibit 16.3 for an example from Macy's). Financing and purchase options (cash, credit card, checks) are important financial services consumers expect but they require a significant investment by the retailer. In many retail environments, consumers want advice in evaluating product options, which means having trained personnel available to answer questions and provide customer service. The opportunity to test product before purchase enhances the purchase experience but requires retailers to plan for the service and allocate resources.[13] Clothing stores, for example, allocate space for dressing rooms to allow people to try on the product before purchase.

These critical functions add value to the purchase for the consumer and provide an effective customer interface for the supply chain. As a result, retailing, despite profound changes, remains critical to the supply chain and consumer marketing.

EXHIBIT 16.3	Range of Services Offered by Macy's Department Stores
Store, online, catalog orders	Shipping Order status and tracking Furniture and mattress shipping Order history and billing profile access online
Macy's credit card	Account status and payment options online and in-store Star rewards plus 10% savings with new application
Returns and exchanges	In-store By mail

(continued)

Gifts	Gift cards Gift boxes and wrapping Wedding and gift registry
Shopping services	In-store or in-home interior design consultation Fund-raising scrip for schools, nonprofits, etc. Certificates are sold at a discount rate to schools and nonprofit organizations, which can then resell them at face value to earn big profits. Supporters who purchase the Fundraising Scrip Certificates can redeem them at any Macy's store for everything from the latest fashions to beautiful home furnishings. Personal shopper:– • Individual appointments • Personal profile of your gift and wardrobe preferences • Wardrobe consultations, including businesswear • Birthday, anniversary, and special-occasion reminders • Advance notice of exclusive events and promotions • Custom gift wrap • Shopping parties Studio services: styles for television shows, commercials, or films; set decorating needs Macy's shop for education program: Register your Macy's card by phone or at www.escrip.com. From that date on, Macy's will donate up to 6% funding to the school of your choice every time you shop with your Macy's card in store or online! Catalog shopping Bridal salon services
Macy's Event Marketing	Macy's Thanksgiving Day Parade, Passport (fund-raising event to fight HIV/AIDS), Macy's Flower Show, 4th of July Fireworks, Holiday Puppet Theatre, Santaland, Annual Tree Lighting
In-store events	Fashion shows, cooking demos, and more
Corporate sales	Employee gift cards, recognition and incentive programs, corporate gift-giving services
Visitor's services	Macy's Visitor Centers in New York, San Francisco, San Diego, Honolulu, and Las Vegas: • Shopping assistance • Tourist information • Coat & package check • Refreshments • Language assistance **Welcome Savings Pass,** which offers up to 11% savings in all Macy's stores nationwide for five days after validation
Special group programs	Macy's can custom-design an informative and entertaining program to address the particular needs and interests of a group. Programs can provide insights on everything from the newest fashions to beauty, from home styles to cooking seminars.

Source: Macys.com, www1.macys.com/service/index.jsp, accessed October 8, 2008.

Characteristics of Retailers

With more than 1.5 million store-based retailers in the United States it may seem impossible to identify a classification system that would be useful for all retailers. While there is certainly great variety in the number and type of retailers, there are four specific characteristics that define retailers. Understanding these characteristics is essential because they define the retail environment and marketing managers know that creating an effective retail strategy begins with knowledge of merchandise assortment, level of service, and the retail value proposition. Let's consider each element.

Type of Merchandise

One of the most fundamental characteristics used to classify retailers is by type of merchandise. Several years ago the United States, Canada, and Mexico created a unified classification system for all business activity that was based on a system from the 1920s developed by the U.S. Census Bureau. As discussed in Chapter 8, remember that the North American Industry Classification System (NAICS), assigns a hierarchical six-digit code based on the company's products and services. The first two digits of the code identify the business sector while the last four categorize a specific business subdivision. Most merchandise retailers fall into the 44 and 45 sectors while services are in 71 (arts, entertainment, and recreation) and 72 (accommodation and food services).[14]

Assortment

Even within a particular product category, the variety and assortment of products carried by retailers can be very different. **Variety** is the number of product categories offered by a retailer and is referred to as **breadth of merchandise. Assortment** is the number of different product items within a product category and is referred to as the **depth of merchandise.**[15]

It is possible, for example, to purchase a briefcase from a department store, warehouse club or superstore, or luggage store. Wilson's Leather Stores is a specialty clothing and accessories retailer specializing in leather products. Its primary product lines include women and men's clothing as well as travel and business-related leather merchandise. The company carries an extensive line of leather briefcases. Costco, the successful warehouse club, also carries briefcases. However, Wilson's Leather has less variety across product lines but more assortment within a few product lines focused on leather products than Costco, which has a large variety of product categories but very little assortment within each product category. Despite the fact they both carry briefcases, target market differences as well as distinct variations in the products offered suggest the two companies do not compete directly (see Exhibit 16.4).

Services Imparted to Consumers

Consumers expect a minimum level of services from all retailers that generally includes flexible payment options, proper merchandise display, convenient store

EXHIBIT 16.4	Comparison of Wilson's Leather Stores Briefcase Selection versus Costco	
	Number of Styles Offered	**Price Range**
Wilson's Leather Stores	32	$ 79–$199
Costco	2	$68.98–$159.98

hours, and easy access. However, beyond the basic services, retailers have a wide range of options based on their market strategy and consumer needs.[16] Most pharmacies, for example, do not deliver prescriptions to the home. A few local pharmacies in many markets, however, do provide home delivery, and consumers in those markets find the service helpful. While the average grocery store carries thousands of products, some differentiate themselves by providing a little extra service. When a customer does not find a product he wants, chains such as Publix will order and store the product for a customer even if it is not part of their normal inventory.

Differences in the Value Equation

The **value equation,** as we have discussed, defines value in terms of price and delivered benefits to the customer. Retailers make critical decisions about each of these elements in the value equation. A general rule in retailing is that broader, deeper product assortments and expanded service options require a higher price to cover increased costs. In other words, carrying more inventories or providing additional services has a cost that ultimately must be covered by the consumer. At the same time, the growth of warehouse clubs (Costco, Sam's Warehouse) and discount stores (Wal-Mart, Target) reflects a strong consumer focus on lower prices, which means fewer services and limited assortments and variety. Essentially, those retailers are making the decision to focus on price as the driver in the value equation.

Ferguson is a specialty retailer that specializes in a variety of products for the bath and kitchen. The company has trained salespeople that work with builders, contractors and consumers.

Specialty retailers, on the other hand, focus on value-added benefits such as greater product selection, more experienced service personnel, and other services. For those retailers, the focus is on the delivered benefits and, as a result, prices are higher. The trade-off between delivered benefits and price is a critical decision for retailers, and they are constantly evaluating their mix of product/service benefits and pricing strategy based on internal company objectives and comparison shopping against the competition.[17]

STORE RETAILERS

Two broad categories define traditional store retailing in industrialized countries, particularly the United States: food and general merchandise retailers.

Food Retailers

As recently as 20 years ago virtually all food sales in the United States were at conventional supermarkets; today that figure is only 61 percent. General merchandise retailers have become **food retailers** and conventional supermarkets carry more general merchandise. Indeed, the largest food retailer in the world is Wal-Mart with over $100 billion in food and related sales. Exhibit 16.5 lists the world's largest food retailers.

Food retailers occupy a unique retail space and face a number of specific challenges. Much of the food retailer's product mix is perishable (dairy, meat, fruits, vegetables) so companies develop sophisticated supply chains that keep products moving into the store while carefully balancing inventory levels to reduce spoilage. Another unique challenge for food retails is that profit margins are low relative to other retailing concepts with net margins averaging 1 percent of sales.[18]

EXHIBIT 16.5 | **World's Five Largest Food Retailers**

Retail sales rank (FY 06)	Name of company	Country of origin	2006 group sales* (US$mil)	2006 retail sales (US$mil)	2006 group income (loss)* (US$mil)	Formats	Countries of operation
1	Wal-Mart Stores, Inc.	US	$348,650	$344,992	$11,284	Cash & Carry/Warehouse Club, Discount Department Store, Hypermarket/Supercenter/Superstore, Supermarket	Argentina, Brazil, Canada, China, Costa Rica, El Salvador, Guatemala, Honduras, Japan, Mexico, Nicaragua, Puerto Rico, UK, US
2	Carrefour S.A.	France	97,861	97,861	2,850	Cash & Carry/Warehouse Club, Convenience/Forecourt Store, Discount Store, Hypermarket/Supercenter/Superstore, Supermarket	Algeria, Argentina, Belgium, Brazil, China, Colombia, Dominican Republic, Egypt, France, French Polynesia, Greece, Guadeloupe, Indonesia, Italy, Malaysia, Martinique, Oman, Poland, Portugal, Qatar, Reunion, Romania, Saudi Arabia, Singapore, Spain, Switzerland, Taiwan, Thailand, Turkey, Tunisia, UAE
3	Tesco plc	UK	79,976	79,976	3,549	Convenience/Forecourt Store, Department Store, Discount Department Store, Hypermarket/Supercenter/Superstore, Supermarket	China, Czech Rep., Hungary, Japan, Rep. of Ireland, Malaysia, Poland, Slovakia, S. Korea, Thailand, Turkey, UK
4	Metro AG	Germany	75,225	74,857	1,327	Apparel/Footwear Specialty, Cash & Carry/Warehouse Club, Department Store, Electronics Specialty, Hypermarket/Supercenter/Superstore, other Specialty, Supermarket	Austria, Belgium, Bulgaria, China, Croatia, Czech Rep., Denmark, France, Germany, Greece, Hungary, India, Italy, Japan, Luxembourg, Moldova, Morocco, Netherlands, Poland, Portugal, Romania, Russia, Serbia and Montenegro, Slovakia, Spain, Sweden, Switzerland, Turkey, Ukraine, UK, Vietnam
5	The Kroger Co.	US	66,111	66,111	1,115	Convenience/Forecourt Store, Hypermarket/Supercenter/Superstore, other Specialty, Supermarket	US

Source: www.nxtbook.com/nxtbooks/nrfe/stores-globalretail08/, accessed November 2008.

Global wealth from oil, technology, and the financial markets has helped make the London neighborhood of Kensington an expensive place to live. It is perhaps not surprising then that the world's largest organic food chain, Whole Foods, has opened an 80,000-square-foot store in Kensington. The prices are high but not beyond the reach of the average Kensington resident; for example, 2 pounds of asparagus are a bargain at $34.[19]

The growth of low-cost alternatives to conventional supermarkets has created a dramatic shift in the food retail market space. Conventional supermarkets are responding to new competitors with

- Greater emphasis on freshness—using just-in-time delivery and maximizing the advantage of their established supply chain.
- Targeting new markets such as health-conscious consumers—incorporating more organic, low-fat, high-quality food into their product mix.
- Creating a neighborhood atmosphere and upgrading facilities—maximizing the location advantage (being close to the consumer) they have in many communities.[20]

General Merchandise Retailers

There is a great deal of variance in the nature of general merchandise retailers, especially since many have moved aggressively into nonstore retailing, particularly e-retailing.

Advantages of Store Retailing

Personal Contact with Product Test-driving a car, trying on a sweater or dress, and watching a TV in the showroom are all examples of the single greatest benefit of store retailing, the ability to see, touch, and test the product. Sophisticated graphics software programs can take someone inside the car, show the sweater, or simulate the TV picture, but that is not the same as experiencing the product firsthand.

Personal Service In-store retailing offers the option of choosing the service level. For example, consumers don't expect great service when they visit a discount store or warehouse club but still respond favorably when asked about service if the basic minimums (shelves stocked, quick checkout, trained helpful customer service counter employees) are met. Consumers wanting a high level of service in purchasing clothes, for example, can visit boutiques or department store clothing departments and get a much higher level of personal service.

Nordstrom has won many awards for its customer service. With a friendly staff, easy to use Web site and no-hassle return policies, the company has built a loyal following of shoppers who appreciate Nordstrom's customer-friendly approach. The company has continued to explore new technologies that enhance customer service. Salespeople can now access one database to review customer information and search the company's store inventory as well as their online inventory to help customers find what they need. If the store does not have the item the salesperson is directed to help the customer find the product online.[21]

Payment Options In industrialized countries, credit/debit cards are the preferred payment method; however, people appreciate options and the opportunity to choose other payment methods including cash. In-store retailing offers consumers the most payment options and is the only retailing format that easily accommodates cash payment.

Social Experience Of all the retail channels, stores offer the greatest social interaction and entertainment experience. One of the reasons cited for the continued growth of store retailing is the social environment created in a store. Chat rooms, bulletin boards, and other forms of online interaction do not match the experience of interacting with other people in person.[22] Book retailers Barnes & Noble and Borders allocate significant space in their stores to social interaction including coffee shops created specifically to encourage social contact.

Immediate Need Fulfillment Even with overnight delivery offered by catalog and online retailers, there is still a delay between purchase and product acquisition. Store retailing enables the consumer to begin using the product immediately.

Reduced Risk to the Consumer Being able to see the product and knowing there is a physical location where they can go for customer service greatly reduces the risk of the purchase to consumers. Many consumers will do lengthy research on electronic products, searching product reviews and user feedback online; however, retailers such as Best Buy continue to grow because once a decision about the product has been made the consumer wants to purchase the product in a store. They make this decision even though online retailers often offer lower prices.[23]

NON-STORE RETAILING

Marketing managers understand that customers can and will connect with a company in a variety of situations, and while in-store retailing is a very successful and powerful customer interface, an effective retail strategy must consider a wide range of other retail environments. **Non-store retailing** uses alternative methods to reach the customer that do not require a physical location. This allows consumers to purchase from their homes or some other convenient location and includes catalogs, direct selling, television home shopping, vending machines, and electronic retailing.[24]

Catalog Retailers

While consumers visit a store to view merchandise, **catalog retailers** offer their merchandise in the comfort of a consumer's home using a printed or online catalog. One of the oldest forms of retailing, catalog retailing has become extremely popular as two-income households often lack the time for an in-store retail experience and appreciate the convenience of shopping when they choose from home.[25] These households often have sufficient income to purchase a variety of products and services. Exhibit 16.6 lists the world's largest catalog retailers. The two largest catalog retailers (Dell and IBM) sell technology-related products around the world, which suggests people are comfortable ordering technology without necessarily seeing it. As home delivery companies UPS, DHL, and FedEx expand their networks, it becomes easier to purchase products from anywhere.

Catalog retailers face three challenges. First, *getting the catalog in the hands of the right target audience is costly.* Creating, printing, and mailing catalogs is an expensive and time-consuming process taking months and costing $5 to $10 per catalog. Second, *breaking through the clutter to reach the consumer is difficult.* Catalog retailers mail 17 billion catalogs a year. When combined with other direct-mail

A critical element in any direct-selling organization's strategy is connecting customers to sales representatives. Avon, one of the largest direct-selling organizations in the world, uses advertisements to encourage customers to contact their Avon representative.

EXHIBIT 16.6 | World's Largest Catalog Retailers

Rank	Company	2007 Direct Sales (in millions)	2006 Direct Sales (in millions)	Market Segment
1	Dell Round Rock, TX	$56,900.0	$57,420.0	Computers
2	IBM Armonk, NY	10,677.0	9,886.5	Computer hardware, software and service
3	Thermo Fisher Scientific Waltham, MA	9,746.4	8,870.4	Laboratory research supplies
4	CDW Vernon Hills, IL	8,145.9	6,785.0	Computers
5	Staples Framingham, MA	6,614.2	5,908.9	Office supplies
6	Wesco International Pittsburgh, PA	6,003.4	3,192.4	Electrical and mainte-nance supplies
7	Henry Schien Melville, NY	5,920.0	5,048.0	Dental, medical, and veterinary supplies
8	OfficeMax Naperville, IL.	4,816.1	4,714.5	Office supplies
9	United Stationers Deerfield, IL	4,646.4	4,546.9	Office and facility supplies
10	Office Depot Delray Beach, FL	4,518.3	4,576.8	Office supplies

Source: Multichannel Merchant, Multichannel Merchant 100, October 2008, www.multichannelmerchant.com, accessed November 2008.

solicitations and junk mail, the consumer often doesn't take the time to read the cata-log. Finally, *building and maintaining the order fulfillment and CRM systems used by cata-log retailers is expensive.* Most of the $125 billion in catalog sales is generated by large, sophisticated retailers; many small catalog companies do not have the resources to be competitive.[26]

Direct Selling

Avon, Mary Kay, and Tupperware are familiar brands around the world and impor-tant companies in a significant non-store retail channel—direct selling. **Direct selling** involves independent businesspeople contacting consumers directly to demonstrate and sell products or services in a convenient location, often the con-sumer's home or workplace. The order is placed and fulfilled by the salesperson, who usually delivers the product directly to the consumer.[27]

While popular in the United States ($25 billion in sales), the real success of direct selling is in Latin America, Asia, and Europe ($75 billion). Direct selling appeals to many people because it allows them to become independent agents and set their own work schedules. Of the 13 million salespeople in direct selling, more than 80 percent work part time.

Many direct-selling organizations have experienced significant growth in developing countries where women comprise much of their sales forces. Avon, for example, is the largest direct-selling organization in the world and boasts it is the best company for women. At the same time, Tupperware's fastest-growing markets are Russia, Turkey, China, and India. Additionally, direct sellers are reinventing their traditional market models. Tupperware is incorporating new products such as Tupperware's Beauty Control, which features a full line of beauty products.[28]

Television Home Shopping

Often overlooked as a major retail concept, **television home shopping** generates over $10 billion in sales each year. Two networks, QVC and HSN, dominate the market. While the potential market includes almost everyone with cable television in the United States, the actual number of viewers is small. As a result, both networks have allocated resources to their online operations seeking to expand beyond the market of television viewers. The primary advantage of this retail format is the ability to show and demonstrate the product. Unlike catalogs, however, shoppers must wait for the product to show up on the screen, which limits sales. To deal with this limitation, the networks have gone to scheduling products for certain times so consumers know when to plan their viewing.[29]

Vending Machines

Perhaps you haven't thought of vending machines as a retail concept, but sales from vending machines in the United States exceed $16 billion annually. **Vending machine retailing** sells merchandise or services that are stored in a machine then dispensed to the consumer when the payment has been made. An extremely popular form of retailing, vending machines can be found throughout the world. Japan boasts one vending machine for every 23 people.

While popular with consumers, vending machines are not particularly profitable. Rising costs in labor, gasoline, and maintenance, coupled with a very competitive environment that limits price increases, keeps margins low.[30]

Advantages of Non-Store Retailing

Ease of Use Non-store retail channels offer the shopper an easy shopping experience. Consumers may review the product when it is convenient for them at a location of their choosing and make the purchase when it fits their schedule. This experience contrasts sharply with the in-store experience and is a major reason non-store retailing is growing in popularity.

Safe Shopping Environment Higher crime rates for theft and assault in many areas have increased concerns about the safety of in-store shopping. It isn't that people are afraid of crime in the store; rather, the concerns generally involve other activities connected to the in-store shopping experience such as traveling to the store or walking alone in a parking lot. This makes non-store shopping a safer choice for consumers concerned about security and safety issues such as senior citizens, who report safety concerns are a major factor in choosing non-store retailing options.[31]

Quality of Visual Presentation While not as good as seeing the product live, non-store retailing does a good job of presenting products in a positive visual format through well-designed catalogs, direct-mail materials, and online content.[32]

ONLINE-ELECTRONIC COMMERCE

Electronic commerce refers to any action using electronic media to communicate with customers; facilitate the inventory, exchange, and distribution of goods and services; or make payment. It is the fastest-growing customer interface and has fundamentally changed the way companies and customers interact. Electronic commerce has created new business opportunities and enabled existing business models to be more efficient as noted in the FYI. The two critical forms of electronic commerce are business-to-consumer and business-to-business.

FYI

Online movie retailer Netflix pioneered online movie rental and distribution. Linking online ordering with regular mail service, Netflix is a major player in the movie rental business. The company built a strong customer service reputation offering such services as long-term rental, easy ordering, and free delivery. The results have been impressive. Netflix continues to experience consistent double-digit growth with over 100,000 titles available and innovative customer packages.

But Netflix must deal with new technologies that have the potential to disrupt its business model. Apple iTunes, Vudu, and others now offer movies for download over the Internet. While download speeds can vary and the quality may not be as good as a DVD, the ease of use could dramatically alter the market for movie rentals. Netflix has met the challenge by introducing its own streaming movies service that will allow current subscribers to choose between renting the DVD by mail or downloading the movie over the Internet using a device called the Roku, which sells for about $100. The pricing plan is also innovative, a flat monthly fee that allows for unlimited downloads.[33]

Business to Consumer—E-Retailing

Electronic retailing is the communication and sale of products or services to consumers over the Internet. E-retailing is the fastest-growing retail format although it has not eliminated more traditional retailing concepts such as store or catalog retailing as suggested in the late 1990s.[34] Electronic retailing has been growing at double-digit rates and now accounts for a relatively small but rapidly increasing percentage of all retail sales in the United States (see Exhibit 16.7).

E-retailing offers even the smallest entrepreneur the opportunity to open a shop on the Internet. However, although many small companies utilize e-retailing, the vast majority of e-retail sales and Internet traffic is dominated by large traditional retailers. Companies such as Wal-Mart, Merrill Lynch, American Express, and many others offer products and services as well as extensive customer support online. Today, most of these companies coordinate a sophisticated brick (store, physical location) and click (online) strategy that links the retail formats. Williams-Sonoma, for example, allows shoppers to purchase online but return products to the store, offering a seamless shopping experience for its consumers.

The greatest success in electronic retailing has been in products where convenience and price are key drivers in the purchase decision. People do enjoy shopping at Barnes & Noble or Borders, but they also appreciate the convenience of shopping online for books. Companies such as e-Trade and traditional financial organizations such as Merrill Lynch are successful offering low-cost trading options and other services online. As consumers become more comfortable evaluating products and making purchase decisions online, they expand their electronic shopping experience. Apple's iTunes redefined the retail music industry with online music downloads accounting for 10 percent of all music purchased and is the second-largest music retailer behind only Wal-Mart.[35] This change has

EXHIBIT 16.7 | Growth of Electronic Retailing

**U.S. E-Commerce Spending
(Excludes Auctions and
Large Corporate Purchases)**

	Jan–Oct 2006 (in millions)	Jan–Oct 2007 (in millions)	Percent Change
Total	$136,483	$159,802	17%
Non-Travel (Retail)	77,524	93,551	21
Travel	58,958	66,252	12

Source: www.marketingcharts.com/interactive/us-retail-e-commerce-oct-sales-up-19-from-last-year-2371/comscore-q1-q3-retail-ecommerce-spending-2006-vs-2007jpg, accessed November 2008.

been relatively fast and dramatic as music companies develop new business models to accommodate the changes in the marketplace.

Click-only retailers produce a lot of their revenue from non-retail operations. Amazon, for example, actually generates a significant portion of its revenue acting as the "back office" e-commerce fulfillment and Web site development for large retailers such as Target and Borders. Another high-profile online-only consumer Web site is eBay, which is not really a retailer; rather, it brings buyers and sellers together in a sort of shopping bazaar.[36]

Advantages of Electronic Retailing

Extensive Selection No other channel offers the breadth and depth of selection. From information search to purchase, the Internet gives consumers greater access to more choices and different product options. In the time it takes someone to drive to Barnes & Noble and find a book, it is possible to visit the Barnes & Noble Web site, order the book (probably at a lower price), and have it shipped for next-day delivery.[37]

Considerable Information Available for Product Research and Evaluation The Internet has dramatically expanded consumers' knowledge, offering an almost unlimited number of Web sites that research, evaluate, and recommend products and services. From retailers (Best Buy in electronics) to independent testing organizations (CNet in technology) consumers can find information on anything.[38] For example, if a consumer wants to find out more about a 1958 John Deere 420T tractor, all he or she has to do is visit www.antiquetractors.com. If a consumer wants a 1935 Whittall Bird of Paradise rug, he or she can simply check out eBay. Additionally, many sites offer additional tools such as side-by-side product comparisons, video product reviews, or three-dimensional interactive product displays that educate consumers in an entertaining and visually informative manner.

Historically, companies tended to minimize customer feedback on their own Websites for fear of negative customer input. However, a number of companies now embrace customer product reviews. A recent survey suggests nearly 60 percent of consumers prefer Web sites that include customer reviews. Petco, the pet retail chain, reports adding customer feedback (the company gets 200–500 product/store reviews per week) led to an increase in sales and reduced costs as more complete information leads to fewer customer returns. Most customer reviews are written by "empty nest" baby boomers and "young transitionals" under 35 with no kids.[39]

Build Product Communities The Internet brings together groups of individuals with a shared interest to create virtual communities. These communities share information, ideas, and product information. Babycenter.com offers parents a one-stop source for information about babies, children, and parenting. These sites are an excellent communication channel for companies marketing products to relevant target markets. Johnson & Johnson is a primary sponsor of Babycenter.com and refers to the site as a "trusted partner" on its own baby products Web site.[40]

Individualized Customer Experience The Internet allows a great deal of personalization for both the consumer and the company. Consumers can get one-on-one interaction from a customer service representative and create their own Web content based on personal preferences. At the same time, companies can tailor messages and Web content by analyzing consumer Web history. The end result is a more customized, personal experience for the consumer.

Disadvantage of Electronic Retailing

Electronic retailing has a number of advantages; however, there are several drawbacks.

Easier for Customers to Walk Away The customer is in total control of the Web experience and has the opportunity to walk away at any time. In sharp contrast to a personal-selling situation or even a retail store, the customer can simply click to another site. This puts additional pressure on the Web site to attract and then hold on to visitors. In evaluating a Web site, one of the key measures is its "stickiness," which refers to the amount of time visitors remain at the site. A good Web site not only attracts a lot of visitors, but it also gets them to remain and explore the site.

Reduced Ability to Sell Features and Benefits Web sites now incorporate sophisticated tools to display and highlight critical features and benefits. However, unless the customer initiates additional contact via Web live chat, phone, or e-mail, it is not possible to engage the customer to answer questions or deal with objections.

Security of Personal Data While companies work hard to make their Web sites secure and keep personal data such as credit card numbers private, many consumers still have concerns about the security of their data. These concerns lead some consumers to limit their electronic purchases.[41]

Thrifty Rent-A-Car combines an online strategy (clicks) with its retail stores (bricks) to create better service for its business customers.

Courtesy Thrifty Car Rental

Business-to-Business Electronic Commerce

While the Internet has reshaped the way businesses and consumers interact, it has had a much more significant role in the business-to-business customer interface. B2B electronic commerce now accounts for nearly 30 percent of all business transactions and is growing at 17 percent per year. Exhibit 16.8 highlights the importance of B2B activity.

Many companies now require their vendors to do business online. Disney suppliers become part of Disney's EDI (electronic data interchange) network and process orders via the Internet. This requires an initial investment of thousands

US B2B Media Spending, 2005–2010 (in millions)

	2005	2006	2007	2008	2009	2010
Total spending*	$22,285	$23,688	$25,131	$26,740	$28,358	$30,172
Online ad spending	$ 1,537	$ 1,951	$ 2,431	$ 2,912	$ 3,410	$ 3,939
Online ad spending growth	24.9%	26.9%	23.7%	20.7%	17.1%	15.5%
Online ad spending % of total	6.9%	8.2%	9.6%	10.9%	12.0%	13.1%

*Includes B2B magazines, trade shows and exhibitions, online advertising, and online content and communities.

Source: Veronis Suhler Stevenson, PQ Media, AdScope, Agricom, American Business Media, BPA International, Center for Exhibition Research, IMS/TheAuditor, PERQ, SRDS, TNS Media Intelligence/CMR, Tradeshow Week, eMarketer calculations.

Source: www.emarketer.com, accessed November 2008.

of dollars to get the infrastructure (hardware and software) to connect with Disney. Wal-Mart, a pioneer in the application of technology into business processes, directly connects its large suppliers such as Procter & Gamble with its IT network so orders for individual stores are received at P&G and shipped directly to each store.

The IT industry in India is experiencing tremendous growth, averaging increases of more than 40 percent a year from $253 million in 2006 to an expected $1 billion in 2010. Much of the growth is attributed to the expansion of the retail sector in India into medium and smaller cities. The retail industry is moving from small, family-owned stores to more modern retail structures that include larger retailers. Enterprise resource planning systems dominate the big-ticket IT purchases, with SAP the market leader at nearly 30 percent market share. Industry sources report that IT is the third-largest investment for Indian retailers behind real estate and human resources.[42]

The Internet has also increased the efficiency of B2B relationships through dedicated B2B sites that facilitate the exchange of products and services. This has made many markets, such as the wholesale distribution of electricity, more efficient as buyers and sellers get together quickly. Known as **market makers,** these sites (such as Lendingtree.com for mortgage and other loans) bring buyers and sellers together.[43]

Customer communities are, as the name suggests, sites where customers come and share stories about their vendor experiences. These sites enable customers to evaluate vendors and then make better product decisions. Nortel sponsors a customer community program to encourage customer dialogue and deliver the most current information and education on its portfolio of products, solutions, and enabling technologies. The company's goal is to offer customers insight into Nortel while providing a forum for feedback and commentary.[44]

RETAIL STRATEGY

Developing an effective retail strategy involves making a series of decisions on six key factors. In essence, working through these six areas will enable the marketing manager to consider critical questions, such as which markets to target, and then develop specific tactics, such as the store environment, to develop the best retail strategy. Let's examine these six keys to a successful retail strategy.

For years Dunkin Donuts focused on selling a limited line of products (donuts). Recently the company has expanded its products to include breakfast sandwiches, gourmet coffee, even coffee equipment. It is expanding its product assortment to take on the retail coffee market leader, Starbucks.

Retail Target Market

Retail strategy begins with a clear understanding of the **retail target market,** the group of consumers targeted by a retailer. Often multiple retailers will target the same group. For instance Sak's Fifth Avenue and Nieman Marcus both target upscale, fashion-conscious consumers. Retailers identify retail target markets using a variety of characteristics such as geographic location, demographics, lifestyle, product benefits, or buying situation.[45]

Ultimately a retailer's goal is to build a loyal group of customers. The best defense against a strong competitor is a loyal group of customers who want to shop at a particular retailer. **Retail positioning** in the consumer's mind is created through the use of a variety of tools that build a retail brand image. The Gap's image offers reasonably priced clothing with good service. T.J. Maxx is known as being a fashion-oriented clothing store with less service and a lower price. By using perceptual mapping techniques, retailers can see where they stand relative to competitors on key characteristics such as service, price, and product selection.

Retailers also use **loyalty programs** that reinforce benefits of purchasing at the retailer and reward consumers for being loyal. As part of a broader customer relationship management strategy, loyalty programs offer discounts and other benefits to customers that strengthen the relationship. Sophisticated data mining programs allow retailers to develop individual loyalty incentives that address specific customer purchase patterns.[46]

Jared M, is a men's clothing store targeting professional athletes and others too big to find sizes and designs in traditional clothing stores. Suits can cost $6,000 each, and it is not uncommon for one of the regular clients to spend $45,000 a year on clothes. To keep customers coming back, Jared M brings in fabrics from Europe and each client is provided a personal salesperson.[47]

Location

The single most critical decision in store retailing is the physical location of the store for two important reasons. First, research strongly suggests that location is a vital consumer choice factor in selecting a store. Small differences in site location can have a big effect on the success of a given store.[48] For example, it may appear that being on any corner of a busy street intersection would be sufficient for a new Shell gas station. However, choosing the wrong corner (cars don't have access, traffic flow favors another corner) can be more costly than not being there at all.

Second, store retailing requires a complex logistics network to make it work effectively, and a good location strategy is essential in that process. Food Lion grocery stores recently pulled out of several markets in Florida because it was not able to create an efficient network of retail stores in key markets. In central Florida, the company did not have enough stores to support the necessary warehousing and transportation infrastructure. Retailers must be thinking not only of a single store location but also the location strategy for future stores and how that will fit into a logistics network. At the same time, retailers need to be sensitive about cannibalization of existing store sales and do not want to overpopulate a given area with too many stores. That approach effectively takes sales from one location and gives it to another. Over time, retailers must be sensitive to the proper density of stores in an area.

Types of Locations

There are many types of locations for store retailers. Each location has advantages and disadvantages. Retail managers make the location decision after considering a number of trade-offs. For example, large malls bring a lot of people into a location but leasing space is more expensive. In addition, for retailers of large products, such as TVs, the mall may prevent direct store access so customers find it difficult to get the product home.

Site Location Criteria

Three primary criteria for considering a particular location are: (1) characteristics of the specific site, (2) characteristics of the trading area surrounding the site, and (3) estimated sales from a store at a specific location. The first criteria, characteristics of the specific site, are used to assess the viability of the site if developed as proposed. The most fundamental factor is customer access—do a sufficient number of customers (traffic flow) have relatively easy access to the site (accessibility)? Companies seek a balance of sufficient car traffic to bring people to the site but not so much to create congestion and limit access. Other factors such as parking and current (as well as projected) tenants are also evaluated. Finally, it is important to identify any building, tenant, or other code restrictions that must be dealt with before building the store.

The second criterion is an analysis of the trading area, or the geographic area from which customers will be drawn. Retailers are particularly interested in the demographic and lifestyle characteristics of the trading area to assess how well the characteristics of the trading area match the retailer's characteristics. Obviously, the closer the match the greater the likelihood that site is a good fit.

Finally, once information about the trading area is collected it is possible to estimate the potential sales for the store site. Several models available, and many companies use their own proprietary models to estimate sales. Retailers want to be reasonably confident that potential sales opportunity exists before investing in a particular site.

Product Mix Assortment

As we discussed earlier, a retailer's product assortment is an essential characteristic that defines the retailer in the marketplace. As a result, choosing the right product mix that aligns the retailer's corporate objectives with the target market's needs is a critical element in the retail strategy. Initially, the focus is on defining the breadth (how many different product items) and depth (how many variations of a particular product) of the product assortment.

Defining the product assortment, however, is only the first component in developing a product mix assortment. Management must make decisions about specific product items. The analysis begins with an assessment of **merchandise categories,** an assortment of items considered substitutes for each other. A mother, for example, looking to purchase pants for her son might consider a number of options (jeans or corduroys, dress or play). Those options represent a merchandise category. Retailers do not define merchandise categories in the same way but, rather, create categories that fit their sales and strategy.[49] Wal-Mart might break out toothpaste and mouthwash into separate categories while a grocery store chain such as Wegmans combines the two into a category called dental care. When a particular brand accounts for sizable sales, the retailer may even create a category based on the brand such as Macy's does with Ralph Lauren/Polo.

National versus Private-Label Brands

In putting the product assortment together, retailers must decide the mix of national versus private-label brands. **National brands** are products created, manufactured, and marketed by a company and sold to retailers around the country and the world. The manufacturing company is responsible for all aspects of product creation, production, distribution, and marketing. The retailer, in turn, sells the product, making a percentage markup and, in most cases, supporting the marketing efforts of the manufacturer with additional marketing communications.

There are a variety of national brand strategies. In some cases, companies create a family brand (Sony) as well as subbrands (Discman CD players) for specific product categories. In other cases, the manufacturer develops distinct brands that do not share names or any identifiable connection. Most people are not aware that AXE men's grooming products, Country Crock spreads, Ben & Jerry's and Bertolli are all part of Unilever, a global consumer products company (see Exhibit 16.9).

Private-label brands, also known as store or house brands, are products managed and marketed by retailers. Generally, private-label brands offer a lower price point product relative to the national brand. Retailers set design and product characteristics then contract with outside manufacturers. Manufacturers are not identified, and the retailer accepts full responsibility for distribution and marketing of the product. Private-label brands are proprietary to the retailer with some, such as Craftsman, becoming major brands in their own right. Historically, private-label brands were viewed as lower quality but that is changing. Increasingly, consumers see little difference between national and private-label branded products in many product categories such as raisin bran cereal and chocolate chip cookies.

Private-label and national brands both have advantages and disadvantages. National brands tend to be supported with excellent product design, support, and marketing communications by their manufacturers. They enhance the image of the retailer and help generate additional store traffic. As a result, retailers spend relatively less on marketing with national brands than their own private-label brands.[50]

EXHIBIT 16.9	**Selected Global Brands for Unilever**
Axe	Austria, Belgium, Canada, Central & South America, Chile, Czech Republic, Europe, France, Germany, Hungary, Mexico, Netherlands, Poland, Portugal, Slovakia, United Kingdom.
Becel, Flora	Australia, Austria, Belgium, Brazil, Canada, Chile, Czech Republic, Denmark, Europe, Finland, Germany, Greece, Hungary, Italy, South Africa, Spain, Sweden, Switzerland, United Kingdom, United States.
Ben & Jerry's	France, Hong Kong, Ireland, Korea, Netherlands, Sweden, United States.
Bertolli	Austria, Belgium, Canada, Czech Republic, Finland, France, Germany, Global, Hungary, Italy, Netherlands, United Kingdom, United States.
Blue Band, Rama, Country Crock, Doriana	Austria, Belgium, Brazil, Chile, Czech Republic, Europe, Germany, Hungary, Netherlands, Slovakia, Sweden, Switzerland, Turkey, United States.
Close Up	Brazil, India.

At the same time, however, national brand manufacturers charge higher prices to the retailer and exert greater control over final sales prices, which translates into lower gross margins than private-label brands. Since national brands are sold at different retailers, there is always price pressure, and retailers, as a rule, make less money on national brands. Finally, because national brands are not associated with the particular retailer, there is not as much retailer loyalty as brand loyalty.

Private-label brands, when successful, offset many negative issues associated with national brands. Margins tend to be higher and the retailer has greater flexibility in pricing and product design. However, marketing costs are higher as the retailer must spend additional resources to support the private-label brand.

Pricing

There are two basic retail pricing strategies: high/low and every day low pricing (EDLP). Retailers must choose the strategy that best fits their overall corporate strategy. **High/low pricing** offers frequent discounts primarily through sales promotions to stated regular prices. Historically, sales occurred at certain times of the year (after the holidays); however, retail price competition has become relentless, driving many retailers to offer constant sales and promotions. The mix of high and low prices allows retailers to differentiate their pricing to different target markets by charging a higher price to less price-sensitive consumers and lower prices to more price-sensitive shoppers. Another benefit of high/low pricing is that sales and sales promotional activities generate excitement and draw people into the store. Finally, it is much easier to move slow merchandise with significant sales promotions. Pricing has become a significant issue as many retailers compete for the same customers.[51] The Ethical Dimension looks at this issue in the context of the popular Harry Potter books and movies.

Everyday low pricing (EDLP) is the approach used by stores that maintain a price point somewhere between high and deeply discounted sales prices. Supermarkets, home improvement stores, and discount stores have been the primary adopters of this strategy. This approach does not preclude sales promotions that offer lower prices, and many retailers using EDLP pricing also offer a **low price guarantee policy** that guarantees consumers the lowest price for any given product by matching the sales price of competitors. EDLP can help build customer loyalty because customers know they can rely on consistently low prices. Once an EDLP strategy is in place, the retailer spends less on marketing communications and advertising because sales promotions are not a big part of the strategy and, as a result, do not need to be advertised. Finally, inventory tends to fluctuate less, it is easier to manage inventory levels.[52]

IKEA has built a global reputation offering high quality products at low prices in a unique in-store experience. Its retail stores are large, in excess of 100,00 square feet, and many products must be assembled by the customer.

In-Store Experience

A key aspect of the customer's overall satisfaction with a retailer is the in-store experience, which begins before the customer enters the store. The retailer's advertising and Web site create expectations for the customer that will be evaluated during the shopping experience. The in-store experience is based on two factors: services and environment.

As we discussed earlier, the service mix offered by the retailer is a key differentiator in the overall retail experience. Three levels of services must be considered:

- Services that enhance the **shopping experience:** services that make shopping more enjoyable, such as fitting rooms, knowledgeable and helpful sales staff, convenient store hours, store displays.

ETHICAL DIMENSION

The Dark Side of Harry Potter's Magic

The numbers are magical; more than 400 million books sold worldwide, $4 billion plus in box office receipts, a $500 million attraction at Universal Orlando, and an author who is now one of the wealthiest women in the world. The world of Harry Potter has certainly been good to J. K. Rowling; it has generated billions of dollars for publishers and moviemakers; and it has been very entertaining for millions of fans.

Given the worldwide phenomenon that is Harry Potter, one would expect the companies most associated with the wizard to be riding a wave of success. However, in most cases, the opposite is true. Scholastic, Harry's publisher in the United States, has seen its stock fall below pre-Harry levels. Bloomsbury, the publisher of Harry Potter outside the United States, has reported a significant drop in earnings and its stock is down 40 percent in 18 months. Big booksellers including Tesco, Amazon, Wal-Mart, Barnes & Noble, and Borders introduced the books at significant discounts (more than 50 percent). Amazon concedes that it does not make any money selling Harry Potter books. The company suggests, however, that it sold more than 1 million copies of *Harry Potter and the Deathly Hallows* and believes many of those buyers continue to shop at Amazon.

This created problems for smaller, independent booksellers that have been forced to reduce prices and create more interesting ways to bring people into their stores. Historically, retailers sold new books at full price using the profits from the new titles to offset discounted older books. The success of Harry Potter, however,

created an interesting problem as retailers offered each new Harry Potter title at discounted prices just to drive traffic into the stores. This new retail pricing model has created challenges for the book industry and a shakeout of the market.

Independent bookstores have tried to find ways to offset the price advantage offered by Amazon, Wal-Mart, and other large booksellers by offering Harry Potter parties and other incentives to bring Potter fans into their stores. Unfortunately, there are many opportunities for Potter fans to connect including chat rooms, dedicated Potter Web sites, and fan clubs.

No doubt Harry Potter aficionados appreciate buying the books at a discount; however, this new pricing model has created challenging dynamics in the book business. Independent bookstores are finding it difficult to find a niche in the crowded marketplace dominated by brick retailers like Wal-Mart, click retailers like Amazon, and the mega booksellers like Barnes & Noble and Borders, which offer a coffee shop experience inside their stores.[53]

Ethical Perspective

1. **Large bookstore chains:** Should they continue to offer new books at significant discounts to increase foot traffic despite losing money on the books?

2. **Independent bookstores:** How should they respond to new book prices that are lower than their purchase costs?

3. **Consumers:** Should customers encourage market forces to keep prices lower, or should they encourage smaller, independent bookstores?

- Services that enhance the **sales experience:** services that make the sales experience easier, such as policies that make it easy to return merchandise for credit or refund, multiple payment methods, easy shipping and delivery options.

- Services that enhance the **retailer experience:** services that strengthen the customer's perception of the retailer, such as loyalty programs, easy store access, additional facilities like restaurants, support services for young children and infants.

Customers bundle their product purchase with other experiences to develop an overall impression of the retailer. Retailers understand that when the products are similar, as is the case with national branded products, the in-store experience differentiates one retailer from another. Bass Pro Shops offers shoppers the opportunity to try fishing gear in a large tank and test rifles on a shooting range. Bookstores such as Barnes & Noble have

Victoria's Secret offers a pleasant shopping experience with fitting rooms and trained staff to facilitate the purchase.

created special children's sections complete with small tables and chairs to encourage children and their parents to read together. Some stores even have stages that bring children into the store for special events.

The environment is fundamental in setting the tone for the shopping experience. Store layout and displays, interior colors, even the music in the store all work together to create an atmosphere that it is hoped will make the customer feel comfortable. A cluttered or poorly designed store layout, inappropriate interior lighting and colors, music that is not consistent with the product or the target market all dampen the customer's shopping experience. Indeed, research suggests that the tempo of music played in the store affects the amount of time spent shopping and, consequently, the average sale.

> HMV, the U.K.'s largest retailer of music and DVDs, expanded its in-store experience by offering customers the opportunity to burn CDs and download music to their MP3 players from HMV's corporate Web site. Each store allocates existing floor space to a "destination area" for customers to customize their music. With annual sales over $3 billion, the company, which also operates in Asia and Canada, hopes to lift both in-store and online sales.[54]

Marketing Communications

Retailers use a wide range of marketing communications to reach their target markets. As we will explore in Chapters 17 and 18 an effective marketing communications strategy requires careful planning, great execution, and coordination. Generally, retailers focus on two key objectives in their marketing communications. First, marketing communications generate customer traffic. Historically, that meant encouraging people to physically visit the store but, increasingly, that also means sending people to the retailer's Web site. Advertising directed at new products or store specials is designed to stimulate retail traffic. Second, marketing communications drive customer purchases. Coupons, sales promotions, in-store sampling are examples of communications that motivate product purchase. Retailers must make sure their marketing communications are consistent with their store image as well as appropriate for the target market. Wal-Mart, for example, would likely not advertise in *Vanity Fair* or *Esquire*.

SUMMARY

The company customer interface is an essential element in the overall customer value experience. Technology has dramatically changed how, where, and when customers choose to interact with a company. These changes have created a number of opportunities, and companies have had to develop new, innovative tools to enhance their customer service and support.

Despite the growth of electronic retailing, traditional retailing continues to flourish for a number of reasons. Non-store retailing also continues to grow. E-retailing, while still a small percentage of all retail sales, is growing faster than any other form of retailing. Although the growth of business-to-consumer e-retailing has been rapid, business-to-business e-commerce has grown even faster and now accounts for over 30 percent of all business transactions. Developing an effective retail strategy involves assessing six critical areas that consider strategic questions as well as specific tactics to best address those strategic questions.

customer touchpoints 436
retailing 437
variety 442
breadth of merchandise 442
assortment 442
depth of merchandise 442
value equation 443
food retailer 443
non-store retailer 446
catalog retailer 446

direct selling 447
television home shopping 448
vending machine retailing 448
electronic commerce 449
electronic retailing 449
market makers 452
customer communities 452
retail target market 453
retail positioning 453
loyalty programs 453

merchandise category 454
national brands 455
private-label brands 455
high/low pricing 456
everyday low pricing (EDLP) 456
low price guarantee policy 456
shopping experience 456
sales experience 457
retailer experience 457

APPLICATION QUESTIONS

1. You are the merchandise manager for Best Buy electronics and have been asked to expand the assortment of music products. Industry trends suggest more people are downloading their music online. How would you assess whether or not to allocate another 200 square feet in each store to CD sales? Do you think it is a good idea? Why or why not?

2. How many unique product items do you think the average Sam's Club store carries? Develop a product mix map that delineates both the breadth and depth of a Sam's Club product mix.

3. You are the department manager for the sporting goods department at Target. Assess the services offered by your department and compare them to the services offered at a Sports Authority. What services, if any, would you consider adding if you wanted to compete more directly against Sports Authority?

4. You are the director of site location strategy for Burger King. Develop a location strategy for expanding the number of stores in your town. How would you choose a location for the next store?

5. From a student's perspective, what functions are available on your campus Web site (for example, class registration, payment, delivery of course materials)? How would you assess the ease of use for the Web site? What functions does the campus Web site perform well and which does it perform poorly?

MANAGEMENT DECISION CASE: Tesco Serves Up Japanese Expansion

British food retail giant Tesco, the third-largest grocery retailer in the world behind Wal-Mart (U.S.) and Carrefour (France), is looking to expand its global footprint. Building on its success in Britain, the company wants to expand its Tesco Express concept to selected markets around the world. For example, in one year it opened more than 100 Express stores in Arizona, California, and Nevada with plans to move into East Coast markets. Tesco Express is a unique mix of convenience store and supermarket featuring higher-quality fresh food, ready-made meals, and certain supermarket items found in its larger, traditional Tesco Supermarkets. The stores are found in highly populated urban environments and appeal to working families and young professionals looking for quality and convenience in food shopping. Tesco Supermarkets and Express stores combine for over 30 percent of the retail food market in Great Britain.

Tesco has demonstrated the ability to understand and be successful in new markets. Consider Japan, which has proved difficult for many Western retailers because of its complex distribution networks and highly competitive retail environment. Wal-Mart, for example, purchased a 53 percent stake in leading retailer Seiyu in 2002 but has yet to post a profit. Carrefour also opened eight stores in Japan but exited the country selling all its stores to Aeon after reporting more than $250 million in losses. At the other end of the market, some experts cite a saturation point in the convenience market as a reason to question Tesco's strategy. There are over 40,000 convenience stores in Japan, or one for every 3,200 residents.

However, those challenges did not deter Tesco. Based on more than five years of research, the company believes it has identified a niche—convenience stores offering quality, ready-made food and limited supermarket items—not currently served by traditional Japanese convenience stores such as 7-Eleven, Lawson, Circle-K Sunkus, or the larger more traditional grocery stores such as Aeon and Daiei. The company's research suggests the Japanese consumer is willing to pay for higher-quality food that is convenient. Tesco's first move into Japan was the purchase of C Two-Network, a small supermarket company, in 2003. From that purchase, Tesco learned a great deal about the food business including supply chain and distribution as well as food retailing. This has been critical as the company focuses on the delivery of fresh ready-made foods as a key differentiator in the overall retail strategy.

In 2007, the company opened its first store in the fashionable Oizumi Garden district of Tokyo. The store encompasses roughly 1,000 square feet and stocks 2,500 items (about 10 percent of a U.S. retail supermarket) with the emphasis on fresh, quality, ready-made products. Initial rollout of the concept included 35 stores in urban areas such as Tokyo. In conjunction with the rollout of Tesco Express, the company will open 10 larger supermarkets using the C Two-Network's Tsurukame brand in an effort to move into the more traditional supermarket space[55].

Questions for Consideration

1. Given the highly competitive nature of the Japanese retail food market and failure of global leaders Wal-Mart and Carrefour to successfully penetrate the Japanese market, do you believe Tesco's decision to open Tesco Express is a good idea? Why or why not?

2. How would you describe the retail strategy for Tesco Express as it expands in Japan?

MARKETING PLAN EXERCISE

ACTIVITY 16: The Customer Interface

No matter your product experience, it is essential to consider the process by which customers will interface with the product. If, for example, the product is to be marketed through retail channels, identifying possible retailers and channels is essential. Furthermore, no matter what the Web objectives, developing an effective Web strategy is also essential. Specifically, develop a strategy for interfacing with your customer:

1. Define the characteristics of the channel and, more specifically, determine what is the best approach for reaching the customer (retail, online, in-company sales force, distributors).

2. If you are using a retail channel, define your retail strategy:

   a. Who is your target market?

   b. Which retailers best fit your strategy and where are they located?

   c. What is your retail pricing strategy?

   d. What kind of in-store experience do you want for your customer?

   e. What is your marketing communications with retailers?

3. Define the Web strategy for the product:

   a. Functionality of Web site (online purchasing, streaming product demo videos, retail locator or showing the customer where and how the product can be purchased).

   b. Look and feel of the Web site.

If you are using Marketing Plan Pro, a template for this assignment can be accessed at www.mhhe.com/marshall1e.

RECOMMENDED READINGS

1. Willard N. Ander, Jr., and Neil Z. Stern, *Winning at Retailing: Developing a Sustained Model for Retail Success* (Hoboken, NJ: Wiley, 2004).

2. Manfred Krafft and Murali K. Mantrala, *Retailing in the 21st Century: Current and Future Trends* (New York: Springer, 2007).

3. Arthur A. Winters, Peggy Fincher Winters, and Carole Paul, *The Power of Retail Branding: Reinvention Strategies for Empowering the Brand* (New York: Visual Reference Publications, 2006).

4. Paula N. Danziger, *Shopping: Why We Love It and How Retailers Can Create the Ultimate Customer Experience* (New York: Kaplan Business, 2006).

5. Lisa Johnson, *Mind Your X's and Y's: Satisfying the 10 Cravings of a New Generation of Consumers* (New York: Free Press, 2006).

CHAPTER 17

INTEGRATED MARKETING COMMUNICATIONS: PROMOTIONAL STRATEGY, ADVERTISING, SALES PROMOTION, AND PUBLIC RELATIONS

LEARNING OBJECTIVES

- Appreciate the significance of the concept of integrated marketing communications (IMC) and its impact on marketing management.

- Identify the elements of the promotion mix and the pros and cons of each element.

- Connect the concept of the communication process model and the AIDA model to important issues in promotional strategy.

- Describe the components of the marketing manager's role in promotional strategy.

- Understand key concepts of advertising, sales promotion, and public relations as they pertain to marketing management.

EXECUTIVE PERSPECTIVE

Executive Pete Barr, Jr., President/CEO

Company Fry-Hammond-Barr

Business Full-service marketing communications agency

What are the primary sources of value added that a full service advertising agency provides to its clients?

Strategic thinking is at the top of the list. In a healthy agency-client partnership when the agency is accurately compensated for its time, the most valuable value-added service provided is regular ongoing strategic thinking. An agency team should always be thinking about the client's business beyond the bounds of time sheets and billable hours. Agencies must remember that the health of their clients' business is often directly linked to the advertising and marketing. A sharp agency knows this and regularly exchanges ideas, thinking, and strategy with its client partner. Other sources of value added include extra media or promotions negotiated by an agency media team as part of paid media efforts. Agencies can also bring forward new media ideas for their clients to consider, especially during the current rapid shift in media habits.

When deciding on investing in one form of advertising media versus another, what are some things a marketing manager must consider before making the commitment?

Media has become quite a science, and careful target analysis is needed when making media decisions. Today's target audiences can have very fragmented media habits, so reaching them effectively and efficiently can be very challenging. Measurability is important; more and more marketers are demanding

"transactional" media choices such as direct mail/response or Internet so they can truly see the effect on sales. Traditional media planning and buying is based on rating points and the cost per point, which can be negotiated. Media pros like to think in terms of "target rating points" as they plan and buy so that the investment is as efficient as possible. Overall, media plans are sometimes calculated in terms of total gross impressions so that all media can be measured in total.

Buzz—word-of-mouth advertising—is huge today. What tips can you provide on how a marketing manager might generate buzz about a brand?

Creating buzz is every marketer's goal. The fastest way to create buzz is from a total integration of the marketing forces, including Web/Internet activity, public relations, advertising, direct marketing, sampling, guerrilla tactics, a great product, and good timing. Some marketers deploy ground forces of advocates who plant and place products and messages in a blitz fashion to create an assault on the market. This can be challenging on a low budget, but it can be effective if the target and geography are limited. Buzz can be created within small, distinct groups by mobilizing teams of "thought leader/trendsetters" who blitz the market with messages and products creating the "ya gotta have this" craze effect. Ideally, the buzz is sustained with the integrated approach, and as each market's buzz wanes, the forces move on to the next market.

INTRODUCTION TO PROMOTION AND INTEGRATED MARKETING COMMUNICATIONS (IMC)

Marketing managers usually communicated with customers through **promotion,** which involves various forms of communication to inform, persuade, or remind. This communication is accomplished through elements of the **promotion mix—advertising, sales promotion, public relations (PR), personal selling, direct marketing,** and **interactive marketing.** These elements, sometimes also called the marketing communications mix, are defined in Exhibit 17.1 The first three tend to be relatively less personal in nature than the last three. That is, advertising, sales promotion, and PR often are developed for receipt by a mass audience, while personal selling, direct marketing, and interactive marketing by their nature are more one-to-one marketing.

The promotion mix is very important in marketing planning. The development of **promotion mix strategies,** or simply *promotional strategies,* involves decisions about which combination of elements in the promotion mix is likely to best communicate the offering to the marketplace and achieve an acceptable ROI for the marketer, given the product and target markets involved. The effectiveness and efficiency of promotional strategies are often tracked on the basis of a **promotional campaign,** which attributes promotional expenditures to a particular creative execution aimed at a particular product or product line during a specified time period. In fact, much of marketing has operated on a campaign-to-campaign basis for ongoing planning purposes.

EXHIBIT 17.1	Definitions of Elements of the Promotion Mix
Advertising	Paid form of relatively less personal marketing communications often through a mass medium to one or more target markets. Example media include television, radio, magazines, newspapers, and outdoor.
Sales Promotion	Provides an inducement for an end-user consumer to buy your product or for a salesperson or someone else in the channel to sell it. Designed to augment other forms of promotion; rarely used alone. Examples of consumer inducements are coupons, rebates, and sweepstakes. Inducements for channel members often involve special monies or prizes for pushing a particular offering.
Public Relations (PR)	Systematic approach to influencing attitudes, opinions, and behaviors of customers and others. Often executed through publicity, which is an unpaid and relatively less personal form of marketing communications usually through news stories and mentions at public events.
Personal Selling	One-to-one personal communication with a customer by a salesperson, either in person or electronically in some way that provides two-way dialogue.
Direct Marketing	An interactive marketing system that uses one or more advertising media to affect a measurable response and/or transaction at any location. Personal communication with a customer by means other than a salesperson.
Interactive Marketing	An Internet-driven relationship between companies, their brands, and customers. Interactive marketing enables customers to control information flow and encourages customer-company interaction as welll as a higher level of customer service.

Sometimes several media vehicles are used within one company. For example, a new co-promotion between Nike shoes and Apple's iPod uses both TV and the Web to drive sales. Called Nike Plus, the project uses the iPod as a tool for monitoring a runner's pace and style. Customers can go to a Web site that gives them more information as well as a sense of community *and* the opportunity to buy more products! The purpose of the TV commercial is merely to drive traffic to the Web site.[1]

The Rise of Integrated Marketing Communications (IMC)

Within the last decade, the inclusion of electronic marketing channels, more sophisticated research, customer database management, and integrated CRM systems began to enable the management of customer relationships and communication with customers on a more one-on-one basis, creating less dependency on traditional promotion through mass media. At the same time, various traditional media outlets began to become very fragmented; we now have literally thousands of cable and satellite dish television channels, hundreds of specialty magazines, micro-specialty genres in radio programming, and ready access to news, information, and entertainment online. These trends have caused the marketing field to rethink how to do promotion. Don Schultz and his colleagues are widely credited with introducing the concept of integrated marketing communications in the mid-1990s as a new paradigm for communicating offerings to a target market. **Integrated marketing communications (IMC)** is a strategic approach to communicating the brand and company message to targeted customers in ways that are clear, concise, and consistent and yet are customizable as needed to maximize the impact on a particular audience.[2]

Think of the difference in IMC versus more traditional promotion mix strategies along the lines of the illustrations in Exhibits 17.2 and 17.3. Exhibit 17.2

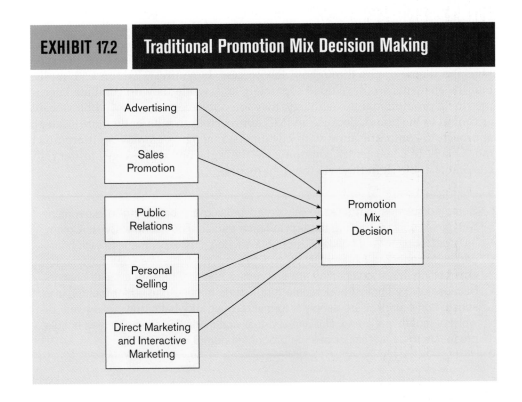

EXHIBIT 17.2 | **Traditional Promotion Mix Decision Making**

Advertising → Promotion Mix Decision
Sales Promotion → Promotion Mix Decision
Public Relations → Promotion Mix Decision
Personal Selling → Promotion Mix Decision
Direct Marketing and Interactive Marketing → Promotion Mix Decision

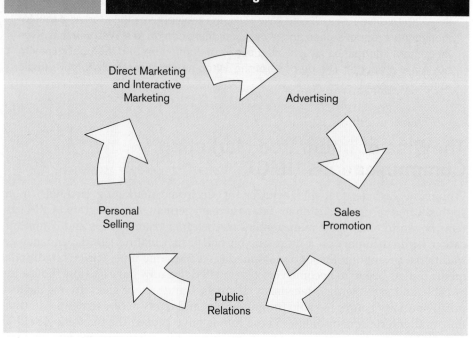

| EXHIBIT 17.3 | IMC Decision Making |

Direct Marketing and Interactive Marketing

Advertising

Sales Promotion

Public Relations

Personal Selling

portrays the concept of a traditional promotion mix decision—separate assessment of whether to invest in promoting the offering through one or more of the promotion mix elements. In contrast, Exhibit 17.3 captures the different nature of IMC decision making—a holistic and interrelated decision process, integrative, connected to the overall brand message, yet still fully customizable to different customer groups.

An IMC approach lends itself to better integration of the communication elements, hence the term *integrated* marketing communications. Exhibit 17.3 connotes that marketing managers' consideration of the elements takes place in a holistic decision process. That is, each element impacts the others and the whole is likely more than the sum of the parts. A strong focus on a unified branding message and theme occurs throughout the process. In contrast, Exhibit 17.2 implies that the elements are developed separately and, while they do combine later to provide a promotional mix strategy, they are not necessarily viewed holistically as central to the brand. Because an IMC approach is an inherently more strategic approach to communicating with customers, managers employing it are much more likely to consistently communicate the right brand messages to the right customers at the right time via the right media.

Some companies that used to rely on advertising are beginning to experiment with direct personal selling through in-home parties. For example, Swiss Colony sells gift foods for the holidays through a catalog. It is experimenting with home parties for goods such as relishes and salsas, which can be used anytime for entertaining. More companies are embracing home parties as a sales channel because of the implied endorsement of friends hosting parties for friends. In a sense, home parties are simply a formalized use of what's now called viral or word-of-mouth marketing. But unlike virtual viral marketing, home parties enable prospects to taste, feel, or see the product firsthand.[3]

IMC and the Promotion Mix

What kinds of decisions are involved in developing and executing IMC strategy? Consider Exhibit 17.4, which assesses the impact of a variety of marketing management factors on the decision of whether to pursue an advertising/sales promotion-driven IMC strategy versus a personal selling-driven approach. As you can see, a gamut of critical issues from buyer information needs to purchase size to the configuration of the marketing mix elements all influence the decision about where to invest promotional budget dollars. In fact, in many marketing planning situations, among all the elements of the marketing mix, promotional budgeting decisions involve the lion's share of the overall marketing budget—often surpassing packaging, distribution, and other marketing elements by a wide margin.

Entertainers use strong IMC, including stylish marquis ads such as these for Cirque du Soleil's *Zumanity* and comedienne Rita Rudner to create buzz about their performances.

The allocation of promotional marketing budget monies across the various elements of the promotion mix is a complex decision. Each promotional form has its own individual pros and cons, and Exhibit 17.5 provides a selection of some of these. Within the IMC approach, it is the *integration* of the elements—not just each individual element—and the resulting *synergies* of the branding message that make the strongest sustainable impact on customers.

| EXHIBIT 17.4 | Illustrative Factors Influencing IMC Strategy |

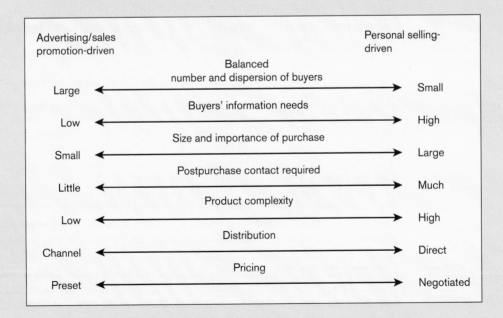

Source: Reprinted from David W. Cravens and Nigel F. Piercy, *Strategic Marketing*, 8th ed., 2006. Copyright © 2006 The McGraw-Hill Companies, Inc.

EXHIBIT 17.5 | Selected Pros and Cons of Individual Promotion Mix Elements

Promotion Mix Element	Pros	Cons
Advertising	• Many media choices • Efficiently reaches large numbers of customers • Great creative flexibility	• Shotgun approach reaches many outside the target • Oversaturation of ads lessens impact • High production costs
Sales Promotion	• Stimulates purchase directly through incentive to buy • Serves as an effective accompaniment to other promotion forms	• Can lead customers to continually wait for the next coupon, rebate, etc. • Brand may be impacted by price-cutting image
Public Relations	• Unpaid communication seen as more credible than paid forms • Association of offering with quality media outlet enhances brand	• Low control of how the message turns out • Highly labor intensive cost of mounting PR campaigns
Personal Selling	• Strong two-way communication of ideas • Directly eases customer confusion and persuades purchase	• Very expensive cost per customer contact • Salesperson may go "off message" from brand to secure the sale
Direct Marketing and Interactive Marketing	• Message customization without high costs of personal selling • Strong relationship building especially when customer can control the interaction	• Spam and other unwanted correspondence when targeting is poorly executed • Reliance on CRM and database marketing requires constant updating

Push and Pull Strategies

Two fundamental approaches to promotional strategy are *push* and *pull* strategies. These are depicted in Exhibit 17.6. The specific promotion mix elements selected for investment will vary depending on the relative degree of push or pull desired.

In a **push strategy,** the focus is on the channel of distribution and in getting the offering into the channel. Members of the channel are targeted for promotion and are depended on to then push the offering into the hands of end users. A push strategy typically relies on a combination of personal selling and sales promotion directed toward channel members.[4] In a **pull strategy,** the focus shifts to stimulating demand for an offering directly from the end user. Advertising, consumer-directed sales promotion, PR, or direct and interactive marketing can be combined in various ways to target end users, creating demand that results in the channel making an offering available for purchase. In practice, push and pull

| EXHIBIT 17.6 | Push and Pull Promotional Strategies |

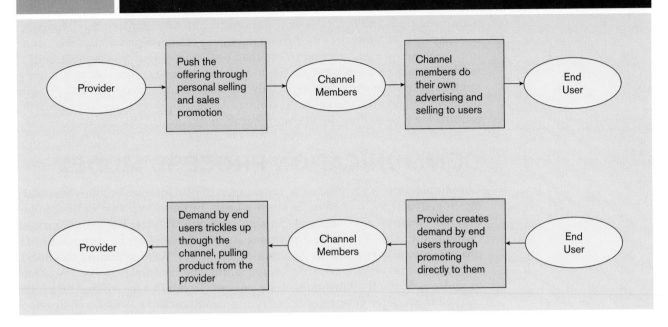

strategies are rarely used mutually exclusively.[5] Rather, a promotional strategy is developed that strikes the best balance of investment of promotional funds in both push and pull strategies that make sense for the product and market involved.

Internal Marketing and IMC

A final critical aspect of IMC that bears mentioning at this point is internal marketing. **Internal marketing** is the application of marketing concepts and strategies inside an organization. Much research has shown that if members of an organization aren't knowledgeable about its offerings, don't understand who the customers are, and can't effectively articulate the branding message, successful marketing management is very difficult. Employees of a firm are potentially its best and most trusted brand and message ambassadors. Properly armed, they can articulate what the firm and its offerings stand for in ways that nobody else can.[6]

Great brand marketers today pay a lot of attention to ensuring that *everybody* in the firm has pride of ownership in its brand, products, and services. From Southwest Airlines to Caterpillar to Apple, great marketing companies are placing a high priority on enabling each and every employee to communicate the marketing message. Most firms successful in internal marketing enlist the help of the human resources department to include indoctrination of all employees in the brand messages beginning with employee orientation programs and continuing when new products are introduced or new markets are entered.

Looking Ahead

This chapter and the next provide a managerially relevant overview of issues involved in promotion mix decision making. In the remainder of this chapter, you will learn about the communication process model, a hierarchy of effect model in promotional strategy development, and the marketing manager's role in promotional strategy. Then, we've divided the chapter coverage of the promotion mix elements by relatively less personal approaches (Chapter 17 includes an introduction to advertising, sales promotion, and PR) and relatively more personal promotional approaches (Chapter 18 covers personal selling, direct marketing, and interactive marketing).

Perhaps more than any other areas of marketing management covered in this book, promotion and IMC as a topic is incredibly broad and specialized. Consider that each of the elements of the promotion mix is often a separate course of study in college, and sometimes even more than one course. Your task as a student of marketing management is to gain an understanding of the process of promotional strategy decision making and especially the basic promotional tools and decision options available for marketing planning. An appropriate place to begin is by introducing a general model of communication.

COMMUNICATION PROCESS MODEL

Communication is the process of exchanging information and conveying meaning from one party to another. Before we begin further discussion of the promotion mix elements, it is important to step back and consider the overall process of communication. Exhibit 17.7 provides a general model of the communication process, based on research in communication theory. Because communication is an integral aspect of a marketer's charge within any organization, it is important to understand the fundamentals of the process. To achieve the desired effect, the marketing manager must consider all of the communication elements in developing the firm's promotional strategies.

The general communication process model identifies the elements in the process of communicating any type of message—marketing communications or otherwise—from a sender through a process of encoding the message, transmitting the message through a channel, decoding the message, receipt of the message by a (hopefully) intended target, and the potential for a response by the target through a feedback loop. Surrounding the entire communication process is noise, or other messages and distractions that reduce the impact and effectiveness of the communication process on the intended target.

Let's translate the elements of the communication process into a marketing management situation.

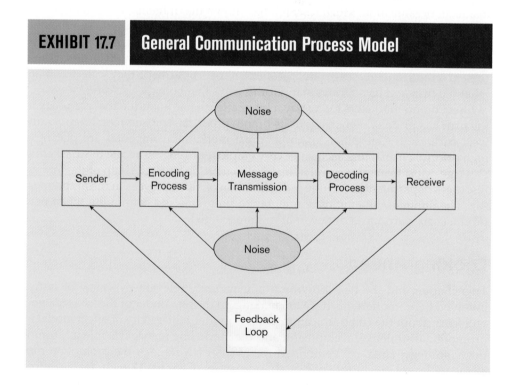

| EXHIBIT 17.7 | General Communication Process Model |

Sender

The **sender** is the source of the message. In a marketing context, the source is generally the organization whose offerings are the subjects of the communication. Often, the identification of the sender is connected more to a brand than to an organization. For example, although some people are aware that Huggies disposable diapers are marketed by Kimberly-Clark, because of Kimberly-Clark's individual branding strategy the message source is intentionally tied to that brand and not to the corporation. However, the issue of **corporate identity** and its impact on customer attitudes and responses toward product offerings now is receiving heightened attention. Research indicates that a growing number of customers pay attention to what organization is behind the message and what its values are, especially in terms of sustainability and social responsibility, when making their purchase decisions.[7]

Importantly, sometimes who the sending firm is and what its brands and offerings are affect the range of choices for managers throughout the remainder of the communication process model. Consider Marriott International, which has a wide range of brands from Fairfield Inn on the economy end to Ritz-Carlton on the luxury end. When executing its marketing communications, to effectively position each of these brands uniquely in the mind of the consumer, Marriott must carefully choose distinct messages for each. This may or may not involve including highlighting the word *Marriott* in the communication; for example, Ritz-Carlton never mentions the Marriott brand but the lower-end offerings do.

Encoding Process

Through the **encoding process,** the sender translates an idea to be communicated into a symbolic message consisting of words, pictures, numbers, and gestures in preparation for transmittal to a receiver. For brands that have developed strong imagery, the encoding process is helped along dramatically. Think about the symbolism of the brand logos for McDonald's, Boeing, and Apple, for example. For many customers, each logo conjures up instant feelings and thoughts about the brands, product line, and company. In this way, branding and marketing communications are inextricably linked—that is, strong investment in brand building almost always pays off through more effective and efficient marketing communications.

The encoding of messages about Fairfield Inn and Ritz-Carlton results in quite a different imagery. Fairfield Inn projects imagery of clean, functional, yet comparatively spartan accommodations. To many, Fairfield Inn equates to business travel on a budget. The imagery involved in encoding messages about Ritz-Carlton is very different. Ritz portrays sumptuous rooms, spa facilities, and exotic locations in its focus on attracting high-end pleasure travelers and businesspeople for whom travel budgets are not an issue.

Message Transmission

After encoding, **message transmission** places the communication into some channel or medium so that it can make its way to the intended receiver. Think of a **channel or medium** as the conduit by which the encoded message travels. Options are wide ranging and include magazines, television, radio, the Internet, newspaper stories, and salespeople. The message arrives at the receiver via some communication channel, but that doesn't necessarily mean that every potential receiver will be equally receptive to the message. Thus, it is the sender's job to select the channel(s) that will reach a maximum number of targeted receivers and a minimum number of nontargeted receivers.

Decoding Process

The message arrives and is sensed (viewed, heard, etc.) by the receiver. But communication does not actually occur until the receiver decodes it. The **decoding process** takes place when the receiver interprets the meaning of the message's symbols as encoded by the sender. A typical challenge for marketers at this stage of the communication process is that different receivers are likely to interpret the message differently based on their own inherent backgrounds and biases. This phenomenon results in **selective perception**–different meanings assigned to the same message by different receivers, based on an array of individual differences.[8]

The potential for selective perception is ubiquitous; to mitigate its impact marketers try mightily to develop messages that are as consistent and unambiguous as possible. To one viewer, an ad for Fairfield Inn intended to feature imagery and words about the brand's economically thrifty qualities might get translated into "cheap motel." To another, the message might be received as "clean, reasonably priced, with free Internet." Obviously, Marriott is hoping the majority receive the second message.

Receiver

The intended **receiver** is the individual who is the target of the communication. Marketers work hard through research to ensure proper identification of targets that are expected to have a high likelihood of connecting with the message based on their needs and wants. Obviously, in a personal selling or direct marketing context, the receivers are identified individually for contact. In the case of less personal marketing communications forms—advertising, sales promotion, and PR—marketing managers attempt to select communication channels and create messages that will have the greatest chance of actually being decoded, and acted upon, by the target receivers.[9]

Feedback Loop

The communication model provides opportunity for two-way communication through a **feedback loop,** in which the receiver can communicate reactions back to the sender. In a personal selling situation, the potential for customer feedback is instantaneous and direct.[10] In fact, one of the prized qualities of successful salespeople is effective listening skills, taking in customer feedback and responding in ways that add value back to the customer. Similarly, as you will learn in Chapter 18, interactive marketing provides a clear two-way electronic conduit for information flow between company and customer. But compared to personal selling and interactive marketing, feedback on marketing communications delivered through advertising, sales promotion, PR, and noninteractive direct marketing is harder to come by. In those cases, marketers have to work hard to solicit customer responses.

For marketers, facilitating the ability of customers to provide feedback is important to success. As you read in Chapter 13 on service, a critical success factor in retaining loyal, satisfied customers is the ability to continually receive information back from customers on their experiences—good or bad—with a firm and its offerings. Investment in ongoing efforts at promoting two-way communication between firm and customer makes sense, given the temptations in today's hypercompetitive marketplace for customers to switch brands at the drop of a hat.

Noise

Most adults remember the child's game in which a group sits in a circle and a parent or teacher whispers a message into the ear of one of the children. Each child in sequence then turns to the next one, whispering the message as he or she heard it. The last child to receive it is then asked to say the message out loud for comparison with the original message, which is usually then revealed in writing on an overhead or blackboard. It's a safe bet that what comes out the other end of that communication process is going to be very different from what went it. The distortion or interference that can occur at any stage of a communication process is referred to as **noise,** and the potential for noise is insidious in marketing communications.[11]

In a perfect world of communication, a decoded message would enter the mind of the receiver exactly the same as the one encoded by the sender. However, it is inevitable that noise will interfere with the purity of the process in the form of conflicting messages, misunderstood terminology, problems or errors in the channel or media used for the communication, or simply the overwhelming din (or clutter) of modern hyper-communication. Too many messages, too many competing media, too many alternative activities for today's customers to partake—all of these factors contribute to a general degrading of the effectiveness of marketing communications. The result is that marketers must be smarter than ever about the way they develop and execute their communications. The ability of TiVo to wipe out an entire genre of advertising is emblematic of the challenges facing marketers' promotional strategies. And the fact that Gen Ys and Millennials tend to shun many traditional promotional forms in favor of communications *they* can control ensures that the noise problem is going to get worse before it gets better.

Even a basic product like Philadelphia Cream Cheese can rise above the noise of the many competing brands by creative execution of its advertisements.

HIERARCHY OF EFFECTS MODEL

Buyers often pass through purchase decision processes in three steps: cognitive (learn), affective (feel), and behavioral (do). These stages are portrayed in various models to illustrate this hierarchy of effects in the context of customer response to

EXHIBIT 17.8

AIDA Model

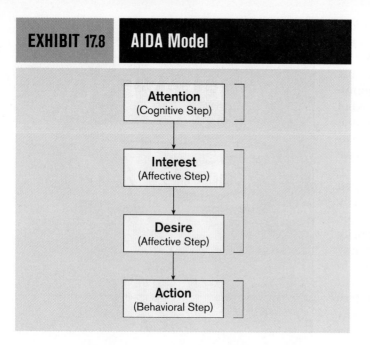

| Attention (Cognitive Step) |
| Interest (Affective Step) |
| Desire (Affective Step) |
| Action (Behavioral Step) |

marketing communications. Here we will illustrate one popular version of such models, the **AIDA model,** so-named because the effects build in this order: **A**ttention (or **A**wareness), **I**nterest, **D**esire, and **A**ction. The attention stage correlates to the cognitive step of buyer decision making, the interest and desire stages to the affective step, and the action stage to the behavioral step.[13] Exhibit 17.8 portrays the AIDA model.

Where the target customers fit on the model is critically important to effective selection and execution of the promotion mix. Recalling the general communication model, different messages and media are required to ensure that the different targets are likely to decode and process the communication successfully. Below are tips for maximizing success in promoting across the various stages of the AIDA model. Exhibit 17.9 rates the general appropriateness of applying each of the promotion mix elements depending on the stage of the hierarchy of effects of the targets.

Attention

If target customers are essentially unaware of an offering, most of the investment in communication must be in raising awareness and gaining their attention. Depending on the situation, this may involve developing awareness for a whole new set of customer needs and wants as well as revealing that your product exists to address those needs and wants. In the initial introduction of the Prius, Toyota put much effort into building awareness of the emerging need for hybrid cars and also into educating potential customers about what a hybrid car actually is. Essentially, the automaker created a product category from scratch, and for a while there was little return on the promotional investment. However, when gas prices began to soar and environmental issues became more prominent, Prius was in a prime position to become the leader in its product category, gaining a first-mover

EXHIBIT 17.9 | **Appropriateness of Promotion Mix Elements at AIDA Stages**

Promotion Mix Element	Attention Stage	Interest Stage	Desire Stage	Action Stage
Advertising	▲ ▲ ▲	▲ ▲ ▲	▲ ▲	▲ ▲
Sales Promotion	▲ ▲	▲ ▲	▲ ▲ ▲	▲ ▲ ▲
Public Relations	▲ ▲ ▲	▲ ▲ ▲	▲ ▲	▲
Personal Selling	▲	▲	▲ ▲ ▲	▲ ▲ ▲
Direct Marketing and Interactive Marketing	▲	▲ ▲	▲ ▲ ▲	▲ ▲

▲ = Generally least appropriate for use
▲ ▲ ▲ = Generally most appropriate for use

advantage and making it difficult for competitors to catch up. Now, every major car manufacturer is jumping into the category.

Gaining attention and building initial awareness can be a daunting task for marketers. Tremendous expenditures may be required to establish a foothold with customers, especially when a brand is relatively unknown or a product category is in its infancy. Chapter 7 covered different categories of adopters depending on how willing a potential customer is to try and buy a new product. At the attention stage of the AIDA model, marketing managers hope to use promotions to gain awareness of their offering with the innovators and early adopters. If marketers can influence these groups to purchase, innovators and early adopters can get others to jump on the bandwagon.

In many cases, gaining attention requires investment in mass appeal forms of promotion, especially advertising and PR. When ultra-premium Voss water was introduced in the United States, marketers relied heavily on PR to create awareness, connecting the water to celebrities and gaining product placements in movies and in magazines sold in outlets frequented by the target customers.

This ad for Aleve gains readers' attention quickly. Notice that the letters are people who are able to move around flexibly, presumably because Aleve has quelled their joint pain.

Interest

To translate customer attention into interest requires persuasive communication. For more technical or complicated products, this means beginning to inform customers more specifically about what a product offering can do for *them*—how it helps fulfill needs and wants. To stimulate interest, the promotion must begin to touch a customer's "hot buttons."

For example, generating awareness about the iPhone was not a problem for Apple; the buildup in the media was gargantuan for months before the initial product introduction. But what would stimulate a person to move beyond just awareness that the product exists to interest in possibly pursuing purchase? Apple masterfully used its early promotion to point out the elegance of the form and integrated functionality of the iPhone to begin to convince customers that any ordinary PDA, let alone a lowly cell phone, simply would not do. Interest was peaked by the communication of product features and benefits, and also by the imagery suggesting that the iPhone was something really different.

Desire

Moving from interest to desire means that a customer has to move past a *need* and begin to really *want* the product. Promotion feeds desire through strong persuasive communication. At this stage, salespeople and customized direct and interactive marketing often enter the promotion mix. Messages are altered to influence customers to feel that they simply can't do without the item. Some of the innovators and early adopters are showing off their purchases to holdouts.

Such was certainly the case with the iPhone. Many people undoubtedly let their friends and co-workers see and touch their prized possession—sharing the experience of its functionality and form. Apple wisely fueled the momentum through targeted direct mailings and e-mailings, inviting potential customers into Apple stores so that salespeople could fully demonstrate the broad spectrum of product virtues. The interest stage of the hierarchy is generally where the emotional part of buyer decision making peaks, and much of the promotional message is centered on creating positive feelings for the brand and product.

Action

The action stage is the purchase itself. To stimulate ultimate purchase, marketers often rely on salespeople, accompanied by some form of sales promotion, to close the sale. Sales promotion, by its nature, stimulates purchase. For the customer, it can be a coupon, rebate, or other special "extra" that pushes them over the edge to buy. Also, the reason sales organizations put so much emphasis on training salespeople in closing techniques is that they are often the final stimulant to purchase.

Growing evidence suggests that Gen Y and Millennials may respond differently from prior generations to promotional strategies. These differences may be attributable to the hierarchy of effects they go through in making purchase decisions. Previous generations, which have been the focus of marketing for years (i.e., Gen X and older), did not grow up with the same level of information availability and access as these younger groups. As a result, marketers have traditionally been placed in the pivotal role of outbound information providers for these customers, largely through promotion. This is true not only in the B2C marketplace, but also in B2B markets where organizational buyers traditionally relied especially on their salespeople for information about products and markets. Gen Y and Millennials have experienced a very different set of circumstances related to information. Because of the Internet and related communication technology, they are accustomed to doing their own research on products, developing their own opinions, and then taking action with less influence from traditional promotional approaches (including salespeople).

This is not to say that the role of the marketing manager in developing promotional strategy is less important when it comes to the younger generation. Rather, the caution is that the response of younger generations to different promotional approaches is not the same as that of previous generations. They are much less likely to want to be "sold to," are generally disinterested in mass advertising, and tend to place high value on objective information for decision making, likely from sources outside of traditional promotion. For example, communication going on in MySpace, blogs, message boards, chat rooms, and other forms of virtual communities carry much more weight than other communication forms. Although many of these qualities make marketing to the younger generations more difficult, their unique attitudes toward marketing also create important opportunities for marketers. For example, they are generally very tuned in to brands, thus affording an opportunity for marketing managers to smartly integrate branding into promotional themes. Ethical Dimension 17 explores some important issues related to the teenage market.

In doing marketing planning in the 21st century, the marketing manager who addresses these preferences among the important Gen Y and Millennial markets will gain a competitive edge over marketers that attempt to capture this business through more traditional promotion forms.

THE MARKETING MANAGER'S ROLE IN PROMOTIONAL STRATEGY

As mentioned at the beginning of the chapter, the field of promotion is very broad and requires much specialization to effectively execute. As a part of the marketing field, the area of promotion more than any other tends to be heavily outsourced. Creative companies such as advertising and PR agencies have the focus and expertise to add substantial value to the execution of a marketer's promotional planning. And because of the unique nature of personal selling, most firms set up the sales organization as virtually a separate entity from marketing or outsource it in the form of external distributors or brokers that represent a company's offerings to customers within the channel. But the proliferation of outsourcing of

ETHICAL DIMENSION 17

The Resourceful Teen and Promotional Ethics

Today's teenagers are more plugged in than any other generation in history. Facebook, MySpace, SMS text messaging, and many more technology tools enable teens to connect with each other and the world in unprecedented ways. More than any other generation, teens have made social networking and, more broadly, an online lifestyle a significant part of their lives. Their online experiences coupled with the new media's ability to track and store user information offers innovative opportunities to connect, communicate, and market to this important demographic. Marketers are empowered as never before by the ability to track individual activities, analyze large amounts of information, and develop unique, individually targeted messaging and products to teens. For example, Facebook now allows advertisers to create display ads using information from individual users posted in their profiles.

However, two critical questions for teen marketers are: How much information should we collect? And what is the most appropriate online marketing strategy from an ethical and business strategy perspective? While the Children's Online Privacy Protection Act (COPPA) requires marketers to get parental consent to collect personal information on anyone younger than 13, no law regulates advertising or direct marketing to teenagers over the age of 13. Marketing managers face difficult ethical and strategic questions as they learn to operate in the online social networking world of teenagers.

A key issue for both marketers and teenagers is the degree to which information presented in the social networking environment should be used by companies. Private details about an individual are available for analysis, but how much and to what degree should marketers use the information to create individual specific messaging. In addition, much of the individual data is self-generated, and there are few checks and balances to validate information. Companies have the ability to connect a sophisticated understanding of teenagers with an individual's personal data to develop targeted communications. However, people on the Internet often make themselves a few years younger (or older in the case of teenagers) or several inches taller. Today's resourceful teenagers create identities that allow them access to age-restricted Web sites such as eBay, which requires a buyer or seller to be 18. Marketers can present messaging to students that may not be appropriate for the individual. For example, someone under 21 may indicate a different age online and receive liquor or beer advertising.

Teenagers do appreciate effective branding and marketing at the same time marketers seek greater access to the teen market. On the surface, it would appear easier than ever to find and speak to the teen market, but things are not always as they seem.[14]

Ethical Perspective

1. **Marketers:** Should a marketer be allowed to use information from an individual's social networking profile? Is targeted messaging based on analysis of personal information ethical?

2. **Teenagers:** Should teenagers be able to provide false information to gain access to Web sites restricted by age or some other characteristic?

---

marketing communications and separation of sales from marketing does not absolve the marketing manager from the need to understand the basics of promotion so that the agency's contributions, as well as those of the sales force, can be properly integrated into the marketing planning process.

Would it be possible to outsource ad creation to product users themselves? Pepsi has! In the United Kingdom, Pepsi created a campaign to reinforce its brand and involve its customers in the brand. Building on the TV campaign featuring Eva Longoria and a ZERO to MAX slider, the concept uses user-generated content to involve consumers with Pepsi MAX, giving them a chance to win £1,000 by creating a winning video.[15]

The seven major elements of the marketing manager's role in managing promotion are identified in Exhibit 17.10 as follows: identify targets for promotion, establish goals for promotion, select the promotion mix, develop the message, select

EXHIBIT 17.10

Elements of the Marketing Manager Role in Promotional Strategy

media for use in promotion, prepare promotion budget, and establish measures of results.

Identify Targets for Promotion

You learned in Chapter 9 that target marketing is a process of evaluating market segments and deciding which are most attractive for investment in development. We also discussed that positioning involves communicating one or more sources of value to customers in ways that the customer can easily make the connection between his or her needs and wants and what the product has to offer. The promotional mix strategy is a crucial element in positioning a firm's offerings effectively. It is not possible for the marketing manager to make sense of developing a promotional strategy until the targets are selected.[16]

Identify Targets for Promotion

↓

Establish Goals for Promotion

↓

Select the Promotion Mix

↓

Develop the Message

↓

Select Media for Use in Promotion

↓

Prepare Promotion Budget

↓

Establish Measures of Results

Establish Goals for Promotion

Before moving forward to develop a promotion mix, the marketing manager must establish goals for promotion. Having a great product but being a best-kept secret is not a favorable position. Earlier we defined promotion as the means by which various forms of communication are used to inform, persuade, or remind potential customers. Exhibit 17.11 summarizes these essential goals of promotion and how each might be achieved.

Goal One: To Inform

How does a customer know that Hilton is running a temporary special on room rates in its Orlando hotels? Or what the store hours are for Macy's annual white sale? Or that a $100 rebate is available on that Canon digital camera you've had your eye on? Or that the next-generation iPhone is about to be released? One important goal of promotion is providing information—about a firm and its offerings. Unless you are fortunate enough to be in the position of Steve Jobs at Apple, where the media start clamoring months in advance for a glimpse of the next new product and are willing to devote prime publication real estate to extolling its virtues (and possibly foibles), chances are you will have to resort to paid forms of promotion to get your information across to potential customers.

Goal Two: To Persuade

Rarely is the communication of facts sufficient for marketers to effectively make their case to potential customers, who are faced with many competing brands and product options. Promotion provides the opportunity to state your offering's advantages and to give the customer a reason to select you over the competition. Why should a construction project lease Caterpillar equipment instead of Kamatsu? What are the advantages of the Toyota Camry over the Honda Accord, and vice versa? Can a person *really* get a healthy meal at McDonald's? Persuasive communication is at the core of marketing and affords companies the chance to put their best foot forward for customers. Of course, persuasion can be taken to extremes, and the potential for crossing an ethical or legal line in promotion is a constant problem for marketers.

EXHIBIT 17.11 | **Goals for Promotion**

Goal One: To Inform
- Indicate features when introducing new products or making product modifications
- Provide explanation of product functionality
- Articulate what a company and its brands stand for in order to develop a clear image
- Discuss various uses and applications for the product

Goal Two: To Persuade
- Impact customer perceptions of a product, especially in comparison to competitor's products
- Get customers to try a product, hopefully resulting in a more permanent switch from a competitor
- Influence customers to purchase right now due to some strong benefit or need
- Drive customers to seek more information online or through a salesperson

Goal Three: To Remind
- Maintain a customer relationship with a brand
- Provide impetus for purchase based on some impending event

The downsides of crossing that line can be severe. In the 1970s, Listerine, playing on its "kills germs" theme, advertised that regular use could "reduce the number and severity of colds," a product claim that was blatantly untrue. The federal government forced the manufacturer to run high-profile retraction ads for several months, severely damaging the public trust and costing substantial revenue and market share to archrival Scope. In promotion, a certain degree of **puffery,** or relatively minor embellishments of product claims to bolster the persuasive message, generally is legal. However, in today's litigious environment, determining the fine line between puffery and making a false claim is best left to attorneys not marketers.

Goal Three: To Remind

For brands that are already top-of-mind for many customers, a primary goal of promotion is to keep the brand and its imagery at the forefront. Essentially, Coca-Cola has 100 percent brand awareness among U.S. consumers (as well as in many other parts of the globe). So why does Coke need to invest in promotion? Marketers must constantly communicate with customers to maintain brand loyalty and reduce the tendency to switch to other brands. For example, the income tax preparation firm Jackson Hewitt starts reminding Americans through a fall promotion that income tax season is right around the corner. Jackson Hewitt wants to plant the seed early so that after the first of the year you will pull together your papers and make an appointment to have your

This ad for Sunny Delight is designed in part to remind readers that they have other choices for a tasty beverage besides soda.

tax return prepared. Reminding customers is a key goal of promotion and often stimulates direct purchase.

A promotional strategy can consist of sponsorship of livestock shows, bass-fishing tournaments, and NASCAR, as Toyota did with its $300 million campaign for the Tundra. The purpose of the campaign was to win over support from customers who in the past have only bought American cars. The tagline is "the all-new, built-in-America Toyota truck." The campaign involves free test drives at chains like Bass Pro Shops and 84 Lumber stores.[17]

Select the Promotion Mix

Promotion mix decisions are dependent on several factors. These include the nature of the offering, stage of the offering in the product life cycle, nature of the market, and available budget.

Nature of the Offering

Some key questions must be answered about the product itself. You learned in Chapters 7 and 8 that B2C products and markets differ in important ways from B2B products and markets. Often, goods and services offered in the B2B marketplace tend to be more complex than those sold to end-user consumers. Also, you learned in Chapter 13 that services possess several distinct characteristics different from physical goods. Whether in the B2B or B2C space, the more complex, intangible, unique, and new an offering, the more challenging the communication about it will be and the more likely that relatively more personal forms of promotion will have to be relied on. In such cases, personal selling and direct or interactive marketing afford a greater opportunity for potential customers to become educated about the offering.[18]

Another related issue to consider is the strength of the brand. Promotion of brands that are already well-known and that carry high positive brand equity allow for more reliance on relatively less personal forms of promotion such as advertising, sales promotion, and PR. The brand itself often carries the day in such communication; for example, when Apple introduced iPhone the equity built up among loyal Apple users made purchase nearly a fait accompli.

Stage of the Offering in the Product Life Cycle

Chapter 10 introduced you to the concept of the product life cycle (PLC). Now it is important to make a connection between the PLC and promotion mix decision making. Exhibit 17.12 portrays the PLC and associated promotion mix considerations.[19]

Nature of the Market

Whether in the B2B or B2C space, the nature of the market served affects promotion mix decisions. Among the important factors:

- *Level of heterogeneity of target customers.* The more target groups and the more diverse the targets, the wider array of promotion mix applications to be developed.[20]

- *Level of geographic dispersion of target customers.* Obviously, online interactive approaches permeate geographic borders much more efficiently than traditional advertising. Geographic constraints are especially challenging for using face-to-face personal selling, since buyers and sellers have to physically get together.

- *Type of purchase decision to be made.* Is the purchase typically a routine, low customer involvement purchase or is it a specialized purchase with higher customer involvement?[21]

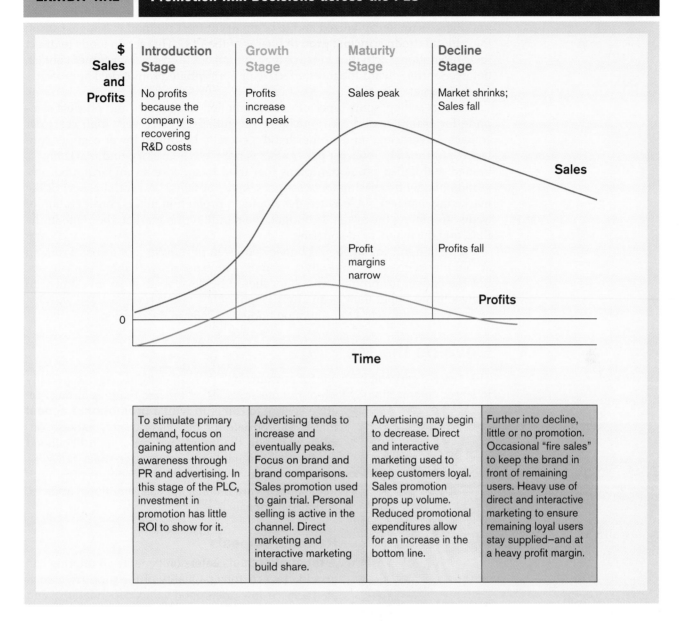

EXHIBIT 17.12 | **Promotion Mix Decisions across the PLC**

$ Sales and Profits

Introduction Stage	Growth Stage	Maturity Stage	Decline Stage
No profits because the company is recovering R&D costs	Profits increase and peak	Sales peak	Market shrinks; Sales fall
		Profit margins narrow	Profits fall

Sales

Profits

0

Time

| To stimulate primary demand, focus on gaining attention and awareness through PR and advertising. In this stage of the PLC, investment in promotion has little ROI to show for it. | Advertising tends to increase and eventually peaks. Focus on brand and brand comparisons. Sales promotion used to gain trial. Personal selling is active in the channel. Direct marketing and interactive marketing build share. | Advertising may begin to decrease. Direct and interactive marketing used to keep customers loyal. Sales promotion props up volume. Reduced promotional expenditures allow for an increase in the bottom line. | Further into decline, little or no promotion. Occasional "fire sales" to keep the brand in front of remaining users. Heavy use of direct and interactive marketing to ensure remaining loyal users stay supplied—and at a heavy profit margin. |

- *Level and type of competition.* If there are many competitors in the same market space, and especially if they are also actively engaged in promoting their offerings, consideration must be given to ensuring your promotion stands out from those of the competition. This may entail going with a promotion mix that seems unusual for the situation but assures notoriety. For example, CUTCO promotes its cutlery only through direct personal selling to consumers. All of its major competitors use more traditional forms of promotion, such as advertising and sales promotion through retail channels.[22] On many occasions CUTCO's management has been asked why it doesn't adopt more traditional promotional forms for household products. The simple answer is that it is the most profitable company in the industry and it wants neither to increase promotional expenditures by turning to advertising nor to risk getting lost among a sea of other brands in department stores.

Available Budget

Ultimately, the budget can constrain decisions about the elements of the promotion mix in which to invest. Costs of different media vary widely. At the high end, costs of making a single face-to-face sales call can easily cost $500 to several thousand dollars depending on the industry. Prime 30-second ads on the Super Bowl go for more than $2 million. It is very common for firms, and especially start-up firms, to find they are undercapitalized and to begin to cut their promotion budget during the critical introductory and growth phases of the PLC. This action tends to direct their promotional activities in ways that minimize the cost per customer contact, not necessarily toward the most effective or appropriate promotional approaches for their target customers.

Personal selling, some types of sales promotion (big rebates and product sampling for example), and labor-intensive PR initiatives carry very high costs per contact. Advertising, on the other hand, generally has much lower cost per contact. Unfortunately, low cost per contact is not the whole story, and marketing is littered with failed promotion plans that tried to squeeze an underfunded promotion budget by chasing low-cost-per-contact options.[23] A central aspect of the marketing manager's role when developing a promotion mix is consideration of trade-offs among the available budget, the nature of the market, the stage in the PLC, and the nature of the offering.

Promotion in general should be viewed as an *investment*, not a cost. From an accounting statement perspective, promotional expenses will show up as costs. But the budget for promotion dollars should be developed as an investment to grow a brand rather than as an afterthought of last year's revenues. We will discuss several approaches to promotion budgeting later in the chapter.

Develop the Message

This task is a very common one for outsourcing by a marketing manager, especially in larger organizations. Much of the message design process requires strong creative energy to come up with a **promotional appeal** that is appropriate for the offering and market, connects well with the brand, and has a high likelihood of ultimately taking the target through the AIDA steps toward purchase.[24] Three broad categories of promotional appeals are rational appeals, emotional appeals, and moral appeals.

Rational Appeals

A **rational appeal** centers on benefits an offering can provide to a customer. Quality of the product, associated service, low price, good value, dependability, and performance are potential benefits that can be communicated.[25] Ads featuring the Maytag repairman, who never has anything to do because a Maytag simply doesn't break down, is a rational appeal (tempered with a good dose of humor) pointing out that nobody likes having to pay to fix an appliance.

Emotional Appeals

In contrast, an **emotional appeal** plays on human nature using humor, drama, joy, adventure, sorrow, love, surprise, guilt, shame, fear—the whole gamut of human emotions and aspirations—in developing promotional messages. Effectively crafted, such message approaches can have a high impact on target customers and can contribute a great deal to defining a brand's personality.[26] The Aflac duck with its humorously timed quacks and physical comedy has done wonders for a previously obscure insurance company

Caresse d'orchidées par Cartier

Cartier

The brand *Cartier* itself evokes emotion, and focusing a fairly simple ad on the product itself serves to augment feelings of prestige and success associated with the brand.

whose brand used to be virtually invisible. Advertisers also use the negative end of the emotional spectrum to tell us about all sorts of things we should *not* want to have—stained teeth, high interest mortgages, insufficient education, 20 extra pounds—you name it, and there's a marketer communicating an emotional appeal and offering you a solution (for the right price).

Most golf balls are pretty much the same; only the very best golfers reap benefits from expensive balls that are supposed to travel farther or spin better. So advertising campaigns often focus on the emotion that the ball conveys. Most golf-ball companies use endorsements from pro players in their ads. Callaway, however, has a different messaging strategy. It sells its Top-Flite balls as appealing to regular guys. Callaway's TV ads for Top-Flite focus on regular guys going for one great shot. Top-Flite intentionally doesn't have any endorsements from golf celebrities. In this way, the message reinforces the brand identity as appealing to everyday golfers.[27]

Moral Appeals

A **moral appeal** in promotional messaging is used to strike a chord with a target customer's sense of right and wrong.[28] Many charities, cause-related marketers, and politicians use moral appeals to elicit support. The Salvation Army uses a tagline "Doing the Most Good" to reflect its reputation of providing more benefits out of donation dollars than many other charities.

Select Media for Use in Promotion

Media selection decisions involve making specific choices about the media, or channel, for the message within each element of the promotion mix selected. Each of the elements of the promotion mix—advertising, sales promotion, PR, personal selling, direct marketing, and interactive marketing—has a variety of media choices available. Attention will be given to those in sections that follow.

Prepare Promotion Budget

As mentioned previously, establishing an appropriate promotion budget sets the stage for a successful promotional strategy. The promotion budget is usually part of the overall marketing budget because the promotion plan is a subset of the overall marketing plan. A variety of typical approaches to promotion budgeting are used. We focus on four types of promotional budgets: the objective-and-task method, percent-of-sales method, comparative parity method, and the all-you-can-afford method.

Objective-and-Task Method

The **objective-and-task method** of promotion budgeting takes an investment approach in that goals are set for the upcoming year and then promotional dollars are budgeted to support the achievement of those goals. Here, the horse is properly before the cart, since the goals drive the budget and the budget enables the execution of the necessary strategies and tactics to achieve those goals. Put another way, the task at hand drives the budget. This approach is very consistent with a market-driving approach to strategic marketing, since investment in opportunistic product and market development requires the support of sufficient and appropriate promotional strategies.

Unfortunately, although this is a superior approach to developing a promotion budget, it is not the most widely used. Many firms are locked into arcane approaches to budgeting that have been in place for years in their firms. Marketing managers must argue the case for objective-and-task driven promotion budgeting. Although it is much more challenging to implement than other methods, the payoff of viewing promotional dollars as an investment rather than an expense opens the door to growing a firm's brands exponentially. Like any investment, the method is not without its risks; there is always the chance that sufficient ROI will not be achieved on the promotional strategy. But in the long run, the objective-and-task approach affords the best opportunity for marketing success.

Percent-of-Sales Method

The **percent-of-sales method** is the most popular approach to promotion budgeting but it is a very constraining model for a firm. There is an undeniable seduction in building a budget off a convenient percentage of revenue, allocated by product or by product line. Product X deserves $500,000 worth of promotion next year because it is forecast to do $10 million in revenue and our firm allocates 5 percent of revenue to promotion expense. The actual percentages of promotional budget to sales employed vary widely by industry and, in fact, vary quite a bit among firms in a particular industry. For example, Wal-Mart has historically spent a far lower percentage of revenues on promotion than Target—less than 2 percent versus close to 5 percent—because their business models and target customers are very different. Firms like the percent-of-sales method because it is considered to be a conservative approach, is easy to administer, and affords maximal budgetary control at higher levels.[29]

But the disadvantages of the percent-of-sales method are compelling. First and foremost, promotion dollar investment should lead to sales; promotion should not be the *result* of sales. Under this method, problems arise when sales are declining because promotion expenditures decline in lockstep, thus exacerbating the downward sales trend and often dooming the product. A firm doesn't really need a professional marketing manager to execute promotional strategy under this budget scenario because the true product-market possibilities will never be achieved.

Comparative-Parity Method

In the **comparative-parity method** of promotion budgeting, the marketing manager focuses on the competitive marketplace and specifically on comparing promotion expenditures across all key competitors in the market to find a budget number that matches. Typically, competitive information is obtained from industry sources, from trade association estimates of promotional spending, or from the public records of the other firms. A budget may be set based on some industry average, on the expenditures of the leading firm, or on the expenditures of the firm most like your own.[30]

This approach does offer some advantage in that it forces a firm to analyze how its competition is developing promotional strategy. But the notion of developing competitor-driven promotion budgets is as flawed and constraining as the percent-of-sales method. In this case, the firm is limiting itself to merely reacting to competitors instead of proactively developing its own strategy. Much research indicates that competitor-driven strategy development almost always leads to missed market opportunities, as the firm is so focused on the competition that it overlooks important changes in the customer marketplace that deserve opportunistic investment of promotion dollars.

An additional problem with the comparative-parity method is its inherent assumption that all the competitive firms are basically apples-to-apples comparatively when it comes to their promotions. Companies differ substantially in how they execute the promotion mix, and these differences are not effectively captured in the firm's raw budget numbers.

All-You-Can-Afford Method

With the **all-you-can-afford method,** a firm simply sets its promotion budget as whatever funds are left over after everything else that's considered a necessity is paid for.[31] Many small business owners and entrepreneurs find themselves using this approach, and it is maximally self-defeating. For years, the Small Business Administration (SBA) has published data on key reasons that business plans fail to gain funding and also key reasons for start-up failures. Consistently, one of the major reasons for both is a poorly conceived and underfunded promotion budget. Such business owners tend to grossly underestimate what it takes to communicate their offering to target customers. The SBA advises that start-ups should capitalize to a level at which they can *comfortably* continue to invest heavily in promotion for the first three to five years of the business, at least. During this early time frame in a business life cycle, most firms do not turn any profit.

Establish Measures of Results

A final role for the marketing manager in promotional strategy is the development of appropriate metrics to determine the success of the promotion plan. The topic of marketing metrics is covered in detail in Chapter 19, with example metrics for various aspects of the marketing planning process including promotion. For now, it is important to note that decisions about which metrics to employ to assess the efficiency and effectiveness of promotion must be selected in the context of the specific goals established for the promotion plan. It is likely that measurement will occur on two levels: first, at the strategic level to determine incremental progress at designated time intervals toward achieving the promotional goals; and second, on a tactical level to assess the effectiveness of various forms of media and the creative execution.

ADVERTISING

Earlier we defined advertising as a paid form of relatively less personal marketing communications, often through a mass medium to one or more target markets. To most of the general public, advertising is synonymous with marketing. Advertising is what most people see as the visible side of marketing—not surprising, since the amount of money spent by firms on advertising is staggering. According to *Advertising Age,* in 2007 spending by the top 100 U.S. advertisers was up 3.1 percent from a year earlier to a total of $105 billion. However, this figure comes with an important caveat; the way this money is being split among different types of advertising media is rapidly changing. The big winner is online advertising, which was up over 15 percent in spending in 2007 versus 2006. The increase in online advertising comes at a bitter cost to print media, especially local newspapers (down nearly 5 percent) and some magazines.

Who spends all this money on advertising? Exhibit 17.13 shows the top 20 U.S. advertisers and data on their total spending on advertising in 2006. These 20 advertisers account for just short of one-third of the total U.S. advertising expenditures for the year.

Several observations can be made based on Exhibit 17.13. First, each of the top 20 U.S. advertisers operates in the *consumer* marketplace. Several (Sony, General Electric, Johnson & Johnson, for example) also have significant B2B operations, but the key issue is that big national advertising tends to be dominated by B2C firms. Second, although the top 20 firms collectively account for about one-third of total U.S. advertising expenditures (the figure spikes to about half when you include the top 50), substantial dollars are invested in various advertising media by firms of all types and sizes across almost every industry. Advertising is ubiquitous promotion, and because it is so visible and seemingly easily understood, many turn to advertising as their promotion mix element of first choice.

There is a danger in overrelying on advertising to the exclusion of other promotional choices. Customers can quickly and easily become bored with any given advertising campaign, a concept referred to as **advertising wearout.** This phenomenon necessitates a constant creation of new ads with new or adjusted themes, resulting in a constant churn of messages.[32] When Wendy's announced in early 2008 that it was pulling its long-running campaign featuring the young girl in red-haired pigtails, it said the decision was made because the advertisements

EXHIBIT 17.13 | **Top 20 U.S. Advertisers**

Rank	Advertiser	Total U.S. Ad Spending in 2006 (billions)	Average Daily Ad Spending in 2006 (millions)
1	Procter & Gamble	$4.9	$13.4
2	AT&T	3.3	9.0
3	General Motors	3.3	9.0
4	Time Warner	3.1	8.5
5	Verizon Wireless	2.8	7.7
6	Ford Motor	2.6	7.1
7	GlaxoSmithKline	2.4	6.6
8	Walt Disney	2.3	6.3
9	Johnson & Johnson	2.3	6.3
10	Unilever	2.1	5.8
11	Toyota Motor	2.0	5.5
12	Sony	2.0	5.5
13	DaimlerChrysler	2.0	5.5
14	General Electric	1.9	5.2
15	Sprint Nextel	1.8	4.9
16	McDonald's	1.7	4.7
17	Sears	1.7	4.7
18	L'Oreal	1.5	4.1
19	Kraft Foods	1.4	3.8
20	Macy's	1.4	3.8
Total		$46.5	$127.7

Source: *Ad Age 2007 Marketing Profiles Yearbook,* June 25, 2007, p. 10.

had run their course. Viewers were "over it." The need for constant renewal of ads is great for advertising agencies, which get paid to create them, but incredibly expensive for marketing managers.

Another problem with advertising is that beyond a certain ad spending level, diminishing returns tend to set in. That is, market share stops growing—or even begins to decline—despite continued spending. This effect is known as the **advertising response function** and leads marketing managers to rely more heavily on advertising early in the PLC, as well as to focus on it during target customers' initial stages of the AIDA model.[33] Spending higher dollars, in this case on advertising, on the promotional goals of *informing* and *persuading* is likely to pay back at a higher level than spending equal dollars on the promotional goal of *reminding*.

Despite these challenges, advertising is not only a potentially highly effective promotional vehicle (when applied properly) but it is also a part of the very fabric of the U.S. culture and, increasingly, of the global culture. The craze associated with the annual Super Bowl advertisements is a testament to the power of advertising to excite the masses.

Types of Advertising

There are two major types of advertising: institutional advertising and product advertising. The choice of which approach to use depends on the promotional goals and the situation.

Institutional Advertising

The goal of **institutional advertising** is to promote an industry, company, family of brands, or some other issues broader than a specific product. Institutional advertising is often used to inform or remind, but to a lesser degree to persuade. Earlier you read about the concept of corporate identity in the context of the sender of communication.[34] Many customers pay a great deal of attention to the organization behind an advertising message, how socially responsible the company is, and what values it stands for. Institutional advertising can help build and enhance a corporate brand or family brand. For instance, P&G runs institutional ads about a charitable cause it supports—the Special Olympics. Certain families of P&G brands (Crest, Pampers, etc.) generally are featured as well. Such an approach helps build the corporate identity of P&G and can enhance its brands through positive association.

Sometimes entire industries will run institutional advertising. Recently, the California Dairy Council has been running national advertising on television. The ad features "happy cows" and carries the tag line "Great cheese comes from happy cows. Happy cows come from California." The council developed a logo that is prominently displayed in the ads, and presumably the expectation is that a consumer would look for that logo on a wedge of cheese in the dairy case, selecting it over cheese from elsewhere, a bit like the famous "Intel Inside" branding on computers. Consider these additional examples of industry-sponsored institutional advertising, manifest through catchy taglines:

- Cotton, the fabric of our lives.
- The incredible edible egg.
- Pork, the other white meat.
- Beef, it's what's for dinner.

Institutional advertising is a particularly smart strategy during the early phases of the PLC and AIDA model in that it can enhance feelings of trust in potential customers with a message that is broader than just "buy me." Institutional advertising is also often employed when a company or industry has a PR problem to dig out from. When JetBlue experienced its operational meltdown at JFK airport in February 2007, leaving hundreds of passengers stranded on their planes on the tarmac for up to 12 hours during a snowstorm, within a few days the firm had already begun an institutional advertising campaign hawking its commitment to a new Passengers' Bill of Rights.

Product Advertising

The vast majority of advertising is **product advertising,** designed to increase purchase of a specific offering (good or service). Three principal types of product advertising are available: pioneering advertising, competitive advertising, and comparative advertising. The decision on which to employ often depends on the stage of the PLC.

Pioneering advertising stimulates primary demand. Hence, it tends to be used during the introductory and early growth stages of the PLC when it is important to

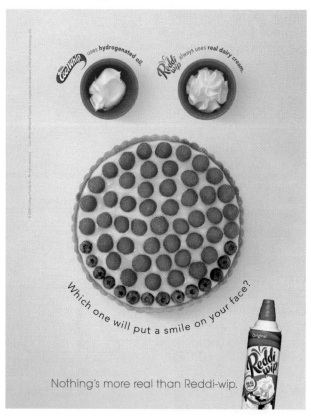

This comparative ad by Reddi Wip takes on rival CoolWhip by pointing out that Reddi Wip always uses real dairy cream, not hydrogenated oil.

gain purchase by innovators and early adopters. From an AIDA model perspective, pioneering advertising seeks to gain awareness and initial interest. Marketing managers introducing new products almost always focus advertising on this form, letting potential customers know what the product is and how it is used. The appeal is usually more rational than emotional.[35]

Marketing managers employ **competitive advertising** to build sales of a specific brand. Here, the appeal often shifts to more emotion and the goal is persuasion as well as providing information. Building a positive customer attitude toward the brand is a key component of competitive advertising, and this approach is heavily used during the growth and early maturity stages of the PLC. Triggering the desire and action stages of the AIDA model is a focus of the message.[36]

In **comparative advertising,** two or more brands are directly compared against each other on certain attributes.[37] Comparative advertising is common during the maturity stage of the PLC, as attempts at shaking out weaker competitors are generally part of a marketing strategy. Obviously, a key to successfully employing this approach is having one or more legitimate claims about your brand that put it in a favorable position against the competition. Apple has run a series of humorous comparative ads on television in which two guys stand side by side and sling barbs back and forth about features of the Mac versus the PC. In one ad, the PC guy stands by a banner proclaiming "Don't give up on Vista." Through IMC, the images of the two actors appear everywhere Apple has messages about itself—online, stores, print ads, and so on.

Comparative advertising works especially well when you are not No. 1 in a product category because you can put the market leader on the defensive. Examples of comparative advertising by a No. 2 brand include Pepsi versus Coke, Avis versus Hertz, and Burger King versus McDonald's. However, it is a very risky advertising approach when you *are* the top brand. Customers may perceive that you are on the defensive, when in reality you are not. The psychology of a top brand stooping to comparisons with a lower brand usually does not make sense. Most experts recommend avoiding comparative advertising if your brand is the leader.

Advertising Execution and Media Types

In selecting which types of advertising media to employ, the marketing manager must consider reach and frequency. **Reach** measures the percentage of individuals in a defined target market that are exposed to an ad during a specified time period. **Frequency** measures the average number of times a person in the target market is exposed to the message. Obviously, the greater the reach and higher the frequency, the more expensive the overall advertising campaign will be. As you might imagine, because advertising budgets are not unlimited, trade-offs are usually required in balancing reach and frequency within budgetary constraints. Goals are generally set and budgeted based on a desired level of reach and frequency. During the course of a campaign, the marketing manager may intentionally vary the reach and frequency. For example, the intensity of the campaign might start heavily to gain initial exposure then be reduced to stave off advertising wearout.

Advertising execution is the way an advertisement communicates the information and image. A variety of different types of advertising execution are available. Earlier in the chapter you learned about three general types of promotional appeals: rational, emotional, and moral. Think of the different approaches to advertising execution as the creative operationalization of these different types of appeal. Exhibit 17.14 presents several of the more common advertising execution approaches.

Seven broad categories of advertising media are available: television, radio, newspapers, magazines, outdoor (billboard, bus and train signs, etc.), direct mail, and the Internet. Each of these media types has a variety of pros and cons that must be considered by marketing managers in deciding how to allocate advertising dollars. Exhibit 17.15 summarizes some of the more important issues when making media choices.

In reviewing the pros and cons of each of the major media choices, it becomes apparent that decisions on media selection always involve trade-offs. One issue inherent to most media forms is some degree of **clutter**—the level of competing messages on that medium. Clutter is sometimes described in the context of the overall din of advertising, meaning that consumers are bombarded by so many messages that they become confused or have difficulty distinguishing what ad goes with what brand. Rising above the din is an overarching goal in media selection and creative execution of the message.

Perfect home baked pastry every time

The Pillsbury Doughboy is a long-standing animated spokesperson for the company's dinner rolls.

The Role of the Creative Agency

Advertising and PR are among the most outsourced functions in marketing, and with good reason. Most organizations naturally focus on their own product or service expertise; thus, developing sufficient internal expertise in the creative side of promotion would be extremely costly and could reduce their focus on their core business. For many marketing managers, the relationship with their firm's creative agency is an important part of the job. Agencies vary from specialized firms that focus on an industry or on a particular area of promotion, such as print media or product placement. Others are full-service shops that manage all aspects of their clients' IMC strategy. Because of the proliferation of an IMC approach in many firms today, the trend is toward more full-service creative agencies and even toward integration of marketing planning and branding services with traditional agency tasks. Almost always a client is billed an hourly rate, plus the costs of media purchases.

Over the past several years, another major trend has been the development of strategic partnerships between creative agencies and full-service Web builders. For many marketers, the Web site is the core of their marketing communications strategy. Often a new-product introduction or rebranding initiative focuses largely on the Web site, with print and other media types used primarily to drive customers to the Web. Some of the very largest agencies have even established their own comprehensive Web operations and are able to perform a full gamut of Web services for clients including Web site building and maintenance, hosting,

EXHIBIT 17.14 | **Common Approaches to Advertising Execution**

Slice of Life	Portrays regular people in everyday settings. The college student doing laundry with Tide in the Laundromat.
Humor	Gains attention and interest through humorous portrayal. Budweiser's famous frogs are not soon forgotten.
Mood/Affect	Sets a positive tone around the offering. Sandals Resorts provides visual images to back the theme of "Luxury Included."
Research Based	Often used in comparative ads, a brand provides scientific evidence of its superiority. Listerine Whitening Strips dissolve faster than Crest Whitestrips.
Demonstration	Physically shows how the product works. Efferdent tablets dropped into a glass of water to clean dentures.
Musical	Uses music or a specific song to connect directly to a brand or product. Mazda's famous "Zoom, zoom, zoom" jingle became an integral part of its advertising.
Endorser	Connects a celebrity, actor posing as an authority figure (with appropriate disclaimer), company officer, or everyday consumer with the product to sanction and support its use. Sally Field endorsing Boniva, the anti-osteoporosis drug.
Lifestyle	Portrays ways a product will connect with a target customer's lifestyle. Dodge Ram pickup trucks navigating through the back roads of America.
Fantasy Creation	Offers a fantasy look at how it might be if a customer purchases the product. Lamisil for toenail fungus portrays an idyllic social life for users once they stamp out that pesky fungus.
Animation and Animal	An animated character or an animal is featured in the ads, sometimes as a spokesperson. The GEICO Gecko.

management of direct e-mail correspondence with customers, and management of the client's overall CRM system.

It is likely that the importance of the outsourced full-service marketing agency will continue to grow into the next decade. As marketing itself becomes more strategic within organizations, more and more of the tactical or programmatic aspects of marketing that were formerly handled in-house will be outsourced. In such a scenario, the importance of the marketing manager role is heightened, as that individual will be the frontline person in a firm that is charged with managing all aspects of the outsourced agency relationship.

Catalog retailer HSN Home Improvements used customer sales data to create personal e-mail campaigns and its personalized ImprovementsCatalog.com's home page to relate one-on-one with each visitor. For example, it used customer data to identify which product category a given customer purchased from the most. Then, it e-mailed suggested additional products in that same category and in other similar categories to the customer. The result? Overall sales increased 130 percent.[38]

EXHIBIT 17.15 Pros and Cons of Key Advertising Media

Type of Media	Pros	Cons
Television	• Combines multimedia • Appeals to multiple senses • Works for both mass coverage or selected markets • Infomercial option	• Impressions are fleeting • Short shelf life • Din (clutter) of competing ads • TiVo effect—cutting out ads • High cost
Radio	• Quick placement and high message immediacy • Easy selectivity by market and station programming • Low cost • Geographic flexibility	• Audio only • Short shelf life • Din of competing ads
Newspapers	• Flexible • Timely • Highly credible medium	• Short shelf life • Big city and national papers can be very costly • Poor reproduction quality, especially in color • Low pass-along rate
Magazines	• Many titles; high geographic, demographic, and lifestyle selectivity • Good reproduction quality and color • High pass-along rate	• Long lead time for ad placement due to production • Final location of ad within the publication often cannot be guaranteed
Outdoor	• Repeat exposure in heavy traffic areas • Relatively low cost • Fewer competing ads • Easy geographic targeting	• Space and structure limits creative execution • Sometimes requires longer than desired commitments to a location • Public discontent over environmental clutter
Direct Mail	• High audience selectivity • Creates feel of one-to-one marketing • Flexible	• Overuse and "junk mail" image • Too many competing ads • Relatively high cost
Internet	• Interactive capabilities • Flexible • Timely • Low cost per exposure	• Reader in control of exposure (click-through) • Spam • Variations in connectivity speed and computers

SALES PROMOTION

Sales promotion was defined earlier as a promotion mix element that provides an inducement for an end-user consumer to buy a product or for a salesperson or someone else in the channel to sell it. Sales promotion is designed to augment other forms of promotion and is rarely used alone. This is because sales promotion initiatives rely on other media forms such as advertising and direct or interactive marketing as a communication vehicle. Think of sales promotion as prompting a "buy now" response; that is, it is squarely aimed at the action (behavior) stage of the AIDA model.

Sales promotion can be aimed directly at end-user consumers, or it can be targeted to members of a channel on which a firm relies to sell product. In the latter case, sales promotion is an important element of a push strategy. One additional potential target for sales promotion is a firm's own sales force. Bonus payments, prizes, trips, and other incentives to induce a salesperson to push one product over another are forms of internal sales promotion. Salesperson incentives will be discussed further in Chapter 18. For now, let's look at sales promotion to consumers and to channel members.

> Retailer Right Start has experienced a 20 percent improvement in its in-store promotions by sending e-mail notifications to its customers. The store chain gives customers an e-mail coupon that they can redeem at a local store. Using e-mail not only drives traffic to the stores but also helps Right Start track click-through and open rates to measure how effective a given advertising campaign is.[39]

Sales Promotion to Consumers

When a firm is looking to gain product trial, spike distribution, shore up sagging quarterly sales, or rekindle interest in a waning brand, sales promotion can be an appropriate choice for investment of promotion dollars. Exhibit 17.16 summarizes nine popular consumer sales promotion approaches.

As with most promotional elements, marketing managers rarely select only one form of consumer sales promotion for execution. Many of the sales promotion options complement each other and all are potentially complementary of the overall promotion mix. One potential downside to sales promotion is a tendency by some firms and industries to overrely on sales promotion to bring in sales on a regular basis. This occurs because of sales promotion's power to elicit an actual purchase. Consider the proliferation of rebates on new-car purchases. Car manufacturers essentially "train" car shoppers not to look for a new vehicle unless a rebate is being offered. Ultimately, if sales promotion becomes institutionalized in such a manner, firms simply build in a hefty cushion into the "everyday" price of the product, thus negating any real benefit to the customer of the promotion. Overuse of sales promotion is not a good promotional strategy and can lead to a general cheapening of brand image and distrust by customers.

This ad ties into a 7Up sales promotion by featuring the winner of their contest "America's Next Top Model 7UP Challenge."

Sales Promotion to Channel Members

Several sales promotion approaches are available for use with members of a firm's channel of distribution. Typically, these channel members would be distributors, brokers, agents, and other forms of middlemen.

EXHIBIT 17.16 | **Consumer Sales Promotion Options**

Sales Promotion Approach	Description	Comments	Example
Product sampling	A physical sample of the product is given to consumers.	Excellent for inducing trial. Sample can be received by mail or in a store.	Gillette sends out a free razor to induce switching from an older model.
Coupons	An instant price reduction at point of sale, available in print media, online, or in-store.	Coupon usage is generally down among consumers. Still a good inducement to "buy now."	Inside the free razor from Gillette is a coupon for $1.00 off the purchase of a pack of blades.
Rebates	A price reduction for purchase of a specific product during a specific time period.	Possibly instant at point of sale, but more frequently requires submission and delay in processing.	Sharp offers a $100 rebate through Best Buy for purchase of a flat-screen television during February.
Contests and sweepstakes	Appeal to consumers' sense of fun and luck. May suggest a purchase but legally must be offered without a purchase requirement.	Contests require some element of skill beyond mere chance. Sweepstakes are pure chance.	McDonald's famous Monopoly game—the more you eat, the more you play (and vice versa!).
Premiums	Another product offered free for purchasing the brand targeted in the promotion.	Gives the customer a bonus for purchase. Products may be complementary or unrelated.	Burger King offers the latest Spider-Man toy with purchase of a meal.
Multiple-purchase offers	Incentive to buy more of the brand at a special price.	Typically "buy 2, get 1 free" or similar.	Centrum Vitamin offer—buy a bottle of 100, get an extra mini-bottle of 20.
Point-of-purchase materials	Displays set up in a retail store to support advertising and remind customers to purchase.	Especially good at driving purchase toward a featured brand in a product category at the store aisle.	Stand-up display and front window poster in Blockbuster of the latest DVD release.
Product placements	Having product images appear in movies, on television, or in photographs in print media.	Strong connections with the show or story, as well as to any associated celebrities.	Coca-Cola cups always on the desks of the American Idol judges.
Loyalty programs	Accumulate points for doing business with a company. Designed to strengthen long-term customer relationships and reduce switching.	Especially popular among the airline and hospitality industry. Credit card providers often facilitate.	American Airlines AAdvantage program, facilitated by CitiCard, MasterCard, and American Express cards.

The purpose is to stimulate them to push your product, resulting in more sales in the channel and ultimately to end users.

Trade shows can be a very fruitful form of sales promotion. A **trade show** is an industry- or company-sponsored event in which booths are set up for the dissemination of information about offerings to members of a channel. Sometimes actual sales occur at a trade show, but often the primary purpose is promotion to attendees. Sales leads are obtained and passed along to the firm's sales organization for follow-up after the trade show.[40]

Another form of sales promotion to a channel is **cooperative advertising and promotion.** In cooperative advertising, a manufacturer provides special incentive money to channel members for certain performances such as running advertisements for one of the manufacturer's brands or doing product demonstrations with potential customers. The idea of cooperative advertising and promotion is that the manufacturer shares promotional expenses with channel members in the process of marketing to end-user consumers.[41]

Sometimes money is made available for a channel member in the form of a special payment for selling certain products, making a large order, or other specific performance. This form of channel-focused sales promotion is called an **allowance.** In addition, as with the consumer market, contests and displays with point-of-purchase materials are also frequently used as sales promotion approaches in the channel.[42]

PUBLIC RELATIONS (PR)

Earlier in the chapter we defined public relations (PR) as a systematic approach to influencing attitudes, opinions, and behaviors of customers and others. PR is often executed through **publicity,** which is an unpaid and relatively less personal form of marketing communications usually through news stories and mentions at public events.[43]

PR is a specialized field. Usually, undergraduate and graduate marketing programs do not include training in PR. Many PR professionals receive specialized training in communication, and outstanding PR people are highly sought after. Some firms have in-house PR departments, while others outsource much or all of the PR function to external agencies. Major responsibilities of a PR department might include any of the following activities:

- Gaining product publicity and buzz.
- Securing event sponsorships (for the company and its brands).
- Managing a crisis.
- Managing and writing news stories.
- Facilitating community affairs.
- Managing relationships with members of the local, national, and global media (media relations).
- Serving as organizational spokesperson.
- Educating consumers.
- Lobbying and governmental affairs.
- Handling investor relations.

However, few PR departments perform all of these functions; some of the above functions are often spread across other areas of a firm, such as investor relations to the finance department and lobbying and governmental affairs to the legal department.

We'll focus on the three core functions of PR that are most closely aligned with the role of the marketing manager: gaining product publicity and buzz, securing event sponsorships, and crisis management.

New companies like BuzzFeed and BuzzLogic are springing up with new tools to create buzz on the Web. As buzz starts circulating around the Web about your company/product on various blogs and forums, BuzzFeed does a search and generates a report that tells you what people are saying, how much is being said, and who are the most important and influential people that are saying it. Armed with that information, you can start working on your next PR move. Also, BuzzFeed finds "high velocity" headlines from bloggers and forums on the Web and then inserts them, on the fly, into banner ads for related products. The buzz is similar to the critics' reviews that are shown in movie ads. The goal is that this quasi-user-generated copy will lead to more click-throughs.[44]

Gaining Product Publicity and Buzz

Especially when it comes to new product offerings, gaining publicity in news outlets and other public forums can provide a major boost to sales. During the introductory phase of the PLC, communication of information is a central promotional goal. The most credible and trusted information sources for potential customers are those that write or tell about a product for free. Newspaper and magazine articles, Web postings and blogs, social marketing Web sites, news stories on television and radio—all of these forms of communication can be cultivated through an active PR program. Many new products have benefited from the initial awareness generated by a well-placed story in a publication or on a Web site frequented by targeted customers.

Although the media employed are free, by no means is the process of securing the story placements free. In fact, PR can account for a great deal of money in a promotion budget due to the work hours required to constantly be writing stories and cultivating media outlets. But the payoff on that investment can be substantial due to the buzz generated among everyday consumers about a brand. **Buzz,** or word-of-mouth communication, is the communication generated about a brand in the marketplace. Buzz is not limited to current customers or even potential customers; when buzz about a brand hits the marketplace, it can even permeate pop culture. The case at the end of this chapter provides a vivid example of the power of buzz based on the experience of Chipotle Mexican Grill. The restaurant chain, like other buzz disciples, is convinced that investment in buzz-generating publicity is a sound promotional strategy, and, in Chipotle's case, it has greatly reduced the need for costly advertising spending.

Social networking sites such as Digg.com, Reddit.com, Del.icio.us, and StumbleUpon.com have created a new generation of influencers with unprecedented power—something like "word of mouth on steroids." "I was in awe," said the chief technology officer of Famster, a family-focused MySpace-like site, "when a mention on Digg generated 50,000 additional unique visitors a day." Although Digg and others seem like democratic mobs, they often have a core group of ultra-active power-users who create much of the site's content and traffic. A mere 30 of Digg's 900,000 users are responsible for one-third of the site's front-page stories.[45]

Securing Event Sponsorships

Event sponsorships, having your brand and company associated with events in the sports, music, arts, and other entertainment communities, can add tremendous brand equity and also provide substantial exposure with the right target customers. Event sponsorships have become a mainstay of promotional strategy. A huge success story for marketers in event sponsorship is NASCAR, which appeals to millions of loyal and passionate racing fans. Consumers transfer the loyalty and passion about NASCAR directly to the brands represented by the sponsorships. No wonder NASCAR cars are referred to as "speeding billboards."[46]

Closely related to event sponsorship is issue sponsorship, in which a firm and its brands connect with a cause or issue that is especially important to its customers. McDonald's achieved a huge PR coup several years ago when it discarded its styrofoam sandwich containers for more environmentally friendly cardboard boxes. This action was well-received by members of the green movement and generated a great deal of positive buzz for McDonald's. Like publicity, the right sponsorships can generate positive buzz in the marketplace that enhances brand image.

FYI

ITT Corp., an engineering and manufacturing company, is a big believer in event sponsorships as an element of promotional strategy. "Events are a key component of our corporate marketing strategy," said Tom Martin, a spokesman for ITT. The company manufactures electronics components, fluid technology systems, and motion and flow control products. "We have limited marketing budgets and have to use them wisely," Martin said. "We came to the conclusion a few years ago that generic print advertising was not reaching our targets efficiently. We have had significant success with our strategy of identifying key industry trade shows and conferences, and projecting a dominating ITT presence." Working with its ad agency, Doremus, New York, ITT has created unique media opportunities at trade shows to project a strong corporate presence. For example, it built an ITT-branded water fountain that it displays outside fluid industry trade shows, placed a 60-by-18-foot three-dimensional banner at the entrance to the Aquatech water industry convention in Amsterdam, and wrapped buses with ITT advertising at the National Space Symposium in Colorado Springs.[47]

Crisis Management

Crisis management is a planned, coordinated approach for disseminating information during times of emergency and for handling the effects of unfavorable publicity.[48] When Hurricane Charley hit Orlando, Florida, in 2004, the Orlando Utility Commission (OUC), Orlando's main electric provider, mobilized its crisis management team immediately, putting into action a plan team members had practiced many times. Although power was out for some residents for more than a week, customer feedback on how OUC handled the crisis was far superior to that of other utilities and governmental entities in the region. Roseanne Harrington, vice president for marketing communications and community relations at OUC, attributes the positive customer attitude to constant updates provided to patrons, being truthful and realistic in setting expectations for return of service (not overpromising), and diligent attention to getting customers back in service as quickly as possible. All firms should have a crisis management plan in place for contingencies that are relevant to their industry and customers.

One way to gain media attention is to tie your promotion to a topic people are naturally interested in. For example, Virgin Trains launched a campaign called "Go greener, go cheaper." The campaign says that not only is train travel cheaper than flying, but it also is better for the environment. Virgin claims that its Pendolino trains emit 78 percent less carbon dioxide than flights inside the United Kingdom. To encourage customers to take the train rather than fly, Virgin Trains let passengers swap their used airplane boarding pass for a free Virgin Trains ticket.[49]

SUMMARY

Developing promotional strategies is an integral part of marketing management and marketing planning. A firm's investment in promotion often involves a substantial amount of money. Fostering an integrated marketing communications (IMC) approach in an organization ensures consistency in communication of the brand and promotional messages across all internal and external communication channels. Although marketing managers are rarely experts in all areas of promotion, they must be well-versed in the process of IMC and how it connects to the overall marketing plan.

KEY TERMS

promotion 464
promotion mix 464
advertising 464
sales promotion 464
public relations (PR) 464
personal selling 464
direct marketing and interactive marketing 464
promotion mix strategies 464
promotional campaign 464
integrated marketing communications (IMC) 465
push strategy 468
pull strategy 468
internal marketing 469
communication 470
sender 471
corporate identity 471
encoding process 471

message transmission 471
channel or medium 471
decoding process 472
selective perception 472
receiver 472
feedback loop 472
noise 473
AIDA model 474
puffery 479
promotional appeal 482
rational appeal 482
emotional appeal 482
moral appeal 483
objective-and-task method 483
percent-of-sales method 484
comparative-parity method 484
all-you-can-afford method 484
advertising wearout 485

advertising response function 486
institutional advertising 487
product advertising 487
pioneering advertising 487
competitive advertising 488
comparative advertising 488
reach 488
frequency 488
advertising execution 489
clutter 489
trade show 494
cooperative advertising and promotion 494
allowance 494
publicity 494
buzz 495
event sponsorship 496
crisis management 496

APPLICATION QUESTIONS

1. Consider the concept of integrated marketing communications (IMC). Select a company and investigate its use of IMC in developing and executing promotional strategies. Look for evidence through its media and messages.

   a. What evidence leads you to conclude the company is or is not successfully practicing an IMC approach? Be specific and connect the evidence to the discussion of IMC in the chapter.

   b. Is there evidence that the firm practices internal marketing? If so, please share what leads you to this conclusion. If not, speculate on how internal marketing would be of value to the organization.

   c. For this or any firm, what are the major advantages of taking an IMC approach? What are the downsides of not practicing IMC?

2. Think of a situation you've experienced in which some communication process you were involved in did not go as well as it might have (it doesn't have to be marketing communications). Using the communication process model (Exhibit 17.7) and accompanying discussion as a guide, systematically retrace the steps of that communication experience through the elements of the model and identify *(a)* where the problems occurred and *(b)* what could have been done differently at each problem step to make the communication experience better.

3. Consider a major purchase you have made recently. Review the AIDA model (Exhibit 17.8) and accompanying discussion.

   a. Think back on the process that led up to your purchase and reconstruct the types of promotion that you experienced during each stage of the AIDA model. Which of the promotional forms was most effective in your situation, and why?

   b. As you reconstruct this purchase experience and the promotional messages you received during it, what other promotion mix elements that you did *not* experience at the time might have been effective in convincing you to make the purchase? At what stage of the AIDA model would they have been helpful, and in what ways do you believe they might have impacted your decision process?

4. The chapter discusses the role of the marketing manager in promotional strategy (Exhibit 17.10 and accompanying discussion). The trend today in both large and small firms is for much of the promotion function to be outsourced.

   a. Comment on this outsourcing trend. What are the major reasons for the trend? What are the pros and cons? What is your personal view about outsourcing all or part of promotion?

   b. Assume you are a marketing manager for a firm that outsources promotion to a creative agency. In what ways does this arrangement impact your job? In particular, concentrate on how it impacts your marketing planning (being mindful that promotion planning is a key element). How would you interact with the agency as a manager representing your firm (assume you have responsibility for the agency relationship with your company)? That is, what are the key things you should do to ensure a productive relationship?

5. Review the Common Approaches to Advertising Execution (Exhibit 17.14) and Pros and Cons of Key Advertising Media (Exhibit 17.15). Review some ads in any three of the seven different types of media identified, watching for examples of the different execution approaches.

   a. Make notes about the ads you reviewed and the different types of media execution you witnessed. Which ads do you think were the most effective? Why?

b. For the same ads, based on the chapter's list of pros and cons for each, identify specific examples of ads for which one or more of the pros and cons apply.

c. Share your findings with another student or with the class.

MANAGEMENT DECISION CASE:
How Chipotle Keeps Sales Climbing with a Minuscule Advertising Budget

It is deep-freezer cold outside—just 5 degrees—and the snow is coming down hard. Never mind. Trey Parrott has just trudged up Chicago's Michigan Avenue to Chipotle Mexican Grill for lunch. Parrott, 25, figures he has eaten at Chipotle every week since a friend first took him to one seven years ago, when he was a high school senior in Kansas City, Missouri. Today he has brought along a couple of co-workers who've never been in a Chipotle before. Their initial review? Two thumbs-up.

Most fast-food chains drum up traffic by barraging consumers with mass-media ads, trumpeting their newest product or latest deal. Chipotle Mexican Grill Inc. plays by different rules. The Denver-based company eschews TV commercials and most other traditional advertising. It spends less in a year on advertising than McDonald's Corp., its former parent, spends in 48 hours. "Advertising is not believable," declares M. Steven Ells, Chipotle's founder and chief executive. Instead, Chipotle banks on customers to spread the word, and customers like Parrott routinely oblige.

This all-volunteer army has helped make Chipotle one of the hottest properties in the restaurant industry. For example, same-store sales have a more than 10-year history of double-digit increases. Consumers consistently rank the chain tops among all quick-serve Mexican places. Chipotle can also brag about the biggest bang of any initial public offering back in 2006. Since then its share price has more than quadrupled, to over $100 in early 2008.

Fittingly, Chipotle is also generating buzz for word-of-mouth marketing. These days the typical consumer is exposed to so many paid pitches—estimates range from 600 to 3,000 a day—that people tend to tune them out. People also dismiss almost anything that comes from big companies, notes Dan Buczaczer, senior vice president of Denuo, a new-media consulting division of Publicis Groupe. But if people hear the same message from a friend or even a stranger, he adds, they'll probably believe it since the tipster has nothing to gain. "Chipotle so far has got it nailed," Buczaczer says. "You have people evangelizing the brand because they love it."

What advertising Chipotle does is mostly on billboards or radio, touting the ample size or fresh ingredients of its burritos and tacos, though with a dash of irony. But its marketing budget is minimal. Over the first 11 months of 2006, McDonald's spent $818.9 million on traditional media advertising in the United States, while Yum! Brand Inc.'s Taco Bell unit spent $252.4 million, according to Nielsen Monitor-Plus. Chipotle's outlay over the same span: $4.5 million. Looked at another way, Chipotle spent less than 1 percent of its full-year revenue on ads compared to 4 percent or more by its larger rivals.

The thriftiness goes back to Chipotle's start in 1993, when Ells opened a cramped outlet in a Denver storefront. With only $85,000 to cover everything, he recalls, even a single ad seemed too costly. Besides, Ells, a white-tablecloth chef who trained at the Culinary Institute of America, thought customers should be swayed first and foremost by the food. So instead of telling people about Chipotle's burritos, he gave them away. When dozens of reporters were camped out in Denver in 1997 as Timothy J. McVeigh was tried for the 1995 Oklahoma City bombing, Chipotle regularly delivered free food to the courthouse.

The handouts are now part of Chipotle's strategy. When Chipotle came to midtown Manhattan, it gave burritos away to 6,000 people, some of whom stood in line for two hours. The stunt cost $35,000, figures James W. Adams, Chipotle's marketing director. In return, the company landed 6,000 new spokespeople. "You could spend that same amount on an ad in *The New York Times* and you wouldn't have that many people talking about you," Adams points out. "The response to the food is almost always positive. It's unique and it's tasty." But don't just take it from him; any Chipotle regular would probably say the same thing.

Questions for Consideration

1. Chipotle relies heavily on free samples as a way to get new customers. How could it make this sales promotion strategy more effective by using other elements of the promotion mix?

2. Do you think event marketing would work as part of Chipotle's marketing mix? Why or why not?

3. What are some other ways (besides sampling) that Chipotle could generate buzz or PR without spending a lot of money? Do you, personally, find these strategies to be more persuasive than traditional advertising messages?

Source: Michael Arndt, "Burrito Buzz–And So Few Ads," *Business-Week,* March 12, 2007. Reprinted with permission.

MARKETING PLAN EXERCISE

ACTIVITY 17: Promoting Your Offering

The promotion plan is an integral part of any marketing plan, and often carries a significant portion of the marketing budget. Develop the following elements for promoting your offering:

1. Review the promotion mix elements and begin to develop goals for promotion and a promotional strategy utilizing the elements of the mix that are most appropriate for your offering.

2. Link the promotional strategy to PLC stages as well as the stages your customers will go through on the AIDA model.

3. Decide how you intend to manage promotion for the offering. Decide on outsourced elements versus elements that will be handled in-house. Establish a structure and process for promotion management.

If you are using Marketing Plan Pro, a template for this assignment can be accessed at www.mhhe.com/marshall1e.

RECOMMENDED READINGS

1. Robyn Blakeman, *Integrated Marketing Communication: Creative Strategy from Idea to Implementation* (Landham, MD: Rowman & Littlefield Publishers, Inc., 2007).

2. Lois Kelly, *Beyond Buzz: The Next Generation of Word-of-Mouth Marketing* (New York: AMACOM, 2007).

3. Roddy Mullin and Julian Cummins, *Sales Promotion: How to Create, Implement, and Integrate Campaigns That Really Work* (Philadelphia: Kogan Page Publishers, 2008).

4. Mario Pricken, *Creative Advertising: Ideas and Techniques from the World's Best Campaigns* (London: Thames and Hudson, 2004).

5. Mark Weiner, *Unleashing the Power of PR: A Contrarian's Guide to Marketing and Communication* (San Francisco: Jossey-Bass, 2006).

CHAPTER 18

INTEGRATED MARKETING COMMUNICATIONS: PERSONAL SELLING, DIRECT MARKETING, AND INTERACTIVE MARKETING

LEARNING OBJECTIVES

- Learn the process of relationship selling.

- Understand the major job responsibilities of sales management.

- Recognize the most significant challenges facing personal communication.

- Identify the major tools in direct marketing.

- Value the use of direct marketing communications in an integrated communications strategy.

- Understand the limitations of direct marketing.

- Learn how to create an effective Internet marketing campaign.

EXECUTIVE PERSPECTIVE

Executive Ken Alloway, Global Product & Marketing Manager

Company ABB Inc.

Business Power products, power systems, automation products, process automation and robotics.

How important is the role of your sales force in building and maintaining customer relationships?

Our sales force is critical in driving our business because the salespeople are our local representation with each customer on a daily basis. The relationship that is built over time allows us to obtain important information such as market-level pricing, customer input for new-product development, and quick resolution of issues.

In addition, the local sales force has the ability to organize a meeting between the customer's decision makers and our product specialists from one of our many factories. These meetings allow us to present to the customer our new products and features and receive valuable feedback. Without the local sales force, the ability to identify and obtain a meeting with key decision makers is nearly impossible.

Who handles prospecting for new clients in your firm? Where do leads come from?

The responsibility of prospecting for new clients lies primarily with the sales force. Each product group or service group, however, has a marketing team that works in conjunction with the sales force. Typically, the specific product group members are located in the factory.

Our leads come from a variety of sources. For instance, we receive quite a number of inquiries through the Internet. These inquiries are assigned to the respective marketing manager for that particular product and are tracked to ensure the customer receives the right information on a timely basis. In addition, we utilize several sales tools such as mobile product trailers that travel from customer to customer on a daily basis. Trade shows also provide a number of new leads through the demonstration of our products.

What are some key success factors that characterize the top salespeople in your company?

I see a greater success when the sales force has a technical understanding of our products and services. Our customers are extremely busy and have little time for vendor meetings and outings. Therefore, in the time a customer will provide, our sales force must be able to communicate our value proposition, which typically is centered on technical features. A customer will provide more time to a salesperson who can provide personal assistance rather than a salesperson who must rely on product experts in the factory for day-to-day issues.

Success also comes from a salesperson's ability to obtain and understand what an individual customer's unique value drivers are. This requires discussions with the customer about the business and various scenarios to solve issues. This allows us to present a bid to a customer that focuses on the value drivers and helps differentiate our products or services from our competition, thus avoiding price wars.

TOWARD A MORE PERSONAL COMMUNICATION WITH THE CUSTOMER

Advertising, sales promotion, and public relations are essential tools in an integrated marketing communications strategy. However, they are all, for the most part, unidirectional. In other words, the company communicates with the customer but the customer has limited ability to provide feedback. Companies know that it is important to communicate directly with the customer and, in turn, enable the customer to communicate directly with the company. As a result, effective integrated marketing communications incorporates interactive, personal communication elements.

The three personal communication methods most widely adopted are personal selling, direct marketing, and interactive marketing. They have the potential to connect the company with the customer as well as encourage the customer to interact with the company in a way that significantly strengthens the relationship. However, if managed poorly, they can profoundly harm the relationship with the customer. Companies know that interactive communication is critical to long-term success and dedicate resources to ensure the quality of the relationship between the company and customer.

Astra-Zeneca has been a technology pioneer in the pharmaceutical industry. One of the challenges has been to better integrate technology with improved sales call effectiveness. Partnering with service provider Fingertip Formulary, Astra-Zeneca introduced a new handheld platform that allows salespeople to create custom formulary tables for doctors during the sales call. The company's entire marketing effort is now more interactive allowing physicians to better access specific information when needed rather than more generic market messaging.[1]

PERSONAL SELLING–THE MOST PERSONAL FORM OF COMMUNICATION

With the average cost of a sales call exceeding $300 and the Internet's interactive capabilities, some people have predicted the decline of personal selling as an effective marketing communications tool. However, this has not been the case; indeed, IBM, Pfizer, and other companies are expanding their sales forces. While there is no question that selling is among the most expensive forms of marketing communication, personal selling offers three distinct advantages over other marketing communications methods:

- *Immediate feedback to the customer.* Customers don't want to wait for information. Increasingly, they demand accurate information quickly, putting pressure on companies for immediate, personal communication with a salesperson or customer service representative.[2]

- *Ability to tailor the message to the customer.* No other marketing communication method does a better job of creating personal, unique customer messages in real time. Salespeople generate distinctive sales messages that directly address customer problems and concerns.[3]

- *Enhance the personal relationship between company and customer.* Salespeople and the personal selling function are the single most effective approach for establishing and enhancing the personal relationship between company and customer. In particular, business-to-business (B2B) customers appreciate the efficiency of the Internet and other communication tools but expect a personal relationship with their suppliers. There is no substitute for a salesperson working with the customer one-on-one to solve problems.[4]

Activities in Personal Selling

Personal selling is a two-way communication process between salesperson and buyer with the goal of securing, building, and maintaining long-term relationships with profitable customers. To be successful in this process, salespeople need a variety of skills that change all the time. Research suggests salespeople today are expected to be more skilled, available, as well as better communicators than ever before. Four basic selling activities composed of dozens of individual tasks define the salesperson's job: communicate, sell, build customer relationships, and manage information. The challenge for many companies is defining the correct mix of activities and then adapting the activities as the selling environment changes.[5] Exhibit 18.1 identifies the four major selling activities and specific tasks associated with each activity.

Personal selling offers three distinct advantages: immediate customer feedback, ability to create unique customer messages, and enhancing the customer relationship. The selling function can be a strategic advantage for the company.

Communicate

Effective communication is an essential selling activity. As the point of contact between customer and company, a salesperson must communicate effectively with both. With the customer, the salesperson needs good verbal communication skills

EXHIBIT 18.1	**Matrix of Selling Activities**			
	Communicate	**Sell**	**Build Customer Relationships**	**Manage Information**
Technology	1. E-mail 2. Make telephone calls/leave voicemail messages	1. Script sales pitch 2. Create customer-specific content 3. Provide relevant technology to customer	1. Create useful company Web page content 2. Develop good team skills inside the company	Develop database management skills to manage customer database
Non-technology	1. Enhance language and overall communication skills 2. Develop effective presentation skills	1. Learn relationship selling skills 2. Conduct research of customer's business 3. Define and sell value-added services to customer 4. Follow up after customer contact 5. Identify and target key customer accounts 6. Listen effectively	1. Develop strong supplier alliances 2. Build rapport with all members of the customer's buying center 3. Network inside the company and throughout the customer's business 4. Build trust 5. Coordinate customer relationships inside the company	1. Develop time management skills 2. Organize information flow to maximize the effectiveness and reduce irrelevant data

to present the sales message. Equally important are good presentation skills that incorporate technology (PowerPoint, wireless access) into the sales presentation. Finally, customers expect near constant access to the company so the salesperson must also have mobile communications skills.[6]

Communication with the company is also important. As discussed in Chapter 5, salespeople represent an excellent source of market information; they are familiar with customers and their needs. Customer feedback is also an excellent source of new-product ideas. Finally, field salespeople frequently find out about competitor or marketplace changes before anyone else in the company. All this information needs to be collected, analyzed, and disseminated to appropriate marketing managers.

Sell

Everyone agrees that the basic activity of a salesperson is selling, but what exactly does that mean? Selling requires a complex set of tasks to reach the point where the customer agrees to purchase the product. From customer research early in the process through the sales presentation and customer support after purchase, the sales process is difficult.[7] We will explore the sales process a little later in the chapter.

Build Customer Relationships

Customers demand a close, strategic relationship with suppliers, and, as the primary point of contact with the company, salespeople are expected to build and support the customer relationship. This means spending time with the customer, developing excellent customer relationship management skills, and ultimately building trust with a customer.[8]

Information Management

Salespeople today must be excellent information managers, collecting information from a variety of sources (their own company, customers, competitors, and independent information sources), determining what is relevant, and then presenting it to the customer. For example, managing the flow of customer information inside the company to ensure the right people get the right information at the right time takes time and follow-up. Often, information is collected from customers and other external sources such as transportation companies to facilitate an order inside the company. Customers will have preferred shipping times that need to be coordinated with transportation companies to ensure on-time arrival. At the same time, being sensitive to customer security concerns means controlling access to information.[9]

Key Success Factors

Because selling involves such a diverse set of activities, it is considered one of the most difficult careers in business. While the variety of sales jobs makes it impossible to generalize to every situation, research has identified the following critical success factors:[10]

- *Listening.* Many people have the impression that salespeople are great talkers. While it is important to be a good communicator, the reality is that great salespeople are skillful listeners. They know that to really learn the customer's needs and then create a value-based solution it is essential to listen.

- *Follow-up.* When a salesperson commits to doing something, the customer expects it to be done. Follow-up and addressing customer concerns is a critical skill.

- *Ability to adapt sales style from situation to situation.* Being able to adjust the sales style from one sales situation to another in real time based on customer feedback, called **adaptive selling,** is critical to long-term success. The "one size fits all" approach does not work with customers expecting personalized service.

- *Persistence.* Building customer relationships takes time and effort. Long-term success is not based on a single sale but, rather, a relationship, which makes the salesperson (and company) a critical partner with the customer in the customer's success.
- *Good verbal communication skills.* Effective communication skills have never been more important. Customers expect a salesperson to be good at verbal communications and incorporate appropriate technologies into the presentation.
- *Effective personal planning and time management.* Customers demand it and good salespeople recognize the importance of effective time management. As salespeople take on more activities and customer expectations increase, managing time becomes essential in relationship building.
- *Ability to interact with individuals at every level of the organization.* Salespeople interact with a wide range of people inside their customer organizations. As a result, they must be just as comfortable in front of C level executives (CEOs) as well as lower-level managers.

Business schools have been criticized for focusing on quantitative "hard" skills at the expense of "soft skills" such as decision making. A recent study surveyed managers across more than 50 industries. Six broad management skill areas were identified: managing human capital, logistics/technology, decision-making processes, administration and control, strategy/innovation, and task environment. Managers reported the two most important skills were managing human capital and decision-making processes. This same study then examined 373 B-school curricula and found that decision-making processes ranked fifth while administration and control was most important (managers ranked this skill fifth).[11]

Sales in B2C versus B2B Markets

In terms of sheer numbers, most salespeople are employed in various kinds of retail selling, or B2C. These jobs involve selling products to end users for their personal use. Examples of these types of sales positions are direct sellers such as Mary Kay and Tupperware, residential real estate agents, and retail store salespeople. However, much more relationship selling is done by salespeople in B2B markets.

Some personal characteristics and sales activities are similar across both B2C and B2B markets. Good interpersonal and communication skills, excellent knowledge of the products being sold, an ability to discover customer needs and solve their problems are common characteristics to both sales environments. Similarly, managers must recruit and train appropriate people no matter what the sales job, provide them with objectives that match the firm's overall marketing program, then supervise, motivate, and finally evaluate their performance.[12]

But B2C and B2B selling also differ in some important ways. Many of the goods and services sold by B2B salespeople are more expensive and technically complex than those in B2C. In addition, B2B customers tend to be larger and engage in extensive decision-making processes involving many people

Classifying Sales Positions

While retail selling employs more people, personal selling plays a more important and strategic purpose in business-to-business markets. Because of the important strategic function of personal selling in business-to-business markets, our discussion of sales positions will focus on different sales positions in the B2B market. There are many different types of sales jobs that require a variety of specific and unique skills. However, no matter what the job title, the salesperson's primary responsibility is to increase business from current and potential customers by providing a good value proposition to customers and effectively dealing with their concerns. The four major types of sales positions are trade servicer, missionary seller, technical seller, and solutions seller.

Trade Servicer

Trade servicers are the group of resellers such as retailers or distributors with whom the sales force does business. Their primary responsibility is to increase business from current or potential customers by providing them with merchandising and promotional assistance. For example, the Procter & Gamble salesperson selling soap products to individual store managers at a large grocery is an example of a trade servicer.

Missionary Seller

Missionary salespeople often do not take orders from customers directly but persuade customers to buy their firm's product from distributors or other suppliers. Anheuser-Bush does missionary selling when its salespeople call on bar owners and encourage them to order a particular brand of beer from the local distributor. Although the sales model is changing, pharmaceutical reps, or detailers, historically called on doctors as representatives of the pharmaceutical manufacturers. When Pfizer introduced Zyrtec, a top-selling allergy drug, its salespeople communicated with physicians to alert them to the efficacy of the product, explain its advantages over other allergy medication such as Allegra and Clarinex, and to influence them to prescribe it to their patients. Keep in mind that the Pfizer salesperson does not "sell" any product directly to the patient.[13]

Technical Seller

An example of **technical selling** is the sales engineer from General Electric who calls on Boeing to sell the GE90 jet engine to be used in Boeing aircraft. The trend is for most technical selling to be done in cross-functional teams. The complexity of many of the products and associated services involved in technical selling makes it difficult for any one salesperson to master all aspects of the sale. Cross-functional teams often include someone who is technically competent in the product (engineer), a customer service specialist, a financial analyst, and an account manager responsible for maintaining the customer-company relationship.

Solution Seller

More and more customers look for strategic partners who provide comprehensive solutions to their business problems. **Key account salespeople,** those responsible for managing large accounts, are skilled in developing complex solutions to a particular customer problem.[14] In addition, in industries such as information technology, customers look to suppliers for wide-ranging solutions from IT infrastructure design to defining product specifications, to purchase and installation of equipment or software, and support after the sale. A Hewlett-Packard or IBM salesperson, for example, needs to know not only a great deal about hardware and software but also the customer's business in order to develop a solution to the customer's IT problems.

Technical selling often involves trained specialists available to address customer concerns in the field.

The Personal Selling Process

Because personal selling is so important in establishing and maintaining customer relationships, particularly in B2B markets, many companies create a separate personal selling function that operates independently from the rest of marketing. As a result, marketing managers often do not have salespeople reporting directly to them. However, marketing managers need to understand the personal selling process for two reasons. First, in companies where salespeople play an important role, personal selling is the single most critical connection to the customer. From selling to customer service, salespeople are often the customer's primary contact point with the company. Marketing managers need a clear understanding of the selling process because it has such a profound effect on the customer relationship. Second, a number of marketing activities such as customer service and marketing communications will be affected by the personal selling function. Understanding the selling process helps marketing managers better plan a marketing communications strategy and coordinate other marketing activities such as customer service.

Exhibit 18.2 shows the six stages in the personal selling process. Although the selling process involves only a few steps, the specific activities involved at each step vary greatly depending on the type of sales position and the firm's overall customer relationship strategy. Consequently, marketing managers must ensure that a firm's sales program incorporates sufficient policies to guide each salesperson while at the same time coordinating the selling effort with the firm's marketing and relationship strategy. The same selling process is used by B2C and B2B salespeople, although how the process works varies greatly between the two environments. For example, B2C salespeople generally do not actively prospect for customers, since the customer is visiting the store, or follow up with the customer after the sale.

| EXHIBIT 18.2 | The Personal Selling Process |

Prospecting for Customers
↓
Opening the Relationship
↓
Qualifying the Prospect
↓
Making the Sales Presentation
↓
Handling Customer Objections
↓
Follow-up with Customers

Prospecting for Customers

Prospecting is critical because recruiting new customers is an essential element in a company's growth strategy. Marketing managers encourage salespeople to use a variety of sources to identify relevant prospects including trade association and industry directories, other customers and suppliers, and referrals from company marketing efforts.

Telemarketing and other direct marketing efforts, which we will discuss in the next section, are also used to generate prospective customers. **Outbound telemarketing** involves calling potential customers at their home or office, either to make a sales call via telephone or to set up an appointment for a field salesperson. **Inbound telemarketing,** where prospective customers call a toll-free number for more information, is also used to identify and qualify prospects. When prospects call for more information, a telemarketing representative determines the extent of interest and assesses the prospect qualifications, then passes the contact information on to the appropriate salesperson. The Internet also generates potential new customer leads. Many companies, particularly those selling complex products, use the Internet to provide technical product information to customers. Then salespeople follow up on legitimate inquiries with a traditional sales call.

In coordinating the marketing effort, marketing managers must understand how much emphasis salespeople give to prospecting for new customers versus calling on existing customers. The appropriate policy depends on the selling and customer relationship strategy of the company, the nature of the product, and the firm's customers. Working with sales managers, the marketing manager considers the right mix of activities for the salesperson. For example, firms that have established customer relationships or products that require substantial service after the sale generally encourage salespeople to devote most of their effort to servicing existing customers.[15]

Prospecting for new customers is a critical function in maintaining company growth. A recent study reported that the more well known a company is in the marketplace, the better it is at generating new sales leads. New customers tend to trust companies they know even if they have not purchased from them before. This reinforces the importance of branding in building customer awareness.[16]

Opening the Relationship

In the initial approach to the prospective customer, the sales representative should try to determine who has the greatest influence or authority in the purchase. For example, when the firm's product is inexpensive and purchased routinely, salespeople are frequently instructed to deal with the purchasing department. At the other end of the continuum, complex, technical products generally require an extensive sales effort calling on influencers and decision makers in various departments and different managerial levels. When the purchase involves people across the customer's organization, the salesperson often works with a team.

Qualifying the Prospect

Before salespeople spend much time trying to establish a relationship with the prospective account, it is important to qualify the prospect to determine if the company is a legitimate potential customer. The process involves answering five questions:

- Does the prospect have a need for the company's products?
- Can the prospect derive added value from the product in ways that the company can deliver?
- Can the salesperson effectively contact, communicate, and work with the prospect over an extended time period (the time it takes to complete the sale and follow up after the sale)?
- Does the prospect have the financial ability and authority to make the sale?
- Will the sale be profitable for the company?

Sales Presentation

Communicating the Sales Message The **sales presentation** is the delivery of information relevant to meet the customer's needs and is the heart of the selling process. It is the process salespeople use to transition customers from interest in the product to purchase of the product. The stereotype of a sales presentation is a salesperson talking in front of a customer or group of customers. In reality, sales presentations are carefully choreographed interactions in which the salesperson tries to discern the customer's real needs while at the same time providing critical information in a persuasive way so the customer appreciates the benefits and advantages of the product. Remember, the goal is not simply to make the sale but to create a strong value proposition that will lead to a mutually beneficial long-term relationship.[17]

Setting Goals and Objectives Ultimately, the goal of the presentation is to secure a purchase commitment from the customer. However, the salesperson does not just walk in asking for the purchase order. Successful salespeople understand that the purchase order does not come until customers believe the company's products offer the best solution to their needs. In defining the goal, salespeople consider where the customer is in the buying process and have a clear understanding of the customer relationship.[18] New customers, for example, generally need more information about company products, policies, and procedures than existing customers. Based on an analysis of these factors, salespeople identify at least one of five principal goals for the presentation. At some point, however, the goal of the presentation will be to obtain customer action.

- Educate the customer by providing enough knowledge about the company's products.
- Get the customer's attention.
- Build interest for the company's products.
- Nurture the customer's desire and conviction to purchase.
- Obtain a customer commitment to action (purchase).

Characteristics of a Great Sales Presentation

How would you respond if someone asked you, "What makes a great sales presentation?" Many people can give examples of a bad presentation, such as not listening to the customer, but not the characteristics of a great sales presentation.[19] Exhibit 18.3 identifies the four characteristics of a great presentation.

Steps in a Sales Presentation

Much of the work for the presentation is done before meeting the customer. However, invariably the customer offers new information, presents a different problem, disagrees with the value proposition, or presents the salesperson with any one of a hundred other challenges. This means that while salespeople need to be well-prepared, they must also have the flexibility to adjust the presentation in real time. An effective sales presentation consists of three steps:

1. *Identify the customer needs.* Research suggests that being able to correctly identify customer needs is one of the key characteristics that distinguish high-performing salespeople. Selling is based, in large part, on the salesperson's ability to identify those needs and develop win-win solutions that benefit both the company and customer.

2. *Apply knowledge to customer needs.* This step, providing solutions that solve customer problems, is the essence of a salesperson's role in the relationship-selling process and is a critical link between what the company has to offer and the customer's needs. Good salespeople can explain product performance characteristics, service turnaround times, and many other important features. Those facts are important, but customers, whether they are consumers or other businesses, do not buy features. They buy solutions to problems. So it is fundamental that salespeople link knowledge of

EXHIBIT 18.3	**Characteritics of a Great Sales Presentation**

Characteristic	Answers the Customer Question
Explains the value proposition	What is the value-added of the product?
Asserts the advantages and benefits of the product	What are the advantages and benefits of the product?
Enhances the customer's knowledge of the company, product, and services	What are the key points I should know about this company, product, and services?
Creates a memorable experience	What should I remember about this presentation?

Source: Adapted from Mark W. Johnston and Greg W. Marshall, *Relationship Selling,* 2nd ed, 2008. Copyright © 2008 The McGraw-Hill Companies, Inc.

the company's products to customer need solutions. This process is often referred to as **FAB (Features, Advantages, and Benefits).**

The FAB approach is designed to make the company's products more relevant for customers. A **feature** is any material characteristic or specification of a product. Antilock brakes on a Cadillac Escalade are an example of a feature. An **advantage** is the particular product/service characteristic that helps meet the customer's needs. The Escalade's antilock brakes help the SUV stop faster than normal brake systems. A **benefit** is the advantageous outcome from the advantage found in the product feature. The SUV will provide greater security for the driver and passengers.

3. *Satisfy customer needs.* No matter how much negotiating is involved before the final purchase decision or how tough it is to close the sale, customer satisfaction is the desired objective of every sales presentation. The nature of the sales presentation creates stress for the customer. The salesperson is asking the customer to choose change by selecting the company's product. As a result, salespeople understand the importance of minimizing **change conflict** for the customer. The best way to manage customer change conflict is to manage the customer's expectations.[20] Salespeople learn to clearly define the value proposition and deliver on all promises made during the presentation.

Handling Objections–Negotiating Win-Win Solutions

Casual observation may suggest there are many different customer concerns; however, when you look closely, customer anxieties fall into four areas. Customers often mask true concerns with general problems, but successful salespeople know how to identify and clarify true objections.[21] Exhibit 18.4 identifies common customer concerns.

Product Need

The customer may not be convinced there is a need for the product. The customer's perspective can be summarized as, "We've always done it one way; why should we start something new now?" Key to the answer is a well-conceived value proposition that explains clearly how the product will benefit the customer and how it will be better than the existing solution.[22] It is important to remember that customers are generally not risk takers.

A much more common concern is whether the customer views the salesperson's product as a better solution than existing options. The customer is already familiar with the current products and change means learning a new product. Careful preparation is critical in dealing with questions about competitors, which is why salespeople spend a great deal of time learning about competitor products.

Cisco has developed an excellent reputation with its customers. It is leveraging that reputation with a sophisticated line of teleconferencing products. Business customers have confidence in Cisco which translates into business opportunities.

Company Trust

Personal selling is based, in part, on mutual trust between the buyer and seller. As we discussed, most customers already have a supplier, and while they may not be totally satisfied, they are familiar with them. For example, they know the process for resolving a problem (who to call, expected wait times, costs, etc.). If the customer is unaware of the company, a common concern is the company's ability to deliver what is needed, when it's needed, and where it's needed.[23] This is a legitimate concern as the customer puts the company at risk by choosing the salesperson's company as the supplier. In other situations,

EXHIBIT 18.4	Common Customer Concerns

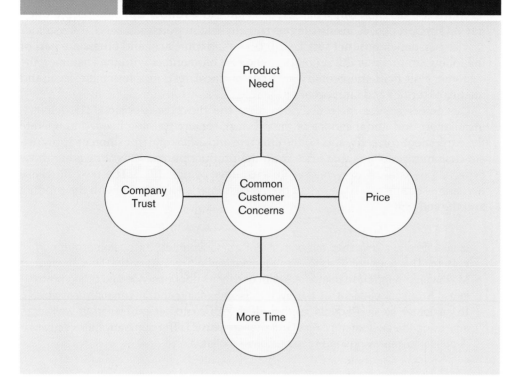

customers may not object to the salesperson's company but are happy with their existing supplier.

More Time

One of the most common customer objections is, "I need more time to consider the proposal." Certainly, concern about making a purchase decision too quickly is legitimate; however, the most likely scenario is that the value proposition has not been sufficiently developed.

Price

Salespeople consistently report that price is the most common customer apprehension. In many cases, the customer has legitimate objections about the price of a product. Nevertheless, the price objection usually means the customer has not accepted the value proposition. In essence, if the customer does not perceive that the product benefits exceed the price, there will be no sale. The salesperson is left with two options. Lower the price until it is below the product's perceived benefits, or raise the perceived benefits until they exceed the price.[24]

Closing the Sale

Closing the sale is obtaining commitment from the customer to make the purchase. The close is not a discrete event but rather a nonlinear process that begins with the approach to the customer. Research suggests salespeople make four critical mistakes in closing. First, a negative attitude about the customer or situation can affect the sales presentation and customer relationship. Second, the failure to conduct an effective pre-approach shows a lack of preparation that turns off customers. Third, too much talking and not enough listening demonstrates a lack of interest in finding out the customer's real needs. Fourth, using a "one size fits all" approach indicates the salesperson lacks creativity and is unwilling to focus on the customer's unique situation.[25]

Follow-up after the Sale

One of the most critical aspects to the selling process is not what happens before the purchase decision but what happens after, the **follow-up.** Salespeople often rely on support people inside the company to help in post-sales service. Customer service personnel, product service call centers, technicians, and others are part of the follow-up process. But no matter who else has contact with the customer, the customer will hold the primary salesperson most responsible for the level and quality of service and support after the sale.

Customers expect three activities after the purchase decision: (1) delivery, installation, and initial service of the product, (2) any training needed to operate the equipment correctly, and (3) the effective and efficient disposition of appropriate customer problems that arise from the product purchase. Not meeting those expectations is a primary reason for customer complaints.[26] The next purchase decision is based to a large extent on the customer's experience with the product and the company.

> British Telecom invested millions of dollars to upgrade its customer support system. The new knowledge management system provides real-time "Instant Messaging" support to customers with questions about service and billing problems. A critical element of the system is enhancing the information available to customer service agents as they deal with customer problems as well as improving the customer's overall experience with BT. The company believes this is critical to improving long-term customer satisfaction.[27]

Organizing the Sales Force

Since salespeople work closely with many departments inside the company, marketing managers have a real interest in working with sales managers to organize the sales force to maximize the efficiency and effectiveness of not only the sales force but also everyone in the company that interacts with the customer. The best sales structures are based on the company's objectives and strategies. In addition, as the firm's environment, objectives, or marketing strategy changes, its sales force must be flexible enough to change as well.[28]

Company Sales Force or Independent Agents

Maintaining a sales force is expensive, and companies are constantly assessing the most practical method to reach customers. One option is to use independent agents instead of company salespeople. It is not unusual for a company, such as IBM, to use both company salespeople and independent agents. Using independent sales agents is referred to as **outsourcing the sales force.**

The decision to use independent agents or a company sales force involves four factors.

- *Economic:* Basic analysis of the costs and expected revenue associated with maintaining a sales force is weighed against outsourcing to independent agents.

- *Control:* A critical factor is the amount of control senior management believes is necessary for the sales function. A company sales force offers complete control in key areas such as recruiting, training, and compensation. On the other hand, independent agents operate without direct company management supervision.

- *Transaction costs:* Finding a good replacement for a poor-performing independent sales agent can be difficult, and once one is found, it is often months before the new agent learns enough about the product and its applications to be effective in the sales job. **Transaction cost analysis (TCA)** states that when substantial transaction-specific assets are necessary to sell a manufacturer's product, the cost of using and administering independent agents is likely higher than the cost of hiring and managing a company's sales force.[29]

- *Strategic flexibility:* In general, a vertically integrated distribution system incorporating a company sales force is less flexible than outsourcing. Independent agents can be added or dismissed at short notice, especially if no specialized assets are needed to sell the product. Furthermore, it is not necessary to sign a long-term contract with independent agents. Firms facing uncertain and rapidly changing competitive or market environments and industries characterized by shifting technology or short product life cycles often use independent agents to preserve flexibility in the distribution channel.

Geographic Orientation

The simplest and most common method of organizing a company sales force is geographic orientation, as illustrated in Exhibit 18.5. Individual salespeople are assigned to separate geographic territories. In this type of organization, each salesperson is responsible for performing all the sales activities in a given territory. The geographic sales organization has several advantages. First, and most importantly, it tends to have the lowest cost because (1) there is only one salesperson in each territory, (2) territories tend to be smaller than other organizational structures so travel time and expenses are minimized, and (3) fewer managerial levels are required for coordination so sales administration and overhead expenses are lower. Second, the simplicity of the geographical structure minimizes customer confusion because each customer is called on by one salesperson. The major disadvantage is that it does not encourage or support any division or specialization of labor. Each salesperson is expected to be good at many things (various customer needs, product applications and specifications).

Product Organization

Some companies have a separate sales force for each product or product category (see Exhibit 18.6). The primary advantage of a product organization is that individual salespeople can develop familiarity with the technical attributes, applications, and most effective selling methods associated with a single product. Also, there

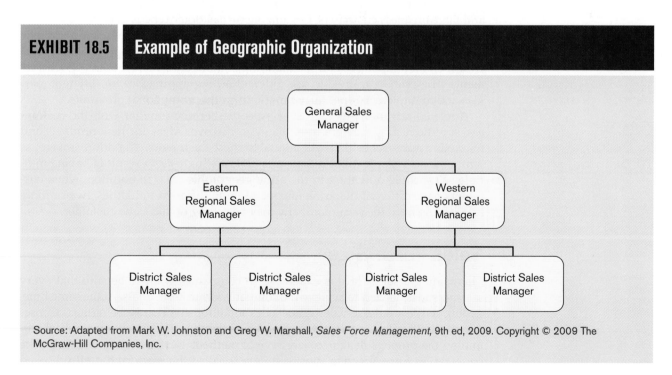

EXHIBIT 18.5 **Example of Geographic Organization**

Source: Adapted from Mark W. Johnston and Greg W. Marshall, *Sales Force Management*, 9th ed, 2009. Copyright © 2009 The McGraw-Hill Companies, Inc.

EXHIBIT 18.6 | **Example of Product Orientation**

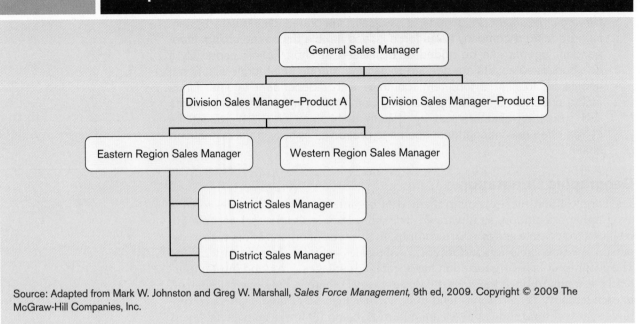

Source: Adapted from Mark W. Johnston and Greg W. Marshall, *Sales Force Management*, 9th ed, 2009. Copyright © 2009 The McGraw-Hill Companies, Inc.

tends to be a closer relationship between sales and engineering, product development, and manufacturing when salespeople focus on one product or product category. Finally, this structure enables greater control in the allocation of selling effort across various products. Management can then adjust sales assets based on the needs of individual products. The major disadvantage is the duplication of effort with salespeople across different products assigned to the same geographic territory. This generally leads to higher sales costs.

Customer Type or Market Organization

It has become increasingly popular for organizations to structure their sales force by customer type as IBM did when it created separate sales teams to call on small and large business customers. Organizing by customer type is a natural extension of creating value for the customer and reflects a market segmentation strategy (see Exhibit 18.7). When salespeople specialize in calling on a particular type of customer, they gain a better understanding of those customers' needs and requirements. They can be trained to use different selling approaches for different markets and to implement specialized marketing and promotional programs.[30]

A related advantage is that as salespeople become familiar with the customers' specific needs, they are more likely to discover ideas for new products and marketing approaches that will appeal to those customers. The disadvantage, as with product organization, is that sales costs are higher as a result of having multiple salespeople operating in the same geographic area. In addition, when customers have different departments operating in different industries, two or more salespeople from the same company may be calling on the same customer.

Sales Force Size

Maintaining a sales force is expensive so companies want to be sure that every salesperson is needed to achieve the company's long-term goals. At the same time, having too few salespeople means sales are almost certainly being lost. Consequently, both sales and marketing managers have a significant interest in determining the proper sales force size. Several methods can be used to determine the correct sales force size. The most common is called the **workload method** based

EXHIBIT 18.7 | Example of Customer Orientation

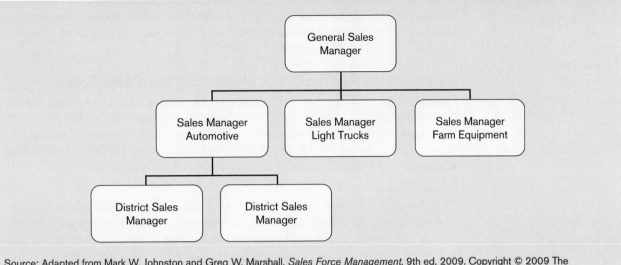

Source: Adapted from Mark W. Johnston and Greg W. Marshall, *Sales Force Management*, 9th ed, 2009. Copyright © 2009 The McGraw-Hill Companies, Inc.

on the premise that all salespeople should undertake an equal amount of work. The method has advantages and disadvantages. First, it is easy to understand and recognizes that different types of accounts should be called on with different frequencies. Second, the data to estimate the sales force are readily available. But the method does not allow for differences in sales response among customers that receive the same sales effort. Also, it assumes all salespeople use their time with equal efficiency, which is not the case.

The method involves six steps.

- *Classify all the company's customers into categories.* Often the classification is based on the sales to each customer and to prioritize accounts as A, B, C based on sales volume

- *Determine the frequency with which each type of account should be called on and the desired length of each sales call.* This analysis is based on management insights or a more formal analysis of historical data.

- *Calculate the workload involved in covering the entire market.* This calculation should include the total amount of work involved in covering each class of account.

- *Determine the time available for each salesperson.* Estimate the number of hours a typical salesperson works per week, and then multiply that by the number of weeks the salesperson works during the year.

- *Apportion the salesperson's time by task performed.* Not all the salesperson's time is involved in direct selling to the customer. A great deal of time is spent on nonselling activities such as making reports, meetings, and service calls.

- *Calculate the number of salespeople needed.* The number of salespeople the company will need is determined by dividing the total number of hours required to service the entire market by the number of hours available per salesperson for direct selling activities.

Managing the Sales Force

Sales and marketing work together to deliver value to the customer and achieve company objectives. While primary responsibility for managing a sales force generally falls to sales managers, integrating the marketing and sales function requires a coordinated effort with marketing managers. Understanding how salespeople are managed helps marketing managers better understand the selling function and coordinate sales with the rest of the marketing department. The sales function is unique in the organization and requires talented management to maximize its efficiency and effectiveness. Managing a sales force involves five primary responsibilities: salesperson performance, recruitment and selection, training, compensation and rewards, and performance evaluation.

Salesperson Performance: Motivating the Sales Force

Understanding salesperson performance is important to sales managers because almost everything they do influences sales performance one way or another. For example, how the manager selects salespeople and the kind of training they receive affects their aptitude and skills. The compensation program and the way it is administered influences motivation and overall sales performance.

> Generation Y entered the workforce with a different set of rules than their baby boomer parents. While still focused on high performance and high-paying jobs, they also look for positions that are fun and exciting. In essence, they are not just looking for a job but an opportunity to both enjoy their job and be well-rewarded in the process. Generation Y places a higher priority on finding the right life-work balance so the 60-hour workweek does not appeal to them, but working remotely and with flexible schedules does.[31]

As presented in Exhibit 18.8, salesperson performance is a function of five factors: (1) role perceptions, (2) aptitude, (3) skill level, (4) motivation, and (5) personal, organizational, and environment factors.

Role Perceptions The role of a salesperson is the set of activities or behaviors to be performed by the salesperson. This role is largely defined through the

EXHIBIT 18.8   Model of Salesperson Performance

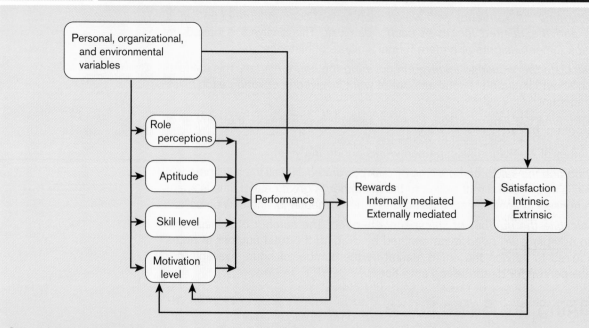

Source: Adapted from Mark W. Johnston and Greg W. Marshall, *Sales Force Management*, 9th ed, 2009. Copyright © 2009 The McGraw-Hill Companies, Inc.

expectations, demands, and pressure communicated to the salesperson by role partners. These partners include people inside as well as outside the company with a vested interest in how a salesperson performs the job—top management, the salesperson's sales manager, customers, and family members. How salespeople perceive their roles has significant consequences that affect job satisfaction and motivation, which, in turn, have the potential to increase sales force turnover and hurt performance.[32]

Sales Aptitude: Are Good Salespeople Born or Made? Sales ability has historically been considered a function of (1) physical factors such as age and physical attractiveness, (2) aptitude factors such as verbal skills and sales expertise, and (3) personality characteristics such as empathy. However, there is no proof these measures, by themselves, affect sales performance. As a result, most managers believe the things a company does to train and develop its salespeople are the most important determinants of success.

Sales skill levels **Sales skill levels** are the individual's learned proficiency at performing necessary sales tasks. They include such learned abilities as interpersonal skills, leadership, technical knowledge, and presentation skills. The relative importance of each of these skills and the need for other skills depends on the selling situation.[33]

Motivation **Motivation** is how much the salesperson wants to expend effort on each activity or task associated with the sales job. Sales managers constantly try to find the right mix of motivation elements that direct salespeople to perform sales activities. Unfortunately, motivational factors that work well with one person may not motivate another. For example, an autocratic managerial style may work with a midcareer salesperson but have a profound negative effect on a senior salesperson. In addition, a number of motivational factors are not directly under the sales manager's control such as personal family issues or general economic conditions.[34]

Organizational, Environmental, and Personal Factors Organizational factors include company marketing budget, current market share for the company's products, and the degree of sales management supervision. Personal and organizational variables such as job experience, the manager's interaction style, and performance feedback all affect the amount of role conflict and ambiguity salespeople perceive.[35] In addition, the desire for job-related rewards (such as higher pay or promotion) differs with age, education, family size, career stage, and organizational climate.

Rewards A company bestows a variety of rewards on any given level of performance. There are two types of rewards—extrinsic and intrinsic. **Extrinsic rewards** are those controlled and given by people other than the salesperson such as managers and customers. They include pay, financial incentives, security, recognition, and promotion. **Intrinsic rewards** are those salespeople primarily attain for themselves and include feelings of accomplishment, personal growth, and self-worth.[36]

Satisfaction Salesperson job satisfaction refers to all the characteristics of the job that salespeople find rewarding, fulfilling, and satisfying—or frustrating and unsatisfying. Satisfaction is a complex job attitude and salespeople can be satisfied or dissatisfied with many different aspects of the job.[37]

Recruiting and Selecting Salespeople

Hiring the right people is important to long-term success, so there is a great deal of focus on recruiting and selecting qualified salespeople. The recruitment and selection process has three steps: (1) analyze the job and determine selection criteria, (2) find and attract a pool of applicants, and (3) develop and apply selection procedures to evaluate applicants.

Firms often compete against competitors and other industries for the best candidates. As a result, companies develop a well-coordinated recruiting strategy

EXHIBIT 18.9	Sales Training Topics

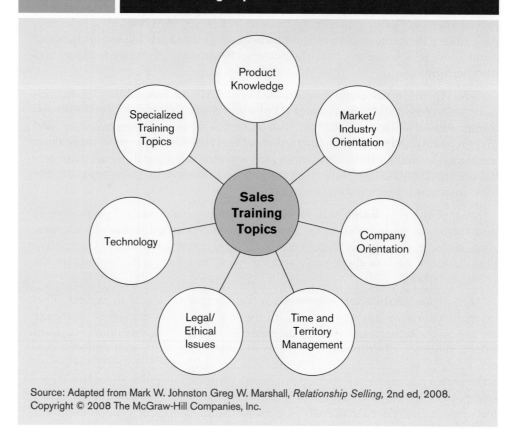

Source: Adapted from Mark W. Johnston Greg W. Marshall, *Relationship Selling*, 2nd ed, 2008. Copyright © 2008 The McGraw-Hill Companies, Inc.

that, contrary to popular belief, does not seek to maximize the number of applicants. Having too many recruits overloads the selection process. The true objective of a successful recruiting strategy is to identify a few exceptionally qualified recruits.[38]

Training

Sales managers often work with marketing managers to identify training objectives that integrate the needs of the salesperson with corporate marketing objectives and include: (1) improved customer relationships, (2) increased productivity, (3) improved morale, (4) lower turnover, and (5) improved selling skills. The challenge for sales managers is measuring the effectiveness of sales training.[39]

Sales training most often involves one or more of the seven topics listed in Exhibit 18.9 ranging from product knowledge to very specialized topics such as communication and customer relationship building. The key for sales managers is fitting the sales training content to the needs of the individual salespeople.

Johnson & Johnson incorporates several online games to help train employees. In one online computer game called 3DU (the U stands for University) new employees become acquainted with company policies, procedures, and benefits including the health care program, diversity networks, and ethics policies. Another online experience is based on Second Life and enables new employees to meet other people in the company including President Garry Neil. Finally, a game called Mission Possible trains new hires on the drug development process and complexity of bringing new products to market.[40]

Compensation and Rewards

The total financial compensation paid to salespeople has several components designed to achieve different objectives. A **salary** is a fixed sum of money paid at regular intervals. Most firms that pay a salary also offer **incentive pay** to encourage better performance. Incentives are generally commissions tied to sales volume or profitability, or bonuses for meeting or exceeding specific performance targets (for example, meeting quotas for a particular product). Such incentives direct salespeople's efforts toward specific strategic objectives during the year, as well as offer additional rewards for top performers. A **commission** is payment based on short-term results, usually a salesperson's dollar or unit sales volume. Since there is a direct link between sales volume and the amount of commission received, commission payments are useful for increasing salespeople's sales efforts.[41] Exhibit 18.10 summarizes the components and objectives of financial compensation plans.

In addition to financial compensation, sales managers (and management across the company) also incorporate a range of **nonfinancial incentives.** Most sales managers consider promotional opportunities second only to financial incentives as effective sales force motivators. This is particularly true for young,

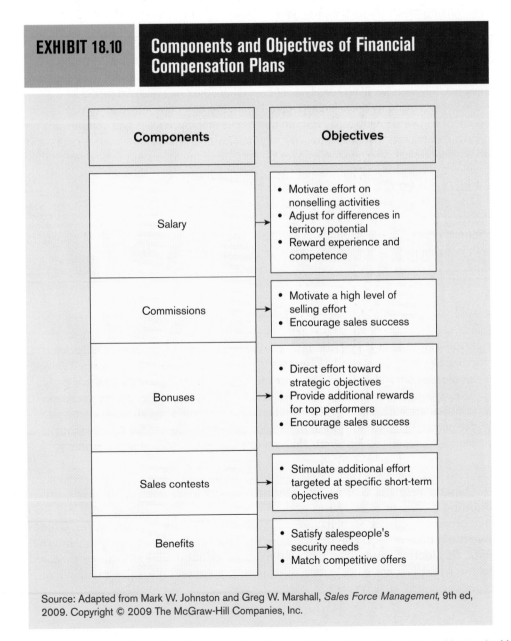

EXHIBIT 18.10	Components and Objectives of Financial Compensation Plans

Components	Objectives
Salary	• Motivate effort on nonselling activities • Adjust for differences in territory potential • Reward experience and competence
Commissions	• Motivate a high level of selling effort • Encourage sales success
Bonuses	• Direct effort toward strategic objectives • Provide additional rewards for top performers • Encourage sales success
Sales contests	• Stimulate additional effort targeted at specific short-term objectives
Benefits	• Satisfy salespeople's security needs • Match competitive offers

Source: Adapted from Mark W. Johnston and Greg W. Marshall, *Sales Force Management*, 9th ed, 2009. Copyright © 2009 The McGraw-Hill Companies, Inc.

well-educated salespeople who tend to view their sales position as a stepping-stone to a senior management position.

Evaluating Salesperson Performance

A fundamental issue is monitoring sales activity and evaluating salesperson performance. Salespeople should be evaluated solely on those elements of the sales process they control. To do this a company develops objective and subjective measures that distinguish between controllable and noncontrollable factors. The FYI highlights the challenges companies face in evaluating salesperson performance.

FYI

A recent study reported that less than 40 percent of employees believe their performance reviews actually help them do their jobs better. However, a number of companies are adopting new technologies and improved communication tools to improve the performance review. Aetna Insurance was experiencing significant problems across a number of key sales metrics including lower than expected revenue, higher levels of customer complaints, and corresponding lower customer satisfaction. Contributing to the problem was a feeling among salespeople that management did not evaluate them properly. They felt they were working hard but not being measured or evaluated properly.

To measure and evaluate salespeople better, the company introduced a new management software dashboard program that tracks employee skills and competency on critical dimensions, evaluates training needs, and charts individual career goals and objectives. Results are positive as over 80 percent of the salespeople now report they understand how they contribute to achieving the company's goals compared with only 59 percent in 2002.

The challenge for many companies is simply finding the right tools that not only measure the right information but also make it available in real time for managers. Programs such as Authoria (Aetna's software package) provide lower-level managers with valuable information that can then be shared with salespeople.[42]

Microsoft, long recognized as a performance-driven, measurement-focused company, has revamped its reward and performance evaluation system. While employees are still ranked on performance and long-term potential, the company no longer uses a forced curve to evaluate performance, which means employee bonuses are not subject to a curve (if an employee performs well, he or she gets the bonus no matter the ranking). The company also offers other perks including Mobile Medicine, which sends doctors to employee homes in an emergency.[43]

The end result is that many activities critical to long-term success such as building customer satisfaction go unmeasured. These other measures fall into two broad categories: (1) objective measures and (2) subjective measures. **Objective measures** reflect statistics the sales manager gathers from the firm's internal data. **Subjective measures** rely on personal evaluations by someone connected to the salesperson's sales process, usually the immediate sales manager or a customer. Objective measures fall into two major categories: (1) output measures and (2) input measures. **Output measures** show the results of the efforts expended by the salesperson while **input measures** focus on the efforts of salespeople during the sales process (see Exhibit 18.11).

DIRECT MARKETING

Chapter 16 discussed direct marketing in terms of its role in the distribution network; here the focus is on direct marketing as a promotional tool. Direct marketing is among the fastest-growing marketing communication methods. As defined by the Direct Marketing Association, **direct marketing** is an interactive marketing system that uses one or more advertising media to affect a measurable response and/or transaction at any location. The term *direct marketing* includes a number of communication channels: direct mail, catalogs, telemarketing, and Internet marketing. Historically, direct mail was the most widely used method; however, that has been replaced by the Internet.[44]

Creating a Direct Marketing Campaign

A direct marketing campaign encompasses a series of specific steps.

EXHIBIT 18.11	Examples of Output and Input Measures

Output Measures	Input Measures

• Orders
  • Number of orders
  • Average size of orders
  • Number of canceled orders
• Accounts
  • Number of active accounts
  • Number of new accounts
  • Number of lost accounts
  • Number of overdue accounts
  • Number of prospective accounts
	• Calls
	  • Total number of calls
	  • Number of planned calls
	  • Number of unplanned calls
	• Time and time utilization
	  • Days worked
	  • Calls per day (call rate)
	  • Selling time versus nonselling time
	• Expenses
	  • Total
	  • By type
	  • As a percentage of sales
	  • As a percentage of quota
	• Nonselling activities
	  • Letters to prospects
	  • Phone calls to prospects
	  • Number of formal proposals developed
	  • Advertising displays set up
	  • Number of meetings held with distributors/dealers
	  • Number of training sessions held with distributor/dealer personnel
	  • Number of calls on distributor/dealer customers
	  • Number of service calls made
	  • Number of overdue accounts collected

Source: Adapted from Mark W. Johnston and Greg W. Marshall, *Sales Force Management*, 9th ed., 2009. Copyright © 2009 The McGraw-Hill Companies, Inc.

Set Strategy for Campaign

As one element of a marketing communications strategy, the direct marketing campaign is incorporated into a broader promotional strategy. As part of that strategy, the direct marketing campaign should specify two criteria. First, what are the specific, quantifiable objectives? Direct marketing, unlike other marketing communications tools, can be measured, and it is important that marketing managers state objectives in specific, quantifiable terms. Second, marketing managers should identify the target market for the campaign and include demographic characteristics, lifestyle, and reasons direct marketing is an appropriate communications methodology for the market. At all times it is essential that the direct marketing campaign is consistent with and supports the overall marketing communications strategy.

Specify Direct Marketing Channels

A number of direct marketing channels are available to marketers. As a result, a key task for marketing managers is aligning the direct marketing strategy with the most effective direct marketing media based on the unique advantages and disadvantages of each one.

Identify Qualified Target Customers

Direct marketing, by nature, is more focused on specific customers than other nonpersonal communication media such as advertising or public relations. As a result, a critical step is to identify, qualify, and target a group of customers for the direct marketing campaign. There are primarily two sources of customers. The first is internally generated prospects that consist of prior customers or inquiries (through direct-mail campaigns or the company Web site). It is important to consider internal contacts first for two reasons. Internal names have demonstrated an interest in the company either through a purchase or inquiry. In addition, internally generated prospects are less expensive than the second customer source—external lists from outside vendors. List companies such as InfoUSA and Dun & Bradstreet specialize in developing and selling lists to direct marketers. In addition, companies sometimes make their customer lists available for purchase for a fee. Recently, however, Yahoo and others have been criticized for this practice.

Develop and Test the Offer for the Campaign

This is the basic element of a direct marketing campaign. Sophisticated database management programs enable companies to create specific offers for individual customers by matching customer information with the offer. One advantage of direct marketing is the ability to easily test alternative offer options. By targeting different individuals with unique offers, it is possible to quickly and accurately understand what messages are working well.

Analyze Results of Offer

Once the campaign is under way it is important to analyze the results. Analysis of the data can discover the revenue, cost, and overall profitability of each individual included in the campaign. No other marketing communications channel has that level of data for analysis.

Direct Marketing Channels

Direct marketing media accessible to marketing managers include direct mail, telemarketing, and e-mail. Other direct media do not allow for individual targeted communication but do enable the prospect to respond immediately; an example of this is television infomercials.

Direct Mail

Direct mail is one of the least expensive direct marketing channels with costs of $.75 to $2.00 per message, and despite frequent complaints about the amount of junk mail (totaling billions each year), it is still an effective channel for reaching targeted customers. Direct mail is much more effective in B2C than B2B markets because reaching the appropriate individual inside an organization is difficult.

Students, alumni, faculty, and staff are able to show their support for their university every time they make a credit-card purchase through the use of "affinity" cards. Financial institutions have long recognized the benefits of co-branding their credit cards with schools, universities, and other nonprofit organizations. Many schools receive millions of dollars in royalties each year for access to their database of potential credit-card users. At Virginia Tech, for example, 20,000 friends of the university have signed up for the VT affinity card through JPMorgan Chase.[45]

One drawback to direct mail is the low response rate. Since it is easily discarded or, if read, not acted upon, the average direct-mail response rate as reported by the Direct Marketing Association is only 2.77 percent. Put another way, a little more than 97 percent of the direct mail is not acted on, making it relatively inefficient.

Components in a Direct-Mail Offer The contents or elements in a direct-mail offer include:

- Outside envelope: The offer comes in an envelope that must get the prospect's attention. Colorful illustrations, a more "personal" address, and a unique envelope feature (size, color, shape) all contribute to the prospect opening the envelope.
- Sales collateral: The offer is conveyed in the sales material inside the envelope. Most often this includes a letter detailing the offer and a brochure that presents a more graphic presentation of the material.
- Contact information: The offer gives contact information in several places. It is also important to provide multiple contact opportunities—toll-free number, response card, and Web site. Companies have found mentioning discounts such as coupons in the direct mail and then posting them on the Web site increases response rates as prospects are moved to additional action. If a response card is included, then a postage-paid return envelope is also included in the packet of material.

Telemarketing

Telemarketing has come under a lot of criticism in recent years. As noted in Chapter 16, the National Do Not Call Registry, as well as state restrictions, severely limits "cold call" telemarketing calls. However, despite its negative reputation and high cost per contact ($1 to $3), research conducted by the Direct Marketing Association suggests telemarketing works; indeed, it had one of the highest response rates of any direct marketing channel—8.55 percent. The challenge for the telemarketer is to break through the negative initial reaction and make a personal connection with the customer. Creating a tailored sales presentation that adjusts to customer feedback is a significant advantage for telemarketers after they have established a relationship.

Successful telemarketing campaigns contain three essential elements. First, access to an accurate list of qualified prospects is very important. Research suggests a good list of prospects boosts the success rate by 60 percent. Second, the offer must persuade the prospect to act immediately. Enhancing the offer to encourage immediate action includes a lower price, discounts on shipping, added product features and benefits. In addition, the offer must convey a sense of exclusivity demonstrating that the product cannot be purchased anywhere else. Finally, the telemarketer must engage the prospect with the highest ethical standards. Given the negative perception of telemarketing and the frequent abuses of unwanted telephone solicitations, most people perceive a high degree of risk in purchasing over the phone. As a result, the telemarketer must offer, and stand behind, money-back guarantees as well as, when possible, nationally recognized brand names.

Catalogs

Catalog marketers use a variety of different types of catalogs including full-line catalogs, specialty catalogs designed for small customer groups, as well as B2B catalogs to target potential buyers. The average consumer catalog purchase is $150, and more than 70 percent of Americans use catalogs. Keys to success include useful lists of customers and prospects to target, precise inventory control to monitor costs and enhance customer satisfaction, and careful brand management to maintain the company's integrity and reputation.

Seamless integration with the company's Web site is indispensable as consumers interact with the company through many channels. For example, the process may begin when a consumer looks at a catalog then orders online, or they may see something online and then call the company.[46] Catalog marketers have expanded globally, taking advantage of the Internet to target customers in Asia and Europe. U.S. catalog companies L.L. Bean and Lands' End have found success, particularly in Japan. The FYI addresses the growth of catalogs despite the number of consumers moving to Internet shopping.

FYI

Outdoor gadgets seller, Smith & Hawken, has experienced explosive growth in its online business. Internet sales now account for over 25 percent of the company's annual $175 million sales. At the same time, sales from the company's catalogs have been declining and now represent less than 15 percent of total sales. Given the growth of online sales and the decline of catalog sales, a strong case could be made to discontinue the catalogs and focus on an online strategy. However, the company disagrees and plans to continue its long-established catalog strategy.

Smith &a Hawken management believes the catalog does more than generate sales. It is one of the most effective tools for building and reinforcing the company's relationship with the customer. In addition, the catalog is considered the single best promotional method for driving customers to the Internet. This view is shared by many retailers and has contributed to significant growth in the catalog business.

Catalogs are changing as companies refine their message and objectives. Smith & Hawken recently conducted a total redesign of their catalog, making it more colorful. The old style displayed page after page of product pictures while the new layout presents lifestyle stories that show the products being used and enjoyed by the target market. The same approach focusing on lifestyle stories using colorful pictures of people enjoying their products is carried into the Web site to present a coordinated message to customers.[47]

INTERACTIVE MARKETING

The Internet has redefined the relationship between companies and customers. In less than 15 years, it has established a powerful new communication channel. **Interactive marketing** is an Internet-driven relationship between companies, their brands, and customers. It enables customers to control information flow and encourages customer-company interaction as well as a higher level of customer service.[48] Even though it represents less than 20 percent of U.S. commerce and less than 10 percent of global business, the Internet and, more broadly, interactive electronic marketing are the future. In both B2C and B2B markets, electronic interactive channels are considered essential elements in an overall marketing communications strategy. Indeed, many companies including Procter & Gamble and General Motors are shifting communication budgets to Internet marketing and away from traditional communication channels, particularly network television.

Customers drive interactive marketing, controlling when, where, and how they interact. While companies expand access to information and explore new methods to facilitate the exchange process, customers define the relationship on their terms. The speed of this transformation has caught many companies by surprise. Finding what works, and equally important what doesn't work, on the Internet presents a number of challenges. For example, as customers become more connected to a company, their expectations about service and the customer-company relationship also increase. In addition, combining traditional marketing communications channels with online, interactive media has proven to be a challenge. Communicating with customers is faster using e-marketing media, which often creates a challenge coordinating online and traditional marketing messages. Ethical Dimension 18 discusses one interactive communication tool, the use of company sponsored Web bloggers to present information about a product, which has come under criticism for misrepresenting the nature of the relationship between company and blogger.

The Online Customer Interface

The company's Web site is the primary point of connection with the online customer. Customers visit a Web site to get information, ask questions, register complaints, develop a sense of community with other users, and purchase the product. As a result, it must do a number of things well. Performing the traditional role of retail storefront, the Web site conveys the company's value proposition to anyone that visits the site. Effective sites are able to draw new potential customers "inside" to check out the company's products and services.

At the same time, the Web site must service existing customers by providing access to customer service and information in an efficient and effective manner. Several researchers define the Web site interface on seven dimensions (see Exhibit 18.12).

Context

Context refers to the overall layout, design, and aesthetic appeal of the site. More and more, broadband and high-speed Internet has led to more graphics, video, and

EXHIBIT 18.12 **Summary of Seven Design Elements of the Customer Interface**

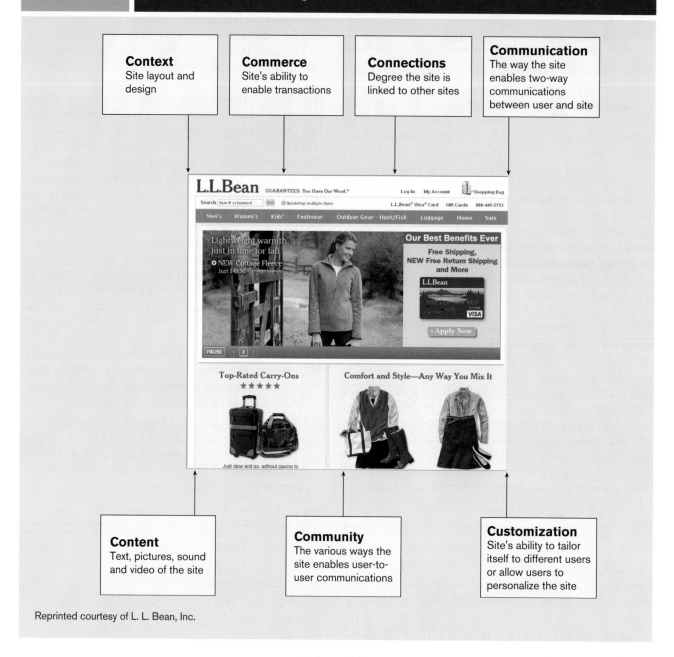

Context
Site layout and design

Commerce
Site's ability to enable transactions

Connections
Degree the site is linked to other sites

Communication
The way the site enables two-way communications between user and site

Content
Text, pictures, sound and video of the site

Community
The various ways the site enables user-to-user communications

Customization
Site's ability to tailor itself to different users or allow users to personalize the site

Reprinted courtesy of L. L. Bean, Inc.

interesting design features that make the Web site more appealing. The challenge for the Web designer is balancing the aesthetic appeal of high graphic content with the download time for graphics and other complex visual elements. The "look and feel" of the site must be consistent with the company or product's overall brand image. For example, visit the L.L. Bean Web site and then go to Lucky Brand jeans to see how different companies approach the layout and design of a Web site.

Content

In the 1990s companies put their existing print materials (catalogs, for example) on the Web site and there was little in the way of original Web content. Today, company Web sites incorporate a great deal of Web-specific content. Volkswagen created ads that ran only on its Web site, while Costco and Best Buy have a specific

Web strategy that displays products not available in stores. Text, photos, charts, and graphics are all part of Web content.

Community

A key advantage of interactive electronic marketing is the opportunity to create a community of users or visitors to the site. Blogs and company bulletin boards encourage a sense of community that enhances the customer's company and product experience. Companies are still learning how to effectively harness the power of community for their products. In many cases, the most powerful online communities have been established by third parties such as Kelly Blue Book, an auto industry site.

Customization

The ability to create a unique individual experience with a company Web site adds great value to the customer interface. Customers appreciate and expect customization of their Web site experience. Simple customization includes turning off the sound to the site and reducing the graphic interface (html versus flash sites). More customized sites enable customers to choose content and context. Yahoo, for example, allows users to create their own Yahoo experience defining the look and content of their Yahoo Web page.

Communication

The interactive electronic channel allows companies to communicate with customers in three ways. First, companies communicate to customers and visitors to the Web site one-on-one through e-mail. Second, customers and interested visitors communicate directly with the company via e-mail through customer service requests. Finally, companies use instant messaging for customer service requests and sales inquiries. Symantec software, for example, has representatives available online to walk customers through questions about service or products.

Connection

The Internet allows for communication among many sources. Information sites such as Edmunds.com (automobiles) and cnet.com (electronics) offer a lot of information at the site but also allow users to access company and retailer Web sites when they need more information or wish to make a purchase. This kind of connectivity greatly expands the usefulness of the site for the user.

Pairup is an online start-up with a unique focus, bringing people together who are headed to the same location for a trade show or conference. It's social networking with a twist. Business travelers upload relevant data on flight itinerary, conferences, or trade show information then wait to be notified through e-mail or desktop widget when the site locates a colleague or client that will be attending the same event. Salespeople and trade show executives believe the concept is a great way to connect a wide range of people.[50]

Commerce

The number of products purchased on the Internet has grown dramatically over the last five years. Some products, such as music, are now purchased primarily over the Internet either through retail sites such as Amazon or music download sites like iTunes. Web designers know that creating a simple, easy to understand, and secure purchase experience is essential for success in online commerce. Customers are still concerned with online purchase security; however, the convenience, pricing, and selection of the online purchase experience have led to significant growth in consumer online purchasing.

Online Advertising Decisions

The Internet offers companies a wide range of advertising options. Companies create sophisticated analysis programs that review an individual's Web traffic, how long people remain on the page, their Web browsing history, and many other characteristics to target specific ads. As a result, companies are changing their advertising strategies to include more interactive electronic media.

Banner ads are small boxes containing graphics and text and have a hyperlink embedded in them. Clicking on a banner ad will take you to the company's Web site. In a response similar to the reaction to telemarketing, there is a growing negative perception toward banner ads. While still prevalent throughout the Internet, the click-through rate is very low and companies have expanded to other forms of Internet advertising.

Search-related ads have shown the greatest growth in the last several years because 35 percent of all Internet searches are for products and services. Companies pay to be included on the page as the results of the search inquiry come up. Complex algorithms developed by Google, Yahoo, and others place ads based on an analysis of keywords. Advertisers pay based on the position of the ad on the search results page as well as the number of click-throughs. While the response rate is low, around 2 percent, the cost is also low (less than $.50 per click-through) compared to more than $1 per lead from an ad in the telephone directory.

Interstitials are more graphic, visually interesting ads that move across the Web page. As with banner ads, people find these ads distracting, and antivirus software from Norton, McAfee, as well as Windows enables users to block them.

High traffic Web sites sell **sponsorships** that enable companies to subsidize some section of Web page on the site. Edmunds.com offers a number of sponsorship opportunities. For example, as customers evaluate vehicles, they are made aware of a "premier dealer" in their area that is helping to sponsor the site.

Internet advertising is growing and there is no indication the demand is slowing. Costs are still low relative to other advertising channels such as television, and, since it is much more targeted and measured, advertisers appreciate the ability to know exactly how well their dollars are working on the Internet.

VIRAL MARKETING

More than a year before the release of *Batman: The Dark Knight,* Warner Bros. created a Web site featuring the fictional character, Harvey Dent, and his political campaign. As the campaign continued, other Web sites such as www.whysoserious.com were created to build interest, although visitors to the sites did not know, at first, the purpose of the sites. The Web sites generated a lot of traffic and over time, visitors realized it was part of the new Batman movie and, more specifically, "The Joker" character, played by deceased actor Heath Ledger, was revealed. With the death of Ledger, Warner Bros. adapted its campaign to offer fans the opportunity to mourn the death of the young star with a Web site to post comments and memorials.[51]

Interest in the movie was created not by spending money on traditional advertising tools such as print or television advertising. Rather, Warner Bros. used a technique called **viral marketing** to create buzz about a product using word of mouth or Internet social networks. The American Marketing Association defines viral marketing as a "marketing phenomenon that facilitates and encourages people to pass along a marketing message. Nicknamed viral because the number of people exposed to a message mimics the process of passing a virus or disease from one person to another."

Marketing managers have known how valuable strong word of mouth can be in a product's success. However, with the growth of social networking on the Internet and the ability of marketers to target individuals more carefully, it is now possible to create marketing communication campaigns that incorporate a word-of-mouth, one-on-one methodology.

Viral Marketing Guidelines

In many respects, successful viral marketing requires a very different approach to marketing communications than, for example, advertising or personal selling. When it works, it can be possible to connect the success of the viral marketing with sales success. One successful viral marketing effort was the Mentos-Diet Coke "geyser" ad, which showed the effect of dropping several Mentos in a bottle of Diet Coke. The Mentos ad generated 5 million views in three months. People viewing the ad were encouraged to participate in "Make your own Mentos geyser" competitions and the company distributed thousands of product samples. The result was a 20 percent sales increase, which it attributes to the ad. However, the link between a viral marketing campaign and sales is often not that easy to establish. Let's consider some guidelines.

Measuring Success

One of the biggest challenges marketing managers face in viral marketing is measurement. While it is certainly easy to know how many hits there are to a particular Web site, translating that into marketing metrics, such as higher unit sales, is more difficult. As a result, marketers often define broad goals for a viral campaign. Another viral campaign started by Mentos, the Mentos-intern, encourages Web site visitors to assign tasks to a 19-year-old student intern named, Trevor. Success for the campaign was not defined in terms of sales but "how well the campaign can integrate the idea of Mentos into pop culture." This more broadly defined goal may be appropriate since more defined metrics such as unit sales are difficult to identify.

Connect People to the Experience

One key to a successful campaign is enabling participants to be part of the experience. In the campaign for *Batman: The Dark Knight,* individuals were encouraged to take pictures of each other dressed as the "The Joker" and submit them to why-soserious.com. Giving people a reason to come back and become engaged connects people to the product.

Target a Younger Demographic

Viral marketing works well with a younger demographic and enables marketers to reach out to a different market segment. For example, Folgers's "Happy Morning" viral video campaign was a creative stretch for the company that has focused primarily on an older market segment. The video, a funny send-up on happy morning commercials, was widely distributed to video Web sites and represented Folgers' first significant attempt to reach younger audiences using a viral marketing strategy. The ability to target younger audiences without offending existing target markets that are not likely to be part of the same social networks gives companies the freedom to experiment.

SUMMARY

Companies understand that successful integrated marketing communications incorporates interactive, personal communication elements. The three personal communication methods most widely adopted are personal selling, direct marketing, and interactive marketing. Together these tools have the potential to connect the company with the customer as well as encourage the customer to interact with the company in ways that appreciably strengthen the relationship. Personal, interactive customer communication is important, and companies dedicate significant resources to ensure the quality of the company-customer communication relationship.

KEY TERMS

personal selling 505

adaptive selling 506

trade servicer 508

missionary salespeople 508

technical selling 508

key account salespeople 508

outbound telemarketing 509

inbound telemarketing 509

sales presentation 510

FAB (Features, Advantages, Benefits) 512

features 512

advantages 512

benefits 512

change conflict 512

closing the sale 513

follow-up 514

outsourcing the sales force 514

transactional cost analysis (TCA) 514

workload method 516

sales skill levels 519

motivation 519

extrinsic rewards 519

intrinsic rewards 519

salary 521

incentive pay 521

commission 521

nonfinancial incentives 521

objective measures 522

subjective measures 522

output measures 522

input measures 522

direct marketing 523

market space 526

banner ads 530

search-related ads 530

interstitials 530

sponsorships 530

viral marketing 530

APPLICATION QUESTIONS

1. You are the vice president of sales for a $30 million manufacturer of home building materials. The company employs 50 salespeople around the country to market the company's products to hardware stores and major building contractors. The CEO believes the company needs to cut costs and wants to reduce the sales force by 50 percent. You have been asked to come in and explain why that is a bad long-term strategy for the company. Discuss why salespeople are critical to the success of the company.

2. Identify three important personal characteristics that a key account salesperson for a global manufacturer of networking hardware would need to be successful. The company sells multimillion-dollar product solutions to telecommunications companies and *Fortune* 100 global organizations.

3. You are marketing manager for Sharp electronics and have been asked to create a sales brochure for a new Sharp Aquos 42-inch LCD TV. Pick one model and identify the features, advantages, and benefits for the product.

4. You are vice president of sales for a medium-sized technology firm and have been asked to design a new compensation package for the company's national sales force of 50 people. Currently, they are paid solely on commission with average compensation of $75,000 to $100,000. The CEO is concerned about customer service and wants the salespeople to focus more on servicing existing customers. What compensation plan would you suggest?

5. You are the marketing director for the local Red Cross chapter. Create a direct marketing campaign to generate money that is needed for a new building. What should be included in the direct marketing campaign?

MANAGEMENT DECISION CASE: Death of the Car Salesperson

Everyone is familiar with the dramatic changes in the automobile industry. The Big Three (GM, Ford, and Chrysler) have experienced significant market share declines to foreign manufacturers such as Honda, Toyota, and BMW. Even Toyota has been forced to discount vehicles to stimulate sales in light of recent economic turbulence.

The painful experiences of the past several years have been felt most by the local front-line retail sales force. Salespeople have seen their income drop by more than 30 percent from the late 1990s when it was not uncommon for car salespeople to make more than $100,000. One Toyota salesperson in Dallas reported his income dropped from $140,000 in 1999 to $94,000 in 2007 despite selling the same number of cars. What led to this decline in car sales commissions? First, online data and other sources such as *Consumer Reports* have educated consumers about the real price of a car. A key source of power for salespeople, namely knowledge of the car's actual cost, has been taken away. This means dealers have to offer greater discounts, with lower margins, than in the past. For example, a $20,000 car from one of the Big Three will have a markup of aproximately 9 percent, or $1,800. After overhead ($300) and the usual customer discount ($1,000) that leaves $500 profit for the dealer. Commissions generally run about 20 percent which returns $100 to the salesperson. Second, manufacturers, particularly the Big Three, have been lowering prices to better reflect the actual cost of the vehicle to the customer. This further reduces the opportunity for salespeople to make a larger commission.

It is perhaps not surprising to find many car salespeople leaving the car business or moving to more popular brands such as Toyota or BMW. Mike J. Jackson, CEO of AutoNation (one of the largest dealer networks in the United States), puts it this way, "I'm seeing a migration of capital and talent away from domestic dealerships that I have never seen before."

At least one vision of the car-buying experience in the future does not include salespeople. Customers would research and negotiate a final price online, then visit the dealer where a salaried customer service agent works out the financing arrangements and delivers the car. A more immediate reality suggests a downsizing of GM, Ford, and Chrysler dealerships, which account for 75 percent (approximately 15,750) of the nearly 21,000 dealerships in the United States. A natural result of a dealer shakeout would be fewer salespeople selling more cars and presumably making more money. Bill Heard Chevrolet, a string of dealerships in the South, closed all its stores in 2008 putting hundreds of salespeople out of work. Clearly, however, the future of the car salesperson is based on an answer to the question, What value do salespeople add to the car buying process? As we have seen in this chapter, there are excellent reasons for salespeople to be part of a company's integrated marketing communications program, but they must add value to the experience for the customer.[52]

Questions for Consideration

1. What role will traditional car salespeople play in the car buying experience of the future?

2. Salespeople offer a personal one-on-one experience for the customer; how should car dealers maintain that experience for the customer without increasing costs?

3. How would you as a car salesperson add value to a customer's purchase experience? A friend is interested in becoming a salesperson at a BMW dealership and asks your opinion, what would you tell your friend?

MARKETING PLAN EXERCISE

ACTIVITY 18: Building the Interpersonal Relationship

A critical component of your company's marketing communications is the interpersonal connection to the customer. Developing an effective interpersonal communications strategy is essential and can include: (1) sales force, (2) Web site, and (3) direct marketing. In this exercise, you will create an interpersonal communications strategy as part of the overall marketing communications plan. The following tasks are part of the strategy:

1. Review the overall marketing communications plan and determine the role of interpersonal marketing communications in communicating with target customers.

2. If personal selling is part of the marketing communications plan, create a sales strategy to include nature of sales force (company sales force or external sales team), sales structure, hiring/recruiting policies, and compensation program.

3. By this point in the marketing plan, you have already spent time considering an interactive Web strategy. Here you will develop the marketing communications element. Specific questions you should address include the following. What are the objectives of the interactive marketing communications program? How much and in what format will the company's products and services be presented

on the Web site? What action do you want someone visiting the Web site to take after viewing the marketing communications?

4. Determine the level of direct marketing for the company. Specifically, define the role of direct marketing in the overall marketing communications plan. Next, identify specific objectives for the direct marketing effort. Finally, create a direct marketing campaign and follow-up plan.

If you are using Marketing Plan Pro, a template for this assignment can be accessed at www.mhhe.com/marshall1e.

RECOMMENDED READINGS

1. Mark W. Johnston and Greg W. Marshall, *Relationship Selling,* 2nd ed. (New York: McGraw-Hill, 2008).

2. Mark W. Johnston and Greg W. Marshall, *Sales Force Management,* 9th ed. (New York: McGraw-Hill, 2009).

3. John DeVincentis, *Rethinking the Sales Force: Redefining Selling to Create and Capture Customer Value* (New York: McGraw-Hill, 1999).

4. Howard Stevens and Theodore Kinni, *Achieve Sales Excellence: The 7 Customer Rules for Becoming the New Sales Professional* (La Crosse, WI: Platinum Press, 2006).

5. David Meerman Scott, *The New Rules of Marketing and PR: How to Use News Releases, Blogs, Podcasting, Viral Marketing, and Online Media to Reach Buyers Directly* (Hoboken, NJ: Wiley, 2007).

6. Chet Meisner; *The Complete Guide to Direct Marketing: Creating Breakthrough Programs that Work* (New York: Kaplan, 2006).

CHAPTER 19

THE MARKETING DASHBOARD: METRICS FOR MEASURING MARKETING PERFORMANCE

LEARNING OBJECTIVES

- Understand the concept of a marketing dashboard and how it improves marketing planning for a firm.

- Explain return on marketing investment (ROMI), including cautions about its use.

- Identify other relevant marketing metrics and how they are applied.

- Develop detailed action plans in support of the overall marketing plan.

- Decide on an appropriate combination of forecasting approaches.

- Prepare a marketing budget.

- Provide controls and contingency plans.

- Conduct a marketing audit.

Executive Rick Rotondo, Chief Marketing Officer

Company Spectrum Bridge Inc.

Business Telecommunications

In years past, marketers got a bit of a "pass" on measuring the success of their activities versus other business functions. Why has this changed today?

First and foremost, everyone is figuring out that the world is *flat!* That is, competition is coming from all directions and there are several low-cost producers out there ready to take your customers. Businesses today have to make every dollar count. Second, your marketing budget is competing for dollars that could just as easily be spent by engineering, customer support, or R&D departments.

Shareholders and senior management want—and in some cases have the obligation—to see the ROI from the dollars they allocate. Remember that resources are finite; resources can and should be shifted to where they deliver the biggest payback. As a marketing professional, you should be proactively evaluating your marketing efforts and campaigns to make sure they are delivering the "best bang for the buck." If you wait until someone else asks you to do it, you're not doing your job as well as you should.

In your view, what types of metrics are most relevant nowadays in assessing marketing's performance?

There are many ways to measure success and effectiveness in marketing. Which ones you choose will depend on what type of product you are selling, your channels to market, your target audience, and your branding objectives.

Because the Web is an essential tool for marketing just about every type of product and service, metrics like unique page visits, click-throughs, and completed checkouts are good measures. More traditional measures like press mentions, analyst rankings, and speaking engagements are also common. The best metrics I have found, however, can come from your own sales force or market channels. These people will tell you if you are reaching the right audience with the right messages. They will know if you are outpositioning the competition and getting top-of-mind with buyers, and they are more than willing to say whether your firm's collateral, presentation, and competitive analysis are hitting the mark. In short, "sales force or channel happiness" is a key metric of your success.

Is it possible that the measurement of marketing's contribution to performance can be taken too far? After all, isn't marketing an art along with a science?

Sure it's possible; in fact, I've seen it many times. Management can get so caught up in the process of measurement that you may end up measuring the wrong things. Metrics that were once relevant but no longer have meaning are still used.

Metrics for one product or business sometimes are force-fit into a completely different business, market, or channel. However, to claim that the "Art of Marketing" cannot be measured is a cop-out! There are many quantitative and qualitative ways of tracking the effectiveness of marketing.

Keep in mind that it's OK if some of your new or innovative ideas don't get the results you want. It's also OK (in fact, I would say mandatory) to fail once in a while. That's how you know you're stretching your marketing muscles. Feedback and measurements can help you course-correct or even kill a program that's gone too far off the rails to salvage. They will also help you learn and do better next time—and that's how you become the best and most sought after marketing talent in the company.

THE MARKETING DASHBOARD

Consider how a dashboard of a car, airplane, or even a video game provides you with a lot of crucial information in real time and in a convenient format. So it should be with a **marketing dashboard,** which is a comprehensive system providing managers with up-to-the-minute information necessary to run their operation including data on actual sales versus forecast, progress on marketing plan objectives, distribution channel effectiveness, sales force productivity, brand equity evolution, and whatever metrics and information are uniquely relevant to the role of the marketing manager in a particular organization.[1] Clearly, a dashboard metaphor for this process of capturing, shaping, and improving marketing effectiveness and efficiency is a good one.[2]

Marketing is vital to the corporation and touches many aspects of a company's operations. Therefore, good metrics programs consider how marketing links to other disciplines of the company and help executives unite all the disciplines to support business goals. VF Corporation, for example, has a multidisciplinary metrics program that has helped alter the apparel company's perception of the value of marketing and how it can be used to grow a brand. Stephen Dull, vice president for strategy, explained: "For us, it is less about how to measure and more about how to interpret and bring multiple disciplines together to drive business decisions. By doing this, we have been able to avoid the 'tyranny of one voice' and make better business decisions."[3]

How does a marketing dashboard manifest itself? It could appear in your inbox weekly or monthly in the form of a color printout, be beamed through cyberspace as e-mail updates, or be accessible on a password-protected Web site on your company intranet. Its physical form and layout should be developed within your organization *by* managers *for* managers. Search the Internet for "Marketing Dashboards" and you will be amazed at how many consulting firms come up, each working hard to convince you that its proprietary approach to a marketing dashboard is the right one for you. To successfully compete in today's market, firms must focus on marketing planning so that managers and executives have the core information about progress toward relevant goals and metrics at their fingertips *at all times.* This is what a dashboard approach delivers.

A marketing dashboard approach to enhance marketing planning delivers five key benefits summarized in Exhibit 19.1.

Goals and Elements of a Marketing Dashboard

An effective dashboard is organic, not static. The dashboard must adapt and change with the organization as objectives are clarified and redefined, as causal relationships are established between metrics and results, and as confidence in predictive measures grows. About the only thing you know for certain about your first version of a marketing dashboard is that it will likely look very different in a year or two.

Two primary goals of any dashboard are diagnostic insight and predictive foresight—with a special emphasis on the latter. Some dashboard metrics are diagnostic, looking at what has happened and trying to discern why. Probably the most important metrics you'll come to rely on, however, are predictive, using the diagnostic experience to better forecast results under various assumptions of circumstances and resource allocations.[4]

A great marketing dashboard is comprised of the nine elements described in Exhibit 19.2.

---

[1]A number of concepts in this section are derived from the following outstanding book, which is the best single source for understanding marketing dashboards. It is highly recommended as a guidebook on the topic for marketing managers: Patrick LaPointe, *Marketing by the Dashboard Light: How to Get More Insight, Foresight, and Accountability from Your Marketing Investments,* New York: ANA, 2005.

1. **Alignment of Marketing with the Firm**
   A marketing dashboard aligns marketing objectives with the company's financial objectives and corporate strategy through the selection of critical metrics and sharing of results.

2. **Development of Internal Relationships with Marketing**
   The marketing dashboard not only creates organizational alignment *within* marketing by linking all expenditures back to a smaller set of focused objectives, but it also clarifies the relationships *between* marketing and other organizational areas. It crystallizes roles and responsibilities to ensure everyone understands the inherent interdependencies. The result of all this alignment fosters greater job satisfaction within a culture of performance and success.

3. **Establishment of Direct Links between Marketing Spending and Profits**
   A dashboard uses graphical representations of crucial metrics in ways that begin to show, often for the first time, the causal relationships between marketing initiatives and financial results. It portrays historical data in a fashion that makes it easier for any manager to grasp and understand the implications. The result is a greater ability to make smart resource allocations and increase both the efficiency and effectiveness of marketing spending.

4. **Facilitation of Smoother Decision Making**
   A marketing dashboard fosters a learning organization whose members make decisions based on hard facts, creativity, and experiential intuition, rather than as a result of battles based on pure subjectivity. The real benefit of this evolution to a culture of "everyone has the information" is a dramatic reduction in time spent in highly politicized arguments, which greatly speeds decision making in organizations.

5. **Enhancement of Marketing's Ability to Contribute**
   A dashboard creates transparency in marketing's goals, operations, and performance, creating stronger alliances between marketing and the rest of the firm. This elevates marketing's perceived accountability, earning greater trust and confidence from the CEO, CFO, board, and other key decision makers and influencers.

Source: Patrick LaPointe, *Marketing by the Dashboard Light: How to Get More Insight, Foresight, and Accountability from Your Marketing Investments* (New York: ANA, 2005). Courtesy of Marketing NPV LLC © 2003–2008. All rights reserved.

Sometimes standard marketing metrics can overshadow other important metrics, like customer service. Curt Tueffert, regional sales vice president of the Gulf Coast region for DXP Enterprises Inc., a Houston-based distributor, believes it's important to have data to measure your level of service. And getting that data can be as easy as asking a few simple questions. "Most people want to provide feedback if asked," he says. "In our high-tech, Web world, it would be easy to go to a Web site and complete a short survey, or have a place to go to submit comments and feedback 24/7."[5]

Potential Pitfalls in Marketing Dashboards

Although taking a dashboard approach to marketing metrics goes a long way toward enabling successful marketing planning, several potential pitfalls exist in its execution, including the following:

- *Overreliance on "inside-out" measurement.* Having too many internal measures puts the focus on what you already know instead of on the unpredictably dynamic external marketplace. A focus on monitoring external factors likely to cause significant changes to the marketing plan is what makes a dashboard especially valuable.

- *Too many tactical metrics; not enough strategic insight.* Because of the focus over the past decade on holding marketing accountable for financial

EXHIBIT 19.2   Elements of Great Marketing Dashboards

1. Goals and Objectives

These are the goals of the company, translated into a set of marketing objectives. All ideas, initiatives, and metrics should be considered in light of these.

2. Initiative ROI and Resource Allocation

An important part of a marketing dashboard is measuring the incremental cash flows generated by marketing programs and action plans in the short term. In addition, the dashboard is an excellent tool to measure the efficiency of resource allocation in dollars, customers, or other appropriate units.

3. Brand and Customer Asset Evolution

At least equal to the short-term results is the longer-term evolution of the corporate assets entrusted to marketing. As you have learned, key marketing assets often include the brand and customer perceptions and relationships. The dashboard can provide a read of how the assets have been growing and how they are likely to progress.

4. Skills

A well-rounded dashboard tracks the skills and competencies of the marketing team against a clear set of proficiency goals.

5. Process

The dashboard also provides insight into the execution of critical business processes requ-ired to deliver on the desired customer value propositions.

6. Tools

Less a metric than an enabler of marketing planning success, successful dashboards employ and continuously refine tools to increase insight and reduce effort in both production and distribution.

7. Diagnostic Insight

The dashboard must push beyond portrayal of *what* is happening to explain *why* it is happening, providing insight into where expectations were inaccurate and helping hone the process of setting expectations and forecasts for the future.

8. Predictive Value

The difference between a helpful dashboard and a truly effective one is the degree to which it uses the diagnostic insight and predicts what is *likely* to happen on critical performance dimensions that have been identified.

9. Efficiency and Effectiveness

The end goal is the enhancement of both the efficiency and the effectiveness of marketing investments, thereby improving return on marketing investment (ROMI).

Source: Patrick LaPointe, *Marketing by the Dashboard Light: How to Get More Insight, Foresight, and Accountability from Your Marketing Investments* (New York: ANA, 2005). Courtesy of Marketing NPV LLC © 2003–2008. All rights reserved.

results, tactical, or "intermediary," metrics have proliferated. Numerous books and articles provide list after list of calculations and ratios to assess all sorts of marketing programmatic results (brand awareness, customer trial, lead conversion, etc.). Although these are valuable and having the right set of intermediary metrics on the dashboard is important, it is critical that they do not overshadow measures of strategic importance to the firm.

- *Forgetting to market the dashboard internally.* One measure of the success of a marketing dashboard is the level at which it is embraced and *used* by managers and executives throughout the firm. As we've emphasized consistently, marketing is not just a department, but rather a part of the strategic and cultural fabric of the enterprise. As such, it is important to market the dashboard internally to key stakeholders, not just to marketers. You want the percentage of senior executives who both believe in and understand what the dashboard is presenting to be very high. Obviously, the CEO should be a target for internal marketing, but just as important is your CFO. The greater the affinity a CFO has for marketing and especially for marketing as a contributor to the firm's long-term success the better.[6]

Toward Your Own Marketing Dashboard

The goals of the remainder of this chapter are somewhat different from the other chapters so far. Here, ideas and resources have been gathered to enhance the measurement side of the marketing planning process you have learned throughout the book, especially to aid in a marketing plan project if you are working on one for the course. Here you will learn about return on marketing investment (ROMI) and will be exposed to a sampling of other marketing metrics for your consideration. We then introduce action plans, forecasting, budgets, controls and contingency planning, and the marketing audit as important tools to enhance marketing planning. Any or all of these elements can be an integral part of, or a key informational input to, your own marketing dashboard that you can develop when you leave this course.

Peter Worster, planning director at creative agency Presky Maves, believes there are a wide range of assessment tools in addition to ROI that advertisers can use to demonstrate the value of a marketing campaign. Companies often measure campaigns through response, conversion, sales, and cost per sale, but other metrics are also important. Speaking the language of business—using terms such as ROI and profitability rather than just the traditional language of marketing—can pay off. Worster gave the example of a customer management program that Presky Maves ran for single malt Scotch whisky Glenfiddich. In addition to all the usual analysis, the agency tracked voucher redemption and profitability and measured things such as engagement in the program by looking at brand preference.[7]

RETURN ON MARKETING INVESTMENT (ROMI)

CEOs today expect to know exactly what impact an investment in marketing has on a firm's success, especially financially. Hence, it has become critical to consider **return on marketing investment (ROMI).**[8] Throughout this book we have focused on marketing as an *investment*, not as an expense, because a goal-driven investment approach to marketing maximizes the opportunity for a firm's offerings to reach their full potential in the marketplace. The alternative viewpoint—approaching marketing as an expense tied to a percentage of historical or forecasted sales—both limits market opportunities and thwarts the ability to meaningfully plan for and measure marketing results.[9]

Similar to other investment decisions, investment decisions in marketing must consider four basic elements:

- Level of investment.
- Returns.
- Risks.
- Hurdle rates.

As with any investment, the projected results (returns minus costs) must exceed a certain investment hurdle rate for a given level of risk (both defined by the firm). Hence, ROMI represents either the revenue or the margin generated by a marketing program divided by the cost of that program at a given risk level. The ROMI hurdle rate is defined as the minimum acceptable, expected return on a program at a given level of risk. Consider an example of a relatively low-risk marketing program with costs of $1 million and new revenue generated of $5 million. This program has a ROMI of 5.0. If the company has a marketing budget of $5 million and needs to generate $20 million in revenue, then the ROMI hurdle rate for any

---

[8]The single best source for understanding ROMI is the following book, which is highly recommended for marketing managers: Guy R. Powell, *Return on Marketing Investment: Demand More from Your Marketing and Sales Investments,* Albuquerque, NM: RPI Press, 2002. The ideas in this section are drawn from this source.

low-risk marketing program is 4.0. This means that any marketing program must generate at a minimum $4.00 in revenue for every $1.00 in marketing expenditure. The example ROMI of 5.0 above surpasses the ROMI hurdle rate and is therefore an acceptable marketing program.[10]

Companies have to set their own hurdle rates based on differing levels of potential risk across marketing programs. Risk also tends to vary quite a bit by industry and by whether the marketing plan involves a start-up or an established product line. At its core, ROMI is a tool to help yield more out of marketing. This tool and the way of thinking promoted by the use of the tool within an organization will help marketing managers better conceptualize and execute marketing plans and programs. It puts them in a much better position to connect their planning, measurement, and results to the firm's goals and expectations and, when successful, provides gravitas for the CMO to go back to the CEO for more investment money for marketing.

Cautions about Overreliance on ROMI

Given the above, it's no wonder that ROMI is the *metric du jour* for many firms' marketing bottom line. Several offshoots of ROMI have been developed that apply the same principles to customers (ROCI), brands (ROBI), and promotion (ROPI).[11] Overall, the trend in boardrooms and executive suites of expecting more quantification of marketing's contributions has been a positive one. But remember that within the marketing dashboard concept, what organizations should be reviewing is an *array of relevant metrics,* selected for inclusion on the dashboard because together they paint a picture of firm performance. Managers should always temper the interpretation of ROMI results with review of other appropriate metrics.

In addition, it is important to remember that ROMI was originally designed for comparing capital projects, where investments are made once and the returns flow in during the periods that follow. In marketing, capital projects are analogous to discrete marketing programs or campaigns that have well-defined goals and clear points of beginning and end. However, in practice, ROMI is often applied in situations that have no clear beginning or end. Here are six other commonly expressed objections about an overreliance on ROMI:

1. While a firm may "talk the talk" of marketing as an investment, not an expense, typically marketing expenditures are not treated as an investment in a company's accounting system.

2. ROMI requires the profit to be divided by expenditure, yet all other bottom-line performance measures consider profit or cash flow *after* deducting expenditures.

3. The truth is, ROMI is maximized during the period when profits are still growing. Pursuit of ROMI during flat periods can be viewed as "causing" underperformance and suboptimal levels of activity, thus firms tend to reduce marketing reinvestment at that time in an attempt to maximize profits and cash flow. The result is a self-fulfilling prophecy of downward performance.

4. Calculating ROMI requires knowing what would have happened if the incremental expenditure hadn't occurred. Few marketers have those figures or can conjure something meaningful up to replace them.

5. ROMI has become a fashionable surrogate for "marketing productivity" in executive suites and boardrooms, yet there is mounting evidence that firms interpret the appropriate calculation of ROMI quite differently. When executives discuss ROMI with different metrics in mind, confusion results and the value of the metric degrades.

6. ROMI by nature ignores the effect of the marketing assets of the firm (for example, its brands) and tends to lead managers toward a more short-term decision perspective. That is, it typically considers only short-term incremental profits and expenditures without looking at longer-term effects or any change in brand equity.[12]

Proceed with Caution

The expectation is that ROMI and other metrics of marketing performance will continue to proliferate, as firms home in on attempting to better quantify marketing's contribution to various dimensions of organizational success. Marketing managers should embrace the opportunity to quantify their contributions, and by taking a more holistic dashboard approach to goal-driven measurement, the potential downsides to focusing on one or a few metrics are largely mitigated.

In the end, marketing management is both a science and an art. The scientific side craves quantification and relishes the ability to provide numeric evidence of success to superiors in a firm and to stockholders. But the artistic side understands that sometimes the difference between an average new-product introduction and a world-class one rests largely on creativity, insight, and the good fortune to have a great idea that is hitting the market at just the right time.

An interesting question, given the current focus in business toward sustainability and socially responsible business practices, is how would metrics related to such aspects (say for example, ROSI, or return on social investment) operate in tandem with other more traditional performance measures? Ethical Dimension 19 provides some insights into this important issue.

Sainsbury's Supermarkets are famous for combining a successful bottom line with a strong sense of social responsibility. The company even has a tagline "Make the Difference Today."

A SAMPLING OF OTHER MARKETING METRICS

This section provides a mix of metrics for your consideration. Because a variety of excellent books exist that provide hundreds of potential metrics for assessing the gamut of marketing planning activities, we provide only a sampling here. In the Recommended Readings section at the end of the chapter, you will find additional resources for seeking out marketing metrics. Throughout the following section these symbols are used: $ = a monetary figure; % = a percentage figure; # = a figure in units; I = an index figure, such as a comparative or average, often interpreted as a percentage.[13]

Cisco is well-known for the computer networking products it sells. Theresa Kushner, of Cisco Systems, believes that in today's world "interruptive marketing"—that is, ads that interrupt the TV or radio program the consumer is enjoying or the Web page they are reading—are becoming less effective. Instead, companies need to expand their marketing mix beyond traditional media. "As marketers, we need to be ready to engage the customer whenever and wherever the customer wants," Kushner says. The metrics used also need to change. In an interactive marketing world, "response rate" may no longer be valid. That is, what qualifies as a "response"? Instead, Kushner says, "The measurements we need to concentrate on are those that show the progression of the contact throughout the buying cycle. Response may no longer be relevant."[14]

---

[13] In this section, the example formulas and descriptions are selected from the following outstanding treatise on marketing metrics, which is a must-have book for marketing managers: Paul W. Farris, Neil T. Bendle, Philip E. Pfeifer, and David J. Reibstein, *Marketing Metrics: 50+ Metrics Every Executive Should Master,* Upper Saddle River, NJ: Wharton School Publishing, 2006.

When the Bottom Line Is Profit *and* Social Responsibility

A new kind of company is emerging that encompasses both profitability and social responsibility in its business model, creating not just one bottom line but two. These hybrid companies, founded by entrepreneurs who are focused as much on doing the right thing as on making a profit, are redefining traditional metrics for success. On the surface, the "do the right thing" and "maximize profit" models might seem to be incompatible, which can create challenges for entrepreneurs looking for funding.

Socially responsible companies today operate in a wide variety of industries and can include environmentally sensitive consumer products companies, organic grocers, fair trade coffee producers, and many others. These firms are often started after the founder is already committed to a social agenda. That is, the company is the tool by which the founder achieves a targeted social objective (better environment, better working conditions for the poor, etc.). Applying a socially responsible agenda frequently increases costs and suggests companies that want to follow a two bottom-line business model need to do business at the premium end of their market or else be relegated to lower expected margins. Melinda Olson, founder of Earth Mama Angel Baby, a manufacturer of premium natural products for young mothers and babies, believes that her gross margins are 12 to 15 percent lower than her competitors' (if she priced at parity).

In addition, if a company is really going to be socially responsible it must "walk the talk." This includes using energy-friendly products and paying living wage rates to employees. While all the choices may be the right thing to do, collectively they add to the cost of running the business.

A significant challenge for entrepreneurs desiring to develop a two bottom-line business model is finding investors who understand and are willing to support such a goal. Most investors are looking for the ROI not the ROSI (return on social investment). As a result, many of these organizations are underfunded and fail. Another challenge is how to measure success. Investors and managers all understand traditional success metrics such as profitability, ROI, and market share. However, when the bottom line also includes a company's social responsibility, the relevant success metrics become more difficult to determine.[15]

Ethical Perspective

1. **Investors:** Should investors be concerned only with a company's profitability? What metrics might an investor use to measure the social responsibility success of a company?

2. **Entrepreneurs:** Is a two bottom-line business model realistic in the long term? Is it sustainable?

3. **You:** Would you invest in a company with a two bottom-line strategy (profitability and social responsibility)?

Market Share

Definition: The percentage of a market (defined in terms of units or revenue) accounted for by a specific product, product line, or brand.

- Unit Market Share (%) = Unit Sales (#) ÷ Estimated Total Market Unit Sales (#)
- Revenue Market Share (%) = Sales Revenue ($) ÷ Estimated Total Market Revenue ($)

Marketers need to be able to translate sales forecasts into the context of market share, which will provide evidence if forecasts are to be attained by growing with the market or by capturing share from competitors. The latter will almost always be more difficult to achieve. Market share is closely monitored for signs of change in the competitive landscape, and it frequently influences strategic or tactical marketing planning. Importantly, market share is highly dependent on how the manager defines his or her market.[16] For example, Diet Coke would report varying market share numbers depending on whether it is comparing itself to all beverages, all carbonated beverages, or diet sodas.

Penetration

Definition: A measure of brand or category popularity. It is defined as the number of people who buy a specific brand or category of goods at least once in a given time period, divided by the size of the relevant market population.

- Market Penetration (%) = Customers Who Have Purchased a Product in the Category (#) ÷ Total Population (#)
- Brand Penetration (%) = Customers Who Have Purchased the Brand (#) ÷ Total Population (#)
- Penetration Share Formula 1 (%) = Brand Penetration (%) ÷ Market Penetration (%)
- Penetration Share Formula 2 (%) = Customers Who Have Purchased the Brand (#) ÷ Customers Who Have Purchased a Product in the Category (#)

Often, marketing managers must decide whether to seek sales growth by acquiring existing category users from their competitors or by expanding the total population of category users, attracting new customers to the market. Penetration metrics help indicate which of these strategies would be most appropriate and also help monitor the success of the strategy.[17]

For established brand-name merchants, Internet visitor-to-customer conversion rates should be 5 percent plus an adjustment upward or downward based on category, price points, and competition. For example, QVC is estimated to have a conversion rate of roughly 6 percent, L.L. Bean 8 percent, and Williams-Sonoma 10 percent.[18]

Margin on Sales

Definition: The difference between selling price and cost. This difference is typically expressed either as a percentage of selling price or on a per-unit basis.

- Unit Margin ($) = Selling Price per Unit ($) − Cost per Unit ($)
- Margin (%) = Unit Margin ($) ÷ Selling Price per Unit ($)

Marketing managers need to know margins for almost all decisions. Margins represent a key factor in pricing, ROMI, earnings forecasts, and analyses of customer profitability.[19]

Cannibalization Rate

Definition: Cannibalization is the reduction in sales (units or dollars) of a firm's existing products due to the introduction of a new product. The cannibalization rate is generally calculated as the percentage of a new product's sales that represents a loss of sales (attributable to the introduction of the new entrant) by a specific existing product or products.

- Cannibalization Rate (%) = Sales Lost from Existing Products (# or $) ÷ Sales of New Product (# or $)

Cannibalization rates represent an important factor in the assessment of new-product strategies, since how robbing some of the sales of Brand X by introducing Brand Y impacts overall sales must be considered in the financial projections for the introduction.[20]

Customer Lifetime Value (CLV)

Definition: The dollar value of a customer relationship based on the present value of the projected future cash flows from the customer relationship. When margins and retention rates are constant, the following formula can be used to calculate CLV:

- CLV ($) = Margin ($) X (Retention Rate [%] ÷ 1 + Discount Rate [%] − Retention Rate [%])

Present value is the discounted sum of future cash flows. The discount rate is usually set at a corporate level, with the goal of compensating for the time value of money and the inherent risk of the particular activity. Generally, the riskier the project, the greater the discount rate to use. Techniques for setting discount rates are beyond the scope of this chapter. Suffice it to say that separate discount rates are appropriate on a by-project basis because the risk varies. A government contract might be a fairly certain project compared to a handshake agreement with a private client.[21]

Overall, CLV is an important concept in that it encourages firms to shift their focus from quarterly profits to the long-term health of their customer relationships. CLV is an important number because it represents an upper limit on spending to acquire new customers.[22]

Sales Force Effectiveness

Definition: By analyzing sales force performance, marketing managers can make changes to optimize sales going forward. Toward that end, there are a number of ways (beyond just sales volume) to gauge the performance of individual salespeople and of the sales force as a whole.[23] Among the sales force effectiveness (SFE) ratios are the following:

- SFE = Sales ($) ÷ Contacts with Clients (Number of Calls) (#)
- SFE = Sales ($) ÷ Potential Accounts (#)
- SFE = Sales ($) ÷ Active Accounts (#)
- SFE = Sales ($) ÷ Customer Buying Power ($)
- SFE = Selling Expenses ($) ÷ Sales ($)

Supply Chain Metrics

Definition: Measures of important indicators of a firm's success in its supply chain.

- Stock-Outs (%) = Outlets Where Brand or Product is Listed but Unavailable (#) ÷ Total Outlets Where Brand or Product is Listed (#)
- Service Level Re: On-Time Delivery (%) = Deliveries Achieved in Time Frame Promised (#) ÷ All Deliveries Initiated in the Period (#)
- Inventory Turns (I) = Product Revenues ($) ÷ Average Inventory (#)

Supply chain tracking helps ensure that companies are meeting demand efficiently and effectively.[24]

Promotions and Pass-Through

Definition: Of the promotional value provided by a manufacturer to its distributors and retailers (often referred to as "the trade"), the pass-through percentage represents the portion that ultimately reaches the end-user consumer.

- Percentage of Sales on Deal (%) = Sales with Any Temporary Discount ($ or #) ÷ Total Sales ($ or #)

- Pass-Through (%) = Value of Temporary Promotional Discounts Provided to End-User Consumers by the Trade ($) ÷ Value of Temporary Discounts Provided to the Trade by the Manufacturer ($)

Manufacturers offer many discounts to the trade with the objective of encouraging them to offer their own promotions, in turn, to their customers. If trade customers or end-user consumers do not find promotions attractive, this will be indicated by a decline in the percentage of sales on a deal. Likewise, low pass-through percentages can indicate that too many deals, or the wrong kinds of deals, are being offered.[25]

Cost per Thousand Impressions (CPM) Rates

Definition: The cost per thousand advertising impressions. This metric is calculated by dividing the cost of an advertising placement by the number of impressions (expressed in thousands) that it generates.

- CPM = Cost of Advertising ($) ÷ Impressions Generated (# in thousands)

CPM is useful in comparing the relative efficiency of different advertising opportunities or media and in evaluating the costs of overall campaigns.[26]

Share of Voice

Definition: Quantifies the advertising "presence" that a specific product or brand enjoys. It is calculated by dividing the brand's advertising by total market advertising, and it is expressed as a percentage.

- Share of Voice (%) = Brand Advertising ($ or #) ÷ Total Market Advertising ($ or #)

For purposes of share of voice, there are at least two ways to measure "advertising": (1) in terms of dollar spending, or (2) in unit terms, through impressions or gross rating points (GRPs). By any of these measures, share of voice represents an estimate of a company's advertising as compared to that of its competitors.[27]

Click-Through Rates

Definition: The percentage of impressions that leads a user to click on an online ad. It describes the fraction of impressions that motivate users to click on a link, causing a redirect to another Web location.

- Click-Through Rate (%) = Click-Throughs (#) ÷ Impressions (#)

Most Internet-based businesses use click-through metrics. Although these metrics are useful, they should not dominate all online marketing analysis. Unless a user clicks on a "Buy Now" button, click-throughs measure only one step along the path toward a final sale.[28]

Online advertising, such as that offered by Yahoo.com, provides unparalleled opportunities for measuring marketing's success. Measurements of click-through and conversion help Yahoo and advertisers reduce the percentage of unwanted and irrelevant ads displayed online. Yahoo carefully selects which ads to display to users of the search engine, sometimes even picking low-revenue ads that Yahoo thinks will be more relevant. The true measure of Yahoo's success is its finding that searchers are now clicking more often on the ads than on the free search results.[29]

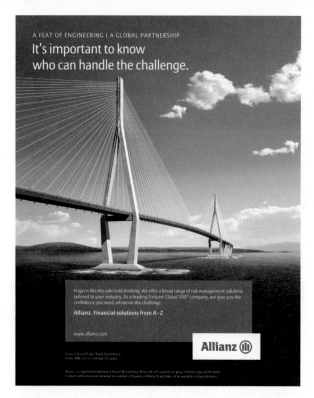

A FEAT OF ENGINEERING | A GLOBAL PARTNERSHIP

It's important to know who can handle the challenge.

Projects like this take bold thinking. We offer a broad range of risk management solutions tailored to your industry. As a leading Fortune Global 500® company, we give you the confidence you need, whatever the challenge.

Allianz. Financial solutions from A–Z

www.allianz.com

Allianz ⑪

The phrase Allianz uses that "projects like this take bold thinking" translates well to the process of developing and executing action plans in marketing.

Allianz SE, Germany. Photo: AMEC/Incheon Bridge Company.

DEVELOPING EFFECTIVE ACTION PLANS

In a marketing plan, every strategy must include an implementation element. Sometimes these are called **action plans** or programs.[30] Each must discuss timing, assign persons responsible for various aspects of implementation, and indicate the resources necessary to make the strategy happen. Budgets for the action plan must be developed based on the forecast. Then, appropriate metrics must be identified for each, along with a control process, to assess along the way to what degree the action plan is on track and contributing to the marketing strategy and achievement of the stated marketing objectives. Exhibit 19.3 provides a format for developing action plans.

Responsibility for the Action Plan

A marketing plan can't be implemented without people. And not everybody who will be involved in implementing a marketing plan is a marketer because marketing plans touch most areas of an organization. Upper management and the human resource department will

EXHIBIT 19.3	Format for Developing Action Plans
Title of Action Plan	Give the action plan a relevant name.
Purpose of Action Plan	What do you hope to accomplish by the action plan—that is, what specific marketing objective and strategy within the marketing plan does it support?
Description of Action Plan	Be succinct, but still thorough, in explaining the action plan. What are the steps involved? This is the core of the action plan. It describes what must be done to accomplish the intended purpose of the action plan.
Responsibility for the Action Plan	What person(s) or organizational unit(s) are responsible for carrying out the action plan? What external parties are needed to make it happen? Most importantly, who specifically has final "ownership" of the action plan—that is, who is accountable for it?
Timing for the Action Plan	Provide a specific timetable of events leading to the completion of the plan. If different people are responsible for different elements of the timeline, provide that information.
Budget for the Action Plan (Based on the Forecast)	How much will implementation of the action plan cost? This may be direct costs only, or may also include indirect costs, depending on the situation. The sum of all the individual action plan budget items will ultimately be aggregated by category to create the overall budget for the marketing plan.
Measurement and Control of the Action Plan	Indicate the appropriate metrics, how and when they will be measured, and who will measure them.

need to be involved in deploying the necessary people to accomplish the plan's objectives. Reviewing the various action plans needed for implementation of a marketing plan is a great way to develop an overall human resource deployment strategy for accomplishing the marketing plan. As you know, marketing isn't just the responsibility of the marketing department and nowhere is this idea more relevant than in market plan implementation. A wide range of organizational functions—sales, production, quality control, shipping, customer service, finance, information technology, and others—will have a stake in making the plan successful. If the functions are outsourced rather than handled internally by the firm, then someone internally still must take responsibility for the outsourced aspect of the action plan.

Timing of the Action Plan

Each action plan must address the timing for accomplishment of its associated tasks. This information can then be aggregated for inclusion in the overall marketing plan. Most marketing plans portray the timing of tasks in flowchart form so that it is easy to visualize when the pieces of the plan will come together. Marketers often use *Gantt charts* or *PERT charts,* popular in operations management, to portray a plan's timeline.[31] These are the same types of tools that might be used by a general contractor to map out the different elements of building a house from the ground up. Ultimately, budgets and the financial management of the marketing plan are developed around the timing of the elements of the plan so that managers know when cash outlays are required.

Budget for the Action Plan

Each action plan carries a budget item, assuming costs are involved in carrying it out. Forecasting the needed expenditures related to a marketing plan can be challenging, but one way to improve accuracy in the budgeting process overall is to ensure that estimates for expenditures for the individual action plans are as accurate as possible.[32] At the overall marketing plan level, a master budget is created and tracked throughout the marketing planning process. Variances from the budget are reported to the parties responsible for each budget item throughout the process. For example, a firm's vice president for sales might receive a weekly or monthly report showing each sales area's performance against its budget allocation. The vice president would note patterns of budget overage and contact affected sales managers to determine what actions, if any, need to be taken to get the budget back on track. The same approach would be repeated across all the functional areas of the firm on which the budget has an impact. In such a manner, the budget itself becomes a critical element of control.

Measurement and Control of the Action Plan

This portion of the action plan establishes a formal process of monitoring progress through measuring actual performance, comparing the performance to the established marketing plan objectives and metrics, and adjusting the plan on the basis of this analysis. The metrics and process a marketer uses to monitor and control individual action plans ultimately forms the overall control process for the marketing plan. Unfortunately, many marketers do not consistently do a good job of measurement and control, which compromises their marketing planning. Controls are discussed in more detail later in this chapter, in the context of the overall marketing plan.

FORECASTING FOR MARKETING PLANNING

The forecast is one of the most important information tools used by marketing managers and lies at the heart of most firms' marketing planning efforts. Top management uses the forecast to allocate resources among functional areas and to control the operations of the overall firm. Finance uses it to project cash flows, to decide on capital appropriations, and to establish operating budgets. Production uses it to determine quantities and schedules and to control inventories. Human resources uses it to plan personnel requirements and also as an input in collective bargaining. Purchasing uses it to plan the company's overall materials requirements and also to schedule their arrival. And in the marketing plan itself, the forecast is used to prepare a budget and to allocate resources among the various action plans that comprise the marketing strategy.

Two broad categories of forecasting approaches are subjective and objective methods, listed in Exhibit 19.4. Each method has advantages and disadvantages in application, which are summarized in Exhibit 19.5. The decision of which method (or methods) to employ is not always as clear as a manager would like. In a typical marketing planning situation, the decision will likely depend on how much time is available, the level of technical sophistication of products, the ready availability of historical sales data, and the level of uncertainty in the external marketplace.

EXHIBIT 19.4 | **Forecasting Approaches**

Sales forecasting methods

Subjective methods
User expectations
Sales force composite
Jury of executive opinion
Delphi technique

Objective methods
Market test
Time-series analysis
  Moving averages
  Exponential smoothing
  Decomposition
Statistical demand analysis

Source: Mark W. Johnston and Greg W. Marshall, *Churchill/Ford/Walker's Sales Force Management*, 9th ed. (New York: McGraw-Hill/Irwin, 2009), p. 140. Copyright © 2009 The McGraw-Hill Companies, Inc.

EXHIBIT 19.5 | Advantages and Disadvantages of Forecasting Approaches

Sales Forecasting Method	Advantages	Disadvantages
Subjective methods		
User expectations	1. Forecast estimates obtained directly from buyers 2. Projected product usage information can be greatly detailed 3. Insights gathered aid in the planning of marketing strategy 4. Useful for new-product forecasting	1. Potential customers must be few and well defined 2. Does not work well for consumer goods 3. Depends on the accuracy of user's estimates 4. Expensive, time-consuming, labor intensive
Sales force composite	1. Involves the people (sales personnel) who will be held responsible for the results 2. Is fairly accurate 3. Aids in controlling and directing the sales effort 4. Forecast is available for individual sales territories	1. Estimators (sales personnel) have a vested interest and therefore may be biased 2. Elaborate schemes sometimes necessary to counteract bias 3. If estimates are biased, process to correct the data can be expensive
Jury of executive opinion	1. Easily done, very quick 2. Does not require elaborate statistics 3. Utilizes collective wisdom of the top people 4. Useful for new or innovative products	1. Produces aggregate forecasts 2. Expensive 3. Disperses responsibility for the forecast 4. Group dynamics operate
Delphi technique	1. Minimizes effects of group dynamics 2. Can utilize statistical information	1. Can be expensive and time-consuming
Objective methods		
Market test	1. Provides ultimate test of consumers' reactions to the product 2. Allows the assessment of the effectiveness of the total marketing program 3. Useful for new and innovative products	1. Lets competitors know what firm is doing 2. Invites competitive reaction 3. Expensive and time-consuming to set up 4. Often takes a long time to accurately assess level of initial and repeat demand
Time-series analysis	1. Utilizes historical data 2. Objective, inexpensive	1. Not useful for new or innovative products 2. Factors for trend, cyclical, seasonal, or product life-cycle phase must be accurately assessed and included 3. Technical skill and good judgment required 4. Final forecast difficult to break down into individual territory estimates 5. Ignores planned marketing effort
Statistical demand analysis	1. Great intuitive appeal 2. Requires quantification of assumptions underlying the estimates 3. Allows management to check results 4. Uncovers hidden factors affecting sales 5. Method is objective	1. Factors affecting sales must remain constant and be accurately identified to produce an accurate estimate 2. Requires technical skill and expertise 3. Some managers reluctant to use method due to its sophistication

Much of Delta's business, as well as that of other airlines, now comes directly from the Internet. This has made tracking sales and customer trends and translating the information into forecasts a more straightforward process than it was when independent travel agents sold most of the tickets.

Subjective Methods of Forecasting

Subjective forecasting methods do not rely primarily on sophisticated quantitative (empirical) analytical approaches in developing the forecast.[34]

User Expectations

The **user expectations** method of forecasting is also known as the *buyers' intentions method* because it relies on answers from customers regarding their expected consumption or purchases of the product. Data are collected through various market research methodologies discussed in Chapter 5.[35]

The user expectations method may provide estimates closer to market or sales *potential* than will other approaches. In reality, user groups would have difficulty anticipating the industry's (or a particular firm's) marketing efforts. Rather, the user estimates reflect their *anticipated needs.* From a marketing planning standpoint, the user expectations approach provides a measure of the opportunities available among a particular segment of users.

Sales Force Composite

The **sales force composite** method of forecasting is so named because the initial input is the opinion of each member of the field sales staff. The idea is that the sales force is the closest organizational unit to the customer and will be able to come close to providing an aggregate of their customers' needs.[36] Each person states how much he or she expects to sell during the forecast period. Subsequently, these estimates are typically adjusted at various higher levels in the firm, depending on historical records of accuracy (if available). That is, when forecasting via sales force composite, organizations typically use historical information about the accuracy of the salespeople's estimates to make adjustments to the raw forecast data provided by the field sales organization. For various reasons, salespeople may be motivated to either underestimate or overestimate what they expect to sell during a period.

Jury of Executive Opinion

The **jury of executive opinion** (or jury of expert opinion) method is a formal or informal internal poll of key executives within the firm to gain their assessment of sales potential. The separate assessments are combined into an overall forecast for inclusion in the marketing plan. Sometimes this is done by simply averaging the individual judgments but other times differing viewpoints are resolved through group discussion toward consensus.[37] The initial views may reflect no more than the executive's hunch about what is going to happen, or the opinion may be based on considerable factual material or perhaps even an initial forecast prepared by other means.

Delphi Technique

In gaining expert opinion, one method for controlling group dynamics to produce a more accurate forecast is the **Delphi technique.** Delphi uses an iterative approach with repeated measurement and controlled anonymous feedback, instead of direct confrontation and debate among the experts preparing the forecast.[38] Each individual involved prepares a forecast using whatever facts, figures, and general knowledge of the environment he or she has available. Then the forecasts are collected and the person supervising the process summarizes the forecasts (protecting the anonymity of participants). The summary is distributed to each person who participated in the initial phase. Typically, the summary lists each forecast figure, the average (median), and some summary measure of the spread of the estimates. Often, those whose initial estimates fell outside the midrange of responses are asked to express their reasons for these extreme positions. These explanations are then incorporated into the summary. The participants study the summary and submit a revised forecast. The process is then repeated. Typically, several rounds of these iterations occur until something close to consensus is achieved. The Delphi method is based on the premise that, with repeated measurements (1) the range of responses will decrease and the estimates will converge, and (2) the total group response or median will move successively toward the "correct" or "true" answer.

Do ads for consumer products turn into sales of those products? Do the consumers exposed to TV and radio ads for specific products then purchase those advertised products more? Media ratings companies Arbitron and Nielsen decided to employ new technology to find the answers. In a joint venture called Project Apollo, they used two devices to monitor the media exposure and product purchases of 11,000 consumers. One device, known as the Portable People Meter, picked up audible advertising messages from radio and television. A second device, called HomeScan, tracked purchases when participants used it to scan the bar code of every item they bought. Apollo found that people exposed to several months' worth of advertising for 13 mid-to-large brands spent 5 to 8 percent more on the brands compared with spending before the ads ran. Consumers in the brands' target demographic boosted their spending even more: 8 to 12 percent.[39]

Objective Methods of Forecasting

Objective forecasting methods rely primarily on more sophisticated quantitative (empirical) analytical approaches in developing the forecast.

Market Test

The typical **market test** (or test market) involves placing a product in several representative geographic areas to see how well it performs and then projecting that experience to the market as a whole. Often this is done for a new product or an improved version of an old product.[40]

Many firms consider the market test to be the final gauge of consumer acceptance of a new product and ultimate measure of market potential. A. C. Nielsen data, for example, has indicated for years that roughly three out of four products that have been test-marketed succeed, whereas four out of five that have not been test-marketed fail. Despite this advantage, market tests have several drawbacks:

- Market tests are costly to administer and are more conducive to testing of consumer products than industrial products.
- The time involved in conducting a market test can be considerable.
- Because a product is being test-marketed, it receives more attention in the market test than it can ever receive on a national scale, giving an unrealistic picture of the product's potential.
- A market test, because it is so visible to competitors, can reveal a firm's hand on its new-product launch strategy, thus allowing competitors time to formulate a market response before full market introduction.

Time-Series Analysis

Approaches to forecasting using **time-series analysis** rely on the analysis of historical data to develop a prediction for the future.[41] The sophistication of these analyses can vary widely. At the most simplistic extreme, the forecaster might predict next year's sales to be equal to this year's sales. Such a forecast might be reasonably accurate for a mature industry that is experiencing little growth or external market turbulence. However, barring these conditions, more sophisticated time-series approaches should be considered. Three of these methods are moving averages, exponential smoothing, and decomposition.

Moving Average   The *moving average* method is conceptually quite simple. Consider the forecast that next year's sales will be equal to this year's sales. Such a forecast might be subject to large error if there is much fluctuation in sales from one year to the next. To allow for such randomness, we might consider using some kind of average of recent values.[42] For example, we might average the last two years' sales, the last three years' sales, the last five years' sales, or any number of other periods. The forecast would simply be the average that resulted. The number of observations included in the average is typically determined by trial and error. Differing numbers of periods are tried, and the number of periods that produces the most accurate forecasts of the trial data is used to develop the forecast model. Once determined, it remains constant. The term *moving average* is used because a new average is computed and used as a forecast as each new observation becomes available.

Exhibit 19.6 presents a moving average forecast example with 16 years of historical sales data and also the resulting forecasts for a number of years using two- and four-year moving averages. Exhibit 19.7 displays the results graphically. The entry 4,305 for 1995, under the two-year moving average method, for example, is the average of the sales of 4,200 units in 1993 and 4,410 units in 1994. Similarly, the forecast of 5,520 units in 2008 represents the average of the number of units sold in 2006 and 2007. The forecast of 5,772 units in 2008 under the four-year moving average method, on the other hand, represents the average number of units sold during the four-year period 2004–2007. Obviously, it takes more data to begin forecasting with four-year than with two-year moving averages. This is an important consideration when starting to forecast sales for a new product.

Exponential Smoothing   The method of moving averages gives *equal weight* to each of the last n values in forecasting the next value, where n represents the number of years used. Thus, when $n = 4$ (the four-year moving average is being used), equal weight is given to each of the last four years' sales in predicting the sales for next year. In a four-year moving average, no weight is given to any sales five or more years previous.

Exponential smoothing is a type of moving average that, instead of weighting all observations equally in generating the forecast, weights the most recent observations heaviest. The reasoning behind this strategy is that the most recent observations contain the most information about what is likely to happen in the future, and they should therefore be given more weight.[43]

The key decision affecting the use of exponential smoothing is the choice of the *smoothing constant,* referred to as α in the algorithm for calculating exponential smoothing, which is constrained to be between 0 and 1. High values of α give great weight to recent observations and little weight to distant sales; low values of α, on the other hand, give more weight to older observations. If sales change slowly, low values of α work fine. However, when a firm experiences rapid changes and fluctuations in sales, high values of α should be used so that the forecast series responds to these changes quickly. The value of α is normally determined empirically. First, various values of α are tried, and then the one that produces the smallest forecast error when applied to the historical series is adopted.

EXHIBIT 19.6 | Moving Average Forecast Example

Year	Actual sales	Forecast sales	
		Two-year moving average	**Four-year moving average**
1993	4,200		
1994	4,410		
1995	4,322	4,305	
1996	4,106	4,366	
1997	4,311	4,214	4,260
1998	4,742	4,209	4,287
1999	4,837	4,527	4,370
2000	5,030	4,790	4,499
2001	4,779	4,934	4,730
2002	4,970	4,905	4,847
2003	5,716	4,875	4,904
2004	6,116	5,343	5,128
2005	5,932	5,916	5,395
2006	5,576	6,024	5,684
2007	5,465	5,754	5,835
2008		5,520	5,772

Source: Mark W. Johnston and Greg W. Marshall, *Churchill/Ford/Walker's Sales Force Management*, 9th ed. (New York: McGraw-Hill/Irwin, 2009), p. 143. Copyright © 2009 The McGraw-Hill Companies, Inc.

Decomposition The *decomposition* method of forecasting is typically applied to monthly or quarterly data where a seasonal pattern is evident and the marketing manager wishes to forecast not only for the whole year but also for each period in the year. It is important to determine what portion of any changes in sales represents an overall, fundamental change in demand and what portion is due to *seasonality* in demand. The decomposition method attempts to isolate four separate portions of a time series: the trend, cyclical, seasonal, and random factors.[44]

- The *trend* reflects the long-run changes experienced in the series when the cyclical, seasonal, and irregular components are removed. It is typically assumed to be a straight line.

- The *cyclical factor* is not always present because it reflects the waves in a series when the seasonal and irregular components are removed. These ups and downs typically occur over a long period, perhaps two to five years.

EXHIBIT 19.7 | Graphical Representation of Moving Average Forecast

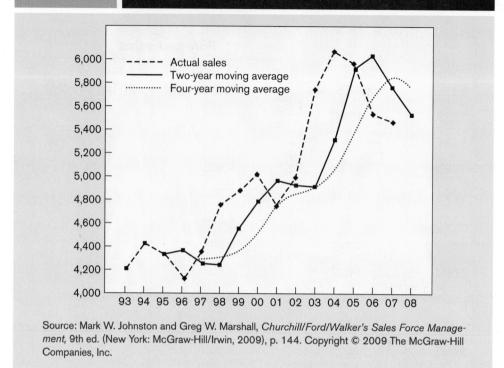

Source: Mark W. Johnston and Greg W. Marshall, *Churchill/Ford/Walker's Sales Force Management*, 9th ed. (New York: McGraw-Hill/Irwin, 2009), p. 144. Copyright © 2009 The McGraw-Hill Companies, Inc.

Some products experience little cyclical fluctuation (canned peas), whereas others experience a great deal (housing starts).

- *Seasonality* reflects the annual fluctuation in the series due to the natural seasons. The seasonal factor normally repeats itself each year, although the exact pattern of sales may be different from year to year.

- The *random factor* is what is left after the influence of the trend, cyclical, and seasonal factors is removed.

Exhibit 19.8 shows the calculation of a simple seasonal index based on five years of sales history. The data suggest definite seasonal and trend components in the series, as the fourth quarter of every year is always the best quarter and the first quarter is the worst. At the same time, sales each year are higher than they were the previous year. One could calculate a seasonal index for each year by simply dividing quarterly sales by the yearly average per quarter. It is much more typical, though, to base the calculation of the seasonal index on several years of data to smooth out the random fluctuations that occur by quarter.

In using the decomposition method, the marketing manager typically first determines the seasonal pattern and removes its impact to identify the trend. Then the cyclical factor is estimated. After the three components are isolated, the forecast is developed by applying each factor in turn to the historical data.

Statistical Demand Analysis

Time-series methods attempt to determine the relationship between sales volume and time as the basis to forecast future sales. *Statistical demand analysis* attempts to determine the relationship between sales and the important factors affecting sales to forecast the future. Typically, regression analysis is used to estimate the relationship. The emphasis is not to isolate all factors that affect sales but simply to identify those that have the most dramatic impact on sales and then to estimate the magnitude of the impact. The predictor variables in statistical demand

EXHIBIT 19.8   Seasonal Index Calculation Example

Year	Quarter				Total	Quarter average
	1	2	3	4		
2004	82.8	105.8	119.6	151.8	460.0	115.0
2005	93.1	117.6	122.5	156.9	490.1	122.5
2006	92.0	122.4	132.6	163.2	510.2	127.6
2007	95.3	129.0	151.3	185.0	560.6	140.2
2008	120.1	138.1	162.2	180.2	600.6	150.2
Five-year average	96.7	122.6	137.6	167.4	524.3	131.1
Seasonal index*	73.8	93.5	105.0	127.7		

* The seasonal index equals the quarterly average divided by the overall quarterly average times 100; for the first quarter, for example, the seasonal index equals $(96.7 \div 131.1) \times 100 = 73.8$.

Source: Mark W. Johnston and Greg W. Marshall, *Churchill/Ford/Walker's Sales Force Management*, 9th ed. (New York: McGraw-Hill/Irwin, 2009), p. 145. Copyright © 2009 The McGraw-Hill Companies, Inc.

analysis often are historical indexes such as leading economic indicators and other similar measures.[45] For example, Home Depot or Lowe's might use housing starts, interest rates, and a seasonal shift in demand during summer months to forecast its sales of construction materials. Today, numerous statistical software packages are available for marketing managers doing statistical demand analysis through regression. Most are user friendly and intuitive in operation. Excel, SPSS, and SAS are three popular types of software that are easily capable of statistical demand analysis.

E-Dialog, an e-mail services provider, can tell its clients when a customer opens a message and can pinpoint what time of day customers tend to open their e-mail. "Response behavior is another important data point to gather for continued relevancy," says John Doub, director of Web engineering and application service provider accounts for e-Dialog. "When the recipient opens his or her e-mail message, you can even track open and click time stamps to score when the best time of the day is to send that customer e-mails."[46]

Selecting the Appropriate Forecasting Method(s)

In preparing the forecast for a marketing plan, the marketing manager must answer two key questions: Which forecasting method(s) should be used and how accurate is the forecast likely to be? The importance of the decision is exacerbated when several methods are tried and the forecasts don't agree, which is the norm rather than the exception.

Over the years, many researchers have assessed forecast accuracy using the various techniques. Some studies have been conducted within individual companies, and others have used existing data sets to which the various forecasting techniques have been systematically applied. One of the most extensive

Today, firms often complete their forecasting and budgeting processes through virtual meetings, facilitated by firms such as GoToMeeting.com that eliminate the need to travel.

comparisons involved 1,001 time series from a variety of sources in which each series was forecast using 24 different extrapolation methods. The general conclusion was that the method used made little difference with respect to forecast accuracy. Similarly, comparisons of forecast accuracy of objective versus subjective methods tend to reach no clear conclusion as to which method is superior. Some of the comparisons seem to favor the quantitative methods, but others indicate that the subjective methods produce more accurate forecasts.

Bottom line, no single method of forecasting is likely to be superior under all conditions. Rather, a number of factors, both analytical and situational, are likely to affect the superiority of any particular technique. Analytical factors include the stability of the data series, the time horizon, the degree of structure imposed on the process, and the seasonal nature of the data. Situational factors include the volatility of the external marketplace, experience and expertise of the marketing manager in forecasting, and access to the necessary information and people required to accomplish the chosen forecasting approach. Overall, the best approach is for marketing managers to utilize multiple methods of forecasting, including a combination of subjective and objective methods, compare the results, and then make a decision on what the actual final forecast will be. Ultimately, in marketing planning the marketing manager cannot expect a final forecast to pop directly out of a statistical model, ready for use in developing strategies, action plans, and budgets. Instead, the manager must create the forecast based on multiple forms of input, ultimately relying on his or her judgment.

THE MARKETING BUDGET

Chapter 17 discussed four principal methods of preparing a promotion budget. These methods are valid for overall marketing plan budgeting as well.

1. *Objective-and-task method*, which takes an investment approach in that marketing goals and objectives are set for the upcoming year and then budget dollars are secured to support the achievement of those goals and objectives. This approach is also sometimes referred to as **zero-based budgeting,** because the marketing manager essentially starts the process with a blank slate and builds the budget based on the level of investment required.[47]

2. *Percent-of-sales method*, which is the most popular approach but is constraining because sales are driving budget dollars rather than marketing investment leading to sales opportunities.

3. *Comparative-parity method*, in which marketing expenditures across key competitors are assessed to arrive at a budget number.

4. *All-you-can-afford method*, which simply sets the marketing budget as whatever funds are left over after other "necessities" are funded.

Because the latter three approaches to budgeting have flaws that make them suboptimal, we encourage marketing managers to adopt a zero-based budgeting approach to marketing planning. The action planning process described earlier in this chapter facilitates the implementation of zero-based budgeting because the manager is required to justify the individual budget elements (based on the forecast) for each action plan within the overall marketing plan. These individual action plan budgets can then be aggregated into an overall budget for the marketing plan. Since these budget items are, by nature, primarily direct costs—costs attributable directly to the action plan and not inclusive of ongoing indirect or overhead costs—when the final marketing plan budget is developed, the overhead costs must be allocated to the plan on whatever basis the company uses in its accounting practices.

The marketing budget must be allocated across the different kinds of media vehicles and promotional tools. Wendy's, the fast-food restaurant, spent about $375 million in measured media in 2006, and it has steadily been increasing the percentage of its marketing budget that it spends online. In 2004, Wendy's spent only 4 percent of its overall marketing budget online, but increased it to 8 percent in 2007 and planned to exceed 10 percent in 2008. The company is investing in online media vehicles such as microsites like hotjuicyburger .com and thisismyburger.com, in an effort to reach its core 18-to-34-year-old consumers.[48]

In practice, most marketing plan budgets are created and maintained through the use of Excel spreadsheets that provide formulaic capabilities to perform scenario analyses on a variety of contingencies and see the impact on the budget. An example of such an interactive marketing plan budget may be accessed online at the following URL: www.mhhe.com/marshall1e. Feel free to manipulate the numbers in the spreadsheet; you will quickly find out that budgets are very sensitive to changes, illustrating the criticality of good forecasting and cost estimation by marketing managers.

CONTROLS AND CONTINGENCY PLANNING

In marketing planning, the assumption is that the marketing manager moves forward to make the best possible decisions with the information that he or she has available at the time. However, a variety of uncontrollable external forces can impact the results of even the best-crafted marketing plan, sometimes very rapidly. To cope with this eventuality, **controls** must be in place from the outset of the planning process that specify the timing, procedure, and persons responsible for systematically monitoring the progress toward the goals and metrics established in the marketing plan.[49] Having goals and metrics in place without a control process to ensure that progress toward them is closely tracked is a fatal error in marketing planning. Exhibit 19.9 provides some tips for effective control.

What happens if it becomes apparent that your marketing plan is not on track to meet its goals or achieve acceptable performance metrics? And alternatively, what if evidence shows that results are *exceeding* those planned? With proper controls in place, a marketing manager should be able to detect either of these scenarios in a timely fashion, while there is still an opportunity to adjust the plan. Remember that marketing plans are not cast in stone, and the marketing manager must be willing and able to be flexible to alter any elements of the plan—from the forecast to the budget to the promotional strategy—based on unanticipated changes in the marketplace.

A convenient way to prepare for the possibility that controls will reveal significant deviations from the plan is through **contingency planning,** also called

EXHIBIT 19.9 **Tips for Effective Control**

1. **Controls should involve only the minimum amount of information needed to give a reliable picture of events.**

   Too many controls create confusion. Focus on the strategic factors by following the 80/20 rule—monitor those 20 percent of the factors that determine 80 percent of the results.

2. **Controls should monitor only meaningful activities and results.**

   Regardless of measurement difficulty, if cooperation between units is important to the performance of the marketing plan, some form of qualitative or quantitative measures should be established to monitor cooperation.

3. **Controls should be timely.**

   Corrective action must be taken before it is too late. Steering controls, which are controls that monitor or measure the factors influencing performance, should be stressed so that advance notice of problems is given.

4. **Controls should be long term and short term.**

   If only short-term measures are emphasized, a short-term managerial orientation is likely.

5. **Controls should pinpoint exceptions.**

   Only those activities or results that fall outside a predetermined tolerance range should call for action.

6. **Controls should be used to reward meeting or exceeding standards rather than to punish failure to meet standards.**

   Heavy punishment of failure typically results in goal displacement. Managers will "fudge" performance reports and lobby for lower standards.

Source: J. David Hunger and Thomas L. Wheelen, *Essentials of Strategic Management,* 4th ed. Copyright © 2007. Reproduced by permission of Pearson Education, Inc., Upper Saddle River, NJ: Prentice Hall, 2007.

When the U.S. bee population began to diminish mysteriously in 2007, Haagen-Dazs faced an unexpected contingency in its planning process—without honey bees many of their products cannot be produced.

Courtesy Dreyer's Grand Ice Cream, Inc.

scenario planning. Contingency planning requires the establishment of different planning options depending on the expected case, best case, or worst case.[50] The expected-case scenario is the one on which the primary plan is based. Essentially, you would prepare a response in advance as to how you would change that plan if a worst- or best-case scenario occurred. Assume that a few months into the execution of your marketing plan an unanticipated competitor enters the market with a product similar to yours at a lower price. The impact is immediate on your sales and undoubtedly you will want to adjust your marketing strategy to better compete. With a contingency plan in place, rather than starting the marketing planning process again from scratch, you can simply shift to the relevant elements of a worst-case plan, losing no time in addressing the competitive threat.

While such worst-case scenarios are certainly common, marketing managers often get caught off guard in best-case scenarios too. What if market response to your product greatly exceeds expectations and you find yourself straining production capacity and facing customers clamoring for product line extensions? A good position to be in, right? Except that without a best-case scenario plan worked out in advance, you will find yourself starting the planning process over midstream. Beginning with the forecast and through to all the planning elements, preparing contingency planning scenarios in advance is well worth the effort.

THE MARKETING AUDIT

A very useful tool to aid in marketing planning is the marketing audit. A **marketing audit** systematically reviews the current state of marketing within an organization including how things are done, by whom, with what controls, and with what level of success. It uncovers what is working well and what is not working well within an organization's marketing activities, providing an invaluable snapshot of the full scope of a firm's marketing. Analysis of the results can reveal key opportunities for improvement.[51] Note that we are distinguishing a marketing audit from a *brand audit,* which includes an additional extensive external research process.

A marketing manager may wish to initiate a marketing audit when any of the following conditions are present:

- The firm is about to undergo a major rebranding initiative.
- Evidence exists of significant marketing inefficiencies and poor ROMI and other metrics.
- A new creative agency is coming onboard.
- A recent change has occurred in top management.
- Marketing has undergone a reorganization within the firm.

All units within a firm that do marketing should participate in the marketing audit. It is best administered under the direct purview of the firm's CMO. Clear objectives should be established for the audit as well as expectations about how the results will be used. This information should be communicated in advance to all participants. Exhibit 19.10 provides an example of a marketing audit instrument. Usually the instrument and instructions would be sent to the participating organizational units in advance, requesting that they gather the necessary background information and materials by a certain date. Then, the CMO or his or her designee should schedule an interview with representatives of each participating unit, either in person or by phone, to go through the audit questions. After the audit results are compiled, a summarizing report should be produced and distributed to all participants.

FYI

Glenda Brungardt, trade show/event manager at Hewlett-Packard Imaging and Printing Group Americas Marketing, incorporates audits into her trade show strategy. "By using audits, HP's Imaging and Printing Group can more accurately calculate ROI/ROO from an event and better understand our audience," Brungardt said. "Audits help us determine the value derived from our participation, add credibility, and make the decision to exhibit easier. They also help us determine what marketing activities to target to the audience." A trade show audit is a report produced by an independent, third-party, certified auditor that reviews registration data to objectively confirm attendance figures and demographics collected in the registration process. Auditing involves contacting attendees to validate attendance and demographic information.[52]

One benefit of a marketing audit is simply getting organization members talking about marketing. It can be very useful not only for sharing best practices but also for internal marketing; for example, setting the stage for a major new branding initiative or in preparation for a change to a new creative agency.

EXHIBIT 19.10 **Marketing Audit Instrument**

Staff and Unit

1. What is your position?
      What are your primary responsibilities?
            If not marketing, what is your involvement in marketing, if any?
      What marketing experience do you have?
      How long have you worked in this position, this unit, and this company?
2. What is the unit's purpose?

Customers

1. Are customers internal, external, or both?
2. Who are your unit's customers?
3. What are your customers' needs?
4. Do you break your customers down into segments?
      How are segments determined?
      Which segments are most important?
      How much attention does each segment receive?
      What methods do you use to communicate with different segments?
5. How often does the unit have contact with its customers?
6. Who makes contact with the customers?
7. Does the unit have a customer database or management system?
      Who is in charge of keeping records?
      What software is the unit currently using, and what does it do?
      How many customers does the unit have?
8. What trends in your customers have you seen in the last year?
      Have there been any recent changes in these trends?
      How has the unit adapted to these changes?
9. What future trends do you think will affect your customer base?
10. What do you know about the buying habits of your customers?
      What external factors have had an impact on these habits?
11. To the best of your knowledge, what is the customers' view of your unit?
      What do you think has shaped these perceptions?
12. What percentage of your target customers are you serving?
13. How many customers does your unit have?

Competition

1. Who do you see as your competition?
2. What are the strengths of your competition?
3. What are the weaknesses of your competition?
4. What do you find yourselves competing on (e.g., lower price, better entertainment, faster response times, etc.)?

Budget

1. Is there a marketing budget?
      How much is allocated for marketing in the budget?
      What percentage of the total unit budget is used for marketing?
      Who manages and decides how to spend this budget?
      What is the process for budget proposal and approval?

(continued)

2. How much money is spent on marketing activities?

How are these expenditures tracked?

3. Do you think the right amount of money is being allocated for marketing?

If not, is it too much or too little, and why?

4. Do you think the money is being used effectively?

If not, what should change?

Process

1. Does the unit have a marketing plan?

What are the unit's marketing objectives and strategies?

2. How are marketing initiatives determined?

Who is responsible for this?

3. How many hours a week does your unit spend on marketing?

4. Does your unit have a formal marketing position?

If so, what is this person responsible for?

5. Could you explain the approval process for marketing activities?

Is the process the same every time?

6. Do marketing activities require the approval of anyone outside the unit?

If so, whose approval is needed and what unit are they in?

7. Does your unit communicate with any other departments?

8. Are there any combined efforts with other departments?

9. How aware are you of other unit's marketing efforts?

10. How are logos decided on and where do they come from?

11. Who produces the content for your unit's marketing communications?

12. Does your unit use outside companies or services for marketing activities?

What vendors are used and what are they used for?

How does your unit decide which vendors to use?

Does your unit have a list of preferred vendors?

How was this list made and where did it come from?

Does your unit have any existing contracts?

With what vendors, for how much money, and for what duration?

13. Is your unit contemplating any new contracts?

Communications Audit

1. What message does your unit attempt to convey?

2. What image are you trying to project?

3. What does your unit attempt to accomplish with all of its communications?

4. Do you think the unit's communication materials are effective?

5. Do you think the unit is successful at communicating your message?

What areas does your unit need to work on with its communications?

6. Do you think the communications are properly timed?

How do you determine when to send out communications?

7. How effective is the unit at reaching its desired audience?

8. How consistent is the unit in the design of its materials?

9. When materials are not consistent, what is the reason for the difference?

10. Are there any special events or annual events that your unit sponsors?

(continued)

| EXHIBIT 19.10 | Marketing Audit Instrument [continued] |

Control

1. What measurements or statistics does your unit use to track marketing activities?
2. What data do you have on response rates or effectiveness of marketing efforts?
3. What forecasting methods do you use?
4. When you use publications, how do you decide how many to send out and when to send them?

Experience and Perceptions

1. How do you see your unit fitting in with the company's overall message?
2. What marketing initiatives have and have not worked for your unit in the past?
3. What is the biggest marketing challenge your unit is currently facing?
4. What current factors are impacting your unit today?
5. What do you believe are your unit's biggest strengths and weaknesses?

Credit: Thanks to Harry Antonio for creating this exhibit for *Marketing Management*.

SUMMARY

Successful marketing planning requires the application of a variety of metrics for assessing performance against the plan's goals. Marketing dashboards provide a comprehensive approach to providing managers relevant, timely, and accurate information in a convenient format for use in decision making. Action plans, forecasts, budgets, and marketing audits are all important tools and processes that marketing managers must master to maximize the potential success in marketing planning.

KEY TERMS

marketing dashboard 538
return on marketing investment
  (ROMI) 541
action plans 548
subjective forecasting methods 552
user expectations 552

sales force composite 552
jury of executive opinion 552
Delphi technique 552
objective forecasting methods 553
market test 553
time-series analysis 554

zero-based budgeting 558
controls 559
contingency planning 559
marketing audit 561

APPLICATION QUESTIONS

1. Pick a firm that interests you and for which you have some knowledge of its offerings.

   a. How would this firm benefit from a marketing dashboard approach?

   b. What elements would you recommend it put onto its dashboard? Why do you recommend the ones you do?

   c. How could the firm avoid some of the pitfalls potentially associated with marketing dashboards?

2. Pick any two of the marketing metrics presented in the chapter. For each, pick any brand or product and discuss how each of those brands or products would benefit from the application of each of the marketing metrics you selected. That is, what will the information reveal that will be useful in marketing planning?

3. Consider the Apple iPhone. Develop one complete action plan that addresses a marketing objective to gain more iPhones purchases from 50-year-old and older consumers. Be sure to complete all the elements of the action plan as shown in Exhibit 19.3 and the accompanying discussion.

4. Identify one product of interest in the B2C market and one in the B2B market. Research the products online. For each, given what you know about the products and their markets, which forecasting approaches do you believe would be most appropriate for use in developing a marketing plan? Which approaches would be least appropriate? What leads you to make these suggestions?

5. Assume that your school has decided to undertake a complete marketing audit. Review the marketing audit instrument (Exhibit 19.10) and accompanying discussion.

    a. List as many areas as you can across the entire institution that engage in marketing activities and thus should participate in the audit.

    b. As you look over the questions on the audit, do any stand out as especially important or potentially problematic when you consider what you know about your school and its marketing initiative?

    c. How would you actually administer the audit?

    d. From your perspective as a student, what aspects of marketing do you believe your school does well, and what aspects could use some improvement? What leads you to these conclusions?

MANAGEMENT DECISION CASE: Sustaining the "Toyota Way"

Toyota, the company that has the rest of the auto industry running scared, is worried. As new hires pour in and top executives approach retirement, the company fears it might lose the culture of frugality, discipline, and constant improvement that has been vital to its success. Consequently, management has launched a slew of education initiatives, and even uses a business school to teach Toyota to be, well, more like Toyota.

Why is management worried? Rapid growth has forced this Japanese company to rely more and more on *gaijin* (foreigners) overseas. Top brass—the ones who transformed a lean upstart into a global powerhouse—are nearing retirement, to be replaced by a whole new generation of managers. And in the past three years, Toyota has hired 40,000 workers new to the company's culture.

To tackle these problems, new hires are sent to work on the assembly line to learn Toyota's production system; even long-time managers who have been hired from outside Toyota are sent to the line as a way to learn the company's culture. In addition, new managers hired from the outside—still a rarity at Toyota—get a mentor. The mentor is typically the new manager's retired predecessor, who gets paid to advise his or her replacement.

Even lifers get the treatment. Randy Pflughaupt has worked at the company since 1982 and in 2007 was promoted to U.S. marketing chief for the flagship Toyota brand. With the promotion, he was handed a stack of books and binders telling him all about the Toyota Way and was packed off to the Toyota Institute in Japan for a week of indoctrination. "Why does a 25-year veteran go to training? I could take it personally," Pflughaupt jokes. "It's to remind me that I don't have all the answers."

At the institute, President Katsuaki Watanabe, Chairman Fujio Cho, family scion Akio Toyoda, and others spend the week telling 50 trainees how they built the company. Cho recalled opening Toyota's first U.S. factory, describing how he dug into the community by joining the local Rotary club, eating in diners, and going bowling. The moral: Reading market data at your desk is great, but you have to leave the office to find out what's really going on, a process everyone at the company calls *Genchi Genbutsu*.

There's another step that growing numbers of newly minted executives must do: Find a problem Toyota faces and come up with a solution, which will be presented to Watanabe. Pflughaupt is figuring out how marketers can analyze the effectiveness of different media (print, television, Web) in various regions. He'll be graded not only on his solution but also on whether he used an eight-step method that's part of the Toyota Way to figure it out. Watanabe has been known to deep-six projects because the problem itself isn't "severe enough." Oh, and the *whole answer* has to fit on a single 11-by-17-inch sheet of paper.

In Japan, a management school instructs white-collar staffers in the company's philosophy. The aim is to apply the same principles that have worked in manufacturing to other areas of the business. One lesson teaches office workers to apply the "five whys"—a tenet of the Toyota Production System that tells engineers to ask continually why a problem is occurring until they can think of no new answers.

With quality slipping, Toyota has redoubled training for factory hands. The company has recently opened centers in the United States, Europe, and Asia where it can train new trainers drawn from across its global staff. This will help Toyota increase the ranks of qualified trainers from today's level of 2,000. In the United States, these trainers will work with every one of Toyota's 31,000 factory employees, coaching new hires and teaching veterans to better focus on quality.

Questions for Consideration

1. As Toyota looks to the future, it is looking inward at how to sustain its famous culture—the Toyota Way—that helped it become the automotive powerhouse it is. What areas does Toyota consider most important to its success?

2. The case mentions a problem facing Toyota: how marketers can analyze the effectiveness of different media (print, TV, Web) in various regions. What metrics would you design to begin to tackle this problem?

3. In what ways might Toyota link what it measures to the principles of the Toyota Way ("Continuous Improvement" and "Respect for People")?

Source: David Welch and Ian Rowley, "Toyota's All-Out Drive to Stay Toyota," *BusinessWeek*, December 3, 2007, pp. 54–55. Reprinted with permission.

MARKETING PLAN EXERCISE

ACTIVITY 19: Metrics

1. Select appropriate metrics for use in your marketing plan.

2. Prepare action plans in support of your marketing plan. For each action plan be sure to list budget items, and then aggregate these into an overall budget for your marketing plan. Also, be sure to specify relevant controls.

3. Select and justify the forecasting approaches you will employ in your marketing plan.

4. Develop expected-case, best-case, and worst-case scenarios for your marketing plan.

If you are using Marketing Plan Pro, a template for this assignment can be accessed at www.mhhe.com/marshall1e.

RECOMMENDED READINGS

1. Tim Ambler, *Marketing and the Bottom Line: The Marketing Metrics to Pump Up Cash Flow*, 2nd ed. (London: FT Prentice Hall, 2003).

2. Paul W. Farris, Neil T. Bendle, Philip E. Pfeifer, and David J. Reibstein, *Marketing Metrics: 50+ Metrics Every Executive Should Master* (Upper Saddle River, NJ: Wharton School Publishing, 2006).

3. Patrick LaPointe, *Marketing by the Dashboard Light: How to Get More Insight, Foresight, and Accountability from Your Marketing Investments* (New York, ANA, 2005).

4. Guy R. Powell, *Return on Marketing Investment: Demand More from Your Marketing and Sales Investments* (Albuquerque, NM: RPI Press, 2002).

5. Carroll Rogé et al., *Improving Marketing ROI: Leading CMOs on Adding Value, Calculating Return on Investments, and Creating a Financial Impact* (Boston: Aspatore Books, 2006).

GLOSSARY

A

acceleration effect When small changes in consumer demand lead to considerable shifts in business product demand.

accumulating bulk A function performed by intermediaries that involves taking product from multiple sources and sorting it into different classifications for sales through the channel.

action plans The implementation element of a marketing plan that discusses issues such as timing, persons responsible, and resources necessary.

adaptive selling Being able to adjust the sales style from one sales situation to another in real time based on customer feedback.

additions to existing product lines An extension to an existing product that has already been developed and introduced to the market.

administered vertical marketing system (VMS) When the channel control of a vertical marketing system is determined by the size and power of one of its channel members.

advantages The particular product/service characteristic that helps meet the customer's needs.

advertising Paid form of relatively less personal marketing communications often through a mass medium to one or more target markets.

advertising execution The way an advertisement communicates the information and image.

advertising response function An effect in which, beyond a certain ad spending level, diminishing returns tend to set in.

advertising wearout When customers become bored with an existing advertising campaign.

agent intermediaries Intermediaries who do not take title to the product during the exchange process.

AIDA model A model designed to illustrate the hierarchy of effects in the context of customer response to marketing communications. It states that the effects build in this order: Attention (or Awareness), Interest, Desire, and Action.

allowances A remittance of monies to the consumer after the purchase of the product.

all-you-can-afford method Method of promotional budgeting that sets the promotional budget as whatever funds are left over after everything else that's considered a necessity is paid for.

ASEAN Founded in 1967, it is the most important Asian market zone and includes 10 countries running the entire length of the Pacific Rim (Brunei Darussalam, Indonesia, Malaysia, Philippines, Cambodia, Laos, Myanmar, Singapore, Thailand, and Vietnam).

aspirational purchases Products bought outside the individual's social standing.

assortment The number of different product items within a product category.

attitude Learned predisposition to respond to an object or class of objects in a consistently favorable or unfavorable way.

attitude-based choice A product choice that relies on an individual's beliefs and values to direct his or her assessment.

attribute-based choice A product choice based on the premise that product choices are made by comparing brands across a defined set of attributes.

auction pricing A pricing tactic in which individuals competitively bid against each other and the purchase goes to the highest bidder.

average-cost pricing A pricing decision made by identifying all costs associated with an offering to come up with what the average cost of a single unit might be.

awareness set A reduced set of possible alternatives a consumer considers after eliminating available options based on gathered information and personal preference.

B

backward integration When a firm merges operations back up the supply chain away from the consumer.

bait and switch When a seller advertises a low price but has no intent to actually make the lower priced item available for sale.

banner ads Internet advertisements that are small boxes containing graphics and text, and have a hyperlink embedded in them.

basket of global marketing themes Global advertising strategy in which distinct ads built around several marketing messages are created that local marketers can select from to best fit their specific market situation.

behavioral data Information about when, what, and how often customers purchase products and services as well as other customer "touches."

behavioral segmentation Dividing consumer groups based on similarities in benefits sought or product usage patterns.

benefits The advantageous outcome from the advantage found in a product feature.

Boston Consulting Group (BCG) Growth-Share Matrix A popular approach for in-firm portfolio analysis that categorizes business units' level of contribution to the overall firm based on two factors: market growth rate and competitive position.

brand A name, term, sign, symbol, or design, or a combination of these elements, intended to identify the goods or services of one seller or groups of sellers and to differentiate them from those of competitors.

brand assets Other assets brands possess such as trademarks and patents that represent a significant competitive advantage.

brand association When customers develop a number of emotional, psychological, and performance associations with a brand. These associations become a primary purchase driver, particularly with brand loyal users.

brand awareness The most basic form of brand equity is simply being aware of the brand. Awareness is the foundation of all other brand relationships.

brand equity A set of assets and liabilities linked to a brand's name and symbol that adds to or subtracts from the value provided by a product or service to a firm or that firm's customers.

brand extensions A firm's use of knowledge of an existing brand when introducing a new product.

brand identity A summary of unique qualities attributed to a brand.

brand loyalty The strongest form of brand equity and reflects a commitment to repeat purchases.

brand personality The association between a brand and an individual's specific personality characteristics.

brand strategy The unique elements of a brand that define the products sold by a firm.

breadth of merchandise The number of different product categories offered by a retailer.

breaking bulk A shipping method used by manufacturers to better match quantities needed in terms of the space constraints and inventory turnover requirements of their buyers.

B-to-B (business-to-business) markets Markets in which a firm's customers are other firms, characterized by few but large customers, personal relationships, complex buying processes, less price sensitive demand.

buying center A number of individuals with a stake in a purchase decision who manage the purchase decision process and ultimately make the decision.

buying decision Decisions made throughout the purchase decision process that vary widely and are based on factors such as nature of the purchase, number of people involved in the decision, understanding of the product being purchased, and time frame for the decision.

Buzz Word-of-mouth communication generated about a brand in the marketplace.

C

capital equipment A firm's significant, long-term investments in critical equipment or technology necessary for its manufacturing and production activities.

capital goods Major purchases in support of significant business functions.

captive pricing (complementary pricing) A pricing tactic of gaining a commitment from a customer to a basic product or system that requires continual purchase of peripherals to operate.

cash discounts A percentage discount off invoice to elicit quicker payment by the customer.

catalog retailer A retailer that offers merchandise in the form of a printed or online catalog.

category extensions When a firm uses its brand to expand into new product categories.

causal research Descriptive research designed to identify associations between variables.

census A comprehensive record of each individual in the population.

change conflict A customer's reluctance to choose change by selecting a company's product.

channel captain (channel leader) The lead player in an administered vertical marketing system (VMS).

channel conflict Disagreements among channel members that can result in their relationship to become strained or even fall apart.

channel of distribution A system of interdependent relationships among a set of organizations that facilitates the exchange process.

channel or medium The conduit by which an encoded message travels.

channel power The degree to which any member of a marketing channel can exercise influence over the other members of the channel.

closed-ended questions Question format that encourages respondents to provide specific responses.

closing the sale Obtaining commitment from the customer to make the purchase.

clutter The level of competing messages on a particular medium.

coercive power An explicit or implicit threat that a channel captain will invoke negative consequences on a channel member if it does not comply with the leader's request or expectations.

cognitive Active learning that involves mental processes that acquire information to work through problems and manage life situations.

commission Payment based on short-term results.

communication The process of exchanging information and conveying meaning from one party to another.

comparative advertising Advertising in which two or more brands are directly compared against each other on certain attributes.

comparative-parity method Method of promotional budgeting that focuses on comparing promotion expenditures across all key competitors in the market to determine a budget number.

competitive advertising Advertising intended to build sales of a specific brand through shifting emotional appeal, persuasion, and providing information.

competitive scenario analysis Analyzing competitors using various scenarios to predict competitor behavior.

competitive strategy An organization-wide strategy designed to increase a firm's performance within the marketplace in terms of its competitors.

complete set The very large set of possible alternatives a consumer considers during the initial search for information.

competitor orientation A reactive marketing strategy that uses competitor analysis as its primary driver.

competitor-based pricing A pricing strategy in which a firm decides to price at some market average price in context with prices of competitors.

concentrated target marketing (focus or niche strategy) The target marketing approach that involves targeting a large portion of a small market.

conditioning The creation of a psychological association between two stimuli.

conformance A product's ability to deliver on features and performance characteristics promised in marketing communications.

consideration (evoked) set A refined list that encompasses the strongest options an individual considers in a purchase decision once he or she has obtained additional information and carried out an evaluation.

consumer marketing The practice of marketing toward large groups of like-minded customers.

contingency planning Also called scenario planning, a planning approach that requires the establishment of different planning options depending on the expected case, best case, or worst case.

contractual agreements Enduring, nonequity relationships with another company that allow a company to expand its participation in a foreign market.

contractual VMS The binding of otherwise independent entities in the vertical marketing system legally through contractual agreements.

controls Elements put in place to ensure progress is being made in the implementation of a marketing plan. Controls must be in place from the outset of the planning process to specify the timing, procedure, and persons responsible for systematically monitoring.

convenience goods Frequently purchased, relatively low-cost products for which customers have little interest in seeking new information about or considering other product options.

cooperative advertising and promotion When a manufacturer provides special incentive money to channel members for certain promotional performance.

core competencies The activities a firm can do exceedingly well.

core product The physical, tangible elements that make up a product's essential benefit.

corporate identity Consumers' perceptions of a corporation that influences their attitudes and responses toward products or services offered by it.

corporate-level strategic plan An umbrella plan for the overall direction of the corporation developed above the strategic business unit (SBU) level.

corporate vertical marketing system (VMS) The investment of a channel member in backward or forward vertical integration by buying controlling interest in other intermediaries.

cost-based price An international pricing strategy in which the firm considers cost plus markup to arrive at a final price.

cost leadership A marketing strategy in which a firm utilizes its core cost advantages to gain an advantage over competitors due to flexibility in pricing strategies as well as its ability to translate cost savings to the bottom line.

cost reduction A specific method for introducing lower-cost products that frequently focuses on value-oriented product price points in the product mix.

cost-plus pricing Building a price by adding standardized markup on top of the costs associated with the offering.

country-of-origin effect The influence of the country of manufacture, assembly, or design on a customer's positive or negative perception of a product.

creating assortments The process of accumulating products from several sources to then make those products available down the channel as a convenient assortment for consumers.

credence attributes Aspects of an offering for which customers cannot make a reasonable evaluation, even after use.

crisis management A planned, coordinated approach for disseminating information during times of emergency and for handling the effects of unfavorable publicity.

cultural values Principles shared by a society that assert positive ideals.

culture A system of values, beliefs, and morals shared by a particular group of people that permeates over time.

customer advocacy A willingness and ability on the part of a customer to participate in communicating the brand message to others within his or her sphere of influence.

customer benefit Some type of utility that a company and its products (and services) provide its customers.

customer communities Web sites where customers come and share stories about their vendor experiences.

customer delight The exceeding of customer expectations.

customer expectations management The process of making sure the firm does not set customer expectations so high that they cannot be effectively met on a consistent basis.

customer loyalty A customers commitment to a company and its products and brands for the long run.

customer marketing The practice of marketing that focuses on developing relationships with individuals.

customer mind-set An individual's belief that understanding and satisfying customers, whether internal or external to the organization, is central to the proper execution of his or her job.

customer orientation Placing the customer at the core of all aspects of the enterprise.

customer relationship management (CRM) A comprehensive business model for increasing revenues and profits by focusing on customers.

customer retention Low propensity among a firm's customer base to consider switching to other providers.

customer satisfaction The level of liking an individual harbors for an offering.

customer-centric Placing the customer at the core of the enterprise and focusing on investments in customers over the long term.

customized (one-to-one) marketing A marketing strategy that involves directing energy and resources into establishing a learning relationship with each customer to increase the firm's customer knowledge.

D

data collection The distribution of a survey to its respondents, recording of the respondents' responses, and making the data available for analysis.

data mining A sophisticated analytical approach to using the massive amounts of data accumulated through a firm's CRM system to develop segments and microsegments of customers either for purposes of market research or development of market segmentation strategies.

data warehouse A compilation of customer data generated through touchpoints that can be transformed into useful information for marketing management decision making and marketing planning.

database marketing Direct marketing involving the utilization of the data generated through CRM practices to create lists of customer prospects who are then contacted individually by various means of marketing communication.

deceptive pricing Knowingly stating prices in a manner that gives a false impression to customers.

decider An individual within the buying center who ultimately makes the purchase decision.

decision-making authority An issue that arises when companies grow internationally and lines of authority become longer and more complicated resulting in difficulty in defining decision-making protocols.

decoding process When a receiver interprets the meaning of the message's symbols as encoded by the sender.

degree of affiliation The amount of interpersonal contact an individual has with the reference group.

degree of centralization The degree to which decisions are made at the firm's home office.

delightful surprises Built-in extras in service delivery not expected by the customer.

Delphi technique A subjective method of forecasting that is done iteratively, employing repeated measurement and controlled anonymous feedback instead of direct confrontation and debate among those preparing the forecast.

demographic segmentation Dividing consumer groups based on a variety of readily measurable descriptive factors about the group.

demographics The characteristics of human populations and population segments, especially when used to identify consumer markets.

depth of merchandise The number of different product items within a product category.

derived demand Demand that originates from the demand for consumer products in business-to-business (B-to-B) marketing.

descriptive research Research designed to explain or illustrate some phenomenon.

desirability The extent and direction of the emotional connection an individual wishes to have with a particular group.

developed economies Specific economies that have fueled world economic growth for much of the 20th century, including Western Europe, the United States, and Japan.

differentiated target marketing The target marketing approach that involves developing different value offerings for different targeted segments.

differentiation Communicating and delivering value in different ways to different customer groups.

dimensions of service quality The five aspects of a service that make up its total quality, including tangibles, reliability, responsiveness, assurance, and empathy.

direct and interactive marketing Personal communication with a customer by means other than a salesperson.

direct channel A channel that has no intermediaries and operates strictly from producer to end-user consumer or business user.

direct competitors Competing firms that produce products considered very close substitutes for those of other firms' current products and services.

direct foreign investment A strategic alliance with long-term implications in which a company moves manufacturing or operations into a foreign market.

direct marketing An interactive marketing system that uses one or more advertising media to affect a measurable response and/or transaction at any location.

direct selling A form of non-store retailing that involves independent businesspeople contacting consumers directly to demonstrate and sell products or services in convenient locations.

discounts Direct, immediate reductions in price provided to purchasers.

disintermediation The shortening or collapsing of marketing channels due to the elimination of one or more intermediaries.

distinctive competencies A firm's core competencies that are superior to those of their competitors.

distribution intensity The number of intermediaries involved in distributing the product.

diversification strategies Strategies designed to seize on opportunities to serve new markets with new products.

dumping A global pricing issue that refers to the practice of charging less than their actual costs or less than the product price in the firm's home markets.

durability The length of product usage.

durable product Products with a comparatively long product life that are often expensive.

E

early adopter A consumer who is a product opinion leader who seeks out new products consistent with his or her personal self-image.

early majority Consumers who are product watchers who want to be convinced of the product's claims and value proposition before making a commitment to it.

electronic commerce (e-commerce) Any action that uses electronic media to communicate with customers, facilitate the inventory, exchange, and distribution of goods and services, or facilitate payment.

electronic data interchange (EDI) Sophisticated programs that link a customer with its suppliers to manage inventories and automatically replenish supplies.

electronic retailing The communication and sale of products or services to consumers over the Internet.

emerging markets Growing economies that have developed over the last 25 years that are projected to contribute toward 75 percent of world economic growth over the next 20 years.

emotional appeal Promotional appeal that plays on human nature using a variety of human emotions and aspirations in developing promotional messages.

emotional choice A product choice based more on emotional attitudes about a product rather than rational thought.

encoding process The process in communication in which the sender translates an idea to be communicated into a symbolic message in preparation for transmittal to a receiver.

end-user purchase A category of products purchased by manufacturers that represents the equipment, supplies, and services needed to keep their business operational.

enhanced product Additional features, designs, or innovations that extend beyond the core product to exceed customer expectations.

enterprise resource planning (ERP) system A software application designed to integrate information related to logistics processes throughout the organization.

e-procurement The process of online business purchasing.

essential benefit The fundamental need met by a product.

European Union A successful regional marketing zone founded more than 50 years ago by six European countries (Belgium, France, Italy, Luxembourg, The Netherlands, and West Germany) with the Treaty of Rome that now includes 25 countries.

even pricing A pricing tactic in which the price is expressed in whole dollar increments.

event sponsorship Having your brand and company associated with events in the sports, music, arts, and other entertainment communities.

everyday low pricing (EDLP) A pricing tactic that entails relatively low, constant prices and minimal spending on promotional efforts.

exchange The giving up of something of value for something desired.

exclusive dealing When a supplier creates a restrictive agreement that prohibits intermediaries that handle its product from selling competing firms' products.

exclusive distribution Distribution strategy built on prestige, scarcity, and premium pricing in which a producer only distributes its products to one or very few vendors.

exclusive territory The protection of an intermediary from having to compete with others selling a producer's goods.

experience attributes Aspects of an offering that can be evaluated only during or after consumption.

expert power A channel member's utilization of its unique competencies and knowledge to influence others in the channel.

exploratory research Research geared toward discovery that can either answer the research question or identify other research variables for further study. It is generally the first step in the marketing research process.

exporting The most common method for entering foreign markets, it offers firms the ability to penetrate foreign markets with minimal investment and very little risk.

extensive information search When a consumer makes a purchase decision based on a thorough process of investigation and research.

external information Additional information an individual seeks from outside sources when internal information is not sufficient to make a purchase decision.

F

FAB A selling approach designed to make the company's products more relevant for customers by explaining the products features, advantages, and benefits.

facilitating functions Activities that help fulfill completed transactions and also maintain the viability of the channel relationships.

fair trade laws Laws designed to allow manufacturers to establish artificially high prices by limiting the ability of wholesalers and retailers to offer reduced or discounted prices.

family A group of two or more people living together and related by birth, marriage, or adoption.

family branding The creation of brands that have synergy between them in terms of the overall company brand.

family life cycle The changes in life stage that transform an individual's buying habits.

features Any product attribute or performance characteristic.

feedback loop Two-way communication in which a receiver can communicate reactions back to the sender.

firing a customer The shifting of investment of resources from a less attractive customer to more profitable ones.

first-mover advantage When a firm introduces a new market offering, thus defining the scope of the competitive marketplace.

fluctuating demand When the level of consumer demand is not constant, having serious implications related to the perishability of services.

FOB (free on board) Determination of title transfer and freight payment based on shipping location.

focus group A qualitative research method that consists of a meeting (either in person or increasingly online) of 6 to 10 people that is moderated by a professional who carefully moves the conversation through a defined agenda in an unstructured, open format.

follow-up A company's actions after the customer has decided to purchase the product.

food retailer Any retailer that includes food as a part of its breadth of merchandise.

form The physical elements of a product, such as size, shape, and color.

formalization The formal establishment of a firm's structure, processes and tools, and managerial knowledge and commitment to support its culture.

forward integration When a firm moves its operations more toward the end user.

franchise organization A contractual relationship between a franchisor who is the grantor of the franchise, and the franchisee who is the independent entity entering into an agreement to perform at the standards required by the franchisor.

franchising A contractual agreement in which a firm provides a contracted company in a foreign market with a bundle of products, systems, services, and management expertise in return for local market knowledge, financial consideration, and local management experience.

frequency The average number of times a person in the target market is exposed to the message.

functional-level plans Plans for each business function that makes up one of the firm's strategic business units (SBUs). These include core business functions within each SBU such as operations, marketing, finance, as well as other pertinent operational areas.

G

gap model A visual tool used in the measurement of service quality that identifies and measures the differences between consumer and marketer perceptions of a provided service.

gatekeeper An individual who controls access to information and relevant individuals in the buying center.

GE business screen A popular approach for in-firm portfolio analysis that categorizes business units' level of contribution to the overall firm based on two factors: business position and market attractiveness.

gender roles Behaviors regarded as proper for men and women in a particular society.

general warranty Broad promises about product performance and customer satisfaction.

generic strategy An overall directional strategy at the business level.

geographic regions An international organizational structure that divides international markets by geography, building autonomous regional organizations that perform business functions in the geographic areas.

geographic segmentation Dividing consumer groups based on physical location.

global marketing themes Global advertising strategy in which a basic template is used for global ads that allows for slight modifications depending on local markets.

global marketing with local content Global advertising strategy in which a firm keeps the same global marketing theme as the home market but adapts it with local content.

goals General statements of what the firm wishes to accomplish in support of the mission and vision.

go-to-market mistake When a company fails to stop a bad product idea from moving into product development.

government Local, state, and federal entities that have unique and frequently challenging purchasing practices for manufacturing firms.

gray market A global pricing issue that references the unauthorized diversion of branded products into global markets.

growth phase A stage of the product life cycle marked by rapid expansion as competitors come into the market and customers learn, understand, and begin to adopt the product.

H

harvesting A product strategy that involves a measured but consistent investment reduction in a product.

high-involvement learning The learning process in which an individual is stimulated to acquire new information.

high mass consumption An economy characterized by rising income levels, creating a large population with discretionary income, which results in consumers that demand higher levels of service and more durable goods.

high/low pricing A pricing strategy in which the retailer offers frequent discounts, primarily through sales promotions, to stated regular prices.

household life cycle (HLC) A structured set of chronological activities a particular household follows over time.

I

impulse goods Goods whose sales rely on the consumer seeing the product, feeling an immediate want, and being able to purchase now.

inbound logistics The process of sourcing materials and knowledge inputs from external suppliers to the point at which production begins.

inbound telemarketing When a prospective customer contacts a company for more information.

incentive pay Generally commissions tied to sales volume or profitability, or bonuses for meeting or exceeding specific performance targets.

in-depth interview A qualitative research method that consists of an unstructured (or loosely structured) interview with an individual who has been chosen based on some characteristic of interest, often a demographic attribute.

indirect channel A channel that contains one or more intermediary levels.

indirect competitors Competing firms that offer products that may be substituted based on the customer's need and choice options.

inelastic demand When changes in demand are not significantly affected by changes in price.

influencer An individual, either inside or outside the organization, with relevant expertise in a particular area who provides information used by the buying center in making a final buying decision.

information search The process consumers use to gather information to make a purchase decision.

initiator The individual who starts the buying decision process.

innovator A consumer who is a product enthusiast who is among the first to try and master a new product.

input measures The efforts of salespeople during the sales process.

inseparability The characteristic of a service in which it is produced and consumed at the same time and cannot be separated from its provider.

insourcing (third-party logistics) Handing over one or more core functions to a third-party supplier with expertise in those areas so the firm can better focus on its core business.

institutional advertising Advertising that promotes industry, company, family of brands, or some other issues broader than a specific product.

institutions Nongovernmental organizations driven by the delivery of service to the target constituency, rather than by profits.

instrumental performance The actual performance features of the product in terms of what it was promised to do.

intangibility The characteristic of a service in which it cannot be experienced through the physical senses of the consumer.

integrated marketing communications (IMC) A strategic approach to communicating the brand and company message to targeted customers in ways that are clear, concise, and consistent and yet are customizable as needed to maximize the impact on a particular audience.

intensive distribution A distribution strategy designed to saturate every possible intermediary, especially retailers.

interactive marketing An Internet-driven relationship between companies, their brands, and customers. Interactive marketing enables customers to control information flow and encourages customer-company interaction as well as a higher level of customer service.

intermediaries Organizations that play a role in the exchange process between producers and consumers.

internal information All information stored in memory and accessed by the individual regarding a purchase decision.

internal marketing The treating of employees as customers and developing systems and benefits that satisfy their needs to promote internal service quality.

international joint ventures A strategic alliance formed by legal entities consisting of a partnership of two or more participating companies that share management duties and a defined management structure in which every partner holds an equity position.

interstitials Graphic, visually interesting Internet advertisements that move across the Web page.

involvement A significant outcome of an individual's motivation that mediates the product choice decision. It is activated by three elements: background and psychological profile, aspirational focus, and the environment at the time of purchase decision.

J

jury of executive opinion Subjective method of forecasting that relies on a formal or informal poll of key executives within the firm to gain their assessment of sales potential.

just-in-time (JIT) inventory control system An inventory management system designed to balance levels of overstock and stock-out in an effort to reduce warehousing costs.

just noticeable difference (JND) The amount of price increase that can be taken without impacting customer demand.

K

key account salespeople Salespeople responsible for the firm's largest customers.

L

laggard A consumer who is a product avoider who evades adoption until there is no other product choice.

language An established system of ideas and phonetics shared by members of a particular culture that serves as their primary communication tool.

late majority Consumers who are product followers who are price sensitive, risk averse, and generally prefer products with fewer features.

learning Any change in the content or organization of long-term memory or behavior.

legitimate power A channel member's ability to influence other members based on contracts or other formal agreements.

licensing When a firm offers other manufacturers the right to use its brand in exchange for a set fee or percentage of sales.

lifestyle An individual's perspective on life that manifests itself in activities, interests, and opinions.

lifetime value of a customer The measurement of important business success factors related to long-term relationships with customers.

limited information search When a consumer makes a purchase decision based on incomplete information and/or lack of personal knowledge.

line extensions Introducing a new product to an existing product line.

line of visibility The separation between activities customers see and those they do not in the process of service delivery.

local market ad generation Global marketing strategy in which a firm allows local marketers to create local ads that do not necessarily coordinate with its global marketing messages.

local market conditions price An international pricing strategy in which the firm assigns a price based on local market conditions with minimal consideration for the actual cost of putting the product into the market.

long-term memory Enduring memory storage that can remain with an individual for years or even a lifetime.

loss-leader products Products sacrificed at prices below costs in an effort to attract shoppers to the retail location.

low-involvement learning The learning process in which an individual is not prompted to value new information, characterized by little or no interest in learning about a new product offering.

low-price guarantee policy A pricing strategy used by retailers that guarantees consumers the lowest price for any given product by matching the sales price of competitors.

loyalty programs Programs that reinforce the customer's benefits of purchasing at the retailer.

M

macroeconomics The study of economic activity in terms of broad measures of output and input as well as the interaction among various sectors of an entire economy.

management research deliverable The definition of what management wants to do with marketing research.

market creation Approaches that drive the market toward fulfilling a whole new set of needs that customers did not realize was possible or feasible before.

market deterioration The third and final phase of the maturity stage of the product life cycle in which the market starts to lose customers and competitors begin to feel the pressure of overcapacity in the market.

market development strategies Strategies designed to allow for expansion of the firm's product line into heretofore untapped markets, often internationally.

market expansion When a firm that operates in closely related markets expands into new markets to compete more directly.

market information system (MIS) A continuing process of identifying, collecting, analyzing, accumulating and dispensing critical information to marketing decision makers.

market makers Web sites that bring buyers and sellers together.

market mavens Individuals who have information about many kinds of products, places to shop, and other facets of markets, and initiate discussions with consumers and respond to requests from consumers for market information.

market orientation The implementation of the marketing concept, based on an understanding of customers and competitors.

market penetration strategies Strategies designed to involve investing against existing customers to gain additional usage of existing products.

market research The methodical identification, collection, analysis, and distribution of data related to discovering then solving marketing problems or opportunities and enhancing good decision making.

market segmentation Dividing a market into meaningful smaller markets or submarkets based on common characteristics.

market share The percentage of total category sales accounted for by a firm.

market space A powerful new communication channel that encourages customer-company interaction and a higher level of customer service.

market stability The second phase of the maturity stage of the product life cycle in which a product experiences no market growth as the market reaches saturation.

market test Objective method of forecasting that involves placing a product in several representative geographic areas to see how well it performs and then projecting that experience to the market as a whole.

market-driven strategic planning The process at the corporate or strategic business unit (SBU) level of a firm that acts to marshal the various resource and functional areas toward a central purpose around the customer.

marketing The activity, set of institutions, and processes for creating, communicating, delivering, and exchanging offerings that have value for customers, clients, partners, and society at large.

Marketing (big M) The dimension of marketing that focuses on external forces that affect the organization and serves as the driver of business strategy.

marketing (little m) The dimension of marketing that focuses on the functional or operational level of the organization.

marketing audit A systematic review of the current state of marketing within an organization.

marketing concept Business philosophy that emphasizes an organization-wide customer orientation with the objective of achieving long-run profits.

marketing control The process of measuring marketing results and adjusting the firm's marketing plan as needed.

marketing dashboard A comprehensive system of metrics and information uniquely relevant to the role of the marketing manager in a particular organization. Dashboards provide managers with up-to-the-minute information necessary to run their operation.

marketing intelligence The collecting, analyzing, and storing of data from the macro environment on a continuous basis.

marketing management The leading and managing of the facets of marketing to improve individual, unit, and organizational performance.

marketing metrics Tools and processes designed to identify, track, evaluate, and provide key benchmarks for improvement of marketing activities.

marketing mix (4Ps of marketing) Product, price, place, and promotion—the fundamental elements that comprise the marketer's tool kit that can be developed in unique combinations to set the product or brand apart from the competition.

marketing plan The resulting document that records the marketing planning process in a useful framework.

marketing planning The ongoing process of developing and implementing market-driven strategies for an organization.

marketing's stakeholders Any person or entity inside or outside a firm with whom marketing interacts, impacts, and is impacted by.

markup on cost The addition to the price of an offering after costs have been considered.

markup on sales price Using the sales price as a basis for calculating the markup percentage.

mass customization Combining flexible manufacturing with flexible marketing to greatly enhance customer choice.

mass marketing The classic style of consumer marketing in which a firm views all consumers as equal reactors to a firm's marketing strategies.

materials Natural or farm products that become part of the final product.

materials requirement planning (MRP) The overall management of the inbound materials from suppliers to facilitate minimal production delays.

materials, repairs, operational (MRO) Products used in everyday business operations that are not typically considered to be a significant expense for the firm.

matrix structure An international organizational structure that encourages regional autonomy among organizations while building product competence in key areas around the world.

maturity An economy that, through private and public investments, has reached the point where it seeks to maintain its growth rates.

maturity stage A stage of the product life cycle in which a product is in the transition from high growth to relative sales decline. There are three phases in the maturity stage: relative market expansion, market stability, and market deterioration.

mechanical observation A variation of observational data that uses a device to chronicle activity.

memory Where people store all past learning events.

merchandise category An assortment of items considered substitutes for each other.

merchant intermediaries Intermediaries who take title to the product during the exchange process.

MERCOSUR Inaugurated in 1995, it is the most powerful market zone in South America and includes the major economies of South America: Argentina, Bolivia, Brazil, Chile, Paraguay, and Uruguay.

message transmission Placing a communication into some channel or medium so that it can make its way to the intended receiver.

microeconomics The study of individual economic activity.

minimal information search When a consumer makes a purchase decision based on very little information or investigation.

minimum markup laws Laws that require retailers to apply a certain percentage of markup to their products for sale.

mission statement The verbal articulation of an organization's purpose, or reason for existence.

missionary salespeople Salespeople who do not take orders from customers directly but persuade customers to buy their firm's product from distributors or other suppliers.

modifications to existing products Creating newer, better, faster versions of existing products that target, for the most part, existing customers.

modified re-buy A buying decision in which a customer is familiar with the product and supplier in a purchase decision, but is looking for additional information because of one or more of three circumstances: the supplier has performed poorly, new products have come into the market, or the customer believes it is time for a change.

moment of truth The face-to-face time between customer and service provider.

monopolistic competition When there are many companies offering unique products in different market segments.

monopoly When a market is controlled by a single company offering one set of products.

moral appeal Promotional appeal that strikes a chord with a target customer's sense of right and wrong.

motivation The stimulating power that induces and then directs an individual's behavior.

MRO supplies (maintenance, repair, operating) The everyday items that a company needs to keep running.

multiattribute model A model that measures an individual's attitudes toward an object by evaluating it on several important attributes.

N

NAFTA The North American Free Trade Agreement: created to eliminate tariffs between Canada, Mexico, and the United States, and which stands as the single largest economic alliance today.

national brands Products created, manufactured, and marketed by a company and sold to retailers around the country and the world.

network organization (virtual organization) Organizations that eliminate many in-house business functions and activities in favor of focusing only on those aspects for which they are best equipped to add value.

new dominant logic for marketing A shift in worldview from the traditional goods versus services dichotomy to recognition of both goods and services as "offerings" that create value for consumers.

new purchase A buying decision in which the purchase of a product or service by a customer is for the first time.

new-to-the-world product A product that has not been available before or bears little resemblance to an existing product.

nimble To be in a position to be maximally flexible, adaptable, and speedy in response to the many key change drivers affecting business.

noise The distortion or interference that can occur at any stage of a communication process.

nondurable product Products that are usually consumed in a few uses and, in general, are of low cost to the consumer.

nonfinancial incentives Sales force motivators beyond financial compensation.

nonprobability sampling The selection of individuals for statistical research in which the probability of everyone in the population being included in the sample is not identified.

non-store retailer A retailer that uses alternative methods to reach the customer that do not require a physical location.

nonverbal communication The means of communicating through facial expressions, eye behavior, gestures, posture, and any other body language.

North American Industrial Classification System (NAICS) A system developed by the United States, Canada, and Mexico that classifies companies on the basis of their primary output to define and segment business markets.

O

objective forecasting methods Forecasting methods that rely primarily on sophisticated quantitative (empirical) analytical approaches.

objective measures Statistics the sales manager gathers from the firm's internal data.

objective-and-task method Method of promotional budgeting that takes an investment approach in that goals are set for the upcoming year and then promotional dollars are budgeted to support the achievement of those goals.

objectives Specific, measurable, and potentially attainable milestones necessary for a firm to achieve its goals.

observational data The documentation of behavioral patterns among the population of interest.

odd pricing A pricing tactic in which the price is not expressed in whole dollar increments.

offering A product or service that delivers value to satisfy a need or want.

oligopoly When a market is controlled by more than one company in an industry that is either standardized or differentiated.

one world price An international pricing strategy in which the firm assigns one price for its products in every global market.

one-price strategy A pricing tactic in which the price marked on a good is what it typically sells for.

one-to-one marketing Directing energy and resources into establishing a learning relationship with each customer and connecting that knowledge with the firm's production and service capabilities to fulfill that customer's needs in as customary a manner as possible.

online database Data stored on a server that is accessed remotely over the Internet or some other telecommunications network.

open-ended questions Question format that encourages respondents to be expressive and offers them the opportunity to provide more detailed, qualitative responses.

opinion leaders Individuals with expertise in certain products or technologies who classify, explain, and then bestow information to a broader audience.

organizational factors Organization-wide beliefs and attitudes that factor into a purchase decision.

organizational learning The analysis and refinement phase of the CRM process that is based on customer response to the firm's implementation strategies and programs.

original equipment manufacturer (OEM) Manufacturing firms that sell products that are used as integral manufacturing components by their customer companies.

out supplier A company that is not on a firm's list of approved suppliers.

outbound logistics The process of a product's movement from production by the manufacturer to purchase by the end-user consumer.

outbound telemarketing Calling potential customers at their home or office, either to make a sales call via telephone or to set up an appointment for a field salesperson.

output measures The results of the efforts expended by the salesperson.

outsourcing the sales force Using independent sales agents to sell a company's products.

P

partner relationship management (PRM) strategies A strategic alliance that includes connectivity of inventory, billing systems, and market research among marketing channel members.

parts Equipment that is either fully assembled or in smaller pieces that will be assembled in larger components and then used in the production process.

penetration pricing A pricing strategy in which a firm's objective is to gain as much market share as possible.

perceived quality The conveyed perception of quality of a brand that is either positive or negative.

percent-of-sales method Method of promotional budgeting that allocates funding for promotional activities to certain products as a function of their forecasted sales revenues.

perception A system to select, organize, and interpret information to create a useful, informative picture of the world.

perceptual maps A visual tool used in positioning that allows for comparing attributes to gauge consumer perceptions of each competitor's delivery against those attributes.

perishability The characteristic of a product or service in which it cannot be stored or saved for future use.

personal factors The needs, desires, and objectives of those involved in a purchase decision.

personal selling A two-way communication process between salesperson and buyer with the goal of securing, building, and maintaining long-term relationships with profitable customers.

personality An individual's set of unique personal qualities that produce distinctive responses across similar situations.

physical distribution (logistics) The integrated process of moving input materials to the producer, in-process inventory through the firm, and finished goods out of the firm through the channel of distribution.

pioneering advertising Advertising intended to stimulate primary demand, typically during the introductory or early growth stages of an offering.

portfolio analysis A tool used in strategic planning for multibusiness corporations that views SBUs, and sometimes even product lines, as a series of investments from which it expects maximization of returns.

positioning The communication of sources of value to customers so they can easily make the connection between their needs and wants and what the product has to offer.

postpurchase dissonance A feeling of doubt or anxiety following a recent purchase, generally attributed with high-involvement, large purchases.

preferred state An individual's desires that reflect how he or she would like to feel or live in the present time.

prestige pricing A pricing tactic that lends prestige to a product or brand by virtue of a price relatively higher than the competition.

price bundling A pricing tactic in which customers are given the opportunity to purchase a package deal at a reduced price compared to what the individual components of the package would cost separately.

price elasticity of demand The measure of customers' price sensitivity estimated by dividing relative changes in quantity sold by relative changes in price.

price fixing When companies collude to set prices at a mutually beneficial high level.

price points Prices established to convey the differences in benefits offered as the customer moves up and down the product line.

price skimming A pricing strategy in which a firm enters a market at a relatively high price point, usually in an effort to create a strong price-quality relationship for the product.

price war When a company purposefully makes pricing decisions to undercut one or more competitors and gain sales and net market share.

pricing objectives The desired or expected results associated with a pricing strategy that is consistent with other marketing-related objectives.

primary data Data collected specifically for a particular research question.

primary group A reference group an individual has frequent contact with.

primary target markets Market segments that clearly have the best chance of meeting ROI goals and the other attractiveness factors.

private-label brands Products managed and marketed by retailers, also known as store or house brands.

probability sampling The specific protocol used to identify and select individuals from the population in which each population element has a known non-zero chance of being selected.

product advertising Advertising designed to increase purchase of a specific offering.

product choice The end result of evaluating product alternatives in the purchase decision process.

product deletion Discontinuing the production of a product.

product demand Demand within business markets affected by three critical dimensions: derived demand, fluctuating demand, and inelastic demand.

product development strategies Strategies designed to recognize the opportunity to invest in new products that will increase usage from the current customer base.

product expansion When a firm leverages its existing expertise (technical product experience or supply chain) to create new products for existing or new markets.

product line A group of products linked through usage, customer profile, price points, and distribution channels or needs satisfaction.

product line pricing (price lining) A pricing tactic in which a firm affords the marketing manager an opportunity to develop a rational pricing approach across a complete line of related items.

product mix The combination of all the products offered by a firm.

production orientation The maximization of production capacity through improvements in products and production activities without much regard for what is going on in the marketplace.

professional services Services that require specialized training and certification that are typically self-regulated by industry or trade groups.

profitability analysis A thorough analysis that accounts for all costs associated with bringing a product to market to determine short- and long-term product profitability.

promotion Various forms of communication to inform, persuade, or remind.

promotion mix The elements of promotion, including advertising, sales promotion, public relations (PR), personal selling, direct marketing, and interactive marketing.

promotion mix strategies Decisions about which combination of elements in the promotion mix is likely to best communicate the offering to the marketplace and achieve an acceptable ROI for the marketer.

promotional allowances Sales promotions initiated by the manufacturer and carried out by the retailer, who is then compensated by the manufacturer.

promotional appeal The connection an offering establishes with customers. includes rational appeals, emotional appeals, and moral appeals.

promotional campaign Promotional expenditures to a particular creative execution aimed at a particular product or product line during a specified time period.

psychographic segmentation Dividing consumer groups based on variables such as personality and AIOs: activities, interests, and opinions.

psychological pricing Creating a perception about price merely from the image the numbers provide the customer.

public relations (PR) Systematic approach to influencing attitudes, opinions, and behaviors of customers and others.

publicity An unpaid and relatively less personal form of marketing communications, usually through news stories and mentions at public events.

puffery Relatively minor embellishments of product claims to bolster the persuasive message.

pull strategy Promotional and distribution strategy in which the focus is on stimulating demand for an offering directly from the end user.

pure competition When there are many companies offering essentially the same product in the market.

push strategy Promotional and distribution strategy in which the focus is on stimulating demand within the channel of distribution.

Q

qualitative research Less structured research not meant to be used for statistical analysis that can employ methods such as surveys and interviews to collect data.

quantitative research Research used to develop a measured understanding using statistical analysis to assess and quantify the results.

quantity discounts Discounts taken off an invoice price based on different levels of product purchased.

R

rational appeal Promotional appeal that centers on the benefits an offering can provide to a customer.

reach The percentage of individuals in a defined target market that are exposed to an ad during a specific time period.

real state An individual's perceived reality of present time.

receiver The individual who is the target of the communication.

reducing transactions The process of lowering the number of purchasing transactions carried out by a firm by utilizing the services of intermediaries.

reference group A group of individuals whose beliefs, attitudes, and behavior influence (positively or negatively) the beliefs, attitudes, and behavior of an individual.

reference pricing A pricing strategy in which a firm gives customers comparative prices when considering purchase of a product so they are not viewing a price in isolation from prices of other choices.

referent power A channel member's ability to influence other members based on respect, admiration, or reverence.

regional marketing zones A group of countries that create formal relationships for mutual economic benefit through lower tariffs and reduced trade barriers.

relationship orientation Investing in keeping and cultivating profitable current customers instead of constantly having to invest in gaining new ones.

relationship-based enterprise A firm that strives to facilitate long-term, win-win relationships between buyers and sellers.

relative market expansion The first phase in the maturity stage of the product life cycle in which product category sales continue to grow but at a rate significantly less than the growth stage.

reliability The percentage of time a product works without failure or stoppage.

repairability The ease of fixing a problem with a product.

repeat purchase A function of total demand that considers the number of products purchased by the same customer.

replacement purchase A function of total demand that considers the number of products purchased to replace existing products that have either become obsolete or malfunctioned.

repositioning Using the marketing mix approach to change present consumer perceptions of a firm's product or service.

request for proposal (RFP) The document distributed to potential vendors that outlines an organization's product or service needs. It serves as a starting point from which vendors put together their product solution.

research design A framework for a study that directs the identification of a problem and collection and analysis of data.

research problem The definition of what information is needed to help management in a particular situation.

resellers Companies that buy products and then resell them to other businesses or consumers for a profit.

retail positioning The retailer's brand image in the consumer's mind.

retail target market The group of consumers targeted by a retailer.

retailer cooperative (co-op) The binding of retailers across a variety of product categories to gain cost and operating economies of scale in the channel.

retailer experience The overall experience a consumer has shopping at a retail location or online.

retailing Any business activity that creates value in the delivery of goods and services to consumers for their personal, nonbusiness consumption and is an essential component of the supply chain.

return on customer investment (ROCI) A calculation that estimates the projected financial returns from a customer. It is a useful strategic tool for deciding which customers deserve what levels of investment of various resources.

return on marketing investment (ROMI) What impact an investment in marketing has on a firm's success, especially financially.

reverse auctions When sellers bid prices to buyers and the purchase typically goes to the lowest bidder.

reverse logistics The process of moving goods back to the manufacturer or intermediary after purchase.

reward power A channel member's ability to coerce vendors by offering them incentives.

S

salary A fixed sum of money paid at regular intervals.

sales contests Short-term incentive programs designed to motivate salespeople to accomplish specific sales objectives.

sales experience The level of ease a consumer experiences in purchasing and returning merchandise at a retailer.

sales force composite Subjective method of forecasting that relies on the opinion of each member of the field sales staff.

sales orientation The increase of sales and consequently production capacity utilization by having salespeople "push" product into the hands of customers.

sales presentation The delivery of information relevant to meet the customer's needs.

sales promotion An inducement for an end-user consumer to buy a product or for a salesperson or someone else in the channel to sell it.

sales skill levels The individual's learned proficiency at performing necessary sales tasks.

sample A subgroup of the population selected for participation in research.

SBU-level strategic plan Planning that occurs within each of the firm's strategic business units (SBUs) designed to meet individual performance requirements and contribute satisfactorily to the overall corporate plan.

search attributes Aspects of an offering that are physically observable before consumption.

search-related ads Paid advertisements featured in Internet search engine results based on analysis of keywords entered in the search field.

seasonal discounts Discounts that reward the purchaser for shifting part of the inventory storage function away from the manufacturer.

SEC 10-K report A document filed with the Securities and Exchange Commission (SEC) that reports detailed information about a firm's operations and strategies.

secondary data Data collected for some other purpose than the problem currently being considered.

secondary group A reference group with which an individual has limited contact.

secondary target markets Market segments that have reasonable potential but for one reason or another are not best suited for development immediately.

selective awareness A psychological tool an individual uses to help focus on what is relevant and eliminate what is not relevant.

selective distortion The process in which an individual can misunderstand information or make it fit existing beliefs.

selective distribution A distribution strategy in which goods are distributed only to a limited number of intermediaries.

selective perception Different meanings assigned to the same message by different receivers that are based on an array of individual differences.

selective retention The process of placing in one's memory only those stimuli that support existing beliefs and attitudes about a product or brand

sender The source of the message in communication.

service A product that represents a bundle of benefits that can satisfy customer wants and needs without having physical form.

service blueprints Complete pictorial designs and flow charts of all of a service's activities from the first customer contact to the actual delivery of the service.

service economy An economy that is predominantly comprised of service-related jobs.

service encounter The time period during which a customer interacts in any way with a service provider.

service failure When a service fails to meet the quality level promised by the provider.

service quality The formalization of the measurement of customer expectations of a service compared to perceptions of actual service performance.

service recovery The restoring of service quality to a level at or above customer's expectations following a service failure.

service sector The portion of an economy that is comprised of service-related jobs.

service-profit chain The formalization of linkages between employee and customer aspects of service delivery.

SERVQUAL A measurement instrument designed to reflect the five dimensions of service quality.

shopping experience The consumer's holistic experience while looking for and evaluating products during the purchase decision process.

shopping goods Products that require consumers to do research and compare across product dimensions like color, size, features, and price.

short-term memory The information an individual recalls at the present time. Sometimes referred to as working memory.

situation analysis An analysis of the macro-and micro-level environment within which a firm's marketing plan is being developed.

SKU (stock keeping unit) Unique identification numbers used in tracking products through a distribution system, inventory management, and pricing.

slotting allowance (shelf fee) Extra incentives paid to wholesalers or retailers by the manufacturer for placing a particular product into inventory.

social class A ranking of individuals into harmonized groups based on demographic characteristics such as age, education, income, and occupation.

societal marketing The concept that, at the broadest level, members of society at large can be viewed as a stakeholder for marketing.

sorting The process of classifying products for sale through different channels.

specialty goods Unique products in which consumers' purchase decision is based on a defining characteristic.

specific warranty Explicit product performance promises related to components of the product.

sponsorships Spaces sold on high traffic Web sites that enable companies to subsidize some section of the Web page on the site.

stability pricing A pricing strategy in which a firm attempts to find a neutral set point for price that is neither low enough to raise the ire of competition nor high enough to put the value proposition at risk with customers.

stand-alone brands Brands created to be separate from a company brand that can insulate the company if there is a problem with the brand.

stock-out When an item is not in stock.

stop-to-market mistake When a product that is a good idea is prematurely eliminated during the screening process and ultimately never introduced to the market.

store brands Brands created by retailers for sale only in their store locations.

straight re-buy A buying decision that requires little evaluation because the products are purchased on a consistent, regular basis.

strategic alliances A market entry strategy designed to spread the risk of foreign investment among its partners. Examples of strategic alliances would be international joint ventures or direct foreign investment.

strategic marketing The long-term, firm-level commitment to investing in marketing–supported at the highest organization level–for the purpose of enhancing organizational performance.

strategic type Firms of a particular strategic type have a common strategic orientation and a similar combination of structure, culture, and processes consistent with that strategy. Four strategic types are prospectors, analyzers, defenders, and reactors–depending on a firm's approach to the competitive marketplace.

strategic vision Often included within a firm's mission statement, it is a discussion of what the company would like to become in the future.

strategy A comprehensive plan stating how the organization will achieve its mission and objectives.

style The look and feel of a product.

subculture A group within a culture that shares similar cultural artifacts created by differences in ethnicity, religion, race, or geography.

subjective forecasting methods Forecasting methods that do not rely primarily on sophisticated quantitative (empirical) analytical approaches.

subjective measures Personal evaluations by someone connected to the salesperson's sales process.

supplier choice Selecting between multiple suppliers offering similar product configurations by examining their qualifications.

supply chain A complex logistics network characterized by high levels of coordination and integration among its members.

supply chain management The process of managing the aspects of the supply chain.

survey A quantitative research method that employs structured questionnaires given to a sample group of individuals representing the population of interest and that are intended to solicit specific responses to explicit questions.

sustainability The practicing of business that meets humanity's needs without harming future generations.

sustainable competitive advantage The resulting advantage a firm has when it invests in distinctive competencies.

SWOT analysis A convenient framework used to summarize key findings from a firm's situational analysis into a matrix of strengths, weaknesses, opportunities, and threats.

symbolic performance The image-building aspects of the product in terms of how it makes the consumer feel after purchase.

T

tactical marketing Marketing activities that take place at the functional or operational level of a firm.

tangibility The physical aspects of a product.

target marketing Evaluating market segments and making a decision about which among them shows the most promise for development.

target return on investment (ROI) A pricing strategy in which a bottom-line profit is established first and then pricing is set to achieve that target.

target return pricing A pricing decision made by considering fixed and variable costs and then demand forecasting to determine the price per unit.

technical selling Selling that requires a salesperson to have technical understanding of the product or service.

television home shopping A form of non-store retailing that involves showcasing products on a television network that can be ordered by the consumer.

tertiary target markets Market segments that may develop emerging attractiveness for investment in the future but that do not appear attractive at present.

time-series analysis Objective method of forecasting that relies on the analysis of historical data to develop a prediction for the future.

total demand The cumulative demand for a product over a given time period.

touchpoints The intersection of a selling firm with a customer via a media channel.

trade discounts An incentive to a channel member for performing some function in the channel that benefits the seller.

trade servicer Resellers such as retailers or distributors with whom the sales force does business.

trade show An industry- or company-sponsored event in which booths are set up for the dissemination of information about offerings to members of a channel.

traditional society A society dependent on agriculture as the primary driver of the economy, these economies lack the capabilities to industrialize and have high rates of illiteracy, which hinders advances in technology.

transactional cost analysis (TCA) A tool that measures cost of using different types of selling agents.

transfer pricing The cost companies charge internally to move products between subsidiaries or divisions.

transportation and storage Commonly provided intermediary functions for producers that do not perform these functions themselves.

tying contract A formal requirement by the seller of an intermediary to purchase a supplementary product to qualify to purchase the primary product the intermediary wishes to buy.

U

undifferentiated target marketing (mass market) The broadest approach to target marketing that involves offering a product or service that can be perceived as valuable to a very generalized group of consumers.

uniform delivered pricing When the same delivery fee is charged to customers regardless of geographic location within a set area.

unsought goods Products that consumers do not seek out and often would rather not purchase at all.

user Actual customers of a product or service who have a great deal of input at various stages of the buying decision process, but are typically not decision makers.

user expectations Subjective method of forecasting that relies on answers from customers regarding their expected consumption or purchase of a product.

utility The want-satisfying power of a good or service. There are four types of utility: form utility, time utility, place utility, and ownership utility.

V

VALS™ (Values and Lifestyles) A psychographic instrument developed by SRI Consulting that divides U.S. adults into groups based on their primary motivation and resources.

value A ratio of the bundle of benefits a customer receives from an offering compared to the costs incurred by the customer in acquiring that bundle of benefits.

value chain The synthesis of activities within a firm involved in designing, producing, marketing, delivering, and supporting its products or services.

value co-creation The combining of capabilities among members of a value network to create value.

value equation Value in terms of price and delivered benefits to the customer.

value network An overarching system of formal and informal relationships within which the firm participates to procure, transform, and enhance, and ultimately supply its offerings in final form within a market space.

value pricing A pricing strategy in which a firm attempts to take into account the role of price as it reflects the bundle of benefits sought by the customer.

value proposition The whole bundle of benefits a company promises to deliver to the customer, not just the benefits of the product itself.

value-creating activities Activities within a firm's value chain that act to increase the value of its products and services for its customers. These can take the form of either primary activities or support activities.

variability The characteristic of a service in which its service quality can only be as good as that of its provider.

variable pricing A pricing tactic in which customers are allowed or encouraged to haggle about prices.

variety The number of different product categories offered by a retailer.

vending machine retailing The selling of merchandise or services that are stored in a machine then dispensed to the consumer when the payment has been made.

vendor reliability A vendor's ability to meet contractual obligations including delivery time and service schedules.

vertical marketing system (VMS) Vertically aligned networks behaving and performing as a unified system.

viral marketing Entertaining and informative messaging created by a firm intended to be passed among individuals and delivered through online and other media channels.

W

wholesaler cooperative When retailers contract for varying degrees of exclusive dealings with a particular wholesaler.

workload method A method for determining the correct size of a company's sales force based on the premise that all salespeople should undertake an equal amount of work.

Z

zero-based budgeting An investment approach in that marketing goals and objectives are set for the upcoming year and then budget dollars are secured to support the achievement of those goals and objectives.

zone pricing When shippers set up geographic pricing zones based on the distance from the shipping location.

ENDNOTES

CHAPTER 1

1. www.marketingpower.com, accessed May 17, 2008.

2. Carol Hymowitz, "All Companies Need Innovation," *Wall Street Journal*, February 26, 2007, p. B1.

3. Vanessa O'Connell, "Bubble Gum at Bergdorf's," *Wall Street Journal*, February 15, 2007, p. B1.

4. Pola B. Gupta, Paula M. Saunders, and Jeremy Smith, "Traditional Master of Business Administration (MBA) versus the MBA With Specialization: A Disconnection Between What Business Schools Offer and What Employers Seek," *Journal of Education for Business* 82, no. 8 (2007), pp. 307–12.

5. David W. Stewart, "How Marketing Contributes to the Bottom Line," *Journal of Advertising Research* 48, no. 1 (2008), p. 94.

6. Malcolm A. McNiven, "Plan for More Productive Advertising," *Harvard Business Review* 58, no. 2 (1980), p. 130.

7. Mitchell J. Lovett and Jason B. MacDonald, "How Does Financial Performance Affect Marketing? Studying the Marketing-Finance Relationship from a Dynamic Perspective," *Journal of the Academy of Marketing Science* 33, no. 4 (2005), pp. 476–85; and Ramesh K.S. Rao and Neeraj Bharadwaj, "Marketing Initiatives, Expected Cash Flows, and Shareholders' Wealth," *Journal of Marketing* 72, no. 1 (2008), pp. 16–26.

8. Jehangir S. Pocha, "Chi-Fi," *Forbes Global*, January 29, 2007, p. 58.

9. Peter F. Drucker, *The Practice of Management* (New York: Harper and Row, 1954), pp. 37–38.

10. Peter F. Drucker, *Management: Tasks, Responsibilities, Practices* (New York: Harper and Row, 1973), p. 63.

11. Shaun Powell, "The Management and Consumption of Organisational Creativity," *Journal of Consumer Marketing* 25, no. 3 (2008), pp. 158–66.

12. Rosa Chun and Gary Davies, "The Influence of Corporate Character on Customers and Employees: Exploring Similarities and Differences," *Journal of the Academy of Marketing Science* 34, no. 2 (2006), pp. 138–47.

13. John Grant, "Green Marketing," *Strategic Direction* 24, no. 6 (2008), pp. 25–27.

14. Stanley Holmes, "Nike Goes Green," *BusinessWeek*, September 25, 2006, pp. 106–08.

15. Michael J. Barone, Kenneth C. Manning, and Paul W. Miniard, "Consumer Response to Retailers' Use of Partially Comparative Pricing," *Journal of Marketing* 68, no. 3 (2004), pp. 37–47; and Dhruv Grewal and Joan Lindsey-Mullikin, "The Moderating Role of the Price Frame on the Effects of Price Range and the Number of Competitors on Consumers' Search Intentions," *Journal of the Academy of Marketing Science* 34, no. 1 (2006), pp. 55–63.

16. Jyh-shen Chiou and Cornelia Droge, "Service Quality, Trust, Specific Asset Investment, and Expertise: Direct and Indirect Effects in a Satisfaction-Loyalty Framework," *Journal of the Academy of Marketing Science* 34, no. 4 (2006), pp. 613–28.

17. Mike Bierne, "Q&A: Randy Wagner CMO, Orbitz," *Brandweek*, January 22, 2007, pp. 17–22.

18. "Henry Ford Quotes," UBR Inc., www.people.ubr.com/historical-figures/by-first-name/h/henry-ford/henry-ford-quotes.aspx, accessed May 15, 2008.

19. Louis E. Boone and David L. Kurtz, *Contemporary Marketing* (Hinsdale, IL: The Dryden Press, 1974), p. 14.

20. General Electric Company, *1952 Annual Report* (New York: General Electric Company, 1952), p. 21.

21. Neil H. Borden, "The Concept of the Marketing Mix," *Journal of Advertising Research* 4 (June 1964), pp. 2–7; and E. Jerome McCarthy, *Basic Marketing: A Managerial Approach* (Homewood, IL: Irwin, 1960).

22. Bernard Cova and Robert Salle, "Marketing Solutions in Accordance with the S-D Logic: Co-creating Value with Customer Network Actors," *Industrial Marketing Management* 37, no. 3 (2008), pp. 270–77.

23. Evangelia D. Fassoula, "Transforming the Supply Chain," *Journal of Manufacturing Technology Management* 17, no. 6 (2006), pp. 848–60.

24. Mary Jo Bitner and Bernard H. Booms, "Marketing Strategies and Organizational Structures for Service Firms," in *Marketing of Services*, J. Donnelly and W. George, eds. (Chicago: American Marketing Association, 1981), pp. 47–51.

25. V. Kumar and J. Andrew Petersen, "Using a Customer-Level Marketing Strategy to Enhance Firm Performance: A Review of Theoretical and Empirical Evidence," *Journal of the Academy of Marketing Science* 33, no. 4 (2005), pp. 504–20; and Stephen L. Vargo and Robert F. Lusch, "Evolving to a New Dominant Logic for Marketing," *Journal of Marketing* 68, no. 1 (2004), pp. 1–17.

26. Jena McGregor, "Customer Service Champs," *BusinessWeek*, March 5, 2007, p. 63.

27. Sundar Bharadwaj, Terry Clark, and Songpol Kulviwat, "Marketing, Market Growth, and Endogenous Growth Theory: An Inquiry into the Causes of Market Growth," *Journal of the Academy of Marketing Science* 33, no. 3 (2005), pp. 347–60.

28. Ray A. Smith, "(Strong Entrepreneurs) + (Financial Controls) = Growth," *Wall Street Journal*, January 22, 2007, p. R4.

29. Vargo and Lusch, "Evolving to a New Dominant Logic for Marketing."

30. Mark W. Johnston and Greg W. Marshall, *Relationship Selling*, 2nd ed. (New York: McGraw-Hill/Irwin, 2008), p. 5.

31. George S. Day, "Managing Market Relationships," *Journal of the Academy of Marketing Science* 28, no. 1 (2000), pp. 24–31.

32. Robert Berner, "Detergent Can Be So Much More," *BusinessWeek*, May 1, 2006, pp. 66–68.

33. Simon J. Bell, Seigyoung Auh, and Karen Smalley, "Customer Relationship Dynamics: Service Quality and Customer Loyalty in the Context of Varying Levels of Customer Expertise and Switching Costs," *Journal of the Academy of Marketing Science* 33, no. 2 (2005), pp. 169–84; and Girish Ramani and V. Kumar, "Interaction Orientation and Firm Performance," *Journal of Marketing* 72, no. 1 (2008), pp. 27–45.

34. Don Peppers and Martha Rogers, *The One-to-One Manager: Real World Lessons in Customer Relationship Management* (New York: Doubleday Business, 2002).

35. Jagdish N. Sheth, Rajendra S. Sisodia, and Arun Sharma, "The Antecedents and Consequences of Customer-Centric Marketing," *Journal of the Academy of Marketing Science* 28, no. 1 (2000), pp. 55–67.

36. www.dell.com, accessed May 15, 2008.

37. Fred Wiersema, *The New Market Leaders: Who's Winning and How in the Battle for Customers* (New York: Free Press, 2001), pp. 48–58.

38. Michael Arndt, "Burrito Buzz–And So Few Ads," *BusinessWeek,* March 12, 2007, pp. 84–85.

39. Michael Arndt, "McDonalds 24/7," *BusinessWeek,* February 5, 2007, pp. 65–72.

40. Efhymios Constantinides and Stefan J. Fountain, "Web 2.0: Conceptual Foundations and Marketing Issues," *Journal of Direct, Data and Digital Marketing Practice* 9, no. 3 (2008), pp. 231–45.

41. Anonymous, "Search and Seizure," *Marketing Health Services* 28, no. 1 (2008), p. 6.

42. Barton Goldenberg, "Conquering Your 2 Biggest CRM Challenges,*"* *Sales & Marketing Management* 159, no. 3 (2007), p. 35.

43. Bonnie McGeer, "Podcasts, Debit Cards Good Youth Strategy," *American Banker,* October 17, 2006, p. 10A.

44. Ruth Maria Stock and Wayne D. Hoyer, "An Attitude-Behavior Model of Salespeople's Customer Orientation," *Journal of the Academy of Marketing Science* 33, no. 4 (2005), pp. 536–53.

45. Marco Vriens, "Strategic Research Design," *Marketing Research* 15, no. 4 (2003), p. 20.

46. Lovett and MacDonald, "How Does Financial Performance Affect Marketing?"; and Steven H. Seggie, "Assessing Marketing Strategy Performance,*"* *Journal of the Academy of Marketing Science* 34, no. 2 (2006), pp. 267–69.

47. www.msi.org, accessed May 17, 2008.

48. Jacqueline Durett, "A Matter of Trust," *Sales & Marketing Management,* January-February 2007, p. 36.

49. Thomas S. Gruca and Lopo L. Rego, "Customer Satisfaction, Cash Flow, and Shareholder Value," *Journal of Marketing* 69, no. 3 (2005), pp. 115–30.

CHAPTER 2

1. Peter C. Verhoef, "Understanding the Effect of Customer Relationship Management Efforts on Customer Retention and Customer Share Development," *Journal of Marketing,* Vol. 67, Iss. 4, October 2003, pp. 30–45.

2. Stephanie Coyles and Timothy C. Gokey, "Customer Retention Is Not Enough,*"* *Journal of Consumer Marketing,* Vol. 22, Iss. 2/3, 2005, pp. 101–06.

3. Kathie Canning, "All Together Now," *Refrigerated & Frozen Foods,* July 2006, pp. 10–18.

4. Anders Gustafsson, Michael D. Johnson, and Inger Roos, "The Effects of Customer Satisfaction, Relationship Commitment Dimensions, and Triggers on Customer Retention," *Journal of Marketing,* Vol. 69, Iss. 4, October 2005, pp. 210–18.

5. Seongjae Yu, "The Growth Pattern of Samsung Electronics: A Strategy Perspective," *International Studies of Management & Organization,* Vol. 28, Iss. 4, Winter 1998/1999, pp. 57–73.

6. Michael D. Johnson, Andreas Herrman, and Frank Huber, "The Evolution of Loyalty Intentions," *Journal of Marketing,* Vol. 70, Iss. 2, April 2006, pp. 122–32.

7. Jena McGregor, "Customer Service Champs," *BusinessWeek,* March 5, 2007, p. 63.

8. Kusum L. Ailawadi and Bari Harlam, "An Empirical Analysis of the Determinants of Retail Margins: The Role of Store-Brand Share," *Journal of Marketing,* Vol. 68, Iss. 1, January 2004, pp. 147–65.

9. Frederick F. Reichheld, *Loyalty Rules! How Leaders Build Lasting Relationships in the Digital Age.* Cambridge, MA: Harvard Business School Press, 2001.

10. "The Customer Service Elite," *BusinessWeek* Online, www.businessweek.com/interactive_reports/customer_satisfaction/index.asp, accessed July 22, 2007.

11. Michael E. Porter, *Competitive Advantage.* New York: Simon & Schuster, 1985.

12. J. David Hunger and Thomas H. Wheelen, *Essentials of Strategic Management* 4th edition. Upper Saddle River, NJ: Prentice Hall, 2007.

13. Eric M. Olson, Stanley F. Slater and G. Tomas M. Hult, "The Performance Implications of Fit among Business Strategy, Marketing Organization Structure, and Strategic Behavior," *Journal of Marketing* Vol. 69, Iss. 3, July 2005, pp. 49–65.

14. Thomas L. Friedman, *The World is Flat: A Brief History of the Twenty-First Century.* New York: Farrar, Stratus and Giroux, 2005.

15. Wayne McPhee and David Wheeler, "Making the Case for the Added-Value Chain," *Strategy and Leadership* Vol. 34, Iss. 4, 2006, pp. 39–48.

16. Roland T. Rust, Katherine N. Lemon, and Valarie A. Zeithaml, "Return on Marketing: Using Customer Equity to Focus Marketing Strategy;" *Journal of Marketing,* Vol. 68, Iss. 1, January 2004, pp. 109–27.

17. Richard W. Mosley, "Customer Experience, Organisational Culture, and the Employer Brand," *Journal of Brand Management,* Vol. 15, Iss. 2, November 2007, pp. 123–35.

18. Steven Power, "Worry Over the Climate, Regulation Has Group Backing Shift in Focus," *Wall Street Journal,* February 23, 2007, p. B3.

19. P. Rajan Varadarajan, Satish Jayachandran, and J. Chris White, "Strategic Interdependence in Organizations: Deconglomeration and Marketing Strategy," *Journal of Marketing,* Vol. 65, Iss. 1, January 2001, pp. 15–29.

20. Karen Norman Kennedy, Jerry R. Goolsby, and Eric. J. Arnold, "Implementing a Customer Orientation: Extension of Theory and Application," *Journal of Marketing* Vol. 67, Iss. 4, October 2003, pp. 67–81.

21. Jena McGregor, "Customer Service Champs," *BusinessWeek,* March 5, 2007, pp. 52–64.

22. Roland T. Rust, Katherine N. Lemon, and Valarie A. Zeithaml, "Return on Marketing: Using Customer Equity to Focus Marketing Strategy," *Journal of Marketing* Vol. 68, Iss. 1, January 2004, pp. 109–27.

23. Karen Dubinsky, "Brand is Dead," *Journal of Business Strategy,* Vol. 24, Iss. 2, March/April 2003, pp. 42–43.

24. "GE Business Screen," *Business Resource Software* Online, www.brs-inc.com/pwxcharts.asp?32, accessed May 16, 2008.

25. "The Experience Curve–Reviewed: IV. The Growth Share Matrix or The Product Portfolio," *Boston Consulting Group* Online, www.bcg.com/impact_expertise/publications/files/Experience_Curve_IV_Growth_Share_Matrix_1973.pdf, accessed May 16, 2008.

26. Andrew E. Polcha, "A Complex Global Business' Dilemma: Long Range Planning vs. Flexibility," *Planning Review,* Vol. 18, Iss. 2, March/April 1990, pp. 34–40.

27. Robert Slater, *Jack Welch and the GE Way: Management Insights and Leadership Secrets of the Legendary CEO.* Boston: McGraw-Hill, 1998.

28. J. David Hunger and Thomas H. Wheelen, *Essentials of Strategic Management* 4th edition. Upper Saddle River, NJ: Prentice Hall, 2007.

29. "Customer Service Commitment," *Southwest Airlines* Company Web site, www.southwest.com/travel_center/customer_service_commitment.html, accessed May 18, 2008; "Mission Statement," City of Clearwater, FL

Web site, www.myclearwater.com/services/customer_service/mission.asp, accessed May 19, 2008.

30. Noel Tichy and Ram Charan, "Speed, Simplicity, Self-Confidence: An Interview with Jack Welch," *Harvard Business Review,* September-October 1989, p. 113.

31. Mohanbir Sawhney and Jeff Zabin, "Managing and Measuring Relational Equity in the Network Economy," *Journal of the Academy of Marketing Science,* Vol. 30, Iss. 4, Fall 2002, pp. 313–33.

32. Lorraine Woellert, "HP's Hunsaker Papers," *BusinessWeek* Online, October 4, 2006, www.businessweek.com/technology/content/oct2006/tc20061003_396787.htm, accessed May 22, 2008.

33. Bishnu Sharma, "Marketing Strategy, Contextual Factors, and Performance: An Investigation of their Relationship," *Marketing Intelligence & Planning,* Vol. 22, Iss. 2/3, 2004, pp. 128–44.

34. Bill Stopper, "Innovation at Whirlpool," *Human Resources Planning,* September 2006, pp. 28–31.

35. Mark B. Houston, Beth A. Walker, Michael D. Hutt, and Peter H. Reingen, "Cross-unit Competition for Market Charter: The Enduring Influence of Structure," *Journal of Marketing,* Vol. 65, Iss. 2, April 2001, pp. 19–35.

36. David Mercer, *Marketing Strategy: The Challenge of the External Environment.* Thousand Oaks, CA: Sage, 1998.

37. Robert L. Cardy, "Employees as Customers?," *Marketing Management,* Vol. 10, Iss. 3, September/October 2001, pp. 12–14.

38. Regina D. Woodall, Charles L. Colby, and A. Parasuraman, "Evolution" to Revolution," *Marketing Management,* Vol. 16, Iss. 2, March/April 2007, p. 29.

39. Marc Graser, "Toyota Hits Touch Points as It Hawks Yaris to Youth," *Advertising Age,* May 1, 2006, p. 28.

40. Chaman L. Jain, "Benchmarking the Forecasting Process," *Journal of Business Forecasting Methods & Systems,* Vol. 21, Iss. 3, Fall 2002, pp. 12–16.

41. Rajdeep Grewal and Patriya Tansuhaj, "Building Organizational Capabilities for Managing Economic Crisis: The Role of Market Orientation and Strategic Flexibility," *Journal of Marketing,* Vol. 65, Iss. 2, April 2001, pp. 67–81.

42. Hunger and Wheelen, *Essentials of Strategic Management.*

43. Gary Chaison, "Airline Negotiations and the New Concessionary Bargaining," *Journal of Labor Research,* Vol. 28, Iss. 4, September 2007, pp. 642–57.

44. Kennedy, Goolsby and Arnold, "Implementing a Customer Orientation."

45. Ross Goodwin and Brad Ball, "What Marketing Wants the CEO to Know," *Marketing Management,* Vol. 12, Iss. 5, September/October 2003, pp. 18–23.

46. Robert Inglis and Robert Clift, "Market-oriented Accounting: Information for Product-level Decisions," *Managerial Auditing Journal,* Vol. 23, Iss. 3, 2008, pp. 225–39.

47. Jena McGregor, "Customer Service Champs," *BusinessWeek,* March 5, 2007, p. 55.

48. Mya Frazier, "Ad Spending Booms in War of Car Insurers," *Advertising Age* March 13, 2006, p. 4.

49. Denis Smith, "Business (not) as Usual: Crisis Management, Service Recovery, and the Vulnerability of Organisations," *Journal of Services Marketing,* Vol. 19, Iss. 5, 2005, pp. 309–21.

50. Tobin Hensgen, Kevin C. Desouza, and Maryann Durland, "Initial Crisis Agent-Response Impact Syndrome (ICARIS)," *Journal of Contingencies and Crisis Management,* Vol. 14, Iss. 4, December 2006, pp. 190–98.

51. Robert Liodice, "No Rest for Brands," *Advertising Age,* May 1, 2006, p. 17.

52. William B. Locander, "Staying Within the Flock," *Marketing Management,* Vol. 14, Iss. 2, March/April 2005, pp. 52–55.

53. Henry Mintzberg, *The Rise and Fall of Strategic Planning.* New York: Financial Times Prentice Hall, 2000.

54. Andrew E. Polcha, "A Complex Global Business' Dilemma: Long Range Planning vs. Flexibility," *Planning Review,* Vol. 18, Iss. 2, March/April 1990, pp. 34–40.

CHAPTER 3

1. Peter Gabrielsson, Mika Gabrielsson, John Darling, and Reijo Luostarinen, "Globalizing Internationals: Product Strategies of ICT Manufacturers," *International Marketing Review,* London, 2006, Vol. 23 (6), pp. 650–67.

2. M. Theodosiou, and L.C. Leonidou, "International Marketing Policy: A Integrative Assessment of the Empirical Research," International Business Review, 2003, Vol. 12 (2), pp. 141–71.

3. David C. Michael, "China and the U.S.: The Ties That Bind," *BusinessWeek Online,* July 18, 2007, http://www.businessweek.com/print/globalbiz/content/jul2007/gb20070718_614386.htm; and Michael Arndt, and Dexter Roberts, "A Finger Lickin' Good Time in China," *BusinessWeek Online,* October 30, 2006, http://www.businessweek.com/magazine/content/06_44/b4007074.htm?chan=search.

4. Katrijn Gielens, Marnik G. Dekimpe, "The Entry Strategy of Retail Firms into Transition Economies," *Journal of Marketing,* 2007, Vol. 71 (2), pp. 196–210; and Jasmine E.M. Williams, "Export Marketing Information-gathering and Processing in Small and Medium-sized Companies," *Marketing Intelligence and Planning,* 2006, Vol. 24 (5), pp.477–92.

5. Kerry Capell, "Wal-Mart with Wings," *BusinessWeek Online,* November 26, 2006, http://www.businessweek.com/globalbiz/content/nov2006/gb20061116_574456.htm?chan=search.

6. Geri Smith and Michael Arndt, "Wrapping the Globe in Tortillas," *BusinessWeek Online,* February 26, 2007, http://www.businessweek.com/magazine/content/07_09/b4023055.htm?chan=search.

7. Kristian Moller, and Senja Svahn, "Crossing East-West boundaries: Knowledge Sharing in Intercultural Business Networks," *Industrial Marketing Management,* 2004, Vol. 33 (3), pp.219–28.

8. Eric Ellis, "Iran's Cola War," *Fortune,* March 5, 2007, Vol. 155 (4), p. 35.

9. Thane Peterson, "First Drive: 2007 Toyota Tundra," *BusinessWeek* Online, January 30, 2007 and Norihiko Shirouzu, Gina Chon, "Toyota Plays Copy with Tundra Push," *Wall Street Journal,* February 5, 2007, A11.

10. "Growth Still Strong Quite Strong: Inflation Remains the Key Concerns for Emergers, with Many Countries Still Tightening Policies," *Emerging Marketing Weekly,* April 14, 2008, pp. 1–13; and Luiz F. Mesquita and Sergio G. Lazzarini, "Horizontal and Vertical Relationships in Developing Economies: Implications for SME's Access to Global Markets," *Academy of Management Journal,* 2008, Vol. 51 (2), pp. 359–71.

11. Reena Jana, "Silverjet Enters Business–Class Warfare, " *BusinessWeek* Online, January 3, 2007, http://www.businessweek.com/innovate/content/jan2007/id20070103_588790.htm?chan=search.

12. Jennifer Hoyt, "Innovations in Beauty," *The Prague Post* online, April 7, 2005.

13. Cristina del Campo, Carlos M.F. Monteiro, Joao Oliveira Soares, "The European Regional Policy and the Socioeconomic Diversity of European Regions: A Multivariate Analysis," *European Journal of Operational Research,* 2008, Vol. 187 (2), pp. 600–612; and David Floyd, "Have "European Politics" and EU

Policymaking Replaced the Politics of Member State Countries," *International Journal of Social Economics,* 2008, Vol. 35 (5), pp. 338–43.

14. "Wal-Mart Banks on the "Unbanked," *BusinessWeek* Online, December 13, 2007 and www.giganteusa.com.

15. BBC News Online, "Profile Mercosur–Common Market of the South, May 20, 2008. http://news.bbc.co.uk/1/hi/world/americas/5195834.stm.

16. Kerry Campbell, "McDonald's Offers Ethics with Those Fries," *BusinessWeek* online, January 7, 2007, accessed May 20, 2008 http://www.businessweek.com/globalbiz/content/jan2007/gb20070109_958716.htm?chan=search.

17. BBC News Online, "Profile Mercosur–Association of Southeast Asian Nations," May 20, 2008, http://news.bbc.co.uk/2/hi/asia-pacific/country_profiles/4114415.stm.

18. Jason Overdorf, "Hooray for Bollywood," *Newsweek* online, November 30, 2007, http://www.newsweek.com/id/72719/output/print.

19. Richard A. Owusu, Maqsood Sandhu, Soren Kock, "Project Business: A Distinct Mode of Internationalization," *International Marketing Review,* 2007, Vol. 24 (6), pp. 695–714; and Terence Fan and Phillip Phan, "International New Ventures: Revisiting the Influences behind the "Born-Global" Firm," *Journal of International Business Studies,* 2007, Vol. 38 (7), pp. 1113–32.

20. Judith Crown and Carol Matlack, "Boeing Delays Dreamliner Again," *BusinessWeek* Online, April 9, 2008 http://www.businessweek.com/print/bwdaily/dnflash/content/apr2008/db2008049_424569.htm, and Carol Matlack, "Airbus Cost-Cuts Don't Fly," *BusinessWeek* Online, May 7, 2008. http://www.businessweek.com/globalbiz/content/may2008/gb2008057_379072.htm?chan=search.

21. "L.L. Bean, Inc. Reports 2007 Net Sales Results," March 7, 2008, www.llbean.com http://www.llbean.com/customerService/aboutLLBean/newsroom/stories/03072008_LLBean_News.html.

22. "Nichia and Sony Cross-License Blue Laser-diode Patents," *Laser Focus World,* April 23, 2004, http://www.laserfocusworld.com/articles/print.html?id=203343&bPool=LFW.pennnet.com%2farticle_tool_bar; and Tom Lowry and Ronald Grover "Blu-Ray Isn't Getting Much Traction," *Business-Week* Online, May 8, 2008, http://www.businessweek.com/print/magazine/content/08_20/b4084050513499.htm.

23. "Helsinn Healthcare SA; Pharmaceutical Company Granted Distribution Rights for Aloxi in Indonesia, "*Biotech Week,* Feb. 9. 2005, p. 350.

24. B. Elango, "Are Franchisors with International Operations Different from Those Who Are Domestic Market Oriented?" *Journal of Small Business Management,* 2007, Vol. 45 (2), pp. 179–85.

25. Sergio G. Lazzarini, "The Impact of Membership in Competing Alliance Constellations: Evidence on the Operational Performance of Global Airlines," *Strategic Management Journal,* 2007, Vol. 28 (4), pp 345–60; and Kerry Capell, "Skirmishing in the Open Skies," *BusinessWeek* Online, January 14, 2008, http://www.businessweek.com/print/globalbiz/content/jan2008/gb20080114_431564.htm.

26. Jane W. Lu and Xufei Ma, "The Contingent Value of Local Partners' Business Group Affiliations," *Academy of Management Journal,* 2008, Vol. 51 (2), pp. 295–305; and Eric Rodriguez, "Cooperative Ventures in Emerging Economies," *Journal of Business Research,* 2008, Vol. 61 (6), pp. 640–55.

27. "SABMiller Joint Venture Makes China Acquisitions in Liaoning, Anhui, and Hunan Provinces," SABMiller press release, August 2007; and Adrienne Carter with Bruce Einhorn, "It's Miller Time in China," *BusinessWeek* Online, November 27, 2006, http://www.businessweek.com/magazine/content/06_48/b4011082.htm?chan=search.

28 Lance Eliot Brouthers, Yan Gao, Jason Patrick McNicol, "Corruption and Market Attractiveness Influences on Different Types of FDI," *Strategic Management Journal,* 2008, Vol. 29 (6), pp. 673–81; and Jan Hendrik Fisch, "Investment in New Foreign Subsidiaries under Receding Perception of Uncertainty, *Journal of International Business Studies,* 2008, Vol. 39 (3), pp. 370–87.

29. Riki Takeuichi, Jeffrey P. Shay, Jiatao Li, "When Does Decision Autonomy Increase Expatriate Managers' Adjustment" An Empirical Test," *Academy of Management Journal,* 2008, Vol. 51 (1), pp. 45–60.

30. Andrea Dossi, Lorenzo Patelli, "The Decision-Influencing use of Performance Measurement Suystems in Relationships between Headquarters and Subsidiaries," *Management Accounting Research,* 2008, Vol. 19 (2), pp. 126–39.

31. Michael G. Harvey, David A. Griffith, "The Role of Globalization, Time Acceleration, and Virtual Global Teams in Fostering Successful Global Product Launches, *The Journal of Product Innovation Management,* 2007, Vol. 24 (5), pp. 486–501; and Thomas L. Powers and Jeffrey J. Loyka, "Market, Industry, and Company Influences on Global Product Standardization," *International Marketing Review,* 2007, Vol. 24 (6), pp. 678–94.

32. Pitsinee Jitpleecheep, "Samsonite Aims to Double Sales in Three Years," *McClatchy–Tribune Business News,"* February 28, 2008; and Susan Berfield, "Sleek. Stylish, Samsonite? The Brand Has Been Kicked around for Years. Now Marchello Bottoli Wants to Take It Upscale," *BusinessWeek,* February 26, 2007, pp. 106–8.

33. Sadrudin A. Ahmed and Alain d'Astous, "Antecedents, Moderators, and Dimensions of Country-of-Origin Evaluations," *International Marketing Review,* 2008, Vol. 25, (1), pp. 75–84; and Saikat Banerjee, "Strategic Brand-Culture Fit: A Conceptual Framework for Brand Management," *Journal of Brand Management,* 2008, Vol. 15 (5), pp. 312–22.

34. "Made in the USA? The Truth Behind the Labels," *Consumer Reports,* 2008, Vol. 73 (3), pp. 12.

35. Eric (Er) Gang, Robert W. Paimatier, Lisa K. Scheer, and Ning Li, "Trust at Different Organizational Levels," *Journal of Marketing,* 2008, Vol. 72 (2), pp. 80–98; Janice M. Payan, Richard G. McGarland, "Decomposing Influence Strategies: Argument Structure and Dependence as Determinants of the Effectiveness of Influence Strategies in Gaining Channel Member Compliance, *Journal of Marketing,* 2005, Vol. 69 (3), pp 66–79; Eric M. Olson, Stanley F. Slater, G. Tomas M. Hult, "The Performance Implications of Fit Among Business Strategy, Marketing Organization Structure, and Strategic Behavior," *Journal of Marketing,* 2005, Vol. 69 (3), pp. 49–65; and Carlos Niezen and Julio Rodriguez, "Distribution Lessons from Mom and Pop," 2008, *Harvard Business Review,* Vol. 86 (4), pp. 23–46.

36. Abel P. Jeuland, Steven M. Shugan, "Managing Channel Profits," *Marketing Science,* Vol. 27 (1), pp. 49–54.

37. Neil Herndon, "Effective Ethical Response: A New Approach to Meeting Channel Stakeholder Needs for Ethical Behavior and Socially Responsible Conduct," *Journal of Marketing Channels,* 2005, Vol. 13 (1), pp 63–67; and Emma Kambewa, Paul Ingenbleek, and Aad Van Tilbury, "Improving Income Positions of Primary Producers in International Marketing Channels: The Lake Victoria–DU Nile Perch Case," *Journal of Macromarketing,* 2008, Vol. 28 (1), pp. 53–64.

38. Michelle R. Nelson, Hye-Jin Paek, "A Content Analysis of Advertising in a Global Magazine Across Seven Countries: Implications for Global Advertising Strategies," *International Marketing Review,* 2007, Vol. 24 (1), pp. 64–78.

39. Wagner A. Kamakura and Wooseong Kang, "Chain Wide and Store Level Analysis for Cross Category Management," *Journal of Retailing,* 2007, Vol. 83 (2), pp. 159–70.

40. Piet Verhoeven, "Who's In and Who's Out?; Studying the Effects of Communication Management on Social Cohesion," *Journal of Communication Management,* 2008, Vol. 12 (2), pp.124–30; and Tom Watson, "Public Relations Research Priorities: A Delphi Study," *Journal of Communication Management,* 2008, Vol. 12 (2), pp. 104–11.

41. George S. Yip, Audrey J.M. Bink, "Managing Global Accounts," *Harvard Business Review,* 2007, Vol. 85 (9), pp. 102–19; and Kenneth D. Ko, "Optimal Pricing Model," *Journal of Global Business Issues,* 2008, Vol. 2 (1), pp. 143–48.

42. David Welch, David Kiley, and Moon Ihiwan, "My Way of the Highway at Hyundai," *BusinessWeek* Online, March 6, 2008. http://www.businessweek .com/print/magazine/content/08_11/ b4075048450463.htm; and Moon Ihiwan, "Hyundai Pitches Luxury in the U.S.," *BusinessWeek* Online, April 2, 2007, http://www.businessweek. com/print/globalbiz/content/apr2007/ gb20070402_949571.htm.

43. Magda Kandil, The Asymmetric Effects of Exchange Rate Fluctuations on Output and Prices: Evidence from Developing Countries," *The Journal of International Trade and Economic Development,* 2008, Vol. 17 (2), pp. 257–70.

44. Benjamin Eden, "Inefficient Trade Patterns: Excessive Trade, Cross-Hauling and Dumping," *Journal of International Economics,* 2007, vol. 73 (1), pp. 175–87.

45. William Vetter, C. Jeanne Hill, "The Hunt for Online Trademark Infringers: The Internet, Gray Markets, and the Law Collide," *Journal of the Academy of Marketing Science,* 2006, Vol. 34 (1), pp. 85–88; Jen-Hung Huang, Bruce C.Y. Lee, and Shu Hsun Ho, "Consumer Attitudes Toward Gray Market Goods" *International Marketing Review,* 2004, Vol. 21 (6), pp. 598–611; and Barry Berman, "Strategies to Combat the Sale of Gray Market Goods," *Business Horizons,* 2004, Vol. 47 (4), pp. 51–70.

46. Bruce Einhorn, "Lenovo Has Less to Lose in the U.S.," *BusinessWeek* Online, January 28 , 2008, http://www .businessweek.com/print/globalbiz/ content/jan2008/gb20080128_593717 .htm; Jane Spencer, "Lenovo Seeks Higher U.S. Profile, *Wall Street Journal,* February 2, 2007 p A14; and Steve Hamm and Dexter Roberts, "China's First Global Capitalist, *BusinessWeek,* December 11, 2006, pp 52–58.

CHAPTER 4

1. Bob Thompson, *What Is CRM?* http://www.customerthink.com, CRM Knowledge Item.

2. Adrian Payne and Pennie Frow, "A Strategic Framework for Customer Relationship Management," *Journal of Marketing,* Vol. 69, Iss. 4, October 2005, pp. 167–76.

3. George Day, "Capabilities for Forging Customer Relationships," *MSI Report* #00–118. Cambridge, MA, Marketing Science Institute, 2000.

4. John Adams, "Event-Based Marketing," *Bank Technology News,* June 2006, p. 26.

5. Ronald S. Swift, *Accelerating Customer Relationships: Using CRM and Relationship Technologies.* Upper Saddle River, NJ: Prentice Hall PTR, 2001.

6. Don Peppers and Martha Rogers, *Managing Customer Relationships: A Strategic Framework.* Hoboken, NJ: John Wiley & Sons, Inc., 2004.

7. Payne and Frow, "A Strategic Framework."

8. Swift, *Accelerating Customer Relationships.*

9. Stephen F. King and Thomas F. Burgess, "Understanding Success and Failure in Customer Relationship Management," *Industrial Marketing Management,* Vol. 37, Iss. 4, June 2008, pp. 421–31.

10. Stanley A. Brown, ed., *Customer Relationship Management: A Strategic Imperative in the World of E-Business.* Toronto: John Wiley & Sons Canada, 2000, pp. 8–9.

11. "Direct Mail: FMCGs Tap Loyalty Medium," *Marketing,* September 27, 2006, p. 48.

12. Anders Gustafsson, Michael D. Johnson, and Inger Roos, "The Effects of Customer Satisfaction, Relationship Commitment Dimensions, and Triggers on Customer Retention," *Journal of Marketing,* Vol. 69, Iss. 4, October 2005, pp. 210–18.

13. Mohanbir Sawhney and Jeff Zabin, "Managing and Measuring Relational Equity in the Network Economy," *Journal of the Academy of Marketing Science,* Vol. 30, Iss. 4, Fall 2002, pp. 313–33.

14. Frederick F. Reichheld, *Loyalty Rules! How Leaders Build Lasting Relationships in the Digital Age.* Cambridge, MA: Harvard Business School Press, 2001.

15. Paul Caris, "Turning Home Buyers into Partners," *Professional Builder,* August 1, 2006, p. 37.

16. Day, "Capabilities for Forging Customer Relationships."

17. Timothy W. Aurand, Linda Gorchels, and Terrence R. Bishop, "Human Resource Management's Role in Internal Branding: An Opportunity for Cross-functional Brand Messaging Synergy," *The Journal of Product and Brand Management,* Vol. 14, Iss. 2/3, 2005, pp. 163–70; and Scott Davis, "Marketers Challenged to Respond to Changing Nature of Brand Building," *Journal of Advertising Research,* Vol. 45, Iss. 2, June 2005, pp. 198–200.

18. Sawhney and Zabin, "Managing and Measuring Relational Equity."

19. Maria Woehr, "Time for Your Close-up," *Insurance and Technology,* January 2007, pp. 28–33.

20. Naveen Donthu and Boonghee Yoo, "Marketing Management Support Systems: Principles, Tools, and Implementation," *Journal of Marketing,* Vol. 65, Iss. 4, October 2001, pp. 122–25.

21. Werner Reinartz, Jacquelyn S. Thomas, and V. Kumar, "Balancing Acquisition and Retention Resources to Maximize Customer Profitability," *Journal of Marketing,* Vol. 69, Iss. 1, January 2005, pp. 63–79.

22. Nicole E. Coviello, Roderick J. Brodie, Peter J. Danaher, and Wesley J. Johnston, "How Firms Relate to their Markets: An Empirical Examination of Contemporary Marketing Practices," *Journal of Marketing,* Vol. 66, Iss. 3, July 2002, pp. 33–47.

23. Peter C. Verhoef, Understanding the Effect of Customer Relationship Management Efforts on Customer Retention and Customer Share Development," *Journal of Marketing,* Vol. 67, Iss. 4, October 2003, pp. 30–45.

24. Neil A. Morgan, Eugene W. Anderson, and Vikas Mittal, "Understanding Firm's Customer Satisfaction Information Usage," *Journal of Marketing,* Vol. 69, Iss. 3, July 2005, pp. 131–51.

25. Connie Robbins Gentry, "Personal Recognition," *Chain Store Age,* January 2007, p. 78.

26. Dan Warmenhoven, "Protect Me, Protect My Data," *BusinessWeek* Online, June 8, 2006, www.businessweek

.com/technology/content/jun2006/tc20060608_894982.htm, accessed May 27, 2008.

27. James E. Richard, Peter C. Thirkell, and Sid L. Huff, "An Examination of Customer Relationship Management (CRM) Technology Adoption and Its Impact on Business-to-Business Customer Relationships," *Total Quality Management & Business Excellence,* Vol. 18, Iss. 8, October 2007, pp. 927–45.

28. Bob Lewis, "The Customer is Wrong," *InfoWorld,* Vol. 24, Iss. 2, January 14, 2002, pp. 40–41.

29. "Subway Merges Payment, Loyalty, and CRM Programs," *eWeek,* August 10, 2006.

30. Jena McGregor, "Customer Service Champs," *BusinessWeek,* March 5, 2007, pp. 52–64.

31. Leonard L. Berry, *On Great Service: A Framework for Action.* New York: The Free Press, 1995.

32. Coviello et al., "How Firms Relate to Their Markets."

33. Peppers and Rogers, *Managing Customer Relationships.*

34. "Targeted Tactics Drive Response" *B to B,* October 9, 2006, p. 1.

35. Swift, *Accelerating Customer Relationships* p. 42.

36. David Stodder, "Walking in a Data Wonderland," *Intelligent Enterprise,* December 2006, p. 4.

37. Payne and Frow, "A Strategic Framework."

38. Day, "Capabilities for Forging Customer Relationships."

39. The Chally Group, *The Customer-Selected World Class Sales Excellence Research Report.* Dayton, OH: The H.R. Chally Group, 2002.

40. Patricia Kilgore, "Personalization Provides a Winning Hand for Borgata," *Printing News,* December 11, 2006, pp. 7–8.

41. Karen Norman Kennedy, Felicia G. Lassk, and Jerry R. Goolsby, "Customer Mind-Set of Employees throughout the Organization," *Journal of the Academy of Marketing Science,* 30, Spring 2002, pp. 159–71.

42. Ibid.

43. Kimberly Griffiths, "Got Satisfaction?" *Industrial Distribution,* October 1, 2006, p. 34.

44. Chuck Chakrapani, "The Relationship-Based Enterprise," *Marketing Research,* Vol. 13, Iss. 1, Spring 2001, pp. 39–40.

45. McKenzie, pp. 7–8.

46. Kelly Shermach, "Cram for CRM Effectiveness," *Sales & Marketing Management,* May 2006, p. 20.

47. Kathleen Cholewka, "CRM: The Failures Are Your Fault," *Sales & Marketing Management,* 154, January 2002, pp. 23–24.

CHAPTER 5

1. Anne L. Souchon, John W. Cagogan, David B. Procter, and Belinda Dewsnap, "Marketing Information Use and Organizational Performance: The Mediating role of Responsiveness," *Journal of Strategic Marketing,* 2004, Vol. 12 (4), pp. 231–42.

2. "J.D. Power and Associates Reports: Del Webb Ranks Highest in Satisfying Buyers of Homes in Active Adult Communities," *PR Newswire,* September 13, 2006.

3. Cliff Edwards and Bruce Einhorn, "So Maybe Apple was Onto Something," *BusinessWeek,* April 14, 2008, p. 51.

4. Roger Bennett, "Sources and Use of Marketing Information by Marketing Managers," *Journal of Documentation,* 2007, Vol. 63, (5), p. 702; and Hean Tat Keh, Thi Mai Nguyen, Hwei Ping Ng, "The Effects of Entrepreneurial Orientation and Marketing Information on the Performance of SME's," *Journal of Business Venturing,* 2007, Vol. 22 (4), pp. 592–611.

5. Paul Ingenbleek, "Value-Informed Pricing in Its Organizational Context: Literature Review, Conceptual Framework, and Directions for Future Research," *Journal of Product and Brand Management,* 2007, Vol. 16 (7), 441–58.

6. Deborah Kong, "Design That Captures the Buzz," *Business 2.0,* 2007, Vol. 8 (2), pp. 46–47.

7. Gerrit H. Van Bruggen, Ale Smidts, Berend Wierenga, "The Powerful Triangle of Marketing Data, Managerial Judgment, and Marketing Management Support Systems," *European Journal of Marketing,* 2001, Vol. 35 (7), pp. 796–816.

8. Stephen F. King and Thomas F. Burgess, "Understanding Success and Failure in Customer Relationship Management," *Industrial Marketing Management,* 2008, Vol. 37 (4), pp. 421–39.

9. Joao F Proenca, Teresa M. Fernandez, P.K. Kannan, "The Relationship in Marketing: Contribution of a Historical Perspective," *Journal of Macromarketing,* 2008, Vol. 28 (1), pp. 90–106.

10. Sandra S. Liu and Lucette B. Comer, "Salespeople as Information Gatherers: Associated Success Factors," *Industrial Marketing Management,* 2007, Vol. 36 (5), pp. 565–79.

11. Joel Le Bon, Dwight Merunka," The Impact of Individual and Managerial Factors on Salespeople's Contribution to Marketing Intelligence Activities,"

International Journal of Research in Marketing, 2006, Vol. 23 (4), pp. 395–412.

12. Jean Michel Moutot, Ganael Bascoul, "Effects of Sales Force Automation Use on Sales Force Activities and Customer Relationship Management Process," *The Journal of Personal Selling and Sales Management,* Vol. 28 (2), pp. 167–182.

13. Louis Lee, "Paul Pressler's Fall from the The Gap," *BusinessWeek,* February, 28, 2007, pp. 80–82.

14. Daniel Lyons, "Zune's New Tune," *Forbes,* Jan. 28, 2008, Vol. 181 (2), p. 53 and Stephen H. Wildstrom, "Zune 2.0: Playing Tomorrow's Tune?," *BusinessWeek,* November 28, 2007, pp. 87–88.

15. Craig Stedman, "Failed ERP Gamble Haunts Hershey," *Computerworld,* Nov. 1, 1999, Vol. 33 (44), pp. 1–2.

16. Sajjad Matin, "Clicks Ahoy! Navigating Online Advertising in a Sea of Fraudulent Clicks," *Berkeley Technology Law Journal,* 2007, Vol. 22 (1), pp. 533–55; and Brian Grow and Ben Elgin, "Click Fraud," *BusinessWeek,* October 2, 2006, pp. 46–57.

17. Connie R. Bateman and JoAnn Schmidt, "Do Not Call Lists: A Cause for Telemarketing Extinction or Evolution," *Academy of Marketing Studies Journal,* 2007, Vol. 11 (1), pp. 83–107; and Herbert Jack Rotfeld, "Misplace Marketing: Do-not-Call as the U.S. Government's Improvement to Telemarketing Efficiency," *The Journal of Consumer Marketing,* 2004, vol. 21 (4/5), pp. 242–59.

18. Siobham Gorman, "Politics and Economics: Intelligence Sharing Still Lacking: Home Security Cites New Efforts to Fill Local Needs," *The Wall Street Journal* (Eastern Edition), February 26, 2008, A12.

19. Thomas W. Miller, "At the Junction," *Marketing Research,* 2007, Vol. 19 (4), pp. 8–14.

20. Alan Tapp, "A Call to Arms for Applied Marketing Academics," *Marketing Intelligence and Planning,* 2004, Vol. 22 (5), pp. 579–96.

21. Dianne Altman Weaver, "The Right Questions," *Marketing Research,* 2006, Vol. 18 (1), pp. 17–18.

22. Janice Denegri-Knott, Detiev Zwick, Jonathan E. Schroeder, "Mapping Consumer Power: An Integrative Framework for Marketing and Consumer Research," *European Journal of Marketing,* 2006, Vol. 40 (9/10), pp. 950–71.

23. Margaret Cross, "PDA's Chase Workflow Improvements," *Health Data Management,* 2006, Vol. 14 (5), pp. 61–62.

24. Gordon A. Wyner, "Redefining Data," *Marketing Research,* 2004, Vol. 16 (4), pp 6–7.

25. Naomi R. Henderson, "Twelve Steps to Better Research," *Marketing Research,* 2005, Vol. 17 (2), pp. 36–37.

26. David Stokes and Richard Bergin, "Methodology or "Methodolatry"? An Evaluation of Focus Groups and Depth Interviews?" *Qualitative Market Research,* 2006, Vol. 9 (1), pp. 26–38.

27. Clive Boddy, "A Rose by Any Other Name May Smell as Sweet but Group 'Group Discussion' is Not Another Name for a 'Focus Group' Nor Should It Be," *Qualitative Market Research,* 2005, Vol. 8 (3), pp. 248–56.

28. Jennifer Comiteau, "Why the Traditional Focus Group Is Dying," *Adweek,* October 31, 2005, pp. 24–27.

29. Gordon Wyner, "Survey Errors," *Marketing Research,* 2007, (Vol. 19 (1), pp. 6–7.

30. Catherine A. Roter, Robert A. Rogers, George C. Hozier, Jr., Kenneth G. Baker, and Gerald Albaum, "Management of Marketing Research Projects: Does Delivery Method Matter Anymore in Survey Research," *Journal of Marketing Theory and Practice,* 2007, Vol. 15 (2), pp. 127–145; and Sharon Loane, Jim Bell, and Rob McNaughton, "Employing Information Communication Technologies to Enhance Qualitative International Marketing Enquiry," *International Marketing Review,* 2006, Vol. 23 (4), pp. 438–53.

31. Sudhir N. Kale and Peter Klugsberger, "Reaping Rewards," *Marketing Management,* 2007, Vol. 16 (4), pp. 14–16; and Phil Bligh and Doug Turk, "Cashing in on Customer Loyalty," *Customer Relationship Management,* 2004, Vol. 8 (6), pp. 48–52.

32. David Tiltman, "The Only Question You Need to Ask," *Marketing,* Feb. 21, 2007, pp. 30–33; and Damon Darlin, "The Only Question That Matters, Surveys are Tedious, Focus Groups are Fickle. That's Why Intuit and GE Use a Radical New Research Technique to Keep Customers Happy and Revenue Growing," *Business 2.0,* 2005, Vol. 6 (8), pp. 50–53.

33. Edward Blair, and George M. Zinkhan, "Nonresponse and Generalizability in Academic Research," *Academy of Marketing Science Journal,* 2006, Vol. 34 (1), pp. 4–8.

34. Peter Keliner, "Can Online Polls Produce Accurate Findings," *International Journal of Market Research,* 2004, Vol. 46, pp. 3–15; and Olivier Furrer and D. Sudharshan, "Internet Marketing Research: Opportunities and Problems," *Qualitative Market Research,* 2001, Vol. 4 (3), pp 123–30.

35. N.L. Reynolds, A.C. Siminitiras, and A. Diamantopoulos, "Theoretical Justification of Sampling Choices in International Marketing Research: Key Issues and Guideliens for Researchers," 2003, Vol. 34 (1), pp. 80–90.

36. Pallavi Gogoi, "The New Science of Siting Stores," *BusinessWeek,* July 6, 2005, http://www.businessweek .com/technology/content/jul2005/ tc2005076_7033.htm?chan=search, May 24, 2008.

37. Bill Blyth, "Mixed Mode: The Only 'Fitness' Regime?", *International Journal of Marketing Research,* 2008, Vol. 50 (2), pp. 241–56.

38. Nick Sparrow, "Quality Issues in Online Research," *Journal of Advertising Research,* 2007, Vol. 47 (2), pp. 179–91; and Elisabeth Deutskens, Ad de Jong, Ko de Ruyter, and Martin Wetzels, "Comparing the Generalizability of Online and Mail Surveys in Cross National Service Quality Research," *Marketing Letters,* 2006, Vol. 17 (2), pp. 119–32.

39. Kai Wehmeyer, "Aligning IT and Marketing–The Impact of Database Marketing and CRM," *Journal of Database Marketing & Customer Strategy Management,* 2005, Vol. 12 (3), pp. 243–57; Joshua Weinberger, "Database Marketers Mine for Perfect Customer Segmentation," *Customer Relationship Management,* 2004, Vol. 8 (10), p. 19; and Hoda McClymont and Graham Jocumsen, "How to Implement Marketing Strategies using Database Approaches, "*Journal of Database Marketing and Customer Strategy Management,* 2003, Vol. 11 (2), pp. 135–49.

40. R. Dale Wilson, "Developing New Business Strategies in B2B Markets by Combining CRM Concepts and Online Databases," *Competitiveness Review,* 2006, Vol. 16 (1), pp. 38–44.

41. David Ward, "Master of All You Survey," *PRweek,* 2006, Vol. 9 (38), pp. 22.

42. Steve Ranger, "How Firms Use Business Intelligence," *BusinessWeek* Online, May 24, 2007, http://www .businessweek.com/globalbiz/ content/may2007/gb20070524_ 006085.htm?chan=search, May 24, 2008 and Colin Beasty, "Minimizing Customer Guesswork," *Customer Relationship Management,* 2006, Vol. 10 (6), p. 45.

43. "Efficient Frontier Releases Q! Search Engine Performance Report," *Business Wire,* April 17, 2008; and Robert D. Hof, "Efficient Frontier: Hacking Madison Avenue," *BusinessWeek,* July 24, 2006, p. 52.

44. Moom Ihiwan, "Why Samsung and LG Scare Motorola," *BusinessWeek* Online, May 2008, and http://www .businessweek.com/print/globalbiz/ content/apr2008/gb20080430_ 178487.htm; and Pallavi Gogoi, "Six Sigma Still Pays Off at Motorola," *BusinessWeek,* December 4, 2006, p. 46.

45. Randall Frost, "Feeling Your Way in a Global Market," *BusinessWeek,* February 24, 2006, p. 53–54.

46. Ian Rowley and Hiroko Tashiro, "Japan's Cybercafés Go Up Market," *BusinessWeek* Online, September 11, 2007, http://www.businessweek .com/print/globalbiz/content/sep2007/ gb20070911_834445.htm, May 24, 2008.

47. Christopher Palmeri, "Green Homes: The Price Still Isn't Right," *BusinessWeek,* February 12, 2007, pp. 54–55.

CHAPTER 6

1. "Airlines in a Tailspin," *BusinessWeek* Online, May 23, 2008, http:// www.businessweek.com/globalbiz/ content/may2008/gb20080523_ 828225.htm?chan=search, May 27, 2008.

2. Jim F. Infanger, "The Southwest Perspective," *Airport Business,* 2008, Vol. 22 (3), pp. 11–15.

3. Arie De Geus and Peter M. Senge, "The Living Company," *Harvard Business School Press,* 1997.

4. Javier Oubina, Natalia Rubio, Maria Jesus Yague, "Effect of Strategy, Structure, and Performance Variables on the Store Brand Market Share," *Journal of Marketing Management,* 2007, Vol. 23 (9/10), pp. 1013–27.

5. Haig Simonian, "New Breed of Buyer Comes to the Fore," *Financial Times,* April 4, 2008, p. 1; and Jessica E. Vascellaro, "The Times They Are Changing; Watch Sales Slip as Teens, Young Adults Use Cell Phones, Other Gadgets to Tell Time" *The Wall Street Journal,* January 18, 2006, p. D1.

6. Steven Ward and Aleksandra Leweandowska, "Is the Marketing Concept Always Necessary? The Effectiveness of Customer, Competitor, and Societal Strategies in Business Environment Types," *European Journal of Marketing,* 2008, Vol. 42 (1/2), pp. 222–39.

7. Kira R. Fabrizio, Nancy L. Rose, and Catherine D. Wolfram, "Do Markets Reduce Costs? Assessing the Impact of Regulatory Restructuring on U.S. Electric Generation Efficiency," *The American Economic Review,* 2007, Vol. 97 (4), pp. 1250–68.

8. Joshua Chaffin and Stephanie Kirchgaessner, "XM and Sirius Merger Approved," *Financial Times,* March 26, 2008, p. 19.

9. Prasad A. Naik, Ashtosh Prasad, Suresh P. Sethi, "Building Brand Awareness in Dynamic Oligopoly Markets," *Management Science,* 2008, Vol. 54 (1), 129–40; Morihiro Yomogida, "Competition, Technology, and Trade in Oligopolistic Industries," *International Review of Economics and Finance,* 2008, Vol. 17 (1), pp. 127–40; and Susanna Esteban and Matthew Shum, "Durable Goods Oligopoly with Secondary Markets: The Case of Automobiles," *The Rand Journal of Economics,* 2007, Vol. 38 (2), pp. 332–55.

10. Ron Ruggless, "Up for the Challenge," *Nation's Restaurant News,* 2008, Vol. 42 (7), pp. 51–54.

11. Sylvie Laforet, "Size, Strategic, and Market Orientation Affects on Innovation," *Journal of Business Research,* 2008, Vol. 61 (7), pp. 753–64.

12. David J. Ketchen, Jr., William Rebarick, G. Tomas, M. Hult, David Meyer, "Best Value Supply Chains: A Key Competitive Weapon for the 21st Century," *Business Horizons,* 2008, Vol. 51 (3), pp. 235–43; and John Brodie, "It's Ralph's World," *Fortune,* 2007, Vol. 150 (6), pp. 64–71.

13. Jack Neff, "Huggies Finds Pampers-free Ad Platforms," *Advertising Age,* 2007, Vol. 78 (45), p. 24; and "For P&G, Success Lies in More Than Merely a Drier Diaper," *Advertising Age,* 2007, Vol. 78 (41), p. 30.

14. David Carey, "The MP3 That Broke New Ground," *Electronic Engineering Times,* 2007, Iss. 1465, pp. 43–44; and Antony Bruno, "No More Rio," *Billboard,* 2005, Vol. 117 (37), p. 6.

15. "Creative Unveils New Product Line of iPod Speakers," *Wireless News,* May 28, 2008; and Jessica Tan, "If You Can't Beat Em . . . " *Forbes,* 2007, Vol. 179 (4), p. 52.

16. Matthew Boyle and Jim Collins, "Interview with Jim Collins," *Fortune,* 2007, Vol. 155 (3), pp. 50–53; and "Sony History," *Marketing Week,* March 17, 2005, p. 29.

17. Jena McGregor, "The World's Most Innovative Companies," *BusinessWeek,* 2008, Iss. 4081, p. 61.

18. Chad P. Bown and Rachel McCulloch, "Trade Adjustments in the WTO System: Are More Safeguards the Answer?," *Oxford Review of Economic Policy,* 2007, Vol. 23, (3), pp. 415–35.

19. Steve Hamm, "Rivals Say HP is Using Hardball Tactics," *BusinessWeek,* 2007, Iss. 4022, pp. 48–49.

20. Jack Neff, "Crest Is King: Brand Wrests No. 1 Spot from Colgate," *Advertising Age* (Midwest Edition), 2007, Vol. 78 (20), pp. 3–5.

21. Barbara White-Sax, "Manufacturers Ride the Bottles Water Wave," *Drug Store News,* 2007, Vol. 29 (9), pp. 47–48.

22. Beth A. Walker, Dimitri Kapelianis, and Michael D. Hutt, "Competitive Cognition," *MIT Sloan Management Review,* 2005, Vol. 46 (4), pp. 10–19.

23. "Business: Coffee Wars: Starbucks vs. McDonald's," *The Economist,* 2008, Vol. 386 (8562), p. 58.

24. "Leaders: Is Google the New Microsoft? Information Technology," *The Economist,* 2006, Vol. 379 (8477), pp. 10–11.

25. Bruce Greenwald and Judd Kahn, "All Strategy Is Local," *Harvard Business Review,* 2005, Vol. 83 (9), pp. 94–104.

26. Jonathan Birchall, "Wal-Mart Unveils First New Format in a Decade with Small Store Brand," *Financial Times,* May 16, 2008, p. 1; and Matthew Boyle and Michael V. Copeland, "Tesco Reinvents the 7–Eleven," *Fortune,* 2007, Vol. 156 (1), pp. 34–35.

27. Elizabeth Rigby, "Breakthrough Year Begins on French Soil," *Financial Times* (Asia Edition), November 26, 2007, p. 19; and "Business Crossroads: Carrefour," *The Economist,* 2007, Vol. 382 (Issue 8520), p. 87.

28. Ronald Grover, "MYSpaceTV: Teaching New Media Old Tricks; News Corp Aims to Make Its New Web-TV Venture a Stripped Down Version of Fox," *BusinessWeek,* May 12 2008, Issue 4083, pp. 50–51.

29. Tom Lowry and Ronald Grover, "Blu-Ray Isn't Getting Much Traction," *BusinessWeek* Online, May 8, 2008. http://www.businessweek.com/print/magazine/content/08_20/b4084050513499.htm, May 29, 2008; and Kenji Hall, "Sony's Blu-Ray Breakthrough," *BusinessWeek* Online, January 8, 2008, http://www.businessweek.com/print/globalbiz/content/jan2008/gb2008018_681920.htm, May 29, 2008.

30. David Welch, "GM: Live Green or Die; The Lumbering, Money-Losing Giant Finally Sees That Gas Engines Are a Losing Bet. But Is It Too Late?," *BusinessWeek,* May 26, 2008, Issue 4085, pp. 36–41.

31. Katrina Brooker, "The Chairman of the Board Looks Back," *Fortune,* May 28, 2001, Vol. 143 (11), pp. 62–71.

32. David Whitford, "Hanging It Up," *Fortune,* May 5, 2007, Vol. 155, (4), pp. 29–34.

33. Richard Waters, "Chief of SAP Unit in U.S. Quits in Spy Scandal," *Financial Times,* November 21, 2007, p. 20; and Aaron Ricadela, "Oracle vs. SAP: Sound or Fury?; and "Larry Ellison's High-Profile Shares May Be Only PR, but That May Be All He Wants," *BusinessWeek,* April 9, 2007, Issue 4029, p. 38.

34. "Jack Welch on Jeff Immelt," *BusinessWeek,* April 17, 2008, http://www.businessweek.com/print/magazine/content/08_17/b4081138464667.htm, May 29, 2008; and Interview with Jack Welch, April 18, 2008, CNBC. http://www.cnbc.com/id/24158810/site/14081545, May 29, 2008.

35. "L.L. Bean Tops Customer-Service Survey," *Chain Store Age,* 2008, Vol. 84 (2), p. 24; and Aaron Pressman, "Want Some Pajamas with That Kayak?" *BusinessWeek,* 2006, Iss. 4010, p. 76.

36. Douglas W. Vorhies and Neil A. Morgan, "Benchmarking Marketing Capabilities for Sustainable Competitive Advantage," *Journal of Marketing,* 2005, Vol. 69 (1), pp. 80–96.

37. Anna Lund Jepsen, "Factors Affecting Consumer Use of the Internet for Information Search," *Journal of Interactive Marketing,* 2007, Vol. 21 (3), pp. 21–33.

38. Catherine Holahan, "EBay: Take That, Google!" *BusinessWeek* Online, June 22, 2007, http://www.businessweek.com/print/technology/content/jun2007/tc20070623_273469.htm, May 29, 2008; and Robert Hof, "Google's eBay Challenge," *BusinessWeek* Online, June 28, 2006, http://www.businessweek.com/print/investor/content/jun2006/pi20060628_081708.htm, May 29, 2008.

39. Jay Greene, "Inside Microsoft's War Against Google," *BusinessWeek* Online, May 8, 2008, http://www.businessweek.com/print/magazine/content/08_20/b4084036492860.htm, May 29, 2008; Jay Greene, "Microsoft's New Best on Search," *BusinessWeek* Online, September 27, 2007, http://www.businessweek.com/print/technology/content/sep2007/tc20070926_626712.htm, May 29, 2008; Jay Greene, "Microsoft's Latest, Best Hope in Search," *BusinessWeek* Online, June 26, 2007, http://www.businessweek.com/print/technology/content/jun2007/tc20070625_001418.htm; and Jay Greene, "Where Is Microsoft Search," *BusinessWeek,* April 2, 2007, pp. 30–32.

CHAPTER 7

1. S. Mark Young, James J. Gong, and Wim A Van der Stede, "The Business of Selling Movies," *Strategic Finance,* 2008, Vol. 89 (9), pp. 35–42; and Jon Silver and John McDonnell, "Are Movie Theaters Doomed? Do Exhibitors See the Big Picture as Theaters Lose Their Competitive Advantage?" *Business Horizons,* 2007, Vol. 50 (6), pp. 491–501.

2. P. Sullivan and J. Heitmeyer, "Looking at Gen Y Shopping Preferences and Intentions: Exploring the Role of Experience and Apparel Involvement," *International Journal of Consumer Studies,* 2008, Vol. 32 (3), pp. 285–99.

3. Lisa Sanders, "Major Marketers Get Wise to the Power of Assigning Personas," *Advertising Age,* 2007, Vol. 78 (15), pp. 36–37; and Colleen Bohen, "Geek Squad Posts Web Video Tutorials," *Twice,* 2008, Vol. 23 (1), pp. 112–13.

4. Frank Hobbs and Nicole Stoops, "Demographic Trends in the 20th Century," U.S Census Bureau, 2002.

5. Suzanne Vranica, "Can Dove Promote a Cause and Sell Soap? Web Site is Devoted to "Real Beauty"…and Product Placement," *The Wall Street Journal,* April 10, 2008, p. B6; and Carlos Grande, "Beating Rivals When It Comes to Risk-Taking Marketing," *Financial Times,* May 16, 2007, p. 21.

6. Paul G. Patterson, "Demographic Correlates of Loyalty in a Service Context," *Journal of Services Marketing,* 2007, Vol. 21 (2), pp. 112–21.

7. Lisa E. Bolton, Americus Reed II, Kevin G. Volpp, Katrina Armstrong, "How Does Drug and Supplement Marketing Affect a Healthy Lifestyle? *Journal of Consumer Research,* 2008, Vol. 34 (5), pp. 713–26.

8. Cara Peters, Christie H. Amato, and Candice R. Hollenbeck, "An Exploratory Investigation of Consumers' Perceptions of Wireless Advertising," *Journal of Advertising,* 2007, Vol. 36 (4), pp. 129–46; "A Pocketful of Marketing," *Inc.* 2008, p. 79; and Catherine Holahan, "The "Sell" Phone Revolution," *BusinessWeek,* April 23, 2007, pp. 94–97.

9. Maureen E. Hupfer and Brian Detlor, "Beyond Gender Differences: Self-Concept Orientation and Relationship-Building Orientation on the Internet," *Journal of Business Research,* 2007, Vol. 60 (6), pp. 613–28; and J. Michael Pearson, Ann Pearson, and David Green, "Determining the Importance of Key Criteria in Web Usability," *Management Research News,* 2007, Vol. 30 (11), pp. 816–29.

10. Parimal S. Bhagat, Jerome D. Williams, "Understanding Gender Differences in Professional Service Relationships," *Journal of Consumer Marketing,* 2008, Vol. 25 (1), pp. 16–29.

11. Oliver M. Freestone and Patrick J. McGoldrick, "Motivations of the Ethical Consumer," *Journal of Business Ethics,* 2008, Vol. 79 (4), pp. 445–68.

12. Matthew Boyle, "The Fast Food Capital of America," *Fortune* Online, April 12, 2007. www.money.cnn .com/2007/04/12/magazines/fortune/ pluggedin_boyle_fastfood.fortune/index .html, June 3, 2008

13. M. Fishbein and I. Ajzen, *Belief, Attitude, Intention, and Behavior: An Introduction to Theory and Research,* Reading MA: Addison–Wesley. 1975.

14. Maxwell Winchester and Jenni Romaniuk, "Positive and Negative Brand Beliefs and Brand Defection/Update," *European Journal of Marketing,* 2008, Vol. 42 (5/6), pp. 553–68.

15. John Davis, "Did Seth Go to the Dark Side," *Inc.,* May 2008, pp. 21–24.

16. Pamela Miles Horner, "Perceived Quality and Image: When All Is Not "Rosy", *Journal of Business Research,*" 2008, Vol. 61 (7), pp. 715–31.

17. Louise Story, "Anywhere the Eye Can See, It's Likely to See an Ad," *New York Times,* 2007, January 15, B1.

18. "The Caveman: Evolution of a Character," *Adweek,* 2007, Vol. 48 (11), p. 9.

19. Joseph B. White, "Eyes on the Road: Good News, Bad News at Buick; Models Get Safer, Says J.D. Power, Then Get Dumped," *The Wall Street Journal,* August 14, 2007, p. D5.

20. Elizabeth Cowley, "How Enjoyable Was It? Remembering an Affective Reaction to a Previous Consumption Experience," *Journal of Consumer Research,* 2007, Vol. 34 (4), pp. 494–510, Moonhee Yang and David R. Roskos-Ewoldsen, "The Effectiveness of Brand Placements in the Movies: Levels of Placements, Explicit and Implicit Memory, and Brand Choice Behavior," *Journal of Communication,* 2007, Vol. 57 (3), pp. 469–82.

21. Rance Crain, "Objections to Objects! Is There Any Safe Endorser Anymore," *Advertising Age,* 2007, Vol. 78 (8), p. 13; and Gene Marcial, "Staples: No. 1 in the World's Offices," *BusinessWeek,* November 26, 2007, Issue 4060, p. 109.

22. Ming-tiem Tsai, Wen-ko Liang, and Mei-Ling Liu, "The Effects of Subliminal Advertising on Consumer Attitudes and Buying Intentions, *International Journal of Management,* 2007, Vol. 24 (1), pp. 3–15; and Sheri J. Broyles, "Subliminal Advertising and the Perpetual Popularity of Playing to People's Paranoia," *Journal of Consumer Affairs,* 2006, Vol. 40 (2), pp. 392–407.

23. Brian D. Till and Sarah M. Stanley, "Classical Conditioning and Celebrity Endorsers: An Examination of Belongingness and Resistance to Extinction," *Psychology and Marketing,* 2008, Vol. 25 (2), pp. 179–94.

24. Gordon R. Foxall, M. Mirella, and Yani de Soriano, "Situational Influences on Consumers' Attitudes and Behaviors," *Journal of Business Research,* 2005, Vol. 58 (4), pp. 518–33.

25. Marcus Cunha Jr., Chris Janiszewski, and Juliano Laran, "Protection of Prior Learning in Complex Consumer Learning Environments," *Journal of Consumer Research,* 2008, Vol. 34 (6), pp. 850–68.

26. Jennifer L. Aaker, "Dimensions of Brand Personality," *Journal of Marketing Research,* 1997, Vol. 34 (3), pp. 347–363, Jennifer Aaker, Susan Fournier, and S. Adam Brasel, "When Good Brands Do Bad," *Journal of Consumer Research,* 2004, Vol. 31(10), pp. 1–17; and Robert Madrigal, David M. Boush, "Social Responsibility as a Unique Dimension of Brand Personality and Consumers' Willingness to Reward," *Psychology and Marketing,* Vol. 25 (6) , pp. 538–52.

27. Alex Markels, "Croc and Roll: The Maker of the Popular Funky Footwear Is on the Hunt for the Next Big Hit," *U.S. News and World Report,* 2007, Vol. 143 (10). P. 54; and *Crocs 2007 Annual Report.*

28. Katja Magion-Muller and Malcolm Evans, "Culture, Communications, and Business: The Power of Advanced Semiotics," *International Journal of Marketing Research,* 2008, Vol. 50 (2), pp. 169–82.

29. David Pearson, "French Language Purists Put Brakes on Car Makers," *The Wall Street Journal,* April 4, 2007, p. B5b.

30. Mark W. Johnston and Greg. W. Marshall, *Relationship Selling,* 2e, McGraw-Hill, p. 183.

31. Lauren Foster, "Ethnic Shopper Sets Tone for Beauty Contest: Cosmetics Giants Need to Woo Consumers across Color Spectrum," *Financial Times,* April 12, 2005, p. 27.

32. Deborah Kong, "The 5-Star Hospital," *Business 2.0,* 2007, Vol. 8 (3), p. 46.

33. Alexandra Montgomery, "U.S. Families 2025: In Search of Future Families," *Futures,* 2008, Vol. 40 (4), pp. 377–89.

34. Julie Tinson, Clive Nancarrow, and Ian Brace, "Purchase Decision Making and the Increasing Significance of Family Types," *The Journal of Consumer Marketing,* Vol. 25 (1), pp. 45–56.

35. Rex Y. Du and Wagner A. Kamakura, "Household Life Cycles and Lifestyles in the United States," *Journal of Marketing Research,* 2006, Vol. 43 (1), pp. 121–32.

36. Palaniappan Thiagarajan, Jason E. Lueg, Nicole Ponder, Sheri Lokken Worthy and Ronald D. Taylor, "The Effect of Role Strain on the Consumer Decision Process of Single Parent Households," *American Marketing Association, Conference Proceedings,* Summer 2006, Vol. 17, p. 124.

37. Alan Deutschman, "The Kingmaker," *Wired,* May 2004, http://www.wired.com/wired/archive/12.05/mossberg.html, June 3, 2008.

38. Caroline Goode and Robert East, "Testing the Marketing Maven Concept," *Journal of Marketing Management,* 2008, Vol. 24 (3/4), pp. 265–81; and Lawrence F. Feick and Linda L. Price, "The Market Maven: A Diffuser of Marketplace Information," *Journal of Marketing,* 1987, Vol. 51 (1), pp. 83–98.

39. Katherine White and Darren W. Dahl, "Are All Out-Groups Created Equal? Consumer Identity and Dissociative Influence," *Journal of Consumer Research,* 2007, Vol. 34 (4), pp. 525–40, Jennifer Edson Escalas and James R. Bettman, "Self-Construal, Reference Groups, and Brand Meaning," *Journal of Consumer Research,* 2005, Vol. 32 (3), pp. 378–90; and Terry L. Childers and Akshay R. Rao, "The Influrnce of Familiar and Peer-Based Reference Groups on Consumer Decisions," *Journal of Consumer Research,* 1992, Vol. 19 (2) pp. 198–212.

40. Brian Hindo, "Toys with a Second Life; Can Ganz's Webkins-Plush Animals with Online Alter Egos Stay Ahead of the Copycats?, *BusinessWeek,* December 31, 2007, Issue 4065, p. 91; and Carleen Hawn, "Time to Play, Money to Spend," *Business 2.0,* 2007, April 2007, Vol. 8 (3), p. 43.

41. Hans H. Baurer, Nicola E. Sauer, and Christine Becker, "Investigating the Relationship Between Product Involvement and Consumer Decision Making Styles," *Journal of Consumer Behavior,* 2006, Vol. 5 (4), pp. 342–55; Salvador Miquel, Eva M. Capillure, and Joaquin Aldas-Maznazo, "The Effect of Personal Involvement on the Decision to Buy Store Brands," *The Journal of Product and Brand Management,* 2002, Vol. 11 (1) , pp. 6–19; and Laurent Gilles and Jean-Noel Kapferer, "Measuring Consumer Involvement Profiles," *Journal of Marketing Research,* 1985, Vol. 22 (1), pp. 41–54.

42. Diane Brady and Alli McConnon, edited by Deborah Stead," Booking a Room in Cyberspace," *BusinessWeek,* September 11, 2006, Issue 4000, p. 12; and *Business Wire,* "Aloft Hotels to Unveil Updated Design Strategy in Second Life," May 7, 2007.

43. Zafar U. Ahmed, James P. Johnson, Xiz Yang, and Chen Kehng Fatt, "Does Country of Origin Matter for Low Involvement Products? *International Marketing Review,* 2004, Vol. 21 (1), pp. 102–15; and Wayne D. Hoyer, "An Examination of Consumer Decision Making for Common Repeat Purchase Product," *Journal of Consumer Research,* 1984, Vol. 11 (3), pp. 822–30.

44. Girish N. Punj and Robert Moore, "Smart Versus Knowledgeable Online Recommendation Agents," *Journal of Interactive Marketing,* 2007, Vol. 21 (4), pp. 46–60; Teemu Yikoski, "A Sequence Analysis of Consumers' Online Searches," *Internet Research,* 2005, Vol. 15 (2), pp. 181–95; and Donnavieve Smith, Satya Menon, K. Sivakumar, "Online Peer and Editorial Recommendations, Trust and Choice in Virtual Markets," *Journal of Interactive Marketing,* Vol. 19 (3), pp. 15–38.

45. Carrie Coolidge, "Discount Chic," *Forbes,* April 7, 2008, Vol. 181 (7), p. 108.

46. On Amir and Jonathan Levan, "Choice Construction versus Preference Construction" The Instability of Preferences Learned in Context," *Journal of Marketing Research,* 2008, Vol. 45 (2), pp. 145–61.

47. Mohammed M. Nadeem, "Post Purchase Dissonance: The Wisdom of 'Repeat' Purchase," *Journal of Global Business Issues,* 2007, Vol. 1 (2), pp. 183–94.

48. Mark Borden, Jeff Chu, Charles Fishman, Michael A. Prospero, and Daniell Sacks, "50 Ways to Green Your Business," *Fast Company,* Nov. 2007, Issue 120, pp. 90–99; and "Coca-Cola Enterprises Forms Recycling Unit for Package Recycling," *Automatic Merchandiser,* October 2007, Vol. 49 (10), p. 12.

49. Jeffrey M. O'Brien, "What's Your House Really Worth?" *Fortune,* 2007, Vol. 155 (3), pp. 56–61.

CHAPTER 8

1. Kenji Hall, "Sharp's Mega-Wager on LCD TV's," *BusinessWeek,* August 1, 2007, pp. 35–37.

2. Thomas L. Powers and Jay U. Sterling, "Segmenting Business-to-Business Markets: A Micro-Macro Linking Methodology," *The Journal of Business and Industrial Marketing,* 2008, Vol. 23 (3), pp. 170–86.

3. Brian N. Rutherford, James S. Boles Hiram C. Barksdale, Jr. and Julie T. Johnson, "Buyer's Relational Desire and Numbers of Suppliers Used: The Relationship between Perceived Commitment and Continuance," *Journal of Marketing Theory and Practice,* 2008, Vol. 16 (3), pp. 247–58.

4. Jewel Gopwani, "Honda Alliance Rescues Shop in Grand Rapids," *Knight Ridder Tribune Business News,* September 23, 2007.

5. Ruben Chumpitaz Caceres and Nicholas G. Paparoidamis, "Service Quality, Relationship Satisfaction, Trust, Commitment and Business-to-Business Loyalty," *European Journal of Marketing,* 2007, Vol. 41 (7/8), pp. 836–48; and Papassapa Rauyruen and Kenneth E. Miller, "Relationship Quality as Predictor of B2B Customer Loyalty," *Journal of Business Research,* 2007, Vol. 60 (1), pp. 21–35.

6. Srilata Zaheer and Shalini Manrakhan, "Concentration and Dispersion in Global Industries: Remote Electronic Access and Location of Economic Activities," *Journal of International Business Studies,* 2001, Vol. 32 (4), pp. 667–87.

7. Tao Gao, M. Joseph Sirgy, and Monroe M. Bird, "Reducing Buyer Decision Making Uncertainty in Organizational Purchasing: Can Supplier Trust, Commitment, and Dependency Help?" *Journal of Business Research,* 2005, Vol. 58 (4). pp. 397–409.

8. Rachel Smolker, "Go Ahead, Blame Biofuels," *BusinessWeek,* May 20, 2008, p. 24; and John Carey and Adrienne Carter with Assif Shammen, "Food vs. Fuel," *BusinessWeek,* February 5, 2007, pp. 58–61.

9. Juro Osawa and Hiroyuki Kachi, "International Business: Boeing Braces for Claims: Dreamliner Delay May Bring Calls for Compensation," *The Wall Street Journal,* April 11, 2008, B4; and J. Lynn Lunsford, "High Design: Boeing Lets Airlines Browse: A New Showroom Displays Options for Outfitting 787's; Seats, Wide or Less Wide," *The Wall Street Journal,* February 14, 2007, p. B1.

10. Leonidas C. Leonidou, "Industrial Manufacturer-Customer Relationships" the Discriminating role of the Buying Situation," *Industrial Marketing Management,* 2004, Vol. 33 (8), pp. 731–45.

11. Ray A. Smith, "Weekend Jouranl; Style—Mensware: China's Challenge to Italy; Now a Rival to European High End Suits," *The Wall Street Journal,* May 29, 2008, W4; and Richard Nailey, "Big Changes at the High End," *The Wall Street Journal,* August 16, 2007, p. D7.

12. G. Tomas M. Hult, David J. Ketchen, Jr. and Brian R. Chabowski, "Leadership, the Buying Center, and Supply Chain Performance: A Study of Linked Users, Buyers, and Suppliers," *Industrial Marketing Management,* 2007, vol. 36 (3), pp. 393–408.

13. Marcel Paulssen and Matthias M. Birk, "Satisfaction and Repurchase Behavior in a Business to Business Setting: Investigating the Moderating Effect of Manufacturer, Company and Demographic characteristics," *Industrial Marketing Management,* 2007, Vol. 36 (7), pp. 983–95.

14. Marydee Ojala, "SIC Those NAICS on Me: Industry Classification Codes for Business Research," *Online,* 2005, Vol. 29 (1), pp. 42–45; and Robert P. Parker, "More U.S. Economic Data Series Incorporate the North American Industry Classification System," *Business Economics,* 2003, vol. 38 (2), pp. 57–60.

15. Kun Liao and Paul Hong, "Building Global Supplier Networks: A Supplier Portfolio Entry Model," *Journal of Enterprise Information Management,* 2007, Vol. 20 (5), pp. 511–23; and Chiaho Chang, "Procurement Policy and Supplier Behavior-OEM vs. ODM," *Journal of Business and Management,* 2002, Vol. 8 (2), pp. 181–98.

16. Masaaki Kotabe, Michael J. Mol and Janet Y. Murray, "Outsourcing, Performance, and the Role of E-Commerce: A Dynamic Perspective," *Industrial Marketing Management,* 2008, Vol. 37 (1), pp. 37–48 and Bruno Schilli and Fan Dai, "Collaborative Life Cycle Management Between Suppliers and OEM," *Computers in Industry,* 2006, Vol. 57 (8/9), pp. 725–29.

17. "S&T Trends," *Air Safety Week,* March 31, 2008, Vol. 22, p. 13; and Susan Carey, "Calculating Costs in the Clouds: How Flight Planning Software Helps Airlines Balance Fuel, Distance, Wind and "Overfly" Fees," *The Wall Street Journal,* March 6, 2007, p. B1.

18. Robert S. Dudney, "Beyond the F-22 Problem" *Air Force Magazine,* 2008, Vol. 91 (3), p. 2.

19. Diane Sears, "Joining Forces," *Florida Trend,* 2008, Vol. 50 (13), p. 66.

20. Dan Risch, "Kite Powered Cargo," *Science World,* 2008, Vol. 64 (13), p. 3; and Matthew Power, "Kite-Sailing Tankers," *New York Times Magazine,* April 20, 2008, p. 70.

21. Jesus Cerquides, Maite Lopex-Sanchez, Antonio Reyes-Moro, and Juan A. Rodruguez-Aguilar, "Enabling Assisted Strategy Negotiations in Actual World Procurement Scenarios," *Electronic Commerce Research,* 2007, Vol. 7 (3/4), pp. 189–221; and Mike Brewster, "Perfecting the RFP," *Inc.,* 2005, p. 38.

22. Stephen Copestake, "Getting Your Website noticed," *Personal Computer World,* July 2008; and Marshall Lager, "The Dark Side of the Search Engine," *Customer Relationship Management,* 2007, Vol. 11 (12), p. 50.

23. S.Y. Chou, C.Y. Shen and Y.H. Chang, "Vendor Selection in a Modified Re-Buy Situation Using a Strategy Aligned Fuzzy Approach," *International Journal of Production Research,* 2007, Vol. 45 (14), pp. 3113–24.

24. Ian Rowley, "Facing an Auto Slump, Japan Lifts Capacity," *BusinessWeek,* June 9, 2008, p. 64.

25. S. Sen, H. Basligil, C.G. Sen, and H. Baracli, "A Framework for Defining both Qualitative and Quantitative Supplier Selection Criteria Considering the Buyer-Supplier Integration Strategies," *International Journal of Production Research,* 3008, Vol. 46 (7), pp. 1825–39.

26. Felix T.S. Chan and Niraj Kumar, "Global Supplier Development Considering Risk Factors Using Fuzzy Extended AHP-based Approach," *Omega,* 2007, Vol. 35 (4), pp. 417–31; and Donna Gill and B. (Ram) Ramaseshan, "Influences on Supplier Repurchase Selection of UK Importers," *Marketing Intelligence and Planning,* " 2007, Vol. 25 (6), pp. 597–611.

27. Ruth N. Bolton, Katherine N. Lemon, and Peter C. Verhoef, "Expanding Business to Business Customer Relationships: Modeling the Customer's Upgrade Decision," *Journal of Marketing,* 2008, Vol. 72 (1), pp. 46–60; and James M. Barry, Paul Dion, and William Johnson, "A Cross Cultural Examinations of Relationship Strength in B2B Services," Journal *of Services Marketing,* 2008, Vol. 22 (2), pp. 114–31.

28. Maria Holmlund, "A Definition, Model and Empirical Analysis of Business to Business Relationship Quality," *International Journal of Service Industry Management,* 2008, Vol. 19 (1), pp. 32–46.

29. Havard Hansen, Bendik M. Samuelsen, and Pal R. Siseth, "Customer Perceived Value in B-to-b Service Relationships: Investigating the Importance of Corporate Reputation," *Industrial Marketing Management,* 2008, Vol. 37 (2), pp. 206–20; and Jeffrey E. Lewin and Wesley J. Johnston, "The Impact of Supplier Downsizing on Performance, Satisfaction over Time, and Repurchase Decisions," *Journal of Business and Industrial Marketing,* 2008, Vol. 23 (4), pp. 249–63.

30. David Barboza, China Getting Intel Factory to Build Sophisticated Chips, *New York Times,* March 27, 2007, p. C3; and Jason Dean, "Intel May Expand Technology in New China Plant," *The Wall Street Journal,* March 27, 2007, B4.

31. Wayne A. Neu and Stephen W. Brown, "Manufacuers Forming Successful Complex Business Services: Designing an Organization to Fit the Market," *International Journal of Service Industry Management,* 2008, Vol. 19 (2), pp. 232–39.

32. Samantha Stainburn, "M&A Top Ten: Mapping A New Strategy," *Crain's Chicago Business,* January 21, 2008, Vol. 31 (3), pp. 25; and Alison Edwards, "The Map Knows All," *Calliope,* 2007, Vol. 18 (3), pp. 48–50.

33. Blanca Hernandez Ortega, Julio Jimenez Martinez, and Ja Jose Martin De Hoyos, "The Role of Information Technology Knowledge, in B2B Development," *International Journal of E-Business Research,* 2008, Vol. 4 (1), pp. 40–55.

34. Christian Tanner, Ralf Wolffle, Petra Schubert, and Michael Quade, "Current Trends and Challenges in Electronic Procurement: An Empirical Study," *Electronic Markets,* 2008, Vol. 18 (1), pp. 8–19.

35. Juha Mikka Nurmilaakso, "Adoption of e-Business Functions Migration from EDI Based on XML Based e-Business Frameworks in Supply Chain Integration," *International Journal of Production Economics,* 2008, Vol. 113 (2), pp. 721–41,

36. T. Ravichandran, S. Pant, and D. Chatterjee, "Impact of Industry Structure and Product Characteristics on the Structure of Be2 Vertical Hubs," *IEEE Transactions on Engineering Management,* 2007, Vol. 54 (3), p. 506.

37. Michelle Conlin, "The Waning Days of the Road Warrior: Why the Current Slowdown in Business Travel May Not End When the Economy Recovers," *BusinessWeek,* June 2, 2008, Issue 4086, pp. 65–66, Rachael King, "Cisco Pays Big for New Idea, *BusinessWeek*

Online, June 2, 2008, http://www
.businessweek.com/print/technology/
content/may2008/tc20080529_968185
.htm; June 10, 2008; and Bobby White
and Roger Cheng, "Cisco to Acquire
WebEx: Appeal of Internet for Services
Fuels $3.2 Billion Accord, *The Wall
Street Journal,* March 16, 2007, p. B4.

CHAPTER 9

1. Nicole E. Coviello, Roderick J.
Brodie, Peter J. Danaher, and Wesley J.
Johnston, "How Firms Relate to their
Markets: An Empirical Examination of
Contemporary Marketing Practices,"
Journal of Marketing, Vol. 66, Iss. 3,
pp. 33–57.

2. Jacquelyn S. Thomas and Ursula Y.
Sullivan, "Managing Marketing Com-
munications with Multichannel Custom-
ers," *Journal of Marketing* Vol. 69, Iss.
4, October 2005, pp. 239–51; and
Stephen L. Vargo and Robert F. Lusch,
"Evolving to a New Dominant Logic for
Marketing," *Journal of Marketing,*
Vol. 68, Iss. 1, January 2004, pp. 1–17.

3. Javier Rodriguez-Pinto, Ana Isabel
Rodriguez-Escudero, and Jesus
Gutierrez-Cilian, "Order, Positioning,
Scope, and Outcomes of Market Entry,"
Industrial Marketing Management,
Vol. 37, Iss. 2, April 2008, pp. 154–66.

4. Anders Gustafsson, Michael D.
Johnson, and Inger Roos, "The Effects
of Customer Satisfaction, Relationship
Commitment Dimensions, and Triggers
on Customer Retention," *Journal of Mar-
keting,* Vol. 69, Iss. 4, October 2005,
pp. 210–18; and Ajay Kalra and
Ronald C. Goodstein, "The Impact of
Advertising Positioning Strategies on
Consumer Price Sensitivity," *Journal of
Marketing Research,* Vol. 35, Iss. 2, May
1998, pp. 210–25.

5. Cenk Koca and Jonathan D.
Bohlmann, "Segmented Switchers and
Retailer Pricing Strategies," *Journal of
Marketing,* Vol. 72, Iss. 3, May 2008,
pp. 124–42.

6. Allan D. Shocker, Barry L. Bayus,
and Namwoon Kim, "Product Comple-
ments and Substitutes in the Real World:
The Relevance of "Other Products,"
Journal of Marketing, Vol. 68, Iss. 1,
January 2004, pp. 28–40.

7. Arik Hesseldahl, "The iPhone
Legacy: Pricier Smartphones?" *BusinessWeek* Online, November 1, 2007,
www.businessweek.com/technology/
content/oct2007/tc20071031_825744.
htm?chan=search, accessed: May 22,
2008.

8. Leonard M. Lodish, "Another Reason
Academics and Practitioners Should

Communicate More," *Journal of Marketing Research,* Vol. 44, Iss. 1, February
2007, pp. 23–25.

9. Tat Y. Chan, V. Padmanabhan, and
P. B. Seetharaman, "An Econometric
Model of Location and Pricing in the
Gasoline Market," *Journal of Marketing
Research* Vol. 44, Iss. 4, November 2007,
pp. 622–35; and Jeff Wang and Melanie
Wallendorf, "Materialism, Status Signal-
ing, and Product Satisfaction," *Journal of
the Academy of Marketing Science,*
Vol. 34, Iss. 4, Fall 2006, pp. 494–506.

10. Subim Im, Barry L. Bayus, and
Charlotte H. Mason, "An Empirical Study
of Innate Consumer Innovativeness,
Personal Characteristics, and New-
product Adoption Behavior," *Journal of the
Academy of Marketing Science,* Vol. 31,
Iss. 1, Winter 2003, pp. 61–74; and Sud-
hir N. Kale and Peter Klugsberger, "Reap-
ing Rewards," *Marketing Management,*
Vol. 16, Iss. 4, July/August 2007, p. 14.

11. "Grand Theft Auto IV Breaks Guinness World Records with Biggest
Entertainment Release of All Time," ING.
com, May 13, 2008, http://ps3.ign.com/
articles/873/873531p1.html, accessed
May 29, 2008.

12. "2007 Essential Facts about the
Computer and Video Game Industry,"
Sales, Demographic, and Usage Data,
Entertainment Software Association.
www.theesa.com/facts/pdfs/ESA_EF_
2007.pdf, accessed May 27, 2008.

13. Vauhini Vara, "EBay Bids for Younger
Auction Crowd at Social-Network Sites,"
Wall Street Journal, March 1, 2007, p. B1.

14. Charles D. Schewe and Geoffrey
Meredith, "Segmenting Global Markets
by Generational Cohorts: Determining
Motivations by Age," *Journal of Consumer Behaviour,* Vol. 4, Iss. 1, October
2004, pp. 51–64.

15. Sara Silver, "How Match.com Found
Love among Boomers," *Wall Street
Journal,* January 27, 2007, p. A1.

16. Anne L. Balazs, "Expenditures of
Older Americans," *Journal of the Acad-
emy of Marketing Science,* Vol. 28, Iss. 4,
Fall 2000, pp. 543–46; and Christopher
D. Hopkins, Catherine A. Roster, and
Charles M. Wood, "Making the Transition
to Retirement: Appraisals, Post-transition
Lifestyle, and Changes in Consumption
Patterns," *Journal of Consumer Market-
ing,* Vol. 23, Iss. 2, 2006, pp. 89–101.

17. Stuart Van Auken, Thomas E. Barry,
and Richard P. Bagozzi, "A Cross-Country
Construct Validation of Cognitive Age,"
*Journal of the Academy of Marketing
Science,* Vol. 34, Iss. 3, Summer 2006,
pp. 439–56.

18. Mark Andrew Mitchell, Piper
McLean, and Gregory B. Turner, "Under-
standing Generation X . . . Boom or Bust
Introduction," *Business Forum,* Vol. 27,
Iss. 1, 2005, pp. 26–31.

19. Qimei Chen, Shelly Rodgers, and
William D. Wells, "Better than Sex," *Marketing Research,* Vol. 16, Iss. 4, Winter
2004, pp. 16–22.

20. www.gillettevenus.com/us/,
accessed May 29, 2008.

21. Rex Y. Du and Wagner A Kamakura,
"Household Life Cycles and Lifestyles in
the United States," *Journal of Marketing
Research,* Vol. 43, Iss. 1, February 2006
pp. 121–32.

22. Andrew Lindridge and Sally Dibb,
"Is 'Culture' a Justifiable Variable for
Market Segmentation? A Cross-cultural
Example," *Journal of Consumer
Behaviour,* Vol. 2, Iss. 3, March 2003,
pp. 269–87.

23. Frederick A. Palumbo and Ira Teich,
"Market Segmentation Based on Level of
Acculturation," *Marketing Intelligence &
Planning,* Vol. 22, Iss. 4, 2004,
pp. 472–84.

24. Frederick A. Palumbo and Ira Teich,
"Segmenting the U.S. Hispanic Market
Based on Level of Acculturation," *Journal
of Promotion Management,* Vol. 12,
Iss. 1, 2005, pp. 151–73.

25. Mark R. Forehand and Rohit Desh-
pande, "What We See Makes Us Who
We Are: Priming Ethnic Self-awareness
and Advertising Response," *Journal of
Marketing Research,* Vol. 38, Iss. 3,
August 2001, pp. 336–4.

26. Carmen DeNavas-Walt, Bernadette D.
Proctor, and Jessica Smith, "Income,
Poverty, and Health Insurance Coverage
in the United States: 2006," *US Census
Online,* August 2007, www.census.gov/
prod/2007pubs/p60-233.pdf, accessed
May 23, 2008.

27. C. B. Bhattacharya and Sankar Sen,
"Consumer-Company Identification: A
Framework for Understanding Consum-
ers' Relationships with Companies,"
Journal of Marketing, Vol. 67, Iss. 2, April
2003, pp. 76–88.

28. Ben Levisohn and Brian Burnsed,
"The Credit Rating in Your Shoe Box,"
BusinessWeek Online, April 10, 2008,
www.businessweek.com/magazine/
content/08_16/b4080052299512.
htm?chan=search, accessed May 23,
2008.

29. Christopher Hinton and Nicole
Urbanowicz, "Diageo Seeks Blue Label
Niche," *Wall Street Journal,* February 28,
2007, p. B3E.

30. http://www.census.gov.

31. Paul G. Patterson, "Demographic Correlates of Loyalty in a Service Context," *Journal of Services Marketing* Vol. 21, Iss. 2, 2007, pp. 112–21.

32. Madhubalan Viswanathan, Jose Antonio Rosa, and James Edwin Harris, "Decision Making and Coping of Functionally Illiterate Consumers and Some Implications for Marketing Management," *Journal of Marketing,* Vol. 69, Iss. 1, January 2005, pp. 15–31.

33. Robert D. Hof, "How to Hit a Moving Target," *BusinessWeek,* August 21/28, 2006, p. 82.

34. Charles M. Schaninger and Sanjay Putrevu, "Dual Spousal Work Involvement: An Alternative Method to Classify Households/Families," *Academy of Marketing Science Review,* Vol. 2006, 2006, pp. 1–21.

35. Rob Lawson and Sarah Todd, "Consumer Lifestyles: A Social Stratification Perspective," *Marketing Theory* Vol. 2, Iss. 3, September 2002, pp. 295–308.

36. David J. Faulds and Stephan F. Gohmann, "Adapting Geodemographic Information to Army Recruiting: The Case of Identifying and Enlisting Private Ryan," *Journal of Services Marketing,* Vol. 15, Iss. 3, 2001, pp. 186–211.

37. David Reed, "Attitude Problem," *Precision Marketing,* January 26, 2007, p. 27.

38. Geraldine Fennell, Greg M. Allenby, Sha Yang, and Yancy Edwards, "The Effectiveness of Demographic and Psychographic Variables for Explaining Brand and Product Category Use," *Quantitative Marketing and Economics,* Vol. 1, Iss. 2, June 2003, pp. 223–44.

39. Ray A. Smith, "At Levi Strauss, Dockers Are In," *Wall Street Journal,* February 14, 2007, p. A14.

40. "VALS Survey," *SRI Consulting Business Intelligence* Online, www.sric-bi.com/VALS/, accessed May 25, 2008.

41. "The Price is Right," *Brand Strategy,* June 14, 2006, p. 25.

42. James Frederick, "Walgreens Leaders Reaffirm Strategy, Outlook," *Drug Store News,* February 16, 2004.

43. Florian V. Wangenheim and Tomas Bayon, "Behavioral Consequences of Overbooking Service Capacity," *Journal of Marketing,* Vol. 71, Iss. 4, October 2007, pp. 36–47; and Ruth N. Bolton, Katherine N. Lemon, and Peter C. Verhoef, "The Theoretical Underpinnings of Customer Asset Management: A Framework and Propositions for Future Research," *Journal of the Academy of Marketing Science,* Vol. 32, Iss. 3, Summer 2004, pp. 271–93.

44. Sarah Plaskitt, "Listerine Boosts Sales by 20%," *B&T Magazine* Online, May 22, 2003, www.bandt.com.au/news/49/0c016749.asp, accessed May 25, 2008.

45. Yuping Liu, "The Long-Term Impact of Loyalty Programs on Consumer Purchase Behavior and Loyalty," *Journal of Marketing,* Vol. 71, Iss. 4, October 2007, pp. 19–35.

46. V. Kumar and J. Andrew Petersen, "Using Customer-Level Marketing Strategy to Enhance Firm Performance: A Review of Theoretical and Empirical Evidence," *Journal of the Academy of Marketing Science,* Vol. 33, Iss. 4, Fall 2005, pp. 504–20; and David Feldman, "Segmentation Building Blocks," *Marketing Research,* Vol. 18, Iss. 2, Summer 2006, p. 23.

47. Larry Selden and Yoko S. Selden, "Profitable Customer," *Advertising Age,* July 10, 2006, p. 7.

48. Thomas L. Powers and Jay U. Sterling, "Segmenting Business-to-Business Markets: A Micro-Macro Linking Methodology," *Journal of Business & Industrial Marketing* Vol. 23, Iss. 3, 2008, pp. 170–77.

49. Peter R. Dickson, Paul W. Farris, and Willem J. M. I. Verbeke, "Dynamic Strategic Thinking," *Journal of the Academy of Marketing Science,* Vol. 29, Iss. 3, Summer 2001, pp. 216–38.

50. Eric Almquist and Gordon Wyner, "Boost Your Marketing ROI with Experimental Design," *Harvard Business Review,* Vol. 79, Iss. 9, October 2001, pp. 135–47.

51. Kate Maddox, "Vertical Variety," *B to B,* June 26, 2006, p. 4.

52. Gary L. Frazier, "Organizing and Managing Channels of Distribution," *Journal of the Academy of Marketing Science,* Vol. 27, Iss. 2, Spring 1999, pp. 226–51; and Darren W. Dahl and Page Moreau, "The Influence and Value of Analogical Thinking during New Product Ideation," *Journal of Marketing Research,* Vol. 39, Iss. 1, February 2002, pp. 47–61.

53. Amol Sharma, "Cricket' Still Clears Bar for Leap," *Wall Street Journal,* December 26, 2006, p. C1.

54. J. David Hunger and Thomas H. Wheelen, *Essentials of Strategic Management,* 4th edition. Upper Saddle River, NJ: Prentice Hall, 2007.

55. Subin Im and John P. Workman Jr., "Market Orientation, Creativity, and New Product Performance in High-Technology Firms," *Journal of Marketing,* Vol. 68, Iss. 2, April 2004, pp. 114–32.

56. Bruce Buskirk, Stacy M. P. Schmidt, and David L. Ralph, "Patterns in High-Tech Firms Growth Strategies by Seeking Mass Mainstream Customer Adaptations," *The Business Review, Cambridge,* Vol. 8, Iss. 1, Summer 2007, pp. 34–40.

57. Don Peppers and Martha Rogers, *The One-to-One Manager: Real World Lessons in Customer Relationship Management.* New York: Doubleday Business, 2002.

58. Robert D. Hof, "How to Hit a Moving Target," *BusinessWeek,* August 21/28, 2006, p. 82.

59. David A. Schweidel, Eric T. Bradlow, and Patti Williams, "A Feature-Based Approach to Assessing Advertisement Similarity," *Journal of Marketing Research,* Vol. 43, Iss. 2, May 2006, pp. 237–43.

60. "Dylon in 'Colour-Care' Shift," *Marketing,* February 21, 2007, p. 11.

61. Andrew Curry, Gill Ringland, and Laurie Young, "Using Scenarios to Improve Marketing," *Strategy & Leadership,* Vol. 34, Iss. 6, 2006, pp. 30–39.

62. "Burger King's Monster 923 Calorie Burger," *Metro News* Online, November 6, 2006, www.metro.co.uk/news/article.html?in_article_id=23982&in_page_id=34, accessed May 25, 2008.

63. Detelina Marinova, "Actualizing Innovation Effort: The Impact of Market Knowledge Diffusion in a Dynamic System of Competition," *Journal of Marketing,* Vol. 68, Iss. 3, July 2004, pp. 1–20.

64. Michael E. Porter, *Competitive Advantage.* New York: Simon & Schuster, 1985.

65. David W. Cravens and Nigel F. Piercy, *Strategic Marketing,* 9/e. Boston: McGraw-Hill/Irwin, 2009.

CHAPTER 10

1. David Welch, "GM: Live Green or Die", *BusinessWeek,* May 26, 2008, Issue 4085, pp. 36–39.

2. Albert M. Muniz Jr. and Hope Jensen Schau, "Religiosity in the Abandoned Apple Newton Brand Community," *Journal of Consumer Research,* 2005, Vol. 31 (4), pp. 737–48; and Hope Jensen Schau and Albert Muniz, "A Tale of Tales: The Apple Newton Narratives," *Journal of Strategic Marketing,* 2006, Vol. 14 (1), pp. 19–28.

3. Julee Kaplan, "Aeropostale Targets Teen Charities," *WWD,* 2008, Vol. 195 (13), p. 14.

4. Jack Neff, "Tide's Washday Miracle: Not Doing Laundry," *Advertising Age,* 2007, Vol. 78 (45), p. 12.

5. Andreas B. Eisingerich and Tobias Kretschmer, "In E-Commerce, More Is More," *Harvard Business Review*, 2008, Vol. 86 (3), pp. 20–35.

6. Lance A. Bettencourt and Anthony W. Ulwick, "The Customer-Centered Innovation Map," *Harvard Business Review*, 2008, Vol. 86 (5), p. 109.

7. Moon Ihlwan, "LG Closes in on Motorola," *BusinessWeek*, May 19, 2008, Issue 4084, pp. 30.

8. Yukair Iwatani Kane, "Sony, Sharp Form Venture to Make LCD-TV Panels," *Wall Street Journal*, February 27, 2008, p. B2; and Yukari Iwatani Kane and Evan Ramstad, "Sharp Grabs LCD-TV sales lead," *Wall Street Journal*, Nov. 2, 2007, p. B6.

9. Stephen L. Vargo and Robert F. Lusch, "From Goods Go Service(s): Divergences and Convergences of Logics," *Industrial Marketing Management*, 2008, Vol. 37 (3), pp. 254–68.

10. Preyas S. Desai, Oded Koenigsberg, and Devarat Purohit, "The Role of Production Lead Time and Demand Uncertainty in Marketing Durable Goods," *Management Science*, 2007 vol. 53 (1), pp. 150–59.

11. "Earnings Rise 40% at J&J," *Financial Times*, April 16, 2008, p. 27; and Arlene Weintraub and Bruce Einhorn, "J&J's New Baby," *BusinessWeek*, 2007, Issue 4039, pp. 48–50.

12. Jena McGregor, "USAA: Better Service for Those Who Serve," *BusinessWeek*, March 3, 2008, p. 48.

13. Robert Wright, "Big Order for Trains Expected to Cost 1.4 billion Pounds," *Financial Times*, April 9, 2008, p. 4; and Kerry A. Dolan, "The Great Train Catch-Up," *Forbes*, 2007, Vol. 179 (7), p. 98.

14. Marc Abrahams, "A Pointed Lesson about Product Features," *Harvard Business Review*, 2006, Vol. 84 (3), pp. 21–23.

15. Carol Matlack, "What Airbus Learned from the Dreamliner," *BusinessWeek*, April 28, 2008, Issue 4081, p. 92; and Kevin Done, "Boeing and Airbus Hit New Highs," *Financial Times*, January 5, 2008, p. 8.

16. Rob Sabin, "The Great Flat Panel Face-Off," *Sound & Vision*, Feb./Mar. 2008, Vol. 73 (2), p. 68.

17. Ben Levisohn, "Keep That Rolex Ticking," *BusinessWeek*, March 24, 2008, Issue 4076, p. 21; and Stacy Meichtry, "How Timex Plans to Upgrade Its Image," *Wall Street Journal*, June 21, 2007, p. B6.

18. Djoko Setijono, Jens J. Dahlgaard, "The Value of Quality Improvements," *The International Journal of Quality and Reliability Management*, 2008, Vol. 25, (3), pp. 292–306; and Gavriel Melirovich, "Quality of Design and Quality of Conformance: Contingency and Synergistic Approaches," *Total Quality Management and Business Excellence*, 2008, Vol. 17 (2), pp. 205–20.

19. Rajeev K. Goel, "Uncertain Innovation with Uncertain Product Durability," *Applied Economics Letters*, "2006, Vol. 13 (13), pp. 829–42.

20. Chuniai Chen, Jun Yang, Christopher Findlay, "Measuring the Effect of Food Standards on China's Agricultural Exports," *Review of World Economics*, 2008, Vol. 144 (1), 83–107; and David Kesmodel and Nicholas Zamiska, "China Curbs Garlic, Ginger Exports to U.S., "*Wall Street Journal*, September 18, 2007, p. D7.

21. Kamalini Ramdas and Taylor Randall, "Does Component Sharing Help or Hurt Reliability? An Empirical Study in the automotive Industry," *Management Science*, 2008, Vol. 54 (5), pp. 922–39; and Niranjan Pati and Dayr Reis, "The Quality Learning Curve: An Approach to Predicting Quality Improvement in Manufacturing and Services," *Journal of Global Business Issues*, Vol. 1 (2), pp. 129–41.

22. Bimai Nepal, Leslie Monplaisir, and Nanua Singh, "A Framework to Integrate Design for Reliability and Maintainability in Modular Product Design, *International Journal of Product Development*, 2007, Vol. 4 (5), pp. 459–674.

23. Rita Som, "Luxe Evian Bottle for Fine Dining Segment," *Packaging*, 2007, p. 4; and "Evian Place Bottle Puts on Pedestal for Innovative Packaging," PR Newswire, April 7, 2008.

24. Ravinda Chitturi, Rajagopal Raghunathan and Vijar Mahajan, "Delight By Design: The Role of Hedonic Versus Utilitarian Benefits, *Journal of Marketing*, 2008, Vol. 72 (3), pp. 48–61.

25. Penelope Green, "While You Were Out, the Post-It Went Home," *New York Times*, June 28, 2007, p. F1.

26. Julie Jargon, "Boss Talk: Campbell's Chief Looks for Splash of Innovation," *Wall Street Journal*, May 30, 2008, p. B8; and David Jacobson, "Hits and Misses", *Business 2.0*, 2007, Vol. 8 (3), p. 118.

27. Stephanie Kang, "Nike Gets Back to Basics, Reinventing the T-Shirt," *Wall Street Journal*, April 2, 2007, B1.

28. Muhammad A. Noor, Rick Rabiser, and Paul Grunbacher, "Agile Product Line Planning: A Collarborative Approach and a Case Study," *The Journal of Systems and Software*, 2008, Vol. 81 (6), pp. 868–81.

29. Mike Bieme, "A-B Redefines Marketplace to Stay Ahead of the Pack," *Brandweek*, 2008, Vol. 49 (14), p. 9; and Matthew Maier, "$100 Bottles of Beer on the Wall," *Business 2.0*, 2006, Vol. 7 (1), p. 26.

30. Peter N. Golder and Gerald J. Tellis, "Growing, Growing, Gone: Cascades, Diffusion, and Turning Points in the Product Life Cycle," *Marketing Science*, 2004, Vol. 23 (2), pp. 207–21.

31. Kate Niederhoffer, Rob Mooth, David Wiesenfeld, Jonathon Gordon, "The Origin and Impact of CPG New Product Buzz: Emerging Trends and Implications," *Journal of Advertising*, 2007, Vol. 47 (4), pp. 420–36.

32. Aric Chen, "Get a Room," *Interior Design*, 2008, Vol. 79 (1), p. 248; and Laura Koss-Feder, "At Your Service," *Time*, 2007, Vol. 169 (24), pp. P1–P4.

33. Ming-Jung Hsiet, Huen-Hung Tsai, Jun-Ren Wang, "The Moderating Effect of Marketing Orientation and Launch Proficiency on the Product Advantage Performance Relationship", *Industrial Marketing Management*, 2008, Vol. 37 (5), pp. 580–97.

34. Khaleed Aboulnasr, Om Harasimhan, Edward and Rajesh Chandy, "Competitive Response to Radical Product Innovations," *Journal of Marketing*, 2008, Vol. 72 (3), pp. 94–110.

35. Paul Matthyssens, and Koen Vandenbempt, "Moving from Basic Offerings to Value Added Solutions: Strategies, Barriers and Alignment," *Industrial Marketing Management*, Vol. 37 (3), pp. 316–31.

36. Manak C. Gupta and C. Anthony Di Benedetto, "Optimal Pricing and Advertising Strategy for Introducing a New Business Product with Threat of Competitive Entry," *Industrial Marketing Management*, 2007, Vol. 36 (4), pp. 540–57.

37. J. Alberto Castaneda, Francisco J. Montoso and Teodoro Luque, "The Dimensionality of Customer Privacy Concerns on the Internet," *Online Information Review*, 2007, Vol. 31 (4), pp. 420–37.

38. Bar J. Bronnenberg and Carl F. Mela, "Market Roll-Out and Retailer Adoption for New Brands," *Marketing Science*, 2004, Vol. 23 (4), pp. 500–19.

39. Stefan Stremersch, Gerard J. Tellis, Philip Hans Franses and Jeroen L.G. Binken, "Indirect Network Effects In New Product Growth," *Journal of Marketing*, 2007, Vol. 71 (3), pp. 52–68.

40. John R. Hauser and Steven M. Shugan, "Defensive Marketing Strategies," *Marketing Science,* 2008, Vol. 27 (1), pp. 88–113.

41. Pia Hurmelinna-Laukkanen, Liisa-Maija Sainio, and Tiina Jauhiainen, "Appropriability Regime for Radical and Incremental Innovations," *R&D Management,* 2008, Vol. 38 (3), pp. 278–94.

42. Venkatesh Bala, Jason Green, "Charge What Your Products Are Worth," *Harvard Business Review,* 2007, Vol. 85 (9), pp. 22–31.

43. Erin D. Parrish, Nancy L. Cassill, and William Oxenham, "Niche Marketing Strategy for A Mature Market Place," *Marketing Intelligence and Planning,* 2006, Vol. 24 (7), pp. 694–709.

44. Gila E. Fruchter and Ariel Fligler, "The Various Brands in the Optimal Product Line versus the Optimal Single Product," *Innovative Marketing,* 2007, Vol. 3 (1), pp. 15–24.

45. Debanjan Mitra and Peter N. Golder, "Quality Is in the Eye of the Beholder," *Harvard Business Review,* 2007, Vol. 85 (4), pp. 26–41.

46. Dexter Roberts, "Scrambling to Bring Crest to the Masses," *Business-Week,* 2007, Issue 4040, p. 72.

47. Joseph W. K. Chan, "Product End of Life Options Selection: Grey Relational Analysis Approach," *International Journal of Production Research,* 2008, Vol. 46 (11), pp. 2889–2901.

48. Drew Winter, "Audi 5000 to Success," *Ward's Auto World,* 2005, Vol. 41 (6), p. 5.

49. William M. Bulkeley, ""Inkjet Presses by H-P, Kodak May Challenge Xerox," *Wall Street Journal,* March 29, 2008, B.5; and Stephen H. Wildstrom, "Kodak Moments for Less," *Business-Week,* May 14, 2007, Issue 4034, pp. 24–27.

50. Alex Taylor III, "Gentlemen, Start Your Turnaround," *Fortune,* 2008, Vol. 157 (1), pp. 70–73; and David Welch, "Putting Designers in the Driver's Seat," *BusinessWeek,* 2007, Issue 4039, pp. 72–75.

CHAPTER 11

1. Jonathan Birchall, "Ralph Lauren Aims to Double Sales in Asia and Europe," *Financial Times,* May 29, 2008, p. 17; and John Brodie, "It's Ralph's World," *Fortune,* 2007, Vol. 156, (6), pp 64–68.

2. DeWayne Bevil, "Simpsons Ride Opens at Universal," *Orlando Sentinel,* April 29, 2008, p. B1; and Kara Newman, "How to Sell with Smell," *Business 2.0,* April 2007, p. 36.

3. Arch G. Woodside, Suresh Sood, Kenneth E. Miller, "When Consumers and Brands Talk: Storytelling Theory and Research in Psychology and Marketing," *Psychology & Marketing,* 2008, Vol. 25 (2), pp. 97–111.

4. Franz Rudolf Esch, Tobia Langner, Bernd H. Schmitt, and Patrick Gaus, "Are Brands Forever? Brand Knowledge and Relationship Affect Current and Future Purchases," *The Journal of Product and Brand Management,* 2006, Vol. 15 (2), pp. 98–105.

5. William Kingston, "Trademark Registration Is Not a Right," *Journal of Macromarketing,* 2006, Vol. 26 (1), pp. 17–26.

6. Madhubalan Viswanathan and Terry L. Childers, "Understanding How Product Attributes Influence Product Categorization: Development and Validation of Fuzzy Set–based Measures of Gradedness in Product Categories," *Journal of Marketing Research,* 1999, Vol. 36, (1), pp. 75–95.

7. Arik Hesseldahl, "The iPhone Eyes BlackBerry's Turf," *BusinessWeek* Online, June 11, 2008, http://www.businessweek.com/print/magazine/content/08_25/b4089038650669.htm; and Peter Burrows, "Apple's iPhone Goes Corporate," March 4, 2008, *BusinessWeek* Online, http://www.businessweek.com/print/magazine/content/08_11/b4075000707492.htm, June 19, 2008.

8. Pamela Miles Homer, "Perceived Quality and Image: When All Is Not "Rosy," *Journal of Business Research,* 2008, Vol. 61 (6), pp. 715–30.

9. Julie Manning Magid, Anthony D. Cox, and Dena S. Cox, "Quantifying Brand Image: Empirical Evidence of Trademark Dilution," *American Business Law Journal,* 2006, Vol. 43 (1), pp. 1–43.

10. Bing Jing, "Product Differentiation Under Imperfect Information: When Does Offering a Lower Quality Pay?" *Quantitative Marketing and Economics,* 2007, Vol. 5 (1), pp. 35–62.

11. Andy McCue, "Virtual Booze: Diageo Taps Second Life," *BusinessWeek* Online, June 11, 2007, http://www.businessweek.com/globalbiz/content/jun2007/gb20070611_608713.htm?chan=search; and Jenny Wiggins, "Emerging Markets Are Also Crucial Target Areas," *Financial Times,* February 15, 2008, p. 21.

12. Elizabeth Woyke, "Flunking Brand Geography," *BusinessWeek,* 2007, Issue 4039, p. 14.

13. William B. Locander and David L. Luechauer, "Building Equity," *Marketing Management,* 2005, Vol. 14 (3), pp. 45–48.

14. David Aaker, *Managing Brand Equity,* Free Press, 1991.

15. Saikat Banaerjee, "Strategic Brand-culture Fit: A Conceptual Framework for Brand Management," *Journal of Brand Management,* 2008, Vol. 15 (5), pp. 312–22.

16. "The New Brand Landscape," *Marketing Health Services,* 2008, Vol. 28 (1), p. 14; and Helen Stride and Stephen Lee, "No Logo? No Way, Branding in the Non-Profit Sector," *Journal of Marketing Management,* 2007, Vol. 23 (1/2), pp. 107–22.

17. Matthew Yeung and Bala Ramasamy, "Brand Value and Firm Performance Nexus: Further Empirical Evidence," *Journal of Brand Management,* 2008, Vol. 15 (5), pp. 322–36.

18. Jane Simms, "Brand on the Run," *Computing,* May 30, 2007, http://www.computing.co.uk/financial-director/features/2190915/brand-run., June 19, 2008.

19. B. Ramaseshan and Hsiu-Yuan Tsao, "Moderating Effects of the Brand Concept on the Relationship Between Brand Personality and Perceived Quality," *Journal of Brand Management,* 2007, Vol. 14, (6), pp. 458–67; and Joel Espejel, Carmina Fandos and Carlos Flavian, "The Role of Intrinsic and Extrinsic Quality Attributes on Consumer Behavior for Traditional Food Products," *Managing Service Quality,* 2007, Vol. 17 (6), pp. 681–99.

20. Keith Walley, Paul Custance, Sam Taylor, Adam Lindgreen, and Martin Hinghley, "The Importance of Brand in the Industrial Purchase Decision: A Case Study of the UK Tractor Market," *Journal of Business & Industrial Marketing,* 2007, Vol. 22 (6), pp. 383–99.

21. Karen E. Klein, "A Practical Guide to Branding," *BusinessWeek Online,* June 9, 2008, http://www.businessweek.com/print/smallbiz/content/jun2008/sb2008069_694225.htm, June 19, 2008.

22. Natalie Mizik and Robert Jacobson, "The Financial Value Impact of Perceptual Brand Attributes," *Journal of Marketing Research,* 2008, Vol. 45 (1), pp. 15–31.

23. David Ballantyne and Robert Aitken, "Branding in B2B Markets: Insights from the Service Dominant Logic of Marketing," *The Journal of Business & Industrial Marketing,* 2007, Vol. 22 (6), pp. 363–81.

24. Avinash V. Mainkar, Michael Lubatkin, and William S. Schulze, "Toward a

riers," *Academy of Management Review,* 2006, Vol. 31 (4), pp. 1062–79.

25. Rong Huang and Emine Sarigollu, "Assessing Satisfaction with Core and Secondary Attributes," *Journal of Business Research,* 2008, Vol. 61 (9), pp. 942–59.

26. Suraksah Gupta, Susan Grant, and T.C. Melewar, "The Expanding Role of Intangible Assets of the Brand," *Management Decision,* 2008, Vol. 46 (6), pp. 948–61.

27. Bob Lutz, "The Way Ahead for Cars," *Newsweek,* 2008, Vol. 151 (18), p. 18; and Stephen Baker and Heather Green, "Beyond Blogs," *BusinessWeek,* June 2, 2008, pp. 45–50.

28. Brad D. Carlson, Tracy A. Suter, and Tom J. Brown, "Social versus Psychological Brand Community: The Role of Psychological Sense of Brand Community," *Journal of Business Research,* 2008, Vol. 61 (4), pp. 284–301.

29. Jing Lei, Niraj Dawar, and Jos Lemmink, "Negative Spillover in Brand Portfolios: Exploring the Antecedents of Asymmetric Effects," *Journal of Marketing,* Vol. 72 (3), pp. 111–29.

30. Satish Nambisan and Priya Nambisan, "How to Profit from a Better 'Virtual Customer Environment," *MIT Sloan Management Review,* 2008, Vol. 49 (3), pp. 53–70.

31. Ingrid M. Martin, David W. Stewart and Shashi Matta, "Branding Strategies, Marketing Communication, and Perceived Brand Meaning: the Transfer of Purposive, Goal Oriented Brand Meaning to Brand Extensions," *Journal of the Academy of Marketing Science,* 2005, Vol. 33 (3), pp. 275–95.

32. Burt Helm, "OK Kids, Name that Chip," *BusinessWeek,* 2007, Issue 4040, p. 14.

33. N.Amrouche, G. Martin-Herran, and G. Zaccour, "Pricing and Advertising of Private and National Brands in a Dynamic Marketing Channel," *Journal of Optimization Theory and Applications,* Vol. 137 (3), pp. 465–84.

34. Tsung-Chi Liu and Chung-Yu Want, "Factors Affecting Attitudes toward Private Labels and Promoted Brands," *Journal of Marketing Management,* 2008, Vol. 24 (3/4), pp. 283–99; and Kyong-Nan Kwon, Mi-Hee Lee and Yoo Jin Kin, "The Effect of Perceived Product Characteristics on Private Brand Purchases," *The Journal of Consumer Marketing,* 2008, Vol. 25 (2), pp. 105–22.

35. Najam Saqib, Rajesh V. Manchanda, "Consumers Evaluations of Co-Branded

Products, the Licensing Effect," *The Journal of Product and Brand Management,* 2008, Vol. 17 (2), pp. 73–89.

36. Klaus-Peter Wiedmann and Dirk Ludewig, "How Risky Are Brand Licensing Strategies in View of Customer Perceptions and Reactions?" *Journal of General Management,* 2008, Vol. 33, (3), pp. 31–50.

37. Alokparna Basu, Monga, Loraine Lau-Gesk, "Blending Co Brand Personalities; An Examination of the Complex Self," *Journal of Marketing Research,* 2007, Vol. 44 (3), pp. 389–402.

38. Wei-Lun Chang, "A Typology of Co-branding Strategy: Position and Classification," *Journal of the American Academy of Business,* March 2008, Vol. 12 (2), pp. 220–27.

39. Randi Schmelzer, "Nickelodeon, Marriott Pair on Branded Family Resorts," *PRweek,* 2007, Vol. 10 (24), p. 2

40. "P&G to Replace Bold and Lenor with Premium Line," *Marketing Week,* November 22, 2207, p. 3.

41. "Symbian Fights Against Google and Apple," *SinoCast China Business News,* April 9, 2008; and "Symbian", *Hoovers,* June 18, 2008.

42. Carolyn Walkup, "Yum Studies McD's Strengths in Bid to Boost U.S. Sales," *Nation's Restaurant News,* 2008, Vol. 42 (1), pp. 1–3.

43. Gene Marcial, "Document Security: A Deadeye for Knockoffs," *BusinessWeek,* July 2, 2007, p. 21.

44. Pinya Silayoi and Mark Speece, "The Importance of Packaging Attributes: A Conjoint Analysis Approach," *European Journal of Marketing,* 2007, Vol. 41 (11/12), pp. 1495–1508.

45. Jessie Scanlon, "Pushing the Boundaries of Design," *BusinessWeek,* June 12, 2007, pp. 38–39.

46. Ulrich R. Orth and Keven Malkewitz, "Holistic Package Design and Consumer Brand Impressions," *Journal of Marketing,* 2008, Vol. 72 (3), pp. 64–81.

47. Thomas J. Madden, Kelly Hewett, and Martin S. Roth, "Managing Images in Different Cultures: Across National Study of Color Meanings and Preferences," *Journal of International Marketing,* 2000, Vol. 8 (4), pp. 90–108.

48. "Konami and Nestle Waters North America Announce the 'Green with Envy' National Promotion, *Business Wire,* September 17, 2007.

49. Eric F. Shaver and Curt C. Braun, "Caution: How to Develop an Effective Product Warning," *Risk Management,* 2008, Vol. 55 (6), pp. 46–52.

50. Matthew Boyle, "Microsoft and GE Are Not Old and in the Way," *Fortune,* 2007, Vol. 156 (10), pp. 28; and Ellen McGirt, "Breakaway Brands," *Fortune,* 2006, Vol. 154 (6), pp. 27–29.

51. Rebecca J. Slotegraaf and J. Jeffrey Inman, "Longitudinal Shifts in the Drivers of Satisfaction with Product Quality: The Role of Attribute Resolvability," *Journal of Marketing Research,* 2004, Vol. 41 (3), pp. 269–83.

52. D.N.P. Murthy, O. Solem, and T. Roren, "Product Warranty Logistics: Issues and Challenges," *European Journal of Operational Research,* 2004, Vol. 156 (1), pp. 110–25.

53. Shallendra Pratap Jain, Rebecca J. Slotegraaf, and Charles D. Lindsey, "Towards Dimensionalizing Warranty Information: The Role of Consumer Costs of Warranty Information," *Journal of Consumer Psychology,* 2007, Vol. 17 (1), pp. 70–88.

54. Jena McGregor, "Customer Service Champs," *BusinessWeek,* 2008, Issue 4073, p. 37; and David Welch, "Cadillac: Looser Rules, Happier Clients," *BusinessWeek,* 2007, Issue 4024, p. 62.

55. Daniel Lyons, "Still Spinning," *Forbes,* 2007, Vol. 179 (12), pp. 64–65.

CHAPTER 12

1. Mark Scott, "Ocean Power: Europe's Next Green Thing," *BusinessWeek Online,* March 14, 2008, http://www.businessweek.com/globalbiz/content/mar2008/gb20080314_838407.htm; Vaughan Scully, "Wave Power Attracts Investors," *BusinessWeek Online,* August 27, 2007, http://www.businessweek.com/investor/content/aug2007/pi20070824_560536.htm; and Melanie Haiken, "The Next Wave in Clean Energy," *Business 2.0,* Vol. 8 (7), pp. 30.

2. Glen M. Schmidt and Cheryl T. Druehl, "When Is a Disruptive Innovation Disruptive?", *Journal of Product Innovation Management,* 2008, 25 (4), pp. 347–62; and Lee G. Demuth III, "A Viewpoint on Disruptive Innovation," *Journal of American Academy of Business,* 2008, Vol. 13 (1), pp. 86–92.

3. Geoffrey A. Moore, "Darwin and the Demon: Innovating within Established Enterprises," *Harvard Business Review,* 2005, Issue 82 (7/8), pp. 86–98.

4. Arlene Weintraub, "It's on the Tip of Your Tongue," *BusinessWeek,* 2006, Issue 2995, pp. 32–33.

5. Kenneth J. Petersen, Robert B. Handfield, and Gary L. Ragatz, "Supplier Integration into New Product Development: Coordinating Product, Process

and Supply Chain Design," *Journal of Operations Management,* Vol. 23 (3/40), pp. 371–89.

6. Alex Taylor III, "Can This Care Save Ford?" *Fortune,* 2008, Vol. 157 (9), pp. 170–72; and David Kiley, One World, One Car," *BusinessWeek,* 2008, Issue 4076, p. 63.

7. Cornelia Droge, Roger Calantone, and Nukhet Harmancioglu, "New Product Success: Is It Really Controllable by Managers in Highly Turbulent Environments?" *Journal of Production Innovation Management,* 2008, Vol. 25 (3), pp. 272–90.

8. "Innovation Is More Than Just a Good Idea," *Strategic Direction,* Vol. 24 (8), p. 25.

9. Serkan Aydin, Ayse Tanbsel Cetin, and Gokhan Ozer, "The Relationship between Marketing and Product Development Process and Their Effects on Firm's Performance," *Journal of Academy of Marketing Studies,* 2007, Vol. 11 (10), pp. 53–69.

10. "Ford's European Arm Lends a Hand: Cars," *The Economist,* March 8, 2008, Vol. 385 (Issue 8570), p. 82.

11. Jennifer Ordonez, "Taking the Junk out of Junk Food," *Newsweek,* 2007, (Vol. 150 (15), pp. 46–47; and Russell Flannery, "China's Is a Big Prize," *Forbes,* 2004, (Issues 173 (10), pp. 163–64.

12. Peter Huber, "Toyota's MPG Game," *Forbes,* 2007, Vol. 180 (13), pp. 100.

13. "Wind Powered Ethanol," *Farm Industry News,* 2007, Vol. 40 (2), p. 5; and Duff McDonald, "John Deere Reaps the Wind," *Business 2.0,* 2006, Vol. 7 (2), p. 32.

14. "Eclipse 500 Wins Export Approvals," *Flight International,* 2008, Vol. 173 (5137), p. 12; and Bruce Nussbuam, "The Best Product Design of 2007," *BusinessWeek,* 2007, Issue 4044, pp. 52.

15. Rajesh Sethi and Zafar Iqbal, "State Gate Controls, Learning Failure, and Adverse Effect on Novel New Products," *Journal of Marketing,* 2008, Vol. 72 (1), pp. 118–32.

16. Pfizer Pipeline, "Our Medicines in Development," www.pfizer.com/research/pipeline/pipeline.psp, June 21, 2008.

17. Maria Bartiromo, "Chris DeWolfe on MySpace's Widening Web of Users," *BusinessWeek,* 2008, (Issue 5086), p. 25.

18. "Cadbury Launches Trident Xtra care," *Business Wire,* May 28, 2008 and Jenny Wiggins, "Take a Bite from the Gum Market Wrigley Is Going on the Defensive as Cadbury Plans an Aggressive Launch," *Financial Times,* Jan. 29, 2007, p. 21.

19. "Odyssey Software's Athena Add-In for Microsoft's System Center Configuration Manager 2007 Names "Best of Tech Ed 2008 IT Professional Awards Finalist," *PR Newswire,* June 3, 2008.

20. "KidCare Medical Television Network Launches Digital Television Network," *Wireless News,* December 26, 2007, p. 1.

21. John Saunders, Veronica Wong, Chris Stagg, and Mariadel Mar Souza Fontana, "How Screening Criteria Change during Brand Management," *Journal of Product and Brand Management,* 2005, Vol. 14 (4/5), pp. 239–50.

22. "Apple Prototypes: 5 Product We Never Saw," Applegazette, June 20, 2008, www.applegazette.com/mac.

23. Raul O. Chao and Stylianon Kavadias, "A Theoretical Framework for Managing the New Product Development Portfolio: When and How to Use Strategic Buckets," Management Science, 2008, Vol. 54 (5), pp. 907–22.

24. Dean Richard Prebble, Gerritt Anton De Waal, and Cristiaan de Groot, "Applying Multiple Perspectives to the Design of a Commercialization Process," R&D Management, 2008, Vol. 38 (3), pp. 311–27.

25. Karan Girotra, Christian Terwiesch and Karl T. Ulrich, "Valuing R&D Projects in a Portfolio: Evidence from the Pharmaceutical Industry," *Management Science,* 2007, Vol. 53 (9), pp. 1452–66.

26. Barry Fox, "Hi-Fi Failure helps to Brighten Beer," *New Scientist,* 2004, Vol. 183 (2455), p. 21; and Gail Edmondson, "Philips Needs Laser Speed," 1994, Issue 3375, pp 46–48.

27. Lenny H. Pattikawa, Ernst Verwaal and Harry R. Commandeur, "Understanding New Product Project Performance," *European Journal of Marketing,* 2006, Vol. 40 (11/12), pp. 1178–93.

28. Harold Sirkin and Jim Hemerling, "Price Trumps Quality in Emerging Markets," *BusinessWeek,* June 4, 2008, www.businessweek.comp/globalbiz/content/june2008/gb2008064_293370.htm; and Nandini Lakshman, "Nokia's Global Design Sense," *BusinessWeek,* August 10, 2007, www.businessweek.com/innovate/content/aug2007/id20070810_686743.htm, June 22, 2008.

29. Nukhel Armancioglu, Regina C. McNally, Roger J. Calantone, and Serdar S. Durmusoglu, "Your New Product Development (NPD) Is Only as Good as Your Process; an Exploratory Analysis of New NPD Process Design and Implementation," *R&D Management,* 2007, Vol. 37 (95), pp. 399–415.

30. Glen L. Urban and John R. Hauser, "Listening In to Find and Explore New Combinations of Customer Needs," *Journal of Marketing,* 2004, Vol. 68 (2), pp. 72–90.

31. B. Sorescu and Jelena Spanjol, "Innovation's Effect on Firm Value and Risk: Insights from Consumer Packaged Goods," *Journal of Marketing,* 2008, Vol. 72 (2), pp. 114–131.

32. Roger O. Crockett, "Motorola Sets Its Phone Unit Free," *BusinessWeek,* 2008, Issue 4078, p. 36; and Roger O. Crockett, "Honing the RAZR Edge," *BusinessWeek,* 2007, Issue 4038, p. 38.

33. J. Brock Smith and Mark Colgate, "Customer Value Creation: A Practical Framework," *Journal of Marketing Theory and Practice,* 2007, Vol. 15 (1), pp. 7–24.

34. Sanjiv Erat and Stylianos Kavadias, "Sequential Testing of Product Designs: Implications for Learning," *Management Science,* 2008, Vol. 54 (5) pp. 956–69.

35. Quentin Hardy and Evan Hessel, "GooTube," *Forbes,* 2008, Vol. 181 (12), p. 50; and Bharat Mediratta and Julie Bick, "The Google Way: Give Engineers Room," *New York Times,* October 21, 2007, p. 3.1.

36. Wei-Lun Chang, "A Typology of Co-Branding Strategy: Position and Classification," *Journal of the Academy of Business,* 2008, Vol. 12 (92) pp. 220–27.

37. Sharan Jagpal, Kamel Jedidi, and M. Jamil, "A Multibrand Concept Testing Methodology for New Product Strategy," *Journal of Product Innovation Management,* 2007, Vol. 24 (1), pp. 34–51.

38. Destan Kandemir, Roger Calantone and Rosanna Garcia, "An Exploration of Organizational Factors in New Product Development Success," *Journal of Business and Industrial Marketing,* 2006, Vol. 21 (5), pp. 300–18.

39. Robert G. Cooper, "Perspective: The Stage Gate Idea to Launch Process–Update, What's New and NexGen systems," *Journal of Product Innovation Management,* 2008, vol. 25 (3), pp. 213–29; and Ming-hung Hsieh, Kuen-Hung, and Jun-Ren Wang, "The Moderating Effects of Market Orientation and Launch Proficiency on the Product Advantage Performance Relationship," *Industrial Marketing Management,* 2008, Vol. 37 (5), pp. 580–99; and

Susan Jung Grant and Alice M. Tybout, "The Effect of Temporal Frame Information Considered in New Product Evaluation: The Role of Uncertainty," *Journal of Consumer Research,* 2008, Vol. 34 (6), pp. 897–912.

40. Aaron Ricadela, "Big Business Starts to Sour on Vista," *BusinessWeek,* 2008, Issue 4085, p. 48.

41. Henrik Sjodin, "Upsetting Brand Extensions: An Enquiry into Current Customer Inclination to Spread Negative Word of Mouth," *Journal of Brand Management,* 2008, Vol. 15 (4), pp. 258–62; and Kate Niederhoffer, Rob Mooth, David Wiesenfield, and Jonathan Gordon, "The Origin and Impact of CPG New Product Buzz: Emerging Trends and Implications," *Journal of Advertising Research,* 2007, Vol. 467 (4), pp. 420–38.

42. Christophe Van Den Butte and Yogesh V. Joshi, "New Product Diffusion with Influentials and Imitators," *Marketing Science,* 2007, Vol. 26 (3), pp. 400–24.

43. Joe Wilkie and Nick Sorvillo, "Targeting Early Adopters: A Means for New Product Survival," A.C. Nielsen, June 23, 2008.

44. Kapil Bawa and Robert Shoemaker, "The Effects of Free Sample Promotions on Incremental Brand Sales," *Marketing Science,* 2004, Vol. 23 (3), pp. 345–64.

45. Morris Kalliny, Angela Hausman, "The Impact of Cultural and Religious Vaues on Consumer's Adoption of Innovation," *Journal of the Academy of Marketing Studies,* Vol. 11 (1), pp. 125–37; and Stacy L. Wood and C. Page Moreau, From Fear to Loathing? How Emotion Influences the Evaluation and Early Use of Innovations," *Journal of Marketing,* Vol. 70 (3), pp. 44–60.

46. Peter Burrows, "Smoothing the Way for Web Video," *BusinessWeek* Online, March 21, 2008, www.businessweek.com/technology/content/mar2008/tc20080321.685942.htm; and Scott Woodley, "Building the Infinite Internet," *Forbes,* 2007, Vol. 179 (9), p. 68.

47. Kevin P. Coyne, "A Green and Bumpy Road for CEO's," *BusinessWeek* Online, April 3, 2008, www.businessweek.com/managing/content/apr2008/ca20080403_909948/htm; and Stacy Perman, "After Burt's Bees, What?" *BusinessWeek* Online, January 16, 2007, www.businessweek.com/smallbiz/content/jan2007/sb20070116_026260.htm, June 23, 2008.

CHAPTER 13

1. Leonard L. Berry, *On Great Service: A Framework for Action,* New York, The Free Press, 1995.

2. Stephen L. Vargo and Robert F. Lusch, "Evolving to a New Dominant Logic for Marketing," *Journal of Marketing,* Vol. 68, Iss. 1, January 2004, pp. 1–17.

3. Michael K. Brady, Brian L. Bourdeau, and Julia Heskel, "The Importance of Brand Cues in Intangible Service Industries: An Application to Investment Services," *Journal of Services Marketing,* Vol. 19, Iss. 6/7, 2005, pp. 401–11.

4. Carol Krol, "Web 2.0: Join the Revolution," *B to B,* November 13, 2006, p. 1.

5. Harvir S. Bansal, Shirley F. Taylor, and Yannik St. James, "Migrating' to New Service Providers: Toward a Unifying Framework of Customers' Switching Behaviors," *Journal of the Academy of Marketing Science,* Vol. 33, Iss. 1, Winter 2005, pp. 96–116.

6. "Steve Case's New Health Portal Offers Early Mix of Free and Paid Services," *InformationWeek,* January 24, 2007.

7. Jeremy J. Sierra and Shaun McQuitty, "Service Providers and Customers: Social Exchange Theory and Service Loyalty," *Journal of Services Marketing,* Vol. 19, Iss. 6/7, 2005, pp. 392–401.

8. Howard Riell, "Stir Up Customer Thrills with Display Cooking," *Food Service Director,* February 15, 2007, pp. 48–49.

9. Don Kuehnast, "Customer Relationship Management Solution Energizes Bank Sales Environment," *Microsoft Business Solutions CRM Customer Case Study,* 2004.

10. Christian Homburg, Wayne D. Hoyer, and Martin Fassnacht, "Service Orientation of a Retailer's Business Strategy: Dimensions, Antecedents, and Performance Outcomes," *Journal of Marketing,* Vol. 66, Iss. 4, October 2002, pp. 86–102; and Medhi Mourali, Michael Laroche, and Frank Pons, "Individualistic Orientation and Customer Susceptibility to Interpersonal Influence," *Journal of Services Marketing,* Vol. 19, Iss. 3, 2005, pp. 164–74.

11. William J. Holstein, "At Southwest, the Culture Drives Success," *BusinessWeek* Online, February 21, 2008, www.businessweek.com/managing/content/feb2008/ca20080221_179423.htm?chan=search, accessed May 28, 2008.

12. Jena McGregor, "Customer Service Champs," *BusinessWeek,* March 3, 2008, pp. 37–50.

13. Rajshekhar G. Javalgi, Thomas W. Whipple, Amit K Ghosh, and Robert B. Young, "Market Orientation, Strategic Flexibility, and Performance: Implications for Services Providers," *Journal of Services Marketing,* Vol. 19, Iss. 4, 2005, pp. 212–22.

14. Kenneth J. Klassen and Thomas R. Rohleder, "Combining Operations and Marketing to Manage Capacity and Demand in Services," *Service Industries Journal,* Vol. 21, Iss. 2, April 2001, pp. 1–30.

15. Kimberly Griffiths, "Got Satisfaction?" *Industrial Distribution,* October 1, 2006, p. 34.

16. D. Todd Donovan, Tom J. Brown, and John C. Mowen, "Internal Benefits of Service-Worker Customer Orientation: Job Satisfaction, Commitment, and Organizational Citizenship Behaviors," *Journal of Marketing,* Vol. 68, Iss. 1, January 2004, pp. 128–46.

17. Margaret Littman, "Playing for Keeps," *ABA Journal,* Vol. 91, June 2005, pp. 71–72.

18. Ceridwyn King and Debra Grace, "Exploring the Role of Employees in the Delivery of the Brand: A Case Study Approach," *Qualitative Market Research,* Vol. 8, Iss. 3, 2005, pp. 277–96.

19. Brad Perriello, "8 Tips To Improver Your Customer Service," *Industrial Distribution,* March 1, 2007, p. 34.

20. Deepak Sirdeshmukh, Jagdip Singh, and Barry Sabol, "Customer Trust, Value, and Loyalty in Relational Exchanges," *Journal of Marketing,* Vol. 66, Iss. 1, January 2002, pp. 15–38.

21. Lawrence A. Crosby and Brian Lunde, "Loyalty Linkage," *Marketing Management* Vol. 16, Iss. 3, May/June 2007, p. 12; and James H. McAlexander, John W. Schouten, and Harold F. Koening, "Building Brand Community," *Journal of Marketing,* Vol. 66, Iss. 1, January 2002, pp. 38–55.

22. Nancy Michael, "Customer Loyalty," *ABA Banking Journal,* February 2007, pp. 42–45.

23. "Targeted Tactics Drive Response," *B to B,* October 9, 2006, p. 1.

24. Sudhir N. Kale and Peter Klugsberger, "Reaping Rewards," *Marketing Management* Vol. 16, Iss. 4, July/August 2007, p. 14.

25. Kimberly Griffiths, "Got Satisfaction?" *Industrial Distribution,* October 1, 2006, p. 34.

26. Anita Goyal, "Consumer Perceptions towards the Purchase of Credit Cards," *Journal of Service Research,* Vol. 6, July 2006, pp. 179–91.

27. Minakshi Trivedi, Michael S. Morgan, and Kalpesh Kaushik Desai, "Consumer's Value for Informational Role of Agent in Service Industry," *Journal of Services Marketing* Vol. 22, Iss. 2, 2008, pp. 149–59.

28. Bruce Einhorn, "Stem Cell Refugees," *BusinessWeek*, February 12, 2007, pp. 40–41; and Steven Reinberg, "U.S. Health Care Spending to Double by 2017, Report Predicts," *BusinessWeek* Online, February 26, 2008, www.businessweek.com/print/lifestyle/content/healthday/612998.html, accessed June 2, 2008.

29. Frances X. Frei, "The Four Things a Service Business Must Get Right," *Harvard Business Review* Vol. 86, Iss. 4, April 2008, pp. 70–80.

30. Paul Cardis, "Manage Your Stock in Customer Loyalty," *Professional Builder*, March 1, 2007, p. 21.

31. Kevin M. McNeilly and Terri Feldman Barr, "I Love my Accountants–They're Wonderful: Understanding Customer Delight in the Professional Services Arena," *Journal of Services Marketing*, Vol. 20, Iss. 3, 2006, pp. 152–59.

32. Kenneth R. Evans, Simona Stan, and Lynn Murray, "The Customer Socialization Paradox: The Mixed Effects of Communicating Customer Role Expectations," *Journal of Services Marketing*, Vol. 22, Iss. 3, 2008, pp. 213–23; and Amy K. Smith and Ruth N. Bolton, "The Effect of Customers' Emotional Responses to Service Failures on their Recovery Effort Evaluations and Satisfaction Judgments," *Journal of the Academy of Marketing Science*, Vol. 30, Iss. 1, Winter 2002, pp. 5–23.

33. Chris T. Sullivan, "A Stake in the Business," *Harvard Business Review*, Vol. 83, Iss. 9, September 2005, p. 57.

34. "Takeout Trend," *BusinessWeek* Online, August 24, 2007, www.businessweek.com/mediacenter/video/businessweektv/f3dcbeb754a244fb3ad7082bfe62af0362e7d167.html?chan=search, accessed May 29, 2008.

35. "Is Customer Delight a Viable Goal?" *Businessline*. March 23, 2007, p. 1.

36. Jena McGregor, "An Extraordinary Stumble at JetBlue," *BusinessWeek*, March 5, 2007, pp. 58–59.

37. Airline Quality Rating, AQR Report Card, http://www.aqr.aero/track/index.htm, accessed June 4, 2008.

38. Astute Solutions, *British Airways Case Study*, March 28, 2006, pp. 1–4.

39. Teck H. Ho and Yu-Sheng Zheng, "Setting Customer Expectation in Service Delivery: An Integrated Marketing-Operations Perspective," *Management Science*, Vol. 50, Iss. 4, April 2004, pp. 479–89.

40. A. Parasuraman, Valarie A. Zeithaml, and Leonard L. Berry, "A Conceptual Model of Service Quality and its Implications for Future Research," *Journal of Marketing*, Fall 1985, pp. 41–50.

41. Robert D. Hof, "How to Hit a Moving Target," *BusinessWeek*, August 21/28, 2008, p. 82.

42. A. Parasuraman, Leonard L. Barry, and Valarie A. Zeithaml, "SERVQUAL: A Multiple-Item Scale for Measuring Consumer Perceptions of Service Quality," *Journal of Retailing*, 64:1, 1988, pp. 12–40; and A. Parasuraman, Leonard L. Barry, and Valarie A. Zeithaml, "Refinement and Reassessment of the SERVQUAL Scale," *Journal of Retailing*, 67:4, 1991, pp. 420–50.

43. A. Parasuraman, Leonard L. Berry and Valarie A. Zeithaml, "Perceived Service Quality as a Customer-Based Performance Measure: An Empirical Examination of Organizational Barriers Using an Extended Service Quality Model," *Human Resource Management* Vol. 30, Iss. 3, New York, Fall 1991, pp. 335–42.

44. Brad Perriello, "8 Tips to Improve Your Customer Service," *Industrial Distribution*, March 1, 2007, p. 34.

45. Pao-Tiao Chuang, "Combining Service Blueprint and FMEA for Service Design," *The Service Industries Journal* Vol. 27, Iss. 2, London, March 2007, pp. 91–105.

CHAPTER 14

1. Richard G. Netemeyer, Balaji Krishnan, Chris Pullig, and Guangping Wang, "Developing and Validating Measures of Facets of Customer-based Brand Equity," *Journal of Business Research*, Vol. 57, Iss. 2, February 2004, pp. 209–24.

2. Richard J. Speed, "Oh Mr. Porter! A Re-Appraisal of Competitive Strategy," *Marketing Intelligence & Planning*, Vol. 7, Iss. 5,6, 1989, pp. 8–11.

3. "The Price is Right," *Brand Strategy*, June 14, 2006, p. 25.

4. Bruce Einhorn, "Intel Inside the Third World," *BusinessWeek*, July 9 & 16, 2007, pp. 38–40; and Reena Jana, "Behind the Intel/OLPC Breakup," *BusinessWeek* Online, January, 8, 2008, www.businessweek.com/print/innovate/content/jan2008/id2008018_145303.htm, accessed June 2, 2008.

5. Roy W. Ralston, "The Effects of Customer Service, Branding, and Price on the Perceived Value of Local Telephone Service," *Journal of Business Research*, Vol. 56, Iss. 3, March 2003, pp. 201–13.

6. Kent B. Monroe, "Pricing Practices that Endanger Profits," *Marketing Management*, Vol. 10, Iss. 3, September/October 2001, pp. 42–46.

7. George J. Avlonitis and Kostis A. Indounas, "Pricing Objectives and Pricing Methods in the Services Sector," *Journal of Services Marketing*, Vol. 19, Iss. 1, 2005, pp. 47–57.

8. Anita Hamilton, "Brand New Buzz," *Time* Online, March 9, 2007, www.time.com/time/magazine/article/0,9171,1597466,00.html, accessed March 15, 2007.

9. Yikuan Lee and Gina Colarelli O'Connor, "New Product Launch Strategy for Network Effects Products," *Journal of the Academy of Marketing Science*, Vol. 31, Iss. 3, Summer 2003, pp. 241–55.

10. Angel F. Villarejo-Ramos and Manuel J. Sanchez-Franco, "The Impact of Marketing Communication and Price Promotion on Brand Equity," *Journal of Brand Management*, Vol. 12, Iss. 6, August 2005, pp. 431–44.

11. Ana Garrido-Rubio and Yolanda Polo-Redondo, "Tactical Launch Decisions: Influence on Innovation Success/Failure," *Journal of Product and Brand Management*, Vol. 14, Iss. 1, 2005, pp. 29–38.

12. Laurie Flynn, "Upgraded Version of Xbox 360 to be Introduced by Microsoft," *New York Times*, March 28, 2007, p. C5.

13. Ioana Popescu and Yaozhong Wu, "Dynamic Pricing Strategies with Reference Effects," *Operations Research*, Vol. 55, Iss. 3, May/June 2007, pp. 413–32.

14. Mark Burton and Steve Haggett, "Rocket PLAN," *Marketing Management*, Vol. 16, Iss. 5, September/October 2007, p. 32.

15. Tulin Erdem, Michael P. Keane, and Baohong Sun, "The Impact of Advertising on Consumer Price Sensitivity in Experience Goods Markets," *Quantitative Marketing and Economics*, Vol. 6, Iss. 2, June 2008, pp. 139–76.

16. Harun Ahmet Kuyumcu, "Emerging Trends in Scientific Pricing," *Journal of Revenue and Pricing Management*, Vol. 6, Iss. 4, December 2007, pp. 293–99.

17. Tina Seeley, "CFTC Targets Shipping, Storage in Oil Investigation (Update2)," *Bloomberg*, May 30, 2008.

18. Tridib Mazumdar, S. P. Raj, and Indrajit Sinha, "Reference Price Research:

Review and Propositions," *Journal of Marketing,* Vol. 69, Iss. 4, October 2005, pp. 84–102; and Xueming Luo, Aric Rindfleisch, and David K. Tse, "Working with Rivals: The Impact of Competitor Alliances on Financial Performance," *Journal of Marketing Research,* Vol. 44, Iss. 1, February 2007, pp. 73–83.

19. Marc Vanhuele and Xavier Dreze, "Measuring the Price Knowledge Shoppers Bring to the Store," *Journal of Marketing,* Vol. 66, Iss. 4, October 2002, pp. 72–85.

20. Kusum Ailawadi, Donald R. Lehmann, and Scott A. Neslin, "Market Response to a Major Policy Change in the Marketing Mix: Learning from Procter & Gamble's Value Pricing Strategy," *Journal of Marketing* Vol. 65, Iss. 1, January 2001, pp. 44–61.

21. Timothy Aeppel, "Seeking Perfect Prices, CEO Tears Up the Rules," *Wall Street Journal,* March 27, 2007, p. A1.

22. Stephan Zielke and Thomas Dobbelstein, "Customers' Willingness to Purchase New Store Brands," *Journal of Product and Brand Management,* Vol. 16, Iss. 2, 2007, pp. 112–21.

23. Michaela Draganska and Dipak C. Jain, "Consumer Preferences and Product-Line Pricing Strategies: An Empirical Analysis," *Marketing Science,* Vol. 25, Iss. 2, March/April 2006, pp. 164–75.

24. "The Price is Right."

25. Baba Shiv, Ziv Carmon, and Dan Ariely, "Placebo Effects of Marketing Actions: Consumers May Get What They Pay For," *Journal of Marketing Research,* Vol. 42, Iss. 4, November 2005, pp. 383–93.

26. Michael Levy, Dhruv Grewal, Praveen K. Kopalle, and James D. Hess, "Emerging Trends in Retail Pricing Practice: Implications for Research," *Journal of Retailing,* Vol. 80, Iss. 3, 2004, pp. 13–21.

27. Chris Janiszewski and Marcus Cunha Jr., "The Influence of Price Discount Framing on the Evaluation of a Product Bundle," *Journal of Consumer Research* Vol. 30, Iss. 4, March 2004, pp. 534–46.

28. Nick Wingfield, "Apple Introduces Album Discount," *Wall Street Journal,* March 30, 2007, p. B3.

29. Daniel J. Howard and Roger A. Kerin, "Broadening the Scope of Reference Price Advertising Research: A Field Study of Consumer Shopping Involvement," *Journal of Marketing,* Vol. 70, Iss. 4, October 2006, pp. 185–204.

30. James McClure and Erdogan Kumcu, "Promotions and Product Pricing: Parsimony versus Veblenesque Demand," *Journal of Economic Behavior & Organization* Vol. 65, Iss. 1, January 2008, pp. 105–17.

31. "The Price is Right."

32. Robert M. Schindler and Alan R. Wiman, "Effects of Odd Pricing on Price Recall," *Journal of Business Research,* Vol. 19, Iss. 3, November 1989, pp. 165–77.

33. John Huston and Nipoli Kamdar, "$9.99: Can "Just-Below" Pricing Be Reconciled with Rationality?" *Eastern Economic Journal,* Vol. 22, Iss. 2, Spring 1996, pp. 137–45.

34. Kathleen Seiders and Glenn B. Voss, "From Price to Purchase," *Marketing Management,* Vol. 13, Iss. 6, November/December 2004, pp. 38–43.

35. Jenny McTaggart, "Pump up the Volume," *Progressive Grocer,* September 1, 2006, pp. 20–25.

36. Christian Terwiesch, Sergei Savin, and Il-Horn Hann, "Online Haggling at a Name-Your-Own-Price Retailer: Theory and Application," *Management Science* Vol. 51, Iss. 3, March 2005, pp. 339–52.

37. Louise Story, "Double Click to Set up an Exchange for Buying and Selling Digital Ads," *The New York Times* Online, April 4, 2007, www.nytimes .com/2007/04/04/business/media/ 04adco.html?n=Top%2fReference%2 fTimes%20Topics%2fPeople%2fS%2f Story%2c%20Louise, accessed May 8, 2007.

38. Chris Guilding, Colin Drury, and Mike Tayles, "An Empirical Investigation of the Importance of Cost-plus Pricing," *Managerial Auditing Journal,* Vol. 20, Iss. 2, 2005, pp. 125–37.

39. J. Isaac Brannon, "The Effects of Resale Price Maintenance Laws on Petrol Prices and Station Attrition: Empirical Evidence from Wisconsin," *Applied Economics,* Vol. 35, Iss. 3, February 2003, pp. 343–49.

40. Chuan He and Yuxin Chen, "Managing e-Marketplace: A Strategic Analysis of Nonprice Advertising," *Management Science,* Vol. 25, Iss. 2, March/April 2006, pp. 175–87.

41. Ben Vinod, "Retail Revenue Management and the New Paradigm of Merchandise Optimisation," *Journal of Revenue and Pricing Management,* Vol. 3, Iss. 4, January 2005, pp. 358–68.

42. "Cadbury to Cut Down on Price Promotion Activity," *Marketing,* June 14, 2006, p. 4.

43. George J. Avlonitis and Kostis A. Indounas, "Pricing Practices of Service Organizations," *Journal of Services Marketing,* Vol. 20, Iss. 5, 2006, pp. 346–57.

44. Keith S. Coulter, "Decreasing Price Sensitivity Involving Physical Product Inventory: A Yield Management Application," *Journal of Product and Brand Management* Vol. 10, Iss. 4/5, 2001, pp. 301–17.

45. Kusum L. Ailawadi and Bari Harlam, "An Empirical Analysis of the Determinants of Retail Margins: The Role of Store-Brand Share;" *Journal of Marketing,* Vol. 68, Iss. 1, January 2004, pp. 147–65.

46. Fred S. McChesney and William F. Shughart, II, "Delivered Pricing in Theory and Policy Practice," *The Antitrust Bulletin,* Vol. 52, Iss. 2, Summer 2007, pp. 205–28.

47. Hiroshi Ohta, Yan-Shu Lin, and Masa K. Naito, "Spatial Perfect Competition: A Uniform Delivered Pricing Model," *Pacific Economic Review,* Vol. 10, Iss. 4, December 2005, pp. 407–20.

48. Pradeep K. Chintagunta, Jean-Pierre Dube, and Vishal Singh, "Balancing Profitability and Customer Welfare in a Supermarket Chain," *Quantitative Marketing and Economics,* Vol. 1, Iss. 1, March 2003, pp. 111–46.

49. Lynn Henderson, "The Monsanto Miracle," *Agri Marketing,* September 2006, pp. 48–51.

50. John M. Connor, "Forensic Economics: An Introduction with Special Emphasis on Price Fixing," *Journal of Competition Law & Economics,* Vol. 4, Iss. 1, March 2008, pp. 21–59.

51. Siva Viswanathan, Jason Kuruzovich, Sanjay Gosain, and Ritu Agarwal, "Online Infomediaries and Price Discrimination: Evidence from the Automotive Retailing Sector," *Journal of Marketing,* Vol. 71, Iss. 3, July 2007, pp. 89–107.

52. Allan J. Kimmel, "Deception in Marketing Research and Practice: An Introduction," *Psychology & Marketing,* Vol. 18, Iss. 7, July 2001, pp. 657–61.

53. Jules Stuyck, Evelyne Terryn, and Tom van Dyck, "Confidence through Fairness? The New Directive on Unfair Business-to-Consumer Commercial Practices in the Internal Market," *Common Market Law Review,* Vol. 43, Iss. 1, February 2006, pp. 107–52.

54. Patrick DeGraba, "The Loss Leader Is a Turkey: Targeted Discounts from Multi-product Competitors," *International Journal of Industrial Organization,* Vol. 24, Iss. 3, May 2006, pp. 613–28.

CHAPTER 15

1. Sjoerd Schaafsma and Joerg Hofstetter, "Raising the Game to a New Level," *ECR Journal: International Commerce Review,* Vol. 5, Iss. 1, Summer 2005, pp. 66–69.

2. Lee G. Cooper, "Strategic Marketing Planning for Radically New Products," *Journal of Marketing,* Vol. 64, Iss. 1, January 2000, pp. 1–16.

3. Bernard Cova and Robert Salle, "Marketing Solutions in Accordance with the S-D Logic: Co-creating Value with Customer Network Actors," *Industrial Marketing Management* Vol. 37, Iss. 3, May 2008, pp. 270–77.

4. Jennifer Rowley, "Synergy and Strategy in E-business," *Marketing Intelligence & Planning,* Vol. 20, Iss. 4/5, 2002, pp. 215–22.

5. Ravi S. Achrol and Michael J. Etzel, "The Structure of Reseller Goals and Performance in Marketing Channels," *Journal of the Academy of Marketing Science,* Vol. 31, Iss. 2, Spring 2003, pp. 146–63.

6. John Kerr, "3PL Metrics Take Root at Scotts," *Logistics Management,* March 1, 2007, p. 37.

7. Arik Hesseldahl, "The iPhone Eyes BlackBerry's Turf," *BusinessWeek* Online, June 11, 2008, www.businessweek.com/print/magazine/content/08_25/b4089038650669.htm, accessed June 13, 2008; and Arik Hesseldahl, "Taking the IPhone Apart," *BusinessWeek* Online, July 3, 2007, www.businessweek.com/print/technology/content/jul2007/tc2007072_957316.htm, accessed June 11, 2008.

8. "Tie Your Own Bow Tie; How to Make Smart Product Management Decisions," *Strategic Direction,* Vol. 23, Iss. 5, 2007, pp. 5–8.

9. Stephen Keysuk Kim, "Relational Behaviors in Marketing Channel Relationships: Transaction Cost Implications," *Journal of Business Research,* Vol. 60, Iss. 11, November 2007, pp. 1125–34.

10. Junhong Chu, Pradeep K. Chintagunta, and Naufel J. Vilcassim, "Assessing the Economic Value of Distribution Channels: An Application to the Personal Computer Industry," *Journal of Marketing Research,* Vol. 44, Iss. 1, February 2007, pp. 29–41.

11. Daniel C. Bello and Nicholas C. Williamson, "The American Export Trading Company: Designing a New International Marketing Institution," *Journal of Marketing* Vol. 49, Iss. 4, Fall 1985, pp. 60–69.

12. Alberto Sa Vinhas and Erin Anderson, "How Potential Conflict Drives Channel Structure (Direct and Indirect) Channels," *Journal of Marketing Research,* Vol. 42, Iss. 4, November 2005, pp. 507–15.

13. Aksel I. Rokkan, Jan B. Heide, and Kenneth H. Wathne, "Specific Investments in Marketing Relationships: Expropriation and Bonding Effects," *Journal of Marketing Research,* Vol. 40, Iss. 2, pp. 210–24.

14. Michael Ketzenberg, Richard Metters, and Vicente Vargas, "Quantifying the Benefits of Breaking Bulk in Retail Operations," *International Journal of Production Economics* Vol. 80, Iss. 3, December 2002, pp. 249–63.

15. Paul Teague, "Supplier Relationships Provide Lift in an Unstable Market," *Purchasing,* November 2, 2006, p. 32B13.

16. E. Bashkansky, S. Dror, R. Ravid, and P. Grabov, "Effectiveness of Product Quality Classifier," *Quality Engineering,* Vol. 19, Iss. 3, July 2007, p. 235.

17. Jason M. Carpenter, "Demographics and Patronage Motives of Supercenter Shoppers in the United States," *International Journal of Retail & Distribution Management,* Vol. 36, Iss. 1, 2008, pp. 5–16.

18. Daisy Whitney, "Cash Registers Ringing as Buyers Migrate Online," *TVWeek,* August 14, 2006, p. 16.

19. Devon S. Johnson and Sundar Bharadwaj, "Digitization of Selling Activity and Sales Force Performance: An Empirical Investigation," *Journal of the Academy of Marketing Science* Vol. 33, Iss. 1, Winter 2005, pp. 3–18.; and Xueming Luo and Naveen Donthu, "The Role of Cyber-intermediaries: A Framework Based on Transaction Cost Analysis, Agency, Relationship Marketing, and Social Exchange Theories," *Journal of Business & Industrial Marketing,* Vol. 22, Iss. 7, 2007, pp. 452–58.

20. Joseph Pancras and K. Sudhir, "Optimal Marketing Strategies for a Customer Data Intermediary," *Journal of Marketing Research* Vol. 44, Iss. 4, November 2007, pp. 452–58.

21. Virpi Havila, Jan Johanson, and Peter Thilenius, "International Business-relationship Triads," *International Marketing Review,* Vol. 21, Iss. 2, 2004, pp. 172–86.

22. Kevin Lane Keller, "Building Customer-based Brand Equity," *Marketing Management* Vol. 10, Iss. 2, July/August 2001 pp. 14–19.

23. Phillip Bond, "Band and Nonbank Financial Intermediation," *Journal of Finance,* Vol. 59, Iss. 6, December 2004, pp. 2489–2530.

24. Joseph Pancras and K. Sudhir.

25. Evan Schuman, "A New Kind of Data Need for a New Kind of Retailer," *eWeek.com,* May 17, 2006, www.eweek.com/c/a/Retail/A-New-Kind-of-Data-Need-for-a-New-Kind-of-Retailer, accessed June 12, 2008.

26. Amal R. Karunaratna and Lester W. Johonson, "Initiating and Maintaining Export Channel Intermediary Relationships," *Journal of International Marketing* Vol. 5, Iss. 2, 1997, pp. 11–32.

27. David Biederman, "Planning for Happy Returns," *Traffic World,* September 4, 2006, pp. 18–22.

28. Bert Rosenbloom, "The Wholesaler's Role in the Marketing Channel: Disintermediation vs. Reintermediation," *International Review of Retail, Distribution, and Consumer Research* Vol. 17, Iss. 4, September 2007, pp. 327–39.

29. David Grossman, "A Lesson from Portugal," *Searcher,* April 2006, pp. 45–48.

30. Kenneth K. Boyer and G. Tomas M. Hult, "Extending the Supply Chain: Integrating Operations and Marketing in the Online Grocery Industry," *Journal of Operations Management,* Vol. 23, Iss. 6, September 2005, pp. 642–61; and Thomas L. Friedman, *The World Is Flat 3.0: A Brief History of the Twenty-First Century.* New York: Picador, 2007.

31. Ravi S. Achrol and Michael J. Etzel.

32. Gilles Corriveau and Robert D. Tamilla, "Comparing Transactional Forms in Administered, Contractual, and Corporate Systems in Grocery Distribution," *Journal of Business Research,* Vol. 55, Iss. 9, September 2002, pp. 771–73.

33. L. Lynn Judd and Bobby C. Vaught, "Three Differential Variables and Their Relation to Retail Strategy and Profitability," *Journal of the Academy of Marketing Science,* Vol. 16, Iss. 3,4, Fall 1988, pp. 30–37.

34. Tim Burkink, "Cooperative and Voluntary Wholesale Groups: Channel Coordination and Interim Knowledge Transfer," *Supply Chain Management,* Vol. 7, Iss. 2, 2002, pp. 60–70.

35. Gilles Corriveau and Robert D. Tamilla.

36. Nancy Nix, Robert Lusch, Zach Zacharia, and Wesley Bridges, "Competent Collaborations," *Marketing Management,* Vol. 17, Iss. 2, March/April 2008, p. 18.

37. Bonnie McCarthy, "On Its Toes," *Apparel,* February 2006, pp. 16–17.

38. John R. P. French and Bertram Raven, *The Bases of Social Power.* Ann Arbor: University of Michigan Press, 1959.

39. Boonghee Yoo, Naveen Donthu, and Sungho Lee, "An Examination of Selected Marketing Mix Elements and Brand Equity," *Journal of the Academy of Marketing Science,* Vol. 28, Iss. 2, Spring 2000, pp. 195–211.

40. Robert Berner, "Chanel's American in Paris," *BusinessWeek,* January 29, 2007, p 70–71.

41. P. Rajan Varadarajan, Satish Jayachandran, and J. Chris White, "Strategic Interdependence in Organizations: Deconglomeration and Marketing Strategy," *Journal of Marketing,* Vol. 65, Iss. 1, January 2001, pp. 15–28.

42. Jennifer Korolishin, "Sweet Leaf Tea," *Beverage Industry,* February 2006, p. 42.

43. Frederick E. Webster Jr., "Understanding the Relationships among Brands, Consumers, and Resellers," *Journal of the Academy of Marketing Science,* Vol. 28, Iss. 1, Winter 2000, pp. 17–23.

44. Vaidyanathan Jayaraman and Yadong Luo, "Creating Competitive Advantages through New Value Creation: A Reverse Logistics Perspective," *Academy of Management Perspectives,* Vol. 21, Iss. 2, May 2007, pp. 56–73.

45. Clyde E. Witt, "Forward Thinking about Reverse Logistics," *Material Handling Management,* February 2007, pp. 24–28.

46. Stanley C. Gardiner, Joe B. Hanna, and Michael S. LaTour, "ERP and the Reengineering of Industrial Marketing Processes: A Prescriptive Overview for the New-age Marketing Manager," *Industrial Marketing Management,* Vol. 31, Iss. 4, July 2002, pp. 357–65.

47. Dale G. Sauers, "Evaluating Just-in-time Projects from a More Focused Framework," *Quality Process,* Vol. 34, Iss. 1, January 2001, p. 160.

48. Alan D. Smith, "Effective Supplier Selection and Management Issues in Modern Manufacturing and Marketing Service Environments," *Services Marketing Quarterly,* Vol. 29, Iss. 2, 2007, pp. 45–65.

49. Thomas J. Ryan, "Pendleton Embraces Multi-Channel Approach," *Apparel,* February 2007, pp. 22–25.

50. Roger Morton, "A European Retailer's Quest for Visibility," *Logistics Today,* October 2006, p. 36.

51. Richard J. Gilbert, "Exclusive Dealing, Preferential Dealing, and Dynamic Efficiency," *Review of Industrial Organization,* Vol. 16, Iss. 2, 2000, pp. 167–84.

52. Howard P. Marvel and Stephen McCafferty, "Comparing Vertical Restraints," *Journal of Economics and Business,* Vol. 48, Iss. 5, December 1996, pp. 473–86.

53. Alan J. Meese, "Tying Meets the New Institutional Economics: Farwell to the Chimera of Forcing," *University of Pennsylvania Law Review,* Vol. 146, Iss. 1, November 1997, pp. 1–98.

CHAPTER 16

1. Jeffery F. Rayport and Bernard J. Jaworski, "Best Face Forward," *Harvard Business Review,* 2004, Vol. 82 (12), pp.47–62.

2. Richard W. Mosley, "Customer Experience, Organizational Culture and Employer Brand," *Journal of Brand Management,* Vol. 15 (2), pp. 123–35.

3. Michael Bumiak, "Cash Management: Finding Middle Ground, In New Jersey, a Retail Power Looks to Catch Up Online with a Small Business Hook", *Bank Technology News,* 2008, Vol. 21 (3), p. 1; and Mike Vogel, "Retail Style," *Florida Trend,* 2007, Vol. 50 (4), p. 54.

4. Tin-Peng Liang, Hung-Jen Lai, Yi-Cheng Ku, "Personalized Content Recommendation and User Satisfaction Theoretical Synthesis and Empirical Findings," *Journal of Management Information Systems,* 2006–2007, Vol. 23 (3), pp. 45–61.

5. Jane W. Licata, Goutam Chakraborty and Balaji C. Krishnan, "The Consumer's Expectation Formation Process Over time," *The Journal of Services Marketing,* 2008, Vol. 22 (3), pp. 176–91.

6. Stuart E. Jackson, "Making Growth Make Sense for Retail and Franchise Businesses," *Journal of Business Strategy,* 2008, Vol. 29 (3), pp. 48–64.

7. Kirthi Kalyanam, Sharad Borle, and Peter Boartwright, "Deconstructing Each Item's Category Contribution," *Marketing Science,* 2007, Vol. 26 (3), pp. 327–44.

8. "Muji Opens NYC Flgship Store," *Home Textiles Today,* Vol. 29 (15), p. 2; and Kenji Hall, "Zen and the Art of Selling Minimalism," *BusinessWeek,* 2007, Iss. 4029, p. 45.

9. Andrew Baxter, "Profile: Tide and Ariel Clean Up," *Financial Times,* April 21, 2008, p. 6; and Robert Berner, "How P&G Pampers New Thinking," *BusinessWeek,* 2008, Issue 4079, p. 73.

10. Chandra K. Jaggi, SK Goyal, SK Goel, "Retailer's Optimal Replenishment Decisions with Credit Linked Demand under Permissible Delay in Payments," *European Journal of Operational Research,* 2008, Vol. 190 (1), pp. 130–48; and R. Glenn Richey Jr., Mert Tokman, and Lauren R. Skinner, "Exploring Collaborative Technology Utilization in Retailer-Supplier Performance," *Journal of Business Research,* 2008, Vol. 61 (8), pp. 842–60.

11. Martin A. Koschat, "Store Inventory Can Affect Demand: Empirical Evidence form Retailing," *Journal of Retailing,* 2008, Vol. 84 (2), pp. 165–81.

12. "Helmut Newton Inspires Topshop Site from Poke," *Design Week,* 2008, Vol. 23 (25), p. 6; and Elizabeth Esfahani, "High Class, Low Price," *Business 2.0,* 2006, Vol. 7 (10), p. 74

13. James G. Maxham III, Richard G. Netemeyer, and Donald R. Lichtenstein, "The Retail Value Chain: Linking Employee Perceptions to Employee Performance, Customer Evaluations and Store Performance, *Marketing Science,* 2008, Vol. 27 (2), p. 147–69; and Aron O'Cass and Debra Grace, "Understanding the Role of Retail Service in Light of Self-image Store Image Congruence," *Psychology and Marketing,* 2008, Vol. 25 (6), pp. 521–39.

14. Christina ML Kelton, Margaret K Pasquale, and Robert P. Rebelein, "Using the North American Industry Classification System (NAICS) to Identify National Industry Cluster Templates for Applied Regional Analysis," *Regional Studies,* 2008, Vol. 42 (3), pp. 305–20.

15. Jie Zhang and Aradhna Krishna, "Brand Level Effects of Stockkeeping Unit Reductions," *Journal of Marketing Research,* 2007, Vol. 44 (4), pp. 545–61 and Felipe Caro and Jeremie Gallien, "Dynamic Assortment with Demand Learning for Season Consumer Goods," *Management Science,* 2007, Vol. 63 (2), pp. 276–83.

16. Dan Padgett and Micahael S. Mulvey, "Differentiation Via Technology: Strategic Positioning of Services Following the Introduction of Disruptive Technology," *Journal of Retailing,* 2007, Vol. 83, (4), pp. 375–91.

17. G.H. Griffiths and A. Howard, "Balancing Clicks and Brands–Strategies for Multichannel Retailers," *Journal of Global Business Issues,* 2008, Vol. 2 (10) pp. 69–74.

18. Sameer Kumar, "A Study of the Supermarket Industry and Its Growing Logistics Capabilities," *International Journal of Retail & Distribution Management,* 2008, Vol. 36 (3), pp. 192–210.

19. Emily Bryson York, "Retail: Whole Foods," *Advertising Age,* 2008, Vol. 79 (23), p. S6; and Elizabeth Rigby, "Whole Foods Opens Flagship Store," *Financial Times,* June 7, 2007, p. 4

20. Susan Reda, "Wegman of My Dreams," *Stores,* 2008, Vol. 90 (3), p. 10; and "Tesco's American Dream: Doing It Differently," *Strategic Direction,* 2008, Vol. 24 (2), p.11.

21. Philip Elmer-DeWitt, Jon Birger, Geoff Colvin, and Josh Quittner, "A Look Inside the Top 20,*" Fortune,* 2008, Vol. 157 (5), pp. 109–111; and Vanessa O'Connell, "Weekend Journal: Style: Nordstrom's Makeover Man, Boutique Star Tries to Keep Chain Ahead in Hip Race," *Wall Street Journal,* February 23, 2008, W1.

22. Haiyan Hu and Cynthia R. Jasper, "Social Cues in the Store Environment and Their Impact on Store Image," *International Journal of Retail and Distribution Management,* 2006, Vol. 34 (1), p. 25–49.

23. Peter J. McGoldrick and Matalie Collins, "Multichannel Retailing: Profiling the Multichannel Shopper," *The International Review of Retail, Distribution and Consumer Research,* 2007, Vol. 17 (2), pp. 139–52.

24. Asim Ansari, Carl F. Mela, and Scott A. Neslin, "Customer Channel Migration," *Journal of Marketing Research,* 2008, Vol. 45 (1), pp. 60–77.

25. Bill Merrilees and Tino Fenech, "From Catalog to Web: B2B Multichannel Marketing Strategy," *Industrial Marketing Management,* 2007, Vol. 36 (1), pp. 44–61.

26. Ruby Roy Dholakia, Miao Zhao, and Nikhilesh Dholakia, "Multichannel Retailing: A Case Study of Early Experiences," *Journal of Interactive Marketing,* 2005, Vol. 19 (2), pp. 63–75.

27. Dennis L. Duffy, "Direct Selling as the Next Channel," *Journal of Consumer Marketing,* 2005, Vol. 22 (1), pp. 43–46.

28. David Sterrett, "Spotlight: Gina Boswell; Putting a New Shine on Established Brands," *Crain's Chicago Business,* 2008, Vol. 31 (8), p. 6; and "Redeeming Direct Sales," *Financial Times,* April 12, 2008, p. 14.

29. Clyde A. Warden, Stephen Chi-Tsun Huang, Tsung Chi Liu, and Wann-Yih Wu, "Global Media, Local Metaphor: Television Shopping and Marketing as Relationship in America, Japan and Taiwan," *Journal of Retailing,* 2008, Vol. 84 (1), pp. 119–34; and Enrique Bigne Alcaniz, Silvia Sanz Blas, and Francisco Toran Torres, "Dependency in Consumer Media Relations: An Application to the Case of Teleshopping," *Journal of Consumer Behavior,* 2006, Vol. 5 (5), pp. 397–411.

30. Eliot Maras, "In the Face of Challenge, Opportunity Beckons," *Automatic Merchandiser,* May 2008, Vol. 50 (5), p. 6; and Eliot Maras, "Badly Needed Consumer Research Is Here, So Use It," *Automatic Merchandiser,* Jan. 2007, Vol. 49 (1), p. 4

31. David R. Bowes, "A Two-Stage Model of the Simultaneous Relationship Between Retail Development and Crime," *Economic Development Quarterly,* 2007, Vol. 21 (1), pp. 79–92; and Richard Peiser and Jiaqui Xioong, "Crime and Town Centers: Are Downtowns More Dangerous than Suburban Shopping Nodes?" *Journal of Real Estate Research,* 2003, Vol. 25 (4), pp. 577–89.

32. Eric M. Olson, Stanley F. Slater and Christine SH Olson, "Dolls and Sense," *Marketing Management,* 2006, Vol. 15 (5) pp. 14–20; and Leigh Sparks, "A Catalogue of Success? Argos and Catalogue Showroom Retailing," *The Services Industry Journal,* 2003, Vol. 23 (2) pp. 79–89.

33. Stephen H. Wildstrom, "Streaming Movies–From Netflix," *BusinessWeek,* 2008, Issue 4086, p. 88; and Michael V. Copeland, "Netflix Lives," *Fortune,* 2008, Vol. 157 (8), p. 40.

34. "Online Sales to Climb Despite Struggling Economy," *National Retail Federation,* April 8, 2008, www.nrf.com/modules.php?name=news&sp_id=499.

35. Jim Dalrymple, "Apple Is Number Two Music Retailer in the United States," *MacWorld,* 2008, Vol. 25 (5), p. 28.

36. "Business: The Three Survivors; Yahoo, eBay, and Amazon," *The Economist,* 2008, Vol. 387 Issue 8585, pp. 69–90.

37. Pearl Pu, Li Chen, Pratyush Kumar, "Evaluating Product Search and Recommender Systems for E-Commerce Environments," *Electronic Commerce Research,* 2008, Vol. 8 (1/2), pp. 1–28.

38. Andreas B. Eisingerich and Tobia Kretschmer, "In E-Commerce, More is More," *Harvard Business Review,* 2008, Vol. 86 (3), pp. 20–38; and Amanda Spink, Bernard J. Jansen, "Trends in Searching for Commerce Related Information on Web-Search Engines," *Journal of Electronic Commerce Research,* 2008, Vol. 9 (2), pp. 154–60.

39. Mylene Mangalindan, "Business Technology: Web Stores Tap Product Reviews," *Wall Street Journal,* September 11, 2007, p. B3.

40. Christy M.K. Cheung, Matthew K.O. Lee, and Neil Rabojohn, "The Impact of Electronic Work of Mouth: The Adoption of Online Opinions in Online Customer Communities," *Internet Research,* 2008, Vol. 18 (3), pp. 229–41; Dina Mayzlin, "Promotional Chat on the Internet," *Marketing Science,* 2006, Vol. 25 (2), pp. 155–65.

41. Kyosti Pennanen, Tarja Tiainen, and Harri T. Luomala, "A Qualitative Exploration of a Consumer's Value Based e-Trust Building Process: A Framework Development," *Qualitative Market Research,* 2007, Vol. 10 (1), pp. 28–42.

42. Michael Maiello, "India a Tiger at IT Outsourcing," *Better Investing,* 2008, Vol. 57 (6), pp. 34–35; and "Business: Gravity's Pull; Information Technology in India," *The Economist,* 2007, Vol. 385 (8559), p. 75.

43. Myonung Soo Kim and Jae Hyeon Ahn, "Comparison of Trust Sources of an Online Market Maker in the E-Marketplace: Buyers and Seller's Perspectives," *Journal of Computer Information Systems,*" 2006, Vol. 47 (1), pp. 84–95.

44. Rene Algesheimer and Paul M. Dholakia, "Do Customer Communities Pay Off?" *Harvard Business Review,* 2006, Vol. 84 (11), pp. 26–41.

45. Yasemin Boztu and Thomas Reutterer, "A Combined Approach for Segment Specific Market Basket Analysis," *European Journal of Operational Research,* 2008, Vol. 187 (1), pp. 294–310.

46. Lars Meyer Waarden, "The Influence of Loyalty Programme Members on Customer Purchase Behaviour," *European Journal of Marketing,* 2008, Vol. 42 (1/2), pp. 87–102; and Jennifer Rowley, "Reconceptualizing the Strategic Role of Loyalty Schemes," *Journal of Consumer Marketing,* 2007, Vol. 24 (6), pp. 366–80.

47. Paliavi Gogoi, "Causal Male: Combining Fit and Fashion," *BusinessWeek,* February 5, 2007, p. 59.

48. Dinesh K. Gauri, K. Sudhir, and Debabrata Talukdar, "The Temporal and Spatial Dimensions of Price Search: Insights from Matching Household Survey and Purchase data," *Journal of Marketing Research,* 2008, Vol. 45 (2), pp. 226–41.

49. Vishal Gaur and Dorothee Honhon, "Assortment Planning and Inventory Decisions under a Locational Choice Model," *Management Science,* 2006, Vol. 52 (10) pp. 1528–44.

50. Miguel I. Gomez, Vithala R. Rao, and Edward W. McLaughlin, "Empirical Analysis of Budget and Allocation of Trade Promotions in the U.S. Supermarket Industry," *Journal of Marketing Research,* 2007, Vol. 44 (3), pp. 410–27.

51. Ruiliang Yan, Pricing Strategy for Companies with Mixed Online and Traditional Retailing Distribution Markets," *Journal of Product and Brand Management,* 2008, Vol. 17 (1) pp. 48–62.

52. Joydeep Srivastava and Nicholas H. Lurie, "Price Matching Guarantees as Signals of Low Store Prices: Survey and experimental evidence," *Journal of Retailing,* 2004, Vol. 80 (2), pp. 117–31.

53. Sarah Arnott, "Potter Publisher Sees New Magic," *BusinessWeek Online,* April 2, 2008, http://www.businessweek.com/print/globalbiz/content/apr2008/gb2008042_889246.htm; and Diane Brady, "The Twisted Economics of Harry Potter," *BusinessWeek,* July 2, 2007, pp. 46–47.

54. "HMV to Launch MP3 Download Store," *Music Week,* May 3, 2008, p. 6; and "HMV Launches Blogging Site," June 14, 2008, p. 6.

55. Ian Rowley, "Tesco Takes a Fresh Look at Japan," *BusinessWeek Online,* 2007, May 24, 2008 http://www.businessweek.com/print/globalbiz/content/may2007/gb20070523_237538.htm; and Michiyo Makamoto, "Tesco Confronts Zen Puzzle of Japanese Retailing," *Financial Times,* April 19, 2007, p. 16.

CHAPTER 17

1. Bob Garfield, "The Post Advertising Age," *Ad Age,* March 26, 2007.

2. Don E. Schultz and Phillip J. Kitchen, "Integrated Marketing Communications in U.S. Advertising Agencies: An Exploratory Study," *Journal of Advertising Research,* Vol. 37, Iss. 5, September/October 1997 pp. 7–18.

3. Tim Parry, "Get in on the Party," *MultichannelMerchant.com,* January 1, 2007, http://multichannelmerchant.com/crosschannel/marketing/party_2/, accessed June 19, 2008.

4. P. Rajan Varadarajan, Satish Jayachandran, and J. Chris White, "Strategic Interdependence in Organizations: Deconglomeration and Marketing Strategy," *Journal of Marketing,* Vol. 65, Iss. 1, January 2001, pp. 15–28.

5. Frederick E. Webster Jr., "Understanding the Relationships among Brands, Consumers, and Resellers," *Journal of the Academy of Marketing Science,* Vol. 28, Iss. 1, Winter 2000, pp. 17–23.

6. Emim Babakus, Ugar Yavas, Osman M. Karatepe, and Turgay Avci, "The Effect of Management Commitment to Service Quality on Employees' Affective and Performance Outcomes," *Journal of the Academy of Marketing Science,* Vol. 31, Iss. 3, Summer 2003, pp. 272–86.

7. C. B. Bhattacharya and Sankar Sen, "Consumer-Company Identification: A Framework for Understanding Consumers' Relationships with Companies," *Journal of Marketing,* Vol. 67, Iss. 2, April 2003, pp. 76–88.

8. Charles R. Taylor, George R. Franke, and Hae-Kyong Bang, "Use and Effectiveness of Billboards," *Journal of Advertising,* Vol. 35, Iss. 4, Winter 2006, pp. 21–34.

9. Charles R. Taylor, George R. Franke, and Hae-Kyong Bang.

10. Susan Powell Mantel, Ellen Bolman Pullins, David A. Reid, and Richard E. Buehrer, "A Realistic Sales Experience: Providing Feedback by Integrating Buying, Selling, and Managing Experiences," *Journal of Personal Selling & Sales Management,* Vol. 22, Iss. 1, Winter 2002, pp. 33–40.

11. Bob T. Wu and Stephen J. Newell, "The Impact of Noise on Recall of Advertisements," *Journal of Marketing Theory and Practice,* Vol. 11, Iss. 2, Spring 2003, pp. 56–65.

12. Brian Steinberg, "NBC Turns 'Fresh Eyes' to Its Ad Sales," *Wall Street Journal,* February 12, 2007, p. B5.

13. Yu-Shan Lin and Jun-Ying Huang, "Internet Blogs as a Tourism Marketing Medium: A Case Study," *Journal of Business Research,* Vol. 59, Iss. 10/11, October 2006, pp. 1201–05.

14. Anastasia Goodstein, "Marketing to Teens Online," *BusinessWeek* Online, November 7, 2007, www.businessweek.com/print/technology/content/nov2007/tc2007117_522831.htm, accessed June 11, 2008.

15. www.maxyourlife.co.uk/, accessed December 12, 2007.

16. Thomas Reutterer, Andreas Mild, Martin Natter, and Alfred Taudes, "A Dynamic Segmentation Approach for Targeting and Customizing Direct Marketing Campaigns," *Journal of Interactive Marketing* Vol. 20, Iss. 3/4, Summer/Fall 2006, pp. 43–57.

17. David Welch, "Why Toyota Is Afraid of Being #1," *BusinessWeek,* March 5, 2007, p. 49.

18. Chatterjee, Subimal, Yong Soon Kang and Debi Prasad Mishra, "Market Signals and Relative Preference: The Moderating Effects of Conflicting Information, Decision Focus, and Need for Cognition," *Journal of Business Research,* Vol. 58, Iss. 10, October 2005, pp. 1362–70.

19. Mark Burton and Steve Haggett, "Rocket PLAN," *Marketing Management* Vol. 16, Iss. 5, September/October 2007, p. 32.

20. Davod A. Schweidel, Peter S. Fader, and Eric T. Bradlow, "Understanding Service Retention within and across Cohorts Using Limited Information," *Journal of Marketing,* Vol. 72, Iss. 1, January 2008, pp. 82–94.

21. Brian Wansink, Robert J. Kent, and Stephen J. Hoch, "An Anchoring and Adjustment Model for Purchase Quantity Decisions," *Journal of Marketing Research,* Vol. 35, Iss. 1, February 1998, pp. 71–81.

22. "Illinois State Continues Sales Curriculum Incorporating Cutco, Vector Marketing Program," *PRWeb.com,* March 4, 2008, www.prweb.com/releases/cutco/vector/prweb741974.htm, accessed June 19, 2008.

23. John I. Coppett and Roy Dale Voorhees, "Telemarketing: Supplement to Field Sales," *Industrial Marketing Management,* Vol. 14, Iss. 3, August 1985, pp. 213–16.

24. Joo-Gim Heaney, Ronald E. Goldsmith, and Wan Jamaliah Wan, "Status Consumption among Malaysian Consumers: Exploring Its Relationships with Materialism and Attention-to-Social-Comparison-Information," *Journal of International Consumer Marketing,* Vol. 17, Iss. 4, 2005, pp. 83–98.

25. Hae-Kyong Bang, Mary Anne Raymond, Charles R. Taylor, and Young Sook Moon, "A Comparison of Service Quality Dimensions Conveyed in Advertisements for Service Providers in the USA and Korea: A Content Analysis," *International Marketing Review,* Vol. 22, Iss. 3, 2005, pp. 309–27.

26. Kathleen Mortimer, "Identifying the Components of Effective Service Advertisements," *Journal of Services Marketing,* Vol. 22, Iss. 2, 2008, pp. 104–13.

27. Brian Steinberg, "Callaway Shifts Its Stance on Top-Flite Golf-Ball Brand," *Wall Street Journal,* February 20, 2007, p. B10.

28. Ziad Swaidan, Mohammed Y. A. Rawwas, and Scott J. Vitell, "Culture and Moral Ideologies of African Americans," *Journal of Marketing Theory and Practice,* Vol. 16, Iss. 2, Spring 2008, pp. 127–37.

29. David C. Carlson and Paul McDevitt, "Budgeting Promotional Expenditures: Theory and Practice," *Managerial Finance,* Vol. 11, Iss. 1, 1985, pp. 1–4.

30. Boonghee Yoo and Rujirutana Mandhachitara, "Estimating Advertising

Effects on Sales in a Competitive Setting," *Journal of Advertising Research,* Vol. 43, Iss. 3, September 2003, pp. 310–21.

31. Nicolaos E. Synodinos, Charles F. Keown, and Laurences W. Jacobs, "Transnational Advertising Practices: A Survey of Leading Brand Advertisers in Fifteen Countries," *Journal of Advertising Research,* Vol. 29, Iss. 2, April/May 1989, pp. 43–50.

32. Margaret Henderson Blair, "An Empirical Investigation of Advertising Wearin and Wearout," *Journal of Advertising Research,* Vol. 40, Iss. 6, November/December 2000, pp. 95–100.

33. John R. Hauser and Steven M. Shugan, "Defensive Marketing Strategies," *Marketing Science,* Vol. 27, Iss. 1, January/February 2008, pp. 88–112.

34. Janas Sinclair and Tracy Irani, "Advocacy Advertising for Biotechnology," *Journal of Advertising,* Vol. 34, Iss. 3, Fall 2005, pp. 59–63.

35. Glen L. Urban, Theresa Carter, Steven Gaskin, and Zofia Mucha, "Market Share Rewards to Pioneering Brands: An Empirical Analysis and Strategic Implications," *Management Science,* Vol. 32, Iss. 6, June 1986, pp. 645–59.

36. Peter J. Danaher, André Bonfrer, and Sanjay Dhar, "The Effect of Competitive Advertising Interference on Sales for Packaged Goods," *Journal of Marketing Research,* Vol. 45, Iss. 2, April 2008, pp. 211–25.

37. Chingching Chang, "The Relative Effectiveness of Comparative and Non-comparative Advertising: Evidence for Gender Differences in Information-Processing Strategies," *Journal of Advertising,* Vol. 36, Iss. 1, Spring 2007, pp. 21–35.

38. Connie Robbins Gentry, "Personal Recognition" *Chain Store Age,* January 2007, p. 78.

39. "Point-and-Click Marketing," *Chain Store Age,* July 2006 p. 70.

40. Li Ling-yee, "The Effects of Firm Resources on Trade Show Performance: How Do Trade Show Marketing Processes Matter?" *Journal of Business & Industrial Marketing,* Vol. 23, Iss. 1, 2008, pp. 35–47.

41. Salma Karray and Georges Zaccour, "Could Co-op Advertising Be a Manufacturer's Counterstrategy to Store Brands?" *Journal of Business Research,* Vol. 59, Iss. 9, September 2006, pp. 1008–15.

42. Sang Yong Kim and Richard Staelin, "Manufacturer Allowances and Retailer Pass-through Rates in a Competitive Environment," *Marketing Science,* Vol. 18, Iss. 1, 1999, pp. 59–77.

43. Hyun Seung Jin, Jaebeom Suh, and D. Todd Donavan, "Salient Effects of Publicity in Advertised Brand Recall and Recognition: The List-Strength Paradigm," *Journal of Advertising* Vol. 37, Iss. 1, Spring 2008, pp. 45–57.

44. Oliver Ryan, "The Buzz around Buzz," *Fortune,* March 19, 2007. pp. 46–48.

45. Jamin Warren and John Jurgensen, "The Wizards of Buzz," *Wall Street Journal,* February 10, 2007, p. 1.

46. "Win Sunday, Sell Monday," *LoganRacing.com,* www.loganracing.com/Marketing/NASCAR_General.html, accessed June 10, 2008.

47. Kate Maddox, "The Future Looks Bright, with Marketing Expanding and Online Exploding," *B to B,* v91, December 11, 2006, p. 28.

48. Joseph Eric Massey and John P. Larsen, "Qualitative Research–Case Studies–Crisis Management in Real Time: How to Successfully Plan for and Respond to a Crisis," *Journal of Promotion Management,* Vol. 12, Iss. 3/4, 2006, pp. 63–97.

49. "Virgin Trains Push on with Environmental and Value for Money Positioning with Second Wave of 'Go Greener, Go Cheaper' Marketing Campaign," www.virgin.com/News/Articles/VirginTrains/2007/190907.aspx, September 19, 2007, accessed June 19, 2008.

CHAPTER 18

1. Stephen McGuire, "Rep. 2.0," *Medical Marketing and Media,* 2008, Vol. 43 (3), pp. 40–44.

2. David Mayer and Herbert M. Greenberg, "What Makes a Good Salesperson," *Harvard Business Review,*" 2006, Vol. 84 (7/8) pp. 164–79.

3. Mark C. Johlke, "Sales Presentation Skills and Salesperson Job Performance," *Journal of Business and Industrial Marketing,*" Vol. 21 (5), pp. 311–29.

4. Chia-Chi Chang, "What Service Fails: The Role of the Salesperson and the Customer," *Psychology & Marketing,* 2006, Vol. 23 (3), pp. 203–18; and Julia T. Johnson, Hiram C. Barksdale Jr., and James S. Boles, "The Strategic Role of the Salesperson in Reducing Customer Defection in Business Relationships," *Journal of Personal Selling and Sales Management,* vol. 21 (2), pp. 123–35.

5. Richard G. McFarland, Gautam N. Challagalla, Tasadduq A. Shervani, "Influence Tactics for Effective Adaptive Selling," *Journal of Marketing,* 2006, Vol. 70 (4), pp. 103–17.

6. David T. Norris, "Sales Communication in a Mobile World: Using the Latest Technology and Retaining the Personal Touch," *Business Communication Quarterly,* 2007, Vol. 70 (4), pp. 492–510.

7. Philippe Declos, Rodolfo Luzardo and Yasir H. Mirza, "Refocusing the Sales Force to Cross-Sell," *The McKinsey Quarterly,* 2008, (1), pp. 13–15; and Robert M. Peterson and George H. Lucas, "What Buyers Want Most from Salespeople: A View from the Senior Level," *Business Horizons,* 2001, Vol. 44 (5), 39–45.

8. Robert W. Palmatier, Lisa K. Scheer, and Jan-Benedict E.M. Steenkamp, "Customer Loyalty to Whom? Managing the Benefits and Risks of Salesperson-Owned Loyalty," *Journal of Marketing Research,* 2007, Vol. 44 (2), pp. 185–201.

9. Sandra S. Liu and Lucette B. Comer, "Salespeople as Information Gatherers: Associated Success Factors," *Industrial Marketing Management,* 2007, Vol. 36 (5), pp. 565–79; and Leroy Robinson Jr., Greg W. Marshall, and Miriam B. Stamps, "An Empirical Investigation of Technology Acceptance in a Field Sales Force Setting," *Industrial Marketing Management,* 2005, Vol. 34 (4), pp. 407–22.

10. David Mayer and Herbert M. Greenberg, "What Makes a Good Salesperson," *Harvard Business Review,*" 2006, Vol. 84 (7/8) pp. 164–79; Fernando Jaramillo and Greg. W. Marshall, "Critical Success Factors in the Personal Selling Process: An Empirical Investigation of Ecuadorian Salespeople in the Banking Industry," *International Journal of Bank Marketing,* 2004, Vol. 22 (1), pp. 9–21; and Sean Dwyer, John Hill, and Warren Martin, "An Empirical Investigation of Critical Success Factors in the Personal Selling for Homogenous Goods," *Journal of Personal Selling & Sales Management* 2000, Vol 20 (3), pp. 151–60.

11. Jane Porter, "B-Schools Soft on "Soft Skills," *BusinessWeek* Online, August 3, 2007, www.businessweek.com/bschools/content/aug2007/bs2007082_280172.htm.

12. Jagdish N. Sheth and Arun Sharma, "The Impact of the Product to Service Shift in Industrial Markets and the Evolution of the Sales Organization," *Industrial Marketing Management,* 2008, Vol. 37 (3), pp. 260–77; and Philip Kriendler and Goapl Rajguru, "What B2B Customers Really Expect," *Harvard Business Review,* 2006, vol. 84 (40), pp. 22–37.

13. "The Doctor Won't See You Now," *BusinessWeek,* 2007, issue 4020, p. 30.

14. Paolo Guenzi, Cahterine Pardo, Laurent Georges, "Relational Selling Strategy and Key Account Managers Relational Behaviors: An Exploratory Study," *Industrial Marketing Management,* 2007, Vol. 36 (1), pp. 121–38.

15. Dian Ledingham, Mark Kovac, Heidi Locke Smith, "The New Science of Sales Force Productivity," *Harvard Business Review,* 2006, Vol. 84 (9), pp. 124–40.

16. Christina Sichtmann, "An Analysis of Antecedents and Consequences of Trust in Corporate Brand," *European Journal of Marketing,* 2007, Vol. 41 (9/10), pp. 999–1115.

17. Lewis Hershey, "The Role of Sales Presentations in Developing Customer Relationships," *Services Marketing Quarterly,* 2005, Vol. 26 (3), pp. 41–59.

18. Joshua Rossman, "Value Selling at Cisco," *Marketing Management,* 2004, Vol. 13 (2), pp. 16–23.

19. Mark C. Johlke, "Sales Presentation Skills and Salesperson Job Performance," *Journal of Business and Industrial Marketing,* 2006, Vol. 21 (5), pp. 311–28.

20. Thomas N. Ingram, "Future Themes In Sales and Sales Management: Complexity, Collaboration, and Accountability," *Journal of Marketing Theory and Practice,* 2004, Vol. 12 (40), pp. 18–29.

21. Kim Sydow Campbell, Lenita Davis and Lauren Skinner, "Rapport Management During the Exploration Phase of the Salesperson Customer Relationship," *Journal of Personal Selling & Sales Management,* 2006, Vol. 26 (4), pp. 359–72.

22. Jim Braselton and Bruce Blair, "Cementing Relationships," *Marketing Management,* 2007, Vol. 16 (3), pp. 14–29.

23. John E. Swan, Michael R. Bowers, Lynne D. Richardson, "Customer Trust in the Salesperson: An Integrative Review of Meta Analysis of the Empirical Literature," *Journal of Business Research,* 1999, Vol. 44 (2), pp. 93–108; and Jackie L.M. Tam and Y.J. Wong," Interactive Selling: A Dynamic Framework for Services," *Journal of Services Marketing,* 2001, Vol. 15 (4/5), pp. 379–95.

24. Tom Nagle and John Hogan, "Is Your Sales Force a Barrier to More Profitable Pricing . . . or Is It You?" *Business Strategy Series,* Vol. 8 (5), pp. 365–79.

25. Joseph J. Belonax Jr. , Stephen J. Newell, and Richard E. Plank, "The Role of Purchase Importance on Buyer Perceptions of the Trust and Expertise Components of Supplier and Salesperson Credibility in Business to Business

Relationships," *Journal of Personal Selling & Sales Management,* 2007, Vol. 27 (3), pp. 247–60; Thomas V. Bonoma, "Major Sales: Who Really Does the Buying," *Harvard Business Review,* 2006, Vol. 84 (7/8), pp. 172–90; and Edward C. Bursk, " Low Pressure Selling," *Harvard Business Review,* 2006, Vol. 84 (7/8), pp. 150–69.

26. Gordon A. Wyner, "The Customer," *Marketing Management,* 2005, Vol. 14 (1), pp. 8–10.

27. Tim Furguson, "BT to Boost Online Customer Support," *BusinessWeek Online,* August 22, 2007, http://www .businessweek.com/print/globalbiz/ content/aug2007/gb20070822_ 202845.htm.

28. Andris A. Zoltners, Prabhakant Sinha, and Sally E. Lorimer, "Match Your Sales Force Structure to Your Business Life Cycle," *Harvard Business Review,* 2006, Vol. 84 (7/8), pp. 80–97.

29. Erin Anderson, "The Salesperson as Ouside Agent or Employee: A Transaction Cost Analysis," *Marketing Science,* 2008, Vol. 27 (1), pp. 70–86.

30. Ernest Waaser, Marshall Dahneke, Michael Pekkarinen, and Micahel Weissel, "How You Slice It: Smarter Segmentation of Your Sales Force," *Harvard Business Review,* 2004, Vol. 82 (3), pp. 105–22.

31. Marshall Goldsmith, "Getting to Know Gen Why," *BusinessWeek Online,* February 28, 2008, http://www .businessweek.com/print/managing/ content/feb2008/ca20080226_ 921853.htm.

32. C Fred Miao and Ken R. Evans, "The Impact of Salesperson Motivation on Role Perceptions and Job Performance: A Cognitive and Affective Perspective, "*Journal of Personal Selling & Sales Management,* 2007, Vol. 27 (1), pp. 89–103.

33. Willem J. Verbeke, Frank D. Belschak, Arnold B. Bakker, and Bart Dietz, "When Intelligence Is (Dys) Functional Achieving Sales Performance," *Journal of Marketing,* 2008, Vol. 72 (4), pp. 44–57.

34. Fernando Jaramillo and Jay Prakas Mulki, "Sales Effort: The Intertwined Roles of the Leader, Customers, and the Salesperson," *Journal of Personal Selling & Sales Management,* 2008, Vol. 28 (1), pp 37–51; and C. Fred Miao, Kenneth R. Evans and Zou Shaoming, "The Role of Salesperson Motivation in Sales Control Systems—Intrinsic and Extrinsic Motivation Revisited,*" Journal of Business Research,* 2007, Vol. 60 (5), pp. 417–32.

35. Clive Muir, "Relationship Building and Sales Success: Are Climate and Leadership Key?" *The Academy of Management Perspectives,* 2007, Vol. 21 (1), pp. 71–89; and Ken LeMeunier-FitzHugh and Nigel F. Piercy, "Does Collaboration between Sales and Marketing Affect Business Performance,*" Journal of Personal Selling & Sales Management,* 2007, Vol. 27 (3), pp. 207–20.

36. Dong Hwan Lee, "The Moderating Effect of Salesperson Reward Orientation on the Relative Effectiveness of Alternative Compensation Plans, "*Journal of Business Research,* 1998, vol. 43 (2), pp. 63–78.

37. George R. Franke, Jeong-Eun Park, "Salesperson Adapative Selling Behavior and Customer Orientation: A Meta-Analysis, *Journal Of Marketing Research,* 2006, Vol. 43 (4), pp. 34–50; and Charles E. Pettijohn, Linda S. Pettijohn, and A.J. Taylor, "Does Salesperson Perception of the Importance of Sales Skills Improve Sales Performance, Customer Orientation, Job Satisfaction, and Organizational Commitment, and Reduce Turnover," *Journal of Personal Selling & Sales Management,* 2007, Vol. 27 (1), p. 75.

38. Rene Y. Darmon, "Controlling Sales Force Turnover Costs Through Optimal Recruiting Training Policies," *European Journal of Operational Research,* 2004, Vol. 154 (10) pp. 291–308; and Phan Tej Adidam, "Causes and Consequences of High Turnover by Sales Professionals," *Journal of American Academy of Business,* 2006, Vol. 10 (1), pp. 137–42.

39. Joe M. Ricks, Jr., Jacqueline A. Williams, and William A. Weeks, "Sales Trainer Roles, Competencies, Skills, and Behaviors: A Case Study," *Industrial Marketing Management,* 2008, Vol. 37 (5), pp. 593–610; and Mark P. Leach and Annie H. Liu, "Investigating Interrelationships Among Sales Training Methods," *Journal of Personal Selling & Sales Management,* 2003, Vol. 23 (4), pp. 327–40.

40. Aili McConnon, "The Name of the Game Is Work" *BusinessWeek* Online, August 13, 2007, www.businessweek .com/innovate/content/august2007/ id20070813_467743.htm.

41. Tara Burnthorne Jopez, Chirstopher D. Hopkins, and Mary Anne Raymond, "Reward Preferences of Salespeople: How Do Commissions Rate,*" Journal of Personal Selling & Sales Management,* 2006, Vol. 26 (4), pp. 381–87; and Sridhar N. Ramaswami and Jagdip Singh, "Antecedents and Consequences

of Merit Pay Fairness for Industrial Sales-people," *Journal of Marketing,* 2003, Vol. 67 (4), pp. 46–60.

42. Michael Myser, "Bosses Get a Helping Hand," *Business 2.0,* 2007, Vol. 8 (6), p. 31–32.

43. Kevin McKeough, "Best Places to Work: Benefits, Benefits, Microsoft," *Crain's Chicago Business,* 2008, Vol. 31 (9), p. 24; and Michelle Conlin and Jay Greene, "How to Make a Microserf Smile," *BusinessWeek,* 2007, Issue 4049, pp. 56–59.

44. Raquel Ortega, "Impact of Direct to Consumers Marketing Strategies on Firm Market Value," *International Journal of Consumer Studies,* 2004, Vol. 28 (5), pp. 466–80; and Jacquelyn S. Thomas, Werner Reinartz, and V. Kumar, "Getting the Most Out of All Your Customers," *Harvard Business Review,* 2004, Vol. 82 (7/8), pp. 116–29.

45. Jessica Silver-Greenberg, "The Dirty Secret of Campus Credit Cards," *BusinessWeek* Online, September 6, 2007, www.businessweek.com/bwdaily/content/sep2007/db2007095_053822.htm.

46. Asim Ansari, Carl F. Mela, and Scott A. Neslin, "Customer Chan-nel Migration," *Journal of Marketing Research,* 2008, Vol. 45 (1), pp. 60–75.

47. Louise Lee, "Catalogs, Catalogs, Everywhere," *BusinessWeek* Online, November 22, 2006, www.businessweek.com/bwdaily/content/nov2006/db20061121_706666.htm.

48. George M. Zinkhan, "The Market-place, Emerging Technology and Market-ing Theory," *Marketing Theory,* 2005, Vol. 5 (1), pp. 105–16.

49. Dee Gill, "Blogging Ethics 101," *Crain's Chicago Business,* 2007, Vol. 30 (46), p. 33; and Jon Fine, "Polluting the Blogosphere," *Business-Week Online,* July 10, 2006, www.businessweek.com/magazine/content/06_28/b3992034.htm.

50. Lindsay Blakely, "The (Less) Lonely Life of the Road Warrior," *Business 2.0,* 2007, Vol. 8 (4), p. 104; and Matt Villano, "Information Please: the Kindness of Travel Minded Strangers," *International Herald Tribune,* April 16, 2007, p. 14.

51. Marshall Crook and Peter Sanders, "Will Marketing Change after Star's Death?" *Wall Street Journal,* Jan. 24 2008, B1.

52. John F. Tanner Jr., Christophe Fournier, Jorge A. Wise, Sandrine Hollet, and Juliet Poujoi, "Executives Perspec-tives of the Changing Role of the Sales Profession: Views from France, United States, and Mexico," *Journal of Business & Industrial Marketing,* 2008,

Vol. 23 (3), pp. 193–207; and David Welch, "Death of the Car Salesman," *Busi-nessWeek,* November 27, 2006, p. 33.

CHAPTER 19

1. A number of concepts in this section are derived from the following outstand-ing book, which is the best single source for understanding marketing dash-boards. It is highly recommended as a guidebook on the topic for marketing managers: Patrick LaPointe, *Marketing by the Dashboard Light: How to Get More Insight, Foresight, and Account-ability from Your Marketing Investments,* New York: ANA, 2005.

2. Gail J. McGovern, David Court, John A. Quelch, and Blair Crawford, "Bringing Customers into the Board-room," *Harvard Business Review,* Vol. 82, Iss. 11, November 2004, pp. 70–80.

3. John Nardone, "Free Yourself from the Tyranny of Metrics," *Advertising Age,* Nov. 20, 2006, Vol. 77, Iss. 47, p. 12.

4. Thorsten Wiesel, Bernd Skiera, and Julián Villanueva, "Customer Equity: An Integral Part of Financial Reporting," *Journal of Marketing,* Vol. 72, Iss. 2, March 2008, pp. 1–14.

5. Brad Perriello, "8 Tips to Improve Your Customer Service," *Industrial Distri-bution,* March 1, 2007, p. 34.

6. Leigh McAlister, Raji Srinivasan, and MinChung Kim, "Advertising, Research, and Development, and Systematic Risk of the Firm," *Journal of Marketing,* Vol. 71, Iss. 1, January 2007, pp. 35–49.

7. "Customer Management: Hitting the Target," *Precision Marketing,* September 22, 2006, p. 39.

8. The single best source for under-standing ROMI is the following book, which is highly recommended for mar-keting managers: Guy R. Powell, *Return on Marketing Investment,* Albuquerque, RBI Press, 2002. Many of the key con-cepts in this section emanate from this book. The ideas in this section are drawn from that source.

9. Claes Fornell, Sunil Mithas, Forrest V. Morgeson III, and M.S. Krishnan, "Cus-tomer Satisfaction and Stock Prices: High Returns, Low Risk," *Journal of Marketing,* Vol. 70, Iss. 1, January 2006, pp. 3–14; and Roland T. Rust, Katherine Lemon, and Valarie A. Zeithaml, "Return on Marketing: Using Customer Equity to Focus Marketing Strategy," *Journal of Marketing,* Vol. 68, Iss. 1, January 2004, pp. 109–27.

10. Behram Hansotia and Brad Rukstales, "Incremental Value Modeling," *Journal of Interactive Marketing,* Vol. 16, Iss. 3, Summer 2002, pp. 35–46.

11. Dominique M. Hanssens, Daniel Thorpe, and Carl Finkbeiner, "Market-ing When Customer Equity Matters," *Harvard Business Review,* Vol. 86, Iss. 5, May 2008, p. 117; and Rick Ferguson, "Word of Mouth and Viral Marketing: Taking the Temperature of the Hottest Trends in Marketing," *Journal of Consumer Marketing* Vol. 25, Iss. 3, 2008, pp. 179–82.

12. Don E. Schultz, "The New Branding Lingo," *Marketing Management,* Vol. 12, Iss. 6, November/December 2003, pp. 8–9.

13. In this section, the example formulas and descriptions are selected from the following outstanding treatise on market-ing metrics, which is a must-have book for marketing managers: Paul W. Farris, Neil T. Bendle, Phillip E. Pfeifer, and David J. Reibstein, *Marketing Metrics: 50 + Metrics Every Executive Should Master,* Upper Saddle River, NJ: Pear-son/Wharton School Publishing, 2006.

14. "Targeted Tactics Drive Response," *B to B,* Oct 9, 2006, Vol. 90 Iss. 13, p. 1.

15. Anne Field, "Strategies: Mission Possible," *BusinessWeek* Online, December 14, 2007, www.businessweek.com/print/magazine/content/07_72/s0712038774148.htm, accessed June 11, 2008.

16. William O. Bearden, R. Bruce Money, and Jennifer L. Nevins, "A Mea-sure of Long-Term Orientation: Devel-opment and Validation," *Journal of the Academy of Marketing Science,* Vol. 34, Iss. 3, Summer 2006, pp. 456–67.

17. Kusum L. Ailawadi, Donald R. Lehmann, and Scott A. Neslin, "Market-ing Response to a Major Policy Change in the Marketing Mix: Learning from Proctor & Gamble's Value Pricing Strat-egy," *Journal of Marketing,* Vol. 65, Iss. 1, January 2001, pp. 44–61.

18. Goel Love, "MC3 and the Leadership Gap," *MultichannelMerchant .com,* November 1, 2006, http://multichannelmerchant.com/crosschannel/leadership_gap_112006/index.html, accessed June 20, 2008.

19. Kusum L. Ailawadi, Karen Gedenk, Christian Lutzky, and Scott A. Neslin, "Decomposition of the Sales Impact of Promotion-Induced Stockpiling," *Journal of Marketing Research,* Vol. 44, Iss. 3, August 2007, pp. 450–67.

20. Thorsten Henning-Thurau, Victor Henning, and Henrik Sattler, "Consumer File Sharing of Motion Pictures," *Journal of Marketing,* Vol. 71, Iss. 4, October 2007, pp. 1–18; and Raghavan Srinivasan, Sreeram Ramakrishnan Sundara, and

Scott E. Grasman, "Identifying the Effects of Cannibalization on the Product Portfolio," *Marketing Intelligence & Planning,* Vol. 23, Iss. 4/5, 2005, pp. 359–71.

21. Paul W. Farris, Neil T. Bendle, Phillip E. Pfeifer, and David J. Reibstein, *Marketing Metrics: 50 + Metrics Every Executive Should Master.* Upper Saddle River, NJ: Pearson/Wharton School Publishing, 2006, p. 317.

22. Lynette Ryals, "Making Customer Relationship Management Work: The Measurement and Profitable Management of Customer Relationships," *Journal of Marketing,* Vol. 69, Iss. 4, October 2005, pp. 252–61.

23. Gary K. Hunter and William D. Perreault, Jr., "Making Sales Technology Effective," *Journal of Marketing,* Vol. 71, Iss. 1, January 2007, pp. 16–34.

24. Cristina Gimenez and Eva Ventura, "Logistics-Production, Logistics-Marketing and their External Integration: Their Impact on Performance," *International Journal of Operations & Production Management,* Vol. 25, Iss. 1, 2005, pp. 20–38.

25. Robert C. Blattberg, Richard Briesch, and Edward J. Fox, "How Promotions Work," *Marketing Science,* Vol. 14, Iss. 3, Summer 1995, pp. 122–32.

26. Hsiao-Fan Wang and Wei-Kuo Hong, "Managing Customer Profitability in a Competitive Market by Continuous Data Mining," *Industrial Marketing Management* Vol. 35, Iss. 6, August 2006, pp. 715–23.

27. Vanitha Swaminathan, Richard J. Fox, and Srinivas K. Reddy, "The Impact of Brand Extension Introduction on Choice," *Journal of Marketing,* Vol. 65, Iss. 4, October 2001, pp. 1–15.

28. David W. Stewart and Paul A. Pavlou, "From Consumer Response to Active Consumer: Measuring the Effectiveness of Interactive Media," *Journal of the Academy of Marketing Science,* Vol. 30, Iss. 4, Fall 2002, pp. 376–96.

29. Riva Richmond, "Yahoo Ad-Ranking Tool Clicks With Online Users," *Wall Street Journal,* February 28, 2007, p. B3D.

30. Jose A. Varela and Marisa del Rio, "Market Orientation Behavior: An Empirical Investigation using MARKOR," *Marketing Intelligence & Planning,* Vol. 21, Iss. 1, 2003, pp. 6–15.

31. Fred Anderholm, III, James Gaertner, and Ken Milani, "The Utilization of PERT in the Preparation of Marketing Budgets," *Managerial Planning,* Vol. 30, Iss. 1, July/August 1981, pp. 18–23.

32. Anonymous, "Marketing on a Tight Budget: A 10-point Action Plan," *Management Research News* Vol. 23, Iss. 12, 2000, p. 32.

33. Jordan K. Speer, "The Remaking of Casual Male," *ApparelMag.coml,* July 2006, www.apparelmag.com/ME2/dirmod.asp?sid=&nm=&type=Publishing&mod=Publications%3A%3AArticle&mid=8F3A7027421841978F18BE895F87F791&tier=4&id=EBC599B66F8F4569848E07C1C6557C4D, accessed June 16, 2008.

34. J. Holton Wilson and Hugh G. Daubek, "Marketing Managers Evaluate Forecasting Models," *Journal of Business Forecasting Methods & Systems,* Vol. 8, Iss. 1, 1989, pp. 19–23.

35. Robin T. Peterson, "How Efficient Are Salespeople in Surveys of Buyer Intentions?," *Journal of Business Forecasting Methods & Systems,* Vol. 7, Iss. 1, Spring 1988, pp. 11–12.

36. Kenneth B. Kahn and John T. Mentzer, "Forecasting in Consumer and Industrial Markets," *Journal of Business Forecasting Methods & Systems,* Vol. 14, Iss. 2, Summer 1995, pp. 21–27.

37. Kenneth B. Kahn and John T. Mentzer.

38. Zuhaimy Haji Ismael and Maizah Hura Ahamad, "Delphi Improves Sales Forecasts: Malaysia's Electronic Companies' Experience," *Journal of Business Forecasting Methods & Systems* Vol. 22, Iss. 2, Summer 2003, pp. 22–25.

39. Sarah McBride, "Arbitron-Nielsen Venture Shows Promise," *Wall Street Journal,* February 27, 2007, p. B4.

40. Steve Hoeffler, "Measuring Preferences for Really New Products," *Journal of Marketing Research,* Vol. 40, Iss. 4, November 2003, pp. 406–20.

41. Stefan Stremersch, Gerard J. Tellis, Phillip Hans Franses, and Jeroen L.G. Binken, "Indirect Network Effects in New Product Growth," *Journal of Marketing,* Vol. 71, Iss. 3, July 2007, pp. 52–74.

42. Werner J. Reinartz and V. Kumar, "The Impact of Customer Relationship Characteristics on Profitable Lifetime Duration," *Journal of Marketing,* Vol. 67, Iss. 1, January 2003, pp. 77–99; and Wendy W. Moe and Peter S. Fader, "Modeling Hedonic Portfolio Products: A Joint Segmentation Analysis of Music Compact Disc Sales," *Journal of Marketing Research,* Vol. 38, Iss. 3, August 2001, pp. 376–85.

43. Rebecca J. Slotegraaf, Christine Moorman, and J. Jeffrey Inman, "The Role of Firm Resources in Returns to Market Deployment," *Journal of Marketing Research,* Vol. 40, Iss. 3, August 2003, pp. 295–309.

44. Jim Burruss and Dorothea Kuettner, "Forecasting for Short-lived Products: Hewlett-Packard's Journey," *Journal of Business Forecasting Methods & Systems,* Vol. 21, Iss. 4, Winter 2002/2003, pp. 9–13.

45. Guido Berens, Cees B.M. van Riel, and Gerrit H. van Bruggen, "Corporate Associations and Consumer Product Responses: The Moderating Role of Corporate Brand Dominance," *Journal of Marketing,* Vol. 69, Iss. 3, July 2005, pp. 35–48; and S. M. Musyoka, S. M. Mutyauvyu, J. B. K. Kiema, F. N. Karanja, and D. N. Siriba, "Market Segmentation Using Geographic Information Systems (GIS): A Case Study of the Soft Drink Industry in Kenya," *Marketing Intelligence & Planning,* Vol. 25, Iss. 6, 2007 pp. 632–42.

46. Tim Parry, "Tips for Capturing More Data," *MultichannelMerchant.com,* March 1, 2007, http://multichannelmerchant.com/crosschannel/lists/tips_capturing_data/, accessed June 16, 2008.

47. Myron Gable, Ann Fairhurst, Roger Dickinson, and Lynn Harris, "Improving Students' Understanding of the Retail Advertising Budgeting Process," *Journal of Marketing Education,* Vol. 22, Iss. 2, August 2000, pp. 120–28.

48. Andrew McMains, "To Reach Core Audience, Wendy's Busts Out Online," *Adweek,* Nov. 12, 2007, p. 8.

49. Clark, Bruce H., Andrew V. Abela, and Tim Ambler, "BEHIND the Wheel," *Marketing Management,* Vol. 15, Iss. 3, May/June 2006, p. 18.

50. Denis Smith, "Business (not) as Usual: Crisis Management, Service Recovery and the Vulnerability of Organizations," *Journal of Services Marketing,* Vol. 19, Iss. 5, 2005, pp. 309–20.

51. George Schlidge, "Marketing Audits: Why Principles of Accountability in Marketing Are Useful in Promoting Company Growth," *Journal of Promotion Management,* Vol. 12, Iss. 2, 2006, pp. 49–52.

52. Jonathan Cox, "Why Show Audits are Crucial for Effective Measurement," *B to B,* March 12, 2007, p. 33.

PHOTO CREDITS

COMPANY INDEX

Super 8 Motel, 81
Survey Monkey, 134
Suzuki, 313
Sweet Leaf, 426
Swiss Colony, 466
Swiss International Air Lines, 82
Symantec, 529
Symbian, 318
Systembolaget, 152

T

Taco Bell, 249, 499
TAP Portugal, 82
Target Corp., 25, 155, 246, 250, 397, 405, 419, 439, 443, 450, 484
TargetRx, 22
Technomic, 387
Tesco, 159, 444, 457, 459–460
T.G. Lee, 280
TGI Friday's, 17
Thai Airways International, 82
Thermo Fisher Scientific, 447
Thomas Global Register, 225
3M, 67, 163, 283, 284, 285, 286, 288
Thrifty Car Rental, 451
Tiffany & Company, 424
Timberland, 204
Time Warner, 174, 486
Timex, 151, 281
TJ Maxx, 104, 453
T-Mobile, 179
TMS, 130
Tommy Hilfiger, 304
Tomorrow Now, 163
Topshop, 440
Toshiba, 80, 161, 199, 210
Total, 64
Toyota Motor, 43, 64, 69, 70, 90, 156, 161, 183, 228, 270, 299, 311, 313, 324, 332, 394, 474–475, 478, 480, 486, 532, 533, 565–566

Trader Joe's, 343
Tupperware, 447, 448
Turkish Airlines, 82
Tyson Foods, 65

U

Unilever, 25–26, 90, 177, 349, 455, 486
Union Pacific, 156
United Airlines, 81, 82, 150, 222, 271
United Stationers, 447
Universal Orlando Resort, 173, 174, 435, 457
UNTIL.org, 13
UPS, 78, 260, 418, 420, 426, 446
Urban Outfitters, Inc., 253
US Airways, 82, 150, 271
USAA Insurance, 105, 277, 379–380
UTV Software Communications, 77

V

Verizon Wireless, 86, 179, 185, 486
VF, 15
VF Corporation, 538
Victoria's Secret, 457
Victorinox, 324
Virgin Trains, 497
Visa, 78, 107
Vittel, 263
Volkswagen, 263, 528
Voss Water, 396, 397, 424–425, 475

W

Wachovia Bank, 104
Walgreens, 254, 349, 395, 417
Wallhogs.com, 527
Wal-Mart, 19, 25, 32, 64, 65, 67, 74, 76, 94, 109, 155, 157, 161, 211, 212–213, 240, 254, 259, 263, 282, 314, 316–317, 390, 397, 422, 423, 427–428, 438, 443, 444, 449, 452, 454, 457, 458, 459–460, 484
Walt Disney Company, 21, 117, 158, 174, 186, 311, 314, 353, 357, 451–452, 486
Warner Bros., 530
Washington Mutual, 31
Waste Management, Inc., 9
WebEx Communications, 234
Wegmans, 157, 439, 454
Wella Corporation, 247
Wendy's, 261, 265, 485–486
Wesco International, 447
WhereNet, 339
Whirlpool, 42, 126, 146, 276, 277
White Wave Foods, 314
Whole Foods Markets, 250
Williams-Sonoma, 449, 545
Wilson's Leather Stores, 442
World Bank, 140
WorldCom, 5

X

XL Capital, 215
XM Radio, 152

Y

Yahoo, 128, 170, 193, 335, 347, 524, 529, 530, 547
Yankelovich, Inc., 136, 137
York International, 258
YPB&R, 136
Yum Brands, 318, 499

Z

Zephyrhills Water, 289, 321
Zillow, 206
Zoomerang, 134

NAME INDEX

A

Aaker, David A., 267, 310, E-15
Aaker, Jennifer L., E-9
Abela, Andrew V., E-28
Aboulnasr, Khaleed, E-14
Abrahams, Marc, E-14
Achrol, Ravi S., E-21
Adams, James W., 499
Adams, John, E-5
Adamson, Allen P., 327
Adidam, Phan Tej, E-26
Aeppel, Timothy, E-20
Agarwal, Ritu, E-20
Ahamad, Maizah Hura, E-28
Ahmed, Sadrudin A., E-4
Ahmed, Zafar U., E-10
Ahn, Jae Hyeon, E-23
Ailawadi, Kusum L., E-2, E-20, E-27
Aitken, Robert, E-15
Ajzen, I., E-9
Albaum, Gerald, E-7
Albrecht, Karl, 381
Alcaniz, Enrique Bigne, E-23
Aldas-Maznazo, Joaquin, E-10
Algesheimer, Rene, E-23
Allenby, Greg M., E-13
Alloway, Ken, 63, 503
Almquist, Eric, E-13
Amato, Christie H., E-9
Ambler, Tim, 566, E-28
Amelio, William, 93
Amir, On, E-10
Amrouche, N., E-16
Ander, Willard N., Jr., 461
Anderholm, Fred, III, E-28
Anderson, Erin, E-21, E-26
Anderson, Kristin, 115
Ansari, Asim, E-23, E-27
Ansoff, H. Igor, 47, 48
Antonio, Harry, 564
Ariely, Dan, E-20
Armancioglu, Nukhel, E-17
Armstrong, Katrina, E-9
Arndt, Michael, 266, 500, E-2, E-3
Arnold, Eric J., E-2, E-3
Arnott, Sarah, E-24
Aurand, Timothy W., E-5
Avci, Turgay, E-24
Avlonitis, George J., E-19, E-20
Aydin, Serkan, E-17

B

Babakus, Emin, E-24
Bagozzi, Richard P., E-12
Baker, Kenneth G., E-7
Baker, Ronald J., 408
Baker, Stephen, E-16
Bakker, Arnold B., E-26
Bala, Venkatesh, E-15
Balazs, Anne L., E-12
Ball, Brad, E-3
Ballantyne, David, E-15
Ballmer, Steve, 345
Banerjee, Saikat, E-4, E-15
Bang, Hae-Kyong, E-24
Bansal, Harvir S., E-18
Baracli, H., E-11
Barboza, David, E-11
Bardlow, Eric T., E-13
Barkley, Bruce T., 350
Barksdale, Hiram C., Jr., E-10, E-25
Barone, Michael J., E-1
Barr, Pete, Jr., 303, 463
Barr, Terry Feldman, E-19
Barry, James M., E-11
Barry, Thomas E., E-12
Bartiromo, Maria, E-17
Barton, Richard, 206
Bascoul, Ganael, E-6
Bashkansky, E., E-21
Basligil, H., E-11
Basu, Alokparna, E-16
Bateman, Connie R., E-6
Baurer, Hans H., E-10
Bawa, Kapil, E-18
Baxter, Andrew, E-22
Bayon, Tomas, E-13
Bayus, Barry L., E-12
Bearden, William O., E-27
Beasty, Colin, E-7
Becker, Christine, E-10
Beckham, David, 400
Bell, Jim, E-7
Bell, Marie, 433
Bell, Simon J., E-1
Bello, Daniel C., E-21
Belonax, Joseph J., Jr., E-26
Belschak, Frank D., E-26
Bendle, Neil T., 543, 566,
    E-27, E-28
Bennett, Peter D., 415
Bennett, Roger, E-6

Berens, Guido, E-28
Berfield, Susan, E-4
Bergin, Richard, E-7
Bergman, Todd L., 380
Berman, Barry, E-5
Berner, Robert, E-1, E-22
Berry, Leonard L., 354, 368, 373, 381,
    E-6, E-18, E-19
Bettencourt, Lance A., E-14
Bettman, James R., E-10
Bevil, DeWayne, E-15
Bezos, Jeff, 114
Bhagat, Parimal S., E-9
Bhagwati, Jagdish, 94
Bharadwaj, Neeraj, E-1
Bharadwaj, Sundar, E-1, E-21
Bhattacharya, C. B., E-12, E-24
Bick, Julie, E-17
Biederman, David, E-21
Bieme, Mike, E-14
Bierne, Mike, E-1
Bink, Audrey J. M., E-5
Binken, Jeroen L. G., E-14, E-28
Birchall, Jonathan, E-8, E-15
Bird, Monroe M., E-10
Birger, Jon, E-23
Birk, Matthias M., E-11
Bishop, Terrence R., E-5
Bitner, Mary Jo, E-1
Bjerke, Rune, 327
Blair, Bruce, E-26
Blair, Edward, E-7, E-14
Blair, Margaret Henderson, E-25
Blakely, Lindsay, E-27
Blakeman, Robyn, 500
Blanchard, David, 433
Blattberg, Robert C., E-28
Blenkhorn, David L., 171
Bligh, Phil, E-7
Bliss, Jeanne, 360
Blyth, Bill, E-7
Boartwright, Peter, E-22
Boddy, Clive, E-7
Bohen, Colleen, E-9
Bohlmann, Jonathan D., E-12
Boles, James S., E-10, E-25
Bolton, Lisa E., E-9
Bolton, Ruth N., E-11,
    E-13, E-19
Bond, Phillip, E-21

Simms, Jane, E-15
Simonian, Haig, E-7
Sinclair, Janas, E-25
Singh, Jagdip, E-18, E-26
Singh, Nanua, E-14
Singh, Vishal, E-20
Sinha, Indrajit, E-19
Sinha, Prabhakant, E-26
Sirdeshmukh, Deepak, E-18
Sirgy, M. Joseph, E-10
Siriba, D. N., E-28
Sirkin, Harold, E-17
Siseth, Pal R., E-11
Sisodia, Rajendra S., E-1
Sivakumar, K., E-10
Sjodin, Henrik, E-18
Skiera, Bernd, E-27
Skinner, Lauren, E-26
Skinner, Lauren R., E-22
Slater, Robert, E-2
Slater, Stanley F., E-2, E-4, E-23
Sloan, Julia, 54
Slotegraaf, Rebecca J., E-16, E-28
Smalley, Karen, E-1
Smidts, Ale, E-6
Smith, Alan D., E-22
Smith, Amy K., E-19
Smith, David, 426
Smith, Denis, E-3, E-28
Smith, Donnavieve, E-10
Smith, D.V.L., 147
Smith, Geri, E-3
Smith, Heidi Locke, E-26
Smith, J. Brock, E-17
Smith, Jeremy, E-1
Smith, Jessica, E-12
Smith, Ray A., E-1, E-11, E-13
Smith, Ronald S., 101, 106
Smith, Steve, 398
Smolker, Rachel, E-10
Snow, Charles C., 41, 42, 52
Snyder, Richard, 52
Soares, Joao Oliveira, E-3
Solem, O., E-16
Som, Rita, E-14
Sood, Suresh, E-15
Sorescu, B., E-17
Sorrell, Martin, 327
Sorvillo, Nick, E-18
Souchon, Anne L., E-6
Souza Fontana, Mariadel Mar, E-17
Spanjol, Jelena, E-17
Sparks, Leigh, E-23
Sparrow, Nick, E-7
Spath, Ron, 14
Speece, Mark, E-16
Speed, Richard J., E-19
Speer, Jordan K., E-28

Spencer, Jane, E-5
Spink, Amanda, E-23
Srinivasan, Raghavan, E-27
Srinivasan, Raji, E-27
Srivastava, Joydeep, E-24
St. James, Yannik, E-18
Staelin, Richard, E-25
Stagg, Chris, E-17
Stainburn, Samantha, E-11
Stallings, Angie, 266
Stamps, Miriam B., E-25
Stan, Simona, E-19
Stanley, Sarah M., E-9
Stead, Deborah, E-10
Stedman, Craig, E-6
Steenkamp, Jan-Benedict E. M., E-25
Steinberg, Brian, E-24
Sterling, Jay U., E-10, E-13
Stern, Neil Z., 461
Stern, Paula, 431
Sterrett, David, E-23
Stevens, Howard, 534
Stewart, David W., E-1, E-16, E-28
Stiger, Steve, 209, 237, 255
Stock, Ruth Maria, E-2
Stodder, David, E-6
Stokes, David, E-7
Stoopes, Nicole, E-9
Stopper, Bill, E-3
Storbacka, Kaj, 115
Story, Louise, E-9, E-20
Stremersch, Stefan, E-14, E-28
Stride, Helen, E-15
Stuyck, Jules, E-20
Sudharshan, D., E-7
Sudhir, K., E-21, E-23
Suh, Jaebeom, E-25
Sullivan, Chris T., E-19
Sullivan, P., E-9
Sullivan, Ursula Y., E-12
Sun, Baohong, E-19
Sun, Jeanne-Mey, 408
Sun Tzu, 162
Sundara, Sreeram Ramakrishnan, E-27
Suter, Tracy A., E-16
Svahn, Senja, E-3
Swaidan, Ziad, E-24
Swaminathan, Vanitha, E-28
Swan, John E., E-26
Swift, Ronald S., 98, E-5, E-6
Synodinos, Nicolaos E., E-25

T

Takeuichi, Riki, E-4
Talukdar, Debabrata, E-23
Tam, Jackie L. M., E-26
Tamilla, Robert D., E-21

Tan, Jessica, E-8
Tanner, Christian, E-11
Tanner, John F., Jr., E-27
Tanny, Stephen M., 408
Tansuhaj, Patriya, E-3
Tapp, Alan, E-6
Tashiro, Hiroko, E-7
Taudes, Alfred, E-24
Tayles, Mike, E-20
Taylor, A. J., E-26
Taylor, Alex, III, E-15, E-17
Taylor, Charles R., E-24
Taylor, Ronald D., E-10
Taylor, Sam, E-15
Taylor, Shirley F., E-18
Teague, Paul, E-21
Teich, Ira, E-12
Tellis, Gerald J., E-14, E-28
Terryn, Evelyne, E-20
Terwiesch, Christian, E-17, E-20
Theodosiou, M., E-3
Thiagarajan, Palaniappan, E-10
Thilenius, Peter, E-21
Thirkell, Peter C., E-6
Thomas, Jacquelyn S., E-5, E-12, E-27
Thompson, Bob, 98, E-5
Thorpe, Daniel, E-27
Thull, Jeff, 234
Tiainen, Tarja, E-23
Tichy, Noel, E-3
Till, Brian D., E-9
Tiltman, David, E-7
Tinson, Julie, E-10
Todd, Sarah, E-13
Tokman, Mert, E-22
Toran Torres, Francisco, E-23
Toyoda, Akio, 565
Trivedi, Minakshi, E-19
Tsai, Kuen-Hung, E-14, E-17
Tsai, Ming-tiem, E-9
Tsao, Hsiu-Yuan, E-15
Tse, David K., E-20
Turk, Doug, E-7
Turner, Gregory B., E-12
Tybout, Alice M., E-18

U

Ulrich, Karl, 350, E-17
Ulwick, Anthony W., E-14
Underhill, Paco, 207
Urban, Glen L., E-17, E-25
Urbanowicz, Nicole, E-12

V

Van Auken, Stuart, E-12
Van Bruggen, Gerrit H., E-6, E-28
Van Den Butt, Christophe, E-18

Z

Zabin, Jeff, E-3, E-5
Zaccour, G., E-16
Zaccour, Georges, E-25
Zacharia, Zach, E-21
Zaheer, Srilata, E-10
Zaltman, Gerald, 147, 207

Zamiska, Nicholas, E-14
Zawada, Craig C., 408
Zeithaml, Valarie A., 54, 364, 368, 373, E-2, E-19, E-27
Zemke, Ron, 381
Zhang, Jie, E-22
Zhao, Miao, E-23
Zheng, Yu-Sheng, E-19

Zielke, Stephan, E-20
Zimmer, Jim, 402
Zinkhan, George M., E-7, E-27
Zoltners, Andris A., E-26
Zou Shaoming, E-26
Zwick, Detiev, E-6

SUBJECT INDEX

A

Acceleration effect, 215
Accumulating bulk, 418
Acquisitions, 152, 258
Action plans, 548–549, 559
Action stage, 476
Activities, interests, and opinions (AIOs), 178, 252
Adaptive selling, 506
Additions to existing product lines, 330–331
Administered VMS (vertical marketing systems), 421–422
Advantages, product, 512
Advertising; *see also* Internet advertising
    cooperative, 494
    costs, 482, 488
    cultural mistakes, 86
    customer-created, 477
    definition, 464
    diminishing returns, 486
    effectiveness measures, 553
    execution approaches, 489, 490
    in foreign markets, 86, 89–90
    frequency, 488–489
    institutional, 487
    interruptive, 543
    largest advertisers, 90, 485, 486
    location-based targeted, 179
    low-involvement settings, 195–196
    media selection, 488–489, 491
    metrics, 541, 547
    music, 184
    opinion leaders in, 193
    overreliance on, 485–486
    product, 487–488
    pros and cons, 468
    reach, 488–489
    spending, 485
    subliminal stimuli, 184
    television, 482, 491, 543
    in video games, 244
Advertising agencies; *see* Creative agencies
Advertising execution, 489
Advertising response function, 486
Advertising wearout, 485–486
Aesthetics, package design, 320
African Americans
    marketing to, 188, 247
    population, 247, 248

Age groups; *see* Generational groups
Age segmentation, 243
Agent intermediaries, 415
AIDA model, 474–476
AIOs; *see* Activities, interests, and opinions
Airlines
    competition, 150
    efficiency, 222
    market shares, 150
    service recovery, 369–370
    strategic alliances, 81, 82
Allowances, 400–402
    promotional, 401–402, 419, 494
    slotting, 425, 426
All-you-can-afford method, 484–485, 558
AMA; *see* American Marketing Association
American Academy of Pediatrics, 336
American Indians, 248
American Marketing Association (AMA)
    brand definition, 304
    historical definitions of marketing, 9
    marketing definition, 4, 8, 11, 30
    viral marketing definition, 530
Annual reports, 165
ASEAN (Association of Southeast Asian Nations), 76
Asia, cultural differences, 125–126
Asian Americans, 247–249
Aspirational purchases, 192
Association of Southeast Asian Nations; *see* ASEAN
Assortments, product, 418, 438–439, 442
Assurance, 374
Attention, 474–475
Attitude-based choices, 201
Attitudes, 181–182
Attribute-based choices, 201
Auction pricing, 398
Audits
    marketing, 561, 562–564
    trade show, 561
Auto industry
    luxury carmakers, 152, 153, 192
    product development, 332
    regulations, 333
    salespeople, 532–533
    warranties, 324–325
Average-cost pricing, 399–400
Awareness set, 200

B

B2B; *see* Business-to-business markets
B2C; *see* Business-to-consumer marketing
Baby boomers, 176, 177, 245, 246
Backward integration, 160
Bait and switch practices, 404
Banner ads, 530
Basket of global marketing themes, 89
Behavioral data, 134
Behavioral segmentation, 254–255
Beliefs, of consumers, 181–182
Benchmarking, 166
Benefits
    definition, 30
    essential, 271, 272
    features, advantages, and, 512
    sought by consumers, 254
Big M marketing, 20–21, 33
Biofuels, 214
Blogs, 314, 476, 495, 526–527
Boston Consulting Group (BCG) Growth-Share Matrix, 35–36
Bottled water industry, 157, 158
Brand assets, 310
Brand associations, 310, 471
Brand awareness, 310, 479
Brand connections, 312–313
Brand equity
    benefits, 312–314
    dimensions, 310–311
Brand experience, role of scent, 304
Brand identity, 308
Brand loyalty, 310
    benefits, 313–314
    brand strategies and, 310–311
    maintaining, 479–480
Brand personalities, 185–186
Brand sponsors, 306
Brand strategies
    for global marketing, 86–87
    importance, 304
    increasing brand equity, 310–311
Branding decisions
    co-branding, 317–318
    licensing, 317
    national or store brands, 316–317
    stand-alone or family branding, 314–316
Brands; *see also* Products
    boundaries, 308

late majority, 347
sales promotion to, 492, 493, 550
Contingency plans, 49, 559–560
Contractual agreements
    in foreign markets, 80–81
    franchising, 80–81, 421, 423
    licensing, 80, 317
Contractual VMS (vertical marketing systems), 421, 425
Controls, 549, 559, 560; see also Audits
Convenience goods, 275–276, 424
Cooperative advertising and promotion, 494
Cooperatives, 421
Core competencies, 40–41, 42
Core products, 271–272
Corporate identity, 471
Corporate VMS (vertical marketing systems), 421, 425
Corporate-level strategic planning, 35
Cost leadership strategy, 41, 384, 391–392
Cost per thousand impressions (CPM) rates, 547
Cost reduction, 331
Cost-based price strategy, 91
Cost-plus pricing, 398–399
Costs; see also Budgets
    average-cost pricing, 399–400
    channel, 88
    distribution, 91–92
    of international distribution, 88, 91–92
    transportation, 91–92, 428
Counterfeit packaging, 318
Counterfeit products, 308
Countries; see also Cultures, foreign
    developing, 385
    economic development stages, 70–72
    emerging markets, 70–72
    fastest-growing, 70, 71
    Internet access, 79
    top five economies, 68
Country-of-origin effect, 87
CPM; see Cost per thousand impressions
Creating assortments, 418, 438–439
Creative agencies
    full-service, 489, 490
    public relations, 494
    roles, 489–490
    value added, 476
    Web site development, 489–490
Credence attributes, 365
Crisis management, 496–497
CRM; see Customer relationship management
Cultures
    definition, 186
    influence on consumer decisions, 186–188

subcultures, 187–188
    values, 187
Cultures, company
    of competitors, 155–156, 162–164
    customer-centric, 108–109
    strategic decisions and, 155–156
Cultures, foreign
    differences, 86, 125–126
    language differences, 86, 144
    researching, 68
    similarities, 73
Customer acquisition, 100
Customer advocacy, 361
Customer communities, 452
Customer delight, 367
Customer expectations
    actual, 368–369, 372–373
    gap analysis, 368–369, 372–373
    management's perceptions of, 368–369
    for product experience, 271–272
Customer expectations management, 361, 371–372
Customer interface, changing rules of, 436–437
Customer lifetime value (CLV), 100–101, 546
Customer loyalty
    definition, 100
    measuring, 135
    programs, 255, 363, 453, 493
    satisfaction and, 100, 361–363
    segmentation by degree, 255
    value proposition and, 31
Customer marketing
    advantages, 107
    distinction from consumer marketing, 105–107
Customer mind-set, 109, 110, 360
Customer orientation, 15, 17, 109, 150; see also Cultures, customer-centric
Customer profitability, 100, 122
Customer relationship management (CRM)
    characteristics, 99, 108–111
    core concepts, 108
    customer-centric culture, 108–109
    data mining, 102, 134
    data security, 104, 105
    definitions, 98–99
    implementation, 99–100
        failures, 99, 111–112, 127
        success factors, 112–113
    importance, 99
    integration into marketing planning, 100, 102
    metrics, 100–101

objectives, 100
    process cycle, 101–103
        analysis and refinement, 103
        customer interaction, 103
        knowledge discovery, 102
        marketing planning, 102
        relationship-based enterprises, 110–111
    sales proposals, 227
    uses of data, 122
Customer retention, 31, 100, 361
Customer satisfaction
    assessing, 203
    definition, 100
    loyalty and, 100, 361–363
    measuring, 31, 372
    product evaluation, 204
Customer service and support, 436–437, 440; see also Services
Customer switching, 31
Customer touchpoints, 102, 103–105, 436
Customer-centric culture, 108–109
Customer-centric enterprises, 14, 34, 359
Customers; see also Consumers
    brand roles for, 304–306
    feedback, 472
    firing, 101
    information power, 18–19
    new product ideas, 335
    shortages, 16–18
    as source of competitor information, 167–168
    switching behavior, 361
    as value network members, 414–415
    views of competitors, 156–158
Customized (one-to-one) marketing, 260

D

Dashboard; see Marketing dashboard
Data; see also Information
    behavioral, 134
    confidential, 103–104, 120, 477
    observational, 134
    primary, 133
    secondary, 133, 136–138
Data collection, 133–134, 138
Data mining, 102, 134
Data warehouses, 102
Database marketing, 102
Databases, online, 140, 167
Deceptive pricing, 404
Deciders, 219–220
Decision-making authority, in global marketing, 83–84

Interviews, in-depth, 133
Intrinsic rewards, 519
Introduction phase, product life cycle, 290–293
Inventory
    just-in-time, 427–428
    management, 427–428
    of retailers, 439–440
    stock-outs, 427, 546
    turns, 546
Investment
    direct foreign, 82–83
    marketing as, 541
    promotion as, 482, 483–484
Issue sponsorships, 496

J

JIT; see Just-in-time inventory management
JND; see Just noticeable differences
Jobbers, 415
Joint ventures, 81–82, 317
Jury of executive opinion, 551, 552
Just noticeable differences (JND), 403
Just-in-time (JIT) inventory management, 427–428

K

Key account salespeople, 508
Knowledge discovery, 102

L

Labeling; see also Packaging
    information included, 322–323
    legal requirements, 322
    marketing role, 323
Laggards, 346, 347
Language
    culture and, 186–187
    differences, 86, 144
    Spanish, 249
Late entrants, 294
Late majority, 347
Latin America, MERCOSUR, 74–76
Learning
    definition, 184
    high-involvement, 195
    influence on consumer decisions, 184–185
    low-involvement, 195–196
    organizational, 103
Legal environments of foreign markets, 68–69
Legal issues
    collecting information on, 128
    counterfeit products, 308
    data security, 104, 105

identity theft, 104
    labeling, 322
    pricing practices, 401, 404–405
    privacy, 103–104, 477
    supply chain management, 429
    telemarketing restrictions, 128, 525
    trademarks, 306, 307, 308, 319
Legitimate power, 423
Licensing
    brands, 317
    in foreign markets, 80
Life cycles
    family, 176–177, 190, 247
    product; see Product life cycle
Lifestyles
    gender roles, 178–179, 190
    influence on consumer decisions, 178–180
    psychographic segmentation, 252–253
    trends, 178
Lifetime value of customer, 100–101, 546
Limited information search, 198
Line extensions, 314–315
Line of visibility, 377
Literacy rates, 144
Little m marketing, 21–22, 33
Local governments, 167
Local market ad generation, 89
Local market conditions price strategy, 91
Logistics, 417
    inbound, 426
    inventory management, 427–428
    order processing, 427
    outbound, 426
    reverse, 426, 427
    for store retailing, 453–454
    third-party providers, 413, 421
    transportation, 428
    warehousing and materials handling, 427
Logos, 304, 319, 471; see also Brands; Labeling
Long-term memory, 183, 184
Loss leader products, 405
Low price guarantee policies, 456
Loyalty; see also Brand loyalty; Customer loyalty
    employee, 360
    programs, 255, 363, 453, 493

M

Macroeconomics, 126–127
Magazine advertising, 491
Management research deliverable, 130

Manufacturers
    in China, 229–230, 414
    as customers, 210–211, 221–222, 278
Manufacturers' agents, 415
Margin on sales, 545
Market channels
    discounts and allowances, 400–402, 425, 547
    in foreign markets, 87–89
    integration, 160
Market creation, 21
Market deterioration, 294
Market development strategies, 47
Market entry strategies, 78
    contractual agreements, 80–81
    direct foreign investment, 82–83
    exporting, 78–79, 91–92
    strategic alliances, 81–82
Market exits, 295
Market expansion, 159–160, 294
Market followers, 290–292
Market information systems (MISs)
    definition, 119
    external information, 123
        competition, 129
        demographic data, 123–126
        economic conditions, 126–127
        natural world, 127
        political/legal environment, 128
        technology, 127
    internal information sources, 120–123
Market makers, 452
Market mavens, 193
Market orientation, 15
Market penetration pricing strategy, 292, 387–388
Market penetration strategies, 47
Market research; see Marketing research
Market research companies, 130, 136–137
Market segmentation; see Segmentation
Market share, 387
Market skimming pricing strategy, 292, 388, 392
Market space, 160, 526
Market stability, 294
Market testing, 342–344, 551, 553
Market-driven strategic planning, 35
Marketing
    AMA definition, 4, 8, 9, 11, 30
    Big M, 20–21, 33
    definition, 8
    history, 11–14
    as investment, 541
    little m, 21–22, 33
    misconceptions, 4–7
    strategic, 20–21, 33
    tactical, 21–22, 33
    visibility, 5–6

Networks, value, 412–415
New dominant logic for marketing, 354–355
New products; *see also* Product development
    business case analysis, 340
    cannibalization rates, 545
    company perspective, 330–331
    consumer adoption, 345–347
    customer's perspective, 331
    definition, 330–331
    failures, 290, 291
    idea sources, 334–335
    launching, 344
    marketing strategies, 292, 338
    pricing strategies, 292, 387
    reasons for success or failure, 332–333
    screening ideas, 335–337
New purchase situations, 217, 224, 340
Newspaper advertising, 491
New-to-the-world products, 330
Niche strategy, 41, 259, 260, 388
Nimble operations, 413–414
Noise, 472–473
Nondurable products, 274–275
Nonfinancial incentives, 521–522
Nonprobability sampling, 135, 136
Non-store retailers, 446
    advantages, 448
    catalog retailers, 446–447, 525–526
    direct selling, 447–448
    television home shopping, 448
    vending machines, 448
Nonverbal communication, 187
North American Free Trade Agreement (NAFTA), 74, 75
North American Industrial Classification System (NAICS), 220–221, 442

O

Objective measures, 522
Objective-and-task method, 483–484, 558–559
Objectives, 38, 47
Observational data, 134
Occupational segmentation, 249–250
Occupations, 177
Odd pricing, 396–397
OEM; *see* Original equipment manufacturer
Offerings, 13
Oligopolies, 152
One world price strategy, 90–91
One-price strategy, 397
One-to-one marketing, 15–16
Online advertising; *see* Internet advertising

Online databases, 140, 167
Open-ended questions, 135
Operant conditioning, 184
Opinion leaders, 192–193
Order processing, 427
Organizational factors, 230
Organizational learning, 103
Organizational structure
    for global marketing, 83–84
    sales forces, 514–516
Original equipment manufacturer (OEM) customers, 221–222; *see also* Manufacturers
Out suppliers, 217
Outbound logistics, 426
Outbound telemarketing, 509, 525
Outdoor advertising, 491
Output measures, 523
Outsourcing
    call centers, 437
    ethical issues, 414
    functions, 413
    global, 414
    logistics, 413, 421
    sales forces, 419, 477, 514–515
Ownership utility, 30

P

Packaging
    aesthetics, 320
    colors, 320, 322
    costs, 318
    counterfeit, 318
    designing, 320, 342
    effective, 319–322
    environmentally sensitive, 318
    importance, 318
    information communicated, 319, 321–322
    innovative designs, 319, 320–321
    labeling, 322–323
    objectives, 318–319
    security, 318
    testing, 342
Partner relationship management (PRM) strategies, 422, 427
Parts, 278
Pass-through percentage, 546–547
Patents, 166–167
Penetration, 545
Penetration pricing, 292, 387–388
Perceived quality
    brands and, 310, 312
    in foreign markets, 85–86
Percent-of-sales method, 484, 558
Perceptions
    definition, 182

    influence on consumer decisions, 182–184
    selective, 472
    selective awareness, 182–183
    selective distortion, 183
    selective retention, 183
    subliminal stimuli, 184
Perceptual maps, 261–262
Perishability of services, 358
Personal factors, 230
Personal selling
    activities, 505–506
    advantages, 504
    in B2B markets
        relationships, 212, 225, 504
        sales positions, 507–508
    in consumer markets, 507
    costs, 504
    customer needs, 511, 512
    definition, 464
    in foreign markets, 90
    key success factors, 506–507
    process, 508–509
        closing sales, 513
        follow-up, 514
        handling objections, 512–513
        opening relationships, 510
        prospecting, 509–510
        qualifying prospects, 510
        sales presentations, 510–512
        stages, 509
    pros and cons, 468
Personality
    brand, 185–186
    definition, 185
    influence on consumer decisions, 185–186
    theories, 185
Physical distribution, 417–418; *see also* Distribution; Logistics
Physical surroundings
    influence on consumer decisions, 188–189, 201–202
    of retail stores, 458
Pioneering advertising, 487–488
Pioneers, 290, 292
Place utility, 30
Planning; *see* Marketing planning
PLC; *see* Product life cycle
Politics
    collecting information on, 128
    in foreign markets, 68–69
    influence on formation of regional market zones, 73
Population growth; *see also* Demographics
    in cities, 125, 240, 242
    in less developed countries, 124
Portfolio analysis, 35–37

T

Tactical marketing, 21–22
Tangibility, of products, 274
Tangibles, in services, 373
Target marketing; *see also* Positioning; Segmentation
  approaches
    concentrated, 260
    customized, 260
    differentiation, 259–260
    undifferentiated, 259
  definition, 238, 256
  evolution to customer marketing, 106
  steps, 256
    approach selection, 259–260
    market segment analysis, 257–258
    profiles of target markets, 258
Target markets
  abandoning, 258
  primary, 258
  profiles, 258
  promotion mix decisions, 480–481
  retail strategy, 453
  secondary, 258
  tertiary, 258
Target return on investment, 388–389
Target return pricing, 400
TCA; *see* Transaction cost analysis
Technical selling, 508
Technology
  in B2B markets, 212, 231–232, 451–452
  changes caused by, 127
  electronic data interchange, 231, 232, 451–452
  marketing research, 139–141
  new products, 330
Teenagers, 477
Telemarketing
  costs, 525
  customer prospecting, 509
  inbound, 509
  offshore call centers, 437
  outbound, 509, 525
  regulations, 128, 525
  response rates, 525
  success factors, 525
Television
  advertising, 482, 491, 543
  in pediatricians' waiting rooms, 336
  ratings, 136, 553
Television home shopping, 448
10-K reports, 165
Tertiary target markets, 258
Test markets, 342–344, 551, 553
Third-party logistics, 421

Time, influence on consumer decisions, 189, 202
Time utility, 30
Time-series analysis, 551, 554–556
Touchpoints, 102, 103–105, 436
Trade discounts, 401
Trade servicers, 508
Trade shows, 225, 494, 561
Trademarks, 306, 307, 308, 319
Training, sales, 520
Transaction cost analysis (TCA), 514–515
Transfer pricing, 91
Transportation
  costs, 91–92, 428
  in foreign markets, 88
  intermediaries, 418
  methods, 428
Trust, 104, 229, 512–513
Tying contracts, 429

U

Undifferentiated target marketing, 259; *see also* Mass marketing
Uniform delivered pricing, 402
Unions, 44
Unit sales, 340
U.S. Army, 33
U.S. Census Bureau, 136, 143, 175, 248, 442
U.S. Department of Defense, 223
U.S. Justice Department, 152
U.S. Patent and Trademark Office, 166–167
U.S. Postal Service (USPS), 219, 402
Unsought goods, 276
Upgrades or modifications to existing products, 330
Usage patterns, segmentation by, 255; *see also* Product usage
User expectations method, 551, 552
Users, 219
Utility, 30

V

VALS (Values and Lifestyles), 252–254
Value
  benefits-cost ratio, 30
  definition, 10
Value chain, 31–33, 412
Value co-creation, 413
Value equation, 443
Value networks, 412–415
Value offering; *see* Pricing; Products; Services
Value pricing, 390–392
Value propositions, 30–31, 85–86; *see also* Positioning

Value-creating activities, 31–32
Values
  of consumers, 181
  cultural, 187
  generational, 19–20, 246
Values and Lifestyles (VALS), 252–254
Variability, of services, 357–358
Variable pricing, 397
Variety, product, 438–439, 442
Vending machines, 448
Vendors; *see* Business-to-business markets; Suppliers
Vertical marketing systems (VMSs), 421–422
Video gaming, 244, 388
Viral marketing, 530–531
Virtual organizations, 413
Visions, strategic, 38
VMSs; *see* Vertical marketing systems

W

Warehousing, 427
Warranties
  brands and, 324
  costs and benefits, 324–325
  general, 323
  message conveyed to customer, 324
  specific, 323–324
Web site advertising; *see* Internet advertising
Web sites, company; *see also* Electronic commerce; Internet
  community, 529
  of competitors, 166
  content, 528–529
  context, 527–528
  conversion rates, 545
  customer interface dimensions, 527–529
  customization, 529
  development, 489–490
  integration with print catalogs, 525–526
Wholesaler cooperatives, 421
Wholesalers, 415
Women; *see also* Gender roles
  Internet use, 179–180
  purchasing roles, 178–179
Word-of-mouth advertising, 495; *see also* Buzz; Viral marketing
Workload method, 516–517
World Trade Organization (WTO), 92, 156

Z

Zero-based budgeting, 558–559
Zone pricing, 402

ONLINE LEARNING CENTER

Students using this text will have access to resources located on the Online Learning Center, including Chapter Quizzes and a Marketing Plan Guide.

The online learning center also contains password protected instructor supplements including the Instructor's Manual, PowerPoint Presentation Slides, and **BusinessWeek Video Monthly Newsletters**. Each month instructors will receive an electronic newsletter from the authors including synopses of current BusinessWeek videos as well as discussion questions that correlate to relevant topics in the textbook.